Green type indicates global example. 🍁 indicates Canadian feature.

P9-ELG-581

SECOND CANADIAN EDITION
MACROECONOMICS

Paul Krugman
PRINCETON UNIVERSITY

Robin Wells

Iris Au
UNIVERSITY OF TORONTO

Jack Parkinson
UNIVERSITY OF TORONTO

WORTH PUBLISHERS
A Macmillan Higher Education Company

Sr. Vice President, Editorial and Production: Catherine Woods

Publisher: Charles Linsmeier

Marketing Manager: Tom Digiano

Development Editors: A. Robert Templeton and Bradley T. Smith of First Folio Resource Group Inc.

Marketing Assistant: Tess Sanders

Senior Media Editor: Marie McHale

Director of Digital and Print Development: Tracey Kuehn

Associate Managing Editor: Lisa Kinne

Coordinating Editor: Debbie Smith of First Folio Resource Group Inc.

Managing Editor: Julie Kretchman of First Folio Resource Group Inc.

Art Director: Babs Reingold

Interior Designer: Babs Reingold

Cover Designer: Kevin Kall

Copy Editor: Arleane Ralph

Photo Editors: Cecilia Varas and Maria Decambra

Photo Researchers: Elyse Rieder and Maria Decambra

Production Manager: Barbara Anne Seixas

Composition: Kim Hutchinson of First Folio Resource Group Inc.

Printing and Binding: RR Donnelley

ISBN-13: 978-1-4292-4006-2
ISBN-10: 1-4292-4006-7

Library of Congress Control Number: 2012930400

Printed in the United States of America

First printing 2013

Worth Publishers
41 Madison Avenue
New York, NY 10010
www.worthpublishers.com

To beginning students everywhere,
which we all were at one time.

And, to Sophia & Jon and
Dora, Alena, & Hanna

Iris & Jack

Paul Krugman, recipient of the 2008 Nobel Memorial Prize in Economic Sciences, is Professor of Economics at Princeton University, where he regularly teaches the principles course. He received his BA from Yale and his PhD from MIT. Prior to his current position, he taught at Yale, Stanford, and MIT. He also spent a year on the staff of the Council of Economic Advisers in 1982–1983. His research is mainly in the area of international trade, where he is one of the founders of the "new trade theory," which focuses on increasing returns and imperfect competition. He also works in international finance, with a concentration in currency crises. In 1991, Krugman received the American Economic Association's John Bates Clark medal. In addition to his teaching and academic research, Krugman writes extensively for nontechnical audiences. He is a regular op-ed columnist for the *New York Times*. His latest trade books, both bestsellers, are *End this Depression Now!*, a look at the recent global financial crisis and recovery, and *The Return of Depression Economics and the Crisis of 2008*, a history of recent economic troubles and their implications for economic policy. His earlier books, *The Conscience of a Liberal*, *Peddling Prosperity*, and *The Age of Diminished Expectations*, have become modern classics.

Robin Wells was a Lecturer and Researcher in Economics at Princeton University. She received her BA from the University of Chicago and her PhD from the University of California at Berkeley; she then did postdoctoral work at MIT. She has taught at the University of Michigan, the University of Southampton (United Kingdom), Stanford, and MIT. The subject of her teaching and research is the theory of organizations and incentives.

Iris Au is a Senior Lecturer in Economics at the University of Toronto Scarborough (UTSC). She received her BA, MA, and PhD from Simon Fraser University, British Columbia. She taught at Simon Fraser University and Kwantlen University College (now known as Kwantlen Polytechnic University) before joining UTSC. Currently, she teaches introductory and intermediate macroeconomics, international finance, economics of public policy, and topics on financial crises on a regular basis.

Jack Parkinson is a Senior Lecturer in Economics at the University of Toronto Scarborough (UTSC). He received his Hons. BA from Western University and his MA and PhD from the University of Toronto. He has worked as a corporate tax policy analyst for the Ontario Ministry of Finance while teaching during his lunchtime or evenings. Over the past twenty years he has taught on all three campuses of the University of Toronto. Currently, he teaches introductory microeconomics, intermediate and advanced macroeconomics, money and banking, economics of organization, and applied economic statistics.

BRIEF CONTENTS

CONTENTS

PREFACE

FROM PAUL AND ROBIN

More than a decade ago, when we began writing the first edition of this textbook, we had many small ideas: particular aspects of economics that we believed weren't covered the right way in existing textbooks. But we also had one big idea: the belief that an economics textbook could and should be built around narratives, that it should never lose sight of the fact that economics is, in the end, a set of stories about what people do.

Many of the stories economists tell take the form of models—for whatever else they are, economic models are stories about how the world works. But we believed that students' understanding of and appreciation for models would be greatly enhanced if they were presented, as much as possible, in the context of stories about the real world, stories that both illustrate economic concepts and touch on the concerns we all face as individuals living in a world shaped by economic forces.

Those stories have been integrated into every edition, including this one, which contains more stories than our earlier editions. Once again, you'll find them in the chapter opening stories, in boxed features like Economics in Action, For Inquiring Minds, and Global Comparisons, but now in our new Business Cases as well.

As in the previous edition, we've made extensive changes and updates in coverage to reflect current events—events that have come thick and fast in a turbulent, troubled world economy, which is affecting the lives and prospects of students everywhere. Currency is very important to us.

We have also expanded our coverage of business issues, both because business experience is a key source of economic lessons and because most students will eventually find themselves working in the business world. We are especially pleased with how the new Business Cases have turned out and how they augment the overall number and richness of our stories.

As you'll see, there's a great deal of new material, and there are some significant changes (and, we hope, improvements) in pedagogy. But we've tried to keep the spirit the same. This is a book about economics as the study of what people do and how they interact, a study very much informed by real-world experience.

FROM IRIS AND JACK

When we were approached about the possibility of adapting the latest edition of Paul and Robin's wonderful book for the Canadian market we were incredibly excited. The U.S. edition of the text, which started out as a top-tier product, has only improved with each new edition.

We believe the narratives approach adopted by Paul and Robin is an excellent way to expose students to the beauty of economics and its power to explain and understand the world we all live in.

Many of the narratives contained in the chapter opening stories, Economics in Action, For Inquiring Minds, Global Comparisons, and Business Cases have been altered, sometimes significantly, so as to infuse them with content relevant to Canadians. Of course Canadians, living in an open economy that is quite dependent on trade, are used to thinking about global economic issues and linkages. With that in mind a few of the narratives have not changed much from what appeared in the third U.S. edition. Throughout we have taken great care whenever altering the text so as to maintain the quality of the underlying narratives.

Chapters 14 and 15, the two chapters that deal with money, banking, the central banking system, and monetary policy have been almost entirely rewritten so as to properly cover this material from the Canadian perspective. Of course discussion of other government policies, such as fiscal and trade policy, and other facets of the economy have also been given a Canadian treatment as well.

We are extremely pleased to be able to do our part to bring these narratives to a Canadian audience. If, after reading this text, some students decide that economics is really interesting and go on to take additional economics courses, we would be happy. But most importantly, we hope that all students feel this text greatly enhances and assists their study of economics.

What's New

Although the second U.S. edition was a resounding success, further establishing *Macroeconomics* as one of the bestselling macroeconomics textbooks in the United States, we learn with each new edition that there is always room for improvement. So, for the second Canadian edition, we undertook each revision with four goals in mind:

1. To make the book more relevant to a Canadian audience
2. To expand the book's appeal to business students
3. To be as current and cutting edge as possible in the topics covered and the examples included
4. To make the book more teachable and accessible

We hope that the following revisions lead to a more successful teaching experience for you.

Selected Canadian Examples

- Introduction: Opener: Any Given Sunday (p. 1): Halifax's Spring Garden Road as an example of the market economy in action.

- Chapter 2: Economics in Action: Economists, Beyond the Ivory Tower (p. 43): Looking at jobs for Canadian economists outside academia.

- Chapter 3: Global Comparison: Pay More, Pump Less (p. 70): Comparing European fuel costs and consumption with those of Canada and the United States.

- Chapter 4: Economics in Action: The Lobsters of Atlantic Canada (p. 136): How quotas control the supply of lobster coming from Atlantic Canada.

- Chapter 5: For Inquiring Minds: Softwood Lumber Dispute (p. 169): A history of the contentious softwood lumber trade between Canada and the United States.

- Chapter 5: Economics in Action: Freeing Canada's Trade with the World (p. 171): Discussion of the Canada–Chile Free Trade Agreement and Canada's current free trade negotiations.

- Chapter 7: Figure 7-3: Canada's GDP in 2011 (p. 208): Two Methods of Calculating GDP.

- Chapter 8: The Unemployment Rate (p. 232): Determining various unemployment rates in Canada and comparing them to the real GDP growth rate.

- Chapter 9: Business Case: Sources of Canada's Labour Productivity Growth, 1970–2010 (p. 296): How different Canadian industry sectors have fared since 1970.

- Chapter 10: Economics in Action: A Housing Bubble in Vancouver? (p. 331): A bursting housing bubble in the United States triggered the financial crisis of 2008. Is a similar bubble, with the same potential for crisis, now building in Canada?

- Chapter 11: Opener: In Cod We Trusted—The Cod Fishery in Newfoundland and Labrador (p. 339): How the moratorium on cod fishing affected the economy of Atlantic Canada.

- Chapter 12: Economics in Action: Is Stabilization Policy Stabilizing? (p. 406): How the Bank of Canada has responded to different recessions.

- Chapter 13: Business Case: KIP Goes to School: Action Plan Spending on Knowledge Infrastructure (p. 443): The beneficial effect of Canada's 2009 Economic Action Plan on educational infrastructure.

- Chapter 14: The Evolution of the Canadian Banking System (p. 483): How our banking system came to be as it is today, including the creation of the Bank of Canada.

- Chapter 15: For Inquiring Minds: Eight Fixed Dates for the BOC Policy Interest Rate Announcements (p. 508): When the Bank of Canada announces its interest rate policy and why these announcements are so important.

- Chapter 17: Regulation in the Wake of the Crisis (p. 578): How the Canadian government changed mortgage regulations after the banking crisis of 2008, which began in the U.S., to reduce the likelihood of such an event happening here.

- Chapter 18: Economics in Action: When Did the Business Cycle Begin? (p. 589): How Canada's economy changed from predominantly agricultural to industrial.

New Business Cases

Now, more than ever, students entering the business community need a strong understanding of economic principles and their applications to business decisions. To meet this demand, almost every chapter now concludes with a real-world Business Case, showing how the economic issues discussed in the chapter play out in the world of entrepreneurs and bottom lines.

The cases range from the 2009 bankruptcy of General Motors, once the symbol of North American economic success, and its rebound in 2010, to a look at how small businesses in Newfoundland adapted in order to survive during the recent recession, to an examination of the productivity surge in retailing driven by improvements in global logistics at Loblaws and Walmart. They also place the individual consumer and firm in the macroeconomy with examples that illustrate the changing job market during a recession (Workopolis.com and Monster.ca), the role of gift cards in secondary markets (CardSwap.ca), and the value of "breakage" when individual consumers fail to use up their gift cards completely.

Each case is followed by critical thinking questions that prompt students to apply the economics they learned in the chapter to real-life business situations (answers to these questions are found in the Instructor's Resource Manual). See a full list of the Business Cases on the inside front cover.

An Emphasis on Currency

The second Canadian edition has been updated to remain the most current textbook on the market in its content, data, and examples.

New Chapter: "Crises and Consequences" This new chapter provides an up-to-date look at the recent financial crisis and the aspects of the U.S. banking system that allowed it to take place. Starting with the story of the Lehman Brothers collapse, the chapter integrates coverage of the dangers of banking, the trade-off between liquidity and rate of return, the emergence of "shadow banks," and the early bank runs of the recession. Also covered: asset bubbles, financial contagion, financial panic, a comparison of the Canadian and U.S. banking systems, and a look at how the financial crisis of 2008 fits into a long history of economic crises. The chapter concludes with a discussion of why banking crises are so bad for so many, and the role governments and regulations play in crises.

Economics in Action: A Richer Story to Be Told

Students and instructors alike have always championed *Macroeconomics* for its applications of economic principles, especially our Economics in Action feature. In the second Canadian edition, we have revised or replaced a significant number of Economics in Action applications in every chapter to ensure that the book remains fresh and cutting edge. We believe this provides the richness of content that drives student and instructor interest. All Economics in Action features are listed on the inside cover.

Opening Stories We have always taken great care to ensure that each chapter's opening story illustrates the key concepts of that chapter in a compelling and accessible way. And, as always, we update most of these in each edition and provide many completely new stories. New openers include the story of Facebook and the huge amounts of funding needed to obtain its large server farms; the story behind Canada's Economic Action Plan and the reactions to the stimulus; the story of China's economic rise, surpassing Japan as the world's second largest economy, and the method economists use to measure such trends; and the story of Mark Carney and his high profile roles, first as Governor of the Bank of Canada, then as Governor of the Bank of England.

A More Teachable and Accessible Presentation

Streamlined Chapters Because less is often more, we've streamlined the exposition in a number of places where our desire for thoroughness got a little ahead of our pedagogy. The chapters on fiscal policy and monetary policy, in particular, are a lot smoother in this edition.

A More Focused Treatment of the Keynesian Cross The main coverage of the Keynesian cross in the chapters on aggregate expenditure and *AD/AS* has been retained, but coverage of the integrated 45-degree diagrams in later chapters on fiscal policy and monetary policy has been cut back. This change was made in response to input from instructors who were vocal in their request for less integrated coverage of the Keynesian cross to make our book more accessible to their students. Keynesian coverage remains as important as ever in these chapters. But the treatment is now more focused and, we hope, free of unnecessary complexity.

A More Visual Exposition The research tells us that students read more online, in shorter bursts, and respond better to visual representations of information than ever before. In the second Canadian edition, we've worked hard to present information in the format that best teaches students.

We've shortened our paragraphs for easier reading and included numbered and bulleted lists whenever content would allow. You will find helpful new summary tables in this edition. And, most helpful, are the visual displays in the book, including dynamic representations that turn paragraphs of text into a more accessible, and appealing, visual presentation.

Advantages of This Book

Our basic approach to textbook writing remains unchanged:

- **Chapters build intuition through realistic examples.** In every chapter, we use real-world examples, stories, applications, and case studies to teach the core concepts and motivate student learning. The best way to introduce concepts and reinforce them is through real-world examples; students simply relate more easily to them.

- **Pedagogical features reinforce learning.** We've crafted a genuinely helpful set of features, our "tools for learning," that are presented in a visual walk-through format starting on the next page.

- **Chapters are accessible and entertaining.** We use a fluid and friendly writing style to make concepts accessible and, whenever possible, we use examples that are familiar to students.

- **Although easy to understand, the book also prepares students for further coursework.** There's no need to choose between two unappealing alternatives: a textbook that is "easy to teach" but leaves major gaps in students' understanding, or a textbook that is "hard to teach" but adequately prepares students for future coursework. We offer the best of both worlds.

CHAPTER 14

Money, Banking, and the Central Banking System

FUNNY MONEY

Paul Chiasson/CP Images

Phuong Anh Ho Huu, a senior representative for the Bank of Canada in Quebec, holds up a new $100 banknote. Issued in November 2011, the $100 bill was the first in Canada's polymer banknote series, which features a wealth of anti-counterfeiting components.

IN 2008, THE ROYAL CANADIAN Mounted Police (RCMP) dismantled a major counterfeiting plant in Surrey, British Columbia, that was believed to be responsible for a significant portion of the counterfeit Canadian paper bills in B.C. between 2006 and 2008. A year later, the RCMP seized $130 000 worth of fake Canadian banknotes. In 2011, following a tip provided to Crime Stoppers and after a two-week investigation, the RCMP seized $1.1 million of counterfeit Canadian banknotes in Vancouver. Some of these fake paper bills were of high quality and were very hard to tell from the real thing.

The funny thing is that these elaborately decorated pieces of paper have little or no intrinsic value. Indeed, a $ 0

bill printed with blue or orange ink literally wouldn't be worth the paper it was printed on. But if the ink on that decorated piece of paper is just the right shade of green, people will think that it's money and will accept it as payment for very real goods and services. Why? Because they believe, correctly, that they can do the same thing: exchange that piece of green paper for real goods and services.

In fact, here's a riddle: if a fake $20 bill enters Canada and nobody ever realizes it's a fake, who gets hurt? Accepting a fake $20 bill isn't like buying a car that turns out to be a lemon or a meal that isn't edible; as long as the bill's counterfeit nature remains undiscovered, it will pass from hand to hand just like a real $20 bill. The answer to the riddle, as we'll

ment. Accordingly, the RCMP diligently monitors the integrity of Canadian currency, promptly investigating any reports of counterfeit dollars. The Bank of Canada (BOC) continues to bolster the security features of our paper bills and increase education efforts on note checking. The recent introduction of the polymer series of banknotes with improved security features is an example of the effort by the BOC to reduce counterfeiting.

The activities of the BOC and RCMP attest to the fact that money isn't like assets. It plays a unique role in the economy as the essential channel that links the various parts of the modern economy. In this chapter, we'll look at the role money plays, and then look at how a modern monetary system works and at the institutions that sustain and regulate it. This topic is important in itself, and it's also essential background for the understanding of monetary policy, which we will examine in the next chapter. ■

Global Stamps identify which boxes, cases, and applications are global in focus.

ECONOMICS ▶ IN ACTION

ONLY CREATURES SMALL AND PAMPERED

During the 1970s, British television featured a popular show titled *All Creatures Great and Small*. It chronicled the real life ...led to cows, pigs, ...n under arduous ... The show made ...itical member of ...nals and helping ...that Mr. Herriot ... the United States ...of farm vets over the past two decades. The source of the problem is competition. As the number of household pets has increased and the incomes of pet owners have grown, the demand for pet vets has increased sharply. As a result, vets are being drawn away from the business of caring for farm animals into the more lucrative business of caring for pets. As one American vet stated, she began her career caring for farm animals but changed her mind after "doing a C-section on a cow and it's 50 bucks. Do a C-section on a Chihuahua and you get $300. It's the money. I hate to say that." Add to this the relatively long hours and greater need for travel required of farm vets and it's easy to see why this choice less appealing than being a pet vet in an urban centre.

How can we translate this into supply and demand curves? Farm veterinary services and pet veterinary services are like gasoline and fuel oil: they're related goods that are substitutes in production. A vet typically specializes in one type of practice or the other, and that decision often depends on the going price for the service. The growing pet population in North America, combined with the increased willingness of doting owners to spend on their companions' care, has driven up the price of pet veterinary services. As a result, fewer and fewer vets have gone i... ... vets has shifted leftward—f... ... price.

In the e... ...rs and cents; they get fewer ve... ... one farmer, who had recently... ..., stated, "The fact that there's... ...e now. You didn't used to. If y... ...deadstock."

Higher spending on pets means fewer veterinarians are available to tend to farm animals.

Economics in Action cases conclude every major text section. This much-lauded feature lets students immediately apply concepts they've read about to real phenomena.

Check Your Understanding questions allow students to immediately test their understanding of a section. Solutions appear at the back of the book.

CHECK YOUR UNDERSTANDING 3-2

1. Explain whether each of the following events represents (i) a *shift of* the supply curve or (ii) a *movement along* the supply curve.
   a. More homeowners put their houses up for sale during a real estate boom that causes house prices to rise.
   b. Many strawberry farmers open temporary roadside stands during harvest season, even though prices are usually low at that time.
   c. Immediately after the school year begins, fast-food chains must raise wages, which represent the price of labour, to attract workers.
   d. Due to favourable growing conditions, wheat farmers in the Prairie provinces experience bumper crops.
   e. Since new technologies have made it possible to build larger cruise ships (which are cheaper to run per passenger), Caribbean cruise lines offer more cabins, at lower prices, than before.

Solutions...

▼ Quick Review

- The **supply schedule** shows how, all other things equal, the **quantity supplied** depends on the price. The **supply curve** illustrates this relationship.

- Supply curves are normally upward sloping: at a higher price, all other things equal, producers are willing to supply more of a good or service.

- A change in price, all other things equal, results in a **movement along the supply curve** and a change in the quantity supplied.

- Increases or decreases in supply lead to **shifts of the supply curve**. An increase in supply is a rightward shift: the quantity supplied rises for any given price. A decrease in supply is a leftward shift: the quantity supplied falls for any given price.

- The six main factors that can shift the supply curve are changes in (1) **input** prices, (2) prices of related goods or services, (3) technology, (4) weather, (5) expectations about future prices, and (6) number of producers.

- The mark... supply curve is the horizontal s... the **individual supply curve**... ...ducers in the market.

Quick Reviews offer students a short, bulleted summary of key concepts in the section to aid understanding.

GLOBAL COMPARISON

PAY MORE, PUMP LESS

For a real-world illustration of the law of demand, consider how gasoline consumption varies according to the prices consumers pay at the pump. Because of high taxes, gasoline and diesel fuel are more expensive in most European countries than in Canada and the United States. According to the law of demand, this should lead Europeans to buy less gasoline than Canadians and Americans—and they do. As you can see from the figure, Europeans consume less than half as much fuel per person as their counterparts in North America, mainly because they drive smaller cars with better fuel economy.

Prices aren't the only factor affecting fuel consumption, but they're a significant cause of the difference between European and North American fuel consumption per person.

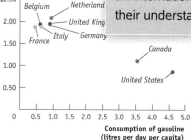

Sources: U.S. Energy Information Administration; Natural Resources Canada, 2010.

Global Comparison boxes use real data from several countries and colourful graphs to illustrate how and why countries reach different economic outcomes. The boxes give students an international perspective that will expand their understanding of economics.

FOR INQUIRING MINDS

MORE ON NATIONAL INCOME

For Inquiring Minds boxes apply economic concepts to real-world events in unexpected and sometimes surprising ways, generating a sense of the power and breadth of economics. The feature furthers the book's goal of helping students build intuition with real-world examples.

...NP? This term refers to the total ...me earned by residents of a ... *excludes* the factor income ... foreigners, like profits paid to ...estors who own Canadian stocks ...nts to foreigners who work ...y in Canada. It *includes* the fac... earned abroad by Canadians, ...ts of the European operations ...ccrue to Blackberry's ...ders, and the wages of ...who work abroad temporarily. ...nship between GDP and GNP is: ... + (factor income earned abroad ...ns – factor income earned by ...in Canada). ...Canadian GDP was about 1.9%

higher than its GNP, mainly because of foreign companies operating in Canada.

Statistics Canada releases Canada's national income data monthly. But occasionally Statistics Canada will revise these data months afterward. Why? It is because whenever Statistics Canada releases data, there is a trade-off between accuracy and timeliness. It wants to release data in a timely fashion so people can use the most recent information to formulate economic decisions. However, these initial estimates are based on information that may be incomplete at the time of release. As time passes, more reliable and complete data become available and Statistics Canada can revise its initial estimates accordingly.

GNP, the value of output produced within a country's borders, is typically smaller than GDP, the value of output produced worldwide that is owned by a country's citizens and firms such as this Tim Hortons in Dubai. This is because GDP includes the GNP.

PITFALLS

DEMAND VERSUS QUANTITY DEMANDED

When economists say "an increase in demand," they mean a rightward shift of the demand curve, and when they say "a decrease in demand," they mean a leftward shift of the demand curve—that is, when they're being careful. In ordinary speech, most people, including professional economists, use the word *demand* casually. For example, an economist might say "the

demand for air travel has do... past 15 years, partly because of ... fares" when he or she really means th... *quantity demanded* has doubled.

Pitfalls boxes clarify concepts that are easily misunderstood by students new to economics.

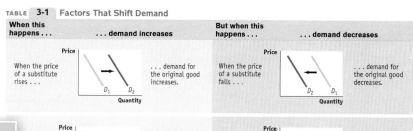

TABLE **3-1** Factors That Shift Demand

When this happens . . .	. . . demand increases	But when this happens . . .	. . . demand decreases
When the price of a substitute rises . . .	. . . demand for the original good increases.	When the price of a substitute falls . . .	. . . demand for the original good decreases.
When the price ... complement ...	. . . demand for the original good increases.	When the price of a complement rises . . .	. . . demand for the original good decreases.

New! Summary Tables serve as a helpful study aid for readers. Many incorporate visuals to help students grasp important economic concepts.

BUSINESS • KIP Goes to School: Action Plan Spending on
CASE • Knowledge Infrastructure

If you were on a Canadian post-secondary campus in 2009 or 20_
chance you may have seen a construction site there with an Econ_
Plan sign. The EAP included the Knowledge Infrastructure Progr_
$2 billion initiative providing funds to universities and colleges to _
and maintain teaching facilities such as lecture halls and laboratorie_
520 projects at colleges and universities across Canada received fu_
this program.

The construction service company EllisDon was awarded _
including George Brown College Waterfront Health Sciences Ca__,
(pictured here); the Schulich School of Engineering in Calgary; and _
Ivey School of Business in London, Ontario. The Canadian authors _
also indirectly benefitted from this spending as their university (the _
Toronto, Scarborough Campus) was a recipient of KIP funds to buil_
ing facilities that would allow students to learn in a better environm_

This spending on building infrastructure has both short-term a_
benefits to the economy. In the short run, it helps to create jobs. In the long run,
better and improved infrastructure should raise the productivity of Canadian
workers and the competitiveness of Canadian business in the world economy; and
this will translate into long-term sustainable economic growth.

How effective was this spending? KIP was just one part of the "Building
Infrastructure to Create Jobs" element of the EAP, which altogether represented
$12 billion in spending (23% of the total stimulus package in 2009 and 2010) on
better transportation networks, cleaner drinking water systems, improving infrastructure at universities and colleges, and so on. According to the Government
of Canada, by December 2010 about 82 000 jobs had been created or maintained
under the "Building Infrastructure to Create Jobs" element (about 37% of all the
jobs that had been created or maintained as a result of the EAP); and the multiplier associated with this spending was around 1.6, the highest among different
elements of the EAP. EllisDon and other companies in the construction business,
their employees, and suppliers were clearly getting some benefit from the EAP.

QUESTIONS FOR THOUGHT

1. Some opponents of fiscal expansion have accused it of consisting of make-work projects
   ___ little social value. What ___ ___ KIP story say about this view?

New!
Business Cases
close each chapter, applying
key economic principles to
real-life business situations
in both Canadian and
international companies. Each
case concludes with critical
thinking questions.

SUMMARY

1. The **supply and demand model** illustrates how
   a **competitive market,** one with many buyers
   and seller_ none of whom can influence the market
   price, w_

2. The d_ _chedule shows the **quantity**
   _ _ _ _ _ _ ented graphi-
   _ _ _ **demand** says
   _ _ hat is, a higher
   _ _ to demand a
   _e occurs

ing supply, they mean **shifts of the supply curve**—a
change in the quantity supplied at any given price. An
increase in supply causes a rightward shift of the supply curve. A decrease in supply causes a leftward shift.

8. There are six main factors that shift the supply curve:
   • A change in **input** prices
   • A change in the prices of related goods and services
   • A change in technology
   • A change in weather
   • A change in expectations
   _ _ _ _ _ ducers

End-of-Chapter Reviews include a brief but
complete summary of key concepts, a list of key terms,
and a comprehensive, high-quality set of end-of-
chapter Problems.

PROBLEMS

1. A survey indicated that chocolate is Canadians' favourite
   ice-cream flavour. For each of the following, indicate the
   possible effects on demand, supply, or both as well as
   equilibrium price and quantity of chocolate ice cream.
   a. A severe drought in Ontario causes dairy farmers
      to reduce the number of milk-producing cattle in
      their herds by a third. These dairy farmers supply
      cream that is used to manufacture chocolate
      ice cream.
   b. A new report by the Canadian Medical Association
      reveals that chocolate does, in fact, have significant
      health benefits.

Case 2: There is a big news event in your town,
which is rep_
   b. The market _
      Case 1: The _
      Case 2: The _
   c. The market _
      Case 1: Peop_
      Case 2: Peop_
      cooked brea_
   d. The market _
      ___kinson e_

KEY TERMS

Competitive market, p. 68	Substitutes, p. 73
Supply and demand model, p. 68	Complements, p. 73
Demand schedule, p. 69	Normal good, p. 74
Quantity demanded, p. 69	Inferior good, p. 74
Demand curve, p. 70	Individual demand curve, p. 75
Law of demand, p. 70	Quantity supplied, p. 78
Shift of the demand curve, p. 71	Supply schedule, p. 78
Movement along the demand curve, p. 71	Supply curve, p. 78
	Shift of the supply curve, p. 79

Organization of This Book: What's Core, What's Optional

We realize that some of our chapters will be considered optional. Below and on the facing page is a list of what we view as core chapters and those that could be considered optional. We've annotated the list of chapters to indicate what they cover should you wish to incorporate them.

Core	Optional
	Introduction: The Ordinary Business of Life Initiates students into the study of economics with basic terms and explains the difference between microeconomics and macroeconomics.
1. First Principles Outlines 12 principles underlying the study of economics: principles of individual choice, interaction between individuals, and economy-wide interaction.	
2. Economic Models: Trade-offs and Trade Employs two economic models—the production possibilities frontier and comparative advantage—as an introduction to gains from trade and international comparisons.	**Appendix 2A: Graphs in Economics** Offers a comprehensive review of graphing and math skills for students who would find a refresher helpful to prepare them for better economic literacy.
3. Supply and Demand Covers the essentials of supply, demand, market equilibrium, surplus, and shortage.	**Appendix 3A: The Algebra of Demand, Supply, and Equilibrium** Offers a mathematical approach to the concepts of demand and supply, using algebra to determine the equilibrium price and quantity.
	Appendix 3B: Consumer and Producer Surplus Introduces students to market efficiency, the ways markets fail, the roles of prices as signals, and property rights.
	4. Price Controls and Quotas: Meddling with Markets Covers market interventions and their consequences: price and quantity controls, inefficiency, and deadweight loss.
	5. International Trade Here we trace the sources of comparative advantage, consider tariffs and quotas, and explore the politics of trade protection, including coverage of the controversy over imports from low-wage countries.
6. Macroeconomics: The Big Picture Introduces the big ideas of macroeconomics with an overview of recessions and expansions, employment and unemployment, long-run growth, inflation versus deflation, and the open economy.	
7. GDP and the CPI: Tracking the Macroeconomy Explains how the numbers macroeconomists use are calculated and why, including the basics of national income accounting and price indexes.	
8. Unemployment and Inflation Covers the measurement of unemployment, the reasons why positive employment exists even in booms, and the problems posed by inflation.	
9. Long-Run Economic Growth Emphasizes an international perspective—economic growth is about the world as a whole—and explains why some countries have been more successful than others.	
10. Savings, Investment Spending, and the Financial System Introduces students to financial markets and institutions, loanable funds and the determination of interest rates. Includes new coverage of present value in the chapter proper and in a new appendix.	

Core	Optional
11. Income and Expenditure Addresses the determinants of consumer and investment spending, introduces the famous 45-degree diagram, and explains the logic of the multiplier.	**Appendix 11A: Deriving the Multiplier Algebraically** A rigorous and mathematical approach to deriving the multiplier.
12. Aggregate Demand and Aggregate Supply Provides the traditional focus on aggregate price level using the traditional approach to *AD/AS*. It also covers the ability of the economy to recover in the long run.	
13. Fiscal Policy Provides an analysis of the role of discretionary fiscal policy, automatic stabilizers, and long-run issues of debt and solvency.	**Appendix 13A: Taxes and the Multiplier** A rigorous derivation of the roles of taxes in reducing the size of the multiplier and acting as an automatic stabilizer.
14. Money, Banking, and the Central Banking System Covers the roles of money, the ways in which banks create money, and the structure and role of the Bank of Canada and other central banks.	
15. Monetary Policy Covers the role of the Bank of Canada policy in driving interest rates and aggregate demand. It includes a section bridging the short and long run by showing how interest rates set in the short run reflect the supply and demand of savings in the long run.	**Appendix 15A: Reconciling the Two Models of the Interest Rate** Explains why the loanable funds model (long-run discussions) and the liquidity preference approach (short-run discussions) are both valuable approaches.
16. Inflation, Disinflation, and Deflation Covers the causes and consequences of inflation, the large cost deflation imposes on the economy, and the danger of disinflation leading the economy into a liquidity trap.	
	17. Crises and Consequences Provides an up-to-date look at the recent financial crisis, starting with the Lehman Brothers collapse and integrating coverage of the dangers posed by banking, shadow banking, asset bubbles, and financial contagion.
	18. Macroeconomics: Events and Ideas Provides a unique overview of the history of macroeconomic thought, set in the context of changing policy concerns, and the current state of macroeconomic debates.
19. Open-Economy Macroeconomics Analyzes special issues raised for macroeconomics in an open economy: balance of payments, issues surrounding exchange rates such as floating versus fixed exchange rates.	

Supplements and Media

Worth Publishers is pleased to offer an enhanced and completely revised supplements and media package to accompany this textbook. The package has been crafted to help instructors teach their principles course and to give students the tools to develop their skills in economics.

For Instructors

Instructor's Resource Manual with Solutions Manual The Instructor's Resource Manual is a resource meant to provide materials and tips to enhance the class-room experience. The Instructor's Resource Manual provides the following:

- Chapter-by-chapter learning objectives
- Chapter outlines
- Teaching tips and ideas that include:
  - Hints on how to create student interest
  - Tips on presenting the material in class
- Discussion of the examples used in the text, including points to emphasize with your students
- Activities that can be conducted in or out of the classroom
- Hints for dealing with common misunderstandings that are typical among students

- Web resources (includes tips for using EconPortal)
- Solutions manual with detailed solutions to all of the end-of-chapter Problems in the textbook

Printed Test Bank The Test Bank provides a wide range of questions appropriate for assessing your students' comprehension, interpretation, analysis, and synthesis skills. Totalling over 4500 questions, the Test Bank offers multiple-choice, true/false, and short-answer questions designed for comprehensive coverage of the text concepts. Questions have been checked for continuity with the text content, overall usability, and accuracy.

The Test Bank features include the following:

- To aid instructors in building tests, each question has been categorized according to its general *degree of difficulty*. The three levels are *easy, moderate,* and *difficult.*
  - *Easy* questions require students to recognize concepts and definitions. These are questions that can be answered by direct reference to the textbook.
  - *Moderate* questions require some analysis on the student's part.
  - *Difficult* questions usually require more detailed analysis by the student.
- Each question has also been categorized according to a *skill descriptor*. These include *Fact-Based, Definitional, Concept-Based, Critical Thinking,* and *Analytical Thinking.*
  - *Fact-Based Questions* require students to identify facts presented in the text.
  - *Definitional Questions* require students to define an economic term or concept.
  - *Concept-Based Questions* require a straightforward knowledge of basic concepts.
  - *Critical Thinking Questions* require the student to apply a concept to a particular situation.
  - *Analytical Thinking Questions* require another level of analysis to answer the question. Students must be able to apply a concept and use this knowledge for further analysis of a situation or scenario.
- To further aid instructors in building tests, each question is conveniently cross-referenced to the appropriate topic heading in the textbook. Questions are presented in the order in which concepts are presented in the text.
- The Test Bank includes questions with tables that students must analyze to solve for numerical answers. It also contains questions based on the graphs that appear in the book. These questions ask students to use the graphical models developed in the textbook and to interpret the information presented in the graph. Selected questions are paired with scenarios to reinforce comprehension.

Computerized Test Bank The printed Test Bank is available in CD-ROM format for both Windows and Macintosh users. With this program, instructors can easily create and print tests and write and edit questions. Tests can be printed in a wide range of formats. The software's unique synthesis of flexible word-processing and database features creates a program that is extremely intuitive and capable.

Lecture PowerPoint Presentation The enhanced PowerPoint presentation slides are designed to assist you with lecture preparation and presentations. The slides are organized by topic and contain graphs, data tables, and bulleted lists of key concepts suitable for lecture presentation. Key figures from the text are replicated and animated to demonstrate how they build. The slides have been designed to allow for easy editing of graphs and text. These slides can be customized to suit your individual needs by adding your own data, questions, and lecture notes.

CoursePacks Plug our content into your course management system. Whatever you teach, or whether you use Blackboard, WebCT, Desire2Learn, Angel, Sakai, or Moodle to manage your course, we have free content and support available. Registered instructors can download cartridges with no hassle and no strings attached. Content includes our most popular free resources and book-specific content. For more information, go to http://worthpublishers.com/catalog/Other/Coursepack.

Further Resources Offered

sapling learning
www.saplinglearning.com
Sapling Learning provides the most effective interactive homework and instruction that improves student-learning outcomes for the problem-solving disciplines.

Sapling Learning offers an enjoyable teaching and effective learning experience that is distinctive in three important ways:

- **Ease of Use:** Sapling Learning's easy-to-use interface keeps students engaged in problem solving, not struggling with the software.
- **Targeted Instructional Content:** Sapling Learning increases student engagement and comprehension by delivering immediate feedback and targeted instructional content.
- **Unsurpassed Service and Support:** Sapling Learning makes teaching more enjoyable by providing a dedicated Masters- or PhD-level colleague to service instructors' unique needs throughout the course, including content customization.

CourseSmart eBooks

http://www.coursesmart.com/ourproducts
CourseSmart eBooks offer the complete book in PDF format. Students can save money, up to 60% off the price of print textbooks. With the CourseSmart eBook, students have the ability to take notes, highlight, print pages, and more. A great alternative to renting print textbooks!

Worth Noting Worth Noting keeps you connected to your textbook authors in real time. Whether they were just on CNBC or published in the *New York Times*, this is the place to find out about it. Visit Worth Noting at http://blogs.worthpublishers.com/econblog/.

i>clicker Developed by a team of University of Illinois physicists, i>clicker is the most flexible and reliable classroom response system available. It is the only solution created *for* educators, *by* educators—with continuous product improvements made through direct classroom testing and faculty feedback. You'll love i>clicker, no matter your level of technical expertise, because the focus is on *your* teaching, *not the technology*. To learn more about packaging i>clicker with this textbook, please contact your local sales rep or visit www.iclicker.com.

Acknowledgments

Our deep appreciation and heartfelt thanks to the following reviewers, class-testers, and contributors whose input helped us shape the U.S. third edition.

Carlos Aguilar, *El Paso Community College*
Seemi Ahmad, *Dutchess Community College*
Farhad Ameen, *Westchester Community College*
Dean Baim, *Pepperdine University*
David Barber, *Quinnipiac College*
Janis Barry-Figuero, *Fordham University at Lincoln Center*
Hamid Bastin, *Shippensburg University*
Michael Bonnal, *University of Tennessee, Chattanooga*
Milicia Bookman, *Saint Joseph's University*
Anne Bresnock, *California State Polytechnic University, Pomona*
Colleen Callahan, *American University*
Giuliana Campanelli Andreopoulos, *William Patterson University*
Charles Campbell, *Mississippi State University*
Randall Campbell, *Mississippi State University*
Joel Carton, *Florida International University*
Andrew Cassey, *Washington State University*
Sanjukta Chaudhuri, *University of Wisconsin, Eau Claire*
Eric Chiang, *Florida Atlantic University*
Abdur Chowdhury, *Marquette University*
Chad Cotti, *University of Wisconsin, Oshkosh*
Maria DaCosta, *University of Wisconsin, Eau Claire*
James P. D'Angelo, *University of Cincinnati*
Orgul Demet Ozturk, *University of South Carolina*

Harold Elder, *University of Alabama*
Rudy Fichenbaum, *Wright State University*
Sherman Folland, *Oakland University*
Amanda Freeman, *Kansas State University*
Shelby Frost, *Georgia State University*
Sarah Ghosh, *University of Scranton*
Satyajit Ghosh, *University of Scranton*
Fidel Gonzalez, *Sam Houston State University*
Michael G. Goode, *Central Piedmont Community College*
Alan Gummerson, *Florida International University*
Eran Guse, *West Virginia University*
Don Holley, *Boise State University*
Scott Houser, *Colorado School of Mines*
Russell A. Janis, *University of Massachusetts, Amherst*
Jonatan Jelen, *The City College of New York*
Miles Kimball, *University of Michigan*
Colin Knapp, *University of Florida*
Stephan Kroll, *Colorado State University*
Vicky Langston, *Columbus State University*
Richard B. Le, *Cosumnes River College*
Yu-Feng Lee, *New Mexico State University*
Mary Lesser, *Iona College*
Solina Lindahl, *California Polytechnic State University*
Volodymyr Lugovskyy, *Indiana University*
Mark E. McBride, *Miami University*
Michael Mogavero, *University of Notre Dame*
Gary Murphy, *Case Western Reserve University*
Anna Musatti, *Columbia University*
Christopher Mushrush, *Illinois State University*
ABM Nasir, *North Carolina Central University*
Gerardo Nebbia, *El Camino College*
Pattabiraman Neelakantan, *East Stroudsburg University*
Pamela Nickless, *University of North Carolina, Asheville*
Nick Noble, *Miami University (Ohio)*
Walter Park, *American University*
Brian Peterson, *Central College*
Michael Polcen, *Northern Virginia Community College*
Reza Ramazani, *Saint Michael's College*
Ryan Ratcliff, *University of San Diego*
Robert Rebelein, *Vassar College*
Ken Roberts, *Southwestern University*
Greg Rose, *Sacramento City College*
Jeff Rubin, *Rutgers University, New Brunswick*
Jason C. Rudbeck, *University of Georgia*
Michael Sattinger, *State University of New York, Albany*
Elizabeth Sawyer Kelly, *University of Wisconsin, Madison*
Arzu Sen, *West Virginia University*
Marcia Snyder, *College of Charleston*
Liliana V. Stern, *Auburn University*
Adam Stevenson, *University of Michigan*
Eric Stuen, *University of Idaho*
Christine Tarasevich, *Del Mar College*
Henry S. Terrell, *George Washington University*
Mickey Wu, *Coe College*

We are indebted to the following reviewers for their suggestions and advice on improving the second Canadian edition.

James Feehan, *Memorial University of Newfoundland*

Phillippe Ghayad, *Dawson College*

Michael Leonard, *Kwantlen Polytechnic University*

Michel Mayer, *Dawson College*

Trien Nguyen, *University of Waterloo*

Shadab Qaiser, *York University*

Terri Rizzo, *Lakehead University*

Neil Roberts, *Kwantlen Polytechnic University*

Scott Skjei, *Acadia University*

Vitaly Terekhov, *Marianopolis College*

Greg Tkacz, *St. Francis Xavier University*

Andrew Wong, *University of Alberta*

We owe a huge debt of gratitude to Paul Krugman and Robin Wells who, with the assistance of many of the people named above, have created a wonderful text that is both a pleasure to read and a great tool for learning. We also benefitted from the extensive work undertaken by Anthony Myatt for the first Canadian edition.

We would like to thank all the fine people at Worth Publishers. In particular we are indebted to Chris Spavins who was the Worth sales representative that first recommended us for this project. Charles Linsmeier, publisher, skillfully guided the project along, providing us lots of freedom, but carefully nudging us or others whenever he sensed an improvement could be reached. Julia Jevmenova, field manager in the Canadian market, has provided plenty of support and marketing advice. We would also like to thank Tracey Kuehn, Barbara Seixas, Sharon Balbos, Craig Bleyer, and, of course, Elizabeth Widdicombe for making this project possible.

We have also benefitted greatly from all the hard work of the fantastic team at First Folio. Bob Templeton and Brad Smith patiently edited the drafts and acted as a sounding board for new ideas and refinements. Kim Hutchinson ensured the formatting and illustrating remained clear and concise. Arleane Ralph efficiently copy-edited and proofread the entire manuscript. Julie Kretchman acted as the project manager and helped make sure everyone had what they needed to stay on schedule.

We can honestly say that until you work on a project like this you truly don't understand the impact of the vast array of experts and professionals who are assembled to bring such an undertaking to completion. We are indebted to them all. Their assistance has not only made this text possible, it has made it much better.

Lastly, we would like to thank our families for all the love, support, and understanding they have provided us over the years. We hope that this book can help them and the next generation of students understand why we think economics is so cool.

Iris Au   *Jack Parkinson*

We must also thank the many people at Worth Publishers for their contributions. Elizabeth Widdicombe, president of Freeman and Worth, and Catherine Woods, senior vice president, played an important role in planning for this revision. We have Liz to thank for the idea that became the Business Case in each chapter. Charles Linsmeier, publisher, ably oversaw the revision and contributed throughout. A special thanks to Craig Bleyer, our original publisher at Worth and now national sales director, who put so much of his effort into making each edition a success. His keen instincts showed again in the revision plan for this edition.

Once again, we have had an incredible production and design team on the U.S. third edition, people whose hard work, creativity, and dedication paid off as we developed the Second Canadian Edition. Once again, you have outdone yourselves. Thank you all: Tracey Kuehn, Lisa Kinne, and Anthony Calcara for producing this book; Babs Reingold and Lyndall Culbertson for their beautiful interior design which is the basis for this second Canadian edition; Barbara Seixas, who worked her magic yet again despite the vagaries of the project schedule; Cecilia Varas and Elyse Rieder for photo research; Stacey Alexander for coordinating all the production of the supplemental materials.

Many thanks to Marie McHale for devising and coordinating the impressive collection of media and supplements that accompany our book. Thanks to the incredible team of supplements writers and coordinators who worked with Marie on the supplements and media package; we are forever grateful for your tireless efforts.

And most of all, special thanks to Sharon Balbos, executive development editor on each of our editions. Much of the success of this book is owed to Sharon's dedication and professionalism. As always, she kept her cool through rough spots. Sharon, we're not sure we deserved an editor as good as you, but we're sure that everyone involved as well as our adopters and their students have been made better off by your presence.

Paul Krugman   *Robin Wells*

Introduction: The Ordinary Business of Life

ANY GIVEN SUNDAY

SF photo/Shutterstock

Delivering the goods: the market economy in action.

IT'S SUNDAY AFTERNOON IN MAY of 2013, and Spring Garden Road in downtown Halifax, Nova Scotia, is a busy place. Thousands of people crowd the more than 200 stores as well as the restaurants and coffee shops that line the road, while many more shop in the surrounding nine city blocks that make up the Spring Garden Road area. Most of the shoppers are cheerful—and why not? The stores in this area offer an extraordinary range of choice; you can buy everything from sophisticated electronic equipment to fashionable clothes to organic carrots. There are probably 100 000 distinct items available along that stretch of road and in the surrounding area. And most of these items are not luxury goods that only the rich can afford; they are products that millions of Canadians can and do purchase every day.

The scene along Spring Garden Road on this day is, of course, perfectly ordinary—very much like the scene along hundreds of other stretches of road, all across Canada, that same afternoon. And the discipline of economics is mainly concerned with ordinary things. As the great nineteenth-century economist Alfred Marshall put it, economics is "a study of mankind in the ordinary business of life."

What can economics say about this "ordinary business"? Quite a lot, it turns out. What we'll see in this book is that even familiar scenes of economic life pose some very important questions— questions that economics can help answer. Among these questions are:

- How does our economic system work? That is, how does it manage to deliver the goods?

- When and why does our economic system go astray, leading people into counterproductive behaviour?

- Why are there ups and downs in the economy? That is, why does the economy sometimes have a "bad year"?

- Finally, why is the long run mainly a story of ups rather than downs? That is, why has Canada, along with other advanced nations, become so much richer over time?

Let's take a look at these questions and offer a brief preview of what you will learn in this book.

The Invisible Hand

That ordinary scene in downtown Halifax would not have looked at all ordinary several centuries ago—say, to the people who General Cornwallis brought to the area in 1749 to establish a British community. Halifax has the second largest natural harbour in the world, but at that time the area was mostly unoccupied, and known mainly to the Mi'kmaq First Nations people.

Imagine that you could transport a Nova Scotian from 1749, or even from the time of the Halifax Explosion of 1917, forward in time to our own era. (Isn't that the plot of a movie? Several, actually.) What would this time traveller find amazing?

Surely the most amazing thing would be the sheer prosperity of modern Canada—the range of goods and services that ordinary families can afford. Looking at all that wealth, our transplanted traveller would wonder, "How can I get some of that?" Or perhaps she would ask herself, "How can my society get some of that?"

The answer is that to get this kind of prosperity, you need a well-functioning system for coordinating productive activities—the activities that create the goods and services people want and a means to get them to the people who want them. That kind of system is what we mean when we talk about the **economy.** And **economics** is the social science that studies the production, distribution, and consumption of goods and services.

An economy succeeds to the extent that it, literally, delivers the goods. A time traveller from the eighteenth century—or even from 1950—would be amazed at how many goods and services the modern Canadian economy delivers and at how many people can afford them. Compared with any past economy and with all but a few other countries today, Canada has an incredibly high standard of living.

So our economy must be doing something right, and the time traveller might want to compliment the person in charge. But guess what? There isn't anyone in charge. Canada has a **market economy,** in which production and consumption are the result of decentralized decisions by many firms and individuals. There is no central authority telling people what to produce or where to ship it. Each individual producer makes what he or she thinks will be most profitable; each consumer buys what he or she chooses.

The alternative to a market economy is a *command economy,* in which there *is* a central authority making decisions about production and consumption. Command economies have been tried, most notably in the Soviet Union between 1917 and 1991. But they didn't work very well. Producers in the Soviet Union routinely found themselves unable to produce because they did not have crucial raw materials, or they succeeded in producing but then found that nobody wanted their products. Consumers were often unable to find necessary items—command economies are famous for long lines at shops.

Market economies, however, are able to coordinate even highly complex activities and to reliably provide consumers with the goods and services they want. Indeed, people quite casually trust their lives to the market system: residents of any major city would starve in days if the unplanned yet somehow orderly actions of thousands of businesses did not deliver a steady supply of food. Surprisingly, the unplanned "chaos" of a market economy turns out to be far more orderly than the "planning" of a command economy.

In 1776, in a famous passage in his book *The Wealth of Nations,* the pioneering Scottish economist Adam Smith wrote about how individuals, in pursuing their own interests, often end up serving the interests of society as a whole. Of a businessman whose pursuit of profit makes the nation wealthier, Smith wrote: "[H]e intends only his own gain, and he is in this, as in many other cases, led by an invisible hand to promote an end which was no part of his intention." Ever since, economists have used the term **invisible hand** to refer to the way a market

An **economy** is a system for coordinating society's productive activities.

Economics is the social science that studies the production, distribution, and consumption of goods and services.

A **market economy** is an economy in which decisions about production and consumption are made by individual producers and consumers.

The **invisible hand** refers to the way in which the individual pursuit of self-interest can lead to good results for society as a whole.

economy manages to harness the power of self-interest for the good of society.

The study of how individuals make decisions and how these decisions interact is called **microeconomics.** One of the key themes in microeconomics is the validity of Adam Smith's insight: individuals pursuing their own interests often do promote the interests of society as a whole.

So part of the answer to our time traveller's question—"How can my society achieve the kind of prosperity you take for granted?"—is that her society should learn to appreciate the virtues of a market economy and the power of the invisible hand.

But the invisible hand isn't always our friend. It's also important to understand when and why the individual pursuit of self-interest can lead to counterproductive behaviour.

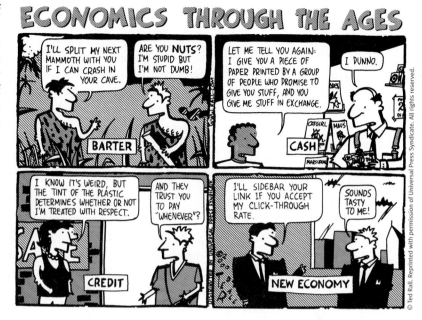

My Benefit, Your Cost

One thing that our time traveller would not admire about the modern Spring Garden Road area is the traffic. In fact, although most things have gotten better in Canada over time, traffic congestion has gotten a lot worse.

When traffic is congested, each driver is imposing a cost on all the other drivers on the road—he is literally getting in their way (and they are getting in his way). This cost can be substantial: in major metropolitan areas, each time someone drives to work instead of taking public transportation or working at home, he can easily impose $15 or more in hidden costs on other drivers. Yet when deciding whether or not to drive, commuters have no incentive to take the costs they impose on others into account.

Traffic congestion is a familiar example of a much broader problem: sometimes the individual pursuit of one's own interest, instead of promoting the interests of society as a whole, can actually make society worse off. When this happens, it is known as **market failure.** Other important examples of market failure involve air and water pollution as well as the overexploitation of natural resources such as fish and forests.

The good news, as you will learn if you study microeconomics, is that economic analysis can be used to diagnose cases of market failure. And often, economic analysis can also be used to devise solutions for the problem.

Good Times, Bad Times

Spring Garden Road was bustling on that day in 2013. But if you'd visited the stores in 2009, the scene wouldn't have been quite as cheerful. That's because Nova Scotia's economy, along with that of Canada as a whole, was depressed in 2009: in late 2008, businesses began laying off workers in large numbers, and employment didn't start bouncing back until the fall of 2009.

Such troubled periods are a regular feature of modern economies. The fact is that the economy does not always run smoothly: it experiences fluctuations, a series of ups and downs. By middle age, a typical Canadian will have experienced two or three downs, known as *recessions.* (The Canadian economy experienced serious recessions beginning in 1982, 1990, and 2008.) During a severe recession, hundreds of thousands of workers may be laid off.

Microeconomics is the branch of economics that studies how people make decisions and how these decisions interact.

When the individual pursuit of self-interest leads to bad results for society as a whole, there is **market failure.**

Macroeconomics is the branch of economics that is concerned with overall ups and downs in the economy.

Economic growth is the growing ability of the economy to produce goods and services.

Like market failure, recessions are a fact of life; but also like market failure, they are a problem for which economic analysis offers some solutions. Recessions are one of the main concerns of the branch of economics known as **macroeconomics,** which is concerned with the overall ups and downs of the economy. As you study macroeconomics, you will learn how economists explain recessions and how government policies can be used to minimize the damage from economic fluctuations.

Despite the occasional recession, however, over the long run the story of the Canadian economy contains many more ups than downs. And that long-run ascent is the subject of our final question.

Onward and Upward

At the beginning of the twentieth century, most Canadians lived under conditions that we would now think of as extreme poverty. Less than 10% of homes had flush toilets or central heating; even fewer had electricity, and almost nobody had a car, let alone a washing machine or modern electrical air conditioning, which did not arrive in homes until the 1920s.

Such comparisons are a stark reminder of how much our lives have been changed by **economic growth,** the growing ability of the economy to produce goods and services. Why does the economy grow over time? And why does economic growth occur faster in some times and places than in others? These are key questions for economics because economic growth is a good thing, as those shoppers on Spring Garden Road can attest, and most of us want more of it.

An Engine for Discovery

We hope we have convinced you that the "ordinary business of life" is really quite extraordinary, if you stop to think about it, and that it can lead us to ask some very interesting and important questions.

In this book, we will describe the answers economists have given to these questions. But this book, like economics as a whole, isn't a list of answers: it's an introduction to a discipline, a way to address questions like those we have just asked. Or as Alfred Marshall, who described economics as a study of the "ordinary business of life," put it: "Economics ... is not a body of concrete truth, but an engine for the discovery of concrete truth."

So let's turn the key and start the ignition.

KEY TERMS

Economy, p. 2
Economics, p. 2
Market economy, p. 2

Invisible hand, p. 2
Microeconomics, p. 3
Market failure, p. 3

Macroeconomics, p. 4
Economic growth, p. 4

First Principles

COMMON GROUND

One must choose.

WHAT YOU WILL LEARN IN THIS CHAPTER

❯ A set of principles for understanding the economics of how individuals make choices

❯ A set of principles for understanding how economies work through the interaction of individual choices

❯ A set of principles for understanding economy-wide interactions

THE ANNUAL MEETING OF THE Canadian Economic Association draws hundreds of economists, young and old, famous and obscure. There are booksellers, business meetings, and sometimes even a few job interviews. But mainly the economists gather to talk and listen. During the busiest times, 30 or more presentations may be taking place simultaneously on questions that range from financial market crises to who does the cooking in two-earner families.

What do these people have in common? An expert on financial markets probably knows very little about the economics of housework, and vice versa. Yet an economist who wanders into the wrong seminar and ends up listening to presentations on some unfamiliar topic is nonetheless likely to hear much that is familiar. The reason is that all economic analysis is based on a set of common principles that apply to many different issues.

Some of these principles involve *individual choice*—for economics is, first of all, about the choices that individuals make. Do you save your money and take the bus or do you buy a car? Do you keep your old smart phone or upgrade to a new one? These decisions involve *making a choice* from among a limited number of alternatives—limited because no one can have everything that he or she wants. Every question in economics at its most basic level involves individuals making choices.

But to understand how an economy works, you need to understand more than how individuals make choices. None of us is Robinson Crusoe, alone on an island. We must make decisions in an environment that is shaped by the decisions of others. Indeed, in a modern economy even the simplest decisions you make—say, what to have for breakfast—are shaped by the decisions of thousands of other people, from the banana grower in Costa Rica who decided to grow the fruit you eat to the farmer in Ontario who provided the corn in your cornflakes.

Because each of us in a market economy depends on so many others—and they, in turn, depend on us—our choices interact. So although all economics at a basic level is about individual choice, in order to understand how market economies behave we must also understand *economic interaction*—how my choices affect your choices, and vice versa.

Many important economic interactions can be understood by looking at the markets for individual goods, like the market for corn. But an economy as a whole has ups and downs, and we therefore need to understand economy-wide interactions as well as the more limited interactions that occur in individual markets.

In this chapter, we will look at twelve basic principles of economics—four principles involving individual choice, five involving the way individual choices interact, and three more involving economy-wide interactions. ∎

Principles That Underlie Individual Choice: The Core of Economics

Every economic issue involves, at its most basic level, **individual choice**—decisions by an individual about what to do and what not to do. In fact, you might say that it isn't economics if it isn't about choice.

Step into a big store like Walmart or Hudson's Bay. There are thousands of different products available, and it is extremely unlikely that you—or anyone else—could afford to buy everything you might want to have. And anyway, there's only so much space in your dorm room or apartment. So will you buy another bookcase or a mini-refrigerator? Given limitations on your budget and your living space, you must choose which products to buy and which to leave on the shelf.

The fact that those products are on the shelf in the first place involves choice—the store manager chose to put them there, and the manufacturers of the products chose to produce them. All economic activities involve individual choice.

Four economic principles underlie the economics of individual choice, as shown in Table 1-1. We'll now examine each of these principles in more detail.

TABLE **1-1**	The Principles of Individual Choice
1. People must make choices because resources are scarce.
2. The opportunity cost of an item—what you must give up in order to get it—is its true cost.
3. "How much" decisions require making trade-offs at the margin: comparing the costs and benefits of doing a little bit more of an activity versus doing a little bit less.
4. People usually respond to incentives, exploiting opportunities to make themselves better off.

Principle #1: Choices Are Necessary Because Resources Are Scarce

You can't always get what you want. Everyone would like to have a beautiful house in a great location (and have help with the housecleaning), a new car or two, and a nice vacation in a fancy hotel. But even in a rich country like Canada, not many families can afford all that. So they must make choices—whether to travel by train through the Rockies this year or buy a better car, whether to make do with a small backyard or accept a longer commute in order to live where land is cheaper.

Limited income isn't the only thing that keeps people from having everything they want. Time is also in limited supply: there are only 24 hours in a day. And because the time we have is limited, choosing to spend time on one activity also means choosing not to spend time on a different activity—spending time studying for an exam means forgoing a night spent watching a movie. Indeed, many people are so limited by the number of hours in the day that they are willing to trade money for time. For example, convenience stores normally charge higher prices than a regular supermarket. But they fulfill a valuable role by catering to time-pressured customers who would rather pay more than travel farther to the supermarket.

This leads us to our first principle of individual choice:

People must make choices because resources are scarce.

A **resource** is anything that can be used to produce something else. Lists of the economy's resources usually begin with land, labour (the time of workers), capital (machinery, buildings, and other manufactured productive assets), and human capital (the educational achievements and skills of workers). A resource is **scarce** when there's not enough of the resource available to satisfy all the ways a society wants to use it. There are many scarce resources. These include natural resources—resources that come from the physical environment, such as minerals, lumber, and petroleum. There is also a limited quantity of human resources—labour, skill, and intelligence. And in a growing world economy with a rapidly increasing human population, even clean air and water have become scarce resources.

Individual choice is the decision by an individual of what to do, which necessarily involves a decision of what not to do.

A **resource** is anything that can be used to produce something else.

Resources are **scarce**—not enough of the resources are available to satisfy all the various ways a society wants to use them.

Just as individuals must make choices, the scarcity of resources means that society as a whole must make choices. One way a society makes choices is by allowing them to emerge as the result of many individual choices, which is what usually happens in a market economy. For example, Canadians as a group have only so many hours in a week: how many of those hours will they spend going to supermarkets to get lower prices, rather than saving time by shopping at convenience stores? The answer is the sum of individual decisions: each of the millions of individuals in the economy makes his or her own choice about where to shop, and the overall choice is simply the sum of those individual decisions.

But for various reasons, there are some decisions that a society decides are best not left to individual choice. For example, the authors live in areas that until recently were mainly farmland but are now being rapidly built up. Most local residents feel that the community would be a more pleasant place to live if some of the land was left undeveloped. But no individual has an incentive to keep his or her land as open space, rather than sell it to a developer. So, a trend has emerged in many communities across Canada of governments either purchasing undeveloped land, or putting restrictions on its use, to preserve it as open space. For example, the federal government created Rouge Park, Canada's first urban national park, in the Greater Toronto area, to protect about 40 square kilometres of wilderness. The Agricultural Land Reserve was created by the provincial government of British Columbia to protect about 47 000 square kilometres of agricultural land. The Ontario government established the 7300 square kilometre greenbelt surrounding the Golden Horseshoe region to protect farmland and natural space from urban development. Similar greenbelts are proposed for Montreal and Quebec City.

We'll see in later chapters why decisions about how to use scarce resources are often best left to individuals but sometimes should be made at a higher, community-wide, level.

Principle #2: The True Cost of Something Is Its Opportunity Cost

It is the last term before you graduate, and your class schedule allows you to take only one elective. There are two, however, that you would really like to take: Intro to Computer Graphics and History of Jazz.

Suppose you decide to take the History of Jazz course. What's the cost of that decision? It is the fact that you can't take the computer graphics class, your next best alternative choice. Economists call that kind of cost—what you must give up in order to get an item you want—the **opportunity cost** of that item. This leads us to our second principle of individual choice:

> *The opportunity cost of an item—what you must give up in order to get it—is its true cost.*

So the opportunity cost of taking the History of Jazz class is the benefit you would have derived from the Intro to Computer Graphics class.

The concept of opportunity cost is crucial to understanding individual choice because, in the end, all decisions dealing with scarcity involve opportunity costs. That's because every choice you make means forgoing some other alternative and these costs can be both monetary and non-monetary.

Let's consider two cases for our elective course example. First, suppose that taking any elective class involves a tuition fee of $750. In this case, you would have to spend that $750 no matter which class you take. So what you give up to take the History of Jazz class is still only the benefit derived from the computer graphics class, period—you would have to spend that $750 either way. But suppose there isn't any fee for the computer graphics class. In that case, what you give up to take the jazz class is the benefit from the computer graphics class *plus* the benefit you could have gained from spending the $750 on other things.

So the opportunity costs of taking the History of Jazz class are both monetary (any additional tuition you paid over the computer graphics class) and

The real cost of an item is its **opportunity cost**: what you must give up in order to get it.

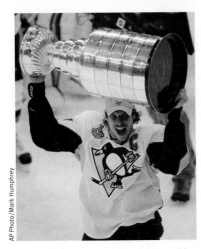

By the time he was eighteen years old, Sidney Crosby was playing in the NHL. He understood the concept of opportunity cost.

non-monetary (the benefits derived from taking the computer graphics class). In other words, the real cost of taking your preferred class is everything you must give up (by not choosing your next best alternative) to get it. As you expand the set of decisions that underlie each choice—whether to take an elective or not, whether to finish this term or not, whether to drop out or not—you'll realize that all costs are ultimately opportunity costs.

Sometimes the money you have to pay for something is a good indication of its opportunity cost. But many times it is not. One very important example of how poorly monetary cost alone can indicate opportunity cost is the cost of attending college or university. Tuition and housing are major monetary expenses for most post-secondary students; but even if these things were free, attending school would still be an expensive proposition because most college and university students, if they were not in school, would have a job. That is, by going to college or university, students *forgo* the income they could have earned if they had worked instead. This means that the opportunity cost of attending a post-secondary institution is what you pay for tuition and housing plus the forgone income you would have earned in a job.

It's easy to see that the opportunity cost of going to a post-secondary institution is especially high for people who could be earning a lot during what would otherwise have been their university or college years. That is why star athletes like Sidney Crosby, entertainers like Celine Dion, and entrepreneurs like Mike Lazardis, founder of BlackBerry, often skip or drop out of college. Other famous people who left school early include Mark Zuckerberg, Bill Gates, Steve Jobs, and Mick Jagger.

Principle #3: "How Much" Is a Decision at the Margin

Some important decisions involve an "either–or" choice—for example, you decide either to go to college or university or to begin working; you decide either to take economics or to take something else. But other important decisions involve "how much" choices—for example, if you are taking both economics and chemistry this semester, you must decide how much time to spend studying for each. When it comes to understanding "how much" decisions, economics has an important insight to offer: "how much" is a decision made at the margin.

Suppose you are taking both economics and chemistry. And suppose you are a pre-med student, so your grade in chemistry matters more to you than your grade in economics. Does that therefore imply that you should spend *all* your study time on chemistry and wing it on the economics exam? Probably not; even if you think your chemistry grade is more important, you should put some effort into studying economics.

Spending more time studying chemistry involves a benefit (a higher expected grade in that course) and a cost (you could have spent that time doing something else, such as studying to get a higher grade in economics). That is, your decision involves a **trade-off**—a comparison of costs and benefits.

How do you decide this kind of "how much" question? The typical answer is that you make the decision a bit at a time, by asking how you should spend the next hour. Say both exams are on the same day, and the night before you spend time reviewing your notes for both courses. At 6:00 P.M., you decide that it's a good idea to spend at least an hour on each course. At 8:00 P.M., you decide you'd better spend another hour on each course. At 10:00 P.M., you are getting tired and figure you have one more hour to study before bed—chemistry or economics? If you are pre-med, it's likely to be chemistry; if you are pre-MBA, it's likely to be economics.

Note how you've made the decision to allocate your time: at each point the question is whether or not to spend *one more hour* on either course. And in deciding whether to spend another hour studying for chemistry, you weigh the costs (an hour forgone of studying for economics or an hour forgone of sleeping) versus

You make a **trade-off** when you compare the costs with the benefits of doing something.

the benefits (a likely increase in your chemistry grade). As long as the benefit of studying chemistry for one more hour outweighs the cost, you should choose to study for that additional hour.

Decisions of this type—whether to do a bit more or a bit less of an activity, like what to do with your next hour, your next dollar, and so on—are **marginal decisions.** This brings us to our third principle of individual choice:

> *"How much" decisions require making trade-offs at the margin: comparing the costs and benefits of doing a little bit more of an activity versus doing a little bit less.*

The study of such decisions is known as **marginal analysis.** Many of the questions that we face in economics—as well as in real life—involve marginal analysis: How many workers should I hire in my shop? After how many kilometres of driving should I change the oil in my car? What is an acceptable rate of negative side effects from a new medicine? Marginal analysis plays a central role in economics because it is the key to deciding "how much" of an activity to do.

Principle #4: People Usually Respond to Incentives, Exploiting Opportunities to Make Themselves Better Off

One day, while listening to the morning financial news, one of the American-based authors of this textbook heard a great tip about how to park cheaply in Manhattan. Garages in the Wall Street area charge as much as $30 per day. But according to the newscaster, some people had found a better way: instead of parking in a garage, they had their oil changed at the Manhattan Jiffy Lube, where it costs $19.95 to change your oil—and they keep your car all day!

It's a great story, but unfortunately it turned out not to be true—in fact, there is no Jiffy Lube in Manhattan. But if there were, you can be sure there would be a lot of oil changes there. Why? Because when people are offered opportunities to make themselves better off, they normally take them—and if they could find a way to park their car all day for $19.95 rather than $30, they would.

In this example economists say that people are responding to an **incentive**—an opportunity to make themselves better off. We can now state our fourth principle of individual choice:

> *People usually respond to incentives, exploiting opportunities to make themselves better off.*

When you try to predict how individuals will behave in an economic situation, it is a very good bet that they will respond to incentives—that is, exploit opportunities to make themselves better off. Furthermore, individuals will *continue* to exploit these opportunities until they have been fully exhausted. If there really were a Manhattan Jiffy Lube and an oil change really were a cheap way to park your car, we can safely predict that before long the waiting list for oil changes would be weeks, if not months, long.

In fact, the principle that people will exploit opportunities to make themselves better off is the basis of *all* predictions by economists about individual behaviour. If the earnings of those who get MBAs soar while the earnings of those who get law degrees decline, we can expect more students to go to business school and fewer to go to law school. If the price of gasoline rises and stays high for an extended period of time, we can expect people to buy smaller cars with better fuel efficiency—making themselves better off in the presence of higher gas prices by driving more fuel-efficient cars.

One last point: economists tend to be skeptical of any attempt to change people's behaviour that *doesn't* change their incentives. For example, a plan that calls on manufacturers to reduce pollution voluntarily probably won't be effective

Decisions about whether to do a bit more or a bit less of an activity are **marginal decisions**. The study of such decisions is known as **marginal analysis**.

An **incentive** is anything that offers rewards to people who change their behaviour.

FOR INQUIRING MINDS

CASHING IN AT SCHOOL

The true reward for learning is, of course, the learning itself. Many students, however, struggle with their motivation to study and work hard. Teachers and policy-makers have been particularly challenged to help students from disadvantaged backgrounds, who often have poor school attendance, high dropout rates, and low standardized test scores. In a 2007–2008 study, Harvard economist Roland Fryer Jr. found that monetary incentives—cash rewards—could improve students' academic performance in schools in economically disadvantaged areas. How cash incentives work, however, is both surprising and predictable.

Fryer conducted his research in four different school districts, employing a different set of incentives and a different measure of performance in each. In New York City, students were paid according to their scores on standardized tests; in Chicago, they were paid according to their grades; in Washington, D.C., they were paid according to attendance and good behaviour as well as their grades; in Dallas, Grade Two students were paid each time they read a book. Fryer evaluated the results by comparing the performance of students who were in the program to other students in the same school who were not.

In New York, the program had no perceptible effect on test scores. In Chicago, students in the program got better grades and attended class more. In Washington, the program boosted the outcomes of the kids who are normally the hardest to reach, those with serious behavioural problems, raising their test scores by an amount equivalent to attending five extra months of school. The most dramatic results occurred in Dallas, where students significantly boosted their reading-comprehension test scores; results continued into the next year, after the cash rewards had ended.

So what explains the various results?

To motivate students with cash rewards, Fryer found that students had to believe that they could have a significant effect on the performance measure. So in Chicago, Washington, and Dallas—where students had a significant amount of control over outcomes such as grades, attendance, behaviour, and the number of books read—the program produced significant results. But because New York students had little idea how to affect their score on a standardized test, the prospect of a reward had little influence on their behaviour. Also, the timing of the reward matters: a $1 reward has more effect on behaviour if performance is measured at shorter intervals and the reward is delivered soon after.

Fryer's experiment revealed some critical insights about how to motivate behaviour with incentives. How incentives are designed is very important: the relationship between effort and outcome, as well as the speed of reward, matters a lot. Moreover, the design of incentives may depend quite a lot on the characteristics of the people you are trying to motivate: what motivates a student from an economically privileged background may not motivate a student

Cash incentives have been shown to improve student performance.

from an economically disadvantaged one. Fryer's insights give teachers and policy-makers an important new tool for helping disadvantaged students succeed in school.

In Canada, using publicly funded cash incentives to motivate at-risk students is a controversial topic. Some educators claim that financial incentives do work, and are needed, citing the success of such a program in Portage la Prairie, Manitoba. Aboriginal students at Portage Collegiate Institute receive $50 per month to attend school regularly and complete their homework. Students who graduate from Grade 12 receive $1000. This program is funded by the Long Plains First Nations. The result? More students are attending and graduating from Portage Collegiate. Similar programs are operating elsewhere in Canada. But many people think that other solutions should be found to encourage students. When, in 2010, the Toronto District School Board suggested paying students from disadvantaged communities, provincial politicians firmly rejected the plan.

because it hasn't changed manufacturers' incentives. In contrast, a plan that gives them a financial reward to reduce pollution or a penalty for not doing so is a lot more likely to work because it has changed their incentives.

So are we ready to do economics? Not yet—because most of the interesting things that happen in the economy are the result not merely of individual choices but of the way in which individual choices interact.

ECONOMICS ▸ IN ACTION

BOY OR GIRL? IT DEPENDS ON THE COST

One fact about China is indisputable: it's a big country with lots of people. As of 2013, the population of China was about 1 349 586 000. That's right: over *one billion three hundred million.*

In 1978, the government of China introduced the "one-child policy" to address the economic and demographic challenges presented by China's large population. China was very, very poor in 1978, and its leaders worried that the country could not afford to adequately educate and care for its growing population. The average Chinese woman in the 1970s was giving birth to more than five children during her lifetime. So the government restricted most couples, particularly those in urban areas, to one child, imposing penalties on those who defied the mandate. As a result, by 2013 the average number of births for a woman in China was only 1.6.

But the one-child policy had an unfortunate unintended consequence. Because China is an overwhelmingly rural country and sons can perform the manual labour of farming, families had a strong preference for sons over daughters. In addition, tradition dictates that brides become part of their husbands' families and that sons take care of their elderly parents. As a result of the one-child policy, China soon had too many "unwanted girls." Some were given up for adoption abroad, but all too many simply "disappeared" during the first year of life, the victims of neglect and mistreatment.

India, another highly rural poor country with high demographic pressures, also has a significant problem with "disappearing girls." In 1990, Amartya Sen, an Indian-born British economist who would go on to win the Nobel Prize in 1998, estimated that there were up to 100 million "missing women" in Asia. (The exact figure is in dispute, but it is clear that Sen identified a real and pervasive problem.)

Demographers have recently noted a distinct turn of events in China, which is quickly urbanizing. In all but one of the provinces with urban centres, the gender imbalance between boys and girls peaked in 1995 and has steadily fallen toward the biologically natural ratio since then. Many believe that the source of the change is China's strong economic growth and increasing urbanization. As people move to cities to take advantage of job growth there, they don't need sons to work the fields. Moreover, land prices in Chinese cities are skyrocketing, making the custom of parents buying an apartment for a son before he can marry unaffordable for many. To be sure, sons are still preferred in the rural areas. But as a sure mark of how times have changed, Internet websites have recently popped up that advise couples on how to have a girl rather than a boy.

The cost of China's "one-child policy" was a generation of "disappeared" daughters—a phenomenon that has itself begun to disappear as economic conditions have changed.

▼ **Quick Review**

- All economic activities involve **individual choice.**
- People must make choices because **resources** are **scarce.**
- The real cost of something is its **opportunity cost**—what you must give up to get it. All costs are opportunity costs. Monetary costs are sometimes a good indicator of opportunity costs, but not always.
- Many choices involve not *whether* to do something but *how much* of it to do. "How much" choices call for making a **trade-off** at the margin. The study of **marginal decisions** is known as **marginal analysis.**
- Because people usually exploit opportunities to make themselves better off, **incentives** can change people's behaviour.

CHECK YOUR UNDERSTANDING   1-1

1. Explain how each of the following situations illustrates one of the four principles of individual choice.
   a. You are on your third trip to a restaurant's all-you-can-eat dessert buffet and are feeling very full. Although it would cost you no additional money, you forgo a slice of coconut cream pie but have a slice of chocolate cake.
   b. Even if there were more resources in the world, there would still be scarcity.
   c. Different teaching assistants teach several Economics 101 tutorials. Those taught by the teaching assistants with the best reputations fill up quickly, with spaces left unfilled in the ones taught by assistants with poor reputations.
   d. To decide how many hours per week to exercise, you compare the health benefits of one more hour of exercise to the effect on your grades of one fewer hour spent studying.

2. You make $45 000 per year at your current job with Whiz Kids Consultants. You are considering a job offer from Brainiacs, Inc., that will pay you $50 000 per year. Which of the following are elements of the opportunity cost of accepting the new job at Brainiacs, Inc.?
   a. The increased time spent commuting to your new job
   b. The $45 000 salary from your old job
   c. The more spacious office at your new job

Interaction: How Economies Work

As we learned in the Introduction, an economy is a system for coordinating the productive activities of many people. In a market economy like we live in, coordination takes place without any coordinator: each individual makes his or her own choices. Yet those choices are by no means independent of one another: each individual's opportunities, and hence choices, depend to a large extent on the choices made by other people. So to understand how a market economy behaves, we have to examine this **interaction** in which my choices affect your choices, and vice versa.

When studying economic interaction, we quickly learn that the end result of individual choices may be quite different from what any one individual intends. For example, over the past century North American farmers have eagerly adopted new farming techniques and crop strains that have reduced their costs and increased their yields. Clearly, it's in the interest of each farmer to keep up with the latest farming techniques.

But the end result of each farmer trying to increase his or her own income has actually been to drive many farmers out of business. Because Canadian farmers have been so successful at producing larger yields, agricultural prices have steadily fallen. These falling prices have reduced the incomes of many farmers, and as a result fewer and fewer people find farming worth doing. That is, an individual farmer who plants a better variety of corn is better off; but when many farmers plant a better variety of corn, the result may be to make farmers as a group worse off.

A farmer who plants a new, more productive corn variety doesn't just grow more corn. Such a farmer also affects the market for corn through the increased yields attained, with consequences that will be felt by other farmers, consumers, and beyond.

Just as there are four economic principles that underlie individual choice, there are five principles that underlie the economics of interaction. These five principles are summarized in Table 1-2. We will now examine each of these principles more closely.

TABLE **1-2**	The Principles of the Interaction of Individual Choices
5.	There are gains from trade.
6.	Because people respond to incentives, markets move toward equilibrium.
7.	Resources should be used as efficiently as possible to achieve society's goals.
8.	Because people usually exploit gains from trade, markets usually lead to efficiency.
9.	When markets don't achieve efficiency, government intervention can improve society's welfare.

Principle #5: There Are Gains from Trade

Why do the choices I make interact with the choices you make? A family could try to take care of all its own needs—growing its own food, sewing its own clothing, providing itself with entertainment, writing its own economics textbooks. But trying to live that way would be very hard. The key to a much better standard of living for everyone is **trade,** in which people divide tasks among themselves and each person provides a good or service that other people want in return for different goods and services that he or she wants.

The reason we have an economy, not many self-sufficient individuals, is that there are **gains from trade:** by dividing tasks and trading, two people (or 7 billion people) can each get more of what they want than they could get by being self-sufficient. This leads us to our fifth principle:

There are gains from trade.

Gains from trade arise from this division of tasks, which economists call **specialization**—a situation in which different people each engage in a different task, specializing in those tasks that they are good at performing. The advantages of specialization, and the resulting gains from trade, were the starting point for Adam Smith's 1776 book *The Wealth of Nations,* which many regard as the beginning of economics as a discipline. Smith's book begins with a description of an eighteenth-

Interaction of choices—my choices affect your choices, and vice versa—is a feature of most economic situations. The results of this interaction are often quite different from what the individuals intend.

In a market economy, individuals engage in **trade:** they provide goods and services to others and receive goods and services in return.

There are **gains from trade:** people can get more of what they want through trade than they could if they tried to be self-sufficient. This increase in output is due to **specialization:** each person specializes in the task that he or she is good at performing.

century pin factory where, rather than each of the 10 workers making a pin from start to finish, each worker specialized in one of the many steps in pin-making:

> One man draws out the wire, another straights it, a third cuts it, a fourth points it, a fifth grinds it at the top for receiving the head; to make the head requires two or three distinct operations; to put it on, is a particular business, to whiten the pins is another; it is even a trade by itself to put them into the paper; and the important business of making a pin is, in this manner, divided into about eighteen distinct operations … . Those ten persons, therefore, could make among them upwards of forty-eight thousand pins in a day. But if they had all wrought separately and independently, and without any of them having been educated to this particular business, they certainly could not each of them have made twenty, perhaps not one pin a day … .

The same principle applies when we look at how people divide tasks among themselves and trade in an economy. *The economy, as a whole, can produce more when each person specializes in a task and trades with others.*

The benefits of specialization are the reason a person typically chooses only one career. It takes many years of study and experience to become a doctor; it also takes many years of study and experience to become a commercial airline pilot. Many doctors might well have had the potential to become excellent pilots, and vice versa; but it is very unlikely that anyone who decided to pursue both careers would be as good a pilot or as good a doctor as someone who decided at the beginning to specialize in that field. So it is to everyone's advantage that individuals specialize in their career choices.

"I hunt and she gathers—otherwise we couldn't make ends meet."

Markets are what allow a doctor and a pilot to specialize in their own fields. Because markets for commercial flights and for doctors' services exist, a doctor is assured that she can find a flight and a pilot is assured that he can find a doctor. As long as individuals know that they can find the goods and services they want in the market, they are willing to forgo self-sufficiency and to specialize. But what assures people that markets will deliver what they want? The answer to that question leads us to our second principle of how individual choices interact.

Principle #6: Markets Move Toward Equilibrium

It's a busy afternoon at the supermarket; there are long lines at the checkout counters. Then one of the previously closed cash registers opens. What happens? The first thing, of course, is a rush to that register. After a couple of minutes, however, things will have settled down; shoppers will have rearranged themselves so that the line at the newly opened register is about the same length as the lines at all the other registers.

How do we know that? We know from our fourth principle that people will exploit opportunities to make themselves better off. This means that people will rush to the newly opened register in order to save time standing in line. And things will settle down when shoppers can no longer improve their position by switching lines—that is, when the opportunities to make themselves better off have all been exploited.

A story about supermarket checkout lines may seem to have little to do with how individual choices interact, but in fact it illustrates an important principle. A situation in which individuals cannot make themselves better off by doing something different—the situation in which all the checkout lines are the same length—is what economists call an **equilibrium.** An economic situation is in equilibrium when no individual would be better off doing something different.

Recall the story about the mythical Jiffy Lube, where it was supposedly cheaper to leave your car for an oil change than to pay for parking. If the opportunity had really existed and people were still paying $30 to park in garages, the situation

An economic situation is in **equilibrium** when no individual would be better off doing something different.

CHOOSING SIDES

Why do people in North America drive on the right side of the road? Of course, it's the law. But long before it was the law, it was an equilibrium.

Before there were formal traffic laws, there were informal "rules of the road," practices that everyone expected everyone else to follow. These rules included an understanding that people would normally keep to one side of the road. In some places, such as England, the rule was to keep to the left; in others, such as France, it was to keep to the right.

Why would some places choose the right and others, the left? That's not completely clear, although it may have depended on the dominant form of traffic. Men riding horses and carrying swords on their left hip preferred to ride on the left (think about getting on or off the horse, and you'll see why). On the other hand, right-handed people walking but leading horses apparently preferred to walk on the right.

In any case, once a rule of the road was established, there were strong incentives for each individual to stay on the "usual" side of the road: those who didn't would keep colliding with oncoming traffic. So once established, the rule of the road would be self-enforcing—that is, it would be an equilibrium. Nowadays, of course, which side you drive on is determined by law; some jurisdictions have even changed sides. British Columbia, New Brunswick,

Nova Scotia, and Prince Edward Island all switched from the left to the right in the 1920s, and Newfoundland switched in 1947, two years before it joined Canada. In Europe, Sweden and Iceland went from left to right in the 1960s.

But what about pedestrians? There are no laws—but there are informal rules. In Canada, urban pedestrians normally keep to the right. But if you should happen to visit a country where people drive on the left, watch out: people who drive on the left also typically walk on the left. So when in a foreign country, do as the locals do. You won't be arrested if you walk on the right, but you will be worse off than if you accept the equilibrium and walk on the left.

---

would *not* have been an equilibrium. And that should have been a giveaway that the story couldn't be true. In reality, people would have seized an opportunity to park cheaply, just as they seize opportunities to save time at the checkout line. And in so doing they would have eliminated the opportunity! Either it would have become very hard to get an appointment for an oil change or the price of a lube job would have increased to the point that it was no longer an attractive option (unless you really needed a lube job). This brings us to our sixth principle:

> ***Because people respond to incentives, markets move toward equilibrium.***

As we will see, markets usually reach equilibrium via changes in prices, which rise or fall until no opportunities for individuals to make themselves better off remain.

The concept of equilibrium is extremely helpful in understanding economic interactions because it provides a way of cutting through the sometimes complex details of those interactions. To understand what happens when a new line is opened at a supermarket, you don't need to worry about exactly how shoppers rearrange themselves, who moves ahead of whom, which register just opened, and so on. What you need to know is that any time there is a change, the situation will move to an equilibrium.

The fact that markets move toward equilibrium is why we can depend on them to work in a predictable way. In fact, we can trust markets to supply us with the essentials of life. For example, people who live in big cities can be sure that the supermarket shelves will always be fully stocked. Why? Because if some merchants who distribute food *didn't* make deliveries, a big profit opportunity would be created for any merchant who did—and there would be a rush to supply food, just like the rush to a newly opened cash register. So the market ensures that food will always be available for city dwellers. And, returning to our fifth principle, this allows city dwellers to be city dwellers—to specialize in doing city jobs rather than living on farms and growing their own food.

A market economy, as we have seen, allows people to achieve gains from trade. But how do we know how well such an economy is doing? The next principle gives us a standard to use in evaluating an economy's performance.

Principle #7: Resources Should Be Used Efficiently to Achieve Society's Goals

Suppose you are taking a course in which the classroom is too small for the number of students—many people are forced to stand or sit on the floor—despite the fact that large, empty classrooms are available nearby. You would say, correctly, that this is no way to run a college or university. Economists would call this an *inefficient* use of resources. But if an inefficient use of resources is undesirable, just what does it mean to use resources *efficiently*? You might imagine that the efficient use of resources has something to do with money, maybe that it is measured in dollars-and-cents terms. But in economics, as in life, money is only a means to other ends. The measure that economists really care about is not money but people's happiness or welfare. Economists say that *an economy's resources are used efficiently when they are used in a way that has fully exploited all opportunities to make everyone better off.* To put it another way, an economy is **efficient** if it takes all opportunities to make some people better off without making other people worse off.

In our classroom example, there clearly was a way to make everyone better off—moving the class to a larger room would make people in the class better off without hurting anyone else in the school. Assigning the course to the smaller classroom was an inefficient use of the school's resources, whereas assigning the course to the larger classroom would have been an efficient use of the school's resources.

When an economy is efficient, it is producing the maximum gains from trade possible given the resources available. Why? Because there is no way to rearrange how resources are used in a way that can make everyone better off. When an economy is efficient, one person can be made better off by rearranging how resources are used *only* by making someone else worse off. In our classroom example, if all larger classrooms were already occupied by large classes, the school would have been run in an efficient way: your class could be made better off by moving to a larger classroom only by making people in the larger classroom worse off by making them move to a smaller classroom.

We can now state our seventh principle:

> ***Resources should be used as efficiently as possible to achieve society's goals.***

Should economic policy-makers always strive to achieve economic efficiency? Well, not quite, because efficiency is only a means to achieving society's goals. Sometimes efficiency may conflict with a goal that society has deemed worthwhile to achieve. For example, in most societies, people also care about issues of fairness, or **equity.** And there is typically a trade-off between equity and efficiency: policies that promote equity often come at a cost of decreased efficiency in the economy, and vice versa.

To see this, consider the case of disabled-designated parking spaces in public parking lots. Many people have difficulty walking due to age or disability, so it seems only fair to assign closer parking spaces specifically for their use. You may have noticed, however, that a certain amount of inefficiency is involved. To make sure that there is always a parking space available should a person with disabilities want one, there are typically more such spaces available than there are people with disabilities who want one. As a result, desirable parking spaces are unused. (And the temptation for people without disabilities to use them is so great that we must be dissuaded by fear of getting a ticket.) So, short of hiring parking valets to allocate spaces, there is a conflict between *equity*, making life "fairer" for people with disabilities, and *efficiency*, making sure that all opportunities to make people better off have been fully exploited by never letting close-in parking spaces go unused.

An economy is **efficient** if it takes all opportunities to make some people better off without making other people worse off.

Equity means that everyone gets his or her fair share. Since people can disagree about what's "fair," equity isn't as well defined a concept as efficiency.

Construction Photography/Corbis

Sometimes equity trumps efficiency.

Exactly how far policy-makers should go in promoting equity over efficiency is a difficult question that goes to the heart of the political process. As such, it is not a question that economists can answer. What is important for economists, however, is always to seek to use the economy's resources as efficiently as possible in the pursuit of society's goals, whatever those goals may be.

Principle #8: Markets Usually Lead to Efficiency

No branch of the Canadian government is entrusted with ensuring the general economic efficiency of our market economy—we don't have agents who go around making sure that brain surgeons aren't plowing fields or that Manitoba farmers aren't trying to grow oranges. The government doesn't need to enforce the efficient use of resources, because in most cases the invisible hand does the job.

The incentives built into a market economy ensure that resources are usually put to good use and that opportunities to make people better off are not wasted. If a university or college were known for its habit of crowding students into small classrooms while large classrooms went unused, it would soon find its enrollment dropping, putting the jobs of its administrators at risk. The "market" for post-secondary students would respond in a way that induced administrators to run the school efficiently.

A detailed explanation of why markets are usually very good at making sure that resources are used well will have to wait until we have studied how markets actually work. But the most basic reason is that in a market economy, in which individuals are free to choose what to consume and what to produce, people normally exploit opportunities for mutual gain—that is, gains from trade. If there is a way in which some people can be made better off, people will usually be able to take advantage of that opportunity. And that is exactly what defines efficiency: all the opportunities to make some people better off without making other people worse off have been exploited. This gives rise to our eighth principle:

> *Because people usually exploit gains from trade, markets usually lead to efficiency.*

As we learned in the Introduction, however, there are exceptions to this principle that markets are generally efficient. In cases of *market failure*, the individual pursuit of self-interest found in markets makes society worse off—that is, the market outcome is inefficient. And, as we will see in examining the next principle, when markets fail, government intervention can help. But short of instances of market failure, the general rule is that markets are a remarkably good way of organizing an economy.

Principle #9: When Markets Don't Achieve Efficiency, Government Intervention Can Improve Society's Welfare

Let's recall from the Introduction the nature of the market failure caused by traffic congestion—a commuter driving to work has no incentive to take into account the cost that his or her action inflicts on other drivers in the form of increased traffic congestion. There are several possible remedies to this situation; examples include charging road tolls, subsidizing the cost of public transportation, and taxing sales of gasoline to individual drivers. All these remedies work by changing the incentives of would-be drivers, motivating them to drive less and use alternative transportation. But they also share another feature: each relies on government intervention in the market. This brings us to our ninth principle:

> *When markets don't achieve efficiency, government intervention can improve society's welfare.*

That is, when markets go wrong, an appropriately designed government policy can sometimes move society closer to an efficient outcome by changing how society's resources are used.

A very important branch of economics is devoted to studying why markets fail and what policies should be adopted to improve social welfare. These problems and their remedies are commonly studied in texts on microeconomics; but, briefly, there are three principal ways in which they fail:

- Individual actions have side effects that are not properly taken into account by the market. An example is an action that causes pollution.

- One party prevents mutually beneficial trades from occurring in an attempt to capture a greater share of resources for itself. An example is a drug company that prices a drug higher than the cost of producing it, making it unaffordable for some people who would benefit from it.

- Some goods, by their very nature, are unsuited for efficient management by markets. An example of such a good is air traffic control.

An important part of your education in economics is learning to identify not just when markets work but also when they don't work, and to judge what government policies are appropriate in each situation.

ECONOMICS ▶ IN ACTION

RESTORING EQUILIBRIUM ON THE FREEWAYS

Back in 1994 a powerful earthquake struck the Los Angeles area, causing several freeway bridges to collapse and thereby disrupting the normal commuting routes of hundreds of thousands of drivers. The events that followed offer a particularly clear example of interdependent decision-making—in this case, the decisions of commuters about how to get to work.

In the immediate aftermath of the earthquake, there was great concern about the impact on traffic, since motorists would now have to crowd onto alternative routes or detour around the blockages by using city streets. Public officials and news programs warned commuters to expect massive delays and urged them to avoid unnecessary travel, reschedule their work to commute before or after the rush, or use mass transit. These warnings were unexpectedly effective. In fact, so many people heeded them that in the first few days following the quake, those who maintained their regular commuting routine actually found the drive to and from work faster than before.

Witness equilibrium in action on a Los Angeles freeway.

Glowimages/Getty Images

Of course, this situation could not last. As word spread that traffic was relatively light, people abandoned their less convenient new commuting methods and reverted to their cars—and traffic got steadily worse. Within a few weeks after the quake, serious traffic jams had appeared. After a few more weeks, however, the situation stabilized: the reality of worse-than-usual congestion discouraged enough drivers to prevent the nightmare of citywide gridlock from materializing. Los Angeles traffic, in short, had settled into a new equilibrium, in which each commuter was making the best choice he or she could, given what everyone else was doing.

This was not, by the way, the end of the story: fears that the city would strangle on traffic led local authorities to repair the roads with record speed. A mere 18 months after the quake, all the freeways were back to normal.

CHECK YOUR UNDERSTANDING 1-2

1. Explain how each of the following situations illustrates one of the five principles of interaction.
   a. Using a university website, any student who wants to sell a used textbook for at least $30 is able to sell it to someone who is willing to pay $30.
   b. At a college tutoring co-op, students can arrange to provide tutoring in subjects they are good in (like economics) in return for receiving tutoring in subjects they are poor in (like philosophy).
   c. The local municipality imposes a law that requires bars and nightclubs near residential areas to keep their noise levels below a certain threshold.
   d. To provide better care for low-income patients, the province has decided to close some underutilized neighbourhood clinics and shift funds to nearby hospitals.
   e. On a university website, books of a given title with approximately the same level of wear and tear sell for about the same price.

2. Which of the following describes an equilibrium situation? Which does not? Explain your answer.
   a. The restaurants across the street from the university dining hall serve better-tasting and cheaper meals than those served at the university dining hall. The vast majority of students continue to eat at the dining hall.
   b. You currently take the bus to work. Although riding your bicycle is cheaper, the ride takes longer. So you are willing to pay the higher transit fare in order to save time.

Solutions appear at back of book.

Economy-Wide Interactions

TABLE 1-3 The Principles of Economy-Wide Interactions

10. One person's spending is another person's income.
11. Overall spending sometimes gets out of line with the economy's productive capacity.
12. Government policies can change overall spending.

As we mentioned in the Introduction, the economy as a whole has its ups and downs. For example, business for Canada's auto dealers and shopping malls was depressed in 2009, because the economy was in a recession. By 2013, the economy had somewhat recovered. To understand recessions and recoveries, we need to understand economy-wide interactions, and understanding the big picture of the economy requires understanding three more important economic principles. Those three economy-wide principles are summarized in Table 1-3.

Principle #10: One Person's Spending Is Another Person's Income

In late 2008, home construction in Canada began a rapid decline because builders found it increasingly hard to make sales. At first the damage was mainly limited to the construction industry. But over time the slump spread into just about every part of the economy, with consumer spending falling across the board.

But why should a fall in home construction mean empty stores in the shopping malls? After all, malls are places where families, not builders, do their shopping. The answer is that lower spending on construction led to lower incomes throughout the economy; people who had been employed either directly in construction, producing goods and services builders need (like drywall), or in producing goods and services new homeowners need (like new furniture), either lost their jobs or were forced to take pay cuts—or expected that these steps might be imminent. And as incomes fell, so did spending by consumers. This example illustrates our tenth principle:

One person's spending is another person's income.

In a market economy, people make a living selling things—including their labour—to other people. If some group in the economy decides, for whatever reason, to spend more, the income of other groups will rise. If some group decides to spend less, the income of other groups will fall.

Because one person's spending is another person's income, a chain reaction of changes in spending behaviour tends to have repercussions that spread through the economy. For example, a cut in business investment spending, like the one that happened in 2009, leads to reduced family incomes; families respond by reducing consumer spending; this leads to another round of income cuts; and so on. These repercussions play an important role in our understanding of recessions and recoveries.

Principle #11: Overall Spending Sometimes Gets Out of Line with the Economy's Productive Capacity

Macroeconomics emerged as a separate branch of economics in the 1930s, when a collapse of consumer and business spending, a crisis in the U.S. banking industry, and other factors led to a plunge in overall spending. This plunge in spending, in turn, led to a period of very high unemployment worldwide known as the Great Depression.

The lesson economists learned from the troubles of the 1930s is that overall spending—the amount of goods and services that consumers and businesses want to buy—sometimes doesn't match the amount of goods and services the economy is capable of producing. In the 1930s, spending fell far short of what was needed to keep Canadian workers employed, and the result was a severe economic slump. In fact, shortfalls in spending are responsible for most, though not all, recessions.

It's also possible for overall spending to be too high. In that case, the economy experiences *inflation*, a rise in prices throughout the economy. This rise in prices occurs because when the amount that people want to buy outstrips the supply, producers can raise their prices and still find willing customers. Taking account of both shortfalls in spending and excesses in spending brings us to our eleventh principle:

> ***Overall spending sometimes gets out of line with the economy's productive capacity.***

Principle #12: Government Policies Can Change Overall Spending

Overall spending sometimes gets out of line with the economy's productive capacity. But can anything be done about that? Yes—which leads to our twelfth and last principle:

> ***Government policies can change overall spending.***

In fact, government policies can dramatically affect overall spending (sometimes referred to as aggregate expenditure).

For one thing, the government itself does a lot of spending on everything from military equipment to employment insurance benefits—and it can choose to do more or less. The government can also vary how much it collects from the public in taxes, which in turn affects how much income consumers and businesses have left to spend. And the government's control of the quantity of money in circulation, it turns out, gives it another powerful tool with which to affect total spending. Government spending, taxes, and control of the money supply are the tools of *macroeconomic policy*.

Modern governments deploy these macroeconomic policy tools in an effort to manage overall spending in the economy, trying to steer it between the perils of recession and inflation. These efforts aren't always successful—recessions still happen, and so do periods of inflation. But it's widely believed that aggressive efforts to sustain spending in 2009 and 2010, such as Canada's Economic Action Plan, helped prevent the financial crisis of 2008 from turning into a full-blown depression.

As participants in a babysitting co-op soon discovered, fewer nights out made everyone worse off.

ECONOMICS > IN ACTION

ADVENTURES IN BABYSITTING

The website sittingaround.com, which offers advice to families on locating babysitting services, suggests that parents consider joining a babysitting co-operative—an arrangement that is common in many walks of life. In a babysitting co-operative, a number of parents exchange babysitting services rather than hire someone to babysit. But how do these organizations make sure that all members do their fair share of the work? As sittingaround.com explains, "Instead of exchanging cash, members simply exchange sitting for sitting. Coops make sure everything nets out equitably by tracking points. You get points when you sit for someone else, and you spend points when others are sitting for you. The Johnsons can sit for the Browns, the Browns can sit for the Smiths, and the Smiths can sit for the Johnsons. Because you are part of a group, you never have to worry about reciprocating directly with those sitting for you—eventually, it all gets around."

In other words, a babysitting co-op is a miniature economy in which people buy and sell babysitting services. And it happens to be a type of economy that can have macroeconomic problems. A famous article titled "Monetary Theory and the Great Capitol Hill Babysitting Co-Op Crisis," published in 1977, described the troubles of a babysitting co-operative that issued too few tickets (its medium for tracking points). Bear in mind that, on average, people in a babysitting co-op want to have a reserve of tickets or points in case they need to go out several times before they can replenish their reserve by doing some more babysitting.

In this case, because there weren't that many tickets out there to begin with, most parents were anxious to add to their reserves by babysitting but reluctant to run them down by going out. But one parent's decision to go out was another's chance to babysit, so it became difficult to earn tickets. Knowing this, parents became even more reluctant to use their reserves except on special occasions.

In short, the co-op had fallen into a recession. Recessions in the larger, non-babysitting economy are a bit more complicated than this, but the troubles of the Capitol Hill babysitting co-op demonstrate two of our three principles of economy-wide interactions. One person's spending is another person's income: opportunities to babysit arose only to the extent that other people went out. And an economy can suffer from too little spending: when not enough people were willing to go out, everyone was frustrated at the lack of babysitting opportunities.

And what about government policies to change spending? Actually, the Capitol Hill co-op did that, too. Eventually, it solved its problem by handing out more tickets, and with increased reserves, people were willing to go out more.

CHECK YOUR UNDERSTANDING   1-3

1. Explain how each of the following examples illustrates one of the three principles of economy-wide interactions.
   a. The prime minister urged Parliament to pass a package of temporary spending increases and tax cuts in early 2009, a time when employment was plunging and unemployment soaring.
   b. Oil companies are investing heavily in projects that will extract oil from the "oil sands" in Alberta. In Edmonton, near the projects, restaurants and other consumer businesses are booming.
   c. In the mid-2000s, Spain, which was experiencing a big housing boom, also had the highest inflation rate in Europe.

Solutions appear at back of book.

iStockphoto

▼ Quick Review

● In a market economy, one person's spending is another person's income. As a result, changes in spending behaviour have repercussions that spread through the economy.

● Overall spending sometimes gets out of line with the economy's capacity to produce goods and services. When spending is too low, the result is a recession. When spending is too high, it causes inflation.

● Modern governments use macroeconomic policy tools to affect the overall level of spending in an effort to steer the economy between recession and inflation.

BUSINESS CASE • How Priceline.com Revolutionized the Travel Industry

In 2001 and 2002, the travel industry was in deep trouble. After the terrorist attacks of September 11, 2001, many people simply stopped flying. As the economy went into a deep slump, airplanes sat empty on the tarmac and airlines around the world lost billions of dollars. When several major U.S. airlines spiralled toward bankruptcy and laid off more than 100 000 workers, the U.S. Congress passed a US$15 billion aid package that was critical in stabilizing the American airline industry. At the same time, Air Canada, sought a government bailout of $2 to $4 billion. In the end, the Canadian government compensated all Canadian air carriers with a bailout package worth $160 million.

This was also a particularly difficult time for Priceline.com, the online travel service. Just four years after its founding, Priceline.com was in danger of going under. The change in the company's fortunes had been dramatic. In 1999, one year after Priceline.com was formed, investors were so impressed by its potential for revolutionizing the travel industry that they valued the company at US$9 billion dollars. But by 2002 investors had taken a decidedly dimmer view of the company, reducing its valuation by 95% to only US$425 million.

To make matters worse, Priceline.com was losing several million dollars a year. Yet the company managed to survive; as of the time of writing in 2013, it was valued by investors at US$40.3 billion. Not only has it survived, it has thrived.

So exactly how did Priceline.com bring such dramatic change to the travel industry? And what has allowed it to survive and prosper as a company in the face of dire economic conditions?

Priceline.com's success lies in its ability to spot exploitable opportunities for itself and its customers. The company understood that when a plane departs with empty seats or a hotel has empty beds, it bears a cost—the revenue that would have been earned if that seat or bed had been filled. And although some travellers like the security of booking their flights and hotels well in advance and are willing to pay for that, others are quite happy to wait until the last minute, risking not getting the flight or hotel they want but enjoying a lower price.

Customers specify the price they are willing to pay for a given trip or hotel location, and then Priceline.com presents them with a list of options from airlines or hotels that are willing to accept that price, with the price typically declining as the date of the trip nears. By bringing airlines and hotels with unsold capacity together with travellers who are willing to sacrifice some of their preferences for a lower price, Priceline.com made everyone better off—including itself, since it charged a small commission for each trade it facilitated.

Priceline.com was also quick on its feet when it saw its market challenged by newcomers Expedia and Orbitz. In response, it began aggressively moving more of its business toward hotel bookings and into Europe, where the online travel industry was still quite small. Its network was particularly valuable in the European hotel market, which is comprised of many more small hotels in comparison to the North American market, which is dominated by nationwide chains. The efforts paid off, and by 2003 Priceline.com had turned its first profit.

Priceline.com now operates within a network of more than 295 000 hotels in over 190 countries and territories globally. As of 2013, its revenues had grown at least 21% over each of the previous three years, even growing during the recession by 24% in 2009 and 32% in 2010.

QUESTION FOR THOUGHT

1. Explain how each of the twelve principles of economics is illustrated in this story.

SUMMARY

1. All economic analysis is based on a set of basic principles that apply to three levels of economic activity. First, we study how individuals make choices; second, we study how these choices interact; and third, we study how the economy functions overall.

2. Everyone has to make choices about what to do and what *not* to do. **Individual choice** is the basis of economics—if it doesn't involve choice, it isn't economics.

3. The reason choices must be made is that **resources**—anything that can be used to produce something else—are **scarce.** Individuals are limited in their choices by money and time; economies are limited by their supplies of human and natural resources.

4. Because you must choose among limited alternatives, the true cost of anything is what you must give up to get it—all costs are **opportunity costs.**

5. Many economic decisions involve questions not of "whether" but of "how much"—how much to spend on some good, how much to produce, and so on. Such decisions must be made by performing a **trade-off** *at the margin*—by comparing the costs and benefits of doing a bit more or a bit less. Decisions of this type are called **marginal decisions,** and the study of them, **marginal analysis,** plays a central role in economics.

6. The study of how people *should* make decisions is also a good way to understand actual behaviour. Individuals usually respond to **incentives**—exploiting opportunities to make themselves better off.

7. The next level of economic analysis is the study of **interaction**—how my choices depend on your choices, and vice versa. When individuals interact, the end result may be different from what anyone intends.

8. Individuals interact because there are **gains from trade:** by engaging in the **trade** of goods and services with one another, the members of an economy can all be made better off. **Specialization**—each person specializes in the task he or she is good at—is the source of gains from trade.

9. Because individuals usually respond to incentives, markets normally move toward **equilibrium**—a situation in which no individual can make himself or herself better off by taking a different action.

10. An economy is **efficient** if all opportunities to make some people better off without making other people worse off are taken. Resources should be used as efficiently as possible to achieve society's goals. But efficiency is not the sole way to evaluate an economy: **equity,** or fairness, is also desirable, and there is often a trade-off between equity and efficiency.

11. Markets usually lead to efficiency, with some well-defined exceptions.

12. When markets fail and do not achieve efficiency, government intervention can improve society's welfare.

13. Because people in a market economy earn income by selling things, including their own labour, one person's spending is another person's income. As a result, changes in spending behaviour can spread throughout the economy.

14. Overall spending in the economy can get out of line with the economy's productive capacity. Spending below the economy's productive capacity leads to a recession; spending in excess of the economy's productive capacity leads to inflation.

15. Governments have the ability to strongly affect overall spending, an ability they use in an effort to steer the economy between recession and inflation.

KEY TERMS

Individual choice, p. 6
Resource, p. 6
Scarce, p. 6
Opportunity cost, p. 7
Trade-off, p. 8

Marginal decisions, p. 9
Marginal analysis, p. 9
Incentive, p. 9
Interaction, p. 12
Trade, p. 12

Gains from trade, p. 12
Specialization, p. 12
Equilibrium, p. 13
Efficient, p. 15
Equity, p. 15

PROBLEMS

1. In each of the following situations, identify which of the twelve principles is at work.

   a. You choose to shop at the local discount store rather than paying a higher price for the same merchandise at the local department store.

   b. On your spring break trip, your budget is limited to $35 a day.

   c. The student union provides a website on which departing students can sell items such as used books, appliances, and furniture rather than give them away to their roommates as they formerly did.

   d. After a hurricane did extensive damage to homes on the island of St. Crispin, homeowners wanted to purchase many more building materials and hire many more workers than were available on the island. As a result, prices for goods and services rose dramatically across the board.

   e. You buy a used textbook from your roommate. Your roommate uses the money to buy songs from iTunes.

   f. You decide how many cups of coffee to have when studying the night before an exam by considering how much more work you can do by having another cup versus how jittery it will make you feel.

   g. There is limited lab space available to do the project required in Chemistry 101. The lab supervisor assigns lab time to each student based on when that student is able to come.

   h. You realize that you can graduate a semester early by forgoing a semester of study abroad.

   i. At the student union, there is a bulletin board on which people advertise used items for sale, such as bicycles. Once you have adjusted for differences in quality, all the bikes sell for about the same price.

   j. You are better at performing lab experiments, and your lab partner is better at writing lab reports. So the two of you agree that you will do all the experiments and she will write up all the reports.

   k. Provincial and territorial governments mandate that it is illegal to drive without passing a driving exam.

   l. Your parents' after-tax income has increased because of a tax cut passed by Parliament. They therefore increase your allowance, which you spend on a spring break vacation.

2. Describe some of the opportunity costs when you decide to do the following.

   a. Attend college or university instead of taking a job

   b. Watch a movie instead of studying for an exam

   c. Ride the bus instead of driving your car

3. Liza needs to buy a textbook for the next economics class. The price at the university bookstore is $65. One online site offers it for $55 and another site, for $57. All prices include sales tax. The accompanying table indicates the typical shipping and handling charges for the textbook ordered online.

Shipping method	Delivery time	Charge
Standard shipping	3–7 days	$3.99
Second-day air	2 business days	8.98
Next-day air	1 business day	13.98

   a. What is the opportunity cost of buying online instead of at the bookstore? Note that if you buy the book online, you must wait to get it.

   b. Show the relevant choices for this student. What determines which of these options the student will choose?

4. Use the concept of opportunity cost to explain the following.

   a. More people choose to get graduate degrees when the job market is poor.

   b. More people choose to do their own home repairs when the economy is slow and hourly wages are down.

   c. There are more parks in suburban than in urban areas.

   d. Convenience stores, which have higher prices than supermarkets, cater to busy people.

   e. Fewer students enroll in classes that meet before 10:00 A.M.

5. In the following examples, state how you would use the principle of marginal analysis to make a decision.

   a. Deciding how many days to wait before doing your laundry

   b. Deciding how much library research to do before writing your term paper

   c. Deciding how many bags of chips to eat

   d. Deciding how many lectures of a class to skip

6. This morning you made the following individual choices: you bought a bagel and coffee at the local café, you drove to school in your car during rush hour, and you typed your roommate's term paper because you are a fast typist—in return for which she will do your laundry for a month. For each of these actions, describe how your individual choices interacted with the individual choices made by others. Were other people left better off or worse off by your choices in each case?

7. The Duguay family lives on the east side of Shediac Bay, and the Legault family lives on the west side. Each family's diet consists of lobster and potatoes, and each is self-sufficient, trapping their own lobsters and growing

their own potatoes. Explain the conditions under which each of the following would be true.

a. The two families are made better off when the Duguays specialize in trapping lobsters, the Legaults specialize in growing potatoes, and the two families trade.

b. The two families are made better off when the Legaults specialize in trapping lobsters, the Duguays specialize in growing potatoes, and the two families trade.

8. Which of the following situations describes an equilibrium? Which does not? If the situation does not describe an equilibrium, what would an equilibrium look like?

a. Many people regularly commute from the suburbs to downtown Pleasantville. Due to traffic congestion, the trip takes 30 minutes when you travel by highway but only 15 minutes when you go by side streets.

b. At the intersection of Victoria and Main are two gas stations. One station charges 135.5¢ per litre for regular gas and the other charges 131.9¢ per litre. Customers can get service immediately at the first station but must wait in a long line at the second.

c. Every student enrolled in Economics 101 must also attend a weekly tutorial. This year there are two sections offered: section A and section B, which meet at the same time in adjoining classrooms and are taught by equally competent instructors. Section A is overcrowded, with people sitting on the floor and often unable to see the board. Section B has many empty seats.

9. In each of the following cases, explain whether you think the situation is efficient or not. If it is not efficient, why not? What actions would make the situation efficient?

a. Electricity is included in the rent at your dorm. Some residents in your dorm leave lights, computers, and appliances on when they are not in their rooms.

b. Although they cost the same amount to prepare, the cafeteria in your dorm consistently provides too many dishes that diners don't like, such as tofu casserole, and too few dishes that diners do like, such as roast turkey with dressing.

c. The enrollment for a particular course exceeds the spaces available. Some students who need to take this course to complete their major are unable to get a space even though others who are taking it as an elective do get a space.

10. Discuss the efficiency and equity implications of each of the following policies. How would you go about balancing the concerns of equity and efficiency in these areas?

a. The government pays the full tuition for every post-secondary student to study whatever subject he or she wishes.

b. When people lose their jobs, the government provides employment income (EI) until they find new ones.

11. Governments often adopt certain policies in order to promote desired behaviour among their citizens. For each of the following policies, determine what the incentive is and what behaviour the government wishes to promote. In each case, why do you think that the

government might wish to change people's behaviour, rather than allow their actions to be solely determined by individual choice?

a. A tax of $5 per pack is imposed on cigarettes.

b. The government pays parents $100 when their child is vaccinated for measles.

c. The government pays college and university students to tutor children from low-income families.

d. The government imposes a tax on the amount of air pollution that a company discharges.

12. In each of the following situations, explain how government intervention could improve society's welfare by changing people's incentives. In what sense is the market going wrong?

a. Pollution from auto emissions has reached unhealthy levels.

b. Everyone in Woodville would be better off if streetlights were installed in the town. But no individual resident is willing to pay for installation of a streetlight in front of his or her house because it is impossible to recoup the cost by charging other residents for the benefit they receive from it.

13. On June 6, 2013, Stephen Poloz, the newly appointed governor of the Bank of Canada, addressed the House of Commons Standing Committee on Finance. In this speech he said, "In the immediate aftermath of the crisis (the Great Recession of 2008), stimulative monetary and fiscal policies proved highly effective in supporting robust growth in domestic demand, particularly household expenditures, which grew to record levels. Yet, as effective as it has been, with domestic demand now slowing, the limits of this growth model are clear." Which two of the three principles of economy-wide interaction are at work in this statement?

14. In 2007, a sharp downturn in the U.S. housing market reduced the income of many who worked in the American home construction industry. In October of that year, a *Conference Board of Canada* report stated falling house prices in parts of the United States, combined with low savings and rising energy costs, would result in weak U.S. consumer spending. Furthermore, U.S. imports of wood and autos would decline because of the slower U.S. economic growth. With this information, use one of the principles of economy-wide interaction to trace a chain of links that explains how reduced spending for U.S. home purchases is likely to affect the performance of the Canadian economy.

15. In 2005, Hurricane Katrina caused massive destruction to the U.S. Gulf Coast. Tens of thousands of people lost their homes and possessions. Even those who weren't directly affected by the destruction were hurt because businesses failed or contracted and jobs dried up. Using one of the principles of economy-wide interaction, explain how government intervention can help in this situation.

16. During the Great Depression, food was left to rot in the fields or fields that had once been actively cultivated were left fallow. Use one of the principles of economy-wide interaction to explain how this could have occurred.

CHAPTER 2

Economic Models: Trade-offs and Trade

FROM KITTY HAWK TO CSERIES

The Wright Brothers' model made modern airplanes, including the CSeries jets, possible.

WHAT YOU WILL LEARN IN THIS CHAPTER

❱ Why **models**—simplified representations of reality—play a crucial role in economics

❱ Two simple but important models: the **production possibility frontier** and **comparative advantage**

❱ The **circular-flow diagram,** a schematic representation of the economy

❱ The difference between **positive economics,** which analyzes how the economy works, and **normative economics,** which prescribes economic policy based on how the world should work

❱ When economists agree and why they sometimes disagree

ON SEPTEMBER 16, 2013, THE CS100, the newest jet in Bombardier's cutting-edge CSeries of aircraft, took its first test flight. It was a game-changing moment: the CS100 is part of a new aerodynamic revolution— an ultra-efficient airplane designed to cut airline operating costs and one of the first to use super-lightweight composite materials. To ensure that the CS100 was sufficiently lightweight and aerodynamic, it underwent more than 4500 hours of wind tunnel tests—tests that resulted in subtle design changes that improved its performance, reducing fuel consumption and CO_2 emissions each by 20% compared to existing passenger jets.

The CSeries is a spectacular advance from the 1903 maiden voyage of the Wright *Flyer,* the first successful powered airplane flight, in Kitty Hawk, North Carolina. Yet the Bombardier engineers—and all aeronautic engineers—owe an enormous debt to the Wright *Flyer's* inventors, Wilbur and Orville Wright. What made the Wrights truly visionary was their wind tunnel, an apparatus that let them experiment with many different designs for wings and control surfaces. Doing experiments with a miniature airplane inside a wind tunnel the size of a shipping crate gave the Wright Brothers the knowledge that would make heavier-than-air flight possible.

Some 110 years later, Bombardier tested the design of its CSeries aircraft using more than 20 sophisticated miniature scale models inside state-of-the-art wind tunnel facilities in six countries. It also augmented its wind tunnel testing with leading-edge computational fluid dynamics testing, made possible through the use of supercomputers that are 100 000 times faster than the computers in use when the aircraft currently serving this market were designed. Thus, while a miniature airplane—whether inside a packing crate, an ultramodern wind tunnel, or a complex simulation scenario—is not the same thing as an actual aircraft in flight, it is clearly a very useful *model* of a flying plane—a simplified representation of the real thing that can be used to answer crucial questions, such as how much lift a given wing shape will generate at a given airspeed.

Needless to say, testing an airplane design in a wind tunnel or with computer simulations is cheaper and safer than building a full-scale version and hoping it will fly. Likewise, models play a crucial role in almost all scientific research— economics very much included.

In fact, you could say that economic theory consists mainly of a collection of models, a series of simplified representations of economic reality that allow us to understand a variety of economic issues. In this chapter, we'll look at two economic models that are crucially important in their own right and also illustrate why such models are so useful. We'll conclude with a look at how economists actually use models in their work. ∎

A **model** is a simplified representation of a real situation that is used to better understand real-life situations.

The **other things equal assumption** (or ceteris paribus) means that all other relevant factors remain unchanged.

Models in Economics: Some Important Examples

A model is any simplified representation of reality that is used to better understand real-life situations. But how do we create a simplified representation of an economic situation?

One possibility—an economist's equivalent of a wind tunnel—is to find or create a real but simplified economy. For example, economists interested in the economic role of money have studied the system of exchange that developed in World War II prison camps, in which cigarettes became a universally accepted form of payment even among prisoners who didn't smoke.

Another possibility is to simulate the workings of the economy on a computer. For example, when changes in tax law are proposed, government officials use *tax models*—large mathematical computer programs—to assess how the proposed changes would affect different types of people.

Models are important because their simplicity allows economists to focus on the effects of only one change at a time. That is, they allow us to hold everything else constant and study how one change affects the overall economic outcome. So an important assumption when building economic models is the **other things equal assumption,** which means that all other relevant factors remain unchanged. In economics, the phrase *ceteris paribus*—Latin for "other things remain the same (or held constant)"—is also often used.

But you can't always find or create a small-scale version of the whole economy, and a computer program is only as good as the data it uses. (Programmers have a saying: "garbage in, garbage out.") For many purposes, the most effective form of economic modelling is the construction of "thought experiments": simplified, hypothetical versions of real-life situations.

In Chapter 1 we illustrated the concept of equilibrium with the example of how customers at a supermarket would rearrange themselves when a new cash register opens. Though we didn't say it, this was an example of a simple model—an imaginary supermarket, in which many details were ignored. (What were customers buying? Never mind.) This simple model can be used to answer a "what if" question: what if another cash register were opened?

As the cash register story showed, it is often possible to describe and analyze a useful economic model in plain English. However, because much of economics involves changes in quantities—in the price of a product, the number of units produced, or the number of workers employed in its production—economists often find that using some mathematics helps clarify an issue. In particular, a numerical example, a simple equation, or—especially—a graph can be key to understanding an economic concept.

Whatever form it takes, a good economic model can be a tremendous aid to understanding. The best way to grasp this point is to consider some simple but important economic models and what they tell us. First, we will look at the *production possibility frontier,* a model that helps economists think about the trade-offs every economy faces. Then we will turn to *comparative advantage,* a model that clarifies the principle of gains from trade—trade both between individuals and between countries. In addition, we'll examine the *circular-flow diagram,* a schematic representation that helps us understand how flows of money, goods, and services are channelled through the economy.

In discussing these models, we make considerable use of graphs to represent mathematical relationships. Graphs play an important role throughout this book. If you are already familiar with the use of graphs, you may feel free to skip the appendix to this chapter, which provides a brief introduction to the use of graphs in economics. If not, this would be a good time to turn to it.

THE MODEL THAT ATE THE ECONOMY

A model is just a model, right? So how much damage can it do? Economists probably would have answered that question quite differently before the financial meltdown of 2008–2009 than after it. The financial crisis continues to reverberate today—a testament to why economic models are so important. The fact is an economic model—a *bad* economic model, it turned out—played a significant role in the origins of the crisis.

"The model that ate the economy" originated in finance theory, the branch of economics that seeks to understand what assets like stocks and bonds are worth. Financial theorists often get hired (at very high salaries, mind you) to devise complex mathematical models to help investment companies decide what assets to buy and sell and at what price.

Finance theory has become increasingly important as major investment companies have shifted from trading simple assets like stocks and bonds to more complex assets— notably, mortgage-backed securities (or MBS's for short). An MBS is an asset that entitles its owner to a stream of earnings based on the payments made by thousands of people on their home loans. Investors wanted to know how risky these complex assets were. That is, how likely was it that an investor would lose money on an MBS?

Although we won't go into the details, estimating the likelihood of losing money on an MBS is a complicated problem. It involves calculating the probability that a significant number of the thousands of homeowners backing your security will stop paying their mortgages. Until that probability could be calculated, investors didn't want to buy MBS's. In order to generate sales, investment firms needed to provide potential MBS buyers with some estimate of their risk.

In 2000, on Wall Street (the district in New York City where nearly all major American investment companies have their headquarters), one financial theorist announced that he had solved the problem by employing a huge statistical abstraction—assuming that current homeowners were no more likely to stop paying their mortgages than in previous decades. With this assumption, he devised a simple model for estimating the risk of buying an MBS. Financial traders loved the model as it opened up a huge and extraordinarily profitable market for them. Using this simple model, Wall Street was able to create and sell billions of MBS's, generating billions in profits for itself.

Or investors *thought* they had calculated the risk of losing money on an MBS. Some financial experts—particularly Darrell Duffie, a Stanford University finance professor— warned from the sidelines that the estimates of risk calculated by this simple model were just plain wrong. He, and other critics, said that in the search for simplicity, the model seriously underestimated the likelihood that many homeowners would stop paying their mortgages at the same time, leaving MBS investors in danger of incurring huge losses.

The warnings fell on deaf ears—no doubt because Wall Street was making so much money. Billions of dollars worth of MBS's were sold to investors both in the United States and abroad. In 2008–2009, the problems critics warned about exploded in catastrophic fashion. Over the previous decade, American home prices had risen too high, and mortgages had been extended to many who were unable to pay. As home prices fell to earth, millions of American homeowners didn't pay their mortgages. With losses mounting for MBS investors all around the world, it became all too clear that the model had indeed underestimated the risks. When investors and financial institutions around the world realized the extent of their losses, the worldwide economy ground to an abrupt halt. To this day, it has not fully recovered.

Trade-offs: The Production Possibility Frontier

The first principle of economics we introduced in Chapter 1 was that resources are scarce and that, as a result, any economy—whether it's an isolated group of a few dozen hunter-gatherers or the 7 billion people making up the twenty-first-century global economy—faces trade-offs. No matter how lightweight the CS100 jet is, no matter how efficient Bombardier's assembly line, producing CSeries

The **production possibility frontier** illustrates the trade-offs facing an economy that produces only two goods. It shows the maximum quantity of one good that can be produced for any given quantity produced of the other.

aircrafts means using resources (labour, land, and capital) that therefore can't be used to produce something else.

To think about the trade-offs that face any economy, economists often use the model known as the **production possibility frontier.** The idea behind this model is to improve our understanding of trade-offs by considering a simplified economy that produces only two goods. This simplification enables us to show the trade-off graphically.

Suppose, for a moment, that Canada was a one-company economy, with Bombardier its sole employer and trains and commercial aircraft its only products. So there is a choice of what kinds of transportation vehicles to produce—say, Toronto Rocket subway trains versus CSeries commercial passenger jets. Figure 2-1 shows a hypothetical production possibility frontier (*PPF*) representing the trade-off this one-company economy would face. The frontier—the line in the diagram— shows the maximum quantity of jets that Bombardier can produce per year *given* the quantity of subway trains it produces per year, and vice versa. That is, it answers questions of the form, "What is the maximum quantity of jets that Bombardier can produce in a year if it also produces 21 (or 35, or 70) subway trains that year?"

There is a crucial distinction between points *inside* or *on* the production possibility frontier (the shaded area) and *outside* the frontier. If a production point lies inside or on the frontier—like point *C*, at which Bombardier produces 10 jets and 21 subway trains in a year—it is feasible. After all, the frontier tells us that if Bombardier produces 10 jets, it could also produce a maximum of 35 subway trains that year, so it could certainly make 21 subway trains. However, a production point that lies outside the frontier—such as the hypothetical production point *D*, where Bombardier produces 20 jets and 70 subway trains—isn't feasible. Bombardier can produce 20 jets and no subway trains, *or* it can produce 70 subway trains and no jets, but it can't do both.

In Figure 2-1 the production possibility frontier intersects the horizontal axis at 20 jets. This means that if Bombardier dedicated all its production capacity[1] to making jets, it could produce 20 jets per year but could produce no subway trains. The production possibility frontier intersects the vertical axis at 70 subway trains. This means that if Bombardier dedicated all its production capacity to making subway trains, it could produce 70 subway trains per year but no jets.

FIGURE **2-1** **The Production Possibility Frontier**

The production possibility frontier illustrates the trade-offs Bombardier faces in producing subway trains and jets. It shows the maximum quantity of one good that can be produced given the quantity of the other good produced. Here, the maximum quantity of subway trains manufactured per year depends on the quantity of jets manufactured that year, and vice versa. Bombardier's feasible production is shown by the area *inside* or *on* the curve. Production at point *C* is feasible but not efficient. Points *A* and *B* are feasible and efficient in production, but point *D* is not feasible.

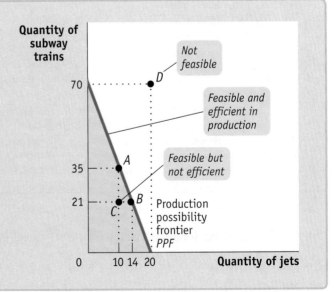

---

[1]The amount of production capacity is determined by the production technology used and amount of productive resources (labour, land, and capital) available.

The figure also shows less extreme trade-offs. For example, if Bombardier's managers decide to make 10 jets this year, they can produce at most 35 subway trains; this production choice is illustrated by point *A*. And if Bombardier's managers decide to produce 14 jets, they can make at most 21 subway trains, as shown by point *B*.

Thinking in terms of a production possibility frontier simplifies the complexities of reality. The real-world Canadian economy produces millions of different goods. Even Bombardier can produce more than two different types of planes and trains. Yet it's important to realize that even in its simplicity, this stripped-down model gives us important insights about the real world.

By simplifying reality, the production possibility frontier helps us understand some aspects of the real economy better than we could without the model: efficiency, opportunity cost, and economic growth.

Efficiency First of all, the production possibility frontier is a good way to illustrate the general economic concept of *efficiency*. Recall from Chapter 1 that an economy is efficient if there are no missed opportunities—there is no way to make some people better off without making other people worse off.

One key element of efficiency is that there are no missed opportunities in production—there is no way to produce more of one good without producing less of other goods. As long as Bombardier operates on its production possibility frontier, its production is efficient. At point *A*, 35 subway trains is the maximum quantity feasible given that Bombardier has also committed to producing 10 jets; at point *B*, 21 subway trains is the maximum number that can be made given the choice to produce 14 jets; and so on. But suppose for some reason that Bombardier was operating at point *C*, making 10 jets and 21 subway trains. In this case, it would not be operating efficiently and would therefore be *inefficient*: using the same resources, it could be producing more of both transportation vehicles.

Although we have used an example of the production choices of a one-firm, two-good economy to illustrate efficiency and inefficiency, these concepts also carry over to the real economy, which contains many firms and produces many goods. If the economy as a whole could not produce more of any one good without producing less of something else—that is, if it is on its production possibility frontier—then we say that the economy is *efficient in production*. If, however, the economy could produce more of some things without producing less of others—which typically means that it could produce more of everything—then it is inefficient in production. For example, an economy in which large numbers of workers are involuntarily unemployed is clearly inefficient in production. And that's a bad thing, because the economy could be producing more useful goods and services.

Although the production possibility frontier helps clarify what it means for an economy to be efficient in production, it's important to understand that efficiency in production is only *part* of what's required for the economy as a whole to be efficient. Efficiency also requires that the economy allocate its resources so that consumers are as well off as possible. If an economy does this, we say that it is *efficient in consumption* (an efficient consumption allocation). To see why efficiency in the consumption allocation is as important as efficiency in production, notice that points *A* and *B* in Figure 2-1 both represent situations in which the economy is efficient in production, because in each case it can't produce more of one good without producing less of the other. But these two situations may not be equally desirable from society's point of view. Suppose that society prefers to have more jets and fewer subway trains than at point *A*; say, it prefers to have 14 jets and 21 subway trains, corresponding to point *B*. In this case, point *A* is an inefficient consumption allocation from the point of view of the economy as a whole because it would rather have Bombardier produce at point *B* than at point *A*.

This example shows that efficiency for the economy as a whole requires *both* efficiency in production and efficiency in consumption: to be efficient, an economy must produce as much of each good as it can given the production of other goods, and it must also produce the mix of goods that people want to consume. (And it must also deliver those goods to the right people: an economy that gives subway trains to airports and commercial passenger jets to intercity transit authorities is inefficient, too.)

In the real world, command economies, such as the former Soviet Union, are notorious for inefficiency in the consumption allocation. For example, it was common in the U.S.S.R. for consumers to find stores well stocked with items few people wanted but lacking such basics as soap and toilet paper.

Opportunity Cost The production possibility frontier is also useful as a reminder of the fundamental point that the true cost of any good isn't the money it costs to buy it, but what must be given up in order to get that good—the *opportunity cost*. If, for example, Bombardier decides to change its production from point A to point B, it will produce 4 more jets but 14 fewer subway trains. So the opportunity cost of 4 jets is 14 subway trains—the 14 subway trains that must be forgone to produce 4 more jets. This means that each jet has an opportunity cost of $^{14}/_4 = ^7/_2$, or, put another way, 3½ subway trains do not get made for each jet that is produced.

Is the opportunity cost of an extra jet in terms of subway trains always the same, no matter how many jets and subway trains are currently produced? In the example illustrated by Figure 2-1, the answer is yes. If Bombardier increases its production of jets from 14 to 20, the number of subway trains it produces falls from 21 to zero. So Bombardier's opportunity cost per additional jet is $^{21}/_6$ or 3½ subway trains, the same as it was when Bombardier went from 10 jets produced to 14. However, the fact that in this example the opportunity cost of a jet in terms of a subway train is always the same is a result of an assumption we've made, an assumption that's reflected in how Figure 2-1 is drawn. Specifically, whenever we assume that the opportunity cost of an additional unit of a good doesn't change regardless of the output mix, the production possibility frontier is a straight line. Note that a linear production possibility frontier implies constant marginal productivity of production for both trains and planes.

Moreover, as you might have already guessed, the absolute value of the slope of a straight-line production possibility frontier is equal to the opportunity cost—specifically, the opportunity cost for the good measured on the horizontal axis in terms of the good measured on the vertical axis.[2] In Figure 2-1, the production possibility frontier has a *constant slope* of $-^7/_2$, implying that Bombardier faces a *constant opportunity cost* for 1 jet equal to 3½ subway trains. (A review of how to calculate the slope of a straight line is found in this chapter's appendix.) This is the simplest case, but the production possibility frontier model can also be used to examine situations in which opportunity costs change as the mix of output changes.[3]

Figure 2-2 illustrates a different assumption, a case in which Bombardier faces *increasing opportunity cost*. Here, the more jets it produces, the more costly it is to produce yet another jet in terms of forgone production of subway trains. And the same holds true in reverse: the more subway trains Bombardier produces, the more costly it is to produce yet another subway train in terms of forgone production of jets. For example, to go from producing zero jets to producing 10, Bombardier has to forgo producing 10 subway trains. That is, the opportunity cost of those 10 jets is 10 subway trains. But to increase its production of jets to

[2]To show this algebraically, suppose we have a production possibility frontier drawn with X on the horizontal axis and Y on the vertical axis. The *opportunity cost of X* (OC_X) is equal to the number of units of Y production we must give up in order to produce 1 more unit of X. So, $OC_X = -(\text{slope of the PPF}) = -\left(\frac{\Delta Y}{\Delta X}\right)$.

Also, the *opportunity cost of Y* (OC_Y) is the inverse of the opportunity cost of X, so $OC_Y = -\left(\frac{\Delta X}{\Delta Y}\right) = \left(\frac{1}{OC_X}\right)$, which is the number of units of X production we must give up to produce 1 more unit of Y.

[3]If the production possibilities frontier is not linear, the opportunity cost at a point continues to be equal to the absolute value of the slope of the production possibilities frontier (at that point). But the slope varies as we move along the production possibility frontier.

FIGURE   **2-2**   Increasing Opportunity Cost

The bowed-out shape of the production possibility frontier reflects increasing opportunity cost. In this example, to produce the first 10 jets, Bombardier must forgo producing 10 subway trains. But to produce an additional 10 jets, Bombardier must forgo manufacturing 60 more subway trains.

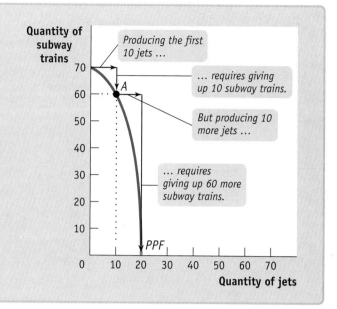

20—that is, to produce an additional 10 jets—it must forgo producing 60 more subway trains, a much higher opportunity cost. As you can see in Figure 2-2, when opportunity costs are increasing rather than constant, the production possibility frontier is a (strictly concave) bowed-out curve rather than a straight line.

Although it's often useful to work with the simple assumption that the production possibility frontier is a straight line, economists believe that in reality opportunity costs are typically increasing. When only a small amount of a good is produced, the opportunity cost of producing that good is relatively low because the economy needs to use only those resources that are especially well suited for its production. For example, if an economy grows only a small amount of corn, that corn can be grown in places where the soil and climate are perfect for corn growing but less suitable for growing anything else, like wheat. So growing that corn involves giving up only a small amount of potential wheat output. Once the economy grows a lot of corn, however, land that is well suited for wheat but isn't so great for corn must be used to produce corn anyway. As a result, the additional corn production involves sacrificing considerably more wheat production. In other words, as more of a good is produced, its opportunity cost typically rises because well-suited inputs are already used up and less adaptable inputs must be used instead.

Economic Growth Finally, the production possibility frontier helps us understand what it means to talk about *economic growth*. We introduced the concept of economic growth in the Introduction, defining it as *the growing ability of the economy to produce goods and services*. As we saw, economic growth is one of the fundamental features of the real economy. But are we really justified in saying that the economy has grown over time? After all, although the Canadian economy produces more of many things than it did a century ago, it produces less of other things—for example, horse-drawn carriages. Production of many goods, in other words, is actually down. So how can we say for sure that the economy as a whole has grown?

The answer is illustrated in Figure 2-3, where we have drawn two hypothetical production possibility frontiers for the economy. In them we have assumed once again that everyone in the economy works for Bombardier and, consequently, the economy produces only two goods, subway trains and jets. Notice how the two curves are nested, with the one labelled "Original *PPF*" lying completely inside the

FIGURE 2-3 Economic Growth

Economic growth results in an *outward shift* of the production possibility frontier because production possibilities are expanded. The economy can now produce more of everything. For example, if production is initially at point *A* (60 subway trains and 10 jets), economic growth means that the economy could move to point *E* (70 subway trains and 12 jets).

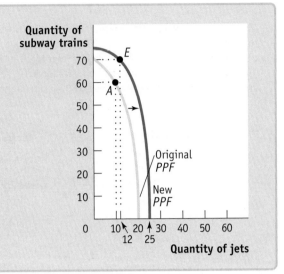

one labelled "New *PPF*." Now we can see graphically what we mean by economic growth of the economy: economic growth means an *expansion of the economy's production possibilities;* that is, the economy can produce more of everything. For example, if the economy initially produces at point *A* (60 subway trains and 10 jets), economic growth means that the economy could move to point *E* (70 subway trains and 12 jets). Point *E* lies outside the original frontier; so in the production possibility frontier model, growth is shown as an outward shift of the frontier.

What can lead the production possibility frontier to shift outward? There are basically two sources of economic growth. One is an increase in the economy's **factors of production,** the resources used to produce goods and services. Economists usually use the term *factor of production* to refer to a resource that is not used up in production. For example, in traditional airplane manufacture, workers used riveting machines to connect metal sheets when constructing a plane's fuselage; the workers and the riveters are factors of production, but the rivets and the sheet metal are not. Once a fuselage is made, a worker and riveter can be used to make another fuselage, but the sheet metal and rivets used to make one fuselage cannot be used to make another.

Broadly speaking, the main factors of production are the resources of land, labour, physical capital, and human capital. Land is a resource supplied by nature; labour is the economy's pool of workers; physical capital refers to created resources such as machines and buildings; and human capital refers to the educational achievements and skills of the labour force, which enhance its productivity. Of course, each of these is really a category rather than a single factor: land in Labrador is quite different from land in southern Ontario.

To see how adding to an economy's factors of production leads to economic growth, suppose that Bombardier builds another construction facility that allows it to increase the number of transportation vehicles—subway trains or CSeries jets or both—it can produce in a year. The new construction facility is a factor of production, a resource Bombardier can use to increase its yearly output. We can't say how many more planes or subway trains Bombardier will produce; that's a management decision that will depend on, among other things, customer demand. But we can say that Bombardier's production possibility frontier has shifted outward because it can now produce more subway trains without reducing the number of CSeries jets it makes, or it can make more CSeries jets without reducing the number of subway trains produced.

Factors of production are resources (labour, land, and capital) used to produce goods and services.

Technology is the technical means for producing goods and services.

The other source of economic growth is progress in **technology,** the technical means for the production of goods and services. Composite and advanced aluminum materials had been used in some parts of aircraft before the Bombardier CSeries was developed. But Bombardier engineers realized that there were large additional advantages to building a whole plane out of composites and advanced aluminum. The plane would be lighter, stronger, and have better aerodynamics than a plane built in the traditional way. It would therefore have longer range, be able to carry more people, and use less fuel, in addition to being able to maintain higher cabin pressure. So in a real sense Bombardier's innovation—a whole plane built out of advanced materials—was a way to do more with any given amount of resources, pushing out the production possibility frontier.

Because improved jet technology has pushed out the production possibility frontier, it has made it possible for the economy to produce more of everything, not just jets and air travel. Over the past 30 years, the biggest technological advances have taken place in information technology, not in construction or food services. Yet Canadians have chosen to buy bigger houses and eat out more than they used to because the economy's growth has made it possible to do so.

The production possibility frontier is a very simplified model of an economy. Yet it teaches us important lessons about real-life economies. It gives us our first clear sense of what constitutes economic efficiency, it illustrates the concept of opportunity cost, and it makes clear what economic growth is all about.

Comparative Advantage and Gains from Trade

Among the twelve principles of economics described in Chapter 1 was the principle of *gains from trade*—the mutual gains that individuals or countries can achieve by specializing in doing different things and trading with one another. Our next illustration of an economic model is a particularly useful model of gains from trade—trade based on *comparative advantage*.

One of the most important insights in all of economics is that there are gains from trade—that it makes sense to produce the things you're especially good at producing and to buy from other people the things you aren't as good at producing. This would be true even if you could produce everything for yourself: even if a brilliant brain surgeon *could* repair her own dripping faucet, it's probably a better idea for her to call in a professional plumber.

How can we model the gains from trade? Let's stay with our mass transportation vehicle example and once again imagine that Canada is a one-company economy in which everyone works for Bombardier, producing airplanes and subway trains. Let's now assume, however, that Canada has the ability to trade with Brazil—another one-company economy in which everyone works for a company that manufactures aircraft and subway trains. (In the real world, the Brazilian company Embraer is an internationally successful producer of small commuter jets. If you fly from one Canadian city to another, your plane is likely to be made by Bombardier; but if you fly within other countries, the odds are equally good that your plane will have been made by Embraer.)

In our example, the only two goods produced are subway trains and jets. Both countries could produce both kinds of mass transportation vehicles. But as we'll see in a moment, they can gain by producing different things and trading with each other. For the purposes of this example, let's return to the simpler case of straight-line production possibility frontiers. Canada's production possibilities are represented by the production possibility frontier in panel (a) of Figure 2-4, which is similar to the production possibility frontier in Figure 2-1. According to this diagram, Canada can produce 70 subway trains if it makes no jets and can manufacture 20 jets if it produces no subway trains. Recall that this means that the slope of the Canadian production possibility frontier is $-7/2$: its opportunity cost of 1 jet is $7/2$ of a subway train (i.e., to make 1 more jet, Canada has to give up making 3.5 subway trains).

Panel (b) of Figure 2-4 shows Brazil's production possibilities. Like Canada, Brazil's production possibility frontier is a straight line, implying a constant opportunity cost of jets in terms of subway trains. Brazil's production possibility

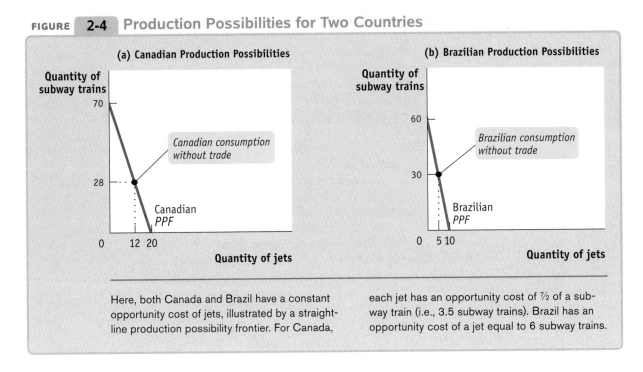

FIGURE **2-4** Production Possibilities for Two Countries

Here, both Canada and Brazil have a constant opportunity cost of jets, illustrated by a straight-line production possibility frontier. For Canada, each jet has an opportunity cost of ⁷⁄₂ of a subway train (i.e., 3.5 subway trains). Brazil has an opportunity cost of a jet equal to 6 subway trains.

frontier has a constant slope of −6. Brazil can't produce as much of anything as Canada can: at most it can produce 60 subway trains or 10 jets. But it is relatively better at manufacturing subway trains than Canada is; whereas Canada sacrifices ²⁄₇ of a jet per subway train produced, for Brazil the opportunity cost of a subway train is only ¹⁄₆ of a jet. Table 2-1 summarizes the two countries' opportunity costs of subway trains and jets.

Now, Canada and Brazil could each choose to make their own subway trains and jets, not trading any airplanes or trains and consuming only what each produced within its own country. (A country "consumes" an airplane or train when it is owned by a domestic resident.) Let's suppose that the two countries start out this way and make the consumption choices shown in Figure 2-4: in the absence of trade, Canada produces and consumes 28 subway trains and 12 jets per year, while Brazil produces and consumes 30 subway trains and 5 jets per year.

But is this the best the two countries can do? No, it isn't. Given that the two producers—and therefore the two countries—have different opportunity costs, Canada and Brazil can strike a deal that makes both of them better off.

TABLE **2-1** Canadian and Brazilian Opportunity Costs of Subway Trains and Jets

	Canadian Opportunity Cost		Brazilian Opportunity Cost
One subway train	²⁄₇ jet	>	¹⁄₆ jet
One jet	⁷⁄₂ subway trains	<	6 subway trains

TABLE **2-2** How Canada and Brazil Gain from Trade

		Without Trade		With Trade		Gains from Trade
		Production	Consumption	Production	Consumption	
Canada	Subway trains	28	28	0	29	+1
	Jets	12	12	20	14	+2
Brazil	Subway trains	30	30	60	31	+1
	Jets	5	5	0	6	+1

FIGURE   2-5   Comparative Advantage and Gains from Trade

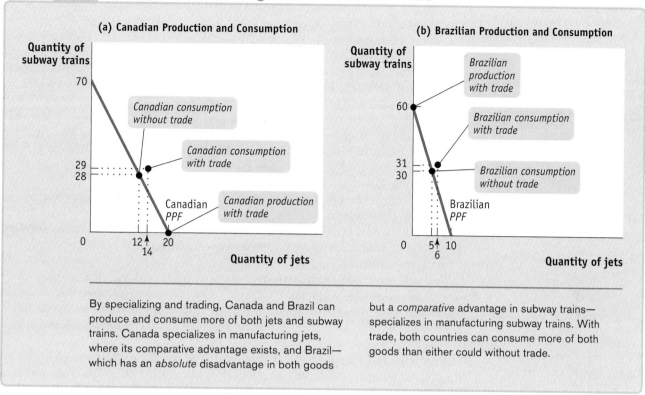

By specializing and trading, Canada and Brazil can produce and consume more of both jets and subway trains. Canada specializes in manufacturing jets, where its comparative advantage exists, and Brazil— which has an *absolute* disadvantage in both goods but a *comparative* advantage in subway trains— specializes in manufacturing subway trains. With trade, both countries can consume more of both goods than either could without trade.

Table 2-2 shows how such a deal works: Canada specializes in the production of jets, manufacturing 20 per year, and sells 6 to Brazil. Meanwhile, Brazil specializes in the production of subway trains, producing 60 per year, and sells 29 to Canada. The result is shown in Figure 2-5. Canada now consumes more of both subway trains and jets than before: instead of 28 subway trains and 12 jets, it now consumes 29 subway trains and 14 jets. Brazil also consumes more, going from 30 subway trains and 5 jets to 31 subway trains and 6 jets. As Table 2-2 also shows, both Canada and Brazil reap gains from trade, consuming more of both types of transportation vehicle than they would have without trade.

Both countries are better off when they each specialize in what they are relatively good at producing and then trade their products. It's a good idea for Canada to specialize in the production of jets because its opportunity cost of a jet is smaller than Brazil's: $7/2 < 6$. Correspondingly, Brazil should specialize in the production of subway trains because its opportunity cost of a subway train is smaller than Canada's: $1/6 < 2/7$.

What we would say in this case is that Canada has a comparative advantage in the production of jets and Brazil has a comparative advantage in the production of subway trains. A country has a **comparative advantage** in producing something if the opportunity cost of that production is lower for that country than for other countries. The same concept applies to firms and people: a firm or an individual has a comparative advantage in producing something if its, his, or her opportunity cost of production is lower than for others.

One point of clarification before we proceed further. You may have wondered why Canada traded 6 jets to Brazil in return for 29 subway trains. Why not some other deal, like trading 6 jets for 20 subway trains? The answer to that question has two parts. First, there may indeed be other trades that Canada and Brazil might agree to. Second, there are some deals that we can safely rule out— one like 6 jets for 20 subway trains.

A country has a **comparative advantage** in producing a good or service if its opportunity cost of producing the good or service is lower than that of other countries. Likewise, an individual has a comparative advantage in producing a good or service if his or her opportunity cost of producing the good or service is lower than for other people.

A country has an **absolute advantage** in producing a good or service if the country can produce more output per worker than other countries. Likewise, an individual has an absolute advantage in producing a good or service if he or she is better at producing it than other people. Having an absolute advantage is not the same thing as having a comparative advantage.

To understand why, re-examine Table 2-1 and consider Canada first. Without trading with Brazil, the Canadian opportunity cost of a subway train is $2/7$ of a jet. So it's clear that Canada will not accept any trade that requires it to give up more than $2/7$ of a jet for a subway train — as doing so would make it worse off. Trading 6 jets in return for 20 subway trains would require Canada to pay an opportunity cost of $6/20 = 3/10$ of a jet for a subway train. Because $3/10$ is *greater than* $2/7$, this is a deal that Canada would reject. Similarly, Brazil won't accept a trade that gives it less than 6 subway trains for a jet.

The point to remember is that Canada and Brazil will be willing to trade only if the "price" of the good each country obtains in the trade is less than its own opportunity cost of producing the good domestically. Moreover, this is a general statement that is true whenever two parties—countries, firms, or individuals—trade voluntarily.

While our story clearly simplifies reality, it teaches us some very important lessons that apply to the real economy, too.

First, the model provides a clear illustration of the gains from trade: through specialization and trade, both countries produce more and consume more than if they were self-sufficient.

Second, the model demonstrates a very important point that is often overlooked in real-world arguments: each country has a comparative advantage in producing something. This applies to firms and people as well: *everyone has a comparative advantage in something, and everyone has a comparative disadvantage in something.*

Crucially, in our example it doesn't matter if, as is probably the case in real life, Canadian workers are just as good as or even better than Brazilian workers at producing subway trains and jets. Suppose that Canada is actually better than Brazil at production of both types of transportation vehicles. In that case, we would say that Canada has an **absolute advantage** in both subway train and jet production: in an hour, a Canadian worker can produce more of either a subway train or jet than a Brazilian worker could. You might be tempted to think that in that case Canada has nothing to gain from trading with the less productive Brazil.

But we've just seen that Canada can indeed benefit from trading with Brazil because *comparative, not absolute, advantage is the basis for mutual gains from trade.*[4] It doesn't matter whether it takes Brazil more resources than Canada to make a subway train; what matters for trade is that for Brazil the opportunity cost of a subway train is lower than the Canadian opportunity cost. So Brazil, despite its absolute disadvantage, even

PITFALLS

MISUNDERSTANDING COMPARATIVE ADVANTAGE

Students do it, pundits do it, and politicians do it all the time: they confuse *comparative* advantage with *absolute* advantage. For example, back in the 1980s, when the North American economy seemed to be lagging behind that of Japan, one often heard commentators warn that if we didn't improve our productivity, we would soon have no comparative advantage in anything.

What those commentators meant was that we would have no *absolute* advantage in anything—that there might come a time

when the Japanese were better at everything than we were. (It didn't turn out that way, but that's another story.) And they had the idea that in that case we would no longer be able to benefit from trade with Japan.

But just as Brazil, in our example, was able to benefit from trade with Canada (and vice versa) despite the fact that Canada was absolutely better at manufacturing both jets and subway trains, in real life nations can still gain from trade even if they are less productive in all industries than the countries they trade with.

---

[4]In 1817, David Ricardo formulated the idea that comparative advantage was the basis of mutually beneficial trade between individuals and nations. It is a very powerful idea that comparative advantage and specialization in production are all that is needed for trade to be beneficial. Before this time, many people mistakenly believed that a nation with an absolute advantage in the production of all goods could not benefit from trade.

GLOBAL COMPARISON

PYJAMA REPUBLICS

Poor countries tend to have low productivity in clothing manufacture, but even lower productivity in other industries (see the upcoming Economics in Action), giving them a comparative advantage in clothing manufacture. As a result, the clothing industry tends to dominate their economies. An official from one such country once joked, "We are not a banana republic—we are a pyjama republic."

The figure to the right plots per capita income (the total income of the country divided by the size of the population) against the share of manufacturing employment devoted to clothing production for several countries. The graph shows just how strongly negative the relationship is between a country's per capita income level and the size of its clothing industry: poor countries have relatively large clothing industries, while rich countries have relatively small ones.

According to the U.S. Department of Commerce, Bangladesh's clothing industry has "low productivity, largely low literacy levels, frequent labor unrest, and outdated technology." Yet Bangladesh devotes most of its manufacturing workforce to clothing, the sector in which it nonetheless has a comparative advantage because its productivity in non-clothing industries is even lower. In

contrast, Costa Rica has "relatively high productivity" in clothing. Yet, a much smaller and declining fraction of Costa Rica's workforce is employed in clothing production. That's because productivity in non-clothing industries is somewhat higher in Costa Rica than in Bangladesh.

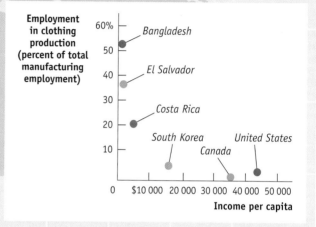

Source: World Bank, World Development Indicators; Nicita A. and M. Olarreaga, "Trade, Production and Protection 1976–2004," *World Bank Economic Review* 21, no. 1 (2007): 165–171.

in subway trains, has a comparative advantage in the manufacture of subway trains. Meanwhile Canada, which can use its resources most productively by manufacturing jets, has a comparative *dis*advantage in manufacturing subway trains.

Comparative Advantage and International Trade, in Reality

Look at the label on a manufactured good sold in Canada, and there's a good chance you will find that it was produced in some other country, such as China or Japan. On the other side, many Canadian industries sell a large fraction of their output overseas. (This is particularly true of agriculture, high technology, and entertainment.)

Should all this international exchange of goods and services be celebrated, or is it cause for concern? Politicians and the public often question the desirability of international trade, arguing that the nation should produce goods for itself rather than buying them from foreigners. Industries around the world demand protection from foreign competition: Japanese farmers want to keep out North American rice, Canadian steelworkers want to keep out European steel. And these demands are often supported by public opinion.

Economists, however, have a very positive view of international trade. Why? Because they view it in terms of comparative advantage. As we learned from our hypothetical example of Canadian jets and Brazilian subway trains, international trade benefits both countries. Each country can consume more than if it didn't trade and remained self-sufficient. Moreover, these mutual gains don't depend on each country being absolutely better than other countries at producing one kind of good. Even if one country has, say, higher output per worker in both industries— that is, even if one country has an absolute advantage in both industries—there are still gains from trade. The above Global Comparison, which explains the pattern of clothing production throughout the global economy, illustrates just this point.

Trade takes the form of **barter** when people directly exchange goods or services that they have for goods or services that they want.

The **circular-flow diagram** represents the transactions in an economy by flows around a circle.

A **household** is a person or a group of people that share their income.

A **firm** is an organization that produces goods and services for sale.

Firms sell goods and services that they produce to households in **markets for goods and services.**

Transactions: The Circular-Flow Diagram

The model economies that we've studied so far—each containing only one firm—are a huge simplification. We've also greatly simplified trade between Canada and Brazil, assuming that they engage only in the simplest of economic transactions, **barter,** in which one party directly trades a good or service for another good or service without using money. In a modern economy, simple barter is rare: usually people trade goods or services for money—pieces of coloured paper with no inherent value—and then trade those pieces of coloured paper for the goods or services they want. That is, they sell goods or services and buy other goods or services.

And they both sell and buy a lot of different things. The Canadian economy is a vastly complex entity, with almost 18 million workers employed by hundreds of thousands of companies, producing thousands of different goods and services. Yet you can learn some very important things about the economy by considering the simple graphic shown in Figure 2-6, the **circular-flow diagram.** This diagram represents the transactions that take place in an economy by two kinds of flows around a circle: flows of things such as goods, services, labour, or raw materials in one direction, and flows of money that pay for these things in the opposite direction. In this case the physical and intangible flows are shown in yellow, the money flows in green.

The simplest circular-flow diagram illustrates an economy that contains only two kinds of inhabitants: **households** and **firms.** A household consists of either an individual or a group of people (usually, but not necessarily, a family) that share their income. A firm is an organization that produces goods and services for sale—and that employs members of households.

As you can see in Figure 2-6, there are two kinds of markets in this simple economy. On one side (here the left side) there are **markets for goods and services** in which households buy the goods and services they want from firms. This produces a flow of goods and services to households and a return flow of money to firms.

FIGURE **2-6** The Circular-Flow Diagram

This diagram represents the flows of money and of goods and services in the economy. In the markets for goods and services, households purchase goods and services from firms, generating a flow of money to the firms and a flow of goods and services to the households. The money flows back to households as firms rent the factors of production (labour, land, and capital) from the households in factor markets.

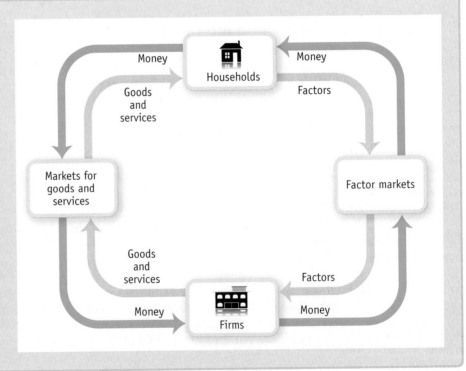

On the other side, there are **factor markets** in which firms buy or rent the resources they need to produce goods and services. Recall from earlier in the chapter that the main factors of production are land, labour, and capital.

The factor market most of us know best is the labour market, in which workers sell their services. In addition, we can think of households as owning, selling, and renting the other factors of production to firms. For example, when a firm buys physical capital in the form of machines, the payment ultimately goes to the households that own the machine-making firm. In this case, the transactions are occurring in the capital market, the market in which capital is bought and sold. As microeconomic analysis reveals, factor markets ultimately determine an economy's **income distribution,** how the total income created in an economy is allocated between less skilled workers, highly skilled workers, and the owners of capital and land.

The circular-flow diagram ignores a number of real-world complications in the interests of simplicity. A few examples:

- In the real world, the distinction between firms and households isn't always that clear-cut. Consider a small, family-run business—a farm, a shop, a small hotel. Is this a firm or a household? A more complete picture would include a separate box for family businesses.

- Many of the sales firms make are not to households but to other firms; for example, steel companies sell mainly to other companies such as auto manufacturers, not to households. A more complete picture would include these flows of goods, services, and money within the business sector.

- The figure doesn't show the government, which in the real world diverts quite a lot of money out of the circular flow in the form of taxes but also injects a lot of money back into the flow in the form of spending.

Figure 2-6, in other words, is by no means a complete picture either of all the types of inhabitants of the real economy or of all the flows of money and physical items and intangible services that take place among these inhabitants.

Despite its simplicity, the circular-flow diagram is a very useful aid to thinking about the economy.

> Firms buy or rent the resources they need to produce goods and services in **factor markets.**
>
> An economy's **income distribution** is the way in which total income is divided among the owners of the various factors of production.

ECONOMICS ► *IN ACTION*

RICH NATION, POOR NATION

Try taking off your clothes—at a suitable time and in a suitable place, of course—and taking a look at the labels inside that say where they were made. It's a very good bet that much, if not most, of your clothing was manufactured overseas, in a country that is much poorer than Canada—say, in El Salvador, Sri Lanka, or Bangladesh.

Why are these countries so much poorer than we are? The immediate reason is that their economies are much less *productive*—firms in these countries are just not able to produce as much from a given quantity of resources as comparable firms in Canada or other wealthy countries. Why countries differ so much in productivity is a deep question—indeed, one of the main questions that preoccupy economists. But in any case, the difference in productivity is a fact.

But if the economies of these countries are so much less productive than ours, how is it that they make so much of our clothing? Why don't we do it for ourselves?

The answer is "comparative advantage." Just about every industry in Bangladesh is much less productive than the corresponding industry in Canada. But the productivity difference between rich and poor countries varies across goods; it is very large in the production of sophisticated goods like aircraft but not that large in the production of simpler goods like clothing. So Bangladesh's

Although less productive than Canadian workers, Bangladeshi workers have a comparative advantage in clothing production.

position with regard to clothing production is like Brazil's position with respect to producing subway trains in our example: it's not as good (absolutely) at it as Canada is, but it's the thing Brazil does comparatively (relatively) well.

Bangladesh, though it is at an absolute disadvantage compared with Canada in almost everything, has a comparative advantage in clothing production. This means that both Canada and Bangladesh are able to consume more because they specialize in producing different things, with Bangladesh supplying our clothing and Canada supplying Bangladesh with more sophisticated goods.

●●◐

▼ Quick Review

- Most economic **models** are "thought experiments" or simplified representations of reality that rely on the **other things equal assumption.**

- The **production possibility frontier** model illustrates the concepts of efficiency, opportunity cost, and economic growth.

- The two sources of economic growth are an increase in the economy's **factors of production** and progress in **technology.**

- Every person and every country has a **comparative advantage** in something, giving rise to gains from trade. Comparative advantage is often confused with **absolute advantage.**

- In the simplest economies people **barter** rather than transact with money. The **circular-flow diagram** illustrates transactions within the economy as flows of goods and services, factors of production, and money between **households** and **firms.** These transactions occur in **markets for goods and services** and **factor markets.** Ultimately, factor markets determine the economy's **income distribution.**

CHECK YOUR UNDERSTANDING 2-1

1. True or false? Explain your answer.
   a. An increase in the amount of resources available to Bombardier for use in producing CSeries jets and subway trains does not change its production possibility frontier.
   b. A technological change that allows Bombardier to build more subway trains for any amount of CSeries jets built results in a change in its production possibility frontier.
   c. The production possibility frontier is useful because it illustrates how much of one good an economy must give up to get more of another good regardless of whether resources are being used efficiently.

2. In Italy, an automobile can be produced by 8 workers in one day and a washing machine by 3 workers in one day. In Canada, an automobile can be produced by 6 workers in one day and a washing machine by 2 workers in one day.
   a. Which country has an absolute advantage in the production of automobiles? In washing machines?
   b. Which country has a comparative advantage in the production of washing machines? In automobiles?
   c. What pattern of specialization results in the greatest gains from trade between the two countries?

3. Using the numbers from Table 2-1, explain why Canada and Brazil are willing to engage in a trade of 7 jets for 29 subway trains.

4. Use the circular-flow diagram to explain how an increase in the amount of money spent by households results in an increase in the number of jobs in the economy. Describe in words what the circular-flow diagram predicts.

Solutions appear at back of book.

Using Models

Economics, we have now learned, is mainly a matter of creating models that draw on a set of basic principles but add some more specific assumptions that allow the modeller to apply those principles to a particular situation. But what do economists actually *do* with their models?

Positive versus Normative Economics

Imagine that you are an economic adviser to the premier of your province. What kinds of questions might the premier ask you to answer?

Well, here are three possible questions:

1. How much revenue will the provincial gasoline tax yield next year?

2. How much would that revenue increase if the tax were raised by 5 percentage points?

3. Should the government increase the tax, bearing in mind that the tax increase will raise much-needed revenue and reduce traffic and air pollution, but will impose some financial hardship on frequent commuters and the trucking industry?

There is a big difference between the first two questions and the third one. The first two are questions about facts. Your forecast of next year's gasoline tax will be proved right or wrong when the numbers actually come in. Your estimate of the impact of a change in the tax is a little harder to check—revenue depends on other factors besides the tax, and it may be hard to disentangle the causes of any change in revenue. Still, in principle there is only one right answer.

But the question of whether the tax on gasoline should be raised may not have a "right" answer—two people who agree on the effects of a higher gasoline tax could still disagree about whether raising this tax is a good idea. For example, someone who takes public transit or walks to work probably won't care about the increased gasoline tax but may care about the reduced traffic and pollution. However, a regular car commuter may have the opposite priorities.

This example highlights a key distinction between two roles of economic analysis. Analysis that tries to answer questions about the way the world works, which have definite right and wrong answers, is known as **positive economics.** In contrast, analysis that involves saying how the world *should* work is known as **normative economics.** To put it another way, positive economics is about objective description; normative economics is about subjective prescription.

Positive economics occupies most of the time and effort of the economics profession. And models play a crucial role in almost all positive economics. As we mentioned earlier, the Canadian government uses computer models to assess proposed changes in federal tax policy, and many provincial and territorial governments have similar models to assess the effects of their own tax policies.

It's worth noting that there is a subtle but important difference between the first and second questions we imagined the premier asking. Question 1 asked for a simple prediction about next year's revenue—a **forecast.** Question 2 was a "what if" question, asking how revenue would change if the tax law were changed. Economists are often called upon to answer both types of questions, but models are especially useful for answering "what if" questions.

The answers to such questions often serve as a guide to policy, but they are still predictions, not prescriptions. That is, they tell you what will happen if a policy is changed; they don't tell you whether or not that result is good. Suppose your economic model tells you that the premier's proposed increase in gasoline taxes will raise inner city property values but will hurt people who must use their cars to get to work. Does that make this proposed tax increase a good idea or a bad one? It depends on whom you ask. As we've just seen, someone who is very concerned about pollution will support the increase, but someone who is very concerned with the welfare of drivers will feel differently. That's a value judgment—it's not a question of economic analysis.

Still, economists often do engage in normative economics and give policy advice. How can they do this when there may be no "right" answer?

One answer is that economists are also citizens, and we all have our opinions. But economic analysis can often be used to show that some policies are clearly better than others, regardless of anyone's opinions.

Suppose that policies A and B achieve the same goal, but policy A makes everyone better off than policy B—or at least makes some people better off without making other people worse off. Then A is clearly more efficient than B. That's not a value judgment: we're talking about how best to achieve a goal, not about the goal itself.

For example, two different policies have been used to help low-income families obtain housing: rent control, which limits the rents landlords are allowed to charge, and rent subsidies, which provide families with additional money to pay rent. Almost all economists agree that subsidies are the more efficient policy. And so the great majority of economists, whatever their personal politics, favour subsidies over rent control.

When policies can be clearly ranked in this way, then economists generally agree. But it is no secret that economists sometimes disagree.

Positive economics is the branch of economic analysis that describes the way the economy actually works.

Normative economics makes prescriptions about the way the economy should work.

A forecast is a simple prediction of the future.

FOR INQUIRING MINDS

WHEN ECONOMISTS AGREE

"If all the economists in the world were laid end to end, they still couldn't reach a conclusion." So goes one popular economist joke. But do economists really disagree that much?

Not according to a classic survey of members of the American Economic Association, reported in the May 1992 issue of the *American Economic Review*. The authors asked respondents to agree or disagree with a number of statements

about the economy; what they found was a high level of agreement among professional economists on many of the statements. At the top, with more than 90 percent of the economists agreeing, were "Tariffs and import quotas usually reduce general economic welfare" and "A ceiling on rents reduces the quantity and quality of housing available." What's striking about these two statements is that many non-economists disagree:

tariffs and import quotas to keep out foreign-produced goods are favoured by many voters, and proposals to do away with rent control in cities like New York and San Francisco have met fierce political opposition.

So is the stereotype of quarrelling economists a myth? Not entirely: economists do disagree quite a lot on some issues, especially in macroeconomics. But there is a large area of common ground.

When and Why Economists Disagree

Economists have a reputation for arguing with each other. Where does this reputation come from, and is it justified?

One important answer is that media coverage tends to exaggerate the real differences in views among economists. If nearly all economists agree on an issue—for example, the proposition that rent controls lead to housing shortages—reporters and editors are likely to conclude that it's not a story worth covering, meaning that professional consensus tends to go unreported. But an issue on which prominent economists take opposing sides—for example, whether cutting taxes right now would help the economy—makes a news story worth reporting. So you hear much more about the areas of disagreement within economics than you do about the large areas of agreement.

It is also worth remembering that economics is, unavoidably, often tied up in politics. On a number of issues powerful interest groups know what opinions they want to hear; they therefore have an incentive to find and promote economists who profess those opinions, giving these economists a prominence and visibility out of proportion to their support among their colleagues.

While the appearance of disagreement among economists exceeds the reality, it remains true that economists often do disagree about important things. For example, some well-respected economists argue vehemently that the Canadian government should replace the income tax with a *consumption tax*. Other equally respected economists disagree. Why this difference of opinion?

One important source of differences lies in values: as in any diverse group of individuals, reasonable people can differ. In comparison to an income tax, a consumption tax typically falls more heavily on people of modest means. So an economist who values a society with more social and income equality for its own sake will tend to oppose a consumption tax. An economist with different values will be less likely to oppose it.

A second important source of differences arises from economic modelling. Because economists base their conclusions on models, which are simplified representations of reality, two economists can legitimately disagree about which simplifications are appropriate—and therefore arrive at different conclusions.

In 2009, British Columbia decided to harmonize its provincial sales tax with the federal Goods and Services Tax (GST) starting in 2010, only to return to the original system after the harmonized sales tax (HST) was defeated in a 2011 referendum. Suppose that two economists were asked for their opinion on the situation. Economist A may focus on the loss of provincial control over the design and collection of sales taxes or the additional sales tax now imposed on certain purchases.[5] But economist B may think that the right way to approach the question is to ignore sovereignty and broadening of the sales tax base and focus on the ways in which the proposed law would change consumption behaviour and the ways in which firms conduct their businesses. This economist might point to studies suggesting that a harmonized sales tax lowers the cost of operating a business, lowers some prices, and promotes more business investment and job creation, all desirable results.

Because the economists have used different models—that is, made different simplifying assumptions about what is most important—they arrive at different conclusions. And so the two economists may find themselves on different sides of the issue.

Behavioural economics, a relatively new approach to modelling that combines concepts from psychology and economics, also leads to different models, which can cause disagreement among economists. Traditional economic models assume that decision-makers are rational, unemotional, and capable of processing large amounts of information in order to make an optimal choice. Meanwhile, behavioural economics acknowledges that economic decision-makers are human beings who can be irrational, emotional, and may not learn from their mistakes. Some might say the traditional approach describes how the world should be (normative economics) while behavioural economics attempts to describe the world as it really is (positive economics).

Both methods of creating models help us better understand economic decision-making, but their differing assumptions can lead to very different results. In finance, for example, the traditional assumptions imply that agents learn from past mistakes and thus do not repeatedly make the same mistakes, resulting in very efficient financial markets, while in behavioural economic models irrational agents can make systematic errors, which can help explain the existence of stock market anomalies.

In most cases such disputes are eventually resolved by the accumulation of evidence showing which of the various models proposed by economists does a better job of fitting the facts. However, in economics, as in any science, it can take a long time before research settles important disputes—decades, in some cases. And since the economy is always changing, in ways that make old models invalid or raise new policy questions, there are always new issues on which economists disagree. The policy-maker must then decide which economist to believe.

The important point is that economic analysis is a method, not a set of conclusions.

ECONOMICS > IN ACTION

ECONOMISTS, BEYOND THE IVORY TOWER

Many economists are mainly engaged in teaching and research. But quite a few economists have a more direct hand in events.

As described earlier in this chapter (For Inquiring Minds, "The Model That Ate the Economy"), one specific branch of economics, finance theory, plays an important role on Bay Street, Wall Street, and other financial centres around the world—not always to good effect. But pricing assets is by no means the only useful function economists serve in the business world. Businesses need forecasts of the future demand for their products, predictions of future raw-material prices, assessments of their future financing needs, and more; for all of these purposes, economic analysis is essential.

Stephen Poloz, the Governor of the Bank of Canada, discusses interest rates as Deputy Governor Tiff Macklem watches. Both men have multiple degrees in economics.

---

[5]Prior to the implementation of BC's HST, newly-constructed homes, restaurant meals, and several services only faced the 5% federal GST. The rate rose to 12% with the HST. A complicated rebate system for new homes meant that purchasers of homes costing less than $525 000 paid no more sales taxes than before, while purchasers of homes costing more than $525 000 paid more sales tax under the HST.

Some of the economists employed in the business world work directly for the institutions that need their input. Top financial institutions like Royal Bank and National Bank maintain high-quality economics groups, which produce analyses of forces and events likely to affect financial markets. Other economists are employed by consulting firms, which sell analysis and advice to a wide range of other businesses.

Last but not least, economists participate extensively in government. Indeed, government agencies at both federal and provincial levels are major employers of economists. This shouldn't be surprising: one of the most important functions of government is to make economic policy, and almost every government policy decision must take economic effects into consideration. So governments around the world employ economists in a variety of roles.

You are likely to find economists working in almost every branch of the Canadian government. Consider the mandates of the departments dealing with Aboriginal affairs, agriculture, environment, immigration, interprovincial relations, natural resources, transportation, or science and technology! No matter what department comes to mind, there is a strong economic dimension involved. However, the strongest concentration of economists is likely to be found in the Department of Finance, which plans and prepares the federal government's budget, and analyzes and designs tax policies. This department also develops policies on international finance and helps design Canada's tariff policies. The Bank of Canada employs economists who help design monetary policy, implement that policy, and regulate chartered banks. And economists play an especially important role in two international organizations headquartered in Washington, D.C.: the International Monetary Fund, which provides advice and loans to countries experiencing economic difficulties, and the World Bank, which provides advice and loans to promote long-term economic development.

In the past, it wasn't that easy to track what all these economists working on practical affairs were up to. These days, however, there is a very lively online discussion of economic prospects and policy, on websites that range from the home page of the International Monetary Fund (www.imf.org), to business-oriented sites like economy.com, to the blogs of individual economists, like that of Mark Thoma (economistsview.typepad.com) or, yes, our own blog, which is among the Technorati top 100 blogs, at krugman.blogs.nytimes.com.

▼ Quick Review

- **Positive economics**—the focus of most economic research—is the analysis of the way the world works, in which there are definite right and wrong answers. If often involves making **forecasts.** But in **normative economics,** which makes prescriptions about how things ought to be, there are often no right answers and only value judgments.

- Economists do disagree—though not as much as legend has it—for two main reasons. One, they may disagree about which simplifications to make in a model. Two, economists may disagree—like everyone else—about values.

CHECK YOUR UNDERSTANDING   2-2

1. Which of the following statements is a positive statement? Which is a normative statement?
   a. Society should take measures to prevent people from engaging in dangerous personal behaviour.
   b. People who engage in dangerous personal behaviour impose higher costs on society through higher medical costs.

2. True or false? Explain your answer.
   a. Policy choice A and policy choice B attempt to achieve the same social goal. Policy choice A, however, results in a much less efficient use of resources than policy choice B. Therefore, economists are more likely to agree on choosing policy choice B.
   b. When two economists disagree on the desirability of a policy, it's typically because one of them has made a mistake.
   c. Policy-makers can always use economics to figure out which goals a society should try to achieve.

Solutions appear at back of book.

BUSINESS CASE • Efficiency, Opportunity Cost, and the Logic of Lean Production

Corbis/Photolibrary

In the summer and fall of 2010, workers were rearranging the furniture in Boeing's final assembly plant in Everett, Washington, in preparation for the production of the Boeing 767. It was a difficult and time-consuming process, however, because the items of "furniture"—Boeing's assembly equipment—weighed on the order of 180 tonnes each. It was a necessary part of setting up a production system based on "lean manufacturing," also called "just-in-time" production. Lean manufacturing, pioneered by Toyota Motors of Japan, is based on the practice of having parts arrive on the factory floor just as they are needed for production. This reduces the amount of parts Boeing holds in inventory as well as the amount of the factory floor needed for production—in this case, reducing the space required for manufacture of the 767 by 40%.

Boeing had adopted lean manufacturing in 1999 in the manufacture of the 737, the most popular commercial airplane. By 2005, after constant refinement, Boeing had achieved a 50% reduction in the time it takes to produce a plane and a nearly 60% reduction in parts inventory. An important feature is a continuously moving assembly line, moving products from one assembly team to the next at a steady pace and eliminating the need for workers to wander across the factory floor from task to task or in search of tools and parts.

Toyota's lean production techniques have been the most widely adopted of all manufacturing techniques and have revolutionized manufacturing worldwide. In simple terms, lean production is focused on organization and communication. Workers and parts are organized so as to ensure a smooth and consistent workflow that minimizes wasted effort and materials. Lean production is also designed to be highly responsive to changes in the desired mix of output—for example, quickly producing more sedans and fewer minivans according to changes in customers' demands.

Toyota's lean production methods were so successful that they transformed the global auto industry and severely threatened once-dominant North American automakers. Until the 1980s, the "Big Three"—Chrysler, Ford, and General Motors—dominated the North American auto industry. In the 1980s, however, Toyotas became increasingly popular in North America due to their high quality and relatively low price—so popular that the Big Three eventually prevailed upon the U.S. government to protect them by restricting the sale of Japanese autos in the United States. A few months later, the Canadian government set a limit on the number of cars Toyota could export to Canada. Over time, Toyota responded by building assembly plants in the United States and in Canada, bringing along its lean production techniques, which then spread throughout North American manufacturing. Toyota's growth continued, and by 2008 it had eclipsed General Motors as the largest automaker in the world.

QUESTIONS FOR THOUGHT

1. What is the opportunity cost associated with having a worker wander across the factory floor from task to task or in search of tools and parts?

2. Explain how lean manufacturing improves the economy's efficiency in production and consumption.

3. Before lean manufacturing innovations, Japan mostly sold consumer electronics to Canada and the United States. How did lean manufacturing innovations alter Japan's comparative advantage vis-à-vis North America?

4. Predict how the shift in the location of Toyota's production from Japan to North America is likely to alter the pattern of comparative advantage in automaking between the two regions.

1. Almost all economics is based on **models,** "thought experiments" or simplified versions of reality, many of which use mathematical tools such as graphs. An important assumption in economic models is the **other things equal assumption,** which allows analysis of the effect of a change in one factor by holding all other relevant factors unchanged.

2. One important economic model is the **production possibility frontier.** It illustrates *opportunity cost* (showing how much less of one good can be produced if more of the other good is produced); *efficiency* (an economy is efficient in production if it produces on the production possibility frontier and efficient in consumption if it produces the mix of goods and services that people want to consume); and *economic growth* (an outward shift of the production possibility frontier). There are two basic sources of growth: an increase in **factors of production**—resources such as land, labour, and capital, inputs that are not used up in production—and improved **technology.**

3. Another important model is **comparative advantage,** which explains the source of gains from trade between individuals and countries. Everyone has a comparative advantage in something—some good or service in which that person has a lower opportunity cost than everyone else. But it is often confused with **absolute advantage,** an ability to produce a particular good or service better than anyone else. This confusion leads some to erroneously conclude that there are no gains from trade between people or countries.

4. In the simplest economies people **barter**—trade goods and services for one another—rather than trade them for money, as in a modern economy. The **circular-flow diagram** represents transactions within the economy as flows of goods, services, and money between **households** and **firms.** These transactions occur in **markets for goods and services** and **factor markets,** markets for factors of production—land, labour, and capital. It is useful in understanding how spending, production, employment, income, and growth are related in the economy. Ultimately, factor markets determine the economy's **income distribution,** how an economy's total income is allocated to the owners of the factors of production.

5. Economists use economic models for both **positive economics,** which objectively describes how the economy works, and for **normative economics,** which prescribes how the economy *should* work. Positive economics often involves making **forecasts.** Economists can determine correct answers for positive questions but typically not for normative questions, which involve value judgments. The exceptions are when policies designed to achieve a certain objective can be clearly ranked in terms of efficiency.

6. There are two main reasons economists disagree. One, they may disagree about which simplifications to make in a model. Two, economists may disagree—like everyone else—about values.

Model, p. 26
Other things equal assumption, p. 26
Production possibility frontier, p. 28
Factors of production, p. 32
Technology, p. 32
Comparative advantage, p. 35

Absolute advantage, p. 36
Barter, p. 38
Circular-flow diagram, p. 38
Household, p. 38
Firm, p. 38
Markets for goods and services, p. 38

Factor markets, p. 39
Income distribution, p. 39
Positive economics, p. 41
Normative economics, p. 41
Forecast, p. 41

1. Two important industries on the island of Bermuda are fishing and tourism. According to data from the Food and Agriculture Organization of the United Nations and the Bermuda Department of Statistics, in the year 2009 the 306 registered fishers in Bermuda caught 387 tonnes of marine fish. And the 2719 people employed by hotels produced 554 400 hotel stays (measured by the number of visitor arrivals). Suppose that this production point is efficient in production. Assume also that the opportunity cost of 1 additional tonne of fish is 2000 hotel stays and that this opportunity cost is constant (the opportunity cost does not change).
   a. If all 306 registered fishers were to be employed by hotels (in addition to the 2719 people already working in hotels), how many hotel stays could Bermuda produce?
   b. If all 2719 hotel employees were to become fishers (in addition to the 306 fishers already working in the fishing industry), how many tonnes of fish could Bermuda produce?

c. Draw a production possibility frontier for Bermuda, with fish on the horizontal axis and hotel stays on the vertical axis, and label Bermuda's actual production point for the year 2009.

2. Atlantis is a small, isolated island in the South Atlantic. The inhabitants grow potatoes and catch fish. The accompanying table shows the maximum annual output combinations of potatoes and fish that can be produced. Obviously, given their limited resources and available technology, as they use more of their resources for potato production, there are fewer resources available for catching fish.

Maximum annual output options	Quantity of potatoes (kilograms)	Quantity of fish (kilograms)
A	1000	0
B	800	300
C	600	500
D	400	600
E	200	650
F	0	675

a. Draw a production possibility frontier with potatoes on the horizontal axis and fish on the vertical axis illustrating these options, showing points *A–F.*

b. Can Atlantis produce 500 kg of fish and 800 kg of potatoes? Explain. Where would this point lie relative to the production possibility frontier?

c. What is the opportunity cost of increasing the annual output of potatoes from 600 to 800 kg?

d. What is the opportunity cost of increasing the annual output of potatoes from 200 to 400 kg?

e. Can you explain why the answers to parts (c) and (d) are not the same? What does this imply about the slope of the production possibility frontier?

3. According to Statistics Canada, 11.0 million hectares of land in Canada were used for wheat or corn farming in 2012. Of those 11.0 million hectares, farmers used 9.6 million hectares to grow 999.62 million bushels of wheat and 1.4 million hectares of land to grow 514.15 million bushels of corn. Suppose that Canada's wheat farming and corn farming are efficient in production. At that production point, the opportunity cost of producing 1 additional bushel of wheat is 1.7 fewer bushels of corn. However, because farmers have increasing opportunity costs at higher levels of wheat production, additional bushels of wheat have an opportunity cost greater than 1.7 bushels of corn. For each of the following production points, decide whether that production point is (i) feasible and efficient in production, (ii) feasible but not efficient in production, (iii) not feasible, or (iv) unclear as to whether or not it is feasible.

a. Farmers use 1.6 million hectares of land to produce 180 million bushels of wheat, and they use 2.4 million hectares of land to produce 900 million bushels of corn. The remaining 7.0 million hectares are left unused.

b. From their original production point, farmers transfer 1.6 million hectares of land from corn to wheat production. They now produce 1009.62 million of bushels of wheat and 497.15 million bushels of corn.

c. Farmers reduce their production of wheat to 950 million bushels and increase their production of corn to 588.58 million bushels. Along the production possibility frontier, the opportunity cost of going from 514.15 million bushels of corn to 588.58 million bushels of corn is 0.666 bushels of wheat per bushel of corn.

4. In the ancient country of Roma, only two goods, spaghetti and meatballs, are produced. There are two tribes in Roma, the Tivoli and the Frivoli. By themselves, the Tivoli each month can produce either 30 kg of spaghetti and no meatballs, or 50 kg of meatballs and no spaghetti, or any combination in between. The Frivoli, by themselves, each month can produce 40 kg of spaghetti and no meatballs, or 30 kg of meatballs and no spaghetti, or any combination in between.

a. Assume that all production possibility frontiers are straight lines. Draw one diagram showing the monthly production possibility frontier for the Tivoli and another showing the monthly production possibility frontier for the Frivoli. Show how you calculated them.

b. Which tribe has the comparative advantage in spaghetti production? In meatball production?

In 100 A.D. the Frivoli discover a new technique for making meatballs that doubles the quantity of meatballs they can produce each month.

c. Draw the new monthly production possibility frontier for the Frivoli.

d. After the innovation, which tribe now has an absolute advantage in producing meatballs? In producing spaghetti? Which has the comparative advantage in meatball production? In spaghetti production?

5. According to the Canadian International Merchandise Trade Database from Statistics Canada, in December 2012, Canada sold aircraft and spacecraft worth $27.23 million to China and bought aircraft and spacecraft worth only $8.1 million from China. During the same month, however, Canada bought $255.1 million worth of apparel and clothing accessories from China but sold only $56 253 worth of apparel and clothing accessories to China. Using what you have learned about how trade is determined by comparative advantage, answer the following questions.

a. Which country has the comparative advantage in aircraft production? In production of apparel and clothing accessories?

b. Can you determine which country has the absolute advantage in aircraft production? In apparel and clothing accessories?

6. Peter Pundit, an economics reporter, states that the European Union (EU) is increasing its productivity very rapidly in all industries. He claims that this productivity advance is so rapid that output from the EU in these industries will soon exceed that of Canada and, as a result, Canada will no longer benefit from trade with the EU.

a. Do you think Peter Pundit is correct or not? If not, what do you think is the source of his mistake?

b. If the EU and Canada continue to trade, what do you think will characterize the goods that the EU sells to Canada and the goods that Canada sells to the EU?

7. You are in charge of allocating residents to your dormitory's baseball and basketball teams. You are down to the last four people, two of whom must be allocated to baseball and two to basketball. The accompanying table gives each person's batting average and free-throw average.

Name	Batting average	Free-throw average
Kelley	70%	60%
Nina	50%	50%
Curt	10%	30%
Yul	80%	70%

a. Explain how you would use the concept of comparative advantage to allocate the players. Begin by establishing each player's opportunity cost of free throws in terms of batting average.

b. Why is it likely that the other basketball players will be unhappy about this arrangement but the other baseball players will be satisfied? Nonetheless, why would an economist say that this is an efficient way to allocate players for your dormitory's sports teams?

8. The inhabitants of the fictional economy of Atlantis use money in the form of cowrie shells. Draw a circular-flow diagram showing households and firms. Firms produce potatoes and fish, and households buy potatoes and fish. Households also provide the land and labour to firms. Identify where in the flows of cowrie shells or physical things (goods and services, or resources) each of the following impacts would occur. Describe how this impact spreads around the circle.

a. A devastating hurricane floods many of the potato fields.

b. A very productive fishing season yields a very large number of fish caught.

c. The inhabitants of Atlantis discover Shakira and spend several days a month at dancing festivals.

9. An economist might say that colleges and universities "produce" education, using faculty members and students as inputs. According to this line of reasoning, education is then "consumed" by households. Construct a circular-flow diagram to represent the sector of the economy devoted to post-secondary education: colleges and universities represent firms, and households both consume education and provide faculty and students to colleges and universities. What are the relevant markets in this diagram? What is being bought and sold in each direction? What would happen in the diagram if the government decided to subsidize 50% of all college and university students' tuition?

10. Your dormitory roommate plays loud music most of the time; you, however, would prefer more peace and quiet. You suggest that she buy some earphones. She responds that although she would be happy to use earphones, she has many other things that she would prefer to spend her money on right now. You discuss this situation with a friend who is an economics major. The following exchange takes place:

He: How much would it cost to buy earphones?

You: $15.

He: How much do you value having some peace and quiet for the rest of the semester?

You: $30.

He: It is efficient for you to buy the earphones and give them to your roommate. You gain more than you lose; the benefit exceeds the cost. You should do that.

You: It just isn't fair that I have to pay for the earphones when I'm not the one making the noise.

a. Which parts of this conversation contain positive statements and which parts contain normative statements?

b. Construct an argument supporting your viewpoint that your roommate should be the one to change her behaviour. Similarly, construct an argument from the viewpoint of your roommate that you should be the one to buy the earphones. If your dormitory has a policy that gives residents the unlimited right to play music, whose argument is likely to win? If your dormitory has a rule that a person must stop playing music whenever a roommate complains, whose argument is likely to win?

11. A representative of the Canadian clothing industry recently made the following statement: "Workers in Asia often work in sweatshop conditions earning only pennies an hour. Canadian workers are more productive and as a result earn higher wages. In order to preserve the dignity of the Canadian workplace, the government should enact legislation banning imports of low-wage Asian clothing."

a. Which parts of this quote are positive statements? Which parts are normative statements?

b. Is the policy that is being advocated consistent with the preceding statements about the wages and productivities of Canadian and Asian workers?

c. Would such a policy make some Canadians better off without making any other Canadians worse off? That is, would this policy be efficient from the viewpoint of all Canadians?

d. Would low-wage Asian workers benefit from or be hurt by such a policy?

12. Are the following statements true or false? Explain your answers.

a. "When people must pay higher taxes on their wage earnings, it reduces their incentive to work" is a positive statement.

b. "We should lower taxes to encourage more work" is a positive statement.

c. Economics cannot always be used to completely decide what society ought to do.

d. "The system of public education in this country generates greater benefits to society than the cost of running the system" is a normative statement.

e. All disagreements among economists are generated by the media.

13. Evaluate the following statement: "It is easier to build an economic model that accurately reflects events that have already occurred than to build an economic model to forecast future events." Do you think this is true or not? Why? What does this imply about the difficulties of building good economic models?

14. Economists who work for the government are often called on to make policy recommendations. Why do you think it is important for the public to be able to differentiate normative statements from positive statements in these recommendations?

15. The mayor of Gotham City, worried about a potential epidemic of deadly influenza this winter, asks an economic adviser the following series of questions. Determine whether a question requires the economic adviser to make a positive assessment or a normative assessment.

a. How much vaccine will be in stock in the city by the end of November?

b. If we offer to pay 10% more per dose to the pharmaceutical companies providing the vaccines, will they provide additional doses?

c. If there is a shortage of vaccine in the city, whom should we vaccinate first—the elderly or the very young? (Assume that a person from one group has an equal likelihood of dying from influenza as a person from the other group.)

d. If the city charges $25 per shot, how many people will pay?

e. If the city charges $25 per shot, it will make a profit of $10 per shot, money that can go to providing poor people with free flu shots. Should the city engage in such a scheme?

16. Assess the following statement: "If economists just had enough data, they could solve all policy questions in a way that maximizes the social good. There would be no need for divisive political debates, such as whether the government should provide free medical care for all."

Graphs in Economics

Getting the Picture

Whether you're reading about economics in the *Globe and Mail* or in your economics textbook, you will see many graphs. Visual images can make it much easier to understand verbal descriptions, numerical information, or ideas. In economics, graphs are the type of visual image used to facilitate understanding. To fully understand the ideas and information being discussed, you need to be familiar with how to interpret these visual aids. This appendix explains how graphs are constructed and interpreted and how they are used in economics.

Graphs, Variables, and Economic Models

One reason to attend university is that a bachelor's degree provides access to higherpaying jobs. Additional degrees, such as MBAs or law degrees, increase earnings even more. If you were to read an article about the relationship between educational attainment and income, you would probably see a graph showing the income levels for workers with different amounts of education. And this graph would depict the idea that, in general, more education increases income. This graph, like most of those in economics, would depict the relationship between two economic variables. A **variable** is a quantity that can take on more than one value, such as the number of years of education a person has, the price of a can of pop, or a household's income.

As you learned in this chapter, economic analysis relies heavily on *models*, simplified descriptions of real situations. Most economic models describe the relationship between two variables, simplified by holding constant other variables that may affect the relationship. For example, an economic model might describe the relationship between the price of a can of pop and the number of cans of pop that consumers will buy, assuming that everything else that affects consumers' purchases of pop stays constant. This type of model can be described mathematically or verbally, but illustrating the relationship in a graph makes it easier to understand. Next we show how graphs that depict economic models are constructed and interpreted.

How Graphs Work

Most graphs in economics are based on a grid built around two perpendicular lines that show the values of two variables, helping you visualize the relationship between them. So a first step in understanding the use of such graphs is to see how this system works.

Two-Variable Graphs

Figure 2A-1 shows a typical two-variable graph. It illustrates the data in the accompanying table on outside temperature and the number of cans of pop a typical vendor can expect to sell at a baseball stadium during one game. The first column shows the values of outside temperature (the first variable) and the second column shows the values of the number of cans of pop sold (the second variable). Five combinations or pairs of the two variables are shown, each denoted by *A* through *E* in the third column.

Now let's turn to graphing the data in this table. In any two-variable graph, one variable is called the *x*-variable and the other is called the *y*-variable.

A quantity that can take on more than one value is called a **variable**.

FIGURE **2A-1** Plotting Points on a Two-Variable Graph

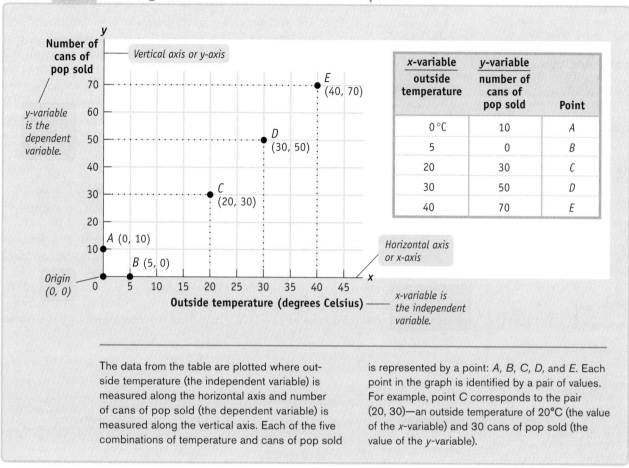

x-variable outside temperature	*y*-variable number of cans of pop sold	Point
0 °C	10	A
5	0	B
20	30	C
30	50	D
40	70	E

The data from the table are plotted where outside temperature (the independent variable) is measured along the horizontal axis and number of cans of pop sold (the dependent variable) is measured along the vertical axis. Each of the five combinations of temperature and cans of pop sold is represented by a point: *A*, *B*, *C*, *D*, and *E*. Each point in the graph is identified by a pair of values. For example, point *C* corresponds to the pair (20, 30)—an outside temperature of 20°C (the value of the *x*-variable) and 30 cans of pop sold (the value of the *y*-variable).

Here we have made outside temperature the *x*-variable and number of cans of pop sold the *y*-variable. The solid horizontal line in the graph is called the **horizontal axis** or ***x*-axis,** and values of the *x*-variable—outside temperature—are measured along it. Similarly, the solid vertical line in the graph is called the **vertical axis** or ***y*-axis,** and values of the *y*-variable—number of cans of pop sold—are measured along it. At the **origin,** the point where the two axes meet, each variable is equal to zero. As you move rightward from the origin along the *x*-axis, values of the *x*-variable are positive and increasing. As you move up from the origin along the *y*-axis, values of the *y*-variable are positive and increasing.

You can plot each of the five points *A* through *E* on this graph by using a pair of numbers—the values that the *x*-variable and the *y*-variable take on for a given point. In Figure 2A-1, at point *C*, the *x*-variable takes on the value 20 and the *y*-variable takes on the value 30. You plot point *C* by drawing a line straight up from 20 on the *x*-axis and a horizontal line across from 30 on the *y*-axis. We write point *C* as (20, 30). We write the origin as (0, 0).

Looking at point *A* and point *B* in Figure 2A-1, you can see that when one of the variables for a point has a value of zero, it will lie on one of the axes. If the value of the *x*-variable is zero, the point will lie on the vertical axis, like point *A*. If the value of the *y*-variable is zero, the point will lie on the horizontal axis, like point *B*.

Most graphs that depict relationships between two economic variables represent a **causal relationship,** a relationship in which the value taken by one variable directly influences or determines the value taken by the other variable. In a causal relationship, the determining variable is called the **independent variable;** the variable it determines is called the **dependent variable.** In our example of pop

The line along which values of the *x*-variable are measured is called the **horizontal axis** or ***x*-axis.** The line along which values of the *y*-variable are measured is called the **vertical axis** or ***y*-axis.** The point where the axes of a two-variable graph meet is the **origin.**

A **causal relationship** exists between two variables when the value taken by one variable directly influences or determines the value taken by the other variable. In a causal relationship, the determining variable is called the **independent variable;** the variable it determines is called the **dependent variable.**

A **curve** is a line on a graph that depicts a relationship between two variables. It may be either a straight line or a curved line. If the curve is a straight line, the variables have a **linear relationship.** If the curve is not a straight line, the variables have a **non-linear relationship.**

sales, the outside temperature is the independent variable. It directly influences the number of cans of pop that are sold, the dependent variable in this case.

By convention, we put the independent variable on the horizontal axis and the dependent variable on the vertical axis. Figure 2A-1 is constructed consistent with this convention; the independent variable (outside temperature) is on the horizontal axis and the dependent variable (number of cans of pop sold) is on the vertical axis. An important exception to this convention is in graphs showing the economic relationship between the price of a product and quantity of the product: although price is generally the independent variable that determines quantity, it is always measured on the vertical axis.

Curves on a Graph

Panel (a) of Figure 2A-2 contains some of the same information as Figure 2A-1, with a line drawn through the points *B, C, D,* and *E.* Such a line on a graph is called a **curve,** regardless of whether it is a straight line or a curved line. If the curve that shows the relationship between two variables is a straight line, or linear, the variables have a **linear relationship.** When the curve is not a straight line, or non-linear, the variables have a **non-linear relationship.**

A point on a curve indicates the value of the *y*-variable for a specific value of the *x*-variable. For example, point *D* indicates that at a temperature of 30°C, a vendor can expect to sell 50 cans of pop. The shape and orientation of a curve reveal

FIGURE 2A-2 **Drawing Curves**

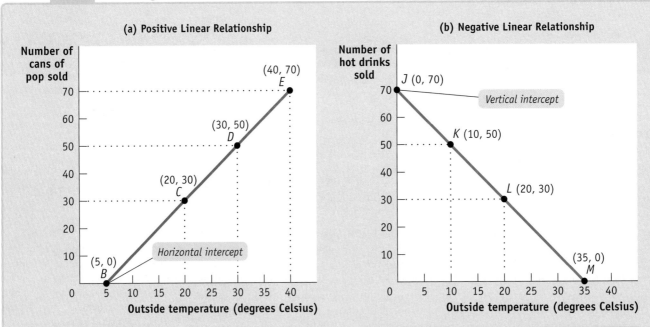

The curve in panel (a) illustrates the relationship between the two variables, outside temperature and number of cans of pop sold. The two variables have a positive linear relationship: positive because the curve has an upward tilt or slope, and linear because it is a straight line. It implies that an increase in the *x*-variable (outside temperature) leads to an increase in the *y*-variable (number of cans of pop sold). The curve in panel (b) is also a straight line, but it slopes (tilts)

downward. The two variables here, outside temperature and number of hot drinks sold, have a negative linear relationship: an increase in the *x*-variable (outside temperature) leads to a decrease in the *y*-variable (number of hot drinks sold). The curve in panel (a) has a horizontal intercept at point *B,* where it hits the horizontal axis. The curve in panel (b) has a vertical intercept at point *J,* where it hits the vertical axis, and a horizontal intercept at point *M,* where it hits the horizontal axis.

the general nature of the relationship between the two variables. The upward tilt of the curve in panel (a) of Figure 2A-2 means that vendors can expect to sell more cans of pop at higher outside temperatures.

When variables are related this way—that is, when an increase in one variable is associated with an increase in the other variable—the variables are said to have a **positive relationship.** It is illustrated by a curve that slopes upward from left to right. Because this curve is also linear, the relationship between outside temperature and number of cans of pop sold illustrated by the curve in panel (a) of Figure 2A-2 is a positive linear relationship.

When an increase in one variable is associated with a decrease in the other variable, the two variables are said to have a **negative relationship.** It is illustrated by a curve that slopes downward from left to right, like the curve in panel (b) of Figure 2A-2. Because this curve is also linear, the relationship it depicts is a negative linear relationship. Two variables that might have such a relationship are the outside temperature and the number of hot drinks a vendor can expect to sell at a baseball stadium.

Return for a moment to the curve in panel (a) of Figure 2A-2 and you can see that it hits the horizontal axis at point *B*. This point, known as the **horizontal intercept,** shows the value of the *x*-variable when the value of the *y*-variable is zero. In panel (b) of Figure 2A-2, the curve hits the vertical axis at point *J*. This point, called the **vertical intercept,** indicates the value of the *y*-variable when the value of the *x*-variable is zero.

A Key Concept: The Slope of a Curve

The **slope** of a curve is a measure of how steep or flat it is and indicates how sensitive the *y*-variable is to a change in the *x*-variable. In our example of outside temperature and the number of cans of pop a vendor can expect to sell, the slope of the curve would indicate how many more cans of pop the vendor could expect to sell with each 1 degree increase in temperature. Interpreted this way, the slope gives meaningful information. Even without numbers for *x* and *y*, it is possible to arrive at important conclusions about the relationship between the two variables by examining the slope of a curve at various points.

The Slope of a Linear Curve

Along a linear curve the slope, or steepness, is measured by dividing the "rise" between two points on the curve by the "run" between those same two points. The rise is the amount that *y* changes, and the run is the amount that *x* changes. Here is the formula:

(2A-1) $\dfrac{\text{Change in } y}{\text{Change in } x} = \dfrac{\Delta y}{\Delta x} = \text{Slope}$

In the formula, the symbol Δ (the Greek uppercase delta) stands for "change in." When a variable increases, the change in that variable is positive; when a variable decreases, the change in that variable is negative.

The slope of a curve is positive when the rise (the change in the *y*-variable) has the same sign as the run (the change in the *x*-variable). That's because when two numbers have the same sign, the ratio of those two numbers is positive. The curve in panel (a) of Figure 2A-2 has a positive slope: along the curve, both the *y*-variable and the *x*-variable increase. The slope of a curve is negative when the rise and the run have different signs. That's because when two numbers have different signs, the ratio of those two numbers is negative. The curve in panel (b) of Figure 2A-2 has a negative slope: along the curve, an increase in the *x*-variable is associated with a decrease in the *y*-variable.

Figure 2A-3 illustrates how to calculate the slope of a linear curve. Let's focus first on panel (a). From point *A* to point *B* the value of the *y*-variable changes from

Two variables have a **positive relationship** when an increase in the value of one variable is associated with an increase in the value of the other variable. It is illustrated by a curve that slopes upward from left to right.

Two variables have a **negative relationship** when an increase in the value of one variable is associated with a decrease in the value of the other variable. It is illustrated by a curve that slopes downward from left to right.

The **horizontal intercept** of a curve is the point at which it hits the horizontal axis; it indicates the value of the *x*-variable when the value of the *y*-variable is zero.

The **vertical intercept** of a curve is the point at which it hits the vertical axis; it shows the value of the *y*-variable when the value of the *x*-variable is zero.

The **slope** of a line or curve is a measure of how steep or flat it is. The slope of a line is measured by "rise over run"—the change in the *y*-variable between two points on the line divided by the change in the *x*-variable between those same two points.

FIGURE **2A-3** Calculating the Slope

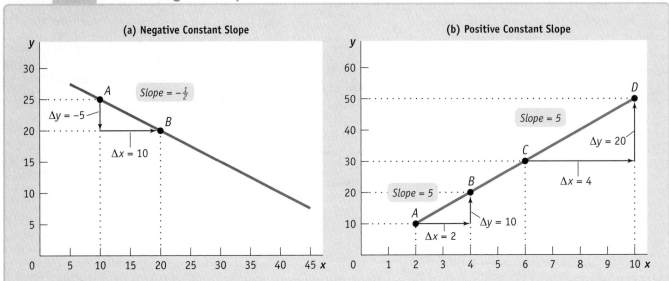

Panels (a) and (b) show two linear curves. Between points A and B on the curve in panel (a), the change in y (the rise) is -5 and the change in x (the run) is 10. So the slope from A to B is $\frac{\Delta y}{\Delta x} = \frac{-5}{10} = -\frac{1}{2} = -0.5$, where the negative sign indicates that the curve is downward sloping. In panel (b), the curve has a slope from A to B of $\frac{\Delta y}{\Delta x} = \frac{10}{2} = 5$. The slope from C to

D is $\frac{\Delta y}{\Delta x} = \frac{20}{4} = 5$. The slope is positive, indicating that the curve is upward sloping. Furthermore, the slope between A and B is the same as the slope between C and D, making this a linear curve. The slope of a linear curve is constant: it is the same regardless of where it is measured along the curve.

25 to 20 and the value of the x-variable changes from 10 to 20. So the slope of the line between these two points is:

$$\frac{\text{Change in } y}{\text{Change in } x} = \frac{\Delta y}{\Delta x} = \frac{-5}{10} = -\frac{1}{2} = -0.5$$

Because a straight line is equally steep at all points, the slope of a straight line is the same at all points. In other words, a straight line has a constant slope. You can check this by calculating the slope of the linear curve between points A and B and between points C and D in panel (b) of Figure 2A-3.

Between A and B: $\qquad \frac{\Delta y}{\Delta x} = \frac{10}{2} = 5$

Between C and D: $\qquad \frac{\Delta y}{\Delta x} = \frac{20}{4} = 5$

Horizontal and Vertical Curves and Their Slopes

When a curve is horizontal, the value of the y-variable along that curve never changes—it is constant. Everywhere along the curve, the change in y is zero. Now, zero divided by any non-zero number is zero. So, regardless of the value of the change in x, the slope of a horizontal curve is always zero.

If a curve is vertical, the value of the x-variable along the curve never changes—it is constant. Everywhere along the curve, the change in x is zero. This means that the slope of a vertical curve is a ratio with zero in the denominator. A ratio with zero in the denominator is equal to infinity—that is, an infinitely large number. So the slope of a vertical curve is equal to infinity.

A vertical or a horizontal curve has a special implication: it means that the x-variable and the y-variable are unrelated. Two variables are unrelated when a change in one variable (the independent variable) has no effect on the other variable (the dependent variable). Or to put it a slightly different way, two variables are unrelated when the dependent variable is constant regardless of the value of the independent variable. If, as is usual, the y-variable is the dependent variable, the curve is horizontal. If the dependent variable is the x-variable, the curve is vertical.

The Slope of a Non-linear Curve

A **non-linear curve** is one in which the slope changes as you move along it. Panels (a), (b), (c), and (d) of Figure 2A-4 show various non-linear curves. Panels (a) and (b) show non-linear curves whose slopes change as you move along them, but the slopes always remain positive. Although both curves tilt upward, the curve in panel (a) gets steeper as you move from left to right in contrast to the curve in panel (b), which gets flatter. A curve that is upward sloping and gets steeper, as in panel (a), is said to have *positive increasing* slope. A curve that is upward sloping but gets flatter, as in panel (b), is said to have *positive decreasing* slope.

When we calculate the slope along these non-linear curves, we obtain different values for the slope at different points. How the slope changes along the curve determines the curve's shape. For example, in panel (a) of Figure 2A-4, the slope of the curve is a positive number that steadily increases as you move from left to right, whereas in panel (b), the slope is a positive number that steadily decreases.

The slopes of the curves in panels (c) and (d) are negative numbers. Economists often prefer to express a negative number as its **absolute value,** which is the value of the negative number without the minus sign. In general, we denote the absolute value of a number by two parallel bars around the number; for example, the absolute value of −4 is written as |−4| = 4. In panel (c), the absolute value of the slope steadily increases as you move from left to right. The curve therefore has *negative increasing* slope (i.e., the absolute value of the slope is increasing, so the curve is getting steeper). And in panel (d), the absolute value of the slope of the curve steadily decreases along the curve. This curve therefore has *negative decreasing* slope.

Calculating the Slope Along a Non-linear Curve

We've just seen that along a non-linear curve, the value of the slope depends on where you are on that curve. So how do you calculate the slope of a non-linear curve? We will focus on two methods: the *arc method* and the *point method*.

The Arc Method of Calculating the Slope
An arc of a curve is some piece or segment of that curve. For example, panel (a) of Figure 2A-4 shows an arc consisting of the segment of the curve between points A and B. To calculate the slope along a non-linear curve using the arc method, you draw a straight line between the two end-points of the arc. The slope of that straight line is a measure of the average slope of the curve between those two end-points. You can see from panel (a) of Figure 2A-4 that the straight line drawn between points A and B increases along the x-axis from 6 to 10 (so that $\Delta x = 4$) as it increases along the y-axis from 10 to 20 (so that $\Delta y = 10$). Therefore the slope of the straight line connecting points A and B is:

$$\frac{\Delta y}{\Delta x} = \frac{10}{4} = 2.5$$

This means that the average slope of the curve between points A and B is 2.5.

A **non-linear curve** is one in which the slope is not the same between every pair of points.

The **absolute value** of a negative number is the value of the negative number without the minus sign.

FIGURE **2A-4** Non-linear Curves

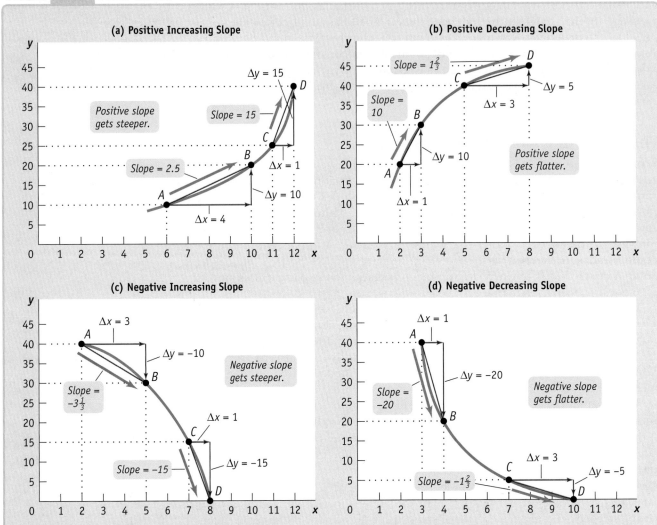

In panel (a) the slope of the curve from A to B is $\frac{\Delta y}{\Delta x} = \frac{10}{4} = 2.5$, and from C to D it is $\frac{\Delta y}{\Delta x} = \frac{15}{1} = 15$. The slope is positive and increasing; the curve gets steeper as you move to the right. In panel (b) the slope of the curve from A to B is $\frac{\Delta y}{\Delta x} = \frac{10}{1} = 10$, and from C to D it is $\frac{\Delta y}{\Delta x} = \frac{5}{3} = 1\frac{2}{3}$. The slope is positive and decreasing; the curve gets flatter as you move to the right. In panel (c) the slope from A to B is $\frac{\Delta y}{\Delta x} = \frac{-10}{3} = -3\frac{1}{3}$, and from C to D it is $\frac{\Delta y}{\Delta x} = \frac{-15}{1} = -15$. The slope is negative and increasing;

the curve gets steeper as you move to the right. And in panel (d) the slope from A to B is $\frac{\Delta y}{\Delta x} = \frac{-20}{1} = -20$, and from C to D it is $\frac{\Delta y}{\Delta x} = \frac{-5}{3} = -1\frac{2}{3}$. The slope is negative and decreasing; the curve gets flatter as you move to the right. The slope in each case has been calculated by using the arc method—that is, by drawing a straight line connecting two points along a curve. The average slope between those two points is equal to the slope of the straight line between those two points.

Now consider the arc on the same curve between points C and D. A straight line drawn through these two points increases along the x-axis from 11 to 12 ($\Delta x = 1$) as it increases along the y-axis from 25 to 40 ($\Delta y = 15$). So the average slope between points C and D is:

$$\frac{\Delta y}{\Delta x} = \frac{15}{1} = 15$$

Therefore the average slope between points *C* and *D* is larger than the average slope between points *A* and *B*. These calculations verify what we have already observed—that this upward-tilted curve gets steeper as you move from left to right and therefore has positive increasing slope.

The Point Method of Calculating the Slope The point method calculates the slope of a non-linear curve at a specific point on that curve. Figure 2A-5 illustrates how to calculate the slope at point *B* on the curve. First, we draw a straight line that just touches the curve at point *B*. Such a line is called a **tangent line:** the fact that it just touches the curve at point *B* and does not touch the curve at any other point on the curve means that the straight line is *tangent* to the curve at point *B*. The slope of this tangent line is equal to the slope of the non-linear curve at point *B*.

You can see from Figure 2A-5 how the slope of the tangent line is calculated: from point *A* to point *C*, the change in *y* is 15 and the change in *x* is 5, generating a slope of:

$$\frac{\Delta y}{\Delta x} = \frac{15}{5} = 3$$

By the point method, the slope of the curve at point *B* is equal to 3.

A natural question to ask at this stage is how to determine which method to use—the arc method or the point method—in calculating the slope of a non-linear curve. The answer depends on the curve itself and the data used to construct it. You use the arc method when you don't have enough information to be able to draw a smooth curve. For example, suppose that in panel (a) of Figure 2A-4 you have only the data represented by points *A*, *C*, and *D* and don't have the data represented by point *B* or any of the rest of the curve. Clearly, then, you can't use the point method to calculate the slope at point *B*; you would have to use the arc method to approximate the slope of the curve in this area by drawing a straight line between points *A* and *C*. But if you have sufficient data to draw the smooth curve shown in panel (a) of Figure 2A-4, then you could use the point method to calculate the slope at point *B*—and at every other point along the curve as well.

A **tangent line** is a straight line that just touches, or is tangent to, a non-linear curve at a particular point. The slope of the tangent line is equal to the slope of the non-linear curve at that point.

FIGURE **2A-5** Calculating the Slope Using the Point Method

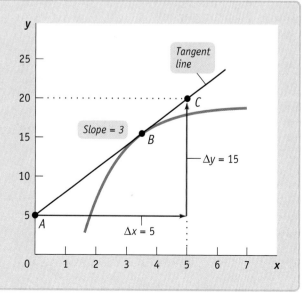

Here a tangent line has been drawn, a line that just touches the curve at point *B*. The slope of this line is equal to the slope of the curve at point *B*. The slope of the tangent line, measuring from *A* to *C*, is $\frac{\Delta y}{\Delta x} = \frac{15}{5} = 3$.

A non-linear curve may have a **maximum** point, the highest point along the curve. At the maximum, the slope of the curve changes from positive to negative.

A non-linear curve may have a **minimum** point, the lowest point along the curve. At the minimum, the slope of the curve changes from negative to positive.

Maximum and Minimum Points

The slope of a non-linear curve can change from positive to negative or vice versa. When the slope of a curve changes from positive to negative, it creates what is called a *maximum* point of the curve. When the slope of a curve changes from negative to positive, it creates a *minimum* point.

Panel (a) of Figure 2A-6 illustrates a curve in which the slope changes from positive to negative as you move from left to right. When x is between 0 and 50, the slope of the curve is positive. At x equal to 50, the curve attains its highest point—the largest value of y along the curve. This point is called the **maximum** of the curve. When x exceeds 50, the slope becomes negative as the curve turns downward. Many important curves in economics, such as the curve that represents how the profit of a firm changes as it produces more output, are hill-shaped like this.

FIGURE **2A-6** Maximum and Minimum Points

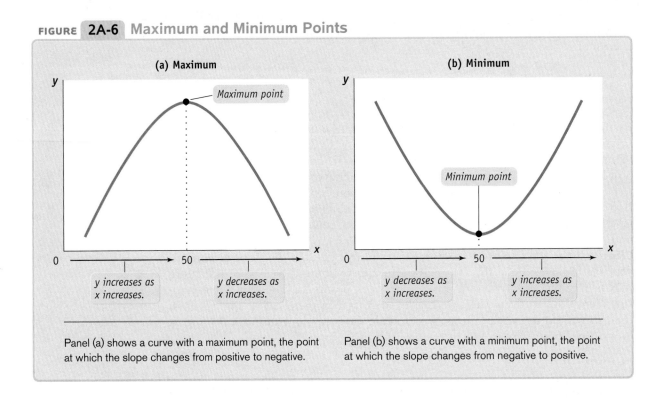

Panel (a) shows a curve with a maximum point, the point at which the slope changes from positive to negative.

Panel (b) shows a curve with a minimum point, the point at which the slope changes from negative to positive.

In contrast, the curve shown in panel (b) of Figure 2A-6 is U-shaped: it has a slope that changes from negative to positive. At x equal to 50, the curve reaches its lowest point—the smallest value of y along the curve. This point is called the **minimum** of the curve. Various important curves in economics, such as the curve that represents how the per-unit costs of some firms change as output increases, are U–shaped like this.

Calculating the Area Below or Above a Curve

Sometimes it is useful to be able to measure the size of the area below or above a curve. We will encounter one such case in an upcoming chapter. To keep things simple, we'll only calculate the area below or above a linear curve.

How large is the shaded area below the linear curve in panel (a) of Figure 2A-7? First note that this area has the shape of a right triangle. A right triangle is a triangle that has two sides that make a right angle with each other. We will refer to one of these sides as the *height* of the triangle and the other side as the *base* of the triangle. For our purposes, it doesn't matter which of these two

FIGURE **2A-7** Calculating the Area Below and Above a Linear Curve

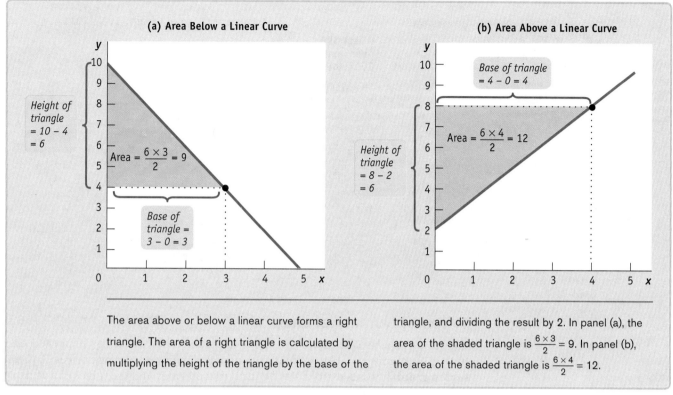

The area above or below a linear curve forms a right triangle. The area of a right triangle is calculated by multiplying the height of the triangle by the base of the triangle, and dividing the result by 2. In panel (a), the area of the shaded triangle is $\frac{6 \times 3}{2} = 9$. In panel (b), the area of the shaded triangle is $\frac{6 \times 4}{2} = 12$.

sides we refer to as the base and which as the height. Calculating the area of a right triangle is straightforward: multiply the height of the triangle by the base of the triangle, and divide the result by 2. The height of the triangle in panel (a) of Figure 2A-7 is $10 - 4 = 6$. And the base of the triangle is $3 - 0 = 3$. So the area of that triangle is:

$$\frac{6 \times 3}{2} = 9$$

How about the shaded area above the linear curve in panel (b) of Figure 2A-7? We can use the same formula to calculate the area of this right triangle. The height of the triangle is $8 - 2 = 6$. And the base of the triangle is $4 - 0 = 4$. So the area of that triangle is:

$$\frac{6 \times 4}{2} = 12$$

Graphs That Depict Numerical Information

Graphs can also be used as a convenient way to summarize and display data without assuming some underlying causal relationship. Graphs that simply display numerical information are called *numerical graphs*. Here we will consider four types of numerical graphs: *time-series graphs*, *scatter diagrams*, *pie charts*, and *bar graphs*. These are widely used to display real, empirical data about different economic variables because they often help economists and policy-makers identify patterns or trends in the economy. But as we will also see, you must be careful not to misinterpret or draw unwarranted conclusions from numerical graphs. That is, you must be aware of both the usefulness and the limitations of numerical graphs.

FIGURE **2A-8** Time-Series Graph

Time-series graphs show successive dates on the x-axis and values for a variable on the y-axis. This time-series graph shows real gross domestic product per capita, a measure of a country's standard of living, in Canada from 1980 to late 2011.

Source: Statistics Canada.

Standard of Living in Canada, 1980–2011

Real GDP per capita (2002 dollars)

Types of Numerical Graphs

You have probably seen graphs in newspapers that show what has happened over time to economic variables such as the unemployment rate or stock prices. A **time-series graph** has successive dates on the horizontal axis and the values of a variable that occurred on those dates on the vertical axis. For example, Figure 2A-8 shows real gross domestic product (GDP) per capita—a rough measure of a country's standard of living—in Canada from 1980 to 2011. A line connecting the points that correspond to real GDP per capita for each calendar quarter during those years gives a clear idea of the overall trend in the standard of living over these years.

A **time-series graph** has dates on the horizontal axis and values of a variable that occurred on those dates on the vertical axis.

Figure 2A-9 is an example of a different kind of numerical graph. It represents information from a sample of 34 countries in a single year on the standard of living,

FIGURE **2A-9** Scatter Diagram

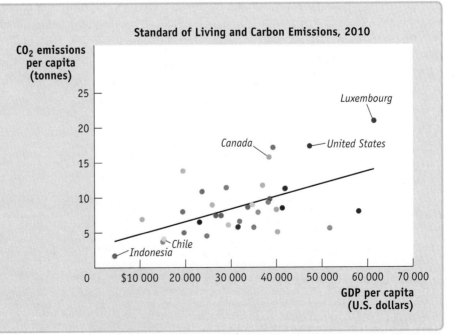

In a scatter diagram, each point represents the corresponding values of the x- and y-variables for a given observation. Here, each point indicates the GDP per capita and the amount of carbon emissions per capita for a given country for a sample of 34 countries in a single year. The upward-sloping fitted line here is the best linear approximation of the general relationship between the two variables.

Source: OECD Factbook, 2012.

Standard of Living and Carbon Emissions, 2010

CO_2 emissions per capita (tonnes)

GDP per capita (U.S. dollars)

again measured by GDP per capita, and the amount of carbon emissions per capita, a measure of environmental pollution. Each point here indicates an average resident's standard of living and his or her annual carbon emissions for a given country. The points lying in the upper right of the graph, which show combinations of a high standard of living and high carbon emissions, represent economically advanced countries such as Canada. Points lying in the bottom left of the graph, which show combinations of a low standard of living and low carbon emissions, represent economically less developed countries such as Indonesia and Chile. The pattern of points indicates that there is generally a positive relationship between living standard and carbon emissions per capita: on the whole, people create more pollution in countries with a higher standard of living. This type of graph is called a **scatter diagram,** a diagram in which each point corresponds to an actual observation of the *x*-variable and the *y*-variable. In scatter diagrams, a curve is typically fitted to the scatter of points; that is, a curve is drawn that approximates as closely as possible the general relationship between the variables. As you can see, the fitted line in Figure 2A-9 is upward sloping, indicating the underlying positive relationship between the two variables. Scatter diagrams are often used to show how a general relationship can be inferred from a set of data.

A **pie chart** shows the share of a total amount that is accounted for by various components, usually expressed in percentages. For example, Figure 2A-10 is a pie chart that depicts what percentage of all unemployed in Canada in 2012 came from different age groups. The fraction of unemployed is the highest among people in the 15 to 24 years age group; about 30% of the unemployed in 2012 fell into this age group.

Bar graphs use bars of various heights or lengths to indicate values of a variable. In the bar graph in Figure 2A-11, the bars show the percent change in the number of unemployed workers in Canada between 2010 and 2011 by different immigrant status—those born in Canada, immigrants

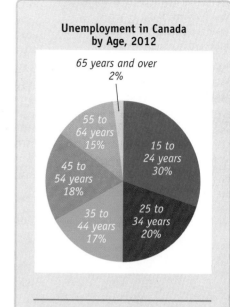

A pie chart shows the percentages of a total amount that can be attributed to various components. This pie chart shows the percentage of the unemployed in Canada in 2012 by age group.
Source: Statistics Canada.

FIGURE **2A-11** Bar Graph

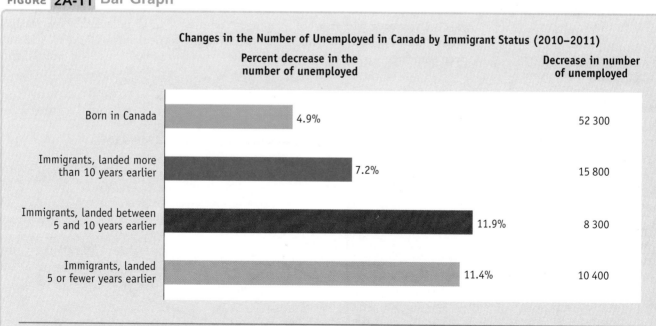

A bar graph measures a variable by using bars of various heights or lengths. This bar graph shows the percent decrease in the number of unemployed workers in Canada between 2010 and 2011 by different immigrant status.
Source: Statistics Canada.

A **scatter diagram** shows points that correspond to actual observations of the *x*- and *y*-variables. A curve is usually fitted to the scatter of points.

A **pie chart** shows how some total is divided among its components, usually expressed in percentages.

A **bar graph** uses bars of varying height or length to show the comparative sizes of different observations of a variable.

An axis is **truncated** when some of the values on the axis are omitted, usually to save space or to make changes to a variable appear larger.

landed in Canada more than 10 years earlier, immigrants landed in Canada between 5 and 10 years earlier, and immigrants landed in Canada fewer than 5 years earlier. Exact values of the variable that is being measured may be written at the end of the bar, as in this figure. For instance, the number of unemployed workers who were born in Canada fell by 4.9% between 2010 and 2011.

Problems in Interpreting Numerical Graphs

Although the beginning of this appendix emphasized that graphs are visual images that make ideas or information easier to understand, graphs can be constructed (intentionally or unintentionally) in ways that are misleading and can lead to inaccurate conclusions. This section raises some issues that you should be aware of when you interpret graphs.

Features of Construction Before drawing any conclusions about what a numerical graph implies, you should pay attention to the scale, or size of increments, shown on the axes. Small increments tend to visually exaggerate changes in the variables, whereas large increments tend to visually diminish them. So the scale used in construction of a graph can influence your interpretation of the significance of the changes it illustrates—perhaps in an unwarranted way.

Take, for example, Figure 2A-12, which shows real GDP per capita in Canada from 1980 to 1984 using increments of $500. You can see that real GDP per capita fell from $26 081 in 1981 to $25 035 in 1982. A decrease, sure, but is it as enormous as the scale chosen for the vertical axis makes it seem? If you go back and re-examine Figure 2A-8, which shows real GDP per capita in Canada from 1980 to 2011, you can see that this would be a misguided conclusion. Figure 2A-8 includes the same data shown in Figure 2A-12, but it is constructed with a scale having increments of $5000 rather than $500. From it, you can see that the fall in real GDP per capita from 1981 to 1982 was, in fact, relatively insignificant. In fact, the story of real GDP per capita—a measure of the standard of living—in Canada is mostly a story of ups, not downs. This comparison shows that if you are not careful to factor in the choice of scale in interpreting a graph, you can arrive at very different, and possibly mistaken, conclusions.

Related to the choice of scale is the use of *truncation* in constructing a graph. An axis is **truncated** when part of the range is omitted. This is indicated by two slashes (//) in the axis near the origin. You can see that the vertical axis of Figure 2A-12 has been truncated—some of the range of values from 0 to $24 000 has been omitted and

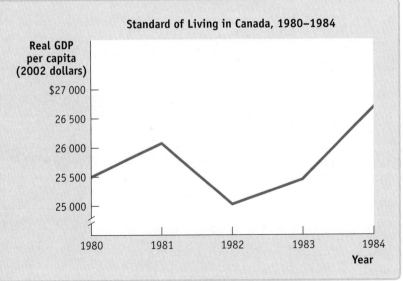

FIGURE 2A-12 Interpreting Graphs: The Effect of Scale

Some of the same data for the years 1980 and 1984 used in Figure 2A-8 are represented here, except that here they are shown using increments of $500 rather than increments of $5000. As a result of this change in scale, changes in the standard of living look much larger in this figure compared to Figure 2A-8.
Source: Statistics Canada.

Standard of Living in Canada, 1980–1984

a // appears in the axis. Truncation saves space in the presentation of a graph and allows smaller increments to be used in constructing it. As a result, changes in the variable depicted on a graph that has been truncated appear larger compared to a graph that has not been truncated and that uses larger increments.

You must also pay close attention to exactly what a graph is illustrating. For example, in Figure 2A-11, you should recognize that what is being shown here are percentage changes in the number of unemployed, not numerical changes. The percentage change in the number of unemployed immigrants landed between 5 and 10 years earlier decreased by the highest percentage, 11.9% in this example. If you were to confuse numerical changes with percentage changes, you would erroneously conclude that the largest absolute reduction of unemployed workers were immigrants landed between 5 and 10 years earlier. But, in fact, Figure 2A-11 shows that the greatest reduction of unemployed workers were those who were born in Canada: the total number of Canadian-born unemployed workers fell by 52 300 workers, which is greater than the decrease in the number of unemployed immigrants landed between 5 and 10 years earlier, which is 8300 in this example.

Omitted Variables From a scatter diagram that shows two variables moving either positively or negatively in relation to each other, it is easy to conclude that there is a causal relationship. But relationships between two variables are not always due to direct cause and effect. Quite possibly an observed relationship between two variables is due to the *unobserved* effect of a third variable on each of the other two variables. An unobserved variable that, through its influence on other variables, creates the erroneous appearance of a direct causal relationship among those variables is called an **omitted variable.** For example, in Manitoba, a greater amount of snowfall during a given week will typically cause people to buy more snow shovels. It will also cause people to buy more lock de-icer. But if you omitted the influence of the snowfall and simply plotted the number of snow shovels sold versus the number of bottles of lock de-icer sold, you would produce a scatter diagram that showed an upward tilt in the pattern of points, indicating a positive relationship between snow shovels sold and lock de-icer sold. To attribute a causal relationship between these two variables, however, is misguided; more snow shovels sold does not cause more lock de-icer to be sold, or vice versa. They move together because they are both influenced by a third, determining, variable—the weekly snowfall, which is the omitted variable in this case. So before assuming that a pattern in a scatter diagram implies a cause-and-effect relationship, it is important to consider whether the pattern is instead the result of an omitted variable. Or to put it succinctly: correlation does not imply causation.

Reverse Causality Even when you are confident that there is no omitted variable and that there is a causal relationship between two variables shown in a numerical graph, you must also be careful that you don't make the mistake of **reverse causality**—coming to an erroneous conclusion about which is the dependent and which is the independent variable by reversing the true direction of causality between the two variables. For example, imagine a scatter diagram that depicts the grade point averages (GPAs) of 20 of your classmates on one axis and the number of hours that each of them spends studying on the other. A line fitted between the points will probably have a positive slope, showing a positive relationship between GPA and hours of studying. We could reasonably infer that hours spent studying is the independent variable and that GPA is the dependent variable. But you could make the error of reverse causality: you could infer that a high GPA causes a student to study more, whereas a low GPA causes a student to study less.

The significance of understanding how graphs can mislead or be incorrectly interpreted is not purely academic. Policy decisions, business decisions, and political arguments are often based on interpretation of the types of numerical graphs that we've just discussed. Problems of misleading features of construction, omitted variables, and reverse causality can lead to very important and undesirable consequences.

An **omitted variable** is an unobserved variable that, through its influence on other variables, may create the erroneous appearance of a direct causal relationship among those variables.

The error of **reverse causality** is committed when the true direction of causality between two variables is reversed.

PROBLEMS

1. Study the four accompanying diagrams. Consider the following statements and indicate which diagram matches each statement. Which variable would appear on the horizontal and which on the vertical axis? In each of these statements, is the slope positive, negative, zero, or infinity?

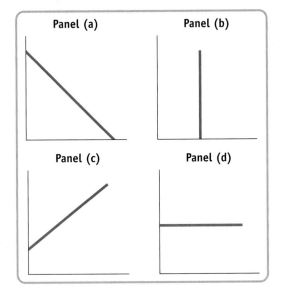

a. If the price of movies increases, fewer consumers go to see movies.

b. More experienced workers typically have higher incomes than less experienced workers.

c. Whatever the temperature outside, Canadians consume the same number of hot dogs per day.

d. Consumers buy more frozen yogourt when the price of ice cream goes up.

e. Research finds no relationship between the number of diet books purchased and the number of kilograms lost by the average dieter.

f. Regardless of its price, Canadians buy the same quantity of salt.

2. In the early 1980s, economist Arthur Laffer argued in favour of lowering income tax rates in order to increase tax revenues. Like most economists, he believed that at tax rates above a certain level, tax revenue would fall because high taxes would discourage some people from working and that people would refuse to work at all if they received no income after paying taxes. This relationship between tax rates and tax revenue is graphically summarized in what is widely known as the Laffer curve. Plot the Laffer curve relationship assuming that it has the shape of a non-linear curve. The following questions will help you construct the graph.

a. Which is the independent variable? Which is the dependent variable? On which axis do you therefore measure the income tax rate? On which axis do you measure income tax revenue?

b. What would tax revenue be at a 0% income tax rate?

c. The maximum possible income tax rate is 100%. What would tax revenue be at a 100% income tax rate?

d. Estimates now show that the maximum point on the Laffer curve is (approximately) at a tax rate of 80%. For tax rates less than 80%, how would you describe the relationship between the tax rate and tax revenue, and how is this relationship reflected in the slope? For tax rates higher than 80%, how would you describe the relationship between the tax rate and tax revenue, and how is this relationship reflected in the slope?

3. In the accompanying figures, the numbers on the axes have been lost. All you know is that the units shown on the vertical axis are the same as the units on the horizontal axis.

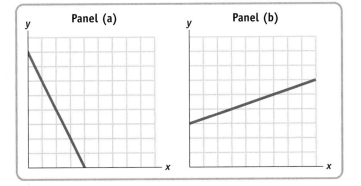

a. In panel (a), what is the slope of the line? Show that the slope is constant along the line.

b. In panel (b), what is the slope of the line? Show that the slope is constant along the line.

4. Answer each of the following questions by drawing a schematic diagram.

a. Taking measurements of the slope of a curve at three points farther and farther to the right along the horizontal axis, the slope of the curve changes from −0.3, to −0.8, to −2.5, measured by the point method. Draw a schematic diagram of this curve. How would you describe the relationship illustrated in your diagram?

b. Taking measurements of the slope of a curve at five points farther and farther to the right along the horizontal axis, the slope of the curve changes from 1.5, to 0.5, to 0, to −0.5, to −1.5, measured by the point method. Draw a schematic diagram of this curve. Does it have a maximum or a minimum?

5. For each of the accompanying diagrams, calculate the area of the shaded right triangle.

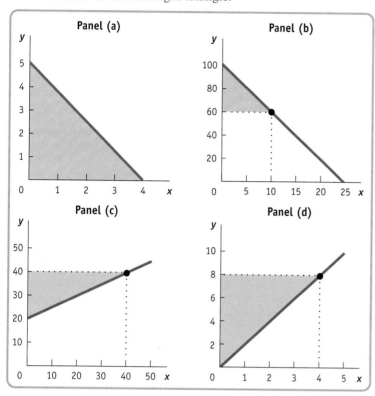

Panel (a)

Panel (b)

Panel (c)

Panel (d)

6. The base of a right triangle is 10, and its area is 20. What is the height of this right triangle?

7. The accompanying table shows the relationship between workers' hours of work per week and their hourly wage rate. Apart from the fact that they receive a different hourly wage rate and work different hours, these five workers are otherwise identical.

Name	Quantity of labour (hours per week)	Wage rate (per hour)
Athena	30	$15
Boris	35	30
Chinedu	37	45
Diego	36	60
Emily	32	75

a. Which variable is the independent variable? Which is the dependent variable?

b. Draw a scatter diagram illustrating this relationship. Draw a (non-linear) curve that connects the points. Put the hourly wage rate on the vertical axis.

c. As the wage rate increases from $15 to $30, how does the number of hours worked respond according to the relationship depicted here? What is the average slope of the curve between Athena's and Boris's data points using the arc method?

d. As the wage rate increases from $60 to $75, how does the number of hours worked respond according to the relationship depicted here? What is the average slope of the curve between Diego's and Emily's data points using the arc method?

8. Studies have found a relationship between a country's yearly rate of economic growth and the yearly rate of increase in airborne pollutants. It is believed that a higher rate of economic growth allows a country's residents to have more cars and travel more, thereby releasing more airborne pollutants.

a. Which variable is the independent variable? Which is the dependent variable?

b. Suppose that in the country of Sudland, when the yearly rate of economic growth fell from 3.0% to 1.5%, the yearly rate of increase in airborne pollutants fell from 6% to 5%. What is the average slope of a non-linear curve between these points using the arc method?

c. Now suppose that when the yearly rate of economic growth rose from 3.5% to 4.5%, the yearly rate of increase in airborne pollutants rose from 5.5% to 7.5%. What is the average slope of a non-linear curve between these two points using the arc method?

d. How would you describe the relationship between the two variables here?

9. An insurance company has found that the severity of property damage in a fire is positively related to the number of firefighters arriving at the scene.

a. Draw a diagram that depicts this finding with number of firefighters on the horizontal axis and amount of property damage on the vertical axis. What is the argument made by this diagram? Suppose you reverse what is measured on the two axes. What is the argument made then?

b. In order to reduce its payouts to policyholders, should the insurance company therefore ask the city to send fewer firefighters to any fire?

10. The accompanying table illustrates annual salaries and income tax owed by five individuals. Apart from the fact that they receive different salaries and owe different amounts of income tax, these five individuals are otherwise identical.

Name	Annual salary	Annual income tax owed
Susan	$22 000	$3 304
Eduardo	63 000	14 317
John	3 000	454
Sheeza	94 000	23 927
Ling	37 000	7 020

a. If you were to plot these points on a graph, what would be the average slope of the curve between the points for Eduardo's and Sheeza's salaries and taxes using the arc method? How would you interpret this value for slope?

b. What is the average slope of the curve between the points for John's and Susan's salaries and taxes using the arc method? How would you interpret that value for slope?

c. What happens to the slope as salary increases? What does this relationship imply about how the level of income taxes affects a person's incentive to earn a higher salary?

CHAPTER 3

Supply and Demand

BLUE JEAN BLUES

How did flood-ravaged cotton crops in Pakistan lead to higher-priced blue jeans and more polyester in T-shirts?

❯ What a **competitive market** is and how it is described by the **supply and demand model**

❯ What the **demand curve** and the **supply curve** are

❯ The factors that determine the demand for, and supply of, a good

❯ The difference between **movements along a curve** and **shifts of a curve**

❯ How the supply and demand curves together determine a market's **equilibrium price** and **equilibrium quantity**

❯ In the case of a **shortage** or **surplus**, how price moves the market back to equilibrium

I F YOU BOUGHT A PAIR OF BLUE jeans in 2011, you may have been shocked at the price. Or maybe not: fashions change, and maybe you thought you were paying the price for being fashionable. But you weren't—you were paying for cotton. Jeans are made of denim, which is a particular weave of cotton, and by late 2010, when jeans manufacturers were buying supplies for the coming year, cotton prices were more than triple their level just two years earlier. The price of cotton continued to rise in early 2011, peaking in March of that year at a price of US$2.30 per pound. (Cotton is traded internationally in U.S. dollars per pound, the equivalent of 0.454 kg). It was the highest level since records began in 1870. The price of cotton softened subsequently but remained relatively high compared to historical standards.

And why were cotton prices so high?

On one side, demand for clothing of all kinds was surging. In 2008–2009, as the world struggled with the effects of a financial crisis, nervous consumers cut back on clothing purchases. But by 2010, with the worst apparently over, buyers were back in force. On the supply side, severe weather events hit world cotton production. Most notably, Pakistan, the world's fourth-largest cotton producer, was hit by devastating floods that put one-fifth of the country under water and virtually destroyed its cotton crop.

Fearing that consumers had limited tolerance for large increases in the price of cotton clothing, apparel makers began scrambling to find ways to reduce costs without offending consumers' fashion sense. They adopted changes like smaller buttons, cheaper linings, and—yes—polyester, doubting that consumers would be willing to pay more for cotton goods. In fact, some experts on the cotton market warned that the sky-high prices of cotton in 2010–2011 might lead to a permanent shift in tastes, with consumers becoming more willing to wear synthetics even when cotton prices came down.

At the same time, it was not all bad news for everyone connected with the cotton trade. In North America, cotton producers had not been hit by bad weather and were relishing the higher prices. Farmers responded to sky-high cotton prices by sharply increasing the farmland devoted to the crop. None of this was enough, however, to produce immediate price relief.

Wait a minute: how, exactly, does flooding in Pakistan translate into higher jeans prices and more polyester in your T-shirts? It's a matter of supply and demand—but what does that mean? Many people use "supply and demand" as a sort of catchphrase to mean "the laws of the marketplace at work." To economists, however, the concept of supply and demand has a precise meaning: it is a *model of how a competitive market behaves.*

In this chapter, we lay out the pieces that make up the *supply and demand model*, put them together, and show how this simple model can be used to understand how many—but not all—markets behave. ■

A **competitive market** is a market in which there are many buyers and sellers of the same good or service, none of whom can influence the price at which the good or service is sold.

The **supply and demand model** is a model of how a competitive market behaves.

Supply and Demand: A Model of a Competitive Market

Cotton sellers and cotton buyers constitute a market—a group of producers and consumers who exchange a good or service for payment. In this chapter, we'll focus on a particular type of market known as a *competitive market*. Roughly, a **competitive market** is a market in which there are many buyers and sellers of the same good or service. More precisely, the key feature of a competitive market is that no individual's actions have a noticeable effect on the price at which the good or service is sold. It's important to understand, however, that this is not an accurate description of every market.

For example, it's not an accurate description of the market for cola beverages. That's because in the market for cola beverages, Coca-Cola and Pepsi account for such a large proportion of total sales that they are able to influence the price at which cola beverages are bought and sold. But it is an accurate description of the market for cotton. The global marketplace for cotton is so huge that even a jeans maker as large as Levi Strauss & Co. accounts for only a tiny fraction of transactions, making it unable to influence the price at which cotton is bought and sold.

It's a little hard to explain why competitive markets are different from other markets until we've seen how a competitive market works. So let's take a rain check—we'll return to that issue at the end of this chapter. For now, let's just say that it's easier to model competitive markets than other markets. When taking an exam, it's always a good strategy to begin by answering the easier questions. In this book, we're going to do the same thing. So we will start with competitive markets.

When a market is competitive, its behaviour is well described by the **supply and demand model.** Because many markets are competitive, the supply and demand model is a very useful one indeed.

There are five key elements in this model:

- The *demand curve*
- The *supply curve*
- The set of factors that cause the demand curve to shift and the set of factors that cause the supply curve to shift
- The *market equilibrium*, which includes the *equilibrium price* and *equilibrium quantity*
- The way the market equilibrium changes when the supply curve or demand curve shifts

To understand the supply and demand model, we will examine each of these elements.

The Demand Curve

How many pounds of cotton, packaged in the form of blue jeans, do consumers around the world want to buy in a given year? You might at first think that we can answer this question by looking at the total number of pairs of blue jeans purchased around the world each day, multiply that number by the amount of cotton it takes to make a pair of jeans, and then multiply by 365. But that's not enough to answer the question, because how many pairs of jeans—in other words, how many pounds of cotton—consumers want to buy depends on the price of a pound of cotton.

When the price of cotton rises, as it did in 2010–2011, some people will respond to the higher price of cotton clothing by buying fewer cotton garments or, perhaps, by switching completely to garments made from other materials, such as synthetics or linen. In general, the quantity of cotton clothing, or of any good or service that people want to buy, depends on the price. The higher the price, the less of the good or service people want to purchase; alternatively, the lower the price, the more they want to purchase.

So the answer to the question "How many pounds of cotton do consumers want to buy?" depends on the price of a pound of cotton. If you don't yet know what the price will be, you can start by making a table of how many pounds of cotton people would want to buy at a number of different prices. Such a table is known as a *demand schedule*. This, in turn, can be used to draw a *demand curve*, which is one of the key elements of the supply and demand model.

A **demand schedule** shows how much of a good or service consumers will want to buy at different prices.

The **quantity demanded** is the actual amount of a good or service consumers are willing and able to buy at some specific price.

The Demand Schedule and the Demand Curve

A **demand schedule** is a table showing how much of a good or service consumers will want to buy at different prices. At the right of Figure 3-1, we show a hypothetical demand schedule for cotton. It's hypothetical in that it doesn't use actual data on the world demand for cotton and it assumes that all cotton is of equal quality.

According to the table, if a pound of cotton costs $1, consumers around the world will want to purchase 10 billion pounds of cotton over the course of a year. If the price is $1.25 a pound, they will want to buy only 8.9 billion pounds; if the price is only $0.75 a pound, they will want to buy 11.5 billion pounds; and so on. The higher the price, the fewer pounds of cotton consumers will want to purchase. So, as the price rises, the **quantity demanded** of cotton—the actual amount consumers are willing to buy at some specific price—falls.

The graph in Figure 3-1 is a visual representation of the information in the table. (You might want to review the discussion of graphs in economics in Appendix 2A.) The vertical axis shows the price of cotton and the horizontal axis shows the quantity of cotton. Each point on the graph corresponds to one of the entries in the

FIGURE   3-1   The Demand Schedule and the Demand Curve

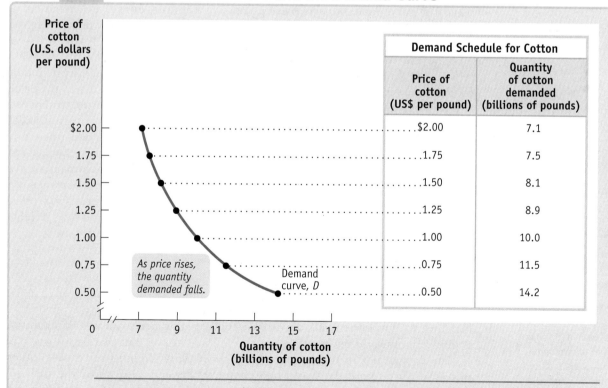

Demand Schedule for Cotton	
Price of cotton (US$ per pound)	Quantity of cotton demanded (billions of pounds)
$2.00	7.1
1.75	7.5
1.50	8.1
1.25	8.9
1.00	10.0
0.75	11.5
0.50	14.2

The demand schedule for cotton yields the corresponding demand curve, which shows how much of a good or service consumers want to buy at any given price. The demand curve and the demand schedule reflect the law of demand: all other things equal, as price rises, the quantity demanded falls. Similarly, all other things equal, a fall in price raises the quantity demanded. As a result, the demand curve is downward sloping.

GLOBAL COMPARISON

PAY MORE, PUMP LESS

For a real-world illustration of the law of demand, consider how gasoline consumption varies according to the prices consumers pay at the pump. Because of high taxes, gasoline and diesel fuel are more expensive in most European countries than in Canada and the United States. According to the law of demand, this should lead Europeans to buy less gasoline than Canadians and Americans—and they do. As you can see from the figure, Europeans consume less than half as much fuel per person as their counterparts in North America, mainly because they drive smaller cars with better fuel economy.

Prices aren't the only factor affecting fuel consumption, but they're a significant cause of the difference between European and North American fuel consumption per person.

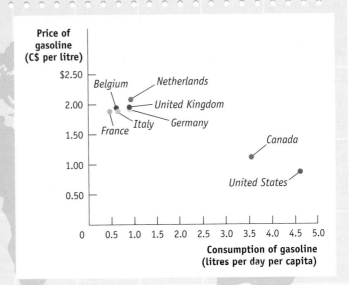

Sources: U.S. Energy Information Administration; Natural Resources Canada, 2010.

---

table. The curve that connects these points is a **demand curve.** A demand curve is a graphical representation of the demand schedule, another way of showing the relationship between the quantity demanded and price.

Note that the demand curve shown in Figure 3-1 slopes downward. This reflects the general proposition that a higher price reduces the quantity demanded. For example, jeans makers know that they will sell fewer pairs when the price of a pair of jeans is higher, reflecting a $2 price for a pound of cotton, compared to the number they will sell when the price of a pair is lower, reflecting a price of only $1 for a pound of cotton. Similarly, someone who buys a pair of cotton jeans when its price is relatively low will switch to synthetic or linen when the price of cotton jeans is relatively high. So in the real world, demand curves almost always *do* slope downward. (The exceptions are so rare that for practical purposes we can ignore them.) Generally, the proposition that a higher price for a good, *other things equal,* leads people to demand a smaller quantity of that good is so reliable that economists are willing to call it a "law"—the **law of demand.**

Shifts of the Demand Curve

Although cotton prices in 2010 and 2011 were higher than they had been in 2007, total world consumption of cotton was higher in 2010. How can we reconcile this fact with the law of demand, which says that a higher price reduces the quantity demanded, other things equal?

The answer lies in the crucial phrase *other things equal.* In this case, other things weren't equal: the world had changed between 2007 and 2010, in ways that increased the quantity of cotton demanded at any given price. For one thing, the world's population, and therefore the number of potential cotton clothing wearers, increased. In addition, the growing popularity of cotton clothing, as well as higher incomes in countries like China that allowed people to buy more clothing than before, led to an increase in the quantity of cotton demanded at any given price. Figure 3-2 illustrates this phenomenon using the

A **demand curve** is a graphical representation of the demand schedule. It shows the relationship between quantity demanded and price.

The **law of demand** says that a higher price for a good or service, other things equal, leads people to demand a smaller quantity of that good or service.

FIGURE **3-2** An Increase in Demand

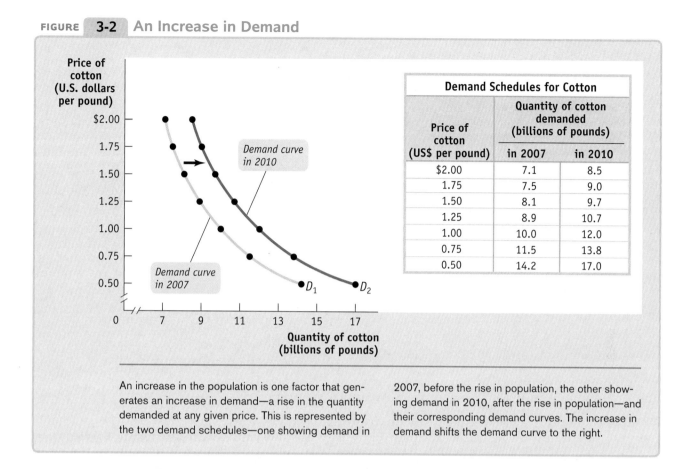

	Demand Schedules for Cotton		
Price of cotton (US$ per pound)	Quantity of cotton demanded (billions of pounds)		
	in 2007	in 2010	
$2.00	7.1	8.5	
1.75	7.5	9.0	
1.50	8.1	9.7	
1.25	8.9	10.7	
1.00	10.0	12.0	
0.75	11.5	13.8	
0.50	14.2	17.0	

An increase in the population is one factor that generates an increase in demand—a rise in the quantity demanded at any given price. This is represented by the two demand schedules—one showing demand in 2007, before the rise in population, the other showing demand in 2010, after the rise in population—and their corresponding demand curves. The increase in demand shifts the demand curve to the right.

demand schedule and demand curve for cotton. (As before, the numbers in Figure 3-2 are hypothetical.)

The table in Figure 3-2 shows two demand schedules. The first is the demand schedule for 2007, the same as shown in Figure 3-1. The second is the demand schedule for 2010. It differs from the 2007 demand schedule due to factors such as a larger population and the increased popularity of cotton clothing, factors that led to an increase in the quantity of cotton demanded at any given price. So at each price the 2010 schedule shows a larger quantity demanded than the 2007 schedule. For example, the quantity of cotton consumers wanted to buy at a price of $1 per pound increased from 10 billion to 12 billion pounds per year, the quantity demanded at $1.25 per pound went from 8.9 billion to 10.7 billion, and so on.

What is clear from this example is that the changes that occurred between 2007 and 2010 generated a *new* demand schedule, one in which the quantity demanded was greater at any given price than in the original demand schedule. The two curves in Figure 3-2 show the same information graphically. As you can see, the demand schedule for 2010 corresponds to a new demand curve, D_2, that is to the right of the demand schedule for 2007, D_1. This **shift of the demand curve** shows the change in the quantity demanded at any given price, represented by the change in position of the original demand curve D_1 to its new location at D_2.

It's crucial to make the distinction between such shifts of the demand curve and **movements along the demand curve,** changes in the quantity demanded of a good arising from a change in that good's price. Figure 3-3 on the next page illustrates the difference.

The movement from point *A* to point *B* is a movement along the demand curve: the quantity demanded rises due to a fall in price as you move down D_1. Here, a fall in the price of cotton from $1.50 to $1 per pound generates a rise in the quantity demanded from 8.1 billion to 10 billion pounds per year. But the quantity demanded can also rise

A **shift of the demand curve** is a change in the quantity demanded at any given price, represented by the change (shift) of the original demand curve to a new position, denoted by a new demand curve.

A **movement along the demand curve** is a change in the quantity demanded of a good arising from a change in the good's price.

The rise in quantity demanded when going from point A to point B reflects a movement along the demand curve: it is the result of a fall in the price of the good. The rise in quantity demanded when going from point A to point C reflects a shift of the demand curve (called an increase in demand): it is the result of a rise in the quantity demanded at any given price.

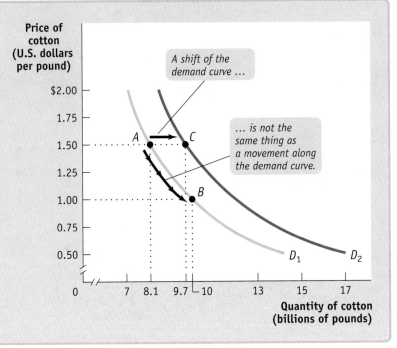

when the price is unchanged if there is an *increase in demand*—a rightward shift of the demand curve. This is illustrated in Figure 3-3 by the shift of the demand curve from D_1 to D_2. Holding the price constant at $1.50 a pound, the quantity demanded rises from 8.1 billion pounds at point A on D_1 to 9.7 billion pounds at point C on D_2.

When economists say "the demand for X increased" or "the demand for Y decreased," they mean that the demand curve for X or Y shifted—not that the quantity demanded rose or fell because of a change in the price.

PITFALLS

DEMAND VERSUS QUANTITY DEMANDED

When economists say "an increase in demand," they mean a rightward shift of the demand curve, and when they say "a decrease in demand," they mean a leftward shift of the demand curve—that is, when they're being careful. In ordinary speech, most people, including professional economists, use the word *demand* casually. For example, an economist might say "the

demand for air travel has doubled over the past 15 years, partly because of falling airfares" when he or she really means that the *quantity demanded* has doubled.

It's okay to be a bit sloppy in ordinary conversation. But when you're doing economic analysis, it's important to make the distinction between changes in the quantity demanded, which involve movements along a demand curve, and shifts of the demand curve (see

Figure 3-3 for an illustration). Sometimes students end up writing something like this: "If demand increases, the price will go up, but that will lead to a fall in demand, which pushes the price down …" and then go around in circles. If you make a clear distinction between changes in *demand*, which mean shifts of the demand curve, and changes in *quantity demanded*, you can avoid a lot of confusion.

Understanding Shifts of the Demand Curve

Figure 3-4 illustrates the two basic ways in which demand curves can shift. When economists talk about an "increase in demand," they mean a *rightward* shift of the demand curve: at any given price, consumers demand a larger quantity of the good or service than before. This is shown by the rightward shift of the original demand curve D_1 to D_2. And when economists talk about a "decrease in demand," they mean a *leftward* shift of the demand curve: at any given price, consumers demand a smaller quantity of the good or service than before. This is shown by the leftward shift of the original demand curve D_1 to D_3.

FIGURE   **3-4**   Shifts of the Demand Curve

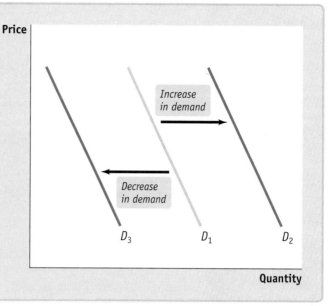

Any event that increases demand shifts the demand curve to the right, reflecting a rise in the quantity demanded at any given price. Any event that decreases demand shifts the demand curve to the left, reflecting a fall in the quantity demanded at any given price.

What caused the demand curve for cotton to shift? We have already mentioned two reasons: changes in population and a change in the popularity of cotton clothing. If you think about it, you can come up with other things that would be likely to shift the demand curve for cotton. For example, suppose that the price of polyester rises. This will induce some people who previously bought polyester clothing to buy cotton clothing instead, increasing the demand for cotton.

Economists believe that there are five principal factors that shift the demand curve for a good or service:

- Changes in the prices of related goods or services
- Changes in income
- Changes in tastes
- Changes in expectations
- Changes in the number of consumers

Although this is not an exhaustive list, it contains the five most important factors that can shift demand curves. So when we say that the quantity of a good or service demanded falls as its price rises, *other things equal*, we are in fact stating that the factors that shift demand are remaining unchanged. Let's now explore, in more detail, how those factors shift the demand curve.

Changes in the Prices of Related Goods or Services Although there's nothing quite like a comfortable pair of all-cotton blue jeans, for some purposes khakis—generally made from polyester blends—aren't a bad alternative. Khakis are what economists call a *substitute* for jeans. Two goods are **substitutes** if a rise in the price of one good (jeans) makes consumers more willing to buy the other good (khakis). Substitutes are usually goods that in some way serve a similar function: coffee and tea, muffins and doughnuts, train rides and air flights. A rise in the price of the alternative good induces some consumers to purchase the original good *instead* of it, shifting demand for the original good to the right.

But sometimes a rise in the price of one good makes consumers *less* willing to buy another good. Such pairs of goods are known as **complements.** Complements are usually goods that in some sense are consumed together: computers and software, cappuccinos and cookies, cars and gasoline. Because consumers like to consume a good and its complement together, a change in the price

Two goods are **substitutes** if a rise in the price of one of the goods leads to an increase in the demand for the other good.

Two goods are **complements** if a rise in the price of one good leads to a decrease in the demand for the other good.

When a rise in income increases the demand for a good—the normal case—it is a **normal good.**

When a rise in income decreases the demand for a good, it is an **inferior good.**

of one of the goods will affect the demand for its complement. In particular, when the price of one good rises, the demand for its complement decreases, shifting the demand curve for the complement to the left. So, for example, when the price of gasoline rose in 2007–2008, the demand for gas-guzzling cars fell.

Changes in Income When individuals have more income, they are normally more likely to purchase a good at any given price. For example, if a family's income rises, it is more likely to take that long-anticipated summer trip to Disney World—and therefore also more likely to buy plane tickets. So a rise in consumer incomes will cause the demand curves for most goods to shift to the right.

Why do we say "most goods," not "all goods"? Most goods are **normal goods**—the demand for them increases when consumer income rises. However, the demand for some products falls when income rises. Goods for which demand decreases when income rises are known as **inferior goods.** Usually an inferior good is one that is considered less desirable than more expensive alternatives—such as a bus ride versus a taxi ride. When they can afford to, people stop buying an inferior good and switch their consumption to the preferred, more expensive alternative. So when a good is inferior, a rise in income shifts the demand curve to the left. And, not surprisingly, a fall in income shifts the demand curve to the right.

One example of the distinction between normal and inferior goods that has drawn considerable attention in the business press is the difference between so-called casual-dining restaurants such as Swiss Chalet or White Spot and fast-food chains such as Harvey's and McDonald's. When Canadians' incomes rise, they tend to eat out more at casual-dining restaurants. However, some of this increased dining out comes at the expense of fast-food venues—to some extent, people visit Harvey's or McDonald's less once they can afford to move upscale. So casual dining is a normal good, whereas fast-food consumption appears to be an inferior good.

Changes in Tastes Why do people want what they want? Fortunately, we don't need to answer that question—we just need to acknowledge that people have certain preferences, or tastes, that determine what they choose to consume and that these tastes can change. Economists usually lump together changes in demand due to fads, beliefs, cultural shifts, and so on under the heading of changes in tastes or preferences.

For example, once upon a time men routinely wore undershirts (or vests). But then came a dramatic moment—American actor Clark Gable removed his shirt in Frank Capra's classic film *It Happened One Night* (1934)—revealing bare skin rather than an undershirt! Reportedly, the sales of vests immediately plummeted. Fashion had changed overnight, and the demand for men's undershirts never recovered.

Economists have relatively little to say about the forces that influence consumers' tastes. (Although marketers and advertisers have plenty to say about them!) However, a change in tastes has a predictable impact on demand. When tastes change in favour of a good, more people want to buy it at any given price, so the demand curve shifts to the right. When tastes change against a good, fewer people want to buy it at any given price, so the demand curve shifts to the left.

Changes in Expectations When consumers have some choice about when to make a purchase, current demand for a good is often affected by expectations about its future price. For example, savvy shoppers often wait for seasonal sales—say, buying next year's holiday gifts during the post-holiday markdowns. In this case, expectations of a future drop in price lead to a decrease in demand today. Alternatively, expectations of a future rise in price are likely to cause an increase in demand today. For example, as cotton prices began to rise in 2010, many textile mills began purchasing more cotton and stockpiling it in anticipation of further price increases.

Expected changes in future income can also lead to changes in demand. If you expect your income to rise in the future, you will typically borrow today and increase your demand for certain goods; if you expect your income to fall in the future, you are likely to save today and reduce your demand for some goods.

Changes in the Number of Consumers As we've already noted, one of the reasons for rising cotton demand between 2007 and 2010 was a growing world population. Because of population growth, overall demand for cotton would have risen even if the demand of each individual wearer of cotton clothing had remained unchanged.

Let's introduce a new concept: the **individual demand curve,** which shows the relationship between quantity demanded and price for an individual consumer. For example, suppose that Darla is a consumer of cotton blue jeans; also suppose that all pairs of jeans are the same, so they sell for the same price. Panel (a) of Figure 3-5 shows how many pairs of jeans she will buy per year at any given price. Then D_{Darla} is Darla's individual demand curve.

The *market demand curve* shows how the combined quantity demanded by all consumers depends on the market price of that good. (Most of the time, when economists refer to the demand curve, they mean the market demand curve.) The market demand curve is the *horizontal sum* of the individual demand curves of all consumers in that market. To see what we mean by the term *horizontal sum*, assume for a moment that there are only two consumers of blue jeans, Darla and Dino. Dino's individual demand curve, D_{Dino}, is shown in panel (b). Panel (c) shows the market demand curve. At any given price, the quantity demanded by the market is the sum of the quantities demanded by Darla and Dino. For example, at a price of $30 per pair, Darla demands 3 pairs of jeans per year and Dino demands 2 pairs per year. So the quantity demanded by the market is 5 pairs per year.

Clearly, the quantity demanded by the market at any given price is larger with Dino present than it would be if Darla were the only consumer. The quantity

An **individual demand curve** illustrates the relationship between quantity demanded and price for an individual consumer.

FIGURE 3-5 Individual Demand Curves and the Market Demand Curve

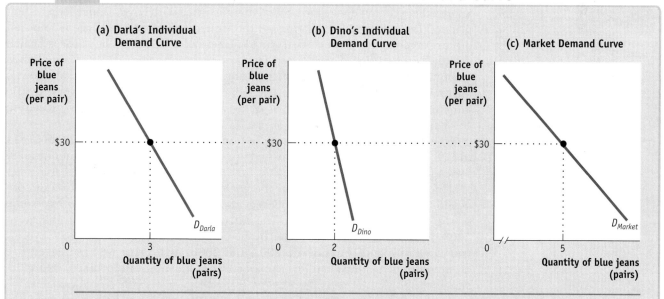

Darla and Dino are the only two consumers of blue jeans in the market. Panel (a) shows Darla's individual demand curve: the number of pairs of blue jeans she will buy per year at any given price. Panel (b) shows Dino's individual demand curve. Given that Darla and Dino are the only two consumers, the *market demand curve*, which shows the quantity of blue jeans demanded by all consumers at any given price, is shown in panel (c). The market demand curve is the *horizontal sum* of the individual demand curves of all consumers. In this case, at any given price, the quantity demanded by the market is the sum of the quantities demanded by Darla and Dino.

demanded at any given price would be even larger if we added a third consumer, then a fourth, and so on. So an increase in the number of consumers leads to an increase in demand.

There are several ways the number of consumers can change on a large scale. For example, demographic trends have seen senior citizens represent a growing percentage of Canada's population, increasing the overall demand for the goods and services seniors tend to demand more than younger people (for example, prescription medicine and assisted care residences). Changes to access to international markets also affect the number of consumers. The demand for Canadian softwood lumber increased after the United States made it easier for Canadians to export lumber to U.S. markets. Conversely, an embargo would reduce the number of consumers.

For a review of the factors that shift demand, see Table 3-1.

ECONOMICS ▸ IN ACTION

BEATING THE TRAFFIC

All big cities have traffic problems, and many local authorities try to discourage driving in the crowded city centre. If we think of a car trip to the city centre as a good that people consume, we can use the economics of demand to analyze anti-traffic policies.

One common strategy is to reduce the demand for car trips by lowering the prices of substitutes. Many Canadian municipalities subsidize bus and rail service, hoping to lure commuters out of their cars. An alternative is to raise the price of complements: several Canadian municipalities impose high taxes on commercial parking garages and impose short time limits on parking meters, both to raise revenue and to discourage people from driving into the city.

A few major cities—including Singapore, London, Oslo, Stockholm, and Milan—have been willing to adopt a direct and politically controversial approach: reducing congestion by raising the price of driving. Under "congestion pricing" (or "congestion charging" in the United Kingdom), a charge is imposed on cars entering the city centre during business hours. Drivers buy passes, which are then debited electronically as they drive by monitoring stations. Compliance is monitored with automatic cameras that photograph license plates. Moscow is currently contemplating a congestion charge scheme to tackle the worst traffic jams of all major cities, with 40% of drivers reporting traffic jams exceeding three hours.

The current daily cost of driving in London ranges from £9 to £12 (about $14 to $19). And drivers who don't pay and are caught pay a fine of £120 (about $189) for each transgression.

Not surprisingly, studies have shown that after the implementation of congestion pricing, traffic does indeed decrease. In the 1990s, London had some of the worst traffic in Europe. The introduction of its congestion charge in 2003 immediately reduced traffic in the city centre by about 15%, with overall traffic falling by 21% between 2002 and 2006. And there was increased use of substitutes, such as public transportation, bicycles, motorbikes, and ride-sharing.

In Canada, some cities have contemplated imposing similar charges. In Vancouver, commuters pay a toll to cross the new Port Mann Bridge. Officials believed the toll would help reduce congestion there, one of the worst traffic bottlenecks in British Columbia. In Toronto, city council has debated the use of tolls and congestion charges. The most common proposal was for the imposition of a road toll on some of the city's busiest roads, such as the Gardiner Expressway and the Don Valley Parkway. At the time of writing, no such charges have been imposed within Toronto.

Cities can reduce traffic congestion by raising the price of driving. This sign tells drivers they are approaching the centre of London.

Global Warming Images/Alamy

TABLE 3-1   Factors That Shift Demand

When this happens …	… demand increases	But when this happens …	… demand decreases
When the price of a substitute rises …	… demand for the original good increases.	When the price of a substitute falls …	… demand for the original good decreases.
When the price of a complement falls …	… demand for the original good increases.	When the price of a complement rises …	… demand for the original good decreases.
When income rises …	… demand for a normal good increases.	When income falls …	… demand for a normal good decreases.
When income falls …	… demand for an inferior good increases.	When income rises …	… demand for an inferior good decreases.
When tastes change in favour of a good …	… demand for the good increases.	When tastes change against a good …	… demand for the good decreases.
When the price is expected to rise in the future …	… demand for the good increases today.	When the price is expected to fall in the future …	… demand for the good decreases today.
When the number of consumers rises …	… market demand for the good increases.	When the number of consumers falls …	… market demand for the good decreases.

- The **supply and demand model** is a model of a **competitive market**—one in which there are many buyers and sellers of the same good or service.

- The **demand schedule** shows how the **quantity demanded** changes as the price changes. A **demand curve** illustrates this relationship.

- The **law of demand** asserts that, all other things equal, a higher price reduces the quantity demanded (and vice versa). Thus, demand curves normally slope downward.

- An increase in demand leads to a rightward **shift of the demand curve:** the quantity demanded rises for any given price. A decrease in demand leads to a leftward shift: the quantity demanded falls for any given price. A change in price results in a change in the quantity demanded and a **movement along the demand curve.**

- The five main factors that can shift the demand curve are changes in (1) the price of a related good, such as a **substitute** or a **complement,** (2) income, (3) tastes, (4) expectations, and (5) the number of consumers.

- As income increases, the demand for **normal goods** increases and the demand for **inferior goods** decreases.

- The market demand curve is the horizontal sum of the **individual demand curves** of all consumers in the market.

CHECK YOUR UNDERSTANDING 3-1

1. Explain whether each of the following events represents (i) a *shift of* the demand curve or (ii) a *movement along* the demand curve.
   a. A store owner finds that customers are willing to pay more for umbrellas on rainy days.
   b. When XYZ Telecom, a long-distance telephone service provider, offered reduced rates on weekends, its volume of weekend calling increased sharply.
   c. People buy more long-stem roses the week of Valentine's Day, even though the prices are higher than at other times during the year.
   d. A sharp rise in the price of gasoline leads many commuters to join carpools in order to reduce their gasoline purchases.

Solutions appear at back of book.

The Supply Curve

Some parts of the world are especially well-suited to growing cotton, and the United States is one of those. But even in the United States, some land is better suited to growing cotton than other land. Whether American farmers restrict their cotton-growing to only the most ideal locations or expand it to less suitable land depends on the price they expect to get for their cotton. Moreover, there are many other areas in the world where cotton could be grown—such as Pakistan, India, Brazil, Turkey, and China. Whether farmers there actually grow cotton depends, again, on the price.

So just as the quantity of cotton that consumers want to buy depends on the price they have to pay, the quantity that producers are willing and able to produce and sell—the **quantity supplied**—depends on the price they are offered.

The Supply Schedule and the Supply Curve

The table in Figure 3-6 shows how the quantity of cotton made available varies with the price—that is, it shows a hypothetical **supply schedule** for cotton.

A supply schedule works the same way as the demand schedule shown in Figure 3-1: in this case, the table shows the number of pounds of cotton farmers are willing to sell at different prices. At a price of $0.50 per pound, farmers are willing to sell only 8 billion pounds of cotton per year. At $0.75 per pound, they're willing to sell 9.1 billion pounds. At $1, they're willing to sell 10 billion pounds, and so on.

In the same way that a demand schedule can be represented graphically by a demand curve, a supply schedule can be represented by a **supply curve,** as shown in Figure 3-6. Each point on the curve represents an entry from the table.

Suppose that the price of cotton rises from $1 to $1.25; we can see that the quantity of cotton farmers are willing to sell rises from 10 billion to 10.7 billion pounds. This is the normal situation for a supply curve, that a higher price leads to a higher quantity supplied. So just as demand curves normally slope downward, supply curves normally slope upward: the higher the price being offered, the more of any good or service producers will be willing to sell (and vice versa).

Shifts of the Supply Curve

Until recently, cotton remained relatively cheap over the past several decades. One reason is that the amount of land cultivated for cotton worldwide expanded more than 35% from 1945 to 2007. However, the major factor accounting for cotton's

---

The **quantity supplied** is the actual amount of a good or service people are willing and able to sell at some specific price.

A **supply schedule** shows how much of a good or service would be supplied at different prices.

A **supply curve** shows the relationship between quantity supplied and price.

FIGURE   **3-6**   The Supply Schedule and the Supply Curve

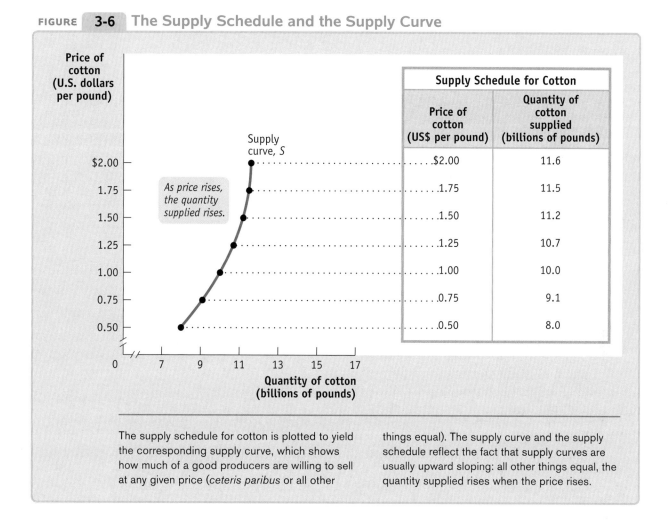

Supply Schedule for Cotton	
Price of cotton (US$ per pound)	Quantity of cotton supplied (billions of pounds)
$2.00	11.6
1.75	11.5
1.50	11.2
1.25	10.7
1.00	10.0
0.75	9.1
0.50	8.0

The supply schedule for cotton is plotted to yield the corresponding supply curve, which shows how much of a good producers are willing to sell at any given price (*ceteris paribus* or all other things equal). The supply curve and the supply schedule reflect the fact that supply curves are usually upward sloping: all other things equal, the quantity supplied rises when the price rises.

relative cheapness was advances in the production technology, with output per hectare more than quadrupling from 1945 to 2007. Figure 3-7 illustrates these events in terms of the supply schedule and the supply curve for cotton.

The table in Figure 3-7 shows two supply schedules. The schedule before improved cotton-growing technology was adopted is the same one as in Figure 3-6. The second schedule shows the supply of cotton *after* the improved technology was adopted. Just as a change in demand schedules leads to a shift of the demand curve, a change in supply schedules leads to a **shift of the supply curve**—a change in the quantity supplied at any given price. This is shown in Figure 3-7 by the shift of the supply curve before the adoption of new cotton-growing technology, S_1, to its new position after the adoption of new cotton-growing technology, S_2. Notice that S_2 lies to the right of S_1, a reflection of the fact that quantity supplied has risen at any given price.

As in the analysis of demand, it's crucial to draw a distinction between such shifts of the supply curve and **movements along the supply curve**—changes in the quantity supplied arising from a change in price (all other things equal). We can see this difference in Figure 3-8. The movement from point A to point B is a movement along the supply curve: the quantity supplied rises along S_1 due to a rise in price. Here, a rise in price from $1 to $1.50 leads to a rise in the quantity supplied from 10 billion to 11.2 billion pounds of cotton. But the quantity supplied can also rise when the price is unchanged if there is an increase in supply—a rightward shift of the supply curve. This is shown by the rightward shift of the supply curve from S_1 to S_2. Holding the price constant at $1, the quantity supplied rises from 10 billion pounds at point A on S_1 to 12 billion pounds at point C on S_2.

A **shift of the supply curve** is a change in the quantity supplied of a good or service at any given price. It is represented by the change (shift) of the original supply curve to a new position, denoted by a new supply curve.

A **movement along the supply curve** is a change in the quantity supplied of a good arising from a change in the good's price.

FIGURE **3-7** An Increase in Supply

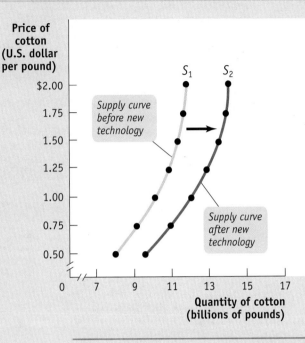

Supply Schedules for Cotton		
Price of cotton (US$ per pound)	Quantity of cotton supplied (billions of pounds)	
	Before new technology	After new technology
$2.00	11.6	13.9
1.75	11.5	13.8
1.50	11.2	13.4
1.25	10.7	12.8
1.00	10.0	12.0
0.75	9.1	10.9
0.50	8.0	9.6

The adoption of improved cotton-growing technology generated an increase in supply—a rise in the quantity supplied at any given price. This event is represented by the two supply schedules—one showing supply before the new technology was adopted, the other showing supply after the new technology was adopted—and their corresponding supply curves. The increase in supply shifts the supply curve to the right.

FIGURE **3-8** Movement Along the Supply Curve versus Shift of the Supply Curve

The increase in quantity supplied when going from point *A* to point *B* reflects a movement along the supply curve: it is the result of a rise in the price of the good. The increase in quantity supplied when going from point *A* to point *C* reflects a shift of the supply curve: it is the result of an increase in the quantity supplied at any given price.

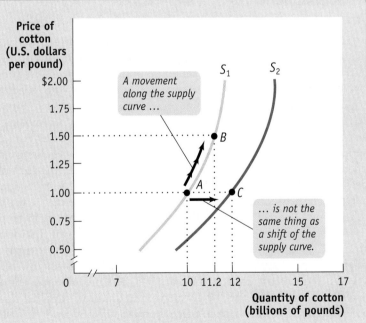

Understanding Shifts of the Supply Curve

Figure 3-9 illustrates the two basic ways in which supply curves can shift. When economists talk about an "increase in supply," they mean a *rightward* shift of the supply curve: at any given price, producers supply a larger quantity of the good than before. This is shown in Figure 3-9 by the rightward shift of the original supply curve S_1 to S_2. And when economists talk about a "decrease in supply," they mean a *leftward* shift of the supply curve: at any given price, producers supply a smaller quantity of the good than before. This is represented by the leftward shift of S_1 to S_3.

FIGURE  **3-9** **Shifts of the Supply Curve**

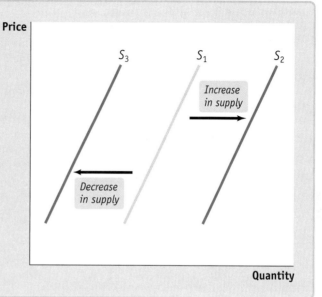

Any event that increases supply shifts the supply curve to the right, reflecting a rise in the quantity supplied at any given price. Any event that decreases supply shifts the supply curve to the left, reflecting a fall in the quantity supplied at any given price.

Economists believe that shifts of the supply curve for a good or service are mainly the result of six factors (though, as in the case of demand, there are other possible causes):

- Changes in input prices
- Changes in the prices of related goods or services
- Changes in technology
- Changes in weather
- Changes in expectations
- Changes in the number of producers

Changes in Input Prices To produce output, you need inputs. For example, to make vanilla ice cream, you need vanilla beans, cream, sugar, and so on. An **input** is any good or service that is used to produce another good or service. Inputs, like outputs, have prices. And an increase in the price of an input makes the production of the final good more costly for those who produce and sell it. So producers are less willing to supply the final good at any given price, and the supply curve shifts to the left. For example, fuel is a major cost for airlines. When oil prices surged in 2007–2008, airlines began cutting back on their flight schedules and some, like Canada's Zoom Airlines, went out of business. Similarly, a fall in the price of an input makes the production of the final good less costly for sellers. They are more willing to supply the good at any given price because they are making more profit than before, and the supply curve shifts to the right.

Changes in the Prices of Related Goods or Services A single producer often produces a mix of goods rather than a single product. For example, an oil refinery produces gasoline from crude oil, but it also produces heating oil

An **input** is a good or service that is used to produce another good or service.

and other products from the same raw material. When a producer sells several products, the quantity of any one good it is willing to supply at any given price depends on the prices of its other co-produced goods.

This effect can run in either direction. An oil refiner will supply less gasoline at any given price when the price of heating oil rises, shifting the supply curve for gasoline to the left. But it will supply more gasoline at any given price when the price of heating oil falls, shifting the supply curve for gasoline to the right. This means that gasoline and other co-produced oil products are *substitutes in production* for refiners.

In contrast, due to the nature of the production process, other goods can be *complements in production*. For example, producers of crude oil—oil-well drillers—often find that oil wells also produce natural gas as a by-product of oil extraction. The higher the price at which a driller can sell its natural gas, the more oil wells it will drill and the more oil it will supply at any given price for oil. As a result, natural gas is a complement in production for crude oil.

Changes in Technology When economists talk about "technology," they don't necessarily mean high technology—they mean all the methods people can use to turn inputs into useful goods and services. In that sense, the whole complex sequence of activities that turn cotton from Pakistan into the pair of jeans hanging in your closet is technology.

Improvements in technology enable producers to spend less on inputs yet still produce the same output. When a better technology becomes available, reducing the cost of production, supply increases, and the supply curve shifts to the right. As we have already mentioned, improved technology enabled farmers worldwide to more than quadruple cotton output per hectare planted over the past several decades. Improved technology is the main reason that, until recently, cotton remained relatively cheap even as worldwide demand grew.

Changes in Weather A change in growing conditions or weather can also affect the supply of a good. For example, when a drought hits the Prairies, the growing conditions for wheat and other grain products becomes unfavourable. As a result, the supply of grain products decreases. Similarly, flooding in Alberta may result in a reduction in supply of grain or other goods due to the disruptions it causes.

Changes in Expectations Just as changes in expectations can shift the demand curve, they can also shift the supply curve. When suppliers have some choice about when they put their good up for sale, changes in the expected future price of the good can lead a supplier to supply less or more of the good today.

For example, consider the fact that gasoline and other oil products are often stored for significant periods of time at oil refineries before being sold to consumers. In fact, storage is normally part of producers' business strategy. Knowing that the demand for gasoline peaks in the summer, oil refiners normally store some of their gasoline produced during the spring for summer sale. Similarly, knowing that the demand for heating oil peaks in the winter, they normally store some of their heating oil produced during the fall for winter sale. In each case, there's a decision to be made between selling the product now versus storing it for later sale. Which choice a producer makes depends on a comparison of the current price versus the expected future price. This example illustrates how changes in expectations can alter supply. An increase in the anticipated future price of a good or service reduces supply today, a leftward shift of the supply curve. But a fall in the anticipated future price increases supply today, a rightward shift of the supply curve.

Changes in the Number of Producers Just as changes in the number of consumers affect the (market) demand curve, changes in the number of producers affect the (market) supply curve. Let's examine the **individual supply curve,** by looking at panel (a) in Figure 3-10. The individual supply curve shows the relationship between quantity supplied and price for an individual producer. For example, suppose that Mr. Silva is a Brazilian cotton farmer and that panel (a) of Figure 3-10 shows how many pounds of cotton he will supply per year at any given price. Then S_{Silva} is his individual supply curve.

The *market supply curve* shows how the combined total quantity supplied by all individual producers in the market depends on the market price of that good. Just as the market demand curve is the horizontal sum of the individual demand curves of all consumers, the market supply curve is the horizontal sum of the individual supply curves of all producers. Assume for a moment that there are only two producers of cotton, Mr. Silva and Mr. Liu, a Chinese cotton farmer. Mr. Liu's individual supply curve is shown in panel (b). Panel (c) shows the market supply curve. At any given price, the quantity supplied to the market is the sum of the quantities supplied by Mr. Silva and Mr. Liu. For example, at a price of $2 per pound, Mr. Silva supplies 3000 pounds of cotton per year and Mr. Liu supplies 2000 pounds per year, making the quantity supplied to the market 5000 pounds.

Clearly, the quantity supplied to the market at any given price is larger with Mr. Liu present than it would be if Mr. Silva were the only supplier. The quantity supplied at a given price would be even larger if we added a third producer, then a fourth, and so on. So an increase in the number of producers leads to an increase in supply and a rightward shift of the supply curve.

For a review of the factors that shift supply, see Table 3-2.

> An **individual supply curve** illustrates the relationship between quantity supplied and price for an individual producer.

FIGURE   3-10   The Individual Supply Curve and the Market Supply Curve

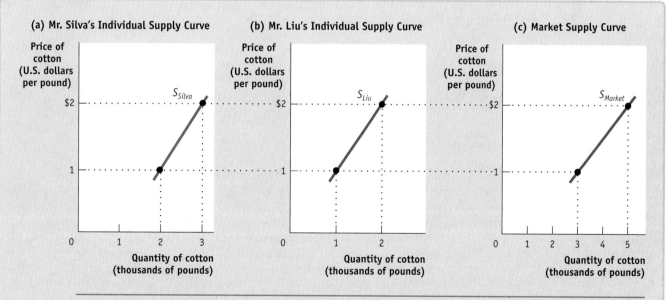

Panel (a) shows the individual supply curve for Mr. Silva, S_{Silva}, the quantity of cotton he will sell at any given price. Panel (b) shows the individual supply curve for Mr. Liu, S_{Liu}. The market supply curve, which shows the quantity of cotton supplied by all producers at any given price, is shown in panel (c). The market supply curve is the horizontal sum of the individual supply curves of all producers.

TABLE 3-2 Factors That Shift Supply

When this happens ...	... supply increases		But when this happens ...	... supply decreases	

When the price of an input falls ...

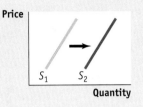

... supply of the good increases.

When the price of an input rises ...

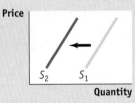

... supply of the good decreases.

When the price of a substitute in production falls ...

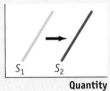

... supply of the original good increases.

When the price of a substitute in production rises ...

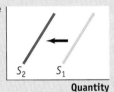

... supply of the original good decreases.

When the price of a complement in production rises ...

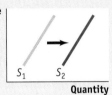

... supply of the original good increases.

When the price of a complement in production falls ...

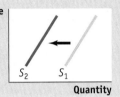

... supply of the original good decreases.

When the technology used to produce the good improves ...

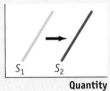

... supply of the good increases.

When the best technology used to produce the good is no longer available ...

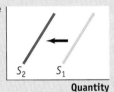

... supply of the good decreases.

When the weather helps production ...

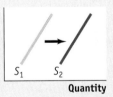

... supply of the good increases.

When the weather disrupts production ...

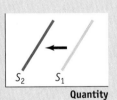

... supply of the good decreases today.

When the price is expected to fall in the future ...

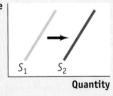

... supply of the good increases today.

When the price is expected to rise in the future ...

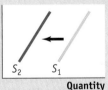

... supply of the good decreases today.

When the number of producers rises ...

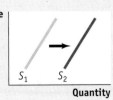

... market supply of the good increases.

When the number of producers falls ...

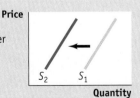

... market supply of the good decreases.

ECONOMICS ➤ IN ACTION

ONLY CREATURES SMALL AND PAMPERED

During the 1970s, British television featured a popular show titled *All Creatures Great and Small*. It chronicled the real life of James Herriot, a country veterinarian who tended to cows, pigs, sheep, horses, and the occasional house pet, often under arduous conditions, in rural England during the 1930s. The show made it clear that in those days the local vet was a critical member of farming communities, saving valuable farm animals and helping farmers survive financially. And it was also clear that Mr. Herriot considered his life's work well spent.

Higher spending on pets means fewer veterinarians are available to tend to farm animals.

But that was then and this is now. Canada and the United States have experienced a severe decline in the number of farm vets over the past two decades. The source of the problem is competition. As the number of household pets has increased and the incomes of pet owners have grown, the demand for pet vets has increased sharply. As a result, vets are being drawn away from the business of caring for farm animals into the more lucrative business of caring for pets. As one American vet stated, she began her career caring for farm animals but changed her mind after "doing a C-section on a cow and it's 50 bucks. Do a C-section on a Chihuahua and you get $300. It's the money. I hate to say that." Add to this the relatively long hours and greater need for travel required of farm vets and it's easy to see why this choice less appealing than being a pet vet in an urban centre.

How can we translate this into supply and demand curves? Farm veterinary services and pet veterinary services are like gasoline and fuel oil: they're related goods that are substitutes in production. A vet typically specializes in one type of practice or the other, and that decision often depends on the going price for the service. The growing pet population in North America, combined with the increased willingness of doting owners to spend on their companions' care, has driven up the price of pet veterinary services. As a result, fewer and fewer vets have gone into farm animal practice. So the supply curve of farm vets has shifted leftward—fewer farm vets are offering their services at any given price.

In the end, farmers understand that it is all a matter of dollars and cents; they get fewer vets because they are unwilling or unable to pay more. As one farmer, who had recently lost an expensive cow due to the unavailability of a vet, stated, "The fact that there's nothing you can do, you accept it as a business expense now. You didn't used to. If you have livestock, sooner or later you're going to have deadstock."

CHECK YOUR UNDERSTANDING   3-2

1. Explain whether each of the following events represents (i) a *shift of* the supply curve or (ii) a *movement along* the supply curve.
   a. More homeowners put their houses up for sale during a real estate boom that causes house prices to rise.
   b. Many strawberry farmers open temporary roadside stands during harvest season, even though prices are usually low at that time.
   c. Immediately after the school year begins, fast-food chains must raise wages, which represent the price of labour, to attract workers.
   d. Due to favourable growing conditions, wheat farmers in the Prairie provinces experience bumper crops.
   e. Since new technologies have made it possible to build larger cruise ships (which are cheaper to run per passenger), Caribbean cruise lines offer more cabins, at lower prices, than before.

Solutions appear at back of book.

▼ **Quick Review**

● The **supply schedule** shows how, all other things equal, the **quantity supplied** depends on the price. The **supply curve** illustrates this relationship.

● Supply curves are normally upward sloping: at a higher price, all other things equal, producers are willing to supply more of a good or service.

● A change in price, all other things equal, results in a **movement along the supply curve** and a change in the quantity supplied.

● Increases or decreases in supply lead to **shifts of the supply curve.** An increase in supply is a rightward shift: the quantity supplied rises for any given price. A decrease in supply is a leftward shift: the quantity supplied falls for any given price.

● The six main factors that can shift the supply curve are changes in (1) **input** prices, (2) prices of related goods or services, (3) technology, (4) weather, (5) expectations about future prices, and (6) number of producers.

● The market supply curve is the horizontal sum of the **individual supply curves** of all producers in the market.

A competitive market is in equilibrium when price has moved to a level at which the quantity of a good or service demanded equals the quantity of that good or service supplied. The price at which this takes place is the **equilibrium price,** also referred to as the **market-clearing price.** The quantity of the good or service bought and sold at that price is the **equilibrium quantity.**

Supply, Demand, and Equilibrium

We have now covered the first three key elements in the supply and demand model: the demand curve, the supply curve, and the set of factors that shift each curve. The next step is to put these elements together to show how they can be used to predict the actual price at which the good is bought and sold, as well as the actual quantity transacted.

In the basic model of a competitive market we normally assume that all buyers and sellers have full information about the product and its price. In addition, it is usually assumed that the good being sold is standardized (i.e., all units are identical).

What determines the price at which a good or service is bought and sold? What determines the quantity transacted of the good or service? In Chapter 1 we learned the general principle that *markets move toward equilibrium,* a situation in which no individual would be better off taking a different action. In the case of a competitive market, we can be more specific: a competitive market is in equilibrium when the price has moved to a level at which the quantity of a good demanded equals the quantity of that good supplied. At that price, no individual seller could make herself better off by offering to sell either more or less of the good and no individual buyer could make himself better off by offering to buy more or less of the good. In other words, at the competitive market equilibrium, price has moved to a level that exactly matches the quantity demanded by consumers to the quantity supplied by sellers.

The price that matches the quantity supplied and the quantity demanded is the **equilibrium price;** the quantity bought and sold at that price is the **equilibrium quantity.** The equilibrium price is also known as the **market-clearing price:** it is the price that "clears the market" by ensuring that every buyer willing to pay that price finds a seller willing to sell at that price, and vice versa. So how do we find the equilibrium price and quantity?

Finding the Equilibrium Price and Quantity

The easiest way to determine the equilibrium price and quantity in a market is by putting the supply curve and the demand curve on the same diagram. Since the supply curve shows the quantity supplied at any given price and the demand curve shows the quantity demanded at any given price, the price at which the two curves cross is the equilibrium price: the price at which quantity supplied equals quantity demanded.

Figure 3-11 combines the demand curve from Figure 3-1 and the supply curve from Figure 3-6. They *intersect* at point *E,* which is the equilibrium of this market; $1 is the equilibrium price and 10 billion pounds is the equilibrium quantity.

⚠ **PITFALLS**

BOUGHT AND SOLD?
We have been talking about the price at which a good or service is bought *and* sold, as if the two were the same. But shouldn't we make a distinction between the price received by sellers and the price paid by buyers? In principle, yes; but it is helpful at this point to sacrifice a bit of realism in the interest of simplicity—by assuming away the difference between the prices received by sellers and those paid by buyers.

In reality, there is often an intermediary—someone who brings buyers and sellers together. The intermediary buys from suppliers, then sells to consumers at a markup—for example, cotton brokers who buy from cotton farmers and sell to textile mills—which turn the cotton into clothing for you and me. The farmers generally receive less than the

mills, who eventually buy their bales of cotton, pay. No mystery there: that difference is how cotton brokers or any other intermediaries make a living. In many markets, however, the difference between the buying and selling price is quite small. So it's not a bad approximation to think of the price paid by buyers as being the *same* as the price received by sellers. And that is what we assume in this chapter.

FIGURE **3-11** Market Equilibrium

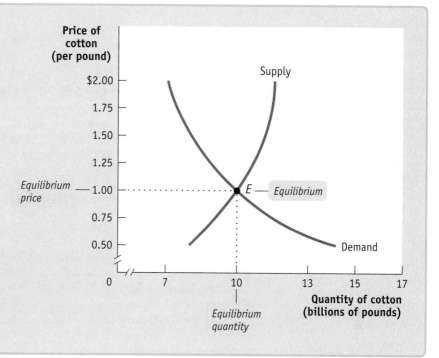

Market equilibrium occurs at point *E*, where the supply curve and the demand curve intersect. In equilibrium, the quantity demanded is equal to the quantity supplied. In this market, the equilibrium price is $1 per pound and the equilibrium quantity is 10 billion pounds per year.

Let's confirm that point *E* fits our definition of equilibrium. At a price of $1 per pound, cotton farmers are willing to sell 10 billion pounds a year and cotton consumers want to buy 10 billion pounds a year. So at the price of $1 a pound, the quantity of cotton supplied equals the quantity demanded. Notice that at any other price the market would not clear: every willing buyer would not be able to find a willing seller, or vice versa. More specifically, if the price were more than $1, the quantity supplied would exceed the quantity demanded; if the price were less than $1, the quantity demanded would exceed the quantity supplied.

The model of supply and demand, then, predicts that given the demand and supply curves shown in Figure 3-11, 10 billion pounds of cotton would change hands at a price of $1 per pound. But how can we be sure that the market will arrive at the equilibrium price? We begin by answering three simple questions:

1. Why do all sales and purchases in a market take place at the same price?

2. Why does the market price fall if it is above the equilibrium price?

3. Why does the market price rise if it is below the equilibrium price?

Why Do All Sales and Purchases in a Market Take Place at the Same Price?

There are some markets where the same good can sell for many different prices, depending on who is selling or who is buying. For example, have you ever bought a souvenir in a "tourist trap" and then seen the same item on sale somewhere else (perhaps even in the shop next door) for a lower price? Because tourists don't know which shops offer the best deals and don't have time for comparison shopping, sellers in tourist areas can charge different prices for the same good.

There is a **surplus** of a good or service when the quantity supplied exceeds the quantity demanded. Surpluses occur when the price is above its equilibrium level.

But in any market where the buyers and sellers have both been around for some time, sales and purchases tend to converge at a generally uniform price, so we can safely talk about *the* market price. It's easy to see why. Suppose a seller offered a potential buyer a price noticeably above what the buyer knew other people to be paying. The buyer would clearly be better off shopping elsewhere—unless the seller were prepared to offer a better deal. Conversely, a seller would not be willing to sell for significantly less than the amount he knew most buyers were paying; he would be better off waiting to get a more reasonable customer. So in any well-established, ongoing market, all sellers receive and all buyers pay approximately the same price. This is what we call the *market price*.

Why Does the Market Price Fall if It Is Above the Equilibrium Price?

Suppose the supply and demand curves are as shown in Figure 3-11 but the market price is above the equilibrium level of $1—say, $1.50. This situation is illustrated in Figure 3-12. Why can't the price stay there?

As the figure shows, at a price of $1.50 there would be more pounds of cotton available than consumers wanted to buy: 11.2 billion pounds versus 8.1 billion pounds. The difference of 3.1 billion pounds is the **surplus**—also known as the *excess supply*—of cotton at $1.50.

This surplus means that some cotton farmers are frustrated: at the current price, they cannot find consumers who want to buy their cotton. The surplus offers an incentive for those frustrated would-be sellers to offer a lower price in order to poach business from other producers and entice more consumers to buy. Similarly, in this situation, as buyers become aware of the surplus, they will offer less than the prevailing price in order to buy this output. Either way, the result of this price cutting will be to push the prevailing price down until it reaches the equilibrium price. So the price of a good will fall whenever there is a surplus—that is, whenever the market price is above its equilibrium level.

FIGURE **3-12** Price Above Its Equilibrium Level Creates a Surplus

The market price of $1.50 is above the equilibrium price of $1. This creates a surplus: at a price of $1.50, producers would like to sell 11.2 billion pounds but consumers want to buy only 8.1 billion pounds, so there is a surplus of 3.1 billion pounds. This surplus will push the price down until it reaches the equilibrium price of $1 (at which point the excess supply has been eliminated).

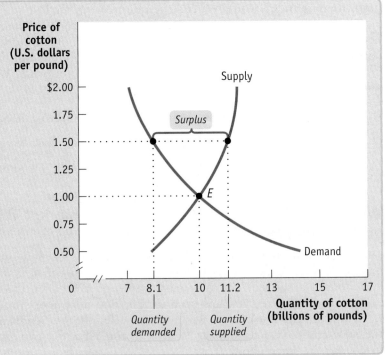

Why Does the Market Price Rise if It Is Below the Equilibrium Price?

Now suppose the market price is below its equilibrium level—say, at $0.75 per pound, as shown in Figure 3-13. In this case, the quantity demanded, 11.5 billion pounds, exceeds the quantity supplied, 9.1 billion pounds, implying that there are would-be buyers who cannot find cotton: there is a **shortage,** also known as an *excess demand,* of 2.4 billion pounds.

When there is a shortage, there are frustrated would-be buyers—people who want to purchase cotton but cannot find willing sellers at the current price. In this situation, either buyers will offer more than the prevailing price or sellers will realize that they can charge higher prices. Either way, the result is to drive up the prevailing price. This bidding up of prices happens whenever there are shortages—and there will be shortages whenever the price is below its equilibrium level. So the market price will always rise if it is below the equilibrium level.

> There is a **shortage** of a good or service when the quantity demanded exceeds the quantity supplied. Shortages occur when the price is below its equilibrium level.

FIGURE 3-13 Price Below Its Equilibrium Level Creates a Shortage

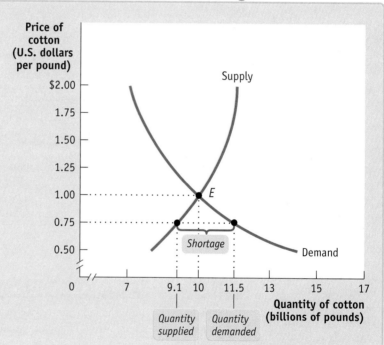

The market price of $0.75 is below the equilibrium price of $1. This creates a shortage: consumers want to buy 11.5 billion pounds, but only 9.1 billion pounds are for sale, so there is a shortage of 2.4 billion pounds. This shortage will push the price up until it reaches the equilibrium price of $1 (at which point the excess demand has been eliminated).

Using Equilibrium to Describe Markets

We have now seen that a market tends to have a single price, the equilibrium price. If the market price is above the equilibrium level, the ensuing surplus leads buyers and sellers to take actions that lower the price. And if the market price is below the equilibrium level, the ensuing shortage leads buyers and sellers to take actions that raise the price. So the market price always *moves toward* the equilibrium price, the price at which there is neither surplus nor shortage.

ECONOMICS ▶ IN ACTION

THE PRICE OF ADMISSION

The market equilibrium, so the theory goes, is pretty egalitarian because the equilibrium price applies to everyone. That is, all buyers pay the same price—the equilibrium price—and all sellers receive that same price. But is this realistic?

The competitive market model determines the price you pay for concert tickets.

The market for concert tickets is an example that seems to contradict the theory—there's one price at the box office, and there's another price (typically much higher) for the same event on Internet sites where people who already have tickets resell them, such as StubHub.com or eBay. For example, compare the box office price for a recent Drake concert in Vancouver, British Columbia, to the StubHub.com price for seats in the same seating area: $75.80 versus $167.15.

Puzzling as this may seem, there is no contradiction once we take opportunity costs and tastes into account. For major events, buying tickets from the box office means waiting in very long lines. Ticket buyers who use Internet resellers have decided that the opportunity cost of their time is too high to spend waiting in line. And tickets for major events being sold at face value by online box offices often sell out within minutes. In this case, some people who want to go to the concert badly but have missed out on the opportunity to buy cheaper tickets from the online box office are willing to pay the higher Internet reseller price.

Not only that—perusing the StubHub.com website, you can see that markets really do move to equilibrium. You'll notice that the prices quoted by different sellers for seats close to one another are also very close: $235.50 versus $240.75 for seats in the same row on the main floor of the Drake concert. As the competitive market model predicts, units of the same good end up selling for the same price. And prices move in response to demand and supply. According to an article in *Canadian Business*, tickets on StubHub.com can sell for less than the face value for events with little appeal, but prices can skyrocket for events that are in high demand. (The article quotes a price of $0.01 for a ticket to a New Jersey Nets game three months before the team moved to Brooklyn, while an article in the *Edmonton Journal* quotes asking prices as high as $2000 for tickets to a local concert by Pink.) Even StubHub.com's chief executive says his site is "the embodiment of supply-and-demand economics."

So the theory of competitive markets isn't just speculation. If you want to experience it for yourself, try buying tickets to a concert.

▼ Quick Review

- Price in a competitive market moves to the **equilibrium price,** or **market-clearing price,** where the quantity supplied is equal to the quantity demanded. This quantity is the **equilibrium quantity.**

- All sales and purchases in a market take place at the same price. If the price is above its equilibrium level, there is a **surplus** that drives the price down to the equilibrium level. If the price is below its equilibrium level, there is a **shortage** that drives the price up to the equilibrium level.

CHECK YOUR UNDERSTANDING 3-3

1. In the following three situations, the market is initially in equilibrium. Explain the changes in either supply or demand that result from each event. After each event described below, does a surplus or shortage exist at the original equilibrium price? What will happen to the equilibrium price as a result?
   a. 2012 was a very good year for Ontario wine-grape growers, who produced a bumper crop.
   b. After a large snowstorm, Ottawa hoteliers often find that many people cancel their upcoming vacations, leaving them with empty hotel rooms.
   c. After a heavy snowfall, many people want to buy second-hand snow blowers at the local hardware store.

Solutions appear at back of book.

Changes in Supply and Demand

The 2010 floods in Pakistan came as a surprise, but the subsequent increase in the price of cotton was no surprise at all. Suddenly there was a decrease in supply: the quantity of cotton available at any given price fell. Predictably, a decrease in supply raises the equilibrium price.

The flooding in Pakistan is an example of an event that shifted the supply curve for a good without having much effect on the demand curve. There are many such events. There are also events that shift the demand curve without shifting the supply curve. For example, a medical report that chocolate is good for you increases the demand for chocolate but does not affect the supply. Events often shift either the supply curve or the demand curve, but not both; it is therefore useful to ask what happens in each case.

We have seen that when a curve shifts, the equilibrium price and quantity change. We will now concentrate on exactly how the shift of a curve alters the equilibrium price and quantity.

What Happens When the Demand Curve Shifts

Cotton and polyester are substitutes: if the price of polyester rises, the demand for cotton will increase, and if the price of polyester falls, the demand for cotton will decrease. But how does the price of polyester affect the *market equilibrium* for cotton?

Figure 3-14 shows the effect of a rise in the price of polyester on the market for cotton. The rise in the price of polyester increases the demand for cotton. Point E_1 shows the equilibrium corresponding to the original demand curve, with P_1 the equilibrium price and Q_1 the equilibrium quantity bought and sold.

An increase in demand is indicated by a *rightward* shift of the demand curve from D_1 to D_2. At the original market price P_1, this market is no longer in equilibrium: a shortage occurs because the quantity demanded exceeds the quantity supplied. So the price of cotton rises and generates an increase in the quantity supplied, an upward *movement along the supply curve*. A new equilibrium is established at point E_2, with a higher equilibrium price, P_2, and higher equilibrium quantity, Q_2. This sequence of events reflects a general principle: *When demand for a good or service increases, the equilibrium price and the equilibrium quantity of the good or service both rise.*

What would happen in the reverse case, a fall in the price of polyester? A fall in the price of polyester reduces the demand for cotton, shifting the demand

FIGURE   **3-14** ## Equilibrium and Shifts of the Demand Curve

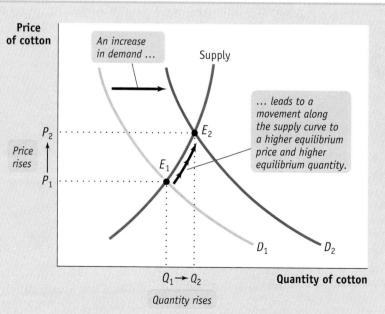

The original equilibrium in the market for cotton is at E_1, at the intersection of the supply curve and the original demand curve, D_1. A rise in the price of polyester, a substitute, shifts the demand curve rightward to D_2. A shortage exists at the original price, P_1, causing both the price and quantity supplied to rise, a movement along the supply curve. A new equilibrium is reached at E_2, with a higher equilibrium price, P_2, and a higher equilibrium quantity, Q_2. When demand for a good or service increases, the equilibrium price and the equilibrium quantity of the good or service both rise.

An increase in demand ...

Supply

... leads to a movement along the supply curve to a higher equilibrium price and higher equilibrium quantity.

Price of cotton

Price rises

P_2

E_2

E_1

P_1

D_1 D_2

$Q_1 \rightarrow Q_2$

Quantity rises

Quantity of cotton

curve to the *left*. At the original price, a surplus occurs as quantity supplied exceeds quantity demanded. The price falls and leads to a decrease in the quantity supplied, resulting in a lower equilibrium price and a lower equilibrium quantity. This illustrates another general principle: *When demand for a good or service decreases, the equilibrium price and the equilibrium quantity of the good or service both fall.*

To summarize how a market responds to a change in demand: *An increase in demand leads to a rise in both the equilibrium price and the equilibrium quantity. A decrease in demand leads to a fall in both the equilibrium price and the equilibrium quantity.*

What Happens When the Supply Curve Shifts

In the real world, it is a bit easier to predict changes in supply than changes in demand. Physical factors that affect supply, like weather or the availability of inputs, are easier to get a handle on than the fickle tastes that affect demand. Still, with supply as with demand, what we can best predict are the *effects* of shifts of the supply curve.

As we mentioned in this chapter's opening story, devastating floods in Pakistan sharply reduced the supply of cotton in 2010. Figure 3-15 shows how this shift affected the market equilibrium. The original equilibrium is at E_1, the point of intersection of the original supply curve, S_1, and the demand curve, with an equilibrium price P_1 and equilibrium quantity Q_1. As a result of the bad weather, supply falls and S_1 shifts *leftward* to S_2. At the original price P_1, a shortage of cotton now exists and the market is no longer in equilibrium. The shortage causes a rise in price and a fall in quantity demanded, an upward movement along the demand curve. The new equilibrium is at E_2, with an equilibrium price P_2 and an equilibrium quantity Q_2. In the new equilibrium, E_2, the price is higher and the equilibrium quantity lower than before. This can be stated as a general principle: *When supply of a good or service decreases, the equilibrium price of the good or service rises and the equilibrium quantity of the good or service falls.*

FIGURE **3-15** Equilibrium and Shifts of the Supply Curve

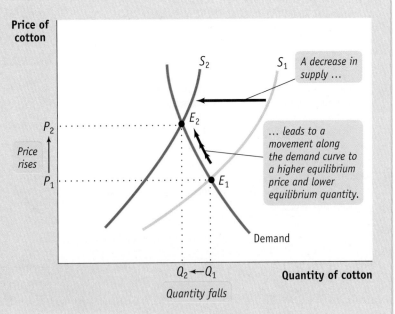

The original equilibrium in the market for cotton is at E_1. Bad weather in cotton-growing areas causes a fall in the supply of cotton and shifts the supply curve leftward from S_1 to S_2. A new equilibrium is established at E_2, with a higher equilibrium price, P_2, and a lower equilibrium quantity, Q_2.

What happens to the market when supply increases? An increase in supply leads to a *rightward* shift of the supply curve. At the original price, a surplus now exists; as a result, the equilibrium price falls and the quantity demanded rises. This describes what happened to the market for cotton as the use of new technology increased cotton yields. We can formulate a general principle: *When supply of a good or service increases, the equilibrium price of the good or service falls and the equilibrium quantity of the good or service rises.*

To summarize how a market responds to a change in supply: *An increase in supply leads to a fall in the equilibrium price and a rise in the equilibrium quantity. A decrease in supply leads to a rise in the equilibrium price and a fall in the equilibrium quantity.*

Simultaneous Shifts of Supply and Demand Curves

Finally, it sometimes happens that events shift *both* the demand and supply curves at the same time. This is not unusual; in real life, supply curves and demand curves for many goods and services shift quite often because the economic environment continually changes. Figure 3-16 illustrates two examples of simultaneous shifts. In both panels there is an increase in demand—that is, a rightward shift of the demand curve, from D_1 to D_2—say, for example, representing an increase in the demand for cotton due to changing tastes. Notice that the rightward shift in panel (a) is larger than the one in panel (b): we can suppose that panel (a) represents a year in which many more people than usual choose to buy jeans and cotton T-shirts and panel (b) represents a normal year. Both panels also show a decrease in supply—that

⚠ **PITFALLS**

WHICH CURVE IS IT, ANYWAY?
When the price of some good or service changes, in general, we can say that this reflects a change in either supply or demand. But it is easy to get confused about which one. A helpful clue is the direction of change in the quantity. If the quantity sold changes in the *same* direction as the price—for example, if both the price and the quantity rise—this suggests that the demand curve has shifted. If the price and the quantity move in *opposite* directions, the likely cause is a shift of the supply curve.

FIGURE   3-16   Simultaneous Shifts of the Demand and Supply Curves

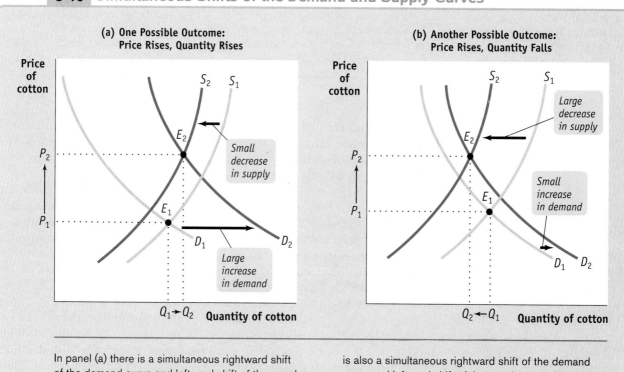

In panel (a) there is a simultaneous rightward shift of the demand curve and leftward shift of the supply curve. Here the increase in demand is relatively larger than the decrease in supply, so the equilibrium price and equilibrium quantity both rise. In panel (b) there

is also a simultaneous rightward shift of the demand curve and leftward shift of the supply curve. Here the decrease in supply is relatively larger than the increase in demand, so the equilibrium price rises and the equilibrium quantity falls.

FOR INQUIRING MINDS

TRIBULATIONS ON THE RUNWAY

You probably don't spend much time worrying about the trials and tribulations of fashion models. Most of them don't lead glamorous lives; in fact, except for a lucky few, life as a fashion model today can be very trying and not very lucrative. And it's all because of supply and demand.

Consider the case of Bianca Gomez, a willowy 18-year-old from Los Angeles, with green eyes, honey-coloured hair, and flawless skin, whose experience was detailed in a *Wall Street Journal* article. Bianca began modelling while still in high school, earning about $30 000 in modelling fees during her senior year. Having attracted the interest of some top designers in New York, she moved there after graduation, hoping to land jobs in leading fashion houses and photo-shoots for leading fashion magazines.

But once in New York, Bianca entered the global market for fashion models. And it wasn't very pretty. Due to the ease of transmitting photos over the Internet and the relatively low cost of international travel, top fashion centres such as New York and Milan are now deluged with beautiful young women from all over the world, eagerly trying to make it as models. Although Russians, other Eastern Europeans,

Bianca Gomez on the runway before intense global competition got her thinking about switching careers.

and Brazilians are particularly numerous, some hail from places such as Kazakhstan and Mozambique. As one designer said, "There are so many models now … . There are just thousands every year."

Returning to our (less glamorous) economic model of supply and demand, the influx of aspiring fashion models from around the world can be represented

by a rightward shift of the supply curve in the market for fashion models, which would by itself tend to lower the price paid to models. And that wasn't the only change in the market. Unfortunately for Bianca and others like her, the tastes of many of those who hire models have changed as well. Over the past few years, fashion magazines have come to prefer using celebrities such as Angelina Jolie on their pages rather than anonymous models, believing that their readers connect better with a familiar face. This amounts to a leftward shift of the demand curve for models—again reducing the equilibrium price paid to them.

This was borne out in Bianca's experiences. After paying her rent, her transportation, all her modelling expenses, and 20% of her earnings to her modelling agency (which markets her to prospective clients and books her jobs), Bianca found that she was barely breaking even. Sometimes she even had to dip into savings from her high school years. To save money, she ate macaroni and hot dogs; she travelled to auditions, often four or five in one day, by subway. As the *Wall Street Journal* reported, Bianca was seriously considering quitting modelling altogether.

---

is, a leftward shift of the supply curve from S_1 to S_2. Also notice that the leftward shift in panel (b) is relatively larger than the one in panel (a): we can suppose that panel (b) represents the effect of particularly bad weather in Pakistan and panel (a) represents the effect of a much less severe weather event.

In both cases, the equilibrium price rises from P_1 to P_2, as the equilibrium moves from E_1 to E_2. But what happens to the equilibrium quantity, the quantity of cotton bought and sold? In panel (a) the increase in demand is large relative to the decrease in supply, and the equilibrium quantity rises as a result. In panel (b), the decrease in supply is large relative to the increase in demand, and the equilibrium quantity falls as a result. That is, when demand increases and supply decreases, the actual quantity bought and sold in equilibrium can rise, fall, or remain the same, depending on *how much* the demand and supply curves have shifted.

In general, when supply and demand shift in opposite directions, we can't predict what the ultimate effect will be on the quantity bought and sold. What we can say is that a curve that shifts a disproportionately greater distance than the other curve will have a disproportionately greater effect on the equilibrium quantity bought and sold. That said, we can make the following prediction about the outcome when the supply and demand curves shift in opposite directions:

- When demand increases and supply decreases, the equilibrium price rises but the change in the equilibrium quantity is ambiguous.

- When demand decreases and supply increases, the equilibrium price falls but the change in the equilibrium quantity is ambiguous.

But suppose that the demand and supply curves shift in the same direction. Before 2010, this was the case in the global market for cotton, where both supply and demand had increased over the past decade. Can we safely make any predictions about the changes in price and quantity? In this situation, the change in quantity bought and sold can be predicted, but the change in price is ambiguous. The two possible outcomes when the supply and demand curves shift in the same direction (which you should check for yourself) are as follows:

- When both demand and supply increase, the equilibrium quantity rises but the change in equilibrium price is ambiguous.

- When both demand and supply decrease, the equilibrium quantity falls but the change in equilibrium price is ambiguous.

ECONOMICS ➤ IN ACTION

THE RICE RUN OF 2008

In April 2008, the price of rice exported from Thailand—a global benchmark for the price of rice traded in international markets—reached $1029 per tonne, up from $398 per tonne at the beginning of 2008. Within hours, prices for rice at major rice-trading exchanges around the world were breaking record levels. The factors that lay behind the surge in rice prices were both demand-related and supply-related: growing incomes in China and India, traditionally large consumers of rice; drought in Australia; and pest infestation in Vietnam. But it was also hoarding by farmers, panic buying by consumers, and an export ban by India, one of the largest exporters of rice, that explained the breathtaking speed of the rise in price.

In much of Asia, governments are major buyers of rice. They buy rice from their rice farmers, who are paid a government-set price, and then sell it to the poor at subsidized prices (prices lower than the market equilibrium price). In the past, the government-set price was better than anything farmers could get in the private market.

Now, even farmers in rural areas of Asia have access to the Internet and can see the price quotes on global rice exchanges. And as rice prices rose in response to changes in demand and supply, farmers grew dissatisfied with the government price and instead hoarded their rice in the belief that they would eventually get higher prices. This was a self-fulfilling belief, as the hoarding shifted the supply curve leftward and raised the price of rice even further.

At the same time, India, one of the largest growers of rice, banned Indian exports of rice in order to protect its domestic consumers, causing yet another leftward shift of the supply curve and pushing the price of rice even higher.

As shown in Figure 3-17, the effects even spilled over to North America, which had not suffered any fall in its rice production. North American rice consumers grew alarmed when large retailers limited some bulk rice purchases by consumers in response to the turmoil in the global rice market.

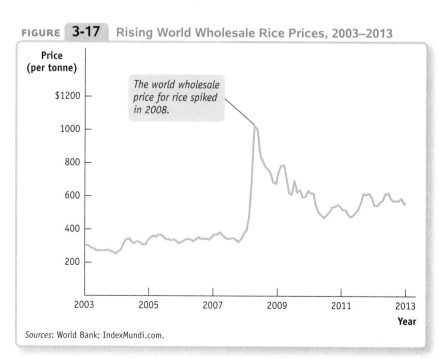

FIGURE **3-17**   Rising World Wholesale Rice Prices, 2003–2013

The world wholesale price for rice spiked in 2008.

Sources: World Bank; IndexMundi.com.

Fearful of paying even higher prices in the future, panic buying set in. As one woman who was in the process of buying 30 pounds of rice said, "We don't even eat that much rice. But I read about it in the newspaper and decided to buy some." According to Canwest, Bruce Cran, president of the Consumers Association of Canada, said he was getting calls in British Columbia that store shelves were being emptied of rice by panicked buyers: "I was in one of the national chains and there was one packet of rice left on the shelf." And, predictably, this panic buying led to even higher prices as it shifted the demand curve rightward, further feeding the buying frenzy. As one market owner said, "People are afraid. We tell them, 'There's no shortage yet' but it was crazy in here."

● ● ◁

CHECK YOUR UNDERSTANDING   3-4

1. In each of the following examples, determine (i) the market in question; (ii) whether a shift in demand or supply occurred, the direction of the shift, and what induced the shift; and (iii) the effect of the shift on the equilibrium price and the equilibrium quantity.
   a. As the price of gasoline fell in Canada during the 1990s, more people bought large cars.
   b. As technological innovation has lowered the cost of recycling used paper, fresh paper made from recycled stock is used more frequently.
   c. When a local cable company offers cheaper on-demand films, local movie theatres have more unfilled seats.

2. When a new, faster computer chip is introduced, demand for computers using the older, slower chips decreases. Simultaneously, computer makers increase their production of computers containing the old chips in order to clear out their stocks of old chips.
   Draw two diagrams of the market for computers containing the old chips:
   a. one in which the equilibrium quantity falls in response to these events and
   b. one in which the equilibrium quantity rises.
   What happens to the equilibrium price in each diagram?

Solutions appear at back of book.

Competitive Markets—And Others

Early in this chapter, we defined a competitive market and explained that the supply and demand framework is a model of competitive markets. But we took a rain check on the question of why it matters whether or not a market is competitive. Now that we've seen how the supply and demand model works, we can offer some explanation.

To understand why competitive markets are different from other markets, compare the problems facing two individuals: a wheat farmer who must decide whether to grow more wheat and the president of a giant aluminum company—say, Rio Tinto Alcan—who must decide whether to produce more aluminum.

For the wheat farmer, the question is simply whether the extra wheat can be sold at a price high enough to justify the extra production cost. The farmer need not worry about whether producing more wheat will affect the price of the wheat he or she was already planning to grow. That's because the wheat market is competitive. There are thousands of wheat farmers, and no one farmer's decision will have any impact on the market price.

For the Rio Tinto Alcan executive, things are not that simple because the aluminum market is *not* competitive. There are only a few big producers, including Rio Tinto Alcan, and each of them is well aware that its actions *do* have a noticeable impact on the market price. This adds a whole new level of complexity to the decisions producers have to make. Rio Tinto Alcan can't decide whether or not to produce more aluminum just by asking whether the additional product will sell for more than it costs to make. The company also has to ask whether producing more aluminum will drive down the market price and reduce its *profit,* its net gain from producing and selling all its output.

When a market is competitive, individuals can base decisions on less complicated analyses than those used in a non-competitive market. This in turn means that it's easier for economists to build a model of a competitive market than of a non-competitive market.

Don't take this to mean that economic analysis has nothing to say about non-competitive markets. On the contrary, economists can offer some very important insights into how other kinds of markets work. But those insights require other models, which are studied in microeconomics.

Good Exchanges Make Great Cities

Chuck Eckert/Alamy

Around the world, commodities are bought and sold on "exchanges," markets organized in a specific location, where buyers and sellers meet to trade. But it wasn't always like this.

The first modern commodity exchange was the Chicago Board of Trade, founded in 1848. At the time, the United States was already a major wheat producer. And St. Louis, not Chicago, was the leading city of the American West and the dominant location for wheat trading. But the St. Louis wheat market suffered from a major flaw: there was no central marketplace, no specific location where everyone met to buy and sell wheat. Instead, sellers would sell their grain from various warehouses or from stacked sacks of grain on the river levee. Buyers would wander around town, looking for the best price.

In Chicago, however, sellers had a better idea. The Chicago Board of Trade, an association of the city's leading grain dealers, created a much more efficient method for trading wheat. There, traders gathered in one place—the "pit"—where they called out offers to sell and accepted offers to buy. The Board guaranteed that these contracts would be fulfilled, removing the need for the wheat to be physically in place when a trade was agreed upon.

This system meant that buyers could very quickly find sellers and vice-versa, reducing the cost of doing business. It also ensured that everyone could see the latest price, leading the price to rise or fall quickly in response to market conditions. For example, news of bad weather in a wheat-growing area hundreds of miles away would send the price in the Chicago pit soaring in a matter of minutes.

The Winnipeg Grain Exchange, later called the Winnipeg Commodity Exchange, opened in 1887 and operated in much the same manner as the Chicago Board of Trade. It helped make Winnipeg one of the fastest growing cities in North America in the early 1900s, earning it the nickname "The Chicago of the North." Its head office building, opened in 1907, was one of the largest office buildings in the British Empire for more than twenty years. By 1911, assisted by the thriving business of selling and shipping commodities, Winnipeg had grown to become the third largest city in Canada. Just as the Chicago Board of Trade was integral to the rise of Chicago, so also did the Grain Exchange have a central role in Winnipeg's rapid growth. Establishing a successful market, it turns out, is very good for business indeed.

QUESTIONS FOR THOUGHT

1. In the chapter we mention how prices can vary in a tourist trap. Which market, St. Louis or Chicago, was more likely to behave like a tourist trap? Explain.

2. What was the advantage to buyers from buying their wheat in the Chicago pit instead of in St. Louis? What was the advantage to sellers?

3. Based on what you have learned from this case, explain why eBay is like a commodity exchange. Why has it been so successful as a marketplace for second-hand items compared to a market composed of various flea markets and dealers?

SUMMARY

1. The **supply and demand model** illustrates how a **competitive market,** one with many buyers and sellers, none of whom can influence the market price, works.

2. The **demand schedule** shows the **quantity demanded** at each price and is represented graphically by a **demand curve.** The **law of demand** says that demand curves slope downward; that is, a higher price for a good or service leads people to demand a smaller quantity, other things equal.

3. A **movement along the demand curve** occurs when a price change leads to a change in the quantity demanded. When economists talk of increasing or decreasing demand, they mean **shifts of the demand curve**—a change in the quantity demanded at any given price. An increase in demand causes a rightward shift of the demand curve. A decrease in demand causes a leftward shift.

4. There are five main factors that shift the demand curve:
   - A change in the prices of related goods or services, such as **substitutes** or **complements**
   - A change in income: when income rises, the demand for **normal goods** increases and the demand for **inferior goods** decreases.
   - A change in tastes
   - A change in expectations
   - A change in the number of consumers

5. The market demand curve for a good or service is the horizontal sum of the **individual demand curves** of all consumers in the market.

6. The **supply schedule** shows the **quantity supplied** at each price and is represented graphically by a **supply curve.** Supply curves usually slope upward.

7. A **movement along the supply curve** occurs when a price change leads to a change in the quantity supplied. When economists talk of increasing or decreas-ing supply, they mean **shifts of the supply curve**—a change in the quantity supplied at any given price. An increase in supply causes a rightward shift of the supply curve. A decrease in supply causes a leftward shift.

8. There are six main factors that shift the supply curve:
   - A change in **input** prices
   - A change in the prices of related goods and services
   - A change in technology
   - A change in weather
   - A change in expectations
   - A change in the number of producers

9. The market supply curve for a good or service is the horizontal sum of the **individual supply curves** of all producers in the market.

10. The supply and demand model is based on the prin-ciple that the price in a competitive market moves to its **equilibrium price,** or **market-clearing price,** the price at which the quantity demanded is equal to the quantity supplied. This quantity is the **equilibrium quantity.** When the price is above its market-clearing level, there is a **surplus** that pushes the price down. When the price is below its market-clearing level, there is a **shortage** that pushes the price up.

11. An increase in demand increases both the equilib-rium price and the equilibrium quantity; a decrease in demand has the opposite effect. An increase in supply reduces the equilibrium price and increases the equilibrium quantity; a decrease in supply has the opposite effect.

12. Shifts of the demand curve and the supply curve can happen simultaneously. When they shift in opposite directions, the change in equilibrium price is predict-able but the change in equilibrium quantity is not. When they shift in the same direction, the change in equilibrium quantity is predictable but the change in equilibrium price is not. In general, the curve that shifts the greater distance has a greater effect on the changes in equilibrium price and quantity.

KEY TERMS

PROBLEMS

1. A survey indicated that chocolate is Canadians' favourite ice-cream flavour. For each of the following, indicate the possible effects on demand, supply, or both as well as equilibrium price and quantity of chocolate ice cream.

   a. A severe drought in Ontario causes dairy farmers to reduce the number of milk-producing cattle in their herds by a third. These dairy farmers supply cream that is used to manufacture chocolate ice cream.

   b. A new report by the Canadian Medical Association reveals that chocolate does, in fact, have significant health benefits.

   c. The discovery of cheaper synthetic vanilla flavouring lowers the price of vanilla ice cream.

   d. New technology for mixing and freezing ice cream lowers manufacturers' costs of producing chocolate ice cream.

2. In a supply and demand diagram, draw the shift of the demand curve for hamburgers in your hometown due to the following events. In each case, show the effect on equilibrium price and quantity.

   a. The price of tacos increases.

   b. All hamburger sellers raise the price of their french fries.

   c. Income falls in town. Assume that hamburgers are a normal good for most people.

   d. Income falls in town. Assume that hamburgers are an inferior good for most people.

   e. Hot dog stands cut the price of hot dogs.

3. The market for many goods changes in predictable ways according to the time of year, in response to events such as holidays, vacation times, seasonal changes in production, and so on. Using the supply and demand model, explain the change in price in each of the following cases. Note that supply and demand may shift simultaneously.

   a. Lobster prices usually fall during the summer peak lobster harvest season, despite the fact that people like to eat lobster during the summer more than at any other time of year.

   b. The price of a Christmas tree is lower after Christmas than before but fewer trees are sold.

   c. The price of a round-trip ticket to Paris on Air France falls by more than $200 in September, after summer vacation. This happens despite the fact that generally worsening weather increases the cost of operating flights to Paris, and Air France therefore reduces the number of flights to Paris at any given price.

4. Show in a diagram the effect on the demand curve, the supply curve, the equilibrium price, and the equilibrium quantity of each of the following events.

   a. The market for newspapers in your town
   Case 1: The salaries of journalists go up.

Case 2: There is a big news event in your town, which is reported in the newspapers.

   b. The market for Montreal Canadiens cotton T-shirts
   Case 1: The Canadiens win the Stanley Cup.
   Case 2: The price of cotton increases.

   c. The market for bagels
   Case 1: People realize how fattening bagels are.
   Case 2: People have less time to make themselves a cooked breakfast.

   d. The market for the Krugman, Wells, Au, and Parkinson economics textbook
   Case 1: Your professor makes it required reading for all of his or her students.
   Case 2: Printing costs for textbooks are lowered by the use of synthetic paper.

5. Statistics Canada reported that in 2009 each person in Canada consumed an average of 85 L of soft drinks at an average price of $0.72 per litre. Assume that, at a price of $0.55 per litre, each individual consumer would demand 102 L of soft drinks. The Canadian population in 2009 was 33.7 million. From this information about the individual demand schedule, calculate the market demand schedule for soft drinks for the prices of $0.55 and $0.72 per litre.

6. Suppose that the supply schedule of Nova Scotia lobsters is as follows:

Price of lobster (per pound)*	Quantity of lobster supplied (pounds)
$25	800
20	700
15	600
10	500
5	400

*Commercially, lobsters are priced in dollars per pound.

Suppose that Nova Scotia lobsters can be sold only in Canada. The Canadian demand schedule for Nova Scotia lobsters is as follows:

Price of lobster (per pound)	Quantity of lobster demanded (pounds)
$25	200
20	400
15	600
10	800
5	1000

   a. Draw the demand curve and the supply curve for Nova Scotia lobsters. What are the equilibrium price and quantity of lobsters?

Now suppose that Nova Scotia lobsters can be sold in France. The demand schedule for Nova Scotia lobsters in France is as follows:

Price of lobster (per pound)	Quantity of lobster supplied (pounds)
$25	100
20	300
15	500
10	700
5	900

b. What is the new demand schedule for Nova Scotia lobsters? Draw a supply and demand diagram that illustrates the new equilibrium price and quantity of lobsters. What will happen to the price at which fishers can sell lobster? What will happen to the price paid by Canadian consumers? What will happen to the quantity consumed by Canadian consumers?

7. Find the flaws in reasoning in the following statements, paying particular attention to the distinction between shifts of and movements along the supply and demand curves. Draw a diagram to illustrate what actually happens in each situation.

a. "A technological innovation that lowers the cost of producing a good might seem at first to result in a reduction in the price of the good to consumers. But a fall in price will increase demand for the good, and higher demand will send the price up again. It is not certain, therefore, that an innovation will really reduce price in the end."

b. "A study shows that eating a clove of garlic a day can help prevent heart disease, causing many consumers to demand more garlic. This increase in demand results in a rise in the price of garlic. Consumers, seeing that the price of garlic has gone up, reduce their demand for garlic. This causes the demand for garlic to decrease and the price of garlic to fall. Therefore, the ultimate effect of the study on the price of garlic is uncertain."

8. The following demand schedule is for a normal good.

Price	Quantity demanded
$23	70
21	90
19	110
17	130

a. Do you think that the increase in quantity demanded (say, from 90 to 110 in the table) when price decreases (from $21 to $19) is due to a rise in consumers' income? Explain clearly (and briefly) why or why not.

b. Would the demand schedule still be valid if it was for an inferior good?

c. Lastly, assume you do not know whether the good is normal or inferior. Devise an experiment that would allow you to determine which one it was. Explain.

9. According to the *New York Times* (November 18, 2006), the number of car producers in China is increasing rapidly. The newspaper reports that "China has more car brands now than the United States. ... But while car sales have climbed 38 percent in the first three quarters of this year, automakers have increased their output even faster, causing fierce competition and a slow erosion in prices." At the same time, Chinese consumers' incomes have risen. Assume that cars are a normal good. Use a diagram of the supply and demand curves for cars in China to explain what has happened in the Chinese car market.

10. Aaron Hank is a star hitter for his baseball team. It is widely anticipated that in the next game he will break the major league record for home runs hit during one season. As a result, tickets for the team's next game have been a hot commodity. But today it is announced that, due to a knee injury, he will not in fact play in the team's next game. Assume that season ticket-holders are able to resell their tickets if they wish. Use supply and demand diagrams to explain the following.

a. Show the case in which this announcement results in a lower equilibrium price and a lower equilibrium quantity than before the announcement.

b. Show the case in which this announcement results in a lower equilibrium price and a higher equilibrium quantity than before the announcement.

c. What accounts for whether case a or case b occurs?

d. Suppose that a scalper had secretly learned before the announcement that Aaron Hank would not play in the next game. What actions do you think he would take?

11. In *Rolling Stone* magazine, several fans and rock stars, including Pearl Jam, were bemoaning the high price of concert tickets. One superstar argued, "It just isn't worth $75 to see me play. No one should have to pay that much to go to a concert." Assume this star sold out arenas around the country at an average ticket price of $75.

a. How would you evaluate the argument that ticket prices are too high?

b. Suppose that due to this star's protests, ticket prices were lowered to $50. In what sense is this price too low? Draw a diagram using supply and demand curves to support your argument.

c. Suppose Pearl Jam really wanted to bring down ticket prices. Since the band controls the supply of its services, what do you recommend they do? Explain using a supply and demand diagram.

d. Suppose the band's next album was a total dud. Do you think they would still have to worry about ticket prices being too high? Why or why not? Draw a supply and demand diagram to support your argument.

e. Suppose the group announced their next tour was going to be their last. What effect would this likely have on the demand for and price of tickets? Illustrate with a supply and demand diagram.

12. The accompanying table gives the annual Canadian demand and supply schedules for pickup trucks.

Price of truck	Quantity of trucks demanded (millions)	Quantity of trucks supplied (millions)
$20 000	2.0	1.4
25 000	1.8	1.5
30 000	1.6	1.6
35 000	1.4	1.7
40 000	1.2	1.8

a. Plot the demand and supply curves using these schedules. Indicate the equilibrium price and quantity on your diagram.

b. Suppose the tires used on pickup trucks are found to be defective. What would you expect to happen in the market for pickup trucks? Show this on your diagram.

c. Suppose that Environment Canada imposes costly regulations on manufacturers that cause them to reduce supply by one-third at any given price. Calculate and plot the new supply schedule. Indicate the new equilibrium price and quantity on your diagram.

13. After several years of decline, the market for handmade acoustic guitars is making a comeback. These guitars are usually made in small workshops employing relatively few highly skilled luthiers. Assess the impact on the equilibrium price and quantity of handmade acoustic guitars as a result of each of the following events. In your answers indicate which curve(s) shift(s) and in which direction.

a. Environmentalists succeed in having the use of Brazilian rosewood banned in Canada, forcing luthiers to seek out alternative, more costly woods.

b. A foreign producer re-engineers the guitar-making process and floods the market with identical guitars.

c. Music featuring handmade acoustic guitars makes a comeback as audiences tire of heavy metal and alternative rock music.

d. The country goes into a deep recession and the income of the average Canadian falls sharply.

14. *Demand twisters:* Sketch and explain the demand relationship in each of the following statements.

a. I would never buy a Justin Bieber CD! You couldn't even give me one for nothing.

b. I generally buy a bit more coffee as the price falls. But once the price falls to $10 per kilogram, I'll buy out the entire stock of the supermarket.

c. I spend more on orange juice even as the price rises. (Does this mean that I'm violating the law of demand?)

d. Due to a tuition rise, most students at a college find themselves with less disposable income. Almost all of them eat more frequently at the school cafeteria and less often at restaurants, even though prices at the cafeteria have risen, too. (This one requires that you draw both the demand and the supply curves for school cafeteria meals.)

15. The small town of Middling experiences a sudden doubling of the birth rate. After three years, the birth rate returns to normal. Use a diagram to illustrate the effect of these events on the following.

a. The market for an hour of babysitting services in Middling today

b. The market for an hour of babysitting services 14 years into the future, after the birth rate has returned to normal, by which time children born today are old enough to work as babysitters

c. The market for an hour of babysitting services 30 years into the future, when children born today are likely to be having children of their own

16. Use a diagram to illustrate how each of the following events affects the equilibrium price and quantity of pizza. Assume that pizza is an inferior good.

a. The price of mozzarella cheese rises.

b. A new study reveals hamburgers are unhealthy.

c. The price of tomato sauce falls.

d. The incomes of consumers rise.

e. Consumers expect the price of pizza to fall next week.

17. Although he was a prolific artist, Pablo Picasso painted only 1000 canvases during his "Blue Period." Picasso is now dead, and all of his Blue Period works are currently on display in museums and private galleries throughout Europe, Asia, and North America.

a. Draw a supply curve for Picasso Blue Period works. Why is this supply curve different from ones you have seen?

b. Given the supply curve from part (a), the price of a Picasso Blue Period work will be entirely dependent on what factor(s)? Draw a diagram showing how the equilibrium price of such a work is determined.

c. Suppose rich art collectors decide that it is essential to acquire Picasso Blue Period art for their collections. Show the impact of this on the market for these paintings.

18. Draw the appropriate curve in each of the following cases. Is it like or unlike the curves you have seen so far? Explain.

a. The demand for cardiac bypass surgery, given that the government pays the full cost for any patient

b. The demand for elective cosmetic plastic surgery, given that the patient pays the full cost

c. The supply of reproductions of Rembrandt paintings

The Algebra of Demand, Supply, and Equilibrium

Often algebraic models are employed in economics to convey the essence of what is being investigated. In particular these models often assume that the curves being studied are nice, linear expressions so that our analysis is easier and we don't get bogged down with less important details and end up getting nowhere.

The Demand Curve

The law of demand says that, other things equal, a higher price for a good or service leads people to demand a smaller quantity of that good or service. On a graph, this means the demand curve is a downward sloping function of the price of the good or service being studied. For each quantity, the demand curve reveals the maximum price consumers are willing (and able) to pay. Similarly, at each level of the price, the demand curve reveals the maximum quantity that consumers are willing (and able) to purchase. In the case of a linear expression, a demand curve in its simplest form would be:

(3A-1) $P = a - b \times Q^d$

where P is the price, Q^d is the quantity, and a and b are positive constants.[1] That $b \times Q^d$ is *subtracted* from a constant tells us the law of demand holds here—as price rises, all else constant, a lower level of quantity is demanded and vice versa (the demand curve slopes downward). The b term describes how sensitive the price is to changes in the quantity demanded (i.e., the slope of the demand curve). If b takes on a larger value, then the demand curve becomes relatively steeper— the same change in quantity results in a larger change in the maximum price consumers are willing to pay. If b takes on a smaller value, the effect is opposite—the demand curve becomes relatively flatter and the same change in quantity results in a smaller change in the maximum price consumers are willing to pay.

Although Equation 3A-1 looks straightforward, there is a lot more going on beneath the surface. The constant a contains information on the factors that shift the demand curve: changes in the price(s) of related goods and services, changes in income, changes in tastes, changes in expectations, and changes in the number of consumers. For example, the annual demand for maple syrup, with the price in dollars per litre and the quantity in millions of litres, may be given by a linear demand curve such as:

$$P = a_0 + a_1 \times P_{corn\ syrup} - a_2 \times P_{pancake\ mix} + a_3 \times Y + a_4 \times Tastes + a_5 \times P^e_{future} + a_6 \times Pop - b \times Q^d$$

with a expanded to include several factors multiplied by constants that are summarized in Table 3A-1. These factors are all multiplied by positive constants that, like b, describe how sensitive the demand curve is to changes in those factors. The constant a_0 picks up the impact of all other determinants of the demand for maple syrup that have been left out of the equation of the demand curve.

---

[1] The price term P should be interpreted as the maximum price consumers are willing to pay (this is sometimes called the *demand price*). Naturally, they would be happy to pay less than this price.

TABLE 3A-1   Variable Factors That Shift Maple Syrup Demand

Factor	Denoted by	Change to the demand curve
Price of corn syrup	$P_{corn\ syrup}$	As the price of a substitute increases (decreases), the demand for maple syrup increases (decreases).
Price of pancake mix	$P_{pancake\ mix}$	As the price of a complement increases (decreases), the demand for maple syrup decreases (increases).
Average consumer income	Y	As the income of consumers increases (decreases), the demand for normal goods increases (decreases) and the demand for inferior goods decreases (increases).[2]
Consumer preference index	$Tastes$	As consumer preference for maple syrup increases (decreases), the demand for maple syrup increases (decreases).
Expected future price	P^e_{future}	As the expected future price of maple syrup increases (decreases), the demand for maple syrup increases (decreases).
Population of potential consumers	Pop	As the population of potential consumers increases (decreases), the demand for maple syrup increases (decreases).

Note that the "other things equal" assumption means that everything in the demand curve equation, except P and Q^d, are being held constant. So, other things equal, when we move along the demand curve as P and Q^d change—the *quantity demanded* either increases or decreases. If one of these other factors does change, then the *entire* demand curve shifts either to the right (up) or left (down)—*demand* either increases or decreases. Figure 3A-1 examines a shift in the demand curve using algebra.

FIGURE 3A-1   Shifts of the Demand Curve

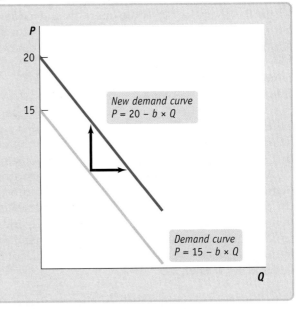

According to geometry, if the value of *a* increases, then the demand curve should shift up. But in economics, an increase in the value of *a* leads to an increase in demand, which shifts the demand curve to the right. Both interpretations are correct because the new demand curve is shifted to the right and shifted up. In this diagram, the value of *a* changes from 15 to 20.

Note that if demand decreases (i.e., *a* decreases), the demand curve shifts down (or to the left).

New demand curve
$P = 20 - b \times Q$

Demand curve
$P = 15 - b \times Q$

Let us simplify the expanded equation. Suppose the following values apply for factors that affect the demand curve for maple syrup: $P_{corn\ syrup} = \$10$, $P_{pancake\ mix} = \$5$, $Y = \$40$, which represents the average income of a Canadian (in thousands of dollars), $Tastes = 9$, $P^e_{future} = \$20$ (per litre), and $Pop = 34$, which is the population of Canada (in millions of people). Suppose also the values for the constants are $a_0 = \$5$, $a_1 = 0.25$, $a_2 = 2$, $a_3 = 0.5$, $a_4 = \$0.45$, $a_5 = 1.5$, $a_6 = \$0.05$, and $b = 1.25$.

Given these assumed values, the demand curve for maple syrup becomes:

$$P = 5 + 0.25(10) - 2(5) + 0.5(40) + 0.45(9) + 1.5(20) + 0.05(34) - 1.25Q^d$$
$$P = 53.25 - 1.25Q^d$$

---

[2]Here we have assumed that maple syrup is a normal good.

The Supply Curve

Usually, in the short run, other things equal, the supply curve is an upward sloping function of the price of the good or service being studied. For each level of output, the supply curve reveals the minimum price at which suppliers are willing to sell. Similarly, at each level of the price the supply curve reveals the maximum quantity that suppliers are willing to sell. In the case of linear expressions, a supply curve in its simplest form would be:

(3A-2) $P = c + d \times Q^S$

where P is the price, Q^S is the quantity, and c and d are positive constants.[3] That $d \times Q^S$ is *added* to a constant tells us that as price rises, all else constant, a higher level of quantity is supplied and vice versa (the supply curve slopes upward). The d term describes how sensitive the price is to changes in the quantity supplied (i.e., the slope of the supply curve). If d takes on a larger value then the supply curve becomes relatively steeper—the same change in quantity results in a larger change in the minimum price at which suppliers are willing to sell. If d takes on a smaller value, the effect is opposite—the demand curve becomes relatively flatter and the same change in quantity results in a smaller change in the minimum price at which suppliers are willing to sell.

Again, the simple appearance of Equation 3A-2 hides enormous amounts of information. The constant c contains information on the factors that shift the supply curve: changes in the prices of inputs, changes in the prices of related goods and services, changes in technology, changes in weather, changes in expectations, and changes in the number of producers. For example, the supply of maple syrup, again with the price in dollars per litre and the quantity in millions of litres, might be represented by a linear supply curve such as:

$$P = c_0 + c_1 \times P_{input} + c_2 \times P_{lumber} - c_3 \times P_{tourism} - c_4 \times Tech - c_5 \times Weather$$
$$+ c_6 \times P^e_{future} - c_7 \times N - d \times Q^S$$

with c expanded to include several factors multiplied by constants that are summarized in Table 3A-2. These factors are all multiplied by positive constants that, like d, describe how sensitive the supply curve is to change in those factors. The constant c_0 picks up the impact of all other determinants of the supply of maple syrup that have been left out of the equation of the supply curve. Like the demand curve, if any of these values change, then the supply curve changes too. Figure 3A-2 examines a shift in the supply curve using algebra.

TABLE **3A-2**   Variable Factors That Shift Maple Syrup Supply

Factor	Denoted by	Change to the supply curve
Input costs	P_{input}	As the price of an input increases (decreases), the supply of maple syrup decreases (increases).
Price of maple lumber	P_{lumber}	As the price of a substitute in production increases (decreases), the supply of maple syrup decreases (increases).
Income from maple farm tourism	$P_{tourism}$	As the income from a complement in production increases (decreases), the supply of maple syrup increases (decreases).
Technology index	$Tech$	As technology improves, the supply of maple syrup increases.
Weather-impact index	$Weather$	As the benefits from the weather increases (decreases), the supply of maple syrup increases (decreases).
Expected future price	P^e_{future}	As the expected future price of maple syrup increases (decreases), the supply of maple syrup decreases (increases).
Number of producers	N	As the number of producers increases (decreases), the supply of maple syrup increases (decreases).

[3]The price term P should be interpreted as the minimum price suppliers are willing to charge (this is sometimes called the *supply price*). Naturally, they would be happy to charge more than this price.

As with the demand curve in Figure 3A-1, there are two ways to interpret a shift in the supply curve. In economics, a decrease in the value of c represents an increase in supply, which shifts the supply curve to the right. The shift right can also be seen as a shift down because the constant term decreased. In this diagram, the value of c changes from 10 to 5.

Note that if supply decreases (i.e., c increases), the supply curve shifts up (or to the left).

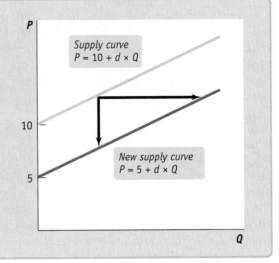

Suppose that, given a set of values for all the factors and constants, we get the following supply curve for maple syrup:

$$P = 12.75 + 0.25Q^S$$

Before we use the demand and supply curves for maple syrup to find the equilibrium price and quantity, let's look at Figure 3A-3, which provides a visual summary of the demand and supply curves. For a summary of how to interpret points along these curves, see Table 3A-3.

FIGURE **3A-3** Demand and Supply Curves

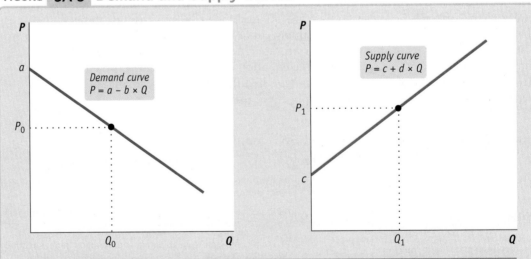

In the demand curve, the term a is the P-axis intercept. This is the lowest price with zero demand. If the price falls below a, then the quantity demanded rises above zero. Similarly, in the supply curve, the term c is the P-axis intercept. This is the price that is so low, the quantity supplied falls to zero. If the price increases from c, then the quantity supplied rises above zero. The slope of the demand curve is equal to −b and the slope of the supply curve is equal to d. Table 3A-3 provides a summary of alternative interpretations of the points along the demand and supply curves.

TABLE **3A-3**   Interpreting Points along Demand and Supply Curves

Curve	Along the Q-axis	Along the P-axis
Demand Curve	At each given price level, the demand curve reveals the maximum quantity that consumers are willing (and able) to buy.	For each given level of output, the demand curve reveals the maximum price consumers are willing (and able) to pay.
	So at the price $P = P_0$, the quantity demanded is equal to $Q^d = Q_0$.	Thus at the output level $Q = Q_0$, the maximum price consumers are willing to pay is $P = P_0$.
Supply Curve	At each level of the price, the supply curve reveals the maximum quantity that suppliers are willing (and able) to sell.	For each level of output, the supply curve reveals the minimum price at which suppliers are willing to sell.
	So at the price $P = P_1$, the quantity supplied is equal to $Q^S = Q_1$.	So at the output level $Q = Q_1$, the minimum price at which suppliers are willing to sell is $P = P_1$.

Market Equilibrium

Along the demand curve, all consumers have voluntarily chosen how much to buy at each specific price to maximize their level of utility or satisfaction. Similarly, along the supply curve all suppliers have voluntarily chosen the quantity they are willing to sell at each specific price to maximize their level of profit. Recall that the market equilibrium occurs where the demand and supply curves intersect. At this intersection, the market outcome is efficient—nobody can be made better off. Figure 3A-4 shows the point of intersection for our maple syrup example.

FIGURE **3A-4**   Market Equilibrium for Maple Syrup

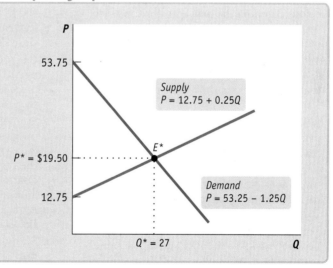

By graphing the pair of lines, we can see that they intersect at E^*, the equilibrium. At this point, $Q^* = 27$ (millions of litres) and $P^* = \$19.50$ per litre. We can use these values to check our answer when we solve for the equilibrium price and quantity algebraically.

Supply
$P = 12.75 + 0.25Q$

E^*

$P^* = \$19.50$

Demand
$P = 53.25 - 1.25Q$

$Q^* = 27$

In the same way we find the intersection of two lines in geometry, we can determine the equilibrium quantity by equating the supply and demand curves. At equilibrium, P^S and P^d should both be equal to the equilibrium price, P^*. Likewise, Q^S and Q^d should both be equal to the equilibrium quantity, Q^*. So in our maple syrup example, we can say:

$$12.75 + 0.25Q^* = 53.25 - 1.25Q^*$$

and solve for Q^*:

$$1.50Q^* = 40.50$$
$$Q^* = 27$$

Knowing that the equilibrium quantity is 27 million litres per year, we can now determine the equilibrium price using either the demand curve or the supply curve:

$$P^* = 53.25 - 1.25Q^* \qquad\qquad P^* = 12.75 + 0.25Q^*$$
$$= 53.25 - 1.25(27) \qquad\qquad = 12.75 + 0.25(27)$$
$$= \$19.50 \qquad\qquad\qquad = \$19.50$$

The equilibrium price is $19.50 per litre of maple syrup.

Since the market is based on voluntary exchanges at the equilibrium point (Q^*, P^*), it is not possible to make either consumers (buyers) or suppliers (sellers) better off without making the other group worse off. For example, consumers would like to buy more maple syrup at a lower price per litre, as this would raise their level of utility or satisfaction. The problem with this is that such a move would result in a reduction in the profits of suppliers, which makes them worse off. Neither group would voluntarily do something that would harm themselves. Thus once we have arrived at the equilibrium intersection, this outcome is a stable situation—stable until such a time that there is a shift in one or both of the curves. Such shifts drive the market to a new equilibrium.

PROBLEMS

1. Suppose that the demand and supply for maple syrup are given by the following equations?

$$P = 53.25 - 1.25Q^d \qquad \text{Demand Curve}$$
$$P = 12.75 + 0.25Q^S \qquad \text{Supply Curve}$$

In each case below, compute the new equilibrium price and quantity exchanged. Has there been an increase/decrease in demand or supply? An increase/decrease in the quantity supplied or demanded? Show in a diagram the initial and new equilibrium locations.

a. Improved weather conditions shift the supply curve to $P = 5.25 + 0.25Q^S$.

b. Increased use of corn to make gasoline additives causes the price of corn syrup to increase, and as a result, the demand curve shifts to $P = 60 - 1.25Q^d$.

c. A new labour contract results in a significant increase in the wages of workers in the maple syrup industry, causing the supply curve to shift to $P = 15.45 + 0.25Q^S$.

d. The income of consumers rises, which shifts the demand curve to $P = 55.50 - 1.25Q^d$; and at the same time an improvement in technology shifts the supply curve to $P = 7.50 + 0.25Q^S$.

2. Suppose the monthly demand and supply for iPods are given by the following equations:

$$P = 500 - 0.001Q^d \qquad \text{Demand Curve}$$
$$P = 200 + 0.0005Q^S \qquad \text{Supply Curve}$$

a. Use the demand and supply curves to solve for the equilibrium price and quantity. Create a diagram to depict this equilibrium.

b. Rewrite the demand curve as an expression that shows quantity demanded (Q^d) in terms of the price.

c. Rewrite the supply curve as an expression that shows quantity supplied (Q^S) in terms of the price.

d. Use the demand and supply curves you derived in parts (b) and (c) to solve for the equilibrium levels of price and quantity. How does this result differ from part (a)? Briefly explain why this is so.

e. Suppose the introduction of new low cost smart phones that also play music causes the demand curve for iPods to shift to $P = 425 - 0.001Q^d$. Derive the resulting new equilibrium levels of price and quantity. Show in a diagram this new equilibrium along with the initial equilibrium location. Are Apple shareholders pleased by this outcome? Briefly explain why or why not.

f. Suppose instead that the offshoring of the production of iPods to a lower cost country causes the supply curve to shift to $P = 140 + 0.0005Q^S$. Derive the resulting new equilibrium levels of price and quantity. Show in a diagram this new equilibrium along with the initial equilibrium location. Are Apple shareholders pleased by this outcome? Briefly explain why or why not.

Consumer and Producer Surplus

The concepts of consumer surplus and producer surplus are extremely useful for analyzing a wide variety of economic issues. They let us calculate how much benefit producers and consumers receive from the existence of a market. They also allow us to calculate how the welfare of consumers and producers is affected by changes in market prices. Such calculations play a crucial role in evaluating many economic policies, and they are especially useful in understanding the effects of trade.

All we need in order to calculate consumer surplus are the demand and supply curves for a good. That is, the supply and demand model isn't just a model of how a competitive market works—it's also a model of how much consumers and producers gain from participating in that market. Our starting point for developing the concepts of consumer and producer surplus is the market in used textbooks.

Consumer Surplus and the Demand Curve

There is a lively market in used university and college textbooks. At the end of each term, some of the students who took a course decide that the money they can get by selling their used books is worth more to them than keeping the books. And some students who are taking the course next term prefer to buy a somewhat battered but cheaper used textbook than a new textbook at full price.

Textbook publishers and authors may not be happy about these transactions because they cut into sales of new books. But both the students who sell used books and those who buy them clearly benefit from the existence of the resale market. That is why many campus bookstores facilitate the trade in used textbooks, buying and selling them alongside the new books.

So, can we put a number on the benefit that used textbook buyers and sellers gain from these transactions? Can we answer the question *"How much* do the buyers and sellers of textbooks gain from the existence of the used book market?" Yes, we can.

Let's start with the buyers. The key point, as we'll see in a minute, is that the demand curve is derived from buyers' tastes or preferences—and that those same preferences also determine how much they gain from the opportunity to buy used books.

Willingness to Pay and the Demand Curve

A used book is not as good as a new book—it will be scuffed up and coffee-stained, may include someone else's highlighting, and may not be completely up to date. How much this bothers you depends on your preferences. Some potential buyers would prefer to buy the used book even if it is only slightly cheaper than a new one; others would buy the used book only if it is considerably cheaper. Let's define a potential buyer's **willingness to pay** as the maximum price at which he or she would buy a good, in this case a used textbook. An individual won't buy the book if it costs more than this amount but will be eager to do so if it costs less. If the price is just equal to an individual's willingness to pay, he or she is indifferent to buying or not buying.

Table 3B-1 shows five potential buyers of a used book that costs $100 new, listed in order of their willingness to pay. At one extreme is Aleisha, who will buy a second-hand book even if the price is as high as $59. Brad is less willing to have

An individual consumer's **willingness to pay** for a good is the maximum price at which he or she would buy that good.

TABLE **3B-1** Consumer Surplus If Price of a Used Textbook = $30

Potential buyer	Willingness to pay	Price paid	Individual consumer surplus = Willingness to pay − Price paid
Aleisha	$59	$30	$29
Brad	45	30	15
Claudia	35	30	5
Darren	25	—	—
Emiko	10	—	—
All buyers			**Total consumer surplus = $49**

a used book and will buy one only if the price is $45 or less. Claudia is willing to pay only $35; Darren, only $25. And Emiko, who really doesn't like the idea of a used book, will buy one only if it costs no more than $10.

How many of these five students will actually buy a used book? It depends on the price. If the price of a used book is $55, only Aleisha will buy one; if the price is $40, Aleisha and Brad will both buy used books, and so on. So the information in the table also defines the *demand schedule* for used textbooks.

Willingness to Pay and Consumer Surplus

Suppose that the campus bookstore makes used textbooks available at a price of $30. In that case Aleisha, Brad, and Claudia will buy used books. Do they gain from their purchases, and if so, how much?

The answer, also shown in Table 3B-1, is that each student who purchases a used book does achieve a net gain but that the amount of the gain differs among students.

Aleisha would have been willing to pay $59, so her net gain is $59 − $30 = $29. Brad would have been willing to pay $45, so his net gain is $45 − $30 = $15. Claudia would have been willing to pay $35, so her net gain is $35 − $30 = $5. Darren and Emiko, however, wouldn't be willing to buy a used book at a price of $30, so they would neither gain nor lose.

The net gain that a buyer achieves from the purchase of a good is called that buyer's **individual consumer surplus.** What we learn from this example is that whenever a buyer pays a price less than his or her willingness to pay, the buyer achieves some individual consumer surplus.

The sum of the individual consumer surpluses achieved by all the buyers of a good is known as the **total consumer surplus** achieved in the market. In Table 3B-1, the total consumer surplus is the sum of the individual consumer surpluses achieved by Aleisha, Brad, and Claudia: $29 + $15 + $5 = $49.

Economists use the term **consumer surplus** to refer to both individual and total consumer surplus. We will follow this practice; it will always be clear in context whether we are referring to the consumer surplus achieved by an individual or by all buyers.

Total consumer surplus can be represented graphically. As we saw in this chapter, we can use the demand schedule to derive the market demand curve shown in Figure 3B-1. Because we are considering only a small number of consumers, this curve doesn't look like the smooth demand curves of this chapter, where markets contained hundreds or thousands of consumers. Instead, this demand curve is stepped, with alternating horizontal and vertical segments. Each horizontal segment—each step—corresponds to one potential buyer's willingness to pay. Each step in that demand curve is one used book wide and represents one consumer. For example, the height of Aleisha's step is $59, her willingness to pay. This step forms the top of a rectangle, with $30—the price she actually pays for a used book—forming the bottom. The area of Aleisha's rectangle, ($59 − $30) × 1 = $29, is her consumer surplus from purchasing one used book at $30. So the individual consumer surplus Aleisha gains is the *area of the dark blue rectangle* shown in Figure 3B-1.

In addition to Aleisha, Brad and Claudia will also each buy a used book when the price is $30. Like Aleisha, they will benefit from their purchases, though not as much, because they each have a lower willingness to pay. Figure 3B-1 also shows the consumer surplus gained by Brad and Claudia; again, this can be measured by the areas of the appropriate rectangles. Darren and Emiko, because they do not buy used books at a price of $30, receive no consumer surplus.

Individual consumer surplus is the net gain to an individual buyer from the purchase of a good. It is equal to the difference between the buyer's willingness to pay and the price paid.

Total consumer surplus is the sum of the individual consumer surpluses of all the buyers of a good in a market.

The term **consumer surplus** is often used to refer to both individual and total consumer surplus.

FIGURE **3B-1** Consumer Surplus in the Used-Textbook Market

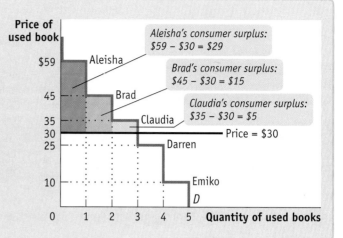

At a price of $30, Aleisha, Brad, and Claudia each buy a used book but Darren and Emiko do not. Aleisha, Brad, and Claudia get individual consumer surpluses equal to the difference between their willingness to pay and the price, illustrated by the areas of the shaded rectangles. Both Darren and Emiko have a willingness to pay less than $30, so they are unwilling to buy a book in this market; they receive zero consumer surplus. The total consumer surplus is given by the entire shaded area—the sum of the individual consumer surpluses of Aleisha, Brad, and Claudia—equal to $29 + $15 + $5 = $49.

The total consumer surplus achieved in this market is the sum of the individual consumer surpluses received by Aleisha, Brad, and Claudia. So total consumer surplus is equal to the combined area of the three rectangles—the entire shaded area in Figure 3B-1. Another way to say this is that total consumer surplus is equal to the area below the demand curve but above the price.

This illustrates the following general principle: *the total consumer surplus generated by purchases of a good at a given price is equal to the area below the demand curve but above that price*. The same principle applies regardless of the number of consumers.

For large markets, this graphical representation of consumer surplus becomes extremely helpful. Consider, for example, the sales of tablet computers to millions of potential buyers. Each potential buyer has a maximum price that he or she is willing to pay. With so many potential buyers, the demand curve will be smooth, like the one shown in Figure 3B-2.

Suppose that at a price of $500, a total of 1 million tablets are purchased. How much do consumers gain from being able to buy those 1 million tablets? We could answer that question by calculating the consumer surplus of each individual buyer and then adding these numbers up to arrive at a total. But it is much easier just to look at Figure 3B-2 and use the fact that the total consumer surplus is equal to the shaded area. As in our original example, consumer surplus is equal to the area below the demand curve but above the price. (You can refresh your memory on how to calculate the area of a right triangle by reviewing Appendix 2A.)

FIGURE **3B-2**   Consumer Surplus

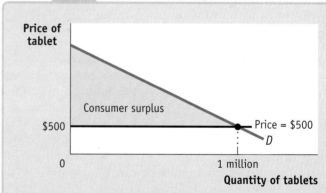

The demand curve for tablets is smooth because there are many potential buyers. At a price of $500, 1 million tablets are demanded. The consumer surplus at this price is equal to the shaded area: the area below the demand curve but above the price. This is the total net gain to consumers generated from buying and consuming tablets when the price is $500.

Producer Surplus and the Supply Curve

Just as some buyers of a good would be willing to pay more for their purchase than the price they actually pay, some sellers of a good would be willing to sell it for less than the price they actually receive. So just as there are consumers who receive consumer surplus from buying in a market, there are producers who receive producer surplus from selling in a market.

Cost and Producer Surplus

Consider a group of students who are potential sellers of used textbooks. Because they have different preferences, the various potential sellers differ in the price at which they are willing to sell their books. Table 3B-2 shows the prices at which several different students would be willing to sell. Andrew is willing to sell his book as long as he can get at least $5; Bahira won't sell unless she can get at least $15; Carlos, unless he can get $25; Donna, unless she can get $35; Etienne, unless he can get $45.

The lowest price at which a potential seller is willing to sell has a special name in economics: it is called the seller's **cost.** So Andrew's cost is $5, Bahira's is $15, and so on.

Using the term *cost*, which people normally associate with the monetary cost of producing a good, may sound a little strange when applied to sellers of used textbooks. The students don't have to manufacture the books, so it doesn't cost the student who sells a used textbook anything to make that book available for sale, does it?

Yes, it does. A student who sells a book won't have it later, as part of his or her personal collection. So there is an *opportunity cost* to selling a textbook, even if the owner has completed the course for which it was required. And remember that one of the basic principles of economics is that the true measure of the cost of doing something is always its opportunity cost. That is, the real cost of something is what you must give up to get it.

Getting back to the example, suppose that Andrew sells his book for $30. Clearly he has gained from the transaction: he was willing to sell for only $5, so he has gained $25. This net gain, the difference between the price he actually gets and his cost, is known as his **individual producer surplus.**

As in the case of consumer surplus, we can add the individual producer surpluses of sellers to calculate the **total producer surplus,** the total net gain to all sellers in the market. Economists use the term **producer surplus** to refer to either individual or total producer surplus. Table 3B-2 shows the net gain to each of the students who would sell a used book at a price of $30: $25 for Andrew, $15 for Bahira, and $5 for Carlos. The total producer surplus is $25 + $15 + $5 = $45.

As with consumer surplus, the producer surplus gained by those who sell used books can be represented graphically. Just as we derived the demand curve from the willingness of different consumers to pay, we derive the supply curve from the cost of different producers. The step-shaped curve in Figure 3B-3 shows the supply curve implied by the cost shown in Table 3B-2. Each step in the supply curve

TABLE 3B-2   Producer Surplus If Price of a Used Textbook = $30

Potential seller	Cost	Price received	Individual producer surplus = Price received − Cost
Andrew	$5	$30	$25
Bahira	15	30	15
Carlos	25	30	5
Donna	35	—	—
Etienne	45	—	—
All sellers			Total producer surplus = $45

An individual seller's **cost** is the lowest price at which he or she is willing to sell a good.

Individual producer surplus is the net gain to an individual seller from selling a good. It is equal to the difference between the price received and the seller's cost.

Total producer surplus is the sum of the individual producer surpluses of all the sellers of a good in a market.

Economists use the term **producer surplus** to refer to either total or individual producer surplus.

FIGURE 3B-3   Producer Surplus in the Used-Textbook Market

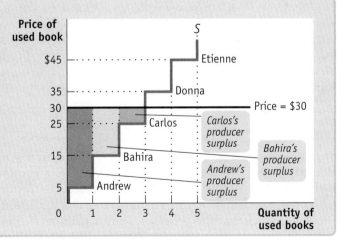

At a price of $30, Andrew, Bahira, and Carlos each sell a used book but Donna and Etienne do not. Andrew, Bahira, and Carlos get individual producer surpluses equal to the difference between the price and their cost, illustrated here by the shaded rectangles. Donna and Etienne each have a cost that is greater than the price of $30, so they are unwilling to sell a used book and so receive zero producer surplus. The total producer surplus is given by the entire shaded area—the sum of the individual producer surpluses of Andrew, Bahira, and Carlos—equal to $25 + $15 + $5 = $45.

is one used book wide and represents one seller. The height of Andrew's step is $5, his cost. This forms the bottom of a rectangle, with $30, the price he actually receives for his book, forming the top. The area of this rectangle, ($30 – $5) × 1 = $25, is his producer surplus. So the producer surplus Andrew gains from selling his book is the *area of the dark red rectangle* shown in the figure.

Let's assume that the campus bookstore is willing to buy all the used copies of this book that students are willing to sell at a price of $30. Then, in addition to Andrew, Bahira and Carlos will also sell their books. They will also benefit from their sales, though not as much as Andrew, because they have higher costs. Andrew, as we have seen, gains $25. Bahira gains a smaller amount: since her cost is $15, she gains only $15. Carlos gains even less, only $5.

Again, as with consumer surplus, we have a general rule for determining the total producer surplus from sales of a good: *the total producer surplus from sales of a good at a given price is the area above the supply curve but below that price.*

This rule applies both to examples like the one shown in Figure 3B-3, where there are a small number of producers and a step-shaped supply curve, and to more realistic examples, where there are many producers and the supply curve is smooth.

Consider, for example, the supply of wheat. Figure 3B-4 shows how producer surplus depends on the price per bushel. Suppose that, as shown in the figure, the price is $5 per bushel and farmers supply 1 million bushels. What is the benefit to the farmers from selling their wheat at a price of $5? Their producer surplus is equal to the shaded area in the figure—the area above the supply curve but below the price of $5 per bushel.

FIGURE **3B-4** Producer Surplus

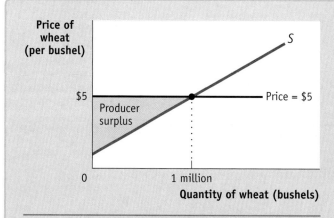

Here is the supply curve for wheat. At a price of $5 per bushel, farmers supply 1 million bushels. The producer surplus at this price is equal to the shaded area: the area above the supply curve but below the price. This is the total gain to producers—farmers in this case—from supplying their product when the price is $5.

The Gains from Trade

Let's return to the market for used textbooks, but now consider a much bigger market—say, one at a large university. There are many potential buyers and sellers, so the market is competitive. Let's line up incoming students who are potential buyers of a used book in order of their willingness to pay, so that the entering student with the highest willingness to pay is potential buyer number 1, the student with the next highest willingness to pay is number 2, and so on. Then we can use their willingness to pay to derive a demand curve like the one in Figure 3B-5. Similarly, we can line up outgoing students, who are potential sellers of used books, in order of their cost, starting with the student with the lowest cost, then the student with the next lowest cost, and so on, to derive a supply curve like the one shown in the same figure.

As we have drawn the curves, the market reaches equilibrium at a price of $30 per used book, and 1000 used books are bought and sold at that price. The two shaded triangles show the consumer surplus (blue) and the producer surplus (red) generated by this market. The sum of consumer and producer surplus is known as the **total surplus** generated in a market.

The striking thing about this picture is that both consumers and producers gain—that is, both consumers and producers are better off because there is a market for this good. But this should come as no surprise—it illustrates another core principle of economics: *there are gains from trade.* These gains from trade are the reason everyone is better off participating in a market economy than they would be if each individual tried to be self-sufficient.

The **total surplus** generated in a market is the total net gain to consumers and producers from trading in the market. It is the sum of the consumer and the producer surpluses.

FIGURE **3B-5** Total Surplus

In the market for used textbooks, the equilibrium price is $30 and the equilibrium quantity is 1000 used books. Consumer surplus is given by the blue area, the area below the demand curve but above the price. Producer surplus is given by the red area, the area above the supply curve but below the price. The sum of the blue and the red areas is total surplus, the total benefit to society from the production and consumption of the good.

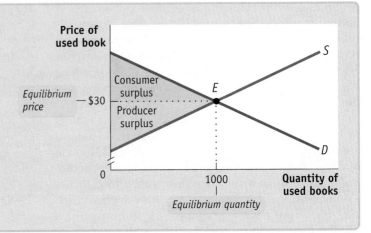

PROBLEMS

1. Determine the amount of consumer surplus generated in each of the following situations.

   a. Leon is willing to pay up to $10 for a new T-shirt. He picks out one he likes with a price tag of exactly $10. When he is paying for it, he learns that the T-shirt has been discounted by 50%.

   b. Alberto goes to a store hoping to find a used copy of The Tragically Hip's *Yer Favourites* for up to $10. The store has one copy selling for $10, which he buys.

   c. After soccer practice, Stacey is willing to pay $2 for a bottle of mineral water. The 7-Eleven sells mineral water for $2.25 per bottle, so she declines to purchase it.

2. Determine the amount of producer surplus generated in each of the following situations.

   a. Gordon lists his old Lionel electric trains on eBay. He sets a minimum acceptable price, known as his *reserve price*, of $75. After five days of bidding, the final high bid is exactly $75. He accepts the bid.

   b. So-Hee advertises her car for sale in the used-car section of the student newspaper for $2000, but she is willing to sell the car for any price higher than $1500. The best offer she gets is $1200, which she declines.

   c. Sanjay likes his job so much that he would be willing to do it for free. However, his annual salary is $80 000.

3. You are the manager of Fun World, a small amusement park. The accompanying diagram shows the demand curve of a typical customer at Fun World.

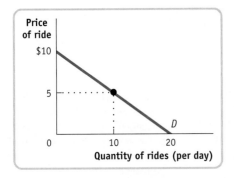

a. Suppose that the price of each ride is $5. At that price, how much consumer surplus does an individual consumer get? (Recall that the area of a right triangle is ½ × the height of the triangle × the base of the triangle.)

b. Suppose that Fun World considers charging an admission fee, even though it maintains the price of each ride at $5. What is the maximum admission fee it could charge? (Assume that all potential customers have enough money to pay the fee.)

c. Suppose that Fun World lowered the price of each ride to zero. How much consumer surplus does an individual consumer get? What is the maximum admission fee Fun World could charge?

4. The accompanying diagram illustrates a taxi driver's individual supply curve (assume that each taxi ride is the same distance).

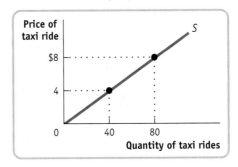

a. Suppose the city sets the price of taxi rides at $4 per ride, and at $4 the taxi driver is able to sell as many taxi rides as he desires. What is this taxi driver's producer surplus? (Recall that the area of a right triangle is ½ × the height of the triangle × the base of the triangle.)

b. Suppose that the city keeps the price of a taxi ride set at $4, but it decides to charge taxi drivers a "licensing fee." What is the maximum licensing fee the city could extract from this taxi driver?

CHAPTER 4

Price Controls and Quotas: Meddling with Markets

BIG CITY, NOT-SO-BRIGHT IDEAS

New York City: an empty taxi is hard to find.

❭ The meaning of **price controls** and **quantity controls,** two kinds of government intervention in markets

❭ How price and quantity controls create problems and can make a market inefficient

❭ Why the predictable side effects of intervention in markets often lead economists to be skeptical of its usefulness

❭ Who benefits and who loses from market interventions, and why they are used despite their well-known problems

IMAGINE YOURSELF IN DOWNTOWN Calgary or Montreal, eager to get a taxi to avoid being late for an important appointment—it is difficult to find an empty cab, especially during peak hours. Or think about the challenges in finding a rental apartment in an urban area—in major Canadian cities, the percentage of apartments that are available to rent is declining. But if you think the conditions are bad in Canada, then you definitely don't want to try to travel by taxicab or to get a decent, affordable rental apartment in New York City because it is almost impossible to do so. Why does this happen in the Big Apple? You might think that New York's notorious shortages of cabs and apartments are the inevitable price of big-city living. However, they are largely the product of government policies—specifically, of government policies that have, one way or another, tried to prevail over the market forces of supply and demand.

In Chapter 3, we learned the principle that a market moves to equilibrium—that the market price rises or falls to the level at which the quantity of a good that people are willing to supply is equal to the quantity that other people demand.

But sometimes governments try to defy that principle. Whenever a government tries to dictate either a market price or a market quantity that's different from the equilibrium price or quantity, the market strikes back in predictable ways. Our ability to predict what will happen when governments try to defy the forces of supply and demand shows the power and usefulness of supply and demand analysis itself.

The shortages of apartments and taxicabs in New York are particular examples that illuminate what happens when the logic of the market is defied. New York's housing shortage is the result of *rent control,* a law that prevents landlords from raising rents except when specifically given permission. Rent control in New York was introduced during World War II to protect the interests of tenants, and it still remains in force. Many other North American cities have had rent control at one time or another, but with the notable exceptions of New York and San Francisco, these controls have largely been done away with. In much of Canada rent controls have been eliminated or, in fact, never existed in

the first place. Where they still exist, in British Columbia, Manitoba, Ontario, Quebec, and Prince Edward Island, rent controls are significantly weaker than they were several decades ago.

Similarly, New York's limited supply of taxis is the result of a licensing system introduced in the 1930s. New York taxi licences are known as "medallions," and only taxis with medallions are allowed to pick up passengers. Although this system was originally intended to protect the interests of both drivers and customers, it has generated a shortage of taxis in the city. The number of medallions remained fixed for nearly 60 years, with no significant increase until 2004.

In this chapter, we begin by examining what happens when governments try to control prices in a competitive market, keeping the price in a market either below its equilibrium level—a *price ceiling* such as rent control—or above it—a *price floor* such as the minimum wage paid to workers in many countries. We then turn to schemes such as agricultural quotas and taxi medallions that attempt to dictate the quantity of a good bought and sold. ■

Price controls are legal restrictions on how high or low a market price may go. They can take two forms: a **price ceiling,** a maximum price sellers are allowed to charge for a good or service, or a **price floor,** a minimum price buyers are required to pay for a good or service.

Why Governments Control Prices

You learned in Chapter 3 that a market moves to equilibrium—that is, the market price moves to the level at which the quantity supplied equals the quantity demanded. But this equilibrium price does not necessarily please either buyers or sellers.

After all, buyers would always like to pay less if they could, and sometimes they can make a strong moral or political case that they should pay lower prices. For example, what if the equilibrium between supply and demand for apartments in a major city leads to rental rates that an average working person can't afford? In that case, a government might well be under pressure to impose limits on the rents landlords can charge.

Sellers, however, would always like to get more money for what they sell, and sometimes they can make a strong moral or political case that they should receive higher prices. For example, consider the labour market: the price to rent an hour of a worker's time is the wage rate. What if the equilibrium between supply and demand for less skilled workers leads to wage rates that yield an income below the poverty level? In that case, a government might well be pressured to require employers to pay a rate no lower than some specified minimum wage.

In other words, there is often a strong political demand for governments to intervene in markets. And powerful interests can make a compelling case that a market intervention favouring them is "fair." When a government intervenes to regulate prices, we say that it imposes **price controls.** These controls typically take the form either of an upper limit, a **price ceiling,** or a lower limit, a **price floor.**

Unfortunately, it's not that easy to tell a market what to do. As we will now see, when a government tries to legislate prices—whether it legislates them *down* by imposing a price ceiling or *up* by imposing a price floor—there are certain predictable and unpleasant side effects.

We make an important assumption in this chapter: the markets in question are efficient before price controls are imposed. But, markets can sometimes be inefficient—for example, a market dominated by a monopolist, a single seller that has the power to influence the market price. When markets are inefficient, price controls don't necessarily cause problems and can potentially move the market closer to efficiency. In practice, however, price controls are often imposed on efficient markets—like the New York apartment market. And so the analysis in this chapter applies to many important real-world situations.

Price Ceilings

Rent control continues to exist to some degree in Ontario, Quebec, British Columbia, Manitoba, and Prince Edward Island. In Ontario, units that were built, or came onto the rental market, after November 1, 1991 are exempt from rent controls. Units on the market prior to that date tend to have rent increases tied to the growth rate of the consumer price index (CPI), but when a tenant moves out rents can be raised to whatever the market will bear. (The Ontario New Democratic Party (NDP) has recently proposed extending rent controls to all Ontario rental apartments.) In Quebec, rent increases are tied to landlord cost increases, but can be lower than these cost increases and, as in Ontario, once a unit is vacated the landlord has some ability to raise the rent. In British Columbia, provincial government guidelines cap rent increases at the growth rate of the CPI plus 2%. In Manitoba, the government mandated maximum rent increase is usually set below the growth rate of the CPI. In Prince Edward Island, maximum percent rent increases are set annually based on the type of dwelling.

Aside from rent control, there are other price ceilings in Canada today. Currently some form of price controls exists in Canadian markets for pharmaceutical drugs, electricity, basic residential phone services, and agricultural commodities (such as eggs, chicken, turkey, and dairy). In the case of patented prescription drug prices, there are two stages of control. The federal government grants monopoly rights to the patent holder to be the sole supplier of a particular drug formulation, but in return the government imposes a price ceiling that the supplier can't exceed. The provincial and territorial governments, which are responsible for delivering health care services within their borders, use their market power as purchasers of large volumes of drugs to negotiate prices that can be well below the ceiling price.

At times, price ceilings have been widespread. They are typically imposed during crises—wars, harvest failures, natural disasters—because these events often lead to sudden price increases that hurt many people but produce big gains for a lucky few. The Canadian government imposed ceilings on many prices during World War II: the war sharply increased demand for raw materials (such as aluminum and steel) and necessities (such as home rentals, sugar, milk, and coal), and price controls prevented those who supplied these goods and services from earning huge profits. World oil prices spiked in 1979–1980 due to uncertainty caused by the Iranian revolution in 1979 and the 1980 outbreak of war between Iran and Iraq (both large oil producing nations). Price controls on oil were imposed in 1980, when Prime Minister Pierre Trudeau's government introduced the National Energy Program to help Canada achieve energy self-sufficiency, redistribute the wealth from non-renewable energy production to all parts of the country, and increase Canadian ownership of the oil industry.

Rent control in New York City is a legacy of World War II: it was imposed because wartime production produced an economic boom, which increased demand for apartments at a time when the labour and raw materials that might have been used to build them were being used to fight the war instead. Although most price controls were removed soon after the war ended, New York's rent limits were retained and gradually extended to buildings not previously covered, leading to some very strange situations.

You can rent a one-bedroom apartment in Manhattan on fairly short notice—if you are able and willing to pay several thousand dollars a month and live in a less-than-desirable area. Yet some people pay only a small fraction of this for comparable apartments, and others pay hardly more for bigger apartments in better locations.[1]

Aside from producing great deals for some renters, however, what are the broader consequences of New York's rent-control system? To answer this question, we turn to the model we developed in Chapter 3: the supply and demand model.

Modelling a Price Ceiling

To see what can go wrong when a government imposes a price ceiling on an efficient market, consider Figure 4-1, which shows a simplified model of the market for apartments in a large city. For the sake of simplicity, we imagine that all apartments are exactly the same and so would rent for the same price in an

---

[1]Being a tenant in a rent-controlled apartment is very desirable since the tenant could have the right to live in the unit until he or she dies. Landlords have been known to pay tens of thousands of dollars in order to get tenants to move out and abandon their claim to a unit. The landlord is then able to rent out the apartment at a much higher market rent. In fact, the value of removing a rent-controlled tenant is so high that some truly exceptional landlords have hired thugs to attack or even murder tenants to free up units.

FIGURE **4-1** **The Market for Apartments in the Absence of Price Controls**

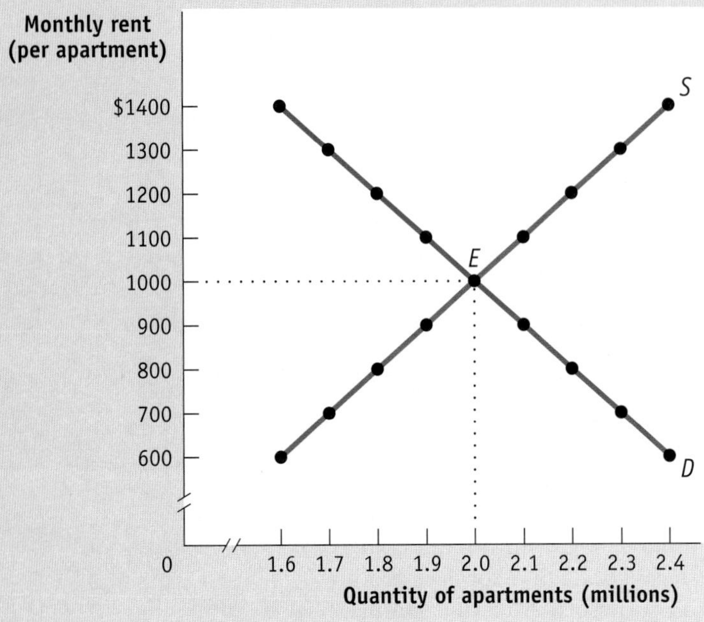

Monthly rent (per apartment)	Quantity of apartments (millions)	
	Quantity demanded	Quantity supplied
$1400	1.6	2.4
1300	1.7	2.3
1200	1.8	2.2
1100	1.9	2.1
1000	2.0	2.0
900	2.1	1.9
800	2.2	1.8
700	2.3	1.7
600	2.4	1.6

Without government intervention, the market for apartments reaches equilibrium at point *E* with a market rent of $1000 per month and 2 million apartments rented.

unregulated market. The table in the figure shows the demand and supply schedules; the demand and supply curves are shown on the left. We show the quantity of apartments on the horizontal axis and the monthly rent per apartment on the vertical axis. You can see that in an unregulated market the equilibrium would be at point *E:* two million apartments would be rented for $1000 each per month.

Now suppose that the government imposes a price ceiling, limiting rents to a price below the equilibrium price—say, no more than $800.

Figure 4-2 shows the effect of the price ceiling, represented by the line at $800. At the enforced rental rate of $800, landlords have less incentive to offer apartments, so they won't be willing to supply as many as they would at the equilibrium rate of $1000. They will choose point *A* on the supply curve, offering only 1.8 million apartments for rent, 200 000 fewer than in the unregulated market. At the same time, more people will want to rent apartments at a price of $800 than at the equilibrium price of $1000; as shown at point *B* on the demand curve, at a monthly rent of $800 the quantity of apartments demanded rises to 2.2 million, 200 000 more than in the unregulated market and 400 000 more than are actually available at the price of $800. So there is now a persistent shortage of rental housing: at that price, 400 000 more people want to rent than are able to find apartments.

Do price ceilings always cause shortages? No. If a price ceiling is set at or above the equilibrium price, it won't have any effect. Suppose that the equilibrium rental rate on apartments is $1000 per month and the city government sets a ceiling of $1200. Who cares? In this case, the price ceiling won't be *binding*—it won't actually constrain market behaviour—and it will have no effect.

Over time, a binding price ceiling can become non-binding if the demand and/or supply curves shift enough to make the equilibrium price less than or equal to the price ceiling. In our rental apartment example, a decrease in demand due to falling house prices, making owning a home more attractive than renting, would shift the demand curve to the left. Similarly, if more apartment buildings are constructed,

FIGURE   **4-2**   The Effects of a Price Ceiling

The black horizontal line represents the government-imposed price ceiling on rents of $800 per month. This price ceiling reduces the quantity of apartments supplied to 1.8 million, point *A*, and increases the quantity demanded to 2.2 million, point *B*. This creates a persistent shortage of 400 000 units: 400 000 people who want apartments at the legal rent of $800 but cannot get them.

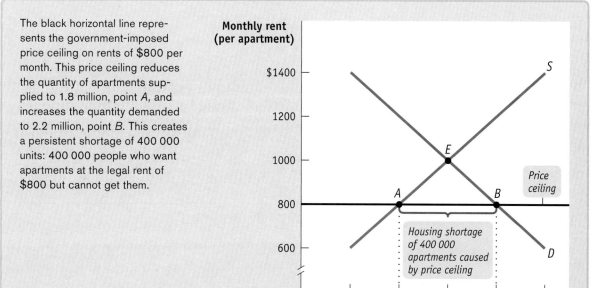

then the supply of rental apartments increases, shifting the supply curve to the right. In Figure 4-2, if these shifts move the intersection of the demand and supply curves to $800 or less, then the rent control is a non-binding price ceiling.

How a Price Ceiling Causes Inefficiency

The housing shortage shown in Figure 4-2 is not merely annoying: like any shortage induced by price controls, it can be seriously harmful because it leads to inefficiency. In other words, there are gains from trade that go unrealized. Rent control, like all price ceilings, creates inefficiency in at least four distinct ways. It reduces the quantity of apartments rented below the efficient level; it typically leads to misallocation of apartments among would-be renters; it leads to wasted time and effort as people search for apartments; and it leads landlords to maintain apartments in inefficiently low quality or condition. In addition to inefficiency, price ceilings give rise to illegal behaviour as people try to circumvent them.

Inefficiently Low Quantity Because a price ceiling reduces the price of a good, it reduces the quantity that sellers are willing to supply. Buyers can't buy more units of a good than sellers are willing to sell; a price ceiling reduces the quantity of a good bought and sold below the competitive or free market equilibrium quantity. Because rent control reduces the number of apartments supplied, it reduces the number of apartments rented, too. The low quantity sold is an inefficiency due to missed opportunities: price ceilings prevent mutually beneficial transactions from occurring, transactions that would benefit both buyers and sellers. Figure 4-3 shows the inefficiently low quantity of apartments supplied with rent control.

Inefficient Allocation to Consumers Rent control doesn't just lead to too few apartments being available. It can also lead to misallocation of the apartments that are available: people who badly need a place to live may not be able to find an apartment, but some apartments may be occupied by people with much less urgent needs.

FIGURE **4-3** A Price Ceiling Causes Inefficiently Low Quantity

A price ceiling reduces the quantity supplied below the market equilibrium quantity. Because buyers can't buy more units of a good than sellers are willing to sell, a price ceiling reduces the quantity of a good bought and sold.

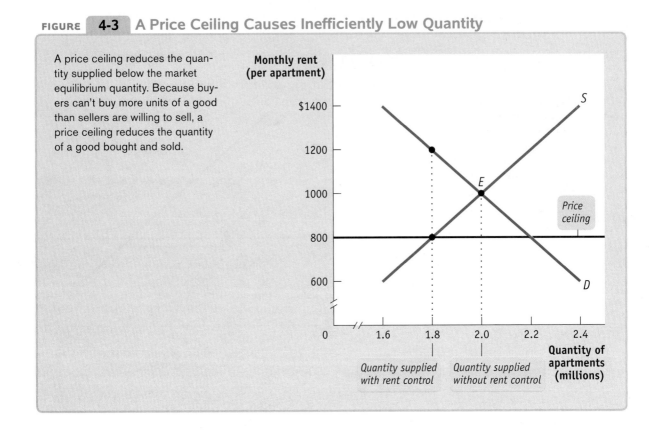

In the case shown in Figure 4-2, 2.2 million people would like to rent an apartment at $800 per month, but only 1.8 million apartments are available. Of those 2.2 million who are seeking an apartment, some want an apartment badly and are willing to pay a high price to get one. Others have a less urgent need and are only willing to pay a low price, perhaps because they have alternative housing. An efficient allocation of apartments would reflect these differences: people who really want an apartment will get one and people who aren't all that anxious to find an apartment won't. In an inefficient distribution of apartments, the opposite will happen: some people who are not especially anxious to find an apartment will get one and others who are very anxious to find an apartment won't.

Because people usually get apartments through luck or personal connections under rent control, it generally results in an **inefficient allocation to consumers** of the few apartments available.

To see the inefficiency involved, consider the plight of the Lees, a family with young children who have no alternative housing and would be willing to pay up to $1500 for an apartment—but are unable to find one. Also consider George, a retiree who lives most of the year in Florida but still has a lease on the New York City apartment he moved into 40 years ago. George pays $800 per month for this apartment, but if the rent were even slightly more—say, $850—he would give it up and stay with his children when he is in the city.

This allocation of apartments—George has one and the Lees do not—is a missed opportunity: there is a way to make the Lees and George both better off at no additional cost. The Lees would be happy to pay George, say, $1200 a month to sublet his apartment, which he would happily accept since the apartment is worth no more than $849 a month to him. George would prefer the money he gets from the Lees to keeping his apartment; the Lees would prefer to have the apartment rather than the money. So both would be made better off by this transaction—and nobody else would be made worse off.

Generally, if people who really want apartments could sublet them from people who are less eager to live there, both those who gain apartments and those who

Price ceilings often lead to inefficiency in the form of **inefficient allocation to consumers:** some people who want the good badly and are willing to pay a high price don't get it, and some who care relatively little about the good and are only willing to pay a low price do get it.

trade their occupancy for money would be better off. However, subletting is illegal under rent control because it would occur at prices above the price ceiling.

The fact that subletting is illegal doesn't mean it never happens. In fact, chasing down illegal subletting is a major business for New York City private investigators. An article in the *New York Times* described how private investigators use hidden cameras and other tricks to prove that the legal tenants in rent-controlled apartments actually live in the suburbs, or even in other states, and have sublet their apartments at two or three times the controlled rent. This subletting is a kind of illegal activity, which we will discuss shortly. For now, just note that landlords and legal agencies actively discourage the practice of illegal subletting. As a result, the problem of inefficient allocation of apartments remains.

Wasted Resources Another reason a price ceiling causes inefficiency is that it leads to **wasted resources:** people expend money, effort, and time to cope with the shortages caused by the price ceiling. Back in 1979, U.S. price controls on gasoline led to shortages that forced millions of Americans to spend hours each week waiting in lines at gas stations. The opportunity cost of the time spent in gas lines—the wages not earned, the leisure time not enjoyed—constituted wasted resources from the point of view of consumers and of the economy as a whole.

Because of rent control, the Lees will spend all their spare time for several months searching for an apartment, time they would rather spend working or in family activities. That is, there is an opportunity cost to the Lee's prolonged search for an apartment—the leisure or income they would have to forgo. If the market for apartments worked freely, the Lees would quickly find an apartment at the equilibrium rent of $1000, leaving them time to earn more or to enjoy themselves—an outcome that would make them better off without making anyone else worse off. Again, rent control creates missed opportunities.

Indeed, in the long run, the time and resources that families like the Lees spend searching for a rental apartment might increase as the city population rises. All other things equal, a larger population increases the demand for rental apartments. Following an increase in demand, the shortage of units grows and renters find it more difficult to locate a rental unit. Also, it is often the case that the demand and supply curves become flatter over time (i.e., for a given price change, the quantity supplied or demanded changes more in the long run than it does in the short run). So in the long run, the size of a shortage caused by a price ceiling tends to grow—with or without an increase in demand.

Inefficiently Low Quality Yet another way a price ceiling creates inefficiency is by causing goods to be of inefficiently low quality. **Inefficiently low quality** means that sellers offer low-quality goods at a low price even though some buyers would rather have higher quality and would be willing to pay a higher price for it.

Again, consider rent control. Landlords have no incentive to provide better conditions because they cannot raise rents to cover their repair costs but are able to find tenants easily. In many cases, tenants would be willing to pay much more for improved conditions than it would cost for the landlord to provide them—for example, the upgrade of an antiquated electrical system that cannot safely run air conditioners or computers. But any additional payment for such improvements would be legally considered a rent increase, which is prohibited. Indeed, rent-controlled apartments are notoriously badly maintained, rarely painted, subject to frequent electrical and plumbing problems, and sometimes even hazardous to inhabit. As one former manager of Manhattan buildings described the situation: "At unregulated apartments we'd do most things that the tenants requested. But on the rent-regulated units, we did absolutely only what the law required. ... We had a perverse incentive to make those tenants unhappy."

Price ceilings typically lead to inefficiency in the form of **wasted resources:** people expend money, effort, and time to cope with the shortages caused by the price ceiling.

Price ceilings often lead to inefficiency in that the goods being offered are of **inefficiently low quality:** sellers offer low-quality goods at a low price even though some buyers would prefer a higher quality at a higher price.

FOR INQUIRING MINDS

RENT CONTROL, MUMBAI STYLE

How far would you go to keep a rent-controlled apartment? Some tenants in the city of Mumbai, India, went very far indeed. According to a *Wall Street Journal* article, three people were killed when four floors in a rent-controlled apartment building in Mumbai collapsed. Despite demands by the city government to vacate the deteriorated building, 58 other tenants refused to leave. They stayed put even after having their electricity and water shut off, being locked out of their apartments, and surviving a police raid. Tenants camped out on the building's veranda, vowing not to give up.

Not all of these tenants were desperately poor and lacking other options. One rent-controlled tenant, the owner of a thriving textile business, paid a total of $8.50 a month for a spacious two-bedroom apartment. (Luxury apartments in Mumbai can go for thousands of dollars a month.)

Although it's a world away, the dynamics of rent control in Mumbai are a lot like those in North America (although Mumbai has clearly had a much more extreme experience). Rent control began in Mumbai in 1947, to address a critical shortage of housing caused by a flood of refugees fleeing conflict between Hindus and Muslims. Clearly intended to be a temporary measure, it was so popular politically that it has been extended 20 times and now applies to about 60% of the buildings in the city's centre. Tenants pass apartments on to their heirs or sell the right to occupy to other tenants.

Despite the fact that home prices in Mumbai surged more than 60% between 2007 and 2010, landlords of rent-controlled buildings have suffered financially, with the result that across the city prime buildings have been abandoned to decay, even though half of the city's 12 million residents live in slums because of a lack of new housing.

This whole situation is a missed opportunity—some tenants would be happy to pay for better conditions, and landlords would be happy to provide them for payment. But such an exchange would occur only if the market were allowed to operate freely.

Black Markets And that leads us to a last aspect of price ceilings: the incentive they provide for illegal activities, specifically the emergence of **black markets.** We have already described one kind of black market activity—illegal subletting by tenants. But it does not stop there. Clearly, there is a temptation for a landlord to say to a potential tenant, "Look, you can have the place if you slip me an extra few hundred in cash each month"—and for the tenant to agree if he or she is one of those people who would be willing to pay much more than the maximum legal rent. Let's look again at Figure 4-3. If there is subletting, then the monthly rent for a sublet apartment would be $1200—the so-called demand price given the number of units available. Alternatively, the landlord could demand an extra cash payment of $400 each month as a "bribe" to rent out the apartment—thereby making the total rental payment actually $1200 per month.

What's wrong with black markets? In general, it's a bad thing if people break any law, because it encourages disrespect for the law in general. Worse yet, in this case illegal activity worsens the position of those who are honest. If the Lees are scrupulous about upholding the rent-control law, but other people—who may need an apartment less than the Lees—are willing to bribe landlords, the Lees may never find an apartment.

So Why Are There Price Ceilings?

We have seen three common results of price ceilings:

- A persistent shortage of the good

- Inefficiency arising from this persistent shortage in the form of inefficiently low quantity transacted, inefficient allocation of the good to consumers, resources wasted in searching for the good, and the inefficiently low quality of the good offered for sale

- The emergence of illegal, black market activity

A **black market** is a market in which goods or services are bought and sold illegally—either because it is illegal to sell them at all or because the prices charged are legally prohibited by a price control (either a price ceiling or floor).

Given these unpleasant consequences, why do governments still sometimes impose price ceilings? Why does rent control, in particular, persist in New York City?

One answer is that although price ceilings may have adverse effects, they do benefit some people. In practice, New York's rent-control rules—which are more complex than our simple model—hurt most residents but give a small minority of renters much cheaper housing than they would get in an unregulated market. And those who benefit from the controls are typically better organized and more vocal than those who are harmed by them.

Also, when price ceilings have been in effect for a long time, buyers may not have a realistic idea of what would happen without them. In our previous example, the rental rate in an unregulated market (Figure 4-1) would be only 25% higher than in the regulated market (Figure 4-2): $1000 instead of $800. But how would renters know that? Indeed, they might have heard about black market transactions at much higher prices—the Lees or some other family paying George $1200 or more—and would not realize that these black market prices are much higher than the price that would prevail in a fully unregulated market.

A last answer is that government officials often do not understand supply and demand analysis! It is a great mistake to suppose that economic policies in the real world are always sensible or well informed.

ECONOMICS ▶ IN ACTION

HUNGER AND PRICE CONTROLS IN VENEZUELA

Something was rotten in the state of Venezuela—specifically, more than 25 000 tonnes of decomposing food in Puerto Cabello in June 2010. The discovery was particularly embarrassing for the then president Hugo Chávez. He was elected in 1998 on a platform denouncing the country's economic elite and promising policies favouring the poor and working classes. Among those policies were price controls on basic foodstuffs, which led to shortages that began in 2003 and had become severe by 2006.

Generous government policies led to higher spending by consumers and sharply rising prices for goods that weren't subject to price controls or which were bought on the black market. The result was a big increase in the demand for price-controlled goods. But a sharp decline in the value of Venezuela's currency led to a fall in imports of foreign food, and the result was empty shelves in the nation's food stores.

Venezuela's food shortages offer a lesson in why price ceilings, however well intentioned, are usually not a good idea.

As the shortages persisted and inflation of food prices worsened (in the first five months of 2010, the prices of food and drink rose by 21%), Chávez declared "economic war" on the private sector, berating it for "hoarding and smuggling." The government expropriated farms, food manufacturers, and grocery stores, creating in their place government-owned ones, which were corrupt and inefficient—it was the government-owned food-distribution company, PDVAL, that left tens of thousands of tonnes of food to rot in Venezuelan ports. Food production also fell; Venezuela must now import 70% of its food.

Not surprisingly, the shelves have been far more bare in government-run grocery stores than in those still in private hands. The food shortages were so severe that they greatly diminished Chávez's popularity among working-class Venezuelans and halted his expropriation plans. As an old Venezuelan saying has it, "Love with hunger doesn't last."

After the death of President Chávez in March 2013, Vice President Nicolás Maduro took over before a special presidential election was held in April to pick a new president. Maduro promised to continue Chávez's socialist revolution while the opposition candidate, Henrique Capriles, argued that this regime had put the country on the road to ruin. During the campaign, shortages of food and basic household items hit a five-year high, and partly as a result, Maduro barely won the election. In May 2013, monthly inflation peaked at 6.1%, the highest monthly rate in 17 years, contributing to an annual rate of inflation of 35.1%. However, according to the central bank, in May shortages were becoming less severe, as the "shortage indicator," which measures the difficulties to obtain a basket of basic goods, declined from 21.3% to 20.5%. Regrettably, some of the decline in shortages may actually be due to the widespread existence and use of black markets. The inefficiency of the price ceilings continues.

● ● ◀

CHECK YOUR UNDERSTANDING **4-1**

1. On game nights, homeowners near Middletown Arena used to rent parking spaces in their driveways to fans at a going rate of $11. A new town ordinance now sets a maximum parking fee of $7. Use the accompanying supply and demand diagram to explain how each of the following corresponds to a price-ceiling concept.
   a. Some homeowners now think it's not worth the hassle to rent out spaces.
   b. Some fans who used to carpool to the game now drive alone.
   c. Some fans can't find parking and leave without seeing the game.

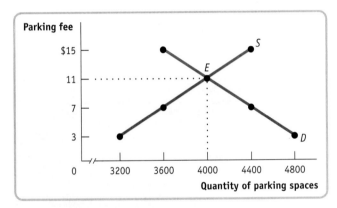

Explain how each of the following adverse effects arises from the price ceiling.

   d. Some fans now arrive several hours early to find parking.
   e. Friends of homeowners near the stadium regularly attend games, even if they aren't big fans. But some serious fans have given up because of the parking situation.
   f. Some homeowners rent spaces for more than $7 but pretend that the buyers are non-paying friends or family.

2. True or false? Explain your answer. A price ceiling below the equilibrium price of an otherwise efficient market does the following:
   a. Increases quantity supplied
   b. Makes some people who want to consume the good worse off
   c. Makes all producers worse off

Solutions appear at back of book.

Price Floors

Sometimes governments intervene to push market prices up instead of down. *Price floors* have been widely legislated for agricultural products, such as wheat and milk, as a way to support the incomes of farmers. (In 2012, the federal government ended the monopoly position of the Canadian Wheat Board (CWB), which used government subsidies to guarantee farmers a minimum price for wheat and barley.[2]) Historically, there were also price floors on such services as trucking and air travel, although these were phased out by the government of Canada in the 1970s and 1980s. If you have ever worked in a fast-food restaurant, you are likely to have encountered a price floor: governments in Canada, the

---

[2]The CWB generally paid farmers in two parts. A first payment (or initial payment) equal to a portion of the expected grain price was made when farmers delivered their grain to the board. A second payment (or the final payment) could occur at the end of a crop year if prices were high enough—that is, higher than the initial payment. If the grain was actually sold at a lower price than the initial payment, the farmers received no final payment. In such cases, the federal government covered any CWB deficit so that farmers did not have to pay back a portion of their earlier payment, so the first payment acted as a price floor.

United States, and many other countries maintain a lower limit on the hourly wage rate of a worker's labour; that is, a floor on the price of labour—called the **minimum wage.**

Just like price ceilings, price floors are intended to help some people but generate predictable and undesirable side effects. Figure 4-4 shows hypothetical supply and demand curves for butter. Left to itself, the market would move to equilibrium at point *E*, with 10 million kilograms of butter bought and sold at a price of $1 per kilogram.

Now suppose that the government, in order to help dairy farmers, imposes a price floor on butter of $1.20 per kilogram. Its effects are shown in Figure 4-5, where the line at $1.20 represents the price floor. At a price of $1.20 per kilogram, producers would want to supply 12 million kilograms (point *B* on the supply curve) but consumers would want to buy only 9 million kilograms (point *A* on the demand curve). So the price floor leads to a persistent surplus of 3 million kilograms of butter.

Does a price floor always lead to an unwanted surplus? No. Just as in the case of a price ceiling, the floor may not be binding—that is, it may be irrelevant. If the equilibrium price of butter is $1 per kilogram but the floor is set at only $0.80, the floor has no effect. And sometimes, a surplus can be saved in order to maintain the price floor in later years. For example, the Federation of Quebec Maple Syrup Producers regulates the production and marketing of maple syrup in Quebec, the source of more than 75% of the world's supply. Besides setting production limits and quality, it holds a strategic reserve of maple syrup equal to about 42% of the world's 2011 production. During high production years the reserve grows in order to limit sales and maintain higher prices, and during years of lower production reserves are sold off at higher prices.

But suppose that a price floor is binding and the surplus is unwanted: what happens to it? The answer depends on government policy. In the case of agricultural

> The **minimum wage** is a legal floor on the wage rate, which is the market price of labour.

FIGURE **4-4** The Market for Butter in the Absence of Government Controls

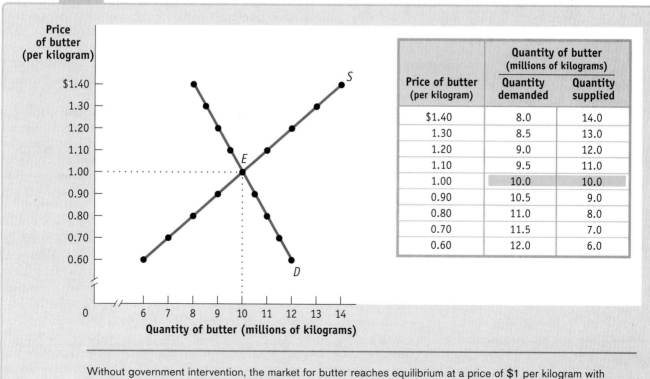

Price of butter (per kilogram)	Quantity of butter (millions of kilograms)	
	Quantity demanded	Quantity supplied
$1.40	8.0	14.0
1.30	8.5	13.0
1.20	9.0	12.0
1.10	9.5	11.0
1.00	10.0	10.0
0.90	10.5	9.0
0.80	11.0	8.0
0.70	11.5	7.0
0.60	12.0	6.0

Without government intervention, the market for butter reaches equilibrium at a price of $1 per kilogram with 10 million kilograms of butter bought and sold.

FIGURE **4-5** The Effects of a Price Floor

The black horizontal line represents the government-imposed price floor of $1.20 per kilogram of butter. The quantity of butter demanded falls to 9 million kilograms, and the quantity supplied rises to 12 million kilograms, generating a persistent surplus of 3 million kilograms of butter.

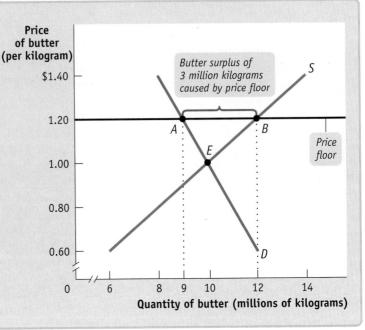

price floors, governments buy up unwanted surplus. (The European Commission, which administers price floors for a number of European countries, once found itself the owner of a so-called butter mountain, equal in weight to the entire population of Austria.) The government then has to find a way to dispose of these unwanted goods.

Some countries pay exporters to sell products at a loss overseas; this is standard procedure for the European Union. Sometimes Canada gives surplus food away as foreign aid to less developed countries. In some cases, governments have actually destroyed the surplus production. For example, in 1975 about 90 million surplus eggs were destroyed in Canada. To avoid the problem of dealing with the unwanted surplus, the Canadian government typically either pays farmers not to produce the products at all or limits their ability to produce more output.

When the government is not prepared to purchase the unwanted surplus, a price floor means that would-be sellers cannot find buyers. This is what happens when there is a price floor on the wage rate paid for an hour of labour, the minimum wage: when the minimum wage is above the equilibrium wage rate, some people who are willing to work—that is, sell labour—cannot find buyers—that is, employers—willing to give them jobs. These people are unemployed thanks in part to the binding minimum wage constraint.

As we said earlier, price floors don't always create a surplus: if a price floor is set below the equilibrium price, it is non-binding and won't have any effect. However, a binding price floor can become non-binding if shifts in the demand and/or supply curves cause the equilibrium price to be greater than or equal to the price floor. In our butter example, the price floor of $1.20 per kilogram may no longer be a binding price floor if there is an increase in the demand for butter due to a change in consumers' preferences. If the demand curve in Figure 4-5 shifts far enough to the right to raise the equilibrium price to $1.20 per kilogram or more, then the price floor is no longer binding. Similarly, if the supply of butter decreases, causing the equilibrium price to increase to $1.20 per kilogram or more, then the price floor will be non-binding.

How a Price Floor Causes Inefficiency

The persistent surplus that results from a price floor creates missed opportunities—inefficiencies—that resemble those created by the shortage that results from a price ceiling. These include an inefficiently low quantity transacted, inefficient allocation of sales among sellers, wasted resources, inefficiently high quality, and the temptation to break the law by selling below the legal price.

Inefficiently Low Quantity Because a price floor raises the price of a good to consumers, it reduces the quantity of that good demanded; because sellers can't sell more units of a good than buyers are willing to buy, a price floor reduces the quantity of a good bought and sold below the market equilibrium quantity. Notice that this is the *same* effect as a price ceiling. You might be tempted to think that a price floor and a price ceiling have opposite effects, but both have the effect of reducing the quantity of a good bought and sold (see Pitfalls at right).

As in the case of a price ceiling, the low quantity sold is an inefficiency due to missed opportunities: price floors prevent mutually beneficial transactions from occurring, transactions that would benefit both buyers and sellers. Figure 4-6 shows the inefficiently low quantity of butter sold with a price floor on the price of butter.

Inefficient Allocation of Sales Among Sellers Like a price ceiling, a price floor can lead to *inefficient allocation*—but in this case **inefficient allocation of sales among sellers** rather than inefficient allocation to consumers.

An episode from the Belgian movie *Rosetta*, a realistic fictional story, illustrates the problem of inefficient allocation of selling opportunities quite well. Like many European countries, Belgium has a high minimum wage, and jobs for young people are scarce. At one point Rosetta, a young woman who is very

PITFALLS

CEILINGS, FLOORS, AND QUANTITIES
A price ceiling pushes the price of a good *down*. A price floor pushes the price of a good *up*. So it's easy to assume that the effects of a price floor are the opposite of the effects of a price ceiling. In particular, if a price ceiling reduces the quantity of a good bought and sold, doesn't a price floor increase the quantity?

No, it doesn't. In fact, both floors and ceilings reduce the quantity bought and sold. Why? When the quantity of a good supplied isn't equal to the quantity demanded, the actual quantity sold is determined by the "short side" of the market—whichever quantity is less. If sellers don't want to sell as much as buyers want to buy, it's the sellers who determine the actual quantity sold, because buyers can't force unwilling sellers to sell. If buyers don't want to buy as much as sellers want to sell, it's the buyers who determine the actual quantity sold, because sellers can't force unwilling buyers to buy.

Price floors lead to **inefficient allocation of sales among sellers:** those who would be willing to sell the good at the lowest price are not always those who actually manage to sell it.

FIGURE 4-6 A Price Floor Causes Inefficiently Low Quantity

A price floor reduces the quantity demanded below the market equilibrium quantity. Because sellers can't sell more units of a good than buyers are willing to buy, a price floor reduces the quantity of a good bought and sold.

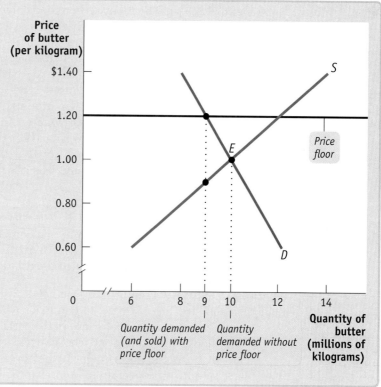

anxious to work, loses her job at a fast-food stand because the owner of the stand replaces her with his son—a very reluctant worker. Rosetta would be willing to work for less money, and with the money he would save, the owner could give his son an allowance and let him do something else. But to hire Rosetta for less than the minimum wage would be illegal.

Wasted Resources Also like a price ceiling, a price floor generates inefficiency by *wasting resources*. The most graphic examples involve government purchases of the unwanted surpluses of agricultural products caused by price floors. The surplus production is sometimes destroyed, which is pure waste; in other cases the stored produce goes, as officials euphemistically put it, "out of condition" and must be thrown away.

Price floors also lead to wasted time and effort. Consider the minimum wage. Would-be workers who spend many hours searching for jobs, or waiting in line in the hope of getting jobs, play the same role in the case of price floors as hapless families searching for apartments in the case of price ceilings.

Inefficiently High Quality Again like price ceilings, price floors lead to inefficiency in the quality of goods produced.

We saw that when there is a price ceiling, suppliers produce products that are of inefficiently low quality: some buyers prefer higher-quality products and are willing to pay for them, but sellers refuse to improve the quality of their products because the price ceiling prevents their being compensated for doing so. Of course, a binding price ceiling means excess demand is created, so some sellers are able to sell all their low-quality units. This same logic applies to price floors, but in reverse: suppliers offer goods of **inefficiently high quality.** A binding price floor creates excess supply, so some sellers must offer higher quality to avoid being shut out of the market.

How can this be? Isn't high quality a good thing? Yes, but only if it is worth the cost. Suppose that some suppliers spend a lot to make goods of very high quality but that this quality isn't worth much to some consumers, who would rather receive the money spent on that quality in the form of a lower price. This represents a missed opportunity: suppliers and buyers could make a mutually beneficial deal in which buyers got goods of lower quality for a much lower price.

A good example of the inefficiency of excessive quality comes from the days when transatlantic airfares were set artificially high by international treaty. Forbidden to compete for customers by offering lower ticket prices, airlines instead offered expensive services, like lavish in-flight meals that went largely uneaten. At one point the regulators tried to restrict this practice by defining maximum service standards—for example, that snack service should consist of no more than a sandwich. One airline then introduced what it called a "Scandinavian Sandwich," a towering affair that forced the convening of another conference to define *sandwich*. All of this was wasteful, especially considering that what passengers really wanted was less food and lower airfares.

Since the deregulation of North American airlines in the 1970s and 1980s, Canadian passengers have experienced a large decrease in ticket prices accompanied by a decrease in the quality of in-flight service—smaller seats, lowerquality food, and so on. Everyone complains about the service—but thanks to lower fares, the number of people flying on Canadian carriers has grown several hundred percent since airline deregulation.

Illegal Activity Finally, like price ceilings, price floors provide incentives for illegal activity. For example, in countries where the minimum wage is far above the equilibrium wage rate, workers desperate for jobs sometimes agree to work off the books for employers who conceal their employment from the government—or bribe the government inspectors. This practice, known in Europe as "black labour," is especially common in southern European countries such as Italy and Spain (see the upcoming Economics in Action).

Price floors often lead to inefficiency in that goods of **inefficiently high quality** are offered: some sellers offer high-quality goods at a high price, even though some buyers would prefer a lower quality at a lower price.

GLOBAL COMPARISON

CHECK OUT THESE LOW WAGES!

As you can see in the graph below, the minimum wage rate in Canada is actually quite reasonable compared with that of other rich countries. Since minimum wages are set in national currency—the British minimum wage is set in British pounds, the French minimum wage is set in euros, and so on—the comparison depends on the exchange rate on any given day. As of July 16, 2013, Australia had a minimum wage over twice as high as the U.S. rate, with France, Ireland, and Canada not far behind. You can see one effect of this difference in the supermarket checkout line. In Canada and Europe, shoppers usually bag their own groceries. In the United States, where hiring a bagger is a lot less expensive, there is usually someone to bag the groceries for you.

The accompanying data reveals that of these countries, the United States had the greatest percentage of workers employed in low-paying jobs. In 2009, about one in four American workers earned the minimum wage. Also, according to the Organisation for Economic Co-operation and Development (OECD), in 2011 the U.S. minimum wage was only 38% of the median wage of American workers. Unfortunately, Canadian workers did not fare much better in respect to either measure, implying a relatively high degree of income inequality in Canada compared to France where many fewer workers are paid the minimum wage and this minimum wage is a much larger percentage of the median wage.

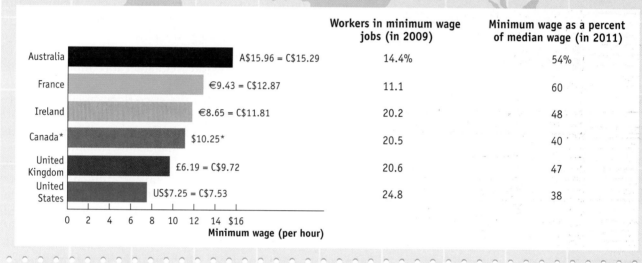

	Minimum wage (per hour)	Workers in minimum wage jobs (in 2009)	Minimum wage as a percent of median wage (in 2011)
Australia	A$15.96 = C$15.29	14.4%	54%
France	€9.43 = C$12.87	11.1	60
Ireland	€8.65 = C$11.81	20.2	48
Canada*	$10.25*	20.5	40
United Kingdom	£6.19 = C$9.72	20.6	47
United States	US$7.25 = C$7.53	24.8	38

Sources: OECD; Bank of Canada.

*The Canadian minimum wage varied by province and territory in 2013, ranging from $9.50 to $11.00.

So Why Are There Price Floors?

To sum up, a price floor creates various negative side effects:

- A persistent surplus of the good
- Inefficiency arising from the persistent surplus in the form of inefficiently low quantity transacted, inefficient allocation of sales among sellers, wasted resources, and an inefficiently high level of quality offered by some suppliers
- The temptation to engage in illegal activity, particularly bribery and corruption of government officials

So why do governments impose price floors when they have so many negative side effects? The reasons are similar to those for imposing price ceilings. Government officials often disregard warnings about the consequences of price floors either because they believe that the relevant market is poorly described by the supply and demand model or, more often, because they do not understand the model. Above all, just as price ceilings are often imposed because they benefit some influential buyers of a good, price floors are often imposed because they benefit some influential sellers.

ECONOMICS > IN ACTION

"BLACK LABOUR" IN SOUTHERN EUROPE

The best-known example of a price floor is the minimum wage. Most economists believe, however, that the minimum wage has relatively little effect on the job market if the floor is relatively low. For example, in the United States, the minimum wage was 53% of the average wage of blue-collar production workers in 1964; by 2010, despite several recent increases, it had fallen to about 44%.

Comunidad de Madrid

OFICINA DE EMPLEO

CONSEJERÍA DE EMPLEO Y MUJER

The generous minimum wage in many European countries has contributed to a high rate of unemployment and the flourishing of an illegal labour market.

The situation is different, however, in many European countries, where minimum wages have been set much higher than in Canada and the United States. This has happened despite the fact that workers in most European countries are somewhat less productive than their North American counterparts, which means that the equilibrium wage in Europe—the wage that would clear the labour market—is probably lower in Europe than in North America. Moreover, European countries often require employers to pay for health and retirement benefits, which are more extensive and so more costly than comparable American and even Canadian benefits. These mandated benefits make the actual cost of employing a European worker considerably more than the worker's paycheque.

The result is that in Europe the price floor on labour is definitely binding: the minimum wage is well above the wage rate that would make the quantity of labour supplied by workers equal to the quantity of labour demanded by employers.

The persistent surplus that results from this price floor appears in the form of high unemployment—millions of workers, especially young workers, seek jobs but cannot find them.

In countries where the enforcement of labour laws is lax, however, there is a second, entirely predictable result: widespread evasion of the law. In both Italy and Spain, officials believe there are hundreds of thousands, if not millions, of workers who are employed by companies that pay them less than the legal minimum, fail to provide the required health and retirement benefits, or both. In many cases the jobs are simply unreported: Spanish economists estimate that about a third of the country's reported unemployed are in the black labour market—working at unreported jobs. In fact, Spaniards waiting to collect cheques from the unemployment office have been known to complain about the long lines that keep them from getting back to work!

Employers in these countries have also found legal ways to evade the wage floor. For example, Italy's labour regulations apply only to companies with 15 or more workers. This gives a big cost advantage to small Italian firms, many of which remain small in order to avoid paying higher wages and benefits. And sure enough, in some Italian industries there is an astonishing proliferation of tiny companies. For example, one of Italy's most successful industries is the manufacture of fine woollen cloth, centred in the Prato region. The average textile firm in that region employs only four workers!

▼ Quick Review

- The most familiar price floor is the **minimum wage.** Price floors are also commonly imposed on agricultural goods.

- A price floor above the equilibrium price benefits successful sellers but causes predictable adverse effects such as a persistent surplus, which leads to four kinds of inefficiencies: inefficiently low quantity transacted, **inefficient allocation of sales among sellers,** wasted resources, and **inefficiently high quality.**

- Price floors encourage illegal activity, such as workers who work off the books, often leading to official corruption.

CHECK YOUR UNDERSTANDING 4-2

1. A provincial legislature mandates a price floor for gasoline of P_F per litre. Assess the following statements and illustrate your answer using the figure provided.

a. Proponents of the law claim it will increase the income of gas station owners. Opponents claim it will hurt gas station owners because they will lose customers.

b. Proponents claim consumers will be better off because gas stations will provide better service. Opponents claim consumers will be generally worse off because they prefer to buy gas at cheaper prices.

c. Proponents claim that they are helping gas station owners without hurting anyone else. Opponents claim that consumers are hurt and will end up doing things like buying gas across the border or on the black market.

Solutions appear at back of book.

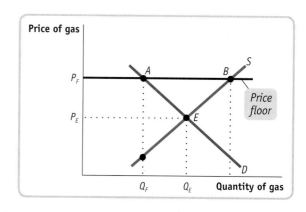

Controlling Quantities

In the 1930s, New York City instituted a system of licensing for taxicabs: only taxis with a special **licence** called a "medallion" were allowed to pick up passengers. Because this system was intended to ensure quality, medallion owners were supposed to maintain certain standards, including safety and cleanliness. A total of 11 787 medallions were issued, with taxi owners paying $10 for each medallion.

In 1995, there were still only 11 787 licensed taxicabs in New York, even though the city had meanwhile become the financial capital of the world, a place where hundreds of thousands of people in a hurry tried to hail a cab every day. (An additional 400 medallions were issued in 1995, and after several rounds of sales of additional medallions, today there are 13 128 medallions.)

The result of this restriction on the number of taxis was that a New York City taxi medallion became very valuable: if you wanted to operate a taxi in New York, you had to lease a medallion from someone else or buy one for a going price of several hundred thousand dollars.

It turns out that this story is not unique; other cities introduced similar medallion systems in the 1930s and, like New York, have issued few new medallions since. In San Francisco and Boston, as in New York, taxi medallions trade for six-figure prices.

In Toronto, standard taxi licences come in the form of a special numbered plate that, like a New York City taxi medallion, must be affixed to the cab. Fifteen hundred of these standard taxi licences were issued in 1953 and no new plates were issued until 1961. New licensing rules in 1963 allowed these licences to be sold on the open market—making them a capital asset for the licence holder, rather than the issuer. By 1973, the number of licences had risen to about 2100 and the following year the leasing of taxi licences was allowed. The limited supply of licences coupled with the transferability and leasing options resulted in the market price of a taxi plate rising significantly while encouraging the decline in taxicab quality. Many plate owners leased out their licences, rather than drive their own cabs. These owners sought to maximize their leasing revenues by setting lease fees as a high percentage of the driver's revenue, which encouraged drivers to keep operating costs as low as possible. Of course, low operating costs meant that cab maintenance was minimized and replacement of the cars was usually delayed as long as legally permitted. Many customers complained about cars in bad or unsafe condition operated by overworked, stressed-out drivers.

In 1998, Toronto decided to introduce a new class of licence with the sale of 1400 new Ambassador taxi licences, and going forward, no new standard licences would ever be issued. Unlike a standard licence, Ambassador licences can't be sold, leased, or otherwise transferred— a licence holder is the owner and operator of the taxi—and the licence remains the property of the city. The aim was to allow these drivers to be entrepreneurs who cared about the quality of their car since they couldn't lease from some other party—so if everything worked as intended, quality in the market would rise.

A **licence** gives its owner the right to supply a good.

A **quantity control,** or **quota,** is an upper limit on the quantity of some good that can be bought or sold. The total amount of the good that can be legally transacted is the **quota limit.**

By 2013, there were about 4850 taxi licences in Toronto of both types. Standard licences sold for about $300 000 and most owners of Ambassador licences wished they too could sell or lease their plates to someone else. Interestingly, a 2013 report to the city licensing commission recommended moving to a single "harmonized" licence that could not be sold or leased for long periods of time. If adopted, this proposal could improve customer service by ensuring that owner-operators are driving full time.

In Vancouver, the city issues taxi licences to only four companies, charging them $522 for each licence. These companies then sell shares in the licence, dividing them into two shares: one for the day shift and one for the night shift. Each share comes with the right to drive a car, but also pays dividends from real estate the taxi company owns. These shares cost about $300 000 to $400 000, making the cost of acquiring rights to an entire car (two shares) about as costly as obtaining a taxi medallion in New York.

A taxi licensing or medallion system is a form of **quantity control,** or **quota,** by which the government regulates the quantity of a good that can be bought and sold rather than the price at which it is transacted. The total amount of the good that can be transacted under the quantity control is called the **quota limit.** Typically, the government limits quantity in a market by issuing licences; only people with a licence can legally supply the good.

There are many other cases of quantity controls, ranging from limits on how much foreign currency (for instance, British pounds or Mexican pesos) people are allowed to buy to the quantity of snow crabs Newfoundland and Labrador fishing boats are allowed to catch. Notice, by the way, that although there are price controls on both sides of the equilibrium price—price ceilings and price floors—in the real world, quantity controls always set an upper, not a lower, limit on quantities. After all, nobody can be forced to buy or sell more than they want to!

Some attempts to control quantities are undertaken for good economic reasons, some for bad ones. In many cases, as we will see, quantity controls introduced to address a temporary problem become politically hard to remove later because the beneficiaries don't want them abolished, even after the original reason for their existence is long gone. But whatever the reasons for such controls, they have certain predictable—and usually undesirable—economic consequences.

The Anatomy of Quantity Controls

To understand why a New York City taxi medallion is worth so much money, we consider a simplified version of the market for taxi rides, shown in Figure 4-7. Just as we assumed in the analysis of rent control that all apartments are the same, we now suppose that all taxi rides are the same—ignoring the real-world complication that some taxi rides are longer, and so more expensive, than others. The table in the figure shows supply and demand schedules. The equilibrium—indicated by point E in the figure and by the shaded entries in the table—is a fare of $5 per ride, with 10 million rides taken per year. (You'll see in a minute why we present the equilibrium this way.)

The New York medallion system limits the number of taxis, but each taxi driver can offer as many rides as he or she can manage. (Now you know why New York taxi drivers are so aggressive!) To simplify our analysis, however, we will assume that a medallion system limits the number of taxi rides that can legally be given to 8 million per year.

Until now, we have derived the demand curve by answering questions of the form: "What is the maximum number of taxi rides passengers will want to take if the price is $5 per ride?" But it is possible to reverse the question and ask instead: "What is the maximum price per ride consumers will pay to buy 10 million rides per year?" The price at which consumers want to buy a given quantity—in this case,

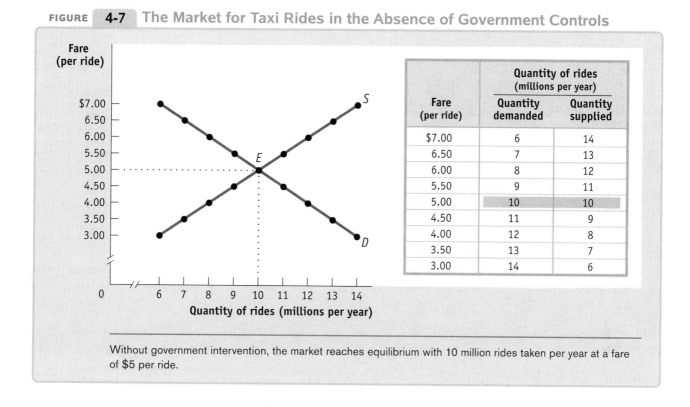

FIGURE **4-7** The Market for Taxi Rides in the Absence of Government Controls

Fare (per ride)	Quantity of rides (millions per year)	
	Quantity demanded	Quantity supplied
$7.00	6	14
6.50	7	13
6.00	8	12
5.50	9	11
5.00	10	10
4.50	11	9
4.00	12	8
3.50	13	7
3.00	14	6

Without government intervention, the market reaches equilibrium with 10 million rides taken per year at a fare of $5 per ride.

10 million rides at $5 per ride—is the **demand price** of that quantity. You can see from the demand schedule in Figure 4-7 that the demand price of 6 million rides is $7 per ride, the demand price of 7 million rides is $6.50 per ride, and so on.

Similarly, the supply curve represents the answer to questions of the form: "What is the maximum number of taxi rides drivers are willing to supply at a price of $5 each?" But we can also reverse this question to ask: "What is the minimum price at which suppliers would be willing to supply 10 million rides per year?" The price at which suppliers will supply a given quantity—in this case, 10 million rides at $5 per ride—is the **supply price** of that quantity. We can see from the supply schedule in Figure 4-7 that the supply price of 6 million rides is $3 per ride, the supply price of 7 million rides is $3.50 per ride, and so on.

Now we are ready to analyze a quota. We have assumed that the city government limits the quantity of taxi rides to 8 million per year. Medallions, each of which carries the right to provide a certain number of taxi rides per year, are made available to selected people in such a way that a total of 8 million rides will be provided. Medallion-holders may then either drive their own taxis or rent their medallions to others for a fee.

Figure 4-8 shows the resulting market for taxi rides, with the black vertical line at 8 million rides per year representing the quota limit. Because the quantity of rides is limited to 8 million, consumers must be at point *A* on the demand curve, corresponding to the shaded entry in the demand schedule: the demand price of 8 million rides is $6 per ride. Meanwhile, taxi drivers must be at point *B* on the supply curve, corresponding to the shaded entry in the supply schedule: the supply price of 8 million rides is $4 per ride.

But how can the price received by taxi drivers be $4 when the price paid by taxi riders is $6? The answer is that in addition to the market in taxi rides, there is also a market in medallions. Medallion-holders may not always want to drive their taxis: they may be ill or on vacation. Those who do not want to drive their own taxis will sell the right to use the medallion to someone else. So we need to consider two sets of transactions here, and so two prices: (1) the transactions

The **demand price** of a given quantity is the price at which consumers will demand that quantity.

The **supply price** of a given quantity is the price at which producers will supply that quantity.

FIGURE **4-8** Effect of a Quota on the Market for Taxi Rides

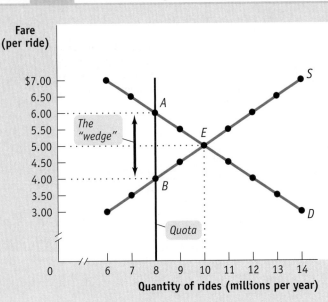

Fare (per ride)	Quantity of rides (millions per year)	
	Quantity demanded	Quantity supplied
$7.00	6	14
6.50	7	13
6.00	8	12
5.50	9	11
5.00	10	10
4.50	11	9
4.00	12	8
3.50	13	7
3.00	14	6

The table shows the demand price and the supply price corresponding to each quantity: the price at which that quantity would be demanded and supplied, respectively. The city government imposes a quota of 8 million rides by selling licences for only 8 million rides, represented by the black vertical line. The price paid by consumers rises to $6 per ride, the demand price of 8 million rides, shown by point A. The supply price of 8 million rides is only $4 per ride, shown by point B. The difference between these two prices is the quota rent per ride, the earnings that accrue to the owner of a licence. The quota rent drives a wedge between the demand price and the supply price, and the quota discourages mutually beneficial transactions.

in taxi rides and the price at which these will occur, and (2) the transactions in medallions and the price at which these will occur. It turns out that since we are looking at two markets, the $4 and $6 prices will both be right.

To see how this all works, consider two imaginary taxi drivers, Sunil and Harriet. Sunil has a medallion but can't use it because he's recovering from a severely sprained wrist. So he's looking to rent his medallion out to someone else. Harriet doesn't have a medallion but would like to rent one. Furthermore, at any point in time, there are many other people like Harriet who would like to rent a medallion. Suppose Sunil agrees to rent his medallion to Harriet. To make things simple, assume that any driver can give only one ride per day and that Sunil is renting his medallion to Harriet for one day. What rental price will they agree on?

To answer this question, we need to look at the transactions from the viewpoints of both drivers. Once she has the medallion, Harriet knows she can make $6 per day—the demand price of a ride under the quota. And she is willing to rent the medallion only if she makes at least $4 per day—the supply price of a ride under the quota. So Sunil cannot demand a rent of more than $2—the difference between $6 and $4. And if Harriet offered Sunil less than $2—say, $1.50—there would be other eager drivers willing to offer him more, up to $2. So, in order to get the medallion, Harriet must offer Sunil at least $2. Since the rent can be no more than $2 and no less than $2, it must be exactly $2.

It is no coincidence that $2 is exactly the difference between $6, the demand price of 8 million rides, and $4, the supply price of 8 million rides. In every case in which the supply of a good is legally restricted, there is a **wedge** between the demand price of the quantity transacted and the supply price of the quantity

A quantity control, or quota, drives a **wedge** between the demand price and the supply price of a good; that is, the price paid by buyers ends up being higher than that received by sellers.

transacted. This wedge, illustrated by the double-headed arrow in Figure 4-8, has a special name: the **quota rent.** It is the earnings that accrue to the licence-holder from ownership of a valuable commodity, the licence. In the case of Sunil and Harriet, the quota rent of $2 goes to Sunil because he owns the licence, and the remaining $4 from the total fare of $6 goes to Harriet.

So Figure 4-8 also illustrates the quota rent in the market for taxi rides. The quota limits the quantity of rides to 8 million per year, a quantity at which the demand price of $6 exceeds the supply price of $4. The wedge between these two prices, $2, is the quota rent that results from the restrictions placed on the quantity of taxi rides in this market.

But wait a second. What if Sunil doesn't rent out his medallion? What if he uses it himself? Doesn't this mean that he gets a price of $6? No, not really. Even if Sunil doesn't rent out his medallion, he could have rented it out, which means that the medallion has an *opportunity cost* of $2: if Sunil decides to use his own medallion and drive his own taxi rather than renting his medallion to Harriet, the $2 represents his opportunity cost of not renting out his medallion. That is, the $2 quota rent is now the rental income he forgoes by driving his own taxi.

In effect, Sunil is in two businesses—the taxi-driving business and the medallion-renting business. He makes $4 per ride from driving his taxi and $2 per ride from renting out his medallion. It doesn't make any difference that in this particular case he has rented his medallion to himself! So regardless of whether the medallion owner uses the medallion himself or herself, or rents it to others, it is a valuable asset. And this is represented in the going price for a New York City taxi medallion: in June 2013, some traded for more than $1 million. Since 1980, medallion prices are up more than 2200%, much more than the Dow Jones Industrial Average (1750%), the Toronto Stock Exchange S&P/TSX index (565%), and gold (150%). Plus leasing out a medallion can bring the owner more than $1000 per week.

Notice, by the way, that quotas—like price ceilings and price floors—don't always have a real effect. If the quota were set at 12 million rides—that is, above the equilibrium quantity in an unregulated market—it would have no effect because it would not be binding.

The Costs of Quantity Controls

Like price controls, quantity controls can have some predictable and undesirable side effects. The first is the by-now-familiar problem of inefficiency due to missed opportunities: quantity controls prevent mutually beneficial transactions from occurring, transactions that would benefit both buyers and sellers. Looking back at Figure 4-8, you can see that starting at the quota limit of 8 million rides, New Yorkers would be willing to pay at least $5.50 per ride for an additional 1 million rides and that taxi drivers would be willing to provide those rides as long as they got at least $4.50 per ride. These are rides that would have taken place if there were no quota limit.

The same is true for the next 1 million rides: New Yorkers would be willing to pay at least $5 per ride when the quantity of rides is increased from 9 to 10 million, and taxi drivers would be willing to provide those rides as long as they got at least $5 per ride. Again, these rides would have occurred without the quota limit.

Only when the market has reached the unregulated market equilibrium quantity of 10 million rides are there no "missed-opportunity rides"—the quota limit of 8 million rides has caused 2 million "missed-opportunity rides."

Generally, *as long as the demand price of a given quantity exceeds the supply price, there is a missed opportunity.* A buyer would be willing to buy the good at a price that the seller would be willing to accept, but such a transaction does not occur because it is forbidden by the quota.

The difference between the demand and supply price at the quota limit is the **quota rent,** the earnings that accrue to the licence-holder from ownership of the right to sell the good. It is equal to the rental market price of the licence when the licences are traded (rented).

Dangerous, unlicensed cabs are one cost of quantity controls.

And because there are transactions that people would like to make but are not allowed to, quantity controls generate an incentive to evade them or even to break the law. New York's taxi industry again provides clear examples. Taxi regulation applies only to those drivers who are hailed by passengers on the street. A car service that makes prearranged pickups does not need a medallion. As a result, such hired cars provide much of the service that might otherwise be provided by taxis, as in other cities. In addition, there are substantial numbers of unlicensed cabs that simply defy the law by picking up passengers without a medallion. Because these cabs are illegal, their drivers are completely unregulated, and they generate a disproportionately large share of traffic accidents in New York City.[3]

In fact, in 2004 the hardships caused by the limited number of New York taxis led city leaders to authorize an increase in the number of licensed taxis. In a series of sales, the city sold 900 new medallions, to bring the total number up to the current 13 128 medallions—a move that certainly cheered New York riders.

But those who already owned medallions were less happy with the increase; they understood that the 900 new taxis would reduce or eliminate the shortage of taxis. As a result, taxi drivers anticipated a decline in their revenues because they would no longer always be assured of finding willing customers. And, in turn, the value of a medallion would fall. So to placate the medallion owners, city officials also raised taxi fares: by 25% in 2004, by 11% in 2006, and again by 17% in 2012. Although taxis are now easier to find, a ride now costs more—and that price increase slightly diminished the newfound cheer of New York taxi riders.

In sum, quantity controls typically create the following undesirable side effects:

- Inefficiencies, or missed opportunities, in the form of mutually beneficial transactions that don't occur
- Incentives for illegal activities

ECONOMICS › IN ACTION

THE LOBSTERS OF ATLANTIC CANADA

Forget the various finned species of fish. When it comes to Canada's fisheries, lobster truly is the "King of Seafood." This industry employs thousands of people in New Brunswick, Newfoundland and Labrador, Nova Scotia, Prince Edward Island, and Quebec, and contributed more than

---

[3]In Toronto, there are a significant number of unlicensed cabs for hire, especially for trips to Pearson International Airport, Canada's busiest airport, which is situated mostly outside of Toronto in Mississauga, Ontario. Legally, taxis with a licence from Toronto can drop off fares at the airport but are not allowed to pick up another fare there unless prearranged. In order to pick up fares both in the city and at the airport, a driver with a municipal taxi licence must also have a second licence issued by the Greater Toronto Airport Authority (the body that runs the airport). So we have a complex collection of rules coupled with the high volume of demand for taxi rides that are often quite profitable, easily running $50 or more for one trip. This has resulted in not only some Toronto cabs breaking these rules, but the rise of a large fleet of unlabelled taxicabs servicing this large and lucrative market to and from the airport.

$1 billion in export sales in 2012. According to the federal government, lobsters are exported to more than 50 countries worldwide and are one of the exports most closely associated with Canada.

But all is not well in this fishery, which has been hit by several negative shocks in recent years. First, usually about 80% of Canadian lobster exports go to the United States, but demand there has softened since the start of the 2008–2009 recession. This situation is worsened by the appreciation of the Canadian dollar against the U.S. dollar, which put additional downward pressure on the value of Canadian exports. At the same time, landings of lobster in Atlantic Canada and the United States (mostly in the state of Maine) have risen almost 50% in the past 12 years. Catches in 2012 and 2013 have been described as the best seen in years. And while the number of lobster fishing licences is limited and, under current rules, licensed Canadian fishers are restricted in the number of traps they can operate, there is no quota on the number of lobsters they can bring in from those traps.

Fishers sort the lobster haul on the warf in Pointe-Sapin, New Brunswick.

So demand is down and supply is up, and together these have resulted in prices plummeting from about $9–14/kg in 2005 to about $7.15/kg (or $3.25/lb) in 2013. Nova Scotian fisher Leonard LeBlanc told the CBC that he couldn't remember prices this low in 30 years. "At $3.25 [per pound], we're not covering our costs; we're just trying to mitigate the expenses—at least pay some of them—not all of them and we're praying we don't have any major repairs."

The low prices hurt more than just fishers according to Merill MacInnis, also of Nova Scotia, who told the CBC, "at one time, Nova Scotia boat builders, for example, were going flat out building new boats, because money was good and fishers were investing in the industry. Well now, when you're just making enough to make your payments, people are not going to do that; they're going to keep going with what they have, and it'll have an effect on everybody, whether it be car dealers, boat builders, restaurant owners, whatever. It all has an effect; it all trickles down."

Of course, limiting the number of lobster fishing licences is a form of a quota, but unfortunately, with low demand and high supply (due to the high volume caught per trap), this quota had become a non-binding constraint. As a result, the price of lobster is not supported above the current low level at the intersection of the supply and demand curves.

The continuation of such low prices has led to calls for the introduction of either new rules that would effectively lower the quota or measures geared toward finding additional demand in other markets at home or abroad, so as to help raise the price of lobster. One way the government has reacted to this situation is via the Atlantic Lobster Sustainability Measures program, which is buying back and retiring about 600 lobster fishing licences. This measure will remove more than 200 000 traps from the water by March 2014.

In 2013, some processing plants, overwhelmed by large catches and hoping to help deal with low prices, imposed their own daily quotas on the volume of lobster per boat they would accept. In other cases, fishers either voluntarily stayed home to reduce supply or agreed to limit catches. Many have called upon the government to buy back even more licences and to impose new rules limiting the daily catch of every licensed boat, a much stronger and clearer quota system.

Notice, by the way, that this is an example of a proposed quota that is probably justified by broader economic and environmental considerations—unlike the New York taxicab quota, which has long since lost any economic rationale. Still, whatever its rationale, the proposed Atlantic Canada lobster quota would work the same way as any other quota.

Once the quota system is established, many boat owners will stop fishing for lobsters. They will realize that rather than operating a boat, it is more profitable to sell or rent their licences to someone else. The value of a licence required to fish for lobsters will easily be worth more than the boat itself.

CHECK YOUR UNDERSTANDING 4-3

1. Suppose that the supply and demand for taxi rides is given by Figure 4-7 but the quota is set at 6 million rides instead of 8 million. Find the following and indicate them on Figure 4-7.
   a. The price of a ride
   b. The quota rent

2. Suppose the quota limit on taxi rides is increased to 9 million. What happens to the quota rent?

3. Assume that the quota limit is 8 million rides. Suppose demand decreases due to a decline in tourism. What is the smallest parallel leftward shift in demand that would result in the quota no longer having an effect on the market? Illustrate your answer using Figure 4-7.

Solutions appear at back of book.

BUSINESS CASE : Medallion Financial: Cruising Right Along

Owaki/Kulla/Corbis

Back in 1937, before New York City froze its number of taxi medallions, Andrew Murstein's immigrant grandfather bought his first one for $10. Over time, the grandfather accumulated 500 medallions, which he rented to other drivers. Those 500 taxi medallions became the foundation for Medallion Financial: the company that would eventually pass to Andrew, its current president.

With a market value of over $300 million in mid-2013, Medallion Financial has shifted its major line of business from renting out medallions to financing the purchase of new ones, lending money to those who want to buy a medallion but don't have the sizable amount of cash required to do so. Murstein believes that he is helping people who, like his Polish immigrant grandfather, want to buy a piece of the American dream.

Andrew Murstein carefully watches the value of a New York City taxi medallion: the more one costs, the more demand there is for loans from Medallion Financial, and the more interest the company makes on the loan. A loan from Medallion Financial is secured by the value of the medallion itself. If the borrower is unable to repay the loan, Medallion Financial takes possession of his or her medallion and resells it to offset the cost of the loan default. As of 2013, the value of a medallion had risen faster than stocks, oil, and gold. Over the past three decades, from 1980 through mid-2013, the value of a medallion rose an average of 6.8% per year, faster than U.S. and Canadian stock market indexes.

But medallion prices can fluctuate dramatically, threatening profits. During periods of a very strong economy, such as 1999 and 2001, the price of New York taxi medallions fell as drivers found jobs in other sectors. When the New York economy tanked in the aftermath of 9/11, the price of a medallion fell to $180 000, its lowest level in 12 years. In 2004, medallion owners were concerned about the impending sale by the New York City Taxi and Limousine Commission of an additional 900 medallions. As Peter Hernandez, a worried New York cabdriver who financed his medallion with a loan from Medallion Financial, said at the time: "If they pump new taxis into the industry, it devalues my medallion. It devalues my daily income, too."

Yet Murstein has always been optimistic that medallions would hold their value. He believed that a 25% fare increase would offset potential losses in their value caused by the sale of new medallions. In addition, more medallions would mean more loans for his company. As of 2013, Murstein's optimism had been justified. Because of the financial crisis of 2007–2009, many New York companies cut back the limousine services they ordinarily provided to their employees, forcing them to take taxis instead. As a result, the price of a medallion rose to an astonishing $1 million in early 2013. And investors have noticed the value in Medallion Financial's line of business: from July 2012 to July 2013, shares of Medallion Financial have rose 31%.

QUESTIONS FOR THOUGHT

1. How does Medallion Financial benefit from the restriction on the number of New York taxi medallions?

2. What will be the effect on Medallion Financial if New York companies resume widespread use of limousine services for their employees? What is the economic motivation that prompts companies to offer this perk to their employees? (Note that it is very difficult and expensive to own a personal car in New York City.)

3. Predict the effect on Medallion Financial's business if New York City eliminates restrictions on the number of taxis.

SUMMARY

1. Even when a market is efficient, governments often intervene to pursue greater fairness or to please a powerful interest group. Interventions can take the form of **price controls** or **quantity controls,** both of which generate predictable and undesirable side effects consisting of various forms of inefficiency and illegal activity.

2. A **price ceiling,** a maximum market price below the equilibrium price, benefits successful buyers but creates persistent shortages. Because the price is maintained below the equilibrium price, the quantity demanded is increased and the quantity supplied is decreased compared to the equilibrium quantity. This leads to predictable problems: inefficiencies in the form of inefficiently low quantity transacted, **inefficient allocation to consumers, wasted resources,** and **inefficiently low quality.** It also encourages illegal activity as people turn to **black markets** to get the good. Because of these problems, price ceilings have generally lost favour as an economic policy tool. But some governments continue to impose them either because they don't understand the effects or because the price ceilings benefit some influential group.

3. A **price floor,** a minimum market price above the equilibrium price, benefits successful sellers but creates persistent surplus. Because the price is maintained above the equilibrium price, the quantity

demanded is decreased and the quantity supplied is increased compared to the equilibrium quantity. This leads to predictable problems: inefficiencies in the form of inefficiently low quantity transacted, **inefficient allocation of sales among sellers,** wasted resources, and **inefficiently high quality.** It also encourages illegal activity and black markets. The most well known kind of price floor is the **minimum wage,** but price floors are also commonly applied to agricultural products.

4. Quantity controls, or **quotas,** limit the quantity of a good that can be bought or sold. The quantity allowed for sale is the **quota limit.** The government issues **licences** to individuals, the right to sell a given quantity of the good. The owner of a licence earns a **quota rent,** earnings that accrue from ownership of the right to sell the good. It is equal to the difference between the **demand price** at the quota limit, what consumers are willing to pay for that quantity, and the **supply price** at the quota limit, what suppliers are willing to accept for that quantity. Economists say that a quota drives a **wedge** between the demand price and the supply price; this wedge is equal to the quota rent. Quantity controls lead to inefficiencies in the form of mutually beneficial transactions that do not occur, in addition to encouraging illegal activity.

KEY TERMS

Price controls, p. 116
Price ceiling, p. 116
Price floor, p. 116
Inefficient allocation to consumers, p. 120
Wasted resources, p. 121
Inefficiently low quality, p. 121

Black markets, p. 122
Minimum wage, p. 125
Inefficient allocation of sales among sellers, p. 127
Inefficiently high quality, p. 128
Licence, p. 131
Quantity control, p. 132

Quota, p. 132
Quota limit, p. 132
Demand price, p. 133
Supply price, p. 133
Wedge, p. 134
Quota rent, p. 135

PROBLEMS

1. Suppose it is decided that rent control in a city will be abolished and that market rents will now prevail. Assume that all rental units are identical and so are offered at the same rent. To address the plight of residents who may be unable to pay the market rent, an income supplement will be paid to all low-income households equal to the difference between the old controlled rent and the new market rent.

   a. Use a diagram to show the effect on the rental market of the elimination of rent control. What will happen to the quality and quantity of rental housing supplied?

   b. Use a second diagram to show the additional effect of the income-supplement policy on the market.

   What effect does it have on the market rent and quantity of rental housing supplied in comparison to your answers to part (a)?

   c. Are tenants better or worse off as a result of these policies? Are landlords better or worse off?

   d. From a political standpoint, why do you think cities have been more likely to resort to rent control rather than a policy of income supplements to help low-income people pay for housing?

2. In order to ingratiate himself with voters, the mayor of Gotham City decides to lower the price of taxi rides. Assume, for simplicity, that all taxi rides are the same

distance and therefore cost the same. The accompanying table shows the demand and supply schedules for taxi rides.

	Quantity of rides (millions per year)	
Fare (per ride)	Quantity demanded	Quantity supplied
$7.00	10	12
6.50	11	11
6.00	12	10
5.50	13	9
5.00	14	8
4.50	15	7

a. Assume that there are no restrictions on the number of taxi rides that can be supplied (there is no licensing system). Find the equilibrium price and quantity.

b. Suppose that the mayor sets a price ceiling at $5.50. How large is the shortage of rides? Illustrate with a diagram. Who loses and who benefits from this policy?

c. Suppose that the stock market crashes and, as a result, people in Gotham City are poorer. This reduces the quantity of taxi rides demanded by 6 million rides per year at any given price. What effect will the mayor's new policy have now? Illustrate with a diagram.

d. Suppose that the stock market rises and the demand for taxi rides returns to normal (that is, returns to the demand schedule given in the table). The mayor now decides to ingratiate himself with taxi drivers. He announces a policy in which operating licences are given to existing taxi drivers; the number of licences is restricted such that only 10 million rides per year can be given. Illustrate the effect of this policy on the market, and indicate the resulting price and quantity transacted. What is the quota rent per ride?

3. In the mid-eighteenth century, the government of New France (modern-day Quebec) controlled the price of bread, which was set at a predetermined price below the free market price.

a. Draw a diagram showing the effect of the policy. Did the policy act as a price ceiling or a price floor?

b. What kinds of inefficiencies were likely to have arisen when the controlled price of bread was below the market price? Explain in detail.

Suppose that one year during this period, a large wheat harvest caused a rightward shift in the supply of bread and therefore a decrease in its free market price. Bakers found that, as a result, the controlled price of bread was above the free market price.

c. Draw a diagram showing the effect of the price control on the market for bread during this one-year

period. Did the policy act as a price ceiling or a price floor?

d. What kinds of inefficiencies do you think occurred during this period? Explain in detail.

4. The Canadian Dairy Commission (CDC) administers the price floor for butter, which was set at $7.28 per kilogram in 2012. At that price, according to data from the CDC, the quantity of butter supplied in 2012 was 114.3 million kilograms, and the quantity demanded was 97.5 million kilograms. To support the price of butter at the price floor, the CDC therefore had to buy up 16.8 million kilograms of butter. The accompanying diagram shows supply and demand curves illustrating the market for butter.

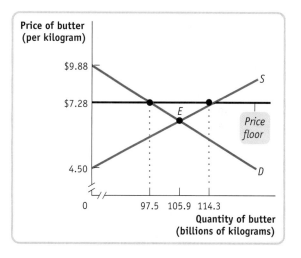

a. In the absence of a price floor, how much consumer surplus is created? How much producer surplus? What is the total surplus?

b. With the price floor at $7.28/kg of butter, consumers buy 97.5 million kilograms of butter. How much consumer surplus is created now?

c. With the price floor at $7.28/kg of butter, producers sell 114.3 million kilograms of butter (some to consumers and some to the CDC). How much producer surplus is created now?

d. How much money does the CDC spend on buying up surplus butter?

e. Suppose the federal government covers the cost of surplus butter using tax revenue, as they do in the United States.[4] As a result, total surplus (producer plus consumer) is reduced by the amount the CDC spent on buying surplus butter. Using your answers for parts (b)–(d), what is the total surplus when there is a price floor? How does this compare to the total surplus without a price floor from part (a)?

---

[4]In reality, with the help of provincial marketing boards, the CDC uses a number of supply management techniques to help ensure that it is not buying butter and ultimately destroying it. The CDC and the marketing boards set the price floor based on supplier costs so that suppliers can earn a fair rate of return and use production quotas to attempt to limit supply. The CDC buys and sells butter at the support price so as to eliminate seasonal price fluctuations; any surplus butter bought one year is sold in the following year when demand is firmer. This eliminates the need for the CDC to use government tax revenue to subsidize its buying activities. Part (e) of this question asks you to imagine that this is not how the CDC actually operates.

5. The accompanying table shows hypothetical demand and supply schedules for milk per year. The Canadian government decides that the incomes of dairy farmers should be maintained at a level that allows the traditional family dairy farm to survive. So it implements a price floor of $1 per litre by buying surplus milk until the market price is $1 per litre.

Price of milk (per litre)	Quantity of milk (millions of litres per year)	
	Quantity demanded	Quantity supplied
$1.20	550	850
1.10	600	800
1.00	650	750
0.90	700	700
0.80	750	650

a. How much surplus milk will be produced as a result of this policy?

b. What will be the cost to the government of this policy?

c. Since milk is an important source of protein and calcium, the government decides to provide the surplus milk it purchases to elementary schools at a price of only $0.60 per litre. Assume that schools will buy any amount of milk available at this low price. But parents now reduce their purchases of milk at any price by 50 million litres per year because they know their children are getting milk at school. How much will the dairy program now cost the government?

d. Explain how inefficiencies in the form of inefficient allocation of sales among sellers and wasted resources arise from this policy.

6. European governments tend to make greater use of price controls than does the Canadian government. For example, the French government sets minimum starting yearly wages for new hires who have completed *le bac*, certification roughly equivalent to a high school diploma. The demand schedule for new hires with *le bac* and the supply schedule for similarly credentialed new jobseekers are given in the accompanying table. The price here—given in euros, the currency used in France—is the same as the yearly wage.

Wage (per year)	Quantity demanded (new job offers per year)	Quantity supplied (new jobseekers per year)
€45 000	200 000	325 000
40 000	220 000	320 000
35 000	250 000	310 000
30 000	290 000	290 000
25 000	370 000	200 000

a. In the absence of government interference, what are the equilibrium wage and number of graduates hired per year? Illustrate with a diagram. Will there be anyone seeking a job at the equilibrium wage who is unable to find one—that is, will there be anyone who is involuntarily unemployed?

b. Suppose the French government sets a minimum yearly wage of €35 000. Is there any involuntary unemployment at this wage? If so, how much? Illustrate with a diagram. What if the minimum wage is set at €40 000? Also illustrate with a diagram.

c. Given your answer to part (b) and the information in the table, what do you think is the relationship between the level of involuntary unemployment and the level of the minimum wage? Who benefits from such a policy? Who loses? What is the missed opportunity here?

7. Until recently, the standard number of hours worked per week for a full-time job in France was 39, just as in Canada. But in response to social unrest over high levels of involuntary unemployment, the French government instituted a 35-hour workweek—a worker could not work more than 35 hours per week even if both the worker and employer wanted it. The motivation behind this policy was that if current employees worked fewer hours, employers would be forced to hire more new workers. Assume that it is costly for employers to train new workers. French employers were greatly opposed to this policy and threatened to move their operations to neighbouring countries that did not have such employment restrictions. Can you explain their attitude? Give an example of both an inefficiency and an illegal activity that are likely to arise from this policy.

8. For the last 70 years the Canadian government has used price supports to provide income assistance to Canadian farmers. To implement these price supports, at times the government has used price floors, which it maintains by buying up the surplus farm products. At other times, it has used target prices, a policy by which the government gives the farmer an amount equal to the difference between the market price and the target price for each unit sold. Consider the market for corn depicted in the accompanying diagram.

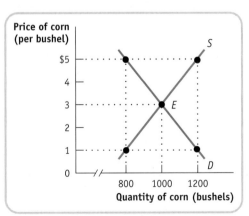

a. If the government sets a price floor of $5 per bushel, how many bushels of corn are produced? How many are purchased by consumers? By the government? How much does the program cost the government? How much revenue do corn farmers receive?

b. Suppose the government sets a target price of $5 per bushel for any quantity supplied up to 1000 bushels. How many bushels of corn are purchased by consumers and at what price? By the government? How much does the program cost the government? How much revenue do corn farmers receive?

c. Which of these programs (in parts (a) and (b)) costs corn consumers more? Which program costs the government more? Explain.

d. Is one of these policies less inefficient than the other? Explain.

9. The waters off the North Atlantic coast were once teeming with fish, but because of overfishing by the commercial fishing industry, the stocks of fish became seriously depleted. In 1991, the International Commission for the Conservation of Atlantic Tunas (ICCAT) implemented an international set of quotas to allow Atlantic tuna and swordfish stocks to recover. The quota limited the amount of swordfish caught per year by all Canadian-licensed fishing boats to 2 million kilograms. As soon as the Canadian fishing fleet had met the quota limit, the swordfish catch was closed down for the rest of the year. The accompanying table gives the hypothetical demand and supply schedules for swordfish caught in Canada per year.

Price of swordfish (per kilogram)	Quantity of swordfish (millions of kilogram per year)	
	Quantity demanded	Quantity supplied
$40	1	10
36	2	8
32	3	6
28	4	4
26	5	2

a. Use a diagram to show the effect of the quota on the market for swordfish in 1991.

b. How do you think fishers changed how they fished in response to this policy?

10. In the Atlantic provinces and Quebec, you must have a licence to harvest lobster commercially; these licences are issued yearly. Suppose the federal Department of Fisheries and Oceans is concerned about the dwindling supplies of lobsters. This department decides to place a yearly quota of 80 000 kg of lobsters harvested in all Canadian waters. It also decides to give licences this year only to those fishers who had licences last year. The accompanying diagram shows the demand and supply curves for Canadian lobsters.

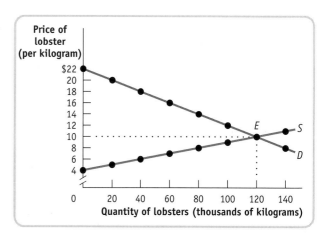

a. In the absence of government restrictions, what are the equilibrium price and quantity?

b. What is the *demand price* at which consumers wish to purchase 80 000 kg of lobsters?

c. What is the *supply price* at which suppliers are willing to supply 80 000 kg of lobsters?

d. What is the *quota rent* per kilogram of lobster when 80 000 kg are sold?

e. Explain a transaction that benefits both buyer and seller but is prevented by the quota restriction.

11. The accompanying diagram shows data from the U.S. Bureau of Labor Statistics on the average price of an airline ticket in the United States from 1975 until 1985, adjusted to eliminate the effect of *inflation* (the general increase in the prices of all goods over time). In 1978, the United States Airline Deregulation Act removed the price floor on airline fares, and it also allowed the airlines greater flexibility to offer new routes. (*Note:* Canada experienced similar airline deregulation in 1978.)

Source: U.S. Bureau of Labor Statistics.

a. Looking at the data on airline ticket prices in the diagram, do you think the price floor that existed before 1978 was binding or non-binding? That is, do you think it was set above or below the equilibrium price? Draw a supply and demand diagram, showing where the price floor that existed before 1978 was in relation to the equilibrium price.

b. Most economists agree that the average airline ticket price per mile travelled actually *fell* as a result of the Airline Deregulation Act. How might you reconcile that view with what you see in the diagram?

12. In Canada, all provinces except Alberta have a minimum legal retail price for beer (a price floor). Part of the rationale for this policy is to discourage immoderate consumption of alcohol.

Suppose the fictitious province of Beerlandia has the following annual demand and supply schedule for beer (sold in cases of 24 bottles).

Price (per case)	Quantity demanded (thousands of cases)	Quantity supplied (thousands of cases)
$16	1040	800
18	1000	1000
20	960	1200
22	920	1400
24	880	1600

a. Find the equilibrium price and quantity of cases of beer in Beerlandia. Draw a diagram representing the market for beer in the province of Beerlandia. Clearly label the price paid by consumers, the quantity of beer exchanged, and the price received by suppliers in equilibrium.

b. Suppose the provincial government of Beerlandia decides to impose a legal minimum price of $28.00 per case of 24 bottles of beer. Briefly describe the winners and losers of this minimum price law.

c. Suppose the majority of the residents of Beerlandia live close to the border and have access to beer at a lower price either in another province or in the United States. What do you expect to occur? What does this imply about the ability of the provincial government of Beerlandia to independently set their tax and alcohol/beer pricing policy? Which jurisdiction is likely to be more problematic, other Canadian provinces or U.S. states?

13. This question uses the algebraic method of determining equilibrium from Appendix 3A. In Canada, producers of milk, poultry, and eggs are protected by government-imposed supply management rules. This supply management system is made up of a combination of import controls, production planning quotas, and minimum prices for these products.

Suppose, for simplicity, the Canadian market for turkeys is described by the following demand and supply curves.

$$P = 30 - 0.125Q^d \qquad \text{Demand Curve}$$
$$P = 1.48 + 0.03Q^S \qquad \text{Supply Curve}$$

where Q represents the monthly quantity of turkey in thousands of kilograms and the price P is the price per kilogram.

a. Suppose Canada does not have any supply management for turkey farmers. Derive the equilibrium price and quantity of turkey. Draw a diagram representing the market for turkey. Clearly label the equilibium price and quantity.

b. Suppose, to support the incomes of farmers who raise turkeys, the government imposes a price floor for turkeys at $9.00 per kilogram. Determine the resulting price paid by consumers, quantity of turkeys exchanged, and the price received by suppliers in equilibrium. Sketch this into your diagram from part (a).

c. Briefly explain how this price floor supports the income of farmers.

d. Why might the government need to also impose limitations on the quantity of turkeys imported? Explain.

e. Show that the imposition of a production quota of 168 000 kg of turkey per month results in the same price paid by consumers as the price floor in part (b). What are the resulting demand price, supply price, and quota rent?

f. Would the government (or a supply management authority) need to have the means to impose penalties for violating the price floor and/or the supply quota? Explain why or why not.

g. Would farmers who were unable to get a turkey production quota licence be pleased by this supply management system? Explain why or why not. Suppose, if they wish, these farmers could rent a production quota licence from another farmer who was awarded one. Would this make these other farmers extremely happy? Explain why or why not.

CHAPTER 5

International Trade

CAR PARTS AND SUCKING SOUNDS

International trade improves the welfare of Mexican producers of auto parts as well as Canadian and American car buyers and sellers.

WHAT YOU WILL LEARN IN THIS CHAPTER

❱ How comparative advantage leads to mutually beneficial international trade

❱ The sources of international comparative advantage

❱ Who gains and who loses from international trade, and why the gains exceed the losses

❱ How **tariffs** and **import quotas** cause inefficiency and reduce total surplus

❱ Why governments often engage in **trade protection** and how **international trade agreements** counteract this

STOP IN AN AUTO SHOWROOM, and odds are that the majority of cars on display were produced in either Canada or the United States. Even if they're foreign brands like Toyotas, Hondas, or Volkswagens, most cars sold in Canada were made here either by the Big Three U.S. auto firms or by subsidiaries of foreign firms. Canadian-made cars are assembled mostly in southern Ontario, within the corridor from Windsor to Oshawa.[1]

Although that car you're looking at may have been made in Canada or the United States, a significant part of what's inside was probably made elsewhere, very likely in Mexico. Since the 1980s, auto production in North America has increasingly relied on factories in Mexico to produce *labour-intensive* auto parts, such as seat parts—products that use a relatively high amount of labour in their production.

Changes in economic policy over the years have contributed greatly to the emergence of large-scale Canadian and U.S. imports of auto parts from Mexico. Until the 1980s, Mexico had a system of *trade protection*—taxes and regulations limiting imports—that both kept out foreign manufactured goods and

encouraged Mexican industry to focus on selling to Mexican consumers rather than to a wider market. In 1985, however, the Mexican government began dismantling much of its trade protection, boosting trade with its trading partners. A further boost came in 1993, when Canada, the United States, and Mexico signed the North American Free Trade Agreement (NAFTA), which eliminated most taxes on trade among the three nations and provided guarantees that business investments in Mexico would be protected from arbitrary changes in government policy.

NAFTA was deeply controversial when it went into effect: Mexican workers were paid only a fraction of what their Canadian and American counterparts were paid, and many workers, especially in the United States, expressed concern that jobs would be lost to low-wage competition. Ross Perot, a U.S. presidential candidate in 1992, warned that there would be a "giant sucking sound" as U.S. manufacturing moved south of the border. And although apocalyptic predictions about NAFTA's impact haven't come to pass, the agreement remains controversial even now.

Most economists disagreed with those who saw NAFTA as a threat to the Canadian economy. We saw in Chapter 2 how international trade can lead to mutual *gains from trade*. Economists, for the most part, believed that the same logic applied to NAFTA, that the treaty would make both Canada and Mexico richer. But making a nation as a whole richer isn't the same thing as improving the welfare of everyone living in a country, and there were and are reasons to believe that NAFTA hurts some Canadian citizens.

Until now, we have analyzed the economy as if it were self-sufficient, as if the economy produces all the goods and services it consumes, and vice versa. This is, of course, true for the world economy as a whole. But it's not true for any individual country. Assuming self-sufficiency would have been far more accurate 50 years ago, when Canada exported only a small fraction of what it produced and imported only a small fraction of what it consumed. Since then, however, Canadian imports and exports have grown much faster than the Canadian economy as a whole. Nowadays, to have a full picture of

[1]Industry Canada provides a list of vehicles made in Canada. For the list of cars made in 2012, see www.ic.gc.ca/eic/site/auto-auto.nsf/eng/am02365.html and for a list of the Canadian assembly plants in 2012, see www.ic.gc.ca/eic/site/auto-auto.nsf/eng/am00767.html.

145

how national economies work, we must understand international trade.

This chapter examines the economics of international trade. We start from the model of comparative advantage, which, as we saw in Chapter 2, explains why there are gains from international trade. We will briefly recap that model here, and then extend our study to address deeper questions about international trade, such as why some individuals can be hurt by international trade while the country, as a whole, gains. At the conclusion of the chapter, we'll examine the effects of policies that countries use to limit imports or promote exports as well as how governments work together to overcome barriers to trade. ■

Goods and services purchased from other countries are **imports;** goods and services sold to other countries are **exports.**

Globalization is the phenomenon of growing economic linkages among countries.

Comparative Advantage and International Trade

Canada buys auto parts—and many other goods and services—from other countries. At the same time, it sells many goods and services to other countries. Goods and services purchased from abroad are **imports;** goods and services sold abroad are **exports.**

As illustrated by the opening story, imports and exports have taken on an increasingly important role in the Canadian economy. Over the last 50 years, both imports into and exports from Canada have grown faster than the Canadian economy. Panel (a) of Figure 5-1 shows how the values of Canadian imports and exports have grown as a percentage of gross domestic product (GDP). Panel (b) shows imports and exports as a percentage of GDP for a number of countries. It shows that foreign trade is more important for some countries than it is for Canada.

Foreign trade isn't the only way countries interact economically. In the modern world, investors from one country often invest funds in another nation; many companies are multinational, with subsidiaries operating in several countries; and a growing number of individuals work in a country different from the one in which they were born. The growth of all these forms of economic linkages among countries is often called **globalization.**

FIGURE **5-1** The Growing Importance of International Trade

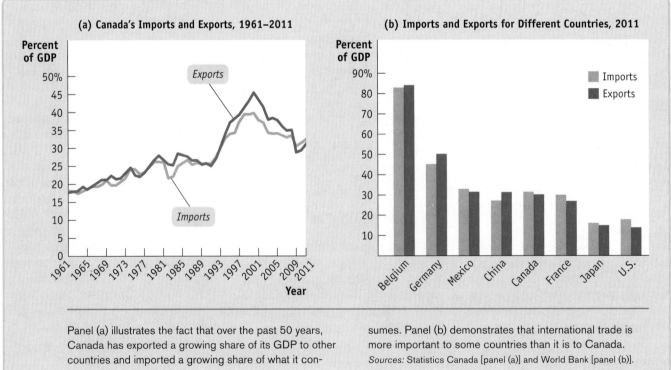

(a) Canada's Imports and Exports, 1961–2011

(b) Imports and Exports for Different Countries, 2011

Panel (a) illustrates the fact that over the past 50 years, Canada has exported a growing share of its GDP to other countries and imported a growing share of what it consumes. Panel (b) demonstrates that international trade is more important to some countries than it is to Canada.
Sources: Statistics Canada [panel (a)] and World Bank [panel (b)].

In this chapter, however, we'll focus mainly on international trade. To understand why international trade occurs and why economists believe it is beneficial to the economy, we will first review the concept of comparative advantage.

Production Possibilities and Comparative Advantage, Revisited

To produce auto parts, any country must use resources—land, labour, capital, and so on—that could have been used to produce other things. The potential production of other goods a country must forgo to produce an auto part is the opportunity cost of that part.

In some cases, it's easy to see why the opportunity cost of producing a good is especially low in a given country. Consider, for example, shrimp—much of which now comes from seafood farms in Vietnam and Thailand. It's a lot easier to produce shrimp in Vietnam, where the climate is nearly ideal and there's plenty of coastal land suitable for shellfish farming, than it is in Canada. Conversely, other goods are not produced as easily in Vietnam as in Canada. For example, Vietnam doesn't have the base of skilled workers and technological know-how that makes Canada so good at producing high-technology goods. So the opportunity cost of a tonne of shrimp, in terms of other goods such as aircraft, is much less in Vietnam than it is in Canada.

In other cases, matters are a bit less obvious. It's as easy to produce auto parts in Canada as it is in Mexico, and Mexican auto parts workers are, if anything, less efficient than their Canadian counterparts. But Mexican workers are a *lot* less productive than Canadian workers in other areas, such as aircraft and chemical production. This means that diverting a Mexican worker into auto parts production reduces output of other goods less than diverting a Canadian worker into auto parts production. That is, the opportunity cost of producing auto parts in Mexico is less than it is in Canada.

So we say that Mexico has a comparative advantage in producing auto parts. Let's repeat the definition of comparative advantage from Chapter 2: *A country has a comparative advantage in producing a good or service if the opportunity cost of producing the good or service is lower for that country than for other countries.*

Figure 5-2 provides a hypothetical numerical example of comparative advantage in international trade. We assume that only two goods are produced and consumed, auto parts and airplanes, and that there are only two countries in the world, Canada and Mexico. (In real life, auto parts aren't worth much without auto bodies to put them in, but let's set that issue aside). The figure shows hypothetical production possibility frontiers for Canada and Mexico.

As in Chapter 2, we simplify the model by assuming that the production possibility frontiers are straight lines, as shown in Figure 2-1, rather than the more realistic bowed-out shape shown in Figure 2-2. The straight-line shape implies that the opportunity cost of an auto part in terms of airplanes in each country is constant—it does not depend on how many units of each good the country produces. The analysis of international trade under the assumption that opportunity costs are constant, which makes production possibility frontiers straight lines, is known as the **Ricardian model of international trade,** named after the English economist David Ricardo, who introduced this analysis in the early nineteenth century.

In Figure 5-2 we have grouped auto parts into bundles of 10 000, so, for example, a country that produces 500 bundles of auto parts is producing 5 million individual auto parts. You can see in the figure that Canada can produce 2000 airplanes if it produces no auto parts, or 1000 bundles of auto parts if it produces no airplanes. Thus, the slope of Canada's production possibility frontier, or PPF, is $-2000/1000 = -2$. That is, to produce an additional bundle of auto parts, Canada must forgo the production of 2 airplanes.

Similarly, Mexico can produce 1000 airplanes if it produces no auto parts or 2000 bundles of auto parts if it produces no airplanes. Thus, the slope of Mexico's

The **Ricardian model of international trade** analyzes international trade under the assumption that opportunity costs are constant.

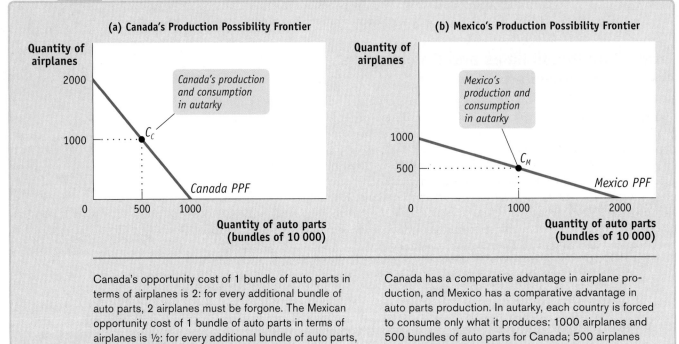

Canada's opportunity cost of 1 bundle of auto parts in terms of airplanes is 2: for every additional bundle of auto parts, 2 airplanes must be forgone. The Mexican opportunity cost of 1 bundle of auto parts in terms of airplanes is ½: for every additional bundle of auto parts, only ½ of an airplane must be forgone. As a result,

Canada has a comparative advantage in airplane production, and Mexico has a comparative advantage in auto parts production. In autarky, each country is forced to consume only what it produces: 1000 airplanes and 500 bundles of auto parts for Canada; 500 airplanes and 1000 bundles of auto parts for Mexico.

Autarky is a situation in which a country does not trade with other countries.

PPF is $-1000/2000 = -1/2$. That is, to produce an additional bundle of auto parts, Mexico must forgo the production of 1/2 an airplane.

Economists use the term **autarky** to refer to a situation in which a country does not trade with other countries—it is self-sufficient. We assume that in autarky Canada chooses to produce and consume 500 bundles of auto parts and 1000 airplanes. We also assume that in autarky Mexico produces 1000 bundles of auto parts and 500 airplanes.

The trade-offs facing the two countries when they don't trade are summarized in Table 5-1. As you can see, Canada has a comparative advantage in the production of airplanes because it has a lower opportunity cost in terms of auto parts than Mexico has: producing an airplane costs Canada only ½ a bundle of auto parts, while it costs Mexico 2 bundles of auto parts. Correspondingly, Mexico has a comparative advantage in auto parts production: 1 bundle costs it only ½ an airplane, while it costs Canada 2 airplanes.

TABLE **5-1** Canadian and Mexican Opportunity Costs of Auto Parts and Airplanes

	Canadian Opportunity Cost		Mexican Opportunity Cost
1 bundle of auto parts	2 airplanes	>	1/2 airplane
1 airplane	1/2 bundle of auto parts	<	2 bundles of auto parts

As we learned in Chapter 2, each country can do better by engaging in trade than it could by not trading. A country can accomplish this by specializing in the production of the good in which it has a comparative advantage and exporting that good, while importing the good in which it has a comparative *dis*advantage. Let's see how this works.

The Gains from International Trade

Figure 5-3 illustrates how both countries can gain from specialization and trade, by showing a hypothetical rearrangement of production and consumption that allows *each* country to consume more of *both* goods. Again, panel (a) represents Canada and panel (b) represents Mexico. In each panel we indicate again the

FIGURE **5-3** The Gains from International Trade

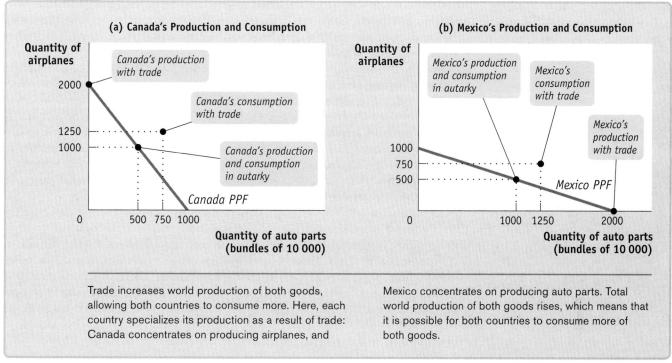

(a) Canada's Production and Consumption

(b) Mexico's Production and Consumption

Trade increases world production of both goods, allowing both countries to consume more. Here, each country specializes its production as a result of trade: Canada concentrates on producing airplanes, and

Mexico concentrates on producing auto parts. Total world production of both goods rises, which means that it is possible for both countries to consume more of both goods.

autarky production and consumption assumed in Figure 5-2. Once trade becomes possible, however, everything changes. With trade, each country can move to producing only the good in which it has a comparative advantage—airplanes for Canada and auto parts for Mexico. Because the world production of both goods is now higher than in autarky, trade makes it possible for each country to consume more of both goods.

Table 5-2 sums up the changes as a result of trade and shows why both countries can gain. The left part of the table shows the autarky situation, before trade, in which each country must produce the goods it consumes. The right part of the table shows what happens as a result of trade. After trade, Canada specializes in the production of airplanes, producing 2000 airplanes and no auto parts; Mexico specializes in the production of auto parts, producing 2000 bundles of auto parts and no airplanes.

TABLE **5-2** How Canada and Mexico Gain from Trade

		In Autarky		With Trade		
		Production	Consumption	Production	Consumption	Gains from trade
Canada	Bundles of auto parts	500	500	0	750	+250
	Airplanes	1000	1000	2000	1250	+250
Mexico	Bundles of auto parts	1000	1000	2000	1250	+250
	Airplanes	500	500	0	750	+250

The result is a rise in total world production of both goods. As you can see in Table 5-2, with trade, Canada is able to consume both more airplanes and more auto parts than before, even though it no longer produces auto parts, because it can import parts from Mexico. Mexico can also consume more of both goods, even though it no longer produces airplanes, because it can import airplanes from Canada.

The key to this mutual gain is the fact that trade liberates both countries from self-sufficiency—from the need to produce the same mixes of goods they consume. Because each country can concentrate on producing the good in which it has a comparative advantage, total world production rises, making a higher standard of living possible in both nations.

Now, in this example we have simply assumed the post-trade consumption bundles of the two countries. In fact, the consumption choices of a country reflect both the preferences of its residents and the *relative prices*—the prices of one good in terms of another in international markets. Although we have not explicitly given the price of airplanes in terms of auto parts, that price is implicit in our example: Mexico sells Canada the 750 bundles of auto parts Canada consumes in return for the 750 airplanes Mexico consumes, so 1 bundle of parts is traded for 1 airplane. This tells us that the price of an airplane on world markets must be equal to the price of one bundle of 10 000 auto parts in our example.

One requirement that the relative price must satisfy is that no country pays a relative price greater than its opportunity cost of obtaining the good in autarky. That is, Canada won't pay more than 2 airplanes for each 1 bundle of 10 000 auto parts from Mexico, and Mexico won't pay more than 2 bundles of 10 000 auto parts for each 1 airplane from Canada. Once this requirement is satisfied, the actual relative price in international trade is determined by supply and demand—and we'll turn to supply and demand in international trade in the next section. However, first let's look more deeply into the nature of the gains from trade.

Comparative Advantage versus Absolute Advantage

It's easy to accept the idea that Vietnam and Thailand have a comparative advantage in shrimp production: they have a tropical climate that's better suited to shrimp farming than that of Canada, and they have a lot of usable coastal area. So Canada imports shrimp from Vietnam and Thailand. In other cases, however, it may be harder to understand why we import certain goods from abroad.

Canadian imports of auto parts from Mexico is a case in point. There's nothing about Mexico's climate or resources that makes it especially good at manufacturing auto parts. In fact, it almost surely takes *fewer* hours of labour to produce an auto seat or wiring harness in Canada than in Mexico.

Why, then, do we buy Mexican auto parts? Because the gains from trade depend on *comparative advantage*, not *absolute advantage*. Yes, it takes less labour to produce a wiring harness in Canada than in Mexico. That is, the productivity of Mexican auto parts workers is less than that of their Canadian counterparts. But what determines comparative advantage is not the amount of resources used to produce a good but the opportunity cost of that good—here, the quantity of other goods forgone in order to produce an auto seat. And the opportunity cost of auto parts is lower in Mexico than in Canada.

Here's how it works: Mexican workers have low productivity compared with Canadian workers in the auto parts industry. But Mexican workers have even lower productivity compared with Canadian workers in other industries. Because Mexican labour productivity in industries other than auto parts is relatively very low, producing a wiring harness in Mexico, even though it takes a lot of labour, does not require forgoing the production of large quantities of other goods.

In Canada, the opposite is true: very high productivity in other industries (such as high-technology goods) means that producing

With their tropical climate, Vietnam and Thailand have a comparative advantage in shrimp production.

an auto seat in Canada, even though it doesn't require much labour, requires sacrificing lots of other goods. So the opportunity cost of producing auto parts is less in Mexico than in Canada. Despite its lower labour productivity, Mexico has a comparative advantage in the production of many auto parts, although Canada has an absolute advantage.

Mexico's comparative advantage in auto parts is reflected in global markets by the wages Mexican workers are paid. That's because a country's wage rates, in general, reflect its labour productivity. In countries where labour is highly productive in many industries, employers are willing to pay high wages to attract workers, so competition among employers leads to an overall high wage rate. In countries where labour is less productive, competition for workers is less intense and wage rates are correspondingly lower.

As the accompanying Global Comparison shows, there is indeed a strong relationship between overall levels of productivity and wage rates around the world. Because Mexico has generally low productivity, it has a relatively low wage rate. Low wages, in turn, give Mexico a cost advantage in producing goods where its productivity is only moderately low, like auto parts. As a result, it's cheaper to produce these parts in Mexico than in Canada.

The kind of trade that takes place between low-wage, low-productivity economies like Mexico and high-wage, high-productivity economies like Canada and the United States gives rise to two common misperceptions. One, the *pauper labour fallacy*, is the belief that when a country with high wages imports goods produced by workers who are paid low wages, this must hurt the standard of living of workers in the importing country. The other, the *sweatshop labour fallacy*, is the belief that trade must be bad for workers in poor exporting countries because those workers are paid very low wages by our standards.

Both fallacies miss the nature of gains from trade: it's to the advantage of *both* countries if the poorer, lower-wage country exports goods in which it has

GLOBAL COMPARISON   PRODUCTIVITY AND WAGES AROUND THE WORLD

Is it true that both the pauper labour argument and the sweatshop labour argument are fallacies? Yes, it is. The real explanation for low wages in poor countries is low overall productivity.

The graph shows estimates of labour productivity, measured by the value of output (GDP) per worker, and wages, measured by the monthly compensation of the average worker, for several countries in 2009. Both productivity and wages are expressed as percentages of U.S. productivity and wages; for example, productivity and wages in Japan were 79% and 91%, respectively, of their U.S. levels. You can see the strong positive relationship between productivity and wages. The relationship isn't perfect. For example, Germany has higher wages than its productivity might lead you to expect. But simple comparisons of wages give a misleading sense of labour costs in poor countries: their low-wage advantage is mostly offset by low productivity.

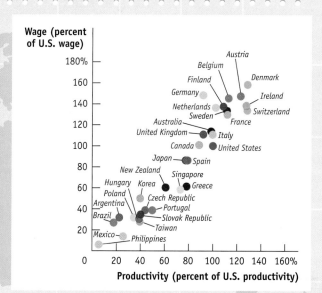

Sources: Bureau of Labor Statistics; International Monetary Fund.

a comparative advantage, even if its cost advantage in these goods depends on low wages. That is, both countries are able to achieve a higher standard of living through trade.

It's particularly important to understand that buying a good made by someone who is paid much lower wages than most Canadian workers doesn't necessarily imply that you're taking advantage of that person. It depends on the alternatives. Because workers in poor countries have low productivity across the board, they are offered low wages whether they produce goods exported to Canada or goods sold in local markets. A job that looks terrible by rich-country standards can be a step up for someone in a poor country.

International trade that depends on low-wage exports can nonetheless raise a country's standard of living. This is especially true of very-low-wage nations. For example, Bangladesh and similar countries would be much poorer than they are—their citizens might even be starving—if they weren't able to export goods such as clothing based on their low wage rates.

Sources of Comparative Advantage

International trade is driven by comparative advantage, but where does comparative advantage come from? Economists who study international trade have found three main sources of comparative advantage: international differences in *climate*, international differences in *factor endowments,* and international differences in *technology*.

Differences in Climate One key reason the opportunity cost of producing shrimp in Vietnam and Thailand is less than in Canada is that shrimp need warm water—Vietnam has plenty of that, but Canada doesn't. In general, differences in climate play a significant role in international trade. Tropical countries export tropical products like coffee, sugar, bananas, and shrimp. Countries in the temperate zones export crops like wheat and corn. Some trade is even driven by the difference in seasons between the northern and southern hemispheres: winter deliveries of Chilean grapes and New Zealand apples have become commonplace in North American and European supermarkets.

Differences in Factor Endowments Canada is a major exporter of forest products—lumber and products derived from lumber, like pulp and paper—to the United States. These exports don't reflect the special skill of Canadian lumberjacks. Canada has a comparative advantage in forest products because its forested area is much greater compared to the size of its labour force than the ratio of forestland to the labour force in the United States.

Forestland, like labour and capital, is a *factor of production:* an input used to produce goods and services. (Recall from Chapter 2 that the factors of production are land, labour, and capital.) Due to history and geography, the mix of available factors of production differs among countries, providing an important source of comparative advantage. The relationship between comparative advantage and factor availability is found in an influential model of international trade, the *Heckscher–Ohlin model,* developed by two Swedish economists in the first half of the twentieth century.

Two key concepts in the model are *factor abundance* and *factor intensity*. Factor abundance refers to how large a country's supply of a factor is relative to its supply of other factors. Factor intensity refers to the fact that producers use different ratios of factors of production in the production of different goods. For example, oil refineries use much more capital per worker than clothing factories. Economists use the term **factor intensity** to describe this difference among goods: oil refining is capital-intensive, because it tends to use a high ratio of capital

The **factor intensity** of production of a good is a measure of which factor is used in relatively greater quantities than other factors in production.

to labour, but auto seats production is labour-intensive, because it tends to use a high ratio of labour to capital.

According to the **Heckscher–Ohlin model,** *a country that has an abundant supply of a factor of production will have a comparative advantage in goods whose production is intensive in that factor.* So a country that has a relative abundance of capital will have a comparative advantage in capital-intensive industries such as oil refining, but a country that has a relative abundance of labour will have a comparative advantage in labour-intensive industries such as auto seats production.

The basic intuition behind this result is simple and based on opportunity cost. The opportunity cost of a given factor—the value that the factor would generate in alternative uses—is low for a country when it is relatively abundant in that factor. Relative to Canada, Mexico has an abundance of low-skilled labour. As a result, the opportunity cost of the production of low-skilled, labour-intensive goods is lower in Mexico than in Canada.

The most dramatic example of the validity of the Heckscher–Ohlin model is world trade in clothing. Clothing production is a labour-intensive activity: it doesn't take much physical capital, nor does it require a lot of human capital in the form of highly educated workers. So you would expect labour-abundant countries such as China and Bangladesh to have a comparative advantage in clothing production. And they do.

That much international trade is the result of differences in factor endowments helps explain another fact: international specialization of production is often *incomplete.* That is, a country often maintains some domestic production of a good that it imports. A good example of this is Canada and oil. Saudi Arabia exports oil to Canada because Saudi Arabia has an abundant supply of oil relative to its other factors of production; Canada exports medical devices to Saudi Arabia because it has an abundant supply of expertise in medical technology relative to its other factors of production. But Canada also produces some oil domestically because the size of its domestic oil reserves in Alberta makes it economical to do so.

In our supply and demand analysis in the next section, we'll consider incomplete specialization by a country to be the norm. We should emphasize, however, that the fact that countries often incompletely specialize does not in any way change the conclusion that there are gains from trade.

Differences in Technology   In the 1970s and 1980s, Japan became by far the world's largest exporter of automobiles, selling large numbers to North America and the rest of the world. Japan's comparative advantage in automobiles wasn't the result of climate. Nor can it easily be attributed to differences in factor endowments: aside from a scarcity of land, Japan's mix of available factors is quite similar to that in other developed countries. Instead, as we discussed in the Chapter 2 Business Case on lean production at Toyota and Boeing, Japan's comparative advantage in automobiles was based on the superior production techniques developed by its manufacturers, which allowed them to produce more cars with a given amount of labour and capital than their North American or European counterparts.

Japan's comparative advantage in automobiles was a case of comparative advantage caused by differences in technology—the techniques used in production.

The causes of differences in technology are somewhat mysterious. Sometimes they seem to be based on knowledge accumulated through experience—for example, Switzerland's comparative advantage in watches reflects a long tradition of watchmaking. Sometimes they are the result of a set of innovations that for some reason occur in one country but not in others. Technological advantage,

According to the **Heckscher–Ohlin model,** a country has a comparative advantage in a good whose production is intensive in the factors that are abundantly available in that country.

FOR INQUIRING MINDS

INCREASING RETURNS TO SCALE AND INTERNATIONAL TRADE

Most analysis of international trade focuses on how differences between countries—differences in climate, factor endowments, and technology—create national comparative advantage. However, economists have also pointed out another reason for international trade: the role of *increasing returns to scale*.

Production of a good is characterized by increasing returns to scale if the average productivity of labour and other resources used in production rise with the quantity of output. For example, in an industry characterized by increasing returns to scale, increasing output by 10% might require only 8% more labour and 9% more raw materials. Examples of industries with increasing returns to scale include auto manufacturing, oil refining, and the production of jumbo jets, all of which require large outlays of capital. Increasing returns to scale (sometimes also called economies of scale) can give rise to monopoly, a situation in which an industry is composed of only one producer, because it gives large firms a cost advantage over small ones.

But increasing returns to scale can also give rise to international trade. The logic runs as follows: If production of a good is characterized by increasing returns to scale, it makes sense to concentrate production in only a few locations, so each location has a high level of output. But that also means production occurs in only a few countries that export the good to other countries. A commonly cited example is the North American auto industry: although both Canada and the United States produce automobiles and their components, each particular model or component tends to be produced in only one of the two countries and exported to the other.

Increasing returns to scale probably play a large role in the trade in manufactured goods between advanced countries, which is about 25% of the total value of world trade.

---

however, is often transitory. As we also discussed in the Chapter 2 Business Case, by adopting lean production, auto manufacturers in North America have now closed much of the gap in productivity with their Japanese competitors. In addition, a technological advantage can be acquired or supported by government funding for research and development. For instance, government support for nuclear and aerospace industries has helped Canada occupy a niche in the world markets for these products. At any given point in time, however, differences in technology are a major source of comparative advantage.

ECONOMICS > IN ACTION

SKILL AND COMPARATIVE ADVANTAGE

In 1953 U.S. workers were clearly better equipped with machinery than their counterparts in other countries. Most economists at the time thought that America's comparative advantage lay in capital-intensive goods. But economist Wassily Leontief made a surprising discovery: America's comparative advantage was in something other than capital-intensive goods. In fact, goods that the United States exported were slightly less capital-intensive than goods the country imported. This discovery came to be known as the Leontief paradox, and it led to a sustained effort to make sense of U.S. trade patterns.

The main resolution of this paradox, it turns out, depends on the definition of *capital*. U.S. exports aren't intensive in *physical* capital—machines and buildings. Instead, they are *skill-intensive*—that is, they are intensive in *human* capital. U.S. exporting industries use a substantially higher ratio of highly educated workers to other workers than is found in U.S. industries that compete against imports. For example, one of America's biggest export sectors is aircraft; the aircraft industry employs large numbers of engineers and other people with graduate degrees relative to the number of manual labourers. Conversely, the United States imports a lot of clothing, which is often produced by workers with little formal education.

In general, countries with highly educated workforces tend to export skill-intensive goods, while countries with less educated workforces tend to export goods whose production requires little skilled labour. Figure 5-4 illustrates this point by comparing the goods the United States imports from Germany, a country with a highly educated labour force, with the goods the United States imports from Bangladesh, where about half of the adult population is still illiterate. In each country industries are ranked, first, according to how skill-intensive they are. Next, for each industry, we calculate its share of exports to the United States. This allows us to plot, for each country, various industries according to their skill intensity and their share of exports to the United States.

In Figure 5-4, the horizontal axis shows a measure of the skill intensity

FIGURE 5-4 Education, Skill Intensity, and Trade

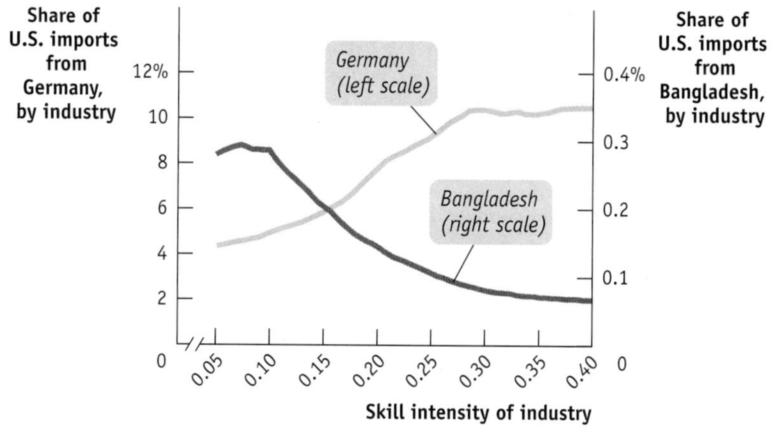

Source: John Romalis, "Factor Proportions and the Structure of Commodity Trade," *American Economic Review* 94, no. 1 (2004): 67–97.

of different industries, and the vertical axes show the share of U.S. imports in each industry coming from Germany (on the left) and Bangladesh (on the right). As you can see, each country's exports to the United States reflect its skill level. The curve representing Germany slopes upward: the more skill-intensive a German industry is, the higher its share of exports to the United States. In contrast, the curve representing Bangladesh slopes downward: the less skill-intensive a Bangladeshi industry is, the higher its share of exports to the United States.

CHECK YOUR UNDERSTANDING 5-1

1. In Canada, the opportunity cost of 1 tonne of wheat is 50 bicycles. In China, the opportunity cost of 1 bicycle is 0.01 tonne of wheat.
   a. Determine the pattern of comparative advantage.
   b. In autarky, Canada can produce 200 000 bicycles if no wheat is produced, and China can produce 3000 tonnes of wheat if no bicycles are produced. Draw each country's production possibility frontier assuming constant opportunity cost, with tonnes of wheat on the vertical axis and bicycles on the horizontal axis.
   c. With trade, each country specializes its production. Canada consumes 1000 tonnes of wheat and 200 000 bicycles; China consumes 3000 tonnes of wheat and 100 000 bicycles. Indicate the production and consumption points on your diagrams, and use them to explain the gains from trade.

2. Explain the following patterns of trade using the Heckscher–Ohlin model.
   a. France exports wine to Canada, and Canada exports lumber to France.
   b. Brazil exports shoes to Canada, and Canada exports shoe-making machinery to Brazil.

Solutions appear at back of book.

▼ **Quick Review**

- **Imports** and **exports** account for a growing share of the Canadian economy and the economies of many other countries.

- The growth of international trade and other international linkages is known as **globalization.**

- International trade is driven by comparative advantage. The **Ricardian model of international trade** shows that trade between two countries makes both countries better off than they would be in **autarky**—that is, there are gains from international trade.

- The main sources of comparative advantage are international differences in climate, factor endowments, and technology.

- The **Heckscher–Ohlin model** shows how comparative advantage can arise from differences in factor endowments: goods differ in their **factor intensity,** and countries tend to export goods that are intensive in the factors they have in abundance.

Supply, Demand, and International Trade

Simple models of comparative advantage are helpful for understanding the fundamental causes of international trade. However, to analyze the effects of international trade at a more detailed level and to understand trade policy, it helps to return to the supply and demand model. We'll start by looking at the effects of imports on domestic producers and consumers, then turn to the effects of exports.

The **domestic demand curve** shows how the quantity of a good demanded by domestic consumers depends on the price of that good.

The **domestic supply curve** shows how the quantity of a good supplied by domestic producers depends on the price of that good.

The **world price** of a good is the price at which that good can be bought or sold abroad.

The Effects of Imports

Figure 5-5 shows the Canadian market for auto seats, ignoring international trade for a moment. It introduces a few new concepts: the *domestic demand curve*, the *domestic supply curve*, and the domestic or autarky price.

The **domestic demand curve** shows how the quantity of a good demanded by residents of a country depends on the price of that good. Why "domestic"? Because people living in other countries may demand the good, too. Once we introduce international trade, we need to distinguish between purchases of a good by domestic consumers and purchases by foreign consumers. So the domestic demand curve reflects only the demand of residents of our own country. Similarly, the **domestic supply curve** shows how the quantity of a good supplied by producers inside our own country depends on the price of that good. Once we introduce international trade, we need to distinguish between the supply of domestic producers and foreign supply—supply brought in from abroad.

In autarky, with no international trade in auto seats, the equilibrium in this market would be determined by the intersection of the domestic demand and domestic supply curves, point A. The equilibrium price of auto seats would be P_A, and the equilibrium quantity of auto seats produced and consumed would be Q_A. As always, both consumers and producers gain from the existence of the domestic market. Economists refer to the net gain that buyers receive from the purchase of a good as *consumer surplus*. Likewise, *producer surplus* is the net gain to sellers from selling a good. *Total surplus* is the sum of consumer and producer surplus. We analyzed these three concepts in detail in Appendix 3B. In autarky, consumer surplus would be equal to the area of the blue-shaded triangle in Figure 5-5. Producer surplus would be equal to the area of the red-shaded triangle. And total surplus would be equal to the sum of these two shaded triangles.

Now let's imagine opening up this market to imports. To do this, we must make an assumption about the supply of imports. The simplest assumption, which we will adopt here, is that unlimited quantities of auto seats can be purchased from abroad at a fixed price, known as the **world price** of auto seats. Figure 5-6 shows a situation in which the world price of an auto seat, P_W, is lower than the price of an auto seat that would prevail in the domestic market in autarky, P_A.

FIGURE 5-5 **Consumer and Producer Surplus in Autarky**

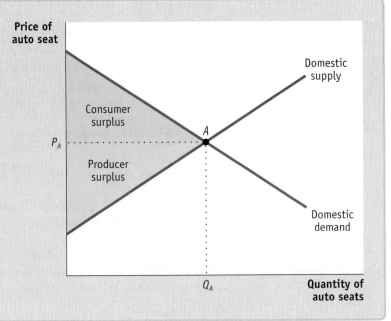

In the absence of trade, the domestic price is P_A, the autarky price at which the domestic supply curve and the domestic demand curve intersect. The quantity produced and consumed domestically is Q_A. Consumer surplus is represented by the blue-shaded area, and producer surplus is represented by the red-shaded area.

FIGURE **5-6**   The Domestic Market with Imports

Here the world price of auto parts, P_W, is below the autarky price, P_A. When the economy is opened to international trade, imports enter the domestic market, and the domestic price falls from the autarky price, P_A, to the world price, P_W. As the price falls, the domestic quantity demanded rises from Q_A to Q_D and the domestic quantity supplied falls from Q_A to Q_S. The difference between domestic quantity demanded and domestic quantity supplied at P_W, the quantity $Q_D - Q_S$, is filled by imports.

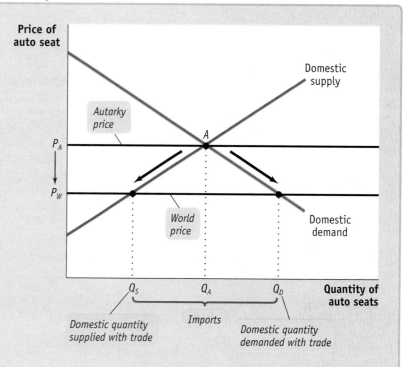

Given that the world price is below the domestic price of an auto seat, it is profitable for importers to buy auto seats abroad and resell them domestically. The imported auto seats increase the supply of auto seats in the domestic market, driving down the domestic market price. Auto seats will continue to be imported until the domestic price falls to a level equal to the world price.

The result is shown in Figure 5-6. Because of imports, the domestic price of an auto seat falls from P_A to P_W. The quantity of auto seats demanded by domestic consumers rises from Q_A to Q_D, and the quantity supplied by domestic producers falls from Q_A to Q_S. The difference between the domestic quantity demanded and the domestic quantity supplied, $Q_D - Q_S$, is filled by imports.

Now let's turn to the effects of imports on consumer surplus and producer surplus. Because imports of auto seats lead to a fall in their domestic price, consumer surplus rises and producer surplus falls. Figure 5-7 shows how this works. We label four areas: W, X, Y, and Z. The autarky consumer surplus we identified in Figure 5-5 corresponds to W, and the autarky producer surplus corresponds to the sum of X and Y. The fall in the domestic price to the world price leads to an increase in consumer surplus; it increases by X and Z, so consumer surplus now equals the sum of W, X, and Z. At the same time, producers lose X in surplus, so producer surplus now equals only Y.

The table in Figure 5-7 summarizes the changes in consumer and producer surplus when the auto seats market is opened to imports. Consumers gain surplus equal to the areas $X + Z$. Producers lose surplus equal to X. So the sum of producer and consumer surplus—the total surplus generated in the auto seats market—increases by Z. As a result of trade, consumers gain and producers lose, but the gain to consumers exceeds the loss to producers.

This is an important result. We have just shown that opening up a market to imports leads to a net gain in total surplus, which is what we should have

FIGURE **5-7** The Effects of Imports on Surplus

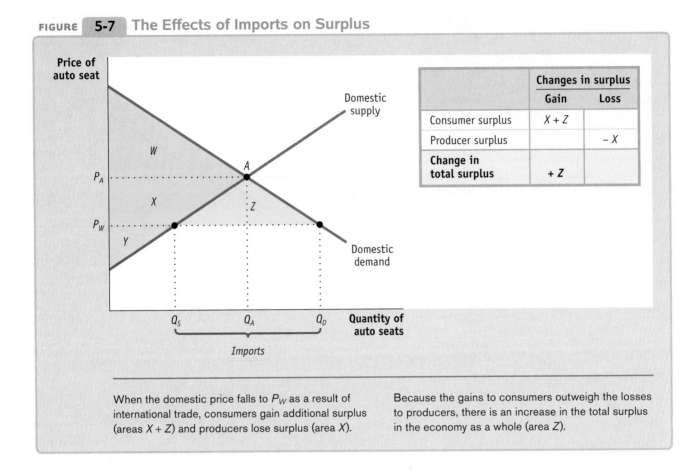

When the domestic price falls to P_W as a result of international trade, consumers gain additional surplus (areas $X + Z$) and producers lose surplus (area X).

Because the gains to consumers outweigh the losses to producers, there is an increase in the total surplus in the economy as a whole (area Z).

expected given the proposition that there are gains from international trade. However, we have also learned that although the country as a whole gains, some groups—in this case, domestic producers of auto parts—lose as a result of international trade. As we'll see shortly, the fact that international trade typically creates losers as well as winners is crucial for understanding the politics of trade policy.

We turn next to the case in which a country exports a good.

The Effects of Exports

Figure 5-8 shows the effects on a country when it exports a good, in this case airplanes. For this example, we assume that unlimited quantities of airplanes can be sold abroad at a given world price, P_W, which is higher than the price that would prevail in the domestic market in autarky, P_A.

The higher world price makes it profitable for exporters to buy airplanes domestically and sell them overseas. The purchases of domestic airplanes drive the domestic price up until it is equal to the world price. As a result, the quantity demanded by domestic consumers falls from Q_A to Q_D and the quantity supplied by domestic producers rises from Q_A to Q_S. This difference between domestic production and domestic consumption, $Q_S - Q_D$, is exported.

Like imports, exports lead to an overall gain in total surplus for the exporting country but also create losers as well as winners. Figure 5-9 shows the effects of airplane exports on producer and consumer surplus. In the absence of trade, the price of each airplane would be P_A. Consumer surplus in the absence of trade is the sum of areas W and X, and producer surplus is area Y. As a result of trade, price rises from P_A to P_W, consumer surplus falls to W, and producer surplus rises to $Y + X + Z$. So producers gain $X + Z$, consumers lose X, and, as shown in the

FIGURE **5-8** The Domestic Market with Exports

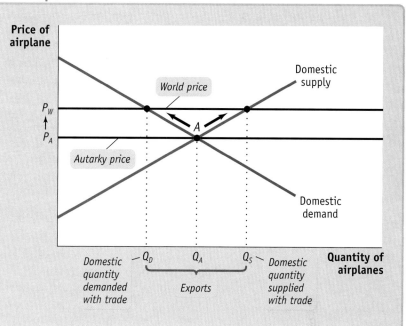

Here the world price, P_W, is greater than the autarky price, P_A. When the economy is opened to international trade, some of the domestic supply is now exported. The domestic price rises from the autarky price, P_A, to the world price, P_W. As the price rises, the domestic quantity demanded falls from Q_A to Q_D and the domestic quantity supplied rises from Q_A to Q_S. The portion of domestic production that is not consumed domestically, $Q_S - Q_D$, is exported.

table accompanying the figure, the economy as a whole gains total surplus in the amount of Z.

We have learned, then, that imports of a particular good hurt domestic producers of that good but help domestic consumers, whereas exports of a particular good hurt domestic consumers of that good but help domestic producers. In each case, the gains are larger than the losses.

FIGURE **5-9** The Effects of Exports on Surplus

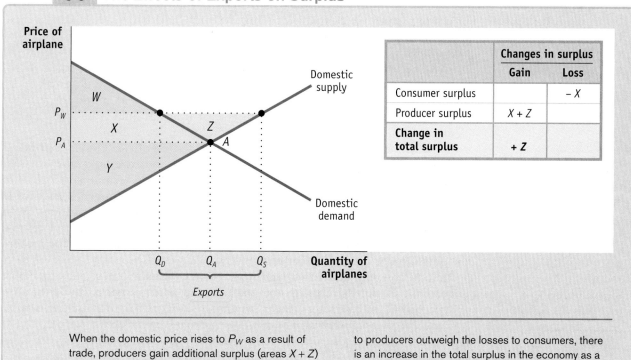

	Changes in surplus	
	Gain	Loss
Consumer surplus		– X
Producer surplus	X + Z	
Change in total surplus	**+ Z**	

When the domestic price rises to P_W as a result of trade, producers gain additional surplus (areas $X + Z$) but consumers lose surplus (area X). Because the gains to producers outweigh the losses to consumers, there is an increase in the total surplus in the economy as a whole (area Z).

International Trade and Wages

So far we have focused on the effects of international trade on producers and consumers in a particular industry. For many purposes this is a very helpful approach. However, producers and consumers are not the only parts of society affected by trade—so are the owners of factors of production. In particular, the owners of labour, land, and capital employed in producing goods that are exported, or goods that compete with imported goods, can be deeply affected by trade.

Moreover, the effects of trade aren't limited to just those industries that export or compete with imports because *factors of production can often move between industries.* So now we turn our attention to the long-run effects of international trade on income distribution—how a country's total income is allocated among its various factors of production.

To begin our analysis, consider the position of Maria, an accountant at Ontario Auto Parts, Inc. If the economy is opened up to imports of auto parts from Mexico, the domestic auto parts industry will contract, and it will hire fewer accountants. But accounting is a profession with employment opportunities in many industries, and Maria might well find a better job in the aircraft industry, which expands as a result of international trade. So it may not be appropriate to think of her as a producer of auto parts who is hurt by competition from imported parts. Rather, we should think of her as an accountant who is affected by auto part imports only to the extent that these imports change the wages of accountants in the economy as a whole.

The wage rate of accountants is a *factor price*—the price employers have to pay for the services of a factor of production. One key question about international trade is how it affects factor prices—not just narrowly defined factors of production like accountants, but broadly defined factors such as capital, unskilled labour, and post-secondary-educated or skilled labour.

Earlier in this chapter we described the Heckscher–Ohlin model of trade, which states that comparative advantage is determined by a country's factor endowment. This model also suggests how international trade affects factor prices in a country: compared to autarky, international trade tends to raise the prices of factors that are abundantly available and reduce the prices of factors that are scarce.

We won't work this out in detail, but the idea is simple. The prices of factors of production, like the prices of goods and services, are determined by supply and demand. If international trade increases the demand for a factor of production, that factor's price will rise; if international trade reduces the demand for a factor of production, that factor's price will fall.

Now think of a country's industries as consisting of two kinds: **exporting industries,** which produce goods and services that are sold abroad, and **import-competing industries,** which produce goods and services that are also imported from abroad. Compared with autarky, international trade leads to higher production in exporting industries and lower production in import-competing industries. This indirectly increases the demand for the factors used by exporting industries and decreases the demand for factors used by import-competing industries.

In addition, the Heckscher–Ohlin model says that a country tends to export goods that are intensive in its abundant factors and to import goods that are intensive in its scarce factors. So *international trade tends to increase the demand for factors that are abundant in our country compared with other countries, and to decrease the demand for factors that are scarce in our country compared with other countries. As a result, the prices of abundant factors tend to rise, and the prices of scarce factors tend to fall as international trade grows.* In other words, international

Exporting industries produce goods and services that are sold abroad.

Import-competing industries produce goods and services that are also imported.

trade tends to redistribute income toward a country's abundant factors and away from its less abundant factors.

The Economics in Action at the end of the preceding section pointed out that U.S. exports tend to be human-capital-intensive and U.S. imports tend to be unskilled-labour-intensive. This suggests that the effect of international trade on U.S. factor markets is to raise the wage rate of highly educated American workers and reduce the wage rate of unskilled American workers.

This effect has been a source of much concern in recent years. Wage inequality—the gap between the wages of high-paid and low-paid workers—has increased substantially over the last 30 years. Some economists believe that growing international trade is an important factor in that trend. If international trade has the effects predicted by the Heckscher–Ohlin model, its growth raises the wages of highly educated North American workers, who already have relatively high wages, and lowers the wages of less educated North American workers, who already have relatively low wages. But keep in mind another phenomenon: trade reduces the income inequality *between* countries as poor countries improve their standard of living by exporting to rich countries.

How important are these effects? In some historical episodes, the impacts of international trade on factor prices have been very large. As we explain in the following Economics in Action, the opening of transatlantic trade in the late nineteenth century had a large negative impact on land rents in Europe, hurting landowners but helping workers and owners of capital.

The effects of trade on wages in Canada and the United States have generated considerable controversy in recent years. Most economists who have studied the issue agree that growing imports of labour-intensive products from newly industrializing economies, and the export of high-technology goods in return, have helped cause a widening wage gap between highly educated and less educated workers in developed nations like Canada and the United States. However, most economists believe that it is only one of several forces explaining the growth in North American wage inequality.

ECONOMICS ▸ IN ACTION

TRADE, WAGES, AND LAND PRICES IN THE NINETEENTH CENTURY

Beginning around 1870, there was an explosive growth of world trade in agricultural products, based largely on the steam engine. Steam-powered ships could cross the ocean much more quickly and reliably than sailing ships. Until about 1860, steamships had higher costs than sailing ships, but after that costs dropped sharply. At the same time, steam-powered rail transport made it possible to bring grain and other bulk goods cheaply from the interior to ports. The result was that land-abundant countries—Canada, the United States, Argentina, and Australia—began shipping large quantities of agricultural goods to the densely populated, land-scarce countries of Europe.

This opening up of international trade led to higher prices of agricultural products, such as wheat, in exporting countries and a decline in

International trade redistributes income toward a country's abundant factors and away from its less abundant factors.

their prices in importing countries. Notably, the difference between wheat prices in western Canada and England plunged.

The change in agricultural prices created winners and losers on both sides of the Atlantic as factor prices adjusted. In England, land prices fell by half compared with average wages; landowners found their purchasing power sharply reduced, but workers benefitted from cheaper food. In Canada, the reverse happened: land prices doubled compared with wages. Landowners did very well, but workers found the purchasing power of their wages dented by rising food prices.

CHECK YOUR UNDERSTANDING 5-2

1. Due to a strike by truckers, trade in food between Canada and Mexico is halted. In autarky, the price of Mexican grapes is lower than that of Canadian grapes. Using a diagram of the Canadian domestic demand curve and the Canadian domestic supply curve for grapes, explain the effect of these events on the following.
   a. Canadian grape consumers' surplus
   b. Canadian grape producers' surplus
   c. Canadian total surplus
2. What effect do you think this event will have on Mexican grape producers? Mexican grape pickers? Mexican grape consumers? Canadian grape pickers?

Solutions appear at back of book.

The Effects of Trade Protection

Ever since David Ricardo laid out the principle of comparative advantage in the early nineteenth century, most economists have advocated **free trade.** That is, they have argued that government policy should not attempt either to reduce or to increase the levels of exports and imports that occur naturally as a result of supply and demand. Despite the free-trade arguments of economists, however, many governments use taxes and other restrictions to limit imports. Less frequently, governments offer subsidies to encourage exports. Policies that limit imports, usually with the goal of protecting domestic producers in import-competing industries from foreign competition, are known as **trade protection** or simply as **protection.**

Let's look at the two most common protectionist policies, tariffs and import quotas, then turn to the reasons governments follow these policies.

The Effects of a Tariff

A **tariff** is a form of excise tax, one that is levied only on sales of imported goods. For example, the Canadian government could declare that anyone bringing in auto seats must pay a tariff of $100 per unit. In the distant past, tariffs were an important source of government revenue because they were relatively easy to collect. But in the modern world, tariffs are usually intended to discourage imports and protect import-competing domestic producers rather than as a source of government revenue.

The tariff raises both the price received by domestic producers and the price paid by domestic consumers. Suppose, for example, that our country imports auto seats, and an auto seat costs $200 on the world market. As we saw earlier, under free trade the domestic price would also be $200. But if a tariff of $100 per

An economy has **free trade** when the government does not attempt either to reduce or to increase the levels of exports and imports that occur naturally as a result of supply and demand.

Policies that limit imports are known as **trade protection** or simply as **protection.**

A **tariff** is a tax levied on imports.

FIGURE   **5-10**   The Effect of a Tariff

FIGURE   **5-10**   The Effect of a Tariff

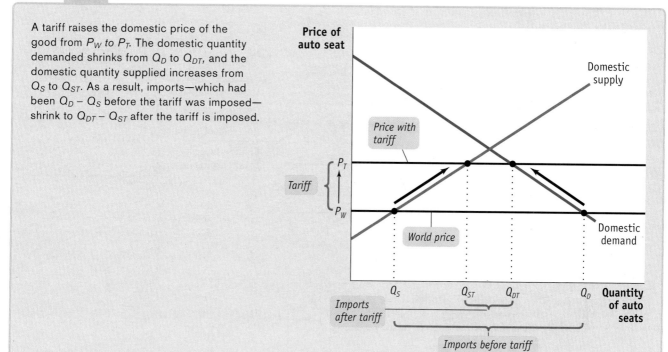

A tariff raises the domestic price of the good from P_W to P_T. The domestic quantity demanded shrinks from Q_D to Q_{DT}, and the domestic quantity supplied increases from Q_S to Q_{ST}. As a result, imports—which had been $Q_D - Q_S$ before the tariff was imposed—shrink to $Q_{DT} - Q_{ST}$ after the tariff is imposed.

unit is imposed, the domestic price will rise to $300, because it won't be profitable to import auto seats unless the price in the domestic market is high enough to compensate importers for the cost of paying the tariff.

Figure 5-10 illustrates the effects of a tariff on imports of auto seats. As before, we assume that P_W is the world price of an auto seat. Before the tariff is imposed, imports have driven the domestic price down to P_W, so that pre-tariff domestic production is Q_S, pre-tariff domestic consumption is Q_D, and pre-tariff imports are $Q_D - Q_S$.

Now suppose that the government imposes a tariff on each auto seat imported. As a consequence, it is no longer profitable to import auto seats unless the domestic price received by the importer is greater than or equal to the world price *plus* the tariff. So the domestic price rises to P_T, which is equal to the world price, P_W, plus the tariff. Domestic production rises to Q_{ST}, domestic consumption falls to Q_{DT}, and imports fall to $Q_{DT} - Q_{ST}$.

A tariff, then, raises domestic prices, leading to increased domestic production and reduced domestic consumption compared to the situation under free trade. Figure 5-11 shows the effects on surplus. There are three effects:

1. The higher domestic price increases producer surplus, a gain equal to area *A*.

2. The higher domestic price reduces consumer surplus, a reduction equal to the sum of areas *A*, *B*, *C*, and *D*.

3. The tariff yields revenue to the government. How much revenue? The government collects the tariff—which, remember, is equal to the difference between P_T and P_W on each of the $Q_{DT} - Q_{ST}$ units imported. So total revenue is $(P_T - P_W) \times (Q_{DT} - Q_{ST})$. This is equal to area *C*.

The welfare effects of a tariff are summarized in the table in Figure 5-11. Producers gain, consumers lose, and the government gains. But consumer losses are greater than the sum of producer and government gains, leading to a net reduction in total surplus equal to areas *B* + *D*.

FIGURE **5-11** A Tariff Reduces Total Surplus

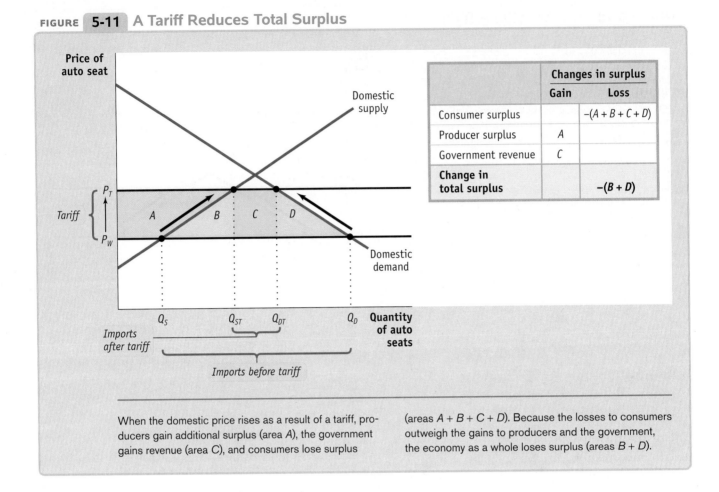

		Changes in surplus	
		Gain	Loss
Consumer surplus			$-(A + B + C + D)$
Producer surplus		A	
Government revenue		C	
Change in total surplus			$-(B + D)$

When the domestic price rises as a result of a tariff, producers gain additional surplus (area A), the government gains revenue (area C), and consumers lose surplus (areas $A + B + C + D$). Because the losses to consumers outweigh the gains to producers and the government, the economy as a whole loses surplus (areas $B + D$).

A tariff creates inefficiency, or **deadweight loss,** because it prevents mutually beneficial trades from occurring. The deadweight loss imposed on society is equal to the loss in total surplus represented by areas $B + D$.

Tariffs generate deadweight losses because they create inefficiencies in two ways:

1. Some mutually beneficial trades go unexploited: some consumers who are willing to pay more than the world price, P_W, do not purchase the good, even though P_W is the true cost of a unit of the good to the economy. The cost of this inefficiency is represented in Figure 5-11 by area D.

2. The economy's resources are wasted on inefficient production: some producers whose cost exceeds P_W produce the good, even though an additional unit of the good can be purchased abroad for P_W. The cost of this inefficiency is represented in Figure 5-11 by area B.

The Effects of an Import Quota

Deadweight loss is the loss in total surplus that occurs whenever an action or a policy reduces the quantity transacted below the efficient market equilibrium quantity.

An **import quota** is a legal limit on the quantity of a good that can be imported.

An **import quota,** another form of trade protection, is a legal limit on the quantity of a good that can be imported. For example, a Canadian import quota on Mexican auto seats might limit the quantity imported each year to 50 000 units. Import quotas are usually administered through licences: a number of licences are issued, each giving the licence-holder the right to import a limited quantity of the good each year.

An import quota has the same effect as a tariff, with one difference: the money that would otherwise have been government revenue becomes quota rents to licence-holders ("Quota rent" was defined in Chapter 4). Look again at Figure 5-11. An import quota that limits imports to $Q_{DT} - Q_{ST}$ will raise the domestic price of auto parts by the same amount as the tariff we considered previously. That is, it will raise the domestic price from P_W to P_T. However, area C will now represent quota rents rather than government revenue.

Who receives import licences and so collects the quota rents? In the case of Canadian import protection, the answer may surprise you: the most important import licences—mainly for textiles and clothing—are granted to foreign governments.

Because the quota rents for most Canadian import quotas go to foreigners, the cost to Canada of such quotas is larger than that of a comparable tariff (a tariff that leads to the same level of imports). In Figure 5-11, the net loss to Canada from such an import quota would be equal to areas $B + C + D$, the difference between consumer losses and producer gains.

When a country imposes trade barriers (import tariffs or import quotas), it has economic impacts on foreign countries. Both types of barriers, in effect, raise the price of foreign products in the importing country and lower the domestic demand for foreign goods. This reduction of domestic demand for foreign goods could lead to job losses and reduced export revenues in foreign countries. In the case of poor or developing countries, the impact of such barriers on their exports may have profound negative effects on their economies.

ECONOMICS > IN ACTION

TRADE PROTECTION IN CANADA

Canada was created as a nation by the British North America Act of 1867. At that time, Canada's western provinces were barely settled, most of the country's trading links were north–south, there was no transcontinental railway, and Canada's fledgling manufacturing industry faced stiff competition from the United States and Britain.

In an attempt to forge Canada's small, diverse, and far-flung people into a single nation, the government of Sir John A. Macdonald implemented a "National Policy" in 1879. This policy had several pillars. It involved encouraging western settlement with homestead grants of free land. It involved building a transcontinental railway to transport manufactured goods from the East and to route food from the West. And, most significantly, it involved a system of high tariffs designed to protect and promote Canadian manufacturing. The aim of the National Policy was to replace existing north–south trading relationships with newly created east–west ones, to create a national market, and to achieve a truly east–west transcontinental union. The tariffs were part of this nation-building enterprise.

Since then, Canada and its infant industries have grown up. In 1947, Canada and 22 other countries signed the General Agreement on Tariffs and Trade (GATT) with the aim of reducing trade barriers. Successive waves of negotiations resulted in additional rounds of GATT, the most notable being the Uruguay Round, completed in 1994. This round had success on four broad fronts. First, it succeeded in reducing world tariffs by about 40%. Second, while Canada and the European Union (EU) prevented an agreement on liberalizing trade in agricultural goods, both were forced to replace agricultural quotas with "tariff equivalents." Those countries pushing for free trade in agricultural goods hoped that pressure would build for reduction of the high tariffs over subsequent decades. Third, quotas restricting trade in textiles and garments had to be phased out over a 10-year period ending January 1, 2005. Fourth, and perhaps most significant, the Uruguay Round eliminated the GATT structure and replaced it with the World Trade Organization (WTO), which has a formal dispute settlement mechanism and whose rulings are binding on member governments.

Besides these multilateral agreements toward trade liberalization, Canada has also negotiated separately with the United States. In 1989 Canada and the United States signed a Free Trade Agreement (FTA), and in 1994 the North American Free Trade Agreement (NAFTA) extended the original agreement to include Mexico.

In recent years, Canada has negotiated with the EU toward a comprehensive economic and trade agreement (CETA), a very ambitious trade initiative because of the size of the EU. These trade negotiations covered many sectors, from agricultural to manufacturing, from the lumber industry to the information technology industry. Even though it is not easy to enter into such an agreement (since it is very difficult for countries to reach consensus on the various issues), Canada and the EU finally signed a free trade agreement in principle on October 18, 2013. For the deal to start in 2015, it requires ratification by all Canadian provinces and territories and all EU member countries. Once the CETA is implemented, most tariffs between Canada and the EU will be eliminated.

Canada today generally follows a policy of free trade, at least in comparison with other countries and in comparison with its own past. Most manufactured goods are subject to either no tariff or a low tariff. However, Canada does still limit imports of many agricultural goods, textiles, and clothing, and has export controls on some agricultural products and strategic goods. According to the Department of Foreign Affairs, Trade, and Development, the federal department that is responsible for issues related to Canada's international trade, import and export controls are justified for the following reasons:

- To protect national security
- To protect domestic industries that are deemed strategic or vulnerable
- To fulfill other international obligations
- To implement United Nations Security Council trade sanctions

▼ Quick Review

- Most economists advocate **free trade,** although many governments engage in **trade protection** of import-competing industries. The two most common protectionist policies are tariffs and import quotas. In rare instances, governments subsidize exporting industries.

- A **tariff** is a tax on imports. It raises the domestic price above the world price, leading to a fall in trade and domestic consumption and a rise in domestic production. Domestic producers and the government gain, but domestic consumer losses more than offset this gain, leading to **deadweight loss.**

- An **import quota** is a legal quantity limit on imports. Its effect is like that of a tariff, except that revenues—the quota rents—accrue to the licence-holder, not to the domestic government.

CHECK YOUR UNDERSTANDING 5-3

1. Suppose the world price of butter is $2.00 per kilogram and the domestic price in autarky is $4.00 per kilogram. Use a diagram similar to Figure 5-10 to show the following.
   a. If there is free trade, domestic butter producers want the government to impose a tariff of no less than $2.00 per kilogram.
   b. A tariff greater than $2.00 per kilogram is imposed.

2. Suppose the government imposes an import quota rather than a tariff on butter. What quota limit would generate the same quantity of imports as a tariff of $2.00 per kilogram?

Solutions appear at back of book.

The Political Economy of Trade Protection

We have seen that international trade produces mutual benefits to the countries that engage in it. We have also seen that tariffs and import quotas, although they produce winners as well as losers, reduce total surplus. Yet many countries continue to impose tariffs and import quotas as well as to enact other protectionist measures.

To understand why trade protection takes place, we will first look at some common justifications for protection. Then we will look at the politics of trade protection. Finally, we will look at an important feature of trade protection in today's world: tariffs and import quotas are the subject of international negotiation and are policed by international organizations.

Arguments for Trade Protection

Advocates for tariffs and import quotas offer a variety of arguments. Three common arguments are *national security, job creation,* and the *infant industry argument.*

The national security argument is based on the proposition that overseas sources of goods are vulnerable to disruption in times of international conflict; therefore, a country should protect domestic suppliers of crucial goods, with the aim to be self-sufficient in those goods. In the 1960s, the United States—which had begun to import oil as domestic oil reserves ran low—had an import quota on oil, justified on national security grounds. Currently, Canada imposes import restrictions on agricultural products to protect Canadian farmers, ensure a stable domestic supply of food, and prevent price fluctuations.

The job creation argument points to the additional jobs created in import-competing industries as a result of trade protection.[2] Economists argue that these jobs are offset by the jobs lost elsewhere, such as industries that use imported inputs and now face higher input costs. But non-economists don't always find this argument persuasive.

Finally, the infant industry argument, often raised in newly industrializing countries, holds that new industries require a temporary period of trade protection to get established. For example, in the 1950s many countries in Latin America imposed tariffs and import quotas on manufactured goods, in an effort to switch from their traditional role as exporters of raw materials to a new status as industrial countries.

In theory, the argument for infant industry protection can be compelling, particularly in high-tech industries that increase a country's overall skill level. Reality, however, is more complicated: it is most often industries that are politically influential that gain protection. In addition, governments tend to be poor predictors of the best emerging technologies. Finally, it is often very difficult to wean an industry from protection when it should be mature enough to stand on its own.

The Politics of Trade Protection

In reality, much trade protection has little to do with the arguments just described. Instead, it reflects the political influence of import-competing producers.

We've seen that a tariff or import quota leads to gains for import-competing producers and losses for consumers. Producers, however, usually have much more influence over trade policy decisions. The producers who compete with imports of a particular good are usually a smaller, more cohesive group than the consumers of that good.

An example is trade protection for eggs: Canada has a limit on how many eggs can be imported, which on average causes our domestic price to be higher than the world price, so Canadian families pay more for the eggs they consume. For example, according to the *National Post,* a carton of eggs cost about $3.19 in Vancouver but only $2.09 in Washington State in 2012 (the higher price was mostly caused by an import quota and supply management policies). This quota is difficult to rationalize in terms of any economic argument. However, consumers rarely complain about the quota because they are unaware that it exists. According to Agriculture and Agri-Food Canada, Canadian egg consumption was 16.1 dozen per person in 2009. At that rate, the average Canadian would pay about $18 more a year for eggs

[2]Advocates of "buy local" policies encourage domestic households, firms, and governments to buy from domestic producers rather than foreign producers. To support their position, they sometimes appeal to the job-creation angle, in addition to citing the benefits from less pollution and greater environmental sustainabiity that buying local will bring.

International trade agreements are treaties in which a country promises to engage in less trade protection against the exports of other countries in return for a promise by other countries to do the same for its own exports.

The **North American Free Trade Agreement, or NAFTA,** is a trade agreement between Canada, the United States, and Mexico.

The **World Trade Organization, or WTO,** oversees international trade agreements and rules on disputes between countries over those agreements.

than an American with similar egg consumption would, a difference small enough to not attract notice. But, according to Egg Farmers of Canada, although there are only a few thousand egg farmers in Canada, the Canadian egg industry employs 16 800 people across the country and contributes $1.4 billion to Canada's output. They are very aware of the benefits they receive from the quota and they make sure that their interest in the matter is heard in Parliament.

Given these political realities, it may seem surprising that trade is as free as it is. For example, Canada has low tariffs, and its import quotas are mainly confined to clothing and a few agricultural products. It would be nice to say that the main reason trade protection is so limited is that economists have convinced governments of the virtues of free trade. A more important reason, however, is the role of *international trade agreements.*

International Trade Agreements and the World Trade Organization

When a country engages in trade protection, it hurts two groups. We've already emphasized the adverse effect on domestic consumers, but protection also hurts foreign export industries. This means that countries care about one anothers' trade policies: the Canadian lumber industry, for example, has a strong interest in keeping U.S. tariffs on forest products low.

Because countries care about one anothers' trade policies, they enter into **international trade agreements:** treaties in which a country promises to engage in less trade protection against the exports of another country in return for a promise by the other country to do the same for its own exports. Most world trade is now governed by such agreements.

Some international trade agreements involve just two countries or a small group of countries. As we mentioned in the opening story, Canada, the United States, and Mexico are joined together by the **North American Free Trade Agreement, or NAFTA.** This agreement, signed in 1993, will eventually remove all barriers to trade among the three nations. In Europe, as of July 1, 2013, 28 nations are part of an even more comprehensive agreement, the European Union, or EU. In NAFTA, the member countries set their own tariff rates against imports from other non-member countries. The EU, however, is a *customs union:* tariffs are levied at the same rate on goods from outside the EU entering the union.

There are also global trade agreements covering most of the world. Such global agreements are overseen by the **World Trade Organization, or WTO,** an international organization composed of 151 member countries, accounting for the bulk of world trade. The WTO plays two roles. First, it provides the framework for the massively complex negotiations involved in a major international trade agreement (the full text of the last major agreement, approved in 1994, was 24 000 pages long). Second, the WTO resolves disputes between its members. These disputes typically arise when one country claims that another country's policies violate its previous agreements.

The WTO is sometimes, with great exaggeration, described as a world government. In fact, it has no army, no police, and no direct enforcement power. The grain of truth in that description is that when a country joins the WTO, it agrees to accept the organization's judgments—and these judgments apply not only to tariffs and import quotas but also to domestic policies that the organization considers trade protection disguised under another name. So in joining the WTO a country does give up some of its sovereignty.

Trade disputes among countries usually take a long time to get resolved. By the time a settlement or a resolution has been reached, a significant amount of costs or hardships may have been incurred. As seen in the For Inquiring Minds on the next page, countries may not follow the intent of the agreements. Having an agreement and abiding by that agreement are not necessarily the same thing.

SOFTWOOD LUMBER DISPUTE

The softwood lumber dispute between Canada and the United States has a long history. Since 1982, there have been several points of contention between the two nations, but at the core of the dispute have been American claims regarding Canada's system of stumpage, a fee that provincial governments set and charge logging companies for the right to harvest lumber from public land (the logging right). The United States has argued that the fee is too low and has viewed it as a subsidy to Canadian-based lumber producers. According to this view, Canadian lumber producers could sell lumber at a price lower than the American lumber producers, constituting unfair trade and hurting the American lumber industry.

In response to these complaints from the U.S. lumber industry, the U.S. Department of Commerce imposed countervailing duties on Canadian softwood lumber.[3] At the Canadian government's request, a dispute-resolution panel of five experts was selected according to the Canada–U.S. Free Trade Agreement. Rulings were in Canada's favour. However, the U.S. government challenged the rulings and delayed the removal of the countervailing duties. On May 29, 1996, Canada and the United States finalized the Softwood Lumber Agreement 1996, covering the five-year period to March 31, 2001. The essence of this agreement was a tariff rate quota administered by Canada whereby 14.7 billion board feet of lumber could be shipped duty-free to the United States annually. Amounts over 14.7 billion board feet were subject to increasingly prohibitive tariff rates. Also, exports from Atlantic Canada were unrestricted.

As the agreement approached its end in 2001, the U.S. lumber industry lobbied to the U.S. Department of Commerce again for the imposition of countervailing duties. This time the United States imposed a 27% duty on Canadian softwood lumber based on the claims that Canada unfairly subsidized lumber producers and that Canadian lumber was sold at a lower price in the United States than in Canada (referred to as *dumping* in international trade). Once again, Canada appealed this 27% duty to NAFTA and WTO panels, and again, many of the rulings were in favour of Canada. The settlement breakthrough came in 2006, when Canada and the United States reached an agreement to provide a resolution to the softwood lumber dispute. In the 2006 Softwood Lumber Agreement, the United States was to remove the countervailing and anti-dumping duties, and to return over US$4 billion in duties collected from Canadian importers since 2002. The agreement had a seven-year term, with a possible two-year extension.

The signing of the 2006 Softwood Lumber Agreement did not really end the softwood lumber dispute. In recent years, the United States has filed several cases to the London Court of International Arbitration regarding the implementation of the agreement by Canada. Some of the rulings from the London Court of International Arbitration favoured Canada and some did not, so the future of Canada's softwood lumber industry remains uncertain.

New Challenges to Globalization

The forward march of globalization over the past century is generally considered a major political and economic success. Economists and policymakers alike have viewed growing world trade, in particular, as a good thing. We would be remiss, however, if we failed to acknowledge that many people are having second thoughts about globalization. To a large extent, these second thoughts reflect two concerns shared by many economists: worries about the effects of globalization on inequality and worries that new developments, in particular the growth in *offshore outsourcing,* are increasing economic insecurity.

Globalization and Inequality We've already mentioned the implications of international trade for factor prices, such as wages: when wealthy countries like Canada export skill-intensive products like aircraft while importing labour-intensive products like clothing, they can expect to see the wage gap between more educated and less educated domestic workers widen. Thirty years ago, this wasn't a significant concern, because most of the goods wealthy countries imported from poorer countries were raw materials or goods where comparative advantage depended on climate. Today, however, many manufactured goods are imported from relatively poor countries, with a potentially much larger effect on the distribution of income.

[3]A government imposes countervailing duties on imported goods that it feels are unfairly subsidized by the exporting nation; the reason for imposing countervailing duties is to minimize the negative effects of a subsidized imported good on the domestic industry.

Offshore outsourcing takes place when businesses hire people in another country to perform various tasks.

Trade with China, in particular, raises concerns among labour groups trying to maintain wage levels in rich countries. Although China has experienced spectacular economic growth since the economic reforms that began in the late 1970s, it remains a relatively poor, low-wage country. In 2012, wages of Chinese manufacturing workers were only about 14% of their Canadian counterparts' wages. Meanwhile, imports from China have soared. In 1992, only 1.67% of Canada's imports came from China; by 2012, the figure had risen to 11%. There's not much question that these surging imports from China put at least some downward pressure on the wages of less educated Canadian workers.

Outsourcing Chinese exports to Canada overwhelmingly consist of labour-intensive manufactured goods. However, some Canadian workers have recently found themselves facing a new form of international competition. *Outsourcing,* in which a company hires another company to perform some task, such as running the corporate computer system, is a long-standing business practice. Until recently, however, outsourcing was normally done locally, with a company hiring another company in the same city or country.

Now, modern telecommunications increasingly makes it possible to engage in **offshore outsourcing,** in which businesses hire people in another country to perform various tasks. The classic example is call centres: the person answering the phone when you call a company's 1-800 help line may well be in India, which has taken the lead in attracting offshore outsourcing. Offshore outsourcing has also spread to fields such as software design/programming and the financial sector. In April 2013, the Royal Bank of Canada (RBC) came under fire when the public found out the bank had outsourced 45 of its information technology (IT) jobs to foreign workers. Although the number of positions being outsourced seems small, it was sufficient to cause concerns among Canadians. According to International Data Corporation (IDC) Canada, this recent outsourcing of 45 IT jobs by RBC is just the tip of an iceberg. An IDC Canada survey found that 6 out of 10 Canadian firms would use outsourcing as a means to cut costs. It is not surprising then that some economists have warned that millions or even tens of millions of North American workers who have never thought they could face foreign competition for their jobs may face unpleasant surprises in the not-too-distant future.

Concerns about income distribution and outsourcing, as we've said, are shared by many economists. There is also, however, widespread opposition to globalization. In 1999, an attempt to start a major round of trade negotiations failed in part because the WTO meeting, in Seattle, was disrupted by antiglobalization demonstrators. However, the more important reason for its failure was disagreement among the countries represented. Another round of negotiations that began in 2001 in Doha, Qatar, known as the "Doha development round," stalled in 2008, mainly because of disagreements over agricultural trade rules. No significant progress has been made since then.

What motivates the antiglobalization movement? To some extent it's the sweatshop labour fallacy: it's easy to get outraged about the low wages paid to the person who made your shirt, and harder to appreciate how much worse off that person would be if denied the opportunity to sell goods in rich countries' markets. It's also true, however, that the movement represents a backlash against supporters of globalization who have oversold its benefits. Countries in Latin America, in particular, were promised that reducing their tariff rates would produce an economic takeoff; instead, they have experienced disappointing results. Some groups, such as poor farmers facing new competition from imported food, ended up worse off.

Do these new challenges to globalization undermine the argument that international trade is a good thing? The great

To some extent, the antiglobalization movement is motivated by the sweatshop labour fallacy.

Justin Lane/epa/Corbis

majority of economists would argue that the gains from reducing trade protection still exceed the losses. However, it has become more important than before to make sure that the gains from international trade are widely spread. And the politics of international trade is becoming increasingly difficult as the extent of trade has grown.

ECONOMICS ▶ IN ACTION

FREEING CANADA'S TRADE WITH THE WORLD

On December 5, 1996, government officials from Canada and Chile signed the Canada–Chile Free Trade Agreement (CCFTA). This bilateral trade agreement covering trade in both goods and services significantly liberalized trade between Canada and Chile. It was Canada's first free trade agreement with a South American country and was Chile's first comprehensive free trade agreement. The agreement, which was implemented on July 5, 1997, eliminated tariffs on 75% of the trade between the two countries and contained commitments to reduce non-tariff barriers.

Between 1997 and 2012, bilateral trade increased 350% and Canadian direct investment in Chile grew by over 300%. According to the Chilean government, Canada is the third largest investor overall in Chile—first in the mining sector—and the largest source of new direct investment in Chile in the past decade.

On April 16, 2012, Prime Minister Stephen Harper and Chilean president Sebastian Pinera signed an expanded CCFTA document.

Prime Minister Stephen Harper and Chilean president Sebastian Pinera at the signing of the expanded CCFTA.

This amended agreement contains a section that will ensures Canadian financial services firms, such as banks and insurance companies, will enjoy preferential access to the Chilean market. It also contains new dispute settlement procedures and provisions on government procurement and customs procedures.

The government of Canada continues to negotiate other potential important trade agreements. For example, after years of negotiation, an agreement in principle on a CETA between Canada and the European Union (EU) was reached in late 2013. The EU is home to more than 500 million people and the world's largest economy, producing more than $16 trillion worth of output in 2012. In the joint press conference with EU president Jose Manuel Barroso, Prime Minister Harper said that the CETA "is the biggest deal our country has ever made. This is a historic win for Canada." Canada has also joined the Trans-Pacific Partnership (TPP), which consists of twelve Pacific nations: Australia, Brunei, Canada, Chile, Japan, Malaysia, Mexico, New Zealand, Peru, Singapore, the United States, and Vietnam. The TPP represents a population of almost 800 million people and a combined output of $27.5 trillion, more than 38% of the world's economy. These countries have held 18 rounds of talks on the possibility of reaching a comprehensive free trade agreement among all 12 member countries.

CHECK YOUR UNDERSTANDING   5-4

1. In Canada, over half of the steel consumed domestically is imported and steel is an input in many Canadian industries. The federal government has imposed import controls on steel and a variety of consumer goods. Explain why political lobbying to eliminate import controls on steel is more likely to be effective than lobbying to eliminate import controls on consumer goods such as clothing and eggs.

2. Over the years, the WTO has increasingly found itself adjudicating trade disputes that involve not just tariffs or quota restrictions but also restrictions based on quality, health, and environmental considerations. Why do you think this has occurred? What method would you, as a WTO official, use to decide whether a quality, health, or environmental restriction is in violation of a free trade agreement?

Solutions appear at back of book.

▼ Quick Review

● The three major justifications for trade protection are national security, job creation, and protection of infant industries.

● Despite the deadweight losses, import protections are often imposed because groups representing import-competing industries are more influential than groups of consumers.

● To further trade liberalization, countries engage in **international trade agreements.** Some agreements are among a small number of countries, such as the **North American Free Trade Agreement (NAFTA)** and the European Union (EU). The **World Trade Organization (WTO)** seeks to negotiate global trade agreements and referee trade disputes between members.

● Resistance to globalization has emerged in response to a surge in imports from relatively poor countries and the **offshore outsourcing** of many jobs that had been considered safe from foreign competition.

• Li & Fung: From Guangzhou to You

Daniel J. Groshong/Bloomberg via Getty Images

It's a very good bet that as you read this, you're wearing something manufactured in Asia. And if you are, it's also a good bet that the Hong Kong company Li & Fung was involved in getting your garment designed, produced, and shipped to your local store. From Levi's to Aéropostale to Walmart, Li & Fung is a critical conduit from factories around the world to the shopping mall nearest you.

The company was founded in 1906 in Guangzhou, China. According to Victor Fung, the company's chairman, his grandfather's "value added" was that he spoke English, allowing him to serve as an interpreter in business deals between Chinese and foreigners. When Mao's Communist Party seized control in mainland China, the company moved to Hong Kong. There, as Hong Kong's market economy took off during the 1960s and 1970s, Li & Fung grew as an export broker, bringing together Hong Kong manufacturers and foreign buyers.

The real transformation of the company came, however, as Asian economies grew and changed. Hong Kong's rapid growth led to rising wages, making Li & Fung increasingly uncompetitive in garments, its main business. So the company reinvented itself: rather than being a simple broker, it became a "supply chain manager." Not only would it allocate production of a good to a manufacturer, it would also break production down, allocate production of the inputs, and then allocate final assembly of the good among its 12 000+ suppliers around the globe. Sometimes production would be done in sophisticated economies like those of Hong Kong or even Japan, where wages are high but so is quality and productivity; sometimes it would be done in less advanced locations like mainland China or Thailand, where labour is less productive but cheaper.

For example, suppose you own a Canadian retail chain and want to sell garment-washed blue jeans. Rather than simply arrange for production of the jeans, Li & Fung will work with you on their design, providing you with the latest production and style information, like what materials and colours are hot. After the design has been finalized, Li & Fung will arrange for the creation of a prototype, find the most cost-effective way to manufacture it, and then place an order on your behalf. Through Li & Fung, the yarn might be made in Korea and dyed in Taiwan, and the jeans sewn in Thailand or mainland China. And because production is taking place in so many locations, Li & Fung provides transport logistics as well as quality control.

Li & Fung has been enormously successful. In 2012 the company had a market capitalization of approximately US$14.8 billion and business turnover of US$20.2 billion, with offices and distribution centres in more than 40 countries. Li & Fung employs more than 28 000 people worldwide and has access to a sourcing network of over 15 000 suppliers.

QUESTIONS FOR THOUGHT

1. Why do you think it was profitable for Li & Fung to go beyond brokering exports to becoming a supply chain manager, breaking down the production process and sourcing the inputs from various suppliers across many countries?

2. What principle do you think underlies Li & Fung's decisions on how to allocate production of a good's inputs and its final assembly among various countries?

3. Why do you think a retailer prefers to have Li & Fung arrange international production of its jeans rather than purchase them directly from a jeans manufacturer in mainland China?

4. What is the source of Li & Fung's success? Is it based on human capital, on ownership of a natural resource, or on ownership of capital?

SUMMARY

1. International trade is of growing importance to Canada and of even greater importance to most other countries. International trade, like trade among individuals, arises from comparative advantage: the opportunity cost of producing an additional unit of a good is lower in some countries than in others. Goods and services purchased abroad are **imports;** those sold abroad are **exports.** Foreign trade, like other economic linkages between countries, has been growing rapidly, a phenomenon called **globalization.**

2. The **Ricardian model of international trade** assumes that opportunity costs are constant. It shows that there are gains from trade: two countries are better off with trade than in **autarky.**

3. In practice, comparative advantage reflects differences between countries in climate, factor endowments, and technology. The **Heckscher–Ohlin model** shows how differences in factor endowments determine comparative advantage: goods differ in **factor intensity,** and countries tend to export goods that are intensive in the factors they have in abundance.

4. The **domestic demand curve** and the **domestic supply curve** determine the price of a good in autarky. When international trade occurs, the domestic price is driven to equality with the **world price,** the price at which the good is bought and sold abroad.

5. If the world price is below the autarky price, a good is imported. This leads to an increase in consumer surplus, a fall in producer surplus, and a gain in total surplus. If the world price is above the autarky price, a good is exported. This leads to an increase in producer surplus, a fall in consumer surplus, and a gain in total surplus.

6. International trade leads to expansion in **exporting industries** and contraction in **import-competing industries.** This raises the domestic demand for abundant factors of production, reduces the demand for scarce factors, and so affects factor prices, such as wages.

7. Most economists advocate **free trade,** but in practice many governments engage in **trade protection.** The two most common forms of **protection** are tariffs and quotas. In rare occasions, export industries are subsidized.

8. A **tariff** is a tax levied on imports. It raises the domestic price above the world price, hurting consumers, benefitting domestic producers, and generating government revenue. As a result, total surplus falls and this loss of surplus is called **deadweight loss.** An **import quota** is a legal limit on the quantity of a good that can be imported. It has the same effects as a tariff, except that the revenue goes not to the government but to those who receive import licences.

9. Although several popular arguments have been made in favour of trade protection, in practice the main reason for protection is probably political: import-competing industries are well organized and well informed about how they gain from trade protection, while consumers are unaware of the costs they pay. Still, Canadian trade is fairly free, mainly because of the role of **international trade agreements,** in which countries agree to reduce trade protection against one anothers' exports. The **North American Free Trade Agreement (NAFTA)** and the European Union (EU) cover a small number of countries. In contrast, the **World Trade Organization (WTO)** covers a much larger number of countries, accounting for the bulk of world trade. It oversees trade negotiations and adjudicates disputes among its members.

10. In the past few years, many concerns have been raised about the effects of globalization. One issue is the increase in income inequality due to the surge in imports from relatively poor countries over the past 20 years. Another concern is the increase in **offshore outsourcing,** as many jobs that were once considered safe from foreign competition have been moved abroad.

KEY TERMS

Imports, p. 146
Exports, p. 146
Globalization, p. 146
Ricardian model of international trade, p. 147
Autarky, p. 148
Factor intensity, p. 152
Heckscher–Ohlin model, p. 153

Domestic demand curve, p. 156
Domestic supply curve, p. 156
World price, p. 156
Exporting industries, p. 160
Import-competing industries, p. 160
Free trade, p. 162
Trade protection, p. 162
Protection, p. 162

Tariff, p. 162
Deadweight loss, p. 164
Import quota, p. 164
International trade agreements, p. 168
North American Free Trade Agreement (NAFTA), p. 168
World Trade Organization (WTO), p. 168
Offshore outsourcing, p. 170

1. Assume Saudi Arabia and Canada face the production possibilities for oil and cars shown in the accompanying table.

Saudi Arabia		Canada	
Quantity of oil (millions of barrels)	Quantity of cars (millions)	Quantity of oil (millions of barrels)	Quantity of cars (millions)
0	4	0	10.0
200	3	100	7.5
400	2	200	5.0
600	1	300	2.5
800	0	400	0

   a. What is the opportunity cost of producing a car in Saudi Arabia? In Canada? What is the opportunity cost of producing a barrel of oil in Saudi Arabia? In Canada?

   b. Which country has the comparative advantage in producing oil? In producing cars?

   c. Suppose that in autarky, Saudi Arabia produces 200 million barrels of oil and 3 million cars; similarly, Canada produces 300 million barrels of oil and 2.5 million cars. Without trade, can Saudi Arabia produce more oil *and* more cars? Without trade, can Canada produce more oil *and* more cars?

2. The production possibilities for Canada and Saudi Arabia are given in Problem 1. Suppose now that each country specializes in the good in which it has the comparative advantage, and the two countries trade. Also assume that for each country the value of imports must equal the value of exports.

   a. What is the total quantity of oil produced? What is the total quantity of cars produced?

   b. Is it possible for Saudi Arabia to consume 400 million barrels of oil and 5 million cars and for Canada to consume 400 million barrels of oil and 5 million cars?

   c. Suppose that, in fact, Saudi Arabia consumes 300 million barrels of oil and 4 million cars and Canada consumes 500 million barrels of oil and 6 million cars. How many barrels of oil does Canada import? How many cars does Canada export? Suppose a car costs $10 000 on the world market. How much, then, does a barrel of oil cost on the world market?

3. Both Canada and the United States produce lumber and music CDs with constant opportunity costs. The United States can produce either 10 tonnes of lumber and no CDs, or 1000 CDs and no lumber, or any combination in between. Canada can produce either 8 tonnes of lumber and no CDs, or 400 CDs and no lumber, or any combination in between.

   a. Draw the U.S. and Canadian production possibility frontiers in two separate diagrams, with CDs on the horizontal axis and lumber on the vertical axis.

   b. In autarky, if the United States wants to consume 500 CDs, how much lumber can it consume at most? Label this point *A* in your diagram. Similarly, if Canada wants to consume 1 tonne of lumber, how many CDs can it consume in autarky? Label this point *C* in your diagram.

   c. Which country has the absolute advantage in lumber production?

   d. Which country has the comparative advantage in lumber production?

   Suppose each country specializes in the good in which it has the comparative advantage, and there is trade.

   e. How many CDs does the United States produce? How much lumber does Canada produce?

   f. Is it possible for the United States to consume 500 CDs and 7 tonnes of lumber? Label this point *B* in your diagram. Is it possible for Canada at the same time to consume 500 CDs and 1 tonne of lumber? Label this point *D* in your diagram.

4. For each of the following trade relationships, explain the likely source of the comparative advantage of each of the exporting countries.

   a. Canada exports BlackBerry smart phones to Venezuela, and Venezuela exports oil to Canada.

   b. Canada exports airplanes to China, and China exports clothing to Canada.

   c. Canada exports wheat to Colombia, and Colombia exports coffee to Canada.

5. Industry Canada provides statistics on Canada's imports and exports on its website. The following steps will take you to the foreign trade statistics. Use them to answer the questions below.

   i. Go to Industry Canada's website at www.ic.gc.ca

   ii. At the top of the page, under All topics, look for the subheading "Import, export and investment," and then select "Find import/export statistics"

   iii. Once you reach the Trade Data Online page, click on "Search by industry"

   iv. In the drop-down menu "Trade Type," select "Total Exports" if you are looking for data on exports or "Total Imports" if you are looking for data on imports

   v. In the drop-down menu "Trading Partner," select "TOP 10 countries"

   vi. In the drop-down menu "Time Period," select "Specific Year(s)" and choose the year(s) you want. Try 2012 and any other year you desire.

   vii. In the drop-down menu "Industry Options," select "Browse List of Industries"

   viii. In the drop-down menu "Browse for an industry," select the good or service you are interested in, or use the North American Industry Classification System (NAICS) code, then hit "View Industries"

ix. In the "Industry List," choose the industry you are interested in and hit "Add to Selected Industries"

x. Click on "Run Report"

a. Look up recent data for Canadian imports of clothing accessories and other clothing manufacturing (NAICS code 3159). From which country do we import the most clothing accessories? Which of the three sources of comparative advantage (climate, factor endowments, and technology) accounts for that country's comparative advantage in clothing accessories?

b. Look up recent data for Canadian imports of fruits (NAICS code 1113). From which country do we import the most fruit? Which of the three sources of comparative advantage (climate, factor endowments, and technology) accounts for that country's comparative advantage in fruit?

c. Look up recent data for Canadian imports of industrial machinery (NAICS code 3332). From which country do we import the most industrial machinery? Which of the three sources of comparative advantage (climate, factor endowments, and technology) accounts for that country's comparative advantage in industrial machinery?

6. Compare the data for Canadian imports of clothing accessories from China in 2012 that you found in Problem 5 with the same data for the year 2002.

a. What happened to the value of Canadian imports of clothing accessories from China in this 10-year period?

b. What prediction does the Heckscher–Ohlin model make about the wages received by labour in China?

7. Shoes are labour-intensive and satellites are capital-intensive to produce. Canada has abundant capital. China has abundant labour. According to the Heckscher–Ohlin model, which good will China export? Which good will Canada export? In Canada, what will happen to the price of labour (the wage) and to the price of capital?

8. Before the North American Free Trade Agreement (NAFTA) gradually eliminated import tariffs on goods, the autarky price of tomatoes in Mexico was below the world price and in Canada was above the world price. Similarly, the autarky price of poultry in Mexico was above the world price and in Canada was below the world price. Draw diagrams with domestic supply and demand curves for each country and each of the two goods. As a result of NAFTA, Canada now imports tomatoes from Mexico and Canada now exports poultry to Mexico. How would you expect the following groups to be affected?

a. Mexican and Canadian consumers of tomatoes. Illustrate the effect on consumer surplus in your diagram.

b. Mexican and Canadian producers of tomatoes. Illustrate the effect on producer surplus in your diagram.

c. Mexican and Canadian tomato workers.

d. Mexican and Canadian consumers of poultry. Illustrate the effect on consumer surplus in your diagram.

e. Mexican and Canadian producers of poultry. Illustrate the effect on producer surplus in your diagram.

f. Mexican and Canadian poultry workers.

9. The accompanying table indicates the Canadian domestic demand schedule and domestic supply schedule for commercial jet airplanes. Suppose that the world price of a commercial jet airplane is $100 million.

Price of jet (millions)	Quantity of jets demanded	Quantity of jets supplied
$120	100	1000
110	150	900
100	200	800
90	250	700
80	300	600
70	350	500
60	400	400
50	450	300
40	500	200

a. In autarky, how many commercial jet airplanes does Canada produce, and at what price are they bought and sold?

b. With trade, what will the price for commercial jet airplanes be? Will Canada import or export airplanes? How many?

10. The accompanying table shows the Canadian domestic demand schedule and domestic supply schedule for apples. Suppose that the world price of apples is $0.30 per apple.

Price of apples	Quantity of apples demanded (thousands)	Quantity of apples supplied (thousands)
$1.00	2	11
0.90	4	10
0.80	6	9
0.70	8	8
0.60	10	7
0.50	12	6
0.40	14	5
0.30	16	4
0.20	18	3

a. Draw the Canadian domestic supply curve and domestic demand curve.

b. With free trade, how many apples will Canada import or export?

Suppose that the Canadian government imposes a tariff on apples of $0.20 per apple.

c. How many apples will Canada import or export after introduction of the tariff?

d. In your diagram, shade the gain or loss to the economy as a whole from the introduction of this tariff.

11. The Canadian domestic demand schedule and domestic supply schedule for apples was given in Problem 10. Suppose that the world price of apples is $0.30. Canada introduces an import quota of 3000 apples and assigns the quota rents to foreign apple exporters.

a. Draw the domestic demand and supply curves.

b. What will the domestic price of apples be after introduction of the quota?

c. What is the value of the quota rents that foreign exporters of apples receive?

12. The accompanying diagram illustrates the Canadian domestic demand curve and domestic supply curve for textiles.

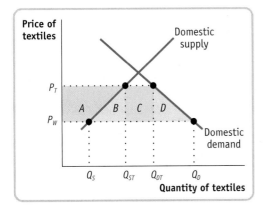

The world price of textiles is P_W. Canada currently imposes an import tariff on textiles, so the price of textiles is P_T. The Canadian government decides to eliminate the tariff. In terms of the areas marked in the diagram, answer the following questions.

a. What is the gain/loss in consumer surplus?

b. What is the gain/loss in producer surplus?

c. What is the gain/loss to the government?

d. What is the gain/loss to the economy as a whole?

13. As Canada has opened up to trade, it has lost many of its low-skill manufacturing jobs, but it has gained jobs in high-skill industries, such as the software industry. Explain whether Canada as a whole has been made better off by trade.

14. Canada is highly protective of its agricultural industry, imposing import tariffs and import quotas on imports of agricultural goods. This chapter presented three arguments for trade protection. For each argument, discuss whether it is a valid justification for trade protection of Canadian agricultural products.

15. In World Trade Organization (WTO) negotiations, if a country agrees to reduce trade barriers (tariffs or quotas), it usually refers to this as a *concession* to other countries. Do you think that this terminology is appropriate?

16. Producers in import-competing industries often make the following argument: "Other countries have an advantage in production of certain goods purely because workers abroad are paid lower wages. In fact, Canadian workers are much more productive than foreign workers. So import-competing industries need to be protected." Is this a valid argument? Explain your answer.

17. In Canada, producers of milk, poultry, and eggs are protected by government imposed supply management rules. This supply management system is made up of a combination of import controls, production planning quotas, and minimum prices for these products.

a. Suppose the goal of the government is to design a supply management system for agricultural products that works to support the incomes of farmers. Explain how the use of production quotas and/or price floors would help to achieve this goal. Briefly explain who benefits and who loses under such a system and why this is so.

b. Why might the supply management system use a combination of a price floor and a production quota?

c. One important facet of this supply management system are restrictions limiting the import of agricultural products. Explain why such import limits are necessary.

d. These Canadian import restrictions are generally not welcomed by foreign suppliers (i.e., farmers in the rest of the world). In fact, this is one of the main reasons that talks between Canada and the European Union (EU) on a trade pact were so slow (a free trade agreement in principle was reached in 2013). Explain why the imposition of Canadian import restrictions on many agricultural products is viewed negatively by some of our trading partners.

e. Suppose European and American farmers are subsidized by their governments in a way that reduces the farmers' costs. Would the existence of such subsidies strengthen or weaken the need for Canadian import restrictions (to protect the incomes of Canadian farmers)? Explain why or why not.

CHAPTER 6

Macroeconomics: The Big Picture

MACROECONOMIC FLUCTUATIONS

During the Depression, many people had to rely on soup kitchens, like this one in Montreal, which offered food either for free or at a very low cost.

WHAT YOU WILL LEARN IN THIS CHAPTER

❱ What makes macroeconomics different from microeconomics

❱ What a **business cycle** is and why policy-makers seek to diminish the severity of business cycles

❱ How **long-run economic growth** determines a country's standard of living

❱ The meaning of **inflation** and **deflation** and why **price stability** is preferred

❱ The importance of **open-economy macroeconomics** and how economies interact through **trade deficits** and **trade surpluses**

ECONOMIC EXPANSIONS AND contractions (often called the business cycle) are common features in all economies around the world—no country can escape them. However, people tend to pay more attention to bad times, like recessions, than to the good times of expansions because of the pain and economic losses associated with slowdowns and recessions.

The Great Depression of the 1930s was by far the harshest recession Canada has ever endured. Life was hard as the unemployment rate rose from less than 2% to almost 20% and many Canadians had to rely on relief. From 1928 to 1930, Canada's economic output fell 42%, from $6050 million to $3492 million. Not until 1939, more than a decade after the Depression began, was the national level of output restored to pre-Depression levels.

When the Great Depression hit the country, the federal government simply had no idea what to do. What happened during the Great Depression, and on a smaller scale on many subsequent occasions (most recently between 2008 and 2009), was a blow to the economy as a whole. In any economic environment at any given moment there are always some industries laying off workers. But workers who lose their jobs in one industry generally have a good chance of finding new jobs elsewhere, because other industries are expanding. Unfortunately, this did not hold true in the Great Depression. Every industry was headed downward.

Although we suffered greatly during the Great Depression, we learned a lot from it. Governments realized that they could and should play a more active role in smoothing out business cycles. The Bank of Canada was created in 1934 to help stabilize the banking system; the Canadian Wheat Board was established in 1935 to help wheat farmers promote their crops and stabilize their incomes. Macroeconomics came into its own as a branch of economics as a result of the Great Depression. Economists realized that to recover from the catastrophe that had overtaken Canada and most of the world, and to learn how to avoid such catastrophes in the future, they needed to understand what had happened. To this day, the effort to understand economic fluctuations, especially slumps, and to find ways to prevent them, is at the core of macroeconomics. Over time, however, the study of macroeconomics has expanded to encompass other subjects, such as *long-run economic growth, inflation,* and *open-economy macroeconomics.*

This chapter offers an overview of macroeconomics. We start with a general description of the difference between macroeconomics and microeconomics, and then we briefly describe some of the field's major concerns. ∎

The Nature of Macroeconomics

What makes macroeconomics different from microeconomics? The distinguishing feature of macroeconomics is that it focuses on the behaviour of the economy as a whole.

Macroeconomic Questions

Table 6-1 lists some typical questions that involve economics. A microeconomic version of the question appears on the left paired with a similar macroeconomic question on the right. By comparing the questions, you can begin to get a sense of the difference between microeconomics and macroeconomics.

TABLE 6-1 **Microeconomic versus Macroeconomic Questions**

Microeconomic Questions	Macroeconomic Questions
Should I go to business school or take a job right now?	How many people are employed in the economy as a whole this year?
What determines the salary offered by Royal Bank (RBC) to Cherie Camajo, a new MBA?	What determines the overall salary levels paid to workers in a given year?
What determines the cost to a university or college of offering a new course?	What determines the overall level of prices in the economy as a whole?
What government policies should be adopted to make it easier for low-income students to attend university or college?	What government policies should be adopted to promote employment and growth in the economy as a whole?
What determines whether Royal Bank (RBC) opens a new office in Shanghai?	What determines the overall trade in goods, services, and financial assets between Canada and the rest of the world?

As these questions illustrate, microeconomics focuses on how decisions are made by individuals and firms and the consequences of those decisions. For example, we use microeconomics to determine how much it would cost a university or college to offer a new course, which includes the instructor's salary, the cost of class materials, and so on. The school can then decide whether or not to offer the course by weighing the costs and benefits. Macroeconomics, in contrast, examines the *overall* behaviour of the economy—how the actions of all the individuals and firms in the economy interact to produce a particular economy-wide level of economic performance. For example, macroeconomics is concerned with the general level of prices in the economy and how high or how low it is relative to prices last year, rather than with the price of one particular good or service.

You might imagine that macroeconomic questions can be answered simply by adding up microeconomic answers. For example, the model of supply and demand we introduced in Chapter 3 tells us how the equilibrium price of an individual good or service is determined in a competitive market. So you might think that applying supply and demand analysis to every good and service in the economy, then summing the results, is the way to understand the overall level of prices in the economy as a whole.

But that turns out not to be right: although basic concepts such as supply and demand are as essential to macroeconomics as they are to microeconomics, answering macroeconomic questions requires an additional set of tools and an expanded frame of reference.

Macroeconomics: The Whole Is Greater Than the Sum of Its Parts

If you occasionally drive on a highway, you probably know what a rubbernecking traffic jam is and why it is so annoying. Someone pulls over to the side of the road for something minor, such as changing a flat tire, and, pretty soon, a long traffic jam occurs as drivers slow down to take a look. What makes it so annoying is that the length of the traffic jam is greatly out of proportion to the minor event that precipitated it. Because some drivers hit their brakes in order to rubberneck, the drivers behind them must also hit their brakes, those behind them must do the same, and so on. The accumulation of all the individual hitting of brakes eventually leads to a long, wasteful traffic jam as each driver slows down a little bit more than the driver in front of him or her. In other words, each person's response leads to an amplified response by the next person.

Understanding a rubbernecking traffic jam gives us some insight into one very important way in which macroeconomics is different from microeconomics: many thousands or millions of individual actions compound upon one another to produce an outcome that isn't simply the sum of those individual actions.

Consider, for example, what macroeconomists call the *paradox of thrift:* when families and businesses are worried about the possibility of economic hard times, they prepare by cutting their spending. This reduction in spending depresses the economy as consumers spend less and businesses react by laying off workers. As a result, families and businesses may end up worse off than if they hadn't tried to act responsibly by cutting their spending. This is a paradox because seemingly virtuous behaviour—preparing for hard times by saving more—ends up harming everyone. And there is a flip side to this story: when families and businesses are feeling optimistic about the future, they spend more today. This stimulates the economy, leading businesses to hire more workers, which further expands the economy. Seemingly profligate behaviour leads to good times for all.

Or consider what happens when something causes the quantity of cash circulating through the economy to rise. An individual with more cash on hand is richer. But if everyone has more cash, the long-run effect is simply to push the overall level of prices higher, taking the purchasing power of the total amount of cash in circulation right back to where it was before.

A key insight of macroeconomics, then, is that the combined effect of individual decisions can have results that are very different from what any one individual intended, results that are sometimes perverse. The behaviour of the macroeconomy is, indeed, greater than the sum of individual actions and market outcomes.

The behaviour of the macroeconomy is greater than the sum of individual actions and market outcomes.

Macroeconomics: Theory and Policy

To a much greater extent than microeconomists, macroeconomists are concerned with questions about *policy,* about what the government can do to make macroeconomic performance better. This policy focus was strongly shaped by history, in particular by the Great Depression of the 1930s.

Before the 1930s, economists tended to regard the economy as **self-regulating:** they believed that problems such as unemployment would be corrected through the working of the invisible hand and that government attempts to improve the economy's performance would be ineffective at best—and would probably make things worse.

In a **self-regulating economy,** problems such as unemployment are resolved without government intervention, through the working of the invisible hand.

FIGURE **6-1** Percentage Change in Real Gross Domestic Product and the Canadian Unemployment Rate, 1927–1950

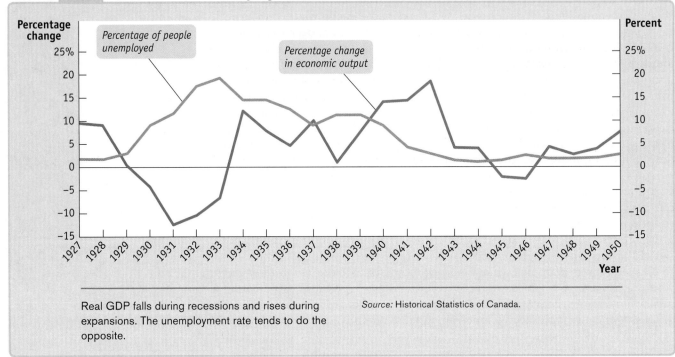

Real GDP falls during recessions and rises during expansions. The unemployment rate tends to do the opposite.

Source: Historical Statistics of Canada.

According to **Keynesian economics,** economic slumps are caused by inadequate spending, and they can be mitigated by government intervention.

Monetary policy uses the quantity and/or the growth rate of money to affect economic activity.

Fiscal policy uses changes in taxes and government spending to affect overall economic activity.

The Great Depression changed all that. The effects of this catastrophe were devastating. From 1929 to 1933, Canada's *real gross domestic product (GDP)* fell by more than 30% and unemployment rose enormously (see Figure 6-1). The gross domestic product and the unemployment rate will be discussed in more detail later on; for now you just need to know that a low GDP and a high unemployment rate are bad for the economy. Furthermore, the Depression threatened the political stability of many countries—it is widely believed to have been a major factor in the Nazi takeover of Germany. All of these effects created a demand for action.

The Depression also led to a major effort on the part of economists to understand economic slumps and find ways to prevent them. In 1936, the British economist John Maynard Keynes (pronounced "canes") published *The General Theory of Employment, Interest, and Money,* a book that transformed macroeconomics. According to **Keynesian economics,** a depressed economy is the result of inadequate spending. In addition, Keynes argued that government intervention can help a depressed economy through *monetary policy* and *fiscal policy.* **Monetary policy** uses the quantity and/or the growth rate of money to affect economic activity. This policy influences the inflation rate, interest rates, exchange rates, and other important short-run economic variables. The Bank of Canada, Canada's central bank, is responsible for the design and implementation of Canadian monetary policy. It also serves as the bank for large domestic banks and helps manage the (bank) accounts of the federal government. More details about the role and functions of the Bank of Canada will be discussed in Chapters 14 and 15. **Fiscal policy** uses changes in taxes and government spending to affect overall economic activity. The federal, provincial, and municipal governments also design and implement fiscal policy. Details on how fiscal policy affects economic activity will be discussed in Chapter 13.

In general, Keynes established the idea that managing the economy is a government responsibility. Keynesian ideas continue to have a strong influence on both economic theory and public policy: in 2008 and 2009, the federal government and the Bank of Canada took steps that were clearly Keynesian in spirit to fend off an economic slump, as described in the following Economics in Action.

ECONOMICS ►IN ACTION

FENDING OFF DEPRESSION

In 2008, the world economy experienced a severe financial crisis that was all too reminiscent of the early days of the Great Depression. Major banks teetered on the edge of collapse; world trade slumped. In the spring of 2009, the economic historians Barry Eichengreen and Kevin O'Rourke, reviewing the available data, pointed out that "globally we are tracking or even doing worse than the Great Depression."

But the worst did not, in the end, come to pass. Figure 6-2 shows one of Eichengreen and O'Rourke's measures of economic activity, world industrial production, during the Great Depression and during "the Great Recession," the now widely used American term for the slump that followed the 2008 financial crisis. During the first year, the two crises were indeed comparable. But this time, fortunately, world production levelled off and turned around. Why?

At least part of the answer is that policy-makers responded very differently. During the Great Depression, it was widely argued that the slump should simply be allowed to run its course. Any attempt to mitigate the ongoing catastrophe, declared Joseph Schumpeter— the Austrian-born Harvard economist now famed for his work on innovation—would "leave the work of depression undone." In the early 1930s, some countries' monetary authorities actually raised interest rates in the face of the slump, while governments cut spending and raised taxes—actions that, as we'll see in later chapters, deepened the recession.

In the aftermath of the 2008 crisis, by contrast, interest rates were slashed, and a number of countries, Canada and the United States included, used temporary increases in spending and reductions in taxes in an attempt to sustain spending. Governments also moved to shore up their banks with loans, aid, and guarantees. For example, the federal government rolled out the Economic Action Plan, while the Bank of Canada lowered interest rates to historically low levels to stimulate the economy.

Many of these measures were controversial, to say the least. But most economists believe that by responding actively to the Great Recession—and doing so using the knowledge gained from the study of macroeconomics—governments helped avoid a global economic catastrophe.

FIGURE 6-2 Measures of Economic Activity and World Industrial Production During the Great Depression and the Great Recession

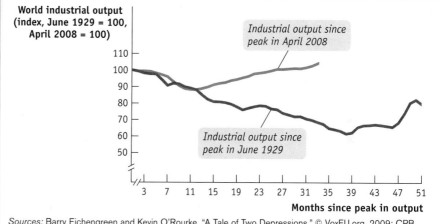

Sources: Barry Eichengreen and Kevin O'Rourke, "A Tale of Two Depressions." © VoxEU.org, 2009; CPB Netherlands Bureau for Economic Policy Analysis World Trade Monitor.

▼ Quick Review

- Microeconomics focuses on decision-making by individuals and firms and the consequences of the decisions made. Macroeconomics focuses on the overall behaviour of the economy.

- The combined effect of individual actions can have unintended consequences and lead to worse or better macroeconomic outcomes for everyone.

- Before the 1930s, economists tended to regard the economy as **self-regulating.** After the Great Depression, **Keynesian economics** provided the rationale for government intervention through **monetary policy** and **fiscal policy** to help a depressed economy.

CHECK YOUR UNDERSTANDING 6-1

1. Which of the following questions involve microeconomics, and which involve macroeconomics? In each case, explain your answer.
   a. Why did consumers switch to smaller cars in 2008?
   b. Why did overall consumer spending slow down in 2008?
   c. Why did the standard of living rise more rapidly in the first generation after World War II than in the second?

    d. Why have starting salaries for students with geology degrees risen sharply of late?

    e. What determines the choice between rail and road transportation?

    f. Why has salmon gotten cheaper over the past 20 years?

    g. Why did inflation fall in the 1990s?

2. In 2008, problems in the financial sector led to a drying up of some types of credit around the country: some homebuyers were unable to get mortgages, and some businesses were unable to get loans.

    a. Explain how the drying up of credit can lead to compounding effects throughout the economy and result in an economic slump.

    b. If you believe the economy is self-regulating, what would you advocate that policy-makers do?

    c. If you believe in Keynesian economics, what would you advocate that policy-makers do?

Solutions appear at back of book.

The Business Cycle

The Great Depression was by far the worst economic crisis in Canadian history. But although the economy managed to avoid catastrophe for the rest of the twentieth century, it has experienced many ups and downs.

    On the positive side, the ups have consistently been bigger than the downs: most chart indicators used to track the Canadian economy show strong upward trends over time. For example, Figure 6-3a shows the levels of real GDP and employment (the number of adults who have paid jobs) between 1961 and 2011. Both real GDP and employment were much higher at the end of the period than at the beginning, and in most years both measures rose.

FIGURE 6-3 Growth, Interrupted, 1961–2011

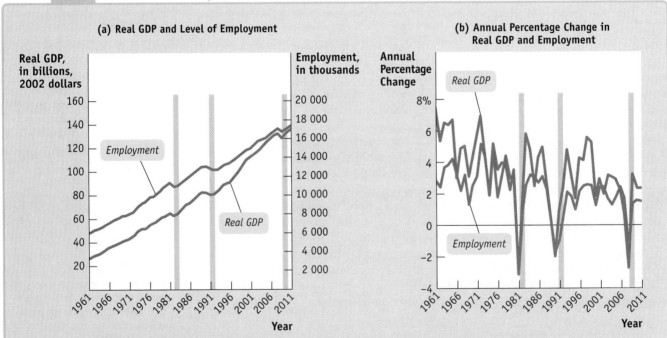

Panel (a) shows two important economic numbers, the levels of real GDP and employment. Both numbers grew substantially from 1961 to 2011, but they didn't grow steadily. Instead, both suffered from three downturns associated with recessions, which are indicated by the shaded areas in the figure. Panel (b) emphasizes those downturns by showing the annual rate of change of real GDP and employment, that is, the percentage increase over the previous year. The simultaneous downturns in both numbers during the three recessions are clear.

Source: Statistics Canada.

But they didn't rise steadily. As you can see from the figure, there were three periods—in the early 1980s, in the early 1990s, and again in late 2008—when the percentage changes of both real GDP and employment turned negative. Figure 6-3b emphasizes these stumbles by showing the rate of change of real GDP and employment over the previous year. For example, the percent changes in real GDP and employment for 2007 were 2.2 and 2.4 respectively, because the levels of real GDP and unemployment in 2007 were 2.2% and 2.4% higher than they had been in 2006. The three big downturns stand out clearly. What's more, a detailed look at the data makes it clear that in each period the stumble wasn't confined to only a few industries: in each downturn, just about every sector of the Canadian economy cut back on production and on the number of people employed.

The economy's forward march, in other words, isn't smooth. And the uneven pace of the economy's progress, its ups and downs, is one of the main preoccupations of macroeconomics.

Charting the Business Cycle

Figure 6-4 shows a stylized representation of the way the economy evolves over time. The vertical axis shows either employment or an indicator of how much the economy is producing, such as industrial production or real gross domestic product (real GDP), which will be discussed in the next chapter. As the data in Figure 6-3 suggest, these two measures tend to move together. Their common movement is the starting point for a major theme of macroeconomics: the economy's alternation between short-run downturns and upturns.

A broad-based downturn, in which output and employment fall in many industries, is called a **recession** (sometimes referred to as a *contraction*). When the economy isn't in a recession, when most economic numbers are following their normal upward trend, the economy is said to be in an **expansion** (sometimes referred to as a *recovery*). The alternation between recessions and expansions is known as the **business cycle.** The point in time at which the economy shifts from expansion to recession is known as a **business-cycle peak;** the point at which the economy shifts from recession to expansion is known as a **business-cycle trough.**

Recessions, or contractions, are periods of economic downturn when output and employment are falling.

Expansions, or recoveries, are periods of economic upturn when output and employment are rising. Many countries use data on a single variable, output, as a proxy for overall economic activity.

The **business cycle** is the short-run alternation between recessions and expansions.

The point at which the economy turns from expansion to recession is a **business-cycle peak.**

The point at which the economy turns from recession to expansion is a **business-cycle trough.**

"Please stand by for a series of tones. The first indicates the official end of the recession, the second indicates prosperity, and the third the return of the recession."

FIGURE   6-4   The Business Cycle

This is a stylized picture of the business cycle. The vertical axis measures either employment or total output in the economy. Periods when these two variables turn down are *recessions*; periods when they turn up are *expansions*. The point at which the economy turns down is a *business-cycle peak*; the point at which it turns up again is a *business-cycle trough*.

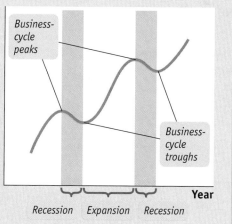

The business cycle is an enduring feature of the economy. As Figure 6-3 shows, the Canadian economy experienced expansions and recessions during the period between 1961 and 2011. Whenever there is a prolonged expansion, as there was in the 1960s and again in the 1990s, books and articles come out proclaiming the end of the business cycle. Such proclamations have always proved wrong: the cycle always comes back. But why does it matter?

The Pain of Recession

Not many people complain about the business cycle when the economy is expanding. Recessions, however, create a great deal of pain.

The most important effect of a recession is its effect on the ability of workers to find and hold jobs. The most widely used indicator of conditions in the labour market is the *unemployment rate*. We'll explain how that rate is calculated in Chapter 7, but for now it's enough to say that a high unemployment rate tells us that jobs are scarce and a low unemployment rate tells us that jobs are easy to find. Figure 6-5 shows the unemployment rate from 1960 to 2011. As you can see, the unemployment rate surged during and after each recession but eventually fell during periods of expansion. For example, it rose sharply in the early 1980s, the early 1990s, and late 2008, during periods of recession.

Because recessions cause many people to lose their jobs and also make it hard to find new ones, recessions hurt the standard of living of many families. Recessions are usually associated with a rise in the number of people living below the poverty line, an increase in the number of people unemployed and collecting employment insurance (EI), a rise in bankruptcies, and an increase in the number of homeowners who lose their homes because they can no longer afford their mortgage payments.

You should not think, however, that workers are the only group that suffers during a recession. Recessions are also bad for firms: like employment and wages, profits suffer during recessions, with many small businesses failing, and do well during expansions.

All in all, then, recessions are bad for almost everyone. Can anything be done to reduce their frequency and severity?

FIGURE **6-5** The Canadian Unemployment Rate, 1960–2011

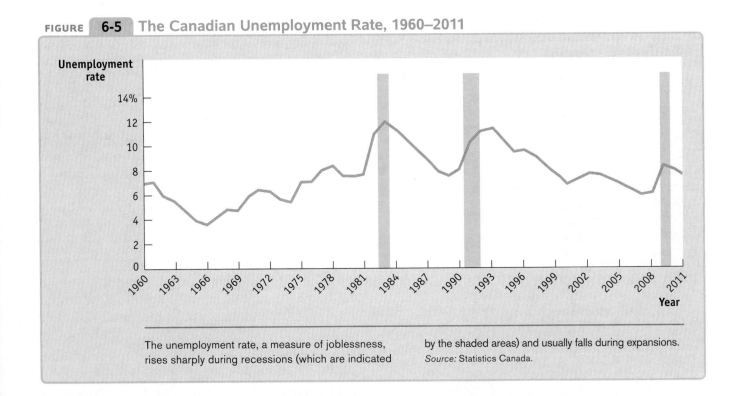

The unemployment rate, a measure of joblessness, rises sharply during recessions (which are indicated by the shaded areas) and usually falls during expansions.

Source: Statistics Canada.

FOR INQUIRING MINDS

DEFINING RECESSIONS AND EXPANSIONS

Some readers may be wondering exactly how recessions and expansions are defined. The answer is that there is no exact definition!

In Canada and many other countries, economists adopt the rule that a recession is a period of at least two consecutive quarters (a quarter is three months) during which the total output of the economy shrinks. The two-consecutive-quarters requirement is designed to avoid classifying brief hiccups in the economy's performance, with no lasting significance, as recessions.

Sometimes, however, this definition seems too strict. For example, an economy that has three months of sharply declining output, then three months of slightly positive growth, then another three months of rapid decline, should surely be considered to have endured a nine-month recession. However, this kind of output growth would not be considered a recession according to this rule. Consequently, other countries use other methods to identify episodes of recession. The most notable example is the United States, in which an independent panel of experts at the National Bureau of Economic Research (NBER) determines when a recession begins and ends.

This panel looks at a variety of economic indicators, with the main focus on employment and production. But, ultimately, the panel makes a judgment call, often with quite a time lag.

Sometimes this judgment is controversial. In fact, there is lingering controversy over the 2001 U.S. recession. According to the NBER, that recession began in March 2001 and ended in November 2001 when output began rising. Some critics argue, however, that the recession really began several months earlier, when industrial production began falling. Other critics argue that the recession didn't really end in 2001 because employment continued to fall and the job market remained weak for another year and a half.

Taming the Business Cycle

Modern macroeconomics largely came into being as a response to the worst recession in history—the 43-month downturn that began in 1929 and continued into 1933, ushering in the Great Depression. The havoc wreaked by the 1929–1933 recession spurred economists to search both for understanding and for solutions: they wanted to know how such things could happen and how to prevent them.

As we explained earlier in this chapter, the work of John Maynard Keynes, published during the Great Depression, suggested that monetary and fiscal policies

INTERNATIONAL BUSINESS CYCLES

This figure shows the annual rate of growth in industrial production—the percent change since the same month the previous year—for four economies from 1991 to 2011: Canada, Japan, the United States, and the eurozone. Do other economies have business cycles similar to those in Canada?

The answer, which is clear from the figure, is yes. Furthermore, business cycles in different economies are often, although not always, synchronized. The downturn of Canadian industrial production of 2001 was paralleled by the recessions in the other three economies; the U.S. Great Recession of 2007–2009 caused a severe slump around the world, including Canada. But not all business cycles are international phenomena. Japan suffered a fairly severe recession in 1998, even as the economies of Canada, the United States, and the eurozone continued to expand.

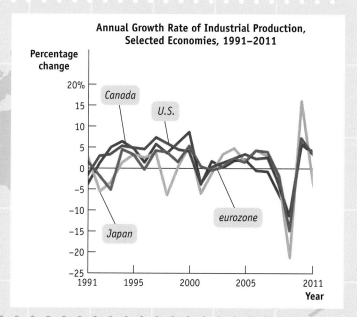

Sources: OECD, Dataset: Production and Sales (MEI).

could be used to mitigate the effects of recessions, and to this day governments turn to Keynesian policies when recession strikes. Later work, notably that of another great macroeconomist, Milton Friedman, led to a consensus that it's important to rein in booms as well as to fight slumps. So modern policy-makers try to "smooth out" the business cycle. They haven't been completely successful, as a look at Figure 6-6 makes clear. It's widely believed, however, that policy guided by macroeconomic analysis has helped make the economy more stable.

Although the business cycle is one of the main concerns of macroeconomics and historically played a crucial role in fostering the development of the field, macroeconomists are also concerned with other issues. We turn next to the question of long-run growth.

ECONOMICS > IN ACTION

COMPARING RECESSIONS

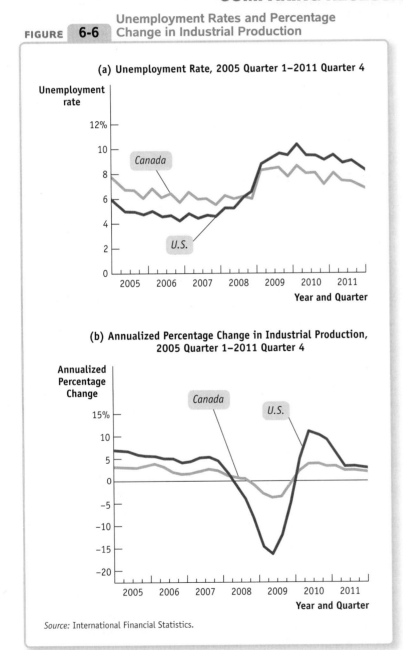

FIGURE **6-6** Unemployment Rates and Percentage Change in Industrial Production

(a) Unemployment Rate, 2005 Quarter 1–2011 Quarter 4

(b) Annualized Percentage Change in Industrial Production, 2005 Quarter 1–2011 Quarter 4

Source: International Financial Statistics.

The alternation of recessions and expansions seems to be an enduring feature of economic life. However, not all business cycles are created equal. Similarly, the same business cycle may have a quite different impact on distinct economies. Let's talk about how the "Great Recession" began and how it affected the economies of Canada and the United States.

The recession began in the U.S. in 2007 and in Canada in late 2008. It was precipitated by a crisis in the U.S. sub-prime mortgage market. Basically, during the 2000s, a large number of U.S. mortgage lenders, fighting for greater market share and profits, undertook riskier and riskier loans. In some cases, loans were made to people with no income, job, or assets—loans that only made any sense as long as house prices continued to rise. In 2006, U.S. house prices began to fall. Fearing the increased risk this fall in prices entailed, lenders tightened lending criteria. Consequently, some borrowers could not renew their loans or obtain a loan easily. So, they were forced to sell their homes, and housing prices dropped even further. Many financial institutions that held significant amounts of assets backed by mortgages suddenly feared for their future. The crisis intensified significantly when Lehman Brothers, the fourth largest investment bank in the U.S. at that time, filed for Chapter 11 Bankruptcy Protection on September 15, 2008.

The shockwaves from the crisis quickly spread to other sectors in the American economy and the rest of the world. It became a full-blown financial crisis that pushed the world economy into its worst recession since the Great Depression (see Chapter 17 for detailed discussion on this financial crisis). However, the severity of the crisis varied between countries, as this comparison between Canada and the United States shows.

Figure 6-6a shows the unemployment rates for Canada and the U.S. from the first quarter of 2005 to the fourth quarter of 2011. Figure 6-6b shows the annualized rates of change in industrial production for these two countries for the same period. From these graphs, it appears the Canadian and American economies had similar experiences during this time; that is, they moved up and down at roughly the same time. But there are important differences.

Before the 2007–2009 recession, the U.S. had a lower unemployment rate and a higher growth rate in industrial production than Canada did. However, when the crisis hit, the U.S. experienced a much larger increase in its unemployment rate. So, while both countries' unemployment rates peaked in the first quarter of 2010, the increase in the unemployment rates was quite divergent. For example, Canada's unemployment rate increased by 3.2 percentage points compared to its lowest level in this seven-year period, while the U.S. unemployment rate rose by 6.2 percentage points. Also, by the end of 2011, Canada's unemployment rate had decreased almost to its pre-recession level, while America's unemployment rate remained well above its pre-recession level and the rate in Canada. (Note that in Canada unemployment statistics include people who are 15 years of age and older, while in the U.S. they include people who are 16 years and older, so the comparison is not quite exact.)

The story for industrial production is similar. Starting in the fourth quarter of 2007, both economies experienced a slowdown in their industrial production, but the growth rate turned negative sooner in the U.S. (in the second quarter of 2008) than in Canada (the fourth quarter of 2008). Moreover, Canada experienced a smaller drop in the growth rate of industrial production and thus in industrial production itself, than the U.S. did.

So the recent financial crisis and the recession it spawned had less impact on Canada than it did on the U.S. Furthermore, Canada was able to recover from the crisis more quickly than the U.S. could.

▼ Quick Review

- The **business cycle,** the short-run alternation between **recessions** and **expansions,** is a major concern of modern macroeconomics.

- The point at which expansion shifts to recession is a **business-cycle peak.** The point at which recession shifts to expansion is a **business-cycle trough.**

CHECK YOUR UNDERSTANDING   6-2

1. Why do we talk about business cycles for the economy as a whole, rather than just talking about the ups and downs of particular industries?

2. Describe who gets hurt in a recession, and how.

Solutions appear at back of book.

Long-Run Economic Growth

Although 2008 was a difficult year for Canadians seeking jobs, the jobs that were on offer paid extremely well by historical standards. In fact, just before this recession, Canadians believed that they were better off than they ever had been before and they had good reason to feel this way. Almost one hundred years earlier, in 1912, there was less than one telephone per 200 people in Canada. By 1952, there were almost 23 telephones per 100 people, and in 1962, almost 34 telephones per 100 people. According to Statistics Canada, in 2010, when cellular phones are included, more than 99% of all households had a telephone. But it was not just telephones that more Canadians could now afford. They could afford automobiles, televisions, washers, dryers, home computers, air conditioning, and so on. For example, in 1997 only about 40% of households had a home computer and about 17% had Internet access. By 2010, about 83% of households had a home computer and 78% had Internet access.

Why can so many Canadians now afford to buy products that they could not afford in the past? The answer is **long-run economic growth,** the sustained rise

Long-run economic growth is the sustained upward trend in the economy's output over time.

FIGURE 6-7 Growth, the Long View

Over the long run, growth in real GDP per capita has dwarfed the ups and downs of the business cycle. Except for the recession that began the Great Depression, recessions are almost invisible until 2009.

Source: Statistics Canada.

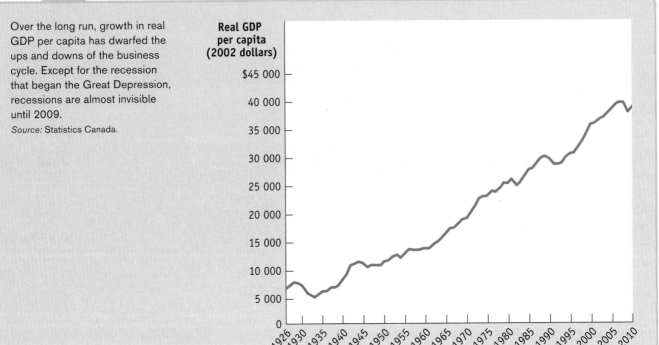

in the quantity of goods and services the economy produces. Figure 6-7 shows the growth since 1926 in Canadian real GDP per capita, a measure of total output per person in the economy. The severe recession of 1929–1933 stands out, but business cycles between World War II and 2007 are almost invisible, dwarfed by the strong upward trend. Part of the long-run increase in total output is accounted for by the fact that we have a growing population and workforce. But, as the upward trending curve demonstrates, the economy's overall production has increased by much more than the population. On average, in 2010 the Canadian economy produced about $38 800 worth of goods and services per person, about twice as much as in 1971, more than three times as much as in 1951, and almost six times as much as in 1926.

Long-run economic growth is fundamental to many of the most pressing economic questions today. Responses to key policy questions, like various levels of government's ability to bear the future costs of health care, education, public pensions, and other programs, depend in part on how fast the Canadian economy grows over the next few decades. More broadly, the public's sense that the country is making progress depends crucially on success in achieving long-run growth. When growth slows, as it did in the 1970s, it can help feed a national mood of pessimism. In particular, *long-run growth per capita*—a sustained upward trend in output per person—is the key to higher wages and a rising standard of living. A major concern of macroeconomics—and the theme of Chapter 9—is trying to understand the forces behind long-run growth.

Long-run growth is an even more urgent concern in poorer, less developed countries. In these countries, which would like to achieve a higher standard of living, the question of how to accelerate long-run growth is the central concern of economic policy.

As we'll see, macroeconomists don't use the same models to think about long-run growth that they use to think about the business cycle. It's always important to keep both sets of models in mind, because what is good in the long run can be

⬤FOR INQUIRING MINDS

WHEN DID LONG-RUN GROWTH START?

Today, Canada is much richer than it was in 1955; in 1955, it was much richer than it had been in 1905. But how did 1905 compare with 1855? Or 1805? How far back does long-run economic growth go?

Of course, Canada is a relatively recent creation; we didn't exist as a country before 1867. And our rapid growth in the latter half of the nineteenth century was partly the result of large-scale immigration to the lands that were to become the Western provinces. But if we cast our net wider and look around the world, we find that long-run growth is a relatively modern phenomenon. If we go back to the period before 1800, we find a world economy that grew extremely slowly by contemporary standards. Between the years 1000 and 1800, according to the best available estimates, the world economy grew by less than 0.2% per year. Furthermore, the population grew almost as fast as the total real output, so that there was hardly any increase in real output per capita (the average amount of real output per person, equal to total real output divided by the total population).

This economic stagnation was

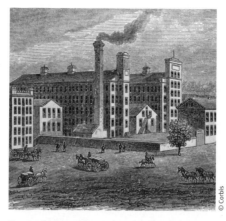

Economic stagnation and unchanging living standards prevailed for centuries until the Industrial Revolution in the mid-1800s ushered in a new era of wealth and sustained increases in living standards.

matched by unchanged living standards. For example, information on prices and wages from sources such as monastery records shows that workers in England weren't significantly better off in the early eighteenth century than they had been five centuries earlier. And it's a good bet they weren't much better off than Egyptian peasants in the age of the pharaohs. From examining historical records of birth and death rates, demographers know that in both cases human beings were living right on the edge of subsistence. However, long-run real economic growth has increased significantly in many countries since 1800.

Over the long-run, real aggregate output rises fairly steadily; in Canada it grew more than 20-fold over the 84 years from 1926 to 2010. In the last 50 years or so, Canadian real GDP per capita has grown by about 2.1% per year.

bad in the short run, and vice versa. For example, we've already mentioned the paradox of thrift: an attempt by households to increase their savings can cause a recession. But a higher level of savings, as we'll see in Chapter 10, plays a crucial role in encouraging long-run economic growth.

ECONOMICS ▸ IN ACTION

A TALE OF TWO COUNTRIES

Many countries have experienced long-run growth, but not all have done equally well. One of the most informative contrasts is between Canada and Argentina, two countries that, at the beginning of the twentieth century, seemed to be in a good economic position.

From today's vantage point, it's surprising to realize that Canada and Argentina looked rather similar before World War I. Both were major exporters of agricultural products; both attracted large numbers of European immigrants; both also attracted large amounts of European investment, especially in the railroads that opened up their agricultural hinterlands. Economic historians believe that the average level of per capita income was about the same in the two countries as late as the 1930s.

After World War II, however, Argentina's economy performed poorly, largely due to political instability and bad macroeconomic policies. (Argentina experienced several periods of extremely high inflation, during which the cost of living soared.) Meanwhile, Canada made steady progress. Thanks to the fact that Canada has achieved sustained long-run growth since 1930, but Argentina has not, Canada's standard of living is about three times as high as Argentina's.

CHECK YOUR UNDERSTANDING 6-3

1. Many poor countries have high rates of population growth. What does this imply about the long-run growth rates of total output that they must achieve in order to generate a higher standard of living per person?

2. Argentina used to be as rich as Canada; now it's much poorer. Does this mean that Argentina is poorer than it was in the past? Explain.

Solutions appear at back of book.

Inflation and Deflation

In 1991, a Canadian worker who was paid by the hour earned $14.01 per hour, on average. By 2011, the average wage had risen to $21.75 per hour. Similarly, in 1991, a Canadian worker on a fixed salary earned the equivalent of $18.70 per hour, on average. By 2011, this salary had risen to $31.64 per hour, on average.

But wait. Canadian workers were paid much more in 2011, but they also faced a much higher cost of living. For example, from 1991 to 2011 the price of coffee rose by 56% and the price of gasoline rose by 118%. Figure 6-8 compares the percentage increase in hourly earnings between 1991 and 2011 with the increases in the prices of some standard items: the average worker's paycheque went further in terms of some goods, but less far in terms of others. Although income for both types of workers increased more than the overall increase in the cost of living (45%),

FIGURE 6-8 Rising Prices

Between 1991 and 2011, the wages of workers who were paid by the hour rose by 55% and the pay of salaried workers rose by 69%. But the prices of goods and services also rose, by varying amounts. The Consumer Price Index (CPI) rose by 45%. Consequently, real income increased for salaried workers and for workers who were paid by the hour, but by different amounts.
Source: Statistics Canada.

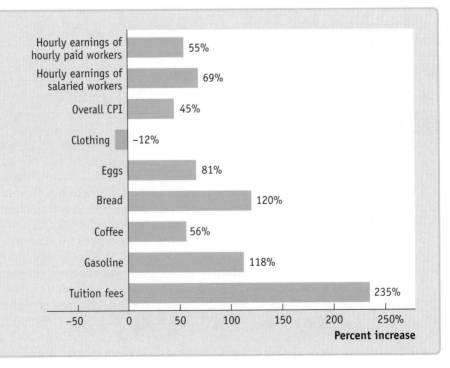

salaried workers fared better than hourly paid workers. Salaried workers' hourly pay rose by 24 percentage points more than the Consumer Price Index (CPI) did over this period compared to only a 10 percentage point gain for their hourly paid counterparts over the CPI.

The point is that between 1991 and 2011 the economy experienced substantial **inflation:** a rise in the overall level of prices. Understanding the causes of inflation and its opposite, **deflation**—a fall in the overall level of prices—is another main concern of macroeconomics.

A rising overall level of prices is **inflation.**

A falling overall level of prices is **deflation.**

The economy has **price stability** when the overall level of prices changes slowly or not at all.

The Causes of Inflation and Deflation

You might think that changes in the overall level of prices are just a matter of supply and demand. For example, higher gasoline prices reflect the higher price of crude oil, and higher crude oil prices reflect such factors as the exhaustion of major oil fields, growing demand from China and other emerging economies as more people grow rich enough to buy cars, and so on. Can't we just add up what happens in each of these markets to find out what happens to the overall level of prices?

The answer is no, we can't. Supply and demand can only explain why a particular good or service becomes more expensive *relative to other goods and services*. It can't explain why, for example, the price of chicken has risen over time in spite of the facts that chicken production has become more efficient (you don't want to know) and that chicken has become substantially cheaper compared to other goods.

What causes the overall level of prices to rise or fall? As we'll learn in Chapter 8, in the short run, movements in inflation are closely related to the business cycle. When the economy is depressed and jobs are hard to find, inflation tends to fall; when the economy is booming, inflation tends to rise. For example, prices of most goods and services fell sharply during the terrible recession of 1929–1933.

In the long run, by contrast, the overall level of prices is mainly determined by changes in the *money supply*, the total quantity of assets that can be readily used to make purchases. As we'll see in Chapter 16, *hyperinflation*, in which prices rise by thousands or hundreds of thousands of percent, invariably occurs when governments print money to pay a large part of their bills.

The Pain of Inflation and Deflation

Both inflation and deflation can pose problems for the economy. Here are two examples: inflation discourages people from holding on to cash, because cash loses value over time if the overall price level is rising. That is, inflation causes the amount of goods and services you can buy with a given amount of cash to fall. In extreme cases, people stop holding cash altogether and turn to barter. Deflation can cause the reverse problem. If the price level is falling, cash gains value over time as it buys more and more goods and services than previously. In other words, the amount of goods and sevices you can buy with a given amount of cash increases. So holding on to it can become more attractive than spending on some goods or investing in new factories and other productive assets. This can deepen a recession.

We'll describe other costs of inflation and deflation in Chapters 8 and 16. For now, let's just note that, in general, economists regard **price stability**—in which the overall level of prices is changing, if at all, only slowly—as a desirable goal. Price stability is a goal that seemed far out of reach for much of the post–World War II period but was achieved to most macroeconomists' satisfaction in the 1990s.

Even though a burger costs almost four times more than it did in 1967, it is still a good bargain compared to other consumer goods.

▼ **Quick Review**

● A dollar today doesn't buy what it did in 1991, because the prices of most goods have risen. This rise in the overall price level has wiped out most, if not all, of the wage increases received by the typical Canadian worker over the past 20 years.

● One area of macroeconomic study is in the overall level of prices. Because either **inflation** or **deflation** can cause problems for the economy, economists typically advocate maintaining **price stability**.

ECONOMICS ▶ IN ACTION

A FAST (FOOD) MEASURE OF INFLATION

The first McDonald's in Canada opened in Richmond, British Columbia, in 1967. It offered fast service—it was, indeed, one of Canada's original fast-food restaurants. And it was also very inexpensive: a hamburger cost about $0.39. By 2012, a hamburger at a typical Canadian McDonald's cost almost four times as much, about $1.39. Has McDonald's lost touch with its fast-food roots? Have burgers become luxury cuisine?

No. In fact compared with other consumer goods, a burger is a better bargain today than it was in 1967. Burger prices were almost four times as high in 2012 as they were in 1967. But according to the Bank of Canada inflation calculator, most goods costing $0.39 in 1967 cost $2.65 in 2012, which is almost seven times as much as in 1967.

CHECK YOUR UNDERSTANDING   6-4

1. Which of these sound like inflation, which sound like deflation, and which are ambiguous?
   a. Gasoline prices are up 10%, food prices are down 20%, and the prices of most services are up 1–2%.
   b. Gas prices have doubled, food prices are up 50%, and most services seem to be up 5% or 10%.
   c. Gas prices haven't changed, food prices are way down, and services have gotten cheaper, too.

Solutions appear at back of book.

International Imbalances

Canada is an **open economy:** an economy that trades goods and services with other countries. There have been times when our trade was more or less balanced—when Canada sold about as much to the rest of world as it bought. But this isn't one of those times.

From the late 1990s until 2008, Canada had a **trade surplus** with other countries. That is, the goods and services it sold to other countries were worth more than the goods and services it bought from them. But, starting in 2009, Canada ran a **trade deficit,** so that the goods and services Canada sold were worth less than the goods and services it bought. The United States was in a similar position, with an even larger deficit than Canada's. Meanwhile, some other countries were in the exact opposite position, going into a trade surplus. Figure 6-9 shows the exports and imports of goods for four important economies in 2011: Canada, the United States, Germany, and China. As you can see, Canada and the United States imported more than they exported, while Germany and China did the reverse: they ran a trade surplus. Was Canada's trade deficit a sign that something was wrong with our economy—that we couldn't make things that other countries wanted to buy?

No, not really. Trade deficits and their opposite, trade surpluses, are macroeconomic phenomena. They're the result of situations in which the whole is very different from the sum of its parts. You might think that countries with

An **open economy** is an economy that trades goods and services with other countries.

A country runs a **trade surplus** when the value of goods and services bought from other countries is less than the value of the goods and services it sells to them. It runs a **trade deficit** when the value of goods and services bought from other countries is more than the value of goods and services it sells to them.

FIGURE **6-9** Unbalanced Trade

In 2011, the goods and services Canada bought from other countries were worth slightly more than the goods and services we sold abroad. The United States had an even larger trade deficit. Germany and China were in the reverse position. Trade deficits and trade surpluses reflect macroeconomic forces, especially differences in savings and investment spending.
Source: World Trade Organization.

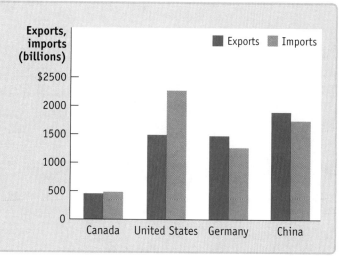

highly productive workers or widely desired products and services to sell run trade surpluses while countries with unproductive workers or poor-quality products and services run deficits. But the reality is that there's no simple relationship between the success of an economy and whether it runs trade surpluses or deficits.

Microeconomic analysis tells us why countries trade but not why they run trade surpluses or deficits. In Chapter 2 we learned that international trade is the result of comparative advantage: countries export goods they're relatively good at producing and import goods they're not as good at producing. That's why Canada exports wheat and imports pineapples. One important thing the concept of comparative advantage doesn't explain, however, is why the value of a country's imports is sometimes much larger than the value of its exports, or vice versa.

So what does determine whether a country runs a trade surplus or a trade deficit? In Chapter 19 we'll learn the surprising answer: the determinants of the overall balance between exports and imports lie in decisions about savings and investment spending—spending on goods like machinery and factories that are in turn used to produce goods and services for consumers. Countries with high investment spending relative to savings run trade deficits; countries with low investment spending relative to savings run trade surpluses.

ECONOMICS › IN ACTION

BALTIC BALANCING ACT

The Soviet Union, once the second-largest world power, broke up into 15 independent countries in 1991. Many of these countries have had a hard time finding a new place in the world, both politically and economically. However, the three small nations of Estonia, Latvia, and Lithuania—often referred to as the "Baltics" because they all have coastlines on the Baltic Sea—were quick both to establish democratic institutions and to move to market economies, building strong ties to the democratic market economies of Western Europe.

What has this meant for their international trade? Figure 6-10 shows the current account balances of the three countries—a broad definition of their trade balances—from 2000 to 2010. As you can see, in the middle years of

FIGURE **6-10** Baltic Current Account Balances, 2000–2010

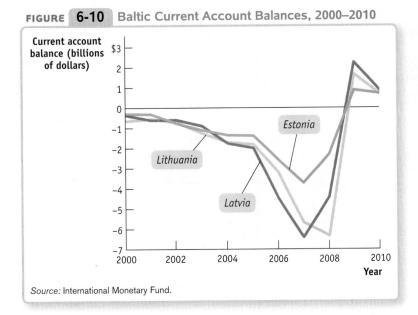

Source: International Monetary Fund.

that decade, all three countries began running sizable deficits (amounting in each case to more than 10% of the total value of goods and services they produced). Then, after 2008, all three suddenly moved into surplus.

Does this mean that these economies were doing badly around 2005 or 2006 and that they rapidly improved late in the decade? Actually, it was the opposite. During the period from 2000 to 2007, financial markets were extremely optimistic about the economic prospects of the Baltic nations and poured money into the countries, allowing them to engage in high rates of investment spending and, correspondingly, to run large trade deficits. When the world plunged into financial crisis, this inflow of funds dried up, forcing the Baltics to move into trade surplus. The adjustment was hard on the three countries, all of which saw unemployment rates rise to Depression-era levels.

▼ Quick Review

- Comparative advantage can explain why an **open economy** exports some goods and services and imports others, but it can't explain why a country imports more than it exports, or vice versa.

- **Trade deficits** and **trade surpluses** are macroeconomic phenomena, determined by decisions about investment spending and savings.

CHECK YOUR UNDERSTANDING 6-5

1. Which of the following reflect comparative advantage, and which reflect macroeconomic forces?
   a. Thanks to the development of huge oil sands in Alberta, Canada has become an exporter of oil and an importer of manufactured goods.
   b. Like many consumer goods, the Apple iPod is assembled in China, although many of the components are made in other countries.
   c. Since 2002, Germany has been running huge trade surpluses, exporting much more than it imports.
   d. Canada, which had a trade surplus beginning in the late 1990s, started running trade deficits in 2009, as the 2008 financial crisis took hold.

Solutions appear at back of book.

General Motors—The Demotion of a General

Christinne Muschi/Reuters/Landov

On June 1, 2009, General Motors (GM) filed for bankruptcy. It was a sad come-down for a company that had once been the leading symbol of North American automobile success. General Motors Canada had just finished celebrating its 100th anniversary in the auto business a year earlier.

The 2009 bankruptcy didn't mean that GM shut down; the company was able to continue operating, thanks to the more than $60 billion in aid that it received from the governments of Canada, Ontario, and the United States. In return for that aid, these governments received stock in the restructured company. The government's intention was to avoid the economic catastrophe that liquidation might cause, preserve some jobs, and sell off that stock once the company was profitable again.

But why did government officials believe GM had a reasonable prospect of returning to profitability? Their case was based on an observation and a prediction.

The observation was that GM's troubles weren't unique. To be sure, the company had been badly run and needed both to make better cars and to reduce its costs. But all North American automakers were in trouble: overall car sales had slumped and, beyond that, overall manufacturing production had slumped. The association of weak auto sales with a general manufacturing slump fit the historical pattern. Figure 6-11 shows Canadian auto sales and total Canadian manufacturing production as a percentage of capacity; the two series have often, although not always, moved together.

The prediction was that both manufacturing production and auto sales would soon rebound, improving GM's bottom line. And this indeed proved to be the case: as the economy bounced back, so did General Motors, which returned to profitability in 2010. By late 2010, the governments were able to start selling off their stock, and expectations were that taxpayers would eventually get most of their money back.

In this case, the governments were able to save a company and preserve some jobs in the auto sector. In fact, in return for their aid to GM Canada, the Canadian and Ontario governments were assured that GM would maintain at least a certain percentage of their annual North American production in Canada.

FIGURE 6-11 Canadian Auto Sales and Total Canadian Manufacturing Production as a Percentage of Capacity

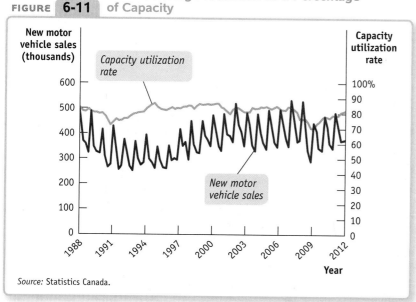

Source: Statistics Canada.

QUESTIONS FOR THOUGHT

1. Why do overall manufacturing production and auto sales often move together?

2. Why was it reasonable to predict in June 2009 that auto sales would improve in the near future?

3. Why were the governments especially lucky that they stepped in to rescue GM in June 2009 rather than, say, six months earlier?

SUMMARY

1. Macroeconomics is the study of the behaviour of the economy as a whole, which can be different from the sum of its parts. Macroeconomics differs from microeconomics in the type of questions it tries to answer. Macroeconomics also has a strong policy focus: **Keynesian economics,** which emerged during the Great Depression, advocates the use of **monetary policy** and **fiscal policy** to fight economic slumps. Prior to the Great Depression, the economy was thought to be **self-regulating.**

2. One key concern of macroeconomics is the **business cycle,** the short-run alternation between **recessions,** periods of falling employment and output, and **expansions,** periods of rising employment and output. The point at which expansion turns to recession is a **business-cycle peak.** The point at which recession turns to expansion is a **business-cycle trough.**

3. Another key area of macroeconomic study is **long-run economic growth,** the sustained upward trend in the economy's output over time. Long-run economic growth is the force behind long-term increases in living standards and is important for financing some economic programs. It is especially important for poorer countries.

4. When the prices of most goods and services are rising, so that the overall level of prices is going up, the economy experiences **inflation.** When the overall level of prices is going down, the economy is experiencing **deflation.** In the short run, inflation and deflation are closely related to the business cycle. In the long run, prices tend to reflect changes in the overall quantity of money. Because both inflation and deflation can cause problems, economists and policy-makers generally aim for **price stability.**

5. Although comparative advantage explains why **open economies** export some things and import others, macroeconomic analysis is needed to explain why countries run **trade surpluses** or **trade deficits.** The determinants of the overall balance between exports and imports lie in decisions about savings and investment spending.

KEY TERMS

Self-regulating economy, p. 179
Keynesian economics, p. 180
Monetary policy, p. 180
Fiscal policy, p. 180
Recession, p. 183
Expansion, p. 183

Business cycle, p. 183
Business-cycle peak, p. 183
Business-cycle trough, p. 183
Long-run economic growth, p. 187
Inflation, p. 191
Deflation, p. 191

Price stability, p. 191
Open economy, p. 192
Trade surplus, p. 192
Trade deficit, p. 192

PROBLEMS

1. Which of the following questions are relevant for the study of macroeconomics and which for microeconomics?

   a. How will Ms. Martin's tips change when a large manufacturing plant near the restaurant where she works closes?

   b. What will happen to spending by consumers when the economy enters a downturn?

   c. How will the price of apples change when a late frost damages Ontario's apple orchards?"

   d. How will wages at a manufacturing plant change when its workforce is unionized?

   e. What will happen to Canadian exports as the dollar becomes less expensive in terms of other currencies?

   f. What is the relationship between a nation's unemployment rate and its inflation rate?

2. When one person saves more, that person's wealth is increased, meaning that he or she can consume more in the future. But when everyone saves more, everyone's income falls. If everyone's income falls, then the nation's wealth might actually fall, meaning that the nation might be forced to consume less in the future. Explain this seeming contradiction.

3. Before the Great Depression, the conventional wisdom among economists and policy-makers was that the economy is largely self-regulating.

   a. Is this view consistent or inconsistent with Keynesian economics? Explain.

   b. What effect did the Great Depression have on conventional wisdom?

   c. Contrast the response of policy-makers during the 2007–2009 recession to the actions of policy-makers during the Great Depression. What would have been the likely outcome of the 2007–2009 recession if policy-makers had responded in the same fashion as policy-makers during the Great Depression?

4. How do economists in Canada determine whether or not a recession is occurring? How do economists in the United States determine when a recession begins and when it ends?

5. Statistics Canada reports statistics on employment and earnings that are used as key indicators by many economists to gauge the health of the economy. Figure 6-5 in the text plots historical data on the unemployment rate. Noticeably, the numbers were high during the recessions in the early 1980s, early 1990s, and 2008–2009.

   a. Locate the latest data on the national unemployment rate. (*Hint:* Go to the website of Statistics Canada, www.statcan.gc.ca, and locate the latest release of the Labour Force Survey, which can be easily accessed in either the Latest Indicators or Labour sections.)

   b. Compare the current numbers with the recessions in the early 1980s, early 1990s, and 2008–2009 as well as with the periods of relatively high economic growth just before the recessions. Are the current numbers indicative of a recessionary trend?

6. The accompanying figure shows the annual rate of growth in employment for the United Kingdom and Japan from 1991 to 2010. (The annual growth rate is the percent change in each year's employment over the previous year.)

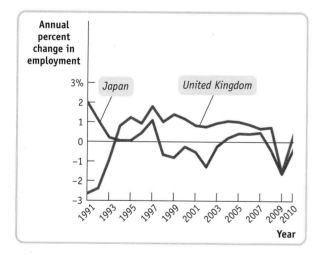

   a. Comment on the business cycles of these two economies. Are their business cycles similar or dissimilar?

   b. Use the accompanying figure and the figure in the Global Comparison on international business cycles in the chapter to compare the business cycles of each of these two economies with those of Canada and the eurozone.

7. a. What three measures of the economy tend to move together during the business cycle? Which way do they move during an upturn? During a downturn?

   b. Who in the economy is hurt during a recession? How?

   c. How did Milton Friedman alter the consensus that had developed in the aftermath of the

Great Depression on how the economy should be managed? What is the current goal of policy-makers in managing the economy?

8. Why do we consider a business-cycle expansion different from long-run economic growth? Why do we care about the size of the long-run growth rate of real GDP versus the size of the growth rate of the population?

9. In 1798, Thomas Malthus's *Essay on the Principle of Population* was published. In it, he wrote: "Population, when unchecked, increases in a geometrical ratio. Subsistence increases only in an arithmetical ratio … . This implies a strong and constantly operating check on population from the difficulty of subsistence." Malthus was saying that the growth of the population is limited by the amount of food available to eat; people will live at the subsistence level forever. Why didn't Malthus's description apply to the world after 1800?

10. University tuition has risen significantly in the last few decades. The average full-time undergraduate paid $1706 in tuition in 1991–1992 and $4917 in 2009–2010, an average rise of 5.9% per year. In contrast, over the same time, on average, the Consumer Price Index rose by 1.8% per year and families' real after-tax income rose by 1.3% per year. Have these tuition increases made it more difficult for the average student to afford higher education?

11. Each year, *The Economist* publishes data on the price of the Big Mac in different countries and exchange rates. The accompanying table shows some data used for the index from 2007 and 2011. Use this information to answer the following questions.

Economy	2007		2011	
	Price of Big Mac (in local currrency)	Price of Big Mac (in Cdn dollars)	Price of Big Mac (in local currency)	Price of Big Mac (in Cdn dollars)
Argentina	peso8.25	$3.12	peso20.0	$4.58
Canada	C$3.63	$3.63	C$4.73	$4.73
eurozone	€2.94	$4.50	€3.44	$4.66
Japan	¥280	$2.72	¥320	$3.86
United States	US$3.22	$3.80	US$4.07	$3.85

   a. Where was it cheapest to buy a Big Mac in Canadian dollars in 2007?

   b. Where was it cheapest to buy a Big Mac in Canadian dollars in 2011?

   c. Using the increase in the local currency price of the Big Mac in each country to approximate the percent change in the overall price level from 2007 to 2011, which nation experienced the most inflation? Did any of the nations experience deflation?

12. The accompanying figure illustrates the current account balance for Canada from 1986 to 2010. A positive balance represents a trade surplus, while a negative one represents a trade deficit. While Canada often ran a trade surplus over this time period, it has also been running a growing trade deficit with China. Which of the following statements are valid possible explanations of this fact? Explain.

a. Many products, such as televisions, that were formerly manufactured in Canada are now manufactured in China.

b. The wages of the average Chinese worker are far lower than the wages of the average Canadian worker.

c. Investment spending in Canada is high relative to its level of savings.

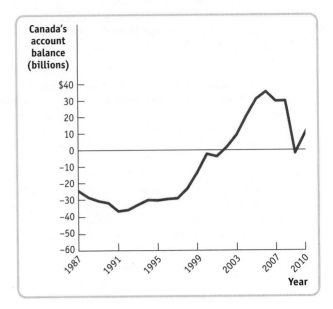

CHAPTER 7

GDP and the CPI: Tracking the Macroeconomy

THE NEW #2

The 2010 economic data showed that China had become an economic superpower, surpassing Japan.

REUTERS/Aly Song

> **WHAT YOU WILL LEARN IN THIS CHAPTER**
>
> ❭ How economists use aggregate measures to track the performance of the economy
>
> ❭ What **gross domestic product,** or **GDP,** is and the three ways of calculating it
>
> ❭ The difference between **real GDP** and **nominal GDP** and why real GDP is the appropriate measure of real economic activity
>
> ❭ What a **price index** is and how it is used to calculate the **inflation rate**

"CHINA PASSES JAPAN AS Second-Largest Economy." That was the headline in the *New York Times* on August 15, 2010. Citing economic data suggesting that Japan's economy was weakening while China's was roaring ahead, the article predicted—correctly, as it turned out—that 2010 would mark the first year in which the surging Chinese economy finally overtook Japan's, taking second place to the United States on the world economic stage. "The milestone," wrote the *Times,* "though anticipated for some time, is the most striking evidence yet that China's ascendance is for real and that the rest of the world will have to reckon with a new economic superpower."

But wait a minute—what does it mean to say that China's economy is larger than Japan's? The two economies are, after all, producing very different mixes of goods. Despite its rapid advance, China is still a fairly poor country whose greatest strength is in relatively low-tech production. Japan, by contrast, is very much a high-tech nation, and it dominates world output of some sophisticated goods, like electronic sensors for automobiles. That's why the 2011 earthquake in northeastern Japan, which put many factories out of action, temporarily caused major production disruptions for auto factories around the world.

How can you compare the sizes of two economies when they aren't producing the same things?

The answer is that comparisons of national economies are based on the *value* of their production. When news reports declared that China's economy had overtaken Japan's, they meant that China's *gross domestic product,* or *GDP*—a measure of the overall value of goods and services produced—had surpassed Japan's GDP.

GDP is one of the most important measures used to track the macroeconomy—that is, to quantify movements in the overall level of output and prices. Measures like GDP and *price indexes* play an important role in formulating economic policy, since policy-makers need to know what's going on, and anecdotes are no substitute for hard data. They're also important for business decisions—to such an extent that, as the business case at the end of the chapter illustrates, corporations and governments are willing to pay for early reads on what official economic measurements are likely to find.

In this chapter, we explain how macroeconomists measure key aspects of the economy. We first explore ways to measure the economy's total output and total income. We then turn to the problem of how to measure the level of prices and the change in prices in the economy. ∎

The **national income and product accounts,** or **national accounts,** keep track of the flows of money between different sectors of the economy.

Consumer spending, or **consumption,** is household spending on goods and services.

A **stock** is a share in the ownership of a company held by a shareholder.

A **bond** is borrowing in the form of an IOU that pays interest.

Government transfers are payments by the government to individuals for which no good or service is provided in return.

Disposable income, equal to income plus government transfers minus taxes, is the total amount of household income available to spend on consumption and to save.

The National Accounts

Almost all countries calculate a set of numbers known as the *national income and product accounts.* In fact, the accuracy of a country's accounts is a remarkably reliable indicator of its state of economic development—in general, the more reliable the accounts, the more economically advanced the country. When international economic agencies seek to help a less developed country, typically the first order of business is to send a team of experts to audit and improve the country's accounts.

In Canada, these numbers are calculated by Statistics Canada. The **national income and product accounts,** often referred to simply as the **national accounts,** keep track of the spending of consumers, sales of producers, business investment spending, government purchases, and a variety of other flows of money between different sectors of the economy. Let's see how they work.

The Circular-Flow Diagram, Revisited and Expanded

To understand the principles behind the national accounts, it helps to look at Figure 7-1, a revised and expanded *circular-flow diagram* similar to the one we introduced in Chapter 2. Recall that in Figure 2-6 we showed the flows of money, goods and services, and factors of production through the economy. Here we restrict ourselves to flows of money but add extra elements that allow us to show the key concepts behind the national accounts. As in our original version of the circular-flow diagram, the underlying principle is that the inflow of money into each market or sector is equal to the outflow of money coming from that market or sector.

Figure 2-7 showed a simplified world containing only two kinds of "inhabitants," households and firms. And it illustrated the circular flow of money between households and firms, which remains visible in Figure 7-1. In the markets for goods and services, households engage in **consumer spending** (or **consumption**), buying goods and services from domestic firms and from firms in the rest of the world. Households also own factors of production—labour, land, physical capital, human capital, and financial capital. They sell the use of these factors of production to firms, receiving wages, profit, interest payments, and rent in return. Firms buy and pay households for the use of those factors of production in the factor markets. Most households derive the bulk of their income from wages earned by selling labour and human capital. But households derive additional income from their indirect ownership of the physical capital used by firms, mainly in the form of **stocks,** shares in the ownership of a company, and from **bonds,** by borrowing in the form of an IOU that pays interest. So the income households receive from the factor markets includes profits distributed to shareholders known as *dividends,* and the interest payments on bonds held by bondholders. Finally, households receive rent in return for allowing firms to use land or structures that they own. So households receive income in the form of wages, profit, interest payments, and rent via factor markets.

In our original, simplified circular-flow diagram, households spent all the income they received via factor markets on goods and services. Figure 7-1, however, illustrates a more complicated but more realistic diagram. There we see two reasons why goods and services don't in fact absorb all of households' income. First, households don't get to keep all the income they receive via the factor markets. They must pay part of their income to the government in the form of taxes, such as income taxes and sales taxes. In addition, some households receive **government transfers**—payments by the government to individuals for which no good or service is provided in return, such as Canadian public pension benefits and employment insurance payments. The total income households have left after paying taxes and receiving government transfers is **disposable income.**

Second, households normally don't spend all their disposable income on goods and services. Instead, a portion of their income is typically set aside as

An Expanded Circular-Flow Diagram: The Flows of Money
FIGURE   **7-1**   **Through the Economy**

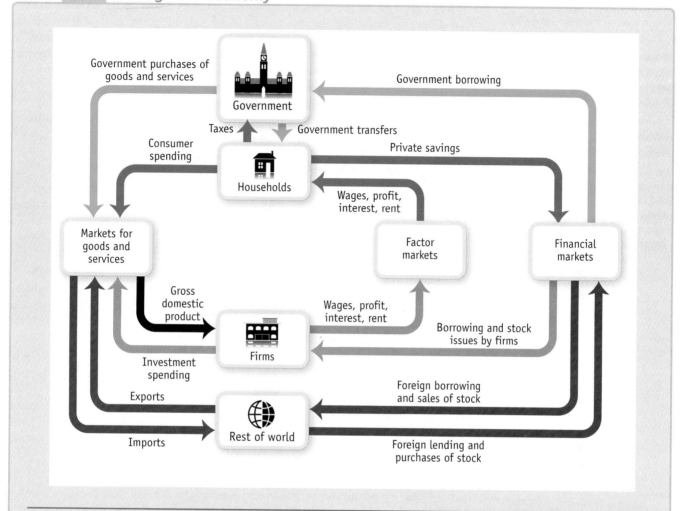

A circular flow of funds connects the four sectors of the economy—households, firms, government, and the rest of the world—via three types of markets: the factor markets, the markets for goods and services, and the *financial markets*. Funds flow from firms to households in the form of wages, profit, interest, and rent through the factor markets. After paying taxes to the government and receiving *government transfers*, households allocate the remaining income—*disposable income*—to private savings and consumer spending. Via the financial markets, *private savings* and funds from the rest of the world are channelled into investment spending by firms, government borrowing, foreign borrowing and lending, and foreign transactions of stocks. In turn, funds flow from the government and households to firms to pay for purchases of goods and services. Finally, exports to the rest of the world generate a flow of funds into the economy and imports lead to a flow of funds out of the economy. If we add up consumer spending on goods and services, investment spending by firms, government purchases of goods and services, and exports, then subtract the value of imports, the total flow of funds represented by this calculation is total spending on final goods and services produced in Canada. Equivalently, it's the value of all the final goods and services produced in Canada—that is, the *gross domestic product* of the economy.

private savings, which goes into **financial markets** where individuals, banks, and other institutions buy and sell stocks and bonds as well as make loans. As Figure 7-1 shows, the financial markets also receive funds from the rest of the world and provide funds to the government, to firms, and to the rest of the world.

Before going further, we can use the box representing households to illustrate an important general feature of the circular-flow diagram: the total sum of flows of money out of a given box is equal to the total sum of flows of money into that box. It's simply a matter of accounting: what goes in must come out. So, for example, the total flow of money out of households—the sum of taxes paid, consumer spending,

Private savings, equal to disposable income minus consumer spending, is disposable income that is not spent on consumption.

The banking, stock, and bond markets, which channel private savings and foreign lending into investment spending, government borrowing, and foreign borrowing, are known as the **financial markets.**

Government borrowing is the total amount of funds borrowed by federal, provincial, and municipal governments in the financial markets.

Government purchases of goods and services are total expenditures on goods and services by federal, provincial, and municipal governments.

Inventories are stocks of goods and raw materials held to facilitate business operations.

Investment spending, or **investment,** is spending on productive physical capital—such as on new machinery and equipment and on construction of buildings—and on changes to inventories.

and private savings—must equal the total flow of money into households—the sum of wages, profit, interest payments, rent, and government transfers.

Now let's look at the other types of inhabitants we've added to the circular-flow diagram, including the government—all federal, provincial, and municipal governments—and the rest of the world. The government returns a portion of the money it collects from taxes to households in the form of government transfers. However, it uses much of its tax revenue, plus additional funds borrowed in the financial markets through **government borrowing,** to buy goods and services. **Government purchases of goods and services,** the total purchases by federal, provincial, and municipal governments, include everything from military spending on UN peacekeeping duties to your local public school's spending on chalk, erasers, and teacher salaries.

The rest of the world participates in the Canadian economy in three ways:

1. Some of the goods and services produced in Canada are sold to residents of other countries. For example, Canada is the world's largest exporter of durum, a type of wheat that is an important ingredient in making pasta. It is also a major exporter of other products such as canola and softwood lumber. Goods and services sold to other countries are known as exports. Export sales lead to a flow of funds from the rest of the world into Canada to pay for them.

2. Some of the goods and services purchased by residents of Canada are produced abroad. For example, many consumer goods are now made in China. Goods and services purchased from residents of other countries are known as imports. Import purchases lead to a flow of funds out of Canada to pay for them.

3. Foreigners can participate in Canadian financial markets by making transactions. Foreign lending—lending by foreigners to borrowers in Canada, and purchases by foreigners of domestic assets, such as shares of stock in Canadian companies—generates a flow of funds into Canada from the rest of the world. Conversely, foreign borrowing—borrowing by foreigners from Canadian lenders and purchases by Canadians of foreign assets, such as stock in foreign companies—leads to a flow of funds out of Canada to the rest of the world.

Finally, let's go back to the markets for goods and services. In Chapter 2 we focused only on purchases of goods and services by households. We now see that there are other types of spending on goods and services, including government purchases, *investment spending* by firms, imports, and exports.

Notice that firms also buy goods and services in our expanded economy. For example, an automobile company that is building a new factory will buy investment goods—machinery like stamping presses and welding robots that are used to produce goods and services for consumers—from companies that manufacture these items. It will also accumulate an inventory of finished cars in preparation for shipment to dealers. **Inventories,** then, are stocks of goods and raw materials that firms hold to facilitate their operations. The national accounts count this **investment spending** (or **investment**)—spending on productive physical capital, such as on new machinery and equipment and on construction of buildings, and on changes to inventories—as part of total spending on goods and services.

You might ask why *changes* to inventories are included in investment spending—finished cars aren't, after all, used to produce more cars. Changes to inventories of finished goods are counted as investment spending because, like machinery, they change the ability of a firm to make future sales. So spending on additions to inventories is a form of investment spending by a firm. Conversely, a drawing-down of inventories is counted as a fall in investment spending because it leads to lower future sales. It's also important to understand that investment spending includes spending on construction of any structure, regardless of whether it is an assembly plant or a new house. Why include construction of homes? Because, like a plant, a new house produces a future stream of output—housing services for its occupants.

Suppose we add up consumer spending on goods and services, investment spending, government purchases of goods and services, and the value of exports, and then subtract the value of imports. This gives us a measure of the overall market value of the goods and services the economy produces. That measure has a name: it's a country's *gross domestic product*. But before we can formally define gross domestic product, or GDP, we have to examine an important distinction between classes of goods and services: the difference between *final goods and services* versus *intermediate goods and services*.

Gross Domestic Product

A consumer's purchase of a new car from a dealer is one example of a sale of **final goods and services:** goods and services sold to the final, or end, user. But an automobile manufacturer's purchase of steel from a steel foundry or glass from a glassmaker is an example of purchasing **intermediate goods and services:** goods and services that are inputs for production of other goods and services. In the case of intermediate goods and services, the purchaser—another firm—is *not* the final user.

Gross domestic product, or **GDP,** is the total value of all *final goods and services* produced in an economy during a given period, usually a year. In 2011, the GDP in Canada was $1721 billion, or about $49 902 per person. If you are an economist trying to construct a country's national accounts, *one way to calculate GDP is to calculate it directly: survey firms and add up the total value of their production of final goods and services.* We'll explain in detail in the next section why intermediate goods, and some other types of goods as well, are not included in the calculation of GDP.

But adding up the total value of final goods and services produced isn't the only way of calculating GDP. There is another way, based on total spending on final goods and services. Since GDP is equal to the total value of final goods and services produced in the economy, it must also equal the flow of funds received by firms from sales in the goods and services market.

If you look again at the circular-flow diagram in Figure 7-1, you will see that the arrow going from markets for goods and services to firms is indeed labelled "Gross domestic product." According to our basic rule of accounting, flows out of any box are equal to flows into the box; so the flow of funds out of the markets for goods and services to firms is equal to the total flow of funds into the markets for goods and services from other sectors. And as you can see from Figure 7-1, the total flow of funds into the markets for goods and services is total or **aggregate expenditure** on domestically produced final goods and services—the sum of consumer spending, investment spending, government purchases of goods and services, and exports minus imports. *So a second way of calculating GDP is to add up aggregate expenditure on domestically produced final goods and services in the economy.*

And there is yet a third way of calculating GDP, based on total income earned by factors of production (inputs) in the economy. Firms, and the factors of production that they employ, are owned by households. So firms must ultimately pay out what they earn to households. The flow from firms to the factor markets is the factor income paid out by firms to households in the form of wages, profit, interest, and rent. Again, by accounting rules, the value of the flow of factor income from firms to households must be equal to the flow of money into firms from the markets for goods and services. And this last value, we know, is the total value of production in the economy—GDP. Why is GDP equal to the total value of factor income paid by firms in the economy to households? Because each sale in the economy must accrue to someone as income—either as wages, profit, interest, or rent. *So a third way of calculating GDP is to add up all the factor income earned by households from firms in the economy.*

Final goods and services are goods and services sold to the final, or end, user.

Intermediate goods and services are goods and services—bought from one firm by another firm—that are inputs for production of final goods and services.

Gross domestic product, or **GDP,** is the total value of all final goods and services produced in the economy during a given year.

Aggregate expenditure, the sum of consumer spending, investment spending, government purchases of goods and services, and exports minus imports, is the total spending on domestically produced final goods and services in the economy.

"You wouldn't think there'd be much money in potatoes, chickens, and woodchopping, but it all adds up."

Calculating GDP

We've just explained that there are in fact three methods for calculating GDP:

1. The Value-Added Approach: Add the total value of all final goods and services produced domestically.

2. The Expenditure Approach: Add the spending on all domestically produced goods and services.

3. The Income Approach: Add the income earned by labour and capital from the domestic production of goods and services.

Government statisticians use all three methods. To illustrate how these three methods work, we will consider a hypothetical economy, shown in Figure 7-2. This economy consists of three firms—Canadian Motors, Inc., which produces one car per year; Canadian Steel, Inc., which produces the steel that goes into the car; and Canadian Ore, Inc., which mines the iron ore that goes into the steel. So GDP is $21 500, the value of the one car per year the economy produces. Let's look at how the three different methods of calculating GDP yield the same result.

The Value-Added Approach: Measuring GDP as the Value of Production of Final Goods and Services The first method for calculating GDP is to add up the value of all the final goods and services produced in the economy—a calculation that excludes the value of intermediate goods and services. Why are intermediate goods and services excluded? After all, don't they represent a very large and valuable portion of the economy?

To understand why only final goods and services are included in GDP, look at the simplified economy described in Figure 7-2. Should we measure the GDP of this economy by adding up the total sales of the iron ore producer, the steel producer, and the auto producer? If we did, we would in effect be counting the value of the steel twice—once when it is sold by the steel plant to the auto plant, and again

FIGURE **7-2** Calculating GDP

In this hypothetical economy consisting of three firms, GDP can be calculated in three different ways: 1) measuring GDP as the value of production of final goods and services, by summing each firm's value added; 2) measuring GDP as aggregate expenditure on domestically produced final goods and services; and 3) measuring GDP as factor income earned by households from firms in the economy.

2. Aggregate expenditure on domestically produced final goods and services = $21 500

	Canadian Ore, Inc.	Canadian Steel, Inc.	Canadian Motors, Inc.	Total factor income
Value of sales	$4 200 (ore)	$9 000 (steel)	$21 500 (car)	
Intermediate goods	0	4 200 (iron ore)	9 000 (steel)	
Wages	2 000	3 700	10 000	$15 700
Interest payments	1 000	600	1 000	2 600
Rent	200	300	500	1 000
Profit	1 000	200	1 000	2 200
Total expenditure by firm	4 200	9 000	21 500	
Value added per firm = Value of sales – Cost of intermediate goods	4 200	4 800	12 500	

3. Total payments (income) to factors = $21 500

1. Value of production of final goods and services, sum of value added = $21 500

when the steel auto body is sold to a consumer as a finished car. And we would be counting the value of the iron ore *three* times—once when it is mined and sold to the steel company, a second time when it is made into steel and sold to the auto producer, and a third time when the steel is made into a car and sold to the consumer.

So counting the full value of each producer's sales would cause us to count the same items several times and artificially inflate the calculation of GDP. For example, in Figure 7-2, the total value of all sales, intermediate and final, is $34 700: $21 500 from the sale of the car, plus $9000 from the sale of the steel, plus $4200 from the sale of the iron ore. Yet we know that GDP is only $21 500. The way we avoid double-counting is to count only each producer's **value added** in the calculation of GDP: the difference between the value of its sales and the value of the intermediate goods and services it purchases from other businesses.

That is, at each stage of the production process we subtract the cost of inputs—the intermediate goods—at that stage. In this case, the value added of the auto producer is the dollar value of the cars it manufactures *minus* the cost of the steel it buys, or $12 500. The value added of the steel producer is the dollar value of the steel it produces *minus* the cost of the ore it buys, or $4800. Only the ore producer, which we have assumed doesn't buy any inputs, has value added equal to its total sales, $4200. The sum of the three producers' value added is $21 500, equal to GDP.

In Canada, the value added of goods-producing industries such as manufacturing, construction, and resource extraction account for about 30% of GDP; while the valued added of service-producing industries such as financial and health care industries account for the remaining 70%.

The "Our Imputed Lives" box below discusses the important assumptions the government makes to estimate the value added of households.

The Expenditure Approach: Measuring GDP as Spending on Domestically Produced Final Goods and Services Another way to calculate GDP is by adding up aggregate expenditure on domestically produced final goods and services. That is, GDP can be measured by the flow of funds into firms. Like the method that estimates GDP as the value of domestic production of final goods and services, this measurement must be carried out in a way that avoids double-counting. In terms of our steel and auto example, we don't want

> The **value added** of a producer is the value of its sales minus the value of its purchases of intermediate goods and services.

FOR INQUIRING MINDS

OUR IMPUTED LIVES

An old line says that when a person marries the household cook, GDP falls. And it's true: when someone provides services for pay, those services are counted as a part of GDP. But the services family members provide to each other are not. Some economists have produced alternative measures that try to "impute" the value of household work—that is, assign an estimate of what the market value of that work would have been if it had been paid for. But the standard measure of GDP doesn't contain that imputation.

GDP estimates do, however, include an imputation for the value of "owner-occupied housing" (the imputed rent). That is, if you buy the home you were formerly renting, GDP does not go down.

It's true that because you no longer pay rent to your landlord, the landlord no longer sells a service to you—namely, use of the house or apartment. But the statisticians make an estimate of what you would have paid if you rented whatever you live in, whether it's an apartment or a house. For the purposes of the statistics, it's as if you were renting your dwelling from yourself.

If you think about it, this makes a lot of sense. In a home-owning country like Canada, the pleasure we derive from our houses is an important part of the standard of living. So to be accurate, estimates of

The value of the services that family members provide to each other is not counted as part of GDP.

GDP must take into account the value of housing that is occupied by owners as well as the value of rental housing.

to count both consumer spending on a car (represented in Figure 7-2 by $21 500, the sales price of the car) and the auto producer's spending on steel (represented in Figure 7-2 by $9000, the price of a car's worth of steel). If we counted both, we would be counting the steel embodied in the car twice. We solve this problem by counting only the value of sales to *final buyers,* such as consumers, firms that purchase investment goods, the government, or foreign buyers. In other words, in order to avoid double-counting of spending, we omit sales of inputs from one business to another when estimating GDP using spending data. You can see from Figure 7-2 that aggregate expenditure on final goods and services—the finished car—is $21 500.

As we've already pointed out, the national accounts *do* include investment spending by firms as a part of final spending. That is, an auto company's purchase of steel to make a car isn't considered a part of final spending, but the company's purchase of new machinery for its factory *is* considered a part of final spending. What's the difference? Steel is an input that is used up in production; machinery will last for a number of years. Since purchases of capital goods that will last for a considerable time aren't closely tied to current production, the national accounts consider such purchases a form of final sales.

In later chapters, we will make use of the proposition that GDP is equal to aggregate expenditure on domestically produced goods and services by final buyers. We will also develop models of how final buyers decide how much to spend. With that in mind, we'll now examine the types of spending that make up GDP.

Look again at the markets for goods and services in Figure 7-1, and you will see that one component of sales by firms is consumer spending. Let's denote consumer

⚠ PITFALLS

GDP: WHAT'S IN AND WHAT'S OUT

It's easy to confuse what is included and what is excluded from GDP. So let's stop here for a moment and make sure the distinction is clear. The most likely source of confusion is the difference between investment spending and spending on intermediate goods and services. Investment spending— spending on productive physical capital (including construction of residential and commercial structures) and changes to inventories—is included in GDP. But spending on intermediate goods and services is not.

Why the difference? Recall from Chapter 2 that we made a distinction between resources that are *used up* and those that are *not used up* in production. An input, like steel, is used up in production. An investment good, like a metal-stamping machine, is not. It will last for many years and will be used repeatedly to make many cars. Since spending on new productive physical capital— investment goods—and construction of structures is not directly tied to current output, economists consider such spending to be spending on final goods.

Spending on changes to inventories is considered a part of investment spending, so it is also included in GDP. Why?

Because, like a machine, additional inventory is an investment in future sales. And in a future period when a good is released for sale from inventories, its value is subtracted from the value of inventories and so from GDP.

Used goods are not included in GDP because, as with intermediate inputs, to include them would be to double-count: counting them once when sold as new and again when sold as used.

Also, financial assets such as stocks and bonds are not included in GDP because they don't represent either the production or the sale of final goods and services. Rather, a bond represents a promise to repay with interest, and a stock represents a proof of ownership. And for obvious reasons, foreign-produced goods and services are not included in calculations of GDP.

Since GDP includes mainly market transactions only, it usually does not include transactions that do not go through commercial markets. These transactions include household production such as homemade meals, homegrown vegetables, and some child care services; illegal transactions such as drug dealings; transactions in the underground economy such as home renovation or auto repair work that is

concealed from the government, so as to avoid paying any related taxes; volunteer work; and environmental damage, such as pollution, caused by production or consumption because its value cannot be determined.

Here is a summary of what's included and not included in GDP:

Included

- Domestically produced final goods and services, including capital goods, new construction of structures, and changes to inventories

Not Included

- Intermediate goods and services
- Inputs, such as pre-existing productive physical capital
- Used goods
- Financial assets like stocks and bonds
- Foreign-produced goods and services
- Household production
- Volunteer work
- Underground economy transactions and illegal activities
- Harm done to the environment during the production or consumption of goods

spending with the symbol C. Figure 7-1 also shows three other components of sales: sales of investment goods to other businesses, or investment spending, which we will denote by I; government purchases of goods and services, which we will denote by G; and sales to foreigners—that is, exports—which we will denote by X.

In reality, not all of this final spending goes toward domestically produced goods and services. We must take account of spending on imports, which we will denote by IM. Income spent on imports is income not spent on domestic goods and services—it is income that has "leaked" across national borders. So to accurately value domestic production using spending data, we must subtract spending on imports to arrive at spending on domestically produced goods and services. Putting this all together gives us the following equation that breaks GDP down by the four sources of aggregate expenditure:

(7-1) $GDP = C + I + G + X - IM$

We'll be seeing a lot of Equation 7-1 in later chapters.

The Income Approach: Measuring GDP as Income Earned from Production of Goods and Services A final way to calculate GDP is to add two sources of income: factor incomes and non-factor payments. **Factor incomes** consist of the income earned by factors of production, or inputs. Examples include the wages earned by workers; the interest paid to those who lend their savings to firms; the rent earned by those who lease their land or structures to firms; the dividends paid to shareholders, who own a firm's physical capital; and other income earned by those who are directly involved in the production of goods and services.

Non-factor payments consist of the income earned by the federal government as a result of the production of goods and services. They are the difference between the prices for which final products are sold in the market and the amount actually received (and kept) by the factors of production before income taxes are removed. One example is net indirect taxes, which are indirect taxes, such as provincial and federal sales taxes, less any subsidies paid to purchasers. Another example is capital depreciation, which is the removal of productive physical capital from the capital stock as it wears out or becomes obsolete; such depreciation can be claimed as an income tax deduction.

Figure 7-2 shows how this calculation works for our simplified economy. The shaded column at the far right shows the total wages, interest, and rent paid by all these firms as well as their total profit. Summing up all of these yields total factor income of $21 500—again, equal to GDP.

Here, we'll focus on the expenditure approach and the income approach in calculating GDP. It's important to keep in mind, however, that all the money spent on domestically produced goods and services generates income for someone in the economy because one person's spending is another person's income—that is, there really is a circular flow. Figure 7-3 shows that the economy's total expenditure must equal its total income.

The Components of GDP Now that we know how GDP is calculated in principle, let's see what it looks like in practice.

Figure 7-3 shows the last two methods of calculating GDP side by side. The height of each bar above the horizontal axis represents the GDP of the Canadian economy in 2011: $1721 billion. Each bar is divided to show the breakdown of that total in terms of where the value was added, how the money was spent, and where the income was generated.

The left bar in Figure 7-3 corresponds to the second method of calculating GDP, showing the breakdown by the four types of aggregate expenditure. The total length of the bar on the left is longer than the bar on the right, a difference of $21 billion (which, as you can see, is the amount by which the left bar

Factor incomes are incomes earned by factors of production, which include wages, interest, rent dividends, and profits.

Non-factor payments are the difference between the prices paid for final goods and services and the amount received by factors of production, which include net indirect taxes and capital depreciation.

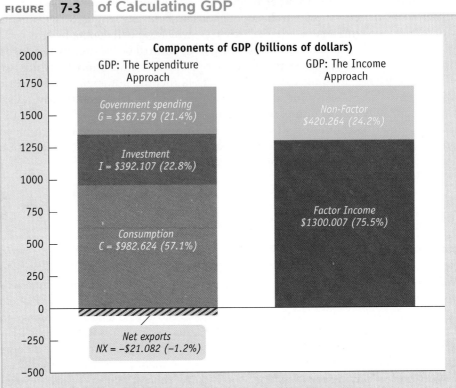

FIGURE 7-3   Canada's GDP in 2011: Two Methods of Calculating GDP

Components of GDP (billions of dollars)

GDP: The Expenditure Approach

Government spending
G = $367.579 (21.4%)

Investment
I = $392.107 (22.8%)

Consumption
C = $982.624 (57.1%)

Net exports
NX = −$21.082 (−1.2%)

GDP: The Income Approach

Non-Factor
$420.264 (24.2%)

Factor Income
$1300.007 (75.5%)

The two bars show two equivalent ways to calculate GDP. The height of each bar above the horizontal axis represents $1720.748 billion, Canada's GDP in 2011. The bar on the left shows Canada's GDP calculated according to the expenditure approach, with the sources of expenditures being consumption, investment, government spending, and net exports. The $21 billion, shown as the area extending below the horizontal axis, is the amount of total spending absorbed by net exports, which means Canada ran a trade deficit in 2011.

The bar on the right shows Canada's GDP according to the income approach, with the sources of income being factor incomes and non-factor payments. Factor incomes include wages, salaries, and supplementary labour income ($889.487 billion, 51.7%); corporation profits, including government enterprises ($255.139 billion, 13.1%), interest, and miscellaneous investment income ($73.794 billion, 4.3%); and unincorporated profits, including rent ($111.587 billion, 6.5%). Non-factor payments include indirect taxes, net of subsidies ($179.980 billion, 10.5%), inventory valuation adjustment (−$1.389 billion, −0.1%), and capital consumption allowances ($241.673 billion, 14.0%).

Source: Statistics Canada.

extends below the horizontal axis). That's because the total length of the left bar represents total spending in the economy, spending on both domestically produced and foreign-produced final goods and services. Within the bar, consumer spending (C), which is 57.1% of GDP, dominates the picture. But some of that spending was absorbed by foreign-produced goods and services. In 2011, **net exports,** the difference between the value of exports and the value of imports ($X - IM$ in Equation 7-1) was negative—Canada was a net importer of foreign goods and services. The 2011 value of $X - IM$ was −$21.1 billion, or −1.2% of GDP. Thus, a portion of the left bar extends below the horizontal axis by $21.1 billion to represent the amount of total spending that was absorbed by net imports and so did not

Net exports are the difference between the value of exports and the value of imports.

lead to higher Canadian GDP. Investment spending (*I*) constituted 22.8% of GDP; government purchases of goods and services (*G*) constituted 21.4% of GDP.

The bar on the right shows Canada's GDP calculated according to the income approach. About 76% of Canada's GDP in 2011, or about $1300 billion, consisted of factor incomes. Of that amount, the labour force earned $889.5 billion, the firms' owners made $366.7 billion, and the owners of capital made $73.8 billion. The remainder of the 2011 GDP, about 24%, or $420.3 billion, comprised non-factor payments, such as the net indirect taxes collected by governments plus the amount of capital depreciation. Adding both numbers yields the incomes estimate of GDP, which in 2011 was 1720.3 billion. This is slightly less than the reported GDP of $1720.748 billion. The difference is due to statistical discrepancy.

FOR INQUIRING MINDS

MORE ON NATIONAL INCOME

What is GNP? This term refers to the total factor income earned by residents of a country. It *excludes* the factor income earned by foreigners, like profits paid to foreign investors who own Canadian stocks and payments to foreigners who work temporarily in Canada. It *includes* the factor income earned abroad by Canadians, like the profits of the European operations of Blackberry that accrue to Blackberry's Canadian shareholders, and the wages of Canadians who work abroad temporarily. The relationship between GDP and GNP is: GNP = GDP + (factor income earned abroad by Canadians − factor income earned by foreigners in Canada).

In 2011, Canadian GDP was about 1.9%

higher than its GNP, mainly because of foreign companies operating in Canada.

Statistics Canada releases Canada's national income data monthly. But occasionally Statistics Canada will revise these data months afterward. Why? It is because whenever Statistics Canada releases data, there is a trade-off between accuracy and timeliness. It wants to release data in a timely fashion so people can use the most recent information to formulate economic decisions. However, these initial estimates are based on information that may be incomplete at the time of release. As time passes, more reliable and complete data become available and Statistics Canada can revise its initial estimates accordingly.

GNP, the value of output produced within a country's borders, is typically smaller than GDP, the value of output produced worldwide that is owned by a country's citizens and firms such as this Tim Hortons in Dubai. This is because GDP includes the GNP.

What GDP Tells Us

Now we've seen the various ways that gross domestic product is calculated. But what does the measurement of GDP tell us?

The most important use of GDP is as a measure of the size of the economy, providing us a scale against which to measure the economic performance of other years or to compare the economic performance of other countries. For example, suppose you want to compare the economies of different nations. A natural approach is to compare their GDPs. In 2011, as we've seen, Canada's GDP was quite large: $1721 billion. But China's GDP was $7126 billion, the U.S. had the biggest national economy at $14 928 billion, and the European Union's GDP was $16 488 billion. (All figures in Canadian dollars.) This comparison tells us that China, although it has the world's second-largest national economy, carries considerably less economic weight than does the United States. Canada's economy is about one-tenth of the size of the American economy. When taken in aggregate, the European Union, which consists of 28 countries, is America's equal or superior.

Still, one must be careful when using GDP numbers, especially when making comparisons over time. That's because part of the increase in the value of GDP over time represents increases in the *prices* of goods and services rather than an increase in output. For example, from 1992 to 2011, Canada's GDP increased in size about 2.5 times, from $700 billion to $1721 billion. But the Canadian economy did not really increase by 2.5 times over that period. To measure actual changes in aggregate output, we need a modified version of GDP that is adjusted for price changes, known as *real GDP*. We'll see next how real GDP is calculated.

ECONOMICS › IN ACTION

CREATING THE NATIONAL ACCOUNTS

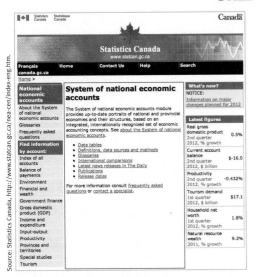

Source: Statistics Canada, http://www.statcan.gc.ca/nea-cen/index-eng.htm.

Statistics Canada maintains a web page devoted to the system of national economic accounts. The information on this page is updated regularly.

Source: Statistics Canada, Retail sales, by industry, (monthly), CANSIM, tables 080-0020.

This Statistics Canada page related to the Monthly Retail Trade Survey shows the retail sales performance for different industries. Other related pages show activities such as general merchandise store sales by province and territory by year and by month, and retail trade by province and territory by year and by month.

The national accounts, like modern macroeconomics, owe their creation to the Great Depression. Before the Depression, many countries had collected some limited data regarding their economic activities. For example, Canada released its first publication dealing with output for selected industries in 1926. Likewise, U.S. government agencies had collected data on that country's economic activities for years. But when the Depression arrived in the 1930s, this information was far from complete; nor was there any systematic way to combine and interpret it. Consequently, as the U.S. economy plunged ever lower during the Depression, lack of adequate economic theories and lack of information hampered American policy-makers in their attempts to formulate policies to smooth out business cycles.

To solve this problem, in 1937, the U.S. Department of Commerce commissioned economist Simon Kuznets to develop a set of national income accounts so there would be a proper, systematic way to collect data on economic activities. Accordingly, Kuznets presented the first version of these accounts to the U.S. Congress in 1937 and in a research report titled *National Income, 1929–35.*

This report lead to the development of national income accounting in the U.S., a policy that has proven so beneficial for economic analysis and policy-making that many countries, including Canada, now use it. Drawing on Kuznets's work, Canada published its first annual estimates of the Income and Expenditure Accounts (IEA) in the latter half of the 1940s. Information about previous years was also collected and this series of reports was "back-dated," so Canada's accounts can be said to have begun in 1926.

Since then, Statistics Canada[1] has collected and published data related to our national accounts regularly. Nowadays, these detailed statistics are given in Canada's System of National Accounts (CSNA), which Statistics Canada describes as "a set of statistical statements, or accounts, each one providing an aggregated portrait of economic activity during a given period."[2] The data used to compile the national accounts are taken from many sources including customs records, income tax returns, government public accounts, surveys conducted by government agencies, statistics collected by departments at all levels of governments, and so on. Once the data are collected, compiled, and tabulated, they are integrated into the CSNA framework for analysis. These data are used extensively. For example, the federal government and the Bank of Canada use them to formulate policies and to assess the country's economic performance. The federal government also uses the data to set the payments it makes to each province under the equalization plan. Under this plan, the federal government makes payments to less wealthy, or "have-not," provinces to "equalize" the provinces' fiscal stability. Businesses and individuals use these data to help them make informed economic decisions.

---

[1]In point of fact, Statistics Canada only came into being in 1971. Before then Canada's central statistical agency was called the Dominion Bureau of Statistics.

[2]*Source:* "Canada's System of National Economic Accounts: An Overview" Statistics Canada, last modified February 25, 2009, www.statcan.gc.ca/nea-cen/about-apropos/index-eng.htm#sources.

The CSNA includes numerous related items, such as the Monthly Retail Trade Survey (MRTS). Retail sales are an important component of gross domestic product, which is a key indicator of consumer purchasing patterns in Canada. This information is valuable to many organizations. Federal and provincial governments use it to gain an understanding of the overall economy and to design tax and spending policies. The Bank of Canada uses it to decide on monetary policy. For example, high retail sales could suggest to the federal government that its economic stimulus programs have been successful and could suggest to the Bank of Canada that it should consider raising interest rates. A business can use this information to compare its own sales performance against the industry standard. Investors may use it to decide whether to invest in a certain industry or not.

CHECK YOUR UNDERSTANDING 7-1

1. Explain why the three methods of calculating GDP produce the same estimate of GDP.

2. What are the various sectors to which firms make sales? What are the various ways in which households are linked with other sectors of the economy?

3. Consider Figure 7-2 and suppose you mistakenly believed that total value added was $30 500, the sum of the sales price of a car and a car's worth of steel. What items would you be counting twice?

Solutions appear at back of book.

Real GDP: A Measure of Aggregate Output

In this chapter's opening story, we described how China passed Japan as the world's second-largest economy in 2010. At the time, Japan's economy was weakening: during the second quarter of 2010, output declined by an annual rate of 6.3%. Oddly, however, GDP was up. In fact, Japan's GDP measured in yen, its national currency, rose by an annual rate of 4.8% during the quarter. How was that possible? The answer is that Japan was experiencing inflation at the time. As a result, the yen value of Japan's GDP rose although output actually fell.

The moral of this story is that the commonly cited GDP number is an interesting and useful statistic, one that provides a good way to compare the size of different economies, but it's not a good measure of the economy's growth over time. GDP can grow because the economy grows, but it can also grow simply because of inflation. Even if an economy's output doesn't change, GDP will go up if the prices of the goods and services the economy produces have increased. Likewise, GDP can fall either because the economy is producing less or because prices have fallen.

In order to accurately measure the economy's growth, we need a measure of real **aggregate output:** the total quantity of final goods and services the economy actually produces. The measure that is used for this purpose is known as *real GDP*. By tracking real GDP over time, we avoid the problem of changes in prices distorting the value of changes in production of goods and services over time. Let's look first at how real GDP is calculated, then at what it means.

Calculating Real GDP

To understand how real GDP is calculated, imagine an economy in which only two goods, apples and oranges, are produced and in which both goods are sold only to final consumers. The outputs and prices of the two fruits for two consecutive years are shown in Table 7-1.

Aggregate output is the economy's total quantity of output of final goods and services.

Real GDP is the total value of all final goods and services produced in the economy during a given year, calculated using the prices of a selected base year.

Nominal GDP is the value of all final goods and services produced in the economy during a given year, calculated using the prices (current) in the year in which the output is produced.

TABLE **7-1** Calculating GDP and Real GDP in a Simple Economy

	Year 1		Year 2	
	Quantity (billions)	Price	Quantity (billions)	Price
Apples	2000	$0.25	2200	$0.30
Oranges	1000	$0.50	1200	$0.70
GDP (billions of dollars)	(2000 × $0.25) + (1000 × $0.50) = **$1000**		(2200 × $0.30) + (1200 × $0.70) = **$1500**	
Real GDP (billions of year 1 dollars)	(2000 × $0.25) + (1000 × $0.50) = **$1000**		(2200 × $0.25) + (1200 × $0.50) = **$1150**	

The first thing we can say about these data is that the nominal value of sales increased from year 1 to year 2. In the first year, the total value of sales was (2000 billion × $0.25) + (1000 billion × $0.50) = $1000 billion; in the second it was (2200 billion × $0.30) + (1200 billion × $0.70) = $1500 billion, which is 50% larger. But it is also clear from the table that this increase in the dollar value of GDP overstates the real growth in the economy. Although the quantities of both apples and oranges increased, the prices of both apples and oranges also rose. So part of the 50% increase in the dollar value of GDP from year 1 to year 2 simply reflects higher prices, not higher production of output.

To estimate the true increase in aggregate output produced, we have to ask the following question: how much would GDP have gone up if prices had *not* changed? To answer this question, we need to find the value of output in year 2 expressed in year 1 prices. In year 1 the price of apples was $0.25 each and the price of oranges $0.50 each. So year 2 output *at year 1 prices* is (2200 billion × $0.25) + (1200 billion × $0.50) = $1150 billion. And output in year 1 at year 1 prices was $1000 billion. So in this example, GDP measured in year 1 prices rose 15%—from $1000 billion to $1150 billion.

Now we can define **real GDP:** it is the total value of final goods and services produced in the economy during a year, calculated as if prices had stayed constant at the level of some given base year. A real GDP number always comes with information about what the base year is. Statistics Canada revises the base year every 10 years, and the current base year is 2002.

Sometimes, GDP is calculated using the prices of the same year in which the output is produced. Economists call this measure **nominal GDP,** GDP at current prices. Nominal GDP has not been adjusted for changes in prices and thus can be distorted by price changes (i.e., inflation or deflation). If we had used nominal GDP to measure the true change in output from year 1 to year 2 in our apples and oranges example, we would have overstated the true growth in output: we would have claimed it to be 50%, when in fact it was only 15%. By comparing output in the two years using the same set of prices—the year 1 prices in this example—we are able to focus solely on changes in the quantity of output by eliminating the influence of changes in prices.

Table 7-2 shows a real-life version of our apples and oranges example. The second column shows the nominal GDP in 1992, 2002, and 2011. The third column shows the real GDP for each year in 2002 dollars. For 2002, the two numbers are the same—as is always the case—in the base year nominal GDP equals real GDP. But the real GDP in 1992 expressed in 2002 dollars was higher than the nominal GDP in 1992, reflecting the fact that prices were in general higher in 2002 than in 1992. However, the real GDP in 2011, expressed in 2002 dollars, was less than the nominal GDP in 2011 because prices in 2002 were lower than in 2011.

TABLE **7-2** Nominal versus Real GDP in 1992, 2002, and 2011

	Nominal GDP (billions of current dollars)	Real GDP (billions of 2002 dollars)
1992	$700.5	$815.1
2002	1152.9	1152.9
2011	1720.7	1356.9

Source: Statistics Canada.

FIGURE **7-4** Canada's Real GDP Growth Rate from 1962 to 2011

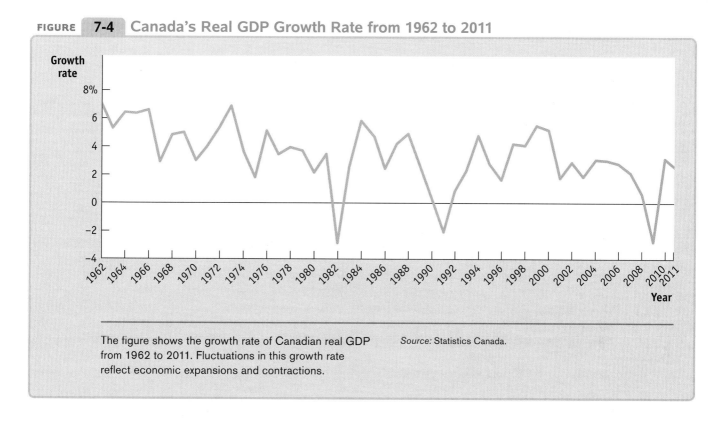

The figure shows the growth rate of Canadian real GDP from 1962 to 2011. Fluctuations in this growth rate reflect economic expansions and contractions.

Source: Statistics Canada.

You might have noticed that there is an alternative way to calculate real GDP using the data in Table 7-1. Why not measure it using the prices of year 2 rather than year 1 as the base-year prices? This procedure seems equally valid. According to that calculation, real GDP in year 1 at year 2 prices is (2000 billion × $0.30) + (1000 billion × $0.70) = $1300 billion; real GDP in year 2 at year 2 prices is $1500 billion, the same as nominal GDP in year 2. So using year 2 prices as the base year, the growth rate of real GDP is equal to ($1500 billion – $1300 billion)/$1300 billion = 0.154, or 15.4%. This is slightly higher than the figure we got from the previous calculation, in which year 1 prices were the base-year prices. In that calculation, we found that real GDP increased by 15%. Neither answer, 15.4% versus 15%, is more "correct" than the other.

In reality, the government economists who put together Canada's national accounts have adopted a method to measure the change in real GDP known as *chain-linking,* which uses the average between the GDP growth rate calculated using an early base year and the GDP growth rate calculated using a late base year. As a result, Canada's statistics on real GDP are always expressed in **chained dollars.**

The Growth Rate of Canada's Real GDP

Now that we know what real GDP is, we can examine the growth rate of Canada's real GDP. It is useful to do so, because real GDP is one of the most closely followed pieces of data that Statistics Canada releases. This is because the real GDP tells whether our economy is slowing down or expanding. Figure 7-4 depicts Canada's real GDP growth rate from 1962 to 2011. As you see, its growth rate fluctuated during that period, showing that business cycles indeed are a common feature for any economy, including our own. As you know from Chapter 6, Canada experienced three recessions during this period: one in the early 1980s, one in the 1990s, and one in 2008–2009. The recession in the 1980s was partly the result of the two oil price shocks in the 1970s, during which the price of oil skyrocketed. The recession in the early 1990s was the result of a U.S. recession

Chained dollars is the method of calculating changes in real GDP using the average between the growth rate calculated using an early base year and the growth rate calculated using a late base year.

GLOBAL COMPARISON

GDP AND THE MEANING OF LIFE

"I've been rich and I've been poor," the actress Mae West famously declared. "Believe me, rich is better." But is the same true for countries?

This figure shows two pieces of information for a number of countries: how rich they are, as measured by GDP per capita, and how people assess their well-being. Well-being was measured by a Gallup world survey that asked people to rate their lives at the current time and their expectations for the next five years. The graph shows the percentage of people who rated their well-being as "thriving." The figure seems to tell us three things:

1. *Rich is better.* Richer countries on average have higher well-being than poor countries.

2. *Money matters less as you grow richer.* The gain in life satisfaction as you go from GDP per capita of $5000 to $20 000 is greater than the gain as you go from $20 000 to $35 000.

3. *Money isn't everything.* We Canadians seem to be more satisfied with our lives, even though we are poorer than Americans or Netherlanders. Japan is richer than most other nations, but by and large, quite miserable.

These results are consistent with the observation that high GDP per capita makes it easier to achieve a good life but that countries aren't equally successful in taking advantage of that possibility.

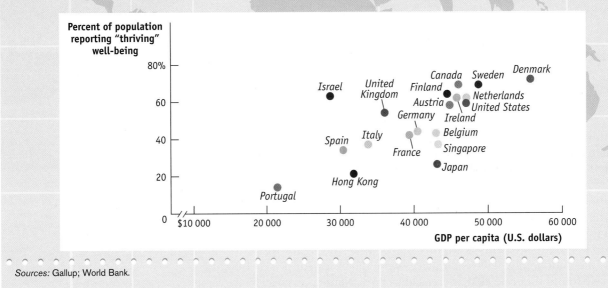

Sources: Gallup; World Bank.

and of a deflationary (contractionary) monetary policy undertaken by the Bank of Canada. The most recent recession was triggered by the financial crises that originated in the United States. During these recessions, the country's real GDP growth turned negative as firms, seeing the demand for their products soften, lowered their production. The diagram clearly shows another important fact—over the last several decades the growth rate of real GDP has been trending downward. Chapter 9 will discuss long-run growth in greater detail.

What Real GDP Doesn't Measure

GDP, nominal or real, is a measure of a country's aggregate output. Other things being equal, a country with a larger population will have higher GDP simply because there are more people working. So if we want to compare GDP across countries but want to eliminate the effect of differences in population size, we use the measure **GDP per capita**—GDP divided by the size of the population, equivalent to the average GDP per person.

GDP per capita is GDP divided by the size of the population; it is equivalent to the average GDP per person.

Real GDP per capita can be a useful measure in some circumstances, such as in a comparison of labour productivity between countries. However, despite the fact that it is a rough measure of the average real output per person, real GDP per capita has well-known limitations as a measure of a country's living standards. Every once in a while economists are accused of believing that growth in real GDP per capita is the only thing that matters—that is, thinking that increasing real GDP per capita is a goal in itself. In fact, economists rarely make that mistake; the idea that economists care only about real GDP per capita is a sort of urban legend. Let's take a moment to be clear about why a country's real GDP per capita is not a sufficient measure of human welfare in that country and why growth in real GDP per capita is not an appropriate policy goal in itself.

One way to think about this issue is to say that an increase in real GDP means an expansion in the economy's production possibility frontier. Because the economy has increased its productive capacity, there are more things that society can achieve. But whether society actually makes good use of that increased potential to improve living standards is another matter. To put it in a slightly different way, your income may be higher this year than last year, but whether you use that higher income to actually improve your quality of life is your choice.

So let's say it again: real GDP per capita is a measure of an economy's average aggregate output per person—and so of what it *can* do. It is not a sufficient goal in itself because it doesn't address how a country uses that output to affect living standards. A country with a high GDP can afford to be healthy, to be well educated, and in general to have a good quality of life. But there is not a one-to-one match between GDP and the quality of life.

ECONOMICS ▸ IN ACTION

MIRACLE IN VENEZUELA?

The South American nation of Venezuela has a distinction that may surprise you: in recent years, it has had one of the world's fastest-growing nominal GDPs. Between 2000 and 2010, Venezuelan nominal GDP grew by an average of 29% each year—much faster than nominal GDP in Canada, the United States or even in booming economies like China.

So is Venezuela experiencing an economic miracle? No, it's just suffering from unusually high inflation. Figure 7-5 shows Venezuela's nominal and real GDP from 2000 to 2010, with real GDP measured in 1997 prices. Real GDP did grow over the period, but at an annual rate of only 3%. This was higher than the growth rate in Canada, which was 1.7% over the same period, but it is far short of China's 10% growth.

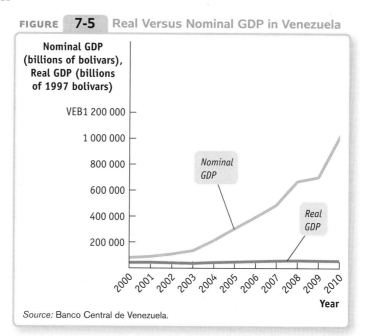

FIGURE **7-5** Real Versus Nominal GDP in Venezuela

Source: Banco Central de Venezuela.

CHECK YOUR UNDERSTANDING   7-2

1. Assume there are only two goods in the economy, french fries and onion rings. In 2011, 1 000 000 servings of french fries were sold at $0.40 each and 800 000 servings of onion rings at $0.60 each. From 2011 to 2012, the price of french fries rose by 25% and the servings sold fell by 10%; the price of onion rings fell by 15% and the servings sold rose by 5%.
   a. Calculate nominal GDP in 2011 and 2012. Calculate real GDP in 2012 using 2011 prices.
   b. Why would an assessment of growth using nominal GDP be misguided?

2. From 2005 to 2010, the price of electronic equipment fell dramatically and the price of housing rose dramatically. What are the implications of this in deciding whether to use 2005 or 2010 as the base year in calculating 2012 real GDP?

Solutions appear at back of book.

Price Indexes and the Aggregate Price Level

In the spring and summer of 2011, Canadians were facing sticker shock at the gas pump: the price of a litre of regular gasoline had risen from an average of $0.765 at the end of December 2008 to close to $1.32. Many other prices were also up. Some prices, though, were heading down: some foods, like oranges, were coming down from a run-up from late 2010, and virtually anything involving electronics was getting cheaper as well. Yet practically everyone felt that the overall cost of living was rising. But how fast?

Clearly, there was a need for a single number summarizing what was happening to consumer prices. Just as macroeconomists find it useful to have a single number representing the overall level of output, they also find it useful to have a single number representing the overall level of prices: the **aggregate price level.** Yet a huge variety of goods and services are produced and consumed in the economy. How can we summarize the prices of all these goods and services with a single number? The answer lies in the concept of a *price index*—a concept best introduced with an example.

Market Baskets and Price Indexes

Suppose that a frost in Ontario destroys several fruit crops. As a result, the price of an apple rises from $0.20 to $0.40, the price of a peach rises from $0.60 to $1.00, and the price of a small bunch of grapes rises from $0.25 to $0.45. How much has the price of fruit increased?

One way to answer that question is to state three numbers—the changes in prices for apples, peaches, and bunches of grapes. But this is a very cumbersome method. Rather than having to recite three numbers in an effort to track changes in the prices of fruit, we would prefer to have some kind of overall measure of the *average* price change.

To measure average price changes for consumer goods and services, economists track changes in the cost of a typical consumer's *consumption bundle*— the typical basket of goods and services purchased by the average household at some point in time. A hypothetical consumption bundle, used to measure changes in the overall price level, is known as a **market basket.**

Suppose that before the frost a typical consumer bought 200 apples, 50 peaches, and 100 small bunches of grapes over the course of a year, our market basket for this example. Table 7-3 shows the pre-frost and post-frost cost of this market basket. Before the frost, it cost $95; after the frost, the same bundle of goods cost $175. Since $175/$95 = 1.842, the post-frost basket costs 1.842 times the cost of the pre-frost basket, a cost increase of 84.2%. In this example, the average

The **aggregate price level** is a measure of the overall level of prices in the economy.

A **market basket** is a hypothetical set of goods and services (purchased or made). The quantities in the basket are weights to be used in a price index.

TABLE 7-3   Calculating the Cost of a Market Basket

	Pre-frost	Post-frost
Price of an apple	$0.20	$0.40
Price of a peach	0.60	1.00
Price of a small bunch of grapes	0.25	0.45
Cost of market basket (200 apples, 50 peaches, 100 small bunches of grapes)	(200 × $0.20) + (50 × $0.60) + (100 × $0.25) = $95.00	(200 × $0.40) + (50 × $1.00) + (100 × $0.45) = $175.00

A **price index** measures the cost of purchasing a given market basket in a given year, where that cost is normalized so that it is equal to 100 in the selected base year.

The **inflation rate** is the annual percentage change in a price index—typically the consumer price index.

price of fruit has increased 84.2% since the base year as a result of the frost, where the base year is the initial year used in the measurement of the price change.

Economists use the same method to measure changes in the overall price level: they track changes in the cost of buying a given market basket. In addition, they perform another simplification in order to avoid having to keep track of the information that the market basket cost, for example, $95 in such-and-such a year. They *normalize* the measure of the aggregate price level, which means that they set the cost of the market basket equal to 100 in the chosen base year. Working with a market basket and a base year, and after performing normalization, we obtain what is known as a **price index,** a normalized measure of the overall price level. It is always cited along with the year for which the aggregate price level is being measured and the base year. A price index can be calculated using the following formula:

(7-2) Price index in a given year $= \dfrac{\text{Cost of market basket in a given year}}{\text{Cost of market basket in base year}} \times 100$

In our example, the fruit market basket cost $95 in the base year, the year before the frost. So by Equation 7-2 we define the price index for fruit as (cost of market basket in current year/$95) × 100, yielding an index of 100 for the period before the frost and 184.2 after the frost. You should note that the price index for the base year always results in a price index equal to 100. This is because the price index in the base year is equal to: (cost of market basket in base year/cost of market basket in base year) × 100 = 100.

Thus, the price index makes it clear that the average price of fruit has risen 84.2% as a consequence of the frost. Because of its simplicity and intuitive appeal, the method we've just described is used to calculate a variety of price indexes to track average price changes among a variety of different groups of goods and services. For example, the *consumer price index*, which we'll discuss shortly, is the most widely used measure of the aggregate price level, the overall price level of final consumer goods and services across the whole economy.

Price indexes are also the basis for measuring inflation. The **inflation rate** is the annual percent change in an official price index. The inflation rate from year

FOR INQUIRING MINDS

WHICH INDEX?

To calculate a price index all we need is the list of prices to be averaged and a list of the weights to be used (one weight for each price to be averaged). The weights are the quantities of items in the market basket, that is, the quantities of goods and services, consumed or produced, either from some fixed (usually past) period or the current period (in time).

Since a price index is a weighted average of the prices of the items in the basket, a price index is either fixed-weighted or current-weighted, depending on what type of weights the market basket holds. A fixed-weighted price index employs a market basket that does not change over time: the quantities of items in the basket are taken from one given point in time.

On the other hand, a current-weighted price index takes its quantities from the current year. It has this name because the quantities are not fixed and these weights are likely to change over time. The example of the market basket with the apples, peaches, and grapes uses a fixed-weighted price index.

The **consumer price index,** or **CPI,** uses the cost of the market basket purchased by a typical Canadian family to gauge what the high average price level is and how quickly it is changing.

1 to year 2 is calculated using the following formula, where we assume that year 1 and year 2 are consecutive years:

(7-3) Inflation rate = $\dfrac{\text{Price index in year 2} - \text{Price index in year 1}}{\text{Price index in year 1}} \times 100$

Typically, a news report that cites "the inflation rate" is referring to the annual percent change in the consumer price index.

The Consumer Price Index

The most widely used measure of prices in Canada is the **consumer price index** (often referred to simply as the **CPI**), which is intended to show how the cost of all the purchases by a typical Canadian family has changed over time. It is calculated by surveying market prices for a market basket constructed to represent the consumption of a typical, or average, Canadian family. Once the basket (weights) and prices are known, we can calculate the expenditure necessary to buy the market basket in a particular year and use this to construct the CPI as:

(7-4) CPI in a given year = $\dfrac{\text{Cost of (fixed) market basket in a given year}}{\text{Cost of (fixed) market basket in base year}} \times 100$

At the time of publication, the base period for the index was 2002; that is, the index is calculated so that the average of consumer prices in 2002 is 100.

The market basket used to calculate the CPI is far more complex than the three-fruit market basket we described above. In fact, about every four years Statistics Canada uses information from their Survey of Household Spending to construct a market basket that contains more than 600 goods and services, ranging from carrots to gasoline to rent, that an average Canadian household purchased during the survey, or base, year. These quantities are the fixed-weights for the index. To calculate the CPI, once the market basket has been set, Statistics Canada employees go out every month to collect information on market prices—the prices that consumers are actually being charged *including* sales taxes *less* subsidies. They survey supermarkets, gas stations, hardware stores, and hundreds of retail outlets in every province, as well as in Iqaluit, Nunavut, Whitehorse, Yukon, and Yellowknife, Northwest Territories. Figure 7-6 shows the weight of major categories in the consumer price index as of April 2011. For example, gasoline accounted for 6% of the CPI in April 2011. So when gas prices rose about 73% from $0.765/L in late 2008 to $1.32/L in May 2011, the effect was to increase the CPI by about 0.73 times 6%—that is, around 4.3%.

Figure 7-7 shows how the CPI has changed since measurement began in 1914. Since 1940, the CPI has risen steadily, although its annual percent increases in recent years have been much

FIGURE 7-6 The Makeup of the Consumer Price Index in 2011

This chart shows the percentage shares of major types of spending in the CPI as of April 2011 (using the 2009 basket at April 2011 prices). Housing (shelter & household operations), food, transportation, and gasoline comprised about 76% of the CPI 2009 market basket.

Source: Statistics Canada.

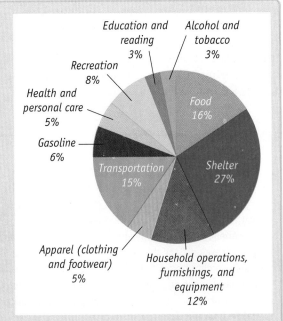

- Education and reading 3%
- Alcohol and tobacco 3%
- Recreation 8%
- Health and personal care 5%
- Food 16%
- Gasoline 6%
- Transportation 15%
- Shelter 27%
- Apparel (clothing and footwear) 5%
- Household operations, furnishings, and equipment 12%

FIGURE **7-7** The CPI, 1914–2011

Since 1914, the CPI has generally risen steadily. But the annual percentage increases in recent years have been much smaller than those of the 1970s and early 1980s. Since the mid-1990s, the inflation rate has fluctuated around 2%, partly owing to the 2% inflation rate target set by the Bank of Canada. (The vertical axis is measured on a logarithmic scale so that equal percent changes in the CPI have the same slope.)

Source: Statistics Canada.

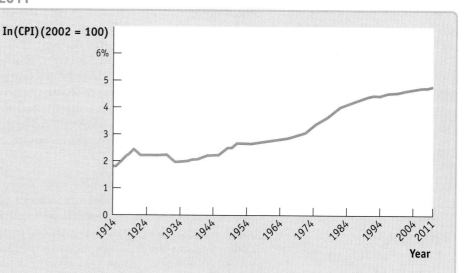

FOR INQUIRING MINDS

TOTAL CPI VS. CORE CPI

There are several versions of the consumer price index: the CPI we have discussed so far is often called the *total,* or *all-items CPI,* because it includes all types of items. Other versions, however, omit some items. For example, the core CPI omits the prices of eight items: fruit, vegetables, gasoline, fuel oil, mortgage interest cost, natural gas, intercity transportation, and tobacco. It omits these prices because they are volatile, which is to say they can fluctuate to such an extent that the CPI can be misleading. Further, the core CPI is adjusted so as to remove the effect of changes in sales taxes on the remaining items. Many economists feel that, for these reasons, the core CPI is a more reliable measure of changes in the inflation rate in the long term than the total CPI. The Bank of Canada uses the percentage change in the core CPI as a guide to determine monetary policy. Figure 7-8a shows the annual levels of the CPI and the core CPI from 1985 to 2011. Clearly these indexes move together over time, which isn't surprising given their large overlap. But now look at Figure 7-8b, which shows the annual percentage change in each index over the same years. As this diagram shows, the two indexes do vary from period to period; the change in total CPI is more volatile than the change in core CPI, even on an annual basis.

FIGURE **7-8** Annual Total CPI and Core CPI

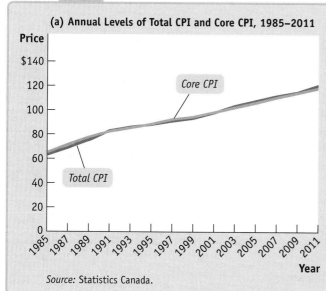

(a) Annual Levels of Total CPI and Core CPI, 1985–2011

Source: Statistics Canada.

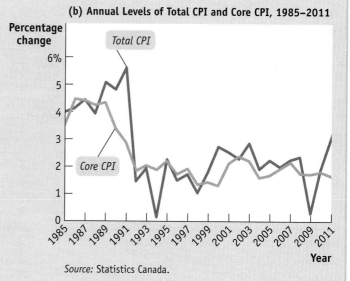

(b) Annual Levels of Total CPI and Core CPI, 1985–2011

Source: Statistics Canada.

The **industrial producer price index,** or **IPPI,** measures changes in the prices of goods purchased by producers.

The **GDP deflator** for a given year is 100 times the ratio of nominal GDP to real GDP in that year.

smaller than those of the 1970s and early 1980s. A logarithmic scale is used so that equal percent changes in the CPI have the same slope.

Canada is not the only country that calculates a consumer price index. In fact, nearly every country has one. As you might expect, the market baskets that make up these indexes differ quite a lot from country to country. In developing countries, where people must spend a high proportion of their income just to feed themselves, food makes up a large share of the price index. Among high-income countries, differences in consumption patterns lead to differences in the price indexes: the Japanese price index puts a larger weight on raw fish and a smaller weight on beef than ours does, and the French price index puts a larger weight on wine.

Other Price Measures

There are two other price measures that are also widely used to track economy-wide price changes. One is the **industrial producer price index (IPPI).** As its name suggests, this index measures the wholesale cost of a typical (fixed) basket of goods—containing raw commodities such as steel, electricity, coal, and so on—purchased by producers. Because commodity producers are relatively quick to raise prices when they perceive a change in overall demand for their goods, the IPPI often responds to inflationary or deflationary pressures more quickly than the CPI. As a result, the IPPI is often regarded as an "early warning signal" of changes in the inflation rate.

The other widely used price measure is the *GDP deflator,* which is a *current-weighted* price index. It employs the current quantities of all goods and services that enter into GDP as weights (market basket quantities) in the weighted average. The **GDP deflator** for a given year is equal to the ratio of nominal GDP for that year to real GDP for that year, multiplied by 100. That is,

$$(7\text{-}5) \quad \text{GDP deflator} = \frac{\text{Nominal GDP for given year}}{\text{Real GDP for given year}} \times 100$$

At the time of writing, real GDP was expressed in 2002 dollars, so the GDP deflator for 2002 is 100. If the nominal GDP were to double and real GDP were to remain the same, then the GDP deflator would indicate that the aggregate price level had doubled.

Perhaps the most important point about the different inflation rates generated by these three measures of prices—CPI, IPPI, and GDP deflator—is that they usually move closely together (although the producer price index tends to fluctuate more than either of the other two measures). Figure 7-9 shows the annual percent changes in the

FIGURE **7-9** The CPI, the IPPI, and the GDP Deflator

As the figure shows, the three different measures of inflation, the IPPI (orange), the CPI (green), and the GDP deflator (purple), usually move closely together. Each reveals a drastic acceleration of inflation during the 1970s and a return to relative price stability in the 1990s.

Source: Statistics Canada.

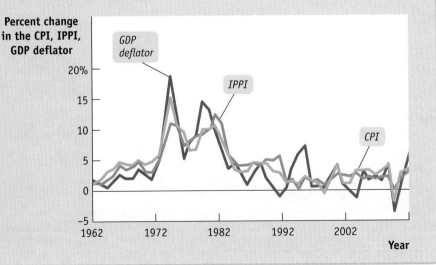

three indexes since the early 1960s. By all three measures, the Canadian economy experienced accelerating inflation during the 1970s and a return to relative price stability in the 1990s. Notice, by the way, the dramatic ups and downs in producer prices from 2000 to 2010 on the graph; this reflects large swings in energy and food prices, which play a much bigger role in the PPI than they do in either the CPI or the GDP deflator. The average price level does not always rise. The economy experienced a falling price level, called *deflation,* after World War I and during the Great Depression as seen by the falling slope of Figure 7-7 in the 1920s and 1930s.

ECONOMICS ▶ IN ACTION

INDEXING TO THE CPI

Although GDP is a very important number for shaping economic policy, official statistics on GDP don't have a direct effect on people's lives. The CPI, by contrast, has a direct and immediate impact on millions of Canadians. The reason is that many payments are tied, or "indexed," to the CPI—the amount paid rises or falls when the CPI rises or falls.

In 2012, more than 5 million people, most of them old or disabled, received payments from the Canada Pension Plan (CPP), Old Age Security (OAS), or a supplemental program. These payments amounted to almost 72 billion dollars. The amount of an individual's CPP payment is determined by a formula that reflects his or her previous payments into the system as well as other factors. In addition, all CPP and OAS payments are adjusted each year to offset any increase in consumer prices over the previous year. The CPI is used to calculate the official estimate of the inflation rate used to adjust these payments yearly. So every percentage point added to the official estimate of the rate of inflation adds 1% to the cheques received by millions of individuals.

Other government payments are also indexed to the CPI. In addition, income tax brackets, the bands of income levels that determine a taxpayer's income tax rate, are also indexed to the CPI. (An individual in a higher income bracket pays a higher income tax rate in a progressive tax system like ours.) Indexing also extends to the private sector, where many private contracts, including some wage settlements, contain cost-of-living allowances (called COLAs) that adjust payments in proportion to changes in the CPI.

Because the CPI plays such an important and direct role in people's lives, it's a politically sensitive number. Statistics Canada, which calculates the CPI, takes great care in collecting and interpreting price and consumption data. It uses a complex method in which households are surveyed to determine what they buy and where they shop, and a carefully selected sample of stores are surveyed to get representative prices.

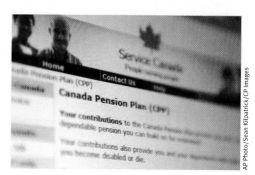

A small change in the CPI has large consequences for those dependent on government pension and social assistance payments.

CHECK YOUR UNDERSTANDING   7-3

1. Consider Table 7-3 but suppose that the market basket is composed of 100 apples, 50 peaches, and 200 small bunches of grapes. How does this change the pre-frost and post-frost price indexes? Explain. Generalize your explanation to how the construction of the market basket affects the price index.

2. For each of the following events, how would an economist using a 10-year-old market basket create a bias in measuring the change in the cost of living today?
   a. A typical family owns more cars than it would have a decade ago. Over that time, the average price of a car has increased more than the average prices of other goods.
   b. Virtually no households had broadband Internet access a decade ago. Now many households have it, and the price has regularly fallen each year.

3. The consumer price index in Canada (2002 base period) was 114.4 in 2009 and 116.5 in 2010. Calculate the inflation rate from 2009 to 2010.

Solutions appear at back of book.

▼ Quick Review

- Changes in the **aggregate price level** are measured by the cost of buying a particular **market basket** during different years. A **price index** for a given year is the cost of the market basket in that year normalized so that the price index equals 100 in a selected base year.

- The **inflation rate** is calculated as the percent change in a price index. The most commonly used price index is the **consumer price index**, or **CPI**, which tracks the cost of a basket of consumer goods and services. The **industrial producer price index**, or **IPPI**, does the same for goods and services used as inputs by firms. The **GDP deflator** measures the aggregate price level as the ratio of nominal to real GDP times 100. These three measures normally behave quite similarly.

BUSINESS • Expectations and the Market for Forecasts
CASE •

Should you sell your stocks and bonds or buy some more? Should your company lay off employees or hire more? Should the Bank of Canada reduce interest rates to stimulate economic growth or should it raise them to slow the growth of the economy, reduce inflationary pressure, and encourage more saving?

These are only a few of the decisions that economic agents need to make on a regular basis. Economic agents are those who make economic decisions, using known data and their own expectations. They may be making decisions on behalf of a household, a business, or a government. And before these agents make their decisions, they need to consider many variables: the levels and rates of change of real output, employment, consumption, government budgetary position (i.e., the size of its deficit or surplus), exchange rates, flows of international trade, housing starts, money supply, and inflation. True, economic variables may not be the only factors considered, but they will have some influence. For example, if the income of a household rises significantly, then the members of the household may consider buying a larger house.

When making decisions, it is helpful to know the past and current levels of these variables, and it is useful to anticipate future levels. An economic agent would likely make one set of decisions if the levels of real output and employment were expected to rise, and make a completely different set of decisions if they were expected to fall. For example, if employment levels are expected to fall, then a household might rule out buying a larger home, even though its own income has risen. This household might be reluctant to buy a new large home if the likelihood of a job loss has arisen.

So important is it to make accurate economic forecasts that agents pay close attention when government agencies, such as Statistics Canada or the Bank of Canada, release their official economic statistics. This is done according to a fixed schedule. For instance, Statistics Canada releases the unemployment rate and other labour market data on the first Friday of each month. The Bank of Canada announces its target for the overnight interest rate on eight predetermined fixed announcement dates (see www.bankofcanada.ca/monetary-policy-introduction/key-interest-rate/schedule/ for the announcement schedule). For the more popular statistics, such as gross domestic product (output), inflation, employment, and unemployment, the lead-up to and the activity immediately following the release can receive significant attention in the media.

As soon as the official economic statistics are released, specialized analysts pore over the data to determine to what extent past expectations were correct or incorrect and, more importantly, to help figure out where the economy is headed. These analysts work for government agencies, banks, investment dealers, stockbrokers, insurance companies, pension funds, credit rating agencies, forecasting groups at think tanks and industry associations, news agencies, and so on, and their expert opinion is fundamental to economic agents' decision-making. For example, knowing the future path of the growth rate of real GDP, the unemployment rate, the inflation rate, interest rates, the exchange rate, and other variables helps governments more accurately forecast tax revenue (from GDP growth and exchange rate movements), program expenditures (from GDP growth and movements in unemployment and inflation), and interest costs of government debt (from interest and exchange rates).

Analysts also examine statistics from reliable private-sector sources, since predictions are likely to be more accurate when data come from more than just one or two sources. Even the federal government itself does this. For example, before the 2012 federal budget, the Department of Finance, which does collect its own statistics, also surveyed the following private-sector economists: Bank of America Merrill Lynch, BMO Capital Markets, Caisse de dépôt et placement du

Québec, CIBC World Markets, the Conference Board of Canada, Desjardins Group, Deutsche Bank of Canada, Laurentian Bank Securities, National Bank Financial Group, Royal Bank of Canada, Scotiabank Group, TD Bank Financial Group, UBS Securities Canada, and the University of Toronto (Policy and Economic Analysis Program).[1] The federal government is not alone in this practice; other governments often survey private-sector forecasts, as well. While developing its 2012 budget, the Ontario Ministry of Finance consulted forecasts from BMO Capital Markets, Central 1 Credit Union, the Centre for Spatial Economics, CIBC World Markets, the Conference Board of Canada, Desjardins Group, HIS Global Insight, Laurentian Bank Securities, National Bank Financial Group, RBC Financial Group, Scotiabank Group, TD Bank Financial Group, and the University of Toronto (Policy and Economic Analysis Program).[2] Governments' consultations of other reliable sources allows them to build and refine their own forecasting models to be as reasonable as possible.

QUESTIONS FOR THOUGHT

1. Why would economic agents, such as firms and households, be interested in the statistics that government agencies release?

2. Briefly explain how an agent's expectation may affect the operation of the economy.

3. Why would the federal government use the services of private economic forecasters, when it already collects its own data about the economy?

---

[1]*Source:* "Chapter 2: Economic Developments and Prospects," Government of Canada, last modified March 29, 2012, www.budget.gc.ca/2012/plan/chap2-eng.html.

[2]*Source:* "2012 Ontario Budget: Chapter II: Ontario's Economic Outlook and Fiscal Review," Ontario Ministry of Finance, last modified March 27, 2012, www.fin.gov.on.ca/en/budget/ontariobudgets/2012/ch2c.html.

SUMMARY

1. Economists keep track of the flows of money between sectors with the **national income and product accounts,** or **national accounts.** Households earn income via the factor markets from wages, interest on **bonds,** profit accruing to owners of **stocks,** and rent on land. In addition, they receive **government transfers** from the government. **Disposable income,** total household income minus taxes plus government transfers, is allocated to **consumer spending** (C) and **private savings.** Via the **financial markets,** private savings and foreign lending are channelled to **investment spending** (I), government borrowing, and foreign borrowing. **Government purchases of goods and services** (G) are paid for by tax revenues and any **government borrowing.** Exports (X) generate an inflow of funds into the country from the rest of the world, but imports (IM) lead to an outflow of funds to the rest of the world. Foreigners can also buy stocks and bonds in Canadian financial markets.

2. **Factor incomes** are incomes earned by factors of production, which include wages, interest, rent dividends, and profits. **Non-factor payments** are the difference between the prices paid for final goods and services and the amount received by factors of production, which include net indirect taxes and capital depreciation.

3. **Gross domestic product,** or **GDP,** measures the value of all **final goods and services** produced in the economy. It does not include the value of **intermediate goods and services,** but it does include **inventories** and **net exports** (X – IM). It can be calculated in three ways: add up the **value added** by all producers; add up all spending on domestically produced final goods and services, leading to the equation $GDP = C + I + G + X - IM$, also known as **aggregate expenditure;** or add up all the income earned from the production of goods and services. These three methods are equivalent because in the economy as a whole, one person's spending will always be another person's income. Thus, total spending on final goods and services must be equal to total income earned from production.

4. **Real GDP** is the value of the final goods and services produced calculated using the prices of a selected base year. Except in the base year, real GDP is not the same as **nominal GDP,** the value of **aggregate output** calculated using current prices. Analysis of the growth rate of aggregate output must use real GDP because doing so eliminates any change in the value of aggregate output due solely to price changes. Real **GDP per capita** is a measure of average aggregate output per person but is not in itself an appropriate policy goal. Canadian statistics on real GDP are always expressed in **chained dollars.**

5. To measure the **aggregate price level,** economists calculate the cost of purchasing a **market basket.** A **price index** is the ratio of the current cost of that market basket to the cost in a selected base year, multiplied by 100.

6. The **inflation rate** is the yearly percent change in a price index, typically based on the **consumer price index,** or **CPI,** the most common measure of the aggregate price level. A similar index for goods and services purchased by firms is the **industrial producer price index,** or **IPPI.** Finally, economists also use the **GDP deflator,** which measures the price level by calculating the ratio of nominal to real GDP times 100.

KEY TERMS

PROBLEMS

1. At right is a simplified circular-flow diagram for the economy of Micronia. (Note that there is no investment in Micronia.)

   a. What is the value of GDP in Micronia?

   b. What is the value of net exports?

   c. What is the value of disposable income?

   d. Does the total flow of money out of households—the sum of taxes paid and consumer spending—equal the total flow of money into households?

   e. How does the government of Micronia finance its purchases of goods and services?

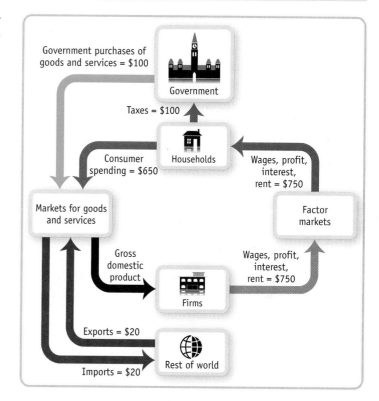

2. A more complex circular-flow diagram for the economy of Macronia is shown at right. (Note that Macronia has investment and financial markets.)

   a. What is the value of GDP in Macronia?

   b. What is the value of net exports?

   c. What is the value of disposable income?

   d. Does the total flow of money out of households—the sum of taxes paid, consumer spending, and private savings—equal the total flow of money into households?

   e. How does the government finance its spending?

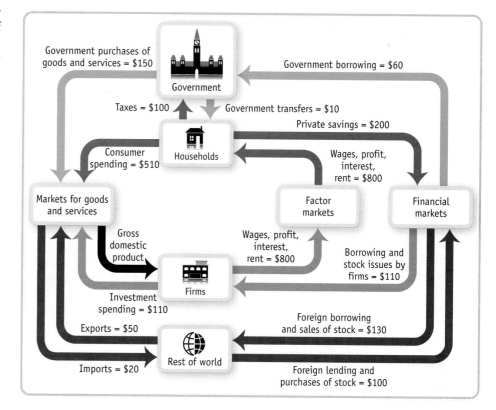

3. Consider the following table for Canada's GDP in 2011.

Category	Components of GDP in 2011 (billions of dollars)
Personal expenditure on consumer goods and services	
Durable goods	$113.7
Semi-durable goods	72.6
Non-durable goods	240.3
Services	556.0
Business gross fixed capital formation	
Residential structures	118.5
Non-residential structures	104.1
Machinery and equipment	97.8
Business investment in inventories	4.7
Government purchases of goods and services and investment spending	
Expenditure on goods and services	367.6
Gross fixed capital formation and inventories	67.0
Exports of goods and services	
Goods	458.2
Services	77.5
Imports of goods and services	
Goods	455.9
Services	100.9

Source: Statistics Canada.

a. Calculate 2011 consumer spending.

b. Calculate 2011 private investment spending.

c. Calculate 2011 net exports.

d. Calculate 2011 government purchases of goods and services and investment spending.

e. Calculate 2011 gross domestic product.

f. Calculate consumer spending on services as a percentage of total consumer spending.

g. Calculate 2011 exports as a percentage of imports.

h. Calculate 2011 exports and imports as a percentage of gross domestic product. Was there a trade surplus or trade deficit in 2011? How large was this as a percentage of GDP?

4. The small economy of Pizzania produces three goods (bread, cheese, and pizza), each produced by a separate company. The bread and cheese companies produce all the inputs they need to make bread and cheese, respectively. The pizza company uses the bread and cheese from the other companies to make its pizzas. All three companies employ labour to help produce their goods, and the difference between the value of goods sold and the sum of labour and input costs is the firm's profit. The accompanying table summarizes the activities of the three companies when all the bread and cheese produced are sold to the pizza company as inputs in the production of pizzas.

	Bread company	Cheese company	Pizza company
Cost of inputs	$0	$0	$50 (bread) 35 (cheese)
Wages	15	20	75
Value of output	50	35	200

a. Calculate GDP as the value added in production.

b. Calculate GDP as spending on final goods and services.

c. Calculate GDP as income earned from production.

5. In the economy of Pizzania (from Problem 4), bread and cheese produced are sold both to the pizza company for inputs in the production of pizzas and to consumers as final goods. The accompanying table summarizes the activities of the three companies.

	Bread company	Cheese company	Pizza company
Cost of inputs	$0	$0	$50 (bread) 35 (cheese)
Wages	25	30	75
Value of output	100	60	200

a. Calculate GDP as the value added in production.

b. Calculate GDP as spending on final goods and services.

c. Calculate GDP as income earned from production.

6. Which of these transactions should be included in Canada's GDP?

a. Canada Dry builds a new bottling plant in Canada.

b. Air Canada sells one of its existing airplanes to Korean Air.

c. Ms. Moneybags buys an existing share of Telus Corporation.

d. A softwood lumber firm in British Columbia sells softwood lumber to a construction firm in California.

e. A Canadian buys a bottle of French perfume in Paris.

f. A Canadian book publisher produces too many copies of a new book. The books don't sell this year, so the publisher adds the surplus books to inventories.

7. The economy of Britannica produces three goods: computers, DVDs, and pizza. The accompanying table shows the prices and output of the three goods for the years 2010, 2011, and 2012.

Year	Computers		DVDs		Pizzas	
	Price	Quantity	Price	Quantity	Price	Quantity
2010	$900	10	$10	100	$15	2
2011	1000	10.5	12	105	16	2
2012	1050	12	14	110	17	3

a. What is the percent change in production of each of the goods from 2010 to 2011 and from 2011 to 2012?

b. What is the percent change in prices of each of the goods from 2010 to 2011 and from 2011 to 2012?

c. Calculate nominal GDP in Britannica for each of the three years. What is the percent change in nominal GDP from 2010 to 2011 and from 2011 to 2012?

d. Calculate real GDP in Britannica using 2010 prices for each of the three years. What is the percent change in real GDP from 2010 to 2011 and from 2011 to 2012?

8. The accompanying table shows data on nominal GDP (in billions of 2002 dollars) and population (in thousands) of Canada in 1960, 1970, 1980, 1990, 2000, and 2010. The Canadian price level rose consistently from 1960 to 2010.

Year	Nominal GDP (billions of dollars)	Real GDP (billions of 2002 dollars)	Population (thousands)
1960	$39.8	$257.2	17 870
1970	90.2	420.4	21 297
1980	314.4	625.4	24 516
1990	679.9	825.3	27 691
2000	1076.6	1100.5	30 686
2010	1624.6	1325.0	34 126

Source: Statistics Canada.

a. Why is real GDP greater than nominal GDP for all years until 2000 and lower for 2010?

b. Calculate the percent change in real GDP from 1960 to 1970, 1970 to 1980, 1980 to 1990, 1990 to 2000, and 2000 to 2010. Which period had the highest growth rate?

c. Calculate real GDP per capita for each of the years in the table.

d. Calculate the percent change in real GDP per capita from 1960 to 1970, 1970 to 1980, 1980 to 1990, 1990 to 2000, and 2000 to 2010. Which period had the highest growth rate?

e. How do the percent change in real GDP and the percent change in real GDP per capita compare? Which is larger? Do we expect them to have this relationship?

9. Kwantlen Polytechnic University is concerned about the rising price of textbooks that students must purchase. To better identify the increase in the price of textbooks, the dean asks you, the Economics Department's star student, to create an index of textbook prices. The average student purchases three English, two math, and four economics textbooks per year. The prices of these books are given in the accompanying table.

	2010	2011	2012
English textbook	$50	$55	$57
Math textbook	70	72	74
Economics textbook	80	90	100

a. What is the percent change in the price of an English textbook from 2010 to 2012?

b. What is the percent change in the price of a math textbook from 2010 to 2012?

c. What is the percent change in the price of an economics textbook from 2010 to 2012?

d. Using 2010 as a base year, create a price index for these books for all years.

e. What is the percent change in the price index from 2010 to 2012?

10. The consumer price index, or CPI, measures the cost of living for a typical household by multiplying the price for each category of expenditure (housing, food, and so on) by a measure of the importance of that expenditure in the average consumer's market basket and summing over all categories. However, using data from the consumer price index, we can see that changes in the cost of living for different types of consumers can vary a great deal. Let's compare the cost of living for a hypothetical retired person and a hypothetical university student. Let's assume that the market basket of a retired person is allocated in the following way: 10% on housing, 15% on food, 5% on transportation, 60% on medical care, 0% on education, and 10% on recreation. The university student's market basket is allocated as follows: 5% on housing, 15% on food, 20% on transportation, 0% on medical care, 40% on education, and 20% on recreation. The accompanying table shows the April 2012 CPI for each of the relevant categories.

	CPI April 2012
Housing	126.6
Food	130.1
Transportation	131.3
Medical care	121.3
Education	141.2
Recreation	95.9

(2002 base year)

Calculate the overall CPI for the retired person and for the university student by multiplying the CPI for each of the categories by the relative importance of that category to the individual and then summing each of the categories. The CPI for all items in April 2012 was 122.2. How do your calculations for a CPI for the retired person and the university student compare to the overall CPI?

11. Each month Statistics Canada releases the Consumer Price Index estimates for the previous month. Go to StatCan's home page at www.statcan.gc.ca. Pick English or French. Click on the "CPI annual inflation" link under the "Latest Indicators" heading. This will open the latest CPI update in StatCan's "Daily." Go to the bottom of the page and click Table 1 for the "not seasonally adjusted figures." What was the CPI for the previous month, that is, the month before this one? How did it change from one month to the next? How does the CPI compare to the same month last year?

12. The accompanying table provides the annual real GDP (in billions of 2002 dollars) and nominal GDP (in billions of dollars) for Canada.

	2007	2008	2009	2010	2011
Real GDP (billions of 2002 dollars)	1311.3	1320.3	1283.7	1325.0	1356.9
Nominal GDP (billions of current dollars)	1529.6	1603.4	1529.0	1624.6	1720.7

Source: Statistics Canada.

a. Calculate the GDP deflator for each year.

b. Use the GDP deflator to calculate the inflation rate for all years except 2007.

13. The accompanying table contains two price indexes for the years 2009, 2010, and 2011: the GDP deflator and the CPI. For each price index, calculate the estimated inflation rate from 2009 to 2010 and from 2010 to 2011. (Note that both price indexes have a 2002 base year.)

Year	GDP deflator	CPI
2009	119.1	114.4
2010	122.6	116.5
2011	126.6	119.9

Source: Statistics Canada.

14. The cost of undergraduate (university) education in Canada has risen in recent years. These tables show the average cost of tuition for Canadian full-time students for the academic years that began in 2010 and 2011, measured in current dollars, and the consumer price index (CPI) in 2010 and 2011.

	Average tuition for Canadian full-time students by province (current dollars)	
	2010	2011
Canada	**$5146**	**$5366**
Newfoundland and Labrador	2649	2649
Prince Edward Island	5131	5258
Nova Scotia	5497	5731
New Brunswick	5647	5853
Quebec	2411	2519
Ontario	6316	6640
Manitoba	3593	3645
Saskatchewan	5431	5601
Alberta	5505	5662
British Columbia	4758	4852

Source: Statistics Canada.

	Consumer Price Index (2002 = 100)	
	2010	2011
Canada	**116.5**	**119.9**
Newfoundland and Labrador	117.4	121.4
Prince Edward Island	119.5	123.0
Nova Scotia	118.2	122.7
New Brunswick	115.9	120.0
Quebec	114.8	118.3
Ontario	116.5	120.1
Manitoba	115.0	118.4
Saskatchewan	118.7	122.0
Alberta	122.7	125.7
British Columbia	113.8	116.5

Source: Statistics Canada.

a. Calculate the percentage change in average tuition from 2010 to 2011 in Canada and in each province.

b. Calculate the percentage change in the CPI from 2010 to 2011 in Canada and in each province.

c. Did an average Canadian undergraduate student find that his or her tuition fees increased faster than the overall cost of living? Does your answer depend on which province the student lived in?

d. Consider this table, which gives the average annual tuition according to discipline. Which disciplines had an increase in tuition that is above the national average increase?

Discipline	Average tuition fees for Canadian full-time students by discipline (current dollars)		
	2010	2011	% change
Agriculture, natural resources, and conservation	$4 803	$5 023	4.6%
Architecture and related technologies	5 179	5 424	4.7
Humanities	4 638	4 791	3.3
Business, management, and public administration	5 386	5 711	6.0
Education	3 850	3 970	3.1
Engineering	5 992	6 326	5.6
Law	8 657	9 214	6.4
Medicine	10 867	11 345	4.4
Visual and performing arts and communications technologies	4 748	4 731	–0.4
Physical and life sciences and technology	5 049	5 247	3.9
Mathematics and computer and information science	5 526	5 811	5.2
Social and behavioural science	4 586	4 759	3.8
Other health, parks, recreation, and fitness	4 698	4 874	3.7
Dentistry	15 062	16 024	6.4
Nursing	4 662	4 809	3.2
Pharmacy	9 014	9 806	8.8
Veterinary medicine	5 612	5 889	4.9

Source: Statistics Canada.

CHAPTER 8

Unemployment and Inflation

AN UNWELCOME DILEMMA

On the left, the Bank of Canada, in Ottawa. On the right, the Bank of England, known as the "Old Lady of Threadneedle Street."

Christopher Pike/Xinhua/Landov

Alex Segre/Alamy

David Levenson/Alamy

FROM THE PERSPECTIVE OF central banks, the past few years have been tough. This is true even if we ignore their role in the bailouts that occurred as a result of the financial crisis that peaked in 2008. Central banks, including the Bank of Canada, have faced other difficult situations, including a higher unemployment rate and rising prices. In Canada, the unemployment rate rose, and remained relatively high, compared to what it was before the crisis. But our inflation rate was also rising— from 0.26% in 2009 to 2.92% in 2011. This posed an unwelcome dilemma for the Bank of Canada. Should it have focused on fighting inflation, or should it have kept trying to bring down unemployment?

Canada was not the only country facing this dilemma. Across the Atlantic Ocean, British inflation was rising too: in February 2011, consumer prices were 4.4 percent higher than they had been a year earlier, a rate of increase far above the comfort level of the Bank of England (the British central bank). At the same time, the British economy was still suffering the after-effects of the recession, and unemployment, especially among young people, was disturbingly high.

So, although the Bank of Canada did face a dilemma, the Bank of England faced one that was much worse, because the inflation rate had risen more than in Canada. Let's take a closer look at what happened in Britain. Opinion on what the Bank of England should do was sharply divided. The Bank of England faced "a genuine problem of credibility," declared Patrick Minford, a professor at Cardiff University, who urged the Bank of England to fight inflation by raising interest rates. The rise in inflation reflected temporary factors and would soon reverse course, countered Adam Posen, a member of the Bank of England's Policy Committee, who argued that any tightening would risk putting Britain into a prolonged slump.

Whoever was right, the dispute highlighted the key concerns of macroeconomic policy. Unemployment and inflation are the two great evils of macroeconomics. So the two principal goals of macroeconomic policy are low unemployment and price stability, usually defined as a low but positive rate of inflation. Unfortunately, those goals sometimes appear to be in conflict with each other: economists often warn that policies intended to fight unemployment run the risk of increasing inflation; con-

- **How unemployment is measured** and how the **unemployment rate is calculated**

- **The significance of the unemployment rate for the economy**

- **The relationship between the unemployment rate and economic growth**

- **The factors that determine the natural rate of unemployment**

- **The economic costs of inflation**

- **How inflation and deflation create winners and losers**

- **Why policy-makers try to maintain a stable rate of inflation**

versely, policies intended to bring down inflation can raise unemployment.

The nature of the trade-off between low unemployment and low inflation, along with the policy dilemma it creates, is a topic reserved for later chapters. This chapter provides an overview of the basic facts about unemployment and inflation: how they're measured, how they affect consumers and firms, and how they change over time. ■

The Unemployment Rate

Britain had an unemployment rate of 7.7 percent in early 2011, up from just 5.7 percent in 2008. That was bad. But the Canadian unemployment rate was slightly worse. Figure 8-1 shows the Canadian unemployment rate annually from 1946 to 2011; as you can see, unemployment soared during the 2008–2009 recession and had fallen only modestly by 2011. What did the rise in the unemployment rate mean, and why was it such a big factor in people's lives? To understand why policy-makers pay so much attention to employment and unemployment, we need to understand how they are both defined and measured.

FIGURE   8-1   The Canadian Unemployment Rate, 1946–2011

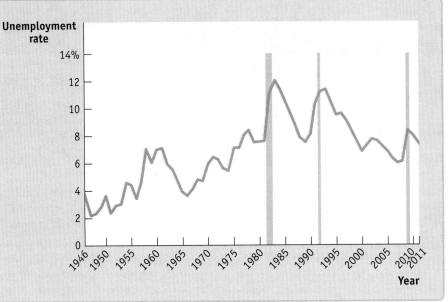

Canada's unemployment rate has fluctuated widely over time. It always rises during recessions, which are shown by the shaded bars. It usually, but not always, falls during periods of economic expansion.

Sources: Statistics Canada; Historical Statistics of Canada.

Defining and Measuring Unemployment

It's easy to define employment: you're employed if and only if you have a paid job. **Employment** is the total number of people aged 15 and older currently employed, either full time or part time.

Unemployment, however, is a more subtle concept. Just because a person isn't working doesn't mean that we consider that person unemployed. For example, as of May 2012, there were just more than 5 million retired workers in Canada receiving Old Age Security benefits. Most of them were probably happy that they were no longer working, so we wouldn't consider someone who has settled into a comfortable, well-earned retirement to be unemployed. There were also about 330 thousand disabled Canadian workers receiving Canadian Pension Plan benefits because they were unable to work. Again, although they weren't working, we wouldn't normally consider them to be unemployed.

By one criterion, Statistics Canada, the federal agency tasked with collecting data on unemployment, considers the unemployed to be those who are "... without work, ... looking for work, and ... available for work." Retired people don't count because they aren't looking for jobs; the disabled don't count because they aren't available for work. More specifically, an individual aged 15 or older is considered to be *unemployed* if he or she

Employment is the total number of people in the economy (aged 15 and older) currently employed, in either a full-time or part-time paid job.

1. does not currently have a paid job (i.e., is *not* employed);

2. is available for work; and

3. has been actively looking for a job during the past four weeks.

Individuals on temporary layoffs and those waiting for a new job to start in the next four weeks or less are considered unemployed if they satisfy conditions 1 and 2. Individuals on either maternity leave or paternity leave are not considered to be unemployed in the official *labour force* statistics. But, if certain conditions are met, these individuals may qualify for employment insurance (EI) benefit payments similar to those received by some unemployed workers.

So **unemployment** is defined as the total number of available people who aged 15 and older are actively looking for work but aren't currently employed. A country's **labour force** is the sum of employment and unemployment—that is, of people who are currently working and people who are currently looking for work, respectively. The **labour force participation rate,** defined as the share of the working-age population that is in the labour force, is calculated as follows:

(8-1) Labour force participation rate $= \dfrac{\text{Labour force}}{\text{Population aged 15 and older}} \times 100$

The **unemployment rate,** defined as the percentage of the total number of people in the labour force who are unemployed, is calculated as follows:

(8-2) Unemployment rate $= \dfrac{\text{Number of unemployed workers}}{\text{Labour force}} \times 100$

To estimate the numbers that go into calculating the unemployment rate, Statistics Canada carries out a monthly survey called the Labour Force Survey, which involves interviewing a random sample of 56 000 households across Canada. People are asked whether they are currently employed. If they are not employed, they are asked whether they have been looking for a job during the past four weeks. The results are then scaled up, using estimates of the total population, to estimate the total number of employed and unemployed Canadians.

> **Unemployment** is the number of available people (aged 15 and older) who are actively looking for paid work but aren't currently employed.
>
> The **labour force** is equal to the sum of the total number of employed people (employment) and the total number of unemployed people (unemployment)—aged 15 or older in all cases.
>
> The **labour force participation rate** is the percentage of the population aged 15 or older that is in the labour force.
>
> The **unemployment rate** is the percentage of the labour force that is unemployed.

The Significance of the Unemployment Rate

In general, the unemployment rate is a good indicator of how easy or difficult it is to find a job given the current state of the economy. When the unemployment rate is low, nearly everyone who wants a job can find one. In 2007, when the unemployment rate averaged 6%, jobs were so abundant that employers spoke of a "mirror test" for getting a job: if you were breathing (therefore your breath would fog a mirror), you could find work. By contrast, in 2011, with the unemployment rate at 7.5%, it was harder to find work. In fact, there were almost six times as many Canadians seeking work as there were job openings.

Although the unemployment rate is a good indicator of current labour market conditions, it's not a literal measure of the percentage of people who want a job but can't find one. That's because in some ways the unemployment rate exaggerates the difficulty people have in finding jobs. But in other ways, the opposite is true—a low unemployment rate can conceal deep frustration over the lack of job opportunities.

How the Unemployment Rate Can Overstate the True Level of Unemployment If you are searching for work, it's normal to take at least a few weeks to find a suitable job. Yet a worker who is quite confident of finding a job, but has not yet accepted a position, is counted as unemployed. As a consequence, the unemployment rate never falls to zero, even in boom times when jobs are plentiful. Even in the buoyant labour market of 2007, when it was easy to find work, the unemployment rate was still 6%. Later in this chapter, we'll discuss in greater depth the reasons that measured unemployment persists even when jobs are abundant.

⚠ PITFALLS

EMPLOYMENT RATE AND UNEMPLOYMENT RATE
Sometimes you may come across the term "employment rate." What is the employment rate? According to Statistics Canada is defined as the ratio of the number of employed workers to the adult population (people who are aged 15 or above). This ratio is usually expressed as a percentage. So:

Employment rate $= \dfrac{\text{Number of employed workers}}{\text{Adult population}} \times 100$

Suppose you know that the unemployment rate is 5%. Does that mean that the employment rate is 100% − 5% = 95%? No, probably not. Why? It is because there are some adults who technically do not fall into either category. That is why the employment rate and the unemployment do not add up to 1, or 100%.

Discouraged workers are non-working people who are capable of working but have given up looking for a job since they believe, given the state of the job market, no work is available (for someone with their qualifications and experience in their region).

Marginally attached workers would like to be employed and have looked for a job in the recent past (more than four weeks ago) but are not currently looking for work as they wait for employment.

Underemployment occurs when workers have jobs that, in certain ways, fall short of what they want.

Visible underemployment is the number of people who involuntarily work part time because they cannot find full-time jobs.

Invisible underemployment is the number of people who have jobs that do not fully use their skills or that have one or more substandard job characteristics, such as low pay.

How the Unemployment Rate Can Understate the True Level of Unemployment Frequently, people who would like to work but aren't working still don't get counted as unemployed. In particular, an individual who has given up looking for a job for the time being because there are no jobs available—say, a laid-off steelworker in a deeply depressed steel town—isn't counted as unemployed because he or she has stopped looking for work. Statistics Canada calculates the official measured unemployment rate. Although accurate, this rate is apt to be understated, because Statistics Canada omits workers in three categories: discouraged workers, marginally attached workers, and underemployed workers.

Discouraged workers are not working and have sought employment within the past 12 months; however, they are not currently seeking work because they feel they have little hope of getting a job in the current job market.

Marginally attached workers are not currently working and have stopped seeking employment, too; however, they have stopped looking because they are waiting for employment to begin. For example, they may be waiting for recall after a layoff, for replies from potential employers, or for a new job to start in the next five or more weeks.

Underemployed workers do work, but not in the desired capacity. **Visibly underemployed workers** have jobs in which they work fewers hours than they would like to do. They may have part-time jobs, but would prefer to be working full time. **Invisibly underemployed workers** have jobs that do not use their skills fully or that are considered to be substandard, owing to low wages or some other disadvantage. Statistics Canada does estimate the number of visibly underemployed workers, but cannot estimate the number of invisibly underemployed workers—they are "invisible."

Statistics Canada does include these three categories of frustrated workers in other "measures of labour underutilization." Figure 8-2 shows what happens to the unemployment rate when these categories are included. The broadest measure of unemployment and underemployment, known as R8, is the sum of these three measures plus the unemployed. It is substantially higher than the rate usually quoted in the media. But R8 and the unemployment rate move very much in parallel, so changes in the unemployment rate remain a good guide to what is happening in the overall labour market, including frustrated workers.

FIGURE **8-2** Supplementary Unemployment Rates, 1997–2011

The unemployment figures usually quoted in the media only include people who have been seeking work during the past four weeks. Broader measures also count discouraged workers, marginally attached workers, and the underemployed. These broader measures show a higher (modified) unemployment rate, but they move closely in parallel with the standard rate.

Source: Statistics Canada.

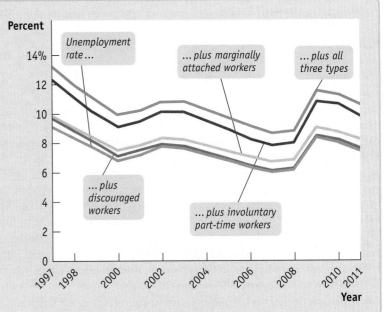

FIGURE **8-3** Unemployment Rates for Different Groups and Regions, August 2012

This graph shows that unemployment rates can differ by group and by region. For example, in August 2012, the unemployment rate for youth in Alberta was less than half that of youth in Newfoundland and Labrador. So, even during periods of low overall unemployment, unemployment remains a serious problem for some groups. Note that even though youths from Alberta and Newfoundland and Labrador had a higher rate of unemployment if they had a university degree, the situation is just the reverse nationally.

Source: Statistics Canada.

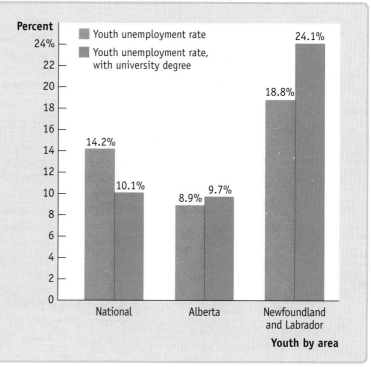

Finally, it's important to realize that the unemployment rate varies greatly by region and among demographic groups. Other things being equal, jobs are generally easier to find for more experienced workers and for workers during their "prime" working years, from ages 25 to 54. For younger workers, as well as workers nearing retirement age, jobs are typically harder to find.

Similarly, at any moment in time, jobs can be easier or harder to find in different regions of the country, regardless of which demographic group is being considered. Just as there is not really one single labour market for all demographic groups nationally, neither is there just one single labour market for all regions. Different regions may well have macroeconomic conditions and trends that differ from those of the nation as a whole. The job market in resource-producing regions of the country, such as Alberta, Saskatchewan, and Manitoba, can boom while job markets in other provinces may trend downward.

Figure 8-3 shows the unemployment rates for different groups in October 2007, when the overall unemployment rate (5.3%) was low by recent historical standards. As you can see, at this time, the unemployment rate for youth (ages 15–24) was double the national average; the unemployment rate for youth with university degrees was two-thirds of the national average. (Bear in mind that a youth is not considered unemployed, even if he or she is not working, unless that youth is looking for work and cannot find it.) Regional factors also play a role. Unemployment rates in the Prairie Provinces tend to be lower than the national average, owing to their economic structure and the high world demand for their output (wheat, oil, and other commodities). For example, in Alberta in 2007, labour market conditions were so strong that the unemployment rates for all groups were significantly below the national rate. On the other hand, unemployment rates in Atlantic Canada were higher than the national average. In October 2007, the average unemployment rate in Newfoundland and Labrador was more than twice the national average, and the youth unemployment rate was also 6.3 percentage points higher than the comparable national one; the only exception was for university graduates, indicating that people who have human capital (more education) are less likely to suffer from unemployment even in a tough job market.

So even at a time when the overall unemployment rate was relatively low, jobs were hard to find for some groups.

So you should interpret the unemployment rate as an indicator of overall labour market conditions, not as an exact, literal measure of the percentage of people unable to find jobs. The unemployment rate is, however, a very good indicator: its ups and downs closely reflect economic changes that have a significant impact on people's lives. Let's turn now to the causes of these fluctuations.

Growth and Unemployment

Compared to Figure 8-1, Figure 8-4 shows the Canadian unemployment rate over a somewhat shorter period, the years from 1976 to 2012. The shaded bars represent periods of recession. As you can see, during every recession, without exception, the unemployment rate rose. The severe recession of 2008–2009, like the earlier two recessions, led to a significant rise in unemployment.

Correspondingly, during periods of economic expansion the unemployment rate usually falls. The long economic expansion of the 1990s eventually brought the unemployment rate down to 6.3%, and the expansion of the mid-2000s brought the rate down to 5.3%. However, it's important to recognize that *economic expansions aren't always periods of falling unemployment*. Look at the periods immediately following the recessions of 1990–1991 in Figure 8-4. The unemployment rate continued to rise for more than a year after the recession was officially over. The explanation is that although the economy was growing, it was not growing fast enough to reduce the unemployment rate.

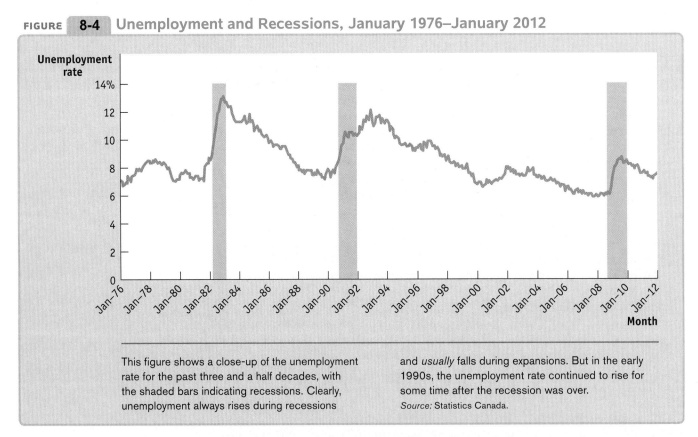

FIGURE **8-4** Unemployment and Recessions, January 1976–January 2012

This figure shows a close-up of the unemployment rate for the past three and a half decades, with the shaded bars indicating recessions. Clearly, unemployment always rises during recessions and *usually* falls during expansions. But in the early 1990s, the unemployment rate continued to rise for some time after the recession was over.

Source: Statistics Canada.

Figure 8-5 is a scatter diagram showing Canadian data for the period from 1946 to 2010. The horizontal axis measures the annual rate of growth in real GDP—the percent by which each year's real GDP changed compared to the previous year's real GDP. (Notice that there were four years in which growth was negative—that is, real GDP shrank.) The vertical axis measures the *change* in the unemployment rate over the previous year in percentage points. Each dot represents the observed growth rate of real GDP and change in the unemployment rate for a given year. For example, in 2000 the average unemployment rate fell to 6.8% from 7.6% in 1999; this is shown as a value of −0.8 along the vertical axis for the year 2000. Over the same period, real GDP grew by 5.2%; this is the value shown along the horizontal axis for the year 2000.

The downward trend of the scatter diagram in Figure 8-5, as indicated by the blue "line of best fit," shows that there is a generally strong negative relationship between growth in the economy and the rate of unemployment. Years of high growth in real GDP were usually years in which the unemployment rate fell, and years of low or negative growth in real GDP were years in which the unemployment rate usually rose.

The green vertical line in Figure 8-5 at the value of 3.62% indicates the average growth rate of real GDP over the period from 1946 to 2010. Points lying to the right of the vertical line are years of above-average growth. In these years, the value on the vertical axis is usually negative, meaning that the unemployment rate fell. That is, years of above-average growth were usually years in which the unemployment rate was falling. Conversely, points lying to the left of the green vertical line were years of below-average growth. In these years, the value on the vertical axis is usually positive, meaning that the unemployment rate rose. That is, years of below-average growth were usually years in which the unemployment rate was rising.

A period in which real GDP is growing, perhaps at a below-average rate, and unemployment is rising (or at least not falling) is called a **jobless recovery** or a "growth recession." Since 1990 there have been two recessions in Canada. The one

A **jobless recovery** is a period in which the real GDP growth rate is positive but the unemployment rate is still rising (or at least not falling).

FIGURE **8-5** Growth and Changes in Unemployment, 1946–2010

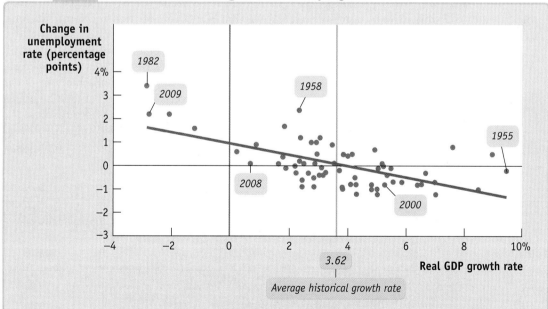

Each dot shows the growth rate of the economy and the change in the unemployment rate for a specific year between 1946 and 2010. For example, in 2000, the economy grew 5.2% and the unemployment rate fell 0.8 of a percentage point, from 7.6% to 6.8%. In general, unemployment fell when growth was above its average rate of 3.62% a year and rose when growth was below average. Unemployment always rose when real GDP fell.

Source: Statistics Canada.

from 1990 to 1991 was followed by a jobless recovery, while the one from 2008 to 2009 was not. The U.S. has had three recessions since 1990, all of which were followed by jobless recoveries. But true recessions, periods when real GDP falls, are especially painful for workers. As illustrated by the points to the left of the purple vertical line in Figure 8-5 (representing years in which the real GDP growth rate is negative), falling real GDP is always associated with a rising rate of unemployment, causing a great deal of hardship to families. The job loss that recessions create lowers the income and standard of living of many families, which can lead to other significant financial, physical, and emotional troubles for members of society.

ECONOMICS > IN ACTION

WE DON'T WANT OUR YOUTH TO BE NEET!

According to Statistics Canada, in 2011 about 904 000 (or 13.3%) of the 6.8 million Canadians aged 15 to 29 were **N**either **E**nrolled in school, nor **E**mployed, nor in **T**raining. People in this group are referred to as "NEET." This concept is meant to measure the percentage of youth who are at risk of becoming discouraged and disengaged, perhaps leading to reduced educational attainment, lack of satisfactory employment opportunities, and other related social problems as a consequence.

Some have argued that the civil unrest and regime changes that occurred in 2010 to 2012 in Tunisia, Egypt, Libya, Yemen, and other countries were fuelled, in part, by limited economic opportunities for the youth of these nations. So, in theory, a high or sharply growing NEET rate could indicate that the future holds the risk of significant economic and political hardship. But not necessarily: the rate may be high because of young people who choose to travel, to engage in leisure activities, to take parental leave, or to do unpaid volunteer work, instead of doing paid work. Some countries may have a high NEET rate for non-economic reasons, such as compulsory military service.

Even though NEET rates may not be absolutely reliable predictors, it is still useful to compare them, either for one country over several years or for several countries during the same year. As Table 8.1 shows, in 2009 Canada had one of the lowest NEET rates in the G7. Furthermore, Canada's NEET percentage has been very stable from 2001 to 2011, and rose only two percentage points as a result of the 2008–2009 recession.[1] Canada's youth fared better in the recession than their peers in other G7 countries, who saw a substantially greater increase. So we can probably look forward to periods of civil stability.

TABLE **8-1** The NEET Rate in G7, 2009

	In education	Employed	Not in Education, Employment, or Training (NEET)		
			Total NEET	Unemployed	Not in labour force
Canada	42.8%	43.9%	13.3%	5.7%	7.6%
France	44.0	40.5	15.6	9.0	6.6
Germany	52.4	36.0	11.6	5.5	6.1
Italy	45.3	33.5	21.2	7.5	13.7
United Kingdom	40.4	43.9	15.6	7.0	8.6
United States	45.7	37.9	16.9	6.7	10.2

Sources: Statistics Canada; OECD database 2009.

---

[1]Canada's NEET rate was 12% during 2006–2008, rose about 1 percentage point in 2009, and peaked at 14% in 2010 before falling back to 13% in 2011.

However, according to the Organisation for Economic Co-operation and Development (OECD), young people, including Canadian youth, are among the demographic groups most at risk of long-term unemployment, which is a concern. Long-term unemployment can harm both the economy of the country and the unemployed workers themselves. Workers often find long-term unemployment (especially when it lasts six months or longer) to be very demoralizing. During these periods, workers may become disheartened by constant rejection and/or they may lose their job market skills. As a result, when the economy does recover and jobs are available, these workers may either be too discouraged to enter the job market or lack the skills to do so. Their absence from the workforce leads to higher structural unemployment, which increases the long-run unemployment rate. Financially, the loss of employment opportunities and skills erosion can put some people on an entirely different employment and career path that may lead to significantly reduced lifetime earnings and standard of living. Psychologically, some people may never quite recover from the experience.

CHECK YOUR UNDERSTANDING 8-1

1. Suppose that the advent of employment websites enables jobseekers to find suitable jobs more quickly. What effect will this have on the unemployment rate over time? Also suppose that these websites encourage jobseekers who had given up their searches to begin looking again. What effect will this have on the unemployment rate?

2. In which of the following cases is a worker counted as unemployed? Explain.
   a. Rosa, an older worker who has been laid off and who gave up looking for work months ago
   b. Anthony, a schoolteacher who is not working during his three-month summer break
   c. Grace, an investment banker who has been laid off and is currently searching for another position
   d. Émile, a classically trained musician who can only find work playing for local parties
   e. Natasha, a graduate student who went back to school because jobs were scarce

3. Which of the following are consistent with the observed relationship between growth in real GDP and changes in the unemployment rate? Which are not?
   a. A rise in the unemployment rate accompanies a fall in real GDP.
   b. An exceptionally strong business recovery is associated with a greater percentage of the labour force being employed.
   c. Negative real GDP growth is associated with a fall in the unemployment rate.

Solutions appear at back of book.

The Natural Rate of Unemployment

Fast economic growth tends to reduce the unemployment rate. So how low can the unemployment rate go? You might be tempted to say zero, but that isn't feasible. Over the past half-century, the annual national unemployment rate has never dropped below 3.6%.

How can there be so much unemployment even when many businesses are having a hard time finding workers? To answer this question, we need to examine the nature of labour markets and why they normally lead to substantial measured unemployment even when jobs are plentiful. Our starting point is the observation that even in the best of times, jobs are constantly being created and destroyed.

Job Creation and Job Destruction

Even during good times, most Canadians know someone who has lost his or her job. In October 2007, the national unemployment rate was only 5.3%, relatively low by historical standards. Yet in that month there were about 450 thousand "job

"At this point, I'm just happy to still have a job"

separations"—terminations of employment that occur because a worker is either fired or quits voluntarily.

There are many reasons for such job loss. One is structural change in the economy: industries rise and fall as new technologies emerge and consumers' tastes change. For example, employment in high-tech industries such as telecommunications surged in the late 1990s but slumped severely after 2000. However, structural change also brings the creation of new jobs: after 2000, the number of jobs in the health care sector surged as new medical technologies and the aging of the population increased the demand for medical care. Poor management performance or bad luck at individual companies also leads to job loss for their employees. For example, in 2005 General Motors announced plans to eliminate 30 000 jobs globally after several years of lagging sales, even as Japanese companies such as Toyota announced plans to open new plants in North America to meet growing demand for their cars. Research in Motion (RIM, now known as BlackBerry) cut about 2000 jobs in the summer of 2011 due to stiffer competition from other smartphone producers such as Apple and Samsung. RIM announced another round of layoffs in July 2012, and this time it planned to cut approximately 5000 jobs.

Continual job creation and destruction are a feature of modern economies, making a naturally occurring amount of unemployment inevitable. Within this naturally occurring amount, there are two types of unemployment—*frictional* and *structural*.

Frictional Unemployment

When a worker loses a job involuntarily due to job destruction, he or she often doesn't take the first new job offered. For example, suppose a skilled programmer, laid off because her software company's product line was unsuccessful, sees a help-wanted ad for clerical work online. She might respond to the ad and get the job—but that would be foolish. Instead, she should take the time to look for a job that takes advantage of her skills and pays accordingly. In addition, individual workers are constantly leaving jobs voluntarily, typically for personal reasons— family moves, dissatisfaction, and better job prospects elsewhere.

Economists say that workers who spend time looking for employment are engaged in **job search.** If all workers and all jobs were alike, job search wouldn't be necessary; if information about jobs and workers was perfect, job search would be very quick. In practice, however, it's normal for a worker who loses a job, or a young worker seeking a first job, to spend at least a few weeks searching.

Frictional unemployment is unemployment due to the time workers spend in job search. A certain amount of frictional unemployment is inevitable due to the constant process of economic change. Thus even in 2007, a year of low unemployment, there were millions of "job separations," in which workers left or lost their jobs. Total employment grew because these separations were more than offset by millions of new hires—with more than 370 thousand net new jobs created in 2007. Inevitably, some of the workers who left or lost their jobs spent at least some time unemployed, as did some of the workers newly entering the labour force.

Figure 8-6 shows the 2007 flows of workers among three categories: employed, unemployed, and not in the labour force. What the figure suggests is how much churning is constantly taking place in the labour market. An inevitable consequence of that churning is a significant number of workers who haven't yet found their next job—that is, frictional unemployment.

A limited amount of frictional unemployment is relatively harmless and may even be a good thing. The economy is more productive if workers take the time to find jobs that are well matched to their skills and workers who are unemployed for

Workers who spend time looking for employment are engaged in **job search.**

Frictional unemployment is unemployment due to the time workers spend in job search.

FIGURE   **8-6**   Net Labour Market Flows in 2007

The labour market is always in flux, as some people move from one category to another. And while only a small fraction of the people may be moving at any one time, there are millions of people in each category, which implies hundreds of thousands of people are shifting from category to category each year. Even in 2007, a year of low unemployment, large numbers of workers moved into and out of employment and unemployment. In net, over the year employment grew by about 370 thousand jobs, unemployment dropped by about 1600 people, and the not-in-labour force category grew by about 2900 people.

Source: Statistics Canada.

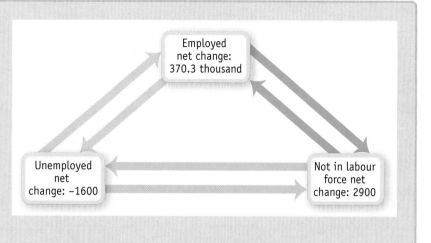

a brief period while searching for the right job don't experience great hardship. In fact, when there is a low unemployment rate, periods of unemployment tend to be quite short, suggesting that much of the unemployment is frictional.

Figure 8-7 shows the composition of unemployment for all of 2007, when the unemployment rate was only 6%. Forty percent of the unemployed had been unemployed for less than 5 weeks, and only 27% had been unemployed for 14 or more weeks. Only about one in eight unemployed workers were considered to be "long-term unemployed"—unemployed for 27 or more weeks.

In periods of higher unemployment, however, workers tend to be jobless for longer periods of time, suggesting that a smaller share of unemployment is frictional. By 2010, the fraction of unemployed workers considered "long-term unemployed" had jumped to 21%.

FIGURE   **8-7**   Distribution of the Unemployed by Duration of Unemployment, 2007

In years when the unemployment rate is low, most unemployed workers are unemployed for only a short period. In 2007, a year of low unemployment, 40% of the unemployed were unemployed for less than five weeks and 68% were unemployed for less than 14 weeks. The short duration of unemployment for most workers suggests that most unemployment in 2007 was frictional. (Statistics Canada no longer tracks the length of unemployment of unemployed people who have a job to start in the next four weeks: they are classified as "Duration unknown.")

Source: Statistics Canada.

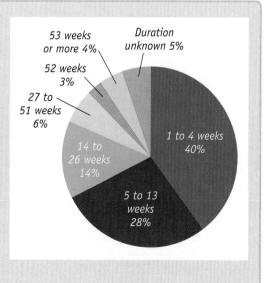

Structural unemployment occurs when workers are unable to fill available jobs because they lack the skills, do not live where jobs are available, or are unwilling to work at the wage rate offered. It arises from the rigidities in the labour market such that some workers are unable to get a job at the prevailing wage, even in the long run.

Structural Unemployment

Frictional unemployment exists even when the number of people seeking jobs is equal to the number of jobs being offered—that is, the existence of frictional unemployment doesn't mean that there is a surplus of labour. Sometimes, however, there is a *persistent surplus* of jobseekers in a particular labour market, even when the economy is at the peak of the business cycle. There may be more workers with a particular skill than there are jobs available using that skill, or there may be more workers in a particular geographic region than there are jobs available in that region, or are unwilling to work at the offered wage. **Structural unemployment** is unemployment that results when there are more people seeking jobs in a particular labour market than there are jobs available at the current wage rate. This unemployment is usually driven by technological change and other demand shocks that create structural differences between job vacancies and the pool of unemployed workers.

The supply and demand model tells us that the price of a good, service, or factor of production tends to move toward an equilibrium level that matches the quantity supplied with the quantity demanded. This is equally true, in general, of labour markets.

Figure 8-8 shows a typical market for labour. The labour demand curve indicates that when the price of labour—the wage rate—increases, employers demand less labour. The labour supply curve indicates that when the price of labour increases, more workers are willing to supply labour at the prevailing wage rate. These two forces coincide to lead to an equilibrium wage rate for any given type of labour in a particular location. That equilibrium wage rate is shown as W_E.

FIGURE 8-8   The Effect of a Minimum Wage on a Labour Market

When the government sets a minimum wage, W_F, that exceeds the market equilibrium wage rate in that market, W_E, the number of workers, Q_S, who would like to work at that minimum wage is greater than the number of workers, Q_D, demanded at that wage rate. This surplus of labour is structural unemployment.

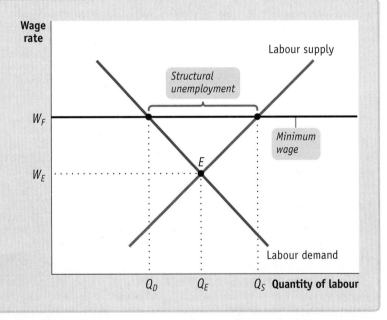

Even at the equilibrium wage rate W_E, there will still be some frictional unemployment. That's because there will always be some workers engaged in job search even when the number of jobs available is equal to the number of workers seeking jobs. But there wouldn't be any structural unemployment in this labour market. *Structural unemployment occurs when the wage rate is, for some reason, persistently above W_E.* Several factors can lead to a wage rate in excess of W_E, the most important being minimum wages, labour unions, *efficiency wages,* the side effects of government policies, and mismatches between employees and employers.

Minimum Wages A minimum wage is a government-mandated floor on the price of labour. In Canada, each province and territory sets its own minimum wage. As Table 8-2 shows, most set it to be about $10 per hour. For many Canadian workers, the minimum wage is irrelevant; the market equilibrium wage for these workers is well above this price floor. But for less skilled workers, the minimum wage may be binding—it affects the wages that people are actually paid and can lead to structural unemployment in particular markets for labour. Other wealthy countries have higher minimum wages; for example, in 2012 the French minimum wage was 9.22 euros an hour, or around $11.53. In these countries, the range of workers for whom the minimum wage is binding is larger.

Figure 8-8 shows the effect of a binding minimum wage. In this market, there is a legal floor on wages, W_F, which is above the equilibrium wage rate, W_E. This leads to a persistent surplus in the labour market: the quantity of labour supplied, Q_S, is larger than the quantity demanded, Q_D. In other words, more people want to work than can find jobs at the minimum wage, leading to structural unemployment.

Given that minimum wages—that is, binding minimum wages—generally lead to structural unemployment, you might wonder why governments impose them. The rationale is to help ensure that people who work can earn enough income to afford at least a minimally comfortable lifestyle. However, this may come at a cost, because it may eliminate the opportunity to work for some workers who would have willingly worked for lower wages. As illustrated in Figure 8-8, not only are there more sellers of labour than there are buyers, but there are also fewer people working at a minimum wage (Q_D) than there would have been with no minimum wage at all (Q_E).

Although economists broadly agree that a high minimum wage has the employment-reducing effects shown in Figure 8-8, there is some question about whether this is a good description of how minimum wage actually works. The minimum wages in Canadian provinces and territories are quite low compared with those of other wealthy countries. For three decades, from the 1970s to the mid-2000s, Canadian minimum wages were so low that they were not binding for the vast majority of workers.

In addition, some researchers have produced evidence that increases in the minimum wage actually lead to higher employment when, as was the case in Canada at one time, the minimum wage is low compared to average wages. They argue that firms that employ low-skilled workers sometimes restrict their hiring in order to keep wages low and that, as a result, the minimum wage can sometimes be increased without any loss of jobs. Most economists, however, agree that a sufficiently high minimum wage *does* lead to structural unemployment.

Labour Unions The actions of *labour unions* can have effects similar to those of minimum wages, leading to structural unemployment. By bargaining collectively for all of a firm's workers, unions can often win higher wages from employers than workers would have obtained by bargaining individually. This process, known as *collective bargaining,* is intended to tip the scales of bargaining power more toward workers and away from employers. Labour unions exercise bargaining power by threatening firms with a *labour strike,* a collective refusal to work. The threat of a strike can have serious consequences for firms. In such cases, workers acting collectively can exercise more power than they could if acting individually.

Employers have acted to counter the bargaining power of unions by threatening and enforcing lockouts—periods in which union workers are locked out and rendered unemployed—while hiring replacement workers.

When workers have increased bargaining power, they tend to demand and receive higher wages. Unions also bargain over benefits, such as health care and pensions,

TABLE 8-2	Minimum Wage by Province/Territory, End of 2012
Province/Territory	**Minimum Wage**
Alberta	$9.75
British Columbia	$10.25
Manitoba	$10.25
New Brunswick	$10.00
Northwest Territories	$10.00
Newfoundland and Labrador	$10.00
Nova Scotia	$10.15
Nunavut	$11.00
Ontario	$10.25
Prince Edward Island	$10.00
Quebec	$9.90
Saskatchewan	$9.50
Yukon	$10.30

which we can think of as additional wages. Indeed, economists who study the effects of unions on wages find that unionized workers earn higher wages and more generous benefits than non-union workers with similar skills. The result of these increased wages can be the same as the result of a minimum wage: labour unions push the wage that workers receive above the equilibrium wage. Consequently, there are more people willing to work at the wage being paid than there are jobs available. Like a binding minimum wage, this leads to structural unemployment. In Canada, however, due to a falling level of unionization over the past 15 years, the amount of structural unemployment generated by union demands has declined.

Efficiency Wages Actions by firms can contribute to structural unemployment. Firms may choose to pay **efficiency wages**—wages that employers set above the equilibrium wage rate as an incentive for their workers to perform better.

Employers may feel the need for such incentives for several reasons. For example, employers often have difficulty observing directly how hard an employee works. They can, however, elicit more work effort by paying above-market wages: employees receiving these higher wages are more likely to work harder to ensure that they aren't fired, which would cause them to lose their higher wages.

When many firms pay efficiency wages, the result is a pool of workers who want jobs but can't find them. So the use of efficiency wages by firms leads to structural unemployment.

Side Effects of Government Policies In addition, government policies designed to help workers who lose their jobs can lead to structural unemployment as an unintended side effect. Most economically advanced countries provide benefits to laid-off workers as a way to tide them over until they find a new job. In Canada, these benefits, called employment insurance (EI) benefits, typically replace up to 55% of a worker's average insured income up to a yearly maximum insurable amount—currently equal to $45 900—and expire after 19 to 45 weeks, depending on the unemployment rate in the region. During the recession of 2008–2009, as a measure to combat hardship caused by more frequent and longer occurrences of unemployment, the federal government temporarily increased the maximum length that employment insurance benefits could be paid by five weeks. In other countries, particularly in Europe, benefits are more generous and last longer. The drawback to this generosity is that it reduces a worker's incentive to quickly find a new job. Generous unemployment benefits in some European countries are often argued to be one of the causes of "Eurosclerosis," the persistent high unemployment that afflicts a number of European economies.

Mismatches between Employees and Employers It takes time for workers and firms to adjust to shifts in the economy. The result can be a mismatch between what employees have to offer and what employers are looking for. A skills mismatch is one form; for example, in the aftermath of the U.S. housing bust of 2006–2009, there were more construction workers looking for jobs than were available. Another form is geographic as in Windsor (Ontario), which has had a long-standing surplus of workers after its auto industry declined. Until the mismatch is resolved through a big enough fall in wages of the surplus workers that induces retraining or relocation, there will be structural unemployment.

The Natural Rate of Unemployment

Because some frictional unemployment is inevitable and because many economies also suffer from structural unemployment, a certain amount of unemployment is normal, or "natural." Actual unemployment fluctuates around this normal level. The **natural rate of unemployment** is the normal unemployment rate around which the actual unemployment rate fluctuates. It is the rate of unemployment that arises from the effects of frictional plus structural unemployment. The natural rate of unemployment is often called the non-accelerating inflation rate of unemployment (NAIRU) because it is the rate of unemployment that will not put any pressure on the inflation

Efficiency wages are wages that employers set above the equilibrium wage rate as an incentive for better employee performance.

The **natural rate of unemployment** is the unemployment rate that arises from the effects of frictional plus structural unemployment.

rate. **Cyclical unemployment** is the deviation of the actual rate of unemployment from the natural rate; that is, it is the difference between the actual and natural rates of unemployment. As the name suggests, cyclical unemployment is the share of unemployment that arises from the downturns and upturns caused by the business cycle. As such, cyclical unemployment can be positive, negative, or zero.

We'll see in Chapter 16 that an economy's natural rate of unemployment is a critical policy variable because government cannot keep the unemployment rate persistently below the natural rate without leading to accelerating inflation.

We can summarize the relationships between the various types of unemployment as follows:

(8-3) Natural unemployment =
Frictional unemployment + Structural unemployment

(8-4) Actual unemployment =
Natural unemployment + Cyclical unemployment

Perhaps because of its name, people often imagine that the natural rate of unemployment is a constant that doesn't change over time and can't be affected by government policy. Neither proposition is true. Let's take a moment to stress two facts: the natural rate of unemployment changes over time, and it can be affected by government policies.

> **Cyclical unemployment** is the deviation of the actual rate of unemployment from the natural rate due to downturns and upturns caused by the business cycle.

GLOBAL COMPARISON

NATURAL UNEMPLOYMENT AROUND THE OECD

The Organisation for Economic Co-operation and Development (OECD) is an association of relatively wealthy countries, in Europe and North America but also including Japan, Korea, New Zealand, and Australia. Among other activities, the OECD collects data on unemployment rates for member nations. The figure shows average unemployment, which is a rough estimate of the natural rate of unemployment, for select OECD members, from 2000–2010. The purple bar in the middle shows the average across all the OECD countries.

The Canadian natural rate of unemployment appears to be slightly above average; those of many European countries (including the major economies of Germany, Italy, and France) are also above average. Many economists think European countries that persistently high unemployment rates that exist in some European countries are the result of government policies, such as high minimum wages and generous unemployment benefits, which discourage employers from offering jobs and discourage workers from accepting jobs, leading to high rates of structural unemployment.

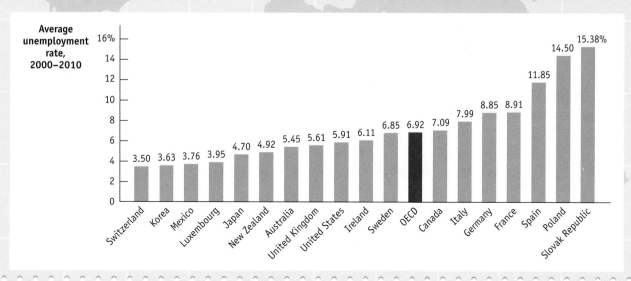

Source: OECD.

Changes in the Natural Rate of Unemployment

Private-sector economists and government agencies sometimes use estimates of the natural rate of unemployment both to make forecasts and to conduct policy analyses. Almost all these estimates show that the Canadian natural rate rises and falls over time. For example, the OECD estimated that Canada's natural rate of unemployment was about 4% in 1960, rose to 5% in 1970, rose to 8% in 1980, and fluctuated between 8 and 10% during the 1980s and 1990s. It declined to less than 8% by the late 1990s. In the late 1990s, the Bank of Canada decided to de-emphasize the gap between the measured unemployment rate and the estimated natural rate of unemployment as a guide for determining the future direction of monetary policy. In fact, in the late 1990s, Canada's unemployment rate fell below the OECD's estimate of the natural rate without causing any significant economic problems, such as inflation. This implies that the OECD estimate may have been too high. According to the OECD, some European countries have experienced even larger swings in their natural rates of unemployment.

What causes the natural rate of unemployment to change? The most important factors are changes in labour force characteristics, changes in labour market institutions, and changes in government policies. Let's look briefly at each factor.

Changes in Labour Force Characteristics In 2007 the overall rate of unemployment in Canada was 6%. Young workers, however, had much higher unemployment rates: 14.8% for teenagers and 8.7% for workers aged 20 to 24. Workers aged 25 years and over had an unemployment rate of only 5.0%.

In general, unemployment rates tend to be lower for experienced than for inexperienced workers. Because experienced workers tend to stay in a given job longer than do inexperienced ones, they have lower frictional unemployment. Also, because older workers are more likely than young workers to be family breadwinners, they have a stronger incentive to find and keep jobs.

One reason the natural rate of unemployment rose during the 1970s was a large rise in the number of new workers—children of the post–World War II baby boom entered the labour force, as did a rising percentage of married women. As Figure 8-9 shows, both the percentage of the labour force less than 25 years old and the percentage of women in the labour force grew rapidly in the 1960s and 1970s. By the end of the 1990s, however, the share of women in the labour force had levelled off and the percentage of workers under 25 had fallen sharply. As a result, the labour force as a whole is more experienced today than it was in the 1970s, one likely reason that the natural rate of unemployment is lower today than in the 1970s.

Changes in Labour Market Institutions As we pointed out earlier, unions that negotiate wages above the equilibrium level can be a source of structural unemployment. Some economists believe that strong labour unions are one reason for the high natural rate of unemployment in Europe, discussed in the Global Comparison. In Canada, a fall in union membership after 1980 may have been one reason the natural rate of unemployment fell between the 1970s and the 1990s.

Other institutional changes may also be at work. For example, some labour economists believe that temporary employment agencies, which have proliferated in recent years, have reduced frictional unemployment by helping match workers to jobs. Furthermore, as discussed in the Business Case at the end of the chapter, Internet websites such as Workopolis.com and Monster.ca may have reduced frictional unemployment.

Technological change, coupled with labour market institutions, can also affect the natural rate of unemployment. Technological change tends to increase the demand for skilled workers who are familiar with the relevant technology and a reduction in the demand for unskilled workers. Economic theory predicts that wages should increase for skilled workers and decrease for unskilled workers. But if wages for unskilled

FIGURE   **8-9** The Changing Makeup of the Canadian
Labour Force, 1946–2011

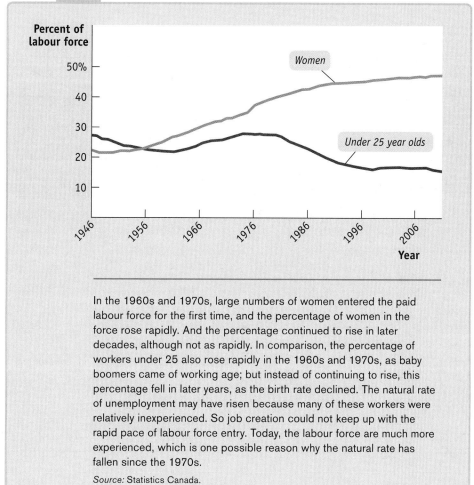

In the 1960s and 1970s, large numbers of women entered the paid
labour force for the first time, and the percentage of women in the
force rose rapidly. And the percentage continued to rise in later
decades, although not as rapidly. In comparison, the percentage of
workers under 25 also rose rapidly in the 1960s and 1970s, as baby
boomers came of working age; but instead of continuing to rise, this
percentage fell in later years, as the birth rate declined. The natural rate
of unemployment may have risen because many of these workers were
relatively inexperienced. So job creation could not keep up with the
rapid pace of labour force entry. Today, the labour force are much more
experienced, which is one possible reason why the natural rate has
fallen since the 1970s.

Source: Statistics Canada.

workers cannot go down—say, due to a binding minimum wage—increased structural
unemployment, and therefore a higher natural rate of unemployment, will result.

Changes in Government Policies A high minimum wage can cause structural unemployment. Generous unemployment benefits can increase both structural
and frictional unemployment. So government policies intended to help workers can
have the undesirable side effect of raising the natural rate of unemployment.

Some government policies, however, may reduce the natural rate. Two examples
are job training and employment subsidies. Job-training programs are supposed
to provide unemployed workers with skills that widen the range of jobs they can
perform. Employment subsidies are payments either to workers or to employers
that provide a financial incentive to accept or offer jobs.

The 1970s represented the height of Canada's Unemployment Insurance (UI)
program in terms of coverage, benefits, and eligibility. This may have contributed
to increased frictional and structural unemployment, thereby raising the natural rate of unemployment during this decade. It is possible that with generous
UI benefits a worker might take longer to find a suitable new job; that is, there
would be higher frictional unemployment. Similarly, generous benefits might
induce a worker to hold out for a higher paying job rather than a lower paying job
that is available; that is, there would be higher structural unemployment. In the

FOR INQUIRING MINDS

MORE ON THE LABOUR MARKET

One may wonder where the supply and demand for labour come from. As shown in the circular-flow diagram in Chapter 7 (Figure 7-1), the labour market is part of the factor markets, where productive inputs are being traded. Given that firms require labour as one of the inputs to produce their products, the demand for labour comes from firms. On the other hand, the supply of labour comes from households. They "sell" their labour services to firms and receive income in the form of wages for their contribution to the production of goods and services.

The labour demand curve slopes downward, showing that there is an inverse relationship between the wage rate and the quantity of labour demanded. This inverse relationship arises because, holding all else constant, an increase in wage rate will make the cost of using labour in the production process more expensive; in an attempt to minimize the cost of production, firms will try to replace some labour with other, now relatively cheaper, productive inputs. As a result, the quantity of labour demanded falls. Changes in technology and the stock of other productive inputs

will shift the labour demand curve. For example, if an improvement in technology raises labour productivity at all wage rates, it makes labour more profitable to firms, which causes the labour demand curve to shift up and to the right.

The labour supply curve slopes upward, showing that the quantity of labour supplied by households rises as the wage rate increases. In economics, we refer to a household's decision to work or not as the labour–leisure choice. Any household is free to choose how to allocate its time, between work on the one hand and leisure (non-work activities) on the other. However, there is a trade-off between these two choices. Households certainly value and enjoy leisure, but there is a cost associated with it (known as opportunity cost)—the wage rate is foregone. When households spend time on leisure, they are not working, and therefore not earning any wage. Thus, the opportunity cost of an hour of leisure is the hourly wage foregone. All else being equal, an increase in wage rate raises the opportunity cost of leisure and makes leisure relatively more expensive. Households may be willing to work more

when wage rate goes up, cutting back on their leisure to work more and earn the higher wage—this is why the labour supply curve slopes upward. Factors that cause a shift in the labour supply curve include changes in wealth and the size of the labour force. For example, workers who suddenly inherit money or win a lottery often respond by cutting back on the amount of work they perform so that they can enjoy more leisure now that their wealth has risen; that is, the labour supply curve has shifted up toward the left.

Government policies may also affect the labour market. For example, policies that discourage the laying off of workers, by making such layoffs costlier to the firm, will lower firms' incentive to hire workers, leading to a downward shift in labour demand. The provision of employment insurance (EI) payments to unemployed workers, or a more generous EI program, may shift the labour supply curve to the right as workers are encouraged to join the labour force. As Figure 8-8 shows, if minimum wage laws are set high enough, they are a structural feature of the labour market that helps to create (more) unemployment in the labour market, even in the long run.

1980s and 1990s, the federal government introduced changes to the UI program, which was renamed the Employment Insurance (EI) program. These changes were designed to reduce payouts in order to help balance the federal budget. As a result, benefits were slashed, and coverage and eligibility were reduced drastically. These changes likely contributed to the fall in Canada's natural rate of unemployment that occurred in the late 1980s and 1990s.

ECONOMICS ▸ *IN ACTION*

STRUCTURAL UNEMPLOYMENT IN EAST GERMANY

In one of the most dramatic events in world history, a spontaneous popular uprising in 1989 overthrew the communist dictatorship in East Germany. Citizens quickly tore down the wall that had divided Berlin, and in short order East and West Germany united into one democratic nation.

Then the trouble started.

After reunification, employment in East Germany plunged and the unemployment rate soared. This high unemployment rate has persisted: despite receiving massive aid from the federal German government, the economy of the former East Germany has remained persistently depressed, with an unemployment rate of more than 16% in 2008. Other parts of formerly communist Eastern Europe have done much better. For example, the Czech Republic, which was often cited along with East Germany as a relatively successful communist economy, had an unemployment rate of only 5.5% in July 2007. What went wrong in East Germany?

The answer is that, through nobody's fault, East Germany found itself suffering from severe structural unemployment. When Germany was reunified, it became clear that workers in East Germany were much less productive than their cousins to the west. Yet unions initially demanded and received wage rates equal to those in West Germany. These wage rates have been slow to come down because East German workers objected to being treated as inferior to their West German counterparts. Meanwhile, productivity in the former East Germany has remained well below West German levels, in part because of decades of misguided investment under the former dictatorship. The result has been a persistently large mismatch between the number of workers demanded and the number of those seeking jobs, and persistently high structural unemployment in the former East Germany.

After reunification in 1989, East Germany found itself suffering from severe structural unemployment that continues to this day.

CHECK YOUR UNDERSTANDING 8-2

1. Explain the following.
   a. Frictional unemployment is higher when the pace of technological advance quickens.
   b. Structural unemployment is higher when the pace of technological advance quickens.
   c. Frictional unemployment accounts for a larger share of total unemployment when the unemployment rate is low.

2. Why does collective bargaining have the same general effect on unemployment as a minimum wage? Illustrate your answer with a diagram.

3. Suppose that at the peak of the business cycle the Government of Canada dramatically increases benefits for unemployed workers. Explain what will happen to the natural rate of unemployment.

Solutions appear at back of book.

Inflation and Deflation

As we mentioned in the opening story, in early 2011 British officials were worried about two things: the unemployment rate was high and so was inflation. And there was a fierce debate about which concern should take priority.

Why is inflation something to worry about? Why do policy-makers even now get anxious when they see the inflation rate moving upward? The answer is that inflation can impose costs on the economy—but not in the way most people think.

The Level of Prices Doesn't Matter ...

The most common complaint about inflation, an increase in the price level, is that it makes everyone poorer—after all, a given amount of money buys less. But inflation does not make everyone poorer. To see why, it's helpful to imagine what would happen if Canada did something other countries have done from time to time—replacing the dollar with a new currency.

An example of this kind of currency conversion happened in 2002, when France, like a number of other European countries, replaced its national currency, the franc, with the new pan-European currency, the euro. People turned in their franc coins

The **real wage** is the wage rate divided by the price level.

Real income is income divided by the price level.

and notes, and received euro coins and notes in exchange, at a rate of precisely 6.55957 francs per euro. (February 17, 2012 was the last day for the French residents to exchange their old French currency for the euro.) At the same time, all contracts were restated in euros at the same rate of exchange. For example, if a French citizen had a home mortgage debt of 500 000 francs, this became a debt of 500 000/6.55957 = 76 224.51 euros. If a worker's contract specified that he or she should be paid 100 francs per hour, it became a contract specifying a wage of 100/6.55957 = 5.2449 euros per hour, and so on. This kind of currency conversion has also happened in other countries, such as Brazil. In an attempt to address the issue of high inflation, Brazil introduced a new currency, the Brazilian real, to replace the old currency, the Brazilian cruzerio, in 1994.

You could imagine doing the same thing here, replacing the dollar with a "new dollar" at a rate of exchange of, say, 7 to 1. If you owed $140 000 on your home, that would become a debt of 20 000 new dollars. If you had a wage rate of $14 an hour, it would become 2 new dollars an hour, and so on. This would bring the overall Canadian price level back to about what it was in 1965, when Lester B. Pearson was the prime minister.

So would everyone be richer as a result because prices would be only one-seventh as high? Of course not. Prices would be lower, but so would wages and incomes in general. If you cut a worker's wage to one-seventh of its previous value, but also cut all prices to one-seventh of their previous level, the worker's **real wage**—the wage rate divided by the price level—hasn't changed. In fact, bringing the overall price level back to what it was during the Pearson administration would have no effect on overall purchasing power because doing so would reduce income exactly as much as it reduced prices.

Conversely, the rise in prices that has actually taken place since the mid-1960s hasn't made Canada poorer because **real income**—nominal income (income that has not been adjusted for inflation and decreasing purchasing power) divided by the price level—has also increased. Real income per person increased at an average rate of 1.9% per year between 1965 and 2011.

The moral of this story is that the *level* of prices doesn't matter: Canada would be no richer than it is now if the overall level of prices was still as low as it was in 1965; conversely, the rise in prices over the past half century hasn't made us poorer.

... But the Rate of Change of Prices Does

The conclusion that the level of prices doesn't matter might seem to imply that the inflation rate doesn't matter either. But that's not true.

To see why, it's crucial to distinguish between the *level of prices* and the *inflation rate:* the percent increase in the overall level of prices per year. Recall from Chapter 7 that the inflation rate is defined as follows:

$$\text{Inflation rate} = \frac{\text{Price index in year 2} - \text{Price index in year 1}}{\text{Price index in year 1}} \times 100$$

Figure 8-10 highlights the difference between the price level and the inflation rate in Canada over the last half-century, with the price level measured along the left vertical axis and the inflation rate measured along the right vertical axis. In the 2000s, the overall level of prices in Canada was much higher than it had been in 1960—but that, as we've learned, didn't matter. The inflation rate in the 2000s, however, was much lower than in the 1970s—and that almost certainly made the economy richer than it would have been if high inflation had continued.

Economists believe that high rates of inflation impose significant economic costs. The most important of these costs are *shoe-leather costs, menu costs,* and *unit-of-account costs.* We'll discuss each in turn.

FIGURE **8-10** The Price Level versus the Inflation Rate, 1960–2011

Over the past half-century the consumer price index has increased almost continuously. But the *inflation rate*—the rate at which consumer prices are rising—has fluctuated, going both up and down.
Source: Statistics Canada.

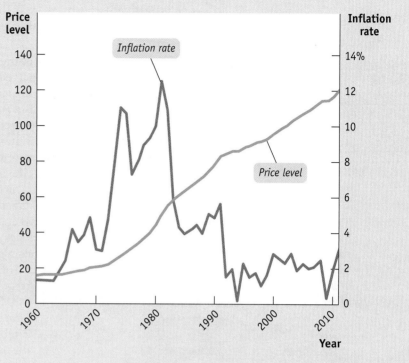

Shoe-Leather Costs People hold money—cash in their wallets and bank deposits on which they can write cheques—for convenience in making transactions. A high inflation rate, however, discourages people from holding money because the purchasing power of the cash in your wallet and the funds in your bank account steadily erodes as the overall level of prices rises. This leads people to search for ways to reduce the amount of money they hold, often at considerable economic cost.

The Economics in Action at the end of this section describes how Israelis spent a lot of time at the bank during the periods of high inflation rates that afflicted Israel in 1984–1985. During the most famous of all inflations, the German *hyperinflation* of 1921–1923, merchants employed runners to take their cash to the bank many times a day to convert it into something that would hold its value, such as a stable foreign currency. In each case, in an effort to avoid having the purchasing power of their money eroded, people used up valuable resources, such as time for Israeli citizens and the labour of those German runners that could have been used productively elsewhere. During the German hyperinflation, so many banking transactions were taking place that the number of employees at German banks nearly quadrupled—from around 100 000 in 1913 to 375 000 in 1923.

More recently, Brazil experienced hyperinflation during the early 1990s; during that episode, the Brazilian banking sector grew so large that it accounted for 15% of GDP, more than twice the size of the financial sector in Canada measured as a share of GDP. The large increase in the Brazilian banking sector needed to cope with the consequences of inflation represented a loss of real resources to its society.

Increased costs of transactions caused by inflation are known as **shoe-leather costs,** an allusion to the wear and tear caused by the extra running around that takes place when people are trying to avoid holding money. Shoe-leather costs are substantial in economies with very high inflation, as anyone

Shoe-leather costs are the increased costs of transactions caused by inflation.

Menu costs refer to the real costs of changing listed prices.

who has lived in such an economy—say, one suffering inflation of 100% or more per year—can attest. Most estimates suggest, however, that the shoe-leather costs of inflation at the rates seen in Canada—which in peacetime has never had inflation above 13%—are quite small.

Menu Costs In a modern economy, most of the things we buy have a listed price. There's a price listed under each item on a supermarket shelf, a price printed on the back of a book, a price listed for each dish on a restaurant's menu. Changing a listed price has a real cost, called a **menu cost.** For example, to change prices in a supermarket requires sending clerks through the store to change the listed price under each item. In the face of inflation, of course, firms are forced to change prices more often than they would if the aggregate price level was more or less stable. This means higher costs for the economy as a whole.

In times of very high inflation, menu costs can be substantial. During the Brazilian inflation of the early 1990s, for instance, supermarket workers reportedly spent half of their time replacing old price stickers with new ones. When inflation is high, merchants may decide to stop listing prices in terms of the local currency and use either an artificial unit—in effect, measuring prices relative to one another—or a more stable currency, such as the U.S. dollar. This is exactly what the Israeli real estate market began doing in the mid-1980s: prices were quoted in U.S. dollars, even though payment was made in Israeli shekels. And this is also what happened in Zimbabwe when, in May 2008, official estimates of the inflation rate reached 1 694 000%. By 2009, the government had suspended the Zimbabwean dollar, allowing Zimbabweans to buy and sell goods using foreign currencies.

Menu costs are also present in low-inflation economies, but they are not severe. In low-inflation economies, businesses might update their prices only sporadically—not daily or even more frequently, as is the case in high-inflation or hyperinflation economies. Also, with technological advances, menu costs are becoming less and less important, since prices can be changed electronically and fewer merchants attach price stickers to merchandise.

When trillion-dollar bills are in circulation as they were in Zimbabwe, menu costs are substantial.

During any period of inflation, not all prices are changing by the same percentage, and this causes a *change in relative prices*. Since consumers and producers use relative prices in decision-making, such changes can create positive and negative welfare impacts for some agents.

Unit-of-Account Costs In the Middle Ages, contracts were often specified "in kind": a tenant might, for example, be obliged to provide his landlord with a certain number of cattle each year (the phrase *in kind* actually comes from an ancient word for *cattle*). This may have made sense at the time, but it would be an awkward way to conduct modern business. Instead, we state contracts in monetary terms: a renter owes a certain number of dollars per month, a company that issues a bond promises to pay the bondholder the dollar value of the bond when it comes due, and so on. We also tend to make our economic calculations in dollars: a family planning its budget, or a small business owner trying to figure out how well the business is doing, makes estimates of the amount of money coming in and going out.

This role of the dollar as a basis for contracts and calculation is called the *unit-of-account* role of money. It's an important aspect of the modern economy.

Yet it's a role that can be degraded by inflation, which causes the purchasing power of a dollar to change over time—a dollar next year is worth less than a dollar this year. The effect, many economists argue, is to reduce the quality of economic decisions: the economy as a whole makes less efficient use of its resources because of the uncertainty caused by changes in the unit of account, the dollar. The **unit-of-account costs** of inflation are the costs arising from the way inflation makes money a less reliable unit of measurement.

Unit-of-account costs may be particularly important in the tax system because inflation can distort the measures of income on which taxes are collected. Here's an example: Assume that the inflation rate is 10%, so the overall level of prices rises 10% each year. Suppose that a business buys an asset, such as a piece of land, for $100 000, then resells it a year later for $110 000. In a fundamental sense, the business didn't make a profit on the deal: in real terms, the value of the land remains unchanged. For example, if the general price level is $5 today and $5.50 a year later (due to 10% inflation), the real value of the land is $20 000 ($100 000/$5) today and $20 000 ($110 000/$5.5) a year from now. But Canada's tax law would say that the business made a capital gain of $10 000, and it would have to pay taxes on that capital ("phantom") gain.

During the 1970s, when Canada had relatively high inflation, the distorting effects of inflation on the tax system were a serious problem. Some businesses were discouraged from productive investment spending because they found themselves paying taxes on phantom gains. Meanwhile, some unproductive investments became attractive because they led to phantom losses that reduced tax bills. When inflation began to fall in the 1980s and since it stabilized around 2% in the 1990s—and tax rates were reduced—these problems became much less important.

The government can reduce some of the problems inflation creates for the income tax system by **indexing** tax brackets to the rate of inflation so that only real income gains, not nominal income gains, will be taxed. In Canada, our tax and welfare systems are indexed to the CPI inflation rate. Both Old Age Security (OAS) benefits and Canada Pension Plan (CPP) benefits are indexed to the consumer price index to reflect changes in the cost of living—this helps maintain the "real" value or purchasing power of these benefit payments. CPP benefit payments are adjusted on an annual basis, while OAS benefits are revised four times a year (in January, April, July, and October).

Winners and Losers from Unexpected Inflation

As we've just learned, a high inflation rate imposes overall costs on the economy. In addition, inflation can produce winners and losers within the economy. The main reason inflation sometimes helps some people while hurting others is that economic transactions often involve contracts that extend over a period of time, such as loans, and these contracts are normally specified in nominal—that is, in dollar—terms.

In the case of a loan, the borrower receives a certain amount of funds at the beginning, and the loan contract specifies the *interest rate* on the loan and when it must be paid off. The **interest rate** is the return a lender receives for allowing borrowers the use of their savings for one year, calculated as a percentage of the amount borrowed.

But what that dollar is worth in real terms—that is, in terms of purchasing power—depends greatly on the rate of inflation over the intervening years of the loan. Economists summarize the effect of inflation on borrowers and lenders by distinguishing between the *nominal* interest rate and the *real* interest rate. The **nominal interest rate** is the interest rate in dollar terms—for example, the interest rate on a student loan. The nominal interest rate is the interest we see in our daily lives. The **real interest rate** is the nominal interest rate minus the rate

Unit-of-account costs arise from the way inflation makes money a less reliable unit of measurement.

Indexing is a way to correct the effect of inflation on the purchasing power of a unit of currency by adjusting the nominal/dollar value of an item to the inflation rate.

The **interest rate** on a loan is the price, calculated as a percentage of the amount borrowed, that a lender charges a borrower for the use of their savings for one year.

The **nominal interest rate** is the interest rate expressed in dollar terms.

The **real interest rate** is the nominal interest rate minus the rate of inflation.

of inflation. For example, if a loan carries an interest rate of 8%, but there is 5% inflation, the real interest rate is 8% − 5% = 3%.

(8-5) Real interest rate = Nominal interest rate − Inflation rate

When a borrower and a lender enter into a loan contract, the contract is normally written in dollar terms—that is, the interest rate it specifies is a nominal interest rate. (And in later chapters, when we say the interest rate we will mean the nominal interest rate unless noted otherwise) But each party to a loan contract has an expectation about the future rate of inflation and therefore an expectation about the real interest rate on the loan. If the actual inflation rate is *higher* than expected, borrowers gain at the expense of lenders: borrowers will repay their loans with funds that have a lower real value than had been expected. Conversely, if the inflation rate is *lower* than expected, lenders will gain at the expense of borrowers: borrowers must repay their loans with funds that have a higher real value than had been expected.

The above example shows that **unexpected inflation,** the difference between the actual and expected rates of inflation, may redistribute wealth arbitrarily among members of the economy, creating unexpected winners and losers. For typical Canadian households, home mortgages are the most important source of gains and losses from unexpected inflation. In the 1970s, inflation was higher than expected, so that in 1983 the purchasing power of a dollar was 41% of what it had been in 1973. As a result, Canadians who took out mortgages in the 1970s benefitted, because their real payments were substantially reduced. But those who took out mortgages in the early 1990s were not so lucky. At that time, inflation occurred at a lower rate than expected, partly because in 2003 the purchasing power of a dollar was 82% of what it had been in 1993.

Because gains for some and losses for others result from inflation that is either higher or lower than expected, yet another problem arises: uncertainty about the future inflation rate discourages people from entering into any form of long-term contract. This is an additional cost of high inflation, because high rates of inflation are usually unpredictable. In countries with high and uncertain inflation, long-term loans are rare, which makes it difficult in many cases to make long-term investments.

Similar to unexpected inflation, unexpected *deflation*—a surprise fall in the price level—creates winners and losers, too. During the Great Depression, Canada experienced deflation. Between 1929 and 1933, the consumer price index fell by 26%. This meant that debtors, including many farmers and homeowners, saw a sharp rise in the real value of their debts, which led to widespread bankruptcy and helped create a banking crisis, as lenders found their customers unable to pay back their loans. Since the Great Depression, Canada's annual inflation rate has generally remained positive with the exception of 1953 when the inflation rate was −1.4%. Figure 8-10 shows that our inflation rate has fluctuated around 2% in recent years, which, as you will see later in the chapter, is due mostly to the successful efforts of the Bank of Canada to maintain this target level. We will discuss the effects of deflation in more detail in Chapter 16.

Inflation Is Easy; Disinflation Is Hard

Unexpected inflation is the difference between the actual and expected inflation rates.

Disinflation is the process of bringing the inflation rate down.

There is not much evidence that a rise in the inflation rate from, say, 2% to 5% would do a great deal of harm to the economy. Still, policy-makers generally move forcefully to bring inflation back down when it creeps above 2% or 3%. Why? Because experience shows that bringing the inflation rate down—a process called **disinflation**—is very difficult and costly once a higher rate of inflation has become well established in the economy.

FIGURE **8-11** The Cost of Disinflation

There were two major periods of disinflation in modern Canadian history, in the early 1980s and in the early 1990s. This figure shows the track of the unemployment rate and the "core" inflation rate, which excludes food and energy, during these two episodes. In each case bringing inflation down required a temporary but very large increase in the unemployment rate, demonstrating the high cost of disinflation.

Source: Statistics Canada.

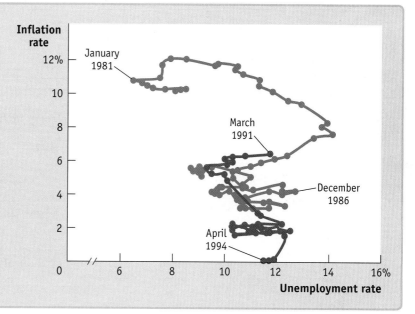

Figure 8-11 shows what happened during two major episodes of disinflation in Canada, in the early 1980s and in the early 1990s. The horizontal axis shows the unemployment rate. The vertical axis shows "core" inflation over the previous year, a measure that excludes volatile food and energy prices and is widely considered a better measure of underlying inflation than overall consumer prices. Each marker represents the inflation rate and the unemployment rate for one month. In each episode, unemployment and inflation followed a sort of clockwise spiral, with high inflation gradually falling in the face of an extended period of very high unemployment.

According to many economists, these periods of high unemployment that temporarily depressed the economy were necessary to reduce inflation that had become deeply embedded in the economy. The best way to avoid having to put the economy through a wringer to reduce inflation, however, is to avoid having a serious inflation problem in the first place. So policy-makers respond forcefully to signs that inflation may be accelerating as a form of preventive medicine for the economy. To alleviate the problems that disinflation and high rates of inflation can cause, Canada adopted, in 1991, the policy of having an inflation-control target that lets the public know what inflation rate is likely to prevail in the economy. As a result, households and firms have the opportunity to reduce their costs by making wiser economic decisions. In November 2011, the inflation target was renewed with a target inflation rate of 2% and a target range of 1 to 3%. The inflation-control target in Canada will be discussed in greater detail in Chapter 16.

ECONOMICS ▶ IN ACTION

ISRAEL'S EXPERIENCE WITH INFLATION

It's often hard to see the costs of inflation clearly because serious inflation problems are often associated with other problems that disrupt economic life, notably war or political instability (or both). In the mid-1980s, however, Israel experienced a "clean" inflation: there was no war, the government was stable, and there was order in the streets. Yet a series of policy errors led to very high inflation, with prices often rising more than 10% a month.

The shoe-leather costs of inflation in Israel: when the inflation rate hit 500% in 1985, people spent a lot of time in line at banks.

As it happens, one of the authors spent a month visiting at Tel Aviv University at the height of the inflation, so we can give a first-hand account of the effects.

First, the shoe-leather costs of inflation were substantial. At the time, Israelis spent a lot of time in lines at the bank, moving money in and out of accounts that provided high enough interest rates to offset inflation. People walked around with very little cash in their wallets; they had to go to the bank whenever they needed to make even a moderately large cash payment. Banks responded by opening a lot of branches, a costly business expense.

Second, although menu costs weren't that visible to a visitor, what you could see were the efforts businesses made to minimize them. For example, restaurant menus often didn't list prices. Instead, they listed numbers that you had to multiply by another number, written on a chalkboard and changed every day, to figure out the price of a dish.

Finally, it was hard to make decisions because prices changed so much and so often. It was a common experience to walk out of a store because prices were 25% higher than at one's usual shopping destination, only to discover that prices had just been increased 25% there, too.

▼ Quick Review

- The **real wage** and **real income** are unaffected by the level of prices.

- Inflation, like unemployment, is a major concern of policy-makers—so much so that in the past they have accepted high unemployment as the price of reducing inflation.

- While the overall level of prices is irrelevant, high rates of inflation impose real costs on the economy: **shoe-leather costs, menu costs,** and **unit-of-account costs.**

- The **interest rate** is the return a lender receives for use of his or her funds for a year. The **real interest rate** is equal to the **nominal interest rate** minus the inflation rate. As a result, unexpectedly high inflation helps borrowers and hurts lenders. With high and uncertain inflation, people will often avoid long-term investments.

- **Indexing** is a way to correct the effect of inflation on the purchasing power of a unit of currency by adjusting the nominal/dollar value of an item to the inflation rate. **Unexpected inflation** is the difference between the actual and expected inflation rates.

- **Disinflation** is very costly, so policy-makers try to avoid getting into situations of high inflation in the first place.

CHECK YOUR UNDERSTANDING 8-3

1. The widespread use of technology has revolutionized the banking industry, making it much easier for customers to access and manage their assets. Does this mean that the shoe-leather costs of inflation are higher or lower than they used to be?

2. Most people in Canada have grown accustomed to a modest inflation rate of around 2%. Who would gain and who would lose if inflation unexpectedly came to a complete stop over the next 15 or 20 years?

Solutions appear at back of book.

BUSINESS CASE : Workopolis and the Duration of Unemployment

The 1990s were famously years of significant business hype and irrational exuberance, a decade in which numerous Internet-based companies were created, providing a wide array of goods and services. Online recruitment was one of the services created during the information technology boom. To capture this business opportunity, Workopolis Canada was founded in 1999. It launched its own recruitment website, workopolis.com, in January 2000, and its French version in September 2001. Workopolis is currently Canada's leading Internet recruitment company and has one of the country's most popular employment and recruitment related websites.

Workopolis and its competitors, such as Monster Canada, use the Internet to sell services to both employers seeking workers and workers seeking jobs. Employers can place job listings, to which workers can respond; jobseekers can also obtain advice on writing effective résumés, improving their interview skills, and other employment related services.

Figure 8-12 shows the average duration of spells (episodes) of unemployment and the share or percentage of the unemployed who were unemployed for 27 weeks or more between 1997 and 2011. Up until the 2008–2009 recession, there was a downward trend in the average duration of spells of unemployment; the average number of weeks of unemployment fell from 26.5 weeks in 1997 to 14.8 weeks in 2008. In addition, the share of the unemployed that suffered from a relatively long spell of unemployment (i.e., 27 or more weeks) fell from 24.9% to 12.8% during this same time period. These downward trends demonstrate that the labour market had become friendlier to jobseekers. Aside from the fact that the Canadian economy was expanding during that period (the average annual growth rate in real GDP between 1997 and 2008 was 3.1%), the surge of online job listings might be partly responsible. By providing screening tools to employers and job notification services to jobseekers, Workopolis and its competitors helped to improve the matching of potential employers and jobseekers in the recruitment process. Such an improvement in matching helped lower

FIGURE 8-12 The Unemployment Spell, 1997–2011

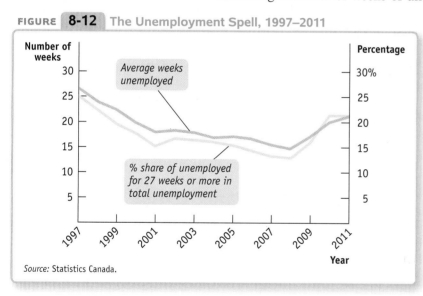

Source: Statistics Canada.

unemployment and, to some extent, supported the fall in the nation's unemployment rate from 9.1% to 6.1% between 1997 and 2008.

With the widespread use of online social networks, such as Twitter and Facebook, online job advertising/recruitment should continue to play an increasingly important role in the labour market, and help make frictional unemployment less "sticky."

QUESTIONS FOR THOUGHT

1. Use the flows in Figure 8-6 to explain the potential role of online job listings in the economy.

2. Briefly explain how online recruitment services might help lower the duration of unemployment.

3. In light of our discussion of the determinants of the unemployment rate, how could improved matching of employers and jobseekers through online job listings help lower the unemployment rate?

SUMMARY

1. Inflation and unemployment are the twin evils of macroeconomics and the main concerns of macroeconomic policy.

2. **Employment** is the number of people employed; **unemployment** is the number of people unemployed and actively looking for work. Their sum is equal to the **labour force,** and the **labour force participation rate** is the percentage of the population age 15 or older that is in the labour force.

3. The **unemployment rate,** the percentage of the labour force that is unemployed and actively looking for work, can both overstate and understate the true level of unemployment. It can overstate because it counts as unemployed those who are continuing to search for a job despite having been offered one. It can understate because it ignores frustrated workers, such as **discouraged workers, marginally attached workers,** and the **underemployed,** including those who are **visibly** and **invisibly underemployed.** In addition, the unemployment rate varies greatly among different groups in the population; it is typically higher for younger workers and for workers near retirement age than for workers in their prime working years.

4. The unemployment rate is affected by the business cycle. The unemployment rate generally falls when the growth rate of real GDP is above average and generally increases when the growth rate of real GDP is below average. A **jobless recovery,** a period in which real GDP is growing but unemployment rises, often follows recessions.

5. Job creation and destruction, as well as voluntary job separations, lead to **job search** and **frictional unemployment.** In addition, a variety of factors, such as minimum wages, unions, **efficiency wages,** government policies designed to help laid-off workers, and mismatch between employees and employers, results in a situation in which there is a surplus of labour at the market wage rate, creating **structural unemployment.** As a result, the **natural rate of**

   unemployment, the sum of frictional and structural employment, is well above zero, even when jobs are plentiful.

6. The actual unemployment rate is equal to the natural rate of unemployment, the share of unemployment that is independent of the business cycle, plus **cyclical unemployment,** the share of unemployment that depends on fluctuations in the business cycle.

7. The natural rate of unemployment changes over time, largely in response to changes in labour force characteristics, labour market institutions, and government policies.

8. Inflation does not, as many assume, make everyone poorer by raising the level of prices. That's because wages and incomes are adjusted to take into account a rising price level, leaving **real wages** and **real income** unaffected. However, a high inflation rate imposes overall costs on the economy: **shoe-leather costs, menu costs,** and **unit-of-account costs.**

9. Inflation can produce winners and losers within the economy, because long-term contracts are generally written in dollar terms. The **interest rate** specified in a loan is typically a **nominal interest rate,** which differs from the **real interest rate** due to inflation. A higher-than-expected inflation rate is good for borrowers and bad for lenders. A lower-than-expected inflation rate is good for lenders and bad for borrowers. **Unexpected inflation** is the difference between the expected rate of inflation and the actual rate. Some pensions are subject to **indexing,** so a retired person's income keeps pace with inflation.

10. Many believe policies that depress the economy and produce high unemployment are necessary to reduce embedded inflation. Because **disinflation** is very costly, policy-makers try to prevent inflation from becoming excessive in the first place.

KEY TERMS

Employment, p. 232
Unemployment, p. 233
Labour force, p. 233
Labour force participation rate, p. 233
Unemployment rate, p. 233
Discouraged workers, p. 234
Marginally attached workers, p. 234
Underemployment, p. 234
Visible underemployment, p. 234
Invisible underemployment, p. 234

Jobless recovery, p. 237
Job search, p. 240
Frictional unemployment, p. 240
Structural unemployment, p. 242
Efficiency wages, p. 244
Natural rate of unemployment, p. 244
Cyclical unemployment, p. 245
Real wage, p. 250
Real income, p. 250
Shoe-leather costs, p. 251

Menu costs, p. 252
Unit-of-account costs, p. 253
Indexing, p. 253
Interest rate, p. 253
Nominal interest rate, p. 253
Real interest rate, p. 253
Unexpected inflation, p. 254
Disinflation, p. 254

PROBLEMS

1. Each month, usually on the first Friday of the month, Statistics Canada releases the Labour Force Survey for the previous month. Go to StatCan's home page at www.statcan.gc.ca. Pick English or French. Click on the "Unemployment rate" link under the "Latest Indicators" heading. This will open the latest unemployment rate update in StatCan's "The Daily." Go to the bottom of the page and click Table 1 for the "Labour force characteristics by age and sex—Seasonally adjusted" figures. How does the unemployment rate compare to the rate one month earlier? How does the unemployment rate compare to the rate one year earlier? Is the labour market improving or worsening?

2. In general, how do changes in the unemployment rate vary with changes in real GDP? After several quarters of a severe recession, explain why we might observe a decrease in the official unemployment rate. Explain why we could see an increase in the official unemployment rate after several quarters of a strong expansion.

3. In each of the following situations, what type of unemployment is Melanie facing?

a. After completing a complex programming project, Melanie is laid off. Her prospects for a new job requiring similar skills are good, and she has signed up with a programmer placement service. She has passed up offers for low-paying jobs.

b. When Melanie and her co-workers refused to accept pay cuts, her employer outsourced their programming tasks to workers in another country. This phenomenon is occurring throughout the programming industry.

c. Due to the current slump, Melanie has been laid off from her programming job. Her employer promises to rehire her when business picks up.

4. Part of the information collected in the Labour Force Survey concerns how long individuals have been unemployed. Go to www.statcan.gc.ca to find the latest report. Using the same technique as in Problem 1 to find the Labour Force Survey, go to the bottom of the page and click CANSIM tables 282-0047 to 282-0063. This will direct you to another page that contains links to these tables of labour market data. Then click on Table 282-0047 for the "duration of unemployment by sex and age group, unadjusted for seasonality, monthly (Persons)" figures.

a. How many workers were unemployed less than 5 weeks? What percentage of all unemployed workers do these workers represent? How do these numbers compare to the previous month's data?

b. How many workers were unemployed for 27 or more weeks? What percentage of all unemployed workers do these workers represent? How do these numbers compare to the previous month's data?

c. How long has the average worker been unemployed (average duration, in weeks)? How does this compare to the average for the previous month's data?

d. Comparing the latest month for which there are data with the previous month, has the problem of long-term unemployment improved or deteriorated?

5. There is only one labour market in Profunctia. All workers have the same skills, and all firms hire workers with these skills. Use the accompanying diagram, which shows the supply of and demand for labour, to answer the following questions. Illustrate each answer with a diagram.

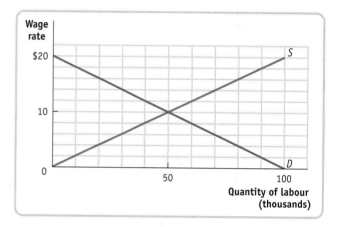

a. What is the equilibrium wage rate in Profunctia? At this wage rate, what are the level of employment, the size of the labour force, and the unemployment rate?

b. If the government of Profunctia sets a minimum wage equal to $12, what will be the level of employment, the size of the labour force, and the unemployment rate?

c. If unions bargain with the firms in Profunctia and set a wage rate equal to $14, what will be the level of employment, the size of the labour force, and the unemployment rate?

d. If the concern for retaining workers and encouraging high-quality work leads firms to set a wage rate equal to $16, what will be the level of employment, the size of the labour force, and the unemployment rate?

6. The accompanying table provides data on the size of the labour force and the number of unemployed workers for the provinces and territories of Canada.

Province/ Territory	Labour force (thousands)		Unemployed (thousands)	
	May 2011	May 2012	May 2011	May 2012
Alberta	2185.6	2255.0	117.3	102.2
British Columbia	2460.6	2503.6	185.4	185.0
Manitoba	659.0	664.5	35.7	33.9
New Brunswick	388.4	393.4	37.2	36.8
Newfoundland and Labrador	258.8	261.8	31.3	31.5
Northwest Territories	2.0	2.1	24.5	24.3
Nova Scotia	493.3	499.5	44.3	46.0
Nunavut	2.3	2.2	14.1	14.0
Ontario	7300.7	7331.9	571.7	570.2
Prince Edward Island	81.2	81.2	9.6	9.2
Quebec	4293.0	4328.5	315.4	338.4
Saskatchewan	554.0	561.7	27.7	25.5
Yukon	1.5	2.0	20.4	20.4

Source: Statistics Canada.

a. Calculate the number of workers employed in each province and territory in May 2011 and in May 2012. Use your answer to calculate the change in the total number of workers employed between May 2011 and May 2012.

b. For each province and territory, calculate the growth in the labour force from May 2011 to May 2012.

c. Compute the unemployment rate in each province and territory in May 2011 and May 2012.

d. From May 2011 to May 2012, which provinces or territories experienced a fall in their unemployment rates? Do you think this fall was caused by a net gain in the number of jobs or by a large fall in the number of people seeking jobs? Explain.

e. The following table shows the population (aged 15 and over) in each province and territory. Calculate the labour force participation for each province in May 2012 and for Canada as a whole in May 2011.

Province/Territory	Population (thousands)	
	May 2011	May 2012
Alberta	3 000.1	3 058.4
British Columbia	3 774.9	3 810.3
Manitoba	951.8	962.2
New Brunswick	619.1	620.3
Newfoundland and Labrador	429.0	427.4
Northwest Territories	32.1	32.1
Nova Scotia	778.8	780.1
Nunavut	21.2	21.0
Ontario	10 909.3	11 054.3
Prince Edward Island	119.1	120.6
Quebec	6 568.5	6 629.1
Saskatchewan	798.5	808.9
Yukon	26.3	26.9

Source: Statistics Canada.

f. The labour force participation rate for Canada as a whole was 66.8% in May 2012. Based on your answer in part (e), which provinces had labour force participation rates that were higher than the national average? Did Canada's labour force rate rise or fall from 2011 to 2012?

7. In which of the following cases is it more likely for efficiency wages to exist? Why?

a. Jane and her boss work as a team selling ice cream.

b. Jane sells ice cream without any direct supervision by her boss.

c. Jane speaks Korean and sells ice cream in a neighbourhood in which Korean is the primary language. It is difficult to find another worker who speaks Korean.

8. How will the following changes affect the natural rate of unemployment?

a. The government reduces the time during which a worker can receive employment insurance.

b. More teenagers focus on their studies and do not look for jobs until after college or university.

c. Greater access to the Internet leads both potential employers and potential employees to use the Internet to list and find jobs.

d. Union membership declines.

9. With its tradition of a job for life for most citizens, Japan once had a much lower unemployment rate than that of Canada; from 1960 to 1995, the unemployment rate in Japan exceeded 3% only once. However, since the crash of its stock market in 1989 and slow economic growth in the 1990s, the job-for-life system has broken down and unemployment rose to more than 5% in 2003.

   a. Explain the likely effect of the breakdown of the job-for-life system in Japan on the Japanese natural rate of unemployment.

   b. As this diagram shows, the rate of growth of real GDP picked up in Japan after 2001 and before the global economic crisis of 2007–2009. Explain the likely effect of this increase in real GDP growth on the unemployment rate. Was the likely cause of the change in the unemployment rate during this period a change in the natural rate of unemployment or a change in the cyclical unemployment rate?

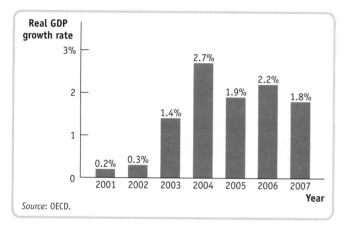

Source: OECD.

10. In the following examples, is inflation creating winners and losers at no net cost to the economy or is inflation imposing a net cost on the economy? If a net cost is being imposed, which type of cost is involved?

   a. When inflation is expected to be high, workers get paid more frequently and make more trips to the bank.

   b. Lanwei is reimbursed by her company for her work-related travel expenses. Sometimes, however, the company takes a long time to reimburse her. So when inflation is high, she is less willing to travel for her job.

   c. Hector Homeowner has a mortgage with a fixed nominal 6% interest rate that he took out five years ago. Over the years, the inflation rate has crept up unexpectedly to its present level of 7%.

   d. In response to unexpectedly high inflation, the manager of Cozy Cottages of Cape Spear must reprint and resend expensive colour brochures correcting the price of rentals this season.

11. The accompanying diagram shows the interest rate on one-year loans and inflation during 1995–2010 in the economy of Albernia. When would one-year loans have been especially attractive and why?

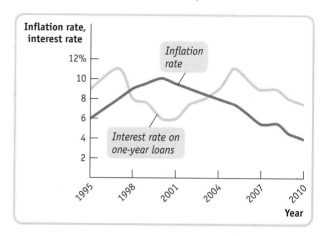

12. The accompanying table provides the inflation rate in the year 2000 and the average inflation rate over the period 2001–2010 for seven different countries.

Country	Inflation rate in 2000	Average inflation rate in 2001–2010
Brazil	7.06	6.70
Canada	2.80	2.02
China	0.4	2.16
Indonesia	3.77	8.55
Japan	−0.78	−0.25
Turkey	55.03	18.51
United States	3.37	2.40

Source: International Monetary Fund.

   a. Given the expected relationship between average inflation and menu costs, rank the countries in descending order of menu costs using average inflation over the period 2001–2010.

   b. Rank the countries in order of inflation rates that most favoured borrowers with ten-year loans that were taken out in 2000. Assume that the loans were agreed upon with the expectation that the inflation rate for 2001 to 2010 would be the same as the inflation rate in 2000.

   c. Did borrowers who took out ten-year loans in Japan gain or lose overall versus lenders? Explain.

13. The accompanying diagram shows the inflation rate in Canada from 1980 to 2011.

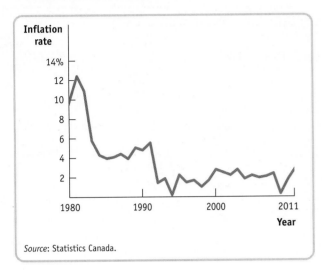

Source: Statistics Canada.

a. From 1980 to 2011, Canada experienced two periods of disinflation—the first between 1980 and 1985 and the second between 1991 and 1994. How would you have expected the unemployment rate to behave during these two periods?

b. Nowadays, policy-makers react forcefully when the inflation rate rises above a target rate of 2%. Why would it be harmful if inflation rose from 1.8% (the level in 2010) to, say, a level of 5%?

14. In 1991, the Bank of Canada adopted an inflation-control target. The current target rate of inflation is 2%, with a target range of 1 to 3%. Many Canadians welcome the adoption of the inflation-control target as it allows them to make better economic decisions. Explain how both creditors and debtors can benefit from having an inflation-control target.

Long-Run Economic Growth

TALL TALES

As China illustrates, there is a positive relationship between a country's rate of long-run economic growth and its average population height.

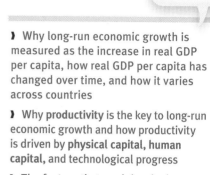

WHAT YOU WILL LEARN IN THIS CHAPTER

❯ Why long-run economic growth is measured as the increase in real GDP per capita, how real GDP per capita has changed over time, and how it varies across countries

❯ Why **productivity** is the key to long-run economic growth and how productivity is driven by **physical capital, human capital,** and technological progress

❯ The factors that explain why long-run growth rates differ so much among countries

❯ How growth has varied among several important regions of the world and why the **convergence hypothesis** applies to economically advanced countries

❯ The question of **sustainability** and the challenges to growth posed by scarcity of natural resources and environmental degradation

CHINA IS GROWING—AND SO are the Chinese. According to official statistics, children in China are almost 6 cm taller now than they were 30 years ago. The average Chinese citizen is still a lot shorter than the average Canadian, but at the current rate of growth the difference may be largely gone in a couple of generations.

If that does happen, China will be following in Japan's footsteps. Older Canadians tend to think of the Japanese as short, but today young Japanese men are more than 12 cm taller on average than they were in 1900, which makes them almost as tall as their Canadian counterparts (and taller, on average, than three of the four authors of this book).

There's no mystery about why the Japanese grew taller—it's because they

grew richer. In the early twentieth century, Japan was a relatively poor country in which many families couldn't afford to give their children adequate nutrition. As a result, their children grew up to be short adults. However, since World War II, Japan has become an economic powerhouse in which food is ample and young adults are much taller than before.

The same phenomenon is now happening in China. Although it is still a relatively poor country, China has made great economic strides over the past 30 years. Its recent history is probably the world's most dramatic example of long-run economic growth—a sustained increase in output per capita. Yet despite its impressive performance, China is currently playing catch-up with economically advanced countries like Canada,

the United States, and Japan. It's still a relatively poor country because these other nations began their own processes of long-run economic growth many decades ago—and in the case of Canada, the United States, and European countries, more than a century ago.

Many economists have argued that long-run economic growth—why it happens and how to achieve it—is the single most important issue in macroeconomics. In this chapter, we present some facts about long-run growth, look at the factors that economists believe determine the pace at which long-run growth takes place, examine how government policies can help or hinder growth, and address questions about the environmental sustainability of long-run growth. ■

Comparing Economies Across Time and Space

Before we analyze the sources of long-run economic growth, it's useful to have a sense of just how much the Canadian economy has grown over time and how large the gaps are between wealthy countries like Canada and countries that have yet to achieve comparable growth. So let's take a look at the numbers.

Real GDP per Capita

The key statistic used to track economic growth is *real GDP per capita*—real GDP divided by the population size. We focus on GDP because, as we learned in Chapter 7, GDP measures the total value of an economy's production of final goods and services as well as the income earned in that economy in a given year. We use *real* GDP because we want to separate changes in the quantity of goods and services from the effects of a rising price level. We focus on real GDP *per capita* because we want to isolate the effect of changes in the population. For example, other things equal, an increase in the population lowers the standard of living for the average person—there are now more people to share a given amount of real GDP. An increase in real GDP that only matches an increase in population leaves the average standard of living unchanged.

Although we also learned in Chapter 7 that growth in real GDP per capita should not be a policy goal in and of itself, it does serve as a very useful summary measure of a country's economic progress over time, or of its progress relative to other countries at one moment in time. Figure 9-1 shows real GDP per capita for Canada, the United States, India, and China, measured in 1990 international dollars, from 1900 to 2011.[1] (We'll talk about India and China in a

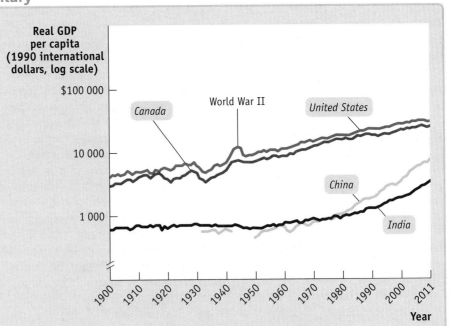

FIGURE 9-1 Economic Growth in Canada, the United States, India, and China over the Past Century

Real GDP per capita from 1900 to 2011, measured in 1990 international dollars, is shown for Canada, the United States, India, and China. Equal percent changes in real GDP per capita are drawn the same size. As the steeper slopes of the lines representing China and India show, since 1980 India and China had a much higher growth rate than Canada and the United States. In 1995, China attained the standard of living achieved in Canada in 1900. In 2011, India still had not attained the standard of living Canadians had in 1900. (Break in China data from 1940 to 1950 is due to war.)

Sources: Angus Maddison, "Statistics on World Population, GDP, and Per Capita GDP, 1–2008 AD," www.ggdc.net/maddison; The Conference Board, Total Economy Database, www.conference-board.org/data/economydatabase/.

[1] An international dollar is a hypothetical unit of currency, created by the World Bank, that has the same real purchasing power that the U.S. dollar had in the United States at a given point in time: 1990 in this case.

moment.) The vertical axis is drawn on a logarithmic scale so that equal percent changes in real GDP per capita across countries have the same sized slope over time in the graph.[2]

To give a sense of how much the Canadian economy grew during the last century, Table 9-1 shows real GDP per capita at selected years, expressed two ways: as a percentage of the 1900 level and as a percentage of the 2011 level. In 1920, the Canadian economy already produced 133% as much per person as it did in 1900. In 2011, it produced 869% as much per person as it did in 1900, a more than eightfold increase. Alternatively, in 1900 the Canadian economy produced only 12% as much per person as it did in 2011. From 1900 to 1920, real GDP per capita grew by three percentage points relative to its level in 2011. During the next 20 years, from 1920 to 1940, the growth rate of real GDP per capital doubled; it grew by six percentage points relative to its level in 2011. During the next 40 years, ending in 1980, real GDP per capita really sped up—it grew by 43 percentage points relative to its level in 2011, or about 22 percentage points per 20-year period.

The income of the typical family normally grows more or less in proportion to per capita income. For example, a 1% increase in real GDP per capita corresponds, roughly, to a 1% increase in the income of the median or typical family—a family at the centre of the income distribution. In 2011, the median Canadian household had an income of about $70 000. Since Table 9-1 tells us that real GDP per capita in 1900 was only 12% of its 2011 level, a typical family in 1900 probably had a purchasing power only 12% as large as the purchasing power of a typical family in 2011. That's around $8400 in 2011's dollars, representing a standard of living that we would now consider severe poverty. Today's typical Canadian family, if transported back to Canada of 1900, would feel quite a lot of deprivation.

Yet many people in the world have a standard of living equal to or lower than that of Canada at the beginning of the last century. That's the message about China and India in Figure 9-1: despite dramatic economic growth in China over the last three decades and the less dramatic acceleration of economic growth in India, China has only recently exceeded the standard of living that Canada enjoyed in the early twentieth century, while India is still poorer than Canada was at that time. And much of the world today is poorer than China or India.

You can get a sense of how poor much of the world remains by looking at Figure 9-2, a map of the world in which countries are classified according to their 2010 levels of GDP per capita, in nominal U.S. dollars. As you can see, large parts of the world have very low incomes. Generally speaking, the countries of Europe and North America, as well as a few in the Pacific, have high incomes. The rest of the world, containing most of its population, is dominated by countries with GDP less than $3976 per capita—and often much less. In fact, today about 50% of the world's people live in countries with a lower standard of living than the Canada had a century ago.

Growth Rates

How did Canada manage to produce over eight times as much per person in 2011 than in 1900? A little bit at a time. Long-run economic growth is normally a gradual process in which real GDP per capita grows at most a few percent per year. From 1900 to 2011, real GDP per capita in Canada increased an average of 1.95% each year.

To have a sense of the relationship between the annual growth rate of real GDP per capita and the long-run change in real GDP per capita, it's helpful to keep in mind the **Rule of 70,** a mathematical formula that tells us how long it

TABLE 9-1   Canadian Real GDP per Capita

Year	Percentage of 1900 real GDP per capita	Percentage of 2011 real GDP per capita
1900	100%	12%
1920	133	15
1940	184	21
1980	556	64
2000	772	89
2011	869	100

Sources: Angus Maddison, "Statistics on World Population, GDP, and Per Capita GDP, 1–2008 AD," www.ggdc.net/maddison; The Conference Board, Total Economy Database, www.conference-board.org/data/economydatabase/.

[2]If $X = \left(\frac{A}{B}\right)$, then $\ln X = \ln\left(\frac{A}{B}\right) = \ln A - \ln B$. The percentage growth rate of X over time is equal to the slope of the $\ln X$ curve. Also, at any moment in time this growth rate of X (slope) is about equal to the percentage growth rate of A (over time) *minus* the percentage growth rate in B (over time).

FIGURE **9-2** Incomes Around the World, 2010

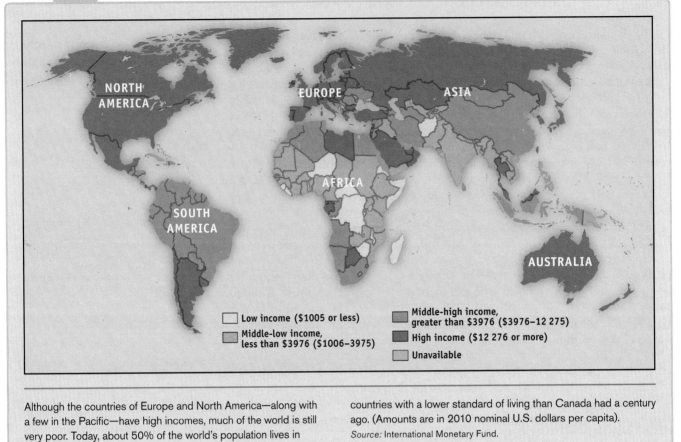

Although the countries of Europe and North America—along with a few in the Pacific—have high incomes, much of the world is still very poor. Today, about 50% of the world's population lives in countries with a lower standard of living than Canada had a century ago. (Amounts are in 2010 nominal U.S. dollars per capita).
Source: International Monetary Fund.

takes real GDP per capita, or any other variable that grows gradually over time, to double. The approximate answer is:

(9-1) Number of years for variable to double $= \dfrac{70}{\text{Annual growth rate of variable}}$

(Note that the Rule of 70 can only be applied to a positive growth rate.) So if real GDP per capita grows at 1% per year, it will take 70 years to double. If it grows at 2% per year, it will take only 35 years to double. In fact, Canadian real GDP per capita rose on average 1.95% per year over the last century. Applying the Rule of 70 to this information implies that it should have taken 36 years for real GDP per capita to double; it would have taken 108 years—three periods of 36 years each—for Canadian real GDP per capita to double three times. That is, the Rule of 70 implies that over the course of 108 years, Canadian real GDP per capita should have increased by a factor of $2 \times 2 \times 2 = 8$. And this does turn out to be a pretty good approximation of reality. Between 1899 and 2007—a period of 108 years—real GDP per capita rose just about eightfold.

Figure 9-3 shows the average annual rate of growth of real GDP per capita for selected countries from 1980 to 2010. Some countries were notable success stories: for example, China, though still quite a poor country, has made spectacular progress. India, although not matching China's performance, has also achieved impressive growth, as discussed in the following Economics in Action.

Some countries, though, have had very disappointing growth. Argentina was once considered a wealthy nation. In the early years of the twentieth century, it was in the same league as Canada and the United States. But since then it has lagged far behind more dynamic economies. And still others, like Zimbabwe, have slid backward.

What explains these differences in growth rates? To answer that question, we need to examine the sources of long-run economic growth.

According to the **Rule of 70,** the time it takes a variable that grows gradually over time to double is approximately 70 divided by that variable's annual growth rate.

FIGURE **9-3** Comparing Recent Growth Rates

The average annual rate of growth of real GDP per capita from 1980 to 2010 is shown here for selected countries. China and, to a lesser extent, India and Ireland achieved impressive growth. Canada, the United States, and France had moderate growth. Once considered an economically advanced country, Argentina had more sluggish growth. Still others, such as Zimbabwe, slid backward.

Source: International Monetary Fund.

*Data for Zimbabwe is average annual growth rate 2000–2010 due to data limitations.

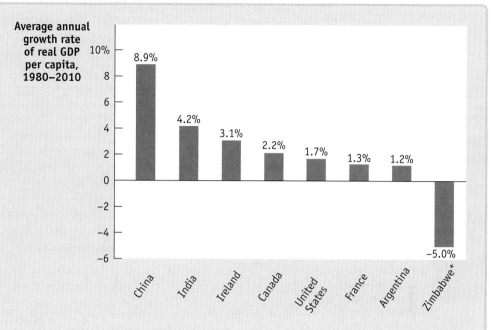

Average annual growth rate of real GDP per capita, 1980–2010

China 8.9%, India 4.2%, Ireland 3.1%, Canada 2.2%, United States 1.7%, France 1.3%, Argentina 1.2%, Zimbabwe* –5.0%

⚠ PITFALLS

CHANGE IN LEVELS VERSUS GROWTH RATE

When studying economic growth, it's vitally important to understand the difference between a change in the level of a variable (a *level change*) and a change in the growth rate of this variable (a *growth rate change*). When we say that real GDP "grew," we mean that the level of real GDP increased. Thus, we might say that Canadian real GDP grew during 2011 by $32 billion.

If we knew the level of Canadian real GDP in 2010, we could also represent the amount of 2011 growth in terms of a rate of change. For example, if Canadian real GDP in 2010 was $1325 billion, then Canadian real GDP in 2011 was $1325 billion + $32 billion = $1357 billion. We could calculate the percentage rate of change, or the growth rate, of Canadian real GDP during 2011 as (($1357 billion – $1325 billion)/$1325 billion) × 100 = ($32 billion/$1325 billion) × 100 = 2.42%. Statements about economic growth over a period of years almost always refer to changes in the growth rate.

When talking about growth or growth rates, economists often use phrases that appear to mix the two concepts and so can be confusing. For example, when we say that "Canadian growth fell during the 1970s," we are really saying that the Canadian growth rate of real GDP was lower in the 1970s in comparison to the 1960s. When we say that "growth decelerated during the 1970s, the 80s, 90s, and 2000s," we are saying that the average growth rate decreased from decade to decade—for example, going from more than 5% to 4.2% to 3.2% to 2.4% to 2.1%.

ECONOMICS ▶*IN ACTION*

INDIA TAKES OFF

India achieved independence from Great Britain in 1947, becoming the world's most populous democracy—a status it has maintained to this day. For more than three decades after independence, however, this happy political story was partly overshadowed by economic disappointment. Despite ambitious economic development plans, India's performance was consistently sluggish. In 1980, India's real GDP per capita was only about 50% higher than it had been in 1947; the gap between Indian living standards and those in wealthy countries like Canada had been growing rather than shrinking.

Since then, however, India has done much better. As Figure 9-3 shows, real GDP per capita has grown at an average rate of 4.2% a year, more than tripling between 1980 and 2010. India now has a large and rapidly

India's high rate of economic growth since 1980 has raised living standards and led to the emergence of a rapidly growing middle class.

growing middle class. And yes, the well-fed children of that middle class are much taller than their parents.

What went right in India after 1980? Many economists point to policy reforms. For decades after independence, India had a tightly controlled, highly regulated economy. Today, things are very different: a series of reforms opened the economy to international trade and freed up domestic competition. Some economists, however, argue that this can't be the main story because the big policy reforms weren't adopted until 1991, yet growth accelerated around 1980.

Regardless of the explanation, India's economic rise has transformed it into a major new economic power—and has allowed hundreds of millions of people to have a much better life, better than their grandparents could have dreamed.

The big question now is whether this growth can continue. Skeptics argue that there are important bottlenecks in the Indian economy that may constrain future growth. They point in particular to the still low education level of much of India's population and inadequate infrastructure—that is, the poor quality and limited capacity of the country's roads, railroads, power supplies, and so on. But India's economy has defied the skeptics for several decades and the hope is that it can continue doing so.

▼ Quick Review

- Economic growth is measured using real GDP per capita.

- In Canada, real GDP per capita increased over eightfold since 1900, resulting in a large increase in living standards.

- Many countries have real GDP per capita much lower than that of Canada. More than half of the world's population currently has living standards worse than those existing in Canada in the early 1900s.

- The long-term rise in real GDP per capita is the result of gradual growth. The **Rule of 70** tells us how many years at a given annual rate of growth it takes to double real GDP per capita.

- Growth rates of real GDP per capita differ substantially among nations.

CHECK YOUR UNDERSTANDING 9-1

1. Why do economists use real GDP per capita to measure economic progress rather than some other measure, such as nominal GDP per capita or real GDP?

2. Apply the Rule of 70 to the data in Figure 9-3 to determine how long it will take each of the countries listed there (except Zimbabwe) to double its real GDP per capita. Would India's real GDP per capita exceed that of Canada in the future if growth rates remain as shown in Figure 9-3? Why or why not?

3. Although China and India currently have growth rates much higher than the Canadian growth rate, the typical Chinese or Indian household is far poorer than the typical Canadian household. Explain why.

Solutions appear at back of book.

The Sources of Long-Run Growth

Long-run economic growth depends almost entirely on one ingredient: rising *productivity*. However, a number of factors affect the growth of productivity. Let's look first at why productivity is the key ingredient and then examine what affects it.

The Crucial Importance of Productivity

Sustained economic growth occurs only when the amount of output produced by the average worker increases steadily. The terms **labour productivity,** or **Average Productivity of Labour (AP_L)** or simply **productivity** for short, are used to refer either to output per worker or, in some cases, to output per hour. (The number of hours worked by an average worker differs to some extent across countries, although this isn't an important factor in the difference between living standards in, say, India and Canada.) In this book we'll focus on output per worker. For the economy as a whole, productivity—output per worker—is simply real GDP divided by the number of people working.

You might wonder why we say that higher productivity is the only source of long-run growth. Can't an economy also increase its real GDP per capita by putting more of the population to work? The answer is, yes, but … . For short periods of time, an economy can experience a burst of growth in output per

Labour productivity, often referred to as **Average Productivity of Labour (AP_L)** or simply **productivity,** is (real) output per worker or, in some cases, output per hour.

capita by putting a higher percentage of the population to work. That happened in Canada during World War II, when hundreds of thousands of women who previously worked only in the home entered the paid workforce. The percentage of adult civilians employed outside the home rose from 51% in 1939 to 61% in 1944, and you can see the resulting bump in real GDP per capita for Canada during those years in Figure 9-1.

Over the longer run, however, the rate of employment growth is never very different from the rate of population growth. Over the course of the twentieth century, for example, Canada's population rose at an average rate of about 1.7% per year and employment rose by 2.1% per year. Real GDP per capita rose 2.0% per year; of that, 1.6%—that is, about 80% of the total—was the result of rising productivity. In general, overall real GDP can grow because of population growth; a higher population increases the number of workers employed, which in turns raises the real amount of goods and services produced. But any large increase in real GDP *per capita* must be the result of increased output *per worker*, that is, it must be due to higher productivity.[3]

So increased productivity is the key to long-run economic growth. But what leads to higher productivity?

Explaining Growth in Productivity

There are three main reasons why the average Canadian worker today produces far more than his or her counterpart a century ago. First, on average, each modern worker has far more *physical capital*, such as machinery and office space, to work with. Second, the modern worker is much better educated and so possesses much more *human capital*. Finally, modern firms have the advantage of a century's accumulation of technical advancements reflecting a great deal of *technological progress*.

Let's look at each of these factors in turn.

Increase in Physical Capital Economists define **physical capital** as manufactured resources such as buildings and machines. Physical capital makes workers more productive. For example, a farmworker operating a tractor can cultivate a lot more farmland per day than one equipped only with a shovel.

The average Canadian private-sector worker today is backed up by more than $190 000 worth of non-residential physical capital—far more than a Canadian worker had 100 years ago and far more than the average worker in most other countries has today.

Increase in Human Capital It's not enough for a worker to have good equipment—he or she must also know what to do with it. **Human capital** refers to the improvement in labour created by the education and knowledge embodied in the workforce.

Canada's human capital has increased dramatically over the past century. A hundred years ago, most Canadians could read and write, but few had an extensive education. In 1920, only 3.2% of Canadians under the age of 25 were enrolled in university or college and about 3% of Canadians between 25 and 29

Physical capital consists of human-made resources such as buildings and machines.

Human capital is the improvement in labour created by the education and knowledge embodied in the workforce.

---

[3]If we denote real output by Y, then we can rewrite real output per capita as:
$$\left(\frac{Y}{\text{population}}\right) = \left(\frac{Y}{\text{number of workers}}\right)\left(\frac{\text{number of workers}}{\text{population}}\right).$$

Recall that since the scale is logarithmic, the growth rate of $A = B \times C$ equals the growth rate of B *plus* the growth rate of C. Further, the growth rate of $D = \dfrac{E}{F}$ equals the growth rate of E *minus* the growth rate of F. Therefore, the growth rate of real output per capita is equal to the growth rate of the amount of real output per worker $\left(\dfrac{Y}{\text{number of workers}}\right)$, plus the growth rate of the number of workers *minus* the growth rate of the population.

had a post-secondary degree. By way of contrast, far more people have a post-secondary education today. In 2009, 88% of Canadians aged 25–64 had a high school education and 55% had a college or university education—it would be impossible to run today's economy with a population as poorly educated as that of a century ago.

Analyses based on *growth accounting,* described later in this chapter, suggest that education—and its effect on productivity—is an even more important determinant of growth than increases in physical capital.

"I remember when you used to look for answers using your astute powers of deduction."

Technological Progress Probably the most important driver of productivity growth is **technological progress,** which is broadly defined as an advance in the technical means of the production of goods and services. We'll see shortly how economists measure the impact of technology on growth.

Workers today are able to produce more than those in the past, even with the same amount of physical and human capital, because technology has advanced over time. It's important to realize that economically important technological progress need not be flashy or rely on cutting-edge science. Historians have noted that past economic growth has been driven not only by major inventions, such as the railroad or the semiconductor chip, but also by thousands of modest innovations, such as the green plastic garbage bag, invented in Canada in 1950, which made collecting garbage easier, and the egg carton, invented in British Columbia in 1911, which allowed eggs to be delivered unbroken. Experts attribute much of the productivity surge that took place in Canada late in the twentieth century to new technology adopted by retail companies like Loblaws and by cultural services firms such as publishers and broadcasters rather than to high-technology companies.

Accounting for Growth: The Aggregate and Per Worker Production Functions

Aggregate real output for an economy is higher, other things equal, when i) more physical capital is used, ii) more labour (workers) is used, iii) more human capital is used, and/or iv) the technology improves. Economists use the **aggregate production function** to demonstrate this relation:

(9-2) $Y = A \times F(K, L, H)$

where
$$Y = \text{aggregate real output (GDP)}$$
$$K = \text{amount of physical capital used}$$
$$L = \text{amount of labour used}$$
$$H = \text{amount of human capital used}$$
$$F(\ldots) = \text{aggregate production function}$$
$$A = \text{total factor productivity}$$

This equation shows that if **total factor productivity** rises, then aggregate real output will also rise, *all else the same*[4]—a result that can be interpreted as an improvement in technology. We assume that a small increase in K, holding all other inputs and technology fixed, causes the amount of aggregate real output

Technological progress is an advance in the technical means of the production of goods and services.

The **aggregate production function** is a relationship that shows how the aggregate real quantity of output is produced using the available factors of production (the inputs: labour, physical capital, and human capital) and technology [A and the function $F(\ldots)$].

Total factor productivity — represented by the parameter A in the aggregate production function $Y = A \times F(K, L, H)$ helps account for output that is not a result of the productive inputs. That is, it captures all inputs and technological features left out of the aggregate production function.

---

[4]This expression is often used with equations. It means that we allow one term on the right side of the equation to change while all the others stay the same. So in this case, A changes, while factors K, L, and H remain the same.

to rise by a marginal amount, called the **positive marginal productivity of physical capital (positive MP_K)**. We also assume that the marginal products of labour and human capital are both positive. If total factor productivity is held constant, then the production function $F(\ldots)$ shows how generous the technology is in increasing productivity, that is, how the technology magnifies the effect of inputs K, L, and H into aggregate real output. Similarly, if the levels of the inputs and the aggregate production remain fixed, then increases in total factor productivity can be interpreted as improvements in technology, since this allows for higher levels of real output to be produced without having to use more inputs.

Likewise, productivity is higher, all else the same, when i) more physical capital is used, ii) human capital increases, and/or iii) the technology improves. In this case we assume that an increase in physical capital per worker causes a rise in real output per worker and that the same holds true for an increase in human capital per worker. So, when total factor productivity rises, then the real output per worker will rise. To quantify these effects, economists use the **per worker production function,** which shows how productivity depends on the quantities of physical capital per worker and human capital per worker as well as the state of technology:

$$(\text{9-3}) \quad \left(\frac{Y}{L}\right) = A \times f\left(\left(\frac{K}{L}\right),\left(\frac{H}{L}\right)\right)$$

where

$\left(\dfrac{Y}{L}\right)$ = real output (GDP) per worker

$\left(\dfrac{K}{L}\right)$ = real physical capital per worker

$\left(\dfrac{H}{L}\right)$ = human capital per worker

A = total factor productivity

In general, all three factors on the right side of the function tend to rise over time, as workers, for example, are equipped with more machinery, receive more education, and benefit from technological advances. What the per worker production function does is allow economists to disentangle the effects of these three factors on overall productivity.

An example of a per worker production function applied to real data comes from a comparative study of Chinese and Indian economic growth by the economists Barry Bosworth and Susan Collins of the Brookings Institution. They used the following aggregate production function:

GDP per worker = A × (Physical capital per worker)$^{0.4}$ × (Human capital per worker)$^{0.6}$

where A represents an estimate of the level of technology and they assumed that each year of education raises workers' human capital by 7%. Using this function, they tried to explain why China grew faster than India between 1978 and 2004. About half the difference, they found, was due to China's higher levels of investment spending, which raised its level of physical capital per worker faster than India's. The other half was due to faster Chinese technological progress (growth in A).

In analyzing historical economic growth, economists have discovered a crucial fact about the estimated per worker production function: it exhibits **diminishing returns to physical capital.** This is often called **diminishing marginal productivity of (physical) capital (dim MP_K).** So when the amount of human capital per worker and the state of technology are held fixed, each successive increase in the amount of physical capital per worker leads to a smaller

The **positive marginal productivity of physical capital (positive MP_K)** is the amount by which productivity is increased as the result of a small increase in physical capital used.

The **per worker production function** is a hypothetical function that shows how productivity (real GDP per worker) depends on the quantities of physical capital per worker and human capital per worker as well as the state of technology.

A per worker production function exhibits **diminishing returns to physical capital** or **diminishing marginal productivity of (physical) capital (dim MP_K)** when, holding the amount of human capital per worker and the state of technology fixed, each successive increase in the amount of physical capital per worker leads to a smaller increase in productivity.

FIGURE   **9-4**   Physical Capital and Productivity

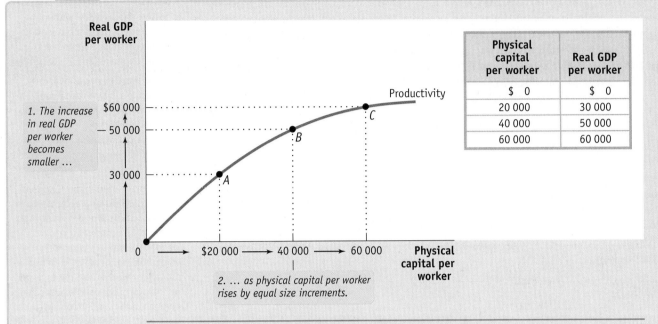

1. The increase in real GDP per worker becomes smaller ...

2. ... as physical capital per worker rises by equal size increments.

Physical capital per worker	Real GDP per worker
$ 0	$ 0
20 000	30 000
40 000	50 000
60 000	60 000

The per worker production function shows how, in this case holding human capital per worker and technology fixed, productivity increases as physical capital per worker rises. Other things equal, a greater quantity of physical capital per worker leads to higher real GDP per worker (positive MP_K, as shown by an upward slope) but is subject to diminishing returns: each successive addition to physical capital per worker produces a smaller increase in productivity (diminishing MP_K, as shown by a decreasing slope as

(K/L) rises). Starting at the origin, 0, a $20 000 increase in physical capital per worker leads to an increase in real GDP per worker of $30 000, indicated by point A. Starting from point A, another $20 000 increase in physical capital per worker leads to an increase in real GDP per worker but only of $20 000, indicated by point B. Finally, a third $20 000 increase in physical capital per worker leads to only a $10 000 increase in real GDP per worker, indicated by point C.

increase in productivity. The graph and table in Figure 9-4 give a hypothetical example of how the level of physical capital per worker might affect the level of real GDP per worker, holding human capital per worker and the state of technology fixed. In this example, we measure the quantity of physical capital in dollars.

To see why the relationship between physical capital per worker and productivity exhibits diminishing returns, think about how having farm equipment affects the productivity of farmworkers. A little bit of equipment makes a big difference: a worker equipped with a tractor can do much more than a worker without one. And a worker using more expensive equipment will, other things equal, be more productive: a worker with a $40 000 tractor will normally be able to cultivate more farmland in a given amount of time than a worker with a $20 000 tractor because the more expensive machine will be more powerful, perform more tasks, or both.

But will a worker with a $40 000 tractor, holding human capital and technology constant, be twice as productive as a worker with a $20 000 tractor? Probably not: there's a huge difference between not having a tractor at all and having even an inexpensive tractor; there's much less difference between having an inexpensive tractor and having a better tractor. And we can be sure that a worker with a $200 000 tractor won't be 10 times as productive: a tractor can be improved only so much. Because the same is true of other kinds of equipment, the per worker production function shows diminishing returns to physical capital.

⚠ PITFALLS

IT MAY BE DIMINISHED ... BUT IT'S STILL POSITIVE
It's important to understand what diminishing returns to physical capital means and what it doesn't mean. As we've already explained, it's an "other things equal" statement: holding the amount of human capital per worker and the technology fixed, each successive increase in the amount of physical capital per worker results in a smaller increase in real GDP per worker. But this doesn't mean that real GDP per worker eventually falls

as more and more physical capital is added. It's just that the *increase* in real GDP per worker gets smaller and smaller, albeit remaining at or above zero. So an increase in physical capital per worker will never reduce productivity. But due to diminishing returns, at some point increasing the amount of physical capital per worker no longer produces an economic payoff: at some point the increase in output is so small that it is not worth the cost of the additional physical capital.

Diminishing returns to physical capital imply a relationship between physical capital per worker and real output per worker like the one shown in Figure 9-4. As the productivity curve for physical capital per worker and the accompanying table illustrate, more physical capital per worker leads to more output per worker. But each $20 000 increment in physical capital per worker adds less to productivity. As you can see from the table, there is a big payoff for the first $20 000 of physical capital: real GDP per worker rises by $30 000. The second $20 000 of physical capital also raises productivity, but not by as much: real GDP per worker goes up by only $20 000. The third $20 000 of physical capital raises real GDP per worker by only $10 000. By comparing points along the curve you can also see that as physical capital per worker rises, output per worker also rises (positive MP_K, as shown by an upward slope)—but at a diminishing rate (diminishing MP_K, as shown by a decreasing slope as (K/L) rises). Going from the origin at 0 to point *A*, a $20 000 increase in physical capital per worker, leads to an increase of $30 000 in real GDP per worker. Going from point *A* to point *B*, a second $20 000 increase in physical capital per worker, leads to an increase of only $20 000 in real GDP per worker. And from point *B* to point *C*, a $20 000 increase in physical capital per worker increased real GDP per worker by only $10 000.

It's important to realize that diminishing returns to physical capital is an "other things equal" phenomenon: additional amounts of physical capital are less productive *when the amount of human capital per worker and the technology are held fixed.*[5] Diminishing returns may disappear if we increase the amount of human capital per worker, or improve the technology, or both at the same time the amount of physical capital per worker is increased.

For example, a worker with a $40 000 tractor who has also been trained in the most advanced cultivation techniques may in fact be more than twice as productive as a worker with only a $20 000 tractor and no additional human capital. But diminishing returns to any one input—regardless of whether it is physical capital, human capital, or number of workers—is a pervasive characteristic of production. Typical estimates suggest that in practice a 1% increase in the quantity of physical capital per worker increases output per worker by only one-third of 1%, or 0.33%.

In practice, all the factors contributing to higher productivity rise during the course of economic growth: both physical capital and human capital per worker increase, and technology advances as well. To disentangle the effects of these factors, economists use **growth accounting,** which estimates the contribution of each major factor in the per worker production function to economic growth. Growth accounting can be applied to either the aggregate or the per

Growth accounting estimates the contribution of each major factor in the per worker production function to economic growth.

---

[5]As we said, the marginal product of capital (MP_K) measures the return to, or change in, output per worker (Y/L) that comes from a small change to capital per worker (K/L), when both the amount of human capital per worker and state of technology are held fixed. If a small increase in the amount of capital per worker used, all else the same, results in an increase in the amount of output per worker, then we have *positive marginal productivity of capital (positive MP_K).* Similarly, if this small increase in the amount of capital per worker used, all else the same, results in a reduction in the MP_K, then the production function exhibits *diminishing marginal returns to capital* or *diminishing MP_K.*

worker versions of the production function. Growth accounting decomposes the growth rate of output per worker into estimated portions that are the results of the growth rates of physical capital per worker, human capital per worker, and total factor productivity owing to technology. For example, suppose the following are true:

- The amount of physical capital per worker grows 3% a year.
- According to estimates of the per worker production function, each 1% rise in physical capital per worker, holding human capital and technology constant, raises output per worker by one-third of 1%, or 0.33%.

In that case, we would estimate that growing physical capital per worker is responsible for 3% × 0.33 = 1 percentage point of productivity growth per year. A similar but more complex procedure is used to estimate the effects of growing human capital. The procedure is more complex because there aren't simple dollar measures of the quantity of human capital.

Growth accounting allows us to calculate the effects of greater physical and human capital on economic growth. But how can we estimate the effects of technological progress? We do so by estimating what is left over after the effects of physical and human capital have been taken into account. For example, let's imagine that there was no increase in human capital per worker so that we can focus on changes in physical capital and in technology.

In Figure 9-5, the lower curve shows the same hypothetical relationship between physical capital per worker and output per worker shown in Figure 9-4. Let's assume that this was the relationship given the technology available in 1940. The upper curve also shows a relationship between physical capital per worker and productivity, but this time given the technology available in 2010. (We've chosen a 70-year stretch to allow us

FIGURE   9-5   Technological Progress and Productivity Growth

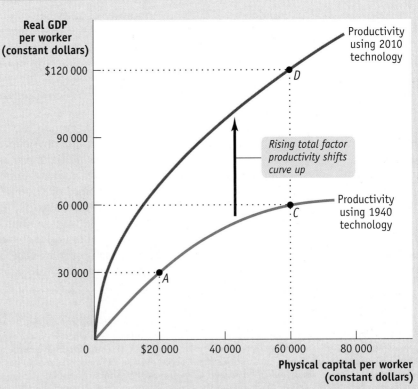

Technological progress raises productivity at any given level of physical capital per worker, and therefore shifts the per worker production function upward. Here we hold human capital per worker fixed. We assume that the lower curve (the same curve as in Figure 9-4) reflects technology in 1940 and the upper curve reflects technology in 2010. Holding technology and human capital fixed, tripling physical capital per worker from $20 000 to $60 000 leads to a doubling of real GDP per worker, from $30 000 to $60 000. This is shown by the movement from point A to point C, reflecting an approximately 1% per year rise in real GDP per worker. In reality, technological progress raised productivity at any given level of physical capital—shown here by the upward shift of the curve—and the actual rise in real GDP per worker is shown by the movement from point A to point D. Real GDP per worker grew 2% per year, leading to a quadrupling during the period. The extra 1% in annual growth of real GDP per worker is due to higher total factor productivity.

to use the Rule of 70.) The 2010 curve is shifted up compared to the 1940 curve because technologies developed over the previous 70 years make it possible to produce more output for a given amount of physical capital per worker than was possible with the technology available in 1940. (Note that the two curves are measured in constant dollars.)

Let's assume that between 1940 and 2010 the amount of physical capital per worker rose from $20 000 to $60 000. If this increase in physical capital per worker had taken place without any technological progress, the economy would have moved from *A* to *C*: output per worker would have risen, but only from $30 000 to $60 000, or 1% per year (using the Rule of 70 tells us that a 1% growth rate over 70 years doubles output). In fact, however, the economy moved from *A* to *D*: output rose from $30 000 to $120 000, or 2% per year. There was an increase in both physical capital per worker and technological progress, which shifted the per worker production function.

In this case, 50% of the annual 2% increase in productivity—that is, 1% in annual productivity growth—is due to higher total factor productivity, which here accounts for any additional output per worker produced that did not come from changes in inputs. So when total factor productivity (*A*) increases, the economy can produce more output with the same quantity of physical capital, human capital, and labour.

Most estimates find that increases in total factor productivity are central to a country's economic growth in the long-run. Economists believe that, on average, observed increases in total factor productivity do measure the economic effects of technological progress. All of this implies that technological change is crucial to long-run economic growth. Statistics Canada estimates the growth rate of both labour productivity and total factor productivity for various business sectors of Canada. According to estimates from Statistics Canada, from 1961 to 2010 Canadian labour productivity rose 2% per year. Only 57% of that rise is explained by increases in physical and human capital per worker; the rest is explained by rising total factor productivity—that is, by technological progress.

Figure 9-6 shows the average annual growth in labour productivity for all provinces and territories up to 2011. The average labour productivity growth was 1.2% for Canada as a whole. All regions experienced positive labour productivity growth during this period, but the amount of growth varied significantly. Nunavut enjoyed the highest growth rate, with an annual growth rate of 3.2%. Newfoundland and Labrador had the second highest growth with an annual growth rate of 2.6%. On the other hand, Alberta had the lowest labour productivity growth, at 0.7%. You may find this surprising, given the significant amount of industry in Alberta. So why is that province's annual growth rate so low?

According to Statistics Canada, the answer lies in the rate of accumulation of productive capital or stock of physical capital and total factor productivity growth. During the time frame in question, all regions saw an increase in their physical capital. In fact, Alberta's (and Saskatchewan's) physical capital increased by much more than that of the other regions. This is to be expected, because these two provinces are engaged in projects, such as the Alberta oil sands, that are extremely capital-intensive. But the effect of increased physical capital intensity on labour productivity was offset because Alberta and Saskatchewan had negative total factor productivity growth. This negative growth might be attributed to the fact that it requires more effort to produce the same amount of oil from the oil sands as from an oil well. In contrast, in Newfoundland and Labrador, the total factor productivity growth was primarily a result of the province moving toward high productivity economic activity, such as onshore and offshore oil production.

The process of extracting oil from the Alberta oil sands could not be done without major technological progress. And as these immense machines indicate, that process requires a great deal of physical capital.

The bars show the average annual labour productivity growth from 1997 to 2011 for the provinces and from 1999 to 2011 for the territories (older data does not exist for the territories). Labour productivity growth varied across Canada; some growth rates were above the national average while some were below. Nunavut experienced the highest average rate of labour productivity growth during this period (3.2%); Newfoundland and Labrador came in second with an annual average growth of 2.6%. On the other hand, Alberta had the lowest labour productivity growth among all provinces and territories.

Source: Statistics Canada.

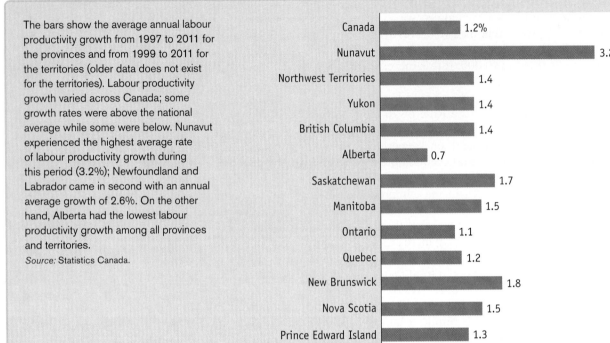

Some regions grew faster while some grew more slowly. But whether the growth is fast or slow, the bottom line is that higher labour productivity transforms into and reflects higher (per capita) economic growth.

What About Natural Resources?

In our discussion so far, we haven't mentioned natural resources, which certainly have an effect on productivity. Other things equal, countries that are abundant in valuable natural resources, such as highly fertile land or rich mineral deposits, have higher real GDP per capita than less fortunate countries. The most obvious modern example is the Middle East, where enormous oil deposits have made a few sparsely populated countries very rich. For example, Kuwait has about the same level of real GDP per capita as Germany, but Kuwait's wealth is based on oil, not manufacturing, the source of Germany's high real output per worker.

But other things are often not equal. In the modern world, natural resources are a much less important determinant of productivity than human or physical capital for the great majority of countries. For example, some nations with very high real GDP per capita, such as Japan, have very few natural resources. Some resource-rich nations, such as Nigeria (which has sizable oil deposits), are very poor.

Historically, natural resources played a much more prominent role in determining productivity. In the nineteenth century, the countries with the highest real GDP per capita were those abundant in rich farmland and mineral deposits: Canada, the United States, Argentina, and Australia. As a consequence, natural resources figured prominently in the development of economic thought. In a famous book published in 1798, *An Essay on the Principle of Population,* the English economist Thomas Malthus made the fixed quantity of land in the world the basis of a pessimistic prediction about future productivity. As population grew, he pointed out, the amount of land per worker would decline. And this, other things equal, would cause productivity to fall.

His view, in fact, was that improvements in technology or increases in physical capital would lead only to temporary improvements in productivity because they would always be offset by the pressure of rising population and more workers on the supply of land. In the long run, he concluded, the great majority of people were condemned to living on the edge of starvation. Only then would death rates be high enough and birth rates low enough to prevent rapid population growth from outstripping productivity growth.

It hasn't turned out that way, although many historians believe that Malthus's prediction of falling or stagnant productivity was valid for much of human history. Population pressure probably did prevent large productivity increases until the eighteenth century. But in the time since Malthus wrote his book, any negative effects on productivity from population growth have been far outweighed by other, positive factors—advances in technology, increases in human and physical capital, and the opening up of enormous amounts of cultivatable land in the New World.

It remains true, however, that we live on a finite planet, with limited supplies of resources such as oil and limited ability to absorb environmental damage. We address the concerns these limitations pose for economic growth in the final section of this chapter.

ECONOMICS > IN ACTION

THE INFORMATION TECHNOLOGY PARADOX

From the early 1970s through the mid-1990s, Canada went through a slump in growth of both output per worker and total factor productivity. Figure 9-7 shows Statistics Canada estimates of annual labour and total factor productivity growth, averaged for each five-year period from 1962 to 2010. Output per worker is commonly used as a simple proxy for the standard of living of members of a society in the long-run. As Figure 9-7 shows, a significant portion of the growth of output per worker comes from total factor productivity growth. Also, as you can see, there was a large fall in the total factor productivity growth rate beginning in the early 1970s. Because higher total factor productivity plays such a key role in long-run growth, the economy's overall growth was also disappointing, leading to a widespread sense that economic progress had ground to a halt.

Many economists were puzzled by the slowdown in total factor productivity growth in the early 1970s, since in other ways the era seemed to be one of rapid technological progress. Modern information technology really began with the development of the first microprocessor—a computer on a chip—in 1971. In the 25 years that followed, a series of inventions that seemed revolutionary became standard equipment in the business world: fax machines, desktop computers, cellphones, and e-mail. Yet the rate of growth of total factor productivity remained stagnant. In a famous remark, MIT economics professor and Nobel laureate Robert Solow, a pioneer in the analysis of economic growth, declared that the information technology revolution could be seen everywhere except in the economic statistics.

Why didn't information technology show large rewards? Paul David, a Stanford University economic historian, offered a theory and a prediction. He pointed out that 100 years earlier another miracle technology—electric power—had spread through the economy, again with surprisingly little impact on productivity growth at first. The reason, he suggested, was that a new technology doesn't yield its full potential if you use it in old ways.

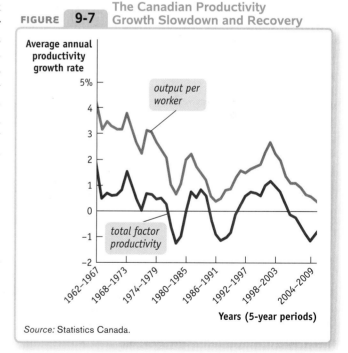

FIGURE **9-7** The Canadian Productivity Growth Slowdown and Recovery

Source: Statistics Canada.

For example, a traditional factory around 1900 was a multi-storey building, with the machinery tightly crowded together and designed to be powered by a steam engine in the basement. This design had problems: it was very difficult to move people and materials around. Yet owners who electrified their factories initially maintained the multi-storey, tightly packed layout. Only with the switch to spread-out, one-storey factories that took advantage of the flexibility of electric power—most famously Henry Ford's auto assembly line—did productivity take off.

David suggested that the same phenomenon was happening with information technology. Productivity, he predicted, would take off when people really changed their way of doing business to take advantage of the new technology—such as replacing letters and phone calls with e-mail. Sure enough, productivity growth accelerated dramatically in the second half of the 1990s as companies began to use information technology more effectively.

CHECK YOUR UNDERSTANDING 9-2

1. Predict the effect of each of the following events on the growth rate of productivity.
   a. The amounts of physical and human capital per worker are unchanged, but there is significant technological progress.
   b. The amount of physical capital per worker grows at a steady pace, but the level of human capital per worker and technology are unchanged.

2. Output in the economy of Erewhon has grown 3% per year over the past 30 years. The labour force has grown at 1% per year, and the quantity of physical capital has grown at 4% per year. The average education level hasn't changed. Estimates by economists say that each 1% increase in physical capital per worker, other things equal, raises productivity by 0.3%. (*Hint:* % change in (X/Y) = % change in X − % change in Y.)
   a. How fast has productivity in Erewhon grown?
   b. How fast has physical capital per worker grown?
   c. How much has growing physical capital per worker contributed to productivity growth? What percentage of productivity growth is that?
   d. How much has technological progress contributed to productivity growth? What percentage of productivity growth is that?

3. Multinomics, Inc., is a large company with many offices around the country. It has just adopted a new computer system that will affect virtually every function performed within the company. Why might a period of time pass before employees' productivity is improved by the new computer system? Why might there be a temporary decrease in employees' productivity?

Solutions appear at back of book.

Why Growth Rates Differ

n 1820, according to estimates by the economic historian Angus Maddison, Mexico had somewhat higher real GDP per capita than Japan. Today, Japan has higher real GDP per capita than most European nations and Mexico is a poor country, though by no means among the poorest. The difference? Over the long run—since 1820—real GDP per capita grew at 1.9% per year in Japan but at only 1.3% per year in Mexico.

As this example illustrates, even small differences in growth rates have large consequences over the long run. So why do growth rates differ across countries and across periods of time?

Explaining Differences in Growth Rates

As one might expect, economies with rapid growth tend to be economies that add physical capital, increase their human capital, or experience rapid technological progress. Striking economic success stories, like Japan in the 1950s and 1960s or China today, tend to be countries that do all three: rapidly add to their physical capital through high savings and investment spending, upgrade their educational level, and make fast technological progress. Evidence also points to the importance of government policies, property rights, political stability, and good governance in fostering the sources of growth.

Savings and Investment Spending One reason for differences in growth rates between countries is that some countries are increasing their stock of physical capital much more rapidly than others, through high rates of investment spending. In the 1960s, Japan was the fastest-growing major economy; it also spent a much higher share of its GDP on investment goods than did other major economies. Today, China is the fastest-growing major economy, and it similarly spends a very large share of its GDP on investment goods. In 2010, investment spending was 38% of China's GDP, compared with only 18% in Canada.

Where does the money for high investment spending come from? From savings. In the next chapter, we'll analyze how financial markets channel savings into investment spending. For now, however, the key point is that investment spending must be paid for either out of domestic (national) savings or out of foreign savings. *Domestic savings* refer to the savings within the country, which can come from households and/or the government. *Foreign savings,* as you might expect, are savings that come from foreign countries. If a country finances its investment with foreign savings, it is borrowing from abroad.

Foreign capital has played an important role in the long-run economic growth of some countries, including Canada, which relied heavily on foreign funds during its early industrialization. For the most part, however, countries that invest a large share of their GDP are able to do so because they have high domestic savings. In fact, China in 2010 saved an even higher percentage of its GDP than it invested at home. The extra savings were invested abroad, largely in the United States. In comparison, Figure 9-8 shows the levels of domestic savings and investment in Canada between 2000 and 2011. Between 2000 and 2008, domestic savings exceeded investment. Canada had saved enough to finance its own investment and the leftover was used to invest (lend)

FIGURE   **9-8**   Domestic Savings and Investment in Canada, 2000–2011

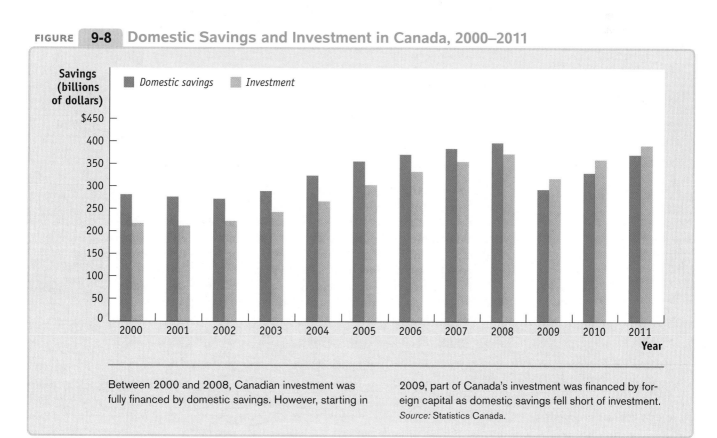

Between 2000 and 2008, Canadian investment was fully financed by domestic savings. However, starting in 2009, part of Canada's investment was financed by foreign capital as domestic savings fell short of investment.
Source: Statistics Canada.

FIGURE   **9-9**   China's Students Are Catching Up

In both China and Argentina, the average educational level—measured by the number of years the average adult aged 25 or older has spent in school—has risen over time. Although China is still lagging behind Argentina, it is catching up—and China's success at adding human capital is one key to its spectacular long-run growth.

Source: Robert Barro and Jong-Wha Lee, "A New Data Set of Educational Attainment in the World, 1950–2010," NBER Working Paper No. 15902, (National Bureau of Economic Research, April 2010).

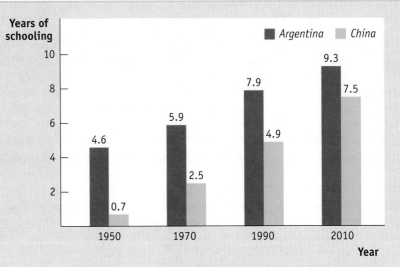

abroad. However, starting in 2009, domestic savings fell below investment and these shortfalls were financed by the inflows of foreign (i.e., borrowed) capital.

One reason for differences in growth rates, then, is that countries add different amounts to their stocks of physical capital because they have different rates of savings and investment spending.

Education   Just as countries differ substantially in the rate at which they add to their physical capital, there have been large differences in the rate at which countries add to their human capital through education.

A case in point is the comparison between Argentina and China. In both countries the average educational level has risen steadily over time, but it has risen much faster in China. Figure 9-9 shows the average years of education of adults in China, which we have highlighted as a spectacular example of long-run growth, and in Argentina, a country whose growth has been disappointing. Compared to China, sixty years ago, Argentina had a much more educated population, while many Chinese were still illiterate. Today, the average educational level in China is still slightly below that in Argentina—but that's mainly because there are still many elderly adults who never received basic education. In terms of secondary and tertiary education, China has outstripped once-rich Argentina.

Research and Development   The advance of technology is a key force behind economic growth. What drives technological progress?

Scientific advances make new technologies possible. To take the most spectacular example in today's world, the semiconductor chip—which is the basis for all modern information technology—could not have been developed without the theory of quantum mechanics in physics.

But science alone is not enough: scientific knowledge must be translated into useful products and processes. And that often requires devoting a lot of resources to **research and development,** or **R&D,** spending to create new technologies and apply them to practical use.

Figure 9-10 breaks down the shares of R&D performed by different sectors in Canada between 2000 and 2011. Although some research and development is conducted by the government and higher education sectors, the largest share of R&D is performed by the business sector. The figure shows that the business sector conducts more than half of the country's R&D, while governments are only responsible for about 10% of the country's R&D. The role of the higher education sector in R&D performance has become more important over time—its share

Research and development, or **R&D,** is spending to create and implement new technologies.

of total R&D spending increased from 28% in 2000 to about 37.5% in 2011. The following For Inquiring Minds describes how the business sector contributes to R&D performance. Developing new technology is one thing; applying it is another. There have been been notable differences in the pace at which different countries take advantage of new technologies, as this chapter's Global Comparison shows.

The Role of Government in Promoting Economic Growth

Governments can play an important role in promoting—or blocking—all three sources of long-term economic growth: physical capital, human capital, and technological progress. They can either affect growth directly through subsidies to factors that enhance growth, or by creating an environment that either fosters or hinders growth.

FIGURE **9-10** The Share of R&D Performed by Different Sectors in Canada, 2000–2011

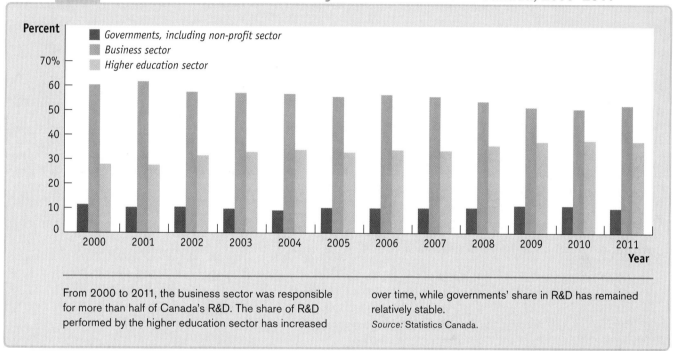

From 2000 to 2011, the business sector was responsible for more than half of Canada's R&D. The share of R&D performed by the higher education sector has increased over time, while governments' share in R&D has remained relatively stable.

Source: Statistics Canada.

FOR INQUIRING MINDS

PRIVATE SECTOR AND R&D

Alexander Graham Bell, one of Canada's most famous scientific innovators, is best known as the inventor of the first telephone, a major milestone in telecommunications technology. His invention stimulated the development of other communication devices, and to some extent, today's smartphones are an extension of his invention.

Bell was also an important early pioneer of research and development. He received his telephone patent from the U.S. Patent and Trademark Office on March 7, 1876. The patent gave him huge financial rewards: it was the most valuable asset of the Bell Telephone Company, the predecessor of American Telephone & Telegraph (AT&T). Bell continued to conduct scientific research throughout the rest of his life. He was particularly interested in technologies to assist deaf and hearing impaired people, like his wife. He also financed other people's research; for instance, he funded the early atomic experiments of American physicist A.A. Michelson. Bell set a good example of how individuals and the private sector can contribute to research and development. Nowadays, the private and business sectors play the predominant role in an economy's R&D.

Roads, power lines, ports, information networks, and other underpinnings for economic activity are known as **infrastructure.**

Government Policies Government policies can increase the economy's growth rate through four main channels.

1. GOVERNMENT SUBSIDIES TO INFRASTRUCTURE Governments play an important direct role in building **infrastructure:** roads, power lines, ports, information networks, and other large-scale physical capital projects that provide a foundation for economic activity. Although some infrastructure is provided by private companies, much of it is either provided by the government or requires a great deal of government regulation and support. Ireland is often cited as an example of the importance of government-provided infrastructure. After the government invested in an excellent telecommunications infrastructure in the 1980s, Ireland became a favoured location for high-technology companies from abroad and its economy took off in the 1990s.

Poor infrastructure, such as a power grid that frequently fails and cuts off electricity, is a major obstacle to economic growth in many countries. To provide good infrastructure, an economy must not only be able to afford it, but it must also have the political discipline to maintain it.

Perhaps the most crucial infrastructure is something we, in Canada rarely think about: basic public health measures in the form of a clean water supply and disease

GLOBAL COMPARISON — OLD EUROPE AND NEW TECHNOLOGY

The accompanying figure shows the five-year average rates of growth in labour productivity in Canada, the United States, and Germany from 1970 to 2011. The figure shows that the productivity growth rates of these countries moved in the same direction most of the time. But there were years in which they drifted apart. All three countries experienced a productivity slowdown in the 1970s, caused partly by the drastic increase in oil prices. However, the United States experienced a burst of productivity growth in the 1990s. Many believe this was caused by the boom in information technology and by the fact that American firms had finally figured out how to use modern information technology more efficiently. By the mid-2000s though, the U.S. productivity growth rate had reverted to the pre-information technology boom level.

Throughout much of the mid-2000s, Canada's productivity grew more slowly than that of its counterparts. This slow growth, and the resulting long-term detrimental impact, may be the result of both the federal and provincial governments reducing their R&D funding from 1995 to 2000. Also, compared to other developed nations, Canada invested a relatively low percentage of its GDP into R&D. According to the Organisation for Economic Co-operation and Development (OECD), Canada's R&D-to-GDP ratio was 1.9% in 2007, far lower than that of the United States (2.7%) and the OECD average (2.3%). Germany has also experienced relatively slower growth than the U.S., but some argue that that is the result of rigid government regulations that

hindered businesses from reorganizing themselves to use new technologies more effectively.

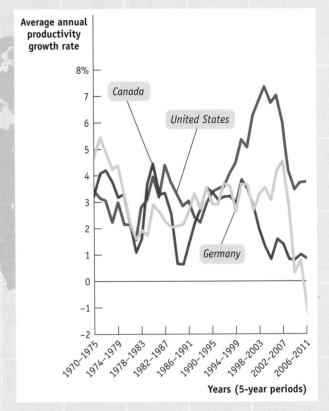

Source: The U.S. Bureau of Labor Statistics.

control. As we'll see in the next section, poor health infrastructure is a major obstacle to economic growth in poor countries, especially those in Africa.

2. GOVERNMENT SUBSIDIES TO EDUCATION In contrast to physical capital, which is mainly created by private investment spending, much of an economy's human capital is the result of government spending on education. In Canada, all levels of government—federal, provincial, and municipal—play an important role in education. In primary and secondary education, more than 90% of the funding comes from governments. Although the share of funding from governments for college and university education has decreased in recent years, governments still finance about 75% and 60% of the direct costs of college and university education, respectively. Differences in the rate at which countries add to their human capital largely reflect government policy. As we saw in Figure 9-9, educational levels in China are increasing much more rapidly than in Argentina. This isn't because China is richer than Argentina; until recently, China was, on average, poorer than Argentina. Instead, it reflects the fact that the Chinese government has made education of the population a high priority.

3. GOVERNMENT SUBSIDIES TO R&D Technological progress is largely the result of private initiative. Governments help promote R&D in the business sector through different programs and initiatives. For example, the federal government funds the Scientific Research and Experimental Development (SR&ED) tax incentive program, which allows businesses to receive cash refunds and/or tax credits and deductions for their spending on R&D in Canada. Governments also directly perform R&D; indeed, some important R&D projects, such as those on water/food safety, health, and environmental stress, are conducted by Canadian government agencies. In the upcoming Economics in Action, we describe Brazil's agricultural boom, which was made possible by government researchers who made discoveries that expanded the amount of arable land in Brazil, as well as developing new varieties of crops that flourish in Brazil's climate.

4. MAINTAINING A WELL-FUNCTIONING FINANCIAL SYSTEM Governments play an important indirect role in making high rates of private investment spending possible. Both the amount of savings and the ability of an economy to direct savings into productive investment spending depend on the economy's institutions, especially its financial system. In particular, a well-regulated and well-functioning financial system is very important for economic growth because in most countries it is the principal way in which savings are channelled into investment spending.

If a country's citizens trust their banks, they will place their savings in bank deposits, which the banks will then lend to their business customers. But if people don't trust their banks, they will hoard gold or foreign currency, keeping their savings in safe deposit boxes or under the mattress, where it cannot be turned into productive investment spending. As we'll discuss later, a well-functioning financial system requires appropriate government regulation to assure depositors that their funds are protected from loss.

Protection of Property Rights *Property rights* are the rights of owners of valuable items to dispose of those items as they choose. A subset, *intellectual property rights*, are the rights of an innovator to accrue the rewards of her innovation. The state of property rights generally, and intellectual property rights in particular, are important factors in explaining differences in growth rates across economies. Why? Because no one would bother to spend the effort and resources required to innovate if someone else could appropriate that innovation and capture the rewards. So, for innovation to flourish, intellectual property rights must receive protection.

Sometimes this is accomplished by the nature of the innovation: it may be too difficult or expensive to copy. But, generally, the government has to protect intellectual property rights. A *patent* is a government-created temporary monopoly given to

FOR INQUIRING MINDS

THE NEW GROWTH THEORY

Until the 1990s, economic models of technological progress assumed that what drove innovation was a mystery—unknown and unpredictable. In the words of economists, the sources of technological progress were *exogenous*—they were outside the models of economics and assumed to "just happen." Then, in a series of influential papers written in the 1980s and 1990s, Paul Romer founded what we now call "the New Growth Theory." In Romer's model, technological progress was explainable because it was in fact *endogenous*—the outcome of economic variables and incentives. And because technological progress was endogenous, policies could be adopted to foster its growth.

At any point in time, an economy has a stock of knowledge capital—the accumulated knowledge generated by past investments in research and development, education, and skill enhancement, as well as knowledge acquired from other economies. And that stock of knowledge capital is spread throughout the economy, so all firms benefit from it. According to the New Growth Theory, a rising stock of knowledge capital creates the foundation for further technological progress as innovation, shared by firms throughout the economy, makes further innovation possible. For example, touchscreen technology—developed in the 1970s and 1980s—became the basis for later developments such as smartphones and tablet computers.

Yet, as Romer pointed out, there is a severe wrinkle in this story: because knowledge is shared throughout the economy, it may be very difficult for an innovator to capture the rewards of his or her innovation as others exploit the innovation for their own interests. So in the New Growth Theory, government protection of intellectual property rights is critical to furthering technological progress. In addition, governments, institutions, and firms can enhance technological progress by subsidizing investments in education and research and development, which, in turn, can increase the stock of knowledge capital.

By giving us a better model of where technological progress comes from, the New Growth Theory makes clear how important the policies of government, institutions, and firms are in fostering it.

an innovator for the use or sale of his or her innovation. It's a temporary rather than permanent monopoly because while it's in society's interests to give an innovator an incentive to invent, it's also in society's interests to eventually encourage competition. The Canadian Intellectual Property Office (CIPO), a federal government agency that is associated with Industry Canada, is responsible for the administration and processing of most of the country's intellectual property. Canadians with new inventions can apply for their patent in Canada through the CIPO.

Political Stability and Good Governance There's not much point in investing in a business if rioting mobs are likely to destroy it, or saving your money if someone with political connections can steal it. Political stability and good governance (including the protection of property rights) are essential ingredients in fostering economic growth in the long run.

Long-run economic growth in successful economies, like that of Canada, has been possible because there are good laws, institutions that enforce those laws, and a stable political system that maintains those institutions. The law must say that your property is really yours so that someone else can't take it away. The courts and the police must be honest so that they can't be bribed to ignore the law. And the political system must be stable so that laws don't change capriciously.

Canadians take these preconditions for granted, but they are by no means guaranteed. Aside from the disruption caused by war or revolution, many countries find that their economic growth suffers due to corruption among the government officials who should be enforcing the law. For example, until 1991 the Indian government imposed many bureaucratic restrictions on businesses, which often had to bribe government officials to get approval for even routine activities—a tax on business, in effect. Economists have argued that a reduction in this burden of corruption is one reason Indian growth has been much faster in recent years.

Even when the government isn't corrupt, excessive government intervention can be a brake on economic growth. If large parts of the economy are supported by government subsidies, protected from imports, subject to unnecessary monopolization, or otherwise insulated from competition, productivity tends to suffer because of a lack of incentives. As we'll see in the next section, excessive government intervention is one often-cited explanation for slow growth in Latin America.

ECONOMICS ▶ IN ACTION

THE BRAZILIAN BREADBASKET

A wry Brazilian joke says that "Brazil is the country of the future—and always will be." The world's fifth most populous country has often been considered as a possible major economic power yet has never fulfilled that promise.

In recent years, however, Brazil's economy has made a better showing, especially in agriculture. This success depends on exploiting a natural resource, the tropical savannah land known as the *cerrado*. Until a quarter-century ago, the land was considered unsuitable for farming. A combination of three factors changed that: technological progress due to research and development, improved economic policies, and greater physical capital.

In Brazil, government-funded R&D has resulted in crucial agricultural technologies and economic reforms that turn unusable land into profitable farmland.

The Brazilian Enterprise for Agricultural and Livestock Research, a government-run agency, developed the crucial technologies. It showed that adding lime and phosphorus made *cerrado* land productive, and it developed breeds of cattle and varieties of soybeans suited for the climate. (Now they're working on wheat.) Also, until the 1980s, Brazilian international trade policies discouraged exports, as did an overvalued exchange rate that made the country's goods more expensive to foreigners. After economic reform, investing in Brazilian agriculture became much more profitable and companies began putting in place the farm machinery, buildings, and other forms of physical capital needed to exploit the land.

What still limits Brazil's growth? Infrastructure. According to a report in the *New York Times,* Brazilian farmers are "concerned about the lack of reliable highways, railways and barge routes, which adds to the cost of doing business." Recognizing this, the Brazilian government is investing in infrastructure, and Brazilian agriculture is continuing to expand. The country has already overtaken the United States as the world's largest beef exporter and may not be far behind in soybeans.

CHECK YOUR UNDERSTANDING   9-3

1. Explain the link between a country's growth rate, its investment spending as a percent of GDP, and its domestic savings.

2. Explain how the accumulation of human capital helps promote long-run economic growth. What should the government do to increase the buildup of human capital?

3. During the 1990s in the former U.S.S.R., a lot of property was seized and controlled by those in power. How might this have affected the country's growth rate at that time? Explain.

Solutions appear at back of book.

▼ **Quick Review**

- Countries differ greatly in their growth rates of real GDP per capita due to differences in the rates at which they accumulate physical capital and human capital as well as differences in technological progress. A prime cause of differences in growth rates is differences in rates of domestic savings and investment spending as well as differences in education levels, and **research and development,** or **R&D,** levels. R&D largely drives technological progress.

- Government actions can promote or hinder the sources of long-term growth.

- Government policies that directly promote growth are subsidies to **infrastructure,** particularly public health infrastructure, subsidies to education, subsidies to R&D, and the maintenance of a well-functioning financial system.

- Governments improve the environment for growth by protecting property rights (particularly intellectual property rights through patents), by providing political stability, and through good governance. Poor governance includes corruption and excessive government intervention.

Success, Disappointment, and Failure

As we've seen, rates of long-run economic growth differ quite a lot around the world. Now let's look at three regions of the world that have had quite different experiences with economic growth over the last few decades.

FIGURE **9-11** Success and Disappointment

Real GDP per capita from 1960 to 2010, measured in 2000 dollars, is shown for Argentina, South Korea, and Nigeria, using a logarithmic scale. South Korea and some other East Asian countries have been highly successful at achieving economic growth. Argentina, like much of Latin America, has had several setbacks, slowing its growth. Nigeria's standard of living in 2010 was only barely higher than it had been in 1960, an experience shared by many African countries. Neither Argentina nor Nigeria exhibited much growth over the 50-year period, although both have had significantly higher growth in recent years.
Source: World Bank.

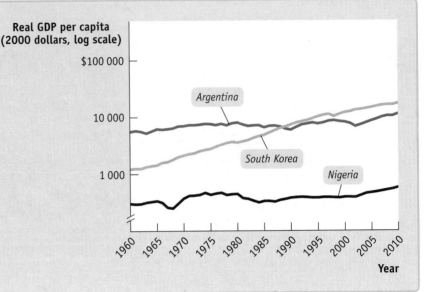

Figure 9-11 shows trends since 1960 in real GDP per capita in 2000 dollars for three countries: Argentina, Nigeria, and South Korea. (As in Figure 9-1, the vertical axis is drawn in logarithmic scale.) We have chosen these countries because each is a particularly striking example of what has happened in its region. South Korea's amazing rise is part of a broad "economic miracle" in East Asia. Argentina's slow progress, interrupted by repeated setbacks, is more or less typical of the disappointing growth that has characterized Latin America. And Nigeria's unhappy story until very recently—with little growth in real GDP until after 2000—was, unfortunately, an experience shared by many African countries.

East Asia's Miracle

In 1960 South Korea was a very poor country. In fact, in 1960 its real GDP per capita was lower than that of India today. But, as you can see from Figure 9-11, beginning in the early 1960s South Korea began an extremely rapid economic ascent: real GDP per capita grew about 7% per year for more than 30 years. Today South Korea, though still somewhat poorer than Canada or the United States, looks very much like an economically advanced country.

South Korea's economic growth is unprecedented in history: it took the country only 35 years to achieve growth that required centuries elsewhere. Yet South Korea is only part of a broader phenomenon, often referred to as the East Asian economic miracle. High growth rates first appeared in South Korea, Taiwan, Hong Kong, and Singapore but then spread across the region, most notably to China. Since 1975, the whole region has increased real GDP per capita by 6% per year, more than three times Canada's historical rate of growth.

How have the Asian countries achieved such high growth rates? The answer is that all of the sources of productivity growth have been firing on all cylinders. Very high savings rates, the percentage of GDP that is saved nationally in any given year, have allowed the countries to significantly increase the amount of physical capital per worker. Very good basic education has permitted a rapid improvement in human capital. And these countries have experienced substantial technological progress.

Why didn't any economy achieve this kind of growth in the past? Most economic analysts think that East Asia's growth spurt was possible because of its *relative* backwardness. That is, by the time that East Asian economies began to move into the modern world, they could benefit from adopting the technological advances that had been generated in technologically advanced countries such as Canada.

In 1900, Canada could not have moved quickly to a modern level of productivity because much of the technology that powers the modern economy, from jet planes to computers, hadn't been invented yet. In 1970, South Korea probably still had lower productivity than Canada had in 1900, but it could rapidly upgrade its productivity by adopting technology that had been developed in Canada, the United States, Europe, and Japan over the previous century. This was aided by a huge investment in human capital through widespread schooling.

The East Asian experience demonstrates that economic growth can be especially fast in countries that are playing catch-up to other countries with higher GDP per capita. On this basis, many economists have suggested a general principle known as the **convergence hypothesis.** It says that differences in real GDP per capita among countries tend to narrow over time because countries that start with lower real GDP per capita tend to have higher growth rates. We'll look at the evidence on the convergence hypothesis in the Economics in Action at the end of this section.

Even before we get to that evidence, however, we can say right away that starting with a relatively low level of real GDP per capita is no guarantee of rapid growth, as the examples of Latin America and Africa both demonstrate.

According to the **convergence hypothesis**, international differences in real GDP per capita tend to narrow over time.

Latin America's Disappointment

In 1900, Latin America was not considered an economically backward region. Natural resources, including both minerals and cultivatable land, were abundant. Some countries, notably Argentina, attracted millions of immigrants from Europe in search of a better life. Measures of real GDP per capita in Argentina, Uruguay, and southern Brazil were comparable to those in economically advanced countries.

Since about 1920, however, growth in Latin America has been disappointing. As Figure 9-11 shows in the case of Argentina, growth has been disappointing for many decades, until 2000 when it finally began to increase. The fact that South Korea is now much richer than Argentina would have seemed inconceivable a few generations ago.

Why did Latin America stagnate? Comparisons with East Asian success stories suggest several factors. The rates of savings and investment spending in Latin America have been much lower than in East Asia, partly as a result of irresponsible government policy that has eroded savings through high inflation, bank failures, and other disruptions. Education—especially broad basic education—has been underemphasized: even Latin American nations rich in natural resources often failed to channel that wealth into their educational systems. And political instability, leading to irresponsible economic policies, has taken a toll.

In the 1980s, many economists came to believe that Latin America was suffering from excessive government intervention in markets. They recommended opening the economies to imports, selling off government-owned companies, and, in general, freeing up individual initiative. The hope was that this would produce an East Asian–type economic surge. So far, however, only one Latin American nation, Chile, has achieved sustained rapid growth. It now seems that pulling off an economic miracle is harder than it looks. Although, in recent years, Brazil and Argentina have seen their growth rates increase significantly as they exported large amounts of commodities to the advanced countries and rapidly developing China.

Africa's Troubles and Promise

Africa south of the Sahara is home to about 780 million people, more than 22 times the population of Canada. On average, they are very poor, nowhere close to Canada's living standards 100 or even 200 years ago. And economic progress has been both slow and uneven, as the example of Nigeria, the most populous nation in the region, suggests. In fact, real GDP per capita in sub-Saharan Africa actually fell 13% from 1980 to 1994, although it has recovered since then. The consequence of this poor growth performance has been intense and continuing poverty.

This is a very disheartening story. What explains it?

Several factors are probably crucial. Perhaps first and foremost is the problem of political instability. In the years since 1975, large parts of Africa have experienced savage civil wars (often with outside powers backing rival sides) that have killed millions of people and made productive investment spending impossible. The threat of war and general anarchy has also inhibited other important preconditions for growth, such as education and provision of necessary infrastructure.

Property rights are also a major problem. The lack of legal safeguards means that property owners are often subject to extortion because of government corruption, making them averse to owning property or improving it. This is especially damaging in a country that is very poor.

While many economists see political instability and government corruption as the leading causes of underdevelopment in Africa, some—most notably Jeffrey Sachs of Columbia University and the United Nations—believe the opposite. They argue that Africa is politically unstable because Africa is poor. And Africa's poverty, they go on to claim, stems from its extremely unfavourable geographic conditions—much of the continent is landlocked, hot, infested with tropical diseases, and cursed with poor soil.

Sachs, along with economists from the World Health Organization, has highlighted the importance of health problems in Africa. In poor countries, worker productivity is often severely hampered by malnutrition and disease. In particular, tropical diseases such as malaria can only be controlled with an effective public health infrastructure, something that is lacking in much of Africa. At the time of writing, economists are studying certain regions of Africa to determine whether modest amounts of aid given directly to residents for the purposes of increasing crop yields, reducing malaria, and increasing school attendance can produce self-sustaining gains in living standards.

Although the example of African countries represents a warning that long-run economic growth cannot be taken for granted, there are some signs of hope. As we noted in Figure 9-11, Nigeria's per capita GDP, after decades of stagnation, turned upward after 2000, achieving a 5.5% real GDP per capita growth rate in 2010. The same is true for sub-Saharan African economies as a whole. In 2011, real GDP per capita growth rates averaged around 5.5% across sub-Saharan African countries. Rising prices for their exports are part of the reason for recent success, but there is growing optimism among development experts that a period of relative peace and better government is ushering in a new era for Africa's economies.

ECONOMICS ▶ IN ACTION

ARE ECONOMIES CONVERGING?

In the 1950s, the United States was the richest country in the world: much of Europe and Canada seemed quaint and backward to American visitors, and Japan seemed very poor. Today, Toronto, Paris, and Tokyo look like cities as rich as New York. Although Americans still enjoy a higher level of real GDP per capita, the differences in the standards of living among the United States, Canada, Europe, and Japan are relatively small.

Many economists have argued that this convergence in living standards is normal; the convergence hypothesis says that relatively poor countries should have higher rates of growth of real GDP per capita than relatively rich countries. And if we look at today's relatively well-off countries, the convergence hypothesis seems to be true. Figure 9-12a shows data for a number of today's wealthy economies measured in 1990 dollars. On the horizontal axis is real GDP per capita in 1955; on the vertical axis is the average annual growth rate of real GDP per capita from 1955 to 2008. There is a clear negative relationship as can be seen from the

FIGURE **9-12** Do Economies Converge?

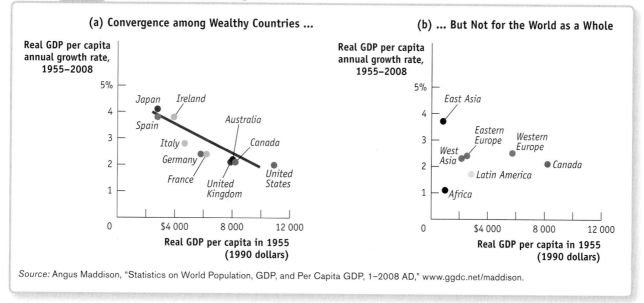

Source: Angus Maddison, "Statistics on World Population, GDP, and Per Capita GDP, 1–2008 AD," www.ggdc.net/maddison.

line fitted through the points. The United States was the richest country in this group in 1955 and had the slowest rate of growth. Japan and Spain were the poorest countries in 1955 and had the fastest rates of growth. These data suggest that the convergence hypothesis is true.

But economists who looked at similar data realized that these results depend on the countries selected. If you look at successful economies that have a high standard of living today, you find that real GDP per capita has converged. But looking across the world as a whole, including countries that remain poor, there is little evidence of convergence. Figure 9-12b illustrates this point using data for regions rather than individual countries (other than Canada). In 1955, East Asia and Africa were both very poor regions. Over the next 53 years, the East Asian regional economy grew quickly, as the convergence hypothesis would have predicted, but the African regional economy grew very slowly. In 1955, Western Europe had substantially higher real GDP per capita than Latin America. But, contrary to the convergence hypothesis, the Western European regional economy grew more quickly over the next 53 years, widening the gap between the regions.

So is the convergence hypothesis all wrong? No: economists still believe that countries with relatively low real GDP per capita tend to have higher rates of growth than countries with relatively high real GDP per capita, *other things equal*. But other things—education, infrastructure, rule of law, and so on—are often not equal. Statistical studies find that when you adjust for differences in these other factors, poorer countries do tend to have higher growth rates. This result is known as *conditional convergence*.

Because other factors differ, such as protection of property rights and political stability, however, there is no clear tendency toward convergence in the world economy as a whole. Western Europe, North America, and parts of Asia are becoming more similar in real GDP per capita, but the gap between these regions and the rest of the world is growing.

▶ ● ●

CHECK YOUR UNDERSTANDING   9-4

1. Some economists think the high rates of growth of productivity achieved by many Asian economies cannot be sustained. Why might they be right? What would have to happen for them to be wrong?

▼ Quick Review

● East Asia's spectacular growth was generated by high savings and investment spending rates, emphasis on education, and adoption of technological advances from other countries.

● Poor education, political instability, and irresponsible government policies are major factors in the slow growth of Latin America.

● In sub-Saharan Africa, severe instability, war, and poor infrastructure—particularly affecting public health—resulted in a catastrophic failure of growth. But economic performance in recent years has been much better than in preceding years.

● The **convergence hypothesis** seems to hold only when other things that affect economic growth—such as education, infrastructure, property rights, and so on—are held equal.

2. Consider Figure 9-12b. Based on the data there, which regions support the convergence hypothesis? Which do not? Explain.

3. Some economists think the best way to help African countries is for wealthier countries to provide more funds for basic infrastructure. Others think this policy will have no long-run effect unless African countries have the financial and political means to maintain this infrastructure. What policies would you suggest?

Solutions appear at back of book.

Is World Growth Sustainable?

Earlier in this chapter we described the views of Thomas Malthus, the early-nineteenth-century economist who warned that the pressure of population growth would tend to limit the standard of living. Malthus was right about the past: for around 58 centuries, from the origins of civilization until his own time, limited land supplies effectively prevented any large rise in real incomes per capita. Since then, however, technological progress and rapid accumulation of physical and human capital have allowed the world to defy Malthusian pessimism.

But will this always be the case? Some skeptics have expressed doubt about whether **sustainable long-run economic growth** is possible—whether it can continue in the face of the limited supply of natural resources and the impact of growth on the environment.

Natural Resources and Growth, Revisited

Sustainable long-run economic growth is long-run growth that can continue in the face of the limited supply of natural resources and the impact of growth on the environment.

In 1972, a group of scientists called The Club of Rome made a big splash with a book titled *The Limits to Growth,* which argued that long-run economic growth wasn't sustainable due to limited supplies of non-renewable resources such as oil and natural gas. These "neo-Malthusian" concerns at first seemed to be validated by a sharp rise in resource prices in the 1970s, then came to seem foolish when resource prices fell sharply in the 1980s. After 2005, however, resource prices rose sharply again, leading to renewed concern about resource limitations to growth. Figure 9-13 shows the real price of oil—the price of oil adjusted for inflation in the rest of the economy. The rise, fall, and rise of concern about resource-based limits to growth have more or less followed the rise, fall, and rise of oil prices shown in the figure.

FIGURE 9-13 The Real Price of Oil, 1949–2010

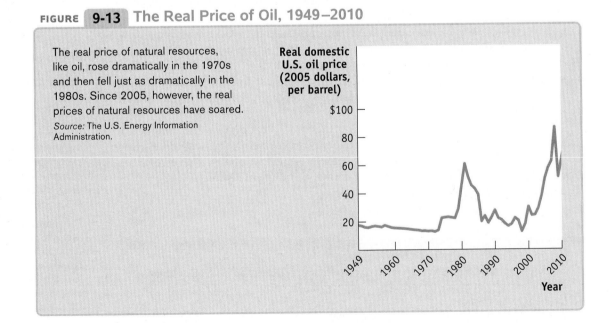

The real price of natural resources, like oil, rose dramatically in the 1970s and then fell just as dramatically in the 1980s. Since 2005, however, the real prices of natural resources have soared.

Source: The U.S. Energy Information Administration.

FIGURE **9-14** Oil Consumption and Growth in Canada, 1980–2011

When oil prices increased in the early 1970s, Canadians responded by lowering their oil consumption in the early 1980s—the switch to more efficient automobiles and technologies takes time, so consumption decreases can occur with a lag. It happened also in the mid-2000s when oil prices again rose sharply. Regardless of whether oil consumption was rising or falling, however, the real GDP continued to grow, which suggests that economies can deal with scarce resources.

Sources: Oil consumption: The U.S. Energy Information Administration; Real GDP per capita: Statistics Canada.

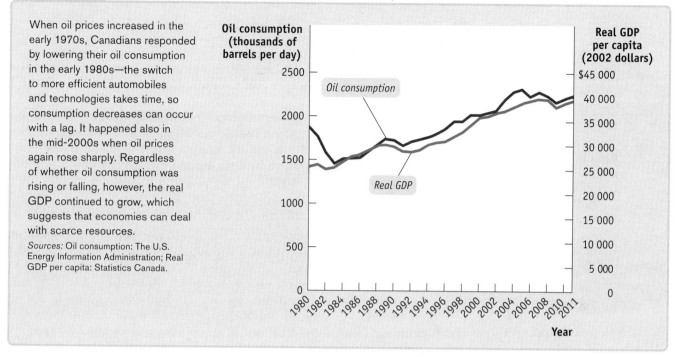

Differing views about the impact of limited natural resources on long-run economic growth turn on the answers to three questions:

- How large are the supplies of key natural resources?
- How effective will technology be at finding alternatives to natural resources?
- Can long-run economic growth continue in the face of resource scarcity?

It's mainly up to geologists to answer the first question. Unfortunately, there's wide disagreement among the experts, especially about the prospects for future oil production. Some analysts believe that there is enough untapped oil in the ground that world oil production can continue to rise for several decades. Others, including a number of oil company executives, believe that the growing difficulty of finding new oil fields will cause oil production to plateau—that is, stop growing and eventually begin a gradual decline—in the fairly near future. Some analysts believe that we have already reached that plateau.

The answer to the second question, whether there are alternatives to natural resources, has to come from engineers. There's no question that there are many alternatives to the natural resources currently being depleted, some of which are already being exploited. For example, "unconventional" oil extracted from the Alberta oil sands is already making a significant contribution to world oil supplies, and electricity generated by wind turbines is rapidly becoming big business.

The third question, whether economies can continue to grow in the face of resource scarcity, is mainly a question for economists. And most, though not all, economists are optimistic: they believe that modern economies can find ways to work around limits on the supply of natural resources. One reason for this optimism is the fact that resource scarcity leads to high resource prices. These high prices in turn provide strong incentives to conserve the scarce resource and to find alternatives.

Figure 9-14 compares Canada's real GDP per capita and oil consumption from 1980 to 2011. Over this 31-year timespan, there seems to have been a close positive relationship between oil consumption and real GDP per capita, with some noticeable exceptions. In the early 1980s and again in the mid-2000s, there were noticeable reductions in oil consumption. These decreases were primarily caused by oil price increases from earlier years. When the oil price increased sharply, as happened in the early 1970s and in the early 2000s, Canadian consumers turned to smaller, more fuel-efficient cars, and Canadian industry also tried to adopt more fuel-efficient technology. However, when the price of oil was low between the mid-1980s and 1990s, the impulse toward conservation lessened; low oil prices made oil a cheap source of energy and encouraged both consumers and firms to once again rely upon it.

Given such responses to prices, economists generally tend to see resource scarcity as a problem that modern economies handle fairly well, and so not a fundamental limit to long-run economic growth. Environmental issues, however, pose a more difficult problem because dealing with them requires effective political action.

Economic Growth and the Environment

Economic growth, other things equal, tends to increase the human impact on the environment. For example, China's spectacular economic growth has also brought a spectacular increase in air pollution in that nation's cities.

Other things, however, aren't necessarily equal: countries can and do take action to protect their environments. In fact, air and water quality in today's developed countries is generally much better than it was a few decades ago. London's famous "fog"—actually a form of air pollution, which killed 4000 people during a two-week episode in 1952—is gone, thanks to regulations that virtually eliminated the use of coal heat. The equally famous smog of Los Angeles, although not extinguished, is far less severe than it was in the 1960s and early 1970s, again thanks to pollution regulations.

While we have seen and heard of local environmental success stories in the past, there is still today widespread concern about the environmental impacts of continuing economic growth. The true scale of the problem, however, has been recognized, and environmental success stories now mainly deal with economic growth and human impact on a national level. In Canada, this includes attempts to reduce greenhouse gas emissions from vehicles, federal and provincial government incentives to induce Canadians to buy more fuel-efficient vehicles, and promotion of environmentally friendly transportation alternatives. Furthermore, nations are now addressing *global* environmental issues—the adverse impacts on the environment of the Earth as a whole by worldwide economic growth. The greatest of these issues involves the impact of fossil fuel consumption on the world's climate.

Burning coal and oil releases carbon dioxide into the atmosphere. There is broad scientific consensus that rising levels of carbon dioxide and other gases are causing a greenhouse effect on the Earth, trapping more of the sun's energy and raising the planet's overall temperature. And rising temperatures may impose high human and economic costs: rising sea levels may flood coastal areas; changing climate may disrupt agriculture, especially in poor countries; and so on.

The problem of climate change is clearly linked to economic growth. Figure 9-15 shows carbon dioxide emission from Canada, the United States, and China between 1980 and 2010. Historically, the wealthy nations have been responsible for the bulk of these emissions because they have consumed far more energy per person than poorer countries. As China and other emerging economies have grown, however, they have begun to consume much more energy and emit much more carbon dioxide.

Is it possible to continue long-run economic growth while curbing the emissions of greenhouse gases? The answer, according to most economists who have studied the issue, is yes. It should be possible to reduce greenhouse gas emissions in a wide variety of ways, ranging from the use of non-fossil-fuel energy sources such as wind, solar, and nuclear power; to preventive measures such as carbon sequestration (capturing the carbon dioxide from power plants and storing it);

FIGURE **9-15** Climate Change and Growth

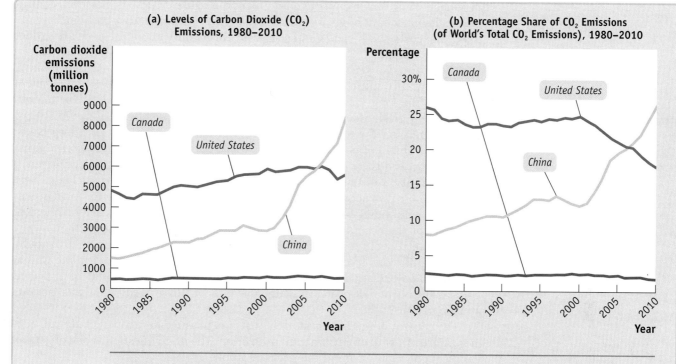

(a) Levels of Carbon Dioxide (CO_2) Emissions, 1980–2010

(b) Percentage Share of CO_2 Emissions (of World's Total CO_2 Emissions), 1980–2010

Greenhouse gas emissions are related positively to economic growth. Panel (a) shows the levels of CO_2 emissions by Canada, the United States, and China from 1980 to 2010. Developed countries have more complex industries and more vehicles in use, plus they consume more non-essential items than less developed countries do. Consequently, developed countries produce far more greenhouse gas emissions. As the economies of China and other emerging nations begin to grow more quickly, these countries will also begin to emit even more CO_2 than they do now. As Panel (b) shows, in recent years China has emitted a greater percent of the world's total CO_2 than the U.S., and hence more CO_2 than the United States, largely as a result of China's rapid transformation over the past three decades into the world's factory. In 2010, China produced about 26% of the world's CO_2 emissions.

We can also look at the level of CO_2 emission on a per capita basis. According to the World Bank, in 2008, the average CO_2 emission per capita was 4.76 tonnes for the world as a whole. China, Canada, and the U.S. were all above the world average in this regard. China produced 5.31 tonnes per capita, Canada produced 16.33 tonnes per capita, and the U.S. produced 17.96 tonnes per capita.

Source: The U.S. Energy Information Administration.

to simpler things like designing buildings so that they're easier to keep warm in winter and cool in summer. Such measures would impose costs on the economy, but the best available estimates suggest that even a large reduction in greenhouse gas emissions over the next few decades would only modestly dent the long-term rise in real GDP per capita.

The problem is how to make all of this happen. Unlike resource scarcity, environmental problems don't automatically provide incentives for changed behaviour. Pollution is an example of a *negative externality,* a cost that individuals or firms impose on others without having to offer compensation. In the absence of government intervention, individuals and firms have no incentive to reduce negative externalities, which is why it took regulation to reduce air pollution in North America's cities. And as Nicholas Stern, the author of an influential report on climate change, put it, greenhouse gas emissions are "the mother of all externalities."

So there is a broad consensus among economists—although there are some dissenters—that government action is needed to deal with climate change. There is also broad consensus that this action should take the form of market-based incentives, either in the form of a carbon tax—a tax per unit of carbon emitted—

or a cap and trade system in which the total amount of emissions is capped, and producers must buy licenses to emit greenhouse gases. There is, however, considerable dispute about how much action is appropriate, reflecting both uncertainty about the costs and benefits and scientific uncertainty about the pace and extent of climate change.

There are also several aspects of the climate change problem that make it much more difficult to deal with than, say, fog in London. One is the problem of taking the long view. The impact of greenhouse gas emissions on the climate is very gradual: carbon dioxide put into the atmosphere today won't have its full effect on the climate for several generations. As a result, there is the political problem of persuading voters to accept pain today in return for gains that will benefit their children, grandchildren, or even great-grandchildren.

There is also a difficult problem of international burden sharing. As Figure 9-15 shows, today's rich economies have historically been responsible for most greenhouse gas emissions, but newly emerging economies like China are responsible for most of the recent growth. Inevitably, rich countries are reluctant to pay the price of reducing emissions only to have their efforts frustrated by rapidly growing emissions from new players. On the other hand, countries like China, which are still relatively poor, consider it unfair that they should be expected to bear the burden of protecting an environment threatened by the past actions of rich nations.

The general moral of this story is that it is possible to reconcile long-run economic growth with environmental protection. The main question is one of getting political consensus around the necessary policies.

ECONOMICS ➤ IN ACTION

THE COST OF CLIMATE PROTECTION

Jonathan Hayward/CP Images

Reducing emissions of greenhouse gases over the long run would have few economic costs and many health benefits.

According to its own brochure, the National Round Table on the Economy and the Environment (NRTEE) has "a direct mandate from Parliament to engage Canadians in the generation and promotion of sustainable development advice and solutions." In 2012, the NRTEE delivered a report called "Reality Check: The State of Climate Progress in Canada." The report was unequivocal: Canada will need to do much more in order to achieve its "2020 GHG (greenhouse gases) emission reductions" target of 17% below 2005 levels.

Most people acknowledge that countries need to take further action to lower harmful emissions—and they must do so now; otherwise, climate change may lead to catastrophic effects on the planet and the economy. According to the NRTEE, global warming could cost Canada about $5 billion a year by 2020 and between $21 and $43 billion a year by the 2050s.[6]

So why are some people or corporations reluctant to take further steps? They may feel that the cost of investing in programs and strategies to reduce greenhouse gas emissions is too high, that there is little incentive to make such investments, or that investment in this area will take away from investment in other areas and thus jeopardize the nation's economic growth. To change this attitude, governments could, for example, provide subsidies and/or tax credits to firms and households that adopt strategies to conserve the environment.

On the brighter side, Environment Canada noted that between 2009 and 2010 greenhouse gas emissions in Canada remained relatively

[6]These estimates depend on the reduction of the global greenhouse gas emissions and on predicted rates of economic and population growth in Canada.

steady, rather than increasing, and that the economy still enjoyed a growth of 3.2%. This result could support the argument that we can tackle climate change without sacrificing economic growth.

CHECK YOUR UNDERSTANDING   9-5

1. Are economists typically more concerned about the limits to growth imposed by environmental degradation or those imposed by resource scarcity? Explain, noting the role of negative externalities in your answer.

2. What is the link between greenhouse gas emissions and growth? What is the expected effect on growth from emissions reduction? Why is international burden sharing of greenhouse gas emissions reduction a contentious problem?

Solutions appear at back of book.

▼ Quick Review

- There's wide disagreement about whether it is possible to have **sustainable long-run economic growth.** However, economists generally believe that modern economies can find ways to alleviate limits to growth from natural resource scarcity through the price response that promotes conservation and the creation of alternatives.

- Overcoming the limits to growth arising from environmental degradation is more difficult because it requires effective government intervention. Limiting the emission of greenhouse gases would require only a modest reduction in the growth rate.

- There is broad consensus that government action to address climate change and greenhouse gases should be in the form of market-based incentives, like a carbon tax or a cap and trade system. It will also require rich and poor countries to come to some agreement on how the cost of emissions reductions will be shared.

Sources of Canada's Labour Productivity Growth, 1970–2010

BUSINESS ● CASE ●

Gunter Marx/Alamy

During the past four decades, the Canadian economy has grown. Figure 9-16 shows the average labour productivity growth between 1970 and 2010 for the whole economy and for different sectors. Most sectors experienced positive productivity growth, with the exception of the mining and oil and gas extraction sector (its average productivity growth rate was –0.36%). The negative growth in that sector may be caused by the fact that these industries are capital-intensive industries and the cost of extracting these resources is high and rising.

On the other hand, the information and cultural industries sector led the country's labour productivity growth. In the past few decades, there have been dramatic innovations in these industries with the widespread use of cheap powerful computers and other new technologies. The agriculture, forestry, fishing, and hunting sector came in second in terms of this metric, experiencing a 3% productivity growth; the surge in the sector's productivity growth is partly due to higher world prices of agricultural products that encourage more investment in the industry, and to the availability of better and improved seeds and planting, maintenance, and harvest techniques. The wholesale trade sector came in third, with an average annual growth rate in productivity of 2.79% over these four decades. Better logistics is the primary reason for the surge in this sector's productivity. Firms like Loblaws and Walmart have figured out how to better use computers to track their inventories (for instance, by using bar-code scanners) and place product orders automatically with their suppliers. These practices gave them a huge advantage over the competitors who failed to innovate—and over previous versions of themselves. Seeing their success, other firms followed in their footsteps, which spread productivity gains to the entire sector and even the economy as a whole.

Thus, we have learned several things from what happened in the past four decades. An economy can enjoy higher productivity in different ways—such as by developing new technologies and equipment (for example, in the case of the information and cultural sector) or by improving existing techniques (as in the lumber and agricultural sector).

FIGURE **9-16** Canada's Average Labour Productivity Growth by Sector, 1970–2010

Sector	Percent increase
Professional, scientific, and technical services	0.61%
Finance, insurance, real estate, and renting and leasing	1.23%
Information and cultural industries	3.37%
Transportation and warehousing	1.73%
Retail trade	2.53%
Wholesale trade	2.79%
Manufacturing	2.53%
Construction	0.85%
Utilities	1.44%
Mining and oil and gas extraction	–0.36%
Agriculture, forestry, fishing, and hunting	3.00%
Overall economy	1.61%

Source: Statistics Canada.

QUESTIONS FOR THOUGHT

1. In this chapter, we described several sources of productivity growth. Which of these sources correspond to the growth in the information and cultural industries sector, in the agriculture, forestry, fishing and hunting sector, and in the wholesale trade sector?

2. How does our description of what happened in the wholesale trade sector tie in with the New Growth Theory?

1. Growth is measured as changes in real GDP per capita in order to eliminate the effects of changes in the price level and changes in population size. Levels of real GDP per capita vary greatly around the world: more than half of the world's population lives in countries that are still poorer than Canada was in 1900. Over the course of the twentieth century, real GDP per capita in Canada increased more than eightfold.

2. Growth rates of real GDP per capita also vary widely. According to the **Rule of 70,** the number of years it takes for real GDP per capita to double is equal to 70 divided by the annual growth rate of real GDP per capita.

3. The key to long-run economic growth is rising **labour productivity,** or **Average Productivity of Labour (AP_L)** or just **productivity,** which is output per worker. Increases in productivity arise from increases in **physical capital** per worker and **human capital** per worker as well as **technological progress.** The **per worker production function** shows how real GDP per worker depends on these three factors. The **aggregate production function** is a relationship that shows how the aggregate real quantity of output is produced using the available factors of production (the inputs: labour, physical capital, and human capital) and technology [A and the function $F(...)$]. The **positive marginal productivity of physical capital (positive MP_K)** is the amount by which productivity is increased as the result of a small increase in physical capital used. Other things equal, there are **diminishing returns to physical capital** or **diminishing marginal productivity of (physical) capital (dim MP_K):** holding human capital per worker and technology fixed, each successive addition to physical capital per worker yields a smaller increase in productivity than the one before. Equivalently, more physical capital per worker results in a lower, but still positive, increase in productivity. **Growth accounting,** which estimates the contribution of each factor to a country's economic growth, has shown that rising **total factor productivity,** the amount of output produced from a given amount of factor inputs, is key to long-run growth. It is usually interpreted as the effect of technological progress. In contrast to earlier times, natural resources are a less significant source of productivity growth in most countries today.

4. The large differences in countries' growth rates are largely due to differences in their rates of accumulation of physical and human capital as well as differences in technological progress. Although inflows of foreign savings from abroad help, a prime factor is dif-

ferences in domestic savings and investment spending rates, since most countries that have high investment spending in physical capital finance it by high domestic savings. Technological progress is largely a result of **research and development,** or **R&D.**

5. Governments can help or hinder growth. Government policies that directly foster growth are subsidies to **infrastructure,** particularly public health infrastructure, subsidies to education, subsidies to R&D, and maintenance of a well-functioning financial system that channels savings into investment spending, education, and R&D. Governments can enhance the environment for growth by protecting property rights (particularly intellectual property rights through patents), by being politically stable, and by providing good governance. Poor governance includes corruption and excessive government intervention.

6. The world economy contains examples of success and failure in the effort to achieve long-run economic growth. East Asian economies have done many things right and achieved very high growth rates. The low growth rates of Latin American and African economies over many years led economists to believe that the **convergence hypothesis,** the claim that differences in real GDP per capita across countries narrow over time, fits the data only when factors that affect growth, such as education, infrastructure, and favourable government policies and institutions, are held equal across countries. In recent years, there has been an uptick in growth among some Latin American and sub-Saharan African countries, largely due to a boom in commodity exports.

7. Economists generally believe that environmental degradation poses a greater challenge to **sustainable long-run economic growth** than does natural resource scarcity. Addressing environmental degradation requires effective governmental intervention, but the problem of natural resource scarcity is often well handled by the market price response.

8. The emission of greenhouse gases is clearly linked to growth, and limiting them will require some reduction in growth. However, the best available estimates suggest that a large reduction in emissions would require only a modest reduction in the growth rate.

9. There is broad consensus that government action to address climate change and greenhouse gases should be in the form of market-based incentives, like a carbon tax or a cap and trade system. It will also require rich and poor countries to come to some agreement on how the cost of emissions reductions will be shared.

PROBLEMS

1. The accompanying table shows data from the World Bank for real GDP per capita (in 2005 U.S. dollars) for Argentina, Ghana, South Korea, and Canada for 1960, 1970, 1980, 1990, 2000, and 2010.

   a. Fill in the empty table cells by expressing each year's real GDP per capita as a percentage of its 1960 and 2010 levels.

   b. How does the growth in living standards from 1960 to 2010 compare across these four nations? What might account for these differences?

	Argentina			Ghana			South Korea			Canada		
	Real GDP per capita (2005 U.S. dollars)	Percentage of		Real GDP per capita (2005 U.S. dollars)	Percentage of		Real GDP per capita (2005 U.S. dollars)	Percentage of		Real GDP per capita (2005 U.S. dollars)	Percentage of	
		1960 real GDP per capita	2010 real GDP per capita		1960 real GDP per capita	2010 real GDP per capita		1960 real GDP per capita	2010 real GDP per capita		1960 real GDP per capita	2010 real GDP per capita
Year												
1960	$6 043	?	?	$1286	?	?	$1 656	?	?	$12 869	?	?
1970	7 617	?	?	1525	?	?	2 808	?	?	18 373	?	?
1980	8 496	?	?	1295	?	?	5 179	?	?	23 621	?	?
1990	6 928	?	?	1273	?	?	11 643	?	?	27 577	?	?
2000	8 909	?	?	1478	?	?	18 729	?	?	33 575	?	?
2010	12 340	?	?	2094	?	?	26 609	?	?	37 104	?	?

2. The accompanying table shows the average annual growth rate in real GDP per capita for the past few decades for Argentina, Ghana, and South Korea using data from the Penn World Table, Version 7.1.

	Average annual growth rate of real GDP per capita		
Years	Argentina	Ghana	South Korea
1960–1970	2.43%	2.21%	5.50%
1970–1980	1.16	−1.46	6.43
1980–1990	−1.89	−0.04	8.46
1990–2000	3.09	1.53	5.05
2000–2010	3.44	3.58	3.60

   a. For each decade and for each country, use the Rule of 70 where possible to calculate how long it would take for that country's real GDP per capita to double.

   b. Suppose that the average annual growth rate that each country achieved over the period 2000–2010 continues indefinitely into the future. Starting from 2000, use the Rule of 70 to calculate, where possible, the year in which a country will have doubled its real GDP per capita.

3. The accompanying table provides approximate statistics on per capita income levels and growth rates for regions defined by income levels. According to the Rule of 70, starting in 2010 the high-income countries are projected to double their per capita GDP in approximately 78 years, in 2088. Throughout this question, assume constant growth rates for each of the regions that are equal to their average value between 2000 and 2010.

Region	GDP per capita (2010)	Average annual growth rate of real GDP per capita (2000–2010)
High-income countries	$38 293	0.9%
Middle-income countries	3 980	4.8
Low-income countries	507	3.0

Source: World Bank.

   a. Calculate the ratio of per capita GDP in 2010 of the following:

      i. Middle-income to high-income countries

      ii. Low-income to high-income countries

      iii. Low-income to middle-income countries

b. Calculate the number of years it will take the low-income and middle-income countries to double their per capita GDP.

c. Calculate the per capita GDP of each of the regions in 2088. (*Hint:* How many times does their per capita GDP double in 78 years, the number of years from 2010 to 2088?)

d. Repeat part (a) with the projected per capita GDP in 2088.

e. Compare your answers to parts (a) and (d). Comment on the change in economic inequality between the regions.

4. You are hired as an economic consultant to the countries of Albernia and Brittania. Each country's current relationship between physical capital per worker and output per worker is given by the curve labelled "Productivity$_1$" in the accompanying diagram. Albernia is at point *A* and Brittania is at point *B*.

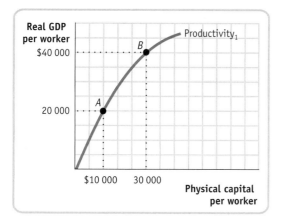

a. In the relationship depicted by the curve Productivity$_1$, what factors are held fixed? Do these countries experience diminishing returns to physical capital per worker?

b. Assuming that the amount of human capital per worker and the technology are held fixed in each country, can you recommend a policy to generate a doubling of real GDP per capita in Albernia?

c. How would your policy recommendation change if the amount of human capital per worker could be changed? Assume that an increase in human capital doubles the output per worker when physical capital per worker equals $10 000. Draw a curve on the diagram that represents this policy for Albernia.

5. The country of Androde is currently using Method 1 for its production function. By chance, scientists stumble onto a technological breakthrough that will enhance Androde's productivity. This technological breakthrough is reflected in another production function, Method 2. The accompanying table shows combinations of physical capital per worker and output per worker for both methods, assuming that human capital per worker is fixed.

Method 1		Method 2	
Physical capital per worker	**Real GDP per worker**	**Physical capital per worker**	**Real GDP per worker**
0	0.00	0	0.00
50	35.36	50	70.71
100	50.00	100	100.00
150	61.24	150	122.47
200	70.71	200	141.42
250	79.06	250	158.11
300	86.60	300	173.21
350	93.54	350	187.08
400	100.00	400	200.00
450	106.07	450	212.13
500	111.80	500	223.61

a. Using the data in the accompanying table, draw the two production functions in one diagram. Androde's current amount of physical capital per worker is 100. In your figure, label that point *A*.

b. Starting from point *A*, over a period of 70 years, the amount of physical capital per worker in Androde rises to 400. Assuming Androde still uses Method 1, in your diagram, label the resulting point of production *B*. Using the Rule of 70, calculate by how many percent per year output per worker has grown.

c. Now assume that, starting from point *A*, over the same period of 70 years, the amount of physical capital per worker in Androde rises to 400, but that during that time period, Androde switches to Method 2. In your diagram, label the resulting point of production *C*. Using the Rule of 70, calculate by how many percent per year output per worker has grown now.

d. As the economy of Androde moves from point *A* to point *C*, what share of the annual productivity growth is due to higher total factor productivity?

6. Statistics Canada regularly releases data on the country's labour productivity and labour cost. Go to StatCan's home page at www.statcan.gc.ca. Pick English or French. Go to the middle section of the home page and click on "Economic accounts" under "Browse by subject." Then click "Productivity accounts" under "Subtopics." Click "Detailed tables from CANSIM" under "Resources," and choose Table 383-0012 (Indexes of labour productivity and related variables, by North American Industry Classification System (NAICS), seasonally adjusted). You should find data on labour productivity for different sectors. What were the percent changes in labour productivity in the goods sector, the services sector, and the non-business sector for the previous quarter? How does the percent change in that quarter's productivity compare to data from the previous quarter?

7. What roles do physical capital, human capital, technology, and natural resources play in influencing long-run economic growth of aggregate output per capita?

8. How have policies and institutions in Canada influenced the country's long-run economic growth?

9. Over the next 100 years, real GDP per capita in Groland is expected to grow at an average annual rate of 2.0%. In Sloland, however, growth is expected to be somewhat slower, at an average annual growth rate of 1.5%. If both countries have a real GDP per capita today of $20 000, how will their real GDP per capita differ in 100 years? [*Hint:* A country that has a real GDP today of x and grows at $y\%$ per year will achieve a real GDP of $\$x \times (1 + (y/100))^z$ in z years. We assume that $0 \leq y < 10$.]

10. The accompanying table shows data from the Penn World Table, Version 7.1 for real GDP per capita (in 2005 U.S. dollars) for Canada, France, Japan, the United Kingdom, and the United States in 1960 and 2010. Complete the table. Have these countries converged economically?

	1960		2010	
	Real GDP per capita (2005 U.S. dollars)	Percentage of U.S. real GDP per capita	Real GDP per capita (2005 U.S. dollars)	Percentage of U.S. real GDP per capita
Canada	$7 084		$31 299	
France	2 787	?	31 447	?
Japan	11 141	?	37 104	?
United Kingdom	8 988	?	34 268	?
United States	13 069	?	41 365	?

11. The accompanying table shows data from the Penn World Table, Version 7.1 for real GDP per capita (in 2005 U.S. dollars) for Argentina, Canada, Ghana, and South Korea om 1960 and 2010. Complete the table by filling in all empty cells. Have the economies of these countries converged?

	1960		2010	
	Real GDP per capita (2005 U.S. dollars)	Percentage of U.S. real GDP per capita	Real GDP per capita (2005 U.S. dollars)	Percentage of Canadian real GDP per capita
Argentina	$6 043	?	$12 340	?
Canada	12 869	?	37 104	?
Ghana	1 286	?	2 094	?
South Korea	1 656	?	26 609	?

12. According to the *Oil & Gas Journal*, the proven oil reserves existing in the world in 2009 consisted of 1342 billion barrels. In that year, the U.S. Energy Information Administration reported that the world daily oil production was 72.26 million barrels a day.

   a. At this rate, for how many years will the proven oil reserves last? Discuss the Malthusian view in the context of the number you just calculated.

   b. In order to do the calculations in part (a), what did you assume about the total quantity of oil reserves over time? About oil prices over time? Are these assumptions consistent with the Malthusian view on resource limits?

   c. Discuss how market forces may affect the amount of time the proven oil reserves will last, assuming that no new oil reserves are discovered and that the demand curve for oil remains unchanged.

13. The accompanying table shows the annual growth rate for the years 2000–2009 in per capita emissions of carbon dioxide (CO_2) and the annual growth rate in real GDP per capita for selected countries.

Country	2000–2009 average annual growth rate of:	
	Real GDP per capita	CO_2 emissions per capita
Argentina	2.81%	1.01%
Bangladesh	4.17	5.47
Canada	0.68	−1.46
China	9.85	11.11
Germany	0.59	−1.23
Ireland	1.05	−2.10
Japan	0.29	−1.03
South Korea	3.48	1.68
Mexico	0.18	0.44
Nigeria	6.07	−2.46
Russia	5.22	0.52
South Africa	2.39	0.80
United Kingdom	0.88	−1.35
United States	0.58	−1.78

Sources: The U.S. Energy Information Administration; International Monetary Fund.

a. Rank the countries in terms of their growth in CO_2 emissions, from highest to lowest. What five countries have the highest growth rate in emissions? What five countries have the lowest growth rate in emissions?

b. Now rank the countries in terms of their growth in real GDP per capita, from highest to lowest. What five countries have the highest growth rate? What five countries have the lowest growth rate?

c. Would you infer from your results that CO_2 emissions are linked to growth in output per capita?

d. Do high growth rates necessarily lead to high CO_2 emissions?

CHAPTER 10

Savings, Investment Spending, and the Financial System

FUNDS FOR FACEBOOK

Rainer Raffalski

Facebook obtained millions of dollars in financing to pay for physical capital like the server farms it needed to expand.

> ❭ The relationship between **savings and investment spending**
>
> ❭ Aspects of the **loanable funds market,** which show how savers are matched with borrowers
>
> ❭ The purpose of the five principal types of **financial assets:** stocks, bonds, **loans,** real estate, and **bank deposits**
>
> ❭ How **financial intermediaries** help investors achieve **diversification**
>
> ❭ Some competing views of what determines asset prices and why asset market fluctuations can be a source of macroeconomic instability

FACEBOOK WENT PUBLIC ON May 18, 2012. Its initial public offering (IPO) captured headlines around the world because it was one of the largest technology sector IPOs in history. Becoming a publicly traded institution allowed Facebook to raise funds from the financial market more easily. Why would a wildly successful business like Facebook need to attract new capital?

Everyone knows Facebook. Founded in 2004, it has gone on to become arguably the biggest business success story of the twenty-first century—so far. According to Socialbakers, one of the most cited and fastest growing social media analytics companies, as of August 2012 there were about 17.7 million Facebook users in Canada. This represents a population penetration rate of 53%. How did Facebook grow so big, so fast?

In large part, of course, the answer is that the company had a good idea. Personalized web pages providing information to friends turned out to be something many people really wanted. Equally important, since advertisers wanted access to the readers of those pages, Facebook could make a lot of money selling advertising space.

But having a good idea isn't enough to build a business. Entrepreneurs need funds: you have to spend money to make money. Although businesses like Facebook seem to exist solely in the virtual world of cyberspace, free of the worldly burdens of brick-and-mortar establishments, the truth is that running such businesses requires a lot of very real and expensive hardware. Like Google, Yahoo!, and other Internet giants, Facebook maintains huge "server farms," arrays of linked computers that track and process all the information needed to provide the user experience.

So where did Facebook get the money to equip these server farms? Some of it came from investors who acquired shares in the business, but much of it was borrowed. As Facebook grew bigger, so did the amount it needed to raise.

The ability of Facebook to raise large sums of money to finance its growth is, in its own way, as remarkable as the company's product. In effect, some young guy with a bright idea was able to lay his hands on hundreds of millions of dollars to build his business. It's an amazing story.

Yet this sort of thing is common in modern economies. The long-run growth we analyzed in the previous chapter depends crucially on a set of markets and institutions, collectively known as the *financial system,* that channels the funds of savers into productive investment spending. Without this system, businesses like Facebook would not be able to purchase much of the physical capital that is an important source of productivity growth. And savers would be forced to accept a lower return on their funds. Historically, financial systems channelled funds into investment spending projects such as railroads and factories. Today, financial systems also channel funds into new sources of growth such as green technology, social media, and investments in human capital. Without a well-functioning financial system, a country will suffer stunted economic growth.

In this chapter, we begin by focusing on the economy as a whole. We will examine the relationship between savings and investment spending. Next, we go behind this relationship and analyze the financial system, the means by which savings is transformed into investment spending. We'll see how the financial system works by creating assets, markets, and institutions that increase the welfare of both savers (those with funds to invest) and borrowers (those with investment spending projects to finance). Finally, we examine the behaviour of financial markets and why they often resist economists' attempts at explanation. ▪

According to the **savings-investment spending identity,** savings and investment spending are always equal for the economy as a whole.

Matching Up Savings and Investment Spending

We learned in the previous chapter that two of the essential ingredients in economic growth are increases in the economy's levels of *human capital* and *physical capital*. Human capital is largely provided by governments through public education. (In countries with a large private education sector, such as Canada, private post-secondary education is also an important source of human capital.) But physical capital, with the exception of infrastructure, is mainly created through private investment spending, that is, spending by firms rather than by the government. (You may also see it referred to simply as "investment.")

Who pays for private investment spending? In some cases it's the people or corporations that actually do the spending—for example, a family that owns a business might use its own savings to buy new equipment or a new building, or a corporation might reinvest some of its own profits to build a new factory. In the modern economy, however, individuals and firms that create physical capital often do it with other people's money—money that they borrow or raise by selling stock.

To understand how investment spending is financed, we need to look first at how savings and investment spending are related for the economy as a whole. Then we will examine how savings are allocated among investment spending projects.

The Savings-Investment Spending Identity

The most basic point to understand about savings and investment spending is that they are always equal. This is not a theory; it's a fact of accounting called the **savings-investment spending identity.**

To see why the savings-investment spending identity must be true, let's look again at the national income accounting that we learned in Chapter 7. Recall that GDP is equal to total spending on domestically produced final goods and services, and that we can write the following equation (which is the same as Equation 7-1):

(10-1) $GDP = C + I + G + X - IM$

where C is spending by consumers, I is investment spending, G is government purchases of goods and services, X is the value of exports to other countries, and IM is spending on imports from other countries.

The Savings-Investment Spending Identity in a Closed Economy

In a closed economy, there are no exports or imports. So $X = 0$ and $IM = 0$, which makes Equation 10-1 simpler. As we learned in Chapter 7, the overall income of this simplified economy would, by definition, equal total spending. Why? Recall one of the basic principles of economics from Chapter 1, that one person's spending is another person's income: the only way people can earn income is by selling something to someone else, and every dollar spent in the economy creates income for somebody. This is represented by Equation 10-2: on the left, GDP represents total income earned in the economy, and on the right, $C + I + G$ represents spending by all sectors in the economy:

(10-2) $$GDP = C + I + G$$
Total income = Total spending by all sectors

As an individual, you can divide your income into two categories: spending (on final goods and services) and savings. The same logic applies to an

---

⚠ **PITFALLS**

FINANCIAL INVESTMENT VERSUS PHYSICAL INVESTMENT

In daily life, when we speak of *investment*, we tend to think of buying assets, such as bonds, stocks, or an existing piece of real estate. That is, we are thinking of financial investment. However, in economics, the term *investment* is used and interpreted much differently. In economics, *investment spending*, or simply *investment*, means buying new physical capital such as machinery, equipment, production plants, and so on. That is, it means *physical investment*.

economy as a whole. Any closed economy can divide its income into consumption spending and savings. Consumption spending comes from households (private sector consumption spending, C) and government (public sector consumption spending, G). The economy's total savings, **national savings ($S_{National}$),** also comes from households and the government. So it must be true that:

(10-3) Total income = Consumption spending by households and government
+ National savings
$$\text{GDP} = (C + G) + S_{National}$$

(10-4) $\qquad\qquad S_{National} = \text{GDP} - C - G$

Since $(\text{GDP} - C - G)$ is the amount of total income left over after consumption spending, it must be equal to savings for the economy as a whole. Making use of Equation (10-2), we get:

(10-5) $\qquad\qquad\qquad\qquad I = S_{National}$
$$\text{Investment spending} = \text{National savings}$$

This is why we can say that it's a basic accounting fact that savings equals investment spending for the economy as a whole.

Now, let's take a closer look at national savings. As mentioned earlier, national savings comes from both households and the government. Thus, another way to look at national savings is to look at savings undertaken by each of these two sectors. Recall from Chapter 7 that the savings undertaken by households is called private savings, $S_{Private}$, and this amount is equal to disposable income minus (private sector) consumption spending:

(10-6) $\qquad\qquad S_{Private} = (\text{GDP} - T + TR) - C$

where GDP represents income, T represents taxes, and TR represents transfers from the government.

As alluded to above, the government can also save. The savings by the government is usually called **public savings, S_{Public},** but you may also see it referred to as government savings. Public savings is the government's **budget balance**—that is, does the budget have a surplus or a deficit, or does total income equal total spending. Like households, the government earns income and has spending on goods and services. The government's income consists of the tax revenues it collects, while its expenditures include spending on final goods and services and making transfer payments to residents. Sometimes, it is convenient to refer to the difference between the tax revenues and transfer payments as *net taxes*, in essence treating transfer payments as negative taxes. Thus, the government's budget balance is the difference between the net tax revenue and government spending on final goods and services. If net taxes *exceed* government spending on final goods and services, then the government is running a **budget surplus.** Since the budget balance is positive, the government has saved the leftover. On the other hand, if the budget balance is negative, the government runs a **budget deficit,** or "dissaves," as the government is engaged in the opposite of savings. Therefore, the budget balance of the government is equivalent to public savings:

(10-7) Budget balance = $(T - TR) - G = S_{Public}$

National savings can be expressed as the sum of private savings and public savings:

(10-8) $S_{National} = S_{Private} + S_{Public}$

National savings is the total amount of domestic savings generated within an economy.

Public savings (or government **budget balance**) is the difference between net tax revenue ($T - TR$) and government spending on goods and services, i.e., $T - TR - G$. If the budget balance is positive, then the government is running a **budget surplus.** If it is negative, then the government is running a **budget deficit.** If it is zero, then the government is running a balanced budget.

Net foreign investment (NFI) is the total outflows of funds out of a country minus the total inflows of funds into that country. It can also be expressed as the difference between the amount of foreign investment undertaken by the country and the amount of domestic investment undertaken by foreigners.

Substituting Equations (10-6) and (10-7) into Equation (10-8), we get back Equation (10-4):

$$S_{National} = (GDP - T + TR - C) + (T - TR - G)$$
$$= GDP - C - G$$

The Savings-Investment Spending Identity in an Open Economy

An open economy is an economy in which goods and money can flow into and out of the country. This changes the savings-investment spending identity because savings need not be spent on investment spending projects in the same country in which the savings are generated, and so the savings of people who live in any one country can be used to finance investment spending that takes place in other countries. Any given country can receive *inflows* of funds—foreign savings that finance investment spending in that country. Any given country can also generate *outflows* of funds—domestic savings that finance investment spending in another country.

The net effect of international outflows and inflows of funds on total savings available for investment in any given country is known as the **net foreign investment (NFI)** of that country. NFI is equal to the total outflows of domestic funds *minus* the total inflows of foreign funds.[1] Like the government budget balance, net foreign investment can be negative—when foreigners invest more money in a country than the country invests in other countries. This has happened in Canada in recent years. In 2010, for example, net foreign investment in Canada was negative C$30.5 billion, meaning that foreigners invested C$30.5 billion more in Canada than Canadians invested in other countries. The negative NFI was, in part, caused by uncertainty in the global economy. At time of writing, Canada had one of the best fiscal positions of all G-7 countries, with an AAA credit rating (the highest available). Owing to the sovereign debt crisis in the European Union and the downgrading of the U.S.'s credit rating from AAA to AA+, foreign investors perceived Canada as a safe place to store their wealth. Also, since 2008–2009, Canada's trade balance has gone from a surplus to a deficit. This implies that the level of national savings fell short of domestic investment, and Canada needed to borrow from the rest of the world to finance a portion of this investment.

It's important to note that, from a national perspective, a dollar generated by national savings and a dollar generated by a foreign capital inflow are not equivalent. Yes, they can both finance the same dollar's worth of investment spending. But any dollar borrowed from a saver must eventually be repaid with interest. A dollar that comes from national savings is repaid with interest to someone domestically—either a private party or the government. But a dollar that comes as a foreign capital inflow must be repaid with interest to a foreigner. So a dollar of investment spending financed by a foreign capital inflow comes at a higher *national* cost—the interest that must eventually be paid to a foreigner—than a dollar of investment spending financed by national savings.

The fact that a *negative* net foreign investment represents funds "borrowed" from foreigners is an important aspect of the savings-investment spending identity in an open economy. Since financial capital can flow freely across national borders, an open economy can allocate in savings in two ways: accumulating

---

[1]An alternate way to look at the international flows of funds is to look at the net inflows of funds (the net capital inflows, NCI). NCI is total inflows of funds into a country minus the total outflows of funds out of a country. A *positive NCI* means more foreign capital is entering a country than domestic capital is leaving the country. Thus, the relationship between NFI and NCI is given by:

Net capital inflows = −Net foreign investment

or, equivalently:

Net foreign investment = −Net capital inflows

physical capital (investing domestically) and acquiring foreign assets (investing abroad). This is equivalent to saying that the funds used to finance domestic investment can come from two sources: domestic funds (via national savings) and foreign funds (via capital inflows, or a negative NFI). It turns out a country's net foreign investment is tied to its net exports. Why? When a country spends more on imports than it earns from exports, it must borrow the difference from foreigners to help pay for its imports. As a consequence, the country's net foreign investment will turn negative. Similarly, when a country earns more from exports than it spends on imports, it must use the excess amount to fund investment abroad. So, it has a positive net foreign investment. As we'll explain in greater detail in Chapter 19, the relationship between net foreign investment and net exports (the trade balance) is given by:

(10-9)
$$\text{NFI} = X - IM = \text{Net exports}$$
$$\text{Net foreign investment} = \text{Exports} - \text{Imports} = \text{Net exports}$$

Rearranging Equation 10-1 we get:

(10-10) $(GDP - C - G) = I + (X - IM)$

The left side of Equation 10-10 is equal to national savings (Equation 10-4), so then:

(10-11)
$$S_{National} = I + (X - IM)$$
$$= I + \text{NFI}$$
$$\text{National savings} = \text{Investment} + \text{Net foreign investment}$$

Equation 10-11 shows that an open economy can split its savings into domestic investment (I) and net foreign investment (NFI). Let's look at some data to demonstrate this. In 2010 in Canada, private savings reached $420.7 billion, while public savings were negative $90.2 billion. So, the government ran a budget deficit. This resulted in national savings of $330.5 billion. However, investment spending totalled $360.7 billion, which was greater than the amount of domestic funds available. The shortfall in funds was supplemented by a trade deficit of $30.5 billion. Thus, in 2010 Canada "borrowed" $30.5 billion from foreigners. You may have noticed these numbers don't quite add up; because data collection isn't perfect, there is a statistical discrepancy of $0.3 billion. But we know that the error lies in the data, not in the theory, because the savings-investment spending identity must hold in reality.

Figure 10-1 shows the savings-investment identity in Canada in 2007 and 2010. To make the comparison easier, we have measured different kinds of savings and investment as a percentage of GDP. In each panel, the bars on the left side show the sum of investment spending and net foreign investment as a percentage of GDP. The bars on the right side show the components of national savings as a percentage of GDP. The levels of investment spending as a percentage of GDP were roughly the same in both years; however, other components in the savings-investment identity changed quite a lot from 2007 to 2010.

Public savings changed from a positive 1.4% in 2007 to a negative 5.6% in 2010, which indicated the government's budget balance changed from a surplus to a deficit. This change in budget balance was the result of an economic slowdown coupled with expansionary fiscal policies such as the Economic Action Plan and other programs implemented in response to the financial crisis. The increase in government spending, the provision of higher transfer payments, and a fall in tax revenues combined to force the federal government to run record-high deficits. In

PITFALLS

THE DIFFERENT KINDS OF CAPITAL
It's important to understand clearly the three different kinds of capital: physical capital, human capital, and financial capital (as explained in the previous chapter):

1. **Physical capital** consists of manufactured resources such as buildings and machines.

2. **Human capital** is the improvement in the labour force generated by education and knowledge.

3. **Financial capital** is funds from savings that are available for investment spending. A country that has a negative net foreign investment is experiencing a positive net flow of funds into that country from abroad, that is, from foreigners. These funds can be used to finance domestic investment spending.

FIGURE 10-1 The Savings-Investment Spending Identity in Canada, 2007 and 2010

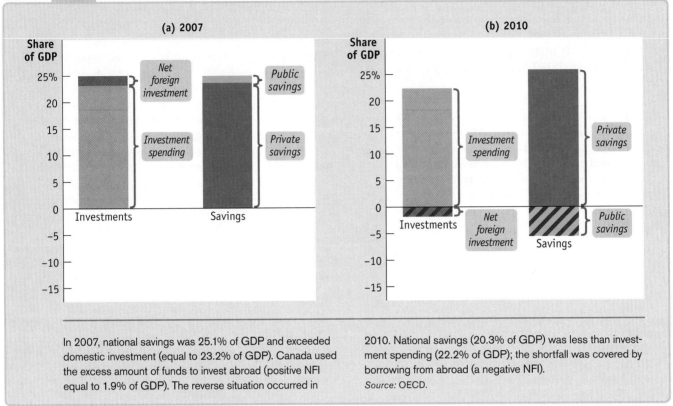

In 2007, national savings was 25.1% of GDP and exceeded domestic investment (equal to 23.2% of GDP). Canada used the excess amount of funds to invest abroad (positive NFI equal to 1.9% of GDP). The reverse situation occurred in

2010. National savings (20.3% of GDP) was less than investment spending (22.2% of GDP); the shortfall was covered by borrowing from abroad (a negative NFI).
Source: OECD.

the 2012 Federal Budget, the federal minister of finance, Jim Flaherty, projected a budget surplus in the fiscal year of 2016–2017, which implied that public savings would remain negative, and the budget would remain in deficit, until 2016.

Similarly, Canada's net foreign investment changed from a positive 1.9% in 2007 to a negative 1.9% in 2010. In 2007, Canada experienced positive NFI and "lent"

FOR INQUIRING MINDS

WHO ENFORCES THE ACCOUNTING?

The savings-investment spending identity is a fact of accounting. By definition, savings equals investment spending for the economy as a whole. But who enforces the arithmetic? For example, what happens if the amount that businesses want to invest in capital equipment is less than the amount households want to save?

The short answer is that actual and *desired* investment spending aren't always equal. Suppose that households suddenly decide to save more by spending less—say, by putting off the purchase of new cars. The immediate effect will be that unsold goods pile up—in this case, in the form of

cars sitting in dealers' lots. And this increase in inventory counts as investment spending, albeit unintended. So the savings-investment spending identity still holds, because auto dealers end up engaging in more investment spending than they intended to. Similarly, if households suddenly decide to save less and spend more, inventories will drop—and this will be counted as *negative* investment spending.

Let's take a look at what happened in 2010. National savings and investment (the sum of domestic and net foreign investment) both increased by $24 billion from the fourth quarter of 2009 to the second quarter of 2010.

On the investment side, $12 billion of that rise took the form of inventory investment spending, showing that when households save more and spend less, the resulting increase in unsold products leads to an increase in firms' inventories. (So, for example, unsold automobiles continued to sit on the dealers' lots.)

Of course, businesses respond to changes in their inventories by altering their production. The increase in inventories in 2010 helped to explain the slower GDP growth in the subsequent quarters, as firms responded by laying off workers and reducing output. We'll examine the special role of inventories in economic fluctuations in Chapter 11.

DIFFERENCES IN NATIONAL SAVINGS

Panel (a) of this figure shows national savings as a percentage of GDP for Canada, the United States, Germany, and the United Kingdom from 1991 to 2010. Canada's and Germany's savings rates were always higher than those of the U.S. and the U.K. The average national savings rates over that period were 22.5% (of GDP) in Canada and 23% in Germany; however, the average national savings rates in the U.S. and the U.K. were 15.2% and 15.4% respectively.

What causes the differences in savings rates among these countries? The main source of these international differences in national savings lies in the relatively low private savings in both the U.S. and the U.K. As panel (b) shows, before the recession of 2008–2009, American and British

citizens saved much less than Canadians and Germans. Why? Economists aren't sure, but one explanation is that U.S. and U.K. households have easier access to credit than Canadian and German households do. When households see that it is relatively easy to borrow to finance the purchase of big-ticket items, there is less incentive to save.

All four countries saw a drop in national savings rates after 2008. As one might expect, this drop was triggered by the financial crisis of 2008–2009; governments in all these countries ran expansionary fiscal policies (and budget deficits) to prevent their economies from taking a drastic downturn. As a result, the recent rise in private savings was more than offset by the fall in public savings.

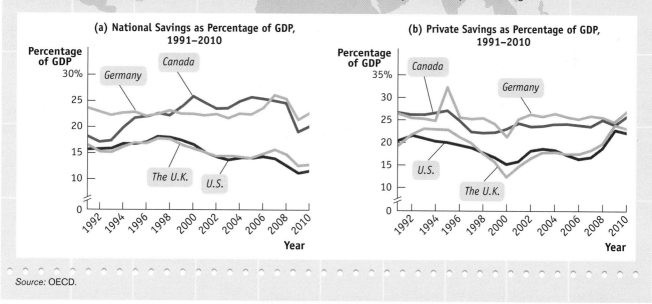

Source: OECD.

money to foreigners; in 2010, Canada experienced negative NFI and "borrowed" from foreigners. The change in the nature of NFI also indicated that Canada's trade balance changed from a surplus to a deficit. This change was caused partly by the recession in the United States, which lowered the demand for exported Canadian goods, and partly by falling oil prices.

On the other hand, the private sector saved more as a percentage of GDP over that period. Private savings increased from 23.7% of GDP in 2007 to 25.9% in 2010. This may have been triggered by heightened uncertainty about the future. Perhaps seeing that economic growth had slowed and firms were laying off workers as a result of the recent recession, households saved more for future rainy days! Although private savings as a percentage of GDP was higher in 2010, national savings actually fell to 20.3% of GDP as the increase in private savings was more than offset by a fall in public savings.

The Domestic Market for Loanable Funds

For the economy as a whole, savings always equals investment spending. In a closed economy, savings is equal to national savings. In an open economy, savings can be split between investment and net foreign investment. At any given time, however,

The **loanable funds market** is a hypothetical market that illustrates the market outcome of the demand for funds generated by borrowers and the supply of funds provided by lenders.

savers, the people with funds to lend, are usually not the same as borrowers, the people who want to borrow to finance their investment spending. How are savers and borrowers brought together?

Savers and borrowers are matched up with one another in much the same way producers and consumers are matched up: through markets governed by supply and demand. In Figure 7-1, the expanded circular-flow diagram, we noted that the *financial markets* channel the savings of households to businesses that want to borrow in order to purchase capital equipment. It's now time to take a look at how those financial markets work.

To do this, it helps to consider a somewhat simplified version of reality. As we noted in Chapter 7, there are a large number of different financial markets in the financial system, such as the bond market and the stock market. However, economists often work with a simplified model in which they assume that there is just one market that brings together those who want to lend money (savers) and those who want to borrow (firms with investment spending projects). This hypothetical market is known as the **loanable funds market.** The price that is determined in the loanable funds market is the interest rate, denoted by i. As we noted in Chapter 8, loans typically specify a nominal interest rate. So although we call i "the interest rate," it is with the understanding that i is a nominal interest rate—an interest rate that is unadjusted for inflation.

We're not quite done simplifying things. There are, in reality, many different kinds of interest rates, because there are many different kinds of loans—short-term loans, long-term loans, loans made to corporate borrowers, loans made to governments, and so on. In the interest of simplicity, we'll ignore those differences and assume that there is only one type of loan.

OK, now we're ready to analyze how savings and investment get matched up.

The Domestic Demand for Loanable Funds The domestic demand for loanable funds (or, for short, the demand for loanable funds) comes from those who need to borrow funds to finance their domestic investment project(s). Figure 10-2 illustrates a hypothetical demand curve for loanable funds, D,

FIGURE 10-2 The Domestic Demand for Loanable Funds

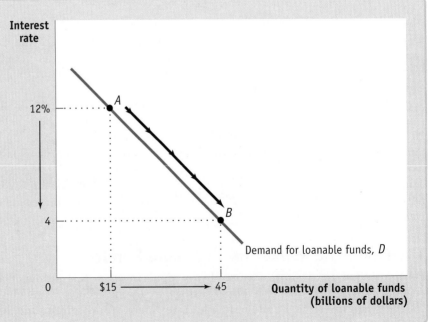

The demand curve for loanable funds slopes downward: the lower the interest rate, the greater the quantity of loanable funds demanded. Here, reducing the interest rate from 12% to 4% increases the quantity of loanable funds demanded from $15 billion to $45 billion.

FOR INQUIRING MINDS

USING PRESENT VALUE

An understanding of the concept of present value shows why the demand curve for loanable funds slopes downward. A simple way to grasp the essence of present value is to consider an example that illustrates the difference in value between having a sum of money today and having the same sum of money a year from now.

Suppose that exactly one year from today you will graduate, and you want to reward yourself by taking a trip that will cost $1000. In order to have $1000 a year from now, how much do you need today? It's not $1000, and the reason why has to do with the interest rate. Let's call the amount you need today X. We'll use i to represent the interest rate you receive on funds deposited in the bank. If you put X into the bank today and earn interest rate i on it, then after one year, the bank will pay you $X \times (1 + i)$. If what the bank will pay you a year from now is equal to $1000, then the amount you need today is

$$X \times (1 + i) = \$1000$$

You can apply some basic algebra to find that

$$X = \$1000/(1 + i)$$

Notice that the value of X depends on the interest rate i, which is always greater than 0. This fact implies that X *is always less than* $1000. For example, if $i = 5\%$ (that is, $i = 0.05$), then $X = \$952.38$. In other words, having

When making financial decisions, individuals and firms must always keep in mind that having $1000 today is worth more than having $1000 a year from now.

$952.38 today is equivalent to having $1000 a year from now when the interest rate is 5%. That is, $952.38 is the present value of having $1000 a year from now when the interest rate is 5%. Now we can define the **present value** of X: it is the amount of money needed today in order to receive X in the future given the interest rate. In this numerical example, $952.38 is the present value of $1000 received one year from now given an interest rate of 5%.

The concept of present value also applies to decisions made by firms.

Think about a firm that has two potential investment projects in mind, each of which will yield $1000 a year from now. However, each project has different initial costs—say, one requires that the firm borrow $900 right now and the other requires that the firm borrow $950. Which, if any, of these projects is worth borrowing money to finance and undertake?

The answer depends on the interest rate, which determines the present value of $1000 a year from now. If the interest rate is 10%, the present value of $1000 delivered a year from now is $909. So only the first project, which has an initial cost of less than $909, is profitable. With an interest rate of 10%, the return on any project costing more than $909 is less than the amount the firm had to repay on its loan and is therefore unprofitable. If the interest rate is only 5%, however, the present value of $1000 rises to $952. At this interest rate, both projects are profitable because $952 exceeds both projects' initial cost. So a firm will want to borrow more (i.e., demand more funds) and engage in more investment spending when the interest rate is lower.

Meanwhile, similar calculations will be taking place at other firms. So a lower interest rate will lead to higher investment spending in the economy as a whole: the demand curve for loanable funds slopes downward.

---

which slopes downward. On the horizontal axis we show the quantity of loanable funds demanded. On the vertical axis we show the interest rate, which is the "price" of borrowing. But why does the demand curve for loanable funds slope downward?

To answer this question, consider what a firm is doing when it engages in investment spending—say, by buying new equipment. Investment spending means laying out money right now, expecting that this outlay will lead to higher profits at some point in the future. In fact, however, the promise of a dollar five or ten years from now is worth less than an actual dollar right now. So an investment is worth making only if it generates a future return that is *greater* than the monetary cost of making the investment today. How much greater? To answer that, we need to take into account the *present value* of the future return the firm expects to get. We examine the concept of present value in the accompanying For Inquiring Minds.

In present value calculations, we use the interest rate to determine how the value of a dollar in the future compares to the value of a dollar today. But the fact is that future dollars are worth less than a dollar today, and they are

The **present value** of Y dollars is the amount of money you would need to invest today at the given interest rate to receive Y dollars at a future date.

worth even less when the interest rate is higher. The intuition behind present value calculations is simple. The interest rate measures the opportunity cost of investment spending that results in a future return: instead of spending money on an investment spending project, a company could simply put the money into the bank and earn interest on it. And the higher the interest rate, the more attractive it is to simply put money into the bank instead of investing it in an investment spending project. In other words, the higher the interest rate, the higher the opportunity cost of investment spending. And, the higher the opportunity cost of investment spending, the lower the number of investment spending projects firms want to carry out, and therefore the lower the quantity of loanable funds demanded. It is this insight (discussed in the accompanying For Inquiring Minds) that explains why the demand curve for loanable funds is downward sloping.

When businesses engage in investment spending, they spend money right now in return for an expected payoff in the future. So, to evaluate whether a particular investment spending project is worth undertaking, a business must compare the present value of the future payoff with the current cost of that project. If the present value of the future payoff is greater than the current cost, a project is profitable and worth investing in. If the interest rate falls, then the present value of any given project rises, so more projects pass that test. If the interest rate rises, then the present value of any given project falls, then fewer projects pass that test. So total investment spending, and hence the demand for loanable funds to finance that spending, is negatively related to the interest rate. Thus, the demand curve for loanable funds slopes downward. You can see this in Figure 10-2. When the interest rate falls from 12% to 4%, the quantity of loanable funds demanded rises from $15 billion (point *A*) to $45 billion (point *B*).

The Domestic Supply of Loanable Funds The domestic supply of loanable funds (or, for short, the supply of loanable funds) comes from those who have extra funds that they are willing to lend. This supply is equal to national savings. Figure 10-3 shows a hypothetical supply curve for loanable funds, *S*. Again, the interest rate plays the same role that the price plays in ordinary supply and demand analysis. But why is this curve upward sloping?

FIGURE **10-3** **The Domestic Supply of Loanable Funds**

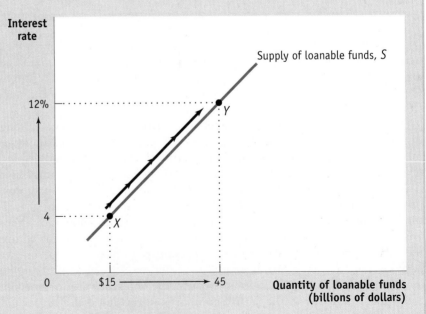

The supply curve for loanable funds slopes upward: the higher the interest rate, the greater the quantity of loanable funds supplied. Here, increasing the interest rate from 4% to 12% increases the quantity of loanable funds supplied from $15 billion to $45 billion.

The answer is that loanable funds are supplied by savers, and savers incur an opportunity cost when they lend to a business: the funds could instead be spent on consumption—say, a nice vacation. Whether a given saver becomes a lender by making funds available to borrowers depends on the interest rate received in return. By saving your money today and earning interest on it, you are rewarded with higher consumption in the future when the loan you made is repaid with interest. So it is a good assumption that more people are willing to forgo current consumption and make a loan to a borrower when the interest rate is higher. As a result, our hypothetical supply curve of loanable funds slopes upward. In Figure 10-3, lenders will supply $15 billion to the loanable funds market at an interest rate of 4% (point X); if the interest rate rises to 12%, the quantity of loanable funds supplied will rise to $45 billion (point Y).

The Equilibrium Interest Rate The equilibrium interest rate is the interest rate at which the quantity of loanable funds supplied equals the quantity of loanable funds demanded. As you can see in Figure 10-4, the equilibrium interest rate, i^*, and the total quantity of lending, Q^*, are determined by the intersection of the supply and demand curves, at point E. Here, the equilibrium interest rate is 8%, at which $30 billion is lent and borrowed. In this equilibrium, only investment spending projects that are profitable if the interest rate is 8% or higher are funded. Projects that are profitable only when the interest rate falls below 8% will not be funded. Correspondingly, only lenders who are willing to accept an interest rate of 8% or less will have their offers to lend funds accepted; lenders who demand an interest rate higher than 8% do not have their offers to lend accepted.

Figure 10-4 shows how the market for loanable funds matches up desired savings with desired investment spending: in equilibrium, the quantity of funds that savers want to lend is equal to the quantity of funds that firms want to borrow (point E). The figure also shows that this match-up is efficient, in two senses. First, the right investments get made: the investment spending projects that are actually financed have higher payoffs (in terms of present value) than those that do not get financed. Second, the right people do the saving and lending: the savers who actually lend funds are willing to lend for lower interest rates than those who do not.

FIGURE 10-4 Equilibrium in the Domestic Loanable Funds Market

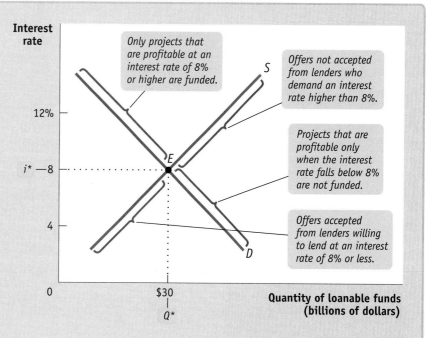

At the equilibrium interest rate, the quantity of loanable funds supplied equals the quantity of loanable funds demanded. Here, the equilibrium interest rate is 8%, with $30 billion of funds lent and borrowed. Lenders who demand an interest rate of 8% or lower have their offers of loans accepted; those who demand a higher interest rate do not. Projects that are profitable at an interest rate of 8% or higher are funded; those that are profitable only when the interest rate falls below 8% are not.

Only projects that are profitable at an interest rate of 8% or higher are funded.

Offers not accepted from lenders who demand an interest rate higher than 8%.

Projects that are profitable only when the interest rate falls below 8% are not funded.

Offers accepted from lenders willing to lend at an interest rate of 8% or less.

The insight that the loanable funds market leads to an efficient use of savings, although drawn from a highly simplified model, has important implications for real life. As we'll see shortly, it is the reason that a well-functioning financial system increases an economy's long-run economic growth rate.

Before we get to that, let's look at how the market for loanable funds responds to shifts of demand and supply. As in the standard model of supply and demand, where the equilibrium price changes in response to shifts of the demand or supply curves, here the equilibrium interest rate changes when there are shifts of the demand curve for loanable funds, the supply curve for loanable funds, or both.

Shifts of the Domestic Demand for Loanable Funds

Let's start by looking at the causes and effects of changes in demand.

The factors that can cause the demand curve for loanable funds to shift include the following:

1. *Changes in perceived business opportunities.* A change in beliefs about the payoff of investment spending can increase or reduce the amount of desired investment spending at any given interest rate. For example, during the 1990s there was great excitement over the business possibilities created by the Internet, which had just begun to be widely used. As a result, businesses rushed to buy computer equipment, put fibre optic cables in the ground, and so on. This shifted the demand for loanable funds to the right. By 2001, the failure of many dot-com businesses had led to disillusionment with technology-related investment; this shifted the demand for loanable funds back to the left.

2. *Changes in government policies that affect investment.* Government policies toward investment can affect business and household incentives to undertake investment. One such policy is a tax credit for investment. A tax credit is a subsidy in the form of lower taxes for those undertaking the targeted type of investment. This policy would promote investment as investment becomes more attractive (less expensive to undertake) for decision-makers. As a result, more investment projects will be undertaken at any given level of the interest rate. So, holding all else constant, the provision of an investment tax credit shifts the demand for loanable funds to the right.

Figure 10-5 shows the effects of an increase in the demand for loanable funds. S is the supply of loanable funds, and D_1 is the initial demand curve. The initial equilibrium interest rate is i_1. An increase in the demand for loanable funds means that the quantity of funds demanded rises at any given interest rate, so the demand curve shifts rightward to D_2. As a result, the equilibrium interest rate rises to i_2.

Shifts of the Domestic Supply of Loanable Funds

Like the demand for loanable funds, the supply of loanable funds can shift. Among the factors that can cause the supply of loanable funds to shift are the following:

1. *Changes in private savings behaviour.* A number of factors can cause the level of private savings to change at any given interest rate. For example, rising home prices in Canada in the past decade made many homeowners feel richer, making them willing to spend more and save less. This had the effect of shifting the supply curve of loanable funds to the left.

2. *Changes in government budget balance.* Recall that national savings come from two sources: the private sector and governments. When the government runs a budget surplus, public savings are positive. These savings from the government can be used to finance investment spending. Similarly, when the government runs a budget deficit, public savings are negative and there will be a reduction in national savings. Thus, changes in the government budget balance can shift the supply of loanable funds. For example, the federal

FIGURE **10-5** An Increase in the Domestic Demand for Loanable Funds

If the quantity of funds demanded by borrowers rises at any given interest rate, the demand for loanable funds shifts rightward from D_1 to D_2. As a result, the equilibrium interest rate rises from i_1 to i_2.

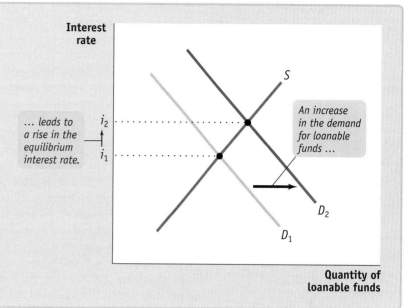

budgetary balance went from a surplus of $15.4 billion in 2007 to a deficit of $33 billion in 2009. This change in budget balance means that the federal government went from being a net saver that provided loanable funds to the market to being a net borrower. Holding all else constant, this change in budget balance will lower national savings and reduce the amount of loanable funds available. As a result, the supply of loanable funds shifts to the left.

Figure 10-6 shows the effects of a decrease in the supply of loanable funds. D is the demand for loanable funds, and S_1 is the initial supply curve. The initial equilibrium interest rate is i_1. A decrease in the supply of loanable funds means that the quantity of funds supplied falls at any given interest rate, so the supply curve shifts leftward to S_2. As a result, the equilibrium interest rate rises to i_2.

FIGURE **10-6** A Decrease in the Domestic Supply of Loanable Funds

If the quantity of funds supplied by lenders falls at any given interest rate, the supply of loanable funds shifts leftward from S_1 to S_2. As a result, the equilibrium interest rate rises from i_1 to i_2.

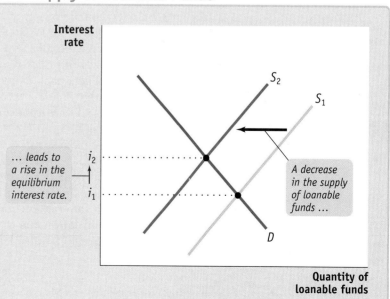

Crowding out occurs when a government budget deficit drives up the interest rate and leads to reduced investment spending.

The fact that a reduction in the supply of loanable funds leads, other things equal, to a rise in the interest rate has one especially important implication: it tells us that increasing or persistent government budget deficits are cause for concern because an increase in the government's deficit shifts the supply curve of loanable funds to the left, which leads to a higher interest rate. If the interest rate rises, businesses and households will cut back on their investment spending. So, other things equal, a rise in the government budget deficit tends to reduce overall investment spending. Economists call the negative effect of government budget deficits on investment spending **crowding out.** It is a key reason for worry about increasing or persistent budget deficits, which explains why a government might put balancing the budget as one of its top priorities.[2]

Inflation and Interest Rates Anything that shifts either the supply of loanable funds curve or the demand for loanable funds curve changes the interest rate. Historically, major changes in interest rates have been driven by many factors, including changes in government policy and technological innovations that created new investment opportunities. However, arguably the most important factor affecting interest rates over time—the reason, for example, that interest rates today are much lower than they were in the late 1970s and early 1980s—is changing expectations about future inflation, which shift both the supply and the demand for loanable funds.

To understand the effect of expected future inflation on interest rates, recall our discussion in Chapter 8 of the way inflation creates winners and losers—for example, the way that higher than expected Canadian inflation in the 1970s and 1980s reduced the real value of homeowners' mortgages, which was good for the homeowners but bad for the banks. In Chapter 8 we learned that economists summarize the effect of inflation on borrowers and lenders by distinguishing between the *nominal interest rate* and the *real interest rate*, where the difference is:

$$\text{Real interest rate} = \text{Nominal interest rate} - \text{Inflation rate}$$

The true cost of borrowing is the real interest rate, not the nominal interest rate. To see why, suppose a firm borrows $10 000 for one year at a 10% nominal interest rate. At the end of the year, it must repay $11 000—the amount borrowed plus the interest. But suppose that over the course of the year the average level of prices increases by 10%, so that the real interest rate is zero. Then the $11 000 repayment has the same purchasing power as the original $10 000 loan. In real terms, the borrower has received a zero-interest loan.

Similarly, the true payoff to lending is the real interest rate, not the nominal rate. Suppose that a bank makes a $10 000 loan for one year at a 10% nominal interest rate. At the end of the year, the bank receives an $11 000 repayment. But if the average level of prices rises by 10% per year, the purchasing power of the money the bank gets back is no more than that of the money it lent out. In real terms, the bank has made a zero-interest loan.

Now we can add an important detail to our analysis of the loanable funds market. Figures 10-5 and 10-6 are drawn with the vertical axis measuring the *nominal interest rate for a given expected future inflation rate*. Why do we use the nominal interest rate rather than the real interest rate? Because in the real world neither borrowers nor lenders know what the future inflation rate will be when they make a deal. Actual loan contracts therefore specify a nominal interest rate rather than a real interest rate. Because we are holding the expected future inflation rate fixed in Figures 10-5 and 10-6, however, changes in the nominal interest rate also lead to changes in the real interest rate.

---

[2]The present discussion of the loanable funds market is applied to a closed economy. The role of net foreign investment in an open economy within the market for loanable funds will be discussed in Chapter 19.

The expectations of borrowers and lenders about future inflation rates are normally based on recent experience. In the late 1970s, after a decade of high inflation, borrowers and lenders expected future inflation to be high. By the late 1990s, after a decade of fairly low inflation, borrowers and lenders expected future inflation to be low. And these changing expectations about future inflation had a strong effect on the nominal interest rate, largely explaining why nominal interest rates were much lower in the early years of the twenty-first century than they were in the early 1980s.

Let's look at how changes in the expected future rate of inflation are reflected in the loanable funds model.

In Figure 10-7, the curves S_0 and D_0 show the supply and demand for loanable funds given that the expected future rate of inflation is 0%. In that case, equilibrium is at E_0 and the equilibrium nominal interest rate is 4%. Because expected future inflation is 0%, the equilibrium expected real interest rate over the life of the loan is also 4%.

Now suppose that the expected future inflation rate rises to 10%. The demand curve for loanable funds shifts upward to D_{10}: borrowers are now willing to borrow as much at a nominal interest rate of 14% as they were previously willing to borrow at 4%. That's because with a 10% inflation rate, a 14% nominal interest rate corresponds to a 4% real interest rate. Similarly, the supply curve of loanable funds shifts upward to S_{10}: lenders require a nominal interest rate of 14% to persuade them to lend as much as they would previously have lent at 4%. The new equilibrium is at E_{10}: the result of an expected future inflation rate of 10% is that the equilibrium nominal interest rate rises from 4% to 14%.

This situation can be summarized as a general principle, known as the **Fisher effect** (after the American economist Irving Fisher, who proposed it in 1930): *In the long run, the expected real interest rate is unaffected by changes in expected future inflation.* According to the Fisher effect, an increase in expected future inflation drives up the nominal interest rate, where each additional percentage point of expected future inflation drives up the nominal interest rate by 1 percentage point. The central point is that both lenders and borrowers base their decisions on the expected real interest rate. As a result, a change in

> According to the **Fisher effect,** an increase in expected future inflation drives up the nominal interest rate, leaving the expected real interest rate unchanged.

FIGURE **10-7** The Fisher Effect

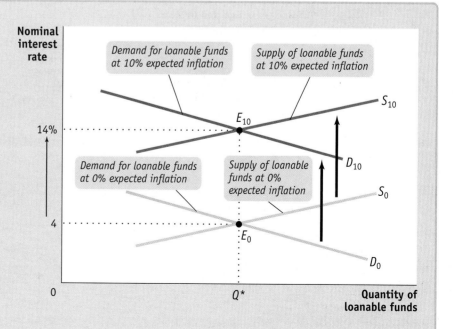

D_0 and S_0 are the demand and supply curves for loanable funds when the expected future inflation rate is 0%. At an expected inflation rate of 0%, the equilibrium nominal interest rate is 4%. An increase in expected future inflation pushes both the demand and supply curves upward by 1 percentage point for every percentage point increase in expected future inflation. D_{10} and S_{10} are the demand and supply curves for loanable funds when the expected future inflation rate is 10%. The 10 percentage point increase in expected future inflation raises the equilibrium nominal interest rate to 14%. The expected real interest rate remains at 4%, and the equilibrium quantity of loanable funds also remains unchanged.

the expected rate of inflation does not affect the equilibrium quantity of loanable funds or the expected real interest rate; all it affects is the equilibrium nominal interest rate.

ECONOMICS ► IN ACTION

FIFTY YEARS OF CANADIAN INTEREST RATES

There have been some large movements in Canada's interest rates over the past half-century. These movements clearly show how changes both in expected future inflation and in the expected return on investment spending move interest rates in the longer term.

Figure 10-8a illustrates the first effect. It shows the average interest rate on bonds issued by the Government of Canada—specifically, bonds for which the government promises to repay the full amount in the longer term (5–10 years later)—from 1960 to 2012, along with the rate of consumer price inflation over the same period. As you can see, the big story about interest rates is the way they soared in the 1970s, before coming back down in the 1980s. It's not hard to see why that happened: inflation shot up during the 1970s, leading to widespread expectations that high inflation would continue. And as we've seen, expected inflation raises the equilibrium (nominal) interest rate. As inflation came down in the 1980s, so did expectations of future inflation, and this brought interest rates down as well.

Figure 10-8b illustrates the second effect: changes in the expected return on investment spending and interest rates, with a "close-up" of interest rates from 2005 to 2012. Notice the sharp drop in interest rate in mid-2007. We know from other evidence that expected inflation didn't change much over those years as the Bank of Canada has an explicitly stated inflation target of 2%. What happened, instead, was a change in the attitudes of businesses (and households) toward investment. In 2007, it was becoming increasingly evident that the housing bubble in the U.S. was about to burst. The economies of Canada and America are closely related, so of course a slowdown in the American economy would cause our

FIGURE **10-8** Changes in Canada's Interest Rates, 1960–2012

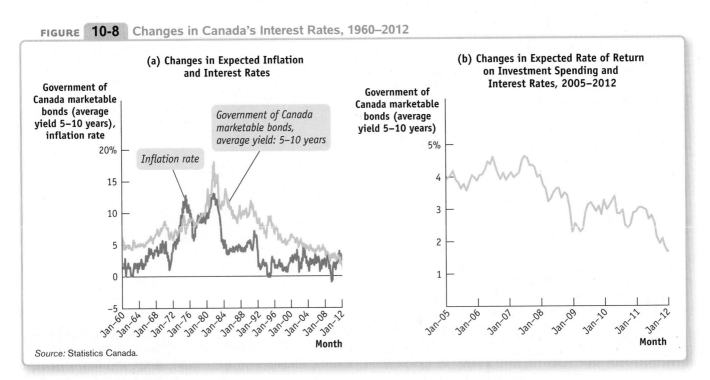

(a) Changes in Expected Inflation and Interest Rates

Government of Canada marketable bonds (average yield 5–10 years), inflation rate

Government of Canada marketable bonds, average yield: 5–10 years

Inflation rate

(b) Changes in Expected Rate of Return on Investment Spending and Interest Rates, 2005–2012

Government of Canada marketable bonds (average yield 5–10 years)

Source: Statistics Canada.

economy to slow down as well. As a result, Canadian businesses became more cautious about investing. They reasoned that if an economic slowdown did occur, the return on investment would be less attractive. When businesses became more pessimistic about the future economic outlook, there was a leftward shift in the demand for loanable funds and a fall in the interest rate.

Throughout this whole process, total savings was equal to total investment spending, and the rise and fall of the interest rate played a key role in matching lenders with borrowers.

CHECK YOUR UNDERSTANDING   10-1

1. Use a diagram of the loanable funds market to illustrate the effect of the following events on the equilibrium interest rate and investment spending.
   a. The government reduces a subsidy to investment.
   b. Retired people generally save less than working people at any interest rate. The proportion of retired people in the population goes up.

2. Explain what is wrong with the following statement: "Savings and investment spending may not be equal in the economy as a whole because when the interest rate rises, households will want to save more money than businesses will want to invest."

3. Suppose that expected inflation rises from 3% to 6%.
   a. How will the real interest rate be affected by this change?
   b. How will the nominal interest rate be affected by this change?
   c. What will happen to the equilibrium quantity of loanable funds?

Solutions appear at back of book.

The Financial System

A well-functioning financial system that brought together the funds of investors and the ideas of brilliant young people made the rise of RIM and Facebook possible. But to think that this is an exclusively modern phenomenon would be misguided. Financial markets raised the funds that were used to develop colonial markets in India, to build canals across Europe, and to finance the Napoleonic wars in the eighteenth and early nineteenth centuries. Capital inflows financed the early economic development of Canada, funding investment spending in mining, railroads, and canals. In fact, many of the principal features of financial markets and assets have been well understood in Europe and North America since the eighteenth century. These features are no less relevant today. So let's begin by understanding exactly what is traded in financial markets.

Financial markets are where households invest their current savings and their accumulated savings, or **wealth,** by purchasing *financial assets*. A **financial asset** is a paper claim that entitles the buyer to future income from the seller. For example, when a saver lends funds to a company, the loan is a financial asset sold by the company that entitles the lender (the buyer of the financial asset) to future income from the company. A household can also invest its current savings or wealth by purchasing a **physical asset,** a tangible object that can be used to generate future income such as a pre-existing house or pre-existing piece of equipment. It gives the owner the right to dispose of the object as he or she wishes (for example, rent it or sell it).

Recall that the purchase of a financial or physical asset is typically called investing. So if you purchase a pre-existing piece of equipment—say, a used airliner—you

A household's **wealth** is the value of its accumulated savings.

A **financial asset** is a paper claim that entitles the buyer to future income from the seller.

A **physical asset** is a tangible object that can be used to generate future income.

A **liability** is a requirement to pay income in the future.

Transaction costs are the expenses of negotiating and executing a deal.

are investing in a physical asset. In contrast, if you spend funds that *add* to the stock of physical capital in the economy—say, purchasing a newly manufactured airplane[3]—you are engaging in investment spending. (See the Pitfalls on financial investment versus physical investment that appears earlier in the chapter.)

If you get a loan from your local bank—say, to buy a new car—you and the bank are creating a financial asset: your loan. A *loan* is one important kind of financial asset in the real world, one that is owned by the lender—in this case, your local bank. In creating that loan, you and the bank are also creating a **liability,** a requirement to pay income in the future. So although your loan is a financial asset from the bank's point of view, it is a liability from your point of view: a requirement that you repay the loan, including any interest. In addition to loans, there are three other important kinds of financial assets: stocks, bonds, and *bank deposits*. Because a financial asset is a claim to future income that someone has to pay, it is also someone else's liability. We'll explain in detail shortly who bears the liability for each type of financial asset. For the time being, you just need to know that a financial asset is an asset to whoever owns it—the buyer who holds the paper claim. It is a liability to whoever initially sold or issued it.

These four types of financial assets—loans, stocks, bonds, and bank deposits—exist because the economy has developed a set of specialized markets, like the stock market and the bond market, and specialized institutions, like banks, that facilitate the flow of funds from lenders to borrowers. In Chapter 7, in the context of the circular-flow diagram, we defined the financial markets and institutions that make up the financial system. A well-functioning financial system is a critical ingredient in achieving long-run growth because it encourages greater savings and investment spending. It also ensures that savings and investment spending are undertaken efficiently. To understand how this occurs, we first need to know what tasks the financial system needs to accomplish. Then we can see how the job gets done.

Three Tasks of a Financial System

Our earlier analysis of the loanable funds market ignored three important problems faced by borrowers and lenders: *transaction costs, risk,* and the desire for *liquidity.* The three tasks of a financial system are to reduce these problems in a cost-effective way. Doing so enhances the efficiency of financial markets: it makes it more likely that lenders and borrowers will make mutually beneficial trades—trades that make society as a whole richer. We'll turn now to examining how financial assets are designed and how institutions are developed to cope with these problems.

Task 1: Reducing Transaction Costs **Transaction costs** are the expenses of actually putting together and executing a deal. For example, arranging a loan requires spending time and money negotiating the terms of the deal, verifying the borrower's ability to pay, drawing up and executing legal documents, and so on. Suppose a large business decided that it wanted to raise $1 billion for investment spending. No individual would be willing to lend that much. And negotiating individual loans from thousands of different people, each willing to lend a modest amount, would impose very large total costs because each individual transaction would incur a cost. Total costs would be so large that the entire deal would probably be unprofitable for the business.

Fortunately, that's not necessary: when large businesses want to borrow money, they either go to a bank or sell bonds in the bond market. Obtaining a loan from a bank avoids large transaction costs because it involves only a single

---

[3]Spending on modifications, repairs, and maintenance to alter the usefulness and/or extend the life of a physical asset adds to the gross stock of physical capital.

borrower and a single lender. We'll explain more about how bonds work in the next section. For now, it is enough to know that the principal reason there is a bond market is that it allows companies to borrow large sums of money without incurring large transaction costs.

Task 2: Reducing Risk A second problem that real-world borrowers and lenders face is **financial risk,** uncertainty about future outcomes that involve financial losses or gains. Financial risk, or simply risk, is a problem because the future is uncertain, containing the potential for losses as well as gains. For example, owning and driving a car entails the financial risk of a costly accident. Most people view potential losses and gains in an *asymmetrical* way: most people experience the loss in welfare from losing a given amount of money more intensely than they experience the increase in welfare from gaining the same amount of money. A person who is more sensitive to a loss than to a gain of an equal dollar amount is called *risk-averse.* Most people are risk-averse, although to differing degrees. For example, people who are wealthy are typically less risk-averse than those who are not so well off.

A well-functioning financial system helps people reduce their exposure to risk, which risk-averse people would like to do. Suppose the owner of a business expects to make a greater profit if she buys additional capital equipment, but she isn't completely sure that this will indeed happen. She could pay for the equipment by using her savings or selling her house. But if the profit is significantly less than expected, she will have lost her savings, or her house, or both. That is, she would be exposing herself to a lot of risk due to uncertainty about how well or poorly the business performs. (This is why business owners, who typically have a significant portion of their own personal wealth tied up in their businesses, are usually people who are more tolerant of risk than the average person.)

So, being risk-averse, this business owner wants to share the risk of purchasing new capital equipment with someone, even if that requires sharing some of the profit if all goes well. How can she do this? By selling shares of her company to other people and using the money she receives from selling shares, rather than money from the sale of her other assets, to finance the equipment purchase. By selling shares in her company, she reduces her personal losses if the profit is less than expected: she won't have lost her other assets. But if things go well, the shareholders earn a share of the profit as a return on their investment.

By selling a share of her business, the owner has achieved *diversification:* she has been able to invest in several things in a way that lowers her total risk. She has maintained her investment in her bank account, a financial asset; in ownership of her house, a physical asset; and in ownership of the unsold portion of her business, a financial asset. These investments are likely to carry some risk of their own; for example, her bank may fail or her house may burn down (though in Canada in modern times it is likely that she is partly protected against these risks by insurance).

But even in the absence of insurance, she is better off having maintained investments in these different assets because their different risks are *unrelated, or independent, events.* This means, for example, that her house is no more likely to burn down if her business does poorly and that her bank is no more likely to fail if her house burns down. To put it another way, if one asset performs poorly, it is very likely that her other assets will be unaffected and, as a result, her total risk of loss has been reduced. But if she had invested all her wealth in her business, she would have faced the prospect of losing everything if the business had performed poorly. By engaging in **diversification**—investing in several assets with unrelated, or independent, risks—our business owner has lowered her total risk of loss.

The desire of individuals to reduce their total risk by engaging in diversification is why we have stocks and a stock market. In the next section on types of financial assets, we'll explain in more detail how certain features of the stock market increase the ability of individuals to manage and reduce risk.

Financial risk is uncertainty about future outcomes that involve financial losses or gains.

An individual can engage in **diversification** by investing in several different things where the possible losses are independent events, so that the risk of total loss is reduced.

Task 3: Providing Liquidity The third and final task of the financial system is to provide investors with *liquidity*, a concern that—like risk—arises because the future is uncertain. Suppose that, having made a loan, a lender suddenly finds himself in need of cash—say, to meet a medical emergency. Unfortunately, if that loan was made to a business that used it to buy new equipment, the business cannot repay the loan on short notice to satisfy the lender's need to recover his money. Knowing in advance that there is a danger of needing to get his money back before the term of the loan is up, our lender might be reluctant to lock up his money by lending it to a business.

An asset is **liquid** if it can be quickly converted into cash with relatively little loss of value, and **illiquid** if it cannot. As we'll see, stocks and bonds are a partial answer to the problem of liquidity. Banks provide an additional way for individuals to hold liquid assets and still finance illiquid investment spending projects.

To help lenders and borrowers make mutually beneficial deals, then, the economy needs ways to reduce transaction costs, to reduce and manage risk through diversification, and to provide liquidity. How does it achieve these tasks?

Types of Financial Assets

In the modern economy there are four main types of financial assets: *loans,* bonds, stocks, and *bank deposits*. In addition, financial innovation has allowed the creation of a wide range of *loan-backed securities*. Each serves a somewhat different purpose. We'll examine loans, bonds, stocks, and loan-backed securities now, reserving our discussion of bank deposits until the following section.

Loans A **loan** is a lending agreement between an individual lender and an individual borrower. Most people encounter loans in the form of a student loan or a bank loan to finance the purchase of a car or a house. And small businesses usually use bank loans to buy new equipment.

A loan is an asset to the lender, who expects or hopes to get repaid. It is a liability to the borrower, who is required or has promised to pay back what was lent to him or her, plus the negotiated amount of interest.

The good aspect of loans is that a given loan is usually tailored to the needs of the borrower. Before a small business can get a loan, it usually has to discuss its business plans, its profits, and so on with the lender. This results in a loan that meets the borrower's needs and ability to pay.

The bad aspect of loans is that making a loan to an individual person or a business typically involves a lot of transaction costs, such as the cost of negotiating the terms of the loan, investigating the borrower's credit history and ability to repay, and so on. To minimize these costs, large borrowers such as major corporations and governments often take a more streamlined approach: they sell (or issue) bonds.

Bonds As we learned in Chapter 7, a bond is an IOU issued by the borrower. Normally, the seller of the bond promises to pay a fixed sum of interest each year and to repay the principal—the value stated on the face of the bond—to the owner of the bond on a particular date. So a bond is a financial asset from its owner's point of view and a liability from its issuer's point of view. A bond issuer sells a number of bonds with a given interest rate and maturity date to whoever is willing to buy them, a process that avoids costly negotiation of the terms of a loan with many individual lenders.

Bond purchasers can acquire information free of charge on the quality of the bond issuer, such as the bond issuer's credit history, from bond-rating agencies rather than having to incur the expense of investigating it themselves. A particular concern for investors is the possibility of **default**, the risk that the bond issuer will fail to make payments as specified by the bond contract. Once a bond's risk of

---

An asset is **liquid** if it can be quickly converted into cash with relatively little loss of value.

An asset is **illiquid** if it cannot be quickly converted into cash with relatively little loss of value.

A **loan** is a lending agreement between an individual lender and an individual borrower.

A **default** occurs when a borrower fails to make payments as specified by the loan or bond contract.

default has been rated, it can be sold on the bond market as a more or less standardized product—a product with clearly defined terms and quality. In general, bonds with a higher default risk must pay a higher interest rate to attract investors.

Another important advantage of bonds is that they are easy to resell. This provides liquidity to bond purchasers. Indeed, a bond will often pass through many hands before it finally comes due. Loans, in contrast, are much more difficult to resell because, unlike bonds, they are not standardized: they differ in size, quality, terms, and so on. This makes them a lot less liquid than bonds.

Loan-Backed Securities **Loan-backed securities,** assets created by pooling individual loans and selling shares in that pool (a process called *securitization*), have become extremely popular over the past two decades. While mortgage-backed securities, in which thousands of individual home mortgages are pooled and shares sold to investors, are the best-known example, securitization has also been widely applied to student loans, credit card loans, and auto loans. These loan-backed securities are traded on financial markets like bonds; they are preferred by investors because they provide more diversification and liquidity than individual loans. However, with so many loans packaged together, it can be difficult to assess the true quality of the asset. That difficulty came to haunt investors during the financial crisis of 2008, when the bursting of the U.S. housing bubble led to widespread defaults on American mortgages and large losses for holders of supposedly "safe" U.S. mortgage-backed securities, pain that spread throughout the financial system worldwide.

> A **loan-backed security** is an asset created by pooling individual loans and selling shares in that pool.

Stocks As we learned in Chapter 7, a stock is a share in the ownership of a company. A share of stock is a financial asset from its owner's point of view and a liability from the issuing company's point of view. Not all companies sell shares of their stock; "privately held" companies are owned by an individual or a few partners, who get to keep all of the company's profit. Most large companies, however, do sell stock. For example, Tim Hortons has about 154 million shares outstanding; if you buy one of those shares, you are entitled to one-154-millionth of the company's profit, as well as one of 154 million votes on company decisions.

Why does Tim Hortons, a profitable company, allow you to buy a share of its ownership? Why didn't the founders (and their families) of Tim Hortons keep complete ownership for themselves and just sell bonds to meet their investment spending needs? The reason, as we have just learned, is risk: few individuals are risk-tolerant enough to face the risk involved in being the sole owner of a large company.

Reducing the risk that business owners face, however, is not the only way in which the existence of stocks improves society's welfare: it also improves the welfare of investors who buy stocks. Shareowners are able to enjoy the higher returns over time that stocks generally offer in comparison to bonds. From 1900 to 2011 in Canada, after adjusting for inflation, stocks have yielded about 5.7% and bonds have yielded only 2.2%. But as investment companies warn you, "past performance is no guarantee of future performance." And there is a downside: owning the stock of a given company is riskier than owning a bond issued by the same company. Why? Loosely speaking, a bond is a promise, while a stock is a hope: by law, a company must pay what it owes its lenders before it distributes any profit to its shareholders. And if the company should fail (that is, be unable to pay its interest obligations and declare bankruptcy), its physical and financial assets go to its bondholders—its lenders—while its shareholders generally receive nothing. So although a stock generally provides a higher return to an investor than a bond, it also carries higher risk.

But the financial system has devised ways to help investors as well as business owners simultaneously manage risk and enjoy somewhat higher returns. It does that through the services of institutions known as *financial intermediaries.*

A **financial intermediary** is an institution that transforms the funds it gathers from many individuals into financial assets.

A **mutual fund** is a financial intermediary that creates a portfolio of financial assets or other physical assets, such as real estate, and then resells shares of this portfolio to individual investors.

Financial Intermediaries

A **financial intermediary** is an institution that transforms funds gathered from many individuals into financial assets. The most important types of financial intermediaries are *mutual funds, pension funds, life insurance companies,* and *banks.* About 70% of the financial assets Canadians own are held through these intermediaries rather than directly.

Mutual Funds As we've explained, owning shares of a company entails accepting risk in return for a higher potential reward. But it should come as no surprise that stock investors can lower their total risk by engaging in diversification. By owning a *diversified portfolio* of stocks—a group of stocks in which risks are unrelated to, or offset, one another—rather than concentrating investment in the shares of a single company or a group of related companies, investors can reduce their risk. In addition, financial advisers, aware that most people are risk-averse, almost always advise their clients to diversify not only their stock portfolio but also their entire wealth by holding other assets in addition to stock—assets such as bonds, real estate, and cash. (And, for good measure, to have plenty of insurance in case of accidental losses!)

However, for individuals who don't have a large amount of money to invest—say $1 million or more—building a diversified stock portfolio can incur high transaction costs (particularly fees paid to stockbrokers) because they are buying a few shares of a lot of companies. Fortunately for such investors, mutual funds help solve the problem of achieving diversification without high transaction costs. A **mutual fund** is a financial intermediary that creates a stock portfolio by buying and holding shares in companies and then selling shares of the stock portfolio to individual investors. By buying these shares, investors with a relatively small amount of money to invest can indirectly hold a diversified portfolio, achieving a better return for any given level of risk than they could otherwise achieve. Table 10-1 shows an example of a diversified mutual fund, the Investors Dividend Fund. It shows the percentage of investors' money invested in the stocks of the largest companies in the mutual fund's portfolio.

Many mutual funds also perform market research on the companies they invest in. This is important because there are more than a thousand stock-issuing Canadian companies (not to mention foreign companies), each differing in terms of its likely profitability, dividend payments, and so on. It would be extremely time-consuming and costly for an individual investor to do adequate research on even a small number of companies. Mutual funds save transaction costs by doing this research for their customers.

The mutual fund industry represents a huge portion of the modern Canadian economy, not just of the Canadian financial system. In total, Canadian mutual funds had assets of more than $800 billion in July 2012. In July 2012, the largest mutual fund company was IGM Financial Inc., the owners of Investors Group, Mackenzie Financial Corporation, and Counsel Group of Funds. Combined, these firms managed more than $110 billion in funds.

We should mention, by the way, that mutual funds charge fees for their services. These fees are quite small for mutual funds that simply hold a diversified portfolio of stocks, without trying to pick winners. But the fees charged by mutual funds that claim to have special expertise in investing your money can be quite high.

TABLE 10-1 Investors Dividend Fund Portfolio Shares, Top Ten Holdings (as of June 2012)

Company	Percent of mutual fund assets invested in a company
Royal Bank of Canada	9.0%
Bank of Nova Scotia	8.4
Bank of Montreal	5.9
TELUS Corp.	5.4
CI Financial Corp.	4.7
TransCanada Corp.	4.7
Power Financial	4.4
Husky Energy, Inc.	4.0
Manulife Financial Corporation	3.6
Sun Life Financial Inc.	3.4
Total for top ten holdings	53.5%

Sources: Morningstar.ca; Investors Group.

Pension Funds and Life Insurance Companies In addition to mutual funds, many Canadians have holdings in **pension funds,** non-profit institutions that collect the savings of their members and invest those funds in a wide variety of assets, providing their members with income when they retire. Although pension funds are subject to some special rules and receive special treatment for tax purposes, they function much like mutual funds. They invest in a diverse array of financial and other assets, allowing their members to achieve more cost-effective diversification and market research than they would be able to achieve individually. In late 2011, pension funds in Canada held a bit more than $1 trillion in assets.

Canadians also have substantial holdings, about $500 billion, in the policies of **life insurance companies,** which guarantee a payment to the policyholder's beneficiaries (typically, the family) when the policyholder dies.[4] By enabling policyholders to cushion their beneficiaries from financial hardship arising from their death, life insurance companies also improve welfare by reducing risk.

Banks Recall the problem of liquidity: other things equal, people want assets that can be readily converted into cash. Bonds and stocks are much more liquid than physical assets or loans, yet the transaction cost of selling bonds or stocks to meet a sudden expense can be large. Furthermore, for many small and moderate-size companies, the cost of issuing bonds and stocks is too large given the modest amount of money they seek to raise. A *bank* is an institution that helps resolve the conflict between lenders' needs for liquidity and the financing needs of borrowers who don't want to use the stock or bond markets.

A bank works by first accepting funds from *depositors:* when you put your money in a bank, you are essentially becoming a lender by lending the bank your money. In return, you receive credit for a **bank deposit**—a claim on the bank, which is obliged to give you your cash if and when you demand it. So a bank deposit is a financial asset owned by the depositor and a liability of the bank that holds it.

A bank, however, keeps only a fraction of its customers' deposits in the form of ready cash. Most of its deposits are lent out to businesses, buyers of new homes, and other borrowers. These loans come with a long-term commitment by the bank to the borrower: as long as the borrower makes his or her payments on time, the loan cannot be recalled by the bank and converted into cash. So a bank enables those who wish to borrow for long lengths of time to use the funds of those who wish to lend but simultaneously want to maintain the ability to get their cash back on demand. More formally, a **bank** is a financial intermediary that provides liquid financial assets in the form of deposits to lenders and uses their funds to finance the illiquid investment spending needs of borrowers.

In essence, a bank is engaging in a kind of mismatch: lending for long periods of time while subject to the condition that its depositors could demand their funds back at any time. How can it manage that?

The bank counts on the fact that, on average, only a small fraction of its depositors will want their cash at the same time. On any given day, some people will make withdrawals and others will make new deposits; these will roughly cancel each other out. So the bank needs to keep only a limited amount of cash on hand to satisfy its depositors. In addition, if a bank becomes financially incapable of paying its depositors, individual bank deposits are guaranteed to depositors up to $100 000 by the Canada Deposit Insurance Corporation, or CDIC, a federal agency. This reduces the risk to a depositor of holding a bank deposit, in turn reducing the incentive to withdraw funds if concerns about the financial state of the bank should arise. So, under normal conditions, banks need hold only a fraction of their depositors' cash.

A **pension fund** is a type of mutual fund that holds assets in order to provide retirement income to its members.

A **life insurance company** sells policies that guarantee a payment to a policyholder's beneficiaries when the policyholder dies.

A **bank deposit** is a claim on a bank that obliges the bank to give the depositor his or her cash when demanded.

A **bank** is a financial intermediary that provides liquid assets in the form of bank deposits to lenders and uses those funds to finance the illiquid investment spending needs of borrowers.

---

[4] As of the end of 2011, Canadians held almost $300 billion worth of regular life insurance policies. They also held another $200 billion worth of segregated funds invested with insurance companies. Segregated funds, as their name implies, are kept completely separate from the insurance company's other investment funds. Segregated funds are in essence a hybrid account type that combines features of a mutual fund with a life insurance policy.

By reconciling the needs of savers for liquid assets with the needs of borrowers for long-term financing, banks play a key economic role. As the following Economics in Action explains, the creation of a well-functioning banking system was a key turning point in South Korea's economic success.

ECONOMICS ▶ IN ACTION

BANKS AND THE SOUTH KOREAN MIRACLE

Seokyong Lee/Bloomberg via Getty Images

South Korea's experience with banks shows how important a good financial system is to economic growth.

South Korea is one of the great success stories of long-run economic growth. In the early 1960s, it was a very poor nation. Then it experienced spectacularly high rates of economic growth. South Korean banks had a lot to do with it.

In the early 1960s, South Korea's banking system was a mess. Interest rates on deposits were very low by government regulation at a time when the country was experiencing high inflation. So savers didn't want to save by putting money in a bank, fearing that much of their purchasing power would be eroded by rising prices. Instead, they engaged in current consumption by spending their money on goods and services or used their wealth to buy physical assets such as real estate and gold. Because savers refused to make bank deposits, businesses found it very hard to borrow money to finance investment spending.

In 1965 the South Korean government reformed the country's banks and increased interest rates to a level that was attractive to savers. Over the next five years the value of bank deposits increased sevenfold, and the national savings rate—the percentage of GDP going into national savings—more than doubled. The rejuvenated banking system made it possible for South Korean businesses to launch a great investment spending boom, a key element in the country's growth surge in the long term.

Many other factors besides banking were involved in South Korea's success, but the country's experience does show how important a good financial system is to long-run economic growth.

▼ Quick Review

- Households can invest their current savings or their **wealth** by purchasing either **financial assets** or **physical assets.** A financial asset is a seller's **liability.**

- A well-functioning financial system reduces **transaction costs,** reduces **financial risk** by enabling **diversification,** and provides **liquid** assets, which investors prefer to **illiquid** assets.

- The four main types of financial assets are **loans,** bonds, stocks, and **bank deposits.** A recent innovation is **loan-backed securities,** which are more liquid and more diversified than individual loans. Bonds with a higher **default** risk typically must pay a higher interest rate.

- The most important types of **financial intermediaries** are **mutual funds, pension funds, life insurance companies,** and **banks.**

- A bank accepts **bank deposits,** which obliges it to return depositors' cash on demand, and lends those funds to borrowers for long lengths of time.

CHECK YOUR UNDERSTANDING 10-2

1. Rank the following assets in terms of (i) level of transaction costs, (ii) level of risk, and (iii) level of liquidity.

   a. A bank deposit with a guaranteed interest rate

   b. A share of a highly diversified mutual fund, which can be quickly sold

   c. A share of the family business, which can be sold only if you find a buyer and all other family members agree to the sale

2. What relationship would you expect to find between the level of development of a country's financial system and its level of economic development? Explain in terms of the country's level of savings and level of investment spending.

Solutions appear at back of book.

Financial Fluctuations

We've learned that the financial system is an essential part of the economy; without stock markets, bond markets, and banks, long-run economic growth would be hard to achieve. Yet the news isn't entirely good: the financial system sometimes doesn't function well and instead is a source of instability in the short run. In fact, the financial consequences of a sharp fall in U.S. housing prices became a major problem for economic policy-makers starting in the summer of 2007. By the fall of 2008, it was clear that the U.S. economy was facing a severe slump as it adjusted to consequences of greatly reduced home values. Canada's economy and those of the many other countries faced significant hardship as this adverse U.S. shock spread around the world. By the end of 2008, our economy experienced a recession owing to the drop in U.S. demand for Canadian exports and uncertainty in financial markets. And in 2012, the time of writing, the economy was only slowly recovering from a severe recession.

We could easily write a whole book on asset market fluctuations. In fact, many people have. Here, we briefly discuss the causes of asset price fluctuations.

The Demand for Stocks

Once a company issues shares of stock to investors, those shares can then be resold to other investors in the stock market. And these days, thanks to cable TV and the Internet, you can easily spend all day watching stock market fluctuations—the movement up and down of the prices of individual stocks as well as summary measures of stock prices like the S&P/TSX Composite Index and the Dow Jones Industrial Average. These fluctuations reflect changes in supply and demand by investors. But what causes the supply and demand for stocks to shift?

 FOR INQUIRING MINDS

WHAT FX THE TSX?

Financial news reports often lead with the day's stock market action, as measured by changes in the S&P/TSX Composite Index, the Dow Jones Industrial Average, the S&P 500, and the NASDAQ. What are these numbers, and what do they tell us?

All four items are stock market indexes. Like the consumer price index, they are numbers constructed as a summary of average prices—in this case, prices of stocks. The S&P/TSX is the headline index and principal broad market measure for Canadian equity (stock) markets. It contains about 95% of the Canadian-based firms listed on the Toronto Stock Exchange (TSX). The Dow, created by the financial analysis company Dow Jones, is an index of the prices of stock in 30 leading U.S.-based companies, such as Microsoft, Walmart, and General Electric. The S&P 500 is an index of 500 American companies, created by Standard and Poor's, another financial company. The NASDAQ is compiled by the National Association of Securities Dealers, which trades the stocks of smaller new companies from North America and around the world, like the satellite radio company SiriusXM Radio,

the computer manufacturer Dell, or the British company Virgin Media.

Because these indexes contain different groups of stocks, they track somewhat different things. The TSX is home to many firms from a wide variety of sectors of the economy, but in terms of market value, almost one half of the index comprises companies operating in the resource sector. The Dow, because it contains only 30 of the largest companies, tends to reflect the "old economy," traditional business powerhouses like Exxon Mobil. The NASDAQ is heavily influenced by technology stocks. The S&P 500, a broad measure, is in between.

Why are these indexes important? Because the movement in an index gives investors a quick, snapshot view of how stocks from certain sectors of the economy are doing. As we'll explain shortly, the price of a stock at a given point in time embodies investors' expectations about the future prospects of the underlying company. By implication, an index composed of stocks drawn from companies in a particular sector embodies investors' expectations of the future prospects of that sector of the economy. So a day on which the NASDAQ

The S&P/TSX Composite Index, the Dow Jones Industrial Average, the S&P 500, and the NASDAQ can all indicate how the stock market is doing. So can the expressions on the faces of the stockbrokers, such as this one on the floor of the Toronto Stock Exchange.

moves up but the S&P/TSX moves down implies that, on that day, prospects appear brighter for the high-tech sector than for the resource sector. The movement in the indexes reflects the fact that investors are acting on their beliefs by selling stocks in the S&P/TSX and buying stocks in the NASDAQ.

Remember that stocks are financial assets: they are shares in the ownership of a company. Unlike a good or service, whose value to its owner comes from its consumption, the value of an asset comes from its expected ability to generate higher future consumption of goods or services. A financial asset allows higher future consumption in two ways. First, many financial assets provide regular income to their owners in the form of interest payments or dividends. But many companies don't pay dividends; instead, they retain their earnings to finance future investment spending. Investors purchase non-dividend-paying stocks in the belief that they will earn income from selling the stock in the future at a profit, the second way of generating higher future income. Even in the cases of a bond or a dividend-paying stock, investors will not want to purchase an asset that they believe will sell for less in the future than today because such an asset will reduce their wealth when they sell it.

So the value of a financial asset today depends on investors' beliefs about the future value or price of the asset. If investors believe that it will be worth more in the future, they will demand more of the asset today at any given price; consequently, today's equilibrium price of the asset will rise. Conversely, if investors believe the asset will be worth less in the future, they will demand less today at any given price; consequently, today's equilibrium price of the asset will fall. Today's stock prices will change according to changes in investors' expectations about future stock prices.

Suppose an event occurs that leads to a rise in the expected future price of a company's shares—say, for example, Bombardier announces that it forecasts higher than expected probability due to a new contract for light rail vehicles in Europe. Demand for Bombardier shares will increase. At the same time, existing shareholders will be less willing to supply their shares to the market at any given price, leading to a decrease in the supply of Bombardier shares. And as we know, an increase in demand or a decrease in supply (or both) leads to a rise in price. Alternatively, suppose that an event occurs that leads to a fall in the expected future price of a company's shares—say, Air Canada announces that it expects lower profitability because a rise in fuel prices has depressed both profit margins and the demand for flights. Demand for Air Canada shares will decrease. At the same time, supply will increase because existing shareholders will be more willing to supply their Air Canada shares to the market. Both changes lead to a fall in the stock price.

So stock prices are determined by the supply and demand for shares—which, in turn, depend on investors' expectations about the future stock price.

Stock prices are also affected by changes in the attractiveness of substitute assets, like bonds. As we learned early on, the demand for a particular good decreases when purchasing a substitute good becomes more attractive—say, due to a fall in its price. The same lesson holds true for stocks: when purchasing bonds becomes more attractive due to a rise in interest rates, stock prices will fall. And when purchasing bonds becomes less attractive due to a fall in interest rates, stock prices will rise.

The Demand for Other Assets

Everything we've just said about stocks applies to other assets as well, including physical assets. Consider the demand for commercial real estate—office buildings, shopping malls, and other structures that provide space for business activities. An investor who buys an office building does so for two reasons. First, because space in the building can be rented out, the owner of the building receives income in the form of rents. Second, the investor may expect the building to rise in value, meaning that it can be sold at a higher price at some future date. As in the case of stocks, the demand for commercial real estate also depends on the attractiveness of substitute assets, especially bonds. When interest rates rise, the demand for commercial real estate decreases; when interest rates fall, the demand for commercial real estate increases.

Most Canadians don't own commercial real estate. A large fraction of the population does not own any stock, not even indirectly through mutual funds, and for most of those people who do own stock, ownership is well under $50 000. However, at the end of 2011 about 70% of Canadian households owned another kind of asset: their own homes. What determines housing prices?

You might wonder whether home prices can be analyzed the same way we analyze stock prices or the price of commercial real estate. After all, stocks pay dividends, commercial real estate yields rents, but when a family lives in its own home, no money changes hands.

In economic terms, however, that doesn't matter very much. To a large extent, the benefit of owning your own home is the fact that you don't have to pay rent to someone else—or, to put it differently, it's as if you were paying rent to yourself. In fact, the Canadian government includes "imputed rent"—an estimate of the amount that homeowners, in effect, pay to themselves—in its estimates of GDP.

The amount people are willing to pay for a house depends in part on the imputed rent they expect to receive from that house. The demand for housing, like the demand for other assets, also depends on what people expect to happen to future prices: they're willing to pay more for a house if they believe they can sell it at a higher price sometime in the future. Last but not least, the demand for houses depends on interest rates: a rise in the interest rate increases the cost of a mortgage and leads to a decrease in housing demand; a fall in the interest rate reduces the cost of a mortgage and causes an increase in housing demand.

All asset prices, then, are determined by a similar set of factors. But we haven't yet fully answered the question of what determines asset prices because we haven't explained what determines investors' *expectations* about future asset prices.

Asset Price Expectations

There are two principal competing views about how asset price expectations are determined. One view, which comes from traditional economic analysis, emphasizes the rational reasons why expectations *should* change. The other, widely held by market participants and also supported by some economists, emphasizes the irrationality of market participants.

The Efficient Markets Hypothesis
Suppose you were trying to assess what Air Canada's stock is really worth. To do this, you would look at the *fundamentals*, the underlying determinants of the company's future profits. These would include factors like the changing vacation habits of the Canadian public and the prospect that competition from other air carriers and travel websites, such as Expedia.ca, could shrink profit margins. You would also want to compare the earnings you could expect to receive from Air Canada with the likely returns on other financial assets, such as bonds.

According to one view of asset prices, the value you would come up with after a careful study of this kind would, in fact, turn out to be the price at which Air Canada stock is already selling in the market. Why? Because all publicly available information about Air Canada's fundamentals is already embodied in its stock price. Any difference between the market price and the value suggested by a careful analysis of the underlying fundamentals indicates a profit opportunity to smart investors, who then sell Air Canada stock if it looks overpriced and buy it if it looks underpriced. The **efficient markets hypothesis** is the general form of this view; it means that asset prices always embody all publicly available information. An implication of the efficient markets hypothesis is that at any point in time stock prices are fairly valued: they reflect all currently available information about fundamentals. So they are neither overpriced nor underpriced.

According to the **efficient markets hypothesis,** asset prices embody all publicly available information.

FOR INQUIRING MINDS

BEHAVIOURAL FINANCE

Individuals often make irrational—sometimes predictably irrational—choices that leave them worse off economically than would other, feasible alternatives. People also have a habit of repeating the same decision-making mistakes. This kind of behaviour is the subject of *behavioural economics*, which includes the rapidly growing subfield of *behavioural finance*, the study of how investors in financial markets often make predictably irrational choices.

Like most people, investors depart from rationality in systematic ways. In particular, they are prone to *overconfidence*, as in having a misguided faith that they are able to spot a winning stock; to *loss aversion*, being unwilling to sell an unprofitable asset and accept the loss; and to a *herd mentality*, buying an asset when its price has already been driven high and selling it when its price has already been driven low.

This irrational behaviour raises an important question: can investors who *are* rational make a lot of money at the expense of those investors who aren't—for example, by buying a company's stock if irrational fears make it cheap?

The answer to this question is sometimes yes and sometimes no. Some professional investors have made huge profits by betting against irrational moves in the market (buying when there is irrational selling and selling when there is irrational buying). For example, the billionaire hedge fund manager John Paulson made

$4 billion by betting against sub-prime mortgages during the U.S. housing bubble of 2007–2008 because he understood that financial assets containing sub-prime mortgages were being sold at inflated prices.

But sometimes even a rational investor cannot profit from market irrationality. For example, a money manager has to obey customers' orders to buy or sell even when those actions are irrational. Likewise, it can be much safer for professional money managers to follow the herd: If they do that and their investments go badly, they have the career-saving excuse that no one foresaw a problem. But if they've gone against the herd and their investments go south, they are likely to be fired for making poor choices. So rational investors can even exacerbate the irrational moves in financial markets.

Some observers of historical trends hypothesize that financial markets alter-

nate between periods of complacency and forgetfulness, which breed bubbles as investors irrationally believe that prices can only go up, followed by a crash, which in turn leads investors to avoid financial markets altogether and renders asset prices irrationally cheap. Clearly, the events of the past decade, with its huge U.S. housing bubble followed by extreme turmoil in financial markets worldwide, have given researchers in the area of behavioural finance a lot of material to work with.

Another implication of the efficient markets hypothesis is that the prices of stocks and other assets should change only in response to new information about the underlying fundamentals. Since new information is by definition unpredictable—if it were predictable, it wouldn't be new information—movements in asset prices are also unpredictable. As a result, the movement of, say, stock prices will follow a **random walk**—the general term for the movement over time of an unpredictable variable.

The efficient markets hypothesis plays an important role in understanding how financial markets work. Most investment professionals and many economists, however, regard it as an oversimplification. Investors, they claim, aren't that rational.

Irrational Markets? Many people who actually trade in the markets, such as individual investors and professional money managers, are skeptical of the efficient markets hypothesis. They believe that markets often behave irrationally and that a smart investor can engage in successful "market timing"—buying stocks when they are underpriced and selling them when they are overpriced.

Although economists are generally skeptical about claims that there are sure-fire ways to outsmart the market, many have also challenged the efficient markets hypothesis. It's important to understand, however, that finding particular examples

A **random walk** is the movement over time of an unpredictable variable.

where the market got it wrong does not disprove the efficient markets hypothesis. If the price of Air Canada stock plunges from $1.80 to $0.70 because of a sudden change in fuel prices and vacation habits, this doesn't mean that the market was inefficient in originally pricing the stock at $1.80. The fact that vacation habits were about to change wasn't publicly available information, so it wasn't embodied in the earlier stock price.

Serious challenges to the efficient markets hypothesis focus instead either on evidence of systematic misbehaviour of market prices or on evidence that individual investors don't behave in the way the theory suggests. For example, some economists believe they have found strong evidence that stock prices fluctuate more than can be explained by news about fundamentals. Others believe they have strong evidence

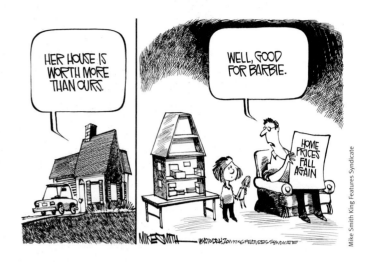

that individual investors behave in systematically irrational ways. For example, people seem to expect that a stock that has risen in the past will keep on rising, even though the efficient markets hypothesis tells us there is no reason to expect this. The same appears to be true of other assets, especially housing: the great U.S. housing bubble arose in large part because homebuyers assumed that home prices would continue rising in the future.

Asset Prices and Macroeconomics

How should macroeconomists and policy-makers deal with the fact that asset prices fluctuate a lot and that these fluctuations can have important economic effects? This question has become one of the major problems facing macroeconomic policy. On one side, policy-makers are reluctant to assume that the market is wrong—that asset prices are either too high or too low. In part, this reflects the efficient markets hypothesis, which says that any information that is publicly available is already accounted for in asset prices. More generally, it's hard to make the general case that government officials are better judges of appropriate prices than private investors who are putting their own money on the line.

On the other side, the past 15 years were marked by not one but two huge asset bubbles, each of which created major macroeconomic problems when it burst. In the late 1990s the prices of technology stocks, including but not limited to dot-com Internet firms, soared to hard-to-justify heights. When the bubble burst, these stocks lost, on average, two-thirds of their value in a short time, helping to cause the 2001 recession and a period of high unemployment in the U.S. A few years later there was a major bubble in U.S. housing prices. The collapse of this bubble in 2008 triggered a severe worldwide financial crisis followed by a deep recession.

These events have led to a fierce debate among economists over whether policy-makers should try to pop asset bubbles before they get too big. We'll describe that debate in Chapter 17.

ECONOMICS ▸ IN ACTION

A HOUSING BUBBLE IN VANCOUVER?

From 2000 to 2006, there was a huge increase in the price of houses in the United States. By the summer of 2006, home prices in a number of major U.S. metropolitan areas had more than doubled since January 2000. By 2004, as the rise in U.S. home prices accelerated, a number of economists (including the authors of this textbook) argued that this price increase was excessive; it was, they believed, a bubble, a rise in asset prices driven by unrealistic expectations about future prices. Ultimately, they were correct, and the bursting of this housing bubble triggered the financial crisis in the U.S. and pushed that nation into its worst recession since the Great Depression. At time of writing, in 2012, the U.S. is still recovering from effects of this housing bubble.

Some people now wonder whether a similar bubble, with the same potential for crisis, is building in Canada. Many would say yes, especially in Vancouver. Figure 10-9a shows the Teranet–National Bank of Canada Housing Price Index between January 2000 and August 2012 for Canada, Vancouver, and Toronto.[5] To make it easier to compare the percentage changes in home prices in different cities, this index was constructed to be equal to 100 in June 2005. As the figure shows, housing prices in Vancouver grew much more rapidly than the national average. From 2000 until 2012, national housing prices rose, on average, by 129%, whereas in Vancouver they rose by 152%. It is worth noting not only the speed at which Vancouver's home prices are rising, but also the heights that they are reaching. By 2012, homes cost far more in Vancouver than anywhere else in Canada. For example, according to the Royal Bank of Canada, in the second quarter of 2012, the average price of a detached bungalow in Vancouver was $846 800, about 132% higher than the national average. Similar trends were evident in other housing types such as standard two-storey houses and condominiums. Why are prices higher in Canada in general and in Vancouver in particular? Economists suggest several reasons. Lower interest rates have encouraged more Canadians to get mortgages. Also, Canada has recovered better from the 2008 recession than other developed countries, making it more financially and politically stable. Consequently, Canada is a safe country in which to invest.

That is why housing prices have risen across Canada. But why have they gone stratospheric in Vancouver? Vancouver is closer to major Asian cities than most other Canadian cities, making it an ideal residence for Asians who wish to immigrate to Canada. Plus, many Canadians hope to retire to this beautiful city with an ocean on one side and mountains on the other. But the ocean and mountains also reduce the amount of space available for building new homes, so the supply is limited.

One rule of thumb is that you should not pay more than 33% of your pre-tax income to make the monthly mortgage payments on your house (although, obviously, some households do pay more than that, by scrimping in other areas). Regrettably, this is rarely the case either in Canada or in Vancouver. Figure 10-9b shows the housing affordability index for a detached bungalow from the first quarter of 2008 to the second quarter of 2012 for Canada and Vancouver.[6] As Figure 10-9b shows, the national average of monthly pre-tax income spent on home ownership has fluctuated around 40%, which puts the cost of owning a detached bungalow above the rule-of-thumb cut-off for families at the median level of income. While the national average shows many Canadian families cannot afford to buy homes, the situation in Vancouver is even worse. At the time of writing, 2012, it definitely cost more to own a house in Vancouver. In fact, in the first few quarters of 2012, the affordability index was over 90%—meaning that it took more than 90% of a typical[7] household's income to own a house. This situation is definitely not sustainable, as incomes in Vancouver are not rising fast enough to keep up with the rise in home prices. Further, it is extremely unlikely that average incomes can or will catch up to average Vancouver home prices, and, as a result, there is a likelihood that Vancouver's housing prices will take a

---

[5]This national composite index consists of 11 Canadian metropolitan areas: Victoria, Vancouver, Calgary, Edmonton, Winnipeg, Hamilton, Toronto, Ottawa, Montreal, Quebec, and Halifax.

[6]The Royal Bank of Canada Housing Affordability Index measures the percentage of pre-tax income required to own a house including mortgage payments, property taxes, and utilities.

[7]The index defines a typical family as one that earns the median level of pre-tax income. This places the typical family in the centre of the family pre-tax income distribution, with 50% of families earning less income and 50% earning more.

FIGURE **10-9** Housing Bubble in Vancouver?

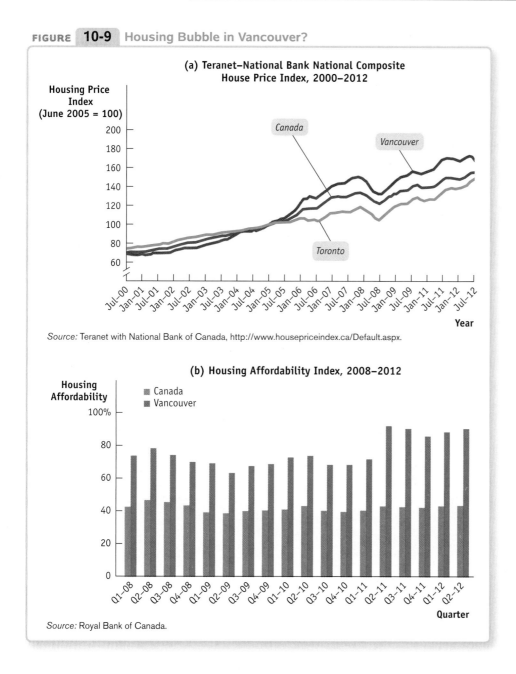

(a) Teranet–National Bank National Composite House Price Index, 2000–2012

Housing Price Index (June 2005 = 100)

Source: Teranet with National Bank of Canada, http://www.housepriceindex.ca/Default.aspx.

(b) Housing Affordability Index, 2008–2012

Housing Affordability

■ Canada
■ Vancouver

Source: Royal Bank of Canada.

significant tumble. In addition, several recent studies have shown that, at time of writing in 2012, the Canadian household debt to income ratio is at a record high level—at a level comparable to levels in the U.S. before its housing bubble burst. Many economists believe that all these factors indicate a dangerous housing bubble in Vancouver, and that a major (negative) adjustment is looming. In 2012, a correction may already be underway in Vancouver—housing demand has softened, sales volume is down, and house prices have begun to decline. The British Columbia Real Estate Association forecasts the unit sales in Vancouver will fall by 15% in 2012. This may further weaken market confidence and cause a more significant slowdown in the real estate market.

If these predictions are correct and a Canadian house price adjustment is inevitable, it is to be hoped the adjustment will be gradual. As the devastating economic hardship in the U.S. demonstrates, less economic harm is caused when a bubble deflates slowly rather than bursts suddenly.

CHECK YOUR UNDERSTANDING 10-3

1. What is the likely effect of each of the following events on the stock price of a company? Explain your answers.
   a. The company announces that although profits are low this year, it has discovered a new line of business that will generate high profits next year.
   b. The company announces that although it had high profits this year, those profits will be less than had been previously announced.
   c. Other companies in the same industry announce that sales are unexpectedly slow this year.
   d. The company announces that it is on track to meet its previously forecast profit target.

2. Assess the following statement: "Although many investors may be irrational, it is unlikely that over time they will behave irrationally in exactly the same way—such as always buying stocks the day after the TSX has risen by 1%."

Solutions appear at back of book.

SUMMARY

1. Investment in physical capital is necessary for long-run economic growth. So in order for an economy to grow, it must channel savings into investment spending.

2. According to the **savings-investment spending identity,** savings and investment spending are always equal for the economy as a whole. The **budget balance** is equal to **public savings,** which is sometimes called government savings. When the government runs a **budget surplus,** public savings is positive and the government is a source of savings. On the other hand, when the government runs a **budget deficit,** then public savings is negative and the government is a source of dissavings. In a closed economy, **national savings,** the sum of private savings plus public savings, must be equal to investment spending. In an open economy, national savings can split between two kinds of investment: (domestic) investment spending and **net foreign investment.** Alternatively, domestic investment can be financed via national savings and/or negative NFI, which represents a net inflow of financial capital from abroad (i.e., in an open economy, the total savings available for investment in any given country, from both domestic and foreign sources, equals investment).

3. The hypothetical **loanable funds market** shows how loans from savers are allocated among borrowers with investment spending projects. By showing how gains from trade between lenders and borrowers are maximized, the loanable funds market shows why a well-functioning financial system leads to greater long-run economic growth. Increasing or persistent government budget deficits can lead to **crowding out:** higher interest rates and reduced investment spending. Changes in perceived business opportunities and government policies that affect investment shift the demand curve for loanable funds; changes in private savings and government budget balance shift the supply curve.

4. In order to evaluate a project in which the return, Y, is realized in the future, you must transform Y into its **present value** using the interest rate, i. The present value of $1 received one year from now is $1 / (1 + i)$, the amount of money you must lend out today to have $1 one year from now. The present value of a given project rises as the interest rate falls and falls as the interest rate rises. This tells us that the demand curve for loanable funds is downward-sloping.

5. Because neither borrowers nor lenders can know the future inflation rate, loans specify a nominal interest rate rather than a real interest rate. For a given expected future inflation rate, shifts of the demand and supply curves of loanable funds result in changes in the underlying real interest rate, leading to changes in the nominal interest rate. According to the **Fisher effect,** an increase in expected future inflation raises the nominal interest rate one-to-one so that the expected real interest rate remains unchanged.

6. Households invest their current savings and their **wealth**—their accumulated savings—by purchasing assets. Assets come in the form of either a **financial asset,** a paper claim that entitles the buyer to future income from the seller, or a **physical asset,** a tangible object that can generate future income. A financial asset is also a **liability** from the point of view of its initial seller (or issuer). There are four main types of financial assets: **loans,** bonds, stocks, and **bank deposits.** Each of them serves a different purpose in addressing the three fundamental tasks of a financial system: reducing **transaction costs**—the cost of making a deal; reducing **financial risk**—uncertainty about future outcomes that involves financial gains and losses; and providing **liquid** assets—assets that can be quickly converted into cash without much loss of value (in contrast to **illiquid** assets, which are not easily converted).

7. Although many small and moderate-size borrowers use bank loans to fund investment spending, larger companies typically issue bonds. Bonds with a higher risk of **default** must typically pay a higher interest rate. Business owners reduce their risk by selling stock. Although stocks usually generate a higher return than bonds, investors typically wish to reduce their risk by engaging in **diversification,** owning a wide range of assets whose returns are based on unrelated, or independent, events. Most people are risk-averse, more sensitive to a loss than to an equal-sized gain. **Loan-backed securities,** a recent innovation, are assets created by pooling individual loans and selling shares of that pool to investors. Because they are more diversified and more liquid than individual loans, bonds are preferred by investors. It can be difficult, however, to assess a bond's quality.

8. **Financial intermediaries**—institutions such as **mutual funds, pension funds, life insurance companies,** and **banks**—are critical components of the financial system. Mutual funds and pension funds allow small investors to diversify, and life insurance companies reduce risk.

9. A bank allows individuals to hold liquid **bank deposits** that are then used to finance illiquid loans. Banks can perform this mismatch because on average only a small fraction of depositors withdraw their funds at any one time. A well-functioning banking sector is a key ingredient of long-run economic growth.

10. Asset market fluctuations can be a source of short-run macroeconomic instability. Asset prices are determined by supply and demand as well as by the desirability of competing assets, like bonds: when the interest rate rises, prices of stocks and physical assets such as real estate generally fall, and vice versa. Expectations drive the supply of and demand for assets: expectations of higher future prices push today's asset prices higher, and expectations of lower future prices drive them lower. One view of how expectations are formed is the **efficient markets hypothesis,** which holds that the prices of assets embody all publicly available information. It implies that fluctuations are inherently unpredictable—they follow a **random walk.**

11. Many market participants and economists believe that, based on actual evidence, financial markets are not as rational as the efficient markets hypothesis claims. Such evidence includes the fact that stock price fluctuations are too great to be driven by fundamentals alone. Policy-makers assume neither that markets always behave rationally nor that they can outsmart them.

KEY TERMS

Savings-investment spending identity, p. 304
National savings, p. 305
Public savings, p. 305
Budget balance, p. 305
Budget surplus, p. 305
Budget deficit, p. 305
Net foreign investment (NFI), p. 306
Loanable funds market, p. 310
Present value, p. 311
Crowding out, p. 316

Fisher effect, p. 317
Wealth, p. 319
Financial asset, p. 319
Physical asset, p. 319
Liability, p. 320
Transaction costs, p. 320
Financial risk, p. 321
Diversification, p. 321
Liquid, p. 322
Illiquid, p. 322
Loan, p. 322

Default, p. 322
Loan-backed securities, p. 323
Financial intermediary, p. 324
Mutual fund, p. 324
Pension fund, p. 325
Life insurance company, p. 325
Bank deposit, p. 325
Bank, p. 325
Efficient markets hypothesis, p. 329
Random walk, p. 330

PROBLEMS

1. Given the following information about the closed economy of Brittania, what is the level of investment spending and private savings, and what is the budget balance? What is the relationship among the three? Is national savings equal to investment spending? There are no government transfers.

   GDP = $1000 million T = $50 million
   C = $850 million G = $100 million

2. Given the following information about the open economy of Regalia, what is the level of investment spending and private savings, and what are the budget balance and net foreign investment? What is the relationship among the four? There are no government transfers. (*Hint:* Net foreign investment equals net exports, or exports minus imports ($X - IM$).)

   GDP = $1000 million G = $100 million
   C = $850 million X = $100 million
   T = $50 million IM = $125 million

3. The accompanying table shows the percentage of GDP accounted for by private savings, investment spending, and net foreign investment in the economies of Capsland and Marsalia. Capsland is currently experiencing a negative net foreign investment and Marsalia, a positive net foreign investment. What is the budget balance (as a percentage of GDP) in both countries? Are Capsland and Marsalia running a budget deficit or surplus?

	Capsland	Marsalia
Investment spending as a percentage of GDP	20%	20%
Private savings as a percentage of GDP	10	25
Net foreign investment as a percentage of GDP	–5	2

4. Assume the economy is open to capital inflows and outflows and therefore net foreign investment equals net exports ($X - IM$).

   a. X = $125 million
   IM = $80 million
   Budget balance = –$200 million
   I = $350 million
   Calculate private savings.

   b. X = $85 million
   IM = $135 million
   Budget balance = $100 million
   Private savings = $250 million
   Calculate I.

   c. X = $60 million
   IM = $95 million
   Private savings = $325 million
   I = $300 million
   Calculate the budget balance.

   d. Private savings = $325 million
   I = $400 million
   Budget balance = $10 million
   Calculate $IM - X$.

5. The accompanying table, taken from Statistics Canada's National Income Accounts tables, shows the various components of Canadian GDP in 2009 and 2010 in billions of dollars.

Year	Gross domestic product	Private consumption	Gross domestic investment	Government purchases of goods and services	Government savings (budget balance)	Net government taxes after transfers
				(billions of dollars)		
2009	$1529.0	$898.2	$319.1	$337.7	−$74.7	?
2010	1624.6	940.6	360.7	353.6	?	263.3

a. Complete the table by filling in the missing figures.

b. For each year, calculate taxes (after transfers) as a percentage of GDP.

c. For each year, calculate national savings and private savings.

6. Use the loanable funds market shown in the accompanying diagram to explain what happens to private savings, private investment spending, and the interest rate if each of the following events occur. Assume that there are no capital inflows or outflows.

a. The government reduces the size of its deficit to zero.

b. At any given interest rate, consumers decide to save more. Assume the budget balance is zero.

c. At any given interest rate, businesses become very optimistic about the future profitability of investment spending. Assume the budget balance is zero.

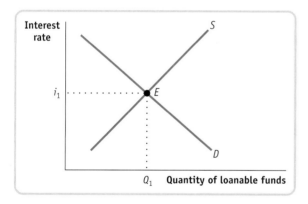

7. The government is running a budget balance of zero when it decides to increase education spending by $200 billion and finance the spending by selling bonds. The accompanying diagram shows the loanable funds market before the government sells the bonds. Assume that there are no capital inflows or outflows. How will the equilibrium interest rate and the equilibrium quantity of loanable funds change? Is there any crowding out in the market?

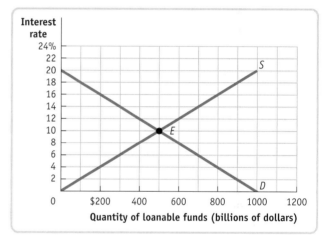

8. Suppose a national early childhood education program for all preschool-aged children has been proposed. The federal government estimates that the program would cost $15 billion to implement. Assume this program would be paid for entirely by the government and financed by government borrowing, which increases the demand for loanable funds without affecting supply. This question considers the likely effect of this government expenditure on the interest rate.

a. Draw typical demand (D_1) and supply (S_1) curves for loanable funds without accounting for the cost of any government measures to fund the education program. Label the vertical axis "Interest rate" and the horizontal axis "Quantity of loanable funds." Label the equilibrium point (E_1) and the equilibrium interest rate (i_1).

b. Now draw a new diagram with the cost of the government measures to fund the education program included in the analysis. Shift the demand curve in the appropriate direction. Label the new equilibrium point (E_2) and the new equilibrium interest rate (i_2).

c. How does the equilibrium interest rate change? Explain.

9. Explain why equilibrium in the loanable funds market maximizes efficiency.

10. How would you respond to a friend who claims that the government should eliminate all purchases that are financed by borrowing because such borrowing crowds out private investment spending?

11. Boris Borrower and Lynn Lender agree that Lynn will lend Boris $10 000 and that Boris will repay the $10 000 with interest in one year. They agree to a nominal interest rate of 8%, reflecting a real interest rate of 3% on the loan and a commonly shared expected inflation rate of 5% over the next year.

a. If the inflation rate is actually 4% over the next year, how does that lower-than-expected inflation rate affect Boris and Lynn? Who is better off?

b. If the actual inflation rate is 7% over the next year, how does that affect Boris and Lynn? Who is better off?

12. Using the accompanying diagram, explain what will happen to the loanable funds market when there is a fall of 2 percentage points in the expected future inflation rate. How will the change in the expected future inflation rate affect the equilibrium quantity of loanable funds?

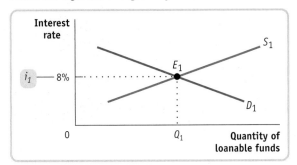

13. The accompanying diagram shows data for the interest rate on 10-year euro area government bonds and inflation rate for the euro area for 1991 through mid-2011, as reported by the European Central Bank. How would you describe the relationship between the two? How does the pattern compare to that of Canada in Figure 10-8?

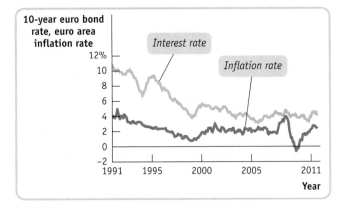

14. For each of the following, is it an example of investment spending, investing in financial assets, or investing in physical assets?

a. Rupert Moneybucks buys 100 shares of existing Coca-Cola stock.

b. Rhonda Moviestar spends $10 million to buy a mansion built in the 1970s.

c. Ronald Basketballstar spends $10 million to build a new mansion with a view of the Pacific Ocean.

d. Rawlings builds a new plant to make catcher's mitts.

e. Russia buys $100 million in Canadian government bonds.

15. Explain how a well-functioning financial system increases savings and investment spending, holding the budget balance and any capital flows fixed.

16. What are the important types of financial intermediaries in the Canadian economy? What are the primary assets of these intermediaries, and how do they facilitate investment spending and saving?

17. Explain the effect on a company's stock price today of each of the following events, other things held constant.

a. The interest rate on bonds falls.

b. Several companies in the same sector announce surprisingly higher sales.

c. A change in the tax law passed last year reduces this year's profit.

d. The company unexpectedly announces that due to an accounting error, it must amend last year's accounting statement and reduce last year's reported profit by $5 million. It also announces that this change has no implications for future profits.

18. Suppose HSBC Canada were to package individual student loans into pools of loans and then sell shares of these pools to investors as HSBC student loan bonds.

a. What is this process called? What effect will it have on investors who previously could only buy and sell individual student loans?

b. What effect do you think HSBC's actions will have on the ability of students to get loans?

c. Suppose that a very severe recession were to occur, and, as a consequence, many graduating students could not get jobs and then had to default on their student loans. What effect would this have on HSBC student loan bonds? Why is it likely that investors would now believe HSBC student loan bonds to be riskier than expected? What will be the effect on the availability of student loans?

CHAPTER 11

Income and Expenditure

IN COD WE TRUSTED—THE COD FISHERY IN NEWFOUNDLAND AND LABRADOR

Even during the boom years of cod fishing, few outport communities were wealthy. But just about every fisher had a boat, and fish plant work (shown on left) sustained over half the population. After the moratorium, that way of life disappeared for many. On the right is the fish processing plant in Burgeo, in decay. Once a thriving operation with hundreds of workers, it is now operational for only about 14 weeks of the year.

WHAT YOU WILL LEARN IN THIS CHAPTER

IN 1497, THERE WERE SO MANY cod off the coast of Newfoundland and Labrador that explorer John Cabot allegedly reported that a person "could walk across their backs." For centuries in Newfoundland and Labrador, "cod was king," providing tens of thousands of jobs and feeding the world. In the early 1980s, annual catches were averaging over 200 000 tonnes, generating huge revenues. And the industry was expanding, with people investing heavily in larger fishing vessels, as well as more powerful machines and equipment. Then, suddenly, the cod industry collapsed. What happened?

By the late 1980s and early 1990s, cod had been overfished to the brink of extinction. Consequently, the federal government declared a moratorium (a temporary suspension) on all commercial cod fishing in Atlantic Canada in 1992. This was the largest industry closure in Canadian history, and it remains in effect to this day.

The impact was devastating. More than 35 000 people lost their jobs, and businesses that had invested in the industry suffered huge financial losses. Local economies began to collapse: as the jobs created by cod fishing disappeared, local spending began to fall, leading to losses of other jobs in the region, leading in turn to further declines in spending, and so on. Realizing cod fishing was unlikely to start up again soon, people had to sell their vessels and equipment at bargain prices. Many folks went to other provinces, territories, or countries to look for work. From 1992 to 2011, Newfoundland and Labrador's population declined by over 72 000 people, or about 12%.

The boom and bust of the cod industry shows how booms and busts can happen in the economy as a whole. The business cycle is often driven by ups or downs in investment spending. Changes in investment spending, in turn, indirectly lead to changes in consumer spending, which magnify—or, as economists usually say, *multiply*—the effect of the investment spending changes on the economy as a whole.

In this chapter we'll study how this process works, showing how a change

❯ The nature of the **multiplier, which** shows how initial changes in spending lead to further changes

❯ The meaning of the **aggregate consumption function,** which shows how current disposable income affects consumer spending

❯ How expected future income and aggregate wealth affect consumer spending

❯ The determinants of investment spending and the distinction between **planned investment spending** and **unplanned inventory investment**

❯ How the inventory adjustment process moves the economy to a new equilibrium after a change in demand

❯ Why investment spending is considered a leading indicator of the future state of the economy

in expenditure would have a multiplier effect on GDP. As a first step, we introduce the concept of the multiplier informally. ∎

The Multiplier: An Informal Introduction

The story of the boom and bust in the cod fishery involves a sort of chain reaction in which an initial rise or fall in aggregate expenditure leads to changes in income, which lead to further changes in aggregate expenditure, and so on. Let's examine that chain reaction more closely, this time thinking through the effects of changes in aggregate expenditure on the economy as a whole.

For the sake of this analysis, we'll make four simplifying assumptions that will have to be reconsidered in later chapters.

1. We assume that *producers are willing to supply additional output at a fixed price.* That is, if consumers or businesses buying investment goods decide to spend an additional $1 billion, that will translate into the production of $1 billion worth of additional goods and services without driving up the overall level of prices. As a result, *changes in aggregate expenditure translate into changes in aggregate output,* as measured by real GDP. As we'll learn in the next chapter, this assumption isn't too unrealistic in the short run, but it needs to be changed when we think about the long-run effects of changes in demand.

2. We take the interest rate as given.

3. We assume that there is no government spending, no taxes, and no transfer payments.

4. We assume that exports and imports are zero.

Given these simplifying assumptions, consider what happens if there is a change in investment spending. Specifically, imagine that for some reason home builders decide to spend an extra $10 billion on home construction over the next year.

The direct effect of this increase in investment spending will be to increase income and the value of aggregate output by the same amount. That's because each dollar spent on home construction translates into a dollar's worth of income for construction workers, suppliers of building materials, electricians, and so on. If the process stopped there, the increase in housing investment spending would raise overall income by exactly $10 billion.

But the process doesn't stop there. The increase in aggregate output leads to an increase in disposable income that flows to households in the form of profits and wages. The increase in households' disposable incomes leads to a rise in consumer spending, which, in turn, induces firms to increase output yet again. This generates another rise in disposable income, which leads to another round of consumer spending increases, and so on. So there are multiple rounds of increases in aggregate output.

How large is the total effect on aggregate output if we sum the effect from all these rounds of spending increases? To answer this question, we need to introduce the concept of the **marginal propensity to consume,** or **MPC:** the increase in consumer spending when disposable income rises by $1. When consumer spending changes because of a rise or fall in disposable income, *MPC* is the change in consumer spending divided by the change in disposable income:

(11-1) $MPC = \dfrac{\Delta \text{ Consumer spending}}{\Delta \text{ Disposable income}}$

where the symbol Δ (delta) means "change in." For example, if consumer spending goes up by $6 billion when disposable income goes up by $10 billion, *MPC* is $6 billion/$10 billion = 0.6.

Because consumers normally spend part but not all of an additional dollar of disposable income, *MPC* is a number between 0 and 1. The additional disposable

The **marginal propensity to consume,** or **MPC,** is the increase in consumer spending when disposable income rises by $1. *MPC* is a positive fraction less than 1, i.e., $0 < MPC < 1$.

income that consumers don't spend is saved; the **marginal propensity to save, or MPS,** is the fraction of an additional dollar of disposable income that is saved. MPS is equal to 1 – MPC.

Because we assumed that there are no taxes and no international trade, each $1 increase in aggregate expenditure raises both real GDP and disposable income by $1. So the $10 billion increase in investment spending initially raises real GDP by $10 billion. This leads to a second-round increase in consumer spending, which raises real GDP by a further $MPC \times \$10$ billion. It is followed by a third-round increase in consumer spending of $MPC \times MPC \times \$10$ billion, and so on. After an infinite number of rounds, the total effect on real GDP is:

> The **marginal propensity to save, or MPS,** is the increase in household savings when disposable income rises by $1. MPS is also a positive fraction less than 1, i.e., $0 < MPS < 1$, and $MPC + MPS = 1$.

$$
\begin{array}{lcl}
\text{Increase in investment spending} & = & \$10 \text{ billion} \\
+ \text{ Second-round increase in consumer spending} & = & MPC \times \$10 \text{ billion} \\
+ \text{ Third-round increase in consumer spending} & = & MPC^2 \times \$10 \text{ billion} \\
+ \text{ Fourth-round increase in consumer spending} & = & MPC^3 \times \$10 \text{ billion} \\
 & \vdots & \\
\end{array}
$$

Total increase in real GDP $= (1 + MPC + MPC^2 + MPC^3 + \ldots) \times \$10$ billion

So the $10 billion increase in investment spending sets off a chain reaction in the economy. The net result of this chain reaction is that a $10 billion increase in investment spending leads to a change in real GDP that is a *multiple* of the size of that initial change in spending.

How large is this multiple? It's a mathematical fact that an infinite series of the form $1 + x + x^2 + x^3 + \ldots$, where x is between 0 and 1, is equal to $1/(1 - x)$. So the total effect of a $10 billion increase in investment spending, I, taking into account all the subsequent increases in consumer spending (and assuming no taxes and no international trade), is given by:

(11-2) Total increase in real GDP from a $10 billion rise in I

$$= \frac{1}{1 - MPC} \times \$10 \text{ billion}$$

Let's consider a numerical example in which $MPC = 0.6$: each $1 in additional disposable income causes a $0.60 rise in consumer spending. In that case, a $10 billion increase in investment spending raises real GDP by $10 billion in the first round. The second-round increase in consumer spending raises real GDP by another $0.6 \times \$10$ billion, or $6 billion. The third-round increase in consumer spending raises real GDP by another $0.6 \times \$6$ billion, or $36 billion. Table 11-1 shows the successive stages of increases, where "…" means the process goes on an infinite number of times. In the end, real GDP rises by $25 billion as a consequence of the initial $10 billion rise in investment spending:

Rounds of Increases of Real GDP When MPC = 0.6

TABLE **11-1**

	Increase in real GDP (billions)	Total increase in real GDP (billions)
First round	$10	$10
Second round	6	16
Third round	3.6	19.6
Fourth round	2.16	21.76
…	…	…
Final round	0	25

$$\frac{1}{1 - 0.6} \times \$10 \text{ billion} = 2.5 \times \$10 \text{ billion} = \$25 \text{ billion}$$

Notice that even though there are an infinite number of rounds of expansion of real GDP, the total rise in real GDP is limited to $25 billion. The reason is that at each stage some of the rise in disposable income "leaks out" because it is saved. How much of an additional dollar of disposable income is saved depends on MPS, the marginal propensity to save.

An **autonomous change in aggregate expenditure** is an initial change in the desired level of spending by firms, households, or government at a given level of real GDP.

The **multiplier** is the ratio of the total change in real GDP caused by an autonomous change in aggregate expenditure to the size of that autonomous change.

We've described the effects of a change in investment spending, but the same analysis can be applied to any other change in aggregate expenditure, such as consumer spending. The important thing is to distinguish between the initial change in aggregate expenditure, before real GDP rises, and the additional change in aggregate expenditure caused by the change in real GDP as the chain reaction unfolds. For example, suppose that a boom in housing prices makes consumers feel richer and that, as a result, they become willing to spend more at any given level of disposable income. This will lead to an initial rise in consumer spending, before real GDP rises. But it will also lead to second and later rounds of higher consumer spending as real GDP rises.

An initial rise or fall in aggregate expenditure at a given level of real GDP is called an **autonomous change in aggregate expenditure.** It's autonomous—which means "self-governing"—because it's the cause, not the result, of the chain reaction we've just described. Formally, the **multiplier** is the ratio of the total change in real GDP caused by an autonomous change in aggregate expenditure to the size of that autonomous change. If we let ΔAE_0 stand for autonomous change in aggregate expenditure and ΔY stand for the change in real GDP, then the multiplier is equal to $\Delta Y/\Delta AE_0$. And we've already seen how to find the value of the multiplier. Assuming no taxes and no trade, the change in real GDP caused by an autonomous change in spending is:

$$\textbf{(11-3)}\ \Delta Y = \frac{1}{1 - MPC} \times \Delta AE_0$$

So the multiplier is:

$$\textbf{(11-4)}\ \text{Multiplier} = \frac{\Delta Y}{\Delta AE_0} = \frac{1}{1 - MPC}$$

Notice that the size of the multiplier depends on *MPC*. If the marginal propensity to consume is high, so is the multiplier. This is true because the size of *MPC* determines how large each round of expansion is compared with the previous round. To put it another way, the higher *MPC* is, the less disposable income "leaks out" into savings at each round of expansion. Let's return to our earlier example of a $100 billion increase in investment. If the *MPC* rises from 0.6 to 0.75, then the multiplier increases from 2.5 to 4, and the total possible increase in real GDP will be equal to $400 billion (an additional $150 billion increase in real GDP).

In later chapters we'll use the concept of the multiplier to analyze the effects of fiscal and monetary policies. We'll also see that the formula for the multiplier changes when we introduce various complications, including taxes and foreign trade. First, however, we need to look more deeply at what determines consumer spending.

ECONOMICS ► IN ACTION

THE MULTIPLIER AND THE GREAT DEPRESSION

The concept of the multiplier was originally devised by economists trying to understand the greatest economic disaster in history, the collapse of output and employment from 1929 to 1933, which began the Great Depression. Most economists believe that the slump during these years was caused by a collapse in investment spending. But as the economy shrank, consumer spending also fell sharply, multiplying the effect on real GDP.

Table 11-2 shows what happened to investment spending, consumer spending, and GDP during those five terrible

TABLE **11-2** Investment Spending, Consumer Spending, and Real GDP in the Great Depression (in billions of 1971 dollars)

	1929	1933	Change
Investment spending	$4.565	$0.858	−$3.707
Consumer spending	10.778	8.827	−1.951
Real GDP	16.894	11.811	−5.083

Source: Historical Statistics of Canada.

years. All data are in 1971 dollars. Both consumer and investment spending fell during this period. Consumer spending fell by 18%, while investment spending plunged by more than 80%. The drastic fall in investment accounted for most of the reduction in real GDP. (The total fall in real GDP was smaller than the combined reduction in consumer and investment spending due to an improvement in the trade balance and technical accounting issues).

The numbers in Table 11-2 suggest that at the time of the Great Depression, Canada's multiplier was around 1.4, whereas today it has risen significantly, to about 3. Why has there been such a change? In 1929, government in Canada was very small by modern standards: taxes were low and major government programs like employment insurance and health care had not yet come into being. In the modern Canadian economy, taxes are much higher, and so is government spending. Why does this matter? It matters since some taxes and government programs act as *automatic stabilizers,* reducing the size of the multiplier. Appendix 13A explains how taxes change the multiplier.

CHECK YOUR UNDERSTANDING   11-1

1. Explain why a decline in investment spending caused by a change in business expectations leads to a fall in consumer spending.

2. What is the multiplier if the marginal propensity to consume is 0.5? What is it if *MPC* is 0.8?

3. As a percentage of GDP, savings accounts for a larger share of the economy in the country of Scania compared to the country of Candia. Which country is likely to have the larger multiplier? Explain.

Solutions appear at back of book.

Consumer Spending

Should you splurge on a restaurant meal or save money by eating at home? Should you buy a new car and, if so, how expensive a model? Should you redo that bathroom or live with it for another year? In the real world, households are constantly confronted with such choices—not just about the consumption mix but also about how much to spend in total. These choices, in turn, have a powerful effect on the economy: consumer spending normally accounts for about 60% of total spending on final goods and services. In particular, as we've just seen, the decision about how much of an additional dollar in income to spend—the marginal propensity to consume—determines the size of the multiplier, which determines the ultimate effect on the economy of autonomous changes in spending.

But what determines how much consumers spend?

Current Disposable Income and Consumer Spending

The most important factor affecting a family's consumer spending is its current disposable income—income after taxes are paid and government transfers are received. It's obvious from daily life that people with high disposable incomes, on average, drive more expensive cars, live in more

During recessions, consumers tend to avoid higher-priced brand-name goods in favour of house brands that cost less.

The **individual consumption function** is an equation showing how an individual household's consumer spending varies with the household's current disposable income.

expensive houses, and spend more on meals and clothing than people with lower disposable incomes. And the relationship between current disposable income and spending is clear in the data.

Statistics Canada collects annual data on family income and spending. Families are grouped by levels of before-tax income, and after-tax income for each group is also reported. Since the income figures include transfers from the government, what Statistics Canada calls a household's after-tax income is equivalent to its current disposable income.

Figure 11-1 is a scatter diagram illustrating the relationship between household current disposable income and household consumer spending for Canadian households by income group in 2010. For example, point *A* shows that in 2010 the middle fifth of the population had an average current disposable income of $66 000 and average spending of $60 946. The pattern of the dots slopes upward from left to right, making it clear that households with higher current disposable income had higher consumer spending.

It's very useful to represent the relationship between an individual household's current disposable income and its consumer spending with an equation. The **individual consumption function** is an equation showing how an individual household's consumer spending varies with the household's current disposable income. The simplest version of a consumption function is a linear equation:

(11-5) $c = ac + MPC \times yd$

where lowercase letters indicate variables measured for an individual household.

In this equation, c is individual household consumer spending and yd is individual household current disposable income. Recall that MPC, the marginal propensity to consume, is the amount by which consumer spending rises if current disposable income rises by $1. Finally, ac is a constant term—individual household *autonomous consumer spending,* the amount of spending a household would do if it had zero disposable income. We assume that ac is greater than zero because a household with zero disposable income is able to fund some consumption by borrowing or using its savings. Notice, by the way, that we're using y for income. That's standard practice in macroeconomics, even though *income* isn't actually spelled "yncome." The reason is that I is reserved for investment spending.

FIGURE **11-1** Current Disposable Income and Consumer Spending for Canadian Households in 2010

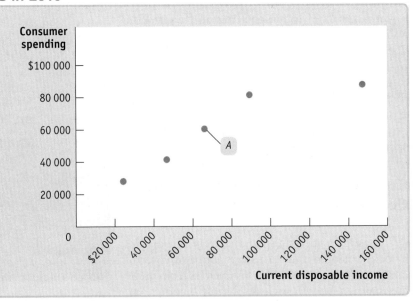

For each income group of households, average current disposable income in 2010 is plotted versus average consumer spending in 2010. For example, the middle income group is represented by point *A*, indicating a household average current disposable income of $66 000 and average household consumer spending of $60 946. The data clearly show a positive relationship between current disposable income and consumer spending: families with higher current disposable income have higher consumer spending.

Source: Statistics Canada.

Recall that we expressed *MPC* as the ratio of a change in consumer spending to the change in current disposable income. We've rewritten it for an individual household as Equation 11-6:

(11-6) $MPC = \Delta c/\Delta yd$

Multiplying both sides of Equation 11-6 by Δyd, we get:

(11-7) $MPC \times \Delta yd = \Delta c$

Equation 11-7 tells us that when *yd* goes up by $1, *c* goes up by $MPC \times \$1$.

Figure 11-2 shows what Equation 11-5 looks like graphically, plotting *yd* on the horizontal axis and *c* on the vertical axis. Individual household autonomous consumer spending, *ac*, is the value of *c* when *yd* is zero—it is the vertical *intercept* of the individual consumption function, *cf*. *MPC* is the *slope* of the line, measured by rise over run. If current disposable income rises by Δyd, household consumer spending, *c*, rises by Δc. Since *MPC* is defined as $\Delta c/\Delta yd$, the slope of the consumption function is:

(11-8) Slope of individual consumption function
    = Rise over run
    = $\Delta c/\Delta yd$
    = *MPC*

FIGURE 11-2 The Individual Consumption Function

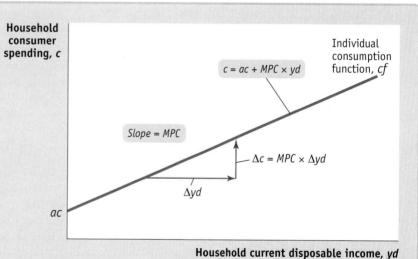

The consumption function relates a household's current disposable income to its consumer spending. The vertical intercept, *ac*, is individual household autonomous consumer spending: the amount of a household's consumer spending if its current disposable income is zero. The slope of the consumption function line, *cf*, is the marginal propensity to consume, or *MPC*; that is, for every additional $1 of current disposable income, $MPC \times \$1$ is spent.

In reality, actual data never fit Equation 11-5 perfectly, but the fit can be pretty good. Figure 11-3 shows the data from Figure 11-1 again, together with a line drawn to fit the data as closely as possible. According to the data on households' consumer spending and current disposable income, the best estimate of *ac* is $23 032 and of *MPC* is 0.50. So the consumption function fitted to the data is:

$$c = \$23\ 032 + 0.50 \times yd$$

That is, the data suggest a marginal propensity to consume of approximately 0.50. This implies that the marginal propensity to save (*MPS*)—the amount of an additional $1 of disposable income that is saved—is approximately 0.50, and the multiplier is approximately 1/0.5 = 2.0.

FIGURE   **11-3**   A Consumption Function Fitted to Data

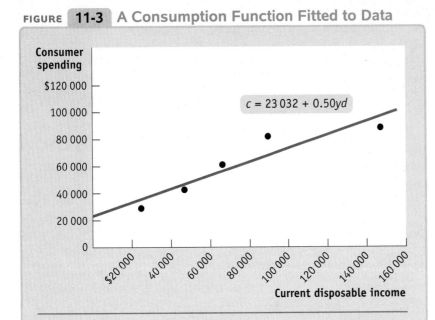

The data from Figure 11-1 are reproduced here, along with a line drawn to fit the data as closely as possible. For Canadian households in 2010, the best estimate of the average household's autonomous consumer spending, ac, is $23 032 and the best estimate of the marginal propensity to consume, or MPC, is about 0.50.

Source: Statistics Canada.

It's important to realize that Figure 11-3 shows a *microeconomic* relationship between the current disposable income of individual households and their spending on goods and services. However, macro-economists assume that a similar relationship holds *for the economy as a whole:* that there is a relationship, called the **aggregate consumption function,** between aggregate current disposable income and aggregate consumer spending. We'll assume that it has the same form as the household-level consumption function:

(11-9) $C = AC + MPC \times YD$

Here, C is aggregate consumer spending (called just "consumer spending"); YD is aggregate current disposable income (called, for simplicity, just "disposable income"); and AC is aggregate autonomous consumer spending, the amount of consumer spending when YD equals zero. This is the relationship represented in Figure 11-4 by CF, analogous to cf in Figure 11-3.

Shifts of the Aggregate Consumption Function

The aggregate consumption function shows the relationship between disposable income and consumer spending for the economy as a whole, other things equal. When things other than disposable income change, the aggregate consumption function shifts. There are two principal causes of shifts of the aggregate consumption function: changes in expected future disposable income and changes in aggregate wealth.

Changes in Expected Future Disposable Income Suppose you land a really good, well-paying job on graduating from college in June—but the job, and the paycheques, won't start until September. So your disposable income hasn't risen yet. Even so, it's likely that you will start spending more on final goods and services right away—maybe buying nicer work clothes than you originally planned—because you know that higher income is coming.

Conversely, suppose you have a good job but learn that the company is planning to downsize your division, raising the possibility that you may lose your job and have to take a lower-paying one somewhere else. Even though your disposable income hasn't gone down yet, you might well cut back on spending even while still employed, to save for a rainy day.

Both of these examples show how expectations about future disposable income can affect consumer spending. The two panels of Figure 11-4, which plot disposable income against consumer spending, show how changes in expected future disposable income affect the aggregate consumption function. In both panels, CF_1 is the initial aggregate consumption function. Panel (a) shows the effect of good news, information that leads consumers to expect higher disposable income in the future than they did before. Consumers will now spend more at any given level of current disposable income, YD, corresponding to an increase in AC, aggregate autonomous consumer spending, from AC_1 to AC_2. The effect is to shift the aggregate consumption function up, from CF_1 to CF_2. Panel (b) shows the effect of bad news, information

The **aggregate consumption function** is the relationship for the economy as a whole between aggregate current disposable income and aggregate consumer spending.

FIGURE **11-4** Shifts of the Aggregate Consumption Function

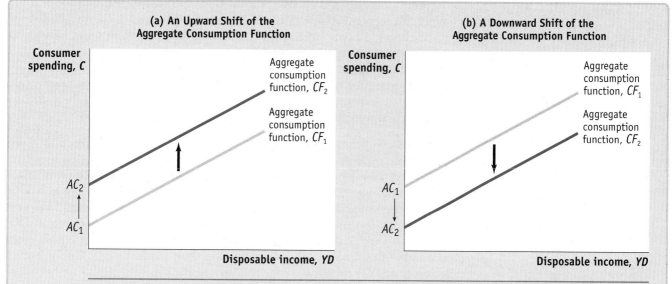

Panel (a) illustrates the effect of an increase in expected aggregate future disposable income. Consumers will spend more at every given level of aggregate current disposable income, *YD*. As a result, the initial aggregate consumption function CF_1, with aggregate autonomous consumer spending AC_1, shifts up to a new position at CF_2 and aggregate autonomous consumer spending AC_2. An increase in aggregate wealth will also shift the aggregate consumption function up. Panel (b), in

contrast, illustrates the effect of a reduction in expected aggregate future disposable income. Consumers will spend less at every given level of aggregate current disposable income, *YD*. Consequently, the initial aggregate consumption function CF_1, with aggregate autonomous consumer spending AC_1, shifts down to a new position at CF_2 and aggregate autonomous consumer spending AC_2. A reduction in aggregate wealth will have the same effect.

that leads consumers to expect lower disposable income in the future than they did before. Consumers will now spend less at any given level of current disposable income, *YD*, corresponding to a fall in *AC* from AC_1 to AC_2. The effect is to shift the aggregate consumption function down, from CF_1 to CF_2.

In a famous 1956 book, *A Theory of the Consumption Function*, Milton Friedman showed that taking the effects of expected future income into account explains an otherwise puzzling fact about consumer behaviour. If we look at consumer spending during any given year, we find that people with high current income save a larger fraction of their income than those with low current income. (This is obvious from the data in Figure 11-3: people in the highest income group spend considerably less than their income; those in the lowest income group spend more than their income.) You might think this implies that the overall savings rate will rise as the economy grows and average current incomes rise; in fact, however, this hasn't happened.

Friedman pointed out that when we look at individual incomes in a given year, there are systematic differences between current and expected future income that create a positive relationship between current income and the savings rate. On one side, people with low current incomes are often having an unusually bad year. For example, they may be workers who have been laid off but will probably find new jobs eventually. They are people whose expected future income is higher than their current income, so it makes sense for them to have low or even negative savings. On the other side, people with high current incomes in a given year are often having an unusually good year. For example, they may have investments that happened

to do extremely well. They are people whose expected future income is lower than their current income, so it makes sense for them to save most of their windfall.

When the economy grows, by contrast, current and expected future incomes rise together. Higher current income tends to lead to higher savings today, but higher expected future income tends to lead to less savings today. As a result, there's a weaker relationship between current income and the savings rate.

Friedman argued that consumer spending ultimately depends mainly on the income people expect to have over the long term rather than on their current income. This argument is known as the *permanent income hypothesis.*

Changes in Aggregate Wealth Imagine two individuals, Maria and Mark, both of whom expect to earn $30 000 this year. Suppose, however, that they have different histories. Maria has been working steadily for the past 10 years, owns her own home, and has $200 000 in the bank. Mark is the same age as Maria, but he has been in and out of work, hasn't managed to buy a house, and has very little in savings. In this case, Maria has something that Mark doesn't have: wealth. Even though they have the same disposable income, other things equal, you'd expect Maria to spend more on consumption than Mark. That is, *wealth* has an effect on consumer spending.

The effect of wealth on spending is emphasized by an influential economic model of how consumers make choices about spending versus saving called the *life-cycle hypothesis.* According to this hypothesis, consumers plan their spending over a lifetime, not just in response to their current disposable income. As a result, people try to smooth their consumption over their lifetimes—they save some of their current disposable income during their years of peak earnings (typically occurring during a worker's 40s and 50s) and during their retirement live off the wealth they accumulated while working. We won't go into the details of this hypothesis but will simply point out that it implies an important role for wealth in determining consumer spending. For example, a middle-aged couple who have accumulated a lot of wealth—who have paid off the mortgage on their house and already own plenty of stocks and bonds—will, other things equal, spend more on goods and services than a couple who have the same current disposable income but still need to save for their retirement.

Because wealth affects household consumer spending, changes in wealth across the economy can shift the aggregate consumption function. A rise in aggregate wealth—say, because of a booming stock market or a booming housing market—increases the vertical intercept AC, aggregate autonomous consumer spending. This, in turn, shifts the aggregate consumption function up in the same way as does an expected increase in future disposable income. A decline in aggregate wealth—say, because of a fall in stock prices as occurred in 2008—reduces AC and shifts the aggregate consumption function down.

ECONOMICS ► *IN ACTION*

FAMOUS FIRST FORECASTING FAILURES

The Great Depression created modern macroeconomics. It also gave birth to the field of econometrics—the use of statistical techniques to fit economic models to empirical data. The aggregate consumption function was one of the first things econometricians studied. And, sure enough, they quickly experienced one of the first major failures of economic forecasting: consumer spending after World War II was much higher than estimates of the aggregate consumption function based on pre-war data would have predicted.

Figure 11-5 tells the story. Panel (a) shows aggregate data on disposable income and consumer spending from 1926 to 1941, measured in millions of current dollars. A simple linear aggregate consumption function, CF_1, seems to fit the data very well. And many economists thought this relationship would continue to hold in the

FIGURE **11-5** Changes in the Aggregate Consumption Function Over Time

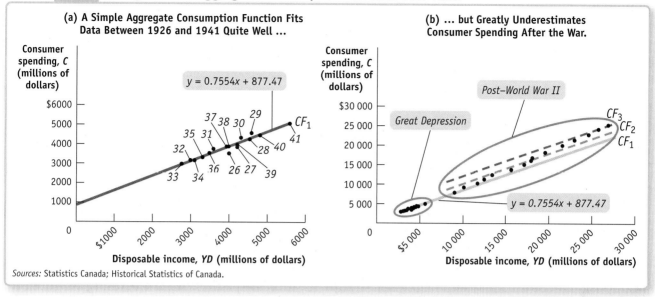

(a) A Simple Aggregate Consumption Function Fits Data Between 1926 and 1941 Quite Well ...

$y = 0.7554x + 877.47$

CF_1

Consumer spending, C (millions of dollars)

Disposable income, YD (millions of dollars)

(b) ... but Greatly Underestimates Consumer Spending After the War.

Post–World War II

Great Depression

CF_3
CF_2
CF_1

$y = 0.7554x + 877.47$

Consumer spending, C (millions of dollars)

Disposable income, YD (millions of dollars)

Sources: Statistics Canada; Historical Statistics of Canada.

future. But panel (b) shows what actually happened in later years. The points in the circle at the left are the data from the Great Depression shown in panel (a). The points in the circle at the right are data from 1946 to 1960. (Data from 1942 to 1945 aren't included because rationing during World War II prevented consumers from spending normally.) The solid line in the figure, CF_1, is the aggregate consumption function fitted to 1926–1941 data. As you can see, post-World War II consumer spending was much higher than the relationship from the Depression years would have predicted. For example, in 1960 consumer spending was 20% higher than the level predicted by CF_1.

Why was extrapolating from the earlier relationship so misleading? The answer is that from 1946 onward, both expected future disposable income and aggregate wealth were steadily rising. Consumers grew increasingly confident that the Great Depression wouldn't re-emerge and that the post-World War II economic boom would continue. At the same time, wealth was steadily increasing. As indicated by the dashed lines in panel (b), CF_2 and CF_3, the increases in expected future disposable income and in aggregate wealth shifted the aggregate consumption function up a number of times.

In macroeconomics, failure—whether of economic policy or of economic prediction—often leads to future intellectual progress. The embarrassing failure of early estimates of the aggregate consumption function to predict post-World War II consumer spending led to important progress in our understanding of consumer behaviour.

▼ **Quick Review**

● The **individual consumption function** shows the relationship between an individual household's current disposable income and its consumer spending.

● The **aggregate consumption function** shows the relationship between disposable income and consumer spending across the economy. It can shift due to changes in expected future disposable income and changes in aggregate wealth.

CHECK YOUR UNDERSTANDING 11-2

1. Suppose the economy consists of three people: Angelina, Felicia, and Marina. The table shows how their consumer spending varies as their current disposable income rises by $10 000.

   a. Derive each individual's consumption function, where *MPC* is calculated for a $10 000 change in current disposable income.

   b. Derive the aggregate consumption function.

2. Suppose that problems in the capital markets make consumers unable either to borrow or to put money aside for future use. What implication does this have for the effects of expected future disposable income on consumer spending?

Current disposable income	Consumer spending		
	Angelina	Felicia	Marina
$0	$8 000	$6 500	$7 250
10 000	12 000	14 500	14 250

Solutions appear at back of book.

Investment Spending

Although consumer spending is much larger than investment spending, booms and busts in investment spending tend to drive the business cycle. In fact, most recessions originate as a fall in investment spending. Figure 11-6 illustrates this point; it shows the annual percent change of investment spending and consumer spending in Canada, measured in real terms, during three recessions between 1980 and the present. As you can see, swings in investment spending are much more dramatic than those in consumer spending real GDP. In addition, due to the multiplier process, economists believe that declines in consumer spending are usually the result of a process that begins with a slump in investment spending. Soon we'll examine in more detail how a slump in investment spending generates a fall in consumer spending through the multiplier process.

Before we do that, however, let's analyze the factors that determine investment spending, which are somewhat different from those that determine consumer spending. The most important ones are the interest rate and expected future real GDP. We'll also revisit a fact that we noted in For Inquiring Minds in Chapter 10: the level of investment spending businesses *actually* carry out is sometimes not the same level as **planned investment spending,** the investment spending that firms *intend* to undertake during a given period. Planned investment spending depends on three principal factors: the interest rate, the expected future level of real GDP, and the current level of production capacity. First, we'll analyze the effect of the interest rate.

The Interest Rate and Investment Spending

Interest rates have their clearest effect on one particular form of investment spending: spending on residential construction—that is, on the construction of homes. The reason is straightforward: home builders only build houses they think they can sell, and houses are more affordable—and so more likely to sell—when the interest rate is low. Suppose you need to borrow $300 000 to buy a house. At an interest rate of 7.5% for 25 years, mortgage payments will cost you $2195 per month, which might not be affordable. But for a rate of 5.3%, you would pay $1796 per month, which is more affordable. As the following Economics in Action relates, from the late 1990s to 2011, mortgage interest rates

Planned investment spending is the investment spending that businesses intend to undertake during a given period.

FIGURE **11-6** Fluctuations in Real GDP, Investment Spending, and Consumer Spending

These bars illustrate the annual percent change in real GDP, investment spending, and consumer spending during three recessions. As the lengths of the bars show, swings in investment spending were much larger in percentage terms than those in consumer spending and real GDP. This pattern has led economists to believe that recessions typically originate as a slump in investment spending.
Source: Statistics Canada.

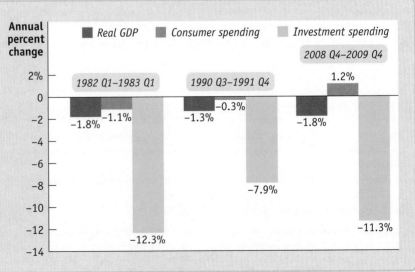

did drop from about 7.5% to 5.3%, which is one reason why housing markets across the country "caught fire" and home prices rose accordingly.

Interest rates also affect other forms of investment spending. Firms with investment spending projects will only go ahead with a project if they expect a rate of return higher than the cost of the funds they would have to borrow to finance that project. As we saw in Chapter 10 when the interest rate rises, fewer projects will pass that test, and as a result investment spending will be lower.

You might think that the trade-off a firm faces is different if it can fund its investment project with its past profits rather than through borrowing. Past profits used to finance investment spending are called *retained earnings*. But even if a firm pays for investment spending out of retained earnings, the trade-off it must make in deciding whether or not to fund a project remains the same because it must take into account the opportunity cost of its funds. For example, instead of purchasing new equipment, the firm could lend out the funds and earn interest. The forgone interest earned is the opportunity cost of using retained earnings to fund an investment project. So the trade-off the firm faces when comparing a project's rate of return to the market interest rate has not changed when it uses retained earnings rather than borrowed funds, which means that regardless of whether a firm funds investment spending through borrowing or retained earnings, a rise in the market interest rate makes any given investment project less profitable. Conversely, a fall in the interest rate makes some investment projects that were unprofitable before profitable at the now lower interest rate. So some projects that had been unfunded before will be funded now.

So planned investment spending—spending on investment projects that firms voluntarily decide whether or not to undertake—is negatively related to the interest rate. Other things equal, a higher interest rate leads to a lower level of planned investment spending.

Expected Future Real GDP, Production Capacity, and Investment Spending

Suppose a firm has enough capacity to continue to produce the amount it is currently selling but doesn't expect its sales to grow in the future. Then it will engage in investment spending only to replace existing equipment and structures that wear out or are rendered obsolete by new technologies (i.e., the depreciation of capital). But if, instead, the firm expects its sales to grow rapidly in the future, it will find its existing production capacity insufficient for its future production needs. So the firm will undertake investment spending to meet those needs. This implies that, other things equal, firms will undertake more investment spending when they expect their sales to grow.

Now suppose that the firm currently has considerably more capacity than necessary to meet current production needs. Even if it expects sales to grow, it won't have to undertake investment spending for a while—not until the growth in sales catches up with its excess capacity. This illustrates the fact that, other things equal, the current level of production capacity has a negative effect on investment spending: other things equal, the higher the current capacity, the lower investment spending.

If we put together the effects on investment spending of growth in expected future sales and the size of current production capacity, we can see one situation in which we can be reasonably sure that firms will undertake high levels of investment spending: when they expect sales to grow rapidly. In that case, even excess production capacity will soon be used up, leading firms to resume investment spending.

What is an indicator of high expected growth of future sales? It's a high expected future growth rate of real GDP. A higher expected future growth rate of real GDP results in a higher level of planned investment spending, but a lower expected future growth rate of real GDP leads to lower planned investment spending. This relationship is summarized in a proposition known as the **accelerator principle.**

According to the **accelerator principle,** a higher growth rate of real GDP leads to higher planned investment spending, but a lower growth rate of real GDP leads to lower planned investment spending.

Inventory investment is the value of the change in total inventories held in the economy during a given period. It can be positive or negative.

Unplanned inventory investment occurs when actual sales are more or less than businesses expected, leading to unplanned changes in inventories.

Actual investment spending is the sum of planned investment spending and unplanned inventory investment.

As we explain in the upcoming Economics in Action, in late 2008, when expectations of future real GDP growth turned negative, planned investment spending—and, in particular, residential investment spending—plunged, accelerating the economy's slide into recession. Generally, the effects of the accelerator principle play an important role in *investment spending slumps*, periods of low investment spending.

Inventories and Unplanned Investment Spending

Most firms maintain inventories, stocks of goods held to satisfy future sales. Firms hold inventories so they can quickly satisfy buyers—a consumer can purchase an item off the shelf rather than waiting for it to be manufactured. In addition, businesses often hold inventories of their inputs to be sure they have a steady supply of necessary materials and spare parts. At the end of the second quarter of 2012, the overall value of inventories in Canada was estimated at $8.9 billion (0.5% of GDP).

As we explained in Chapter 7, a firm that increases its inventories is engaging in a form of investment spending. Suppose, for example, that Canada's auto industry produces 80 000 cars per month but sells only 70 000. The remaining 10 000 cars are added to the inventory at auto company warehouses or car dealerships, ready to be sold in the future. **Inventory investment** is the value of the *change* in total inventories held in the economy during a given period. Unlike other forms of investment spending, inventory investment can actually be negative. If, for example, the auto industry reduces its inventory over the course of a month, we say that it has engaged in negative inventory investment.

To understand inventory investment, think about a manager stocking the canned goods section of a supermarket. The manager tries to keep the store fully stocked so that shoppers can almost always find what they're looking for. But the manager does not want the shelves too heavily stocked because shelf space is limited and products can spoil. Similar considerations apply to many firms and typically lead them to manage their inventories carefully. However, sales fluctuate. And because firms cannot always accurately predict sales, they often find themselves holding more or less inventories than they had intended. These unintended swings in inventories due to unforeseen changes in sales are called **unplanned inventory investment.** They represent investment spending, positive or negative, that occurred but was unplanned.

So in any given period, **actual investment spending** is equal to planned investment spending plus unplanned inventory investment. If we let $I_{Unplanned}$ represent unplanned inventory investment, $I_{Planned}$ represent planned investment spending, and I represent actual investment spending, then the relationship among all three can be represented as:

(11-10) $I = I_{Unplanned} + I_{Planned}$

To see how unplanned inventory investment can occur, let's continue to focus on the auto industry and make the following assumptions. First, let's assume that the industry must determine each month's production volume in advance, before it knows the volume of actual sales. Second, let's assume that it anticipates selling 80 000 cars next month and that it plans neither to add to nor subtract from existing inventories. In that case, it will produce 80 000 cars to match anticipated sales.

Now imagine that next month's actual sales are less than expected, only 70 000 cars. As a result, the value of 10 000 cars will be added to investment spending as unplanned inventory investment.

In 2009, vehicles sat unsold on car dealership lots when the economy slumped and consumer spending plunged.

The auto industry will, of course, eventually adjust to this slowdown in sales and the resulting unplanned inventory investment. It is likely that it will cut next month's production volume in order to reduce inventories. In fact, economists who study macroeconomic variables in an attempt to determine the future path of the economy pay careful attention to changes in inventory levels. Rising inventories typically indicate positive unplanned inventory investment and a slowing economy, as sales are less than had been forecast. Falling inventories typically indicate negative unplanned inventory investment and a growing economy, as sales are greater than forecast. In the next section, we will see how production adjustments in response to fluctuations in sales and inventories ensure that the value of final goods and services actually produced is equal to desired purchases of those final goods and services.

ECONOMICS > IN ACTION

INTEREST RATES AND THE CANADIAN HOUSING MARKET

Many people would say there is a close inverse relationship between interest rates and housing sales: when one goes down, the other goes up. And this makes sense. As we mentioned earlier, when the interest rate falls, mortgage costs also fall, so people are more willing to buy a house, and housing starts rise. As Figure 11-7 shows, this relationship seems to hold true most of the time.

Figure 11-7 compares, from January 2000 to July 2012, the interest rates on five-year home mortgages, which most Canadians use to buy their homes, and the number of housing starts (seasonally adjusted at annual rates). In the early 2000s, the Bank of Canada reduced interest rates to deal with various causes of economic uncertainty in the marketplace, such as the events of 9/11 and an information technology stock price bubble. As a result, five-year mortgage interest rates fell from 8.55% in January 2000 to 5.8% in June 2003. These low rates caused housing starts to surge. In turn, this rise in spending led to overall economic expansion, both directly and through the multiplier process. Indeed, a similar trend happened in the U.S. during the same period. The Federal Reserve lowered interest rates, which lead to a housing boom. This housing boom subsequently went bust, triggering the financial crisis of 2008–2009.

FIGURE 11-7 Mortgage Interest Rates Compared to Housing Starts in Canada

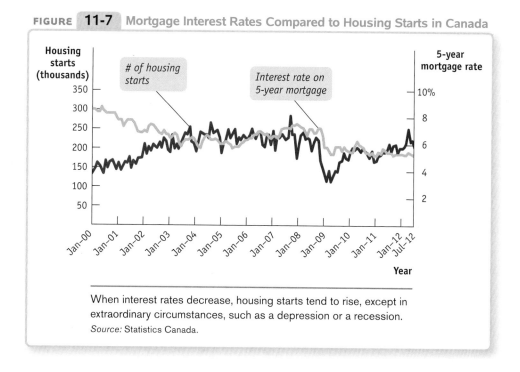

When interest rates decrease, housing starts tend to rise, except in extraordinary circumstances, such as a depression or a recession.
Source: Statistics Canada.

But you may have noticed that the relationship doesn't always seem to hold: when interest rates fell, between late 2008 and early 2009, housing starts also fell, which is just the opposite of what we should expect. Why? Circumstances can alter expectations. These were the years of the Great Recession, when many had lost their jobs. During this time, the Bank of Canada deliberately kept interest rates low to stimulate the sluggish economy. But people were still hesitant to buy homes—it's hard to think about buying a house when you are out of work or are worried about your job security, no matter how attractive the interest rates are. This reluctance caused Canadian home sales and average sale prices to drop in the spring of 2009. As the graph shows, later in 2010 and 2011, as the economic situation stabilized, interest rates remained low, and the number of new housing starts begins to rise again. By the end of the recession, average Canadian home prices once again started to rise. In fact, average prices rose enough that losses caused by the recession were erased. However, this did not happen in the American housing market. Despite interest rates remaining at historically low levels, the number of housing starts remains sluggish and housing prices are still below the pre-crisis levels.

CHECK YOUR UNDERSTANDING 11-3

1. For each event, explain whether planned investment spending or unplanned inventory investment will change and in what direction.
   a. An unexpected increase in consumer spending
   b. A sharp rise in the cost of business borrowing
   c. A sharp increase in the economy's growth rate of real GDP
   d. An unanticipated fall in sales

2. Historically, investment spending has experienced more extreme upward and downward swings than consumer spending. Why do you think this is so? (*Hint:* Consider the marginal propensity to consume and the accelerator principle.)

3. Consumer spending began to slow down in 2008, and economists worried that an *inventory overhang*—a high level of unplanned inventory investment throughout the economy—would make it difficult for the economy to recover anytime soon. Explain why an inventory overhang might, like the existence of too much production capacity, depress current economic activity.

Solutions appear at back of book.

The Income–Expenditure Model

Earlier in this chapter, we described how autonomous changes in spending—such as a fall in investment spending when a housing bubble bursts—lead to a multi-stage process through the actions of the multiplier that magnifies the effect of these changes on real GDP. In this section, we will examine this multi-stage process more closely. We'll see that the multiple rounds of changes in real GDP are accomplished through changes in the amount of output produced by firms—changes that they make in response to changes in their inventories. We'll come to understand why inventories play a central role in macroeconomic models of the economy in the short run as well as why economists pay particular attention to the behaviour of firms' inventories when trying to understand the likely future state of the economy.

Before we begin, let's quickly recap the assumptions underlying the multiplier process.

1. *Changes in overall expenditure (spending) lead to changes in aggregate output.* We assume that producers are willing to supply additional output at a fixed price level. As a result, changes in spending translate into changes in output

rather than moves of the overall price level up or down. A fixed aggregate price level also implies that there is no difference between nominal GDP and real GDP.[1] So we can use the two terms interchangeably in this chapter.

2. *The interest rate is fixed.* We'll take the interest rate as predetermined and unaffected by the factors we analyze in the model. As in the case of the aggregate price level, what we're really doing here is leaving the determinants of the interest rate outside the model. As we'll see, the model can still be used to study the effects of a change in the interest rate.

3. *Taxes, government transfers, and government purchases are all zero.*

4. *Exports and imports are both zero.*

Planned aggregate expenditure is the total amount households, businesses, and governments planned to spend.

In all subsequent chapters, we will drop the assumption that the aggregate price level is fixed. Appendix 13A addresses how taxes affect the multiplier process. We'll explain how the interest rate is determined in Chapter 15 and bring foreign trade back into the picture in Chapter 19.

Planned Aggregate Expenditure and Real GDP

In an economy with no government and no foreign trade, there are only two sources of aggregate expenditure: consumer spending, C, and investment spending, I. And since we assume that there are no taxes or transfers, aggregate disposable income, YD, is equal to nominal GDP (which, since the aggregate price level is fixed, is proportional to real GDP): the total value of final sales of goods and services ultimately accrues to households as income. So in this highly simplified economy, there are two basic equations of national income accounting:

(11-11) $GDP = C + I$

(11-12) $YD = GDP$

As we learned earlier in this chapter, the aggregate consumption function shows the relationship between disposable income and consumer spending. Let's continue to assume that the aggregate consumption function is of the same form as in Equation 11-9:

(11-13) $C = AC + MPC \times YD$

In our simplified model, we will also assume planned investment spending, $I_{Planned}$, is autonomous or fixed.

We need one more concept before putting the model together: **planned aggregate expenditure,** the total amount of planned spending in the economy. Unlike firms, households don't take unintended actions like unplanned inventory investment. So planned aggregate expenditure is equal to the sum of consumer spending and planned investment spending. We denote planned aggregate expenditure by $AE_{Planned}$, so:

(11-14a) $AE_{Planned} = C + I_{Planned}$

Substituting in the aggregate consumption, this becomes:

(11-14b) $AE_{Planned} = AC + MPC \times YD + I_{Planned}$

---

[1]The level (or size) of nominal GDP *is exactly equal* to that of real GDP only if the price level in the current period is the same as in the base period (i.e., the price level has stayed constant since the base period or has returned to the same level as then). If the current price level is different from the base period price level, then nominal GDP *is proportional to* real GDP. In this latter case, percentage changes of real and nominal GDP are equal as long as the price level remains constant—even though the levels are not equal.

This can be rewritten as:

(11-14c) $AE_{Planned} = [AC + I_{Planned}] + MPC \times YD = AE_0 + MPC \times YD$

where AE_0 represents autonomous planned aggregate expenditure, which collects all of the components of aggregate expenditure that are assumed to be autonomous or fixed. This is the intercept in the planned expenditure line—changes in autonomous expenditure will shift the planned expenditure line in a parallel manner. The marginal propensity to consume is the slope of the planned expenditure line—changes in the MPC will make the planned expenditure line either steeper or less steep.

The level of planned aggregate expenditure in a given year depends on the level of real GDP in that year. To see why, let's look at a specific example, shown in Table 11-3. We assume that the aggregate consumption function is:

(11-15) $C = 300 + 0.6 \times YD$

Real GDP, YD, C, $I_{Planned}$, and $AE_{Planned}$ are all measured in billions of dollars, and we assume that the level of planned investment, $I_{Planned}$, is fixed at $500 billion per year. The first column shows possible levels of real GDP. The second column shows disposable income, YD, which in our simplified model is equal to real GDP. The third column shows consumer spending, C, equal to $300 billion plus 0.6 times disposable income, YD. The fourth column shows planned investment spending, $I_{Planned}$, which we have assumed is $500 billion regardless of the level of real GDP. Finally, the last column shows planned aggregate expenditure, $AE_{Planned}$, the sum of aggregate consumer spending, C, and planned investment spending, $I_{Planned}$. (To economize on notation, we'll assume that it is understood from now on that all the variables

TABLE 11-3

Real GDP	YD	C	$I_{Planned}$	$AE_{Planned}$
(billions of dollars)				
$0	$0	$300	$500	$800
500	500	600	500	1100
1000	1000	900	500	1400
1500	1500	1200	500	1700
2000	2000	1500	500	2000
2500	2500	1800	500	2300
3000	3000	2100	500	2600
3500	3500	2400	500	2900

FIGURE 11-8   The Aggregate Consumption Function and Planned Aggregate Expenditure

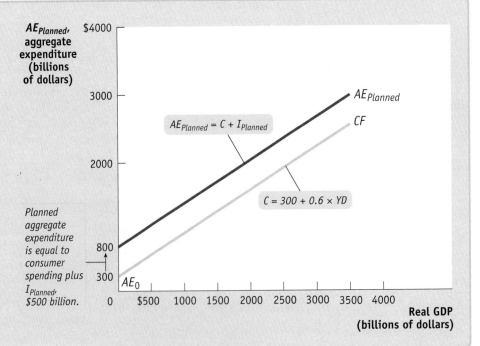

The slope, or steepness of the line depends on the value of MPC. The greater MPC is, the steeper the line will be. AE_0 is the intercept on the vertical axis. The lower line, CF, is the aggregate consumption function constructed from the data in Table 11-3. The upper line, $AE_{Planned}$, is the planned aggregate expenditure line, also constructed from the data in Table 11-3. It is equivalent to the aggregate consumption function shifted up by $500 billion, the amount of planned investment spending, $I_{Planned}$.

Planned aggregate expenditure is equal to consumer spending plus $I_{Planned}$, $500 billion.

in Table 11-3 are measured in billions of dollars per year.) As you can see, a higher level of real GDP leads to a higher level of disposable income: every 500 increase in real GDP raises YD by 500, which in turn raises C by $500 \times 0.6 = 300$ and $AE_{Planned}$ by 300.

Figure 11-8 illustrates the information in Table 11-3 graphically. Real GDP is measured on the horizontal axis. CF is the aggregate consumption function; it shows how consumer spending depends on real GDP. $AE_{Planned}$, the planned aggregate expenditure line, corresponds to the aggregate consumption function shifted up by 500 (the amount of $I_{Planned}$). It shows how planned aggregate expenditure depends on real GDP. Both lines have a slope of 0.6, equal to MPC, the marginal propensity to consume.

But this isn't the end of the story. Table 11-3 reveals that real GDP equals planned aggregate expenditure, $AE_{Planned}$, only when the level of real GDP is at 2000. Real GDP does not equal $AE_{Planned}$ at any other level. Is that possible? Didn't we learn in Chapter 7, with the circular-flow diagram, that total spending on final goods and services in the economy is equal to the total value of output of final goods and services? The answer is that for *brief* periods of time, planned aggregate expenditure can differ from real GDP because of the role of *unplanned* aggregate expenditure—$I_{Unplanned}$, unplanned inventory investment. But as we'll see in the next section, the economy moves over time to a situation in which there is no unplanned inventory investment, a situation called *income–expenditure equilibrium*. And when the economy is in income–expenditure equilibrium, planned aggregate expenditure on final goods and services equals aggregate output.

Income–Expenditure Equilibrium

For all but one value of real GDP shown in Table 11-3, real GDP is either more or less than $AE_{Planned}$, the sum of consumer spending and *planned* investment spending. For example, when real GDP is 1000, consumer spending, C, is 900 and planned investment spending is 500, making planned aggregate expenditure 1400. This is 400 *more* than the corresponding level of real GDP. Now consider what happens when real GDP is 2500; consumer spending, C, is 1800 and planned investment spending is 500, making planned aggregate expenditure only 2300, which is 200 *less* than real GDP.

As we've just explained, planned aggregate expenditure can be different from real GDP only if there is unplanned inventory investment, $I_{Unplanned}$, in the economy. Let's examine Table 11-4, which includes the numbers for real GDP and for planned aggregate expenditure from Table 11-3. It also includes the levels of unplanned inventory investment, $I_{Unplanned}$, that each combination of real GDP and planned aggregate expenditure implies. For example, if real GDP is 2500, planned aggregate expenditure is only 2300. This 200 excess of real GDP over $AE_{Planned}$ must consist of positive unplanned inventory investment. This can happen only if firms have overestimated sales and produced too much, leading to unintended additions to inventories. More generally, any level of real GDP in excess of 2000 corresponds to a situation in which firms are producing more than consumers and other firms want to purchase, creating an unintended increase in inventories.

Conversely, a level of real GDP below 2000 implies that planned aggregate expenditure is *greater* than real GDP. For example, when real GDP is 1000, planned aggregate expenditure is much larger, at 1400. The 400 excess of $AE_{Planned}$ over real GDP corresponds to negative unplanned inventory investment equal to −400. More generally, any level of real GDP below 2000 implies that firms have underestimated sales, leading to a negative level of unplanned inventory investment in the economy.

TABLE **11-4**

Real GDP	$AE_{Planned}$	$I_{Unplanned}$
(billions of dollars)		
$0	$800	−$800
500	1100	−600
1000	1400	−400
1500	1700	−200
2000	2000	0
2500	2300	200
3000	2600	400
3500	2900	

By putting together Equations 11-10, 11-11, and 11-14a, we can summarize the general relationships among real GDP, planned aggregate expenditure, and unplanned inventory investment as follows:

(11-16) $\text{GDP} = C + I$
$$= C + I_{Planned} + I_{Unplanned}$$
$$= AE_{Planned} + I_{Unplanned}$$

So whenever real GDP exceeds $AE_{Planned}$, $I_{Unplanned}$ is positive; whenever real GDP is less than $AE_{Planned}$, $I_{Unplanned}$ is negative.

But firms will act to correct their mistakes. We've assumed that they don't change their prices, but they *can* adjust their output. Specifically, they will reduce production if they have experienced an unintended rise in inventories or increase production if they have experienced an unintended fall in inventories. And these responses will eventually eliminate the unanticipated changes in inventories and move the economy to a point at which real GDP is equal to planned aggregate expenditure. Staying with our example, if real GDP is 1000, negative unplanned inventory investment will lead firms to increase production (by hiring additional workers if necessary), leading to a rise in real GDP. In fact, this will happen whenever real GDP is less than 2000—that is, whenever real GDP is less than planned aggregate expenditure. Conversely, if real GDP is 2500, positive unplanned inventory investment will lead firms to reduce production (perhaps by laying off some of their workers), leading to a fall in real GDP. This will happen whenever real GDP is greater than planned aggregate expenditure.

The only situation in which firms won't have an incentive to change output in the next period is when aggregate output, measured by real GDP, is equal to planned aggregate expenditure in the current period, an outcome known as **income–expenditure equilibrium.** In Table 11-4, income–expenditure equilibrium is achieved when real GDP is 2000, the only level of real GDP at which unplanned inventory investment is zero. From now on, we'll denote the real GDP level at which income–expenditure equilibrium occurs as Y^* and call it the **income–expenditure equilibrium (level of) GDP.**

Figure 11-9 illustrates the concept of income–expenditure equilibrium graphically. Real GDP is on the horizontal axis and planned aggregate expenditure, $AE_{Planned}$, is on the vertical axis. There are two lines in the figure. The solid line is the planned aggregate expenditure line. It shows how $AE_{Planned}$, equal to $C + I_{Planned}$, depends on real GDP; it has a slope of 0.6, equal to the marginal propensity to consume, *MPC*, and a vertical intercept equal to $A + I_{Planned}$ (300 + 500 = 800). The dashed line, which goes through the origin with a slope of 1 (often called a 45-degree line), shows all the possible points at which planned aggregate expenditure is equal to real GDP (i.e., $Y = AE_{Planned}$). This line allows us to easily spot the point of income–expenditure equilibrium, which must lie on both the 45-degree line and the planned aggregate expenditure line. So the point of income–expenditure equilibrium is at E, where the two lines cross. And the income–expenditure equilibrium GDP, Y^*, is 2000—the same outcome we derived in Table 11-4.

Now consider what happens if the economy isn't in income–expenditure equilibrium. We can see from Figure 11-9 that whenever real GDP is less than Y^*, the planned aggregate expenditure line lies above the 45-degree line and $AE_{Planned}$ exceeds real GDP. In this situation, $I_{Unplanned}$ is negative: as shown in the figure, at a real GDP of 1000, $I_{Unplanned}$ is −400. As a consequence, firms will increase their production and then real GDP will rise. In contrast, whenever real GDP is greater than Y^*, the planned aggregate expenditure line lies below the 45-degree line. Here, $I_{Unplanned}$ is positive: as shown, at a real GDP of 2500, $I_{Unplanned}$ is 200. The unanticipated accumulation of inventory will lead firms to lay off some of their workers to reduce levels of output, which leads to a fall in real GDP.

The economy is in **income–expenditure equilibrium** when aggregate output, measured by real GDP, is equal to planned aggregate expenditure.

Income–expenditure equilibrium GDP is the level of real GDP at which real GDP equals planned aggregate expenditure.

FIGURE   **11-9**   Income–Expenditure Equilibrium

Income–expenditure equilibrium occurs at E, the point where the planned aggregate expenditure line, $AE_{Planned}$, crosses the 45-degree line. At E, the economy produces real GDP of $2000 billion per year, the only point at which real GDP equals planned aggregate expenditure, $AE_{Planned}$, and unplanned inventory investment, $I_{Unplanned}$, is zero. This is the level of income–expenditure equilibrium GDP, Y^*. At any level of real GDP less than Y^*, $AE_{Planned}$ exceeds real GDP. As a result, unplanned inventory investment, $I_{Unplanned}$, is negative and firms respond by increasing production. At any level of real GDP greater than Y^*, real GDP exceeds $AE_{Planned}$. Unplanned inventory investment, $I_{Unplanned}$, is positive and firms respond by reducing production.

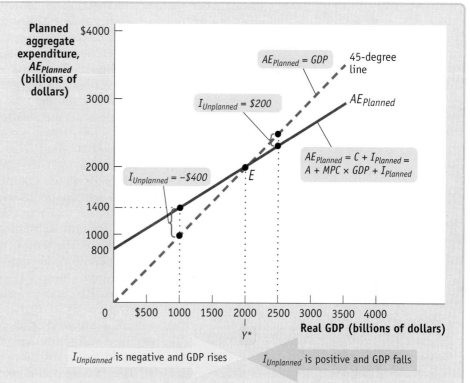

The type of diagram shown in Figure 11-9, which identifies income–expenditure equilibrium as the point at which the planned aggregate expenditure line crosses the 45-degree line, has a special place in the history of economic thought. Known as the **Keynesian cross,** it was developed by Paul Samuelson, one of the greatest economists of the twentieth century (as well as a Nobel Prize winner), to explain the ideas of John Maynard Keynes, the founder of macroeconomics as we know it.

The Multiplier Process and Inventory Adjustment

We've just learned about a very important feature of the macroeconomy: when planned spending by households and firms does not equal the current aggregate output by firms, this difference shows up as (unplanned) changes in inventories. The response of firms to those inventory changes moves real GDP over time to the point at which real GDP and planned aggregate expenditure are equal. That's why, as we mentioned earlier, changes in inventories are considered a leading indicator of future economic activity.

Now that we understand how real GDP moves to achieve income–expenditure equilibrium for a given level of planned aggregate expenditure, let's turn to understanding what happens when there is *a shift of the planned aggregate expenditure line.* How does the economy move from the initial point of income–expenditure equilibrium to a new point of income–expenditure equilibrium? And what are the possible sources of changes in planned aggregate expenditure?

In our simple model there are only two possible sources of a shift of the planned aggregate expenditure line: a change in planned investment spending, $I_{Planned}$, or a shift of the aggregate consumption function, CF. For example, a change in $I_{Planned}$ can occur because of a change in the interest rate. (Remember, we're assuming that the interest rate is fixed by factors that are outside the model. But we can still ask what happens when the interest rate changes.) A shift of the aggregate consumption function (that is, a change in its vertical intercept, AC)

The **Keynesian cross** diagram identifies income–expenditure equilibrium as the point where the planned aggregate expenditure line crosses (or intersects) the 45-degree line.

can occur because of a change in aggregate wealth—say, due to a rise in house prices. When there is a change in autonomous planned aggregate expenditure—when the planned expenditure line shifts (in a parallel manner)—this represents a change in the level of planned aggregate expenditure at any given level of real GDP. Recall from earlier in this chapter that an autonomous change in planned aggregate expenditure is a change in the desired level of spending by firms, households, and government at any given level of real GDP (although we've assumed away the government for the time being). How does an autonomous change in planned aggregate expenditure affect real GDP in income–expenditure equilibrium?

Table 11-5 and Figure 11-10 start from the same numerical example we used in Table 11-4 and Figure 11-9. They also show the effect of an autonomous increase in planned aggregate expenditure of 400, which is what happens when planned aggregate expenditure is 400 higher at each level of real GDP. Look first at Table 11-5. Before the autonomous increase in planned aggregate expenditure, the level of real GDP at which planned aggregate expenditure is equal to real GDP, Y^*, is 2000. After the autonomous change, Y^* has risen to 3000. The same result is visible in Figure 11-10. The initial income–expenditure equilibrium is at E_1, where Y_1^* is 2000. The autonomous rise in planned aggregate expenditure shifts the planned aggregate expenditure line up, leading to a new income–expenditure equilibrium at E_2, where Y_2^* is 3000.

The fact that the rise in income–expenditure equilibrium GDP, from 2000 to 3000, is much larger than the autonomous increase in aggregate expenditure, which is only 400, has a familiar explanation: the multiplier process. In the specific example we have just described, an autonomous increase in planned aggregate expenditure of 400 leads to an increase in Y^* from 2000 to 3000, a rise of 1000. So the multiplier in this example is $\frac{1000}{400} = \left(\frac{1}{1 - MPC}\right) = \left(\frac{1}{0.4}\right) = 2.5$.

TABLE 11-5

Real GDP	$AE_{Planned}$ before autonomous change	$AE_{Planned}$ after autonomous change
	(billions of dollars)	
$0	$800	$1200
500	1100	1500
1000	1400	1800
1500	1700	2100
2000	2000	2400
2500	2300	2700
3000	2600	3000
3500	2900	3300
4000	3200	3600

We can examine in detail what underlies the multi-stage multiplier process by looking more closely at Figure 11-10. First, starting from E_1, the autonomous increase in planned aggregate expenditure leads to a gap between planned aggregate expenditure and real GDP. This is represented by the vertical distance between X, at 2400, and E_1, at 2000. This gap illustrates an unplanned fall in inventory investment: $I_{Unplanned} = -400$. Firms respond by increasing production, leading to a rise in real GDP from Y_1^*. The rise in real GDP translates into an increase in disposable income, YD. That's the first stage in the chain reaction. But it doesn't stop there—the increase in YD leads to a rise in consumer spending, C, which sets off a second-round rise in real GDP. This in turn leads to a further rise in disposable income and consumer spending, and so on. And we could play this process in reverse: an autonomous fall in aggregate expenditure will lead to a chain reaction of reductions in production, causing a fall in real GDP and consumer spending.

We can summarize these results in an equation, where ΔAE_0 represents a change in the autonomous portion of planned expenditure, $AE_{Planned}$, and $\Delta Y^* = Y_2^* - Y_1^*$, the subsequent change in income–expenditure equilibrium GDP:

(11-17) $\Delta Y^* = \text{Multiplier} \times \Delta AE_0 = \left(\frac{1}{1 - MPC}\right) \times \Delta AE_0$

Recalling that the multiplier, $\left(\frac{1}{1 - MPC}\right)$, is greater than 1, Equation 11-17 tells us that the change in income–expenditure equilibrium GDP, ΔY^*, is several

FIGURE **11-10** The Multiplier

This figure illustrates the change in Y^* caused by an autonomous increase in planned aggregate expenditure. The economy is initially at equilibrium point E_1 with an income–expenditure equilibrium GDP, Y_1^*, equal to 2000. An autonomous increase in $AE_{Planned}$ of 400 shifts the planned aggregate expenditure line upward by 400. The economy is no longer in income–expenditure equilibrium: real GDP is equal to 2000 but $AE_{Planned}$ is now 2400, represented by point X. The vertical distance between the two planned aggregate expenditure lines, equal to 400, represents $I_{Unplanned} = -400$—the negative inventory investment that the economy now experiences. Firms respond by increasing production, and the economy eventually reaches a new income–expenditure equilibrium at E_2 with a higher level of income–expenditure equilibrium GDP, Y_2^*, equal to 3000.

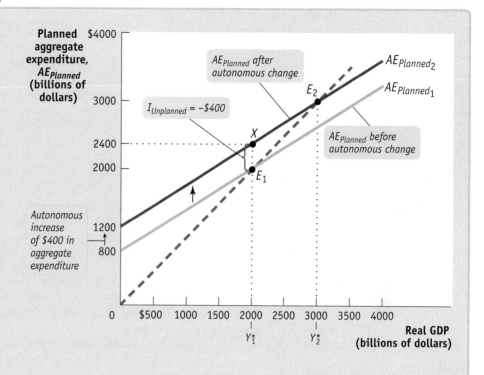

times as large as the autonomous change in planned aggregate expenditure, ΔAE_0. It also helps us recall an important point: because the marginal propensity to consume is less than 1, each increase in disposable income and each corresponding increase in consumer spending is smaller than in the previous round. That's because at each round some of the increase in disposable income leaks out into savings. As a result, although real GDP grows at each round, the increase in real GDP diminishes from each round to the next. At some point the increase in real GDP is negligible, and the economy converges to a new income–expenditure equilibrium GDP at Y_2^*.

The Paradox of Thrift You may recall that in Chapter 6 we mentioned the paradox of thrift to illustrate the fact that in macroeconomics the outcome of many individual actions can generate a result that is different from and worse than the simple sum of those individual actions. In the paradox of thrift, when households and firms anticipate tough(er) economic times, they attempt to save more. These actions depress the economy, leaving households and firms worse off than if they hadn't acted virtuously to prepare for tough times. It is called a paradox because what's usually "good" (saving to provide for your family in hard times) is "bad" (because it can make everyone worse off).

Using the multiplier, we can now see exactly how this scenario unfolds. Suppose that there is a slump in consumer spending or investment spending, or both, just like the slump in residential construction investment spending leading up to the 2008–2009 recession. This causes a fall in income–expenditure equilibrium GDP that is several times larger than the original fall in spending. The fall in real GDP leaves consumers and producers worse off than they would have been if they hadn't cut their spending. Conversely, prodigal behaviour is rewarded: if consumers or

Extravagant spending on the part of producers and consumers makes everyone better off, thanks to the multiplier process.

producers increase their spending, the resulting multiplier process makes the increase in income–expenditure equilibrium GDP several times larger than the original increase in spending. So prodigal spending makes consumers and producers better off than if they had been cautious spenders.

It's important to realize that our result that the multiplier is equal to $1/(1 - MPC)$ depends on the simplifying assumptions that there are no taxes or transfers and that planned investment does not depend directly on GDP, so that disposable income is equal to real GDP. In Appendix 13A, we'll bring taxes into the picture, which makes the expression for the multiplier more complicated and the multiplier itself smaller. But the general principle we have just learned— an autonomous change in planned aggregate expenditure leads to a change in income–expenditure equilibrium GDP, both directly and through an induced change in consumer spending—remains valid.

As we noted earlier in this chapter, declines in planned investment spending are usually the major factor causing recessions, because historically they have been the most common source of autonomous reductions in aggregate expenditure. The tendency of the consumption function to shift upward over time, which we pointed out earlier in Economics in Action, "Famous First Forecasting Failures," means that autonomous changes in both planned investment spending and consumer spending play important roles in expansions. But regardless of the source, there are multiplier effects in the economy that magnify the size of the initial change in aggregate expenditure.

ECONOMICS ➤ IN ACTION

INVENTORIES AND THE END OF A RECESSION

A very clear example of the role of inventories in the multiplier process took place in the 2008–2009 recession. One of the driving forces behind the recession was a slump in business investment spending. It took several quarters before investment spending bounced back in the form of a renewed housing boom and the building of infrastructure funded under the Economic Action Plan.

FIGURE 11-11 Inventories and the End of a Recession

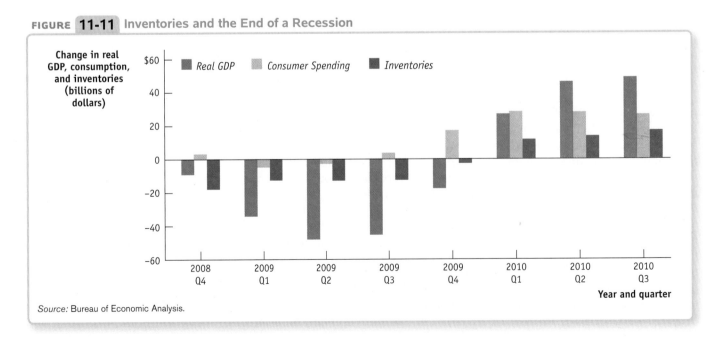

Source: Bureau of Economic Analysis.

Figure 11-11 shows changes in real GDP, real consumer spending, and real inventories by quarter from the fourth quarter of 2008 to the third quarter of 2010. Notice in the last quarter of 2008 how the fall in inventories exceeded the drop in real GDP, showing that this decrease was a driving force behind the recession. Consumer spending began to increase in the second quarter of 2009, but it was not until the first quarter of 2010 that GDP was positive. You might ask, why was that the case? The answer is rather simple. In the third quarter of 2009, the recession was still in full force and suppliers were reluctant to ramp up production too quickly and get caught in a difficult position. It wasn't until the first quarter of 2010 that inventories were positive.

CHECK YOUR UNDERSTANDING   11-4

1. Although economists believe that recessions typically begin as slumps in investment spending, they also believe that consumer spending eventually slumps during a recession. Explain why.

2. **a.** Use a diagram like Figure 11-10 to show what happens when there is an autonomous fall in planned aggregate expenditure. Describe how the economy adjusts to a new income–expenditure equilibrium.
   b. Suppose Y^* is originally $500 billion, the autonomous reduction in planned aggregate expenditure is $300 million ($0.3 billion), and $MPC = 0.5$. Calculate Y^* after such a change.

Solutions appear at back of book.

▼ Quick Review

- The economy is in **income–expenditure equilibrium** when **planned aggregate expenditure** is equal to real GDP.

- At any output level greater than **income–expenditure equilibrium GDP,** real GDP exceeds planned aggregate expenditure and inventories are rising. At any lower output level, real GDP falls short of planned aggregate expenditure and inventories are falling.

- After an autonomous change in planned aggregate expenditure, the economy moves to a new income–expenditure equilibrium through the inventory adjustment process, as illustrated by the **Keynesian cross.** Because of the multiplier effect, the change in income–expenditure equilibrium GDP is a multiple of the autonomous change in aggregate expenditure.

BUSINESS CASE • Keeping Afloat in Newfoundland and Labrador

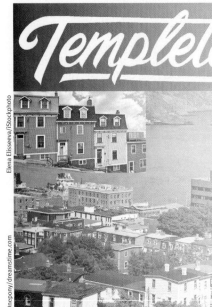

St. John's, the capital of Newfoundland and Labrador, is a large city with many stores and industries that are not related directly to the cod industry. So you might think that the local businesses in St. John's would have been less affected by the moratorium than the small outport fishing communities.

In fact, all of St. John's suffered. Many stores went out of business, and others came close to it. Consider Templeton's, a local family-owned store that has been in operation in St John's for almost a century and a half. Originally an importer of dry goods from Europe and the United States (remember, Newfoundland did not join Canada until 1949), Templeton's decided to specialize in 1922, and since that time it has been the place to shop for paint, wallpaper, and floor coverings. But despite its history and longevity, Templeton's sales fell drastically during the moratorium, and the situation was dire.

The story does have a happy ending though. Templeton's raised its sales by introducing a popular new line of paint in unique colours that reflected the heritage of the province, such as Dory Buff, Iceberg Alley, and Mussels in the Corner. Similarly, other entrepreneurs looked to tourism opportunities in response to the cod moratorium, starting iceberg and whale-watching tours and opening shops featuring local jams and heritage crafts. These businesses have also prospered. But of course the main reason for the economic boom in Newfoundland and Labrador is the development of the huge oil deposits off the coast. In 2012, St. John's economy was described as "sizzling," with a GDP of nearly $52 000 per capita, the second best in Canada.[2] And housing starts, a sure indicator of prosperity, had risen, from a low of 1371 in 1999 to 3488 in 2011.[3]

QUESTIONS FOR THOUGHT

1. Why did a moratorium on cod fishing affect stores like Templeton's, which sells paint and flooring?

2. Why would the number of housing starts be related to the new economic developments in oil and tourism?

---

[2]*Source:* City of St. John's Corporate Plan 2010–2013.
[3]*Sources:* Canada Mortgage and Housing Corporation; Statistics Canada.

SUMMARY

1. An **autonomous change in aggregate expenditure** leads to a chain reaction in which the total change in real GDP is equal to the **multiplier** times the initial change in aggregate expenditure. The size of the multiplier, $\dfrac{1}{1 - MPC}$, depends on the **marginal propensity to consume, *MPC,*** the fraction of an additional dollar of disposable income spent on consumption. The larger the *MPC,* the larger the multiplier and the larger the change in real GDP for any given autonomous change in aggregate expenditure. The **marginal propensity to save, *MPS,*** is equal to $1 - MPC$.

2. The **individual consumption function** shows how an individual household's consumer spending is determined by its current disposable income. The **aggregate consumption function** shows the relationship for the entire economy. According to the life-cycle hypothesis, households try to smooth their consumption over their lifetimes. As a result, the aggregate consumption function shifts in response to changes in expected future disposable income and changes in aggregate wealth.

3. **Planned investment spending** depends negatively on the interest rate and on existing production capacity; it depends positively on expected future real GDP. The **accelerator principle** says that investment spending is greatly influenced by the expected growth rate of real GDP.

4. Firms hold inventories of goods so that they can satisfy consumer demand quickly. **Inventory investment** is positive when firms add to their inventories, and negative when they reduce them. Often, however, changes in inventories are not a deliberate decision but the result of mistakes in forecasts about sales. The result is **unplanned inventory investment,** which can be either positive or negative. **Actual investment spending** is the sum of planned investment spending and unplanned inventory investment.

5. In **income–expenditure equilibrium, planned aggregate expenditure,** which in a simplified model with no government and no trade is the sum of consumer spending and planned investment spending, is equal to real GDP. At the **income–expenditure equilibrium GDP,** or Y^*, unplanned inventory investment is zero. When real GDP is smaller than Y^*, unplanned inventory investment is negative (since planned aggregate expenditure exceeds real GDP and real GDP = $AE_{Planned} + I_{Unplanned}$); there is an unanticipated reduction in inventories and subsequently firms increase production, often by hiring more workers. When real GDP exceeds Y^*, unplanned inventory investment is positive (since planned aggregate expenditure is smaller than real GDP and real GDP = $AE_{Planned} + I_{Unplanned}$); there is an unanticipated increase in inventories and subsequently firms reduce production, usually by laying off some workers. The **Keynesian cross** shows how the economy self-adjusts to income–expenditure equilibrium through inventory adjustments.

6. After an autonomous change in planned aggregate expenditure, the inventory adjustment process moves the economy to a new income–expenditure equilibrium. The change in income–expenditure equilibrium GDP arising from an autonomous change in spending is equal to $\dfrac{1}{1 - MPC} \times \Delta AE_0$.

KEY TERMS

Marginal propensity to consume (*MPC*), p. 340
Marginal propensity to save (*MPS*), p. 341
Autonomous change in aggregate expenditure, p. 342
Multiplier, p. 342

Individual consumption function, p. 344
Aggregate consumption function, p. 346
Planned investment spending, p. 350
Accelerator principle, p. 351
Inventory investment, p. 352
Unplanned inventory investment, p. 352

Actual investment spending, p. 352
Planned aggregate expenditure, p. 355
Income–expenditure equilibrium, p. 358
Income–expenditure equilibrium GDP, p. 358
Keynesian cross, p. 359

1. Due to an increase in consumer wealth, there is a $40 billion autonomous increase in consumer spending in the economies of Westlandia and Eastlandia. Assuming that the aggregate price level is constant, the interest rate is fixed in both countries, and there are no taxes and no foreign trade, complete the accompanying tables to show the various rounds of increased spending that will occur in both economies if the marginal propensity to consume is 0.5 in Westlandia and 0.75 in Eastlandia. What do your results indicate about the relationship between the size of the marginal propensity to consume and the multiplier?

	Westlandia	
Rounds	**Incremental change in GDP**	**Total change in GDP**
1	ΔC = $40 billion	?
2	$MPC \times \Delta C$ =	?	?
3	$MPC \times MPC \times \Delta C$ =	?	?
4	$MPC \times MPC \times MPC \times \Delta C$ =	?	?
...	...	...
Total change in GDP	$(1/(1 - MPC)) \times \Delta C$ = ?	

	Eastlandia	
Rounds	**Incremental change in GDP**	**Total change in GDP**
1	ΔC = $40 billion	?
2	$MPC \times \Delta C$ =	?	?
3	$MPC \times MPC \times \Delta C$ =	?	?
4	$MPC \times MPC \times MPC \times \Delta C$ =	?	?
...	...	...
Total change in GDP	$(1/(1 - MPC)) \times \Delta C$ = ?	

2. Assuming that the aggregate price level is constant, the interest rate is fixed, and there are no taxes and no foreign trade, what will be the change in GDP if the following events occur?

   a. There is an autonomous increase in consumer spending of $2.5 billion; the marginal propensity to consume is 2/3.

   b. Firms reduce investment spending by $4 billion; the marginal propensity to consume is 0.8.

   c. The government increases its purchases of military equipment by $6 billion; the marginal propensity to consume is 0.6.

3. Economists observed the only five residents of a very small economy and estimated each one's consumer spending at various levels of current disposable income. The accompanying table shows each resident's consumer spending at three income levels.

Individual consumer spending by	Individual current disposable income		
	$0	**$20 000**	**$40 000**
Andre	$1000	$15 000	$29 000
Barbara	2500	12 500	22 500
Casey	2000	20 000	38 000
Declan	5000	17 000	29 000
Elena	4000	19 000	34 000

   a. What is each resident's individual consumption function? What is the marginal propensity to consume for each resident?

   b. What is the economy's aggregate consumption function? What is the marginal propensity to consume for the economy?

4. From 2003 to 2008, Eastlandia experienced large fluctuations in both aggregate consumer spending and disposable income, but wealth, the interest rate, and expected future disposable income did not change. The accompanying table shows the level of aggregate consumer spending and disposable income in millions of dollars for each of these years. Use this information to answer the following questions.

Year	Disposable income (millions of dollars)	Consumer spending (millions of dollars)
2003	$100	$180
2004	350	380
2005	300	340
2006	400	420
2007	375	400
2008	500	500

   a. Plot the aggregate consumption function for Eastlandia.

   b. What is the marginal propensity to consume? What is the marginal propensity to save?

   c. What is the aggregate consumption function?

5. Statistics Canada reported, in real terms, that overall consumer spending increased by $9.1 billion during the fourth quarter of 2010.

   a. Suppose this change were due entirely to a change in autonomous consumption and all other autonomous expenditure terms have not changed. Sketch a Keynesian cross (planned aggregate expenditure versus GDP) diagram of the situation. Clearly label the initial and new planned aggregate expenditure lines and the initial and new income–expenditure equilibrium (level of) GDP.

b. If the marginal propensity to consume is 0.52, by how much will real GDP change in response?

c. GDP at the end of the first quarter of 2011 was $1350.4 billion. If GDP were to increase by the amount calculated in part (b), what would be the percent increase in GDP?

6. During the early 2000s, the Case-Shiller U.S. Home Price Index, a measure of average American home prices, rose continuously until it peaked in March 2006. From March 2006 to May 2009, the index lost 32% of its value. Meanwhile, the U.S. stock market experienced similar ups and downs. From March 2003 to October 2007, the Standard and Poor's 500 (S&P 500) stock index, a broad measure of stock market prices, almost doubled, from 800.73 to a high of 1565.15. From that time until March 2009, the index fell by almost 60%, to a low of 676.53.

a. How do you think the movements in U.S. housing prices both influenced the growth in U.S. real GDP during the first half of the decade and added to the concern about maintaining American consumer spending after the collapse in the American housing market that began in 2006? To what extent did the movements in the U.S. stock market hurt or help American consumer spending?

b. How do you think the movements in U.S. housing prices both influenced the growth in Canadian real GDP during the first half of the decade and added to the concern about maintaining Canadian consumer spending after the collapse in the American housing market that began in 2006? To what extent did the movements in the U.S. stock market hurt or help Canadian consumer spending? (Hint: Remember Canada is an open economy that trades with the rest of the world, and that the U.S. is its largest trading partner.)

7. How will planned investment spending change as the following events occur?

a. The interest rate falls as a result of Bank of Canada policy.

b. Environment Canada decrees that corporations must upgrade or replace their machinery in order to reduce their emissions of sulphur dioxide.

c. Baby boomers begin to retire in large numbers and reduce their savings, resulting in higher interest rates.

8. Explain how each of the following actions will affect the level of planned investment spending and unplanned inventory investment. Assume the economy is initially in income–expenditure equilibrium.

a. The Bank of Canada raises the interest rate.

b. There is a rise in the expected growth rate of real GDP.

c. A sizable inflow of foreign funds into the country lowers the interest rate.

9. a. The accompanying table shows gross domestic product (GDP), disposable income (YD), consumer spending (C), and planned investment spending ($I_{Planned}$) in an economy. Assume there is no government or foreign sector in this economy. Complete the table by calculating planned aggregate expenditure ($AE_{Planned}$) and unplanned inventory investment ($I_{Unplanned}$).

GDP	YD	C	$I_{Planned}$	$AE_{Planned}$	$I_{Unplanned}$
(billions of dollars)					
$0	$0	$100	$300	?	?
400	400	400	300	?	?
800	800	700	300	?	?
1200	1200	1000	300	?	?
1600	1600	1300	300	?	?
2000	2000	1600	300	?	?
2400	2400	1900	300	?	?
2800	2800	2200	300	?	?
3200	3200	2500	300	?	?

b. What is the aggregate consumption function?

c. What is Y*, income–expenditure equilibrium GDP?

d. What is the value of the multiplier?

e. If planned investment spending falls to $200 billion, what will be the new Y*?

f. If autonomous consumer spending rises to $200 billion, what will be the new Y*?

10. In an economy with no government and no foreign sectors, autonomous consumer spending is $250 billion, planned investment spending is $350 billion, and the marginal propensity to consume is 2/3.

a. Plot the aggregate consumption function and planned aggregate expenditure.

b. What is unplanned inventory investment when real GDP equals $600 billion?

c. What is Y*, income–expenditure equilibrium GDP?

d. What is the value of the multiplier?

e. If planned investment spending rises to $450 billion, what will be the new Y*?

11. An economy has a marginal propensity to consume of 0.5, and Y^*, income–expenditure equilibrium GDP, equals $500 billion. Given an autonomous increase in planned investment of $10 billion, show the rounds of increased spending that take place by completing the accompanying table. The first and second rows are filled in for you. In the first row, the increase of planned investment spending of $10 billion raises real GDP and YD by $10 billion, leading to an increase in consumer spending of $5 billion ($MPC \times$ change in disposable income) in row 2, raising real GDP and YD by a further $5 billion.

Rounds	Change in $I_{Planned}$ or C	Change in real GDP	Change in YD
		(billions of dollars)	
1	$\Delta I_{Planned} = \$10.00$	$10.00	$10.00
2	$\Delta C = \$ 5.00$	$ 5.00	$ 5.00
3	$\Delta C = ?$	?	?
4	$\Delta C = ?$	?	?
5	$\Delta C = ?$	?	?
6	$\Delta C = ?$	?	?
7	$\Delta C = ?$	?	?
8	$\Delta C = ?$	?	?
9	$\Delta C = ?$	?	?
10	$\Delta C = ?$	?	?

a. What is the total change in real GDP after the 10 rounds? What is the value of the multiplier? What would you expect the total change in Y^* to be, based on the multiplier formula? How do your answers to the first and third questions compare?

b. Redo the table starting from round 2, assuming the marginal propensity to consume is 0.75. What is the total change in real GDP after 10 rounds? What is the value of the multiplier? As the marginal propensity to consume increases, what happens to the value of the multiplier?

12. Although the United States is one of the richest nations in the world, it is also the world's largest debtor nation. We often hear that the problem is the nation's low savings rate. Suppose policy-makers attempt to rectify this by encouraging greater savings in the economy. What effect will their successful attempts have on real GDP?

13. The Canadian economy slowed significantly in 2008, and policy-makers were extremely concerned about lack of growth. To boost the economy, the House of Commons adopted the Economic Action Plan in January 2009. This plan delivered about $64 billion in additional government spending into the economy. Assume, for the sake of argument, this spending was in the form of payments made directly to consumers. The objective was to boost the economy by increasing the disposable income of Canadian consumers.

a. Calculate the initial change in aggregate consumer spending as a consequence of this policy measure if the marginal propensity to consume (MPC) in Canada is 0.5. Then calculate the resulting change in real GDP arising from the $700 billion in payments.

b. Illustrate the effect on real GDP with the use of a graph depicting the income–expenditure equilibrium. Label the vertical axis "Planned aggregate expenditure, $AE_{Planned}$" and the horizontal axis "Real GDP." Draw two planned aggregate expenditure curves ($AE_{Planned1}$ and $AE_{Planned2}$) and a 45-degree line to show the effect of the autonomous policy change on the equilibrium.

Deriving the Multiplier Algebraically

This appendix shows how to derive the multiplier algebraically. First, recall that in this chapter planned aggregate expenditure, $AE_{Planned}$, is the sum of consumer spending, C, which is determined by the consumption function, and planned investment spending, $I_{Planned}$. That is, $AE_{Planned} = C + I_{Planned}$. Rewriting this equation to express all its terms fully, we have:

(11A-1) $AE_{Planned} = AC + MPC \times YD + I_{Planned}$

Because there are no taxes or government transfers in this model, disposable income is equal to GDP, so Equation 11A-1 becomes:

(11A-2) $AE_{Planned} = AC + MPC \times GDP + I_{Planned}$

The income–expenditure equilibrium level of GDP, Y^*, is equal to planned aggregate expenditure:

(11A-3) $Y^* = AE_{Planned}$
$= AC + MPC \times Y^* + I_{Planned}$
   in income–expenditure equilibrium

Just two more steps. Subtract $MPC \times Y^*$ from both sides of Equation 11A-3:

(11A-4) $Y^* - MPC \times Y^* = Y^* \times (1 - MPC) = AC + I_{Planned}$

Finally, divide both sides by $(1 - MPC)$:

(11A-5) $Y^* = \left(\dfrac{1}{1 - MPC}\right) \times [AC + I_{Planned}] = \left(\dfrac{1}{1 - MPC}\right) \times AE_0$

$= \left(\dfrac{1}{1 - MPC}\right) \times [\text{Autonomous Aggregate Expenditure}]$

Equation 11A-5 tells us that a \$1 autonomous change in planned aggregate expenditure—a change in either AC or $I_{Planned}$—causes a \$1/(1 - MPC) change in the income–expenditure equilibrium level of GDP, Y^*. The multiplier in our simple model is therefore:

(11A-6) Multiplier $= 1/(1 - MPC)$

PROBLEMS

1. In an economy without government purchases, transfers, or taxes, and without imports or exports, aggregate autonomous consumer spending is \$500 billion, planned investment spending is \$250 billion, and the marginal propensity to consume is 0.5.

   a. Write the expression for planned aggregate expenditure as in Equation 11A-1.

   b. Solve for Y^* algebraically.

   c. What is the value of the multiplier?

   d. How will Y^* change if autonomous consumer spending falls to \$450 billion?

2. Complete the following table by calculating the value of the multiplier and identifying the change in Y^* due to the change in autonomous expenditure. How does the value of the multiplier change with the marginal propensity to consume?

MPC	Value of multiplier	Change in spending	Change in Y^*
0.5	?	$\Delta C = +$ \$50 million	?
0.6	?	$\Delta I = -$ \$10 million	?
0.75	?	$\Delta C = -$ \$25 million	?
0.8	?	$\Delta I = +$ \$20 million	?
0.9	?	$\Delta C = -$ \$2.5 million	?

Aggregate Demand and Aggregate Supply

SHOCKS TO THE SYSTEM

The Bank of Canada has the options of pumping cash into the economy to fight unemployment or pulling cash out of the economy to fight inflation.

❱ How the **aggregate demand curve** illustrates the relationship between the aggregate price level and the quantity of aggregate output demanded in the economy

❱ How the **aggregate supply curve** illustrates the relationship between the aggregate price level and the quantity of aggregate output supplied in the economy

❱ Why the aggregate supply curve is different in the short run compared to the long run

❱ How the *AD–AS* model is used to analyze economic fluctuations

❱ How monetary policy and fiscal policy can stabilize the economy

SOMETIMES IT'S NOT EASY BEING the boss. The Bank of Canada (BOC) is the institution that sets our monetary policy. Established in 1934, its primary goal is "to promote the economic and financial welfare of Canada."

When the U.S. economy went into a recession in 2001, the BOC rushed cash into the Canadian system—just as its U.S. counterpart the Federal Reserve rushed money into the American system. It was an easy choice: unemployment was rising, and inflation was low and falling. In fact, for much of late 2001 and 2002, the BOC was actually worried about the possibility of *deflation*.

For much of 2008, however, Mark Carney (shown here), then governor of the BOC, faced a much more difficult problem: *stagflation*—a combination of unacceptably high inflation and rising unemployment. Stagflation caused trou-

bles around the world in the 1970s: the two deep U.S. recessions of 1973–1975 and 1979–1982 were both accompanied by soaring inflation. While Canada only had a recession in 1981–1982, our economy experienced much slower real GDP growth and higher unemployment coupled with a high rate of inflation.

Why did the economic difficulties of late 2008 look so different from those of 2001? Because they had different causes. Therefore, they required different policy responses. The U.S. recession of 2001, like many recessions, was caused by a fall in investment and consumer spending. In episodes like this, high inflation isn't a threat. So policy-makers know what they must do: pump cash in, to fight rising unemployment.

The U.S. recessions of the 1970s and slowdowns they brought to Canada, however, were caused largely by sharp

cuts in world oil production and soaring prices for oil and other fuels. Not coincidentally, soaring oil prices also contributed to the economic difficulties of early 2008. In both periods, high energy prices led to a combination of high unemployment and high inflation. They also created a dilemma: should the BOC fight the slump by pumping cash *into* the economy, or should it fight inflation by pulling cash *out* of the economy, which could worsen the slump?

It's worth noting, by the way, that in 2011 the BOC faced some of the same problems it faced in 2008, as rising oil and food prices led to rising inflation despite high unemployment. In 2011, however, the BOC was fairly sure that demand was the main problem. Therefore, it decided to stimulate aggregate demand by keeping interest rate at low levels.

In the previous chapter, we developed the *income–expenditure model,* which focuses on the determinants of aggregate expenditure. This model is extremely useful for understanding events like the U.S. recession of 2001 and the recovery that followed. However, we'll need a more advanced model to understand the problems that the recession of 2008 created for world policy-makers.

In this chapter, we'll develop a model that will help us to distinguish between a *demand* shock, like that of the 2001 U.S. recession, and a *supply shock*, like that of the 2008 recession. To develop this model we'll proceed in three steps. First, we'll develop the concept of *aggregate demand.* Then we'll turn to the parallel concept of *aggregate supply.* Finally, we'll put them together in the *AD–AS model.* ■

The **aggregate demand curve** shows the relationship between the aggregate price level and the quantity of aggregate output demanded by households, businesses, the government, and the rest of the world.

Aggregate Demand

The Great Depression, the great majority of economists agree, was the result of a massive negative, or adverse, demand shock. What does that mean? In Chapter 3 we explained that when economists talk about a fall in the demand for a particular good or service, they're referring to a leftward shift of the demand curve. Similarly, when economists talk about a negative, or adverse, demand shock to the economy as a whole, they're referring to a leftward shift of the **aggregate demand curve,** a curve that shows the relationship between the aggregate price level and the quantity of aggregate output demanded by households, firms, the government, and the rest of the world.

Figure 12-1 shows what the aggregate demand curve may have looked like in 1933, at the end of the 1929–1933 recession. The horizontal axis shows the total quantity of domestic goods and services demanded, measured in 2002 dollars. We use real GDP to measure aggregate output and will often use the two terms interchangeably. The vertical axis shows the aggregate price level, measured by the GDP deflator. With these variables on the axes, we can draw a curve, *AD*, showing how much aggregate output would have been demanded at any given aggregate price level. Since *AD* is meant to illustrate aggregate demand in 1933, one point on the curve corresponds to actual data for 1933, when the aggregate price level was 6.6 and the total quantity of domestic final goods and services purchased was $54.7 billion in 2002 dollars.

As drawn in Figure 12-1, the aggregate demand curve is downward sloping, indicating a negative relationship between the aggregate price level and the quantity of aggregate output demanded. A higher aggregate price level, other things equal, reduces the quantity of aggregate output demanded; a lower aggregate price level, other things equal, increases the quantity of aggregate output demanded. According to Figure 12-1, if the price level in 1933 had been 3.1 instead of 6.6, the total quantity of domestic final goods and services demanded would have been $80 billion in 2002 dollars instead of $54.7 billion.

The first key question about the aggregate demand curve is: why should the curve be downward sloping?

FIGURE 12-1 The Aggregate Demand Curve

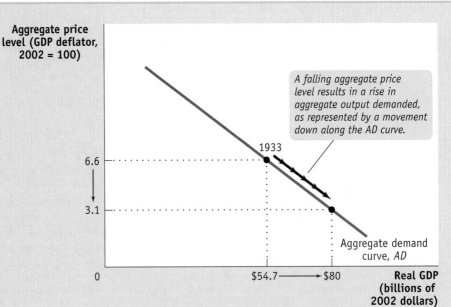

The aggregate demand curve shows the relationship between the aggregate price level and the quantity of aggregate output demanded. The curve is downward sloping due to the wealth effect of a change in the aggregate price level and the interest rate effect of a change in the aggregate price level. Corresponding to the actual 1933 data, here the total quantity of goods and services demanded at an aggregate price level of 6.6 is $54.7 billion in 2002 dollars. According to our hypothetical curve, however, if the aggregate price level had been only 3.1, the quantity of aggregate output demanded would have risen to $80 billion.

Why Is the Aggregate Demand Curve Downward Sloping?

In Figure 12-1, the curve *AD* is downward sloping. But why? Recall the basic equation of national income accounting:

(12-1) GDP = $C + I + G + X - IM$

where C is consumer spending, I is investment spending, G is government purchases of goods and services, X is exports to other countries, and IM is imports. If we measure these variables in constant dollars—that is, in prices of a base year—then $C + I + G + X - IM$ is the real quantity of domestically produced final goods and services demanded during a given period. G is decided by the government, but the other variables are largely from private-sector decisions. To understand why the aggregate demand curve slopes downward, we need to understand why a rise in the aggregate price level reduces C, I, and $X - IM$.

You might think that the downward slope of the aggregate demand curve is a natural consequence of the *law of demand* we defined back in Chapter 3. That is, since the demand curve for any one good is downward sloping, isn't it natural that the demand curve for aggregate output is also downward sloping? This turns out, however, to be a misleading parallel. The demand curve for any individual good shows how the quantity demanded depends on the price of that good, *holding the prices of other goods and services and income constant.* The main reason the quantity of a good demanded falls when the price of that good rises—that is, the quantity of a good demanded falls as we move up the demand curve—is that people switch their consumption to other goods and services.

But when we consider movements up or down the aggregate demand curve, we're considering *a simultaneous change in the prices of all final goods and services.* Furthermore, changes in the composition of goods and services in consumer spending aren't relevant to the aggregate demand curve: if consumers decide to buy fewer clothes but more cars, this doesn't necessarily change the total quantity of final goods and services they demand.

Why, then, does a rise in the aggregate price level lead to a fall in the quantity of all domestically produced final goods and services demanded? There are two main reasons: the *wealth effect* and the *interest rate effect* of a change in the aggregate price level.

The Wealth Effect An increase in the aggregate price level, other things equal, reduces the purchasing power of many assets. Consider, for example, someone who has $5000 in a bank account. If the aggregate price level were to rise by 25%, what used to cost $5000 would now cost $6250, and would no longer be affordable. And what used to cost $4000 would now cost $5000, so that the $5000 in the bank account would now buy only as much as $4000 would have bought previously. With the loss in purchasing power, the owner of that bank account would probably scale back his or her consumption plans. Millions of other people would respond the same way, leading to a fall in real spending on final goods and services, because a rise in the aggregate price level reduces the purchasing power of everyone's bank account. Correspondingly, a fall in the aggregate price level increases the purchasing power of consumers' assets and leads to more consumer demand. The **wealth effect of a change in the aggregate price level** is the effect on consumer spending caused by the effect of a change in the aggregate price level on the purchasing power of consumers' assets. Because of the wealth effect, consumer spending, C, falls when the aggregate price level rises, leading to a downward-sloping aggregate demand curve.

The Interest Rate Effect Economists use the term *money* in its narrowest sense to refer to cash and bank deposits on which people can write cheques and do debit transactions. People and firms hold money because it reduces the cost and inconvenience of undertaking transactions. An increase in the aggregate price level, other things equal, reduces the purchasing power of a given amount of money holdings. To purchase the same basket of goods and services as before, people and firms now need to (and want to) hold more money. So, in response to an increase in the aggregate

The **wealth effect of a change in the aggregate price level** is the effect on consumer spending caused by the effect of a change in the aggregate price level on the purchasing power of consumers' assets.

The **interest rate effect of a change in the aggregate price level** is the effect on consumer spending and investment spending caused by the effect of a change in the aggregate price level on the purchasing power of consumers' and firms' money holdings.

price level, the public tries to increase its money holdings, either by borrowing more or by selling assets such as bonds. This reduces the funds available for lending to other borrowers and drives interest rates up.

In Chapter 10 we learned that a rise in the interest rate reduces investment spending because it makes the cost of borrowing higher. It also reduces consumer spending because households save more of their disposable income. So a rise in the aggregate price level depresses investment spending, I, and consumer spending, C, owing to the rise in interest rates, which is in turn caused by the shrinking real purchasing power of money holdings. This effect is known as the **interest rate effect of a change in the aggregate price level.** This also leads to a downward-sloping aggregate demand curve.

We'll have a lot more to say about money and interest rates in Chapter 15 on monetary policy. We'll also see, in Chapter 19, which covers open-economy macroeconomics, that a higher interest rate indirectly tends to reduce exports (X) and increase imports (IM). The result, which is lower net exports ($X - IM$), further depresses aggregate expenditure on domestically produced final goods and services. For now, the important point is that the aggregate demand curve is downward sloping due to both the wealth effect and the interest rate effect of a change in the aggregate price level.

The Aggregate Demand Curve and the Income–Expenditure Model

In the preceding chapter we introduced the *income–expenditure model,* which shows how the economy arrives at *income–expenditure equilibrium.* Now we've introduced the aggregate demand curve, which relates the overall demand for goods and services to the overall price level. How do these concepts fit together?

Recall that one of the assumptions of the income–expenditure model is that the aggregate price level is fixed. We now drop that assumption. We can still use the income–expenditure model, however, to ask what aggregate expenditure would be *at any given aggregate price level,* which is precisely what the aggregate demand curve shows. So the *AD* curve is actually derived from the income–expenditure model. Economists sometimes say that the income–expenditure model is "embedded" in the *AD–AS* model.

FIGURE 12-2 How Changes in the Aggregate Price Level Affect Income–Expenditure Equilibrium

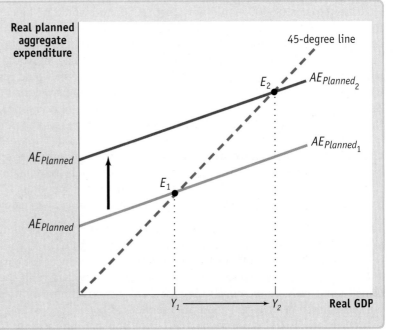

Income–expenditure equilibrium occurs at the point where the curve $AE_{Planned}$, which shows real aggregate planned spending, crosses the 45-degree line. A fall in the aggregate price level causes the $AE_{Planned}$ curve to shift from $AE_{Planned_1}$ to $AE_{Planned_2}$, leading to a rise in income–expenditure equilibrium GDP from Y_1 to Y_2.

Figure 12-2 shows, once again, how income–expenditure equilibrium is determined. Real GDP is on the horizontal axis; real planned aggregate expenditure is on the vertical axis. Other things equal, real planned aggregate expenditure, equal to consumer spending plus planned investment spending, rises with real GDP. This is illustrated by the upward-sloping lines $AE_{Planned_1}$ and $AE_{Planned_2}$. Income–expenditure equilibrium, as we learned in Chapter 11, is at the point where the line representing real planned aggregate expenditure crosses the 45-degree line. For example, if $AE_{Planned_1}$ is the relationship between real GDP and real planned aggregate expenditure, then income–expenditure equilibrium is at point E_1, corresponding to a level of real GDP equal to Y_1.

We've just seen, however, that changes in the aggregate price level change the level of real planned aggregate expenditure *at any given level of real GDP*. This means that when the aggregate price level changes, the $AE_{Planned}$ curve shifts. For example, suppose that the aggregate price level falls. As a result of both the wealth effect and the interest rate effect, the fall in the aggregate price level will lead to higher real planned aggregate expenditure at any given level of real GDP. So the $AE_{Planned}$ curve will shift up, as illustrated in Figure 12-2 by the shift from $AE_{Planned_1}$ to $AE_{Planned_2}$. The increase in real planned aggregate expenditure leads to the multiplier process that moves the income–expenditure equilibrium from point E_1 to point E_2, raising real GDP from Y_1 to Y_2.

Figure 12-3 shows how this result can be used to derive the aggregate demand curve. In Figure 12-3, we show a fall in the aggregate price level from P_1 to P_2. We saw in Figure 12-2 that a fall in the aggregate price level would lead to an upward shift of the $AE_{Planned}$ curve and hence a rise in real GDP. You can see this same result in Figure 12-3 as a movement along the AD curve: as the aggregate price level falls, real GDP rises from Y_1 to Y_2.

So the aggregate demand curve doesn't replace the income–expenditure model. Instead, it's a way to summarize what the income–expenditure model says about the effects of changes in the aggregate price level.

In practice, economists often use the income–expenditure model to analyze short-run economic fluctuations, even though strictly speaking it should be seen as a component of a more complete model. In the short run, in particular, this is usually a reasonable shortcut.

FIGURE 12-3 The Income–Expenditure Model and the Aggregate Demand Curve

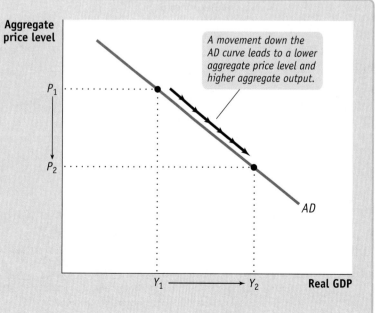

In Figure 12-2 we saw how a fall in the aggregate price level shifts the real planned aggregate expenditure curve up, leading to a rise in real GDP. Here we show that same result as a movement along the aggregate demand curve. If the aggregate price level falls from P_1 to P_2, real GDP rises from Y_1 to Y_2. The AD curve is therefore downward sloping.

A movement down the AD curve leads to a lower aggregate price level and higher aggregate output.

Shifts of the Aggregate Demand Curve

In Chapter 3, where we introduced the analysis of supply and demand in the market for an individual good, we stressed the importance of the distinction between *movements along* the demand curve and *shifts of* the demand curve. The same distinction applies to the aggregate demand curve. Figure 12-1 shows a *movement along* the aggregate demand curve, a change in the aggregate quantity of goods and services demanded as the aggregate price level changes.

But there can also be *shifts of* the aggregate demand curve, changes in the quantity of goods and services demanded at any given price level, as shown in Figure 12-4. When we talk about an increase in aggregate demand, we mean a shift of the aggregate demand curve to the right, as shown in panel (a) by the shift from AD_1 to AD_2. A rightward shift occurs when the quantity of aggregate output demanded increases at any given aggregate price level. A decrease in aggregate demand means that the AD curve shifts to the left, as in panel (b). A leftward shift implies that the quantity of aggregate output demanded falls at any given aggregate price level.

When the aggregate demand curve shifts to the right, it is called a *positive shift*, since it usually has a positive impact on aggregate real income (it rises), employment (more jobs are created), and the unemployment rate (it decreases). Similarly, a shift to the left is called an *adverse shift* because it usually has a negative impact on aggregate real income (it decreases), employment (there are fewer jobs), and the unemployment rate (it increases). When the curve shifts unexpectedly, we refer to it as a *shock*. Positive AD shocks and adverse AD shocks help drive the business cycle, which refers to short-run fluctuations of real economic variables away from long-run (equilibrium) values.

A number of factors that are unrelated to inflation can shift the aggregate demand curve. Among the most important factors are changes in expectations, changes in wealth, and the size of the existing stock of physical capital. In addition, both fiscal and monetary policy can shift the aggregate demand curve. All five factors set the multiplier process in motion. By causing an initial rise or fall in real GDP, they change disposable income, which leads to additional changes in aggregate expenditure, which lead to further changes in real GDP, and so on. For an overview of factors that shift the aggregate demand curve, see Table 12-1.

FIGURE 12-4 Shifts of the Aggregate Demand Curve

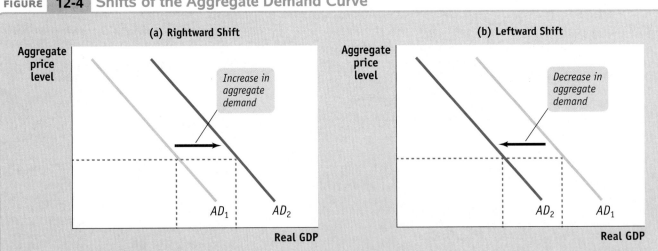

Panel (a) shows the effect of events that increase the quantity of aggregate output demanded at any given aggregate price level, such as improvements in business and consumer expectations or increased government spending. Such changes shift the aggregate demand curve to the right, from AD_1 to AD_2. Panel (b) shows the effect of events that decrease the quantity of aggregate output demanded at any given aggregate price level, such as a fall in wealth caused by a stock market decline. This shifts the aggregate demand curve leftward from AD_1 to AD_2.

TABLE   12-1   Factors That Shift Aggregate Demand

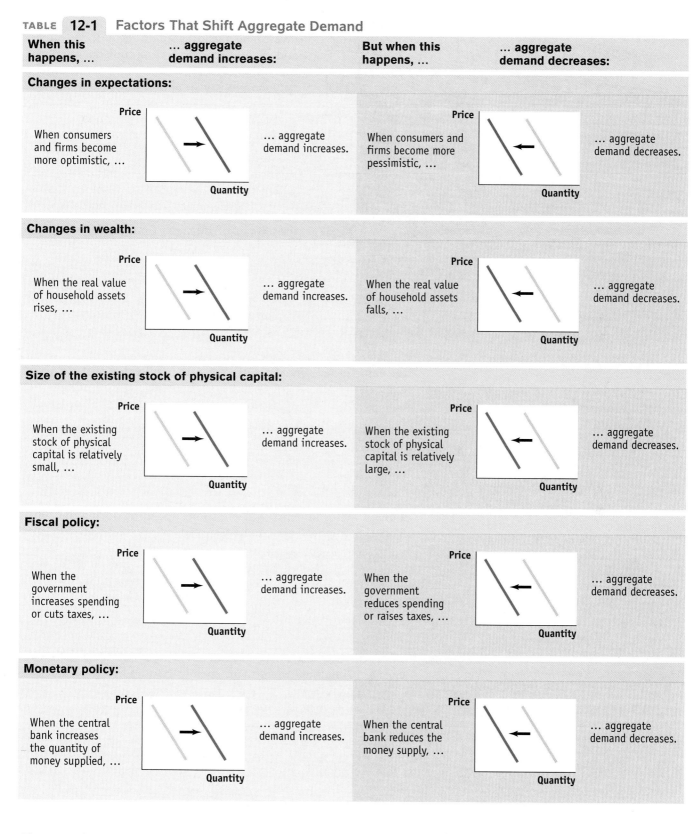

Changes in Expectations As explained in Chapter 11, both consumer spending and planned investment spending depend in part on people's expectations about the future. Consumers base their spending not only on the income they have now but also on the income they expect to have in the future. Firms base their planned investment spending not only on current conditions but also on the sales they expect to make in the future. As a result, changes in expectations

"CONSUMER CONFIDENCE CRISIS IN AISLE 3!"

Jim Borgman

can push consumer spending and planned investment spending up or down. If consumers and firms become more optimistic, aggregate expenditure rises (perhaps due to an increase in autonomous consumption and/or autonomous investment); if they become more pessimistic, aggregate spending falls (as the increased pessimism reduces autonomous consumption and/or autonomous investment). In fact, short-run economic forecasters pay careful attention to surveys of consumer and business sentiment. In particular, forecasters watch for the monthly Index of Consumer Confidence and the quarterly Index of Business Confidence, both from the Conference Board of Canada, and the quarterly Business Outlook Survey from the Bank of Canada. These indexes measure the level of optimism about the economic conditions by consumers and businesses respectively. An increase in the index means that agents are more optimistic about the future while a fall in the index signals a decrease in the level of optimism.

CHANGES IN WEALTH: A MOVEMENT ALONG VERSUS A SHIFT OF THE AGGREGATE DEMAND CURVE

In the last section we explained that one reason the *AD* curve is downward sloping is due to the wealth effect of a change in the aggregate price level: a higher aggregate price level reduces the purchasing power of households' assets and leads to a fall in consumer spending, *C*. But in this section we've just explained that changes in wealth lead to a shift of the *AD* curve. Aren't those two explanations contradictory? Which one is it—does a change in wealth move the economy along the *AD* curve or does it shift the *AD* curve? The answer is both: it depends on the *source* of the change in wealth. A movement along the *AD* curve occurs when a change in the aggregate price level changes the purchasing power of consumers' existing wealth (the real value of their assets). This is the *wealth effect of a change in the aggregate price level*—a change in the aggregate price level is the source of the change in wealth. For example, a fall in the aggregate price level increases the purchasing power of consumers' assets and leads to a movement down the *AD* curve. In contrast, a change in wealth *independent of a change in the aggregate price level* shifts the *AD* curve. For example, a rise in the stock market or a rise in real estate values leads to an increase in the real value of consumers' assets at any given aggregate price level. In this case, the source of the change in wealth is a change in the values of assets without any change in the aggregate price level—that is, a change in asset values holding the prices of all final goods and services constant—as a result the *AD* curve shifts to the right.

Changes in Wealth Consumer spending depends in part on the value of household assets. When the real value of these assets rises, the purchasing power they embody also rises, leading to an increase in aggregate expenditure. For example, in the 1990s there was a significant rise in the stock market that increased aggregate demand. And when the real value of household assets falls—for example, because of a stock market crash—the purchasing power they embody is reduced and aggregate demand also falls. The stock market crash of 1929 was a significant factor leading to the Great Depression. Similarly, a sharp decline in U.S. real estate values was a major factor in depressing consumer spending during the 2007–2008 U.S. financial crisis, which spread to Canada. In late 2008 and early 2009, Canadian consumer and business confidence declined as agents grew more fearful of the worsening worldwide economic climate. The Index of Consumer Confidence fell about 50% and the Index of Business Confidence fell about 30%. Consumers feared the U.S. slowdown would not only lead to job losses in Canada, but might bring falling house prices to Canada as well.

Size of the Existing Stock of Physical Capital Firms engage in planned investment spending to add to their stock of physical capital. Their incentive to spend depends in part on how much physical capital they already have: the more they have, the less they will feel a need to add more, other things equal. The same applies to other types of investment spending—for example, if a large number of houses have been built in recent years, this will depress the demand for new houses and as a result also tend to reduce residential investment spending. In fact, that in part explains why residential investment spending slumped by 13% in the fourth quarter of 2008. The housing boom of the previous few years had created an oversupply of houses: by the spring of 2009, the inventory of unsold houses on the market had risen even though housing starts were down significantly. In early 2009, Canadian resale home prices began to fall. This gave the construction industry little incentive to build even more homes at that time.

Government Policies and Aggregate Demand

One of the key insights of macroeconomics is that the government can have a powerful influence on aggregate demand and that, in some circumstances, this influence can be used to improve economic performance.

The two main ways the government can influence the aggregate demand curve are through fiscal policy and monetary policy. We'll briefly discuss their influence on aggregate demand, leaving a full-length discussion for upcoming chapters.

Fiscal Policy As we learned in Chapter 6, fiscal policy is the use of either government spending—government purchases of final goods and services and government transfers—or tax policy to stabilize the economy. In practice, governments often respond to recessions by increasing spending, cutting taxes, or both. They often respond to inflation by reducing spending or increasing taxes.

The effect of government purchases of final goods and services, G, on the aggregate demand curve is *direct* because government purchases are themselves a component of aggregate demand. So an increase in government purchases shifts the aggregate demand curve to the right and a decrease shifts it to the left. History's most dramatic example of how increased government purchases affect aggregate demand was the effect of wartime government spending during World War II. Because of the war, real government purchases of goods and services surged 570%. This increase in purchases is usually credited with ending the Great Depression. Recent decades offer other examples of the effect of increased government spending. In the 1990s, Japan used large public works projects—such as government-financed construction of roads, bridges, and dams—in an effort to increase aggregate demand in the face of a slumping economy. Similarly, in 2009, to stimulate overall spending, federal and provincial governments in Canada began to spend more than $63 billion, mostly on infrastructure projects such as improving highways, bridges, public transportation, university and college buildings, and so on.

In contrast, changes in either tax rates or government transfers influence the economy *indirectly* through their effect on disposable income. A lower tax rate means that consumers get to keep more of what they earn, increasing their disposable income. An increase in government transfers also increases consumers' disposable income. In either case, this increases consumer spending and shifts the aggregate demand curve to the right. A higher tax rate or a reduction in transfers reduces the amount of disposable income received by consumers. This reduces consumer spending and shifts the aggregate demand curve to the left.

Monetary Policy We opened this chapter by talking about the problems faced by the Bank of Canada, which controls monetary policy—the use of changes in the quantity of money or the interest rate to stabilize the economy. We've just discussed how a rise in the aggregate price level, by reducing the purchasing power of money holdings, causes a rise in the interest rate. That, in turn, reduces both investment spending and consumer spending.

But what happens if the quantity of money in the hands of households and firms changes? In modern economies, the quantity of money in circulation is largely determined by the decisions of a *central bank* created by the government. As we'll learn in Chapter 14, the Bank of Canada, Canada's central bank, is a special institution that is neither exactly part of the government nor exactly a private institution. When the central bank increases the quantity of money in circulation, households and firms have more money, which they are willing to lend out. The effect is to drive the interest rate down at any given aggregate price level, leading to higher investment spending and higher consumer spending. That is, increasing the quantity of money supplied shifts the aggregate demand curve to the right. Reducing the quantity of money supplied has the opposite effect: households and firms have less money holdings than before, leading them to borrow more and lend less. This raises the interest rate, reduces investment spending and consumer spending, and shifts the aggregate demand curve to the left.

ECONOMICS ►IN ACTION

The interest rate effect of a rise in the aggregate price level leads to a drop in consumer and investment spending.

MOVING ALONG THE AGGREGATE DEMAND CURVE, 1979–1982

When looking at data, it's often hard to distinguish between changes in spending that represent *movements along* the aggregate demand curve and *shifts of* the aggregate demand curve. One telling exception, however, is what happened right after the oil crisis of 1979, which we mentioned in this chapter's opening story. Faced with a sharp increase in the aggregate price level—the rate of consumer price inflation reached 12.9% in July of 1981—the Bank of Canada stuck to a policy of increasing the quantity of money slowly. The aggregate price level was rising more steeply, but the quantity of money circulating in the economy was growing slowly. The net result was that the purchasing power of the quantity of money in circulation fell.

This led to an increase in the demand for borrowing and a surge in interest rates. The *prime rate,* which is the interest rate banks charge their best customers, climbed to 22.75% in August 1981. High interest rates, in turn, caused both consumer spending and investment spending to fall: in 1982 purchases of durable consumer goods like cars fell by about 12% and real investment spending fell by 27.5%.

In other words, in 1979–1982 the economy responded just as we'd expect if it were moving upward along the aggregate demand curve from right to left: due to the wealth effect and the interest rate effect of a change in the aggregate price level, the quantity of aggregate output demanded fell as the aggregate price level rose. This does not explain, of course, why the aggregate price level rose. But as we'll see in the section "The *AD–AS* Model," the answer to that question lies in the behaviour of the *short-run aggregate supply curve.*

▼ Quick Review

- The **aggregate demand curve** is downward sloping because of the **wealth effect of a change in the aggregate price level** and the **interest rate effect of a change in the aggregate price level.**

- The aggregate demand curve shows how income–expenditure equilibrium GDP changes when the aggregate price level changes.

- Changes in consumer spending caused by changes in wealth and expectations about the future shift the aggregate demand curve. Changes in investment spending caused by changes in expectations and by the size of the existing stock of physical capital also shift the aggregate demand curve.

- Fiscal policy affects aggregate demand directly through government purchases and indirectly through changes in taxes or government transfers. Monetary policy affects aggregate demand indirectly through changes in the interest rate.

CHECK YOUR UNDERSTANDING   12-1

1. Determine the effect on aggregate demand of each of the following events. Explain whether it represents a movement along the aggregate demand curve (up or down) or a shift of the curve (leftward or rightward).
   a. A rise in the interest rate caused by a change in monetary policy
   b. A fall in the real value of money in the economy due to a higher aggregate price level
   c. News of a worse-than-expected job market next year
   d. A fall in tax rates
   e. A rise in the real value of assets in the economy due to a lower aggregate price level
   f. A rise in the real value of assets in the economy due to a surge in real estate values

Solutions appear at back of book.

Aggregate Supply

Between 1929 and 1933, there was a sharp fall in aggregate demand—a reduction in the quantity of goods and services demanded at any given price level. One consequence of the economy-wide decline in demand was a fall in the prices of most goods and services. By 1933, the GDP deflator (one of the price indexes we defined in Chapter 7) was 18% below its 1929 level, and other indexes were down by similar amounts. A second consequence was a decline in the output of most goods and services: by 1933, real GDP was 30% below its 1929 level. A third consequence, closely tied to the fall in real GDP, was a surge in the unemployment rate from 2.93% to 19.3%.

The association between the plunge in real GDP and the plunge in prices wasn't an accident. Between 1929 and 1933, the Canadian economy was moving down its **aggregate supply curve,** which shows the relationship between the economy's aggregate price level (the overall price level of final goods and services in the economy) and the total quantity of final goods and services, or aggregate output, producers are willing to supply. (As you will recall, we use real GDP to measure aggregate output. So we'll often use the two terms interchangeably.) More specifically, between 1929 and 1933, as a result of a leftward shift of aggregate demand, the economy moved down its (upward-sloping) *short-run aggregate supply curve.*

The Short-Run Aggregate Supply Curve

The period from 1929 to 1933 demonstrated that there is a positive relationship in the short run between the aggregate price level and the quantity of aggregate output supplied. That is, a rise in the aggregate price level is associated with a rise in the quantity of aggregate output supplied, other things equal; a fall in the aggregate price level is associated with a fall in the quantity of aggregate output supplied, other things equal. To understand why this positive relationship exists, consider the most basic question facing a producer: is producing a unit of output profitable or not? Let's define profit per unit:

(12-2) Profit per unit of output = Price per unit of output
                                      – Production cost per unit of output

Thus, the answer to the question depends on whether the price the producer receives for a unit of output is greater or less than the cost of producing that unit of output. At any given point in time, many of the costs producers face are fixed per unit of output and can't be changed for an extended period of time. Typically, the largest source of inflexible production cost is the wages paid to workers. *Wages* here refers to all forms of worker compensation, such as employer-paid health care and retirement benefits in addition to earnings.

Wages are typically an inflexible production cost because the dollar amount of any given wage paid, called the **nominal wage,** in the short run, is often determined by contracts that were signed some time ago. And even when there are no formal contracts, there are often informal agreements between management and workers, making companies reluctant to change wages in response to economic conditions. For example, companies usually will not reduce wages during poor economic times—unless the downturn has been particularly long and severe—for fear of generating worker resentment. Correspondingly, they typically won't raise wages during better economic times—until they are at risk of losing workers to competitors—because they don't want to encourage workers to routinely demand higher wages.

As a result of both formal and informal agreements, then, the economy is characterized by **sticky wages:** nominal wages that are slow to fall even in the face of high unemployment and slow to rise even in the face of labour shortages. It's important to note, however, that nominal wages cannot be sticky forever: ultimately, formal contracts and informal agreements will be renegotiated to take into account changed economic circumstances. As the Pitfalls at the end of this section explains, how long it takes for nominal wages to become flexible is an integral component of what distinguishes the short run from the long run.

To understand how the fact that many costs are fixed in nominal terms gives rise to an upward-sloping short-run aggregate supply curve, it's helpful to know that prices are set somewhat differently in different kinds of markets. In *perfectly competitive markets,* producers take prices as given; in *imperfectly competitive markets,* producers have some ability to choose the prices they charge. In both kinds of markets, there is a short-run positive relationship between prices and output, but for slightly different reasons.

The **aggregate supply curve** shows the relationship between the aggregate price level and the quantity of aggregate output supplied in the economy.

The **nominal wage** is the dollar amount of the wage paid.

Sticky wages are nominal wages that are slow to fall even in the face of high unemployment and slow to rise even in the face of labour shortages.

Let's start with the behaviour of producers in perfectly competitive markets; remember, they take the price as given. Imagine that, for some reason, the aggregate price level falls, which means that the price received by the typical producer of a final good or service falls. Because many production costs are fixed in the short run, production cost per unit of output doesn't fall by the same proportion as the fall in the price of output. So the profit per unit of output declines, inducing perfectly competitive producers to look for ways to alter their production plans so as to limit this decline. Since land, capital, and technology costs cannot be lowered, because they are fixed in the short run, the only way to reduce cost is to reduce the cost of labour. And if wages are fixed, this can be done only by reducing the (profit-maximizing) level of labour employed—that is, by laying off workers. The law of diminishing marginal productivity implies that at some point the marginal product of labour declines as the number of workers employed rises. This implies that layoffs raise the marginal productivity of labour, and this higher productivity works to lower per unit production costs.

But layoffs also reduce the level of output, causing a lower short-run revenue, so why do producers do this? It is because they want to maximize profits, regardless of whether they are operating for the short or long term. So when the aggregate price level falls, reducing the profit per unit, producers want to reduce their per unit production costs because that will push their profit per unit back up, somewhat. In the short run, profit-maximizing producers in a perfectly competitive industry operate where their short-run marginal cost curve is at or above their short-run average variable cost curve. So, at their current production level, their short-run average cost curve slopes upward as the level of output is increased. Consequently, a reduction in level of output will lower the per unit production cost, which will help mitigate the drop in the profit per unit.

On the other hand, suppose that for some reason the aggregate price level rises. As a result, the typical producer receives a higher price for its final good or service. Again, many production costs are fixed in the short run, so production cost per unit of output doesn't rise by the same proportion as the rise in the price of a unit. And since the typical perfectly competitive producer takes the price as given, profit per unit of output rises and producers respond by either hiring workers or increasing the number of hours worked by the existing workers (i.e., more overtime), thus raising the level of output supplied.

Now consider an imperfectly competitive producer that is able to set its own price. If there is a rise in the demand for this producer's product, it will be able to sell more at any given price. Given stronger demand for its products, it will probably choose to increase its prices as well as its output, as a way of increasing profit per unit of output. In fact, industry analysts often talk about variations in an industry's "pricing power": when demand is strong, firms with pricing power are able to raise prices—and they do.

Conversely, if there is a fall in demand, firms will normally try to limit the fall in their sales by cutting prices.

Both the responses of firms in perfectly competitive industries and those of firms in imperfectly competitive industries lead to an upward-sloping relationship between aggregate output and the aggregate price level. The positive relationship between the aggregate price level and the quantity of aggregate output producers are willing to supply during the time period when many production costs, particularly nominal wages, can be taken as fixed is illustrated by the **short-run aggregate supply curve.** The positive relationship between the aggregate price level and aggregate output in the short run gives the short-run aggregate supply curve its upward slope.

Figure 12-5 shows a hypothetical short-run aggregate supply curve, *SRAS*, which matches actual Canadian data for 1929 and 1933. On the horizontal axis is aggregate output (or, equivalently, real GDP)—the total quantity of final goods and services supplied in the economy—measured in 2002 dollars. On the vertical axis is the aggregate price level as measured by the GDP deflator, with the value for the year 2002 equal to 100. In 1929, the aggregate price level was 8.1 and real

The **short-run aggregate supply curve** shows the relationship between the aggregate price level and the quantity of aggregate output supplied that exists in the short run, the time period when many production costs can be taken as fixed.

FIGURE   **12-5**   The Short-Run Aggregate Supply Curve

The short-run aggregate supply curve shows the relationship between the aggregate price level and the quantity of aggregate output supplied in the short run, the period in which many production costs such as nominal wages are fixed. It is upward sloping because a higher aggregate price level leads to higher profit per unit of output and a higher profit-maximizing level of aggregate output supplied given fixed nominal wages. Here we show numbers corresponding to the Great Depression, from 1929 to 1933: when deflation occurred and the aggregate price level fell from 8.1 (in 1929) to 6.6 (in 1933), firms responded by reducing the quantity of aggregate output supplied from $78.3 billion to $54.7 billion measured in 2002 dollars.

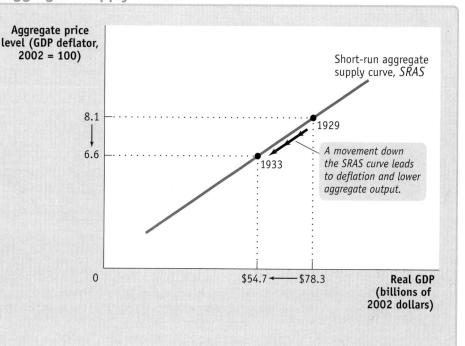

FOR INQUIRING MINDS

WHAT'S TRULY FLEXIBLE, WHAT'S TRULY STICKY

Most macroeconomists agree that the basic picture shown in Figure 12-5 is correct: there is, other things equal, a positive short-run relationship between the aggregate price level and aggregate output. But many would argue that the details are a bit more complicated.

So far we've stressed a difference in the behaviour of the aggregate price level and the behaviour of nominal wages. That is, we've said that the aggregate price level is more flexible than nominal wages, which are sticky in the short run. Although this assumption is a good way to explain why the short-run aggregate supply curve is upward sloping, empirical data on wages and prices don't wholly support a sharp distinction

between flexible prices of final goods and services and sticky nominal wages.

On one side, some nominal wages are in fact flexible even in the short run because some workers are not covered by a contract or informal agreement with their employers. Since some nominal wages are sticky but others are flexible, we observe that the *average nominal wage*—the nominal wage averaged over all workers in the economy—falls when there is a steep rise in unemployment. For example, nominal wages fell substantially in the early years of the Great Depression.

On the other side, some prices of final goods and services are sticky rather than flexible. For example, some

firms, particularly the makers of luxury or name-brand goods, are reluctant to cut prices even when demand falls. Instead they prefer to cut output even if their profit per unit sold hasn't declined.

These complications, as we've said, don't change the basic picture. When the aggregate price level falls, some producers cut output because the nominal wages they pay are sticky. And some producers don't cut their prices in the face of a falling aggregate price level, preferring instead to reduce their output. In both cases, the positive relationship between the aggregate price level and aggregate output is maintained. So, in the end, the short-run aggregate supply curve is still upward sloping.

GDP was $78.3 billion. In 1933, the aggregate price level was 6.6 and real GDP was only $54.7 billion. The movement down the *SRAS* curve corresponds to the deflation and fall in aggregate output experienced over those years.

Shifts of the Short-Run Aggregate Supply Curve

Figure 12-5 shows a *movement along* the short-run aggregate supply curve, as the aggregate price level and aggregate output fell from 1929 to 1933 (perhaps caused by an adverse *AD* shock). But there can also be *shifts of* the short-run

FIGURE **12-6** Shifts of the Short-Run Aggregate Supply Curve

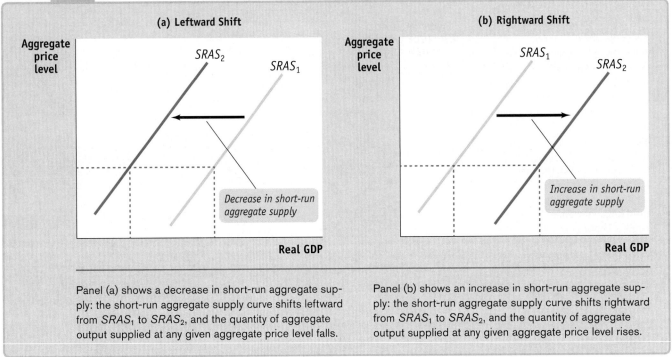

Panel (a) shows a decrease in short-run aggregate supply: the short-run aggregate supply curve shifts leftward from $SRAS_1$ to $SRAS_2$, and the quantity of aggregate output supplied at any given aggregate price level falls.

Panel (b) shows an increase in short-run aggregate supply: the short-run aggregate supply curve shifts rightward from $SRAS_1$ to $SRAS_2$, and the quantity of aggregate output supplied at any given aggregate price level rises.

aggregate supply curve, as shown in Figure 12-6. Panel (a) shows a *decrease in short-run aggregate supply*—a leftward shift of the short-run aggregate supply curve. Aggregate supply decreases when producers reduce the quantity of aggregate output they are willing to supply at any given aggregate price level. Panel (b) shows an *increase in short-run aggregate supply*—a rightward shift of the short-run aggregate supply curve. Aggregate supply increases when producers increase the quantity of aggregate output they are willing to supply at any given aggregate price level.

To understand why the short-run aggregate supply curve can shift, it's important to recall that producers make output decisions based on their profit per unit of output. The short-run aggregate supply curve illustrates the relationship between the aggregate price level and the profit-maximizing level of aggregate output supplied: because some production costs are fixed in the short run, a change in the aggregate price level leads to a change in producers' profit per unit of output and, in turn, leads to a change in the profit-maximizing level of aggregate output supplied. But other factors besides the aggregate price level can affect profit per unit and, in turn, the profit-maximizing level of aggregate output supplied. It is changes in these other factors that will shift the short-run aggregate supply curve.

To develop some intuition, suppose that something happens that raises production costs—say, an increase in the price of oil. At any given price of output, a producer now earns a smaller profit per unit of output. As a result, producers reduce the quantity supplied at any given aggregate price level, and the short-run aggregate supply curve shifts to the left. If, in contrast, something happens that lowers production costs—say, a fall in the nominal wage—a producer now earns a higher profit per unit of output at any given price of output. This leads producers to increase the quantity of aggregate output supplied at any given aggregate price level, and the short-run aggregate supply curve shifts to the right.

Now we'll discuss some of the important factors that affect producers' profit per unit and so can lead to shifts of the short-run aggregate supply curve.

Changes in Commodity Prices In this chapter's opening story, we described how a surge in the price of oil caused problems for the Canadian economy in the 1970s, early in 2008, and again in 2011. Oil is a commodity, a standardized input bought and sold in bulk quantities. An increase in the price of a commodity—oil—raised production costs across the economy and reduced the quantity of aggregate output supplied at any given aggregate price level, shifting the short-run aggregate supply curve to the left. Conversely, a decline in commodity prices reduces production costs, leading to an increase in the quantity supplied at any given aggregate price level and a rightward shift of the short-run aggregate supply curve.

Why isn't the influence of commodity prices already captured by the short-run aggregate supply curve? Because commodities—unlike, say, soft drinks—are not a final good, their prices are not included in the calculation of the aggregate price level. Further, some commodities are a key raw material input and thus represent a significant cost of production to some goods suppliers, just like nominal wages do. So changes in certain commodity prices can have large impacts on production costs. And in contrast to non-commodities, the prices of commodities can sometimes change drastically due to industry-specific shocks to supply—such as wars in the Middle East or rising Chinese demand that leaves less oil, iron, nickel ores, potash, and so on, for Canada and the rest of the world.

Changes in Nominal Wages At any given point in time, the dollar wages of many workers are fixed because they are set by contracts or informal agreements made in the past. Nominal wages can change, however, once enough time has passed for contracts and informal agreements to be renegotiated. Suppose, for example, that there is an economy-wide rise in the cost of health care insurance premiums paid by employers as part of employees' wages. From the employers' perspective, this is equivalent to a rise in nominal wages because it is an increase in employer-paid compensation. So this rise in nominal wages increases production costs and shifts the short-run aggregate supply curve to the left. Conversely, suppose there is an economy-wide fall in the cost of such premiums. This is equivalent to a fall in nominal wages from the point of view of employers; it reduces production costs and shifts the short-run aggregate supply curve to the right.

An important historical fact is that during the 1970s the surge in the price of oil had the indirect effect of also raising nominal wages. This "knock-on" effect occurred because many wage contracts included *cost-of-living allowances* that automatically raised the nominal wage when consumer prices increased. Through this channel, the surge in the price of oil—which led to an increase in overall consumer prices—ultimately caused a rise in nominal wages. So the economy, in the end, experienced two leftward shifts of the aggregate supply curve: the first generated by the initial surge in the price of oil, the second generated by the induced increase in nominal wages. The negative effect on the economy of rising oil prices was greatly magnified through the cost-of-living allowances in wage contracts. Today, automatic cost-of-living allowances in wage contracts are rare.

Changes in Productivity An increase in productivity means that a worker can produce more units of output with the same quantity of inputs. For example, the introduction of bar-code scanners in retail stores greatly increased the ability of a single worker to stock, inventory, and resupply store shelves. As a result, the cost to a store of "producing" a dollar of sales fell and profit rose. And, correspondingly, the quantity supplied increased. (Think of Walmart and dollar stores, such as Dollarama, and the increase in the number of their stores as an increase in aggregate supply.) So a rise in productivity, whatever the source, increases producers' profits and shifts the short-run aggregate supply curve to the right. Conversely, a fall in productivity—say, due to new regulations that require workers to spend more time filling out forms—reduces the number of units of output a worker can produce with the same quantity of inputs. Consequently, the cost per unit of output rises, profit falls, and quantity supplied falls. This shifts the short-run aggregate supply curve to the left.

For a summary of the factors that shift the short-run aggregate supply curve, see Table 12-2.

TABLE **12-2** Factors That Shift Aggregate Supply

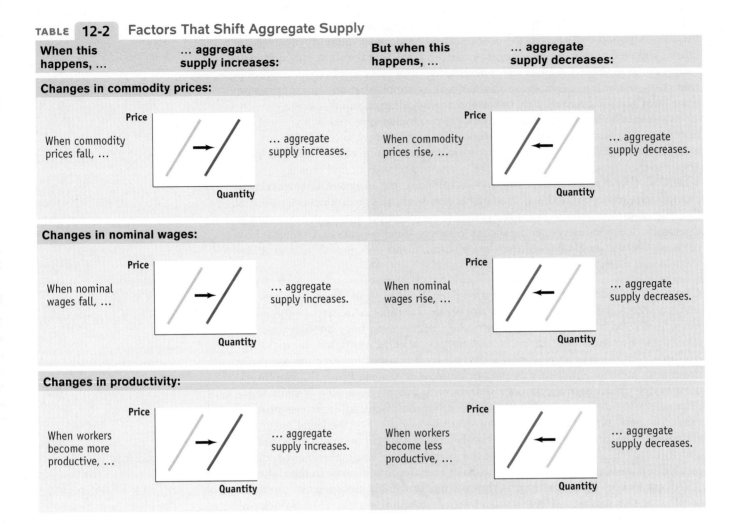

The Long-Run Aggregate Supply Curve

We've just seen that in the short run a fall in the aggregate price level leads to a decline in the quantity of aggregate output supplied because nominal wages are sticky in the short run. But, as we mentioned earlier, contracts and informal agreements are renegotiated in the long run. So in the long run, nominal wages—like the aggregate price level—are perfectly, or fully, flexible, not sticky. This fact greatly alters the long-run relationship between the aggregate price level and aggregate supply. In fact, in the long run the aggregate price level has *no* effect on the quantity of aggregate real output supplied.

To see why, let's conduct a thought experiment. Imagine that you could wave a magic wand—or maybe a magic bar-code scanner—and cut *all prices* in the economy in half at the same time. By "all prices" we mean the prices of all inputs, including nominal wages, as well as the prices of final goods and services. What would happen to aggregate real output, given that the aggregate price level has been halved and all input prices, including nominal wages, have been halved?

The answer is: nothing. Consider Equation 12-2 again: each producer would receive a lower price for its product, but costs would fall by the same proportion. As a result, every unit of output profitable to produce before the change in prices would still be profitable to produce after the change in prices. So a halving of *all* prices in the economy has no effect on the economy's aggregate real level of output. In other words, in the long-run, changes in the aggregate price level have no effect on the quantity of aggregate output supplied.

In reality, of course, no one can change all prices by the same proportion at the same time. But now, we'll consider the *long run, the period of time over which all prices are perfectly, or fully, flexible.* In the long run, inflation or deflation has the same effect as someone changing all prices by the same proportion. *As a result, changes in the aggregate price level do not change the real quantity of aggregate output supplied in the long run.* That's because changes in the aggregate price level will, in the long run, be accompanied by equal proportional changes in *all* input prices, including nominal wages.

The **long-run aggregate supply curve,** illustrated in Figure 12-7 by the *LRAS* curve, shows the relationship between the aggregate price level and the quantity of aggregate output supplied that would exist if all prices, including nominal wages, were perfectly flexible. The long-run aggregate supply curve is vertical because changes in the aggregate price level have *no* effect on aggregate output in the long run. At an aggregate price level of 9.0, the quantity of aggregate output supplied is $80 billion in 2002 dollars. If the aggregate price level falls by 50% to 4.5, the quantity of aggregate output supplied is unchanged in the long run at $80 billion in 2002 dollars.

It's important to understand not only that the *LRAS* curve is vertical but also that its position along the horizontal axis represents a significant measure. The horizontal intercept in Figure 12-7, where *LRAS* touches the horizontal axis ($80 billion in 2002 dollars), is the economy's **potential output,** Y_P: the level of real GDP the economy would produce if all prices, including nominal wages, were perfectly, or fully, flexible.[1]

The **long-run aggregate supply curve** shows the relationship between the aggregate price level and the quantity of aggregate output supplied that would exist if all prices, including nominal wages, were fully flexible.

Potential output is the level of real GDP the economy would produce if all prices, including nominal wages, were perfectly, or fully, flexible.

FIGURE **12-7** The Long-Run Aggregate Supply Curve

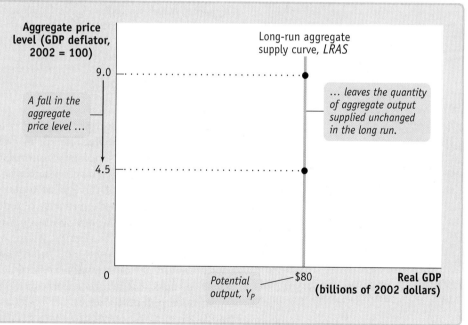

The long-run aggregate supply curve shows the quantity of aggregate output supplied when all prices, including nominal wages, are perfectly flexible. It is vertical at potential output, Y_P, because in the long run a change in the aggregate price level has no effect on the real quantity of aggregate output supplied.

---

[1]Despite what the label might imply, potential output is not the economy's maximum level of output; rather, it is equal to the level of real output the economy would produce when all the factors of production (both inputs and technology) are effectively and fully utilized. Other names for this include the natural rate level of output (Y_{NR}), the full employment level of output (Y_{FE}), or simply the long-run equilibrium level of output (Y_{LR}^*). These names all make sense and are equivalent, since in the longer term all prices become perfectly or fully flexible, which allows the economy to naturally tend toward a long-run equilibrium state in which all factors are fully utilized.

FIGURE **12-8** Actual and Potential Output from 1980 to 2011

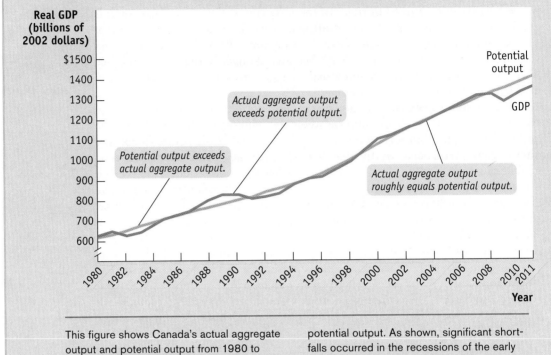

This figure shows Canada's actual aggregate output and potential output from 1980 to 2011. The orange line shows the estimates of potential output made by the office of the Parliamentary Budget Officer. The blue line shows actual aggregate output. The purple-shaded years are periods in which actual aggregate output fell below potential output, and the green-shaded years are periods in which actual aggregate output exceeded

potential output. As shown, significant short-falls occurred in the recessions of the early 1980s and the early 1990s. Actual aggregate output was significantly above potential output in the boom of the late 1980s and in 2000, and a huge shortfall occurred after the recession of 2008–2009.

Sources: Parliamentary Budget Officer (PBO); Statistics Canada.

In reality, the actual level of real GDP is almost always either above or below potential output. We'll see why later in this chapter, when we discuss the *AD–AS* model. Still, an economy's potential output is an important number because it defines the trend around which actual aggregate output fluctuates from year to year.

In Canada, the office of the Parliamentary Budget Officer, or PBO, estimates annual potential output for the purpose of federal budget analysis.[2] In Figure 12-8, the PBO's estimates of Canadian potential output from 1980 to 2011 are represented by the orange line and the actual values of Canadian real GDP over the same period are represented by the blue line. Years shaded purple on the horizontal axis correspond to periods in which actual aggregate output fell short of potential output, while years shaded green correspond to periods in which actual aggregate output exceeded potential output.

The PBO is not the only entity to forecast Canada's potential GDP: the Bank of Canada, the Federal Department of Finance, the OECD, the International Monetary Fund (IMF), and many private sector forecasters, such as the Royal Bank, do likewise. These forecasts are used for several purposes, including the measurement of the *output gap*. The **output gap** is the actual real (measured) GDP minus potential GDP, often calculated and presented as a percentage of potential GDP.

Output gap is the difference between real GDP and potential GDP, often given as a percentage of potential GDP.

[2]The PBO defines potential GDP as "the amount of output that an economy can produce when its capital, labour, and technology are at their respective (long-run) trends."

The output gap helps agents gauge the performance of the economy relative to the long-run (potential) trend. When the output gap is negative, actual real output is below the long-run potential level, so the economy is underperforming relative to the long-run trend. Similarly, when the output gap is positive, actual real output has risen above its long-run potential level, and the economy is booming relative to the long-run trend or potential level of GDP. A positive output gap implies greater inflationary pressure exists in the economy—the larger the gap, the more inflationary pressure is implied.

In 2010, the PBO used its estimates of potential GDP and the associated output gap along with similar estimates calculated by the IMF to conclude that the severity of the 2008–2009 recession in Canada was in line with the experiences of other G-7 countries. That is, the recession did cause our output gap to become negative as actual GDP fell below potential GDP, but we fared no worse than other G-7 countries with respect to the size of our output gap in terms of the percentage and duration of the reduction. On the other hand, the recession hit Japan harder than the rest of the G-7: its output gap fell to almost –7% of potential GDP, about two full percentage points lower than the gap for Canada, the U.K., and the U.S., but Japan's economy was already weaker before the recession.

As you can see, Canadian potential output has risen steadily over time—implying a series of rightward shifts of the *LRAS* curve. What has caused these rightward shifts? The answer lies in the factors related to long-run growth that we discussed in Chapter 9, such as increases in physical capital and human capital, the size of the labour force, and technological progress. Over the very long run, as the amount of both physical and human capital, size of the labour force, and total factor productivity all rise, the level of real GDP that the economy is capable of producing also rises and this causes a rightward shift of the *LRAS* curve. Figure 12-9 shows a rightward shift in the *LRAS* curve. Indeed, one way to think about long-run economic growth is that it is the growth in the economy's potential output. We generally think of the long-run aggregate supply curve as shifting to the right over time as an economy experiences long-run growth.

For a summary of the factors that shift the long-run aggregate supply curve, see Table 12-3.

FIGURE 12-9 Rightward Shift of the Long-Run Aggregate Supply Curve

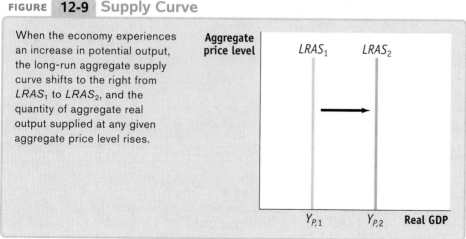

When the economy experiences an increase in potential output, the long-run aggregate supply curve shifts to the right from *LRAS₁* to *LRAS₂*, and the quantity of aggregate real output supplied at any given aggregate price level rises.

From the Short Run to the Long Run

As you can see in Figure 12-8, the economy normally produces more or less than potential output: actual aggregate output was significantly below potential output in the recessions of the early 1980s and the early 1990s, significantly above

TABLE 12-3   Factors That Shift Long-Run Aggregate Supply

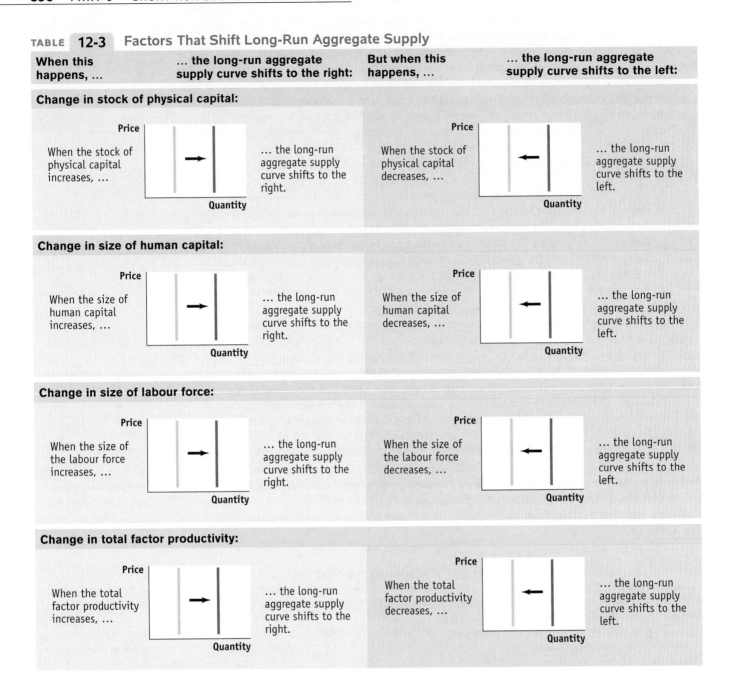

When this happens, ...	... the long-run aggregate supply curve shifts to the right:	But when this happens, ...	... the long-run aggregate supply curve shifts to the left:
Change in stock of physical capital:			
When the stock of physical capital increases, ...	... the long-run aggregate supply curve shifts to the right.	When the stock of physical capital decreases, ...	... the long-run aggregate supply curve shifts to the left.
Change in size of human capital:			
When the size of human capital increases, ...	... the long-run aggregate supply curve shifts to the right.	When the size of human capital decreases, ...	... the long-run aggregate supply curve shifts to the left.
Change in size of labour force:			
When the size of the labour force increases, ...	... the long-run aggregate supply curve shifts to the right.	When the size of the labour force decreases, ...	... the long-run aggregate supply curve shifts to the left.
Change in total factor productivity:			
When the total factor productivity increases, ...	... the long-run aggregate supply curve shifts to the right.	When the total factor productivity decreases, ...	... the long-run aggregate supply curve shifts to the left.

potential output in the boom of the late 1980s and in 2000, and significantly below potential output after the recession of 2008–2009. So the economy is normally on its short-run aggregate supply curve—but not on its long-run aggregate supply curve. So why is the long-run curve relevant? Does the economy ever move from the short run to the long run? And if so, how?

The first step to answering these questions is to understand that the economy is always in one of only two states with respect to the short-run and long-run aggregate supply curves. It can be on both curves simultaneously by being at a point where the curves cross (as in the few years in Figure 12-8 in which actual aggregate output and potential output roughly coincided). Or it can be on the short-run aggregate supply curve but not the long-run aggregate supply curve (as in the years in which actual aggregate output and potential output *did not* coincide). But that is not the end of the story. If the economy is on the short-run but not the long-run aggregate supply curve, the short-run aggregate supply curve will shift over time until the economy is at a point where both curves cross—a point where actual aggregate output is equal to potential output.

FIGURE 12-10 From the Short Run to the Long Run

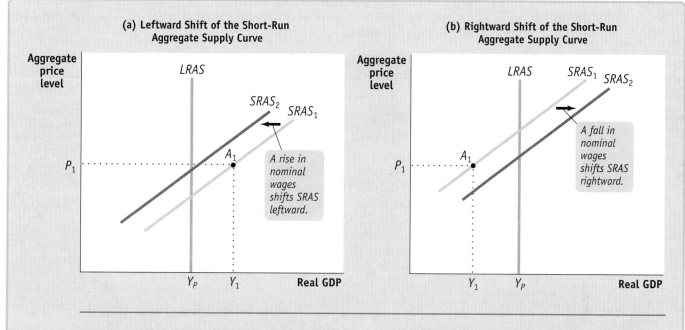

In panel (a), the initial short-run aggregate supply curve is $SRAS_1$. At the aggregate price level, P_1, the quantity of aggregate output supplied, Y_1, exceeds potential output, Y_P. Eventually, low unemployment will cause nominal wages to rise, leading to a leftward shift of the short-run aggregate supply curve from $SRAS_1$ to $SRAS_2$. In panel (b), the reverse happens: at the aggregate price level, P_1, the quantity of aggregate output supplied is less than potential output. High unemployment eventually leads to a fall in nominal wages over time and a rightward shift of the short-run aggregate supply curve.

Figure 12-10 illustrates how this process works. In both panels *LRAS* is the long-run aggregate supply curve, $SRAS_1$ is the initial short-run aggregate supply curve, and the aggregate price level is at P_1. In panel (a) the economy starts at the initial production point, A_1, which corresponds to a quantity of aggregate output supplied, Y_1, that is higher than potential output, Y_P. Producing an aggregate output level (such as Y_1) that is higher than potential output (Y_P) is possible only because nominal wages haven't yet fully adjusted upward. Until this upward adjustment in nominal wages occurs, producers are earning high profits and producing a high level of output. But a level of aggregate output higher than potential output means a low level of unemployment. Because jobs are abundant and workers are scarce, nominal wages will rise over time, gradually shifting the short-run aggregate supply curve leftward. Eventually it will be in a new position, such as $SRAS_2$. (Later in this chapter, we'll show where the short-run aggregate supply curve ends up. As we'll see, that depends on the aggregate demand curve as well.)

In panel (b), the initial production point, A_1, corresponds to an aggregate output level, Y_1, that is lower than potential output, Y_P. Producing an aggregate output level (such as Y_1) that is lower than potential output (Y_P) is possible only because nominal wages haven't yet fully adjusted downward. Until this downward adjustment occurs, producers are earning low (or negative) profits and producing a low level of output. An aggregate output level lower than potential output means high unemployment. Because workers are abundant and jobs are scarce, nominal wages will

⚠️ PITFALLS

ARE WE THERE YET? WHAT THE LONG RUN REALLY MEANS

We've used the term *long run* in two different contexts. In an earlier chapter we focused on *long-run economic growth*: growth that takes place over decades. In this chapter we introduced the *long-run aggregate supply curve*, which depicts the economy's potential output: the level of aggregate output that the economy would produce if all prices, including nominal wages, were perfectly or fully flexible. It might seem that we're using the same term, *long run*, for two different concepts. But we aren't: these two concepts are really the same thing.

Because the economy always tends to return to potential output in the long run, actual aggregate output *fluctuates around* potential output, rarely getting too far from it. As a result, the economy's rate of growth over long periods of time—say, decades—is very close to the rate of growth of potential output. And potential output growth is determined by the factors we analyzed in the chapter on long-run economic growth (i.e., inputs and technology). So that means that the "long run" of long-run growth and the "long run" of the long-run aggregate supply curve coincide.

fall over time, shifting the short-run aggregate supply curve gradually to the right. Eventually it will be in a new position, such as $SRAS_2$.

We'll see shortly that these shifts of the short-run aggregate supply curve will return the economy to potential output in the long run.

ECONOMICS ► IN ACTION

PRICES AND OUTPUT DURING THE GREAT DEPRESSION AND WORLD WAR II

Figure 12-11 shows the actual track of the aggregate price level, as measured by the GDP deflator, and real GDP, from 1929 to 1945. As you can see, aggregate output and the aggregate price level fell together from 1929 to 1933 and generally rose together from 1933 to 1937. This is what we'd expect to see if the economy was moving down the short-run aggregate supply curve from 1929 to 1933 and moving up it (with a brief stall in the growth of real output in 1938) thereafter.

But even in 1941, with the Second World War raging, the aggregate price

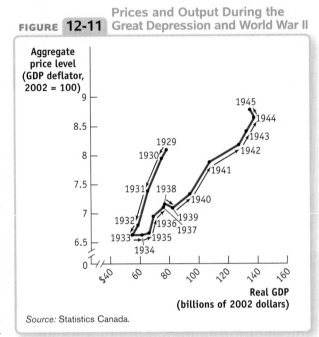

FIGURE 12-11   Prices and Output During the Great Depression and World War II

Source: Statistics Canada.

level was still lower than it was in 1929; yet real GDP was much higher. What happened? The answer is that the short-run aggregate supply curve shifted to the right over time. This shift partly reflected rising productivity—a rightward shift of the underlying long-run aggregate supply curve. But since the Canadian economy was producing below potential output and had high unemployment during this period, the rightward shift of the short-run aggregate supply curve also reflected the adjustment process shown in panel (b) of Figure 12-10. It was not until 1942 that the GDP deflator and the unemployment rate both returned to their 1929 levels. So the movement of aggregate output from 1929 to 1945 reflected both movements along and shifts of the short-run aggregate supply curve.

●◦◄

CHECK YOUR UNDERSTANDING   12-2

1. Determine the effect on short-run aggregate supply of each of the following events. Explain whether it represents a movement along the *SRAS* curve or a shift of the *SRAS* curve.

   a. A rise in the consumer price index (CPI) leads producers to increase output.

   b. A fall in the price of oil leads producers to increase output.

   c. A rise in legally mandated retirement benefits paid to workers leads producers to reduce output.

2. Suppose the economy is initially at potential output and the quantity of aggregate output supplied increases. What information would you need to determine whether this was due to a movement along the *SRAS* curve or a shift of the *LRAS* curve?

Solutions appear at back of book.

▼ Quick Review

- The **aggregate supply curve** illustrates the relationship between the aggregate price level and the quantity of aggregate output supplied.

- The **short-run aggregate supply curve** is upward sloping: a higher aggregate price level leads to higher aggregate output given that **nominal wages** are **sticky**.

- Changes in commodity prices, nominal wages, and productivity shift the short-run aggregate supply curve.

- In the long run, all prices are flexible, and changes in the aggregate price level have no effect on aggregate output. The **long-run aggregate supply curve** is vertical at **potential output.**

- Changes in the stock of physical capital, the stock of human capital, the size of the labour force, and productivity shift the long-run aggregate supply curve.

- The **output gap** measures the difference between actual or measured level of real GDP and potential GDP (output gap = $Y - Y_P$). It is often presented as percentage of potential GDP. A larger gap implies more inflationary pressure, and a smaller gap implies less.

- If actual aggregate output exceeds potential output, nominal wages eventually rise and the short-run aggregate supply curve shifts leftward. If potential output exceeds actual aggregate output, nominal wages eventually fall and the short-run aggregate supply curve shifts rightward.

The *AD–AS* Model

From 1929 to 1933, the Canadian economy moved down the short-run aggregate supply curve as the aggregate price level fell. In contrast, from 1979 to 1982 the Canadian economy moved up the aggregate demand curve as the aggregate price level rose. In each case, the cause of the movement along the curve was a shift of the other curve. In 1929–1933, it was a leftward shift of the aggregate demand curve—a major fall in consumer spending. In 1979–1982, it was a leftward shift of the short-run aggregate supply curve—a dramatic fall in short-run aggregate supply caused by the oil price shock.

So to understand the behaviour of the economy, we must put the aggregate supply curve and the aggregate demand curve together. The result is the **AD–AS model,** the basic model we use to understand economic fluctuations.

Short-Run Macroeconomic Equilibrium

We'll begin our analysis by focusing on the short run. Figure 12-12 shows the aggregate demand curve and the short-run aggregate supply curve on the same diagram. The point at which the *AD* and *SRAS* curves intersect, E_{SR}, is the **short-run macro-economic equilibrium,** the point at which the quantity of aggregate output supplied is equal to the quantity demanded by domestic households, businesses, the government, and the rest of the world. The aggregate price level at E_{SR}, P_E, is the **short-run equilibrium aggregate price level.** The level of aggregate output at E_{SR}, Y_E, is the **short-run equilibrium aggregate output,** which represents real GDP at one given time period.

In the supply and demand model of Chapter 3 we saw that a shortage of any individual good causes its market price to rise but a surplus of the good causes its market price to fall. These forces ensure that the market reaches equilibrium. The same logic applies to short-run macroeconomic equilibrium. If the aggregate price level is above its equilibrium level, the quantity of aggregate output supplied exceeds the quantity of aggregate output demanded. This leads to a fall in the aggregate price level and pushes it toward its equilibrium level. If the aggregate price level is below its equilibrium level, the quantity of aggregate output supplied is less than the quantity of aggregate output demanded. This leads to a rise in the aggregate price level, again pushing it toward its equilibrium

In the **AD–AS model,** the aggregate supply curve and the aggregate demand curve are used together to analyze economic fluctuations.

The economy is in **short-run macroeconomic equilibrium** when the quantity of aggregate output supplied in the short run is equal to the quantity demanded.

The **short-run equilibrium aggregate price level** is the aggregate price level in the short run macroeconomic equilibrium.

Short-run equilibrium aggregate output is the quantity of aggregate output produced in the short-run macroeconomic equilibrium.

FIGURE 12-12 The *AD–AS* Model

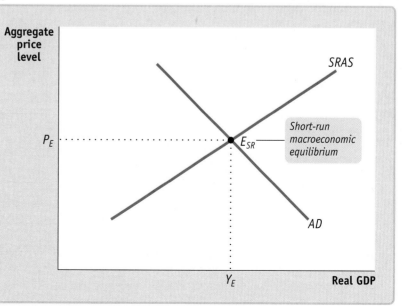

The *AD–AS* model combines the aggregate demand curve and the short-run aggregate supply curve. Their point of intersection, E_{SR}, is the point of short-run macroeconomic equilibrium where the quantity of aggregate output supplied in the short run is equal to the quantity of aggregate output demanded. P_E is the short-run equilibrium aggregate price level, and Y_E is the short-run equilibrium level of aggregate output.

An event that shifts the aggregate demand curve is a **demand shock.**

level. In the discussion that follows, we'll assume that the economy is always in short-run macroeconomic equilibrium.

We'll also make another important simplification based on the observation that in reality there is a long-term upward trend in both aggregate output and the aggregate price level. We'll assume that a fall in either variable really means a fall compared to the long-run trend. For example, if the aggregate price level normally rises 4% per year, a year in which the aggregate price level rises only 3% would count, for our purposes, as a 1% decline. In fact, since the Great Depression there have been very few years in which the aggregate price level of any major nation actually declined—Japan's period of deflation since 1995 is one of the few exceptions. We'll explain why in Chapter 16. There have, however, been many cases in which the aggregate price level fell relative to the long-run trend.

Short-run equilibrium aggregate output and the short-run equilibrium aggregate price level can change either because of shifts of the *AD* curve or because of shifts of the *SRAS* curve. Let's look at each case in turn.

Shifts of Aggregate Demand: Short-Run Effects

An event that shifts the aggregate demand curve, such as a change in expectations or wealth, the effect of the size of the existing stock of physical capital, or the use of fiscal or monetary policy, is known as a **demand shock.** The Great Depression was caused by a negative demand shock, the collapse of wealth and of business and consumer confidence that followed the stock market crash of 1929 and the banking crisis of 1930–1931. The Depression was ended by a positive demand shock—the huge increase in government purchases during World War II. In late 2008 the Canadian economy experienced another significant negative demand shock as consumer and business confidence fell due to the financial crisis that started in the U.S., leading consumers and firms to scale back their spending.

Figure 12-13 shows the short-run effects of negative and positive demand shocks. A negative demand shock shifts the aggregate demand curve, *AD*, to the left, from

FIGURE 12-13 Demand Shocks

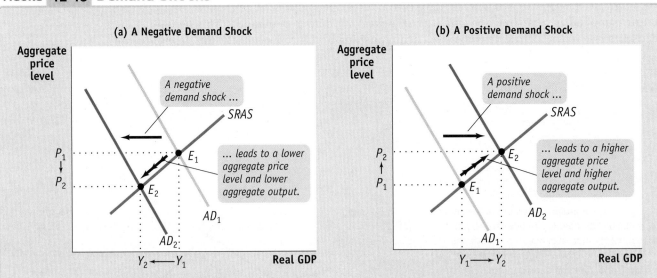

A demand shock shifts the aggregate demand curve, moving the aggregate price level and aggregate output in the same direction. In panel (a), a negative demand shock shifts the aggregate demand curve leftward from AD_1 to AD_2, reducing the aggregate price level from P_1 to P_2 and aggregate output from Y_1 to Y_2. In panel (b), a positive demand shock shifts the aggregate demand curve rightward, increasing the aggregate price level from P_1 to P_2 and aggregate output from Y_1 to Y_2.

AD_1 to AD_2, as shown in panel (a). The economy moves down along the *SRAS* curve from E_1 to E_2, leading to lower short-run equilibrium aggregate output and a lower short-run equilibrium aggregate price level. A positive demand shock shifts the aggregate demand curve, *AD*, to the right, as shown in panel (b). Here, the economy moves up along the *SRAS* curve, from E_1 to E_2. This leads to higher short-run equilibrium aggregate output and a higher short-run equilibrium aggregate price level. Demand shocks cause aggregate output and the aggregate price level to move in the same direction.

> An event that shifts the short-run aggregate supply curve is a **supply shock.**

Shifts of the *SRAS* Curve

An event that shifts the short-run aggregate supply curve, such as a change in commodity prices, nominal wages, or productivity, is known as a **supply shock.** A *negative* or *adverse* supply shock raises production costs and reduces the quantity producers are willing to supply at any given aggregate price level, leading to a leftward shift of the short-run aggregate supply curve. The Canadian economy experienced severe negative supply shocks following disruptions to world oil supplies in 1973 and 1979. In contrast, a *positive* supply shock reduces production costs and increases the quantity supplied at any given aggregate price level, leading to a rightward shift of the short-run aggregate supply curve. Canada experienced a positive supply shock in the late 1990s and early 2000s, when the increasing use of the Internet and other information technologies caused productivity growth to surge.[3]

The effects of a negative supply shock to the short-run aggregate supply curve are shown in panel (a) of Figure 12-14. The initial equilibrium is at E_1, with aggregate

FIGURE **12-14** Supply Shocks That Affect the Short-Run Aggregate Supply Curve Only

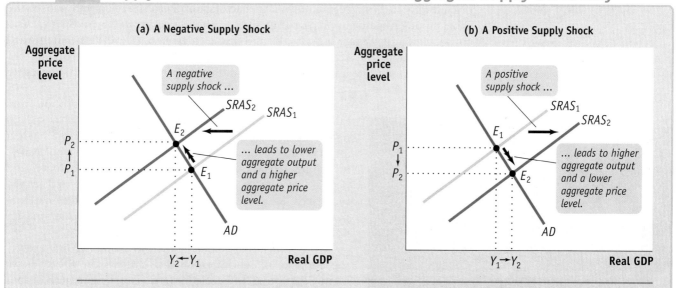

(a) A Negative Supply Shock

A negative supply shock ...

... leads to lower aggregate output and a higher aggregate price level.

$Y_2 \leftarrow Y_1$ Real GDP

(b) A Positive Supply Shock

A positive supply shock ...

... leads to higher aggregate output and a lower aggregate price level.

$Y_1 \rightarrow Y_2$ Real GDP

A supply shock shifts the short-run aggregate supply curve, moving the aggregate price level and aggregate output in opposite directions. Panel (a) shows a negative supply shock, which shifts the short-run aggregate supply curve leftward and causes stagflation—lower aggregate output and a higher aggregate price level. Here the short-run aggregate supply curve shifts from $SRAS_1$ to $SRAS_2$, and the economy moves from E_1 to E_2. The

aggregate price level rises from P_1 to P_2, and aggregate output falls from Y_1 to Y_2. Panel (b) shows a positive supply shock, which shifts the short-run aggregate supply curve rightward, generating higher aggregate output and a lower aggregate price level. The short-run aggregate supply curve shifts from $SRAS_1$ to $SRAS_2$, and the economy moves from E_1 to E_2. The aggregate price level falls from P_1 to P_2, and aggregate output rises from Y_1 to Y_2.

---

[3]The increasing use of the Internet and other information technologies can also shift the *LRAS* curve. The effect of this productivity growth will be discussed in the next section.

SUPPLY SHOCKS OF THE TWENTY-FIRST CENTURY

The price of oil and other raw materials has been highly unstable in recent years, with surging prices in 2007–2008, plunging prices in 2008–2009, and another surge starting in the second half of 2010. There is still controversy as to the reasons for these wild swings, but there is no disagreement about their macroeconomic impact: much of the world has been subjected to a series of supply shocks. There was a negative shock in 2007–2008, a positive shock in 2008–2009, and another negative shock in 2010–2011.

You can see the effect of these shocks in the accompanying figure, which shows the rate of inflation, as measured by the percentage change in consumer prices over the previous year, in three economies. Economic policies have been quite different in Canada, Germany (which shares a currency with another 16 European countries), and China. Yet, in all three countries, inflation rose sharply in 2007–2008, fell dramatically thereafter, and rose sharply again in 2010–2011.

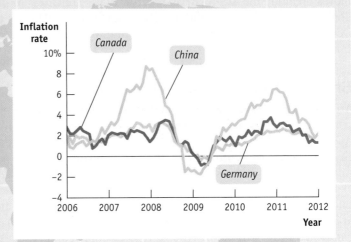

Source: OECD.

price level P_1 and aggregate output Y_1. The disruption in the oil supply causes the short-run aggregate supply curve to shift to the left, from $SRAS_1$ to $SRAS_2$. As a consequence, aggregate output falls and the aggregate price level rises, an upward movement along the AD curve. At the new equilibrium, E_2, the short-run equilibrium aggregate price level, P_2, is higher, and the short-run equilibrium aggregate output level, Y_2, is lower than before.

The combination of rising prices (higher inflation) and falling aggregate output shown in panel (a) has a special name: **stagflation,** for "stagnation plus inflation." When an economy experiences stagflation, it's very unpleasant: falling aggregate output leads to rising unemployment, and people feel that their purchasing power is squeezed by rising prices. Stagflation in the 1970s led to a mood of national pessimism. It also, as we'll see shortly, poses a dilemma for policy-makers.

A positive supply shock, shown in panel (b), has exactly the opposite effects. A rightward shift of the $SRAS$ curve from $SRAS_1$ to $SRAS_2$ results in a rise in aggregate output and a fall in the aggregate price level, a downward movement along the AD curve. The favourable supply shocks of the late 1990s led to a combination of higher employment and lower prices compared with the long-run trend (i.e., declining inflation). This combination produced, for a time, a great wave of national optimism.

The distinctive feature of supply shocks, both negative and positive, is that, unlike demand shocks, they cause the aggregate price level and aggregate output to move in *opposite* directions.

There's another important contrast between supply shocks and demand shocks. As we've seen, monetary policy and fiscal policy enable the government to shift the AD curve, meaning that governments are in a position to create the

As you can see from the faces of these jobseekers, pessimism prevails during stagflation as unemployment and prices rise.

Stagflation is the combination of rising prices (higher inflation) and falling aggregate output.

kinds of shocks shown in Figure 12-13. It's much harder for governments to shift the *AS* curve. Are there good policy reasons to shift the *AD* curve? We'll turn to that question soon.

Simultaneous Shifts of the *SRAS* and *LRAS* Curves

As noted in Tables 12-2 and 12-3, changes in productivity can shift both the *SRAS* and *LRAS* curves simultaneously. Let's examine the effects of such a positive supply shock on the economy. When the economy experiences an increase in total factor productivity, each worker can produce more output for any given level of inputs. For example, the widespread use of information technologies in the past 20 years has greatly increased workers' productivity, and this change has shifted the *SRAS* curve to the right. The *LRAS* curve also shifts to the right because once this new technology has been adopted it will have a long-lasting effect on the economy.

The effects of an increase in productivity are shown in Figure 12-15. The initial equilibrium is at E_1, with aggregate price level P_1 and aggregate output Y_1. Here the rise in productivity causes both the short-run and long-run aggregate supply curves to shift to the right by differing magnitudes from $SRAS_1$ to $SRAS_2$ and from $LRAS_1$ to $LRAS_2$, respectively. As a consequence, aggregate output rises and the aggregate price level falls, a downward movement along the *AD* curve. At the new short-run equilibrium, E_2, the short-run equilibrium aggregate price level, P_2, is lower, and the short-run equilibrium aggregate output level, Y_2, is higher than before.

The level of potential output has risen from Y_1 to Y_3 and the new level of potential output is higher than the new short-run level, Y_2; therefore, even though the economy experienced an increase in aggregate output in the short run, its short-run level of aggregate output is now below the economy's long-run level.

FIGURE 12-15 **Shocks That Affect Both the Short-Run and the Long-Run Aggregate Supply Curves**

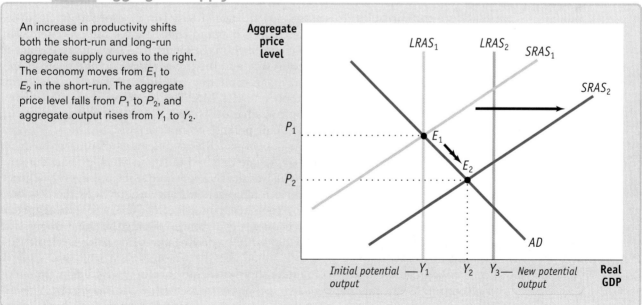

An increase in productivity shifts both the short-run and long-run aggregate supply curves to the right. The economy moves from E_1 to E_2 in the short-run. The aggregate price level falls from P_1 to P_2, and aggregate output rises from Y_1 to Y_2.

Long-Run Macroeconomic Equilibrium

Figure 12-16 combines the aggregate demand curve with both the short-run and long-run aggregate supply curves. The aggregate demand curve, *AD*, crosses the short-run aggregate supply curve, *SRAS*, at E_{LR}. Here we assume that enough

FIGURE **12-16** Long-Run Macroeconomic Equilibrium

Here the point of short-run macroeconomic equilibrium also lies on the long-run aggregate supply curve, *LRAS*. As a result, short-run equilibrium aggregate output is equal to potential output, Y_P. The economy is in long-run macroeconomic equilibrium at E_{LR}.

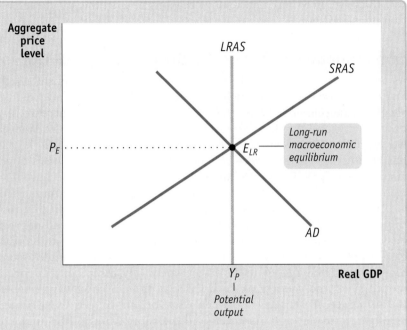

The economy is in **long-run macroeconomic equilibrium** when the point of short-run macroeconomic equilibrium is on the long-run aggregate supply curve.

There is a **recessionary gap** when aggregate output is below potential output.

time has elapsed that the economy is also on the long-run aggregate supply curve, *LRAS*. As a result, E_{LR} is at the intersection of all three curves—*SRAS*, *LRAS*, and *AD*. So short-run equilibrium aggregate output is equal to potential output, Y_P. Such a situation, in which the point of short-run macroeconomic equilibrium is on the long-run aggregate supply curve, is known as **long-run macroeconomic equilibrium.**

Demand Shocks To see the significance of long-run macroeconomic equilibrium, let's consider what happens if a demand shock moves the economy away from long-run macroeconomic equilibrium. In Figure 12-17, we assume that the initial aggregate demand curve is AD_1 and the initial short-run aggregate supply curve is $SRAS_1$. So the initial macroeconomic equilibrium is at E_1, which lies on the long-run aggregate supply curve, *LRAS*. The economy, then, starts from a point of short-run and long-run macroeconomic equilibrium, and short-run equilibrium aggregate output equals potential output at Y_1.

Now suppose that for some reason—such as a sudden worsening of business and consumer expectations—aggregate demand falls and the aggregate demand curve shifts leftward to AD_2. This results in a lower equilibrium aggregate price level at P_2 and a lower equilibrium aggregate output level at Y_2 as the economy settles in the short run at E_2. The short-run effect of such a fall in aggregate demand is what the Canadian economy experienced during the Great Depression and in the recent recession of 2008–2009: a falling aggregate price level and falling aggregate output.

Aggregate output in this new short-run equilibrium, E_2, is below potential output. When this happens, the economy faces a **recessionary gap.** A recessionary gap inflicts a great deal of pain because it corresponds to high unemployment. The large recessionary gap that had opened up in Canada by 1933 caused intense social and political turmoil. And the devastating recessionary gap that opened up in Germany at the same time played an important role in Hitler's rise to power.

But this isn't the end of the story. In the face of high unemployment, nominal wages eventually fall, as do any other sticky prices, ultimately leading producers

FIGURE **12-17** Short-Run versus Long-Run Effects of a Negative Demand Shock

FIGURE **12-17** Short-Run versus Long-Run Effects of a Negative Demand Shock

In the long run the economy is self-correcting: demand shocks have only a short-run effect on aggregate output. Starting at E_1, a negative demand shock shifts AD_1 leftward to AD_2. In the short run the economy moves to E_2 and a recessionary gap arises: the aggregate price level declines from P_1 to P_2, aggregate output declines from Y_1 to Y_2, and unemployment rises. But in the long run nominal wages fall in response to high unemployment at Y_2, and $SRAS_1$ shifts rightward to $SRAS_2$. Aggregate output rises from Y_2 to Y_1, and the aggregate price level declines again, from P_2 to P_3. Long-run macroeconomic equilibrium is eventually restored at E_3.

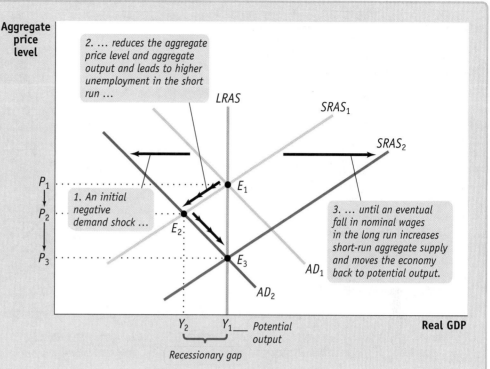

to increase output. As a result, a recessionary gap causes the short-run aggregate supply curve to gradually shift to the right over time. This process continues until $SRAS_1$ reaches its new position at $SRAS_2$, bringing the economy to equilibrium at E_3, where AD_2, $SRAS_2$, and $LRAS$ all intersect. At E_3, the economy is back in long-run macroeconomic equilibrium; it is back at potential output Y_1 but at a lower aggregate price level, P_3, reflecting a long-run fall in the aggregate price level. In the end, the economy is *self-correcting* in the long run.

FOR INQUIRING MINDS

WHERE'S THE DEFLATION?

The *AD–AS* model says that either a negative demand shock or a positive supply shock should lead to a fall in the aggregate price level—that is, deflation. However, since 1945, an actual fall in the aggregate price level has been a rare occurrence in Canada. Similarly, most other countries have had little or no experience with deflation. Japan, which experienced sustained mild deflation in the late 1990s and the early part of the next decade, is the big (and much discussed) exception. What happened to deflation?

The basic answer is that economic fluctuations since World War II have largely taken place around a long-run

inflationary trend. Before the war, it was common for prices to fall during recessions, but since then negative demand shocks have largely been reflected in a *decline in the rate of inflation* rather than an actual fall in prices. For example, the annualized inflation rate fell from 11.3% in January 1982 (the beginning of the recession in the early 1980s) to 5.01% in September 1983 (the end of the recession), but never fell below zero.

All of this changed following the recession of 1990–1991. The annualized inflation rate actually rose from 5.5% in January 1990 to 6.91% in January 1991, before falling to 3.75% in December 1991. Then the annual rate of inflation

fell below 2% for most months during 1992 to 1994. In May, October, and November of 1994, the CPI actually declined on an annual basis—Canada experienced deflation.

Canada experienced deflation again during the recession of 2008–2009. The negative demand shock that followed the 2007–2008 U.S. financial crisis was so severe that, from June 2009 to September 2009, consumer prices in Canada indeed fell, compared to the same period in the previous year. But the deflationary period didn't last long. Starting in October 2009, prices again rose, at a rate of between 1% and 3% per year.

FIGURE **12-18** **Short-Run versus Long-Run Effects of a Positive Demand Shock**

Starting at E_1, a positive demand shock shifts AD_1 rightward to AD_2, and the economy moves to E_2 in the short run. This results in an inflationary gap as aggregate output rises from Y_1 to Y_2, the aggregate price level rises from P_1 to P_2, and unemployment falls to a low level. In the long run, $SRAS_1$ shifts leftward to $SRAS_2$ as nominal wages rise in response to low unemployment at Y_2. Aggregate output falls back to Y_1, the aggregate price level rises again to P_3, and the economy self-corrects as it returns to long-run macroeconomic equilibrium at E_3.

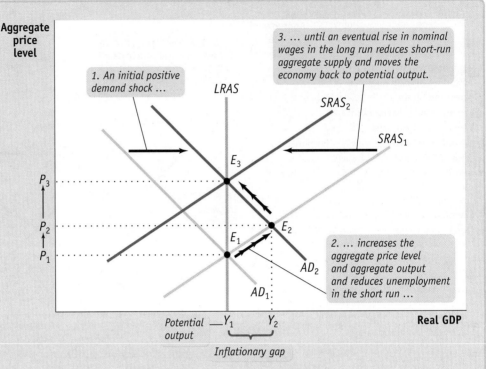

Figure 12-18 shows the results of an increase in aggregate demand. In the short run, a rightward shift in aggregate demand leads to a rise in both aggregate price level and aggregate output. Since the short-run equilibrium level of output, Y_2, is above the level of potential output, the economy is said to be in an **inflationary gap.** Such a gap lowers unemployment and puts upward pressure on nominal wages. This, in the longer term, shifts the short-run aggregate supply curve up to the left. When the economy settles into its new long-run equilibrium, E_3, output falls back to potential output and the aggregate price level increases farther to P_3. Just as in the case of a reduction in aggregate demand, the economy corrects itself.

To summarize the analysis of how the economy responds to recessionary and inflationary gaps, we can focus on the **output gap,** the percentage difference between actual aggregate output and potential output. The output gap is calculated as follows:

$$(12\text{-}3)\ \text{Output gap} = \frac{\text{Actual aggregate output} - \text{Potential output}}{\text{Potential output}} \times 100$$

Our analysis says that the output gap always tends toward zero.

If there is a recessionary gap, so that the output gap is negative, nominal wages eventually fall, moving the economy back to potential output and bringing the output gap back to zero. If there is an inflationary gap, so that the output gap is positive, nominal wages eventually rise, also moving the economy back to potential output and again bringing the output gap back to zero. So in the long run the economy is **self-correcting:** shocks to aggregate demand affect aggregate output in the short run but not in the long run.

Supply Shocks We have examined the long-run adjustment following a demand shock, but what happens if there is supply shock that moves the economy

There is an **inflationary gap** when aggregate output is above potential output.

The **output gap** is the percentage difference between actual aggregate output and potential output.

The economy is **self-correcting** when shocks to aggregate demand affect aggregate output in the short run, but not the long run.

Short-Run versus Long-Run Effects of Positive Shocks to Both
FIGURE **12-19** Short-Run and Long-Run Aggregate Supply

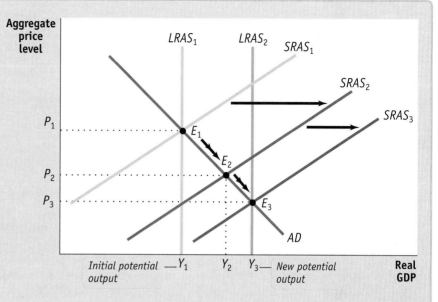

Starting at E_1, a positive productivity shock shifts both *SRAS* and *LRAS* rightward to $SRAS_2$ and $LRAS_2$ respectively, and the economy moves to E_2 in the short-run. This favourable productivity shock results in an increase aggregate output from Y_1 to Y_2 and a fall in the aggregate price level from P_1 to P_2. In the long-run, the *SRAS* shifts farther to the right to $SRAS_3$ as nominal wages fall in response to the fact that the short-run output is below the new level of potential output, Y_3. Aggregate output rises farther to Y_3, while the aggregate price level continues to fall until it reaches P_3, and the economy self-corrects to its new long-run macroeconomic equilibrium at E_3.

An increase in productivity shifts both the short-run and long-run aggregate supply curves to the right. The economy moves from E_1 to E_2 in the short-run. The aggregate price level falls from P_1 to P_2, and aggregate output rises from Y_1 to Y_2.

away from long-run macroeconomic equilibrium? Let's continue with the example of the simultaneous shifts in both the *SRAS* and *LRAS* curves discussed earlier.

The short-run and long-run effects of an increase in productivity are shown in Figure 12-19. The initial equilibrium is at E_1, with aggregate price level P_1 and aggregate output Y_1. The rise in productivity leads to a rightward shift in both the short-run and long-run aggregate supply curves to $SRAS_2$ and $LRAS_2$, respectively. This results in a lower equilibrium aggregate price level at P_2 and a higher equilibrium level of aggregate output at Y_2 as the economy settles in the short-run at E_2. Although the short-run equilibrium level of aggregate output has increased, it is now below the new level of potential output, Y_3. In the longer term, we will observe a fall in nominal wages and other sticky prices. This will further increase output as it causes the short-run aggregate supply curve to gradually shift to the right over time. This process continues until *SRAS* reaches its long-run position, $SRAS_3$, where *AD*, $SRAS_3$, and $LRAS_2$ all intersect. At the new long-run equilibrium, E_3, the economy finds its aggregate output has moved to the new level of potential output Y_3 and the aggregate price level has fallen farther to P_3. Once again, the economy is self-correcting in the long-run.

ECONOMICS ▸ IN ACTION

SUPPLY SHOCKS VERSUS DEMAND SHOCKS IN PRACTICE

How often do supply shocks and demand shocks, respectively, cause recessions? The verdict of most, though not all, macroeconomists is that recessions are mainly caused by demand shocks. But when a negative supply shock does happen, the resulting recession tends to be particularly severe.

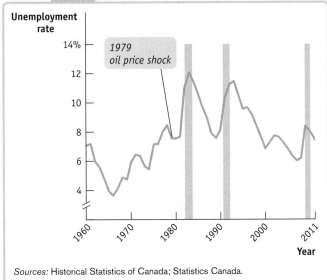

FIGURE 12-20 Negative Supply Shocks: Rare but Nasty

Sources: Historical Statistics of Canada; Statistics Canada.

Let's get specific. Canada has experienced three recessions in the past 50 years: one in 1982–1983, one in 1990–1991, and the third in 2008–2009. The first recession was caused by a supply shock—political turmoil in the Middle East in the late 1970s led to disruption of oil supplies, and oil prices skyrocketed. This recession was the only one to show the distinctive combination of falling aggregate output and a surge in the price level, or in a word, stagflation. Some of the highest unemployment rates since 1960, in fact since the Great Depression, came following this big negative supply shock. In contrast, the last two recessions were caused by demand shocks, and although unpleasant, they were not nearly as bad as the recession in the early 1980s. Although unemployment rates were up, the Canadian economy did not experience a significantly higher rate of inflation. Figure 12-20 shows Canada's unemployment rate since 1960, with the date of the oil price shock in the late 1970s indicated and the periods of recession highlighted in purple.

There's a reason the aftermath of a supply shock tends to be particularly severe for the economy: macroeconomic policy has a much harder time dealing with supply shocks than with demand shocks. For example, the reason the Bank of Canada was having a hard time in 2008, as described in the opening story, was the fact that in early 2008 the Canadian economy was hit by an adverse supply shock (although it was also facing an adverse demand shock). We'll see in a moment why supply shocks present such a problem.

▼ Quick Review

- The **AD–AS model** is used to study economic fluctuations.

- **Short-run macroeconomic equilibrium** occurs at the intersection of the short-run aggregate supply and aggregate demand curves. This determines the **short-run equilibrium aggregate price level** and the level of **short-run equilibrium aggregate output**.

- A **demand shock,** a shift of the *AD* curve, causes the aggregate price level and aggregate output to move in the same direction. A **supply shock,** a shift of the *SRAS* curve, causes them to move in opposite directions. **Stagflation** is the consequence of a negative supply shock.

- A fall in nominal wages occurs in response to a **recessionary gap,** and a rise in nominal wages occurs in response to an **inflationary gap.** Both move the economy to **long-run macroeconomic equilibrium,** where the *AD*, *SRAS*, and *LRAS* curves intersect.

- The **output gap** always tends toward zero because the economy is **self-correcting** in the long run.

CHECK YOUR UNDERSTANDING 12-3

1. Describe the short-run effects of each of the following shocks on the aggregate price level and on aggregate output.
   a. The government sharply increases the minimum wage, raising the wages of many workers.
   b. Solar energy firms launch a major program of investment spending.
   c. The federal government raises taxes and cuts spending.
   d. Severe weather destroys crops around the world.

2. A rise in productivity increases potential output, but some worry that demand for the additional output will be insufficient even in the long run. How would you respond?

Solutions appear at back of book.

Macroeconomic Policy

We've just seen that the economy is self-correcting in the long run: it will eventually trend back to potential output. Most macroeconomists believe, however, that the process of self-correction typically takes a decade or more. In particular, if aggregate output is below potential output, the economy can suffer an extended period of depressed aggregate output and high unemployment before it returns to normal.

This belief is the background to one of the most famous quotations in economics: John Maynard Keynes's declaration, "In the long run we are all dead." We explain the context in which he made this remark in the accompanying For Inquiring Minds.

FOR INQUIRING MINDS

KEYNES AND THE LONG RUN

The British economist Sir John Maynard Keynes (1883–1946), probably more than any other single economist, created the modern field of macroeconomics. We'll look at his role, and the controversies that still swirl around some aspects of his thought, in a later chapter on macroeconomic events and ideas. But for now let's just look at his most famous quote.

In 1923 Keynes published *A Tract on Monetary Reform*, a small book on the economic problems of Europe after World War I. In it he decried the

tendency of many of his colleagues to focus on how things work out in the long run—as in the long-run macroeconomic equilibrium we have just analyzed—while ignoring the often very painful and possibly disastrous things that can happen along the way. Here's a fuller version of the quote:

> This *long run* is a misleading guide to current affairs. *In the long run* we are all dead. Economists set themselves too easy, too useless a task if in tempestuous seasons they can only tell us that when the storm is long past the sea is flat again.

Keynes focused the attention of economists of his day on the short run.

Economists usually interpret Keynes as having recommended that governments and central banks not wait for the economy to correct itself. Instead, it is argued by many economists, but not all, that the governments and central banks should use monetary and fiscal policy to help get the economy back to potential output more quickly in the aftermath of a shift of the aggregate demand curve. This is the rationale for an active **stabilization policy,** which is the use of government policy to reduce the severity and duration of recessions and rein in excessively strong expansions.

Stabilization policy is the use of government policy to reduce the severity and duration of recessions and rein in excessively strong expansions.

Can stabilization policy improve the economy's performance? If we re-examine Figure 12-8, the answer certainly appears to be yes. Under active stabilization policy, the Canadian economy returned to potential output in 1985 after three years of recessionary gap. This happened in a much shorter period than the decade or more that economists believe it would take for the economy to self-correct in the absence of active stabilization policy. However, as we'll see shortly, the ability to improve the economy's performance is not always guaranteed. It depends on the kinds of shocks the economy faces.

Policy in the Face of Demand Shocks

Imagine that the economy experiences a negative demand shock, like the one shown in Figure 12-21. As we've discussed in this chapter, monetary and fiscal policy shift the aggregate demand curve. If policy-makers react quickly to the fall in aggregate demand, they can use monetary or fiscal policy to shift the aggregate demand curve back to the right. And if policy were able to perfectly anticipate shifts of the aggregate demand curve, it could short-circuit the whole process shown in Figure 12-21. Instead of going through a period of low aggregate output and falling prices, the government could manage the economy so that it would stay at E_1.

Why might a policy that short-circuits the adjustment shown in Figure 12-21 and maintains the economy at its original equilibrium be desirable? For two reasons. First, the temporary fall in aggregate output that would happen without policy intervention is a bad thing, particularly because such a decline is associated with high unemployment. Second, as we explained in Chapter 8, *price stability* is generally regarded as a desirable goal. So preventing deflation—a fall in the aggregate price level—is a good thing.

Does this mean that governments and the central bank should always act to offset declines in aggregate demand? Not necessarily. As we'll see in later chapters, some policy measures to increase aggregate demand, especially those that increase budget deficits, may have long-term costs in terms of lower long-run growth due to

FIGURE **12-21** Stabilization Policy under a Negative Demand Shock

Starting at E_1, a negative demand shock shifts AD_1 leftward to AD_2. In the short run the economy moves to E_2 such that aggregate price level falls to P_2 and aggregate output falls to Y_2. If the government responds to the negative demand shock by running an expansionary policy, such as an expansionary fiscal policy or monetary policy, aggregate demand increases back to its initial level, AD_1. The economy returns to its initial equilibrium, E_1: aggregate price level returns to P_1 and aggregate output returns to potential output (Y_1). Thus, stabilization policy can bring the economy back to potential output without causing falling prices and higher unemployment when there is a leftward (negative or adverse) shift in AD curve.

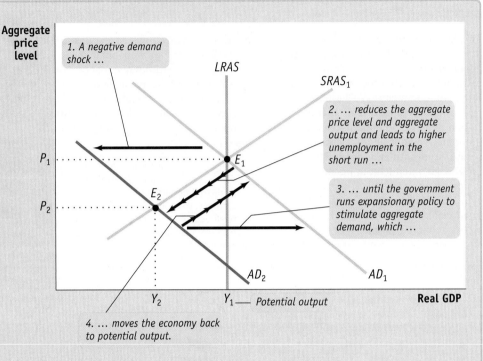

1. A negative demand shock ...

2. ... reduces the aggregate price level and aggregate output and leads to higher unemployment in the short run ...

3. ... until the government runs expansionary policy to stimulate aggregate demand, which ...

4. ... moves the economy back to potential output.

reduced investment. (As discussed in Chapter 10, expansionary fiscal policy causes the interest rate to rise, which crowds out, or lowers, the level of investment spending.) Furthermore, in the real world policy-makers aren't perfectly informed, and the effects of their policies aren't perfectly predictable. This creates the danger that stabilization policy will do more harm than good; that is, attempts to stabilize the economy may end up creating more instability. We'll describe the long-running debate over macroeconomic policy in Chapter 18. Despite these qualifications, most economists believe that a good case can be made for using macroeconomic policy to offset major negative shocks to the AD curve.

Should policy-makers also try to offset positive shocks to aggregate demand? It may not seem obvious that they should. After all, even though inflation may be a bad thing, isn't more output and lower unemployment a good thing? Not necessarily. Most economists now believe that any short-run gains from an inflationary gap must be paid back later. So policy-makers today usually try to offset positive as well as negative demand shocks. For reasons we'll explain in Chapter 15, attempts to eliminate recessionary gaps and inflationary gaps usually rely on monetary rather than fiscal policy. In 2008 the Bank of Canada sharply cut interest rates in an attempt to head off a rising recessionary gap; in the mid-2000s when the Canadian economy seemed headed for an inflationary gap, it raised interest rates to generate the opposite effect.

But how should macroeconomic policy respond to supply shocks?

Responding to Supply Shocks

We've now come full circle to the story that began this chapter. We can now explain why the governor of the Bank of Canada dreads inflation.

Back in panel (a) of Figure 12-14 we showed the effects of a negative supply shock: in the short run such a shock leads to lower aggregate output but a higher aggregate price level. As we've noted, policy-makers can respond to a negative

FIGURE **12-22** Stabilization Policy under a Negative Supply Shock

Starting at E_1, a negative (adverse) supply shock shifts $SRAS_1$ leftward to $SRAS_2$. In the short run the economy moves to E_2 such that aggregate price level rises to P_2, aggregate output falls to Y_2, and unemployment rises. If the government responds to the negative supply shock by running an expansionary policy, such as an expansionary fiscal policy or monetary policy, aggregate demand increases to AD_2. The economy moves to E_3 in the short run: the aggregate price level increases further to P_3 and aggregate output returns to potential output (Y_1). Thus, the government faces a dilemma when the economy experiences an adverse supply shock.

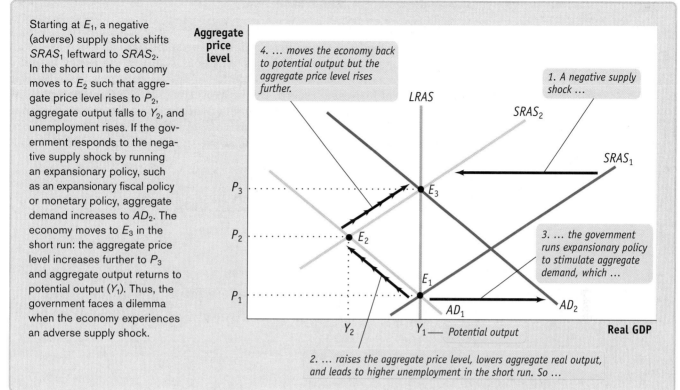

4. ... moves the economy back to potential output but the aggregate price level rises further.

1. A negative supply shock ...

3. ... the government runs expansionary policy to stimulate aggregate demand, which ...

2. ... raises the aggregate price level, lowers aggregate real output, and leads to higher unemployment in the short run. So ...

demand shock by using monetary and fiscal policy to return aggregate demand to its original level. But what can or should they do about a negative *supply* shock?

In contrast to the aggregate demand curve, there are no easy policies that shift the short-run aggregate supply curve. That is, there is no government policy that can easily affect producers' profitability and so compensate for shifts of the short-run aggregate supply curve. So the policy response to a negative supply shock cannot aim to simply push the curve that shifted back to its original position.

And if you consider using monetary or fiscal policy to shift the aggregate demand curve in response to a supply shock, the right response isn't obvious. Two bad things are happening simultaneously: a fall in aggregate output, leading to a rise in unemployment, *and* a rise in the aggregate price level. Any policy that shifts the aggregate demand curve helps one problem only by making the other worse. As shown in Figure 12-22, if the government acts to increase aggregate demand and limit the rise in unemployment, it reduces the decline in output but causes even more inflation. If it acts to reduce aggregate demand, it curbs inflation but causes a further rise in unemployment.

It's a trade-off with no good answer. In the end, Canada and other economically advanced nations suffering from the supply shocks of the 1970s eventually chose to stabilize prices even at the cost of higher unemployment. But being an economic policy-maker in the 1970s, or in early 2008, meant facing even harder choices than usual. When Canada experienced adverse supply shocks in the 1970s and the inflation rate hit double digits, Prime Minister Pierre Trudeau introduced the Anti-Inflation Act in 1975. The aim of this act was to slow the rate of increase in wages and prices. The government hoped that this step would shift the short-run aggregate supply curve to the right, and partially offset the adverse effects of the initial leftward shift in *SRAS*. Unfortunately, this attempt was unsuccessful, as the Canadian economy still suffered from high inflation and high unemployment. Eventually, the wage and price control policy was repealed in 1979.

ECONOMICS ▶ IN ACTION

IS STABILIZATION POLICY STABILIZING?

We've described the theoretical rationale for stabilization policy as a way of responding to demand shocks. But does stabilization policy actually stabilize the economy? One way we might try to answer this question is to look at the long-term historical record. Before World War II, the Canadian government didn't really have a stabilization policy—largely because macroeconomics as we know it didn't exist—and there was no consensus about what to do. Since World War II, and especially since 1960, active stabilization policy has become standard practice.

FIGURE **12-23** Has Stabilization Policy Been Stabilizing?

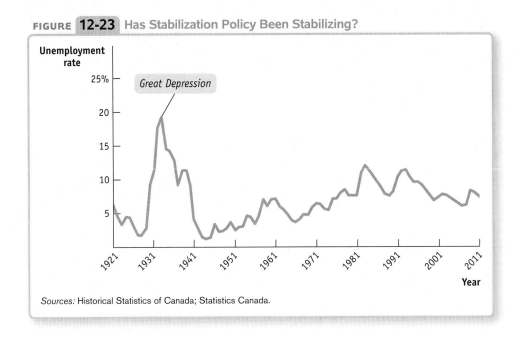

Sources: Historical Statistics of Canada; Statistics Canada.

So here's the question: has the economy actually become more stable since the government began trying to stabilize it? To answer this question, we need to look at the data. Figure 12-23 shows the unemployment rate between 1921 and 2011. Even ignoring the huge spike in unemployment during the Great Depression, unemployment seems to have varied a lot. Since 1960 Canada experienced three recessions—in the early 1980s, in the early 1990s, and again in 2008–2009, and in all these recessions the unemployment rate rose. From this observation one might conclude that stabilization policy fails to reduce fluctuations in unemployment. Is it true? The answer is no, because of the causes of the recessions.

Each of the three recessions we have had since the 1980s had a different cause. The recession in early 1980s was a classic example of an adverse supply-side shock: the economy was pushed into a recession by a significant hike in oil prices. This hike shifted the short-run aggregate supply curve leftward, causing a higher price level and higher unemployment rate. Unfortunately, policy-makers have to choose between fighting the high inflation rate or high unemployment—no stabilization policy deals with both hazards simultaneously. As Figure 12-23 shows, the unemployment rate again rose above double digits in the early 1990s. This time, the recession was caused by a change in the Bank of Canada's monetary policy. The Bank decided that the inflation rate was too high, and it was necessary to pursue a disinflationary policy. This "contractionary" monetary policy lowered aggregate demand and pushed the economy into a recession. This is a good example of how the Bank of Canada's two goals—low unemployment and low, stable prices—can be in conflict with each other. The Bank chose to lower the inflation rate and paid the price of higher unemployment. The 2008–2009 recession was caused mainly by a negative demand-side shock from the U.S., with the bursting of their housing price bubble. Both the federal government and the Bank of Canada reacted to this shock aggressively by using various measures to offset the fall in aggregate demand. The federal government undertook expansionary fiscal policy, by increasing spending on infrastructure, targeting tax cuts, and so on. The Bank of Canada enacted an expansionary monetary policy, slashing the bank interest rate to increase the money supply. Although the unemployment rate did increase on this occasion, it did not increase as much as in the previous two recessions. This suggests that stabilization policy can indeed be stabilizing.

CHECK YOUR UNDERSTANDING   12-4

1. Suppose someone says, "Using monetary or fiscal policy to pump up the economy is counterproductive—you get a brief high, but then you have the pain of inflation."
   a. Explain what this means in terms of the *AD–AS* model.
   b. Is this a valid argument against stabilization policy? Why or why not?

2. In 2008, in the aftermath of the collapse of the U.S. housing bubble and a sharp rise in the price of commodities, particularly oil, there was much internal disagreement within the Bank of Canada about how to properly respond. Some analysts advocated lowering interest rates, but others disagreed, saying that this would set off a rise in inflation. Explain the reasoning behind each one of these views in terms of the *AD–AS* model.

Solutions appear at back of book.

▼ Quick Review

- **Stabilization policy** is the use of fiscal or monetary policy to offset demand shocks. There can be drawbacks, however. Such policies may lead to a long-term rise in the budget deficit and lower long-run growth because of crowding out. And, due to incorrect predictions, a misguided policy can increase economic instability.

- Negative supply shocks pose a policy dilemma because fighting the slump in aggregate output worsens inflation and fighting inflation worsens the slump.

Flying the Ups and Downs of the Business Cycle

Larry MacDougal/CP Images

The airline industry is notoriously "cyclical." That is, instead of making profits all through the business cycle, it tends to plunge into losses during recessions, only regaining profitability sometime after recovery begins. Mainly this is because airlines have large fixed costs that remain high, even if ticket sales slump. The cost of operating a flight from one city to another is pretty much the same whether the flight is fully booked or two-thirds empty, so when business slumps for whatever reason, even highly profitable routes quickly become money-losers. It's true that airlines can to some extent adapt to a decline in business by switching to smaller planes, consolidating flights, and so on, but this process takes time and still tends to leave costs per passenger higher than before.

But some recessions are worse for airlines than for other businesses, because operating costs rise even as demand falls. This was very much the case in 2008. Hit by the global recession and rising fuel prices, Air Canada, our largest airline, suffered a net loss of $132 million (compared to a net income of $273 million a year earlier and net income of $122 million in the previous quarter).

Business travel had started to slacken, but at that point leisure travel was still holding up. So why was Air Canada in so much trouble? Mainly, Air Canada was hurt by the cost of fuel, which soared in late 2007 and 2008. Fuel prices did fall in late 2008, but by that time Air Canada was suffering from a sharp drop in ticket sales. Air Canada finally returned to profitability in 2010, only to see fuel prices take off once again in early 2011, returning it and other airlines to a difficult financial position.

QUESTIONS FOR THOUGHT

1. How did Air Canada's problems in early 2008 relate to our analysis of the causes of recessions?

2. Mark Carney had to choose between fighting two economic evils in 2008. How would his choice affect Air Canada compared with, say, a company producing a service without expensive raw material inputs, like a publisher?

3. In early 2008, business travel was beginning to slacken, but leisure travel was still holding up. Given the situation the overall economy was in, what would you expect to happen to leisure travel as the economy moved further into recession?

SUMMARY

1. The **aggregate demand curve** shows the relationship between the aggregate price level and the quantity of aggregate output demanded.

2. The aggregate demand curve is downward sloping for two reasons. The first is the **wealth effect of a change in the aggregate price level**—a higher aggregate price level reduces the purchasing power of households' wealth and reduces consumer spending. The second is the **interest rate effect of a change in the aggregate price level**—a higher aggregate price level reduces the purchasing power of households' and firms' money holdings, leading to a rise in interest rates and a fall in investment spending and consumer spending.

3. The aggregate demand curve shifts because of changes in expectations, changes in wealth not due to changes in the aggregate price level, and the effect of the size of the existing stock of physical capital. Policy-makers can use fiscal policy and monetary policy to shift the aggregate demand curve.

4. The **aggregate supply curve** shows the relationship between the aggregate price level and the quantity of aggregate output supplied.

5. The **short-run aggregate supply curve** is upward sloping because **nominal wages** are **sticky** in the short run: a higher aggregate price level leads to higher profit per unit of output and increased aggregate output supplied in the short run.

6. Changes in commodity prices, nominal wages, and productivity lead to changes in producers' profits and shift the **short-run aggregate supply curve.**

7. In the long run, all prices, including nominal wages, are flexible and the economy produces at its **potential output.** If actual aggregate output exceeds potential output, nominal wages will eventually rise in response to low unemployment and aggregate output will fall. If potential output exceeds actual aggregate output, nominal wages will eventually fall in response to high unemployment and aggregate output will rise. So the **long-run aggregate supply curve** is vertical at potential output.

8. Changes in the stock of physical capital, the stock of human capital, the size of the labour force, and productivity shift the long-run aggregate supply curve.

9. In the **AD–AS model,** the intersection of the short-run aggregate supply curve and the aggregate demand curve is the point of **short-run macroeconomic equilibrium.** It determines the **short-run equilibrium aggregate price level** and the level of **short-run equilibrium aggregate output.**

10. Economic fluctuations occur because of a shift of the aggregate demand curve (a *demand shock*) or the short-run aggregate supply curve (a *supply shock*). A **demand shock** causes the aggregate price level and aggregate output to move in the same direction as the economy moves along the short-run aggregate supply curve. A **supply shock** causes them to move in opposite directions as the economy moves along the aggregate demand curve. A particularly nasty occurrence is **stagflation**—inflation and falling aggregate output—which is caused by a negative supply shock.

11. Demand shocks and supply shocks have only short-run effects on aggregate output because the economy is **self-correcting** in the long run. In a **recessionary gap,** an eventual fall in nominal wages moves the economy to **long-run macroeconomic equilibrium,** where aggregate output is equal to potential output. In an **inflationary gap,** an eventual rise in nominal wages moves the economy to long-run macroeconomic equilibrium. We can use the **output gap,** the percentage difference between actual aggregate output and potential output, to summarize how the economy responds to recessionary and inflationary gaps. Because the economy tends to be self-correcting in the long run, the output gap always tends toward zero.

12. The high cost—in terms of unemployment—of a recessionary gap and the future adverse consequences of an inflationary gap lead many economists to advocate active **stabilization policy:** using fiscal or monetary policy to offset demand shocks. There can be drawbacks, however, because such policies may contribute to a long-term rise in the budget deficit and crowding out of private investment, leading to lower long-run growth. Also, poorly timed policies can increase economic instability.

13. Negative supply shocks pose a policy dilemma: a policy that counteracts the fall in aggregate output by increasing aggregate demand will lead to higher inflation, but a policy that counteracts inflation by reducing aggregate demand will deepen the output slump.

KEY TERMS

Short-run equilibrium aggregate price
level, p. 393
Short-run equilibrium aggregate
output, p. 393
Demand shock, p. 394

Supply shock, p. 395
Stagflation, p. 396
Long-run macroeconomic equilibrium,
p. 398
Recessionary gap, p. 398

Inflationary gap, p. 400
Output gap, p. 400
Self-correcting, p. 400
Stabilization policy, p. 403

PROBLEMS

1. A fall in the value of the Canadian dollar against other
currencies makes Canadian final goods and services
cheaper to foreigners even though the Canadian aggregate price level stays the same. As a result, foreigners
demand more Canadian aggregate output. Your study
partner says that this represents a movement down
the aggregate demand curve because foreigners are
demanding more in response to a lower price. You,
however, insist that this represents a rightward shift of
the aggregate demand curve. Who is right? Explain.

2. Your study partner is confused by the upward-sloping
short-run aggregate supply curve and the vertical
long-run aggregate supply curve. How would you
explain the difference?

3. Suppose that in Wageland all workers sign annual
wage contracts each year on January 1. No matter
what happens to prices of final goods and services
during the year, all workers earn the wage specified
in their annual contract. This year, prices of final
goods and services fall unexpectedly after the contracts are signed. Answer the following questions
using a diagram and assume that the economy starts
at potential output.

   a. In the short run, how will the quantity of aggregate
   output supplied respond to the fall in prices?

   b. What will happen when firms and workers renegoti-
   ate their wages?

4. In each of the following cases, in the short run, determine whether the events cause a shift of a curve or a
movement along a curve. Determine which curve is
involved and the direction of the change.

   a. As a result of an increase in the value of the Canadian
   dollar in relation to other currencies, Canadian producers now pay less in dollar terms for foreign steel,
   a major commodity used in production.

   b. An increase in the quantity of money by the Bank of
   Canada increases the quantity of money that people
   wish to lend, lowering interest rates.

   c. Greater union activity leads to higher nominal
   wages.

   d. A fall in the aggregate price level increases the
   purchasing power of households' and firms' money
   holdings. As a result, they borrow less and lend
   more.

5. The economy is at point *A* in the accompanying diagram. Suppose that the aggregate price level rises from
P_1 to P_2. How will aggregate supply adjust in the short

run and in the long run to the increase in the aggregate
price level? Illustrate with a diagram.

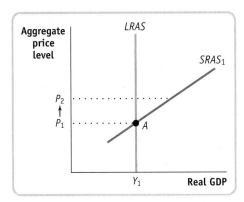

6. Suppose that all households hold all their wealth
in assets that automatically rise in value when the
aggregate price level rises (an example of this is what
is called an "inflation-indexed bond"—a bond whose
interest rate, among other things, changes one-for-one
with the inflation rate). What happens to the wealth
effect of a change in the aggregate price level as a
result of this allocation of assets? What happens to the
slope of the aggregate demand curve? Will it still slope
downward? Explain.

7. Suppose that the economy is currently at potential output. Also suppose that you are an economic
policy-maker and that a college economics student asks
you to rank, if possible, your most preferred to least
preferred type of shock: positive demand shock, negative demand shock, positive supply shock, negative supply shock. How would you rank them and why?

8. Explain whether the following government policies
affect the aggregate demand curve or the short-run
aggregate supply curve and how.

   a. The government reduces the minimum nominal
   wage.

   b. The government increases the size of payments for
   the child care benefit, government transfers to families with dependent children.

   c. To reduce the budget deficit, the government
   announces that households will pay much higher
   taxes beginning next year.

   d. The government reduces military spending.

9. In Wageland, all workers sign an annual wage contract
each year on January 1. In late January, a new computer
operating system is introduced that increases labour

productivity dramatically. Explain how Wageland will move from one short-run macroeconomic equilibrium to another. Illustrate with a diagram.

10. The Conference Board of Canada publishes the Index of Consumer Confidence every month based on a survey of 2000 Canadian households. Many economists use it to track the state of the economy. The latest release showed that the Index of Consumer Confidence increased to 82.2 (2002 = 100) in September 2012, up by 6.7 points from the previous month.

    a. As an economist, do you consider this news encouraging for economic growth?

    b. Explain your answer to part (a) with the help of the *AD–AS* model. Draw a typical diagram showing two equilibrium points (E_1) and (E_2). Label the vertical axis "Aggregate price level" and the horizontal axis "Real GDP." Assume that all other major macroeconomic factors remain unchanged.

    c. How should the federal government respond to this news? What policy measures can it use help neutralize the effect of rising consumer confidence?

11. The Canadian economy suffered two major shocks in 2008, leading to the severe recession of 2008–2009. One shock was related to oil prices; the other was the slump in both consumer and business confidence. This question analyzes the effect of these two shocks on GDP using the *AD–AS* model.

    a. Draw typical aggregate demand and short-run aggregate supply curves. Label the horizontal axis "Real GDP" and the vertical axis "Aggregate price level." Label the equilibrium point E_1, the equilibrium quantity Y_1, and equilibrium price P_1.

    b. Would an increase in oil prices cause a demand shock or a supply shock? Redraw the diagram from part (a) to illustrate the effect of this shock by shifting the appropriate curve.

    c. The New Housing Price Index, published by Statistics Canada, calculates that Canada's home prices fell by an average of 3% in the 12 months between April 2008 and April 2009. Business fixed capital formation fell by 19% during the same period. Would the fall in home prices and business fixed capital formation cause a supply shock or demand shock? Redraw the diagram from part (b) to illustrate the effect of this shock by shifting the appropriate curve. Label the new equilibrium point E_3, the equilibrium quantity Y_3, and equilibrium price P_3.

    d. Compare the equilibrium points E_1 and E_3 in your diagram for part (c). What was the (net) effect of the two shocks on real GDP and the aggregate price level (increase, decrease, or indeterminate)?

12. Using aggregate demand, short-run aggregate supply, and long-run aggregate supply curves, explain the process by which each of the following economic events will

move the economy from one long-run macroeconomic equilibrium to another. Illustrate with diagrams. In each case, what are the short-run and long-run effects on the aggregate price level and aggregate output?

    a. There is a decrease in households' wealth due to a decline in the stock market.

    b. The government lowers taxes, leaving households with more disposable income, with no corresponding reduction in government purchases.

13. Using aggregate demand, short-run aggregate supply, and long-run aggregate supply curves, explain the process by which each of the following government policies will move the economy from one long-run macroeconomic equilibrium to another. Illustrate with diagrams. In each case, what are the short-run and long-run effects on the aggregate price level and aggregate output?

    a. There is an increase in taxes on households.

    b. There is an increase in the quantity of money.

    c. There is an increase in government spending.

14. The economy is in short-run macroeconomic equilibrium at point E_1 in the accompanying diagram. Based on the diagram, answer the following questions.

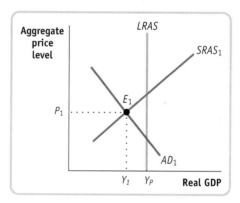

    a. Is the economy facing an inflationary or a recessionary gap?

    b. What policies can the government implement that might bring the economy back to long-run macroeconomic equilibrium? Illustrate with a diagram.

    c. If the government did not intervene to close this gap, would the economy return to long-run macroeconomic equilibrium? Explain and illustrate with a diagram.

    d. What are the advantages and disadvantages of the government implementing policies to close the gap?

15. In the accompanying diagram, the economy is in long-run macroeconomic equilibrium at point E_1 when an oil shock shifts the short-run aggregate supply curve to $SRAS_2$. Based on the diagram, answer the following questions.

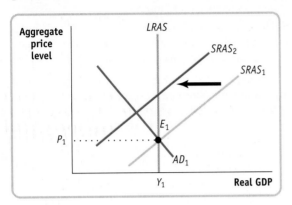

a. How do the aggregate price level and aggregate output change in the short run as a result of the oil shock? What is this phenomenon known as?

b. What fiscal or monetary policies can the government use to address the effects of the supply shock? Use a diagram that shows the effect of policies chosen to address the change in real GDP. Use another diagram to show the effect of policies chosen to address the change in the aggregate price level.

c. Why do supply shocks present a dilemma for government policy-makers?

16. The late 1990s in Canada was characterized by substantial economic growth with low inflation; that is, real GDP increased with little, if any, increase in the aggregate price level. Explain this experience using aggregate demand and aggregate supply curves. Illustrate with a diagram.

Fiscal Policy

TO STIMULATE OR NOT TO STIMULATE?

Anthony Jenkins/The Globe and Mail/CP Images

❭ **What fiscal policy** is and why it is an important tool in managing economic fluctuations

❭ Which policies constitute an **expansionary fiscal policy** and which constitute a **contractionary fiscal policy**

❭ Why fiscal policy has a multiplier effect and how this effect is influenced by **automatic stabilizers**

❭ Why governments calculate the **cyclically adjusted budget balance**

❭ Why a large **public debt** may be a cause for concern

❭ Why **implicit liabilities** of the government are also a cause for concern

N JANUARY 27, 2009, PRIME Minister Harper's government introduced its 2009 Budget Implementation Act. Often called Budget 2009: Canada's Economic Action Plan (EAP), this was a $62 billion package of spending, transfers, and tax cuts intended to help the struggling Canadian economy to reverse a severe recession that began in late 2008. The minister of finance, Jim Flaherty, stated at the time, "It builds on our position of strength. It provides temporary and effective economic stimulus to help Canadian families and businesses deal with short-term challenges. Our investments will build Canada's long-term capacity, so that when the global recession eases, we emerge even stronger."

Others weren't so sure that would be the case. They argued that at a time when Canadian families were suffering, the government should cut spending, not increase it. "Canadians will inevitably see higher taxes as a result of the federal government's plan to stimulate the economy with deficit spending," said financial commentator Evelyn Jacks. "Already, the federal and provincial taxes every Canadian pays on income and capital are by far the largest

destroyer of wealth over a lifetime. These deficits won't help," Jacks said. Some economic analysts were concerned that the so-called temporary measures, such as enhancing employment insurance benefits, would be difficult to reverse and might lead to structural deficits. Others warned that the stimulus bill, as the EAP was often called, would drive up interest rates and increase the burden of our national debt.

Others had the opposite complaint— that the stimulus was too small given the economy's troubles. Toronto mayor David Miller criticized the budget for creating a time-consuming application process for infrastructure funding. He and others also complained that not only might the money come too late, it generally had too many strings attached. Jean Perrault, president of the Federation of Canadian Municipalities and mayor of Sherbrooke, Quebec, said that cities and towns had already set their infrastructure budgets for 2009 and would be hard-pressed to come up with additional funding if they were required to match some or all of Ottawa's contributions.

The passage of time did not resolve these disputes. On one hand, the bill did

not jump-start the economy, as Harper had hoped: the recession did end officially in late 2009, but unemployment remained high above the pre-recession level, by which time the stimulus had largely run its course. On the other hand, interest rates remained low, contrary to what opponents of the stimulus had predicted. But the net effect of the stimulus remained controversial, with opponents arguing that it had failed to help the economy and defenders arguing that things would have been much worse without it.

Whatever the verdict—and this is one of those issues that economists and historians will probably argue about for decades—the Economic Action Plan of 2009 was a classic example of *fiscal policy,* the use of government spending and taxes to manage aggregate demand. In this chapter we'll see how fiscal policy fits into the models of economic fluctuations we studied in Chapters 11 and 12. We'll also see why budget deficits and government debt can be a problem and how short-run and long-run concerns can pull fiscal policy in different directions. ■

Fiscal Policy: The Basics

Let's begin with the obvious: modern governments in economically advanced countries spend a great deal of money and collect a lot in taxes. Figure 13-1 shows government spending and tax revenue as percentages of GDP for a selection of high-income countries in 2007. (We focus on 2007, rather than a more recent year, because it was a largely "normal" year. The numbers for later years were very much affected by the financial crisis of 2008 and its aftermath.) As you can see, the Swedish government sector is relatively large, accounting for more than half of the Swedish economy. The government of Canada may not play quite as large a role in its own national economy as governments of some European countries do in theirs, but it does play a significant role. As a result, changes in the federal budget, such as changes in government spending or in taxation, can have large effects on the Canadian economy.

FIGURE 13-1 Government Spending and Tax Revenue for Some High-Income Countries in 2007

We focus on 2007 because it was a "normal" year, not a year of deep economic slump. Government spending and tax revenue are represented as a percentage of GDP. Sweden has a particularly large government sector, representing more than half of its GDP. The Canadian government sector, while smaller than those of most European countries, is larger than those of Japan or the U.S., mainly owing to more public spending on health and education. *Source:* OECD.

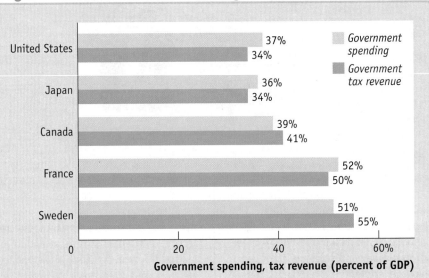

To analyze these effects, we begin by showing how taxes and government spending affect the economy's flow of income. Then we can see how changes in spending and tax policy affect aggregate demand.

Taxes, Purchases of Goods and Services, Government Transfers, and Borrowing

In Figure 7-1 we showed the circular flow of income and spending in the economy as a whole. One of the sectors represented in that figure was the government. Funds flow *into* the government in the form of taxes and government borrowing; funds flow *out* in the form of government purchases of goods and services and government transfers to households.

What kinds of taxes do Canadians pay, and where does the money go? Figure 13-2 shows the composition of Canadian tax revenue in 2007. Taxes, of course, are required payments to the government. In Canada, taxes are collected at the national level by the federal government; at the provincial or territorial level by each provincial or territorial government; and at local levels by counties, cities, and towns. At the federal level, the taxes that generate the greatest revenue are income taxes on both personal income and corporate profits as well as *social insurance* taxes, which we'll explain shortly. At the provincial and local levels, the picture is more complex: these governments rely on a mix of sales taxes, property taxes, income taxes, and fees of various kinds. Overall, taxes on personal income and corporate profits accounted for 48% of total government revenue in 2007; social insurance taxes accounted for 14%; and a variety of other taxes, collected mainly at the provincial and local levels, accounted for the rest.

Figure 13-3 shows the composition of total Canadian government spending in 2007, which, after the payment of interest on government debt, takes two broad forms.[1] One form is purchases of goods and services by government. These direct purchases are counted as part of government purchases of goods and services (the *G* term) in the expenditure approach to measuring GDP (as discussed in Chapter 7). These purchases include everything from diagnostic equipment for hospitals to the salaries of public school teachers (who are treated in the national accounts as providers of a service—education). The big items here are health and education. The fairly large category "Protection of persons and property" consists mainly of federal, provincial, and municipal spending on a variety of security services, from national defence, police and firefighters, correction and rehabilitation services, to legal aid and courts of law. Spending on the construction and maintenance of roads, public transit, and other publicly owned transportation and communications facilities and equipment appears in the "Transportation and communication" category.

The other form of government spending is government transfers, which are payments by the government to households for which no good or service is provided in return. These transfers might be targeted to certain types of activities or spending by households, such as education or health care. Since transfers do not represent direct spending on final output, they are not counted in the *G* term in the expenditure approach. In fact, should the transfer help households finance some of

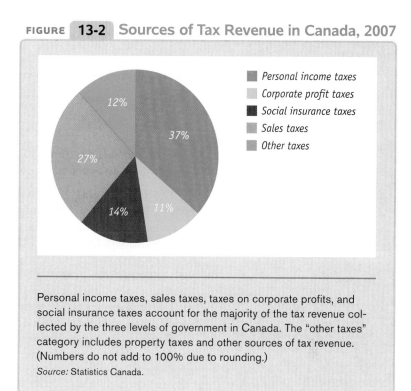

FIGURE 13-2   Sources of Tax Revenue in Canada, 2007

- Personal income taxes
- Corporate profit taxes
- Social insurance taxes
- Sales taxes
- Other taxes

Personal income taxes, sales taxes, taxes on corporate profits, and social insurance taxes account for the majority of the tax revenue collected by the three levels of government in Canada. The "other taxes" category includes property taxes and other sources of tax revenue. (Numbers do not add to 100% due to rounding.)
Source: Statistics Canada.

FIGURE 13-3   Government Spending in Canada, 2007

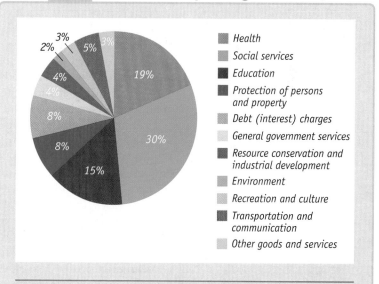

- Health
- Social services
- Education
- Protection of persons and property
- Debt (interest) charges
- General government services
- Resource conservation and industrial development
- Environment
- Recreation and culture
- Transportation and communication
- Other goods and services

After the payment of interest on government debt, the two types of spending by the three levels of government are a) purchases of goods and services and b) government transfers. The big items in government purchases are health care and education. The big items in government transfers are social services, including social assistance transfers, public pension payments (e.g., CPP/QPP, OAS, and GIS), workers' compensation benefits, and veterans' benefits.
Source: Statistics Canada.

---

[1]In 2007, debt charges, the payment of interest on government debt, accounted for 8% of all spending by Canada's three levels of government. About the same amount was spent on the protection of persons and property.

their consumption, this will be captured in the private sector consumption, term *C*, in the expenditure approach.[2] Government transfers represent a huge proportion of Canada's budget, as well as those of the United States and Europe. In Canada, most transfer payments cover two broad areas:

- Public pension plans, which provide guaranteed income to older Canadians, disabled Canadians, and the surviving spouses and dependent children of deceased or retired beneficiaries

- Other social assistance payments, which help individuals and families to maintain an acceptable level of earnings

The term **social insurance** describes government programs intended to protect families against economic hardship. These include payments from public pension plans such as the Canada/Quebec Pension Plan (CPP/QPP), Old Age Security (OAS), Guaranteed Income Supplement (GIS), and so on. Other social assistance payments include general welfare and family allowance payments, as well as smaller programs such as veterans' benefits, motor vehicle accident compensation payments, legal aid, and daycare subsidies. In Canada, social insurance programs are paid for largely with special, dedicated taxes on wages—the social insurance taxes we mentioned earlier.

But how do tax policy and government spending affect the economy? The answer is that taxation and government spending have a strong effect on total aggregate expenditure in the economy.

The Government Budget and Total Spending

Let's recall the basic equation of national income accounting:

(13-1) $GDP = C + I + G + X - IM$

The left-hand side of this equation is GDP, the value of all final goods and services produced in the economy. The right-hand side is aggregate expenditure, total spending on final goods and services produced in the economy. It is the sum of consumer spending (*C*), investment spending (*I*), government purchases of goods and services (*G*), and the value of exports (*X*) minus the value of imports (*IM*). It includes all the sources of aggregate demand.

The government directly controls one of the variables on the right-hand side of Equation 13-1: government purchases of goods and services (*G*). But that's not the only effect fiscal policy has on aggregate expenditure in the economy. Through changes in taxes and transfers, it also may influence consumer spending (*C*) and, in some cases, investment spending (*I*).

To see why the budget affects consumer spending, recall that *disposable income*, the total income households have available to spend, is equal to the total income they receive from wages, dividends, interest, and rent, *minus* taxes, *plus* government transfers. So either an increase in taxes or a reduction in government transfers *reduces* disposable income. And a fall in disposable income, other things equal, leads to a fall in consumer spending. Conversely, either a decrease in taxes or an increase in government transfers *increases* disposable income. And a rise in disposable income, other things equal, leads to a rise in consumer spending.

The government's ability to affect investment spending is a more complex story, which we won't discuss in detail. The important point is that the government

[2]This is done so that spending isn't counted twice when GDP is determined using the expenditure approach. The estimated size of GDP should be a fair and balanced approximation of the amount of activity in the economy at one point in time. Counting spending amounts twice would certainly not be fair and would provide a distorted view of both the pace of economic activity and the percentage shares of *C* and *G* in GDP.

taxes profits and capital goods spending, and changes in the rules that determine how much a business owes can increase or reduce the incentive to spend on investment goods.

Because the government itself is one source of spending in the economy, and because taxes and transfers can affect spending by consumers and firms, the government can use changes in taxes or government spending to *shift the aggregate demand curve*. And as we saw in Chapter 12, there are sometimes good reasons to shift the aggregate demand curve. In early 2009, as this chapter's opening story explained, the Harper government believed it was crucial that the Canadian government act to increase aggregate demand—that is, to move the aggregate demand curve to the right of where it would otherwise be. The 2009 stimulus package was a classic example of *fiscal policy:* the use of taxes, government transfers, or government purchases of goods and services to stabilize the economy by shifting the aggregate demand curve.

Expansionary and Contractionary Fiscal Policy

Why would the government want to shift the aggregate demand curve? Because it wants to close either a recessionary gap, created when aggregate output falls below potential output, or an inflationary gap, created when aggregate output exceeds potential output. Such gaps, created when output is not at the economy's full employment level, are harmful to the welfare of households and firms. The government has the "power" to influence AD, by shifting the AD curve, so as to reduce the gap, thereby making households and firms better off. Governments have found that interventions to influence AS in order to close the gap are not so simple.

Figure 13-4 shows the case of an economy facing a recessionary gap. $SRAS$ is the short-run aggregate supply curve, $LRAS$ is the long-run aggregate supply curve, and AD_1 is the initial aggregate demand curve. At the initial short-run macroeconomic equilibrium, E_1, aggregate output is Y_1, below potential output, Y_P. What the government would like to do is increase aggregate demand, shifting the aggregate demand curve rightward to AD_2. This would increase aggregate output, making it equal to potential output while also raising the price level from P_1 to P_2.

FIGURE 13-4 Expansionary Fiscal Policy Can Close a Recessionary Gap

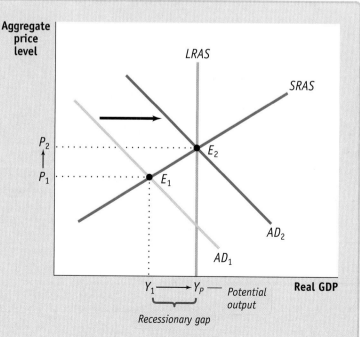

The economy is in short-run macroeconomic equilibrium at E_1, where the aggregate demand curve, AD_1, intersects the $SRAS$ curve. However, it is not in long-run macroeconomic equilibrium. At E_1, there is a recessionary gap of $Y_P - Y_1$. An expansionary fiscal policy—an increase in government purchases of goods and services, a reduction in taxes, or an increase in government transfers—shifts the aggregate demand curve rightward. It can close the recessionary gap by shifting AD_1 to AD_2, moving the economy to a new short-run macroeconomic equilibrium, E_2, which is also a long-run macroeconomic equilibrium.

FIGURE **13-5** Contractionary Fiscal Policy Can Close an Inflationary Gap

The economy is in short-run macroeconomic equilibrium at E_1, where the aggregate demand curve, AD_1, intersects the SRAS curve. But it is not in long-run macroeconomic equilibrium. At E_1, there is an inflationary gap of $Y_1 - Y_P$. A contractionary fiscal policy—such as reduced government purchases of goods and services, an increase in taxes, or a reduction in government transfers—shifts the aggregate demand curve leftward. It closes the inflationary gap by shifting AD_1 to AD_2, moving the economy to a new short-run macroeconomic equilibrium, E_2, which is also a long-run macroeconomic equilibrium.

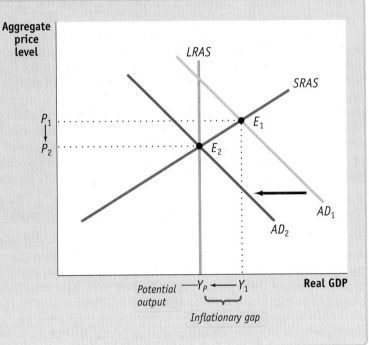

Fiscal policy that increases aggregate demand, called **expansionary fiscal policy,** normally takes one of three forms, or some combination of them:

- An increase in government purchases of goods and services
- A cut in taxes
- An increase in government transfers

The 2009 Economic Action Plan was a combination of all three: a direct increase in federal spending and aid to provincial, territorial, and municipal governments to help them to finance "ready-to-go" infrastructure projects, targeted tax cuts for many families, and increased aid to the unemployed.

Figure 13-5 shows the opposite case—an economy facing an inflationary gap. Again, SRAS is the short-run aggregate supply curve, LRAS is the long-run aggregate supply curve, and AD_1 is the initial aggregate demand curve. At the initial equilibrium, E_1, aggregate output is Y_1, above potential output, Y_P. As we'll explain in later chapters, policy-makers often try to head off inflation by eliminating inflationary gaps. To eliminate the inflationary gap shown in Figure 13-5, fiscal policy must reduce aggregate demand and shift the aggregate demand curve leftward to AD_2. This reduces aggregate output and makes it equal to potential output. This decrease in AD has moved the price level from P_1 to P_2 and closed the inflationary gap. Consequently, there should be less inflation, which is the government's goal. Fiscal policy that reduces aggregate demand, called **contractionary fiscal policy,** is the opposite of expansionary fiscal policy. It is implemented in three possible ways:

- A reduction in government purchases of goods and services
- An increase in taxes
- A reduction in government transfers

Expansionary fiscal policy is fiscal policy that increases aggregate demand.

Contractionary fiscal policy is fiscal policy that reduces aggregate demand.

A classic example of contractionary fiscal policy occurred in 1995, when the federal government grew worried about Canada's large budget deficit and growing debt burden as a percentage of the economy. Things were so bad the *Wall Street Journal* called Canada an honorary member of the third world. As a percent of the economy, the 1995 budget introduced the largest cuts to Canadian federal spending since the end of World War II. This federal budget combined large direct spending cuts, significant reductions in transfer payments to individuals and provinces, along with small tax increases.

Can Expansionary Fiscal Policy Actually Work?

In practice, the use of fiscal policy—in particular, the use of expansionary fiscal policy in the face of a recessionary gap—is often controversial. We'll examine the origins of these controversies in detail in Chapter 17. But for now, let's quickly summarize the major points of the debate over expansionary fiscal policy, so we can understand when the critiques are justified and when they are not.

Broadly speaking, there are three arguments against the use of expansionary fiscal policy:

- Government spending always crowds out private spending
- Government borrowing always crowds out private investment spending
- Government budget deficits lead to reduced private spending

The first of these claims is wrong in principle, but it has nonetheless played a prominent role in public debates. The second is valid under some, but not all, circumstances. The third argument, although it raises some important issues, isn't a good reason to believe that expansionary fiscal policy doesn't work.

Claim 1: "Government Spending Always Crowds Out Private Spending" Some claim that expansionary fiscal policy can never raise aggregate expenditure and therefore can never raise aggregate income, with reasons that go something like this: "Every dollar that the government spends is a dollar taken away from the private sector. So any rise in government spending must be offset by an equal fall in private spending." In other words, every dollar spent by the government *crowds out*, or displaces, a dollar of private spending. So what's wrong with this view? The answer is that the statement is wrong because it assumes that resources in the economy are always fully employed and, as a result, the aggregate income earned in the economy is always a fixed sum—which isn't true. In particular, when the economy is suffering from a recessionary gap, there are unemployed resources in the economy and output, and therefore income, is below its potential level. Expansionary fiscal policy during these periods puts unemployed resources to work and generates higher spending and higher income. So the argument that expansionary fiscal policy always crowds out private spending is wrong in principle.

Claim 2: "Government Borrowing Always Crowds Out Private Investment Spending" In Chapter 10, we discussed the possibility that government borrowing uses funds that would have otherwise been used for private investment spending—that is, it crowds out private investment spending. How valid is that argument?

The answer is "it depends." Specifically, it depends upon whether the economy is depressed or not. If the economy is not depressed, then increased government borrowing, by increasing the demand for loanable funds, can raise interest rates and crowd out private investment spending. However, what if the economy is depressed? In that case, crowding out is much less likely. When the economy is at far less than full employment, a fiscal expansion will lead to higher incomes, which in turn leads to increased savings at any given interest rate. This larger pool of savings allows the government to borrow without driving up interest rates. Canada's Economic Action Plan of 2009 was a case in point: despite high levels of government borrowing, Canadian interest rates stayed near historic lows. This, though, was partly owing to the Bank of Canada's expansionary monetary policy.

Claim 3: "Government Budget Deficits Lead to Reduced Private Spending"

Other things equal, expansionary fiscal policy leads to a larger budget deficit and greater government debt. And higher debt will eventually require the government to raise taxes to pay it off. So, according to the third argument against expansionary fiscal policy, consumers, anticipating that they must pay higher taxes in the future to pay off today's government debt, will cut their spending today in order to save more now—so that they are better able to afford the expected future increases. This argument, first made by the nineteenth-century economist David Ricardo, is known as *Ricardian equivalence*. It is an argument often taken to imply that expansionary fiscal policy will have no effect on the economy because farsighted consumers will undo any attempts at expansion by the government. (And will also undo any contractionary fiscal policy, for that matter.)

In reality, however, it's doubtful that consumers behave with such foresight and budgeting discipline. Most people, when provided with extra cash (generated by the fiscal expansion), will spend at least some of it. So even fiscal policy that takes the form of temporary tax cuts or transfers of cash to consumers probably does have an expansionary effect.

Moreover, it's possible to show that even with Ricardian equivalence, a temporary rise in government spending that involves direct purchases of goods and services—such as a program of road construction—would still lead to a boost in total spending in the near term. That's because even if consumers cut back their current spending in anticipation of higher future taxes, their reduced spending will take place over an extended period as consumers save over time to pay the future tax bill. Meanwhile, the additional government spending will be concentrated in the near future, when the economy needs it. So although the effects emphasized by Ricardian equivalence may reduce the impact of fiscal expansion, the claim that it makes fiscal expansion completely ineffective is neither consistent with how consumers actually behave nor a reason to believe that increases in government spending have no effect. So, in the end, it's not a valid argument against expansionary fiscal policy.

In sum, then, the extent to which we should expect expansionary fiscal policy to work depends upon the circumstances. When the economy has a recessionary gap—as it did when the 2009 Economic Action Plan was passed—economics tells us that this is just the kind of situation in which expansionary fiscal policy helps the economy. However, when the economy is already at full employment, expansionary fiscal policy is the wrong policy and will lead to crowding out, an overheated economy, and higher inflation.

A Cautionary Note: Lags in Fiscal Policy

Looking back at Figures 13-4 and 13-5, it may seem obvious that the government should actively use fiscal policy—always adopting an expansionary fiscal policy when the economy faces a recessionary gap and always adopting a contractionary fiscal policy when the economy faces an inflationary gap. But many economists caution against an extremely active stabilization policy, arguing that a government that tries too hard to stabilize the economy—through either fiscal policy or monetary policy—can end up making the economy less stable.

We'll leave discussion of the warnings associated with monetary policy to Chapter 19. In the case of fiscal policy, one key reason for caution is that there are important *time lags* between when the policy is decided upon and when it is implemented. To understand the nature of these lags, think about what has to happen before the government increases spending to fight a recessionary gap. First, the government has to realize that the recessionary gap exists: economic data take time to collect and analyze, and recessions are often recognized only months after they have begun. Second, the government has to develop a spending plan, which can itself take months, particularly if politicians take time debating how the money should be spent and passing legislation. Finally, it takes time to spend money. For example, a road construction project begins with activities such as surveying that don't involve spending large sums. It may be quite some time before the big spending begins.

Because of these lags, an attempt to increase spending to fight a recessionary gap may take so long to get going that the economy has already recovered on its own. In fact, the recessionary gap may have turned into an inflationary gap by the time the fiscal policy takes effect. In that case, the fiscal policy will make things worse instead of better.

This doesn't mean that fiscal policy should never be actively used. In early 2009 there was good reason to believe that the slump facing the Canadian economy would be both deep and long and that a fiscal stimulus designed to arrive over the next year or two would almost surely push aggregate demand in the right direction. In fact, as we'll see later in this chapter, the 2009 stimulus arguably faded out too soon, leaving the economy still depressed. But the problem of lags makes the actual use of both fiscal and monetary policy harder than you might think from a simple analysis like the one we have just given.

ECONOMICS ▸ IN ACTION

WHAT WAS IN CANADA'S 2009 ECONOMIC ACTION PLAN?

As we've just learned, fiscal stimulus can take three forms: increased government purchases of goods and services, increased transfer payments, and tax cuts. So what form did the government's Economic Action Plan take? Well, it's a bit complicated.

Figure 13-6 shows the composition of the 2009–2010 budget impact of the Action Plan, a measure that adds up the dollar value of tax cuts, transfer payments, and government spending. Here, the numbers are broken down into *four* categories, not three. "Infrastructure and other spending" means spending on roads, bridges, and schools as well as "nontraditional" infrastructure like research and development, all of which fall under government purchases of goods and services. "Tax cuts" are self-explanatory. "Transfer payments to persons" mostly took the form of expanded benefits for the unemployed and additional spending on training programs. But a fourth category, "transfers to lower level governments," accounted for almost a tenth of the funds. Why this fourth category?

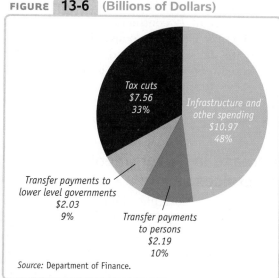

FIGURE 13-6 Canada's Economic Action Plan of 2009 (Billions of Dollars)

Tax cuts
$7.56
33%

Infrastructure and other spending
$10.97
48%

Transfer payments to lower level governments
$2.03
9%

Transfer payments to persons
$2.19
10%

Source: Department of Finance.

It's because Canada has multiple levels of government. The Canadian authors of this book live in the city of Toronto, which has its own budget. But Toronto is part of the province of Ontario, which has its own budget. And Ontario is part of Canada, which of course has its budget. One effect of the recession was a sharp drop in revenues at the provincial/territorial and local levels, which in turn forced

- The main channels of fiscal policy are taxes and government spending. Government spending takes the form of purchases of goods and services as well as transfers.

- In Canada, most government transfers are accounted for by **social insurance** programs designed to alleviate economic hardship—mainly public pensions (e.g., CPP/QPP, OAS, and GIS), and social assistance benefits, such as general welfare and family allowance programs.

- The government controls *G* directly and influences *C* and *I* through taxes and transfers.

- **Expansionary fiscal policy** is implemented by an increase in government spending, a cut in taxes, or an increase in government transfers. **Contractionary fiscal policy** is implemented by a reduction in government spending, an increase in taxes, or a reduction in government transfers.

- Arguments against the effectiveness of expansionary fiscal policy based upon crowding out are valid only when the economy is at full employment. The argument that expansionary fiscal policy won't work because of Ricardian equivalence—that consumers will cut back spending today to offset expected future tax increases—appears to be untrue in practice. What is clearly true is that time lags can reduce the effectiveness of fiscal policy, and potentially render it counterproductive.

these lower levels of government to consider significant spending cuts. Federal aid—those transfers to provincial and local governments—was intended to mitigate these spending cuts.

Perhaps the most surprising aspect of the Action Plan was how little direct federal spending on goods and services was involved. The great bulk of the program involved giving money to other people, one way or another, in the hope that they would spend it.

CHECK YOUR UNDERSTANDING 13-1

1. In each of the following cases, determine whether the policy is an expansionary or contractionary fiscal policy.
   a. Several armed forces bases around the country, which together employ tens of thousands of people, are closed.
   b. The number of weeks an unemployed person is eligible for employment insurance benefits is increased.
   c. The federal tax on gasoline is increased.

2. Explain why federal disaster relief, which quickly disburses funds to victims of natural disasters such as hurricanes, floods, and large-scale crop failures, will stabilize the economy more effectively after a disaster than relief that must be legislated.

3. Is the following statement true or false? Explain. "When the government expands, the private sector shrinks; when the government shrinks, the private sector expands."

Solutions appear at back of book.

Fiscal Policy and the Multiplier

An expansionary fiscal policy, like the 2009 Economic Action Plan, pushes the aggregate demand curve to the right. A contractionary fiscal policy, like Minister of Finance Paul Martin's 1995 federal spending cuts under Prime Minister Jean Chrétien, pushes the aggregate demand curve to the left. For policy-makers, however, knowing the direction of the shift isn't enough: they need estimates of *how much* a given policy will shift the aggregate demand curve. To get these estimates, they use the concept of the multiplier, which we learned about in Chapter 11.

Multiplier Effects of an Increase in Government Purchases of Goods and Services

Suppose that a government decides to spend $50 billion building bridges and roads. The government's purchases of goods and services will directly increase total spending on final goods and services by $50 billion. But as we learned in Chapter 11, there will also be an indirect effect: the government's purchases will start a chain reaction throughout the economy. The firms that produce the goods and services purchased by the government earn revenues that flow to households in the form of wages, profits, interest, and rent. This increase in disposable income leads to a rise in consumer spending. The rise in consumer spending, in turn, induces firms to increase output, leading to a further rise in disposable income, which leads to another round of consumer spending increases, and so on.

As we know, the *multiplier* is the ratio of the change in real GDP caused by an autonomous change in aggregate expenditure to the size of that autonomous change. An increase in government purchases of goods and services is a prime example of such an autonomous increase in aggregate expenditure.

In Chapter 11 we considered a simple case in which there are no taxes or international trade, so that any change in GDP accrues entirely to households.

We also assumed that the aggregate price level is fixed, so that any increase in nominal GDP is also a rise in real GDP, and that the interest rate is fixed. In that case the multiplier is $1/(1 - MPC)$. Recall that *MPC* is the *marginal propensity to consume,* the fraction of an additional dollar in disposable income that is spent. For example, if the marginal propensity to consume is 0.5, the multiplier is $1/(1 - 0.5) = 1/0.5 = 2$. Given a multiplier of 2, a $50 billion increase in government purchases of goods and services would increase real GDP by $100 billion. Of that $100 billion, $50 billion is the initial effect from the increase in *G*, and the remaining $50 billion is the subsequent effect arising from the increase in consumer spending.[3]

What happens if government purchases of goods and services are instead reduced? The math is exactly the same, except that there's a minus sign in front: if government purchases of goods and services fall by $50 billion and the marginal propensity to consume is 0.5, real GDP falls by $100 billion.

Multiplier Effects of Changes in Government Transfers and Taxes

Expansionary or contractionary fiscal policy need not take the form of changes in government purchases of goods and services. Governments can also change transfer payments or taxes. In general, however, a change in government transfers or taxes shifts the aggregate demand curve by *less* than an equal-sized change in government purchases, resulting in a smaller effect on real GDP.

To see why, imagine that instead of spending $50 billion on building bridges, the government simply hands out $50 billion in the form of government transfers. In this case, there is no direct effect on aggregate demand, as there was with government purchases of goods and services. Real GDP goes up only because households spend some of that $50 billion—and they probably won't spend it all.

Table 13-1 shows a hypothetical comparison of two expansionary fiscal policies assuming an *MPC* equal to 0.5

TABLE 13-1   Hypothetical Effects of a Fiscal Policy with Marginal Propensity (*MPC*) of 0.5

Effect on real GDP	$50 billion rise in government purchases of goods and services	$50 billion rise in government transfer payments
First round	$50 billion	$25 billion
Second round	$25 billion	$12.5 billion
Third round	$12.5 billion	$6.25 billion
• • •	• • •	• • •
Eventual effect	$100 billion	$50 billion
Multiplier[4]	$\dfrac{\Delta Y}{\Delta G} = \dfrac{1}{1 - MPC} = \dfrac{1}{1 - 0.5} = 2$	$\dfrac{\Delta Y}{\Delta \text{Transfers}} = \dfrac{MPC}{1 - MPC} = \dfrac{0.5}{1 - 0.5} = 1$

---

[3]Of course in the *AD-AS* model the aggregate price level is not fixed. In this framework, we can say that any change (shift) in *AD* translates perfectly to a change in real GDP given the positive slope of the *SRAS* curve. In the example given, the $50 billion increase in *G* raises *AD* by $100 billion, nominal GDP has risen by $100 billion, and real GDP rises, but by less than $100 billion, as the upward slope to the *SRAS* curve forces the aggregate price level up when the *AD* curve shifts right.

[4]In the case of a change in government spending on goods and services (*G*), since *MPC* is a positive fraction, the cumulative impact to GDP (i.e., ΔY) is equal to the sum, $\Delta G + (MPC) \times \Delta G + (MPC) \times (MPC \times \Delta G) + \ldots = \Delta G[1 + MPC + MPC^2 + MPC^3 + \ldots] = \dfrac{\Delta G}{(1 - MPC)} = \Delta Y$. Therefore, $\left(\dfrac{\Delta Y}{\Delta G}\right) = \left(\dfrac{1}{(1 - MPC)}\right)$, which in the case where *MPC* = 0.5 gives a government spending multiplier of 2. In the case of a change in transfer payments, the sum is similar, but all the terms in the sum are multiplied by *MPC* since households save a portion of the increase in transfer payments; thus, the increase in household spending in the first round is equal to $MPC \times (\Delta\text{Transfers})$, and so on. So, in this case, we get $\Delta Y = MPC \times \Delta\text{Transfers} + (MPC)^2 \times \Delta\text{Transfers} + (MPC)^3 \times \Delta\text{Transfers} + \ldots = (\Delta\text{Transfers}) \times (MPC) \times [1 + MPC + MPC^2 + MPC^3 + \ldots] = \Delta\text{Transfers} \times \left(\dfrac{MPC}{(1 - MPC)}\right)$. Therefore, $\left(\dfrac{\Delta Y}{\Delta\text{Transfers}}\right) = \left(\dfrac{MPC}{(1 - MPC)}\right)$, which in the case where *MPC* = 0.5 gives a multiplier for changes in government transfers of only 1.

and a multiplier equal to 2: one in which the government directly purchases $50 billion in goods and services and one in which the government makes transfer payments instead, sending out $50 billion in cheques to consumers. In each case there is a first-round effect on real GDP, either from purchases by the government or from purchases by the consumers who received the cheques, followed by a series of additional rounds as rising real GDP raises disposable income.

However, the first-round effect of the transfer program is smaller; because we have assumed that the *MPC* is 0.5, only $25 billion of the $50 billion is spent, with the other $25 billion saved. And as a result, all the further rounds are smaller, too. In the end, the transfer payment increases real GDP by only $50 billion. In comparison, a $50 billion increase in government purchases produces a $100 billion increase in real GDP.

Overall, when expansionary fiscal policy takes the form of a rise in transfer payments, real GDP may rise by either more or less than the initial government outlay—that is, the multiplier may be either more or less than 1 depending upon the size of the *MPC*. In Table 13-1, with an *MPC* equal to 0.5, the multiplier is exactly 1: a $50 billion rise in transfer payments increases real GDP by $50 billion. If the *MPC* is less than 0.5, so that a smaller share of the initial transfer is spent, the multiplier on that transfer is *less* than 1. If a larger share of the initial transfer is spent, the multiplier is *more* than 1.

A tax cut has an effect similar to the effect of a transfer. It increases disposable income, leading to a series of increases in consumer spending. But the overall effect is smaller than that of an equal-sized increase in government purchases of goods and services: the autonomous increase in aggregate expenditure is smaller because households save part of the amount of the tax cut.

We should also note that taxes introduce a further complication—they typically change the size of the multiplier. That's because in the real world governments rarely impose **lump-sum taxes,** in which the amount of tax a household owes is independent of its income. With lump-sum taxes there is no change in the multiplier. Instead, the great majority of tax revenue is raised via taxes that are not lump-sum, and so tax revenue depends upon the level of real GDP. As we'll discuss shortly, and analyze in detail in Appendix 13A, non-lump-sum taxes reduce the size of the multiplier.

In practice, economists often argue that the size of the multiplier determines *who* among the population should get tax cuts or increases in government transfers. For example, compare the effects of an increase in employment insurance benefits with a cut in taxes on profits distributed to shareholders as dividends. Consumer surveys suggest that the average unemployed worker will spend a higher share of any increase in his or her disposable income than would the average recipient of dividend income. That is, people who are unemployed tend to have a higher *MPC* than people who own a lot of stocks because the latter tend to be wealthier and tend to save more of any increase in disposable income. If that's true, a dollar spent on employment insurance benefits increases aggregate demand more than a dollar's worth of dividend tax cuts.

How Taxes Affect the Multiplier

When we introduced the analysis of the multiplier in Chapter 11, we simplified matters by assuming that a $1 increase in real GDP raises disposable income by $1. In fact, however, government taxes capture some part of the increase in real GDP that occurs in each round of the multiplier process, since most government taxes depend positively on real GDP. As a result, disposable income increases by considerably less than $1 once we include non-lump-sum taxes in the model.

The increase in government tax revenue when real GDP rises isn't the result of a deliberate decision or action by the government. It's a consequence of the way the tax laws are written, which causes most sources of government revenue to

Lump-sum taxes are taxes that don't depend on the taxpayer's income.

increase *automatically* when real GDP goes up. For example, income tax receipts increase when real GDP rises because the amount each individual owes in taxes depends positively on his or her income, and households' taxable income rises when real GDP rises. Sales tax receipts increase when real GDP rises because people with more income spend more on goods and services. And corporate profit tax receipts increase when real GDP rises because profits increase when the economy expands.

The effect of these automatic increases in tax revenue is to reduce the size of the multiplier. Remember, the multiplier is the result of a chain reaction in which higher real GDP leads to higher disposable income, which leads to higher consumer spending, which leads to further increases in real GDP. The fact that the government siphons off some of any increase in real GDP means that at each stage of this process, the increase in consumer spending is smaller than it would be if non-lump-sum taxes weren't part of the picture. The result is to reduce the multiplier. Appendix 13A shows how to derive the multiplier when taxes that depend positively on real GDP are taken into account.

Many macroeconomists believe it's a good thing that in real life taxes reduce the multiplier. In Chapter 12 we argued that most, though not all, recessions are the result of negative demand shocks. The same mechanism that causes tax revenue to increase when the economy expands causes it to decrease when the economy contracts. Since tax receipts decrease when real GDP falls, the effects of these negative demand shocks are smaller than they would be if there were no taxes. The decrease in tax revenue reduces the adverse effect of the initial fall in aggregate demand—so that output does not fluctuate as much.

The automatic decrease in government tax revenue generated by a fall in real GDP—caused by a decrease in the amount of taxes households pay—acts like an automatic expansionary fiscal policy implemented in the face of contractions and recessions. Similarly, when the economy expands, the government finds itself automatically pursuing a contractionary fiscal policy—a tax increase. Government spending and taxation rules that cause fiscal policy to be automatically expansionary when the economy contracts and automatically contractionary when the economy expands, without requiring any deliberate action by policy-makers, are called **automatic stabilizers.**

The rules that govern tax collection aren't the only automatic stabilizers, although they are the most important ones. Some types of government transfers also play a stabilizing role. For example, more people receive employment insurance (EI) payments when the economy is depressed than when it is booming. The same is true of social assistance programs such as welfare, rent and daycare subsidies, and student assistance grants and loans. So transfer payments tend to rise when the economy is contracting and fall when the economy is expanding. Like changes in tax revenue, these automatic changes in transfers tend to reduce the size of the multiplier because the total change in disposable income that results from a given rise or fall in real GDP is smaller.

As in the case of government tax revenue, many macroeconomists believe that it's a good thing that government transfers reduce the multiplier. Expansionary and contractionary fiscal policies that are the result of automatic stabilizers are widely considered helpful to macroeconomic stabilization because they blunt the extremes of the business cycle.

But what about fiscal policy that *isn't* the result of automatic stabilizers? **Discretionary fiscal policy** is fiscal policy that is the direct result of deliberate actions

Automatic stabilizers are government spending and taxation rules that cause fiscal policy to be automatically expansionary when the economy contracts and automatically contractionary when the economy expands.

Discretionary fiscal policy is fiscal policy that is the result of deliberate actions by policy-makers rather than rules.

Prime Minister Stephen Harper and Saskatchewan Premier Brad Wall in 2009 as they announce funding to twin Highway 11 from Saskatoon to Prince Albert. The federal government paid for nearly half of the $127-million project.

Geoff Howe/CP Images

by policy-makers rather than automatic adjustment. For example, during a recession, the government may pass legislation that cuts taxes and increases government spending in order to stimulate the economy. In general, economists tend to support the use of discretionary fiscal policy only in special circumstances, such as an especially severe recession. We'll explain why, and describe the debates among macroeconomists on the appropriate role of fiscal policy, in Chapter 18.

ECONOMICS > IN ACTION

MULTIPLIERS AND THE 2009 ECONOMIC ACTION PLAN

Canada's Economic Action Plan was the largest peacetime example of discretionary fiscal expansion in Canadian history. The total stimulus was about $62 billion, including all provincial and municipal contributions. But it wasn't spent all at once: only about half, or roughly $29 billion, of the stimulus arrived in 2009, the year of peak impact. Still, even that was a lot—roughly 1.9% of GDP.

The plan was released late in January 2009 and had three guiding principles. It was to be

- timely, to help support the economy within the first 120 days when private demand was weakest;

- targeted to Canadian businesses and families most in need so as to create the largest increase in Canadian jobs and output; and

- temporary, so that the stimulus would be phased out by the time the economy recovered, thus avoiding long-term deficits and/or overstimulating the economy.

Minister of Finance Jim Flaherty presents details of Canada's Economic Action Plan.

Initial government estimates of the economic impact of the proposed plan were generated using the Department of Finance's Canadian Economic and Fiscal Model (CEFM), a complex computer-based economic–statistical model of the Canadian economy. The Model estimated that the stimulus plan would create an estimated 220 000 jobs by the end of 2010. But was that enough? From the beginning, there were some doubts.

By May 2009, Parliamentary Budget Officer (PBO) Kevin Page had begun to question the government's estimates as to the size and timing of the multipliers. He noted that in reality the multipliers varied, sometimes dramatically, across the various kinds of tax and spending options available. The PBO provided this table of estimated multipliers:

Type of fiscal policy change (option)	Estimated size of related multiplier
Corporate income tax rate change	0.3
Employment insurance premium change	0.6
Personal income tax rate change	1.0
Other government spending	1.4
Housing investment	1.5
Infrastructure spending	1.6
Measures for low-income people	1.7

Source: Parliamentary Budget Officer (PBO).

Notice that measures aimed at households and businesses generally have multiplier effects of 1.0 or less. This occurs since these measures are subject to a greater degree of "leakage." That is, some of the change becomes a change in savings or in imports rather than a change in demand for domestically produced output. One notable exception is a measure aimed at low-income households, which has the highest estimated multiplier; every additional dollar put into the hands of these households is thought to result in an increase in equilibrium domestic output of $1.70. This is because low-income households are more likely to spend additional funds right away, on urgent necessities such as food and clothing, rather than save the funds. Also, low-income households are more likely to spend new funds on domestic goods and services. In contrast, high-income households are more likely to save the money from a tax cut or to spend it on imported items.

Other reservations were expressed, too. About three times more of the plan's measures focused on areas with multipliers exceeding 1.0 than those with smaller multipliers. The fact that about one quarter of the stimulus spending was on measures with "small" multipliers led the PBO and others to question whether those most in need were truly being assisted. Critics, including the PBO, also questioned whether the plan could be "rolled out" on a timely basis. They noted that while housing investment and infrastructure projects do have high multiplier effects, these projects tend to start very slowly. Further, the government, hoping to have the plan rolled out within a two-year "window," demanded that the EAP money be spent on "shovel-ready" projects. Many wondered whether enough such projects existed to meet this requirement. If such projects could not be found or encountered delays, then the timeliness and size of stimulus delivered would be reduced.

However, despite the reservations people had about the Plan, it seems to have succeeded. In February 2010, just over a year after the Plan was proposed, the Conference Board of Canada stated that these forecasts and their associated estimated impact on the economy were reasonable and conservative. That is, the assumed or estimated multiplier effects were not too aggressive and thus the estimated stimulus was not being overstated for the intended two-year plan window. And if the Plan had not been introduced, it is likely that Canada would have experienced a far worse recession in 2009 than it did. Total employment did rise by more than 300 000 from January 2009 to January 2011, primarily in Ontario and Quebec. However, there is no way to determine what percentage of this increase was the result of the Plan itself. In fact, about 90 000 more Canadians were classified as unemployed in January 2011 than in January 2009, because as the economy improved, more people joined the labour force to seek work.

▶ CHECK YOUR UNDERSTANDING   13-2

1. Explain why a $500 million increase in government purchases of goods and services will generate a larger rise in real GDP than a $500 million increase in government transfers.

2. Explain why a $500 million reduction in government purchases of goods and services will generate a larger fall in real GDP than a $500 million reduction in government transfers.

3. The country of Boldovia has no employment insurance benefits and a tax system using only lump-sum taxes. The neighbouring country of Moldovia has generous employment benefits and a tax system in which residents must pay a percentage of their income. Which country will experience greater variation in real GDP in response to demand shocks, positive and negative? Explain.

Solutions appear at back of book.

▼ Quick Review

- The amount by which changes in government purchases raise real GDP is determined by the multiplier.

- Changes in taxes and government transfers also move real GDP, but by less than equal-sized changes in government purchases.

- Taxes reduce the size of the multiplier unless they are **lump-sum taxes.**

- Taxes and some government transfers act as **automatic stabilizers** as tax revenue is positively correlated (that is, moves in the same direction) with changes in real GDP and some government transfers are negatively correlated with changes in real GDP. Many economists believe that it is a good thing that they reduce the size of the multiplier. In contrast, the use of **discretionary fiscal policy** is more controversial.

The Budget Balance

Headlines about the government's budget tend to focus on just one point: whether the government is running a surplus or a deficit and, in either case, how big. People usually think of surpluses as good: when the federal government ran a record surplus in 2000, many people regarded it as a cause for celebration. Conversely, people usually think of deficits as bad: when the

Canadian government ran a record deficit in 2010, many people regarded it as a cause for concern.

How do surpluses and deficits fit into the analysis of fiscal policy? Are deficits ever a good thing and surpluses a bad thing? To answer those questions, let's look at the causes and consequences of surpluses and deficits.

The Budget Balance as a Measure of Fiscal Policy

What do we mean by surpluses and deficits? The budget balance, which we defined in Chapter 10, is the difference between the government's revenue, in the form of tax revenue, and its spending, both on goods and services and on government transfers, in a given year. That is, the budget balance—savings by government—is defined by Equation 13-2 (which is the same as Equation 10-7):

(13-2) $S_{Public} = T - TR - G$

where T is the value of tax revenues, G is government purchases of goods and services, and TR is the value of government transfers. As we learned in Chapter 10, a budget surplus is a positive budget balance and a budget deficit is a negative budget balance.

Other things equal, expansionary fiscal policies—increased government purchases of goods and services, higher government transfers, or lower taxes—reduce the budget balance for that year. That is, expansionary fiscal policies make a budget surplus smaller or a budget deficit bigger. Conversely, contractionary fiscal policies—reduced government purchases of goods and services, lower government transfers, or higher taxes—increase the budget balance for that year, making a budget surplus bigger or a budget deficit smaller.

You might think this means that changes in the budget balance can be used to measure fiscal policy. In fact, economists often do just that: they use changes in the budget balance as a "quick-and-dirty" way to assess whether current fiscal policy is expansionary or contractionary. But they always keep in mind two reasons this quick-and-dirty approach is sometimes misleading:

1. Two different changes in fiscal policy that have equal-sized effects on the budget balance may have quite unequal effects on the economy. As we have already seen, changes in government purchases of goods and services have a larger effect on real GDP than equal-sized changes in taxes and government transfers.

2. Often, changes in the budget balance are themselves the result, not the cause, of fluctuations in the economy.

To understand the second point, we need to examine the effects of the business cycle on the budget.

The Business Cycle and the Cyclically Adjusted Budget Balance

Historically there has been a strong relationship between the federal government's budget balance and the business cycle. The budget tends to move into deficit when the economy experiences a recession, but deficits tend to get smaller or even turn into surpluses when the economy is expanding. Figure 13-7 shows the federal budget deficit as a percentage of GDP from 1975 to 2012. Shaded areas indicate major recessions. As you can see, the federal budget deficit increased around the time of each recession and usually declined during expansions. In fact, owing to economic expansions in the mid-1990s and early 2000s, the deficit actually became negative between the 1997–1998 fiscal year and the 2007–2008 fiscal year: the budget deficit turned into a budget surplus.

FIGURE **13-7** The Canadian Federal Budget Deficit and the Business Cycle, 1975–2012

The budget deficit as a percentage of GDP tends to rise during recessions (indicated by shaded areas) and fall during expansions.

Sources: Statistics Canada; Public Accounts of Canada; Department of Finance.

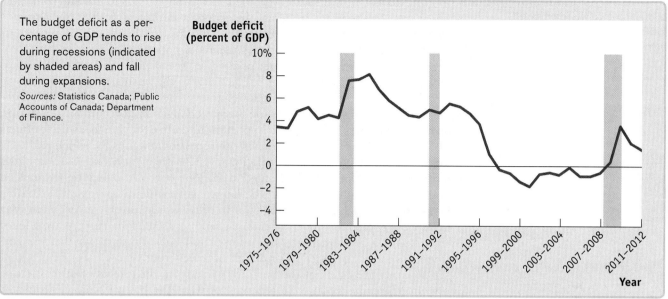

The relationship between the business cycle and the budget balance is even clearer if we compare the budget deficit as a percentage of GDP with the unemployment rate, as we do in Figure 13-8. The budget deficit almost always rises when the unemployment rate rises and falls when the unemployment rate falls.

Is this relationship between the business cycle and the budget balance evidence that policy-makers engage in discretionary fiscal policy, using expansionary fiscal policy during recessions and contractionary fiscal policy during expansions? Not necessarily. To a large extent the relationship in Figure 13-8 reflects automatic stabilizers at work. As we learned in the discussion of automatic stabilizers, government tax revenue tends to rise and some government transfers,

FIGURE **13-8** The Canadian Federal Budget Deficit and the Unemployment Rate, 1975–2012

There is a close relationship between the budget balance and the business cycle: a recession moves the budget balance toward deficit, and an expansion moves it toward surplus. Here, the unemployment rate serves as an indicator of the business cycle, and we should expect to see a higher unemployment rate associated with a higher budget deficit. This is confirmed by the figure: the budget deficit as a percentage of GDP moves closely in tandem with the unemployment rate.

Sources: Statistics Canada; Public Accounts of Canada; Department of Finance.

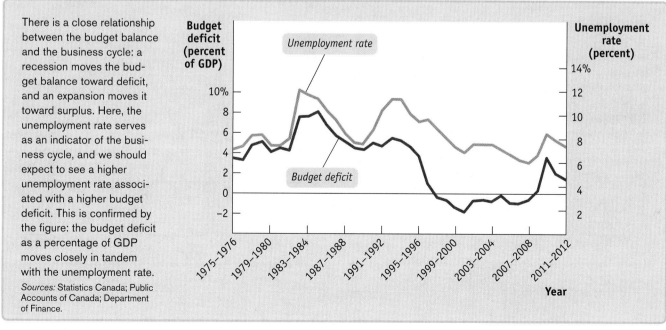

The **cyclically adjusted budget balance** is an estimate of what the budget balance would be if real GDP were exactly equal to potential output.

like employment insurance benefits and welfare payments, tend to fall when the economy expands. Conversely, government tax revenue tends to fall and some government transfers tend to rise when the economy contracts. So the budget tends to move toward surplus during expansions and toward deficit during recessions even without any deliberate action on the part of policy-makers.

In assessing government budget policy (i.e., fiscal policy) it's often useful to separate movements in the budget balance due to the business cycle from movements due to discretionary fiscal policy changes. The former are affected by automatic stabilizers and the latter by deliberate changes in government purchases, government transfers, or taxes. It's important to realize that business-cycle effects on the budget balance are temporary: both recessionary gaps (in which real GDP is below potential output) and inflationary gaps (in which real GDP is above potential output) tend to be eliminated in the long run. Removing their effects on the budget balance sheds light on whether the government's taxing and spending policies are sustainable in the long run. In other words, do the government's tax policies yield enough revenue to fund its spending in the long run? As we'll learn shortly, this is a fundamentally more important question than whether the government runs a budget surplus or deficit in the current year.

To separate the effect of the business cycle from the effects of other factors, many governments produce an estimate of what the budget balance would be if there were neither a recessionary nor an inflationary gap. The **cyclically adjusted budget balance** is an estimate of what the budget balance would be if real GDP were exactly equal to potential output. It takes into account the extra tax revenue the government would collect and the transfers it would save if a recessionary gap were eliminated—or the revenue the government would lose and the extra transfers it would make if an inflationary gap were eliminated.

Figure 13-9 shows the actual budget deficit and the Parliamentary Budget Office estimate of the cyclically adjusted budget deficit, both as a percentage of GDP, from 1975 to 2012. As you can see, the cyclically adjusted budget deficit doesn't fluctuate as much as the actual budget deficit. In particular, large actual deficits, such as those of 1984, 1992, and 2009, are usually caused in part by a depressed economy.

FIGURE **13-9** The Actual Budget Deficit versus the Cyclically Adjusted Budget Deficit

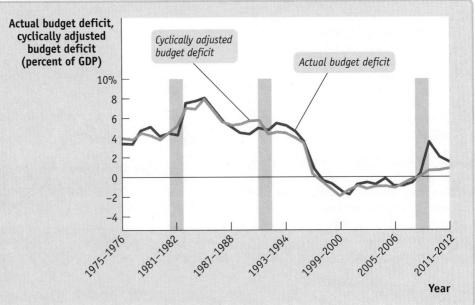

The cyclically adjusted budget deficit is an estimate of what the budget deficit would be if the economy were at potential output. It fluctuates less than the actual budget deficit because large budget deficits tend to occur during the same years when the economy has a large recessionary gap.

Sources: Statistics Canada; Public Accounts of Canada; Department of Finance.

Should the Budget Be Balanced?

As we'll see in the next section, persistent budget deficits can cause problems for both the government and the economy. Yet politicians are always tempted to run deficits because this allows them to cater to voters by cutting taxes without cutting spending or by increasing spending without increasing taxes. As a result, there are occasional attempts by policy-makers to force fiscal discipline by introducing legislation—even a constitutional amendment—forbidding the government from running budget deficits. This is usually stated as a requirement that the budget be "balanced"—that revenues at least equal spending each fiscal year. Would it be a good idea to require a balanced budget annually?

Most economists don't think so. They believe that the government should only balance its budget on average—that it should be allowed to run deficits in bad years, offset by surpluses in good years. They don't believe the government should be forced to run a balanced budget *every year* because this would undermine the role of taxes and transfers as automatic stabilizers. As we learned earlier in this chapter, the tendency of tax revenue to fall and transfers to rise when the economy contracts helps to limit the size of recessions. But falling tax revenue and rising transfer payments generated by a downturn in the economy push the budget toward deficit. If constrained by a balanced-budget rule, the government would have to respond to this deficit with contractionary fiscal policies that would tend to deepen a recession.

Yet policy-makers concerned about excessive deficits sometimes feel that rigid rules prohibiting—or at least setting an upper limit on—deficits are necessary. As the following Economics in Action explains, Europe has had a lot of trouble reconciling rules to enforce fiscal responsibility with the challenges of short-run fiscal policy.

ECONOMICS > IN ACTION

EUROPE'S SEARCH FOR A FISCAL RULE

In 1999 a group of European nations took a momentous step when they adopted a common currency, the euro, to replace their various national currencies, such as the French franc, the German mark, and the Italian lira. Along with the introduction of the euro came the creation of the European Central Bank, which sets monetary policy for the whole region.

As part of the agreement creating the new currency, governments of member countries signed on to the European "stability pact." This agreement required each government to keep its budget deficit—its actual deficit, not a cyclically adjusted number—below 3% of the country's GDP or face fines. The pact was intended to prevent irresponsible deficit spending arising from political pressure that might eventually undermine the new currency. The stability pact, however, had a serious downside: in principle, it would force countries to slash spending and/or raise taxes whenever an economic downturn pushed their deficits above the critical level. This would turn fiscal policy into a force that worsens recessions instead of fighting them.

Nonetheless, the stability pact proved impossible to enforce: European nations, including France and even Germany, with its reputation for fiscal probity, simply ignored the rule during the 2001 recession and its aftermath.

In 2011 the Europeans tried again, this time against the background of a severe debt crisis. In the wake of the 2008 financial crisis, Greece,

François Hollande of France and Angela Merkel of Germany discuss the new EU economic plan.

Ireland, Portugal, Spain, and Italy all lost the confidence of investors, who were worried about their ability and/or willingness to repay all their debt—and the efforts of these nations to reduce their deficits seemed likely to push Europe back into recession. Yet a return to the old stability pact didn't seem to make sense. Among other things, it was clear that the stability pact's rule on the size of budget deficits would not have done much to prevent the crisis—in 2007 all of the problem debtors except Greece were running deficits under 3% of GDP, with Ireland and Spain actually running surpluses.

So the agreement reached in December 2011 was framed in terms of the "structural" budget balance, more or less corresponding to the cyclically adjusted budget balance as defined in the text. According to the new rule, the structural budget balance of each country should be very nearly zero, with deficits not to exceed 0.5% of GDP. This seemed like a much better rule than the old stability pact.

Yet big problems remained. One was the question of how reliable were the estimates of the structural budget balances. Also, the new rule seemed to ban any use of discretionary fiscal policy, under any circumstances. Was this wise?

Unlike the European Union, Canada has no such fiscal rule. Neither the federal government nor many provincial governments are required to run a balanced budget. So the federal and provincial governments could, and did, run an expansionary fiscal policy to stimulate the economy in response to the financial crisis of 2008. This is why Canada was affected less severely than the European Union was.

▼ **Quick Review**

• The budget deficit tends to rise during recessions and fall during expansions. This reflects the effect of the business cycle on the budget balance.

• The **cyclically adjusted budget balance** is an estimate of what the budget balance would be if the economy were at potential output. It varies less than the actual budget deficit.

• Most economists believe that governments should run budget deficits in bad years and budget surpluses in good years. A rule requiring a balanced budget would undermine the role of automatic stabilizers.

CHECK YOUR UNDERSTANDING 13-3

1. Why is the cyclically adjusted budget balance a better measure of whether government policies are sustainable in the long run than the actual budget balance?

2. Explain why a mandatory requirement for the government to balance its budget is likely to cause the economy to experience more severe short-run economic fluctuations.

Solutions appear at back of book.

Long-Run Implications of Fiscal Policy

In 2009 the government of Greece ran into a financial wall. Like most other governments in Europe (and the Canadian government, too), the Greek government was running a large budget deficit, which meant that it needed to keep borrowing more funds, both to cover its expenses and to pay off existing loans as they came due. But governments, like companies or individuals, can only borrow if lenders believe there's a good chance they are willing or able to repay their debts. By 2009 most investors, having lost confidence in Greece's financial future, were no longer willing to lend to the Greek government. Those few who were willing to lend demanded very high interest rates to compensate them for the risk of loss.

Figure 13-10 compares interest rates on 10-year bonds issued by the governments of Greece and Germany. At the beginning of 2007, Greece could borrow at almost the same rate as Germany, widely considered a very safe borrower. By the end of 2011, however, Greece was having to pay an interest rate around 10 times the rate Germany paid.

Why was Greece having these problems? Largely because investors had become deeply worried about the level of its debt (in part because it became clear that the Greek government had been using creative accounting to hide just how much debt it had already taken on). Government debt is, after all, a promise to

FIGURE **13-10** Greek and German Long-Term Interest Rates

As late as 2008, the government of Greece could borrow at interest rates only slightly higher than those facing Germany, widely considered a very safe borrower. But in early 2009, as it became clear that both Greek debt and Greek deficits were larger than previously reported, investors lost confidence, sending Greek borrowing costs sky-high.

Source: European Central Bank.

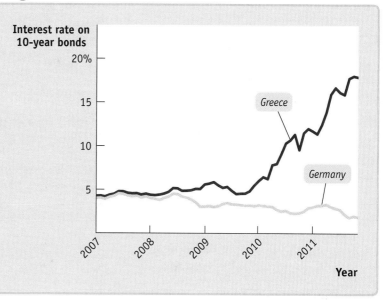

make future payments to lenders. By 2009 it seemed likely that the Greek government had already promised more than it could possibly deliver.

The result was that Greece found itself unable to borrow more from private lenders; it received emergency loans from other European nations and the International Monetary Fund, but these loans came with the requirement that the Greek government make severe spending cuts (commonly called austerity measures), which wreaked havoc with its economy, imposed severe economic hardship on Greeks, and led to massive social unrest. The Greek sovereign debt crisis has caused serious concerns about other members of the eurozone, such as Spain, that face similar problems; this may undermine the long-term viability of the euro.

No discussion of fiscal policy is complete if it doesn't take into account the long-run implications of government budget surpluses and deficits, especially the implications for government debt. We now turn to those long-run implications.

Greeks angered by their government's harsh austerity measures took to the streets in protest.

Deficits, Surpluses, and Debt

When a family spends more than it earns over the course of a year, it has to raise the extra funds either by selling assets or by borrowing. And if a family borrows year after year, it will eventually end up with a lot of debt.

The same is true for governments. With a few exceptions, governments don't raise large sums by selling assets such as national parkland. Instead, when a government spends more than the tax revenue it receives—when it runs a budget deficit—it almost always borrows the extra funds. And governments that run persistent budget deficits end up with substantial debts.

To interpret the numbers that follow, you need to know a slightly peculiar feature of federal government accounting. The Canadian government does not keep its books by calendar year. Instead, budget totals are kept by **fiscal years** that run from April 1 to March 31. For example, the fiscal year that runs from April 1, 2012 to March 31, 2013 is called "fiscal year 2012–2013."

A **fiscal year** runs from April 1 to the end of March.

PITFALLS

DEFICITS VERSUS DEBT

One common mistake—it happens all the time in newspaper reports—is to confuse *deficits* with *debt*. Let's review the difference.

A *deficit* is the difference between the amount of money a government spends and the amount it receives in taxes over a given period—usually, though not always, a year. Deficit numbers always come with a statement about the time period to which they apply, as in "the Canadian budget deficit in the fiscal year of 2011–2012 was $26.2 billion."

A *debt* is the sum of money a government owes at a particular point in time. Debt numbers usually come with a specific date, as in "the Canadian federal debt was at $582.2 billion at the end of the 2011–2012 fiscal year."

Deficits and debt are linked, because government debt grows when governments run deficits. But they aren't the same thing, and they can even tell different stories. For example, Italy, which found itself in debt trouble in 2011, had a fairly small deficit by historical standards, but it had very high debt, a legacy of past policies.

At the end of the fiscal year 2011–2012, the Canadian federal government debt was $582.2 billion—33.8% of the GDP. Part of that debt represented special accounting rules specifying that the federal government owes funds to certain programs, such as Old Age Security. We'll explain those rules shortly. For now, however, let's focus on **public debt:** government debt held by individuals and institutions outside the government. The total federal debt was greater for 2011–2012 than for the previous fiscal year because the government ran a budget deficit. A government that runs persistent budget deficits will a experience a rising level of public debt. Why is this a problem?

Problems Posed by Rising Government Debt

There are two reasons to be concerned when a government runs persistent budget deficits. We described one reason in Chapter 10: when the government runs budget deficits while the economy is at full employment, national savings tends to fall and interest rates tend to rise, owing to a leftward shift in the supply of loanable funds curve. In turn, higher interest rates raise the cost of investment spending, which leads to a decrease in investment spending. In other words, when the government runs budget deficits instead of contributing to national savings, it is borrowing funds in the financial markets and competing with firms and households that plan to borrow funds for investment spending. As a result, when the economy is at full employment, government borrowing may increase interest rates, crowd out private investment spending, and reduce the economy's long-run rate of growth.

But there's a second reason: today's deficits, by increasing the government's debt, place financial pressure on future budgets. The impact of current deficits on future budgets is straightforward. Like individuals, governments must pay their bills, including interest payments on their accumulated debt. When a government is deeply in debt, those interest payments can be substantial. In the 2011–2012 fiscal year, the federal government paid $31 billion in interest on its debts, which is equivalent to 1.8% of GDP. The more heavily indebted government of Italy used 4.7% of its GDP in 2011 to service its debt.

Other things equal, a government paying large sums in interest must raise more revenue from taxes or spend less than it would otherwise be able to afford—or it must borrow even more to cover the gap. And a government that borrows to pay interest on its outstanding debt pushes itself even deeper into debt. This process can eventually push a government to the point where lenders question its ability to repay. Like a consumer who has maxed out his or her credit cards, it will find that lenders are unwilling to lend any more funds. The result can be that the government defaults on its debt—it stops paying what it owes. Default is often followed by deep financial and economic turmoil.

Canadians aren't used to the idea of government default, but such things do happen. In the 1990s Argentina, a relatively high-income developing country, was widely praised for its economic policies—and it was able to borrow large sums from foreign lenders. By 2001, however, Argentina's interest payments were spiralling out of control, and the country stopped paying the sums that were due. In the end, it reached a settlement with most of its lenders under which it paid less than a third of the amount originally due. By late 2011 investors were placing a fairly high probability on Argentine-type default by several European countries— namely, Greece, Ireland, and Portugal—and were seriously worried about Italy

Public debt is government debt held by individuals and institutions outside the government.

THE CANADIAN WAY OF DEBT

How does Canada's public debt stack up internationally? We could answer that question in dollar terms, but that number would not be very useful for purposes of comparison, because the economies of countries can differ so widely in size. A more informative comparison is the ratio of public debt to GDP (the debt-to-GDP ratio, for short), which you will learn more about later.

The accompanying figure shows the *net public debt* of a number of rich countries as a percentage of GDP at the end of 2011. Net public debt is government debt minus any assets governments may have—an adjustment that can make a big difference. What you find is that Canada, compared to other countries, has a relatively low debt-to-GDP ratio, 33.1%, which indicates that our government's finances are in a much better position and our debt is far more manageable than most of the other countries shown.

It may not come as a surprise that Greece heads the list, with the highest debt-to-GDP ratio listed, and most of the other high net debt countries are European nations that have made the headlines for their debt problems. Interestingly, Japan is also high on the list, mainly because it used massive public spending to prop up its economy

in the 1990s. Investors, however, still consider Japan's government reliable, so its borrowing costs remain low despite high net debt.

In contrast, Norway has a large *negative* net public debt. What's going on in Norway? In a word, oil. Thanks to large offshore deposits in the North Sea, Norway is the world's third-largest oil exporter. Like other oil exporters, such as Saudi Arabia, Norway has used its oil revenue to build up an investment fund for future needs, rather than spending it all immediately. As a result, Norway has a huge stock of government assets rather than a large government debt.

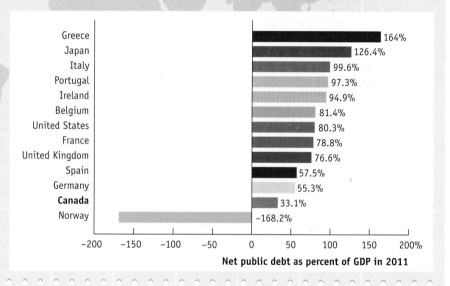

Net public debt as percent of GDP in 2011

Source: International Monetary Fund.

and Spain. Each one was forced to pay high interest rates on its debt by nervous lenders, exacerbating the risk of default.

Default creates havoc in a country's financial markets and badly shakes public confidence in both the government and the economy. Argentina's debt default was accompanied by a crisis in the country's banking system and a very severe recession. And even if a highly indebted government avoids default, a heavy debt burden typically forces it to slash spending or raise taxes, politically unpopular measures that can also damage the economy. In some cases, austerity measures intended to reassure lenders that the government can indeed pay end up depressing the economy so much that lender confidence continues to fall—a process we'll look at more closely in the Economics in Action that follows this section. In addition, the possibility that a country might default on its loans or have a huge, growing debt can cause that country's credit rating to be downgraded. For example, in 2011, the United States was approaching its debt ceiling, the maximum amount it was allowed to borrow. Raising the debt ceiling was controversial, but U.S. Treasury Secretary Timothy Geithner argued that failure to do so would lead to a possible default and catastrophic effects on the global economy. Finally, in the summer of 2011, the U.S. Congress did raise the debt ceiling. Default was avoided, but even so, the timing was a bit late: Standard & Poor's lowered the U.S.'s credit rating from AAA to AA+. This was shocking, because the U.S.'s credit rating had never been downgraded before. People with low credit ratings must pay higher interest rates, and it's just the same for countries. Being downgraded meant the U.S. government and businesses might have to pay higher interest rates on future borrowing.

Similarly, some European countries saw their credit levels downgraded in 2011 and 2012, owing to worries over excessive government borrowing. Greece and Spain were the most notable examples, but Portugal, Italy, France, and Austria were also members of that unfortunate club. Table 13-2 shows long-term interest rates for some European countries in October 2009, before the sovereign debt crisis started, and afterward, in October 2012. Notice that the crisis-stricken countries of Greece, Spain, Portugal, and Italy saw their long-term borrowing costs increase. The interest rate on Greece's long-term government bonds quadrupled. In contrast, Germany, which was not in the same situation, saw its borrowing cost decrease.

TABLE 13-2 Long-Term Interest Rates for Selected Members of the Eurozone

Country	Interest Rates	
	October 2009	October 2012
Germany	3.21%	1.47%
Greece	4.57	17.96
Portugal	3.85	8.17
Spain	3.78	5.64
Italy	4.1	4.95

Source: European Central Bank.

Some may ask why can't a government that has trouble borrowing just print money to pay its bills? Yes, it can if it has its own currency (which the troubled European nations don't). But printing money to pay the government's bills can lead to another problem: inflation. In fact, budget problems are the main cause of very severe inflation, as we'll see in Chapter 16. The point for now is that governments do not want to find themselves in a position where the choice is between defaulting on their debts and inflating those debts away by printing money.

Concerns about the long-run effects of deficits need not rule out the use of expansionary fiscal policy to stimulate the economy when it is depressed. However, these concerns do mean that governments should try to offset budget deficits in bad years with budget surpluses in good years. In other words, governments should run a budget that is approximately balanced over time. Have they actually done so?

Deficits and Debt in Practice

Figure 13-11 shows how Canada's federal government's budget balance and its debt evolved from the 1970–1971 fiscal year to the 2011–2012 fiscal year. The burgundy curve shows the federal budget balance as a percentage of GDP. A positive number means a budget surplus while a negative number means a deficit. As you can see, the federal government normally ran deficits, except from 1997 to 2008, when it ran surpluses. This seems inconsistent with the advice that governments should offset deficits in bad times with surpluses in good times.

To assess a government's ability to pay its debt, economists tend to use the **debt-to-GDP ratio,** the government's debt as a percentage of GDP. We use this measure, rather than simply looking at the size (or stock) of the debt, because GDP, which measures the size of the economy as a whole, is a good indicator of the potential amount of taxes the government can collect. The purple curve shows the country's debt-to-GDP ratio since 1970. As you can see, the (net federal) debt-to-GDP ratio rose until the mid-1990s. This rise was caused by large budget deficits and slower economic growth. Further, the continuing rise of the ratio indicated that Canada's debt burden was increasing—and increasing amounts of resources were needed to service the debt.

The **debt–to–GDP ratio** is the government's debt as a percentage of GDP.

Alarmed by the rising ratio, Canadians demanded that the federal government take appropriate action. So, when the Liberal Party won the federal election of 1993, Prime Minister Jean Chrétien made the reduction of budget deficits and the

FIGURE **13-11** Canada's Federal Deficits and Debt

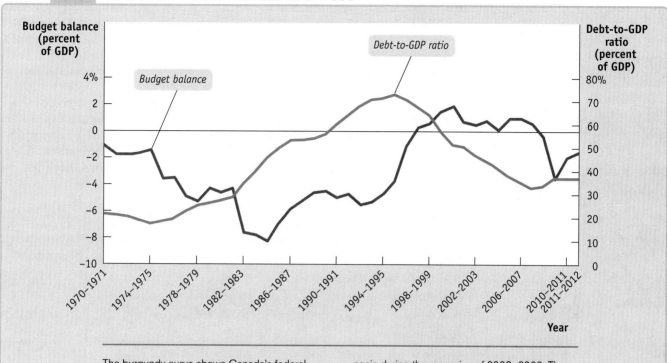

The burgundy curve shows Canada's federal budget balance as a percentage of GDP from 1970 to 2012. The Canadian government ran budget deficits until the mid-1990s. When the government lowered its spending to address the national debt problem, the deficits became surpluses. The government began to run deficits again during the recession of 2008–2009. The purple curve shows Canada's (net federal) debt-to-GDP ratio. Comparing the curves, you can see that the debt-to-GDP ratio often rose when there were budget deficits. The ratio fell when the deficits became surpluses.

Source: The Department of Finance Canada.

national debt one of his top priorities. To do so, government expenditures were cut significantly, particularly by large reductions both in transfer payments to the provinces and in government services. After four years, the federal government finally turned the corner and, in the 1997–1998 fiscal year, it began to run budget surpluses. With these favourable economic conditions, the debt-to-GDP ratio began to fall, and the outlook was positive again.

True, the financial crisis of 2008–2009 did push the budget back into deficits and caused the debt-to-GDP ratio to rise. However, the budget deficits were smaller (as a percentage of GDP) than in past years and the government has projected a balanced budget will return by the 2016–2017 fiscal year. Also, the OECD notes that Canada's debt-to-GDP ratio was the lowest among the G-7, and far below the G-7 average (80.3% in 2011). Therefore, it is not generally expected that our debt burden will skyrocket.

To assess what burden a country's national debt places on the country, look at the debt-to-GDP ratio: a country that persistently runs large deficits will have a rising debt-to-GDP ratio when debt grows faster than GDP. But if its debt is growing more slowly than GDP, then the burden of paying that debt is actually falling compared with potential tax revenue and the debt-to-GDP ratio will fall. In this case, a country can run budget deficits persistently. The For Inquiring Minds feature, which focuses on the large debt the Canadian government ran up during World War II, explains how growth and inflation sometimes allow a government that runs persistent budget deficits to nevertheless have a declining debt-to-GDP ratio.

Table 13-3 shows that in 2007, just before the recession began in 2008, the combined amount of government debt in Canada was about $23 000 per capita, that is, per person. Two thirds of this debt came from the federal government and one third was issued by all the provincial, territorial, and municipal governments combined. At the national level, this debt was about 50% of GDP per capita in 2007. It is interesting to note the great variability in the levels of per capita provincial, territorial, and municipal debt across the nation; this clearly shows that some jurisdictions, especially those in western Canada and the territories, were in better financial shape than others. In fact, based on the strength of revenues from resource exploration and extraction, several jurisdictions, most notably Alberta, Yukon, and Northwest Territories, had a negative level of combined provincial, territorial, and municipal debt, which means these governments actually had more assets than liabilities.

TABLE 13-3 Government Debt Per Capita in 2007

	Provincial, Territorial, and Municipal Governments	Federal Government	All Levels of Government
Canada	$7 600.18	$15 431.53	$23 031.71
Newfoundland and Labrador	19 905.99		35 337.52
Prince Edward Island	9 939.05		25 370.58
Nova Scotia	12 006.63		27 438.16
New Brunswick	8 356.61		23 788.14
Quebec	15 680.89		31 112.42
Ontario	8 485.01		23 916.54
Manitoba	9 858.40		25 289.93
Saskatchewan	7 372.74		22 804.27
Alberta	−10 654.45		4 777.08
British Columbia	2 578.48		18 010.01
Yukon	−12 530.33		2 901.20
Northwest Territories	−4 270.85		11 160.68
Nunavut	1 055.53		16 487.06

Source: Statistics Canada.

FOR INQUIRING MINDS

WHAT HAPPENED TO THE DEBT FROM WORLD WAR II?

The Canadian government paid for World War II by borrowing on a huge scale. By the war's end, the net debt of the federal government was more than 100% of GDP, and many people worried about how it could ever be paid off.

The truth is that it never was paid off. In 1946 net public debt was $13.4 billion; that number dipped slightly in the next few years, as Canada ran post-war budget surpluses, but the government budget went back into deficit in 1952, partly as a result of Canada's involvement in the Korean War. By 1962, the public debt was back up to $13.4 billion.

But by that time nobody was worried about the fiscal health of the Canadian government because the debt-to-GDP ratio had fallen below 40%. The reason? Vigorous economic growth, plus mild inflation, had led to a rapid rise in GDP. The experience was a clear lesson in the peculiar fact that modern governments can run deficits forever, as long as they aren't too large.

Implicit Liabilities

Looking at Figure 13-11, you might be tempted to conclude that until the 2008–2009 financial crisis struck, Canada was in good fiscal shape. The federal government was running budget surpluses and our debt-to-GDP ratio had fallen to a comfortably low level. The ratio did rise slightly in 2008, owing to budget

FIGURE **13-12** Future Demands on the Federal Budget

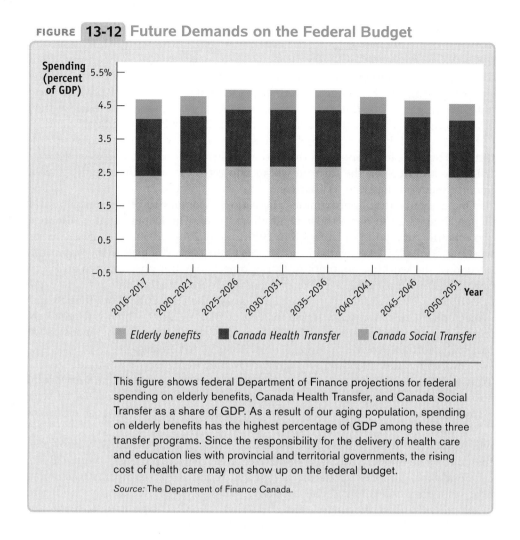

Elderly benefits   Canada Health Transfer   Canada Social Transfer

This figure shows federal Department of Finance projections for federal spending on elderly benefits, Canada Health Transfer, and Canada Social Transfer as a share of GDP. As a result of our aging population, spending on elderly benefits has the highest percentage of GDP among these three transfer programs. Since the responsibility for the delivery of health care and education lies with provincial and territorial governments, the rising cost of health care may not show up on the federal budget.

Source: The Department of Finance Canada.

deficit, but was still low compared both to historical experience and to other wealthy countries such as Japan and the United States. Even so, experts on long-run budget issues tend to view Canada's fiscal position (not to mention that of other countries such as the U.S., Japan, and Italy) with a little alarm. The reason is *implicit liabilities.* **Implicit liabilities** are essentially debts that a government must pay at some future date but that are omitted from the usual debt statistics.

Canada's largest implicit liabilities come from transfer programs, including the Canada Health Transfer (CHT), the Canada Social Transfer (CST), and benefits for retired and elderly people such as Old Age Security (OAS) and Guaranteed Income Supplement and Allowance (GIS). In each of these cases, the government has promised to provide transfer payments to future as well as current beneficiaries. So, these programs represent a future debt that must be honoured, even though it does not show up in the usual statistics. In the fiscal year 2011–2012 for example, spending on these programs reached $76.73 billion, or 28.3% of total federal spending.

The implicit liabilities created by these transfer programs seem worrisome. Figure 13-12 shows why. From 1966 to 2011 actual spending on OAS, CHT, and CST as percentages of GDP has tended to rise, making such promises harder to keep. Figure 13-12 plots projections from the federal Department of Finance presented in *Budget 2012: Economic Action Plan 2010—A Plan for Jobs, Growth and Long-term Prosperity.* According to these projections, the cost as a percentage of GDP for these transfer programs will continue to rise over the next few decades, implying more government resources will be allocated to these programs than others.

Implicit liabilities are spending promises made by governments that are effectively a debt despite the fact that they are not included in the usual debt statistics.

In the case of Old Age Security, what do the demographics reveal? The money for OAS benefits comes from the taxes paid by people who are working now. So, the ratio of workers to retirees is important when it comes to OAS. From 1946 to 1964, there was a huge surge in the birth rate, called the "baby boom." At the time of writing, most "boomers" were of working age, so they were paying taxes, not collecting benefits. But as increasing numbers of boomers start to retire they will stop earning employment (taxable) income and start collecting benefits. Also, Canadians are living longer, which means they may have the opportunity to collect OAS benefits for more years than previous generations did. These two factors will have an effect on the ratio of workers to retirees, and subsequently have a major impact on the system's finances.

One measure that approximates the ratio of workers to retirees is the ratio of people aged 20 to 64 to those aged 65 and over. The Department of Finance projects this ratio will fall from 4.8 in 2011 to only 2.4 in 2050. This means fewer working adults will be available to support retirees, which also increases the burden of the working population. But boomers may not pose a long-run fiscal problem after all. In 2011, the money spent on elderly benefits amounted to 2.2% of GDP. Jean-Claude Ménard, the head actuary at the Department of Finance, has projected that this amount will rise to 2.7% of GDP by 2050, which is a relatively small percentage increase. So although Canada's population is aging, it seems we can still afford to provide promised social benefits to retirees.

How about the spending on Canada Health Transfer and Canada Social Transfer? CHT is the federal government transfer to the provincial and territorial governments to assist in the delivery and funding of health care. CHT is the largest major transfer to provinces and territories. Currently, the CHT cash transfers are set to grow at 6% annually until the fiscal year of 2016–2017; after that they will be reduced to 3% annual growth or a measure of the nominal GDP known as the "three-year moving average," whichever is larger. On the other hand, CST is a federal block transfer to the provincial and territorial governments to support post-secondary education, social assistance and social services, early childhood development, and early learning and child care. The CST is growing at 3% annually. As Figure 13-12 shows, the Department of Finance projects that the shares of CHT and CST as percentage of GDP will be relatively stable, at around 2.3% of GDP.

Based on these estimates, it seems that Canada's implicit liabilities will not pose serious problems for future federal budgets. But the outlook for provincial and territorial budgets is less optimistic. In Canada, provinces and territories, not the federal government, pay for their own health care and education. CHT and CST are just federal transfers that help provinces and territories to fund their programs. Many argue that owing to the planned reductions to CHT funding after 2016–2017, provincial and territorial governments will need to spend more on health care in the future. In fact, according to the Office of the Parliamentary Budget Officer, provincial and territorial health care spending will likely increase from less than 10% of GDP in 2012–2013 to about 14% in 2075–2076. This is a significant percentage increase, and this higher burden on provincial and territorial budgets could easily cause the net debt issued by these governments to rise.

ECONOMICS ▸ IN ACTION

AUSTERITY DILEMMAS

Suppose that a country's economy hits a rough patch and lenders worry if the government, already deeply indebted, will be able to repay its loans. As a result, lenders cut off further lending. What's a government to do?

The usual prescription has been fiscal austerity: cut government spending and raise taxes, to both reduce the need to borrow more funds and to demonstrate to lenders the ability and determination to do what's necessary to honour debts. But besides being painful and politically unpopular, does fiscal austerity really work to extricate a country from a crisis of lender confidence? Both economics and history indicate that the likely answer is no.

Fiscal austerity means contractionary fiscal policy. And we know from our earlier analysis that if an economy is already depressed, contractionary fiscal policy will depress it further. Moreover, the experiences of Argentina and Ireland show that the worsened state of an economy arising from austerity can further undermine the lender confidence that it was supposed to support.

Argentina presents a clear picture of the dynamic. Starting in the 1990s, Argentina was a favourite of foreign lenders and borrowed freely from abroad. But its debts accumulated, and by the late 2000s when the economy hit a downturn, lenders began to get worried. From 1997 to 2001, Argentina tried to reassure lenders that it was credit-worthy by repeatedly raising taxes and cutting government spending. But each round of austerity so weakened the economy that the government was unable to balance its budget. Finally, facing massive popular protests, the government collapsed and defaulted on its debts.

Since 2009, Ireland has gone through a similar experience, although the origins of its troubles were different. Until 2008, Ireland's government ran a more or less balanced budget. But during the 2000s, the Irish economy had a massive real estate bubble, fuelled by excessive bank lending to real estate developers. When the bubble burst, Irish banks were left with massive losses. In order to prop them up, the Irish government guaranteed the banks' losses, making Irish taxpayers responsible for paying off the banks' debts. But, as it turns out, these debts were so large that the government's own solvency came into question, and the interest rate at which it had to borrow rose abruptly. This result can be seen in Figure 13-13, which shows how the interest rate spread between Irish government bonds and German government bonds (which are considered very safe) jumped in late 2008 and early 2009.

In an attempt to regain lender confidence, Ireland imposed severe austerity, even though the economy had already fallen into recession. For example, the government adopted a policy of reducing its workforce by 25 000; calculated as a percentage of the population, this was equivalent to a loss of 250 000 jobs in Canada.

By mid-2010, the Irish austerity policy appeared to be working, as rates on Irish bonds stabilized and even fell a bit from 2009 to 2010. But by 2011, it all fell apart as the size of the banks' losses continued to mushroom and it became clear that the austerity policies were pushing the economy deeper into a recession. By late 2010, Irish GDP was 12% lower than it had been at the end of 2007. The weaknesses

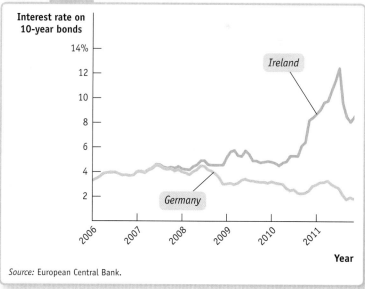

FIGURE 13-13 Interest Rates on Irish and German Bonds

Source: European Central Bank.

of the Irish economy were depressing tax revenues, undoing much of the direct effect of austerity. Simultaneously, the decline in GDP had contributed to a surge in the debt-to-GDP ratio. At the time of writing, Irish officials were still hoping to regain lender confidence through even harsher austerity measures, although prospects did not look encouraging.

So why do lenders advocate, and indebted countries adopt, such self-defeating austerity measures? Because they make the mistake of thinking that an economy is like a household: if the family would just cut back on their

- Persistent budget deficits lead to increases in **public debt.**

- Rising public debt can lead to government default. In less extreme cases, it can crowd out investment spending, reducing long-run growth. This suggests that budget deficits in bad **fiscal years** should be offset with budget surpluses in good fiscal years.

- A widely used indicator of fiscal health is the **debt-to-GDP ratio.** A country with rising GDP can have a stable or falling debt-to-GDP ratio even if it runs budget deficits if GDP is growing faster than the debt.

- In addition to their official public debt, modern governments have **implicit liabilities.** The Canadian government has large implicit liabilities in the form of benefits such as Old Age Security, Guaranteed Income Supplement, Canada Health Transfer, and Canada Social Transfer.

spending, so the thinking goes, then they could pay their credit card bills. But as we know, an economy is not like a family; instead, one person's spending is another person's income. So austerity measures that reduce spending end up reducing income and making it even less likely that a country can repay its debts.

CHECK YOUR UNDERSTANDING 13-4

1. Explain how each of the following events would affect the public debt or implicit liabilities of the Canadian government, other things equal. Would the public debt or implicit liabilities be greater or smaller?
   a. A higher growth rate of real GDP
   b. Retirees live longer
   c. A decrease in tax revenue
   d. Government borrowing to pay interest on its current public debt

2. Suppose the economy is in a slump and the current public debt is quite large. Explain the trade-off of short-run versus long-run objectives that policy-makers face when deciding whether or not to engage in deficit spending.

3. Explain how a policy of fiscal austerity can make it more likely that a government is unable to pay its debts.

Solutions appear at back of book.

BUSINESS CASE • KIP Goes to School: Action Plan Spending on Knowledge Infrastructure

© Tom Ridout/Alamy

If you were on a Canadian post-secondary campus in 2009 or 2010, there's a chance you may have seen a construction site there with an Economic Action Plan sign. The EAP included the Knowledge Infrastructure Program (KIP), a $2 billion initiative providing funds to universities and colleges to build, repair, and maintain teaching facilities such as lecture halls and laboratories. More than 520 projects at colleges and universities across Canada received funding under this program.

The construction service company EllisDon was awarded several KIP projects, including George Brown College Waterfront Health Sciences Campus in Toronto (pictured here); the Schulich School of Engineering in Calgary; and the Richard Ivey School of Business in London, Ontario. The Canadian authors of this book also indirectly benefitted from this spending as their university (the University of Toronto, Scarborough Campus) was a recipient of KIP funds to build new teaching facilities that would allow students to learn in a better environment.

This spending on building infrastructure has both short-term and long-term benefits to the economy. In the short run, it helps to create jobs. In the long run, better and improved infrastructure should raise the productivity of Canadian workers and the competitiveness of Canadian business in the world economy; and this will translate into long-term sustainable economic growth.

How effective was this spending? KIP was just one part of the "Building Infrastructure to Create Jobs" element of the EAP, which altogether represented $12 billion in spending (23% of the total stimulus package in 2009 and 2010) on better transportation networks, cleaner drinking water systems, improving infrastructure at universities and colleges, and so on. According to the Government of Canada, by December 2010 about 82 000 jobs had been created or maintained under the "Building Infrastructure to Create Jobs" element (about 37% of all the jobs that had been created or maintained as a result of the EAP); and the multiplier associated with this spending was around 1.6, the highest among different elements of the EAP. EllisDon and other companies in the construction business, their employees, and suppliers were clearly getting some benefit from the EAP.

QUESTIONS FOR THOUGHT

1. Some opponents of fiscal expansion have accused it of consisting of make-work projects of little social value. What does the KIP story say about this view?

2. Other than construction firms, what other businesses could benefit from the building of infrastructure?

SUMMARY

1. The government plays a large role in the economy, collecting a large share of GDP in taxes and spending a large share both to purchase goods and services and to make transfer payments, largely for **social insurance.** *Fiscal policy* is the use of taxes, government transfers, or government purchases of goods and services to shift the aggregate demand curve.

2. Government purchases of goods and services directly affect aggregate demand, and changes in taxes and government transfers affect aggregate demand indirectly by changing households' disposable income. **Expansionary fiscal policy** shifts the aggregate demand curve rightward; **contractionary fiscal policy** shifts the aggregate demand curve leftward.

3. Only when the economy is at full employment is there potential for crowding out of private spending and private investment spending by expansionary fiscal policy. The argument that expansionary fiscal policy won't work because of Ricardian equivalence—that consumers will cut back spending today to offset expected future tax increases—appears to be untrue in practice. What is clearly true is that very active fiscal policy may make the economy less stable due to time lags in policy formulation and implementation.

4. Fiscal policy has a multiplier effect on the economy, the size of which depends on the fiscal policy. Except in the case of lump-sum taxes, taxes reduce the size of the multiplier. Expansionary fiscal policy leads to an increase in real GDP, and contractionary fiscal policy leads to a reduction in real GDP. Because part of any change in taxes or transfers is absorbed by savings in the first round of spending, changes in government purchases of goods and services have a more powerful effect on the economy than equal-sized changes in taxes or transfers.

5. Rules governing taxes—with the exception of **lump-sum taxes**—and some transfers act as **automatic stabilizers,** reducing the size of the multiplier and automatically reducing the size of fluctuations in the business cycle. In contrast, **discretionary fiscal policy** arises from deliberate actions by policy-makers rather than from the business cycle.

6. Some of the fluctuations in the budget balance are due to the effects of the business cycle. In order to separate the effects of the business cycle from the effects of discretionary fiscal policy, governments estimate the **cyclically adjusted budget balance,** an estimate of the budget balance if the economy were at potential output.

7. Canadian government budget accounting is calculated on the basis of **fiscal years.** Persistent budget deficits have long-run consequences because they lead to an increase in **public debt.** This can be a problem for two reasons. Public debt may crowd out investment spending, which reduces long-run economic growth. And in extreme cases, rising debt may lead to government default, resulting in economic and financial turmoil.

8. A widely used measure of fiscal health is the **debt-to-GDP ratio.** This number can remain stable or fall even in the face of moderate budget deficits if GDP rises over time. However, a stable debt-to-GDP ratio may give a misleading impression that all is well because modern governments often have large **implicit liabilities.** The largest implicit liabilities of the Canadian government come from benefits such as Old Age Security (OAS), Guaranteed Income Supplement (GIS), Canada Health Transfer (CHT), and Canada Social Transfer (CST).

KEY TERMS

Social insurance, p. 416
Expansionary fiscal policy, p. 418
Contractionary fiscal policy, p. 418
Lump-sum taxes, p. 424

Automatic stabilizers, p. 425
Discretionary fiscal policy, p. 425
Cyclically adjusted budget balance, p. 430

Fiscal year, p. 433
Public debt, p. 434
Debt-to-GDP ratio, p. 436
Implicit liabilities, p. 439

PROBLEMS

1. The accompanying diagram shows the current macroeconomic situation for the economy of Albernia. You have been hired as an economic consultant to help the economy move to potential output, Y_P.

    a. Is Albernia facing a recessionary or inflationary gap?

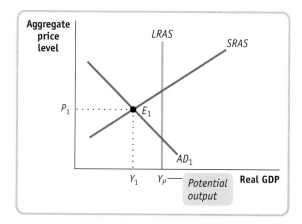

b. Which type of fiscal policy—expansionary or contractionary—would move the economy of Albernia to potential output, Y_P? What are some examples of such policies?

c. Illustrate the macroeconomic situation in Albernia with a diagram after the successful fiscal policy has been implemented.

2. The accompanying diagram shows the current macroeconomic situation for the economy of Brittania; real GDP is Y_1, and the aggregate price level is P_1. You have been hired as an economic consultant to help the economy move to potential output, Y_P.

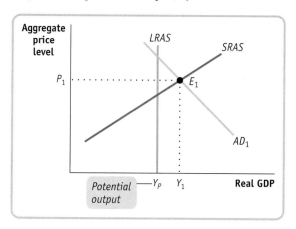

a. Is Brittania facing a recessionary or inflationary gap?

b. Which type of fiscal policy—expansionary or contractionary—would move the economy of Brittania to potential output, Y_P? What are some examples of such policies?

c. Illustrate the macroeconomic situation in Brittania with a diagram after the successful fiscal policy has been implemented.

3. An economy is in long-run macroeconomic equilibrium when each of the following aggregate demand shocks occurs. What kind of gap—inflationary or recessionary—will the economy face after the shock, and what type of fiscal policies would help move the economy back to potential output? How would your recommended fiscal policy shift the aggregate demand curve?

a. A stock market boom increases the value of stocks held by households.

b. Firms come to believe that a recession in the near future is likely.

c. Anticipating the possibility of war, the government increases its purchases of military equipment.

d. The quantity of money in the economy declines and interest rates increase.

4. During an interview in 2008, the German Finance Minister Peer Steinbrück said, "We have to watch out that in Europe and beyond, nothing like a combination of downward economic [growth] and high inflation rates emerges—something that experts call stagflation." Such a situation can be depicted by the movement of the short-run aggregate supply curve from its original position, $SRAS_1$, to its new position, $SRAS_2$, with the new equilibrium point E_2 in the accompanying figure. In this question, we try to understand why stagflation is particularly hard to fix using fiscal policy.

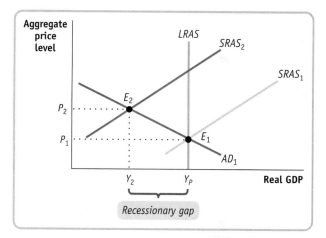

a. What would be the appropriate fiscal policy response to this situation if the primary concern of the government was to maintain economic growth? Illustrate the effect of the policy on the equilibrium point and the aggregate price level using the diagram.

b. What would be the appropriate fiscal policy response to this situation if the primary concern of the government was to maintain price stability? Illustrate the effect of the policy on the equilibrium point and the aggregate price level using the diagram.

c. Discuss the effectiveness of the policies in parts (a) and (b) in fighting stagflation.

5. Show why a $10 billion reduction in government purchases of goods and services will have a larger effect on real GDP than a $10 billion reduction in government transfers by completing the accompanying table for an economy with a marginal propensity to consume (*MPC*) of 0.6. The first and second rows of the table are filled in for you: on the left side of the table, in the first row, the $10 billion reduction in government purchases decreases real GDP and disposable income, *YD*, by $10 billion, leading to a reduction in consumer spending of $6 billion (*MPC* × change in disposable income) in row 2. However, on the right side of the table, the $10 billion reduction in transfers has no effect on real GDP in round 1 but does lower *YD* by

$10 billion, resulting in a decrease in consumer spending of $6 billion in the second round.

	Decrease in G = –$10 billion			Decrease in TR = –$10 billion		
	Billions of dollars			**Billions of dollars**		
Rounds	**Change in G or C**	**Change in real GDP**	**Change in YD**	**Change in TR or C**	**Change in real GDP**	**Change in YD**
1	$\Delta G = $ –$10.00	–$10.00	–$10.00	$\Delta TR = $ –$10.00	$0.00	–$10.00
2	$\Delta C = $ –6.00	–6.00	–6.00	$\Delta C = $ –6.00	–6.00	–6.00
3	$\Delta C = $?	?	?	$\Delta C = $?	?	?
4	$\Delta C = $?	?	?	$\Delta C = $?	?	?
5	$\Delta C = $?	?	?	$\Delta C = $?	?	?
6	$\Delta C = $?	?	?	$\Delta C = $?	?	?
7	$\Delta C = $?	?	?	$\Delta C = $?	?	?
8	$\Delta C = $?	?	?	$\Delta C = $?	?	?
9	$\Delta C = $?	?	?	$\Delta C = $?	?	?
10	$\Delta C = $?	?	?	$\Delta C = $?	?	?

a. When government purchases decrease by $10 billion, what is the sum of the changes in real GDP after the 10 rounds?

b. When the government reduces transfers by $10 billion, what is the sum of the changes in real GDP after the 10 rounds?

c. Using the formula for the multiplier for changes in government purchases and for changes in transfers, calculate the total change in real GDP due to the $10 billion decrease in government purchases and the $10 billion reduction in transfers. What explains the difference? [*Hint:* The multiplier for government purchases of goods and services is $1/(1 - MPC)$. But since each $1 change in government transfers only leads to an initial change in real GDP of $MPC \times \$1$, the multiplier for government transfers is $MPC/(1 - MPC)$.]

6. In each of the following cases, either a recessionary or inflationary gap exists. Assume that the aggregate supply curve is horizontal, so that the change in real GDP arising from a shift of the aggregate demand curve equals the size of the shift of the curve. Calculate both the change in government purchases of goods and services and the change in government transfers necessary to close the gap.

a. Real GDP equals $100 billion, potential output equals $160 billion, and the marginal propensity to consume is 0.75.

b. Real GDP equals $250 billion, potential output equals $200 billion, and the marginal propensity to consume is 0.5.

c. Real GDP equals $180 billion, potential output equals $100 billion, and the marginal propensity to consume is 0.8.

7. Most macroeconomists believe it is a good thing that taxes act as automatic stabilizers and lower the size of the multiplier. However, a smaller multiplier means that the change in government purchases of goods and services, government transfers, or taxes needed to close

an inflationary or recessionary gap is larger. How can you explain this apparent inconsistency?

8. The accompanying table shows how consumers' marginal propensities to consume in a particular economy are related to their level of income.

Income range	Marginal propensity to consume
$0–$20 000	0.9
$20 001–$40 000	0.8
$40 001–$60 000	0.7
$60 001–$80 000	0.6
Above $80 000	0.5

a. Suppose the government engages in increased purchases of goods and services. For each of the income groups in the table, what is the value of the multiplier—that is, what is the "bang for the buck" from each dollar the government spends on government purchases of goods and services in each income group?

b. If the government needed to close a recessionary or inflationary gap, at which group should it primarily aim its fiscal policy of changes in government purchases of goods and services?

9. The government's budget surplus in Macroland has risen consistently over the past five years. Two government policy-makers disagree as to why this has happened. One argues that a rising budget surplus indicates a growing economy; the other argues that it shows that the government is using contractionary fiscal policy. Can you determine which policy-maker is correct? If not, why not?

10. Figure 13-9 shows the actual budget deficit and the cyclically adjusted budget deficit as a percentage of GDP in Canada from 1975–1976 to 2011–2012. Assuming that potential output was unchanged, use this figure to determine in which years from 1989–1990 to 2011–2012 the government used expansionary fiscal policy and in which years it used contractionary fiscal policy.

11. You are an economic adviser to a candidate for national office. She asks you for a summary of the economic consequences of a balanced-budget rule for the federal government and for your recommendation on whether she should support such a rule. How do you respond?

12. In 2012, the policy-makers of the economy of Eastlandia projected the debt-to-GDP ratio and the ratio of the budget deficit to GDP for the economy for the next 10 years under different scenarios for growth in the government's deficit. Real GDP is currently $1000 billion per year and is expected to grow by 3% per year, the public debt is $300 billion at the beginning of the year, and the deficit is $30 billion in 2012.

Year	Real GDP (billions of dollars)	Debt (billions of dollars)	Budget deficit (billions of dollars)	Debt (percent of real GDP)	Budget deficit (percent of real GDP)
2012	$1000	$300	$30	?	?
2013	1030	?	?	?	?
2014	1061	?	?	?	?
2015	1093	?	?	?	?
2016	1126	?	?	?	?
2017	1159	?	?	?	?
2018	1194	?	?	?	?
2019	1230	?	?	?	?
2020	1267	?	?	?	?
2021	1305	?	?	?	?
2022	1344	?	?	?	?

a. Complete the accompanying table to show the debt-to-GDP ratio and the ratio of the budget deficit to GDP for the economy if the government's budget deficit remains constant at $30 billion over the next 10 years. (Remember that the government's debt will grow by the previous year's deficit.)

b. Redo the table to show the debt-to-GDP ratio and the ratio of the budget deficit to GDP for the economy if the government's budget deficit grows by 3% per year over the next 10 years.

c. Redo the table again to show the debt-to-GDP ratio and the ratio of the budget deficit to GDP for the economy if the government's budget deficit grows by 20% per year over the next 10 years.

d. What happens to the debt-to-GDP ratio and the ratio of the budget deficit to GDP for the economy over time under the three different scenarios?

13. Your study partner argues that the distinction between the government's budget deficit and debt is similar to the distinction between consumer savings and wealth.

He also argues that if you have large budget deficits, you must have a large debt. In what ways is your study partner correct and in what ways is he incorrect?

14. In which of the following cases does the size of the government's debt and the size of the budget deficit indicate potential problems for the economy?

a. The government's debt is relatively low, but the government is running a large budget deficit as it builds a high-speed rail system to connect the major cities of the nation.

b. The government's debt is relatively high due to a recently ended deficit-financed war, but the government is now running only a small budget deficit.

c. The government's debt is relatively low, but the government is running a budget deficit to finance the interest payments on the debt.

15. How did or would each action affect the current public debt and implicit liabilities of the Canadian government?

a. In Budget 2012, the federal government announced that it would gradually increase the age of eligibility for Old Age Security (OAS) from 65 to 67.

b. OAS for future retirees is limited to those with low incomes.

c. Because the cost of health care is increasing faster than the three-year moving average of nominal GDP growth rate, the Canada Health Transfer is increased by the annual increase in health care costs rather than the three-year moving average of nominal GDP growth rate.

16. Unlike households, governments are often able to sustain large debts. For example, as of March 31, 2012, the Canadian government's gross debt was $842.7 billion, about 48% of GDP. The government paid an average interest rate of 3.7% on its debt. However, running budget deficits becomes hard when very large debts are outstanding.

a. Calculate the dollar cost of the annual interest on the government's total debt assuming the interest rate and debt figures cited above.

b. If the government operates on a balanced budget before interest payments are taken into account, at what rate must GDP grow in order for the debt-to-GDP ratio to remain unchanged?

c. Calculate the total increase in national debt if the government incurs a deficit of $21 billion in the fiscal year of 2012–2013.

d. At what rate would GDP have to grow in order for the debt-to-GDP ratio to remain unchanged when the budget deficit in 2012–2013 is $21 billion?

e. Why is the debt-to-GDP ratio the preferred measure of a country's debt rather than the dollar value of the debt? Why is it important for a government to keep this number under control?

17. a. What measures does the government have at its disposal to undertake fiscal policy?

b. What is meant by expansionary fiscal policy? How would the government undertake expansionary fiscal policy?

c. What is meant by contractionary fiscal policy? How would the government undertake contractionary fiscal policy?

d. When is expansionary fiscal policy appropriate? When is contractionary fiscal policy appropriate?

e. What are the advantages and disadvantages of expansionary fiscal policy?

f. What are the advantages and disadvantages of contractionary fiscal policy?

g. Should fiscal policy be delivered via automatic rules, such as progressive income taxes, or should it at times be delivered via discretionary measures adopted by the government? Explain.

h. Should fiscal policy measures always be permanent or should they sometimes be temporary, with a known expiry date? Explain.

Taxes and the Multiplier

In the chapter, we described how taxes that depend positively on real GDP reduce the size of the multiplier and act as an automatic stabilizer for the economy. Let's look a little more closely at the mathematics of how this works.

Autonomous Taxation and the Multipliers

An *autonomous* term in an equation is a term that is independent of any (right-hand side) variable. Normally it is the intercept in the equation. An *exogenous* variable means the value of the variable is given and could change when the economy is hit with a shock. Obviously, the autonomous term is an example of an exogenous variable, so they are the slope terms in the equations.

Suppose for simplicity that government spending on goods and services, G, the amount of taxes the government collects, T, and the transfers the government provides, Tr, are all exogenous. Then:

(13A-1) $AE_{Planned} = AC + MPC \times YD + I_{Planned} + G$

Furthermore, since disposable income, YD, is GDP after subtracting taxes and adding transfers, then:

(13A-2) $YD = GDP - T + Tr$

The income–expenditure equilibrium level of GDP, Y^*, is equal to planned aggregate expenditure. So:

(13A-3) $Y^* = AE_{Planned}$
$= AC + MPC(Y^* - T + Tr) + I_{Planned} + G$

With a little algebraic manipulation, we get:

(13A-4) $Y^* = \left(\dfrac{1}{1 - MPC}\right)(AC + I_{Planned} + G - MPC \times T + MPC \times Tr)$

This equation gives us the following three multipliers:

- the autonomous expenditure multiplier (also called simply "the multiplier"):

$$\frac{\Delta Y^*}{\Delta AC} = \frac{\Delta Y^*}{\Delta I_{planned}} = \frac{\Delta Y^*}{\Delta G} = \frac{1}{1 - MPC}$$

- the autonomous taxation multiplier: $\dfrac{\Delta Y^*}{\Delta T} = \dfrac{-MPC}{1 - MPC}$

- the autonomous transfers multiplier: $\dfrac{\Delta Y^*}{\Delta Tr} = \dfrac{-MPC}{1 - MPC}$

So, for example, if the marginal propensity to consume is 0.5, then the autonomous expenditure multiplier is equal to 2. This implies, all else the same, that a \$100 billion increase in autonomous consumption (AC), planned investment ($I_{Planned}$), or government spending on goods and services (G) will result in a \$200 billion increase in the income–expenditure equilibrium level of GDP. Similarly, in this case, the autonomous taxation multiplier is equal to –1, so a \$100 billion increase in taxes will result in a \$100 billion reduction in the income–expenditure equilibrium level of GDP. Also, in this case, the autonomous transfers multiplier is equal to 1, so a \$100 billion increase in transfers results in a \$100 billion increase in the income–expenditure equilibrium level of GDP.

Endogenous Taxation and the Multipliers

In contrast to autonomous taxation, with endogenous taxation the government captures some of the increase in real GDP. Specifically, let's assume that the government "captures" a fraction, t, of any increase in real GDP in the form of taxes, where t, the tax rate, is a fraction between 0 and 1. And let's repeat the exercise we carried out in Chapter 11, where we consider the effects of a $100 billion increase in investment spending. The same analysis holds for *any* autonomous increase in aggregate expenditure—in particular, it is also true for increases in government purchases of goods and services.

The $100 billion increase in investment spending initially raises real GDP by $100 billion (the first round). In the absence of taxes, disposable income would rise by $100 billion. But because part of the rise in real GDP is collected in the form of taxes, disposable income only rises by $(1 - t) \times \$100$ billion. The second-round increase in consumer spending, which is equal to the marginal propensity to consume (MPC) multiplied by the rise in disposable income, is $(MPC \times (1 - t)) \times \$100$ billion. This leads to a third-round increase in consumer spending of $(MPC \times (1 - t)) \times (MPC \times (1 - t)) \times \$100$ billion, and so on. So the total effect on real GDP is:

Increase in investment spending = $100 billion
+ Second-round increase in consumer spending = $(MPC \times (1 - t)) \times \$100$ billion
+ Third-round increase in consumer spending = $(MPC \times (1 - t))^2 \times \$100$ billion
+ Fourth-round increase in consumer spending = $(MPC \times (1 - t))^3 \times \$100$ billion

$$\vdots \qquad\qquad\qquad \vdots$$

$$\text{Total increase in real GDP} = [1 + (MPC \times (1 - t)) + (MPC \times (1 - t))^2 + (MPC \times (1 - t))^3 + \dots] \times \$100 \text{ billion}$$

As we pointed out in Chapter 11, an infinite series of the form $1 + x + x^2 + \dots$, with $0 < x < 1$, is equal to $1/(1 - x)$. In this example, $x = (MPC \times (1 - t))$. So the total effect of a $100 billion increase in investment spending, taking into account all the subsequent increases in consumer spending, is to raise real GDP by:

$$\frac{1}{1 - (MPC \times (1 - t))} \times \$100 \text{ billion}$$

The government captures a fraction of any increase in real GDP, in the form of taxes. That is, if t is the tax rate, then $T = t \times \text{GDP}$. Also, as stated above,

(13A-1) $AE_{Planned} = AC + MPC \times YD + I_{Planned} + G$

Again, since disposable income, YD, is GDP after subtracting taxes and adding transfers, then:

(13A-5) $YD = \text{GDP} - T + Tr = (1 - t) \times \text{GDP} + Tr$

The income–expenditure equilibrium level of GDP, Y^*, is equal to planned aggregate expenditure:

(13A-6) $Y^* = AE\text{Planned}$
$$= AC + MPC((1 - t) \times Y^* + Tr) + I_{Planned} + G$$

Again, with some manipulation, we get:

(13A-7) $Y^* = \left(\dfrac{1}{1 - MPC \times (1 - t)} \right)(AC + I_{Planned} + G + MPC \times Tr)$

This equation gives us the following two multipliers:

- the autonomous expenditure multiplier: $\dfrac{\Delta Y^*}{\Delta AC} = \dfrac{\Delta Y^*}{\Delta I_{planned}} = \dfrac{\Delta Y^*}{\Delta G} = \dfrac{1}{1 - MPC(1 - t)}$

- the autonomous transfers multiplier: $\dfrac{\Delta Y^*}{\Delta T} = \dfrac{MPC}{1 - MPC(1 - t)}$

There is no autonomous taxation multiplier here since taxes now depend on income only. When we calculated the multiplier assuming away the effect of taxes, we found that it was $1/(1 - MPC)$. But when we assume that a fraction, t, of any change in real GDP is collected in the form of taxes, the multiplier is:

$$\text{Multiplier} = \dfrac{1}{1 - (MPC(1 - t))}$$

This is always a smaller number than $1/(1 - MPC)$, and its size diminishes as t grows. Suppose, for example, that $MPC = 0.6$. In the absence of taxes, this implies a multiplier of $1/(1 - 0.6) = 1/0.4 = 2.5$. But now let's assume that $t = 1/3$, that is, that $1/3$ of any increase in real GDP is collected by the government. Then the multiplier is:

$$\dfrac{1}{1 - (0.6 \times (1 - 1/3))} = \dfrac{1}{1 - (0.6 \times 2/3)} = \dfrac{1}{1 - 0.4} = \dfrac{1}{0.6} = 1.667$$

PROBLEMS

1. An economy has a marginal propensity to consume of 0.6, real GDP equals $500 billion, and the government collects 20% of GDP in taxes. If government purchases increase by $10 billion, show the rounds of increased spending that take place by completing the accompanying table. The first and second rows are filled in for you. In the first row, the increase in government purchases of $10 billion raises real GDP by $10 billion, taxes increase by $2 billion, and YD increases by $8 billion; in the second row, the increase in YD of $8 billion increases consumer spending by $4.80 billion (MPC × change in disposable income).

	Change in G or C	Change in real GDP	Change in taxes	Change in YD
Rounds	(billions of dollars)			
1	ΔG = $10.00	$10.00	$2.00	$8.00
2	ΔC = 4.80	4.80	0.96	3.84
3	ΔC = ?	?	?	?
4	ΔC = ?	?	?	?
5	ΔC = ?	?	?	?
6	ΔC = ?	?	?	?
7	ΔC = ?	?	?	?
8	ΔC = ?	?	?	?
9	ΔC = ?	?	?	?
10	ΔC = ?	?	?	?

a. What is the total change in real GDP after the 10 rounds? What is the value of the multiplier? What would you expect the total change in real GDP to be, based on the multiplier formula? How do your two answers compare?

b. Redo the accompanying table, assuming the marginal propensity to consume is 0.75 and the government collects 10% of the rise in real GDP in taxes. What is the total change in real GDP after 10 rounds? What is the value of the multiplier? How do your two answers compare?

2. Calculate the change in government purchases of goods and services necessary to close the recessionary or inflationary gaps in the following cases. Assume that the short-run aggregate supply curve is horizontal, so that the change in real GDP arising from a shift of the aggregate demand curve equals the size of the shift of the curve.

a. Real GDP equals $100 billion, potential output equals $160 billion, the government collects 20% of any change in real GDP in the form of taxes, and the marginal propensity to consume is 0.75.

b. Real GDP equals $250 billion, potential output equals $200 billion, the government collects 10% of any change in real GDP in the form of taxes, and the marginal propensity to consume is 0.5.

c. Real GDP equals $180 billion, potential output equals $100 billion, the government collects 25% of any change in real GDP in the form of taxes, and the marginal propensity to consume is 0.8.

CHAPTER 14

Money, Banking, and the Central Banking System

FUNNY MONEY

Phuong Anh Ho Huu, a senior representative for the Bank of Canada in Quebec, holds up a new $100 banknote. Issued in November 2011, the $100 bill was the first in Canada's polymer banknote series, which features a wealth of anti-counterfeiting components.

WHAT YOU WILL LEARN IN THIS CHAPTER

❱ The various roles **money** plays and the many forms it takes in the economy

❱ How the actions of chartered banks and the Bank of Canada determine the **money supply**

❱ How the Bank of Canada uses **open-market operations** to change the **monetary base**

I N 2008, THE ROYAL CANADIAN Mounted Police (RCMP) dismantled a major counterfeiting plant in Surrey, British Columbia, that was believed to be responsible for a significant portion of the counterfeit Canadian paper bills in B.C. between 2006 and 2008. A year later, the RCMP seized $130 000 worth of fake Canadian banknotes. In 2011, following a tip provided to Crime Stoppers and after a two-week investigation, the RCMP seized $1.1 million of counterfeit Canadian banknotes in Vancouver. Some of these fake paper bills were of high quality and were very hard to tell from the real thing.

The funny thing is that these elaborately decorated pieces of paper have little or no intrinsic value. Indeed, a $20 bill printed with blue or orange ink literally wouldn't be worth the paper it was printed on. But if the ink on that decorated piece of paper is just the right shade of green, people will think that it's money and will accept it as payment for very real goods and services. Why? Because they believe, correctly, that they can do the same thing: exchange that piece of green paper for real goods and services.

In fact, here's a riddle: if a fake $20 bill enters Canada and nobody ever realizes it's a fake, who gets hurt? Accepting a fake $20 bill isn't like buying a car that turns out to be a lemon or a meal that isn't edible; as long as the bill's counterfeit nature remains undiscovered, it will pass from hand to hand just like a real $20 bill. The answer to the riddle, as we'll learn later in this chapter, is that the real victims of counterfeiting are Canadian taxpayers, because counterfeit dollars reduce the revenues available to pay for the operations of the Canadian government. Accordingly, the RCMP diligently monitors the integrity of Canadian currency, promptly investigating any reports of counterfeit dollars. The Bank of Canada (BOC) continues to bolster the security features of our paper bills and increase education efforts on note checking. The recent introduction of the polymer series of banknotes with improved security features is an example of the effort by the BOC to reduce counterfeiting.

The activities of the BOC and RCMP attest to the fact that money isn't like assets. It plays a unique role in the economy as the essential channel that links the various parts of the modern economy. In this chapter, we'll look at the role money plays, and then look at how a modern monetary system works and at the institutions that sustain and regulate it. This topic is important in itself, and it's also essential background for the understanding of monetary policy, which we will examine in the next chapter. ■

Money is any asset that can easily be used to purchase goods and services.

Currency in circulation is cash held by the public.

Chequeable deposits (or demand deposits) are bank accounts on which people can write cheques.

The **money supply** is the total value of financial assets in the economy that are considered money.

The Meaning of Money

In everyday conversation, people often use the word *money* to mean "wealth." If you ask, "How much money does Bill Gates have?" the answer will be something like, "Oh, $50 billion or so, but who's counting?" That is, the number will include the value of the stocks, bonds, real estate, and other assets he owns.

But the economist's definition of money doesn't include all forms of wealth. The dollar bills in your wallet are money; other forms of wealth—such as cars, houses, and stock certificates—aren't money. What, according to economists, distinguishes money from other forms of wealth?

What Is Money?

Money is defined in terms of what it does: **money** is any asset that can easily be used to purchase goods and services. In Chapter 10 we defined an asset as *liquid* if it can easily be converted into cash. Money consists of cash itself, which is liquid by definition, as well as other assets that are highly liquid.

You can see the distinction between money and other assets by asking yourself how you pay for groceries. The person at the cash register will accept dollar bills in return for milk and frozen pizza—but he or she won't accept stock certificates or a collection of vintage baseball cards. If you want to convert stock certificates or vintage baseball cards into groceries, you have to sell them—trade them for money—and then use the money to buy groceries.

Of course, many stores allow you to write a cheque on your bank account in payment for goods (or to pay with a debit card that is linked to your bank account). Does that make your bank account money, even if you haven't converted it into cash? Yes. **Currency in circulation**—actual cash in the hands of the public—is considered money. So are **chequeable deposits**—bank accounts on which people can write cheques.

Are currency and chequeable bank deposits the only assets that are considered to be money? It depends. As we'll see later, there are several widely used definitions of the **money supply,** the total value of financial assets in the economy that are considered money. The narrower definitions consider only the most liquid assets to be money: currency in circulation and chequeable deposits (also called demand deposits). The broader definitions include these two categories plus other assets that are *almost* chequeable, such as saving account deposits at chartered banks, trust and mortgage loan companies, credit unions, and caisses populaires. However, all of the definitions distinguish between assets that can easily be used to buy goods and services and those that can't.

Money plays a crucial role in generating *gains from trade* because it makes indirect exchange possible. Think of what happens when a cardiac surgeon buys a new refrigerator. The surgeon has valuable services to offer—namely, heart operations. The owner of the store has valuable goods to offer—refrigerators and other appliances. It would be extremely difficult for both parties if, instead of using money, they had to directly barter the goods and services they sell. In a barter system, a cardiac surgeon and an appliance store owner could trade only if the store owner happened to want a heart operation and the surgeon happened to want a new refrigerator.

This is known as the problem of finding a "double coincidence of wants": in a barter system, two parties can trade only when each wants what the other has to offer. Money solves this problem: individuals can trade what they have to offer for money and trade money for what they want.

Because the ability to make transactions with money rather than relying on bartering makes it easier to achieve gains from trade, the existence of money increases welfare, even though money does not directly produce anything. In other words, it saves time and resources spent on finding another suitable party that is willing to trade with us. As Adam Smith put it, money "may very properly be compared to a highway, which, while it circulates and carries to market all the grass and corn of the country, produces itself not a single pile of either."

Let's take a closer look at the roles money plays in the economy.

> A **medium of exchange** is an asset that individuals acquire for the purpose of trading goods and services rather than for their own consumption.

Roles of Money

Money plays three main roles in any modern economy: it is a *medium of exchange*, a *store of value*, and a *unit of account*.

1. Medium of Exchange Our cardiac surgeon/refrigerator example illustrates the role of money as a **medium of exchange**—an asset that individuals use to trade for goods and services rather than for consumption. People can't eat dollar bills; rather, they use dollar bills to trade for edible goods and their accompanying services.

In normal times, the official money of a given country—the Canadian dollar in Canada, the U.S. dollar in the U.S., the euro in Germany, and so on —is also the medium of exchange in virtually all transactions in that country. During troubled economic times, however, other goods or assets often play that role instead. For example, during economic turmoil people often turn to other countries' moneys as the medium of exchange: U.S. dollars have played this role in troubled Latin American countries, as have euros in troubled Eastern European countries. In a famous example, cigarettes functioned as the medium of exchange in World War II prisoner-of-war camps: even non-smokers traded goods and services for cigarettes because the cigarettes could in turn be easily traded for other items. During the extreme German inflation of 1923, goods such as eggs and lumps of coal became, briefly, mediums of exchange.

GLOBAL COMPARISON   THE BIG MONEYS

It is not just Americans who consider the U.S. dollar the world's leading currency. Most other countries, including Canada, would agree—and the U.S. dollar is more likely to be accepted around the globe than any other currency. But there are other important currencies, too. One measure of a currency's importance is the quantity that is in circulation worldwide. The accompanying figure shows the value of Canadian dollars, U.S. dollars, euros, Japanese yen, and Chinese yuan in circulation as of September 2012. It is not surprising that far fewer Canadian dollars were in circulation than the other four major currencies. This is because Canadian dollars are used primarily in Canada, and our economy is far smaller than that of the U.S., the eurozone, Japan, or China. But contrary to what you might expect, the U.S. dollar is not the most circulated currency; it is second, just behind the euro. The euro's prominence is not really that surprising though. The eurozone combines the economies of 17 countries, so it is almost as large as the U.S. economy. The Japanese economy, even though it is much

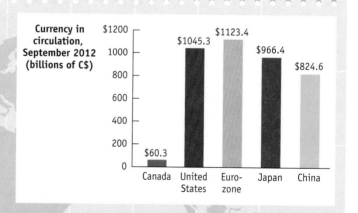

smaller, is close behind the eurozone and American economies in terms of currency in circulation. This is because the Japanese tend to use cash, as opposed to cheques and credit cards, more frequently than either Europeans or Americans do. And now China, with its rapidly growing economy, is moving up the charts.

Sources: Bank of Canada; Federal Reserve Bank of St. Louis; European Central Bank; Bank of Japan; the People's Bank of China.

A **store of value** is a means of holding purchasing power over time.

A **unit of account** is a measure used to set prices and make economic calculations.

Commodity money is a good used as a medium of exchange that has intrinsic value in other uses.

Commodity-backed money is a medium of exchange with no intrinsic value whose ultimate value is guaranteed by a promise that it can be converted into valuable goods.

2. Store of Value In order to act as a medium of exchange, money must also be a **store of value**—a means of holding purchasing power over time. To see why this is necessary, imagine trying to operate an economy in which ice cream cones were the medium of exchange. Such an economy would quickly suffer from, well, monetary meltdown: your medium of exchange would often turn into a sticky puddle before you could use it to buy something else. (As we'll see in Chapter 16, one of the problems caused by high inflation is that, in effect, it causes the value of money to "melt.") Of course, money is by no means the only store of value. Any asset that holds its purchasing power over time is a store of value. So the store-of-value role is a necessary but not distinctive feature of money. Gold is an asset with intrinsic value that can serve as a store of value. During unstable times such as wars or periods of hyperinflation, people often hold gold rather than paper money to better store or preserve their wealth.

3. Unit of Account Finally, money normally serves as the **unit of account**—the commonly accepted measure individuals use to set prices and make economic calculations. To understand the importance of this role, consider a historical fact: during the Middle Ages, peasants typically were required to provide land-owners with goods and labour rather than money. A peasant might, for example, be required to work on the lord's land one day a week and hand over one-fifth of his harvest.

Today, rents, like other prices, are almost always specified in money terms. That makes things much clearer: imagine how hard it would be to decide which apartment to rent if modern landlords followed medieval practice. Suppose, for example, that Mr. Smith says he'll let you have a place if you clean his house twice a week and bring him a kilogram of steak every day, whereas Ms. Jones wants you to clean her house just once a week but wants four kilograms of chicken every day. Who's offering the better deal? It's hard to say. If, instead, Smith wants $600 a month and Jones wants $700, the comparison is easy. In other words, without a commonly accepted measure, the terms of a transaction are harder to determine, making it more difficult to make transactions and achieve gains from trade.

Types of Money

In some form or another, money has been in use for thousands of years. For most of that period, people used **commodity money:** the medium of exchange was a good, normally gold or silver, that had intrinsic value in other uses. These alternative uses gave commodity money value independent of its role as a medium of exchange. For example, the cigarettes that served as money in World War II prisoner-of-war camps were also valuable because many prisoners smoked. Gold was valuable because it was used for jewellery and ornamentation, aside from the fact that it was minted into coins.

In 1776, when Adam Smith wrote *The Wealth of Nations*, there was widespread use of paper money in addition to gold or silver coins. Unlike modern dollar bills, however, this paper money consisted of notes issued by privately owned banks, which promised to exchange their notes for gold or silver coins on demand. So the paper currency that initially replaced commodity money was **commodity-backed money,** a medium of exchange with no intrinsic value whose ultimate value was guaranteed by a promise that it could always be converted into valuable goods on demand.

The big advantage of commodity-backed money over simple commodity money, like gold and silver coins, was that it tied up fewer valuable resources. Although a note-issuing bank still had to keep some gold and silver on hand, it had to keep only enough to satisfy demands for redemption of its notes. And it could rely on the fact that on a normal day only a fraction of its paper notes would be redeemed. So the bank needed to keep only a portion of the total value of its notes in circulation in the form of gold and silver in its vaults. It could lend out the remaining gold and silver to those who wished to use it. This allowed society to use the remaining gold and silver for other purposes, all with no loss in the ability to achieve gains from trade.

In a famous passage in *The Wealth of Nations,* Adam Smith described paper money as a "waggon-way through the air." Smith was making an analogy between money and an imaginary highway that did not absorb valuable land beneath it. An actual highway provides a useful service but at a cost: land that could be used to grow crops is instead paved over. If the highway could be built through the air, it wouldn't destroy useful land. As Smith understood, when banks replaced gold and silver money with paper notes, they accomplished a similar feat: they reduced the amount of real resources used by society to provide the functions of money.

At this point you may ask: why make any use at all of gold and silver in the monetary system, even to back paper money? In fact, today's monetary system goes even further than the system Smith admired, having eliminated any role for gold and silver. A Canadian dollar bill isn't commodity money, and it isn't even commodity-backed. Rather, its value arises entirely from the fact that it is generally accepted as a means of payment, a role that is ultimately decreed by the Canadian government. Money whose value derives entirely from its official status as a means of exchange is known as **fiat money** because it exists by government fiat, a historical term for a policy declared by a ruler.

Fiat money has two major advantages over commodity-backed money. First, it is even more of a "waggon-way through the air"—creating it doesn't use up any real resources beyond the paper it's printed on. Second, the supply of money can be adjusted based on the needs of the economy, instead of being determined by the amount of gold and silver prospectors happen to discover.

Fiat money, though, poses some risks. In this chapter's opening story, we described one such risk—counterfeiting. Counterfeiters usurp a privilege of the Canadian government, which has the sole legal right to print dollar bills. And the benefit that counterfeiters get by exchanging fake bills for real goods and services comes at the expense of the Canadian federal government, which covers a small but non-trivial part of its own expenses by issuing new currency to meet a growing demand for money. According to the RCMP, the estimated value of counterfeit banknotes passed in our economy reached about $2.6 million in 2011, up 0.5% from the 2010 estimates. The $20 bill was the most popular counterfeit paper note, followed by the $100 bill. About 85% of the counterfeit banknotes were passed in Quebec, Ontario, and British Columbia.

The larger risk is that governments that can create money whenever they feel like it will be tempted to abuse the privilege. In Chapter 16 we'll learn how governments sometimes rely too heavily on printing money to pay their bills, leading to high inflation. In this chapter, however, we'll stay focused on the question of what money is and how it is managed.

Measuring the Money Supply

The Bank of Canada (an institution we'll talk more about shortly) calculates the size of several **monetary aggregates,** overall measures of the money supply, which differ in how strictly money is defined. These aggregates are known, rather cryptically, as M1, M1+, M2, M2+, and M3. All of these monetary aggregates include currency in circulation and deposits at financial institutions, but each one includes different types of deposits and financial institutions. In general terms, an aggregate without a "+" sign includes only deposits held at chartered banks. An aggregate with a

> **Fiat money** is a medium of exchange whose value derives entirely from its official status as a means of payment.
>
> A **monetary aggregate** is an overall measure of the money supply.

⚠ PITFALLS

WHAT'S NOT IN THE MONEY SUPPLY

Are financial assets like stocks and bonds part of the money supply? No, not under any definition, because they're not liquid enough.

M1+ consists, roughly speaking, of assets you can use to buy groceries: currency and chequeable deposits (which work as long as your grocery store accepts either cheques or debit cards). Broader definitions of money supply—M2, M2+, and M3—include assets such as savings and term deposits, and other assets that may, at some cost, be converted into M1+.

By contrast, converting a stock or a bond into cash requires selling the stock or bond—something that usually takes some time and also involves paying a broker's fee. That makes these assets much less liquid than bank deposits. So stocks and bonds, unlike bank deposits, aren't considered money.

"+" sign includes the deposits at chartered banks plus the same type(s) of deposits at smaller financial institutions, such as trust companies, mortgage and loan companies, credit unions, and caisses populaires.[1]

More specifically, M1, the narrowest definition, consists only of currency in circulation (cash) and all chequeable (or demand) deposits at chartered banks. As the name suggests, demand deposits are bank deposits that can be withdrawn on demand by, for instance, writing cheques against these accounts, debit transactions, online banking, and accessing ATMs. These deposits pay little or no interest. M1+, a broader definition, consists of M1 plus the demand deposits at trust companies, mortgage and loan companies, credit unions, and caisses populaires. M2, the next step up, includes M1 plus the personal term deposits, non-personal demand deposits, and notice deposits in chartered banks. M2+ includes M2 plus such deposits at trust companies, mortgage and loan companies, credit unions, and caisses populaires as well as life insurance company individual annuities, personal deposits at other financial institutions, and money market mutual funds. M3, one of the broadest definitions of money supply, includes M2 plus bank non-personal term deposits and chartered bank foreign currency deposits

FIGURE **14-1** Value of Monetary Aggregates in Canada as of August 2012

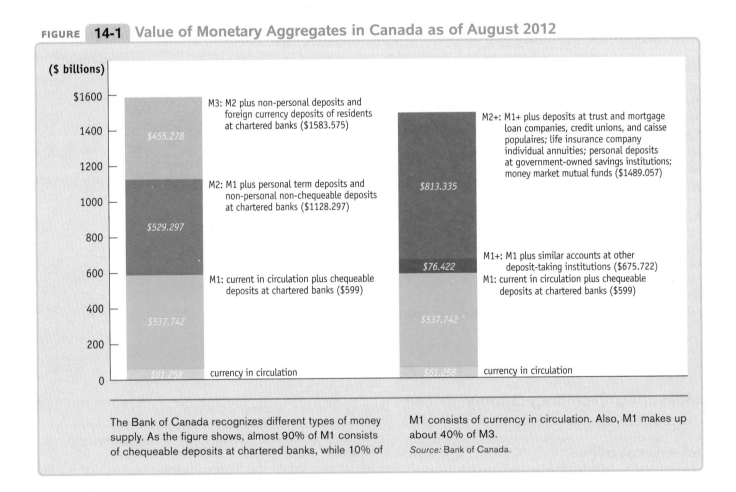

The Bank of Canada recognizes different types of money supply. As the figure shows, almost 90% of M1 consists of chequeable deposits at chartered banks, while 10% of

M1 consists of currency in circulation. Also, M1 makes up about 40% of M3.

Source: Bank of Canada.

---

[1]As a group, and often individually, Canadian chartered banks are much larger than other deposit-taking institutions. Because chartered banks have more branches and greater name recognition, their deposits tend to be more liquid (easier to access and more acceptable as a means of payment). Also, trust companies, mortgage and loan companies, credit unions, and caisses populaires differ from chartered banks in the types of business they can do and the services they can provide their customers. They also differ somewhat in the regulations, such as capital requirements, that they face. Over time, these differences have tended to decline, which makes deposits (assets) held at the other deposit-taking institutions more and more like deposits held at chartered banks.

FOR INQUIRING MINDS

WHAT'S WITH ALL THE CURRENCY?

Alert readers may be a bit startled by one of the numbers in the money supply (in Figure 14-1)—more than $61 billion of currency in circulation. That's about $1756 in cash for every man, woman, and child in Canada. How many people do you know who carry $1756 in their wallets? Not many. So where is all that cash?

Part of the answer is that it isn't in individuals' wallets—it's in cash regis-

ters. Businesses as well as individuals need to hold cash.

Economists believe that cash also plays an important role in transactions that people want to keep hidden. Some small businesses and self-employed individuals may try to avoid paying taxes by accepting cash for their services, thus hiding income from the Canadian Revenue Agency.

Also, drug dealers and other criminals obviously don't want bank records of their dealings. In fact, some analysts have tried to infer the amount of illegal activity in the economy from the total amount of cash holdings held by the public. However, estimates based on this type of analysis range so widely, from very low to very high, that they cannot be considered reliable.

---

of residents. Occasionally the terms of these aggregates may be adjusted, owing to a change in regulations or a merger between two financial institutions.

You may already have noticed that M1 and M1+ include only those assets we use for daily monetary transactions. These assets are the most liquid components of money, or the medium of exchange. However, as the definition of money widens, the monetary aggregates start to include what we call **near-moneys**. These financial assets cannot be used as a medium of exchange but can be converted into cash or chequing deposits readily. An example is a term deposit, which isn't chequeable but can be withdrawn at any time before its maturity date by paying a penalty.

Figure 14-1 shows the actual composition of M1, M1+, M2, M2+, and M3 in Canada as of August 2012, in billions of dollars. M1 was valued at about $599.5 billion, with currency in circulation accounting for about 10% and demand deposits accounting for the remainder. In turn, M2 was valued at $1128.3 billion, with M1 accounting for 53%, and savings deposits, non-personal notice deposits, and demand deposits accounting for the remainder. M2+ was valued at about $1489.1 billion, of which M2 represented about 75%. M3 was valued at about $1583.6, of which M2 represented about 71%. The portions of M2+ and M3 that do not include M2 include different types of near-moneys. These near-moneys typically pay higher interest than chequeable bank deposits do.

Near-moneys are financial assets that can't be directly used as a medium of exchange but can be readily converted into cash or chequeable deposits.

ECONOMICS ▸ IN ACTION

THE HISTORY OF THE CANADIAN DOLLAR[2]

Canadian paper bills are fiat money, which means they have no intrinsic value and are not backed by anything that has value. But money in Canada wasn't always like that. In the 1600s and 1700s, "commodity money" prevailed, that is, the money consisted of coins made of metal, such as gold or silver, that did have intrinsic value. These coins came from many lands, including England, France, Portugal, Spain, and Spain's South American colonies. As you can imagine, this great diversity of currency caused considerable "currency chaos."

The first banknotes issued in Canada were issued by the Bank of Montreal upon its establishment in 1817. These notes could be redeemed in gold and silver coins upon demand. As more banks became incorporated in Upper and Lower Canada during the 1830s and 1840s, they, too, issued their own banknotes. The banking sector lobbied against the issuing of paper notes by the government

---

[2]*Source:* James Powell, *A History of the Canadian Dollar,* (Bank of Canada, 2005), accessed April 2013, www.bankofcanada.ca/publications-research/books-and-monographs/history-canadian-dollar/.

because the banks thought this would erode their right to print money—and printing money has always been a profitable business.

The move to government-issued banknotes occurred gradually, prompted by a series of crises and political events. The first crisis happened when several chartered banks collapsed in the 1850s and 1860s, bringing the banknotes issued by all chartered banks into disrepute. This loss of confidence in the medium of exchange threatened economic prosperity, so the Province of Canada (created in 1841 with the merger of Upper and Lower Canada) began to issue its own paper currency. These notes could be converted into gold on demand.

The next change occurred upon Confederation in 1867, when the Dominion of Canada, consisting of Ontario, Quebec, Nova Scotia, and New Brunswick, was created. Banks were brought under national legislation, but they retained the right to issue their own banknotes.

The next crisis occurred in 1914, when World War I began, causing financial panic. There were heavy withdrawals of gold from banks and real concerns that banks would not be able to meet depositors' demands. To avert a banking collapse, the government temporarily declared banknotes legal tender— that is, the government broke the link between dollars and gold. The government also gave itself the role of "lender of the last resort," which meant it had the power to lend money to the banks at a rate of interest called the "advance rate."

This 25¢ bill is just one of many denominations printed in Canada in the 1800s.

Today, central banks are the lenders of last resort, and the advance rate was the precursor to today's "bank rate."

The Great Depression caused the next major change in Canada's banking system. Public distrust of the banking system and rising political pressure to do something about the depression led the government to create a central bank—the Bank of Canada—in 1934. At this point, the government took on full responsibility for issuing paper bills, and private banknotes were gradually phased out.

Gold backing for Canadian currency was eliminated in 1940, although Canadian paper currency continued to carry the traditional statement "Will pay the bearer on demand" until 1954. Today's Bank of Canada notes simply say "This note is legal tender." They are, in other words, fiat money pure and simple. Their value is backed by the taxing power of the federal government, which helps ensure that not too many notes are issued.

While the Bank of Canada holds the privilege of printing Canadian paper money, it faces the same difficulty that other central banks face with their currencies: people keep trying to make and use fake banknotes. Thus, the Bank of Canada continues to improve the design of banknotes to make them harder to counterfeit. It also works closely with the RCMP to fight counterfeiting.

CHECK YOUR UNDERSTANDING   14-1

1. Suppose you hold a gift certificate, good for certain products at participating stores. Is this gift certificate money? Why or why not?

2. Although most bank accounts do pay some interest, depositors can usually get a higher interest rate by buying a guaranteed investment certificate, or GIC. The difference between a GIC and a bank account is that the depositor pays a penalty for withdrawing the money from a GIC before it comes due—a period of months or even years. GICs are classified as term deposits, so they are counted in M2. Explain why they are not part of M1.

3. Explain why a system of commodity-backed money uses resources more efficiently than a system of commodity money.

Solutions appear at back of book.

The Monetary Role of Banks

R oughly 10% of M1, the narrowest definition of the money supply, consists of currency in circulation—$5 bills, $10 bills, and so on. It's obvious where this currency comes from: it's printed by the Bank of Canada. But the rest of M1 consists of demand deposits. Likewise, bank deposits also account for the bulk of M1+, M2, M2+, and M3, the broader definitions of the money supply. Thus, by any measure, bank deposits are the major component of the money supply.

Bank reserves are the currency banks hold in their vaults plus their deposits at the Bank of Canada.

A **T-account** is a tool for analyzing a business's financial position by showing, in a single table, the business's assets (on the left) and liabilities (on the right).

What Banks Do

As we learned in Chapter 10, a bank is a *financial intermediary* that uses liquid assets in the form of bank deposits to finance the illiquid investments of borrowers. Banks can create liquidity because it isn't necessary for a bank to keep all of the funds deposited with it in the form of highly liquid assets. Except in the case of a *bank run*—which we'll get to shortly—all of a bank's depositors won't want to withdraw their funds at the same time. So a bank can provide its depositors with liquid assets yet still invest much of the depositors' funds in illiquid assets, such as mortgages and business loans.

Banks can't, however, lend out all the funds placed in their hands by depositors because they have to satisfy any depositor who wants to withdraw his or her funds. In order to meet these demands, a bank must keep substantial quantities of liquid assets on hand. In the modern Canadian banking system, these assets take the form either of currency in the bank's vault or deposits held in the bank's own account at the Bank of Canada. As we'll see shortly, the latter can be converted into currency more or less instantly. Currency in bank vaults and bank deposits held at the Bank of Canada are called **bank reserves.** Because bank reserves are in bank vaults and at the Bank of Canada and not held by the public, they are not part of currency in circulation.

To understand the role of banks in determining the money supply, we start by introducing a simple tool for analyzing a bank's financial position: a **T-account.** A business's T-account summarizes its financial position by showing, in a single table, the business's assets and liabilities, with assets on the left and liabilities and equity on the right.

Figure 14-2 shows the T-account for a hypothetical business that *isn't* a bank— Samantha's Smoothies. According to Figure 14-2, Samantha's Smoothies owns a building worth $30 000 and has $15 000 worth of smoothie-making equipment. These are assets, so they're on the left side of the table. To finance its opening, the business borrowed $20 000 from a local bank. That's a liability, so the loan is on the right side of the table. The total assets of Samantha's Smoothies, valued at $45 000, exceed its total liabilities, valued at $20 000, and so Samantha's Smoothies has an equity that is worth $25 000. Equity is the difference between total assets and total liabilities. By looking at the T-account, you can immediately see what Samantha's Smoothies owns and what it owes. Oh, and it's called a T-account because the lines in the table make a T-shape.

FIGURE 14-2 A T-Account for Samantha's Smoothies

A T-account summarizes a business's financial position. Its assets, in this case consisting of a building and some smoothie-making machinery, are on the left side. Its liabilities, consisting of the money it owes to a local bank, are on the right side. Since the value of assets exceeds the value of liabilities, the equity is positive.

Assets		Liabilities and Equity	
Building	$30 000	Loan from bank	$20 000
Smoothie-making machines	$15 000	Equity	$25 000

FIGURE **14-3** Assets and Liabilities of First Street Bank

First Street Bank's assets consist of $1 200 000 in loans and $100 000 in reserves. Its liabilities consist of $1 000 000 in deposits—money owed to people who have placed funds in First Street's hands. The equity of First Street Bank is $300 000. Equity, the gap between assets and other liabilities, represents the value of what the bank owes its shareholders.

Assets		Liabilities and Equity	
Loans	$1 200 000	Deposits	$1 000 000
Reserves	$100 000	Equity	$300 000

Samantha's Smoothies is an ordinary, non-bank business. Now let's look at the T-account for a hypothetical bank, First Street Bank, which is the repository of $1 million in bank deposits.

Figure 14-3 shows First Street Bank's financial position. The loans First Street Bank has made are on the left side because they're assets: they represent funds that those who have borrowed from the bank are expected to repay. The bank's only other assets, in this simplified example, are its reserves, which, as we've learned, can take the form either of cash in the bank's vault or deposits at the Bank of Canada. On the right side we show the bank's liabilities and equity, which in this example consist entirely of deposits made by customers at First Street Bank. These are liabilities because they represent funds that must ultimately be repaid to depositors. First Street Bank's assets are larger than its liabilities and the difference is shown as an equity of $300 000. That's the way it's supposed to be! In fact, we'll see shortly, if the bank's equity is low or turns negative, the bank will suffer a bank run.

In this example, First Street Bank holds reserves equal to 10% of its customers' bank deposits. The fraction of bank deposits that a bank holds as reserves is its **reserve ratio.** At one time, the Bank of Canada required banks to maintain a certain minimum reserve ratio, but this requirement was phased out between 1992 and 1994. In our current system, banks maintain whatever reserve ratio they think is appropriate to avoid running out of cash. Running out of cash could have serious consequences, such as a banking panic or a bank run.

The Problem of Bank Runs

A bank can lend out most of the funds deposited in its care because in normal times only a small fraction of its depositors want to withdraw their funds on any given day. But what would happen if, for some reason, all or at least a large fraction of its depositors did try to withdraw their funds during a short period of time, such as a couple of days?

If a significant share of its depositors demand their money back at the same time, the bank wouldn't be able to raise enough cash to meet those demands. The reason is that banks convert most of their depositors' funds into loans made to borrowers; that's how banks earn revenue—by charging interest on loans.

Bank loans, however, are illiquid: they can't easily be converted into cash on short notice. To see why, imagine that First Street Bank has lent $100 000 to Drive-A-Peach Used Cars, a local dealership. To raise cash to meet demands for withdrawals, First Street Bank can sell its loan to Drive-A-Peach to someone else—another bank or an individual investor. But if First Street Bank tries to sell the loan quickly, potential buyers will be wary: they will suspect that First Street Bank wants to sell the loan because there is something wrong and the loan might not be repaid. As a result, First Street Bank can sell the loan quickly only by offering it for sale at a deep discount—say, a discount of 40%, for a sale price of $60 000.

The **reserve ratio** is the fraction of bank deposits that a bank holds as reserves.

The upshot is that if a significant number of First Street Bank's depositors suddenly decided to withdraw their funds, the bank's efforts to raise the necessary cash quickly would force it to sell off its assets very cheaply. Inevitably, this leads to a *bank failure:* the bank would be unable to pay off its depositors in full.

What might start this whole process? That is, what might lead First Street Bank's depositors to rush to pull their money out? A plausible answer is a spreading rumour that the bank is in financial trouble. Even if depositors aren't sure the rumour is true, they are likely to play it safe and get their money out while they still can. And it gets worse: a depositor who simply thinks that *other* depositors are going to panic and try to get their money out will realize that this could "break the bank." So he or she joins the rush. In other words, fear about a bank's financial condition can be a self-fulfilling prophecy: depositors who believe that other depositors will rush to the exit will rush to the exit themselves.

A **bank run** is a phenomenon in which many of a bank's depositors try to withdraw their funds due to fears of a bank failure. Moreover, bank runs aren't bad only for the bank in question and its depositors. Historically, they have often proved contagious, with a run on one bank leading to a loss of faith in other banks, causing additional bank runs. Canada has not had a major bank run in over a century, not even during the Great Depression. (Two small Western banks did collapse in the 1980s, but these failures had little effect on our banking system.) So we will look at the American experience instead. The upcoming Economics in Action describes a wave of bank runs that swept across the United States in the early 1930s. In response to that experience and similar experiences in other countries, Canada and most other modern governments have established a system of bank regulations that protect depositors and reduce the likelihood of bank runs. We'll encounter bank runs again in Chapter 17, which contains an in-depth analysis of financial crises and their aftermath.

Bank Regulation

Should you worry about losing money in Canada due to a bank run? No. Not only have banking crises been relatively rare in Canadian history and bank runs practically unheard of, but it looks as though that will continue to be the case. The World Economic Forum ranked our banking system as the safest in the world in recent years as our banks remain financially sound and stable in the wake of the Great Recession of 2008.

The financial viability of the Canadian banking system is maintained, in part, through the Bank of Canada's willingness to loan money to banks that are fundamentally sound but temporarily lack cash. The federal agency principally responsible for supervising all financial institutions (not just banks) is the Office of the Superintendent of Financial Institutions (OSFI). The OSFI's role is to administer the regulatory framework—in particular, banks' capital requirements. In Canada, the stability of our financial systems hinges on three main tools at OFSI's disposal: *deposit insurance, capital requirements,* and *reserve requirements.*

1. Deposit Insurance Almost every bank in Canada advertises itself as a "member of the CDIC"—the Canadian Deposit Insurance Corporation. The CDIC is a federal crown corporation created in 1967 to contribute to the stability of Canada's financial system. As we saw in Chapter 10, the CDIC provides **deposit insurance,** a guarantee by the federal government that depositors will be paid even if the bank can't come up with the funds, up to a maximum amount per account. As of 2006 the CDIC guarantees the first $100 000 of each account. It's important to realize that deposit insurance doesn't just protect depositors if a bank actually fails. The insurance also eliminates the main reason for bank runs: since depositors know their funds are safe even if a bank fails, they have

A **bank run** is a phenomenon in which many of a bank's depositors try to withdraw their funds due to fears of a bank failure.

Deposit insurance guarantees that a bank's depositors will be paid even if the bank can't come up with the funds, up to a maximum amount per account.

A government imposes **capital requirements** on a bank to ensure the bank holds more assets than the value of its deposits, thus reducing the possibility of a run on the bank.

Reserve requirements are rules set by the central bank that determine the minimum reserve ratio for banks.

The **desired** (or **voluntary**) **reserve ratio** is the fraction of deposits that banks want to hold as reserves.

no incentive to rush to pull them out because of a rumour that the bank is in trouble. Since the provision of deposit insurance greatly diminishes the possibility of bank runs, this also allows banks to keep their (voluntary) reserve ratio at low levels.

2. Capital Requirements

Deposit insurance does protect us against bank runs, but it also creates a big problem. Since depositors are protected from loss, they have no incentive to monitor their bank's financial health. And, bank owners have an incentive to engage in overly risky investments, such as making speculative loans at high interest. If all goes well, the bank owners make large profits; if things go badly, the federal deposit insurance covers the losses. To reduce the incentive for taking excessive risk, there are **capital requirements.** Regulators require that bank owners hold substantially more assets than the value of their banks' deposits. That way, a bank will still have assets greater than its deposits even if some of its loans go bad, and losses will be paid by the bank owners' assets instead of by the government. The excess of a bank's assets over its bank deposits and other liabilities is called the *bank's capital* (or *equity of the bank*). In Canada, the OSFI requires that a bank's capital is at least a minimum percentage of its assets. Figure 14-3 showed that First Street Bank has an equity of $300 000, or about 23% of its assets. In practice, a bank's capital would be a smaller percent. The OSFI also recognizes that some capital is riskier than others, so it divides the banks' capital into two categories: Tier 1 and Tier 2, with Tier 1 being the safer of the two. As of January 1, 2013, the minimum Tier 1 capital ratio was 4.5% and at least 3.5% of the Tier 1 capital ratio had to be in the form of common equity Tier 1 (CET1) capital. It is planned that by 2015, the percentage of capital requirements in the form of Tier 1 capital and CET1 capital will gradually increase to 6% and 4.5%, respectively. By increasing the Tier 1 capital ratio, the OSFI is increasing the financial strength of our banks. Assets that can be used to satisfy the capital requirements include common shareholders' equity and non-cumulative, perpetual preferred shares. In general, banks hold a significant portion of their assets in the form of loans, mostly residential mortgage loans, but also loans to consumers and businesses, as well as government treasury bills and bonds.

3. Reserve Ratios

At one time, the federal government required Canada's chartered banks to hold a minimum part of their assets as non-interest-bearing reserves (placed on deposit at the Bank of Canada) as another safeguard against bank runs. This set of rules, known as **reserve requirements,** meant that banks had to maintain a higher reserve ratio than they might have held otherwise. However, the banks argued that reserve requirements put them at an unfair disadvantage because their competitors—foreign banks and Canadian non-bank financial institutions—were not subject to this law. The federal government agreed, and phased out reserve requirements by 1994.[3]

Although Canadian banks are no longer required to hold minimum reserves, they continue to do so voluntarily. In general, chartered banks maintain a relatively low **desired** (or **voluntary**) **reserve ratio.** Figure 14-4 shows Canada's chartered banks' desired reserves ratios from August 2003 to August 2012. Before 2008, the ratio was about 3.9%, but during the recession of 2008–2009 it rose to 4.9%. At this time, some of the largest financial institutions in the U.S. faced liquidity and solvency problems, so Canada's chartered banks chose to hold more reserves to protect themselves against unexpected large withdrawals of deposits that might lead to a run. Once the recession was over, the reserve ratios fell back to pre-recession levels.

---

[3]Before 1992, Canadian chartered banks were required to hold reserves equal to 10% of their demand deposits, 2% of their notice deposits totalling less than $500 million, 3% of all notice deposits totalling more than $500 million, and 3% on customers' foreign currency deposits. Between 1992 and 1994, these percentages were reduced gradually to zero.

FIGURE **14-4** Chartered Banks' Desired (or Voluntary) Reserve Ratio, August 2003–August 2012

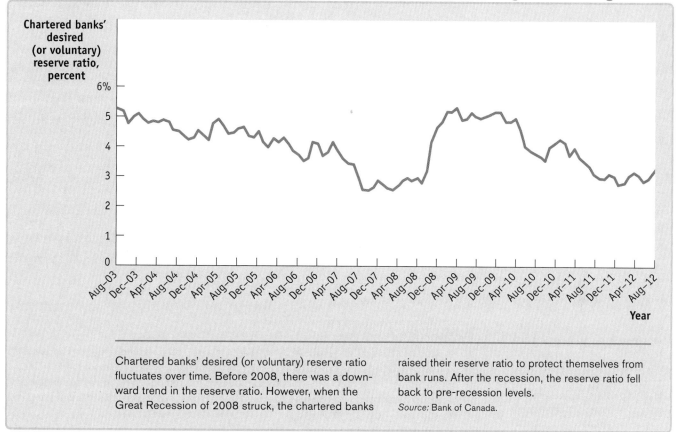

Chartered banks' desired (or voluntary) reserve ratio fluctuates over time. Before 2008, there was a downward trend in the reserve ratio. However, when the Great Recession of 2008 struck, the chartered banks raised their reserve ratio to protect themselves from bank runs. After the recession, the reserve ratio fell back to pre-recession levels.

Source: Bank of Canada.

ECONOMICS ▸ *IN ACTION*

IT'S A WONDERFUL BANKING SYSTEM

Next Christmastime, it's a sure thing that at least one TV channel will show the 1946 film *It's a Wonderful Life,* featuring Jimmy Stewart as George Bailey, a small-town banker whose life is saved by an angel. The movie's climactic scene is a run on Bailey's bank, as fearful depositors rush to take their funds out.

When the movie was made, such scenes were still fresh in Americans' memories. There was a wave of bank runs in late 1930, a second wave in the spring of 1931, and a third wave in early 1933. By the end, more than a third of the nation's banks had failed. To bring the panic to an end, on March 6, 1933, the newly inaugurated president, Franklin Delano Roosevelt, declared a national "bank holiday," closing all banks for a week to give bank regulators time to close unhealthy banks and certify healthy ones.

Since then, regulation has protected the United States and other wealthy countries against most bank runs. In fact, the scene in *It's a Wonderful Life* was already out of date when the movie was made. But recent decades have seen several waves

In July 2008, panicky IndyMac depositors lined up to pull their money out of the troubled California bank.

of bank runs in developing countries. For example, bank runs played a role in an economic crisis that swept Southeast Asia in 1997–1998 and in the severe economic crisis in Argentina that began in late 2001. And as will be explained in Chapter 17, a "panic" with strong resemblance to a wave of bank runs swept world financial markets in 2008.

Notice that we said "most bank runs." There are some limits on deposit insurance; in particular, in the United States currently only the first US\$250 000 of an individual depositor's funds in an insured bank is covered. As a result, there can still be a run on a bank perceived as troubled. In fact, that's exactly what happened to IndyMac in July 2008, a Pasadena-based lender that had made a large number of questionable home loans. As questions about IndyMac's financial soundness were raised, depositors began pulling out funds, forcing federal regulators to step in and close the bank. In Britain the limits on deposit insurance are much lower than the one in the U.S. (The deposit insurance limit in Britain is £85 000, which is around US\$134 100). This exposed the British bank Northern Rock to a classic bank run, also in 2008. Unlike in the bank runs of the 1930s, however, most depositors at both IndyMac and Northern Rock got all their funds back—and the panics at these banks didn't spread to other institutions.

CHECK YOUR UNDERSTANDING 14-2

1. Suppose you are a depositor at First Street Bank. You hear a rumour that the bank has suffered serious losses on its loans. Every depositor knows that the rumour isn't true, but each thinks that most other depositors believe the rumour. Why, in the absence of deposit insurance, could this lead to a bank run? How does deposit insurance change the situation?

2. A con artist has a great idea: he'll open a bank without investing any capital and lend all the deposits at high interest rates to real estate developers. If the real estate market booms, the loans will be repaid and he'll make high profits. If the real estate market goes bust, the loans won't be repaid and the bank will fail—but he will not lose any of his own wealth. How would modern bank regulation frustrate his scheme?

Solutions appear at back of book.

Determining the Money Supply

Without banks, there would be no chequeable deposits, so the quantity of currency in circulation would equal the money supply. In that case, the money supply would be solely determined by whoever controls government minting and printing presses. But banks do exist, and through their creation of chequeable deposits they affect the money supply in two ways. First, banks remove some currency from circulation: dollar bills that are sitting in bank vaults, as opposed to sitting in people's wallets, aren't part of the money supply. Second, and much more importantly, banks create money by accepting deposits and making loans—that is, they make the money supply larger than just the value of currency in circulation. Our next topic is how banks create money and what determines the amount of money they create.

How Banks Create Money

To see how banks create money, let's examine what happens when someone decides to deposit currency in a bank. Consider the example of Silas, a miser, who keeps a shoebox full of cash under his bed. Suppose Silas realizes that it would be safer, as well as more convenient, to deposit that cash in the bank and to use his debit card when shopping. Assume that he deposits $1000 into a chequeable account at First Street Bank. What effect will Silas's actions have on the money supply?

Figure 14-5a shows the initial effect of his deposit. First Street Bank credits Silas with $1000 in his account, so the economy's chequeable deposits rise by $1000. Meanwhile, Silas's cash goes into the vault, raising First Street's reserves by $1000 as well.

This initial transaction has no effect on the money supply. Currency in circulation, part of the money supply, falls by $1000; chequeable deposits, also part of the money supply, rise by the same amount.

But this is not the end of the story because First Street Bank can now lend out part of Silas's deposit. Assume that it holds 10% of Silas's deposit—$100—in reserves and lends the rest out in cash to Silas's neighbour, Maya. The effect of this second stage is shown in Figure 14-5b. First Street's deposits remain unchanged, and so does the value of its assets. But the composition of its assets changes: by making the loan, it reduces its reserves by $900, so that they are only $100 larger than they were before Silas made his deposit. In the place of the $900 reduction in reserves, the bank has acquired an IOU, its $900 cash loan to Maya.

So by putting $900 of Silas's cash back into circulation by lending it to Maya, First Street Bank has, in fact, increased the money supply. That is, the sum of currency in circulation and chequeable deposits has risen by $900 compared to what it had been when Silas's cash was still under his bed. Although Silas is still the owner of $1000, now in the form of a chequeable deposit, Maya has the use of $900 in cash from her borrowings.

And this may not be the end of the story. Suppose that Maya uses her cash to buy a television and a DVD player from Acme Merchandise. What does Anne Acme, the store's owner, do with the cash? If she holds on to it, the money supply doesn't increase any further. But suppose she deposits the $900 into a chequeable deposit— say, at Second Street Bank. Second Street Bank, in turn, will keep only part of that deposit in reserves, lending out the rest, creating still more money.

Assume that Second Street Bank, like First Street Bank, keeps 10% of any bank deposit in reserves and lends out the rest. Then it will keep $90 in reserves and lend out $810 of Anne's deposit to another borrower, further increasing the money supply.

Table 14-1 shows the process of money creation we have described so far. At first the money supply consists only of Silas's $1000. After he deposits the

FIGURE 14-5   Effect on the Money Supply of Turning Cash into a Deposit at First Street Bank

(a) Initial Effect Before Bank Makes a New Loan		(b) Effect When Bank Makes a New Loan	
Assets	**Liabilities and Equity**	**Assets**	**Liabilities and Equity**
Loans No change	Chequeable deposits +$1000	Loans +$900	No change
Reserves +$1000	Equity No change	Reserves –$900	Equity No change

When Silas deposits $1000 (which had been stashed under his bed) into a chequeable bank account, there is initially no effect on the money supply: currency in circulation falls by $1000, but chequeable deposits rise by $1000. The corresponding entries on the bank's T-account, depicted in panel (a), show deposits initially rising by $1000 and the bank's reserves initially rising by $1000. In the second stage, depicted in panel (b), the bank holds 10% of Silas's deposit ($100) as reserves and lends out the rest ($900) to Maya. As a result, its reserves fall by $900 and its loans increase by $900. Its liabilities, including Silas's $1000 deposit, are unchanged. The money supply, the sum of chequeable deposits and currency in circulation, has now increased by $900—the $900 now held by Maya.

TABLE 14-1   **How Banks Create Money**

	Currency in circulation	Chequeable deposits	Money supply
First stage: Silas keeps his cash under his bed.	$1000	$0	$1000
Second stage: Silas deposits cash in First Street Bank, which lends out $900 to Maya, who then pays it to Anne Acme.	900	1000	1900
Third stage: Anne Acme deposits $900 in Second Street Bank, which lends out $810 to another borrower.	810	1900	2710

cash into a chequeable deposit and the bank makes a loan, the money supply rises to $1900. After the second deposit and the second loan, the money supply rises to $2710. And the process will, of course, continue from there. (Although we have considered the case in which Silas places his cash in a chequeable deposit, the results would be the same if he put it into any type of near-money.)

This process of money creation may sound familiar. In Chapter 11 we described the *multiplier process:* an initial increase in real GDP leads to a rise in consumer spending, which leads to a further rise in real GDP, which leads to a further rise in consumer spending, and so on. What we have here is another kind of multiplier—the *money multiplier*. Next, we'll learn what determines the size of this multiplier.

Reserves, Bank Deposits, and the Money Multiplier

In tracing out the effect of Silas's deposit in Table 14-1, we assumed that the funds a bank lends out always end up being deposited either in the same bank or in another bank—so funds disbursed as loans come back to the banking system, even if not to the lending bank itself.

In reality, some of these loaned funds may be held by borrowers in their wallets and not deposited in a bank, meaning that some of the loaned amount "leaks" out of the banking system. Such leaks reduce the size of the money multiplier, just as leaks of real income into savings reduce the size of the real GDP multiplier. (Bear in mind, however, that the "leak" here comes from the fact that borrowers keep some of their funds in currency, rather than the fact that consumers save some of their income.)

But let's set that complication aside for a moment and consider how the money supply is determined in a "chequeable-deposits-only" monetary system, where funds are always deposited in bank accounts and none are held in wallets as currency. That is, in our chequeable-deposits-only monetary system, any and all funds borrowed from a bank are immediately deposited into a chequeable bank account. We'll assume that banks have a desired (or voluntary) reserve ratio of 10% and that every bank lends out all of its **excess reserves,** reserves over and above the amount needed to satisfy the desired reserve ratio.

Now suppose that for some reason a bank suddenly finds itself with $1000 in excess reserves. What happens? The answer is that the bank will lend out that $1000, which will end up as a chequeable deposit somewhere in the banking system, launching a money multiplier process very similar to the process shown in Table 14-1.

In the first stage, the bank lends out its excess reserves of $1000, which becomes a chequeable deposit somewhere. The bank that receives the $1000 deposit keeps 10%, or $100, as reserves and lends out the remaining 90%, or $900, which again becomes a chequeable deposit somewhere. The bank receiving this $900 deposit again keeps 10%, which is $90, as reserves and lends out the remaining $810. The bank receiving this $810 keeps $81 in reserves and lends out the remaining $729, and so on. As a result of this process, the total increase in chequeable deposits is equal to a sum that looks like:

$$\$1000 + \$900 + \$810 + \$729 + \dots$$

Excess reserves are a bank's reserves over and above its desired reserves.

We'll use the symbol rr for the reserve ratio. More generally, the total increase in chequeable deposits that is generated when a bank lends out $1000 in excess reserves is:

(14-1) Increase in chequeable deposits from $1000 in excess reserves =
$1000 + ($1000 \times (1 - rr)) + ($1000 \times (1 - rr)^2) + ($1000 \times (1 - rr)^3) + \ldots$

As we saw in Chapter 11, an infinite series of this form can be simplified to:

(14-2) Increase in chequeable deposits from $1000 in excess reserves =
$1000/$$rr$

Given a reserve ratio of 10%, or 0.1, a $1000 increase in excess reserves will increase the total value of chequeable deposits by $1000/0.1 = $10 000. In fact, in a chequeable-deposits-only monetary system, the total value of chequeable deposits will be equal to the value of bank reserves divided by the reserve ratio. Or to put it a different way, if the reserve ratio is 10%, each $1 of reserves held by a bank supports $1/$$rr$ = $1/0.1 = $10 of chequeable deposits.

The Money Multiplier in Reality

In reality, the determination of the money supply is more complicated than our simple model suggests because it depends not only on the ratio of reserves to bank deposits but also on the fraction of the money supply that individuals choose to hold in the form of currency. In fact, we already saw this in our example of Silas depositing the cash under his bed: when he chose to hold a chequeable deposit instead of currency, he set in motion an increase in the money supply.

To define the money multiplier in practice, it's important to recognize that the Bank of Canada controls the *sum* of bank reserves and currency in circulation, called the *monetary base*, but it does not control the allocation of that sum between bank reserves and currency in circulation. Consider Silas and his deposit one more time: by taking the cash from under his bed and depositing it in a bank, he reduced the quantity of currency in circulation but increased bank reserves by an equal amount—leaving the *monetary base*, on net, unchanged. The **monetary base,** which is the quantity the monetary authorities control, is the sum of currency in circulation and reserves held by banks.

The monetary base is different from the money supply in two ways. First, bank reserves, which are part of the monetary base, aren't considered part of the money supply. A $10 bill in someone's wallet is considered money because it's available for an individual to spend, but a $10 bill held as bank reserves in a bank vault or deposited at the Bank of Canada isn't considered part of the money supply because it's not available for spending. Second, chequeable deposits, which are part of the money supply because they are available for spending, aren't part of the monetary base.

Figure 14-6 shows the two concepts schematically. The circle on the left represents the monetary base, consisting of bank reserves plus currency in circulation. The circle on the right represents the money supply, consisting mainly of currency in circulation plus chequeable or near-chequeable deposits. As the figure indicates, currency in circulation is part of both the monetary base and the money supply. But bank reserves aren't part of the money supply, and chequeable or near-chequeable deposits aren't part of the monetary base. In practice, most of the monetary base actually consists of currency in circulation, which also makes up about half of the money supply.

Now we can formally define the **money multiplier:** it's the ratio of the money supply to the monetary base. The (actual) money multiplier in Canada, using M1 as our measure of money, has fluctuated between 6.1 and 9.1 from August 2003 to August 2012, with the average being 7.3. On the other hand, using M2+ as our

The **monetary base** is the sum of currency in circulation and bank reserves.

The **money multiplier** is the ratio of the money supply to the monetary base.

FIGURE **14-6** The Monetary Base and the Money Supply

The monetary base is equal to bank reserves plus currency in circulation. It is different from the money supply, consisting mainly of chequeable or near-chequeable deposits plus currency in circulation. Each dollar of bank reserves backs several dollars of bank deposits, making the money supply larger than the monetary base.

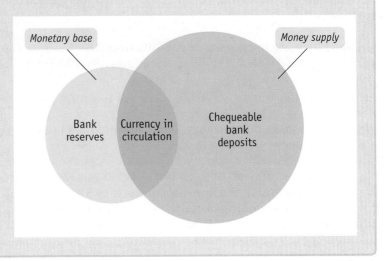

measure of the money supply, during this period, the money multiplier fluctuated between 18.9 and 22.8, with the average being 20.7. How do these numbers compare with our money multiplier formula? The voluntary reserve ratio in Canada during the same time horizon was about 0.04 (i.e., 4%). That implies a money multiplier in a chequeable-deposits-only system of 1/.04, or 25. (Since there is no required reserve ratio, this is the ratio of reserves to deposits that banks desire to hold.) To be precise, that number should be interpreted as the maximum (potential) change in money supply when there is a unit change in monetary base. In this case, with a voluntary reserve ratio of 4%, a unit increase in monetary base will lead to a maximum increase in money supply of 25. As you can see, the actual money multiplier is small because people hold significant amounts of cash, and a dollar of currency in circulation, unlike a dollar in reserves, doesn't support multiple dollars of the money supply. In fact, currency in circulation normally accounts for more than 90% of the monetary base.

That describes what happened during normal times, when the economy was not in a crisis. But during "abnormal" times, the money multiplier can fall dramatically. Take the U.S. as an example. Usually the money multiplier in the United States, using M1 as the measure of money, fluctuates between 1.5 and 3.0. During the U.S. recession of 2007–2009, it fell to about 0.7. What happened? As we explain later in this chapter, and at greater length in Chapter 17, a very abnormal situation developed when Lehman Brothers, a key financial institution in the U.S., failed in September 2008. The American banks, seeing few opportunities for safe, profitable lending, began parking large sums at the Federal Reserve, the U.S. central bank, in the form of deposits—deposits that counted as part of the monetary base. As a result, currency in circulation in January 2012 made up only 40% of the monetary base, and in 2011 the monetary base was actually larger than M1, with the money multiplier therefore less than 1.

ECONOMICS ▷ *IN ACTION*

MULTIPLYING MONEY DOWN

In our hypothetical example illustrating how banks create money, we described Silas the miser taking the currency from under his bed and turning it into a chequeable deposit. This led to an increase in the money supply, as banks engaged in successive waves of lending backed by Silas's funds. It follows that if something happened to make Silas revert to old habits, taking his money out of the bank and putting it back under his bed, the result would be less lending and, ultimately, a decline in the money supply. That's exactly what happened as a result of the bank runs of the 1930s in the U.S.

Table 14-2 shows what happened between 1929 and 1933, as bank failures shook the public's confidence in the American banking system. The second column shows the public's holdings of currency. This increased sharply, as many Americans decided that money under the bed was safer than money in the bank after all. The third column shows the value of chequeable deposits. This fell sharply, through the multiplier process we have just analyzed, when individuals pulled their cash out of banks. Loans also fell because banks that survived the waves of bank runs increased their excess reserves, just in case another wave began. The fourth column shows the value of M1, the first of the monetary aggregates we described earlier. It fell sharply because the total reduction in chequeable or near-chequeable deposits was much larger than the increase in currency in circulation.

TABLE 14-2 The Effects of U.S. Bank Runs, 1929–1933

	Currency in circulation	Chequeable deposits	M1
	(billions of dollars)		
1929	$3.90	$22.74	$26.64
1933	5.09	14.82	19.91
Percent change	+31%	−35%	−25%

Source: U.S. Census Bureau (1975), *Historical Statistics of the United States.*

CHECK YOUR UNDERSTANDING 14-3

1. Assume that total reserves are equal to $200 and total chequeable deposits are equal to $1000. Also assume that the public does not hold any currency. Now suppose that the required reserve ratio falls from 20% to 10%. Trace out how this leads to an expansion in bank deposits.

2. Take the example of Silas depositing his $1000 in cash into First Street Bank and assume that the required reserve ratio is 10%. But now assume that each time someone receives a bank loan, he or she keeps half the loan in cash. Trace out the resulting expansion in the money supply.

Solutions appear at back of book.

▼ Quick Review

- Banks create money when they lend out **excess reserves,** generating a multiplier effect on the money supply.

- In a chequeable-deposits-only system, the money supply would be equal to bank reserves divided by the reserve ratio. In reality, however, the public holds some funds as cash rather than in chequeable deposits, which reduces the size of the multiplier.

- The **monetary base,** equal to bank reserves plus currency in circulation, overlaps but is not equal to the money supply. The **money multiplier** is equal to the money supply divided by the monetary base.

Central Banks

Who decides how large the monetary base will be? For all developed economies, the answer is the **central bank**—an institution that oversees and regulates the banking system and controls the monetary base. Canada's central bank is the Bank of Canada. Other central banks include the Bank of England; the Federal Reserve, of the United States; the Bank of Japan; and the European Central Bank (ECB). The ECB acts as a common central bank for 17 European countries: Austria, Belgium, Cyprus, Estonia, Finland, France, Germany, Greece, Ireland, Italy, Luxembourg, Malta, the Netherlands, Portugal, Slovakia, Slovenia, and Spain. The world's oldest central bank, by the way, is Sweden's Sveriges Riksbank, which awards the Nobel Prize in economics.

The Functions of a Central Bank

In some ways, central banks are just like ordinary banks: they accept deposits and give loans; they have assets and liabilities; and generally they make a profit. But unlike commercial banks, their clientele are not members of the public—central banks allow only domestic commercial banks and the government to open accounts with them. Also, unlike commercial banks, the objective of a central bank is to maximize the national interest, rather than to maximize its profits. A central bank has four main duties: to act as the bankers' bank (the bank for

A **central bank** is an institution that oversees and regulates the banking system and controls the monetary base.

commercial banks); to act as the government's bank; to issue currency; and to conduct monetary policy. We'll discuss these duties in more detail, but first let's consider them in relation to the Bank of Canada, by looking at the BOC's assets and liabilities, as shown in Table 14-3.

TABLE **14-3** The Bank of Canada's Assets and Liabilities, December 2011

Assets ($ millions)		Liabilities and equity ($ millions)	
Government of Canada bonds	$62 098.9	Banknotes in circulation	$61 028.8
Advances to commercial banks	81.5	Government of Canada deposits	1 512.5
Other short-term loans	1 447.7	Deposits of commercial banks	968.5
Foreign currency assets	11.7	Other liabilities	312.8
Other assets	607.4	Equity	424.6
Total assets	64 247.2	Total liabilities and equity	64 247.2

Source: Bank of Canada, Annual Report, 2011.

As with other central banks, the Bank of Canada accepts deposits from, and makes loans to, both the federal government and domestic commercial banks. Deposits from commercial banks are part of the Bank of Canada's reserves. The BOC makes loans to both the government and the commercial banks by buying government bonds. Its greatest asset is Government of Canada bonds and its greatest liability is banknotes in circulation. The sum of the banknotes in circulation and deposits of commercial banks is the monetary base.

The following is a more detailed description of the central bank's four major responsibilities.

1. The Central Bank Acts as Banker for Commercial Banks

Just as you find it convenient to put your money in a bank and to write cheques on that account, so do commercial banks. Depositing cash with the central bank rather than holding cash reserves in their own vaults has another advantage for commercial banks: the central bank will, on order, transfer money from one bank's account to the account of another bank. In this way, commercial bank accounts with the central bank can be used to settle large debts between the commercial banks with a single keystroke. The third row on the right side of Table 14-3 shows that the deposits of commercial banks with the Bank of Canada amounted to $968.5 million in December 2011. This money constitutes an asset owned by the commercial banks—indeed, it is part of their reserves—but it is a liability of the central bank because it promises to pay them on demand.

As banker for the commercial banks, a central bank is also committed to keeping the banking system stable. A central bank will normally act as a "lender of last resort" for a commercial bank with sound investments that is in urgent need of cash and cannot find a lender. More generally, a central bank will loan money on a daily basis to a commercial bank that is short of cash reserves, at a rate known as the bank rate. For example, the second row on the left side of Table 14-3 shows that in December 2011 the Bank of Canada lent $81.5 million to commercial banks for this reason. At the same time, the Bank of Canada made $1447.7 million in short-term loans to these institutions—at a rate known as *the overnight rate*.

2. The Central Bank Acts as Banker for the Federal Government

The federal government also finds it convenient to put its money in a bank and to write cheques on that account. The second row on the right side of Table 14-3 shows that in December 2011, the federal government had $1512.5 million in its chequing account with the Bank of Canada. The federal government also has demand deposits at the large commercial banks, and it is the job of the Bank of Canada to manage these government bank accounts. When the government needs to borrow money, does the central bank lend it money? Yes, occasionally, but not always. When the government needs to borrow money it issues government securities—either short-term treasury bills or longer-term bonds. Occasionally, the Bank of Canada will buy some of these securities and credit the government's account for the amount of the purchase. The top row on the left side of Table 14-3 shows that in December 2011 the Bank of Canada held just over $62 billion in Government of Canada bonds. These bonds are a liability for the government and an asset for the Bank of Canada.

3. The Central Bank Issues Currency It is a central bank's duty to issue currency, prevent counterfeiting, and ensure that the supply of banknotes meets public demand. The top row on the right side of Table 14-3 shows that in December 2011 there were just over $61 billion in banknotes in circulation. These notes are a liability of the Bank of Canada. Before 1940, this liability was clear because these notes could be exchanged for gold. Even though that exchange is no longer in force, the Bank of Canada still has the duty to maintain the viability of these notes as legal tender.

4. The Central Bank Conducts Monetary Policy A central bank has the duty to conduct the nation's monetary policy. This may involve controlling interest rates, the quantity of money, the exchange rate, or some combination of these actions. Since the central bank may occasionally intervene in foreign exchange markets to moderate fluctuations in the value of the Canadian dollar, it needs to hold some foreign currency. Before September 1998, the Bank of Canada's policy was to automatically intervene in the foreign exchange market whenever the Canadian dollar came under significant upward or downward pressure. The BOC also undertook other interventions at its discretion whenever conditions merited it. The Asian financial crisis of 1997 created significant downward pressure on a number of currencies, and not just those of Asian countries. Countries that supplied commodities to these growing Asian countries, such as Canada, found their currencies caught in the downdraft. This contributed to the 1998 Russian financial crisis and default on Russian debt, which in turn caused the failure of the U.S. hedge fund Long-Term Capital Management (LTCM), whose story is highlighted later in this chapter. These developments created significant volatility for the Canadian dollar, too. In response, from mid-1997 until September 1998, the Bank of Canada undertook discretionary interventions in the Canadian dollar to U.S. dollar exchange market on about 25% of all business days. In September 1998, this policy of intervening was altered so that Canada would no longer intervene systematically, but only in exceptional circumstances.[4] The last time the Bank of Canada intervened to influence the Canadian dollar exchange rate was September 1998. The fourth row on the left side of Table 14-3 shows that in December 2011 the Bank of Canada held $11.7 million worth of foreign currency assets.

The Structure of the Bank of Canada

Now we know what central banks do, the next question is "Who controls them?" While all central banks are owned by their governments, most have a degree of autonomy from their government, essentially because it is desirable to separate the power to spend (which the government has) from the power to print money (which the central bank has).

---

[4]According to the Bank of Canada, "intervention might be considered if there were signs of a serious near-term market breakdown (e.g., extreme price volatility with buyers or sellers increasingly unwilling to transact), indicating a severe lack of liquidity in the Canadian-dollar market. It might also be considered if extreme currency movements seriously threatened the conditions that support sustainable long-term growth of the Canadian economy, with the goal of helping to stabilize the currency and to signal a commitment to back up the intervention with further policy actions, as necessary." *Source:* "Backgrounder: Intervention in the Foreign Exchange Market, Bank of Canada, March 2011," www.bankofcanada.ca/wp-content/uploads/2010/11/intervention_foreign_exchange.pdf.

With respect to the Bank of Canada, legally it is a crown corporation owned by the government. As such, any profit it makes is remitted to the government. But despite being owned by the government, it is far from being a typical government department. Just like most central banks, the Bank of Canada is a partially independent institution with considerable autonomy to carry out its responsibilities. This partial autonomy is reflected in its institutional structure.

The Bank of Canada's chief executive officer—the governor—is a government employee and can be fired by the government. But because the governor is appointed for a seven-year term, he or she is insulated from short-term political pressures. The governor and five deputy governors form the Governing Council, and it is this body that implements Canada's monetary policy. All the operations of the Bank of Canada are overseen by a Board of Directors that consists of the governor, the senior deputy governor, the deputy minister of finance (who has no vote), and 12 outside directors drawn from across the country. It is this Board of Directors that appoints the governor of the BOC—not the government.

As we said, the Bank of Canada is only partially autonomous: the government still has considerable influence over it. The minister of finance appoints all members of the Board of Directors, and the federal cabinet must approve the governor's appointment. Also, the minister of finance meets with the governor regularly to express the government's desires regarding monetary policy. If a disagreement over policy occurs, the government can issue written instructions to the governor. If the governor feels these instructions are inappropriate and does not wish to implement them, then the governor must resign (or be fired).

Ultimately, the governor's real power rests with the threat of his or her resignation. When a respected central banker resigns, the world takes notice. Everyone will suspect the government of trying to force unsound and inappropriate monetary policies onto its central bank. In itself this would cause considerable financial uncertainty. The governor of the BOC can use this power to influence monetary policy.

Central Banks' Tools of Monetary Control

In general, central banks have four main tools for monetary control at their disposal: *reserve requirements*, the *bank rate* (or the *discount rate*), *open-market operations*, and *government deposit switching*.

Reserve Requirements Reserve requirements influence how much money the banking system can create with each dollar of reserves. If reserve requirements increase, banks can loan out less of each dollar that is deposited. This lowers the money multiplier and decreases the money supply. Many countries, such as Russia and Turkey, do have reserve requirements, but as noted earlier, Canadian banks do not. As a result, they hold amounts that are consistent with their desire to maximize profits and their experience of sound banking practice. Currently, the voluntary reserve ratio of Canadian banks is around 4%, and on occasions even lower.

The Bank Rate Occasionally, Canadian banks will find themselves short of reserves. On any given day individuals and firms write a great many cheques to finance their purchases. When these cheques are cleared at the end of the day, some banks may gain deposits and some may lose. As we discussed above, settlements between commercial banks can be made with a single keystroke by the Bank of Canada.

But what happens if a commercial bank doesn't have enough in its deposit account with the Bank of Canada to settle its debts? Normally, a bank will borrow additional reserves from other banks. Banks lend money to each other in the *overnight funds market*, at the *overnight rate of interest*. The **overnight funds market** is a financial market that allows banks to borrow reserves

The **overnight funds market** is a financial market in which financial institutions, such as banks that are short of reserves can borrow funds from banks with excess reserves.

from each other, usually just overnight. The interest rate in this market is called the **overnight rate** and is determined by supply and demand, both of which are strongly affected by Bank of Canada actions. As we'll discuss in Chapter 15, the BOC has a *target for the overnight rate* called (appropriately enough) the **target for the overnight rate.** The BOC tries to ensure that the overnight rate stays within a band of half a percentage point of its target; that is, the overnight rate could be a quarter of a percentage point above or below the target. As we'll see in the following Economics in Action, the BOC tends to hit its target almost precisely.

If a bank cannot borrow from other banks in the overnight funds market, it can always borrow from the Bank of Canada, at the *bank rate*. The **bank rate** (or the **discount rate** in some countries) is the rate of interest the BOC charges banks. The bank rate is set as the upper limit of the BOC's operating band for the target for the overnight rate. So, the bank rate is one quarter of a percentage point above the target for the overnight rate.

Incidentally, the lower limit of the BOC's operating band for the overnight rate target is the rate of interest it pays to commercial banks on their accounts (at the BOC). Figure 14-7 illustrates the relationship between the overnight rate, its target, and the upper and lower limits of the band.

If it chooses to do so, the Bank of Canada can change the target for the overnight rate (which would also change the bank rate) and so affect the money supply. If the Bank of Canada were to reduce the target for the overnight rate, banks would increase their lending because the cost of finding themselves short of reserves wouldn't be as high, and as a result the money supply would increase. If the Bank of Canada were to increase the target for the overnight rate, bank lending would fall, as would the money supply.

Nowadays, the target for the overnight rate is the Bank of Canada's main monetary policy tool. When the BOC changes this target, it is sending a clear signal about the direction in which it wants short-term interest rates to go. These changes usually lead to movements in the prime rate at commercial banks, which serves as a benchmark for many commercial bank loans. However, as we'll discuss in the next chapter, influencing the overnight rate involves a bit more than just announcing targets. The BOC will take various *open-market operations* to ensure the overnight rate stays very close to its announced target. An **open-market operation** occurs when a central bank buys or sells assets. In the case of the BOC, these assets are usually Government of Canada bonds, but they may also be foreign exchange.

The **overnight rate** is the interest rate determined in the overnight funds market.

The **target for the overnight rate** is the Bank of Canada's official key policy interest rate.

The **bank rate** is the rate of interest the Bank of Canada charges on loans to banks. In many countries, this rate of interest is known as the **discount rate.**

An **open-market operation** is the purchase or sale of assets by a central bank. For the Bank of Canada, normally these assets are Government of Canada bonds, but they may also be foreign exchange.

FIGURE **14-7** **Example of the Bank of Canada's Operating Band**

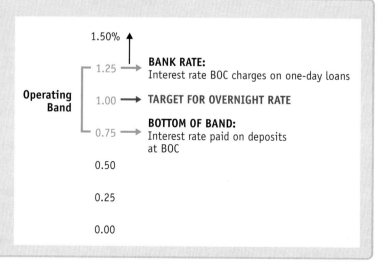

The Bank of Canada's declared policy is to ensure that the actual overnight rate stays within an operating band that is half a percentage point wide and centred at its target rate. The upper limit of the BOC's operating band is the bank rate, which is one quarter of a percentage point above the target for the overnight rate. The lower limit of the BOC's operating band for the overnight rate target is the rate of interest it pays to commercial banks on their accounts. This example shows the operating band when the target for the overnight rate is set at 1%.

Open-Market Operations

Another method central banks use to manage the money supply is open-market operations: central bank purchases and sales of government bonds on the open markets. Refer back to Table 14-3, which shows the Bank of Canada's assets and liabilities. The BOC's most important asset is Government of Canada bonds, which represent 96.6% of its assets. The monetary base consists of two liabilities: currency (banknotes) in circulation and bank reserves (either currency held in bank vaults or commercial bank deposits with the Bank of Canada). Together, these two items constitute 96% of the BOC's liabilities and 100% of the monetary base. Given that most of the BOC's assets and liabilities are treasury bills and monetary base respectively, we can simplify the assets and liabilities of the BOC shown in Table 14-3 into Figure 14-8. When the BOC pursues open-market operations, these transactions will have a direct effect on the monetary base. Let's consider the following examples.

FIGURE **14-8** The BOC's Assets and Liabilities – A Simplified Version

The Bank of Canada holds its assets mostly in short-term government bonds called treasury bills. Its liabilities are the monetary base— currency in circulation plus bank reserves.

Assets	Liabilities
Treasury bills	Monetary base (currency in circulation + bank reserves)

Suppose the Bank of Canada buys $100 million in bonds. It can pay for them using cash if it buys the bonds from the public, in which case banknotes in circulation increase by $100 million. If it buys the bonds from commercial banks, it can credit their accounts at the BOC by $100 million (i.e., bank reserves increase by $100 million). Either way, the monetary base has increased by $100 million. As seen in the previous section, this increases the money supply by a multiple of this $100 million and will shift the aggregate demand curve to the right.

Now let's have a more specific example. Suppose the Bank of Canada buys the bonds from the Bank of Montreal and pays for them by crediting the Bank of Montreal's account at the Bank of Canada with $100 million. Figure 14-9a shows the resulting changes in the financial positions of both institutions. The top of the figure shows the Bank of Canada now has $100 million more assets, consisting of government bonds, and $100 million more in liabilities, consisting of deposits owned by commercial banks—in this case, the Bank of Montreal. The bottom of the figure shows that the Bank of Montreal has reduced its bond holdings by $100 million and increased its reserves by $100 million.

Up to this point the money supply hasn't been affected. However, the Bank of Montreal now has additional reserves. Since the Bank of Montreal earns more from lending money out to clients than having it sit in its account with the Bank of Canada, it will loan this money out. Suppose it loans all of the money. Then, the Bank of Montreal will credit individuals' accounts by an extra $100 million, which they will eventually spend. Some of this money will be deposited back in the banking system, increasing reserves again and permitting a further round of loans, and so on. So an open-market purchase of bonds sets the money multiplier in motion, leading to a rise in the money supply.

Would the process differ if the Bank of Canada bought the bonds from a private individual using cash? Not substantively. The changes to the Bank of Canada's balance sheet would be almost identical. Its assets and liabilities would both increase by $100 million. The only slight difference is that on the liability side of the ledger it would be "banknotes in circulation" that increase by $100 million rather than "deposits of commercial banks." At this point the money supply

FIGURE 14-9 Open-Market Operations by the Bank of Canada

(a) An Open-Market Purchase of $100 Million

	Assets		Liabilities	
Bank of Canada	Treasury bills	+$100 million	Monetary base	+$100 million

	Assets		Liabilities
Bank of Montreal	Treasury bills	−$100 million	No change
	Reserves	+$100 million	

(b) An Open-Market Sale of $100 Million

	Assets		Liabilities	
Bank of Canada	Treasury bills	−$100 million	Monetary base	−$100 million

	Assets		Liabilities
Bank of Montreal	Treasury bills	+$100 million	No change
	Reserves	−$100 million	

In panel (a), the Bank of Canada increases the monetary base by purchasing treasury bills from the Bank of Montreal in an open-market operation. Here, a $100 million purchase of treasury bills by the Bank of Canada is paid for by a $100 million addition to private bank reserves, generating a $100 million increase in the monetary base. This will ultimately lead to an increase in the money supply via the money multiplier as banks lend out some of these new reserves. In panel (b), the Bank of Canada reduces the monetary base by selling treasury bills to the Bank of Montreal in an open-market operation. Here, a $100 million sale of treasury bills by the Bank of Canada leads to a $100 million reduction in private bank reserves, resulting in a $100 million decrease in the monetary base. This will ultimately lead to a fall in the money supply via the money multiplier as banks reduce their loans in response to a fall in their reserves.

has increased by $100 million. However, as soon as the private individual deposits the money in a commercial bank, that bank will find that its deposits and reserves have both increased by $100 million. Apart from the size of the deposit, this process is identical to that described in Table 14-1. In just the same way, the money multiplier process is again set in motion.

Conversely, as Figure 14-9b shows, an open-market sale of bonds by the Bank of Canada has the reverse effect: bank reserves fall, requiring banks to reduce their loans and leading to a fall in the money supply.

Open-Market Operations and the Foreign Exchange Market It is important to understand that it doesn't really matter what asset the Bank of Canada buys or sells when it conducts open-market operations. Instead of buying bonds, the Bank of Canada could just as easily buy $1 million worth of office furniture, using freshly printed banknotes to pay for it. In this case, on the asset side of its balance sheet, other assets (office furniture) would increase by $1 million; and on the liabilities side of its balance sheet, "notes in circulation" would increase by $1 million. When this cash is deposited in commercial banks, a multiple expansion of the money supply is again set in motion.

Of course, the Bank of Canada doesn't often buy (or sell) office furniture. However, there is one other asset (besides bonds) that it does sometimes buy and sell, and that is foreign currency. Suppose the Canadian dollar is appreciating (increasing in value) relative to the U.S. dollar, and this increase is affecting our exports negatively. To prevent the Canadian dollar from appreciating further, the BOC would sell Canadian dollars on the foreign exchange market, receiving foreign currency in exchange. In effect, the BOC is buying foreign currency using Canadian dollars. The BOC's balance sheet would show an increase in assets, in the form of foreign currency, and an increase in liability in the form of banknotes

FOR INQUIRING MINDS

WHO GETS THE INTEREST ON THE BANK OF CANADA'S ASSETS?

As we've just learned, the Bank of Canada owns a lot of assets—mostly treasury bills—that it bought from commercial banks and the federal government in exchange for the monetary base in the form of credits to banks' reserves and government accounts. These assets pay interest. Yet the Bank of Canada's liabilities consist mainly of the monetary base, primarily in the form of banknotes in circulation—liabilities on which the BOC normally doesn't pay interest. So the BOC can, in effect, borrow funds at zero interest and lend them out at a positive interest rate. If that sounds like a pretty profitable business, it's because it is. So who gets the profits?

The answer is, you do—or rather, Canadian taxpayers do. The BOC keeps some of the interest to finance its operations but turns most of it over to the Receiver General of Canada. For example, in 2011 the BOC received $1621 million in interest income (most of it in interest on its holdings of treasury bills), of which $1156 million was returned to the federal government.

We can now finish the chapter's opening story—the impact of those forged $20 bills. When a fake $20 bill enters circulation, it has the same economic effect as a real $20 bill printed by the Canadian government. That is, as long as nobody catches the forgery, the fake bill serves, for all practical purposes, as part of the monetary base.

Meanwhile, the BOC decides on the size of the monetary base based on economic considerations—in particular, the BOC doesn't let the monetary base get too large because that can cause higher inflation. So every fake $20 bill that enters circulation basically means that the BOC prints one less real $20 bill. When the BOC prints a $20 bill legally, however, it gets treasury bills in return—and the interest on those bills helps pay for the Canadian government's expenses. So a counterfeit $20 bill reduces the amount of treasury bills the BOC can acquire and thereby reduces the interest payments going to the BOC and the Receiver General of Canada. Taxpayers, then, bear the real cost of counterfeiting.

in circulation. Since Canada is the only place where these Canadian dollars can be spent, they will eventually find their way into the deposits of commercial banks, leading to a multiple expansion of the money supply. In effect, the BOC has made an open-market purchase of foreign exchange. Whatever asset the BOC buys (bonds, furniture, or foreign exchange), the operation results in a multiple expansion of the money supply.

In contrast, suppose the BOC wishes to prevent the Canadian dollar from depreciating (decreasing in value). Then it would buy Canadian dollars on the foreign exchange market using its foreign currency reserves. Since the Canadian dollars it buys are no longer in private use, the monetary base is reduced. The BOC's balance sheet side would show a decrease in assets in the form of foreign currency, and a decrease in liability in the form of banknotes in circulation. In effect, the Bank of Canada has made an open-market sale that will lead to a multiple contraction of the money supply. Again, it doesn't matter what asset the Bank of Canada sells: bonds, furniture, or foreign exchange. All of them lead to a multiple contraction of the money supply. Note, in real life, the Bank of Canada seldom intervenes in the foreign exchange market to affect the value of the Canadian dollar because of the ineffectiveness in affecting the exchange rate in the face of changes in fundamentals. Nowadays, as noted before, the Bank of Canada's policy on the exchange rate is that it will intervene in the foreign exchange market on a discretionary basis and only in exceptional circumstances.

The key point to all of this is that any attempt the Bank of Canada makes to influence the value of the Canadian dollar necessarily affects the supply of money. An independent monetary policy is possible only when the BOC allows market forces to determine the exchange rate, with no intervention of any sort on its part. Such a policy is called allowing the exchange rate to "float," or a "floating exchange rate." The analogy is to a boat, floating on the sea, buffeted by the waves, moving up and down with the swell.

Similarly, the value of the Canadian dollar, floating on the international exchange market, is buffeted by the forces of demand and supply, appreciating and depreciating as the market sees fit. When the exchange rate is allowed to float, the central bank is under no obligation to make any trades in the foreign exchange market. In this case, open-market operations can be confined to the domestic bond market, and they can be initiated only when domestic monetary policy objectives call for action.

The opposite of a floating exchange rate is a "fixed" exchange rate. When the exchange rate is fixed, the BOC must continually intervene in the foreign exchange market to offset those market forces that would otherwise tend to change the value of the Canadian dollar. It does this through buying and selling foreign currency— through open-market operations in the foreign exchange market. So, if the central bank adopts a fixed exchange rate policy, it loses control over both the timing and magnitude of its open-market operations (those that involve buying and selling foreign currency). Therefore, it also loses control over the domestic monetary base.

We'll talk more about exchange rates in Chapter 19. For now, our bottom line is this: a fixed exchange rate is inconsistent with independent monetary policy. A floating exchange rate is what permits independent monetary policy.

Deposit Switching In addition to open-market operations, the Bank of Canada has another general method for changing the level of reserves in the banking system, called *deposit switching*. As we saw in Table 14-3, the government of Canada holds large deposits at the BOC and at various chartered banks, and it is the Bank of Canada's job to manage these accounts. The BOC can increase or decrease commercial bank reserves by shifting government deposits between itself and the commercial banks. For example, if the BOC were to write cheques on the government accounts that it holds and deposit those cheques into government accounts held with commercial banks, then the commercial bank reserves would be increased. The process used to shift government accounts from the Bank of Canada to the commercial banks, or in the other direction, is called **deposit switching.**

Suppose, for example, that the Bank of Canada transfers $10 million from the government's account at the Bank of Canada to the government's account at the Bank of Nova Scotia. The transactions involved are illustrated in Figure 14-10. From the government's point of view, nothing has changed. However, the Bank of Nova Scotia finds that its deposit liabilities and reserves have each increased by $10 million. With an unchanged desired reserve ratio, the Bank of Nova Scotia will have excess reserves, and will begin expanding its loans and creating more deposit money.

Deposit switching is the shifting of government deposits between the Bank of Canada and the commercial banks. It is a major tool used by the Bank of Canada in its day-to-day operations.

FIGURE 14-10 Deposit Switching Operations by the Bank of Canada

(a) Bank of Canada		(b) Bank of Nova Scotia	
Assets	**Liabilities**	**Assets**	**Liabilities**
No change	Government deposits −$10 million	Reserves +$10 million	Government deposits +$10 million
	Commercial bank deposits +$10 million		

The Bank of Canada can increase or decrease commercial bank reserves by shifting government deposits between itself and the commercial banks. For example, suppose the Bank of Canada writes a $10 million cheque on the government account that it holds, and deposits that cheque into government accounts held with commercial banks, such as the Bank of Nova Scotia. Commercial bank reserves are increased by $10 million, ultimately leading to an increase in the money supply via the money multiplier, as banks lend out some of these new reserves.

Similarly, a switch of government deposits away from chartered banks depletes their reserves—inducing a contraction of loans and so a decrease in the money supply.

Economists often say, loosely, that the Bank of Canada controls the money supply. Actually, it controls only the monetary base. But by increasing or reducing the monetary base, the Bank of Canada can exert a powerful influence on both the money supply and interest rates. This influence is the basis of monetary policy, the subject of our next chapter.

Interest Rate Targets versus Money Supply Targets

In the next chapter, we'll see that all central banks have to make a choice: they can either set the money supply and let the interest rate adjust, or they can set a key interest rate and then adjust the money supply to accommodate the resulting change in desired money holdings. No central bank can set both the money supply and the interest rate independently or simultaneously. But which policy is better?

Currently, the Bank of Canada chooses to set a key interest rate. One reason for this is that the BOC can *influence* the money supply, but not *control* it. In other words, it is possible for the money supply to change without any deliberate change in monetary policy. For example, if households choose to hold more cash, the commercial banks will have less cash to hold as reserves, so the money supply will decrease. Or, if commercial banks feel that the economic environment is too risky, they may choose to increase their desired reserve ratio, and again the money supply will decrease.

FIGURE **14-11** Annual Growth Rates of M1, M2, and M2+, January 1980 to July 2011

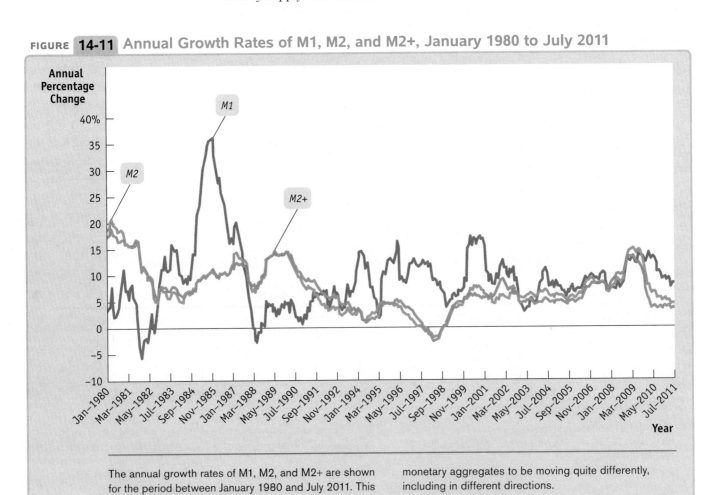

The annual growth rates of M1, M2, and M2+ are shown for the period between January 1980 and July 2011. This shows that, at any given time, it is possible for these monetary aggregates to be moving quite differently, including in different directions.

Source: Statistics Canada.

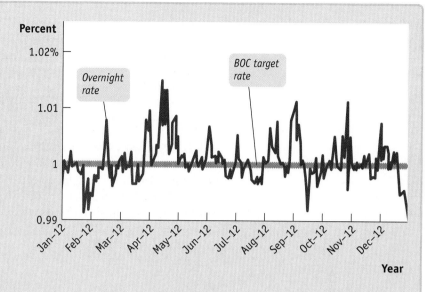

FIGURE 14-12 The Bank of Canada Target Rate and the Overnight Rate, January 3 to December 31, 2012

The Bank of Canada uses open-market operations to make sure that the overnight rate stays close to it target rate. It manages to hit its target extremely accurately. Between January 3 and December 31, 2012, the actual overnight rate differed from its target by one hundredth of a percentage point or less about 98% of the time. It never differed by more than two hundredths of a percentage point.

These reasons explain why, since the late 1980s, the Bank of Canada's policy has been to set a key interest rate rather than set the money supply. An interest rate target has several advantages over a money supply target: it is more easily achieved, and it is more easily explained to and understood by the public.

Source: Bank of Canada.

There is another, more fundamental reason why the BOC can't completely control the money supply: it's not clear what the money supply is. As we have seen, there are several measures of the money supply, including M1, M2, and M2+, which differ in magnitude and in their annual growth rates. At any given time, some measures of the money supply may be increasing, and others may be decreasing. Figure 14-11 shows the annual percentage change in M1, M2, and M2+ from January 1980 to July 2011. It is obvious that, while these different monetary aggregates are highly correlated, their growth rates do not necessarily move together perfectly, let alone even move in the same direction all the time.

But while the BOC may not be able to control the money supply, it can control its key policy interest rate—the overnight rate—almost perfectly. As we have mentioned, the BOC announces a target for the overnight rate and conducts open-market operations in order to keep the overnight rate within an operating band of one quarter of a percentage point above and below that target. As Figure 14-12 shows, the BOC usually hits its target almost precisely. From January 3 to December 31, 2012, the actual overnight rate differed from the target by less than one hundredth of a percentage point about 98% of the time. It never differed from the target by more than two hundredths of a percentage point.

There is another advantage in setting the interest rate instead of the money supply: changes in interest rates tend to be more meaningful to firms and households. For example, if mortgage lending rates at commercial banks have decreased by one percentage point, we can readily understand what this means for our plans to buy a new house. By contrast, if we hear that the money supply has just increased by $5 billion, it is not clear what this means.

ECONOMICS ▸ *IN ACTION*

THE BANK OF CANADA'S BALANCE SHEET, NORMAL AND ABNORMAL

Figure 14-8 showed a simplified version of the BOC's balance sheet. As Figure 14-8 indicated, the liabilities consisted entirely of the monetary base and assets consisted entirely of treasury bills. Of course, in reality, the BOC's balance sheet is much more complicated. But, normally, Figure 14-8 is a reasonable approximation: the monetary base typically accounts for more than 90% of the BOC's liabilities, and almost all its assets are in the form of claims on the Government of Canada (as in Canadian government treasury bills and bonds).

But in late 2007 it became painfully clear that we were no longer in normal times. The source of the turmoil was the bursting of a huge housing bubble in the United States, described in Chapter 10, which led to massive losses for some financial institutions that had made U.S. mortgage loans or held U.S. mortgage-related assets. These losses led to a widespread loss of confidence in the financial system worldwide.

As we'll describe in more detail in the next section, not only standard deposit-taking U.S. banks were in trouble, but also non-depository financial institutions in the U.S.—financial institutions that did not accept customer deposits. Because they carried a lot of debt, faced huge losses from the collapse of the housing bubble, and held illiquid assets, panic hit these "non-bank banks." Within hours, the American financial system was frozen, as financial institutions experienced what were essentially bank runs. For example, early in 2008, many investors became worried about the health of Bear Stearns, a Wall Street non-depository financial institution that engaged in complex financial deals, buying and selling financial assets with borrowed funds. When confidence in Bear Stearns dried up, the firm found itself unable to raise the funds it needed to deliver on its end of these deals and it quickly spiralled into collapse.

The U.S. Federal Reserve (the American central bank, known as "the Fed") sprang into action to contain what was becoming a meltdown across the entire financial sector. It greatly expanded its discount window—making huge loans to deposit-taking banks as well as non-depository financial institutions such as Wall Street financial firms. This gave financial institutions the liquidity that the financial market had now denied them. And as these firms took advantage of the ability to borrow cheaply from the Fed, they pledged their assets on hand as collateral.

As the financial crisis spread around the globe, central banks worldwide found they too faced similar, albeit generally smaller, crises of confidence in their own banks and financial markets. The result was a spread of the freeze-up and liquidity crisis to other nations. These central banks found that they too needed to join the battle, lower their policy interest rates (i.e., bank rates), and increase lending to financial institutions (which increased their money supply). The central banks were forced to supply the liquidity that private markets were afraid to offer so as to avoid the possibility of a complete collapse of world financial markets and the depression this would bring.

Examining Figure 14-13, we see that starting in the fall of 2008, the BOC sharply reduced its holdings of traditional securities like treasury bills, as its lending to financial institutions skyrocketed. "Advances" refer to loans from lenders of last resort made at the bank rate. "Resale agreements" cover purchases by the BOC of assets like mortgages and corporate bonds, which were necessary to keep interest rates on loans to firms from soaring.

By late 2009, the crisis began to subside, but the BOC didn't return to its traditional asset holdings. Instead, it continued to offer substantial amounts of loans via resale agreements throughout much of 2010 and increased its holding of longer-term government debt. The whole episode was very unusual—a major departure from the way in which

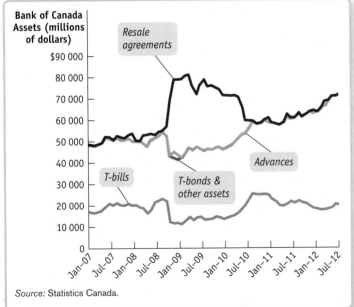

FIGURE 14-13 The Bank of Canada's Assets, 2007–2012

Source: Statistics Canada.

the BOC normally conducts business, but one that it deemed necessary to stave off financial and economic collapse. It was also a graphic illustration of the fact that the BOC does much more than just determine the size of the monetary base.

CHECK YOUR UNDERSTANDING   14-4

1. Assume that any money lent by a bank is always deposited back in the banking system as a chequeable deposit and that the reserve ratio is 10%. Trace out the effects of a $100 million open-market purchase of treasury bills by the Bank of Canada on the value of chequeable deposits. What is the size of the money multiplier?

Solution appears at back of book.

The Evolution of the Canadian Banking System

Up to this point, we have been describing the Canadian banking system[5] and how it works. To fully understand that system, however, it is helpful to understand how and why it was created—a story that is closely intertwined with the story of how and when things went wrong, either here at home or abroad. The twenty-first-century Canadian banking system wasn't created out of thin air; it emerged in response to deeply troubling historical and financial developments, such as global war and depression. This pattern of change in response to negative events has continued. For example, the financial crisis of 2008 has propelled modern financial reform to the forefront and opened the discussion about change to both the regulations that govern banking and the Bank of Canada. This discussion promises to continue reshaping the financial system well into future years.

The First World War—An Early Crisis in Canadian Banking

Many Canadians are aware that Canada "came of age" during World War I (1914–1918). This phrase usually refers to Canada's military and political contribution to the war effort. What is less well known is how Canada matured financially at this time.

Before World War I, Canada was on the gold standard, a complex fixed exchange rate arrangement in which member nations' money was backed by, and exchangeable for, gold. Private Canadian banks in this era were allowed to issue their own banknotes as long as they held a sufficient amount of gold to back their value. These notes circulated along with Dominion of Canada notes to constitute the currency of the country. Also important during this period of our history is the fact that Canada did not have a central bank. In the days just before war was declared, Canadian banks experienced large demands for conversion of currency and deposits into gold, which led to concerns of bank runs. With no lender of last resort, banks were required by law to close if they could not meet depositor demand for gold or Dominion notes.

---

[5]This section draws on material from James Powell's *A History of the Canadian Dollar* (2005). To learn more about this period and other interesting periods in the history of our money, access this publication at www.bankofcanada.ca/publications-research/books-and-monographs/history-canadian-dollar/. Interested readers might also wish to visit the Bank of Canada's Currency Museum (www.currency museum.ca/) in Ottawa, which offers informative and entertaining guided tours in the summer about Canadian and world money.

Rumours that a bank had insufficient gold or Dominion notes to satisfy demands for withdrawal or conversion could quickly lead to a bank run. A bank run could spark a contagion, setting off runs at other nearby banks, sowing widespread panic and devastation in the local economy. So, to protect the banks, the government enacted several laws. First, the government ordered that all the notes issued by Canadian banks were now legal tender. This is important as it gave these notes the same legal status as gold, Dominion of Canada notes, and all metallic coins minted in Canada when it came to settling transactions. Next, the government allowed banks to issue more notes. At the same time, the lender of last resort function was introduced, so the Treasury Board was allowed to make advances, which are loans made to private banks in Dominion notes, against securities these banks pledged as collateral to the minister of finance. Lastly, the government suspended the conversion of Dominion notes into gold—Canada left the gold standard. Now Canada had a floating exchange rate along with a lender of last resort. It was on its way toward creating a full-fledged central bank.

Canada did return to the gold standard temporarily, from 1926 to 1933, but this new standard differed from the pre-war version. Now, private banknotes were no longer legal tender, but the Treasury Board continued to function as the lender of last resort. Thus, banks could use securities that were not backed by gold to obtain Dominion notes, which were backed by gold. As a result, in the late 1920s, quantities of Dominion banknotes grew more quickly than the gold reserves that backed them, leading to a precarious recipe for sustainable currency valuation.

When the Great Depression hit the world in 1929, Canada stuck with the gold standard and the fixed exchange rate it created via international movements of gold. But Canada did try to discourage exports of gold. In 1931, the United Kingdom abandoned the gold standard and let the pound float in currency exchange markets. This created significant turmoil on world financial markets. The world money market froze up, as potential lenders became so fearful of making bad loans they declined to enter into almost all loan requests. Canada found that it could not obtain even short-term loans and the Canadian dollar came under significant downward pressure on foreign exchange markets. Finally, in 1933, Canada once again abandoned the gold standard, and the convertibility of Dominion notes into gold ended.

Following the Wall Street stock market crash of 1929, the Canadian economy shrank significantly. If the federal government had advanced more money to banks, the money supply would have increased; but, as it was, the government provided little or no voluntary monetary stimulus to help the economy recover. **Commercial banks** were allowed to request advances from the government, but chose not to do so. This was because the government did not lower the interest rate on advances, causing banks to fear that they might not be able to repay them. Consequently, the money supply contracted, instead of expanding. Nor did sticking with the gold standard, even notionally, allow the Canadian dollar to depreciate enough to stimulate net exports sufficiently to help expand the economy and create jobs.

Responding to the Great Depression: The Creation of the Bank of Canada

Unfortunately, as is now well understood by economic historians, the falling money supply and shrinking trade balance of the early 1930s acted to significantly worsen and prolong the economic slump now known as the Great Depression. By 1933, the government had realized some of its policy mistakes and attempted to correct them. In this year, Canada left the gold standard, lowered the rate of interest on advances, and set up a royal commission to study the financial system and to consider whether Canada should establish its own central bank.

There were plenty of arguments against a central bank: Canada's existing financial structure was sound but its debt was too high; Canada lacked the constitutional

A **commercial bank** is one that accepts deposits and is covered by deposit insurance.

authority to launch such an entity; creating a central bank during an economic crisis was unwise; such an institution might act as an impediment to the eventual return to the gold standard; the American central bank had been unable to counteract the Depression in the United States; Canada lacked the expertise to operate such as institution; Canada lacked the proper domestic money market that a central bank needs to function; Canadian banks were stable and did not need a central bank to help support them; and so on. In particular, Canadian banks opposed the idea because they feared their profits might fall once a central bank became the sole issuer of domestic banknotes.

However, the commission did recommend the creation of a central bank, and in 1935 the Bank of Canada was established. Now Canada had a single institution with the authority to conduct monetary policy, issue all Canadian banknotes, manage the finances of the federal government, regulate the financial system, and act as the lender of last resort. Authority over monetary policy allowed the central bank to change interest rates via interventions in the money market, initiate loans to banks, intervene in the foreign exchange market to influence the exchange rate, and promote the economic and financial welfare of the nation by attempting to support full employment and stable prices.

It is interesting to note that in 1933 the United States introduced deposit insurance owing to widespread bank runs during the Depression. Why didn't Canada also introduce deposit insurance then? It's because at that time Canada's banking system was much different: our system spread financial risks out more evenly across the nation. As a result, Canada had fewer severe banking disruptions than the U.S. This is why Canadians felt deposit insurance was not needed to stabilize the banking sector, and deposit insurance was not introduced in Canada until 1967.

The U.S. Financial Crisis of 2008

The financial crisis of 2008 had some of the same features of the earlier financial crises. It involved U.S. institutions that were not as strictly regulated as deposit-taking banks, excessive speculation, and a U.S. government that was reluctant to take aggressive action until the scale of the devastation became clear. In addition, by the late 1990s, advances in technology and financial innovation had created yet another systemic weakness that played a central role in 2008. The story of Long-Term Capital Management, or LTCM, highlights these problems.

Long-Term Capital (Mis)Management Created in 1994, LTCM was a U.S. hedge fund, a private investment partnership open only to wealthy individuals and institutions. In the United States, hedge funds are virtually unregulated, allowing for much riskier investments than with mutual funds, which are open to the average investor. Using vast amounts of **leverage**—that is, borrowed money—to increase its returns, LTCM used sophisticated computer models to make money by taking advantage of small differences in asset prices in global financial markets to buy at a lower price and sell at a higher price. In one year, LTCM made a return as high as 40%.

LTCM was also heavily involved in derivatives, complex financial instruments that are constructed—derived—from the obligations of more basic financial assets. Derivatives are popular investment tools because they are cheaper to trade than basic financial assets and can be constructed to suit a buyer's or seller's particular needs. Yet their complexity can make it extremely hard to measure their value. LTCM believed that its computer models allowed it to accurately gauge the risk in the huge bets that it was undertaking in derivatives using borrowed money.

However, LTCM's computer models hadn't factored in a series of financial crises in Asia and in Russia during 1997 and 1998. Through its large borrowing,

A financial institution engages in **leverage** when it finances its investments with borrowed funds.

The **balance sheet effect** is the reduction in a firm's net worth due to falling asset prices.

A **vicious cycle of deleveraging** takes place when asset sales to cover losses produce negative balance sheet effects on other firms and force creditors to call in their loans, forcing sales of more assets and causing further declines in asset prices.

Sub-prime lending is lending to homebuyers who don't meet the usual criteria for being able to afford their payments.

In **securitization,** a pool of loans is assembled and shares of that pool are sold to investors.

LTCM had become such a big player in global financial markets that attempts to sell its assets depressed the prices of what it was trying to sell. As the markets fell around the world and LTCM's panic-stricken investors demanded the return of their funds, LTCM's losses mounted as it tried to sell assets to satisfy those demands. Quickly, its operations collapsed because it could no longer borrow money and other parties refused to trade with it. Financial markets around the world froze in panic.

The Federal Reserve realized that allowing LTCM's remaining assets to be sold at panic-stricken prices presented a grave risk to the entire financial system through the **balance sheet effect:** as sales of assets by LTCM depressed asset prices all over the world, other firms would see the value of their balance sheets fall as assets held on these balance sheets declined in value. Moreover, falling asset prices meant the value of assets held by borrowers on their balance sheets could fall below a critical threshold, leading to a default on the terms of their credit contracts and forcing creditors to call in their loans. This in turn would lead to more sales of assets as borrowers tried to raise cash to repay their loans, more credit defaults, and more loans called in, creating a **vicious cycle of deleveraging.**

The Federal Reserve Bank of New York arranged a $3.625 billion bailout of LTCM in 1998, in which other private institutions took on shares of LTCM's assets and obligations, liquidated them in an orderly manner, and eventually turned a small profit. Quick action by the Federal Reserve Bank of New York prevented LTCM from sparking a contagion, yet virtually all of LTCM's investors were wiped out.

Sub-prime Lending and the Housing Bubble

After the LTCM crisis, U.S. financial markets stabilized. They remained more or less stable even as stock prices fell sharply from 2000 to 2002 and the U.S. economy went into recession. During the recovery from the 2001 recession, however, the seeds for another financial crisis were planted.

The story begins with low interest rates: by 2003, U.S. interest rates were at historically low levels, partly because of Federal Reserve policy and partly because of large inflows of capital from other countries, especially China. These low interest rates helped cause a boom in housing, which in turn led the U.S. economy out of recession. As housing boomed, however, financial institutions began taking on growing risks—risks that were not well understood.

Traditionally, people could only borrow money to buy homes if they could show that they had sufficient income to meet the mortgage payments. **Sub-prime lending,** lending money for buying homes to people who usually wouldn't qualify for such loans, represented only a minor part of overall lending. But in the booming housing market of 2003–2006, sub-prime lending started to seem like a safe bet. Since housing prices kept rising, borrowers who couldn't make their mortgage payments could always pay off their mortgages, if necessary, by selling their homes. As a result, sub-prime lending exploded.

Who was making these sub-prime loans? For the most part, it wasn't American traditional banks that were lending out depositors' money. Instead, most of the loans were being made by "loan originators," who quickly sold mortgages to other investors. These sales were made possible by a process known as **securitization:** financial institutions assembled pools of loans and sold shares in the income from these pools. These shares were considered relatively safe investments, since it was considered unlikely that large numbers of homebuyers would default on their payments all at the same time.

But that's exactly what happened. The housing boom turned out to be a bubble, and when home prices started falling in late 2006, many sub-prime borrowers could neither make their mortgage payments nor sell their houses for enough to pay off their mortgages. As a result, investors in securities backed by sub-prime mortgages started taking heavy losses.

"Honey, we're homeless."

FIGURE **14-14** The TED Spread

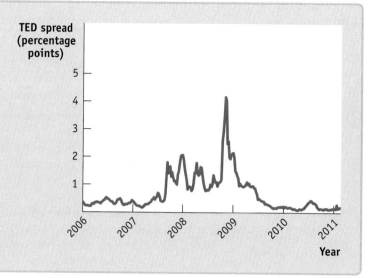

The TED spread is the difference between the interest rate at which banks lend to each other and the interest rate on U.S. government debt. It's widely used as a measure of financial stress. The TED spread soared as a result of the financial crisis of 2007–2008.

Sources: British Bankers' Association; Federal Reserve Bank of St. Louis.

Many of the mortgage-backed assets were held by financial institutions, including banks and other institutions playing bank-like roles. As in previous crises, these "non-bank banks" were less regulated than commercial banks, which allowed them to offer higher returns to investors but left them extremely vulnerable in a crisis. Mortgage-related losses, in turn, led to a collapse of trust in the financial system.

Figure 14-14 shows one measure of this loss of trust: the TED spread, which is the difference between the interest rate on three-month loans that banks make to each other and the interest rate the U.S. federal government pays on three-month bonds. ("TED" is an acronym formed from the "T" of treasury bills and the "ED" of euro dollars.) Since U.S. government bonds are considered extremely safe, the TED spread shows how much risk American banks think they're taking on when lending to each other. Normally the spread is around a quarter of a percentage point, but it shot up in August 2007 and surged to an unprecedented 4.58 percentage points in October 2008, before returning to more normal levels in mid-2009.

Crisis and Response The collapse of trust in the financial system, combined with the large losses suffered by some financial firms, led to a severe cycle of deleveraging and a credit crunch for the U.S. economy as a whole. American firms found it difficult to borrow, even for short-term operations; individuals found home loans unavailable and credit card limits reduced. These symptoms were shared by individuals, firms, and governments worldwide, thanks to our interconnected global financial system.

Overall, the negative economic effect of the financial crisis bore a distinct and troubling resemblance to the effects of the banking crisis of the early 1930s, which helped cause the Great Depression. Policy-makers noticed the resemblance and tried to prevent a repeat performance. Beginning in August 2007, the Federal Reserve engaged in a series of efforts to provide cash to the financial system, lending funds to a widening range of institutions and buying private-sector debt. The Fed and the U.S. Treasury Department also stepped in to rescue individual firms that were deemed too crucial to be allowed to fail, such as the **investment bank** Bear Stearns and the insurance company AIG.

In September 2008, however, American policy-makers decided that one major investment bank, Lehman Brothers, could be allowed to fail. They quickly regretted the decision. Within days of Lehman's failure, widespread panic gripped global financial markets, as illustrated by the surge in the TED spread at this time, as shown in Figure 14-14. In response to the intensified crisis, the U.S. government

An **investment bank** is one that trades in financial assets and is not covered by deposit insurance.

intervened further to support the financial system, as the U.S. Treasury began "injecting" capital into banks. Injecting capital, in practice, meant that the U.S. government would supply cash to banks in return for shares—in effect, partially nationalizing the financial system.

By the fall of 2010, the U.S. financial system appeared to be stabilized, and major institutions had repaid much of the money the U.S. federal government had injected during the crisis. It was generally expected that American taxpayers would end up losing little if any of this stimulus money. However, the recovery of the banks was not matched by a successful turnaround for the overall American economy: although the recession that began in December 2007 officially ended in June 2009, U.S. unemployment remained stubbornly high.

The Federal Reserve responded to this troubled situation with novel forms of open-market operations. Conventional open-market operations are limited to short-term government debt, but the Fed believed that this was no longer enough. It provided massive liquidity through discount window lending, as well as undertaking so-called quantitative easing, the buying of large quantities of other assets, mainly long-term government debt and the debts of Fannie Mae and Freddie Mac, government-sponsored agencies that support home lending.

Like earlier crises, the crisis of 2008 led to changes in U.S. and world banking regulation. Since much of the crisis originated in non-traditional bank institutions, the crisis of 2008 indicated that a wider safety net and broader regulation were needed in the financial sector. And such reforms were implemented. In the U.S., in July 2010, the Wall Street Reform and Consumer Protection Act, known as the Dodd-Frank bill, became law. The biggest U.S. financial reform since the 1930s, this bill resulted in a new agency, the Consumer Financial Protection Bureau, to protect borrowers. In 2012, the Basel Committee on Banking Supervision reached an agreement on detailed measures to strengthen the regulation, supervision, and risk management of the world's banking sector. This package of measures, known as Basel III, will, in a nutshell, require a significant rise in the banking industry's liquid capital requirements so that these institutions will become less prone to banking crises. Will these changes succeed in heading off future banking crises? Time will tell.

ECONOMICS ► IN ACTION

WHY ARE CANADA'S BANKS MORE STABLE?

The 2008 crisis in America's banks caused widespread financial and economic suffering in many nations, including our own. As severe as our downturn was—the most significant slump in Canada since the Great Depression—it easily could have been much worse if not for some important differences in our banking sector.

In 2012, for the fifth year in a row, the World Economic Forum ranked Canada's banking system as the most sound in the world. How is this possible? Is this something new? Not really. Historically the Canadian banking sector has always been very stable. Bank failures have been quite rare in Canada, even during market crashes, depressions, wars, and other financial turmoil. The stability of Canadian banks comes from important structural differences between how banks are set up and operated here relative to other jurisdictions. To quote the Canadian Bankers Association (CBA), speaking on behalf of their members:

Canada's banks are well managed, well regulated, and well capitalized. We play by the rules and our national banking system is a key strength. By diversifying regional risk, a downturn in an individual economic sector is balanced since funds can be moved from areas of excess deposits to regions where growth is creating demand for new credit.

The Canadian Bank of Commerce receives a shipment of gold dust worth $750 000 (about $19 million in today's money) from Dawson, Yukon Territory, September 29, 1899.

Banks in Canada make lending decisions on a case-by-case basis, extending credit to those who have the capacity to repay their loans. This prudent approach is a key reason why banks in Canada have largely avoided the problems that have plagued banks elsewhere.[6]

For more than one hundred years the Canadian banking system has been set up in such a way that it is more concentrated, sometimes called more *oligopolistic,* than those of some other jurisdictions, such as the United States. This means that the Canadian banking system has been dominated for many decades by large national players who are well capitalized and diversified; thus, they are more resilient in the face of financial market fluctuations. The government, in return for allowing such concentration of market power, has demanded that firms face regulatory oversight in order to ensure the system is both sound and meets the needs of society.

The American banking system is considerably different from the Canadian system. Whereas Canada has a few large banks, the U.S. has a great many small ones. This difference may be partly the result of an American desire for greater competition and a distrust of concentrating too much market power in the hands of large firms. Also, until recently, American laws have prevented banks in one state from operating in another. As a result, U.S. banks are often not capitalized or diversified as well as Canadian banks are, so they are more vulnerable to significant financial distress, such as bank runs.

As the CBA notes, Canadian banks have historically acted more conservatively than U.S. banks when it comes to making loans. Key regulatory differences between Canada and the United States generally include the following:

- Canada requires higher minimum credit scores to obtain a mortgage.
- Canada requires higher minimum down payments on mortgages.
- Canada requires mortgage default insurance on all loans with down payments less than 20%.
- Maximum amortization periods are shorter in Canada.
- Interest on mortgages for owner-occupied housing is tax deductible in the U.S., but not in Canada.
- It is more costly to default on a mortgage in Canada than in the U.S. Unlike in the U.S., a Canadian homeowner faced with negative equity cannot "walk away."
- Canada has fewer small (as a percentage of loans made) unregulated mortgage lenders than in the U.S.
- Canadian lenders make fewer sub-prime loans than their American counterparts.
- Canadian lenders are less likely to shift the default risk of their portfolio of mortgage loans to other parties by selling mortgage-backed securities (bonds backed by the cash flow coming from the mortgages). This is partly owing to mortgage default insurance and a less well developed market for asset-backed securities.

These differences make the Canadian financial sector less vulnerable (or more resilient) to any adverse shock in the housing market. First, it is relatively harder for Canadians with low credit ratings or a bad credit history to get mortgages. The relatively higher costs of carrying mortgages, as a result of mortgage default insurance requirements, shorter amortization periods, and the inability to deduct the interest paid on owner-occupied mortgages from taxes, discourage Canadians from borrowing excessively. All these rules help to lower the likelihood of default and to reduce the losses banks may face when defaults occur. These differences help explain why the Canadian market for mortgages is more conservative than

---

[6]*Source:* "Canada's Banks–Made of Canada," Canadian Bankers Association, last modified March 8, 2013, www.cba.ca/en/media-room/50-backgrounders-on-banking-issues/626-canadas-banks-made-of-canada.

the U.S. market, which also explains why U.S. housing prices are more likely to create a harmful financial bubble.

This does not mean that housing price bubbles are unknown in Canada (recall our look in Chapter 10 at the potential housing bubble in Vancouver), but that their risks are lessened. In fact, since the recession of 2008–2009 caused by the bursting of the U.S. housing price bubble in 2006–2007, the Canadian government has been trying to reduce the possibility of a similar bubble bursting here. The Bank of Canada has repeatedly warned Canadians to be aware of the ballooning level of household debt that has, in recent years, climbed higher and higher as a percent of income. To try to slow the market for home sales and, with it, the rise in housing prices, the federal minister of finance has on several occasions adopted measures to make it harder to qualify for a mortgage. These measures have started to take effect: as the volume of home sales has dropped and the rate of increase in home prices has slowed and even declined in some markets.

Were these measures enough? Was there already a nationwide housing bubble and did these measures help to slowly deflate it? Might it still burst at some point? Or, was there no such bubble because these measures helped to prevent its creation? Only the passage of time will reveal whether high Canadian home prices and household indebtedness end up creating significant financial hardship and perhaps another recession.

CHECK YOUR UNDERSTANDING 14-5

1. What structural differences between the Canadian and American banking sectors led to many bank runs in the U.S. and none in Canada during the Great Depression?

2. What is a housing price bubble? Who benefits from the creation of such bubbles? Why should society be concerned about such bubbles arising? What role, if any, might the government play in helping to either create or avoid a housing price bubble?

3. Describe the balance sheet effect. Describe the vicious cycle of deleveraging. Why does the government sometimes need to step in to halt a vicious cycle of deleveraging?

Solutions appear at back of book.

The Perfect Gift: Cash or a Gift Card?

Mario Beauregard/CP Images

On average, Canadians spend about $200 on gift cards per year. What could be more simple and useful, than allowing the recipient to choose what he or she wants? And isn't a gift card more personal than cash or a cheque stuffed in an envelope?

Yet several websites are now making a profit from the fact that gift card recipients are often willing to sell their cards at a discount—sometimes at a fairly sizable discount—to turn them into cold, impersonal dollars and cents.

CardSwap.ca is one such site. At the time of writing, it offers to pay cash to a seller of an Esso Imperial Oil gift card equivalent to 92% of the card's face value (for example, the seller of a card with a value of $100 would receive $92 in cash). But it offers cash equal to only 60% of a Hakim Optical card's face value. CardSwap.ca profits by reselling the card at a premium over what it paid; for example, it buys an Aeropostale card for 70% of its face value and then resells it for almost 100% of its face value. Many consumers are, in fact, willing to sell at a sizable discount to turn their unwanted gift cards into cash.

Retailers are eager to promote the use of gift cards over cash. According to market studies, 10% to 15% of gift cards are never redeemed. Those unredeemed dollars accrue to the retailer, making gift cards a highly profitable line of business. With more than $6 billion worth of gift cards sold in Canada annually, this places the value of "breakage," the amount of a gift card that accrues to the retailer rather than to the cardholder, at more than $600 million in 2012. Breakage also occurs when cardholders redeem only a portion of a gift card. For instance, they spend only $47 of a $50 card, figuring it's not worth the effort to return to the store to spend that last $3.

In addition to breakage, retailers have found that gift cards are profitable in other ways. Retailers benefit when customers intent on using up the value of their gift card actually end up spending more than the card's face value, sometimes spending even more than they would have without the gift card. Customers who use gift cards are more likely to make impulse purchases than customers who use other means of payment. And they are more likely to buy items at full price rather than articles that are on sale. Also, when retailers sell the gift card, they immediately get access to the full amount of the funds provided to charge the card and can use these funds interest free until the card is used. If a retailer goes out of business, the value of any outstanding gift cards disappears with it.

Previously, sellers commonly rewarded customers loyalty with mail-in rebates—actual cheques to the customer that repaid part of the original cost of the purchase. Now retailers often prefer to issue gift cards for the same value instead. As one commentator noted in explaining why, "Nobody neglects to spend cash."

QUESTIONS FOR THOUGHT

1. Why are gift card owners willing to sell their cards for less than their face value?

2. Why do gift cards for Esso sell for a smaller discount than Hakim Optical?

3. Use your answer from Question 2 to explain why cash never "sells" at a discount.

4. Explain why retailers prefer to reward loyal customers with gift cards instead of mail-in rebates.

5. Recent legislation in several provinces has restricted retailers' ability to impose fees and expiration dates on their gift cards and mandated greater disclosure of their terms. Why do you think governments enacted such legislation?

SUMMARY

1. **Money** is any asset that can be used to purchase goods and services easily. **Currency in circulation** and **chequeable (or demand) deposits** are both considered part of the **money supply.** Money plays three roles: it is a **medium of exchange** used for transactions, a **store of value** that holds purchasing power over time, and a **unit of account** in which prices are stated.

2. Over time, **commodity money,** which consists of goods possessing value aside from their role as money, such as gold and silver coins, was replaced by **commodity-backed money,** such as paper currency backed by gold. Today the dollar is pure **fiat money,** whose value derives solely from its official role.

3. The Bank of Canada calculates a number of measures of the money supply. M1 is the narrowest **monetary aggregate,** containing only currency in circulation and demand deposits, such as chequing accounts, held at chartered banks. M2 and M3 includes a wider range of assets called **near-moneys,** mainly other forms of chartered bank deposits that can easily be converted into chequing bank deposits.

4. Banks allow depositors immediate access to their funds, but they also lend out most of the funds deposited in their care. To meet demands for cash, they maintain **desired (or voluntary) reserve ratios** composed of both currency held in their vaults and deposits at the Bank of Canada. **Excess reserves** refer to any reserves above the desired level of reserves. The **reserve ratio** is the ratio of **bank reserves** to bank deposits. A **T-account** summarizes a bank's financial position, with loans and reserves counted as assets and deposits counted as liabilities.

5. Banks have sometimes been subject to **bank runs,** most notably in the early 1930s in the U.S. and briefly just before World War I in Canada. To avert this danger, depositors are now protected by **deposit insurance.** Although Canadian banks are no longer required to meet minimum **reserve requirements,** bank owners still face **capital requirements** that reduce the incentive to make overly risky loans with depositors' funds.

6. When currency is deposited in a bank, it starts a multiplier process in which banks lend out excess reserves, leading to an increase in the money supply—so private banks create money. If the entire money supply consisted of chequeable bank deposits, the money supply would be equal to the value of reserves divided by the reserve ratio. In reality, much of the **monetary base** consists of currency in circulation, and the **money multiplier** is the ratio of the money supply to the monetary base.

7. The monetary base is controlled by the Bank of Canada (BOC), the **central bank** of Canada. The BOC regulates banks and helps to set overnight interest rates. To meet their desired reserve requirements, banks borrow and lend reserves in the **overnight funds market** usually at an interest rate very close to the BOC's **target for the overnight rate.** When banks are unable to borrow funds in the overnight market, they have the option to borrow from the Bank of Canada at the **bank rate.** Such a loan is referred to as a lender of last resort loan.

8. The Bank of Canada's principal tools of monetary policy are **open-market operations** and **deposit switching.** To increase the monetary base, the BOC can buy Canadian treasury bills from commercial banks or switch government deposits from itself to banks. To reduce the monetary base, the BOC can sell Canadian treasury bills to banks or switch government deposits from banks to itself.

9. To counteract a poor monetary policy that had worsened the effects of the Great Depression, the Bank of Canada was created. The BOC's duties were to be the sole issuer of legal tender Canadian banknotes, centralize the holding of reserves, regulate and inspect banks' books, and make the money supply sufficiently responsive to varying economic conditions.

10. The Great Depression sparked widespread bank runs in the United States, which greatly worsened and prolonged it even further. In response, the American government created federal deposit insurance to reduce the risk of bank runs. Public acceptance of deposit insurance finally stopped the American bank runs of the Great Depression. Canada did not experience significant bank runs during the Depression and, as a result, deposit insurance was not set up in Canada until 1967.

11. During the mid-1990s, the U.S. hedge fund LTCM used huge amounts of **leverage** to speculate in global financial markets, incurred massive losses, and collapsed. LTCM was so large that, in selling assets to cover its losses, it caused **balance sheet effects** for firms around the world, leading to the prospect of a **vicious cycle of deleveraging.** As a result, credit markets around the world froze. The New York Fed coordinated a private bailout of LTCM and revived world credit markets.

12. **Sub-prime lending** during the U.S. housing bubble of the mid-2000s spread through the world financial system via **securitization.** When the bubble burst, massive losses by banks and non-bank financial institutions led to widespread collapse in the financial system in the U.S. and elsewhere. To prevent another Great Depression, the U.S. Federal Reserve and the U.S. Treasury expanded lending to banks and non-bank institutions, provided capital through the purchase of bank shares, and purchased private debt. Because much of the crisis originated in non-traditional bank institutions, the crisis of 2008 indicated that a wider safety net and broader regulation are needed in the financial sector. The 2010 Dodd-Frank bill, the biggest American financial reform since the 1930s, is an attempt to prevent another crisis.

13. During the crisis of 2008 and subsequent recession, the Bank of Canada acted much like the Fed, the American central bank. It lowered its target rate for the overnight market, increased lending to Canadian financial institutions, and lengthened the list of securities it would accept as collateral from financial institutions.

KEY TERMS

Money, p. 454

Currency in circulation, p. 454

Chequeable (or demand) deposits, p. 454

Money supply, p. 454

Medium of exchange, p. 455

Store of value, p. 456

Unit of account, p. 456

Commodity money, p. 456

Commodity-backed money, p. 456

Fiat money, p. 457

Monetary aggregate, p. 457

Near-moneys, p. 459

Bank reserves, p. 461

T-account, p. 461

Reserve ratio, p. 462

Bank run, p. 463

Deposit insurance, p. 463

Capital requirements, p. 464

Reserve requirements, p. 464

Desired (or voluntary) reserve ratio, p. 464

Excess reserves, p. 468

Monetary base, p. 469

Money multiplier, p. 469

Central bank, p. 471

Overnight funds market, p. 474

Overnight rate, p. 475

Target for the overnight rate, p. 475

Bank rate, p. 475

Discount rate, p. 475

Open-market operation, p. 475

Deposit switching, p. 479

Commercial bank, p. 484

Leverage, p. 485

Balance sheet effect, p. 486

Vicious cycle of deleveraging, p. 486

Sub-prime lending, p. 486

Securitization, p. 486

Investment bank, p. 487

PROBLEMS

1. For each of the following transactions, what is the initial effect (increase or decrease) on M1? On M2? On M2+?

   a. You sell a few shares of stock and put the proceeds into your savings account in a chartered bank.

   b. You sell a few shares of stock and put the proceeds into your chequing account in a chartered bank.

   c. You transfer money from your savings account to your chequing account in a chartered bank.

   d. You discover $0.25 under the floor mat in your car and deposit it in your chequing account.

   e. You discover $0.25 under the floor mat in your car and deposit it in your savings account in a credit union.

2. There are three types of money: commodity money, commodity-backed money, and fiat money. Which type of money is used in each of the following situations?

   a. Bottles of rum were used to pay for goods in colonial Australia.

   b. Salt was used in many European countries as a medium of exchange.

   c. For a brief time, Germany used paper money (the "Rye Mark") that could be redeemed for a certain amount of rye, a type of grain.

   d. The city of Kamloops, British Columbia, prints its own currency, the Kamloops dollar, which can be used to purchase local goods and services.

3. The table below shows the components of M1, M2, and M2+ in billions of dollars from January 2011 to August 2012 as published in the Bank of Canada's Weekly Financial Statistics on November 16, 2012. Complete the table by calculating M1, M2, M2+, currency in circulation as a percentage of M1, and currency in circulation as a percentage of M2+. What trends or patterns about M1, M2, M2+, currency in circulation as a percentage of M1, and currency in circulation as a percentage of M2+ do you see? What might account for these trends?

4. Indicate whether each of the following is part of M1, M2, M2+, or none of them:

   a. $95 on your campus meal card

   b. $0.55 in the change cup of your car

   c. $1663 in your savings account in a credit union

   d. $459 in your chequing account in a chartered bank

   e. 100 shares of stock worth $4000

   f. A $1000 line of credit on your Sears credit card

5. Tracy Williams deposits $500 that was in her sock drawer into a chequing account at the local bank.

   a. How does the deposit initially change the T-account of the local bank? How does it change the money supply?

   b. If the bank maintains a reserve ratio of 10%, how will it respond to the new deposit?

   c. If every time the bank makes a loan, the loan results in a new chequeable deposit in a different bank equal to the amount of the loan, by how much could the total money supply in the economy expand in response to Tracy's initial cash deposit of $500?

   d. If every time the bank makes a loan, the loan results in a new chequeable deposit in a different bank equal to the amount of the loan and the bank maintains a reserve ratio of 5%, by how much could the money supply expand in response to Tracy's initial cash deposit of $500?

6. Ryan Cozzens withdraws $400 from his chequing account at the local bank and keeps it in his wallet.

   a. How will the withdrawal change the T-account of the local bank and the money supply?

   b. If the bank maintains a reserve ratio of 10%, how will it respond to the withdrawal? Assume that the bank responds to insufficient reserves by reducing the amount of deposits it holds until its level of reserves satisfies its desired reserve ratio. The bank reduces its deposits by calling in some of its loans, forcing borrowers to pay back these loans by taking

Date	Currency outside banks	Chequing deposits at chartered banks	Personal term deposits	Non-personal deposits	Adjustment to M2	Deposits at trust and mortgage loan companies, credit unions, and caisses populaires
Jan. 2011	56.389	470.115	476.357	23.353	−3.175	244.046
Feb. 2011	55.982	465.773	477.576	23.218	−3.171	244.917
Mar. 2011	55.775	464.625	479.753	23.132	−2.999	246.547
Apr. 2011	56.268	472.639	479.544	22.803	−3.418	248.317
May 2011	56.729	476.291	478.246	23.61	−3.246	250.330
Jun. 2011	57.342	487.004	478.349	23.843	−3.579	253.303
Jul. 2011	57.934	490.804	478.241	22.489	−3.639	254.952
Aug. 2011	58.045	490.419	480.214	23.1	−3.772	255.796
Sep. 2011	58.455	503.957	481.148	23.522	−4.239	257.474
Oct. 2011	58.714	511.678	483.737	23.974	−3.664	258.653
Nov. 2011	58.928	510.143	486.697	24.377	0.351	259.550
Dec. 2011	59.898	522.702	488.747	25.022	−0.019	260.148
Jan. 2012	59.316	515.064	491.779	25.64	0.247	260.813
Feb. 2012	58.663	507.281	494.208	25.534	0.454	261.977
Mar. 2012	58.586	504.62	496.562	25.771	−0.598	263.167
Apr. 2012	59.223	515.983	495.581	25.389	0.047	265.303
May 2012	59.689	523.094	495.637	25.788	−0.581	268.076
Jun. 2012	60.481	534.902	498.296	26.833	−0.073	269.812
Jul. 2012	60.913	538.967	500.113	27.423	−0.261	271.267
Aug. 2012	61.258	538.2	504.19	27.965	−3.316	270.263

Source: Bank of Canada.

cash from their chequing deposits (at the same bank) to make repayment.

c. If every time the bank decreases its loans, chequeable deposits fall by the amount of the loan, by how much will the money supply in the economy contract in response to Ryan's withdrawal of $400?

d. If every time the bank decreases its loans, chequeable deposits fall by the amount of the loan and the bank maintains a desired reserve ratio of 20%, by how much will the money supply contract in response to a withdrawal of $400?

7. The government of Eastlandia uses measures of monetary aggregates similar to those used by Canada, and the commercial banks in Eastlandia hold a desired reserve ratio of 10%. Given the following information, answer the questions below.

Bank deposits at the central bank = $200 million
Currency held by public = $150 million
Currency in bank vaults = $100 million
Chequeable deposits = $500 million

a. What is M1?

b. What is the monetary base?

c. Are the commercial banks holding excess reserves?

d. Can the commercial banks increase chequeable deposits? If yes, by how much can chequeable deposits increase?

8. What will happen to the money supply under the following circumstances in a chequeable-deposits-only system?

a. The desired reserve ratio is 25%, and a depositor withdraws $700 from his chequeable deposit.

b. The desired reserve ratio is 5%, and a depositor withdraws $700 from his chequeable deposit.

c. The desired reserve ratio is 20%, and a customer deposits $750 to her chequeable deposit.

d. The desired reserve ratio is 10%, and a customer deposits $600 to her chequeable deposit.

Date	Other deposits	Money market mutual funds	Adjustment to M2+	M1	M2	M2+	Currency in circulation as a percentage of M1	Currency in circulation as a percentage of M2+
Jan. 2011	54.968	39.954	−0.671					
Feb. 2011	54.739	39.023	−0.658					
Mar. 2011	54.521	38.453	−0.601					
Apr. 2011	54.436	37.633	−0.601					
May 2011	54.458	37.125	−0.54					
Jun. 2011	54.448	36.574	−0.585					
Jul. 2011	54.626	36.554	−0.616					
Aug. 2011	54.932	36.52	−0.574					
Sep. 2011	55.273	36.263	−0.587					
Oct. 2011	55.56	35.91	−0.461					
Nov. 2011	55.726	35.263	−0.25					
Dec. 2011	55.891	35.076	−0.168					
Jan. 2012	55.886	34.264	−0.115					
Feb. 2012	55.736	33.471	−0.107					
Mar. 2012	55.563	32.819	−0.018					
Apr. 2012	55.515	32.395	0.047					
May 2012	55.639	32.205	0.016					
Jun. 2012	55.74	32.172	0.069					
Jul. 2012	55.912	31.473	0.185					
Aug. 2012	56.227	31.256	3.014					

Source: Bank of Canada.

9. In Westlandia, the public holds 50% of M1 in the form of currency, and the voluntary reserve ratio is 20%. Estimate how much the money supply will increase in response to a new cash deposit of $500 by completing the accompanying table. (*Hint:* The first row shows that the bank must hold $100 in minimum reserves—20% of the $500 deposit—against this deposit, leaving $400 in excess reserves that can be loaned out. However, since the public wants to hold 50% of the loan in currency, only $400 × 0.5 = $200 of the loan will be deposited in round 2 from the loan granted in round 1.) How does your answer compare to an economy in which the total amount of the loan is deposited in the banking system and the public doesn't hold any of the loan in currency? What does this imply about the relationship between the public's desire for holding currency and the money multiplier?

Round	Deposits	Voluntary reserves	Excess reserves	Loans	Held as currency
1	$500.00	$100.00	$400.00	$400.00	$200.00
2	200.00	?	?	?	?
3	?	?	?	?	?
4	?	?	?	?	?
5	?	?	?	?	?
6	?	?	?	?	?
7	?	?	?	?	?
8	?	?	?	?	?
9	?	?	?	?	?
Total after 10 rounds	?	?	?	?	?

10. Although the Bank of Canada does not impose a minimum reserve ratio on the banking sector, the central bank of Albernia does. The commercial banks of Albernia have $100 million in reserves and $1000 million in chequeable deposits; the initial required reserve ratio is 10%. The commercial banks follow a policy of holding no excess reserves. The public holds no currency, only chequeable deposits in the banking system.

a. How will the money supply change if the required reserve ratio falls to 5%?

b. How will the money supply change if the required reserve ratio rises to 25%?

11. Show the changes to the T-accounts for the Bank of Canada and for commercial banks when the Bank of Canada buys $50 million in treasury bills. If the public holds a fixed amount of currency (so that all loans create an equal amount of deposits in the banking system), the minimum reserve ratio is 10%, and banks hold no excess reserves, by how much will deposits in the commercial banks change? By how much will the money supply change? Show the final changes to the T-account for commercial banks when the money supply changes by this amount.

12. Show the changes to the T-accounts for the Bank of Canada and for commercial banks when the Bank of Canada sells $30 million in treasury bills. If the public holds a fixed amount of currency (so that all new loans create an equal amount of chequeable deposits in the banking system) and the minimum reserve ratio is 5%, by how much will chequeable deposits in the commercial banks change? By how much will the money supply change? Show the final changes to the T-account for the commercial banks when the money supply changes by this amount.

13. In 2011, the RCMP estimated that at least $2.6 million of counterfeit Canadian banknotes were in circulation.

a. Why do Canadian taxpayers lose because of these counterfeit notes?

b. As of December 2011, the interest rate earned on one-year Canadian treasury bills was 1.07%. At a 1.07% rate of interest, what amount of money are Canadian taxpayers losing per year because of these $2.6 million in counterfeit notes?

14. As Figure 14-13 shows, the portion of the Bank of Canada's assets made up of Canadian government treasury bills and bonds declined in late 2008. Go to www.statcan.gc.ca. Under "Search," click on "Specialized search tools" then click on "CANSIM." In the search line enter "Table 176-0010" and click on the search tab. This will provide you a table of the month-end assets and liabilities of the Bank of Canada for the most recent few months. To expand the view to time periods further into the past click on the "Add/Remove data" tab and follow the instructions.

a. Under the "Total assets" portion of the table, look in the "Total assets" row. What amount is displayed next to "Total assets"? What amount is displayed next to "Government of Canada, Treasury Bills"? What amount is displayed next to "Government of Canada, bonds"? What percent of the Bank of Canada's total assets are made up of Canadian government treasury bills? What percent are made up of Canadian government treasury bonds?

b. Do the Bank of Canada's assets consist primarily of Canadian government treasury securities, as they did in January 2007, the beginning of the graph in Figure 14-13, or does the Bank of Canada still own a large number of other assets, as it did in mid-2009, in the middle of the graph in Figure 14-13? In particular, does the Bank of Canada have a figure near zero in the asset rows entitled "Loans and receivables, advances to members of the Canadian Payments Association" and "Loans and receivables, securities purchased under resale agreements"? Or are these two figures a significant percentage of the Bank of Canada's total assets as they were in 2009 and much of 2010?

CHAPTER 15

Monetary Policy

2012 CANADIAN OF THE YEAR

One month into his new job at the Bank of England, and former Bank of Canada governor Mark Carney is front-page news in London.

Toby Melville/Reuters/Corbis

MARK CARNEY, FROM TINY FORT Smith, Northwest Territories, is a popular and well-known figure in Canada. *Time* magazine called him "smart and sexy." In 2009, The *Financial Times* called him one of the 50 people who will "frame the way forward" in the debate on the future of capitalism. In 2012, he was named Canadian of the Year by the Canadian Club of Toronto and Business Newsmaker of the Year by the Canadian Press.

On November 26, 2012, Carney made news headlines by announcing he would leave his current position, as governor of the Bank of Canada, so that he could cross the Atlantic to head up the Bank of England in July 2013. Why does this man generate so much news? The answer is that the governor of the Bank of Canada (BOC) is the head of the organization that controls our country's monetary policy.

Since becoming the governor of the BOC in 2008, Mark Carney has gained considerable popularity and respect, and has been called one of the best central bankers of our generation.

His performance at the BOC was so spectacular and impeccable that the Bank of England offered him its top position. The British chancellor of the exchequer, George Osborne, said about Carney, "he is quite simply the best, most experienced and most qualified person in the world to be the next Governor of the Bank of England." In accepting the offer, Carney becomes the first non-Briton to be the head of the Old Lady of Threadneedle Street.

People sometimes say that the governor of the Bank of Canada decides how much money to print. That's not quite true: for one thing, the Bank of Canada doesn't literally print money, and beyond that, monetary decisions are actually made by a governing council rather than by one person. But as we learned in Chapter 14, the BOC can use actions such as open-market operations and deposit switching to alter the money supply—and the governor of the Bank of Canada has more influence over these actions than anyone else in Canada.

And these actions matter a lot. Of the three recessions Canada has experienced in the past 50 years, two of them were in part either worsened or caused by the decisions of the Bank of Canada to tighten monetary policy conditions to fight inflation.[1] Yet, in a number of other cases, the BOC has played a key role in fighting slumps and promoting recovery. The 2008–2009 recession put the BOC at centre stage. Carney's aggressive response to the recession, which, as we saw in Chapter 14, included lowering its key policy interest rate to a historically low level, inspired both praise (for alleviating the length and the magnitude of

- ❱ What the **money demand curve is**
- ❱ Why the **liquidity preference model** determines the interest rate in the short run
- ❱ How the Bank of Canada implements monetary policy, moving the interest rate to affect aggregate output
- ❱ Why monetary policy is the main tool for stabilizing the economic conditions in a market economy
- ❱ How the behaviour of the Bank of Canada compares to that of other central banks
- ❱ Why economists believe in **monetary neutrality**—that monetary policy affects only the price level, not aggregate output, in the long run
- ❱ Why the Bank of Canada pursues **inflation targeting** and how it uses monetary policy to achieve the inflation target

the recession) and condemnation (for further inflating the housing bubble and increasing household debt).

In this chapter we'll learn how monetary policy works, that is, how actions by the Bank of Canada can have a powerful effect on the nation's economy. We'll start by looking at the *demand for money* from households and firms. Then we'll see how the BOC's ability to change the *supply of money* allows it to move interest rates in the short run and thereby affect real GDP. We'll look at Canada's monetary policy in practice and compare it to the monetary policies of other central banks. We'll conclude by examining the long-run effects of monetary policy. ■

---

[1]The recession of 1981–1982 was caused primarily by adverse supply shocks, but the Bank of Canada's subsequent tightening of monetary policy conditions to fight inflation deepened and prolonged the recession. The Bank of Canada directly caused the recession of 1990–1991 by again using monetary policy to lower the rate of inflation.

The Demand for Money

I n Chapter 14 we learned about the various types of monetary aggregates: M1, the narrowest definition of the money supply, consists of currency in circulation (cash) plus chequeable (demand) deposits at chartered banks. M1+, the next broadest definition, consists of M1 plus the demand deposits at trust companies, mortgage and loan companies, credit unions, and caisses populaires. M2, the next step up, consists of M1 plus personal term deposits and non-personal demand and notice deposits, all at chartered banks. M2+ consists of M2 plus similar deposits at trust companies, mortgage and loan companies, credit unions, and caisses populaires, as well as individual annuities at life insurance companies, personal deposits at other financial institutions, and money market mutual funds. M3, one of the broadest definitions of money supply, consists of M2 plus chartered bank non-personal term deposits and chartered bank foreign currency deposits of residents. We also learned why people hold some of their assets in the form of money—primarily to make it easier to buy goods and services. Other assets lack the liquidity of money, which means they are not as useful for settling transactions. Now we'll go deeper, examining what determines how much money individuals and firms want to hold at any given time.

There is a price to be paid for the convenience of holding money.

The Opportunity Cost of Holding Money

Most economic decisions involve trade-offs at the margin. That is, individuals decide how much of a good to consume by determining whether the benefit they'd gain from consuming a bit more of any given good is worth the cost. The same decision process is used when deciding how much money to hold.

Individuals and firms find it useful to hold some of their assets in the form of money because of the convenience money provides: money can be used to make purchases directly, but other assets can't. But there is a price to be paid for that convenience: money normally yields a lower rate of return than interest-bearing **non-monetary assets**.

As an example of how convenience makes it worth incurring some opportunity costs, consider the fact that even today—with the prevalence of credit cards, debit cards, and ATMs—people continue to keep cash in their wallets rather than leave the funds in an interest-bearing account. They do this because they don't want to have to go to an ATM to withdraw money every time they want to buy lunch from a place that doesn't accept credit cards or won't accept them for small amounts because of the processing fee. In other words, the convenience of keeping some cash in your wallet is more valuable than the interest you would earn by keeping that money in the bank.

Even holding money in a chequing account involves a trade-off between convenience and earning interest. That's because you can earn a higher interest rate by putting your money in assets other than a chequing account. For example, many banks offer guaranteed investment certificates (GICs), which pay a higher interest rate than ordinary bank accounts. But GICs also carry a penalty if you withdraw the funds before a certain amount of time—say, six months—has elapsed. An individual who keeps funds in a chequing account is forgoing the higher interest rate those funds would have earned if placed in a GIC in return for the convenience of having cash readily available when needed.

So making sense of the demand for money is about understanding how individuals and firms trade off the benefit of holding cash—which provides convenience but no interest—versus the benefit of holding interest-bearing non-monetary assets—which provide interest but not convenience. And that trade-off is in part affected by the interest rate. (As before, when we say *the interest rate* it is with the understanding that we mean a nominal interest rate—that is, it's unadjusted for inflation.) Next, we'll

Non-monetary assets are assets that are not made up of money, nor function as money.

vitapix/iStockphoto

examine how that trade-off changed dramatically from April 2008 to April 2009, when there was a big fall in interest rates.

Table 15-1 illustrates the opportunity cost of holding money in a specific month, April 2008. The first row shows what interest rate chartered banks offered on 90-day term deposits—that is, the annual interest rate you could get if you were willing to tie up your funds for 90 days. In April 2008, this rate was 1.55%. The second row shows the interest rate on interest-bearing non-chequeable savings deposits (specifically, those included in M2). The funds in these accounts were much more accessible than those in GICs and term deposits, but the cost of that convenience was a significantly lower interest rate, only 0.1%. Finally, the last row shows the interest rate on currency—the cash in your wallet, which was, of course, zero.

Table 15-1 shows the opportunity cost of holding money at one point in time, but the opportunity cost of holding money changes when the overall level of interest rates changes. Specifically, when the overall level of interest rates falls, the opportunity cost of holding money falls, too.

Table 15-2 illustrates this point by showing how selected interest rates changed between April 2008 and April 2009, a period when the Bank of Canada was slashing rates in an effort to fight off the recession triggered by the financial crisis that originated in the United States. A comparison of the two interest rates illustrates what happens when the opportunity cost of holding money falls sharply. Between April 2008 and April 2009, the bank rate, which the BOC can control, fell by 2.75 percentage points. The interest rate on 90-day prime corporate paper fell 2.55 percentage points, while the rate on 90-day term deposits fell by 1.5 percentage points. These interest rates are **short-term interest rates**—rates on financial assets that come due or mature within less than a year.

TABLE 15-1 Selected Interest Rates, April 2008

Chartered banks' 90-day term deposits	1.55%
Chartered banks' non-chequeable savings deposits	0.10%
Currency	0

Sources: Bank of Canada; Statistics Canada.

TABLE 15-2 Interest Rates and the Opportunity Cost of Holding Money

	April 2008	April 2009
Bank rate	3.25%	0.50%
Prime corporate paper rate: three-month term	3.25%	0.70%
Chartered banks' 90-day term deposits	1.55%	0.05%
Chartered banks' non-chequeable savings deposits	0.1%	0.05%
Chartered Currency	0%	0%
90-day term deposits minus non-chequeable savings deposits (percentage points)	1.45%	0%
90-day term deposits minus currency (percentage points)	1.55%	0.05%

Sources: Bank of Canada; Statistics Canada.

As short-term interest rates fell between April 2008 and April 2009, the interest rates on money didn't fall by the same amount. The interest rate on currency, of course, remained at zero. The interest rate paid on non-chequeable savings accounts did fall, but by much less than short-term interest rates. As a comparison of the two columns of Table 15-2 shows, the opportunity cost of holding money fell. The last two rows of Table 15-2 summarize this comparison: they give the difference between the interest rate on non-chequeable savings accounts and on currency and the interest rate on 90-day term deposits. These differences—the opportunity cost of holding money rather than interest-bearing assets—declined sharply between April 2008 and April 2009. This reflects a general result: *The higher the short-term interest rate, the higher the opportunity cost of holding money; the lower the short-term interest rate, the lower the opportunity cost of holding money.*

It is no coincidence that the bank rate in Table 15-2 and the interest rates on 90-day term deposits for prime corporate paper fell by similar amounts at the

Short-term interest rates are the interest rates on financial assets that mature within less than a year.

same time. Short-term interest rates tend to move together because short-term assets such as term deposits, one-month and three-month treasury bills, and one-year GICs are, in effect, competing for the same business. Investors will sell any short-term asset that offers a lower-than-average interest rate, and buy one that offers a higher yield. Selling these assets, in turn, tends to lower their prices, which forces their interest rates up, because investors must be rewarded with a higher rate to induce them to buy it.

Between April 2008 and April 2009, the annual percentage rate of growth of currency outside of banks and M1 was 8.5% and 13% respectively. In the year before this, the annual growth rate in these monetary aggregates was only 2.6% and 6.9% respectively. So, obviously the growth rate of these narrow measures of the money supply accelerated significantly in 2008; and, as depicted in Figure 15-3, the impact of this increase in the money supply was a significant decrease in short-term nominal interest rates.

Investors will move their wealth into any short-term financial asset that offers an above-average interest rate. The purchase of the asset drives its interest rate down when sellers find they can lower the rate of return on the asset and still find willing buyers. So interest rates on short-term financial assets tend to be roughly the same because no asset will consistently offer a higher-than-average or a lower-than-average interest rate.

Table 15-2 contains only short-term interest rates. At any given moment, **long-term interest rates**—rates of interest on financial assets that mature, or come due, a number of years into the future—may be different from short-term interest rates. The difference between short-term and long-term interest rates is sometimes important as a practical matter. Moreover, it's short-term rates rather than long-term rates that affect money demand, because the decision to hold money involves trading off the convenience of holding cash versus the payoff from holding assets that mature in the short term—a year or less. For the moment, however, let's ignore the distinction between short-term and long-term rates and assume that there is only one interest rate.

The Money Demand Curve

Because the overall level of interest rates affects the opportunity cost of holding money, the quantity of money individuals and firms want to hold is, other things equal, negatively related to the interest rate. In Figure 15-1, the horizontal axis shows the quantity of money demanded and the vertical axis shows the interest rate, i, which you can think of as a representative short-term interest rate such as the rate on 90-day term deposits. (As we discussed in Chapter 10, it is the nominal interest rate, not the real interest rate, that influences people's money allocation decisions. Hence, i in Figure 15-1 and all subsequent figures is the nominal interest rate.)

The relationship between the interest rate and the quantity of money demanded by the public is illustrated by the nominal **money demand curve,** MD, in Figure 15-1. The money demand curve slopes downward because, other things equal, a higher interest rate increases the opportunity cost of holding money, leading the public to reduce the nominal quantity of money it demands. For example, if the interest rate is very low—say, 1%—the interest forgone by holding money is relatively small. As a result, individuals and firms will tend to hold relatively large amounts of money to avoid the cost and nuisance of converting other assets into money when making purchases. Since the interest rates affect the amount of cash agents want to hold, the money demand mentioned here and in the rest of the chapter is the nominal demand for money, whether expressly termed "nominal" or not. Likewise, in Figure 15-1 and all subsequent figures, the quantity of money referred to is the nominal quantity of money, either supplied or demanded.

By contrast, if the interest rate is relatively high—say, 19.5%, a level it reached in Canada for 90-day term deposits in August 1981—the opportunity cost of holding

Long-term interest rates are interest rates on financial assets that mature a number of years in the future.

The **money demand curve** shows the relationship between the interest rate and the (nominal) quantity of money demanded.

FIGURE   **15-1**   The Money Demand Curve

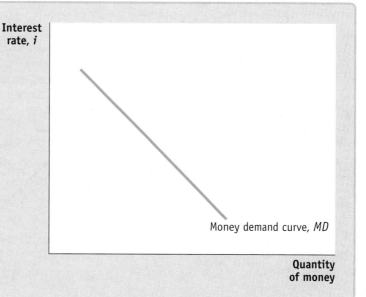

The money demand curve illustrates the relationship between the interest rate and the quantity of money demanded. It slopes downward: a higher interest rate leads to a higher opportunity cost of holding money and reduces the quantity of money demanded. Correspondingly, a lower interest rate reduces the opportunity cost of holding money and increases the quantity of money demanded.

money is high. People will respond by keeping only small amounts in cash and deposits, converting assets into money only when needed.

You might ask why we draw the money demand curve with the interest rate— as opposed to rates of return on other assets, such as stocks or real estate—on the vertical axis. The answer is that for most people the relevant question in deciding how much money to hold is whether to put the funds in the form of other assets that can be turned fairly quickly and easily into money. Stocks don't fit that definition because there are significant transaction fees when you buy and sell stocks (which is why stock market investors are advised not to buy and sell too often). Real estate doesn't fit the definition either because selling real estate involves even larger fees and can take a long time as well. So the relevant comparison is with assets that are "close to" money—fairly liquid assets like GICs. And as we've already seen, the interest rates on all these assets normally move closely together.

Shifts of the Money Demand Curve

A number of factors other than the interest rate affect the demand for money. When one of these factors changes, the money demand curve shifts. Figure 15-2 shows shifts of the money demand curve: an increase in the demand for money corresponds to a rightward shift of the *MD* curve, raising the quantity of money demanded at any given interest rate; a decrease in the demand for money corresponds to a leftward shift of the *MD* curve, reducing the quantity of money demanded at any given interest rate. The most important factors causing the money demand curve to shift are changes in the aggregate price level, changes in real GDP, changes in credit markets and banking technology, and changes in institutions.

Changes in the Aggregate Price Level Canadians keep a lot more cash in their wallets and funds in their chequing accounts today than they did in the 1960s. One reason is that they have to if they want to be able to buy anything: almost everything costs more now than it did when you could get a burger from McDonald's for about 39 cents and a litre of gasoline for about 7 cents. So, other things equal, higher prices increase the demand for money (a rightward shift of the *MD* curve), and lower prices decrease the demand for money (a leftward shift of the *MD* curve).

We can actually be more specific than this: other things equal, the demand for money is *proportional* to the price level. That is, if the aggregate price level rises

FIGURE **15-2** Increases and Decreases in the Demand for Money

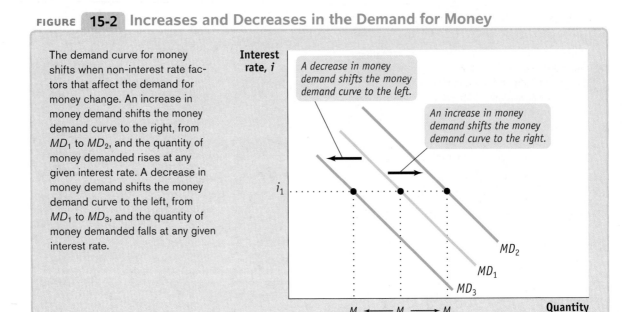

The demand curve for money shifts when non-interest rate factors that affect the demand for money change. An increase in money demand shifts the money demand curve to the right, from MD_1 to MD_2, and the quantity of money demanded rises at any given interest rate. A decrease in money demand shifts the money demand curve to the left, from MD_1 to MD_3, and the quantity of money demanded falls at any given interest rate.

by 20%, the quantity of money demanded at any given interest rate, such as i_1 in Figure 15-2, also rises by 20%—the movement from M_1 to M_2. Why? Because if the price of everything rises by 20%, it takes 20% more money to buy the same basket of goods and services. And if the aggregate price level falls by 20%, at any given interest rate the quantity of money demanded falls by 20%—shown by the movement from M_1 to M_3 at the interest rate i_1. As we'll see later, the fact that money demand is proportional to the price level has important implications for the long-run effects of monetary policy.

Changes in Real GDP Households and firms hold money as a way to facilitate purchases of goods and services. The larger the quantity of goods and services they buy, the larger the quantity of money they will want to hold at any given interest rate. So an increase in real GDP—the total quantity of goods and services produced and sold in the economy—shifts the money demand curve rightward. A fall in real GDP shifts the money demand curve leftward.

Changes in Credit Markets and Banking Technology Credit cards are everywhere in Canadian life today, but it wasn't always so. Credit cards were introduced in Canada in 1968 with the launch of the Chargex card (this brand name was replaced by Visa in the late 1970s). Master Charge, now known as MasterCard, was introduced in the early 1970s. Before then, people would pay for purchases either with cash or a cheque. The invention of credit cards allowed people to hold less money in order to fund their purchases and decreased the demand for money. In addition, changes in banking technology that made credit cards widely available and widely accepted magnified the effect, making it easier for people to make purchases without having to convert funds from their interest-bearing assets, further reducing the demand for money.

Changes in Institutions At one time, chartered banks were virtually synonymous with the Canadian banking system. Other financial institutions, such as credit unions or trust companies, typically offered higher interest rates on savings accounts than banks did, but had a smaller range of financial services. Following major changes to the Bank Act in 1980, the distinction between these financial institutions has become increasingly blurred. As competition has increased, chartered banks have introduced new types of deposits. For example, the introduction of chequeable savings accounts that pay interest has reduced the opportunity cost of holding funds in chequing accounts, leading to a rise in the demand for money.

The recent combination of increased competition in the banking sector and the increased use of new information technologies that permit online banking is reducing the cost of holding money even further. In particular, chartered banks now offer non-chequeable, high-interest savings accounts that combine the features of a chequing account and a GIC. Such accounts appeal to both banks and depositors. The banks like them because they involve less paperwork than GICs. Depositors like them because they can, via the Internet, easily and instantaneously transfer funds from a high-interest savings account to chequeable accounts, at little or no cost. Again, this development is reducing the opportunity cost of holding money, leading to a rise in the demand for money. As these developments, which make money demand rise, occur, the money demand curve is shifted to the right.

As Figure 15-3 shows, M1, M2, and M3, when expressed as percentages of nominal GDP, have generally increased since 1970. One exception to this increase occurred during the 1970s and early 1980s, when M1 declined as a result of the high, and rising, rate of inflation. This downturn made sense, because M1 consists of narrow money: cash in hand, which pays no interest, and demand deposits at chartered banks, which pay little or no interest. The high inflation in the late 1970s and early 1980s raised nominal interest rates considerably, which in turn increased the opportunity cost of holding M1. As a result, people shifted their financial assets to broad money (M2 and M3), which paid higher rates of interest. Subsequently, as inflation declined during the 1980s and 1990s, the demand for M1 rose back up, toward 20% of GDP. The historically low rates of interest experienced since the financial crisis of 2008–2009 have helped to push the demand for M1 above 20% of GDP. The stronger upward drift to M2 and M3 reflects the impact on money demand that is generated by changes to institutions, rules and regulations, and technology. These innovations have tended to make broad money (M2 or M3) more useful and more valuable to people, which has made them willing to hold (demand) a greater amount of broad money (M2 or M3) as a fraction of GDP.

FIGURE   15-3   Canadian Money Supply as a Percent of Nominal GDP

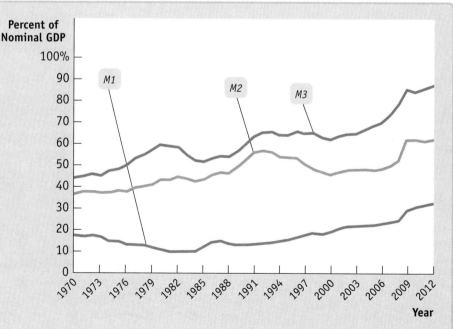

Different measures of money supply as percentages of nominal GDP have generally increased since 1970, with the exception of M1, which decreased as a percentage of GDP between the mid-1970s and the early 1980s. The decline in M1 during that period was caused by a high and rising inflation rate. Later, when the inflation rate became low and stable, the shares of these monetary aggregates as percentage GDP again moved in the same direction.

Source: Statistics Canada.

No matter what they are shopping for, Japanese consumers tend to pay with cash rather than plastic.

ECONOMICS > IN ACTION

A YEN FOR CASH

Japan, say financial experts, is still a "cash society." Visitors from Canada or the United States are surprised at how little use the Japanese make of credit cards and how much cash they carry around in their wallets. Yet Japan is an economically and technologically advanced country and, according to some measures, ahead of Canada in the use of telecommunications and information technology. So why do the citizens of this economic powerhouse still do business the way Canadians did a generation ago? The answer highlights the factors affecting the demand for money.

One reason the Japanese use cash so much is that their institutions never made the switch to heavy reliance on plastic. For complex reasons, Japan's retail sector is still dominated by small mom-and-pop stores, which are reluctant to invest in credit card technology. Japan's banks have also been slow about pushing transaction technology; visitors are often surprised to find that ATMs close early in the evening rather than staying open all night.

But there's another reason the Japanese hold so much cash: there's little opportunity cost to doing so. Short-term interest rates in Japan have been below 1% since the mid-1990s. It also helps that the Japanese crime rate is quite low; you are unlikely to have your wallet full of cash stolen. So why not hold cash?

▼ Quick Review

- Money offers a lower rate of return than other financial assets. We usually compare the rate of return on money with **short-term**, not **long-term, interest rates.**

- Holding money provides liquidity but incurs an opportunity cost that rises with the interest rate, leading to the downward slope of the **money demand curve.**

- Changes in the aggregate price level, real GDP, credit markets and banking technology, and institutions shift the money demand curve. An increase in the demand for money shifts the money demand curve rightward; a decrease in the demand for money shifts the money demand curve leftward.

CHECK YOUR UNDERSTANDING 15-1

1. Explain how each of the following would affect the quantity of money demanded. Does the change cause a movement along the money demand curve or a shift of the money demand curve?
   a. Short-term interest rates rise from 5% to 30%.
   b. All prices fall by 10%.
   c. New wireless technology automatically charges supermarket purchases to credit cards, eliminating the need to stop at the cash register.
   d. In order to avoid paying a sharp increase in taxes, residents of Laguria shift their assets into overseas bank accounts. These accounts are harder for tax authorities to trace but also harder for their owners to tap and convert funds into cash.

2. Which of the following will increase the opportunity cost of holding cash? Reduce it? Have no effect? Explain.
   a. Merchants charge a 1% fee on debit/credit card transactions for purchases of less than $50.
   b. To attract more deposits, banks raise the interest paid on one-year GICs.
   c. It's the holiday shopping season and retailers have temporarily slashed prices to unexpectedly low levels.
   d. The cost of food rises significantly.

Solutions appear at back of book.

Money and Interest Rates

Central Banks Announce Coordinated Interest Rate Reductions

Throughout the current financial crisis, central banks have engaged in continuous close consultation and have cooperated in unprecedented joint actions such as the provision of liquidity to reduce strains in financial markets. Inflationary pressures have started to moderate in a number of countries, partly reflecting a marked decline in energy and other commodity prices. Inflation expectations are diminishing and remain anchored to price stability. The recent intensification of the financial crisis has augmented the downside risks to growth and thus has diminished further the upside risks to price stability.

Some easing of global monetary conditions is therefore warranted. Accordingly, the Bank of Canada, the Bank of England, the European Central Bank, the Federal Reserve, Sveriges Riksbank, and the Swiss National Bank are today announcing reductions in policy interest rates. The Bank of Japan expresses its strong support of these policy actions.

Bank of Canada lowers overnight rate target by ½ percentage point to 2½ per cent.

The Bank of Canada today announced that it is lowering its target for the overnight rate by ½ percentage point to 2½ per cent. The operating band for the overnight rate is correspondingly lowered, and the Bank Rate is now 2¾ per cent.

The intensification of the global financial crisis is having a marked impact on all countries. In recent weeks conditions in global financial markets have deteriorated sharply, the U.S. economy has weakened further, and commodity prices have fallen abruptly.

As a result of these developments, credit conditions in Canada have tightened significantly, despite the relative health of our financial institutions. Weaker growth in the United States and other important trading partners will increase the drag on the Canadian economy coming from net exports. The deterioration of our terms of trade will act to moderate the growth of domestic demand. While the recent depreciation of the Canadian dollar will help cushion the effects of the weaker global outlook on the domestic economy, it will not completely offset them.

Below-potential growth in aggregate demand through 2009, combined with a lower profile for commodity prices, will significantly ease inflation pressures in Canada. Inflation expectations remain well anchored.

In view of these developments, the Bank of Canada decided to join other major central banks and lower its target for the overnight rate by 50 basis points today. This action will provide timely and significant support to the Canadian economy. The Bank will continue to monitor carefully economic and financial developments, along with the evolution of risks, in judging whether any further action might be required to achieve its 2 per cent inflation target over the medium term.[2]

So read a press release from the Bank of Canada issued on October 8, 2008. The BOC lowered the overnight rate by 0.5 percentage points in an attempt to prevent the deepening of the recession.[3] What was special about this announcement was that the BOC lowered its target for the overnight rate on a date that was outside its fixed schedule of dates for policy interest rate announcements. The press release indicated that this surprise interest rate cut was part of a coordinated effort by central banks around the world that were attempting to loosen the tight financial market and to support the weakening global economy. We learned about the overnight rate in Chapter 14: it is the rate at which banks lend excess reserves to each other generally for one business day or less (unless a longer term is negotiated). The BOC sets a target for the overnight rate, and then it's up to the BOC's officials to achieve that target. This is done by open-market operations— buying and selling government bonds, usually short-term bonds.

Once the BOC sets the target for the overnight rate, other key interest rates, such as the prime rate, rates on GICs, and mortgage rates, will move in the same direction, and these interest rates tend to change in proportion to the change in the target for the overnight rate. How does the BOC go about achieving a *target for the overnight rate*? And more to the point, how is the BOC able to affect interest rates at all?

---

[2]*Source:* "Central Banks Announce Coordinated Interest Rate Reductions," Bank of Canada, October 2008, www.bankofcanada.ca/2008.

[3]Sometimes you may hear that the BOC or chartered banks change the interest rates by a certain number of basis points. One basis point is equal to 0.01 percentage point. Thus, 100 basis points is equivalent to one percentage point.

According to the **liquidity preference model of the interest rate,** the interest rate is determined by the supply and demand for money.

The **money supply curve** shows how the quantity of money supplied varies with the interest rate.

The Equilibrium Interest Rate

Recall that, for simplicity, we're assuming there is only one interest rate paid on non-monetary financial assets, both in the short run and in the long run. To understand how the interest rate is determined, consider Figure 15-4, which illustrates the **liquidity preference model of the interest rate;** this model says that the interest rate is determined by the supply and demand for money in the market for money. Figure 15-4 combines the nominal money demand curve, MD, with the nominal **money supply curve,** MS, which shows how the nominal quantity of money supplied by the Bank of Canada varies with the interest rate. As we did with MD, from now on, we drop the word "nominal," with the understanding that "money" in MS, as in MD, represents nominal quantities.

In Chapter 14 we learned how the Bank of Canada can increase or decrease the money supply: it usually does this through *open-market operations*, buying or selling Canadian government bonds (in practice, short-term treasury bills), but it can also lend via the *bank rate* or pursue *government deposit switching*. Let's assume for simplicity that the BOC, using one or more of these methods, simply chooses the level of the money supply that it believes will achieve its interest rate target. Then the money supply curve is a vertical line, MS in Figure 15-4, with a horizontal intercept corresponding to the money supply chosen by the BOC, $\overline{M}$. The money market equilibrium is at E, where MS and MD cross. At this point the quantity of money demanded equals the money supply, $\overline{M}$, leading to an equilibrium interest rate of i_E.

To understand why i_E is the equilibrium interest rate, consider what happens if the money market is at a point like L, where the interest rate, i_L, is below i_E. At i_L the public wants to hold the quantity of money M_L, an amount larger than the actual money supply, $\overline{M}$. This means that at point L, the public wants to shift some of its wealth out of interest-bearing assets such as GICs into money.

This has two implications. One is that the quantity of money demanded is *more* than the quantity of money supplied. The other is that the quantity of interest-bearing money assets demanded is less than the quantity supplied. So those trying to sell non-money assets such as issuers of bonds will find that they have to offer a higher interest rate to attract buyers. As a result, the interest rate will

---

FIGURE **15-4** **Equilibrium in the Money Market**

The money supply curve, MS, is vertical at the money supply chosen by the Bank of Canada, $\overline{M}$. The money market is in equilibrium at the interest rate i_E: the quantity of money demanded by the public is equal to $\overline{M}$, the quantity of money supplied.

At a point such as L, the interest rate, i_L, is below i_E and the corresponding quantity of money demanded, M_L, exceeds the money supply, $\overline{M}$. In an attempt to shift their wealth out of non-money interest-bearing financial assets and raise their money holdings, investors drive the interest rate up to i_E. At a point such as H, the interest rate i_H exceeds i_E and the corresponding quantity of money demanded, M_H, is less than the money supply, $\overline{M}$. In an attempt to shift out of money holdings into non-money interest-bearing financial assets, investors drive the interest rate down to i_E.

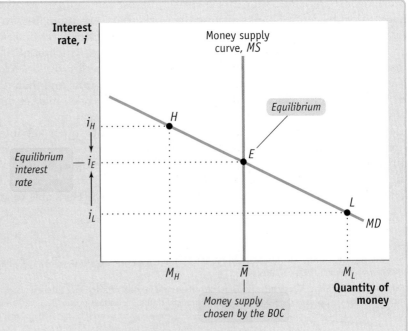

be driven up from i_L until the public wants to hold the quantity of money that is actually available, $\overline{M}$. That is, the interest rate will rise until it is equal to i_E.

Now consider what happens if the money market is at a point such as H in Figure 15-4, where the interest rate i_H is above i_E. In that case the quantity of money demanded, M_H, is less than the quantity of money supplied, $\overline{M}$. Correspondingly, the quantity of interest-bearing non-money assets demanded is greater than the quantity supplied. Those trying to sell interest-bearing non-money assets will find that they can offer a lower interest rate and still find willing buyers. This leads to a fall in the interest rate from i_H. It falls until the public wants to hold the quantity of money that is actually available, $\overline{M}$. Again, the interest rate will end up at i_E.

Two Models of Interest Rates?

You might have noticed that this is the second time we have discussed the determination of the interest rate. In Chapter 10 we studied the *loanable funds model* of the interest rate; according to that model, the interest rate is determined by the equalization of the supply of funds from lenders and the demand for funds by borrowers in the market for loanable funds. But here we have described a seemingly different model in which the interest rate is determined by the equalization of the supply and demand for money in the money market. Which of these models is correct?

The answer is both. We explain how the models are consistent with each other in Appendix 15A. For now, let's put the loanable funds model to one side and concentrate on the liquidity preference model of the interest rate. The most important insight from this model is that it shows us how monetary policy—actions by the Bank of Canada and other central banks—works.

Monetary Policy and the Interest Rate

Let's examine how the Bank of Canada can use changes in the money supply to change the interest rate. Figure 15-5 shows what happens when the BOC increases the money supply from $\overline{M}_1$ to $\overline{M}_2$. The economy is originally in equilibrium at E_1, with an equilibrium interest rate of i_1 and money supply $\overline{M}_1$. An increase in the money supply by the BOC to $\overline{M}_2$ shifts the money supply curve to the right, from MS_1 to MS_2, and leads to a fall in the equilibrium interest rate to i_2. Why? Because i_2 is the only interest rate at which the public is willing to hold the quantity of money actually supplied, $\overline{M}_2$.

So an increase in the money supply drives the interest rate down. Similarly, a reduction in the money supply drives the interest rate up. By adjusting the money supply up or down, the BOC can set the interest rate.

In practice, the Governing Council of the Bank of Canada decides at each meeting what interest rate should prevail until the next fixed announcement date of *the target for the overnight rate*. The BOC sets a target for the overnight rate, which is the desired level for the overnight rate. The BOC then adjusts the money supply by buying and selling treasury bills until the overnight rate reaches the target rate. The BOC can use other tools to reach the target rate, such as monetary policy implemented via government deposit switching, foreign exchange market intervention, and buying and selling of other assets, but these tools are used only rarely.[4]

Figure 15-6 shows how this works. In both panels, i_T is the target for the overnight rate. In panel (a), the initial money supply curve is MS_1 with money

---

[4]As of 1998, Canada no longer has an official policy to systematically intervene in the foreign exchange market so as to achieve some desired exchange rate. So, although we reserve the right to undertake foreign exchange market interventions (i.e., change the money supply) to affect the value of the Canadian dollar exchange rate, we no longer do so. The Bank of Canada last intervened to affect the Canadian dollar in September 1998. However, since 1998 the Bank has intervened to affect the value of a foreign currency. For example, in March 2011 it intervened to help stabilize the Japanese yen and in September 2000 to support the euro.

FIGURE **15-5** The Effect of an Increase in the Money Supply on the Interest Rate

The Bank of Canada can lower the interest rate by increasing the money supply. Here, the equilibrium interest rate falls from i_1 to i_2 in response to an increase in the money supply from $\overline{M}_1$ to $\overline{M}_2$. In order to induce people to hold the larger quantity of money, the interest rate must fall from i_1 to i_2.

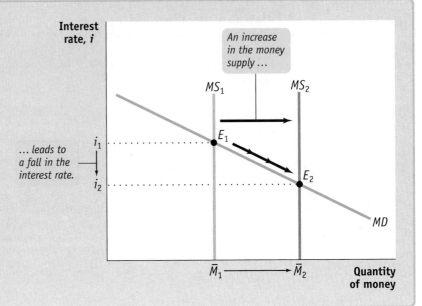

supply $\overline{M}_1$, and the equilibrium interest rate, i_1, is above the target rate. To lower the interest rate to i_T, the BOC makes an open-market purchase of treasury bills. As we learned in Chapter 14, an open-market purchase of treasury bills leads to an increase in the money supply via the money multiplier. This is illustrated in panel (a) by the rightward shift of the money supply curve from MS_1 to MS_2 and an increase in the money supply to $\overline{M}_2$. This drives the equilibrium interest rate down to the target rate, i_T.

FOR INQUIRING MINDS

EIGHT FIXED DATES FOR THE BOC POLICY INTEREST RATE ANNOUNCEMENTS

Eight times a year, in accordance with a pre-announced schedule, and always at 9:00 A.M. Eastern Standard Time, anxiously waiting economists and investors around the country receive a press release from the Bank of Canada. These press releases contain the BOC's analysis of the current performance of the Canadian economy and its view of where the economy is heading. Each press release also reveals whether the Bank of Canada's key policy interest rate, its target for the overnight rate, will be increased, reduced, or left unchanged.

Why is this schedule of announcements important? Because the overnight rate—the rate at which commercial banks lend each other short-term funds—is the *trend-setting interest rate*. When it changes, all short-term interest rates change. So an announced change in the Bank of Canada's target for the overnight rate indicates a change

in monetary policy. And these changes have significant ramifications for financial markets, stock markets, and the economy in general.

In addition, having a schedule of fixed announcement dates ahead of time helps to reduce uncertainty in financial markets and provide transparency for monetary policy. Uncertainty can result in higher interest rates due to investors demanding risk premiums to compensate for additional perceived risk. It also contributes to reluctance on the part of investors to lend and on the part of others to spend and to borrow, and it makes firms wary of hiring additional workers. The consequences are reduced levels of consumption and investment spending, rising unemployment, and shrinking real output. Uncertainty, if high enough, can cause significant economic harm.

It may seem curious that the Bank of Canada commits itself in advance to a schedule of announcements and to

changing its key policy interest rate only eight times a year. However, the BOC does have the option of changing the target for the overnight rate between fixed announcement dates in the event of exceptional circumstances. This last occurred in 2008 when, in light of deteriorating economic conditions stemming from the U.S. financial crisis, the BOC lowered the target rate on October 8 (the press release at the beginning of this section), ahead of the scheduled fixed announcement date of October 21, when it again lowered the rate in response to the economic conditions.

The Bank of Canada is not the only central bank to announce its policy interest rate changes on pre-set dates. The central banks of many countries, including the Federal Reserve of the United States, the Bank of England, the European Central Bank, the Bank of Japan, and the Reserve Bank of Australia, follow the same procedure.

FIGURE **15-6** Setting the Target for the Overnight Rate

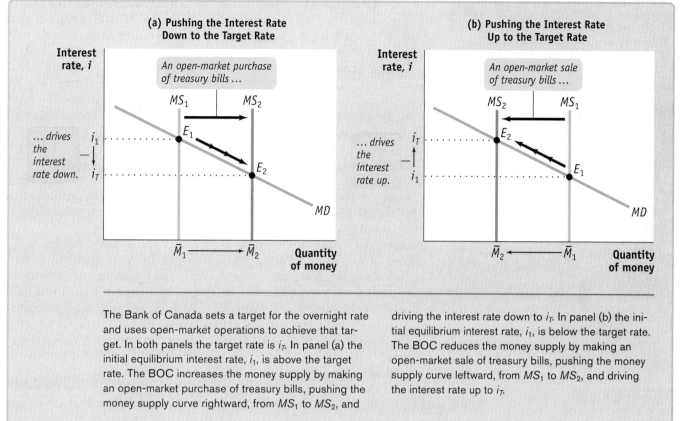

(a) Pushing the Interest Rate Down to the Target Rate

Interest rate, i

An open-market purchase of treasury bills ...

MS_1 MS_2

E_1

... drives the interest rate down.

i_1

i_T

E_2

MD

$\overline{M}_1 \longrightarrow \overline{M}_2$ Quantity of money

(b) Pushing the Interest Rate Up to the Target Rate

Interest rate, i

An open-market sale of treasury bills ...

MS_2 MS_1

E_2

... drives the interest rate up.

i_T

i_1

E_1

MD

$\overline{M}_2 \longleftarrow \overline{M}_1$ Quantity of money

The Bank of Canada sets a target for the overnight rate and uses open-market operations to achieve that target. In both panels the target rate is i_T. In panel (a) the initial equilibrium interest rate, i_1, is above the target rate. The BOC increases the money supply by making an open-market purchase of treasury bills, pushing the money supply curve rightward, from MS_1 to MS_2, and

driving the interest rate down to i_T. In panel (b) the initial equilibrium interest rate, i_1, is below the target rate. The BOC reduces the money supply by making an open-market sale of treasury bills, pushing the money supply curve leftward, from MS_1 to MS_2, and driving the interest rate up to i_T.

Panel (b) shows the opposite case. Again, the initial money supply curve is MS_1 with money supply $\overline{M}_1$. But this time the equilibrium interest rate, i_1, is below the overnight rate, i_T. In this case, the BOC will make an open-market sale of treasury bills, leading to a fall in the money supply to $\overline{M}_2$ via the money multiplier. The money supply curve shifts leftward from MS_1 to MS_2, driving the equilibrium interest rate up to the target for the overnight rate, i_T.

Long-Term Interest Rates

Earlier in this chapter we mentioned that *long-term interest rates*—rates on bonds or loans that mature in several years—don't necessarily move with short-term interest rates. How is that possible, and what does it say about monetary policy?

Consider the case of Millie, who has already decided to place $10 000 in Canadian government bonds for the next two years. However, she hasn't decided whether to put the money in one-year bonds, at a 4% rate of interest, or two-year bonds, at a 5% rate of interest. If she buys the one-year bond, then in one year, Millie will receive the $10 000 she paid for the bond (the *principal*) plus interest earned. If instead she buys the two-year bond, Millie will have to wait until the end of the second year to receive her principal and her interest.

You might think that the two-year bonds are a clearly better deal—but they may not be. Suppose that Millie expects the rate of interest on one-year bonds to rise sharply next year. If she puts her funds in one-year bonds this year, she will be able to reinvest the money at a much higher rate next year. And this could give her a two-year rate of return

⚠ PITFALLS

THE TARGET VERSUS THE MARKET

Over the years, the Bank of Canada has changed the details of how it makes monetary policy. At one point, in the late 1970s and early 1980s, it did so by setting a target level for the money supply and altering the monetary base to achieve that target. Under this policy, the overnight rate fluctuated freely. However, as of December 2000, the Bank of Canada's current policy is to do just the opposite: set a target for the overnight rate eight times a year and allow the money supply to fluctuate as it pursues that target.

It is a common mistake to imagine that these policy changes have changed the way the money market works. That is, you'll sometimes hear people say that the interest rate no longer reflects the supply of and demand for money because the Bank of Canada sets the interest rate.

In fact, the money market works the same way as always: the interest rate is determined by the supply of and demand for money. The only difference is that now the Bank of Canada adjusts the supply of money to achieve its target interest rate. It's important not to confuse a change in the Bank's operating procedure with a change in the way the economy works.

The Canada Premium Bonds are shown coming off the presses at the Canada Bank Note Company in Ottawa.

that is higher than if she put her funds into the two-year bonds today. For example, if the rate of interest on one-year bonds rises from 4% this year to 8% next year, putting her funds in a one-year bond today and in another one-year bond a year from now will give her an annual rate of return over the next two years of about 6%, better than the 5% rate on two-year bonds.

The same considerations apply to all investors deciding between short-term and long-term bonds. If they expect short-term interest rates to rise, investors may buy short-term bonds even if long-term bonds bought today offer a higher interest rate today. If they expect short-term interest rates to fall, investors may buy long-term bonds even if short-term bonds bought today offer a higher interest rate today.

As this example suggests, long-term interest rates largely reflect the average expectation in the market about what's going to happen to short-term rates in the future. When long-term rates are higher than short-term rates, as they were in 2010, the market is signalling that it expects short-term rates to rise in the future.

This is not, however, the whole story: risk is also a factor. Return to the example of Millie, deciding whether to buy one-year or two-year bonds. Suppose that there is some chance she will need to cash in her investment after just one year—say, to meet an emergency medical bill. If she buys two-year bonds, she would have to sell those bonds to meet the unexpected expense. But what price will she get for those bonds? It depends on what has happened to interest rates in the rest of the economy. As we learned in Chapter 10, bond prices and interest rates move in opposite directions: if interest rates rise, bond prices fall, and vice versa.

This means that Millie will face extra risk if she buys two-year rather than one-year bonds, because if a year from now bond prices fall and she must sell her bonds in order to raise cash, she will lose money on the bonds. Owing to this risk factor, long-term interest rates are, on average, higher than short-term rates in order to compensate long-term bond purchasers for the higher risk they face (although this relationship is reversed when short-term rates are unusually high).

As we will see later in this chapter, the fact that long-term rates don't necessarily move with short-term rates is sometimes an important consideration for monetary policy.

ECONOMICS ► IN ACTION

THE BANK OF CANADA REVERSES COURSE

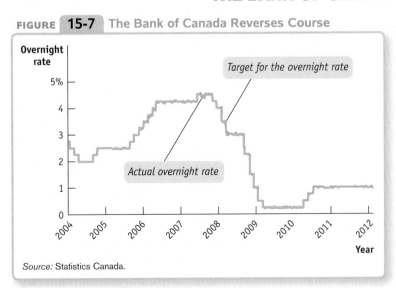

FIGURE 15-7 The Bank of Canada Reverses Course

Source: Statistics Canada.

We began this section with the BOC's press release from October 8, 2008, announcing that it was cutting its target interest rate. This particular action was part of a larger story: a dramatic reversal of the BOC policy that began in December 2007.

Figure 15-7 shows two interest rates from January 2004 to November 2012: the target for the overnight rate, decided by the BOC, and the actual rate in the overnight money market. As you can see, the BOC raised its target rate in a series of steps from mid-2005 until the middle of 2006; it did this to head off the possibility of an overheating economy and rising inflation (more on that later in this chapter). But the BOC dramatically reversed course beginning in December 2007, as the BOC worried that the weakening of the American economy and the increased tightness in world credit markets might have adverse effects on the Canadian economy. The downward trend in the target for the overnight rate continued until it reached its lowest level in history—0.25% on April 21, 2009. From April 2009 to May 2010, the target for the overnight rate was kept at 0.25% in response to a weak economy and high unemployment.

Figure 15-7 also shows that the BOC usually hits its target—the actual and the target for the overnight rates are often very similar. But not always: the BOC missed its target on numerous days in 2007, especially when the actual overnight rate was above or below the target rate. However, these episodes did not last long, and overall the BOC got what it wanted, at least as far as short-term interest rates were concerned.

CHECK YOUR UNDERSTANDING   15-2

1. Assume that there is an increase in the demand for money at every interest rate. Using a diagram, show what effect this will have on the equilibrium interest rate for a given money supply.

2. Now assume that the Bank of Canada is following a policy of targeting the overnight rate. What will the BOC do in the situation described in Question 1 to keep the overnight rate unchanged? Illustrate with a diagram.

3. Frannie must decide whether to buy a one-year bond today and another one a year from now, or buy a two-year bond today. In which of the following scenarios is she better off taking the first action? The second action?
   a. This year, the interest rate on a one-year bond is 4%; next year, it will be 10%. The interest rate on a two-year bond is 5%.
   b. This year, the interest rate on a one-year bond is 4%; next year, it will be 1%. The interest rate on a two-year bond is 3%.

Solutions appear at back of book.

> **Quick Review**
>
> - According to the **liquidity preference model of the interest rate,** the equilibrium interest rate is determined by the money demand curve and the **money supply curve.**
>
> - The Bank of Canada can move the interest rate through open-market operations that shift the money supply curve. In practice, the BOC sets the target for the overnight rate and uses open-market operations to achieve that target.
>
> - Long-term interest rates reflect expectations about what's going to happen to short-term rates in the future. Because of risk, long-term interest rates tend to be higher than short-term rates.

Monetary Policy and Aggregate Demand

In Chapter 13 we saw how fiscal policy can be used to stabilize the economy. Now we will see how monetary policy—changes in the money supply and the interest rate—can play the same role.

Expansionary and Contractionary Monetary Policy

In Chapter 12 we learned that monetary policy shifts the aggregate demand curve. We can now explain how that works: through the effect of monetary policy on the interest rate.

Figure 15-8 illustrates the process. Suppose, first, that the Bank of Canada wants to reduce interest rates, so it expands the money supply. As you can see in the top portion of the figure, a lower interest rate, will lead, other things equal, to more investment spending. This will in turn lead to higher consumer spending, through the multiplier process, and to an increase in aggregate output demanded. In the end, the total quantity of goods and services demanded at any given aggregate price level rises when the quantity of money increases, and the *AD* curve shifts to the right. Monetary policy that increases the demand for goods and services is known as **expansionary monetary policy.**

Suppose, alternatively, that the Bank of Canada wants to increase interest rates, so it contracts the money supply. You can see this process illustrated in the

Expansionary monetary policy is monetary policy that increases aggregate demand.

Contractionary monetary policy is monetary policy that decreases aggregate demand.

The **monetary transmission mechanism** describes the channels through which a change in interest rates (or money supply) will cause a shift in the aggregate demand curve (and ultimately affect the economy's output and inflation rate).

bottom portion of the diagram. Contraction of the money supply leads to a higher interest rate. The higher interest rate leads to lower investment spending, then to lower consumer spending, and then to a decrease in aggregate output demanded. So the total quantity of goods and services demanded falls when the money supply is reduced, and the *AD* curve shifts to the left. Monetary policy that decreases the demand for goods and services is called **contractionary monetary policy.**

Monetary Policy in Practice

How does the Bank of Canada decide whether to use expansionary or contractionary monetary policy? And how does it decide how much is enough? In Chapter 6 we learned that policy-makers try to fight recessions, as well as try to ensure *price stability:* low (though usually not zero) inflation. Actual monetary policy reflects a combination of these goals.

Typically, the Bank of Canada, like most central banks around the world, tends to engage in expansionary monetary policy when the economy is experiencing a recessionary gap (i.e., actual real GDP is below potential output), and engage in contractionary monetary policy when the economy is in an inflationary gap (i.e., actual real GDP is above potential output). Because it is subject to fewer lags than fiscal policy, monetary policy is the main tool for macroeconomic stabilization.

The process in Figure 15-8 that describes how monetary policy affects the economy is a simplified version of the *monetary transmission mechanism*. The **monetary transmission mechanism** describes the process by which a change in monetary policy, or the interest rate, would work its way through the economy, eventually affecting the economy's output and inflation rate. In Canada, the primary objective of monetary policy is to keep the inflation rate close to 2 percent within a target

FIGURE **15-8** **Expansionary and Contractionary Monetary Policy**

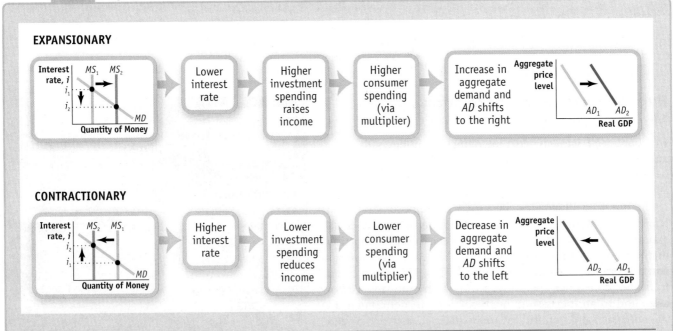

The top portion shows what happens when the BOC adopts an expansionary monetary policy and increases the money supply. Interest rates fall, leading to higher investment spending, which raises income, which, in turn, raises consumer spending and shifts the *AD* curve to the right. The bottom portion shows what happens when the BOC adopts a contractionary monetary policy and reduces the money supply. Interest rates rise, leading to lower investment spending and a reduction in income. This lowers consumer spending and shifts the *AD* curve to the left.

FIGURE **15-9** The Monetary Transmission Mechanism

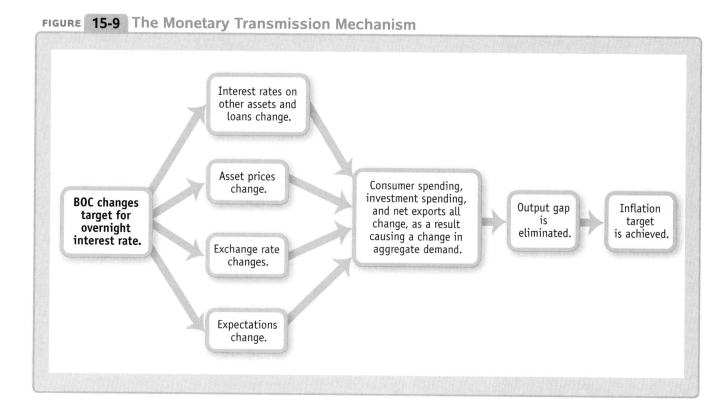

range of 1 to 3 percent. This means that the Bank of Canada will adjust the target for the overnight rate to bring the inflation rate back to its target range. However, if the inflation rate stays within the target range, the Bank of Canada can use monetary policy to smooth out business cycle fluctuations. Details about the inflation-control targeting will be discussed in the later part of this chapter. Now, let's focus on the monetary transmission mechanism, which Figure 15-9 illustrates.

The Bank of Canada believes that changes in the target for the overnight rate can affect the Canadian economy through four different channels: interest rates on other assets and loans, asset prices, the exchange rate, and market expectations.[5] Consider what happens when the economy is in a recessionary gap or in a negative output gap (where actual output is below potential output). To eliminate the recessionary gap, the Bank of Canada will lower the overnight rate target. A fall in the target for the overnight rate affects the economy via the four different channels, as follows:

Interest rates on other assets and loans There is a close link between the target for the overnight rate and interest rates on other assets in the economy, such as the prime rate and mortgage interest rates. Although there may not be a one-for-one relationship between a change in the target for the overnight rate and other commercial interest rates, they do tend to move in the same direction. In other words, we observe a drop in other interest rates when the BOC lowers its overnight rate target. The fall in interest rates makes borrowing less expensive and encourages firms and households to borrow more, resulting in an increase in both consumption and investment spending.

Asset prices As we mentioned in Chapter 10, holding all else constant, there is an inverse relationship between interest rates and asset prices. A fall in interest rates will raise the prices of various assets such as bonds, stocks, and houses.

[5]We will briefly discuss the effect of a change in monetary policy on the exchange rate and net exports here, but will postpone more detailed discussion to Chapter 19.

FIGURE **15-10** Expansionary Monetary Policy in the *AS/AD* Model

Suppose the economy finds itself in a recessionary gap, point E_1 as shown here. When the BOC lowers the target for the overnight rate, this brings about an increase in the money supply, which in turn tends to cause an increase in consumption, investment, and net exports. This increase in the money supply shifts the aggregate demand curve toward the right as shown. This helps to close the negative output gap by moving the economy toward the long-run equilibrium point, E_2, and puts upward pressure on the price level in the short run.

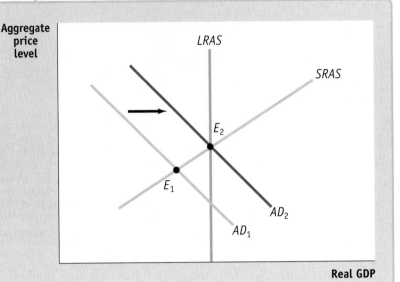

Seeing their wealth increase when asset prices increase, households increase their spending on final goods and services (the wealth effect mentioned in Chapter 12).

The exchange rate A fall in Canadian interest rates will make Canadian assets less attractive to investors. Foreign investors will buy fewer Canadian assets, while Canadian investors will buy more foreign assets. The rise in net foreign investment (or the outflows of financial capital) that results causes the Canadian dollar to depreciate in the foreign exchange market. A weaker currency makes Canadian goods become less expensive and stimulates our net exports.

Market expectations As mentioned in Chapter 7, agents use the available information to form expectations, which they act on. When the BOC lowers the target for the overnight rate, agents would expect the inflation rate to rise in the future. Along with a higher inflation rate, they would also expect future increases in interest rates and wages, all factors that would encourage the agents to increase their spending on investment and consumption now.

In a nutshell, if the economy finds itself in a recessionary gap, point E_1 shown in Figure 15-10, then, when the BOC lowers the target for the overnight rate, this brings about an increase in the money supply, and we would expect to see an increase in consumption, investment, and net exports. These increases raise the aggregate demand for goods and services and help to eliminate a negative output (or, recessionary) gap. Later, when the economy gains momentum, the aggregate price level rises, as does the rate of inflation. This increase in the money supply shifts the aggregate demand curve toward the right, as shown in Figure 15-10. This helps close the negative output gap, moving the economy toward the long-run equilibrium point E_2, and puts upward pressure on the price level in the short-run.

Now consider Figure 15-11, which presents specific data in regard to monetary policy in practice. Panel (a) compares the core inflation rate and target for the overnight rate from 1991 to 2011. Note that they tend to move together: a rise in the core inflation rate generally triggers an increase in the target for the overnight rate. It is also apparent that the BOC has succeeded in keeping the core inflation within the target range, so it can use monetary policy to tackle the output gap. Panel (b) compares, for the same years, the target for the overnight rate and the output gap (the percentage difference between actual real GDP and potential output). (Recall that the output gap is positive when actual real GDP exceeds potential

FIGURE **15-11** Tracking Monetary Policy Using the Core Inflation Rate and the Output Gap

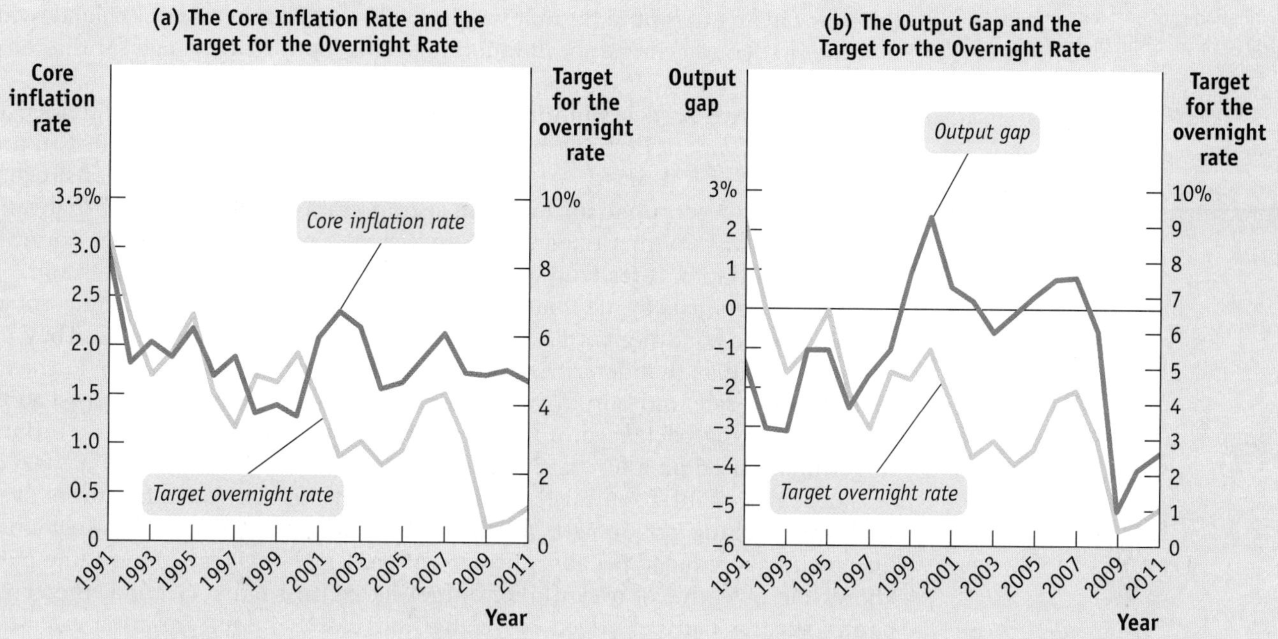

(a) The Core Inflation Rate and the Target for the Overnight Rate

(b) The Output Gap and the Target for the Overnight Rate

Panel (a) shows that the BOC tends to raise the overnight target rate when the inflation rate is high and lower it when inflation is low. Panel (b) shows that the overnight target rate is usually increased when the output gap is positive—that is, when actual real GDP is above potential output—and is decreased when the output gap is negative.

Sources: Parliamentary Budget Officer (PBO); Statistics Canada.

output.) As you can see, the BOC tends to raise interest rates when the output gap is rising—that is, when the economy is developing an inflationary gap—and tends to cut them when the output gap is falling.

Inflation Targeting

In 1991, the Bank of Canada entered into an agreement with the federal government "to reduce inflation, as measured by the total consumer price index (CPI), from a rate of about 5 percent in late 1990 to 2 percent by the end of 1995. Inflation reached the target well ahead of schedule; and so the focus in the 1995 agreement (a renewal) shifted towards keeping it low, stable and predictable over the medium term, at an annual rate of 2 percent—the midpoint of a target or control range of 1 to 3 percent."[6] So now one of the BOC's primary goals is to preserve the value of (Canadian) money by keeping inflation low and stable. Until January 2012, the U.S. Federal Reserve did not explicitly commit itself to achieving a particular inflation rate. However, in January 2012, Ben Bernanke, chairman of the Fed, announced that the Fed would set its policy to maintain an inflation rate of about 2% per year.[7] With that statement, the Fed joined a number of other central banks, like Canada's, that have explicit inflation targets. This method of

[6]*Source:* "Backgrounder: Bank of Canada, Backgrounder on the Inflation-Control Target," Bank of Canada, April 2012, www.bankofcanada.ca/wp-content/uploads/2010/11/inflation_control_target.pdf.

[7]While the Fed did explain in a January 2012 statement that by "price stability" it meant a two percent rate of inflation, it did not say when this rate would be achieved. The Bank of Canada usually tries to achieve its target rate for inflation within six to eight quarters (18 to 24 months), but may alter this length if economic conditions warrant.

Inflation targeting occurs when the central bank sets an explicit target for the inflation rate and sets monetary policy in order to hit that target.

setting monetary policy, called **inflation targeting,** involves having the central bank announce the inflation rate it is trying to achieve—the inflation target—and set policy in an attempt to hit that target. The central bank of New Zealand, which was the first country to adopt inflation targeting, specified a range for that target of 1% to 3%.

Other central banks commit themselves to achieving a specific number. For example, the Bank of England has committed to keeping inflation at 2%. In practice, there doesn't seem to be much difference between these versions: central banks with a target range for inflation seem to aim for the middle of that range, and central banks with a fixed target and no specified upper or lower bound for acceptable inflation rates tend to give themselves considerable wiggle room.

Some economists argue that monetary policy should be based on current and past economic conditions, rather than forecasts of future conditions. They may even use formulas that determine the target interest rate as a function of the current inflation rate and output gap or the unemployment rate. In contrast to this policy of looking backward, inflation targeting looks forward. That is, inflation targeting is based on a forecast of future inflation.

Advocates of inflation targeting argue that it has two key advantages over a backward-looking policy rule: *transparency* and *accountability*. First, economic uncertainty is reduced because the central bank's plan is transparent: the public knows the objective of an inflation-targeting central bank. Second, the central bank's success can be judged by seeing how closely actual inflation rates have matched the inflation target, making central bankers accountable.

Critics of inflation targeting argue that it's too restrictive because there are times when other concerns—like the stability of the financial system—should take priority over achieving any particular inflation rate. Indeed, in late 2007 and early 2008 the BOC cut interest rates much more than either inflation targeting or a backward-looking policy rule would have dictated because it feared that turmoil in the financial markets would lead to a major recession. (In fact, it did.)

To achieve its inflation target, the BOC adjusts (raises or lowers) its target for the overnight interest rate, which, in turn, influences other market interest rates and the exchange rate, thereby shifting the *AD* curve. Changes in monetary policy take between six and eight quarters to fully work their way through the economy and have their cumulative effect on *AD* and inflation. This explains why the BOC

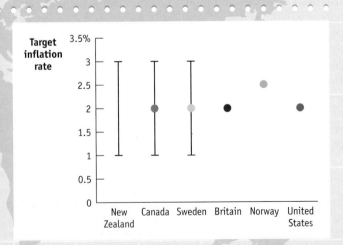

GLOBAL COMPARISON **INFLATION TARGETS**

This figure shows the target inflation rates of six central banks that have adopted inflation targeting. The central bank of New Zealand introduced inflation targeting in 1990. Today it has an inflation target range of 1% to 3%. The central banks of Canada and Sweden have the same target range but also specify 2% as the precise target. The central banks of Britain and Norway have specific targets for inflation, 2% and 2.5%, respectively. Neither states by how much they're prepared to miss those targets. Since 2012, the U.S. Federal Reserve also targets inflation at 2%.

In practice, these differences in detail don't seem to lead to any significant difference in results. New Zealand aims for the middle of its range, at 2% inflation; Britain, Norway, and the United States allow themselves considerable wiggle room around their target inflation rates.

sets its policy rate in a forward-looking fashion, based on what inflation is likely to be in 18 to 24 months, rather than what it is today. According to the BOC, "When demand is too strong, pushing the economy against its capacity limits, and there is a risk that future inflation will move appreciably above the 2 percent target, the Bank raises its policy rate to cool down the economy and bring inflation back to target. When demand is weak, and future inflation pressures are likely to ease, the Bank lowers its policy rate to stimulate the economy, absorb spare production capacity, and return inflation to 2 percent."[8] By construction this tends to keep aggregate demand closer to capacity (potential output), so the inflation-targeting framework creates a monetary policy that acts somewhat like an automatic stabilizer for economic activity.

The Zero Lower Bound Problem

Regardless of whether monetary policy is based on rules that look forward or backward, it will always face one problem: the nominal rate of interest usually has a lower bound of zero. Why? Because people always have the alternative of holding cash, which offers a zero interest rate. Normally, nobody would buy a bond yielding an interest rate less than zero because holding cash would be a better alternative.[9]

The fact that interest rates can't go below zero—called the **zero lower bound for interest rates**—sets limits to the power of monetary policy. In 2009 and 2010, inflation was low and the U.S. economy was operating far below potential, so the U.S. Federal Reserve wanted to increase aggregate demand. Yet it could not do so in the normal way—buying short-term U.S. government debt on the open market to expand the money supply—because short-term U.S. interest rates were already at or near zero percent.

So, in November 2010, the Fed tried to solve this problem using *quantitative easing*. As we have already pointed out, long-term interest rates don't follow short-term rates exactly. The short-term U.S. debt rates, for example on three-month treasury bills, were close to zero percent. But the rates for longer-term debt were higher: for example, five-year or six-year bonds were at about two or three percent. With **quantitative easing (QE),** the Fed began to buy longer-term U.S. government debt. The Fed hoped that buying these longer-term bonds directly would drive down interest rates on long-term debt, thus exerting an expansionary effect on the U.S. economy.

This policy may have given the U.S. economy some boost in 2011, but as of early 2012, recovery remained painfully slow. Over this time period, the Bank of England and the European Central Bank also used quantitative easing to try to solve England and Europe's financial difficulties. At the same time, Canada was in a similar fix: from April 2009 to June 2010, the BOC's target for the overnight interest rate was 0.25 percent. Unlike its counterparts, however, the BOC was not forced to try quantitative easing because our stronger financial system meant that in many ways the impact of the crisis was not as severe in Canada and our recovery was quicker.

The **zero lower bound for interest rates** means that interest rates cannot fall below zero.

Quantitative easing (QE) is a monetary policy in which a government tries to drive down interest rates, thus exerting an expansionary effect on the economy, by buying longer-term government bonds, instead of the shorter-term bonds it would buy usually.

---

[8]*Source:* "Backgrounder: Inflation-Control Target," Bank of Canada, April 2012, www.bankofcanada.ca/wp-content/uploads/2010/11/inflation_control_target.pdf.

[9]Negative nominal interest rates are possible but very rare. In August 2012, yields on two-year government bonds in Germany, Denmark, Finland, and Switzerland fell below zero. In essence, investors were paying these governments to borrow their money. These negative interest rates occurred partly because of the eurozone debt crisis that was stalking several European nations at this time. As a result, the supply of truly safe investment vehicles shrank significantly. For example, Italian government bonds were no longer risk-free, banks deposits were insecure because the banks could fail, and it was not safe for investors to simply "hide their money under their mattresses." With so few good alternatives available, bonds from "good quality" government issuers became popular enough that investors were willing to buy these bonds for more than they would be worth at maturity—creating a negative nominal interest rate.

Most economists felt that the decision to refrain from QE was a positive sign for Canada. It was a sign of Canada's financial strength and of our economy's recovery from the recession. Furthermore, if the Bank had tried QE, longer-term interest rates would have declined, inducing households to increase their debts, which were already at historic highs. Since Canada's longer-term rates remained relatively high, households were induced to decrease their debt.

In contrast, some economists felt that the decision harmed our economy: QE tends to lower the value of the currencies of the countries or regions using it. Consequently, opting out of QE while many of our trading partners were engaged in it raised the value of the Canadian dollar. As a result our trade balance was harmed and jobs in export-oriented sectors of the Canadian economy were killed.

The U.S. Federal Reserve undertook three rounds of QE. The first round, in November 2008, resulted in the Fed's assets swelling by 140% to about $2.2 trillion U.S. This first round of asset purchases helped to lower the 10-year interest rate to 2.93% at the end of November, 1 percentage point lower than the previous month. Subsequent rounds of asset purchases occurred in November 2010 and September 2012. These purchases helped to push the 10-year rate down to 1.57% at the end of September 2012. Unfortunately, even though the Fed bought a significant amount of assets in an attempt to raise the money supply and stimulate the economy, U.S. banks, rather than lending these funds out to others, responded to the fear and uncertainty by raising the amount of reserves they held on account at the Fed by more than 100%. In mid-to late 2009 the (negative) output gap was about 7.5% and the unemployment rate peaked at 10%. The U.S. economy ended 2012 with output almost 6% below potential, an unemployment rate of almost 8% (up 3 percentage points compared to January 2008), and employment still more than 3.2 million below what it had been at the start of 2008. So there is little doubt that without QE the American economy would likely have suffered more. Nonetheless the fact that multiple rounds were undertaken and that the American economy continues to suffer implies that either the degree of QE intervention was too small or that QE itself is not effective enough.

ECONOMICS ▶ IN ACTION

WHAT THE CENTRAL BANK WANTS, THE CENTRAL BANK GETS

What's the evidence that a central bank can actually cause an economic contraction or expansion? You might think that it's just a matter of seeing what happens to the economy when interest rates go up or down. But there's a big problem with that approach: a central bank usually changes interest rates in an attempt to tame the business cycle, raising rates if the economy is expanding (and creating inflationary pressure) and reducing them if the economy is slumping (and creating low inflationary and/or deflationary pressure). So, in the actual data, it often looks as if low interest rates go along with a weak economy and high rates go along with a strong economy.

In a famous 1994 paper titled "Monetary Policy Matters," macroeconomists Christina Romer and David Romer solved this problem by focusing on episodes in which U.S. monetary policy wasn't a reaction to the business cycle. Specifically, they used minutes from

FIGURE **15-12**   When the U.S. Fed Wants a Recession

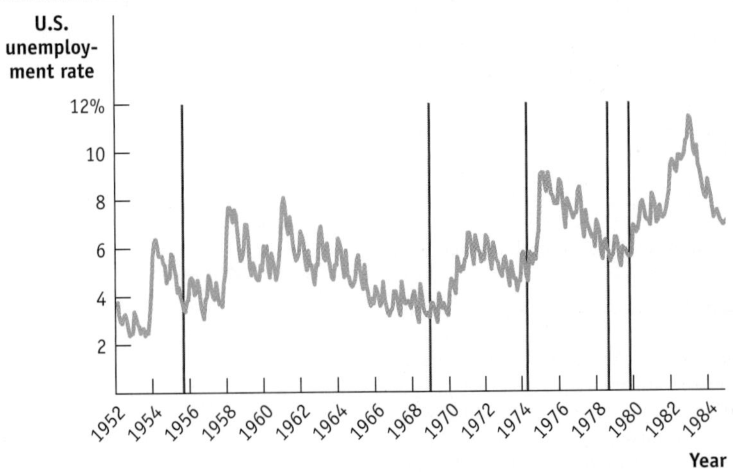

Sources: The U.S. Bureau of Labor Statistics; Christina D. Romer and David H. Romer, "Monetary Policy Matters," *Journal of Monetary Economics* 34 (August 1994): 75–88.

the U.S. Federal Open Market Committee and other sources to identify episodes "in which the Federal Reserve in effect decided to attempt to create a recession to reduce inflation." As we'll learn in Chapter 16, rather than monetary policy just being used as a tool of macroeconomic stabilization, sometimes it is used to eliminate embedded inflation—inflation that people believe will persist into the future. In such a case, the central bank needs to create a recessionary gap—not just eliminate an inflationary gap—to wring *embedded* inflation out of the economy.[10]

Figure 15-12 shows the unemployment rate between 1952 and 1984 (orange) and identifies five dates on which, according to Romer and Romer, the U.S. Federal Reserve decided that it wanted a recession (vertical red lines). In four of the five cases, the decision to contract the economy was followed, after a modest lag, by a rise in the U.S. unemployment rate. On average, Romer and Romer found that the unemployment rate rises by two percentage points after the Fed decides that unemployment needs to go up.

So yes, the Fed and other central banks do get what they want.

CHECK YOUR UNDERSTANDING   15-3

1. Suppose the economy is currently suffering from an output gap and the Bank of Canada uses an expansionary monetary policy to close that gap. Describe the short-run effect of this policy on the following.
   a. The money supply curve
   b. The equilibrium interest rate
   c. Investment spending
   d. Consumer spending
   e. Aggregate output

2. In setting monetary policy, which central bank—one that operates according to a backward-looking policy rule or one that operates by inflation targeting—is likely to respond more directly to a financial crisis? Explain.

Solutions appear at back of book.

Money, Output, and Prices in the Long Run

Through its expansionary and contractionary effects, monetary policy is generally the policy tool of choice to help stabilize the economy. However, not all actions by central banks are productive. In particular, as we'll see in the next chapter, central banks sometimes print money not to fight a recessionary gap but to help the government pay its bills, an action that typically destabilizes the economy.

What happens when a change in the money supply pushes the economy away from, rather than toward, long-run equilibrium? We learned in Chapter 12 that the economy is self-correcting in the long run: a demand shock has only a temporary effect on aggregate output. If the demand shock is the result of a change in the money supply, we can make a stronger statement: in the long run, changes in the quantity of money affect the aggregate price level, but they do not change the long-run levels of either real aggregate output (potential output) or the interest rate. To see why, let's look at what happens if the central bank permanently increases the money supply.

[10]At time of writing, the Bank of Canada has twice been partly responsible for recessions, once in the early 1980s and once in the early 1990s, as it sought to reduce the rate of inflation in the Canadian economy at those times.

> ### ▼ Quick Review
>
> - The Bank of Canada can use **expansionary monetary policy** to increase aggregate demand and **contractionary monetary policy** to reduce aggregate demand. The Bank of Canada and other central banks generally try to tame the business cycle while keeping the inflation rate low but positive.
>
> - Many central banks set monetary policy by **inflation targeting,** a forward-looking policy rule. Although inflation targeting has the benefits of transparency and accountability, some think it is too restrictive.
>
> - Until 2008, when its target interest rate basically hit zero, the U.S. Federal Reserve's behaviour roughly followed a backward-looking policy rule. But starting in early 2012, it began inflation targeting with a target of 2% per year.
>
> - There is a **zero lower bound for interest rates**—they cannot fall below zero—that limits the power of monetary policy.
>
> - In 2010, the Federal Reserve bought longer-term debt, in order to drive interest rates down and exert an expansionary effect on the economy. This policy, called **quantitative easing,** was also tried by the Bank of England and the European Central Bank, in each case with limited success.
>
> - Because it is subject to fewer lags than fiscal policy, monetary policy is the main tool for macroeconomic stabilization.

Short-Run and Long-Run Effects of an Increase in the Money Supply

To analyze the long-run effects of monetary policy, it's helpful to think of the central bank as choosing a target for the money supply rather than the interest rate. In assessing the effects of an increase in the money supply, we return to the analysis of the long-run effects of an increase in aggregate demand, first introduced in Chapter 12.

Figure 15-13 shows the short-run and long-run effects of an increase in the money supply when the economy begins at potential output, Y_1. The initial short-run aggregate supply curve is $SRAS_1$, the long-run aggregate supply curve is $LRAS$, and the initial aggregate demand curve is AD_1. The economy's initial equilibrium is at E_1, a point of both short-run and long-run macroeconomic equilibrium because it is on both the short-run and the long-run aggregate supply curves. Real GDP is at potential output, Y_1.

Now suppose there is an increase in the money supply. Other things equal, an increase in the money supply reduces the interest rate, which increases investment spending, which leads to a further rise in consumer spending, and so on. So an increase in the money supply increases the quantity of goods and services demanded, shifting the AD curve rightward, to AD_2. In the short run, the economy moves to a new short-run macroeconomic equilibrium at E_2. The price level rises from P_1 to P_2, and real GDP rises from Y_1 to Y_2. That is, both the aggregate price level and aggregate output increase in the short run.

But the aggregate output level, Y_2, is above potential output. As a result, in the longer term, nominal wages will rise over time, causing the short-run aggregate supply curve to shift leftward. This process stops only when the $SRAS$ curve ends up at $SRAS_2$ and the economy ends up at point E_3, a point of both short-run and long-run macroeconomic equilibrium. The long-run effect of an increase in the

FIGURE **15-13** The Short-Run and Long-Run Effects of an Increase in the Money Supply

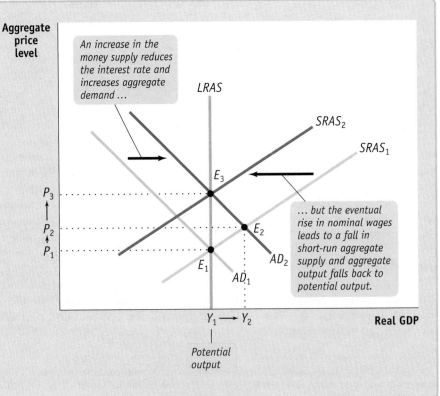

When the economy is already at potential output, an increase in the money supply generates a positive short-run effect, but no long-run effect, on real GDP.

Here, the economy begins at E_1, a point of short-run and long-run macroeconomic equilibrium. An increase in the money supply shifts the AD curve rightward, and the economy moves to a new short-run macroeconomic equilibrium at E_2 and a new real GDP of Y_2. But E_2 is not a long-run equilibrium: Y_2 exceeds potential output, Y_1, leading over time to an increase in nominal wages. In the long run, the increase in nominal wages shifts the short-run aggregate supply curve leftward, to a new position at $SRAS_2$.

The economy reaches a new short-run and long-run macroeconomic equilibrium at E_3 on the $LRAS$ curve, and output falls back to potential output, Y_1. When the economy is again at potential output, the only long-run effect of an increase in the money supply is an increase in the aggregate price level from P_1 to P_3.

money supply, then, is that the aggregate price level has increased from P_1 to P_3, but aggregate output is back at potential output, Y_1. In the long run, a monetary expansion raises the aggregate price level but has no effect on real GDP.

We won't describe the effects of a monetary contraction in detail, but the same logic applies. In the short run, a fall in the money supply leads to a fall in aggregate output as the economy moves down the short-run aggregate supply curve. In the long run, however, the monetary contraction only reduces the aggregate price level, and real GDP returns to potential output.

Monetary Neutrality

How much does a change in the money supply change the aggregate price level in the long run? The answer is that a change in the money supply leads to an equal proportional change in the aggregate price level in the long run. For example, if the money supply falls 25%, the aggregate price level falls 25% in the long run; if the money supply rises 50%, the aggregate price level rises 50% in the long run.

How do we know this? Consider the following thought experiment: Suppose all prices in the economy—prices of final goods and services and also factor prices, such as nominal wage rates—double. And suppose the money supply doubles at the same time. What difference does this make to the economy in real terms? The answer is none. All real variables in the economy—such as real GDP and the real value of the money supply (the amount of goods and services it can buy)—are unchanged. So there is no reason for anyone to behave any differently.

We can state this argument in reverse: If the economy starts out in long-run macroeconomic equilibrium and the money supply changes, restoring long-run macroeconomic equilibrium requires restoring all real values to their original values. This includes restoring the real value of the money supply to its original level. So if the money supply falls 25%, the aggregate price level must fall 25%; if the money supply rises 50%, the price level must rise 50%; and so on.[11]

This analysis demonstrates the concept known as **monetary neutrality,** in which changes in the money supply have no real effects on the economy. In the long run, the only effect of an increase in the money supply is to raise the aggregate price level by an equal percentage. Economists argue that *money is neutral in the long run.*

This is, however, a good time to recall the dictum of John Maynard Keynes: "In the long run we are all dead." In the long run, changes in the money supply don't have any effect on real GDP, interest rates, or anything else except the price level. But it would be foolish to conclude from this that the BOC is irrelevant. Monetary policy does have powerful real effects on the economy in the short run, often making the difference between recession and expansion. And that matters a lot for society's welfare.

Changes in the Money Supply and the Interest Rate in the Long Run

In the short run, an increase in the money supply leads to a fall in the interest rate, and a decrease in the money supply leads to a rise in the interest rate. In the long run, however, changes in the money supply don't affect the interest rate.

Figure 15-14 shows why. It shows the money supply curve and the money demand curve before and after the BOC increases the money supply. We assume that the economy is initially at E_1, in long-run macroeconomic equilibrium at potential output, and with money supply $\overline{M}_1$. The initial equilibrium interest rate,

According to the concept of **monetary neutrality,** changes in the money supply have no real effects on the economy.

---

[11]An expression for the real money supply is $\left(\dfrac{M}{P}\right)$, where M is the nominal money supply and P is the aggregate nominal price level. If the nominal money supply rises by 25%, then the real money supply will rise in the short run, since P has not risen by 25%. In the long run though, the aggregate price level will rise by 25% relative to its initial level, restoring the real money supply to its initial level.

FIGURE **15-14** The Long-Run Determination of the Interest Rate

In the short run, an increase in the money supply from $\overline{M}_1$ to $\overline{M}_2$ pushes the interest rate down from i_1 to i_2 and the economy moves to E_2, a short-run equilibrium. In the long run, however, the aggregate price level rises in proportion to the increase in the money supply, leading to an increase in money demand at any given interest rate in proportion to the increase in the aggregate price level, as shown by the shift from MD_1 to MD_2. The result is that the quantity of money demanded at any given interest rate rises by the same amount as the quantity of money supplied. The economy moves to long-run equilibrium at E_3 and the interest rate returns to i_1.

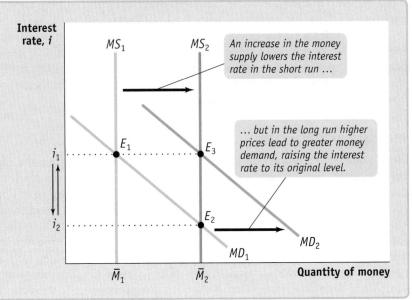

determined by the intersection of the money demand curve MD_1 and the money supply curve MS_1, is i_1.

Now suppose the money supply increases from $\overline{M}_1$ to $\overline{M}_2$. In the short run, the economy moves from E_1 to E_2 and the interest rate falls from i_1 to i_2. Over time, however, the aggregate price level rises, and this raises money demand, shifting the money demand curve rightward from MD_1 to MD_2. The economy moves to a new long-run equilibrium at E_3, and the interest rate rises to its original level at i_1.

And it turns out that the long-run equilibrium nominal interest rate is the original interest rate, i_1. We know this for two reasons. First, due to monetary neutrality, in the long run the aggregate price level rises by the same proportion as the money supply; so if the money supply rises by, say, 50%, the price level will also rise by 50%. Second, the demand for money is, other things equal, proportional to the aggregate price level. So a 50% increase in the money supply raises the aggregate price level by 50%, which increases the quantity of money demanded at any given interest rate by 50%. As a result, the quantity of money demanded at the initial interest rate, i_1, rises exactly as much as the money supply—so that i_1 is still the equilibrium interest rate. In the long run, then, changes in the money supply do not affect the interest rate.

ECONOMICS ▶ IN ACTION

INTERNATIONAL EVIDENCE OF MONETARY NEUTRALITY

These days monetary policy is quite similar among wealthy countries. Each major nation (or, in the case of the euro, the euro area) has a central bank that is insulated from political pressure. All of these central banks try to keep the aggregate price level roughly stable, which usually means inflation of at most 2% to 3% per year.

But if we look at a longer period and a wider group of countries, we see large differences in the growth of the money supply. Between 1970 and the present, the money supply rose only a few percent per year in some countries, such as Canada, Switzerland, and the United States, but rose much more rapidly in some poorer countries, such as South Africa. These differences allow us to see whether it is really true that increases in the money supply lead, in the long run, to equal percent rises in the aggregate price level.

Figure 15-15 shows the annual percentage increases in the money supply and average annual increases in the aggregate price level—that is, the average rate of inflation—for a sample of countries during the period 1970–2010, with each point representing a country. If the relationship between increases in the money supply and changes in the aggregate price level were exact, the points would lie precisely on a 45-degree line. In fact, the relationship isn't exact, because other factors besides money affect the aggregate price level in the short-run.

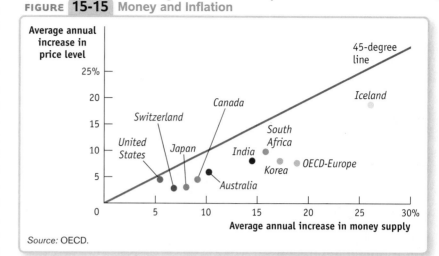

FIGURE 15-15 The Long-Run Relationship Between Money and Inflation

Source: OECD.

But the scatter of points clearly lies close to a 45-degree line, showing a more or less proportional relationship between money and the aggregate price level. That is, the data support the concept of monetary neutrality in the long run.

CHECK YOUR UNDERSTANDING   15-4

1. Assume the central bank increases the quantity of money by 25%, even though the economy is initially in both short-run and long-run macroeconomic equilibrium. Describe the effects, in the short run and in the long run (giving numbers where possible), on the following.
   a. Aggregate output
   b. Aggregate price level
   c. Interest rate

2. Why does monetary policy affect the economy in the short run but not in the long run?

Solutions appear at back of book.

BUSINESS CASE : Was Quantitative Easing A Good Choice?

Courtesy of Camilla Sutton

Usually, central banks set the price of money and attempt to steer the economy using their policy interest rate. But when the overnight interest rate is close to zero percent, or equal to it, the impact of the central bank's target for the overnight rate on the economy becomes limited. In such circumstances, if the central bank wishes to affect the price of money to stimulate the economy it can turn to quantitative easing (QE).

With quantitative easing, the central bank "creates new money," which it then uses to buy assets in the domestic economy: government bonds, stocks, corporate bonds, assets from financial institutions, and so on. When the central bank buys long-term bonds their prices rise, causing their interest rates to fall. Lower interest rates stimulate spending, which should help to pull the economy out of its slump. Thus does the central bank hope to add further stimulus to the economy using QE.

Or so the theory goes. QE can be tricky—if not outright dangerous. A central bank that uses QE might lose money on the assets it buys. Even worse, if the central bank creates too much money, or does not remove the money quickly enough when the economy recovers, then the currency will be devalued by inflation. Furthermore, the fact that QE is being used at all may ruin confidence in an economy rather than build it. According to *Financial Times* economics editor Chris Giles, "This is why central banks cannot use QE willy-nilly, but if you are not aggressive enough QE simply will not work to change other interest rates in the economy and stimulate demand. The trouble is, because the policy is unorthodox and the situation is dramatic no one knows how much QE is too much and how much is not enough."

Unfortunately, so far QE has created a questionable degree of stimulus where it has been used—United States, England, Japan, and the eurozone—and of course, has drawn criticism in each of these places. Indeed, no central bank really does seem to know how much is enough—the U.S., for instance, has rolled out three (or perhaps four) rounds of QE.

Canada's relatively strong economy has meant that the Bank of Canada has not needed to adopt QE. But have we benefitted from QE nonetheless? To an extent, yes. Since the U.S. has used QE to stimulate its economy and create jobs, there is a corresponding increase in demand for exports from nations such as Canada, which is to our benefit. On the other hand, using this expansionary monetary policy puts downward pressure on the U.S. dollar exchange rate, so the Canadian dollar appreciates, which is to our detriment.

Interestingly, Camilla Sutton, the Bank of Nova Scotia's chief currency strategist (pictured here), devised a way that Canadian investors could profit from QE. She calculated that in 2012, investors could have made about a 5.5 percent profit without using any leverage. Her strategy is to sell currencies of countries that are engaging in QE and buy currencies of those that are not. In doing so, the investor is betting that the relative exchange rate will move against countries engaging in QE because they are creating too much money. So it seems the laws of economics do hold: if a central bank prints too much money, then it creates inflation and lowers the exchange rate. And better yet, it seems Canadians might be able to profit from it.

QUESTIONS FOR THOUGHT

1. Why do central banks have difficulty using their policy interest rates to stimulate the economy when these rates are at or near zero?

2. How does quantitative easing (QE) help the central bank to stimulate the economy?

3. What risks does adopting QE bring to an economy?

4. What risks does not adopting QE bring to an economy, when a major trading partner has adopted QE?

SUMMARY

1. The **money demand curve** arises from a trade-off between the opportunity cost of holding money and the liquidity that money provides. The opportunity cost of holding money depends on **short-term interest rates,** not **long-term interest rates.** Changes in the aggregate price level, real GDP, technology, and institutions shift the money demand curve.

2. According to the **liquidity preference model of the interest rate,** the interest rate is determined in the money market by the money demand curve and the **money supply curve.** The Bank of Canada can change the interest rate in the short run by shifting the money supply curve. In practice, the BOC uses open-market operations to achieve a target for the overnight interest rate, which short-term interest rates generally track. Although long-term interest rates don't necessarily move with short-term interest rates, they reflect expectations about what's going to happen to short-term rates in the future.

3. **Expansionary monetary policy** reduces the interest rate by increasing the money supply. This increases investment spending and consumer spending, which in turn increases aggregate demand and real GDP in the short run. **Contractionary monetary policy** raises the interest rate by reducing the money supply. This reduces investment spending and consumer spending, which in turn reduces aggregate demand and real GDP in the short run.

4. The **monetary transmission mechanism** describes the channels through which a change in interest rates (or money supply) will cause a shift in the aggregate demand curve (and ultimately affect the economy's output and inflation rate).

5. The Bank of Canada and other central banks try to stabilize the economy, limiting fluctuations of actual output around potential output, while also keeping inflation low, but positive. To achieve this goal, these banks engage in **inflation targeting,** a forward-looking policy rule, in which they announce the inflation rate that they want to achieve—the inflation target—and set policy in an attempt to hit that target. Because monetary policy is subject to fewer implementation lags than fiscal policy, it is the preferred policy tool for stabilizing the economy. Because interest rates cannot fall below zero—the **zero lower bound for interest rates**—the power of monetary policy is limited.

6. In the U.S., the Fed used a method known as **quantitative easing (QE),** in which it bought longer-term U.S. debt, in the hope that doing so would reduce interest rates and thus exert an expansionary effect on the U.S. economy.

7. In the long run, changes in the money supply affect the aggregate price level but not real GDP or the interest rate. Data show that the concept of **monetary neutrality** holds: changes in the money supply have no real effect on the economy in the long run.

KEY TERMS

Non-monetary assets, p. 498
Short-term interest rates, p. 499
Long-term interest rates, p. 500
Money demand curve, p. 500
Liquidity preference model of the interest rate, p. 506

Money supply curve, p. 506
Expansionary monetary policy, p. 511
Contractionary monetary policy, p. 512
Monetary transmission mechanism, p. 512
Inflation targeting, p. 516

Zero lower bound for interest rates, p. 517
Quantitative easing (QE), p. 517
Monetary neutrality, p. 521

PROBLEMS

1. Go to the schedule of key interest rate announcements page of the Bank of Canada's website (www.bankof-canada.ca/monetary-policy-introduction/key-interest-rate/schedule/) to find the list of the BOC's eight fixed interest rate announcement dates for the current year. Now, to find the most recent press release, click on "Publications and Research" and then select "Press Releases."

   a. What is the BOC's current target for the overnight interest rate?

   b. Is the current target overnight interest rate different from the one on the previous fixed announcement date? If it is, by how much does it differ?

   c. Does the statement comment on current macro-economic conditions in the Canada? How does it describe the Canadian economy?

2. How will the following events affect the demand for money? In each case, specify whether there is a shift of the demand curve or a movement along the demand curve and its direction.

   a. There is a fall in the interest rate from 12% to 10%.

   b. Cold weather arrives and with it, the beginning of the holiday shopping season.

   c. McDonald's and other fast-food restaurants begin to accept credit cards.

   d. The BOC engages in an open-market purchase of Canadian treasury bills.

3. **a.** Go to www.bankofcanada.ca/rates/interest-rates/t-bill-yields/. Find the part of this page that deals with average yields for recent six-month Government of Canada treasury bill auctions. What is the interest rate for the most recently issued six-month T-bills?

   b. Go to the website of your favourite bank. What is the interest rate for six-month GICs?

   c. Why are the rates for six-month GICs higher than for six-month federal treasury bills?

4. Go to www.bankofcanada.ca/rates/interest-rates/canadian-bonds/. Use the most recent data on the list of benchmark bond yields listed there to answer these questions.

   a. What are the interest rates on two-year and ten-year Government of Canada bonds?

   b. How do the interest rates on the two-year and ten-year bonds relate to each other? Why is the interest rate on the ten-year bond higher (or lower) than the interest rate on the two-year bond?

5. An economy is facing the recessionary gap shown in the accompanying diagram. To eliminate the gap, should the central bank use expansionary or contractionary monetary policy? How will the interest rate, investment spending, consumer spending, real GDP, and the aggregate price level change as monetary policy closes the recessionary gap?

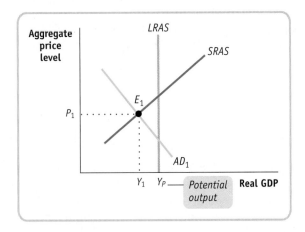

6. An economy is facing the inflationary gap shown in the accompanying diagram. To eliminate the gap, should the central bank use expansionary or contractionary monetary policy? How will the interest rate, investment spending, consumer spending, real GDP, and the aggregate price level change as monetary policy closes the inflationary gap?

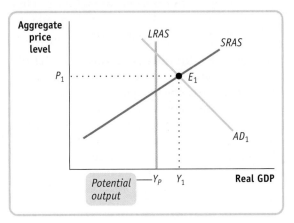

7. In the economy of Eastlandia, the money market is initially in equilibrium when the economy begins to slide into a recession.

   a. Using the accompanying diagram, explain what will happen to the interest rate if the central bank of Eastlandia keeps the money supply constant at $\overline{M}_1$.

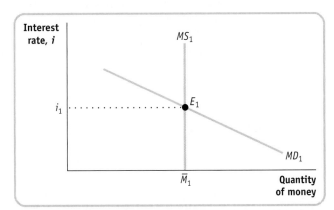

   b. If the central bank is instead committed to maintaining an interest rate target of i_1, then as the economy slides into recession, how should the central bank react? Using your diagram from part (a), demonstrate the central bank's reaction.

8. Suppose that the money market in Westlandia is initially in equilibrium and the central bank decides to decrease the money supply.

   a. Using a diagram like the one in Problem 7, explain what will happen to the interest rate in the short run.

   b. What will happen to the interest rate in the long run?

9. An economy is in long-run macroeconomic equilibrium with an unemployment rate of 5% when the government passes a law requiring the central bank to use monetary policy to lower the unemployment rate to 3% and keep it there. How could the central bank achieve this goal in the short run? What would happen in the long run? Illustrate with a diagram.

10. According to the European Central Bank website, the treaty establishing the European Community "makes clear that ensuring price stability is the most important contribution that monetary policy can make to achieve a favourable economic environment and a high level of employment." If price stability is the only goal of monetary policy, explain how monetary policy would be conducted during recessions. Analyze both the case of a recession that is the result of a demand shock and the case of a recession that is the result of a supply shock.

11. The effectiveness of monetary policy depends on how easy it is for changes in the money supply to change interest rates. By changing interest rates, monetary policy affects investment spending and the aggregate demand curve. The economies of Albernia and Brittania have very different money demand curves, as shown in the accompanying diagram. In which economy will changes in the money supply be a more effective policy tool? Why?

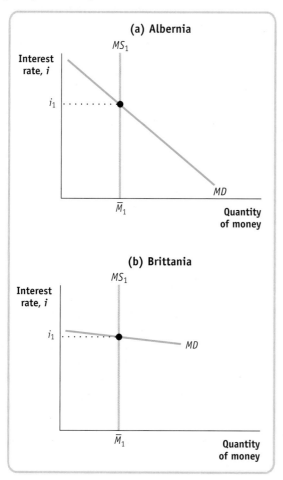

12. During the Great Depression, businesspeople in Canada were very pessimistic about the future of economic growth and reluctant to increase investment spending even when interest rates fell. How did this limit the potential for monetary policy to help alleviate the Depression?

13. Because of the economic slowdown associated with the 2008–2009 recession, the Governing Council of the Bank of Canada, between December 4, 2007 and April 21, 2009, lowered its target for the overnight interest rate in a series of steps from a high of 4.5% to a rate of 0.25%. The idea was to provide a boost to the economy by increasing aggregate demand.

    a. Use the liquidity preference model to explain how the BOC Governing Council lowers the interest rate in the short run. Draw a typical graph that illustrates the mechanism. Label the vertical axis "Interest rate" and the horizontal axis "Quantity of money." Your graph should show two interest rates, i_1 and i_2.

    b. Explain why the reduction in the interest rate causes aggregate demand to increase in the short run.

    c. Suppose that in 2016 the economy is at potential output but that this is somehow overlooked by the BOC, which continues its monetary expansion. Demonstrate the effect of the policy measure on the *AD* curve. Use the *LRAS* curve to show that the effect of this policy measure on the *AD* curve, other things equal, causes the aggregate price level to rise in the long run. Label the vertical axis "Aggregate price level" and the horizontal axis "Real GDP."

Reconciling the Two Models of the Interest Rate

In the liquidity preference model of the interest rate developed in Chapter 15, at the equilibrium interest rate the quantity of money demanded equals the quantity of money supplied. Yet, in the loanable funds model of the interest rate developed in Chapter 10, the equilibrium interest rate matches the quantity of loanable funds supplied by savers with the quantity of loanable funds demanded for investment spending. Can these two models of the interest rate be reconciled? Yes, they can. We will do this in two steps, focusing first on the short run and then on the long run.

The Interest Rate in the Short Run

As explained in Chapter 15, a fall in the interest rate leads to a rise in investment spending, I, which then leads to a rise in both real GDP and consumer spending, C. The rise in real GDP doesn't lead only to a rise in consumer spending, however. It also leads to a rise in savings: at each stage of the multiplier process, part of the increase in disposable income is saved. How much do savings rise? In Chapter 10 we introduced the *savings–investment spending identity:* total savings in the economy is always equal to investment spending. *This tells us that when a fall in the interest rate leads to higher investment spending, the resulting increase in real GDP generates exactly enough additional savings to match the rise in investment spending.* To put it another way, after a fall in the interest rate, the quantity of savings supplied rises exactly enough to match the quantity of savings demanded. Understanding this relationship is the key to reconciling the two models of the interest rate.

Figure 15A-1 illustrates how the two models of the interest rate are reconciled in the short run. Panel (a) shows the liquidity preference model of the interest rate where MS_1 and MD_1 are the initial supply and demand curves for money, and i_1, the initial equilibrium interest rate, equalizes the quantity of money supplied to the quantity of money demanded in the money market. Panel (b) shows the loanable funds model of the interest rate where S_1 is the initial supply curve, D is the demand curve for loanable funds, and i_1, the initial equilibrium interest rate, equalizes the quantity of loanable funds supplied to the quantity of loanable funds demanded in the market for loanable funds.

In Figure 15A-1 both the money market and the market for loanable funds are initially in equilibrium at E_1 with the same interest rate, i_1. You might think that this would only happen by accident, but in fact it will always be true. To see why, consider what happens in panel (a), the money market, when the BOC increases the money supply from $\overline{M}_1$ to $\overline{M}_2$, pushing the money supply curve rightward, to MS_2, reducing the equilibrium interest rate in the market to i_2, and moving the economy to a short-run equilibrium at E_2. What happens in panel (b), the market for loanable funds? In the short run, the fall in the interest rate due to the increase in the money supply leads to a rise in real GDP, which generates a rise in savings through the multiplier process. This rise in savings shifts the supply curve for loanable funds rightward, from S_1 to S_2, moving the equilibrium in the loanable funds market from E_1 to E_2 and reducing the equilibrium interest rate in the loanable funds market. Since the rise in savings must exactly match the rise in investment spending, the equilibrium rate in the loanable funds market must fall to i_2, the same as the new equilibrium interest rate in the money market.

In the short run, then, the supply and demand for money determine the interest rate, and the loanable funds market follows the lead of the money market

FIGURE 15A-1 The Short-Run Determination of the Interest Rate

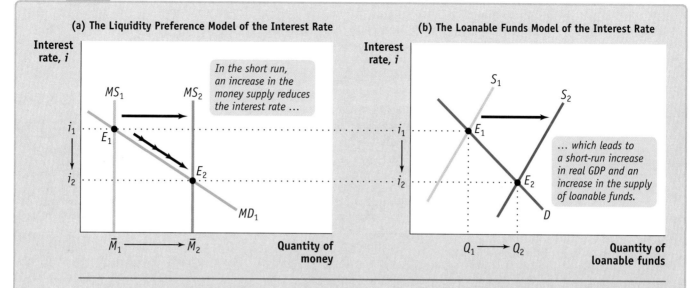

Panel (a) shows the liquidity preference model of the inter-est rate: the equilibrium interest rate matches the money supply to the quantity of money demanded. In the short run, the interest rate is determined in the money market, where an increase in the money supply, from $\bar{M}_1$ to $\bar{M}_2$, pushes the equilibrium interest rate down, from i_1 to i_2. Panel (b) shows the loanable funds model of the interest rate. The fall in the

interest rate in the money market leads, through the multipli-er effect, to an increase in real GDP and savings; to a right-ward shift of the supply curve of loanable funds, from S_1 to S_2; and to a fall in the interest rate, from i_1 to i_2. As a result, the new equilibrium interest rate in the loanable funds mar-ket matches the new equilibrium interest rate in the money market at i_2.

until the equilibrium interest rate in the loanable funds market is the same as the equilibrium interest rate in the money market.

Notice our use of the phrase "in the short run." Changes in aggregate demand affect aggregate output only in the short run. In the long run, aggregate output is equal to potential output. So our story about how a fall in the interest rate leads to a rise in aggregate output, which leads to a rise in savings, applies only to the short run. In the long run, as we'll see next, the determination of the interest rate is quite different, because the roles of the two markets are reversed. In the long run, the loanable funds market determines the equilibrium interest rate, and it is the market for money that follows the lead of the loanable funds market.

The Interest Rate in the Long Run

In the short run an increase in the money supply leads to a fall in the interest rate, and a decrease in the money supply leads to a rise in the interest rate. In the long run, however, changes in the money supply don't affect the interest rate.

Figure 15A-2 shows why. As in Figure 15A-1, panel (a) shows the liquidity pref-erence model of the interest rate and panel (b) shows the supply and demand for loanable funds. We assume that in both panels the economy is initially at E_1, in long-run macroeconomic equilibrium at potential output with the money supply equal to $\bar{M}_1$. The demand curve for loanable funds is D, and the initial supply curve for loanable funds is S_1. The initial equilibrium interest rate in both markets is i_1.

Now suppose the money supply rises from $\bar{M}_1$ to $\bar{M}_2$. As in Figure 15A-1, this initially reduces the interest rate to i_2. According to the neutrality of money, in the long run the aggregate price level rises by the same proportion as the increase in the money supply. And we also know that a rise in the aggregate price level increases money demand by the same proportion. So in the long run the money demand curve shifts out to MD_2 as money demand responds to

FIGURE 15A-2 The Long-Run Determination of the Interest Rate

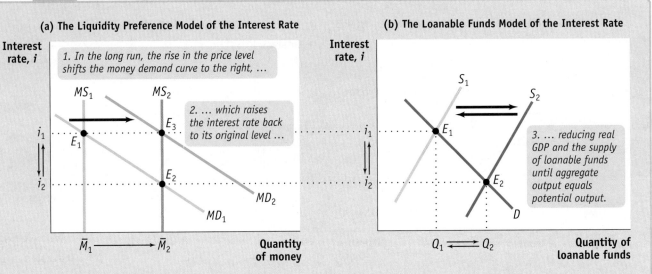

(a) The Liquidity Preference Model of the Interest Rate

(b) The Loanable Funds Model of the Interest Rate

Panel (a) shows the liquidity preference model long-run adjustment to an increase in the money supply from $\overline{M}_1$ to $\overline{M}_2$; panel (b) shows the corresponding long-run adjustment in the loanable funds market. Both panels start from E_1, a long-run macroeconomic equilibrium at potential output and with interest rate i_1. As we discussed in Figure 15A-1, the increase in the money supply reduces the interest rate from i_1 to i_2, increases real GDP, and increases savings in the short run. This is shown in panel (a) and panel (b) as the movement from E_1 to E_2. In the long run, however, the increase in the money supply raises wages and other nominal prices. This shifts the money demand curve in panel (a) from MD_1 to MD_2, leading to an increase in the interest rate from i_2 to i_1 as the economy moves from E_2 to E_3. The rise in the interest rate causes a fall in real GDP and a fall in savings, shifting the loanable funds supply curve back to S_1 from S_2 and moving the loanable funds market from E_2 back to E_1. In the long run, the equilibrium interest rate is determined by matching the supply and demand for loanable funds that arises when real GDP equals potential output.

higher prices, and moving the equilibrium interest rate rises back to its original level, i_1.

Panel (b) of Figure 15A-2 shows what happens in the market for loanable funds. As before, an increase in the money supply leads to a short-run rise in real GDP, and this shifts the supply of loanable funds rightward from S_1 to S_2. In the long run, however, real GDP falls back to its original level as wages and other nominal prices rise. As a result, the supply of loanable funds, S, which initially shifted from S_1 to S_2, shifts back to S_1.

In the long run, then, changes in the money supply do not affect the interest rate. So what determines the interest rate in the long run—i_1 in Figure 15A-2? The answer is the supply and demand for loanable funds. More specifically, in the long run the equilibrium interest rate matches the supply and demand for loanable funds that arise at potential output.

PROBLEMS

1. Using a figure similar to Figure 15A-1, explain how the money market and the loanable funds market react to a reduction in the money supply in the short run.

2. Contrast the short-run effects of an increase in the money supply on the interest rate to the long-run effects

of an increase in the money supply on the interest rate. Which market determines the interest rate in the short run? Which market does so in the long run? What are the implications of your answers for the effectiveness of monetary policy in influencing real GDP in the short run and the long run?

CHAPTER 16

Inflation, Disinflation, and Deflation

WHAT YOU
WILL LEARN
IN THIS
CHAPTER

BRINGING A SUITCASE TO THE BANK

Phillimon Bulawayo/epa/Corbis

In 2008, the Zimbabwe dollar was so devalued by extreme inflation that this much currency was needed to pay for a single loaf of bread.

> **)** Why efforts to collect an **inflation tax** by printing money can lead to high rates of inflation and hyperinflation

> **)** What the **Phillips curve** is and how it describes the short-run trade-off between inflation and unemployment

> **)** Why there is no long-run trade-off between inflation and unemployment

> **)** Why expansionary policies are limited due to the effects of expected inflation

> **)** Why even moderate levels of inflation can be hard to end

> **)** Why deflation is a problem for economic policy and leads policy-makers to prefer a low but positive inflation rate

> **)** Why the nominal interest rate cannot go below the **zero bound** and the danger a **liquidity trap** poses

N 2008, THE AFRICAN NATION OF Zimbabwe achieved a dubious distinction: it exhibited one of the highest inflation rates ever recorded, peaking at around 500 billion percent. Although the government kept introducing ever-larger denominations of the Zimbabwe dollar— for example, in May 2008 it introduced a half-billion-dollar bill—it still took a lot of currency to pay for the necessities of life: a stack of Zimbabwean cash worth $100 weighed about 18 kilograms. Zimbabwean currency was worth so little that some people withdrawing funds from banks brought suitcases along, in order to be able to walk away with enough cash to pay for ordinary living expenses. In the end, the Zimbabwe dollar lost all value—literally. By October 2008, the currency more or less vanished from circulation, replaced by U.S. dollars and South African rands.

Zimbabwe's experience was shocking, but not unprecedented. In 1994 the inflation rate in Armenia hit 27 000%. In 1991 Nicaraguan inflation exceeded 60 000%. And Zimbabwe's experience was more or less matched by history's most famous example of extreme inflation, which took place in Germany in 1922–1923. Toward the end of the German hyperinflation, prices were rising 16% a *day,* which—through compounding—meant an increase of approximately 500 billion percent over the course of five months. People became so reluctant to hold paper money, which lost value by the hour, that eggs and lumps of coal began to circulate as currency. German firms would pay their workers several times a day so that they could spend their earnings before they lost value (lending new meaning to the term *hourly wage*). Legend has it that men sitting down at a bar would order two beers at a time, out of fear that the price of a beer would rise before they could order a second round!

Canada has never experienced that kind of inflation. Canada's worst inflation in the past 60 years occurred in the early 1980s, reaching, at its highest peak, an annual rate of almost 13% in 1981. Yet even that rate of inflation was profoundly troubling to the Canadian public, and the policies the Bank of Canada pursued to get Canada's inflation back down to an acceptable rate contributed to the deepest recession since the Great Depression.

What causes inflation to rise and fall? In this chapter, we'll look at the underlying reasons for inflation. We'll see that the underlying causes of very high inflation, the type of inflation suffered by Zimbabwe, are quite different from the causes of more moderate inflation. We'll also learn why *disinflation,* a reduction in the inflation rate, is often very difficult. Finally, we'll discuss the special problems associated with a falling price level, or deflation. ■

According to the **classical model of the price level,** the real quantity of money is always at its long-run equilibrium level.

Money and Inflation

As we'll see later in this chapter, moderate levels of inflation such as those experienced in Canada—even the double-digit inflation in the early 1980s—can have complex causes. But very high inflation is always associated with rapid increases in the money supply.

To understand why, we need to revisit the effect of changes in the money supply on the overall price level. Then we'll turn to the reasons governments sometimes increase the money supply very rapidly.

The Classical Model of Money and Prices

In Chapter 15, we learned that in the short run an increase in the money supply increases real GDP by lowering the interest rate and stimulating investment spending and consumer spending. However, in the long run, as nominal wages and other sticky prices rise, real GDP falls back to its long-run level (i.e., potential output). So in the long run, an increase in the money supply does not change real GDP. As mentioned in Chapter 8, the long-run level of output is determined by total factor productivity, the stock of physical and human capital used, and the amount of labour employed. Thus, other things equal, an increase in the money supply leads to an equal percent rise in the overall price level; that is, the prices of all goods and services in the economy, including nominal wages and the prices of intermediate goods, rise by the same percent age as the money supply. And when the overall price level rises, the aggregate price level—the prices of all final goods and services—rises as well. As a result, a change in the *nominal* money supply, M, leads in the long run to a change in the aggregate price level that leaves the *real* quantity of money, M/P, at its original level. As a result, there is no long-run effect on aggregate demand or real GDP. For example, when Turkey dropped six zeros from its currency, the Turkish lira, in January 2005, Turkish real GDP did not change. The only thing that changed was the number of zeros in prices: instead of something costing 2 000 000 lira, it cost 2 lira.

This is, to repeat, what happens in the long run. When analyzing large changes in the aggregate price level, however, macroeconomists often find it useful to ignore the distinction between the short run and the long run. Instead, they work with a simplified model in which the effect of a change in the money supply on the aggregate price level takes place instantaneously rather than over a long period of time. You might be concerned about this assumption given that in previous chapters we've emphasized the difference between the short run and the long run. However, for reasons we'll explain shortly, this is a reasonable assumption to make in the case of high inflation.

A simplified model in which the real quantity of money, M/P, is always at its long-run equilibrium level is known as the **classical model of the price level** because it was commonly used by "classical" economists who wrote before the work of John Maynard Keynes. To understand the classical model and why it is useful in the context of high inflation, let's revisit the *AD–AS* model and what it says about the effects of an increase in the money supply. (Unless otherwise noted, we will always be referring to changes in the *nominal* supply of money.)

Figure 16-1 reviews the effects of an increase in the money supply according to the *AD–AS* model. The economy starts at E_1, a point of short-run and long-run macroeconomic equilibrium. It lies at the intersection of the aggregate demand curve, AD_1, and the short-run aggregate supply curve, $SRAS_1$. It also lies on the long-run aggregate supply curve, *LRAS*. At E_1, the equilibrium aggregate price level is P_1.

Now suppose there is an increase in the money supply. This is an expansionary monetary policy, which shifts the aggregate demand curve to the right, to AD_2, and moves the economy to a new short-run macroeconomic equilibrium at E_2. Over time, however, nominal wages adjust upward in response to the rise in

FIGURE   **16-1**   The Classical Model of the Price Level

Starting at E_1, an increase in the money supply shifts the aggregate demand curve rightward, as shown by the movement from AD_1 to AD_2. There is a new short-run macroeconomic equilibrium at E_2 and a higher price level at P_2. In the long run, nominal wages adjust upward and push the *SRAS* curve leftward to $SRAS_2$. The total percent increase in the price level from P_1 to P_3 is equal to the percent increase in the money supply. In the *classical model of the price level*, we ignore the transition period and think of the price level as rising to P_3 immediately. This is a good approximation under conditions of high inflation.

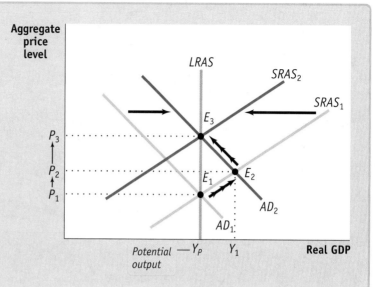

the aggregate price level, and the *SRAS* curve shifts to the left, to $SRAS_2$. The new long-run macroeconomic equilibrium is at E_3, and real GDP returns to its initial level. As we learned in Chapter 15, the long-run increase in the aggregate price level from P_1 to P_3 is proportional to the increase in the money supply. As a result, in the long run changes in the money supply have no effect on the real quantity of money, M/P, or on real GDP. In the long run, money—as we learned—is *neutral*.

The classical model of the price level ignores the short-run movement from E_1 to E_2, assuming that the economy moves directly from one long-run equilibrium to another long-run equilibrium. In other words, it assumes that the economy moves directly from E_1 to E_3 and that real GDP never changes in response to a change in the money supply. In effect, in the classical model the effects of money supply changes are analyzed as if the short-run as well as the long-run aggregate supply curves were vertical.

In reality, this is a poor assumption during periods of low inflation. With a low inflation rate, it may take a while for workers and firms to react to a monetary expansion by raising wages and prices due to the existence of menu costs and long-term contracts. In this scenario, some nominal wages and the prices of some goods are sticky in the short run. As a result, under low inflation there is an upward-sloping *SRAS* curve, and changes in the money supply can indeed change real GDP in the short run.

But what about periods of high inflation such as the one experienced in Zimbabwe? In the face of high inflation, economists have observed that the short-run stickiness of nominal wages and prices tends to vanish. Workers and businesses, sensitized to inflation, are quick to raise their wages and prices in response to changes in the money supply. This implies that under high inflation there is a quicker adjustment of wages and prices of intermediate goods than occurs in the case of low inflation. So the short-run aggregate supply curve shifts leftward more quickly and there is a more rapid return to long-run equilibrium under high inflation. As a result, the classical model of the price level is much more likely to be a good approximation of reality for economies experiencing persistently high inflation.

The consequence of this rapid adjustment of all prices in the economy is that in countries with persistently high inflation, changes in the money supply are quickly translated into changes in the inflation rate. Let's look at Zimbabwe. Figure 16-2 shows the annual rate of growth in the money supply and the annual rate of change of consumer prices from 2003 through April 2008. As

FIGURE **16-2** Money Supply Growth and Inflation in Zimbabwe

This figure, drawn on a logarithmic scale, shows the annual rates of change of the money supply and the price level in Zimbabwe from 2003 through April 2008. The surges in the money supply were quickly reflected in a roughly equal surge in the price level.

Source: International Monetary Fund.

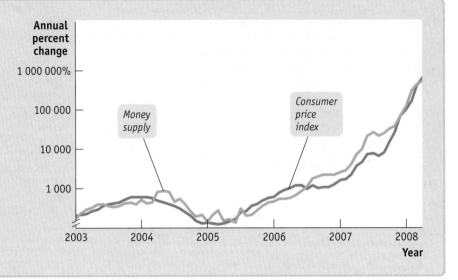

you can see, the surge in the growth rate of the money supply coincided closely with a roughly equal surge in the inflation rate. Note that to fit these very large percentage increases—several thousands of percent—onto the figure, we have drawn the vertical axis using a logarithmic scale that allows us to draw equal-sized percent changes as the same size.

What leads a country to increase its money supply so much that the result is an inflation rate in the millions, or even billions, of percent?

The Inflation Tax

Modern economies use fiat money—pieces of paper that have no intrinsic value but are accepted as a medium of exchange. In Canada and most other wealthy countries, the decision about how many pieces of paper to issue is placed in the hands of a central bank that is somewhat independent of the political process. However, this independence can always be taken away if politicians decide to seize control of monetary policy.

So what is to prevent a government from paying for some of its expenses not by raising taxes or borrowing but simply by printing money? Nothing. In fact, governments, including the Canadian government, do it all the time. How can the Canadian government do this, given that the Bank of Canada issues money, not the Department of Finance Canada? The answer is that the Department of Finance and the Bank of Canada work in concert. The Department of Finance issues debt to finance the government's purchases of goods and services, and the BOC *monetizes* the debt by creating money and buying some of this debt back from the public through open-market purchases of treasury bills. In effect, the Canadian government can and does raise revenue by printing money.

For example, in December 2009 the Canadian monetary base—bank reserves plus currency in circulation—was $4.194 billion larger than it had been a year earlier. This

occurred because, over the course of that year, the Bank of Canada had issued $2.734 billion in money, or its electronic equivalent, and put it into circulation through open-market operations. To put it another way, the BOC created money out of thin air and used it to buy valuable government securities from the private sector. It's true that the Canadian government pays interest on debt owned by the Bank of Canada—but the BOC, by law, hands the interest payments it receives on government debt back to the Receiver General of Canada, keeping only enough to fund its own operations. In effect, then, the BOC's actions enabled the government to pay off $4.194 billion in outstanding government debt by printing money.

An alternative way to look at this is to say that the right to print money is itself a source of revenue. Economists refer to the revenue generated by the government's right to print money as *seigniorage,* an archaic term that goes back to the Middle Ages. It refers to the right to stamp gold and silver into coins, and charge a fee for doing so, that medieval lords—seigneurs, in France—reserved for themselves.

Seigniorage normally accounts for only a tiny fraction, about half a percent, of Canada's budgetary revenue. For example, in 2011, seigniorage was $1.156 billion, or about 0.47% of Canada's total revenue of $245.203 billion. Furthermore, concerns about seigniorage don't have any influence on the Bank of Canada's decisions about how much money to print; the BOC is worried about inflation, not revenue. But there have been many occasions in history when governments turned to their printing presses as a crucial source of revenue. According to the usual scenario, a government finds itself running a large budget deficit—and lacks either the competence or the political will to eliminate this deficit by raising taxes or cutting spending. Furthermore, the government can't borrow to cover the gap because potential lenders won't extend loans given the fear that the government's weakness will continue and leave it unable to repay its debts.

In such a situation, governments end up printing money to cover the budget deficit. But by printing money to pay its bills, a government increases the quantity of money in circulation. And as we've just seen, increases in the money supply sooner or later translate into equally large increases in the aggregate price level. So printing money to cover a budget deficit leads to inflation.

Who ends up paying for the goods and services the government purchases with newly printed money? The people who currently hold money pay. They pay because inflation erodes the purchasing power of their money holdings. In other words, a government imposes an **inflation tax,** the reduction in the value of the money held by the public, by printing money to cover its budget deficit and creating inflation.

It's helpful to think about what this tax represents. If the inflation rate is 5%, then a year from now $1 will buy goods and services worth only $0.95 today. So a 5% inflation rate in effect imposes a tax rate of 5% on the value of all money held by the public.

But why would any government push the inflation tax to rates of hundreds or thousands of percent? We turn next to the logic of hyperinflation.

The Logic of Hyperinflation

Inflation imposes a tax on individuals who hold money. And, like most taxes, it will lead people to change their behaviour. In particular, when inflation is high, people will try to avoid holding money and will instead substitute real goods as well as interest-bearing assets for money. In this chapter's opening story, we described how, during the German hyperinflation, people began using eggs or lumps of coal as a medium of exchange. They did this because lumps of coal maintained their real value over time but money didn't. Indeed, during the peak of German hyperinflation, people often burned paper money, which was less valuable than wood. Moreover, people don't just reduce their nominal money

> The **inflation tax** is the reduction in the value of money held by the public caused by inflation.

In the 1920s, hyperinflation made German currency worth so little that children made kites from banknotes.

holdings—they reduce their *real* money holdings, cutting the amount of money they hold so much that it actually has less purchasing power than the amount of money they would hold if inflation were low. They do this by using the money to buy goods that last over time or assets that hold their value like gold. Why? Because the more real money holdings they have, the greater the real amount of resources the government captures from them through the inflation tax.

We are now prepared to understand how countries can get themselves into situations of extreme inflation. High inflation arises when the government must print a large quantity of money, imposing a large inflation tax, to cover a large budget deficit.

Now, the seigniorage collected by the government over a short period—say, one month—is equal to the change in the money supply over that period. Let's use M to represent the money supply and use the symbol Δ to mean "monthly change in." Then:

(16-1) Seigniorage = ΔM

The money value of seigniorage, however, isn't very informative by itself. After all, the whole point of inflation is that a given amount of money buys less and less over time. So it's more useful to look at *real* seigniorage, the revenue created by printing money divided by the price level, P, as this captures the real purchasing power that the government takes away from money holders:

(16-2) Real seigniorage = $\Delta M/P$

Equation 16-2 can be rewritten by dividing and multiplying by the current level of the money supply, M, giving us:

(16-3) Real seigniorage = $(\Delta M/M) \times (M/P)$

or

Real seigniorage = Rate of growth of the money supply × Real money supply

But as we've just explained, in the face of high inflation the public reduces the real amount of money it holds, so that the far right-hand term in Equation 16-3, M/P, gets smaller. Suppose that the government needs to print enough money to pay for a given quantity of goods and services—that is, it needs to collect a given *real* amount of seignorage. Then, as the real money supply, M/P, falls as people hold smaller amounts of real money, the government has to respond by accelerating the rate of growth of the money supply, $\Delta M/M$. This will lead to an even higher rate of inflation. And people will respond to this new higher rate of inflation by reducing their real money holdings, M/P, yet again. As the process becomes self-reinforcing, it can easily spiral out of control. Although the amount of real seigniorage that the government must ultimately collect to pay off its deficit does not change, the inflation rate the government needs to impose to collect that amount rises. So the government is forced to increase the money supply more rapidly, leading to an even higher rate of inflation, and so on.

Here's an analogy: imagine a city government that tries to raise a lot of money with a special fee on taxi rides. The fee will raise the cost of taxi rides, and this will cause people to turn to easily available substitutes, such as walking or taking the bus. As taxi use declines, the government finds that its tax revenue declines and it must impose a higher fee to raise the same amount of revenue as before. You can imagine the ensuing vicious circle: the government imposes fees on taxi rides, which leads to less taxi use, which causes the government to raise the fee on taxi rides, which leads to even less taxi use, and so on.

Substitute the real money supply for taxi rides and the inflation rate for the increase in the fee on taxi rides, and you have the story of hyperinflation. A race develops between the government printing presses and the public: the presses churn out money at a faster and faster rate, to try to compensate for the fact that the public is reducing its real money holdings. At some point the inflation rate explodes into hyperinflation, and people are unwilling to hold any money at all (and resort to trading in eggs and lumps of coal). The government is then forced to abandon its use of the inflation tax and shut down the printing presses.

ECONOMICS > IN ACTION

ZIMBABWE'S INFLATION

As we noted in this chapter's opening story, Zimbabwe offers a recent example of a country experiencing very high inflation. Figure 16-2 showed that surges in Zimbabwe's money supply growth were matched by almost simultaneous surges in its inflation rate. But looking at rates of change doesn't give a true feel for just how much prices went up.

Figure 16-3 shows Zimbabwe's consumer price index from January 2000 to July 2008, with the January 2000 level set equal to 100. As in Figure 16-2, we also use a logarithmic scale. Over the course of just over eight years, consumer prices rose by approximately 80 trillion percent.

Why did Zimbabwe's government pursue policies that led to runaway inflation? The reason boils down to political instability, which in turn had its roots in Zimbabwe's history. Until the 1970s, Zimbabwe had been ruled by its small white minority; even after the shift to majority rule, many of the country's farms remained in the hands of whites. Eventually Robert Mugabe, Zimbabwe's president, tried to solidify his position by seizing these farms and turning them over to his political supporters. But because this seizure disrupted production, the result was to undermine the country's economy and its tax base. It became impossible for the country's government to balance its budget either by raising taxes or by cutting spending. At the same time, the regime's instability left Zimbabwe unable to borrow money in world markets. Like many others before it, Zimbabwe's government turned to the printing press to cover the gap—leading to massive inflation.

FIGURE 16-3 Consumer Prices in Zimbabwe, 2000–2008

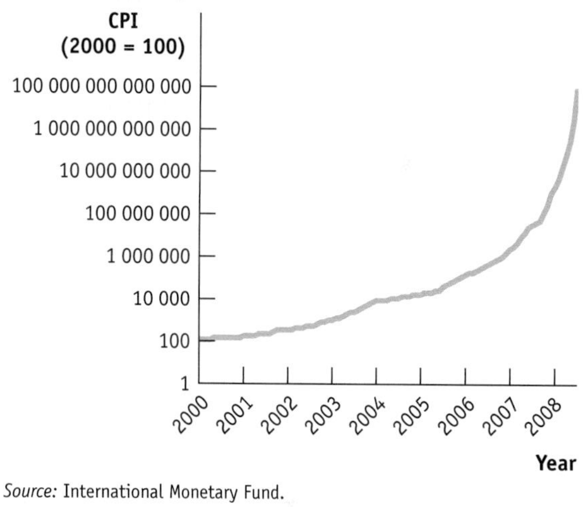

Source: International Monetary Fund.

▼ Quick Review

- The **classical model of the price level** does not distinguish between the short and the long run. It explains how increases in the money supply (growth rate) feed directly into inflation. It is a good description of reality only for countries with persistently high inflation or hyperinflation.

- Governments sometimes print money to cover a budget deficit. The resulting loss in the value of money is called the **inflation tax.**

- A high inflation rate causes people to reduce their real money holdings, leading to the printing of more money and higher inflation in order to collect the inflation tax. This can cause a self-reinforcing spiral into hyperinflation.

CHECK YOUR UNDERSTANDING   16-1

1. Suppose there is a large increase in the money supply in an economy that previously had low inflation. As a consequence, aggregate output expands in the short run. What does this say about situations in which the classical model of the price level applies?

2. Suppose that all wages and prices in an economy are indexed to inflation—that is, wages and prices are automatically adjusted to incorporate the latest inflation figures. Can there still be an inflation tax?

Solutions appear at back of book.

Moderate Inflation and Disinflation

The governments of wealthy, politically stable countries like Canada, the United States, and Britain don't find themselves forced to print large amounts of money to pay their bills. Yet over the past 40 years these countries, along with a number of other nations, have experienced uncomfortable episodes of inflation. In Canada and the United States, the inflation rate peaked at 13% at the beginning of the 1980s. In Britain, the inflation rate reached 26% in 1975. Why did policy-makers allow this to happen?

The answer, in brief, is that in the short run, policies that produce a booming economy also tend to lead to higher inflation, and policies that reduce inflation tend to depress the economy. This creates both temptations and dilemmas for governments.

First, imagine yourself as a politician facing an election in a year or two, and suppose that inflation is fairly low at the moment. You might well be tempted to pursue expansionary policies that will push the unemployment rate down, as a way to please voters, even if your economic advisers warn that this will eventually lead to higher inflation. You might also be tempted to find different economic advisers who will tell you not to worry: in politics, as in ordinary life, wishful thinking often prevails over realistic analysis.

Conversely, imagine yourself as a politician in an economy suffering from inflation. Your economic advisers will probably tell you that the only way to bring inflation down is to push the economy into a recession, which will lead to temporarily higher unemployment. Are you willing to pay that price? Maybe not.

This political asymmetry—inflationary policies often produce short-term political gains, but policies to bring inflation down carry short-term political costs—explains how countries with no need to impose an inflation tax sometimes end up with serious inflation problems. For example, that 26% rate of inflation in Britain was largely the result of the British government's decision in 1971 to pursue highly expansionary monetary and fiscal policies. Politicians disregarded warnings that these policies would be inflationary and were extremely reluctant to reverse course even when it became clear that the warnings had been correct.

But why do expansionary policies lead to inflation? To answer that question, we need to look first at the relationship between output and unemployment.

The Output Gap and the Unemployment Rate

In Chapter 12 we introduced the concept of *potential output*, the level of real GDP that the economy would produce once all prices had fully adjusted. Potential output typically grows steadily over time, reflecting long-run growth. However, as we learned from the aggregate demand–aggregate supply model, actual aggregate output fluctuates around potential output in the short run: a recessionary gap arises when actual aggregate output falls short of potential output; an inflationary gap arises when actual aggregate output exceeds potential output. Recall from Chapter 12 that the percentage difference between the actual level of real GDP and potential output is called the *output gap*. A positive or negative output gap occurs when an economy is producing more than or less than what would be "expected" because all prices have not yet adjusted. And wages, as we've learned, are the prices in the labour market.

Meanwhile, we learned in Chapter 8 that the unemployment rate is composed of cyclical unemployment and natural unemployment, the portion of the unemployment rate unaffected by the business cycle. So there is a relationship between the unemployment rate and the output gap. This relationship is defined by two rules:

1. When actual aggregate output is equal to potential output, the actual unemployment rate is equal to the natural rate of unemployment.

2. When the output gap is positive (an inflationary gap), the unemployment rate is *below* the natural rate. When the output gap is negative (a recessionary gap), the unemployment rate is *above* the natural rate.

In other words, fluctuations of aggregate output around the long-run trend of potential output correspond to fluctuations of the unemployment rate around the natural rate.

This makes sense. When the economy is producing less than potential output—when the output gap is negative—it is not making full use of its productive resources. Among the resources that are not fully utilized is labour, the economy's most important resource. So we would expect a negative output gap to be associated with unusually high unemployment. Conversely, when the economy is producing more than potential output, it is temporarily using resources at higher-than-normal rates. With this positive output gap, we would expect to see lower-than-normal unemployment.

Figure 16-4 confirms this rule. Panel (a) shows the actual and natural rates of unemployment in Canada between 1980 and 2011, as estimated by Statistics Canada and the Organisation for Economic Co-operation and Development (OECD), respectively. Panel (b) shows two series. One is cyclical unemployment: the difference between the actual unemployment rate and the OECD estimate of the natural rate of unemployment. The other is the Parliamentary Budget Officer (PBO) estimate of the output gap. It is obvious that there is an *inverse* relationship between cyclical unemployment and the output gap. When we had negative output gap as happened in the early 1980s, the early 1990s, and in the late 2000s, the cyclical unemployment rate turned positive, indicating that the actual unemployment rate exceeded the natural rate of unemployment. On the other hand,

FIGURE **16-4** Cyclical Unemployment and the Output Gap

Panel (a) shows the actual annual unemployment rate from 1980 to 2011 in Canada, together with the OECD estimate of the natural rate of unemployment. The actual rate fluctuates around the natural rate, often for extended periods. Panel (b) shows cyclical unemployment—the difference between the actual unemployment rate and the natural rate of unemployment—and the output gap, as estimated by the PBO. Cyclical unemployment and the output gap each move in the opposite direction: when the output gap is positive (i.e., actual output is above the natural rate level), the actual unemployment rate is below its natural rate (so the cyclical unemployment rate is low, perhaps even negative); when the output gap is negative, the actual unemployment rate is above its natural rate (so the cyclical unemployment rate is high). The two series track one another closely, showing the strong inverse relationship between the output gap and cyclical unemployment.

Sources: Statistics Canada; OECD; Parliamentary Budget Officer (PBO).

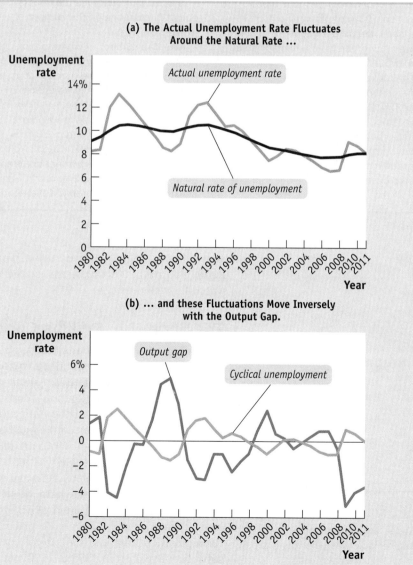

TOLES © 2001 The Washington Post. Reprinted with permission of UNIVERSAL UCLICK. All rights reserved.

FOR INQUIRING MINDS

OKUN'S LAW

Although cyclical unemployment and the output gap move together, cyclical unemployment seems to move *less* than the output gap. For example, the output gap reached −3.04% in 1992, but the cyclical unemployment rate reached only 1.59%. This observation is the basis of an important relationship originally discovered by Arthur Okun, John F. Kennedy's chief economic adviser.

Modern estimates of **Okun's law**—the negative relationship between the output gap and the unemployment rate—typically find that a rise in the output gap of 1 percentage point reduces the unemployment rate by about ½ of a percentage point.

For example, suppose that the natural rate of unemployment is 5.2% and that the economy is currently producing at only 98% of potential output. In that case, the output gap is −2%, and Okun's law predicts an unemployment rate of $5.2\% - \frac{1}{2} \times (-2\%) = 6.2\%$.

The fact that a 1% rise in output reduces the unemployment rate by only ½ of 1% may seem puzzling: you might have expected to see a one-to-one relationship between the output gap and unemployment. Doesn't a 1% rise in aggregate output require a 1% increase in employment? And shouldn't that take 1% off the unemployment rate?

The answer is no: there are several well-understood reasons why the relationship isn't one-to-one. For one thing, companies often meet changes in demand in part by changing the number of hours their existing employees work. For example, a company that experiences a sudden increase in demand for its products may cope by asking (or requiring) its workers to put in longer hours, rather than by hiring more workers. Conversely, a company that sees sales drop will often reduce workers' hours rather than lay off employees. This behaviour dampens the effect of output fluctuations on the number of workers employed.

Also, the number of workers looking for jobs is affected by the availability of jobs. Suppose that the number of jobs falls by 1 million. Measured unemployment will rise by less than 1 million because some unemployed workers become discouraged and give up actively looking for work. (Recall from Chapter 8 that workers aren't counted as unemployed unless they are actively seeking work.) Conversely, if the econ-

omy adds 1 million jobs, some people who haven't been actively looking for work will begin doing so. As a result, measured unemployment will fall by less than 1 million.

Finally, the rate of growth of labour productivity generally accelerates during booms and slows down or even turns negative during busts. The reasons for this phenomenon are the subject of some dispute among economists. The consequence, however, is that the effects of booms and busts on the unemployment rate are dampened.

---

years of a strongly positive output gap like the late 1980s, the late 1990s, early 2000s and mid-2000s were associated with low or even negative rates of cyclical unemployment.

The Short-Run Phillips Curve

We've just seen that expansionary policies lead to a lower unemployment rate. Our next step in understanding the temptations and dilemmas facing governments is to show that there is a short-run trade-off between unemployment and inflation—lower unemployment tends to lead to higher inflation, and vice versa. The key concept is that of the *Phillips curve*.

The origins of this concept lie in a famous 1958 paper by the New Zealand–born economist A.W.H. Phillips. Looking at historical data for Britain, he found that when the unemployment rate was high, the wage rate tended to fall, and when the unemployment rate was low, the wage rate tended to rise. Using data from Britain, the United States, and elsewhere, other economists soon found a similar apparent relationship between the unemployment rate and the rate of inflation—that is, the rate of change in the aggregate price level. For example, Figure 16-5 shows the unemployment rate and the rate of consumer price inflation in Canada over each subsequent year from 1955 to 1970, with each dot representing one year's data.

Okun's law is the negative relationship between the output gap and cyclical unemployment.

FIGURE **16-5** Unemployment and Inflation, 1955–1970

Each point shows the average Canadian unemployment rate for one year and the percentage change in the consumer price index over the subsequent year. Data like these lay behind the initial concept of the Phillips curve.

Sources: Historical Statistics of Canada; Statistics Canada.

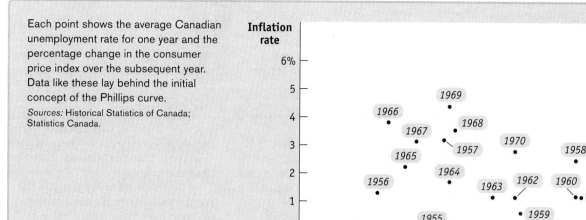

Looking at evidence like Figure 16-5, many economists concluded that there is a negative short-run relationship between the unemployment rate and the inflation rate, which is called the **short-run Phillips curve,** or *SRPC.* (We'll explain the difference between the short-run and the long-run Phillips curves soon.) Figure 16-6 shows a hypothetical short-run Phillips curve.

Early estimates of the short-run Phillips curve for Canada were very simple: they showed a negative relationship between the unemployment rate and the inflation rate, without taking account of any other variables. During the 1950s and 1960s this simple approach seemed, for a while, to be adequate. And this simple relationship is clear in the data in Figure 16-5.

Even at the time, however, some economists argued that a more accurate short-run Phillips curve would include other factors. In Chapter 12 we discussed the effect of *supply shocks,* such as sudden changes in the price of oil, which shift the short-run aggregate supply curve. Such shocks also shift the short-run Phillips curve: surging oil prices were an important factor in the inflation of the

The **short-run Phillips curve** is the negative short-run relationship between the unemployment rate and the inflation rate.

FIGURE **16-6** The Short-Run Phillips Curve

The short-run Phillips curve, *SRPC,* slopes downward because the relationship between the unemployment rate and the inflation rate is negative.

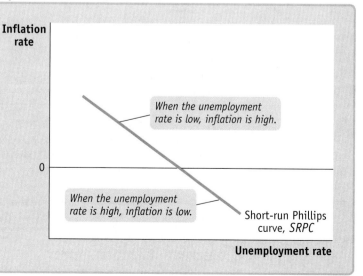

FOR INQUIRING MINDS

THE AGGREGATE SUPPLY CURVE AND THE SHORT-RUN PHILLIPS CURVE

In earlier chapters we made extensive use of the *AD–AS* model, in which the short-run aggregate supply curve—a relationship between real GDP and the aggregate price level—plays a central role. Now we've introduced the concept of the short-run Phillips curve, a relationship between the unemployment rate and the rate of inflation. How do these two concepts fit together?

We can get a partial answer to this question by looking at panel (a) of Figure 16-7, which shows how changes in the aggregate price level and the output gap depend on changes in aggregate demand. Assume that in year 1 the aggregate demand curve is AD_1, the long-run aggregate supply curve is *LRAS*, and the short-run aggregate supply curve is *SRAS*. The initial macroeconomic equilibrium is at E_1, where the price level is 100 and real GDP is $1000 billion. Notice that at E_1, real GDP is equal to potential output, so the output gap is zero.

Now consider two possible paths for the economy over the next year. One is that aggregate demand remains unchanged and the economy stays at E_1. The other is that aggregate demand shifts rightward to AD_2 and the economy moves to E_2.

At E_2, real GDP is $1040 billion, $40 billion more than potential output—a 4% output gap. Meanwhile, at E_2, the aggregate price level is 102—a 2% increase. So panel (a) tells us that in this example a zero output gap is associated with zero inflation and a 4% output gap is associated with 2% inflation.

Panel (b) shows what this implies for the relationship between unemployment and inflation. Assume that the natural rate of unemployment is 6% and that a rise of 1 percentage point in the output gap causes a fall of ½ percentage point in the unemployment rate per Okun's law, described in the previous For Inquiring Minds. In that case, the two cases shown in panel (a)—aggregate demand either

staying put or rising—correspond to the two points in panel (b). At E_1, the unemployment rate is 6% and the inflation rate is 0%. At E_2, the unemployment rate is 4%, because an output gap of 4% reduces the unemployment rate by 4% × 0.5 = 2% below its natural rate of 6%—and the inflation rate is 2%. So there is a negative relationship between unemployment and inflation.

So does the short-run aggregate supply curve say exactly the same thing as the short-run Phillips curve? Not quite. The short-run aggregate supply curve seems to imply a relationship between the *change* in the unemployment rate and the inflation rate, but the short-run Phillips curve shows a relationship between the *level* of the unemployment rate and the inflation rate. Reconciling these views completely would go beyond the scope of this book. The important point is that the short-run Phillips curve is a concept that is closely related, though not identical, to the short-run aggregate supply curve.

FIGURE 16-7 The *AD–AS* Model and the Short-Run Phillips Curve

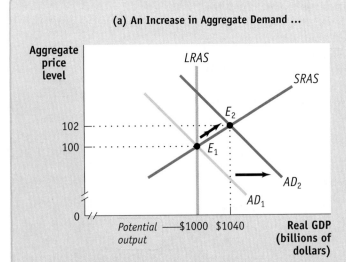

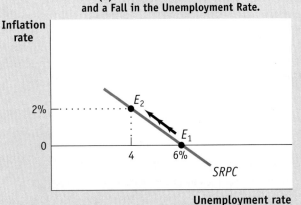

The short-run Phillips curve is closely related to the short-run aggregate supply curve. In panel (a), the economy is initially in equilibrium at E_1, with the aggregate price level at 100 and aggregate output at $1000 billion, which we assume is potential output. Now consider two possibilities. If the aggregate demand curve remains at AD_1, there is an output gap of zero and 0% inflation. If the aggregate demand curve shifts

out to AD_2, there is an output gap of 4%—reducing unemployment to 4%—and 2% inflation. Assuming that the natural rate of unemployment is 6%, the implications for unemployment and inflation are as follows, shown in panel (b): if aggregate demand does not increase, 6% unemployment and 0% inflation will result; if aggregate demand does increase, 4% unemployment and 2% inflation will result.

FIGURE **16-8** The Short-Run Phillips Curve and Supply Shocks

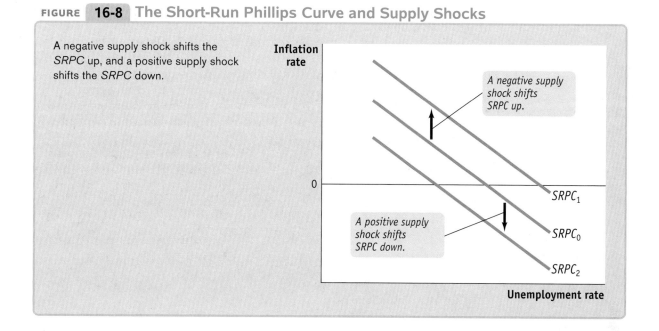

A negative supply shock shifts the *SRPC* up, and a positive supply shock shifts the *SRPC* down.

A negative supply shock shifts *SRPC* up.

A positive supply shock shifts *SRPC* down.

Inflation rate

0

Unemployment rate

$SRPC_1$

$SRPC_0$

$SRPC_2$

1970s and early 1980s and also played an important role in the acceleration of inflation in 2007–2008. In general, a negative supply shock shifts *SRPC* up as the inflation rate increases for every level of the unemployment rate, and a positive supply shock shifts it down as the inflation rate falls for every level of the unemployment rate. Both outcomes are shown in Figure 16-8.

But supply shocks are not the only factors that can change the inflation rate. In the 1950s and early 1960s, Canadians had little experience with inflation because inflation rates had been low. But by the late 1960s, after inflation had been steadily increasing for a number of years, Canadians had come to expect it. In 1968 two economists—Milton Friedman of the University of Chicago and Edmund Phelps of Columbia University—independently set forth a crucial hypothesis: that expectations about future inflation directly affect the present inflation rate. Today most economists accept that the *expected inflation rate*—the rate of inflation that employers and workers expect in the near future—is the most important factor, other than the unemployment rate, affecting inflation.

Inflation Expectations and the Short-Run Phillips Curve

The **expected rate of inflation** is the rate of inflation that employers and workers expect in the near future. One of the crucial discoveries of modern macroeconomics is that changes in the expected rate of inflation affect the short-run trade-off between unemployment and inflation and shift the short-run Phillips curve.

Why do changes in expected inflation affect the short-run Phillips curve? Put yourself in the position of a worker or employer about to sign a contract setting the worker's wages over the next year. For a number of reasons, the wage rate they agree to will be higher if everyone expects high inflation (including rising wages) than if everyone expects prices to be stable. The worker will want a wage rate that takes into account future declines in the purchasing power of earnings. He or she will also want a wage rate that won't fall behind the wages of other workers. And the employer will be more willing to agree to a wage increase now if hiring workers later will be even more expensive. Also, rising prices will make paying a higher wage rate more affordable for the employer because the employer's output will sell for more.

The **expected rate of inflation** is the rate of inflation employers and workers expect in the near future.

For these reasons, an increase in expected inflation shifts the short-run Phillips curve upward: the actual rate of inflation at any given unemployment rate is higher when the expected inflation rate is higher. In fact, macroeconomists believe that the relationship between changes in expected inflation and changes in actual inflation is one-to-one. That is, when the expected inflation rate increases, the actual inflation rate at any given unemployment rate will increase by the same amount. When the expected inflation rate falls, the actual inflation rate at any given level of unemployment will fall by the same amount.

Figure 16-9 shows how the expected rate of inflation affects the short-run Phillips curve. First, suppose that the expected rate of inflation is 0%. $SRPC_0$ is the short-run Phillips curve when the public expects 0% inflation. According to $SRPC_0$, the actual inflation rate will be 0% if the unemployment rate is 6%; it will be 2% if the unemployment rate is 4%.

FIGURE 16-9 Expected Inflation and the Short-Run Phillips Curve

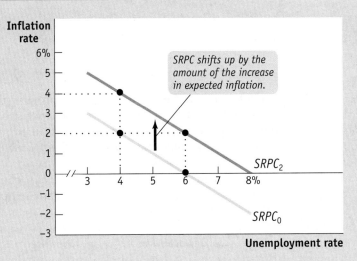

An increase in expected inflation shifts the short-run Phillips curve up. $SRPC_0$ is the initial short-run Phillips curve with an expected inflation rate of 0%; $SRPC_2$ is the short-run Phillips curve with an expected inflation rate of 2%. Each additional percentage point of expected inflation raises the actual inflation rate at any given unemployment rate by 1 percentage point.

Alternatively, suppose the expected rate of inflation is 2%. In that case, employers and workers will build this expectation into wages and prices: at any given unemployment rate, the actual inflation rate will be 2 percentage points higher than it would be if people expected 0% inflation. $SRPC_2$, which shows the Phillips curve when the expected inflation rate is 2%, is $SRPC_0$ shifted upward by 2 percentage points at every level of unemployment. According to $SRPC_2$, the actual inflation rate will be 2% if the unemployment rate is 6%; it will be 4% if the unemployment rate is 4%.

What determines the expected rate of inflation? In general, people base their expectations about inflation on experience. If the inflation rate has hovered around 0% in the last few years, people will expect it to be around 0% in the near future. But if the inflation rate has averaged around 5% lately, people will expect inflation to be around 5% in the near future.

Since expected inflation is an important part of the modern discussion about the short-run Phillips curve, you might wonder why it was not in the original formulation of the Phillips curve. The answer lies in history. Think back to what we said about the early 1960s: at that time, people were accustomed to low inflation rates and reasonably expected that future inflation rates would also be low. It was only after 1965 that persistent inflation became a fact of life. So only then did it become clear that expected inflation would play an important role in price-setting.

ECONOMICS > IN ACTION

FROM THE SCARY SEVENTIES TO THE NIFTY NINETIES

Figure 16-5 showed that the Canadian experience during the 1950s and 1960s supported the belief in the existence of a short-run Phillips curve for the Canadian economy, with a short-run trade-off between unemployment and inflation.

After 1966 or 1967, however, that relationship appeared to fall apart according to the data. Figure 16-10 plots the track of Canadian unemployment and inflation rates from 1961 to 1990. As you can see, the track looks more like a tangled piece of yarn than a smooth curve.

Through much of the 1970s and early 1980s, the economy suffered from a combination of above-average unemployment rates coupled with inflation rates unprecedented in modern Canadian history. This condition came to be known as *stagflation*—for stagnation combined with high inflation. In the late 1990s, by contrast, the economy was experiencing a blissful combination of low unemployment and low inflation. What explains these developments?

Part of the answer can be attributed to a series of negative supply shocks that the Canadian economy suffered during the 1970s. The price of oil, in particular, soared as wars and revolutions in the Middle East led to a reduction in oil supplies and as oil-exporting countries deliberately curbed production to drive up prices. Compounding the oil price shocks, there was also a slowdown in labour productivity growth. Both of these factors shifted the short-run Phillips curve upward. During the 1990s, by contrast, supply shocks were positive. Prices of oil and other raw materials were generally falling, and productivity growth accelerated. As a result, the short-run Phillips curve shifted downward.

Equally important was the role of expected inflation. As mentioned earlier in the chapter, inflation accelerated during the 1960s. During the 1970s the public came to expect high inflation, and this expectation also shifted the short-run Phillips curve up. It took a sustained and costly effort during the 1980s to get inflation back down. The result, however, was that expected inflation was very low by the late 1990s, allowing actual inflation to be low even with low rates of unemployment.

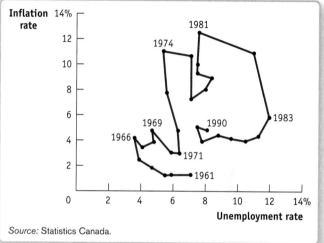

FIGURE 16-10 Unemployment and Inflation, 1961–1990

Source: Statistics Canada.

> ### ▼ Quick Review
>
> - **Okun's law** describes the relationship between the output gap and cyclical unemployment.
>
> - The **short-run Phillips curve** illustrates the negative relationship between unemployment and inflation.
>
> - A negative supply shock shifts the short-run Phillips curve upward, but a positive supply shock shifts it downward.
>
> - An increase in the **expected rate of inflation** pushes the short-run Phillips curve upward: each additional percentage point of expected inflation pushes the actual inflation rate at any given unemployment rate up by 1 percentage point.
>
> - In the 1970s, a series of negative supply shocks and a slowdown in labour productivity growth led to *stagflation* and an upward shift in the short-run Phillips curve.

CHECK YOUR UNDERSTANDING   16-2

1. Explain how the short-run Phillips curve illustrates the negative relationship between cyclical unemployment and the actual inflation rate for a given level of the expected inflation rate.

2. Which way does the short-run Phillips curve move in response to a fall in commodities prices? To a surge in commodities prices? Explain.

Solutions appear at back of book.

Inflation and Unemployment in the Long Run

The short-run Phillips curve says that at any given point in time there is a trade-off between unemployment and inflation. According to this view, policymakers have a choice: they can choose to accept that, in the short run, the price to achieve low unemployment is that the inflation rate must be high. In fact, during the 1960s many economists believed that this trade-off represented a real choice.

However, this view was greatly altered by the later recognition that expected inflation affects the short-run Phillips curve. In the short run, expectations often diverge from reality. In the long run, however, any consistent rate of inflation will be reflected in expectations. If inflation is consistently high, as it was in the 1970s, people will come to expect more of the same; if inflation is consistently low, as it has been in recent years, that, too, will become part of expectations.

So what does the trade-off between inflation and unemployment look like in the long run, when actual inflation is fully incorporated into expectations? Most macroeconomists believe that there is, in fact, no long-run trade-off. That is, it is not possible to achieve lower unemployment in the long run by accepting higher inflation. To see why, we need to introduce another concept: the *long-run Phillips curve*.

The Long-Run Phillips Curve

Figure 16-11 reproduces the two short-run Phillips curves from Figure 16-9, $SRPC_0$ and $SRPC_2$. It also adds an additional short-run Phillips curve, $SRPC_4$, representing a 4% expected rate of inflation. In a moment, we'll explain the significance of the vertical long-run Phillips curve, $LRPC$.

Suppose that the economy has, in the past, had a 0% inflation rate and that this rate is expected to continue into the near future. In that case, the current short-run Phillips curve will be $SRPC_0$, reflecting a 0% expected inflation rate. If the unemployment rate is 6%, the actual inflation rate will be 0%.

Also suppose that policy-makers decide to trade off lower unemployment for a higher rate of inflation. They use monetary policy, fiscal policy, or both to drive the unemployment rate down to 4%. This puts the economy at point A on $SRPC_0$, leading to an actual inflation rate of 2%.

Over time, the public will come to expect a 2% inflation rate. *This increase in inflationary expectations will shift the short-run Phillips curve upward to $SRPC_2$.* Now, when the unemployment rate is 6%, the actual inflation rate will be 2%. Given this new short-run Phillips curve, policies adopted to keep the unemployment rate at 4% will lead to a 4% actual inflation rate—point B on $SRPC_2$—rather than point A with a 2% actual inflation rate.

Eventually, the 4% actual inflation rate gets built into expectations about the future inflation rate, and the short-run Phillips curve shifts upward yet again to $SRPC_4$. To keep the unemployment rate at 4% would now require accepting a 6% actual inflation rate, point C on $SRPC_4$, and so on. In short, a persistent attempt to trade off lower unemployment for higher inflation leads to *accelerating* inflation over time.

To avoid accelerating inflation over time, the unemployment rate must be high enough that the actual rate of inflation matches the expected rate of inflation. This is the situation at E_0 on $SRPC_0$: when the expected inflation rate is 0% and the unemployment rate is 6%, the actual inflation rate is 0%. It is also the situation at E_2 on $SRPC_2$: when the expected inflation rate is 2% and the unemployment rate is 6%, the actual inflation rate is 2%. And it is the situation at E_4 on $SRPC_4$: when the expected inflation rate is 4% and the unemployment rate is 6%, the actual inflation rate is 4%. As we'll learn in Chapter 18, this relationship between accelerating inflation and the unemployment rate is known as the *natural rate hypothesis*.

The unemployment rate at which inflation does not change over time—6% in Figure 16-11—is known as the **non-accelerating inflation rate (level) of unemployment,** or **NAIRU** for short. Keeping the unemployment rate below the NAIRU leads to ever-accelerating inflation and cannot be maintained. Most macroeconomists believe that there is a NAIRU and that there is no long-run trade-off between unemployment and inflation.

We can now explain the significance of the vertical line $LRPC$. It is the **long-run Phillips curve,** the relationship between unemployment and inflation in the long run, after expectations of inflation have had time to fully adjust to experience. It is vertical because any unemployment rate below the NAIRU leads to ever-accelerating inflation. In other words, the long-run Phillips curve shows

The **non-accelerating inflation rate (level) of unemployment,** or **NAIRU,** is the unemployment rate at which inflation does not change over time.

The **long-run Phillips curve** shows the relationship between unemployment and inflation after expectations of inflation have had time to fully adjust to experience.

FIGURE **16-11** The NAIRU and the Long-Run Phillips Curve

$SRPC_0$ is the short-run Phillips curve when the expected inflation rate is 0%. At a 4% unemployment rate, the economy is at point A with an actual inflation rate of 2%. The higher inflation rate will be incorporated into expectations, and the $SRPC$ will shift upward to $SRPC_2$. If policy-makers act to keep the unemployment rate at 4%, the economy will be at B and the actual inflation rate will rise to 4%. Inflationary expectations will be revised upward again, and $SRPC$ will shift to $SRPC_4$. At a 4% unemployment rate, the economy will be at C and the actual inflation rate will rise to 6%. Here, an unemployment rate (level) of 6% is the NAIRU, or non-accelerating inflation rate of unemployment. As long as unemployment is at the NAIRU, the actual inflation rate will match expectations and remain constant. An unemployment rate below 6% requires ever-accelerating inflation. The long-run Phillips curve, $LRPC$, which passes through E_0, E_2, and E_4, is vertical: no long-run trade-off between unemployment and inflation exists.

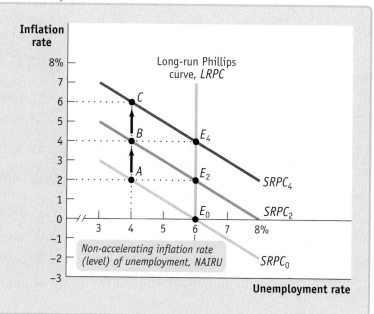

that there are limits to expansionary policies because an unemployment rate below the NAIRU cannot be maintained in the long run. Moreover, there is a corresponding point we have not yet emphasized: any unemployment rate above the NAIRU leads to decelerating inflation.

The Natural Rate of Unemployment, Revisited

Recall the concept of the natural rate of unemployment, the portion of the unemployment rate unaffected by the swings of the business cycle. Now we have introduced the concept of the *NAIRU*. How do these two concepts relate to each other?

The answer is that the NAIRU is another name for the natural rate. The level of unemployment the economy "needs" in order to avoid accelerating inflation, or deflation, is equal to the natural rate of unemployment.

In fact, economists estimate the natural rate of unemployment by looking for evidence about the NAIRU from the behaviour of the inflation rate and the unemployment rate over the course of the business cycle. For example, the way major European countries learned, to their dismay, that their natural rates of unemployment were 9% or more was through unpleasant experience. In the late 1980s, and again in the late 1990s, European inflation began to accelerate as European unemployment rates, which had been above 9%, began to fall, approaching 8%.

In Figure 16-4 we cited OECD estimates of the Canadian natural rate of unemployment. The OECD has a model that predicts changes in the inflation rate based on the deviation of the actual unemployment rate from the natural rate. Given data on actual unemployment and inflation, this model can be used to deduce estimates of the natural rate—and that's where the OECD numbers come from. As of December 2012, the OECD estimate of the Canadian natural rate of unemployment was 6.45%.

The Costs of Disinflation

Through experience, policy-makers have found that bringing inflation down is a much harder task than increasing it. The reason is that once the public has come to expect continuing inflation, bringing inflation down is painful.

A persistent attempt to keep unemployment below the natural rate leads to accelerating inflation that becomes incorporated into expectations. To reduce

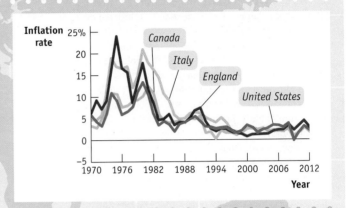

GLOBAL COMPARISON

DISINFLATION AROUND THE WORLD

The great disinflation of the 1980s wasn't unique to Canada. A number of other advanced countries also experienced high inflation during the 1970s, then brought inflation down during the early 1980s at the cost of a severe recession. This figure shows the annual rate of inflation in Canada, England, Italy, and the United States from 1970 to 2012. All four nations experienced high inflation rates following the two oil shocks of 1973 and 1979, with the Canadian inflation rate being the least severe of the four. All four nations then weathered severe recessions in order to bring inflation down. Since the 1980s, inflation has remained low and stable in all wealthy nations.

Source: OECD.

inflationary expectations, policy-makers need to run the process in reverse, adopting contractionary policies that keep the unemployment rate above the natural rate for an extended period of time. Recall that disinflation is the process of bringing down inflation that has become embedded in expectations.

Disinflation can be very expensive. As the following Economics in Action documents, the Canadian retreat from high inflation at the beginning of the 1980s appears to have cost the equivalent of about 11% of a year's real GDP, equivalent to a loss of more than $200 billion today. The justification for paying these costs is that they lead to a permanent gain. Although the economy does not recover the short-term production losses caused by disinflation, it no longer suffers from the costs associated with persistently high inflation. In fact, Canada, the United States, Britain, and other wealthy countries that experienced inflation in the 1970s eventually decided that the longer term benefits of bringing inflation down were worth the required suffering—the large reduction in real GDP in the short term.

Some economists argue that the costs of disinflation can be reduced if policy-makers explicitly state their determination to reduce inflation. A clearly announced, credible policy of disinflation, they contend, can reduce expectations of future inflation and so shift the short-run Phillips curve downward. Some economists believe that the clear determination of the Bank of Canada to combat the inflation of the 1970s was credible enough that the costs of disinflation, huge though they were, were lower than they might otherwise have been.[1]

ECONOMICS ▸ IN ACTION

THE GREAT DISINFLATION OF THE 1980s

As we've mentioned several times in this chapter, Canada ended the 1970s with a high rate of inflation, at least by its own peacetime historical standards—12.5% in 1981. Part of this inflation was the result of one-time events, especially a world oil crisis. But expectations of future inflation at 10% or more per year appeared to be firmly embedded in the economy.

---

[1]In 1991, the Bank of Canada used this same line of reasoning to help explain why it had decided to adopt a policy of explicitly targeting the rate of inflation so as to try to keep inflation at a target of 2% annually. Picking a simple and clearly understood policy goal has allowed the BOC to keep forward-looking inflation expectations well anchored, which helps keep inflation low and stable.

FIGURE 16-12 The Great Disinflation

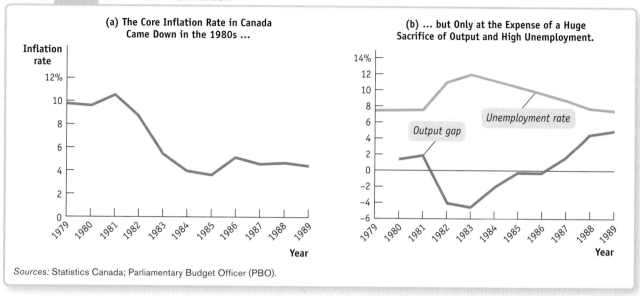

Sources: Statistics Canada; Parliamentary Budget Officer (PBO).

In the early 1980s as the economy slowed down, owing to the disinflationary monetary policy in effect at the time, the output gap became negative, which in turn caused the unemployment rate to rise. By the mid-1980s, however, inflation was running at about 4% per year. Panel (a) of Figure 16-12 shows the annual rate of change in the modified consumer price index (CPI), which helps to measure the *core inflation rate*. This index, which excludes the eight most volatile components of the CPI—categories such as energy and food prices—is widely regarded as a better indicator of underlying inflation trends than the overall CPI. By this measure, inflation fell from about 10% at the end of the 1970s to about 4% by the mid-1980s.

How was this disinflation achieved? At great cost. In 1981, the Bank of Canada imposed strongly contractionary monetary policies, which pushed the economy into its worst recession since the Great Depression. Panel (b) shows the Parliamentary Budget Office estimate of the Canadian output gap from 1980 to 1989 and the unemployment rate from 1979 to 1989: by 1983, actual output was 4.6% below potential output, corresponding to an unemployment rate of 12%. Aggregate output didn't get back to potential output until 1987. The unemployment rate did not return to its pre-recession rate until 1988.

Our analysis of the long-run Phillips curve tells us that a temporary rise in unemployment, like that of the 1980s, is needed to break the cycle of inflationary expectations. Once expectations of inflation are reduced, the economy can return to the natural rate of unemployment at a lower inflation rate. And that's just what happened.

But the cost was huge. If you add up the output gap over 1982–1987, you find that the economy sacrificed approximately 11% of an average year's output over the period. If we had to do the same thing today, that would mean giving up more than $200 billion worth of goods and services.

CHECK YOUR UNDERSTANDING 16-3

1. Why is there no long-run trade-off between unemployment and inflation?

2. British economists believe that the natural rate of unemployment in that country rose sharply during the 1970s, from around 3% to as much as 10%. During that period, Britain experienced a sharp acceleration of inflation, which for a time went above 20%. How might these facts be related?

3. Why is disinflation so costly for an economy? Are there ways to reduce these costs?

Solutions appear at back of book.

▼ Quick Review

- Policies that keep the unemployment rate below the **NAIRU,** the **nonaccelerating rate (level) of inflation,** will lead to accelerating inflation as inflationary expectations adjust to higher levels of actual inflation. The NAIRU is equal to the natural rate of unemployment.

- The **long-run Phillips curve** is vertical and shows that an unemployment rate below the NAIRU cannot be maintained in the long run. As a result, there are limits to expansionary policies.

- Disinflation imposes high costs—unemployment and lost output—on an economy. Governments do it to avoid the costs of persistently high inflation.

Debt deflation is the reduction in aggregate demand arising from the increase in the real burden of outstanding debt caused by deflation.

There is a **zero bound** on the nominal interest rate: it cannot go below zero.

The economy is in a **liquidity trap** when conventional monetary policy is ineffective because nominal interest rates are up against the zero bound.

Deflation

Before World War II, *deflation*—a falling aggregate price level—was almost as common as inflation. In fact, the Canadian consumer price index on the eve of World War II was 33% lower than it had been in 1920. After World War II, inflation became the norm in all countries. But in the 1990s, deflation reappeared in Japan and proved difficult to reverse. Concerns about potential deflation played a crucial role in Canadian monetary policy in the mid-1990s and again in 2009 in the aftermath of the 2008 financial crisis.

Why is deflation a problem? And why is it hard to end?

Debt Deflation

Deflation, like inflation, produces both winners and losers—but in the opposite direction. Due to the falling price level, a dollar in the future has a higher real value than a dollar today. So lenders, who are owed money, gain under deflation because the real value of borrowers' payments increases. Borrowers lose because the real burden of their debt rises.

In a famous analysis at the beginning of the Great Depression, Irving Fisher (who first analyzed the *Fisher effect* of expected inflation on interest rates, described in Chapter 10) claimed that the effects of deflation on borrowers and lenders can worsen an economic slump. Deflation, in effect, takes real resources away from borrowers and redistributes them to lenders. Fisher argued that borrowers, who lose from deflation, are typically short of cash and will be forced to cut their spending sharply when their debt burden rises. Lenders, however, are unlikely to increase spending sharply when the values of the loans they own rise. The overall effect, said Fisher, is that deflation reduces aggregate demand, and the resulting leftward shift of the *AD* (aggregate demand) curve deepens the economic slump, which, in a vicious circle, may lead to further deflation. The effect of deflation in reducing aggregate demand, known as **debt deflation,** probably played a significant role in the Great Depression.

Effects of Expected Deflation

Like expected inflation, expected deflation affects the nominal interest rate. Look back at Figure 10-7, which demonstrated how expected inflation affects the equilibrium interest rate. In Figure 10-7, the equilibrium nominal interest rate is 4% if the expected inflation rate is 0%. Clearly, if the expected inflation rate is –3%—if the public expects deflation at 3% per year—the equilibrium nominal interest rate will be 1%.

But what would happen if the expected rate of inflation is –5%? Would the nominal interest rate fall to –1%, in which lenders are paying borrowers 1% on their debt? No. Nobody would lend money at a negative nominal rate of interest because they could do better by simply holding cash. This illustrates what economists call the **zero bound** on the nominal interest rate: it cannot go below zero.

This zero bound can limit the effectiveness of monetary policy. Suppose the economy is depressed, with output below potential output and the unemployment rate above the natural rate. Normally the central bank can respond by cutting interest rates so as to increase aggregate demand. If the nominal interest rate is already zero, however, the central bank cannot push it down any further. Banks refuse to lend and consumers and firms refuse to spend because, with a negative inflation rate and a 0% nominal interest rate, holding cash yields a positive real return: with falling prices, a given amount of cash buys more over time. Any further increases in the monetary base will either be held in bank vaults or held as cash by individuals and firms, without being spent.

A situation in which conventional monetary policy to fight a slump—cutting interest rates—can't be used because nominal interest rates are up against the zero bound is known as a **liquidity trap.** A liquidity trap can occur whenever there is

FIGURE **16-13** The Zero Bound in Canadian History: 3-Month T-Bill Yields, 1934–2012

This figure shows Canadian short-term interest rates, specifically the interest rate on three-month treasury bills, from 1934 to 2012. As shown by the shaded area on the left, for much of the 1930s and 1940s, interest rates were very close to zero, leaving little room for expansionary monetary policy. After World War II, persistent inflation generally kept interest rates well above zero. However, in late 2008 (the shaded area on the right), in the wake of the worldwide financial crisis caused by the bursting of the U.S. housing bubble, the interest rate on three-month treasury bills was again virtually zero.

Source: Statistics Canada.

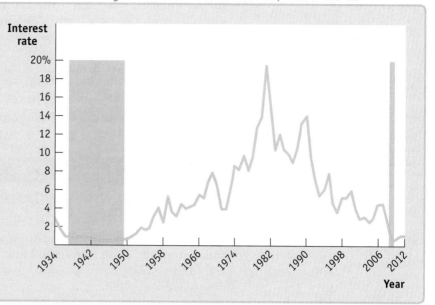

a sharp reduction in demand for loanable funds—which is exactly what happened during the Great Depression. Figure 16-13 shows the interest rate on short-term Canadian government debt from 1934 to the end of 2012. As you can see, from the mid-1930s until World War II brought a full economic recovery, the Canadian economy was either close to or up against the zero bound. After World War II, when inflation became the norm around the world, the zero bound largely vanished as a problem as the public came to expect inflation rather than deflation.

However, the recent history of the Japanese economy, shown in Figure 16-14, provides a modern illustration of the problem of deflation and the liquidity trap. Japan experienced a huge boom in the prices of both stocks and real estate in the late 1980s, then saw both bubbles burst. The result was a prolonged period of economic stagnation, the so-called Lost Decade, which gradually reduced the inflation rate and eventually led to persistent deflation. In an effort to fight the weakness of the economy, the Bank of Japan—the equivalent of the

FIGURE **16-14** Japan's Lost Decade

A prolonged economic slump in Japan led to deflation from the late 1990s on. The Bank of Japan responded by cutting interest rates—but eventually ran up against the zero bound.

Source: OECD.

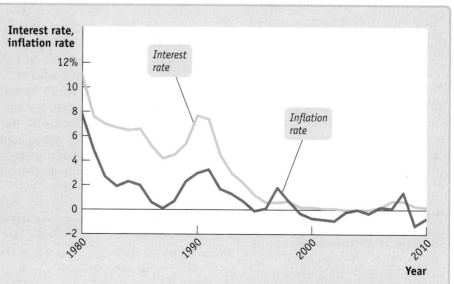

Bank of Canada—repeatedly cut interest rates. Eventually, it arrived at the ZIRP: the zero interest rate policy. The call money rate, the equivalent of the Bank of Canada's bank rate, was literally set equal to zero. Because the economy was still depressed, it would have been desirable to cut interest rates even further. But that wasn't possible: Japan was up against the zero bound.

In the aftermath of the 2008 financial crisis, the U.S. Federal Reserve also found itself up against the zero bound, with the interest rate on short-term U.S. government debt virtually at zero. As discussed in the following Economics in Action, this led to fears of a Japan-type trap and spurred the Fed to take some unconventional action.

ECONOMICS ➤ IN ACTION

THE U.S. DEFLATION SCARE OF 2010

Ever since the financial crisis of 2008, U.S. policy-makers have been worried about the possibility of "Japanification"—that is, they have worried that, like Japan since the 1990s, the United States might find itself stuck in a deflationary trap. Indeed, Ben Bernanke, the chairman of the U.S. Federal Reserve, studied Japan intensively before he went to the Fed and has sought to do better than his Japanese counterparts did.

Fears of deflation were particularly intense in the summer and early fall of 2010. Figure 16-15 shows why, by tracking two numbers the Fed watches carefully when making policy. One of these numbers is the "core" inflation rate over the past year—the percentage rise in a measure of consumer prices (the personal consumption expenditure deflator) that excludes volatile food and energy prices. The Fed normally regards this core inflation rate as its best guide to underlying inflation and tries to keep it at around 2%. The other number is a measure of expected inflation derived by calculating the difference between the interest rate on ordinary government bonds and the rate on government bonds with the same term to maturity whose yield is protected against or indexed to inflation.

FIGURE 16-15 U.S. Expected vs. Actual Inflation, 2010

Sources: The U.S. Bureau of Economic Analysis; Federal Reserve Bank of St. Louis.

As you can see, by the late summer of 2010 both actual inflation and expected inflation were sliding to levels well below the Fed's 2% target. Fed officials were worried, and they took action. In August 2010 Ben Bernanke gave a speech at the annual Fed meeting in Jackson Hole, Wyoming, signalling that he would take special actions to head off the deflationary threat. And in November the Fed, which normally buys only short-term government debt, began a program of long-term bond purchases, in the hope that this would give the economy a boost.

Figure 16-15 shows that Bernanke's speech and the Fed's action led to a major change in expectations, as investors' fears of deflation ebbed. Actual inflation also picked up significantly.

What was far from clear, however, was whether the Fed had achieved more than a temporary reprieve. A year after Bernanke's big speech, expected inflation was sagging again, and deflation fears were again on the rise.

▼ Quick Review

- Unexpected deflation helps lenders and hurts borrowers. This can lead to **debt deflation,** which has a contractionary effect on aggregate demand.

- Deflation makes it more likely that interest rates will end up against the **zero bound.** When this happens, the economy is in a **liquidity trap,** and conventional monetary policy is ineffective.

CHECK YOUR UNDERSTANDING 16-4

1. Why won't anyone lend money at a negative nominal rate of interest? How can this pose problems for monetary policy?

Solution appears at back of book.

BUSINESS CASE : Licences to Print Money

epa european pressphoto agency b.v./Alamy

People sometimes talk about profitable companies as having a "licence to print money." Well, the British firm De La Rue actually does. In 1930, De La Rue, printer of items such as postage stamps, expanded into the money-printing business, producing banknotes for the then-government of China. Today it produces the currencies of about 150 countries.

De La Rue's business received some unexpected attention in 2011 when Moammar Gadhafi, the dictator who had ruled Libya since 1969, was fighting to suppress a fierce popular uprising. To finance his efforts, he turned to seigniorage, ordering around $1.5 billion worth of Libyan dinars printed. But Libyan banknotes weren't printed in Libya; they were printed in Britain at one of De La Rue's facilities. The British Government, an enemy of the Gadhafi regime, seized the new banknotes before they could be flown to Libya, refusing to release them until Gadhafi had been overthrown.

Why do so many countries turn to private companies like De La Rue and its main rival, the German firm Giesecke and Devrient, to print their currencies? The short answer is that printing money isn't as easy as it sounds: producing high-quality banknotes that are hard to counterfeit requires highly specialized equipment and expertise. Some nations, like China, Japan, and the United States, can easily afford to do this for themselves: U.S. currency is printed by the Bureau of Engraving and Printing, a division of the U.S. Treasury Department, on special paper produced by a private supplier. But many countries, even those with rich, advanced economies, feel they do better by turning to experts like De La Rue, which can include high-tech features like security threads and holography to fight counterfeiters.

Canada's banknotes are produced by two private printers located in Ottawa. The Canadian Bank Note Company, a Canadian company, and BA International Inc., a division of Giesecke and Devrient, print all Canadian banknotes for the Bank of Canada. The Bank of Canada designs all the art and security features of the notes. To help prevent counterfeiting, Canada's banknotes are now printed on polymer sheets using technology developed by Australia's central bank.

Recently, De La Rue had problems with quality control: a scandal erupted in 2010, when it emerged that one of its plants had been producing defective security paper and that employees had covered up the problems. Nonetheless, many countries will surely continue relying on expert private firms to produce their currency.

QUESTIONS FOR THOUGHT

1. How can a government obtain revenue by printing money when someone else actually prints the money?

2. Why, exactly, would Gadhafi have resorted to the printing press in early 2011?

3. Were there risks to the Libyan economy in releasing those dinars to the new government?

SUMMARY

1. In analyzing high inflation, economists use the **classical model of the price level,** which says that changes in the money supply lead to proportional changes in the aggregate price level even in the short run.

2. Governments sometimes print money in order to finance budget deficits. When they do, they impose an **inflation tax,** generating tax revenue equal to the inflation rate times the money supply, on those who hold money. Revenue from the real inflation tax, the inflation rate times the real money supply, is the real value of resources captured by the government. In order to avoid paying the inflation tax, people reduce their real money holdings and force the government to increase inflation to capture the same amount of real inflation tax revenue. In some cases, this leads to a vicious circle of a shrinking real money supply and a rising rate of inflation, leading to hyperinflation and a fiscal crisis.

3. The output gap is the percentage difference between the actual level of real GDP and potential output. A positive output gap is associated with lower-than-normal unemployment; a negative output gap is associated with higher-than-normal unemployment. The relationship between the output gap and cyclical unemployment is described by **Okun's law.**

4. Countries that don't need to print money to cover government deficits can still stumble into moderate inflation, either because of political opportunism or because of wishful thinking.

5. At a given point in time, there is a downward-sloping relationship between unemployment and inflation known as the **short-run Phillips curve.** This curve is shifted by changes in the **expected rate of inflation.** The **long-run Phillips curve,** which shows the relationship between unemployment and inflation once expectations have had time to fully adjust, is vertical. It defines the **non-accelerating inflation rate (level) of unemployment,** or **NAIRU,** which is equal to the natural rate of unemployment. *Stagflation,* a combination of high unemployment and high inflation, reflects an upward shift of the short-run Phillips curve.

6. Once inflation has become embedded in expectations, getting inflation back down can be difficult because disinflation can be very costly, requiring the sacrifice of large amounts of aggregate output and imposing high levels of unemployment. However, by the 1980s policy-makers in Canada and other wealthy countries were willing to pay that price of bringing down the high inflation of the 1970s.

7. Deflation poses several problems. It can lead to **debt deflation,** in which a rising real burden of outstanding debt intensifies an economic downturn. Also, interest rates are more likely to run up against the **zero bound** in an economy experiencing deflation. When this happens, the economy enters a **liquidity trap,** rendering conventional monetary policy ineffective.

KEY TERMS

PROBLEMS

1. In the economy of Scottopia, policy-makers want to lower the unemployment rate and raise real GDP by using monetary policy. Using the accompanying diagram, show why this policy will ultimately result in a higher aggregate price level but no change in real GDP.

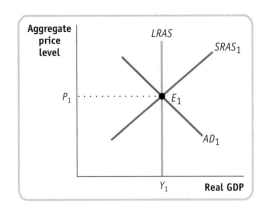

2. In the following examples, would the classical model of the price level be relevant?

a. There is a great deal of unemployment in the economy and no history of inflation.

b. The economy has just experienced five years of hyperinflation.

c. Although the economy experienced inflation in the 10% to 20% range three years ago, prices have recently been stable and the unemployment rate has approximated the natural rate of unemployment.

3. The Bank of Canada and Statistics Canada release data on the Canadian monetary base regularly. You can access that data on Statistics Canada's website. Go to www.statcan.gc.ca/start-debut-eng.html and click on "CANSIM," from the "Features" section. Then enter "v37253" and click the "Search" button, followed by "Continue." Pick a time period that runs for the past 14 months and then click on "Retrieve now."

a. The numbers retrieved show the levels of the monetary base over the past last year. How much did it change in the most recent 12-month period?

b. How did this help in the government's efforts to finance its deficit?

c. Why is it important for the central bank to be independent from the part of the government responsible for spending?

4. Answer the following questions about the (real) inflation tax, assuming that the price level starts at 1.

a. Maria Moneybags keeps $1000 in her sock drawer for a year. Over the year, the inflation rate is 10%. What is the real inflation tax paid by Maria for this year?

b. Maria continues to keep the $1000 in her drawer for a second year. What is the real value of this $1000 at the beginning of the second year? Over the year, the inflation rate is again 10%. What is the real inflation tax paid by Maria for the second year?

c. For a third year, Maria keeps the $1000 in the drawer. What is the real value of this $1000 at the beginning of the third year? Over the year, the inflation rate is again 10%. What is the real inflation tax paid by Maria for the third year?

d. After three years, what is the cumulative real inflation tax paid?

e. Redo parts (a) through (d) with an inflation rate of 25%. Why is hyperinflation such a problem?

5. The inflation tax is often used as a significant source of revenue in developing countries where the tax collection and reporting system is not well developed and tax evasion may be high.

a. Use the numbers in the accompanying table to calculate the inflation tax in Canada, the United States, and India (Rp = rupees).

	Inflation in 2010	Money supply in 2010 (billions)	Federal government total in 2010 (billions)
Canada	1.84%	C$519	C$237
India	1.65%	Rp16 318	Rp7 943
United States	1.4%	US$1 838	US$2 430

Sources: Statistics Canada; Department of Finance Canada; U.S. Bureau of Economic Analysis; Federal Reserve Bank of St. Louis; Controller General of Accounts (India); Reserve Bank of India; International Monetary Fund.

b. How large is the inflation tax for these three countries when calculated as a percentage of government receipts?

6. Concerned about the crowding-out effects of government borrowing on private investment spending, a candidate for member of parliament argues that the Government of Canada should just print money to cover the government's budget deficit. What are the advantages and disadvantages of such a plan?

7. The accompanying scatter diagram shows the relationship between the unemployment rate and the output gap in Canada from 1980 to 2004. Draw a straight line through the scatter of dots in the figure. Assume that this line represents Okun's law:

Unemployment rate = $b - (m \times$ Output gap) where b is the vertical intercept and $-m$ is the slope

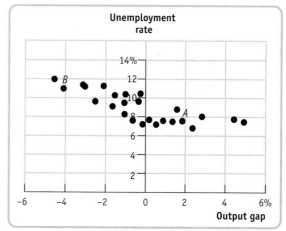

What would the unemployment rate be if the output gap were 1.9%? What if the output gap were −4%? What do these results tell us about the coefficient m in Okun's law? Use this value of m to determine what the unemployment rate would be when aggregate output equals potential output. What does this tell us about the coefficient b in Okun's law?

8. After experiencing a recession for the past two years, the residents of Albernia were looking forward to a decrease in the unemployment rate. Yet after six months of strong positive economic growth, the unemployment rate has fallen only slightly below what it was at the end of the recession. How can you explain why the unemployment rate did not fall as much although the economy was experiencing strong economic growth?

9. Due to historical differences, countries often differ in how quickly a change in actual inflation is incorporated into a change in expected inflation. In a country such as Japan, which has had very little inflation in recent memory, it will take longer for a change in the actual inflation rate to be reflected in a corresponding change in the expected inflation rate. In contrast, in a country such as Zimbabwe, which has recently had very high inflation, a change in the actual inflation rate will immediately be reflected in a corresponding change in the expected inflation rate. What does this imply about the short-run and long-run Phillips curves in these two types of countries? What does this imply about the effectiveness of monetary and fiscal policy to reduce the unemployment rate?

10. **a.** Go to www.statcan.gc.ca/start-debut-eng.html. In the "Latest indicators" window, click on "CPI annual inflation." Scroll to the bottom of the page and click on "326-0020 to 326-0022," then click on "326-0021." What is the value of the percent change in the All-items CPI from 2008 to 2009? Note: You can extend the time span of the data by clicking on "Add/Remove data," scrolling to the bottom of the page, selecting the time frame of your choice from the drop-down menu, and then clicking on "Apply."

   b. Now go to www.bankofcanada.ca. Click on "Rates and Statistics" and select "Interest rates" from the drop-down menu. From there, click on "Selected treasury bill yields" on the left side of the page, and then click on "Selected treasury bill yields: 10-year lookup" on the left side of the page. Then click on "Start (or single date)" and pick start and end dates for the data (select the start and end of 2009 to retrieve all the data for this year). Click "1 month" to select data on 1-month treasury bills. Now click "Submit." Examine the observed yields for 1-month treasury bills in 2009. What is the maximum? The minimum? Follow the same steps to retrieve observed yields for 1-month treasury bills in 2007. How do the data for 2009 and 2007 compare? How would you relate this to your answer in part (a)? From the data on treasury bill interest rates, what would you infer about the level of the inflation rate in 2007 compared to 2009? (You can check your answer by going back to www.statcan.gc.ca/start-debut-eng.html to find the percent change in the CPI from 2006 to 2007.)

   c. How would you characterize the change in the Canadian economy from 2007 to 2009?

11. The accompanying table provides data from Canada on the average annual rates of unemployment and inflation. Use the numbers to construct a scatter plot similar to Figure 16-5. Discuss why, in the short run, the unemployment rate rises when inflation falls.

Year	Unemployment rate	Inflation rate
2000	6.8%	2.69%
2001	7.2	2.52
2002	7.7	2.25
2003	7.6	2.80
2004	7.2	1.85
2005	6.8	2.20
2006	6.3	1.96
2007	6.0	2.20
2008	6.1	2.33
2009	8.3	0.26
2010	8.0	1.84
2011	7.4	2.92

Source: Statistics Canada.

12. The economy of Brittania has been suffering from high inflation with an unemployment rate equal to its natural rate. Policy-makers would like to disinflate the economy with the lowest economic cost possible. Assume that the state of the economy is not the result of a negative supply shock. How can they try to minimize the unemployment cost of disinflation? Is it possible for there to be no cost of disinflation?

13. Who are the winners and losers when a mortgage company lends $100 000 to the Miller family to buy a house worth $105 000 and during the first year prices unexpectedly fall by 10%? What would you expect to happen if the deflation continued over the next few years? How would continuing deflation affect borrowers and lenders throughout the economy as a whole?

CHAPTER 17

Crises and Consequences

FROM PURVEYOR OF DRY GOODS TO DESTROYER OF WORLDS

The collapse of Lehman Brothers, the once-venerable investment bank, set off a chain of events that led to a worldwide financial panic.

Press Association via AP Images

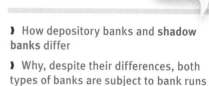

WHAT YOU WILL LEARN IN THIS CHAPTER

❭ How depository banks and **shadow banks** differ

❭ Why, despite their differences, both types of banks are subject to bank runs

❭ What happens during **financial panics** and **banking crises**

❭ Why the effects of panics and crises on the economy are so severe and long-lasting

❭ How regulatory loopholes and the rise of **shadow banking** led to the financial crisis of 2008

❭ How the new American regulatory framework seeks to avoid another crisis

IN 1844 HENRY LEHMAN, A GERMAN immigrant, opened a dry goods store in Montgomery, Alabama. Over time, Lehman and his brothers, who followed him to America, branched out into cotton trading, then into a variety of financial activities. By 1850, Lehman Brothers was established on Wall Street; by 2008, thanks to its skill at trading financial assets, Lehman Brothers was one of America's top investment banks. Unlike commercial banks, investment banks trade in financial assets and don't accept deposits from customers.

In September 2008, Lehman's luck ran out. The firm had invested heavily in sub-prime mortgages—loans to homebuyers with too little income or too few assets to qualify for standard (also called "prime") mortgages. In the summer and fall of 2008, as the

U.S. housing market plunge intensified and investments related to subprime mortgages lost much of their value, Lehman was hit hard.

Lehman had been borrowing heavily in the short-term credit market—often using overnight loans that must be repaid the next business day—to finance its ongoing operations and trading. As rumours began to spread about how heavily Lehman was exposed to the tanking housing market, its sources of credit dried up. On September 15, 2008, the firm declared bankruptcy, the largest bankruptcy to date in the United States. What happened would shock the world.

When Lehman fell, it set off a chain of events that came close to taking down the entire world financial system. Because Lehman had hidden the severity of its vulnerability,

its failure came as a nasty surprise. Through securitization (a concept we defined in Chapter 14) financial institutions throughout the world were exposed to real estate loans that were quickly deteriorating in value as default rates on those loans rose. Credit markets froze because those with funds to lend decided it was better to sit on the funds rather than lend them out and risk losing them to a borrower who might go under like Lehman had. Around the world, borrowers were hit by a global *credit crunch:* they either lost their access to credit or found themselves forced to pay drastically higher interest rates. Stocks plunged, and within weeks the Dow had fallen almost 3000 points.

Nor were the consequences limited to financial markets. The U.S. economy was already in recession when Lehman fell, but the pace of the downturn accelerated drastically in the months that followed. By the time U.S. employment bottomed out in early 2010, more than 8 million jobs had been lost. Canada, Europe, and Japan were also suffering their worst recessions since the 1930s, and world trade plunged even faster than it had in the first year of the Great Depression.

All of this came as a great shock because few people imagined that such events were possible in twenty-first-century America. Yet economists who knew their history quickly recognized what they were seeing: it was a modern version of a *financial panic,* a sudden and widespread disruption of financial markets. Financial panics were a regular feature of the U.S. financial system before World War II. The financial panic that hit the United States in 2008 shared many features

with the American Panic of 1907, whose devastation prompted the creation of the U.S. Federal Reserve system. Financial panics almost always include a *banking crisis,* in which a significant portion of the banking sector ceases to function.

On reflection, the panic following Lehman's collapse was not unique, even in the modern world. The failure of Long-Term Capital Management in 1998 also precipitated a financial panic: global financial markets froze until the Federal Reserve Bank of New York rode to the rescue and coordinated a winding-down of the firm's operations. Because the crisis was resolved quickly, the fall of LTCM didn't result in a blow to the economy at large.

Financial panics and banking crises have happened fairly often, sometimes with disastrous effects on output and employment. Chile's 1981 banking

crisis was followed by a 19% decline in real GDP per capita and a slump that lasted through most of the following decade. Finland's 1990 banking crisis was followed by a surge in the unemployment rate from 3.2% to 16.3%. Japan's banking crisis of the early 1990s led to more than a decade of economic stagnation.

In this chapter, we'll examine the causes and consequences of banking crises and financial panics, expanding on the discussion of this topic in Chapter 14. We'll begin by examining what makes banking vulnerable to a crisis and how this can mutate into a full-blown financial panic. Then we'll turn to the history of such crises and their aftermath, exploring why they are so destructive to the economy. Finally, we'll look at how governments have tried to limit the risks of financial crises.

Banking: Benefits and Dangers

As we learned in earlier chapters, banks perform an essential role in any modern economy. In Chapter 14 we defined commercial banks as financial intermediaries that provide liquid financial assets in the form of deposits to savers and uses its funds to finance the illiquid investment spending needs of borrowers. Deposit-taking banks perform the important functions of providing liquidity to savers and directly influencing the level of the money supply.

Lehman Brothers, however, was not a deposit-taking bank. Instead, it was an investment bank (also defined in Chapter 14)—in the business of speculative trading for its own profit and the profit of its investors. Yet Lehman got into trouble in much the same way that a deposit-taking bank does: it experienced a loss of confidence and something very much like a bank run—a phenomenon in which many of a bank's depositors try to withdraw their funds due to fears of a bank failure. Lehman was part of a larger category of institutions called shadow banks. *Shadow banking,* a term coined by the economist Paul McCulley of the giant bond fund Pimco, is composed of a wide variety of types of financial firms: investment banks like Lehman, hedge funds like Long-Term Capital Management (LTCM), and money market funds. (As we will explain in more detail later, "shadow" refers to the fact that before the 2008 crisis these financial institutions were neither closely watched nor effectively regulated.) Like deposit-taking banks, shadow banks are vulnerable to bank runs because they perform the same economic task: *asset or maturity transformation,* the transformation of short-term liabilities into long-term assets. From now on, we will use the term *depository banks* for banks that accept deposits (so commercial "banks" include chartered banks, trust, mortgage and loan companies, credit unions, and caisses populaires) to better distinguish them from shadow banks (investment banks, hedge funds, and money market funds) which do not.

The Trade-off Between Rate of Return and Liquidity

Imagine that you live in a world without any banks. Further imagine that you have saved a substantial sum of money that you don't plan on spending anytime soon. What can you do with those funds?

One answer is that you could simply store the money—say, put it under your bed or in a safe. The money would always be there if you need it, but it would just sit there, not earning any interest.

Alternatively, you could lend the money out, say, to a growing business. This would have the great advantage of putting your money to work, both for you, since the loan would pay interest, and for the economy, since your funds would help pay for investment spending. There would, however, be a potential disadvantage: if you needed the money before the loan was paid off, you might not be able to recover it.

It's true that we asked you to assume that you had no plans for spending the money soon. But it's often impossible to predict when you will want or need to make cash outlays; for example, your car could break down or you could be offered an exciting opportunity to study abroad. Now, a loan is an asset, and there are ways to convert assets into cash. For example, you can try to sell the loan to someone else. But this can be difficult, especially if you need cash on short notice. So, in a world without banks, it's better to have some cash on hand when an unexpected financial need arises.

In other words, without banks, savers face a trade-off when deciding how much of their funds to lend out and how much to keep on hand in cash: a trade-off between liquidity, the ability to turn one's assets into cash on short notice, and the rate of return, in the form of interest or other payments received for the use of one's assets. Without banks, people would make this trade-off by keeping a large fraction of their wealth idle, sitting in safes rather than helping pay for productive investment spending. Banking, however, changes that by allowing people ready access to their funds even while those funds are being used to make loans for productive purposes.

The Purpose of Banking

Banking, as we know it, emerged from a surprising place: it was originally a sideline business for medieval goldsmiths. By the nature of their business, goldsmiths needed vaults in which to store their gold. Over time, they realized that they could offer safekeeping services for their customers, too, because a wealthy person might prefer to leave his stash of gold and silver with a goldsmith rather than keep it at home, where thieves might snatch it.

Someone who deposited gold and silver with a goldsmith received a receipt that could be redeemed for those precious metals at any time. And a funny thing happened: people began paying for their purchases not by cashing in their receipts for gold and then paying with the gold, but simply by handing over their precious metal receipts to the seller. Thus, an early form of paper money was born.

Meanwhile, goldsmiths realized something else: even though they were obligated to return a customer's precious metals on demand, they didn't actually need to keep all of the treasure on their premises. After all, it was unlikely that all of their customers would want to lay hands on their gold and silver on the same day, especially if customers were using receipts as a means of payment. So a goldsmith could safely put some of his customers' wealth to work by lending it out to other businesses, keeping only enough on hand to pay off the few customers likely to demand their precious metals on short notice—plus some additional reserves in case of exceptional demand.

And so banking was born. In a more abstract form, depository banks today do the same thing those enterprising goldsmiths learned to do: they accept the savings of individuals, promising to return them on demand, but put most of those funds to work by taking advantage of the fact that not everyone will want access to those funds at the same time. A typical bank account lets you withdraw as much of your

Maturity transformation is the conversion of short-term liabilities into long-term assets.

A **shadow bank** is a non-depository financial institution that engages in maturity transformation.

funds as you want, anytime you want[1]—but the bank doesn't actually keep everyone's cash in its safe or even in a form that can be turned quickly into cash. Instead, the bank lends out most of the funds placed in its care, keeping limited reserves to meet day-to-day withdrawals. And because deposits can be put to use, banks don't charge you (or charge very little) for the privilege of keeping your savings safe. Depending on the type of account you have, they might even pay you interest on your deposits.

More generally, what depository banks do is borrow on a short-term basis from depositors (who can demand to be repaid at any time) and lend on a long-term basis to others (who cannot be forced to repay until the end date of their loan). This is what economists call **maturity transformation:** converting short-term liabilities (deposits in this case) into long-term assets (bank loans that earn interest). Shadow banks, such as Lehman Brothers, also engage in maturity transformation, but they do it in a way that doesn't involve taking deposits.

Instead of taking deposits, Lehman borrowed funds in the short-term credit markets and then invested those funds in longer-term speculative projects. Indeed, a **shadow bank** is any financial institution that does not accept deposits but does engage in maturity transformation—borrowing over the short term and lending or investing over the longer term. And just as bank depositors benefit from the liquidity and higher return that banking provides compared to sitting on their money, lenders to shadow banks like Lehman benefit from liquidity (their loans must be repaid quickly, often overnight) and higher return compared to other ways of investing their funds.

A generation ago, depository banks accounted for most banking. After about 1980, however, there was a steady rise in shadow banking, especially in the United States. Shadow banking has grown so popular because it has not been subject to the regulations, such as capital requirements and reserve requirements, that are imposed on depository banking. Shadow banks, facing less regulatory oversight, can offer their customers a higher rate of return on their funds; in that way, they are similar to the unregulated trusts at the start of the twentieth century, which set off the U.S. Panic of 1907. These trusts had attracted large pools of deposits by offering high interest rates. The deposits were channelled into real estate investments during a speculative bubble. When the bubble burst, many trusts failed, which led to a crisis of confidence; this in turn, caused a severe banking crisis and recession. As of July 2007, generally considered the start of the financial crisis that climaxed when Lehman fell in September 2008, the U.S. shadow banking sector was about 1.5 times larger, in terms of dollars, than the formal, deposit-taking banking sector.

As we pointed out in Chapter 14, things are not always simple in banking. There we learned why depository banks can be subject to bank runs. As the cases of Lehman and LTCM so spectacularly illustrate, the same vulnerability afflicts shadow banks. Next we explore why.

Shadow Banks and the Re-emergence of Bank Runs

Because a depository bank keeps on hand just a small fraction of its depositors' funds, a bank run typically results in a bank failure: the bank is unable to meet depositors' demands for their money and closes its doors. Ominously, bank runs can be self-fulfilling prophecies: although a bank may be in fine financial shape, if enough depositors believe it is in trouble and try to withdraw their money, their beliefs end up dooming the bank.

To prevent such occurrences, after the 1930s Canada (and most other countries, including the United States) adopted wide-ranging banking regulations in the form of regular audits by the central bank, capital requirements and reserve

---

[1]A demand deposit is a bank account that can quickly and easily be converted to cash or that can be accessed via cheque writing or debit privileges.

requirements, deposit insurance, and provisions allowing troubled banks to borrow from the central bank in the overnight market.

Shadow banks, though, don't take deposits. So how can they be vulnerable to a bank run? The reason is that a shadow bank, like a depository bank, engages in maturity transformation: it borrows short term and lends or invests longer term. If a shadow bank's lenders suddenly decide one day that it's no longer safe to lend it money, the shadow bank can no longer fund its operations. Unless it can sell its assets immediately to raise cash, it will quickly fail. This is exactly what happened to Lehman.

Lehman borrowed funds in the overnight credit market (also known as the *repo* market), funds that it was required to repay the next business day, in order to fund its trading operations. So Lehman was on a very short leash: every day it had to be able to convince its creditors that it was a safe place to park their funds. And one day, that ability was no longer there. The same phenomenon happened at LTCM: the hedge fund was enormously leveraged (that is, it had borrowed huge amounts of money)—also, like Lehman, to fund its trading operations. One day its credit simply dried up, in its case because creditors perceived that it had lost huge amounts of money during the Asian and Russian financial crises of 1997–1998.

Bank runs are destructive to everyone associated with a bank: its shareholders, its creditors, its depositors and loan customers, and its employees. But a bank run that spreads like a contagion is extraordinarily destructive, causing depositors at other banks to also lose faith, leading to a cascading sequence of bank failures and a banking crisis. This is what happened in the United States during the early 1930s as Americans in general rushed out of bank deposits—the total value of bank deposits fell by 35%—and started holding currency instead. Until 2008, it had never happened again in the United States. Our next topic is to explore how and why bank runs reappeared.

ECONOMICS ▸ *IN ACTION*

THE DAY THE LIGHTS WENT OUT AT LEHMAN

On Friday night, September 12, 2008, an urgent meeting was held in the New York Federal Reserve Bank's headquarters on Wall Street. Attending was the outgoing Bush Administration's Treasury Secretary, Hank Paulson, and Tim Geithner (at that time head of the New York Fed and later the Treasury Secretary in the Obama Administration), along with the heads of the country's largest investment banks. Lehman Brothers was rapidly imploding and Paulson called the meeting in the hope of pressing the investment bankers into a deal that would, like the LTCM bailout described in Chapter 14, avert a messy bankruptcy.

Since the forced sale of the nearly bankrupt investment bank Bear Stearns six months earlier to a healthier bank, Lehman had been under increasing pressure. Like Bear Stearns, Lehman had invested heavily in sub-prime mortgages and other assets tied to real estate. And when Bear Stearns fell as its creditors began calling in its loans and other banks refused to lend to it, many wondered if Lehman would fall next.

In July 2008, Lehman reported a $2.8 billion loss for the second quarter of 2008 (the months April–June), precipitating a 54% fall in its stock price. As its share price fell, Lehman's sources of credit began to dry up and its trading operations withered. CEO of Lehman, Richard Fuld, began a desperate search for a healthier bank to buy shares of Lehman and provide desperately needed funding. By early September 2008, Lehman's loss for the third quarter had risen to $3.9 billion. On September 9, JPMorgan Chase, a far healthier investment bank that had been Lehman's major source of financing for its trades, demanded $5 billion in cash as extra collateral or it would freeze Lehman's accounts and cut off its credit. Unable to come up with the cash, Lehman teetered on the edge of bankruptcy.

Richard Fuld, the head of Lehman, testified before a congressional panel on how the collapse of Lehman precipitated a financial panic.

In the September 12 meeting, U.S. Treasury Secretary Paulson urged the investment bankers to put together a package to purchase Lehman's bad assets. But, fearing for their own survival in an extremely turbulent market, they refused unless Paulson would give them a government guarantee on the value of Lehman's assets. The U.S. Treasury had made the Bear Stearns sale possible by arranging a huge loan from the New York Fed to its purchaser. This time, facing a backlash from Congress over "bailing out profligate bankers," Paulson refused to provide government help. And in the wee hours of Monday morning, September 15, 2008, Lehman went down, declaring the most expensive bankruptcy in history.

Yet, as Fuld had earlier warned Paulson, the failure of Lehman unleashed the furies. That same day the U.S. stock market fell 504 points, triggering an increase in bank borrowing costs and a run on money market funds and financial institutions around the world. By Tuesday, Paulson agreed to an $85 billion bailout of another major corporation, the foundering American International Group, at the time the world's largest insurer. Before the markets stabilized months later, the U.S. government made $250 billion of capital infusions to bolster major U.S. banks. Whether or not Paulson made a catastrophic mistake by not acting to save Lehman is a matter likely to be debated for years to come.

CHECK YOUR UNDERSTANDING 17-1

1. Which of the following are examples of maturity transformations? Which are subject to a bank-run-like phenomenon in which fear of a failure becomes a self-fulfilling prophecy? Explain.

   a. You sell tickets to a lottery in which each ticket holder has a chance of winning a $10 000 jackpot.

   b. Dana borrows on her credit card to pay her living expenses while she takes a year-long course to upgrade her job skills. Without a better-paying job, she will not be able to pay her accumulated credit card balance.

   c. An investment partnership invests in office buildings. Partners invest their own funds and can redeem them only by selling their partnership share to someone else.

   d. The local student union savings bank offers chequing accounts to students and invests those funds in student loans.

   Solutions appear at back of book.

Banking Crises and Financial Panics

While rare in Canada, bank failures are common in some other countries. Even in a good year, several U.S. banks typically go under for one reason or another. And shadow banks sometimes fail, too. **Banking crises**—episodes in which a large part of the depository banking sector or the shadow banking sector fails or threatens to fail—are relatively rare by comparison. Yet they do happen, often with severe negative effects on the broader economy. What would cause so many of these institutions to get into trouble at the same time? Let's take a look at the logic of banking crises, then review some of the historical experiences.

The Logic of Banking Crises

A **banking crisis** occurs when a large part of the depository banking sector or the shadow banking sector fails or threatens to fail.

When many banks—either depository banks or shadow banks—get into trouble at the same time, there are two possible explanations. First, many of them could have made similar mistakes, often due to an *asset bubble*. Second, there may be *financial contagion,* in which one institution's problems spread and create trouble for others.

Shared Mistakes In practice, banking crises usually owe their origins to many banks making the same mistake of investing in an *asset bubble*. In an **asset bubble,** the price of some kind of asset, such as housing, is pushed to an unreasonably high level by investors' expectations of further price gains. For a while, such bubbles can feed on themselves. A good example is the U.S. savings and loan crisis of the 1980s, when there was a huge boom in the construction of commercial real estate, especially office buildings. Many banks extended large loans to real estate developers, believing that the boom would continue indefinitely. By the late 1980s, it became clear that developers had gotten carried away, building far more office space than the country needed. Unable to rent out their space or forced to slash rents, a number of developers, including the Canadian company Olympia & York, which had grown to one of the largest commercial property development firms in the world, defaulted on their loans—and the result was a wave of U.S. bank failures.[2]

A similar phenomenon occurred between 2002 and 2006, in the U.S., when rapidly rising housing prices led many people to borrow heavily to buy a house in the belief that prices would keep rising. This process accelerated as more buyers rushed into the market and pushed housing prices up even faster. Eventually the market runs out of new buyers and the bubble bursts. At this point asset prices fall; in some parts of the United States, housing prices fell by half between 2006 and 2009. This, in turn, undermines confidence in financial institutions that are exposed to losses due to falling asset prices. This loss of confidence, if it's sufficiently severe, can set in motion the kind of economy-wide vicious downward spiral that marks a financial contagion.

Thankfully, no Canadian-based depository banks failed owing to bad commercial loans during these crises. Regrettably though, three of them did fail as the result of outright fraud in the 1980s. In 1982, three Canadian trust companies, Greymac Mortgage, Seaway Mortgage, and Crown Trust, failed when key insiders of these companies orchestrated fraudulent mortgages on about 11 000 apartment units in Toronto. The insiders bought these units for $270 million and then sold them soon afterward to fictitious buyers for $500 million. The insiders attempted to pocket the $230 million in "profits" that were essentially stolen from the three institutions.

Recently, economists have begun to worry about the level of household debt in Canada. In the third quarter of 2012, Statistics Canada reported that Canadian household debt had grown to a record high of 165 percent of disposable income, about the same level reached in the United States before the 2008–2009 financial crisis. This fact, coupled with estimates of slowing Canadian economic growth, led Standard & Poor's (S&P) and Moody's to downgrade the credit ratings for several of Canada's leading banks in late 2012 and early in 2013. "High levels of consumer indebtedness and elevated housing prices leave Canadian banks more vulnerable than in the past to downside risks the Canadian economy faces," said David Beattie, a Moody's vice-president. He added, "Following today's actions, the Canadian banks still rank amongst the highest rated banks in our global rating universe." Nonetheless, the possibility of a severe economic shock does exist, and even if it is remote, such a shock could lead to a loss of confidence in Canadian banks, forced asset sales, a drop in the price of homes, and so on. Such a banking crisis could spark a recession, depress asset and real estate prices, and result in significant economic hardship.

Financial Contagion In especially severe banking crises, a vicious downward spiral of **financial contagion** occurs among depository banks or shadow banks: each institution's failure worsens depositors' or lenders' fears and increases the odds that another bank will fail.

> In an **asset bubble,** the price of an asset is pushed to an unreasonably high level due to expectations of further price gains.
>
> A **financial contagion** is a vicious downward spiral among depository banks or shadow banks: each bank's failure worsens fears and increases the likelihood that another bank will fail.

---

[2]This default affected banks in the United Kingdom and Japan as well, as did the bankruptcies of the U.S. department chains Allied Stores and Federated Department Stores, which were controlled by Canadian entrepeneur Robert Campeau.

A **financial panic** is a sudden and widespread disruption of the financial markets that occurs when people suddenly lose faith in the liquidity of financial institutions and markets.

As already noted, one underlying cause of contagion arises from the logic of bank runs. In the case of depository banks, when one bank fails, depositors are likely to become nervous about others. Similarly in the case of shadow banks, when one fails, lenders in the short-term credit market become nervous about lending to others. The shadow banking sector, because it is largely unregulated, is especially prone to fear- and rumour-driven contagion.

There is also a second channel of contagion: asset markets and the vicious cycle of deleveraging, a phenomenon we learned about in Chapter 14. When a financial institution is under pressure to reduce debt and raise cash, it tries to sell assets. To sell assets quickly, though, it often has to sell them at a deep discount. The contagion comes from the fact that other financial institutions own similar assets, whose prices decline as a result of the "fire sale." This decline in asset prices hurts the other financial institutions' financial positions, too, leading their creditors to stop lending to them—these affected institutions experience a credit or liquidity crunch as available credit dries up. This knock-on effect forces more financial institutions to sell assets, reinforcing the downward spiral of asset prices. This kind of downward spiral was clearly evident in the months immediately following Lehman's fall: prices of a wide variety of assets held by financial institutions, from corporate bonds to pools of student loans, plunged as everyone tried to sell assets and raise cash. Later, as the severity of the crisis abated, many of these assets saw at least a partial recovery in prices.

Combine an asset bubble with a huge, unregulated shadow banking system and a vicious cycle of deleveraging and it is easy to see, as the U.S. economy did in 2008, how a full-blown **financial panic**—a sudden and widespread disruption of financial markets that happens when people suddenly lose faith in the liquidity of financial institutions and markets—can arise. A financial panic almost always involves a banking crisis, either in the depository banking sector, or the shadow banking sector, or both.

Because banking provides much of the liquidity needed for trading financial assets like stocks and bonds, severe banking crises almost always lead to disruptions of the stock and bond markets. Disruptions of these markets, along with a headlong rush to sell assets and raise cash, lead to a vicious circle of deleveraging. As the panic unfolds, the resulting high levels of fear and uncertainty make savers and investors come to believe that the safest place for their money is under their bed, and their hoarding of cash further deepens the distress.

So what can history tell us about banking crises and financial panics?

Historical Banking Crises: The Age of Panics

Between the American Civil War and the Great Depression, the United States had a famously crisis-prone banking system. Even then, banks were regulated: most banking was carried out by "national banks" that were regulated by the federal government and subject to rules involving reserves and capital, of the kind described below. However, there was no system of guarantees for depositors. As a result, bank runs were common, and banking crises, also known at the time as panics, were fairly frequent.

Table 17-1 shows the dates of these nationwide American banking crises and the number of banks that failed in each episode. Notice that the table is divided into two parts. The first part is devoted to the "national banking era," which preceded the 1913 creation of the U.S. Federal Reserve—which was supposed to put an end to such crises. It failed. The second part of the table is devoted to the epic waves of U.S. bank failures that took place in the early 1930s.

The events that sparked each of these panics differed. In the nineteenth century, there was a boom-and-bust cycle in U.S. railroad construction somewhat similar to the boom-and-bust cycle in office building construction during the 1980s. Like modern real estate companies, nineteenth-century railroad companies relied heavily on borrowed funds to finance their investment projects. And railroads, like office buildings, took a long time to build. This meant that there were repeated episodes of overbuilding: competing railroads would invest in expansion, only to find that collectively they had laid more track than the demand for rail transport warranted.

TABLE 17-1   Number of U.S. Bank Failures: National Banking Era and Great Depression

National Banking Era (1863–1912)		Great Depression (1929–1941)	
Panic dates	**Number of failures**	**Panic dates**	**Number of failures**
September 1873	101	November–December 1930	806
May 1884	42	April–August 1931	573
November 1890	18	September–October 1931	827
May–August 1893	503	June–July 1932	283
October–December 1907	73*	February–March 1933	Bank holiday

*This understates the scale of the 1907 crisis because it doesn't take into account the role of trusts.

When the overbuilding became apparent, business failures, debt defaults, and an overall banking crisis followed. The Panic of 1873 began when Jay Cooke and Co., a financial firm with a large stake in the railroad business, failed. The Panic of 1893 began with the failure of the overextended Philadelphia and Reading Railroad.

As we'll see later in this chapter, the major financial panics of the nineteenth and early twentieth centuries were followed by severe economic downturns in the United States. However, the banking crises of the early 1930s made previous crises seem minor by comparison. In four successive waves of bank runs from 1930 to 1932, about 40% of the banks in America failed. In the end, U.S. President Franklin Delano Roosevelt declared a temporary closure of all banks—the so-called "bank holiday"—to put an end to the vicious circle. Meanwhile, the economy plunged, with real GDP shrinking by a third and a sharp fall in prices as well.

There is still considerable controversy about the U.S. banking crisis of the early 1930s. In part, this controversy is about cause and effect: did the banking crisis cause the wider economic crisis, or vice versa? (No doubt causation ran in both directions, but the magnitude of these effects remains disputed.) There is also controversy about the extent to which the banking crisis could have been avoided. Milton Friedman and Anna Schwartz, in their famous study *Monetary History of the United States,* argued that the Federal Reserve could and should have prevented the banking crisis—and that if it had, the Great Depression itself could also have been prevented. However, this view has been disputed by other economists.

In the United States, the experience of the 1930s led to banking reforms that prevented a replay for more than 70 years. Outside the United States, however, there were a number of major banking crises.

A typical scene outside a bank during the banking crises of the Great Depression.

Modern Banking Crises Around the World

Around the world, banking crises are relatively frequent events. However, the ways in which they occur differ according to the banking sector's particular institutional framework. According to a 2008 analysis by the International Monetary Fund (IMF), no fewer than 127 banking crises occurred around the world between 1970 and 2007. Most of these were in small, poor countries that lack the regulatory safeguards found in advanced countries. In poorer countries, banks generally get in trouble in much the same way: insufficient capital, poor accounting, too many loans, and, often, corruption. But banks in advanced countries can also make the same mistakes—for example, there was the savings and loan crisis in the United States during the 1980s (mentioned earlier in this chapter).

In more advanced countries, banking crises almost always occur as a consequence of an asset bubble—typically in real estate. Between 1985 and 1995, three advanced countries—Finland, Sweden, and Japan—experienced banking crises due to the bursting of a real estate bubble. Banks in the three countries lent heavily into a real estate bubble that their lending helped to inflate. Figure 17-1 shows real estate prices, adjusted for inflation, in Finland, Sweden, and Japan from 1985 to 1995. As you can see, in each country a sharp rise was followed by a drastic fall, leading many borrowers to default on their real estate loans, pushing large parts of each country's banking system into insolvency. The Teranet–National Bank Home Price Index (HPI) reveals that the real price of homes in Canada rose by 74% between January 2000 and the end of 2012. This increase in price occurred over a longer time period than similar increases in countries that experienced real estate bubbles. Nonetheless, the magnitude of this increase, along with the fact that home prices grew much more quickly than disposable income over this time span, has caused some to wonder whether Canadian home prices are in bubble territory. And even the possibility of a Canadian residential real estate bubble significantly increases the likelihood of a banking crisis.

FIGURE 17-1 Real Housing Prices in Three Banking Crises

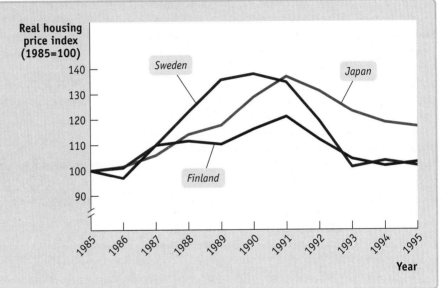

During the period 1985 to 1995, Finland, Sweden, and Japan each experienced a banking crisis due to a real estate bubble. Here you can see how real housing prices (housing prices adjusted for inflation) in each country rose dramatically and then fell sharply. The sharp fall in housing prices pushed a significant part of each country's banking sector into insolvency.

Sources: Bank of Finland; Statistics Sweden; Japan Real Estate Institute; Bank for International Settlements; OECD.

For many years, Bear Stearns had been a respected and successful financial securities firm based in the United States. But in March 2008 investors began to lose confidence in Bear Stearns' ability to repay its debts, resulting in a liquidity crisis for the company. Unable to obtain the capital it needed, Bear Stearns failed. Thanks to a $29 billion government bailout, JPMorgan Chase, a large American bank, was able to take over Bear Stearns. Unfortunately, fear and uncertainty remained in American financial markets. The fall of Lehman in September 2008 precipitated a banking crisis in the shadow banking sector that included financial contagion as well as financial panic, but left the depository banking sector largely unaffected. As we discussed in the opening story, the financial crisis of 2008 was devastating because of securitization, which had distributed sub-prime mortgage loans throughout the entire shadow banking sector throughout the world, especially in the United States.

At the time of writing, the market for securitization has not yet recovered and the shadow banking sector is a shadow of its former self. Since 2008, investors have rediscovered the benefits of regulation, and the depository banking sector has grown at the expense of the shadow banking sector. In the next section, we will learn how troubles in the banking sector soon translate into troubles for the broader economy.

ECONOMICS > IN ACTION

ERIN GO BROKE

For much of the 1990s and 2000s, Ireland was celebrated as an economic success story: the "Celtic Tiger" was growing at a pace the rest of Europe could only envy. But the miracle came to an abrupt halt in 2008, as Ireland found itself facing a huge banking crisis.

Like the earlier banking crises in Finland, Sweden, and Japan, Ireland's crisis grew out of excessive optimism about real estate. Irish housing prices began rising in the 1990s, in part a result of the economy's strong growth. However, real estate developers began betting on ever-rising prices, and Irish banks were all too willing to lend these developers large amounts of money to back their speculations. Housing prices tripled between 1997 and 2007, home construction quadrupled over the same period, and total credit offered by banks rose far faster than in any other European nation. To raise the cash for their lending spree, Irish banks supplemented the funds of depositors with large amounts of "wholesale" funding—short-term borrowing from other banks and private investors.

In 2007 the real estate boom collapsed. Home prices started falling, and home sales collapsed. Many of the loans that banks had made during the boom went into default. Now, so-called ghost estates, new housing developments full of unoccupied, crumbling homes, dot the landscape. In 2008, the troubles of the Irish banks threatened to turn into a sort of bank run—not by depositors, but by lenders who had provided the banks with short-term funding through the wholesale interbank lending market. To stabilize the situation, the Irish government stepped in, guaranteeing repayment of all bank debt.

This created a new problem because it put Irish taxpayers on the hook for potentially huge bank losses. Until the crisis struck, Ireland had seemed to be in good fiscal shape, with relatively low government debt and a budget surplus. The banking crisis, however, led to serious questions about the solvency of the Irish government—whether it had the resources to meet its obligations—and forced the government to pay high interest rates on funds it raised in international markets.

Like most banking crises, Ireland's led to a severe recession. The unemployment rate rose from less than 5% before the crisis, peaking at 15.1% early in 2012 before declining below 15% later in the year.

CHECK YOUR UNDERSTANDING   17-2

1. Regarding the Economics in Action "Erin Go Broke," identify the following:
   a. The asset bubble
   b. The channel of financial contagion

2. Again regarding "Erin Go Broke," why do you think the Irish government tried to stabilize the situation by guaranteeing the debts of the banks? Why was this a questionable policy?

Solutions appear at back of book.

The Consequences of Banking Crises

If banking crises affected only banks, they wouldn't be as serious a concern. In fact, however, banking crises are almost always associated with recessions, and severe banking crises are associated with the worst economic slumps. Furthermore, history shows that recessions caused in part by banking crises inflict sustained economic damage, with economies taking years to recover.

▼ Quick Review

- Although individual bank failures are common in some countries (but not in Canada), a **banking crisis** is a rare event that typically will severely harm the broader economy.

- A banking crisis can occur because depository or shadow banks invest in an **asset bubble** or through **financial contagion,** set off by bank runs or by a vicious cycle of deleveraging. Largely unregulated, the shadow banking sector is particularly vulnerable to contagion.

- In 2008, an asset bubble combined with a huge shadow banking sector and a vicious cycle of deleveraging created a **financial panic** and banking crisis in the United States, as savers cut their spending and investors hoarded their funds, sending the economy into a steep decline.

- Between the American Civil War and the Great Depression, the United States suffered numerous banking crises and financial panics, each followed by a severe economic downturn. The banking reforms of the 1930s prevented another banking crisis until 2008.

- Banking crises usually occur in small, poor countries, although there have been banking crises in rich countries as well. In 2008, the fall of Lehman caused a U.S. banking crisis and a worldwide financial panic in the shadow banking sector, leading investors to shift back into the depository banking sector.

Banking Crises, Recessions, and Recovery

A severe banking crisis is one in which a large fraction of the banking system either fails outright (that is, goes bankrupt) or suffers a major loss of confidence and must be bailed out by the government. Such crises almost invariably lead to deep recessions, which are usually followed by slow recoveries. Figure 17-2 illustrates this phenomenon by tracking unemployment in the aftermath of two banking crises widely separated in space and time: the Panic of 1893 in the United States and the Swedish banking crisis of 1991. In the figure, t represents the year of the crisis: 1893 for the United States, 1991 for Sweden. As the figure shows, these crises on different continents, almost a century apart, produced similarly devastating results: unemployment shot up and came down only slowly and erratically so that, even five years after the crisis, the number of jobless remained high by pre-crisis standards.

FIGURE **17-2** Unemployment Rates, Before and After a Banking Crisis

This figure tracks unemployment in the wake of two banking crises: the Panic of 1893 in the United States and the Swedish banking crisis of 1991. t represents the year of the crisis—1893 for the United States, 1991 for Sweden. $t - 2$ is the date two years before the crisis hit; $t + 5$ is the date five years after. In both cases, the economy suffered severe damage from the banking crisis: unemployment shot up and came down only slowly and erratically. In both cases, five years after the crisis the unemployment rate remained high compared to pre-crisis levels.

Sources: Christina D. Romer, "Spurious Volatility in Historical Unemployment Data," *Journal of Political Economy* 94, no. 1 (1986): 1–37; Eurostat.

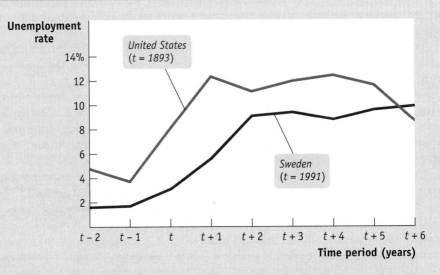

These historical examples are typical. Figure 17-3, taken from a widely cited study by the economists Carmen Reinhart and Kenneth Rogoff, compares employment performance in the wake of a number of severe banking crises. The bars on the left show the rise in the unemployment rate during and following the crisis; the bars on the right show the time it took before unemployment began to fall. The numbers are shocking: on average, severe banking crises have been followed by a 7 percentage point rise in the unemployment rate, and in many cases it has taken four years or more before the unemployment rate even begins to fall, let alone returns to pre-crisis levels.

Why Are Banking-Crisis Recessions So Bad?

It's not difficult to see why banking crises normally lead to recessions. There are three main reasons: a *credit crunch* arising from reduced availability of credit, financial distress caused by a *debt overhang*, and the *loss of monetary policy effectiveness*.

1. *Credit crunch.* The disruption of the banking system typically leads to a reduction in the availability of credit called a **credit crunch,** in which potential borrowers either can't get credit at all or must pay very high interest rates. Unable to borrow or unwilling to pay higher interest rates, businesses and consumers cut back on spending, pushing the economy into a recession.

In a **credit crunch,** potential borrowers either can't get credit at all or must pay very high interest rates.

FIGURE **17-3** Episodes of Banking Crises and Unemployment

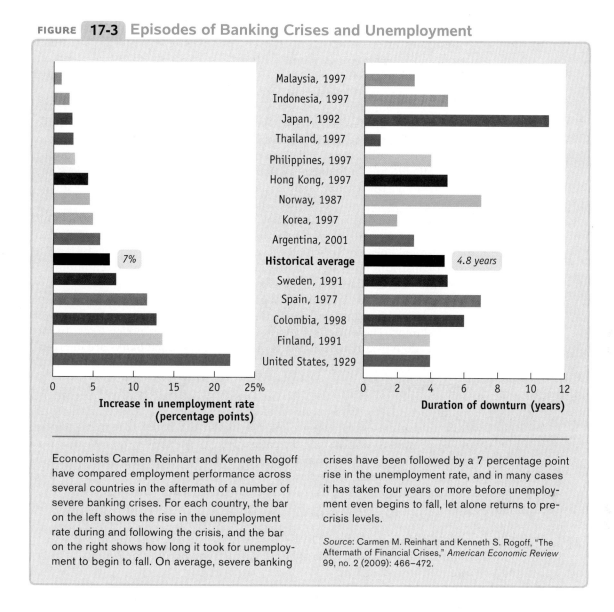

Economists Carmen Reinhart and Kenneth Rogoff have compared employment performance across several countries in the aftermath of a number of severe banking crises. For each country, the bar on the left shows the rise in the unemployment rate during and following the crisis, and the bar on the right shows how long it took for unemployment to begin to fall. On average, severe banking crises have been followed by a 7 percentage point rise in the unemployment rate, and in many cases it has taken four years or more before unemployment even begins to fall, let alone returns to pre-crisis levels.

Source: Carmen M. Reinhart and Kenneth S. Rogoff, "The Aftermath of Financial Crises," *American Economic Review* 99, no. 2 (2009): 466–472.

2. *Debt overhang.* A banking crisis typically pushes down the prices of many assets through a vicious circle of deleveraging, as distressed borrowers try to sell assets to raise cash, pushing down asset prices and causing further financial distress. As we have already seen, deleveraging is a factor in the spread of the crisis, lowering the value of the assets banks hold on their balance sheets and so undermining their solvency. It also creates problems for other players in the economy. To take an example all too familiar from recent U.S. events, falling housing prices can leave consumers substantially poorer, especially because they are still stuck with the debt they incurred to buy their homes. A banking crisis, then, tends to leave consumers and businesses with a **debt overhang**: high debt but diminished assets. Like a credit crunch, this also leads to a fall in spending and a recession as consumers and businesses cut back in order to reduce their debt and rebuild their assets.

3. *Loss of monetary policy effectiveness.* A key feature of banking-crisis recessions is that when they occur, monetary policy—the main tool of policy-makers for fighting negative demand shocks caused by a fall in consumer and investment spending—loses much of its effectiveness. The ineffectiveness of monetary policy makes banking-crisis recessions especially severe and long-lasting.

A **debt overhang** occurs when a vicious circle of deleveraging leaves a borrower with high debt but diminished assets.

Recall from Chapter 14 how the Bank of Canada normally responds to a recession: it engages in open-market operations, purchasing short-term government debt from banks. This leaves banks with excess reserves, which they lend out, leading to a fall in interest rates and causing an economic expansion through increased consumer and investment spending.

Under normal conditions, this policy response is highly effective. In the aftermath of a banking crisis, though, the whole process tends to break down. Banks, fearing runs by depositors or a loss of confidence by their creditors, tend to hold on to excess reserves rather than lend them out. Meanwhile, businesses and consumers, finding themselves in financial difficulty due to the plunge in asset prices, may be unwilling to borrow even if interest rates fall. As a result, even very low interest rates may not be enough to push the economy back to full employment.

In Chapter 16 we described the problem of the economy's falling into a liquidity trap, when even pushing short-term interest rates to zero isn't enough. In fact, all the historical episodes in which the zero bound on interest rates became an important constraint on policy—the 1930s, Japan in the 1990s, and a number of countries after 2008—have occurred after a major banking crisis.

The inability of the usual tools of monetary policy to offset the macroeconomic devastation caused by banking crises is the major reason such crises produce deep, prolonged slumps. The obvious solution is to look for other policy tools. In fact, governments do typically take a variety of special steps when banks are in crisis.

Governments Step In

Before the Great Depression, policy-makers often adopted a laissez-faire attitude toward banking crises, allowing banks to fail in the belief that market forces should be allowed to work. Since the catastrophe of the 1930s, though, almost all policy-makers have believed that it's necessary to take steps to contain the damage from bank failures. In general, central banks and governments take three main kinds of action in an effort to limit the fallout from banking crises:

1. They act as the *lender of last resort*.

2. They offer guarantees to depositors and others with claims on banks.

3. In an extreme crisis, a central bank will step in and provide financing to private credit markets.

1. Lender of Last Resort A **lender of last resort** is an institution, usually a country's central bank, that provides funds to financial institutions when they are unable to borrow from the private credit markets. In particular, the central bank can provide cash to a bank that is facing a run by depositors but is fundamentally solvent, making it unnecessary for the bank to engage in fire sales of its assets to raise cash. This acts as a lifeline, working to prevent a loss of confidence in the bank's solvency from turning into a self-fulfilling prophecy.

Did the U.S. Federal Reserve act as a lender of last resort in the 2008 financial crisis? Very much so. Figure 17-4 shows borrowing by banks from the Fed between 2005 and 2010: commercial banks borrowed negligible amounts from the central bank before the crisis, but their borrowing rose to $700 billion in the months following Lehman's failure. To get a sense of how large this borrowing was, note that total bank reserves before the crisis were less than $50 billion—so these loans were 14 times the banks' initial reserves.

> A **lender of last resort** is an institution, usually a country's central bank, that provides funds to financial institutions when they are unable to borrow from the private credit markets.

2. Government Guarantees There are limits, though, to how much a lender of last resort can accomplish: it can't restore confidence in a bank if there is good reason to believe the bank is fundamentally insolvent. If the public believes that the bank's assets aren't worth enough to cover its debts even if it doesn't have to sell these assets on short notice, a lender of last resort isn't going to help much. And in major banking crises there are often good reasons to believe that many banks are truly bankrupt.

FIGURE **17-4** Total Borrowings of Depository Institutions from the U.S. Federal Reserve

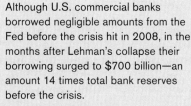

Although U.S. commercial banks borrowed negligible amounts from the Fed before the crisis hit in 2008, in the months after Lehman's collapse their borrowing surged to $700 billion—an amount 14 times total bank reserves before the crisis.

Source: Federal Reserve Bank of St. Louis.

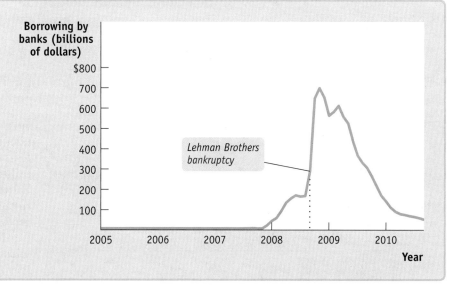

In such cases, governments often step in to guarantee banks' liabilities. In 2007, a bank run hit the British bank Northern Rock, ceasing only when the British government stepped in and guaranteed all deposits at the bank, regardless of size. Ireland's government eventually stepped in to guarantee repayment of not just deposits at all of the nation's banks, but all bank debts. Sweden did the same thing after its 1991 banking crisis. As mentioned earlier, the three Canadian trust companies Greymac Mortgage, Seaway Mortgage, and Crown Trust failed in 1982 as a result of fraudulent mortgages on apartment units in Toronto. In the end, the Ontario government seized these trust companies, forcing them into bankruptcy. In 1983, the Canadian Deposit Insurance Corporation (CDIC) was forced to cover any shortfall to depositors' insured accounts.[3]

When governments take on banks' risk, they often demand a quid pro quo—namely, they often take ownership of the banks they are rescuing. Northern Rock was nationalized in 2008. Sweden nationalized a significant part of its banking system in 1992. In the United States, the Federal Deposit Insurance Corporation routinely seizes banks that are no longer solvent; it seized 140 banks in 2009. Ireland, however, chose not to seize any of the banks whose debts were guaranteed by taxpayers.

These government takeovers are almost always temporary. In general, modern governments want to save banks, not run them. So they "reprivatize" nationalized banks, selling them to private buyers, as soon as they believe they can.

3. Provider of Direct Financing As we learned in Chapter 14, during the depths of the 2008 financial crisis the U.S. Federal Reserve expanded its operations beyond the usual measures of open-market operations and lending to depository banks. It also began lending to shadow banks and buying commercial paper—short-term bonds issued by private companies—as well as buying the debt of Fannie Mae and Freddie Mac, the government-sponsored home mortgage agencies. In this way, the Fed provided credit to keep the economy afloat when private credit markets had dried up.

---

[3]The CDIC paid out about $1.8 billion to the insured depositors of these three companies. After liquidating these companies' assets, the CDIC lost about $360 million. Since the creation of the CDIC in 1967, 43 member institutions have failed. Most of these institutions were small; nonetheless, about $11.5 billion worth of CDIC insurance payouts resulted from these failures, of which only $3.2 billion represented a loss for the CDIC.

ECONOMICS ▷ IN ACTION

U.S. BANKS AND THE GREAT DEPRESSION

FIGURE **17-5** The 1930s U.S. Banking Crisis and Credit Crunch

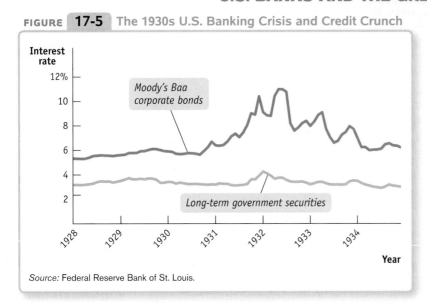

Source: Federal Reserve Bank of St. Louis.

According to the official American business-cycle chronology, the United States entered a recession in August 1929, two months before that year's famous stock market crash. Although the crash surely made the slump worse, through late 1930 it still seemed to be a more or less ordinary recession. Then the bank failures began. A majority of economists believe that the banking crisis is what turned a fairly severe but not catastrophic recession into the Great Depression.

How did the banking crisis hurt the wider economy? Largely by creating a credit crunch, in which businesses in particular either could not borrow or found themselves forced to pay sharply higher interest rates. Figure 17-5 shows one indicator of this credit crunch: the difference between the interest rates—known as the "spread"—at which businesses with good but not great credit could borrow and the borrowing costs of the federal government.

Baa corporate bonds are those that Moody's, the credit rating agency, considers "medium-grade obligations"—debts of companies that should be able to pay but aren't completely reliable. ("Baa" refers to the specific rating assigned to the bonds of such companies.) Until the banking crisis struck, Baa borrowers borrowed at interest rates only about 2 percentage points higher than the interest rates the government borrowed at, and this spread remained low until the summer of 1931. Then it surged, peaking at more than 7 percentage points in 1932. Bear in mind that this is just one indicator of the credit crunch: many would-be borrowers were completely shut out.

One striking fact about the banking

A crowd of unemployed Canadians demanding better welfare payments gather at the York Township Relief Office in Toronto, 1934.

crisis of the early 1930s is that the U.S. Federal Reserve, although it had the legal ability to act as a lender of last resort, largely failed to do so. Nothing like the surge in bank borrowing from the Fed that took place in 2007–2009 occurred. In fact, bank borrowing from the Fed throughout the 1930s banking crisis was at levels lower than those reached in 1928–1929.

Meanwhile, neither the Fed nor the federal government did anything to rescue failing banks until 1933. So the early 1930s offer a clear example of a banking crisis that policy-makers more or less allowed to take its course. It's not an experience anyone wants to repeat.

▼ Quick Review

CHECK YOUR UNDERSTANDING   17-3

1. Explain why, as of late 2010, the U.S. Federal Reserve was able to prevent the crisis of 2008 from turning into another Great Depression but was unable to significantly reduce the surge in unemployment that occurred.

2. Explain why, in the aftermath of a severe banking crisis, a very low interest rate—even as low as 0%—may be unable to move the economy back to full employment.

Solutions appear at back of book.

The 2008 Crisis and Its Aftermath

As we've just seen, banking crises have typically been followed by major economic problems. How did the aftermath of the financial crisis of 2008 compare with this historical experience? The answer, unfortunately, is that history has proved a very good guide: once again, the economic damage from the financial crisis was both large and prolonged. And aftershocks from the crisis continue to shake the world economy today, after Lehman's 2008 fall.

Severe Crisis, Slow Recovery

Figure 17-6 compares how the real GDPs of Canada and the two largest economies, the United States and the European Union (EU), fared during the crisis and its aftermath. For ease of comparison, the peak pre-crisis quarter for each economy has been normalized to 100. For Canada, this was the third quarter of 2008; for the United States, it was the last quarter of 2007; and for the European Union, it was the first quarter of 2008. As you can see, each economy suffered a severe downturn, followed by a slow recovery. However, Canada fared better than the other two economies. Canada's economy declined by 4.2%, whereas the U.S. economy declined by

FIGURE   17-6   Crisis and Recovery in Canada, the U.S., and the European Union

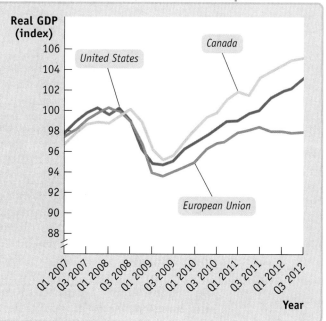

In the aftermath of the 2008 financial crisis, aggregate output in Canada, the European Union, and the United States fell dramatically. Real GDP, shown here as an index with each economy's peak pre-crisis quarter set to 100, declined by more than 4%. Canadian real GDP returned to its pre-crisis level by the fourth quarter of 2010; the United States recovered to pre-crisis levels in the fourth quarter of 2011; as of the third quarter of 2012 though, aggregate output in the European Union had still not reached its pre-crisis peak.

Sources: U.S. Bureau of Economic Analysis; OECD; Statistics Canada.

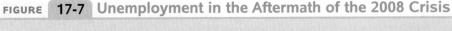

FIGURE **17-7** Unemployment in the Aftermath of the 2008 Crisis

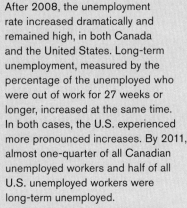

After 2008, the unemployment rate increased dramatically and remained high, in both Canada and the United States. Long-term unemployment, measured by the percentage of the unemployed who were out of work for 27 weeks or longer, increased at the same time. In both cases, the U.S. experienced more pronounced increases. By 2011, almost one-quarter of all Canadian unemployed workers and half of all U.S. unemployed workers were long-term unemployed.

Source: Statistics Canada; U.S. Bureau of Labor Statistics.

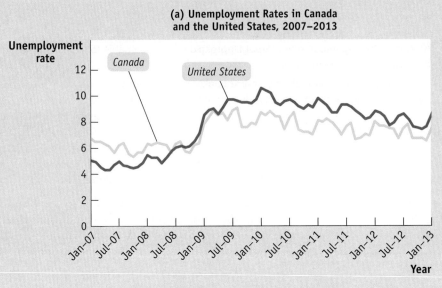

(a) Unemployment Rates in Canada and the United States, 2007–2013

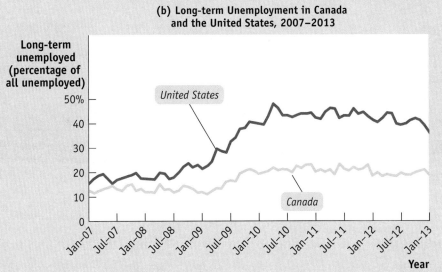

(b) Long-term Unemployment in Canada and the United States, 2007–2013

4.7%, and the EU economy declined by 5.6%. Also, Canada recovered more quickly. As of early 2012, the United States was barely above its pre-crisis peak, and the European Union had yet to regain its pre-crisis level of output.

The severe slump and the slow recovery were very bad news for workers, since a healthy job market depends on an economy growing fast enough to accommodate both a growing workforce and rising productivity. Figure 17-7 shows two indicators of unemployment in Canada and the United States—the overall unemployment rate and the percentage of the unemployed who had been out of work 27 weeks or more. Both measures shot up during the crisis and remained very high years later, indicating a labour market in which it remained hard to find a job.

This outcome was, sad to say, about what one should have expected given the severity of the initial financial shock and the historical experience with such shocks. In fact, in the U.S. experience, unemployment almost exactly matched the average performance of past economies that had suffered major banking disruptions. America, observed Kenneth Rogoff (whose work we cited earlier), was experiencing a "garden variety severe financial crisis." While Canada's labour market performed better than that of the United States, Canadian workers still experienced significant suffering even years after the crisis.

Aftershocks in Europe

One important factor bedevilling hopes for recovery was the emergence of special difficulties in several European nations—difficulties that repeatedly raised the specter of a second financial crisis.

The 2008 crisis was caused by problems with private debt, mainly home loans, which then triggered a crisis of confidence in banks. In 2011 and 2012, fears of a second crisis were focused on public debt, specifically the public debts of Southern European countries plus Ireland.

Europe's troubles first surfaced in Greece, a country with a long history of fiscal irresponsibility. In late 2009, it was revealed that a previous Greek government had understated the size of the budget deficits and the amount of government debt, prompting lenders to refuse further loans to Greece. Other European countries provided emergency loans to the Greek government in return for harsh budget cuts. But these budget cuts depressed the Greek economy, and by late 2011 there was general agreement that Greece could not pay back its debts in full.

By itself, this was probably a manageable shock for the European economy since Greece accounts for less than 3% of European GDP. Unfortunately, foot-dragging by European officials in confronting Greece's problems and the effects of the harsh budget cuts on the Greek economy spooked investors. By the fall of 2011, the crisis had spread beyond the Greek borders, hitting two major European economies: Spain and Italy.

Figure 17-8 shows a measure of pressure on Italy, Spain, Ireland, Portugal, and Greece during the 2008 and 2011 crises: the difference between interest rates on 10-year bonds issued by these five nations' governments and interest rates on German debt, which most people consider a safe investment. Because all six countries use the same currency, the euro, these rates would all be the same if the government debt of Italy, Spain, Ireland, Portugal, and Greece were considered as safe as German government debt. The rise in "spreads" therefore indicates a growing perception of default risk.

Spain's fiscal problems were mainly fallout from the 2008 crisis. Before that crisis, Spain seemed to be in very good fiscal condition, with low debt and a budget surplus. However, Spain, like Ireland, had a huge housing bubble between 2000 and 2007. When the bubble burst, the Spanish economy fell into a deep slump, depressing tax receipts and causing large budget deficits. At the same time, there were worries that the Spanish government might eventually have to spend large amounts bailing out banks. As a result, investors began worrying about the solvency of the Spanish government and a possible default, driving up interest rates.

FIGURE   17-8 Interest Spread Against German 10-Year Bonds

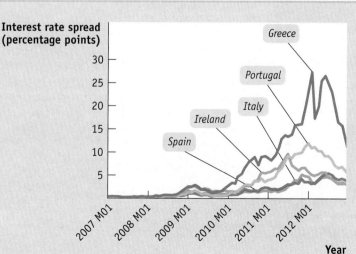

One indicator of investors' perceptions of the risk of government default is the spread of interest rates on government bonds between that country and a country that is perceived as a safe investment. The spread of the interest rates on 10-year government bonds for Italy, Spain, Ireland, Greece, and Portugal, measured against the interest rate on German bonds, rose as investors' fears of default by these countries increased.

Source: Eurostat.

Italy's case was somewhat different. Italy has long had high levels of public debt as a percentage of GDP, but it has not run large deficits in recent years; as late as the spring of 2010 its fiscal position looked fairly stable. At that point, however, investors began to have doubts about the Italian government's solvency, in part because in the aftermath of the 2008 crisis the Italian economy was growing very slowly—too slowly, it was feared, to generate enough tax revenue to repay its public debt. These doubts drove up interest rates on Italian public debt, and this in turn created a vicious circle: higher interest payments, caused by fears about Italian government solvency, worsened Italy's fiscal position even further and pushed it closer to the edge.

At the time of writing, Greece had defaulted on its government bonds twice in 2012; Spanish unemployment had hit 26%, with youth unemployment close to 56%; and it was unclear how much worse the European situation would get. But Europe's difficulties reinforced the sense that the damage from the 2008 financial crisis was by no means over.

The Stimulus–Austerity Debate

The persistence of economic difficulties after the 2008 financial crisis led to fierce debates about appropriate policy responses. Broadly speaking, economists and policy-makers were divided as to whether the situation called for more fiscal stimulus—expansionary fiscal measures such as more government spending and possibly tax cuts to promote spending and reduce unemployment—or for fiscal "austerity," contractionary fiscal measures such as spending cuts and possibly tax increases to reduce budget deficits.

The proponents of more stimulus pointed to the continuing poor performance of major economies, arguing that the combination of high unemployment and relatively low inflation clearly pointed to the need for expansionary policies. And since monetary policy was limited by the zero bound on interest rates, stimulus proponents advocated expansionary fiscal policy to fill the gap.

The austerity camp took a very different view. Strongly influenced by the solvency troubles of Greece, Ireland, Spain, and Italy, they argued that the common source of all the problems were high levels of government deficits and debts. In their view, countries like the United States that continued to run large government deficits several years after the 2008 crisis were at risk of suffering a similar loss of investor confidence in their ability to repay their debts. Moreover, austerity advocates claimed that cuts in government spending would not actually be contractionary because they would improve investor confidence and keep interest rates on government debt low.

Each side of the debate argued that recent experience refuted the other side's claims. Austerity proponents argued that the persistence of high unemployment despite the fiscal stimulus programs adopted by Canada, the United States, and other major economies in 2009 showed that stimulus doesn't work. Stimulus advocates argued that these programs were simply inadequate in size, pointing out that many economists had warned of their inadequacy from the start. Stimulus advocates further argued that warnings about the dangers of deficits were overblown, that far from rising, borrowing costs for Canada, Japan, the United States, and Britain—nations that, unlike the troubled European debtors, still had their own currencies with all the flexibility that implies—had fallen to record lows. And they dismissed claims that spending cuts would raise confidence as mainly fantasy.

The British economy was decimated by the aftermath of the 2008 crisis coupled with government austerity measures.

Oli Scarff/Getty Images

At the time of writing, neither side was giving much ground. Clearly, any resolution of the debate would hinge on future economic developments and how they were interpreted.

The Lesson of the Post-Crisis Slump

Almost all major economies had great difficulty dealing with the aftermath of the 2008 financial crisis—high unemployment, low growth and, for some, solvency concerns, and high interest rates on public debt.

Clearly, then, the best way to avoid the terrible problems that arise after a financial crisis is not to have a crisis in the first place. How can you do that? In part, one might hope, through better regulation of financial institutions. We turn next to attempts at regulatory reform.

ECONOMICS > IN ACTION

AUSTERITY BRITAIN

An election in May 2010 led to a shift in power in Britain, with a Labour Party government replaced by a coalition dominated by the Conservative Party under the new prime minister, David Cameron. The new government was firmly committed to the austerity side of the great post-crisis policy debate, and it changed policy accordingly.

Unlike Greece or Ireland, Britain wasn't under any immediate pressure to slash its budget deficit. Like the Canadian government, the British government was still able to borrow cheaply despite its large deficit. And the British economy was, if anything, even more depressed than the Canadian one, with fewer signs of recovery. The Cameron government believed, however, that pre-emptive cuts in public spending combined with some tax increases were necessary to preserve investor confidence and also that such cuts could boost the economy by improving confidence.

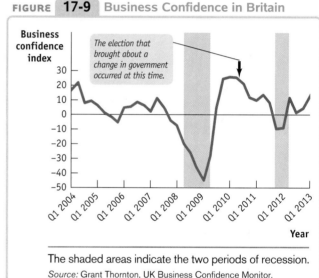

FIGURE 17-9 Business Confidence in Britain

The shaded areas indicate the two periods of recession.

Source: Grant Thornton, UK Business Confidence Monitor.

How have these policies performed? As of 2012 and early 2013, the experiment in austerity had yielded disappointing results. British economic growth was weak—in fact, considerably weaker than in Canada and the United States, even though our own performance was lacklustre. In fact, the United Kingdom suffered another recession from the fourth quarter of 2011 until the end of the second quarter of 2012. And, in early 2013 there was significant concern of the possibility of a third, so-called triple-dip, recession looming, following a drop in real GDP in the last quarter of 2012. As Figure 17-9 shows, the hoped-for surge in business confidence that austerity measures were supposed to generate had failed to materialize.

▼ Quick Review

- Economic damage from the financial crisis of 2008 was both large and prolonged. Aftershocks from the crisis continue to shake the world economy.

- Like Canada, the world's two largest economies, in the United States and the European Union, suffered severe downturns, shrinking more than 4%, followed by relatively slow recoveries. The severe slump and the slow recovery were very bad news for workers.

- The persistence of economic difficulties after the 2008 financial crisis led to severe solvency concerns for several European countries. A fierce debate erupted over whether fiscal stimulus or fiscal austerity was the right policy prescription.

CHECK YOUR UNDERSTANDING 17-4

1. In November 2011, the government of France announced that it was reducing its forecast for economic growth in 2012. It was also reducing its estimates of tax revenue for 2012, since a weaker economy would mean smaller tax receipts. To offset the effect of lower revenue on the budget deficit, the government also announced a new package of tax increases and spending cuts. Which side of the stimulus–austerity debate was France taking?

Solutions appear at back of book.

Regulation in the Wake of the Crisis

By late 2009, interventions by governments and central banks around the world had restored calm to financial markets. However, huge damage had been done to the global economy. In much of the advanced world, countries suffered their deepest slumps since the 1930s. And all indications were that the typical pattern of slow recovery after a financial crisis would be repeated, with unemployment remaining high for years to come.

The banking crisis of 2008 demonstrated, all too clearly, that financial regulation is a continuing process—that regulations will and should change over time to keep up with a changing world. The dependence on very short-term loans (called repo), the lack of regulation, and being outside the lender-of-last-resort system made the shadow banking sector vulnerable to crises and panics. So what changes will the most recent crisis bring? One thing that became all too clear in the 2008 crisis was that the traditional scope of banking regulation was too narrow. Regulating only depository institutions was clearly inadequate in a world in which a large part of banking, properly understood, is undertaken by the shadow banking sector.

In the aftermath of the crisis, then, an overhaul of financial regulation was clearly needed. And in 2010 the U.S. Congress enacted a bill that represented an effort to respond to the events of the preceding years. Like most legislation, the Wall Street Reform and Consumer Protection Act—often referred to as the Dodd-Frank bill—is complex in its details. But it contains four main elements:

1. Consumer protection

2. Derivatives regulation

3. Regulation of shadow banks

4. Resolution authority over non-bank financial institutions that face bankruptcy

1. Consumer Protection One factor in the financial crisis was the fact that many U.S. borrowers accepted offers they didn't understand, such as mortgages that were easy to pay in the first two years but required sharply higher payments later on. In an effort to limit future abuses, the new law creates a special office, the Consumer Financial Protection Bureau, dedicated to policing financial industry practices and protecting borrowers.

2. Derivatives Regulation Another factor in the crisis was the proliferation of derivatives, complex financial instruments that were supposed to help spread risk but arguably simply concealed it. Under the new law, most derivatives have to be bought and sold in open, transparent markets, hopefully limiting the extent to which financial players can take on invisible risk.

3. Regulation of Shadow Banks A key element in the financial crisis, as we've seen, was the rise of institutions that didn't fit the conventional definition of a bank but played the role of banks and created the risk of a banking crisis. How can regulation be extended to such institutions? Dodd-Frank does not offer an explicit new definition of what it means to be a bank. Instead, it offers a sort of financial version of "you know it when you see it." Specifically, it gives a special panel the ability to designate financial institutions as "systemically important," meaning that their activities have the potential to create a banking crisis. Such institutions will be subject to bank-like regulation of their capital, their investments, and so on.

4. Resolution Authority The events of 2008 made it clear that governments would often feel the need to guarantee a wide range of financial institution debts in a crisis, not just deposits. Yet how can this be done without creating huge incentive problems, motivating financial institutions to undertake overly risky behaviour in the knowledge that they will be bailed out by the government if they get into trouble? Part of the answer is to empower the government to seize control of financial institutions that require a bailout, the way it already does with failing commercial banks. (In Canada, depository banks include chartered banks, trust, mortgage and loan companies, credit unions, and caisses populaires.) This new power, known as resolution authority, should be viewed as solving a problem that seemed acute in early 2009, when several major U.S. financial institutions were teetering on the brink. Yet it wasn't clear whether Washington had the legal authority to orchestrate a rescue that was fair to taxpayers.

All this is now law in the United States, but nobody knows for sure how the new regulations will fare in the face of a serious test. For that, we'll just have to wait and see.

Knowing the devastating effect that a bursting housing bubble could have on our economy, the Federal Department of Finance decided to make mortgages harder to obtain and to limit the amount of debt the holder of a mortgage could carry. To achieve these goals, Canadian mortgage rules were changed in four stages: stage 1 in July 2008, stage 2 in February 2010, stage 3 in January 2011, and stage 4 in June 2012. These changes included the following:

- The maximum amortization period on insured mortgages was shortened from 40 years to 35 years (July 2008), then to 30 years (January 2011), and most recently to 25 years (June 2012). Homebuyers who want to have a longer amortization period must make a down payment of at least 20% of the property's value.

- The maximum insured mortgage percentage was reduced from 100% of a home's value to 95% (July 2008), creating a 5% minimum down payment.

- The maximum insured refinancing amount was reduced from 95% to 90% (February 2010), then to 85% (January 2011), and most recently to 80% (June 2012).

- The insurance for home equity lines of credit was withdrawn.

- Minimum credit scores were established. Currently, a borrower who wishes to buy a small rental property (that is, a property that is being bought in order to rent it out) must make a down payment of at least 20% of the property's value. A borrower who obtains a variable-rate mortgage or a fixed-rate mortgage with a term less than five years must qualify for his or her loan based on the posted interest rates for a five-year fixed-rate mortgage.

- The government introduced a cap to limit the amount of mortgage insurance sold by Canada Mortgage and Housing Corporation (CMHC) and by private firms such as Genworth and Canada Guaranty for property values of less than $1 million when the loan-to-value ratio is greater than 0.8 (i.e., 80%).

- Also, for the first time, the government imposed a limit on how much debt can be carried by someone wishing to buy a house: the annual cost of the mortgage payments, property taxes, and applicable condominium fees cannot exceed 39% of the borrower's annual pre-tax income. Furthermore, the borrower's total cost of debt, including credit card payments, car loans, personal loans, and so on, cannot exceed 44% of his or her annual pre-tax income.

The result of these rule changes should be to reduce the number of qualified buyers. Consequently, housing prices should rise more slowly than they have been or perhaps even decline. Jim Flaherty, the minister of finance, said that these changes in mortgage rules were necessary and would help the housing market have a "soft landing" rather than a hard one, which would be beneficial to the Canadian economy. These changes would also help put a brake on the growing level of household debt. On many occasions, Mark Carney, then governor of the Bank of Canada, expressed his concern over the historically high level of indebtedness of Canadian households; he said these mortgage rule changes were "prudent" and "timely" and would reduce the risk of household debt. Last but not least, the Office of the Superintendent of Financial Institutions (OSFI) said these rules would help reduce the default risk on mortgage loans faced by financial institutions because they discouraged institutions from lending to marginal borrowers, who would find it harder to get a mortgage. That being said, the government must prudently tighten the rules while not overly restricting mortgage market conditions; such a balance reduces the likelihood of a significant drop in home prices coming from the rule changes.

But, in fact, some argue that the finance minister has gone too far. Wayne Meon, president of the Canadian Real Estate Association, argues that these new rules were not necessary, as adjustments in the housing market were already underway. These rules might depress the real estate market further, leading to a crash. For example, according to the Royal Bank of Canada's report on housing trends and affordability, the average price of a detached bungalow in Vancouver declined by 4.9% from $846 800 to $805 300 from the second quarter of 2012 to the third quarter of 2012. In the same time period, the housing affordability index for a detached bungalow in Vancouver dropped from 91% to 83%, and similar declines occurred in major cities such as Toronto, Ottawa, Montreal, and Edmonton.[4] Some claim these declines are the result of the new changes, because the changes lowered demand for houses and resulted in homebuyers taking out smaller mortgages. The Canadian Association of Accredited Mortgage Professionals (CAAMP) also argues the new rules are too tough. A report by CAAMP suggests that up to 17% of those who would have qualified as homebuyers under the old rules now do not, and as a result, this lower demand could cause home sales to fall by 9%. This drop in sales will drive home prices downward, and lower the demand for goods and services in related industries, thus causing our still-fragile economy to slow down.

ECONOMICS ▸ IN ACTION

CRISIS IN THE MARKET FOR ABCP: THE CANADIAN SITUATION

In the mid-1980s, private financial institutions found a new way to make a profit: they began to issue short-term promissory notes. These companies supported, or "backed," these notes with long-term assets that they owned (which were held in "trusts" separated from the issuing firms' other assets and liabilities). These long-term assets were often purchased with the very funds raised by selling the notes. Asset-backed commercial paper (ABCP), as these notes were called, quickly became very popular. For instance, the amount of outstanding ABCP grew from about $11 billion in January 1997 to $115 billion in July 2007; over the same period, ABCP grew from being 21% of all the commercial paper issued in Canada to 67% of it. Shadow banks—non-depository financial institutions—can borrow money in the short term (by selling ABCP for high amounts) and lend it in the long term (by buying long-term assets at low amounts). While advantageous for the issuers of ABCP, the situation was risky because, as Canadian economist Frank Milne has noted, the shadow banking sector was largely free of the regulatory and lender-of-last-resort safety net available to deposit-taking banks.[5]

And indeed, trouble lay ahead: from 1997 to 2007, these private financial institutions' portfolios of long-term assets changed to include a greater percent of items that turned out to be financially precarious, such as collat-

---

[4]*Source:* "Housing Trends and Affordability," November 2012, Royal Bank of Canada, www.rbc.com/newsroom/pdf/HA-1122-2012.pdf.

[5]Frank Milne, *Anatomy of the Credit Crisis: The Role of Faulty Risk Management Systems* (C.D. Howe Institute: 2007).

eralized debt obligations and residential and commercial mortgage-backed securities based on U.S. sub-prime mortgages. As economics professor John Chant wrote in a *National Post* article ("Fix ABCP Flaws") on January 23, 2009:

> The 30-to 90-day maturity of the notes issued by the trusts and the longer-term nature of assets forced the trusts to continually seek refinancing for maturing notes, leaving them highly vulnerable to the vagaries of market conditions.
>
> The assets acquired for the trusts by their sponsors included packages of securitized mortgages, many of which contained U.S. subprime mortgages. These packages were not acquired from the parties that originally made the mortgage loans. Rather, the trusts were often several steps removed, as the original lenders had sold the mortgages to others who, in turn, may have repackaged them and sold them on again. Outside observers were unable to determine the quality of the trusts' portfolios because of the many layers separating the trusts from the original mortgage lenders.
>
> The ABCP trusts also held synthetic assets in the form of credit derivatives. Surprisingly, they did not buy derivatives to protect themselves against credit risk but instead wrote them to take on the risks of others. Even more surprising, they did this on a levered basis that magnified their exposure to risk. These transactions also required the trusts to put up additional collateral to back their commitments according to market conditions.
>
> In light of the trusts' asset-liability mismatch, their exposure to subprime mortgages and their credit derivative position, ABCP trusts were essentially hedge funds, albeit with capped returns. They offered investors high risk together with low returns. All in all, they were totally unsuitable for investors seeking a safe haven and would have had few takers had their true nature been known. A broad market developed through a combination of limited information, forbearance from securities administrators and positive credit ratings.[6]

The repayment of ABCP by the issuing trust depends primarily on the cash flow received from the trust's underlying asset portfolio and, due to the maturity mismatch between the notes and the underlying assets, with the trust's ability to issue new ABCP. So, an issuer of ABCP could sustain itself during good financial times, but not during bad ones. During the summer of 2007, negative information about U.S. housing markets, falling resale prices, and rising mortgage default rates caused investors to worry about the true value of mortgage-backed securities and of the entities that had invested in them. This made investors reluctant to purchase newly issued ABCP. In August 2007, the $32 billion market for Canadian non-bank-issued ABCP froze, a circumstance that amounted to what was essentially a run on the shadow banks.[7]

Not only was $32 billion worth of non-bank ABCP held by financial institutions, other firms, and individuals, but an additional $200 billion worth of leveraged derivatives were at risk of unravelling. After 17 months of negotiations, consultation, and stakeholder meetings, a settlement was agreed upon. Under the plan individual investors would get their money back. The rest of the investors were to swap their insolvent ABCP for new notes, most of which matured within eight years. So, finally, investors had access to some of their funds (liquidity).

As part of the settlement, the governments of Canada, Ontario, Quebec, and Alberta agreed that they would provide a $4.5 billion "backstop facility" (essentially a line of credit) to help fund this settlement if private sector funds were unable to do so. Some people referred to this backstop facility as a government bailout. However, the federal government has noted that since the backstop is

---

[6]*Source:* "Fix ABCP flaws," by John Chant, *Financial Post*, Jan. 23, 2009 © John Chant.

[7]This freeze was voluntary, having been selected by the principal investors to buy time to determine the best solution for the market. But with few, if any, willing buyers, the market for non-bank-issued ABCP was practically non-existent. You may recall that the existence of market equilibrium requires the existence and intersection of both a supply curve (representing willing sellers) and a demand curve (representing willing buyers). Unfortunately, after August 2007, there was really only a supply curve and hence no market for these assets. These shadow banks had failed.

- When the panic hit after Lehman's fall, governments and central banks around the world stepped in to fight the crisis and calm the markets. Most advanced economies experienced their worst slump since the 1930s.

- In 2010, the U.S. Congress enacted the Dodd-Frank bill to remedy the regulatory oversights exposed by the crisis of 2007–2009. It created the Consumer Financial Protection Bureau to protect borrowers and consumers, implemented stricter regulation of derivatives, extended the reach of regulation to the shadow banking sector, and empowered the government to seize control of any financial institution requiring a bailout.

- To lessen the possibility of a bursting Canadian housing bubble and the economic distress that would cause, the federal government instituted, from 2008 to 2012, a series of changes designed to make houses more difficult to buy.

unlikely to be required, the risk to taxpayers is low. But one thing is for sure: the financial advisors who helped design this settlement are clearly among the winners, since they earned $200 million in consulting fees. This sad ABCP episode has given us many lessons about financial market regulation and reform. Only time will tell if we were able to enact the changes necessary to avoid another such crisis in the future.

CHECK YOUR UNDERSTANDING 17-5

1. Why does the use of short-term borrowing and being outside of the lender-of-last-resort system make shadow banks vulnerable to events similar to bank runs?

2. How do you think the ABCP crisis of 2008 would have been mitigated if there had been no shadow banking sector but only the formal depository banking sector?

3. Describe the incentive problem facing the U.S. government in responding to the U.S. 2007–2009 crisis with respect to the shadow banking sector. How did the Dodd-Frank bill attempt to address those incentive problems?

Solutions appear at back of book.

SUMMARY

1. Without banks, people would make the trade-off between liquidity and rate of return by holding a large fraction of their wealth in idle cash. Banks engage in **maturity transformation,** transforming short-term liabilities into long-term assets. Banking improves savers' welfare, allowing them immediate access to their funds (liquidity) as well as paying them interest on those funds.

2. **Shadow banks** have grown greatly since 1980. Largely unregulated, they can pay savers a higher rate of return than depository banks. Like depository banks, shadow banks engage in maturity transformation, depending on short-term borrowing to operate and investing in long-term assets. Therefore, shadow banks can also be subject to bank runs.

3. Although **banking crises** are rare, they typically inflict severe damage on the economy. They have two main sources: shared mistakes, such as investing in an **asset bubble,** and **financial contagion.** Contagion is spread through bank runs or via a vicious cycle of deleveraging. When unregulated, shadow banking is particularly vulnerable to contagion. In 2008, a **financial panic** hit the United States, arising from the combination of an asset bubble, a huge shadow banking sector, and a vicious cycle of deleveraging.

4. Banking crises and financial panics are extremely rare in Canada. The United States, however, has suffered many such events, each followed by a severe downturn. The crisis of the 1930s spurred bank reform that prevented another crisis until 2008. Banking crises occur frequently throughout the world, mostly in small, poor countries. In the recent past, though, several advanced countries have had banking crises driven by real estate bubbles.

5. Severe banking crises almost invariably lead to deep and long recessions, with unemployment remaining high for several years after the crisis began. There are three main reasons why banking crises are so damaging to the economy: they result in a **credit crunch,** the vicious circle of deleveraging leads to a **debt overhang,** and monetary policy is rendered ineffective as the economy falls into a liquidity trap. As a result, households and businesses are either unable or unwilling to spend, deepening the downturn.

6. Unlike during the Great Depression, governments now step in to try to limit the damage from a banking crisis by acting as the **lender of last resort** and by guaranteeing the banks' liabilities. Sometimes, but not always, governments nationalize the banks and then later reprivatize them. In an extreme crisis, the central bank may directly finance commercial transactions.

7. Economic damage from the financial crisis of 2008 was large and prolonged. Canada's economy, as well as the world's two largest economies, the United States and the European Union, suffered severe downturns, shrinking more than 4%. These downturns were followed by relatively slow recoveries. The persistence of economic difficulties after 2008 led to fierce debates about appropriate policy responses between economists and policy-makers calling for more fiscal stimulus—more government spending and possibly tax cuts to promote spending and reduce unemployment—and those favouring fiscal austerity—spending cuts and possibly tax increases to reduce budget deficits.

8. The U.S. banking regulatory system put in place during the 1930s has eroded due to the rise of shadow banking. The dependence on short-term financing (repo), the lack of regulation, and being outside the lender-of-last-resort system makes the shadow banking sector vulnerable to a banking panic.

9. The crisis of 2008 began as the shadow banking sector suffered high losses when a real estate bubble in the United States burst. Despite the fact that governments and central banks around the world stepped in to fight the crisis and the downturn, most advanced countries experienced their worst slump since the 1930s. Persistently high unemployment is likely to endure for years to come.

10. In the aftermath of the crisis, the U.S. Congress enacted the Dodd-Frank bill in the hope of preventing a replay of the crisis. The main elements of the new reform are stronger consumer protection, greater regulation of derivatives, regulation of shadow banking, and resolution authority for a variety of financial institutions. We have yet to see whether these changes will be adequate or whether they will also be adopted by other countries.

11. In response to the housing market collapse in the United States, rising Canadian home prices, and the high level of household debt, the Canadian government, in several stages between 2008 and 2012, tightened regulations governing residential mortgages. These new rules include shortening the maximum amortization periods, reducing the percentage of house values that homeowners can borrow, and no longer insuring houses that are worth more than $1 million.

KEY TERMS

Maturity transformation, p. 560
Shadow bank, p. 560
Banking crisis, p. 562

Asset bubble, p. 563
Financial contagion, p. 563
Financial panic, p. 564

Credit crunch, p. 568
Debt overhang, p. 569
Lender of last resort, p. 570

PROBLEMS

1. Which of the following are examples of debt overhang? Which examples are likely to lead to a cutback in spending? Explain.

   a. Your uncle starts a restaurant, borrowing to fund his investment. The restaurant fails, and your uncle must shut down but still must pay his debt.

   b. Your parents take out a loan to buy a house. Your father is transferred to a new city, and now your parents must sell the house. The value of the house has gone up during the time your family has lived there.

   c. Your friend's parents take out a loan to buy her a condo to live in while she is at university. Meanwhile, the housing market plummets. By the time your friend leaves college, the condo is worth significantly less than the value of the loan.

   d. You finish college with an honours degree in a field with many good job prospects and with $25 000 in student loans that you must repay.

2. Which of the following are *not* examples of a vicious cycle of deleveraging? Explain.

   a. Your university decides to sell several commercial buildings in the middle of town in order to upgrade buildings on campus.

   b. A company decides to sell its large and valuable art collection because other asset prices on its balance sheet have fallen below a critical level, forcing creditors to call in their loans to the company because of provisions written into the original loan contract.

   c. A company decides to issue more stock in order to voluntarily pay off some of its debt.

   d. A shadow bank must sell its holdings of corporate bonds because falling asset prices have led to a default on the terms of its loans with some creditors.

3. The following figure shows the Case–Shiller Home Price Index for Canada and the United States from January 2000 to November 2012. For ease of comparison, both indexes have been normalized to equal 100 in January 2000.

   a. Did U.S. housing prices peak before or after the financial crisis in the United States? Explain your answer.

   b. Given the recent experience with U.S. housing prices, and the relative sizes of these two price indexes, does this plot support or undermine the belief that Canadian housing prices are not overvalued? Explain your answer.

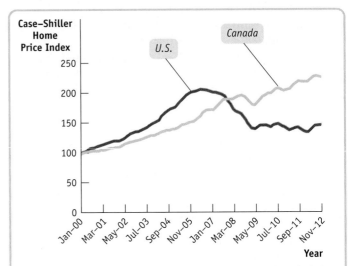

Sources: Teranet–National Bank Home Price Index (www.housepriceindex.ca/Default. aspx); S&P/Case-Shiller 20-City U.S. Composite Home Price Index (us.spindices.com/ indices/real-estate/sp-case-shiller-20-city-composite-home-price-index).

4. Figure 17-2 tracks the unemployment rate in the years before and after the Panic of 1893 in the United States and the banking crisis of 1991 in Sweden.

   a. In Figure 17-2, how many years after the Panic of 1893 did unemployment peak in the United States?

   b. In Figure 17-2, how many years after the banking crisis of 1991 did unemployment peak in Sweden?

5. In 2007–2009, the U.S. Federal Reserve, acting as a lender of last resort, stepped in to provide funds when private markets were unable to do so. The Fed also took over many American banks. In 2007, it seized 3 banks; in 2008, it seized 25 banks; and in 2009, it seized 140 banks.

   a. Go to fdic.gov; under "Bank Closing Information," click on "Complete Failed Bank List." Count the number of American banks that the Federal Reserve has seized so far this year. Have U.S. bank failures decreased since the crisis in 2008?

   b. Go to cdic.ca; under "Where Are My Savings Insured by CDIC?," click on "History of Member Institution Failures." Then count the number of CDIC-insured Canadian depository banks that have failed in the last 10 years, the last 20 years, and the last 30 years.

6. During the financial crisis in October 2008, the U.S. federal government could borrow at a rate of 2.73% (the yield on five-year treasury securities). During October 2008, though, American Baa borrowers (corporate borrowers rated by Moody's as not being completely reliable) had to pay 8.88%.

a. What was the difference in borrowing costs for these American corporate borrowers and the U.S. federal government?

b. In October 2008, the Canadian federal government could borrow at a rate of 2.80% (the yield on five-year Canadian federal treasury bonds). Suppose Canadian BBB borrowers (corporate borrowers rated by the Dominion Bond Rating Service as being not completely reliable) faced the same risk premium—and hence the same yield-spread between federal and corporate bond yields—as similar U.S.-based borrowers did. In this case, what would the interest rate on a five-year bond issued by a Canadian BBB borrower have been in October 2008? Would this encourage more or less borrowing by such firms, relative to similar firms in the United States?

c. Go to research.stlouisfed.org/fred2/categories/22. Click on the link for "Treasury constant maturity" and find the most recent interest rate on 10-year U.S. treasury bonds. Then click on the link for "Corporate bonds" and find the rate for American Baa corporate bonds. What is the current difference in borrowing costs between corporate borrowers and the U.S. government?

d. Has this difference in U.S. borrowing costs increased or decreased since the height of the financial crisis in October of 2008? Why?

7. Go to www.osfi-bsif.gc.ca/ and click on the link "Banks." Then select the link "Financial Data—Banks." Once there, choose the latest release of monthly data.

a. Pick the "Total All Banks" tab and then hit "Submit" and record the total assets figure. Now pick the "Total Domestic Banks" tab and then hit "Submit" and record the total assets figure. What percentage of all Canadian chartered bank assets do domestic chartered banks have versus foreign chartered banks?

b. Now retrieve the consolidated balance sheets for some individual chartered banks by picking their names from the drop-down tab. Which chartered bank has the largest total consolidated assets?

(*Hint:* The big six banks, in order from greatest to smallest, are Royal Bank of Canada, Toronto-Dominion Bank, Bank of Nova Scotia, Bank of Montreal, Canadian Imperial Bank of Commerce, and National Bank of Canada.)

c. Which bank has the largest domestic assets?

d. What percent of Canadian GDP are the consolidated assets of the bank listed in part (b)? (*Hint:* You can find Canadian GDP at www.statcan.gc.ca/start-debut-eng.html using the links "Monthly GDP growth" and then "CSV version of real GDP chart.")

8. Go to fdic.gov and click on the tab "Industry Analysis" and then on the link "Research & Analysis." Under "Historical Perspectives," select "The First Fifty Years: A History of the FDIC 1933–1983." Open Chapter 3, "Establishment of the FDIC," and scroll down to the section entitled "The Banking Crisis of 1933" and the section entitled "Federal Deposit Insurance Legislation." Read the section and then answer these questions.

a. U.S. President Roosevelt was sworn in on March 4, 1933. What was one of his first official acts in response to the banking crisis?

b. How many U.S. banks suspended operations during 1933?

c. Who was the chief proponent of U.S. federal deposit insurance in Congress?

d. How much coverage did the temporary fund for U.S. federal deposit insurance provide?

9. The U.S. Government Accountability Office (GAO) does research to support U.S. congressional decision making. After the Long Term Capital Management (LTCM) crisis, the GAO produced a summary of the events of the crisis located at www.gao.gov/products/GGD-00-3. Read the summary and then answer the following questions.

a. How much of its capital did LTCM lose in 1998?

b. Why did the GAO conclude that LTCM was able to establish leveraged trading positions of a size that posed systemic risk to the banking system?

c. What was the recommendation of the President's Working Group regarding the Securities and Exchange Commission (SEC) and the Commodity Futures Trading Commission (CFTC)?

d. Could the failure of a hedge fund, like LTCM, pose problems for financial markets and the economy of Canada? Would the fund have to be Canadian-based? Explain.

CHAPTER 18

Macroeconomics: Events and Ideas

A TALE OF TWO SLUMPS

The breakthroughs in macroeconomics that occurred in the wake of the Great Depression are being revived today to confront the difficulties created by the Great Recession.

Minnesota Historical Society/Corbis

Andrew Lichtenstein/Corbis

I N NOVEMBER 2002, THE U.S. Federal Reserve held a special conference to honour Milton Friedman on the occasion of his 90th birthday. Among those delivering tributes was Ben Bernanke, who had recently moved to the Fed from Princeton University and would later become the Fed's chairman. In his tribute, Bernanke surveyed Friedman's intellectual contributions, with particular focus on the argument made by Friedman and his collaborator Anna Schwartz that the Great Depression of the 1930s could have been avoided if only the Fed had done its job properly.

At the close of his talk, Bernanke directly addressed Friedman and Schwartz, who were sitting in the audience: "Let me end my talk by abusing slightly my status as an official representative of the Federal Reserve. I would like to say to Milton and Anna: Regarding the Great Depression. You're right, we did it. We're very sorry. But thanks to you, we won't do it again."

Today, in the aftermath of a devastating financial crisis that continues to inflict high unemployment in the United States, those words ring somewhat hollow to Americans. Avoiding severe economic downturns, it turned out, wasn't as easy as Friedman, Schwartz, and Bernanke

had believed. Yet, as bad as they were, the U.S. financial crisis of 2008 and its aftermath were less devastating than the Great Depression.

Canada, like the United States, has also benefitted from the work of Friedman and Schwartz. As was the case with many other nations, Canada suffered greatly from the Great Depression. But we learned a lot from it, as the actions of policy-makers showed during the recession of 2008–2009. When this recession hit, Canadian policy-makers responded quickly and aggressively by rolling out a mix of expansionary fiscal and monetary policies. It was impossible to avoid the economic downturn completely; but, thankfully, perhaps due to the policy intervention, the effects of the recession were less harmful than the Great Depression. Our economy recovered at a faster pace, too. It can be reasonably argued that part of the reason was that macroeconomics had evolved in the 78 years from 1930 to 2008. As a result, policy-makers knew more about the causes of depressions and how to fight them than they did during the Great Depression.

In this chapter we'll trace the development of macroeconomic ideas over the past 80 years. As we'll see, this development has been strongly influ-

WHAT YOU WILL LEARN IN THIS CHAPTER

❯ Why classical macroeconomics was inadequate for the problems posed by the Great Depression

❯ How Keynes and the experience of the Great Depression legitimized **macroeconomic policy activism**

❯ What **monetarism** is and why monetarists claim there are limits to the use of **discretionary monetary policy**

❯ How challenges led to a revision of **Keynesian economics** and the emergence of the **new classical macroeconomics**

❯ Why the **Great Moderation consensus** was challenged by the 2008 financial crisis, leading to fierce debates among economists about the best use of fiscal and monetary policy during challenging economic times

enced by economic events, from the Great Depression of the 1930s, to the stagflation of the 1970s, to the surprising periods of economic stability achieved during the mid-1980s and between the early 1990s and 2007. And as we'll also see, the process continues, as the economic difficulties since 2008 have spurred many macroeconomists to rethink what they thought they knew. ∎

Classical Macroeconomics

The term *macroeconomics* appears to have been coined in 1933 by the Norwegian economist Ragnar Frisch. The date, during the worst year of the Great Depression, is no accident. Still, there were economists analyzing what we now consider macroeconomic issues—the behaviour of the aggregate price level and aggregate output—before then.

Money and the Price Level

In Chapter 16, we described the classical *model of the price level*. According to the classical model, prices are flexible, making the aggregate supply curve vertical even in the short run.[1] In this model, an increase in the money supply leads, other things equal, to an equal proportional rise in the aggregate price level, with no effect on aggregate output. As a result, increases in the money supply lead to inflation, and that's all. Before the 1930s, the classical model of the price level dominated economic thinking about the effects of monetary policy.

Did classical economists really believe that changes in the money supply affected only aggregate prices, without any effect on aggregate output? Probably not. Historians of economic thought argue that before 1930 most economists were aware that changes in the money supply affect aggregate output as well as aggregate prices in the short run—or, to use modern terms, they were aware that the short-run aggregate supply curve slopes upward. But they regarded such short-run effects as unimportant, stressing the long run instead. It was this attitude that led John Maynard Keynes to scoff at the focus on the long run, about which he said the "long run is a misleading guide to current affairs. In the long run we are all dead."

The Business Cycle

Classical economists were, of course, also aware that the economy did not grow smoothly. The American economist Wesley Mitchell pioneered the quantitative study of business cycles. In 1920 he founded the National Bureau of Economic Research, an independent, non-profit organization that to this day has the official role of declaring the beginnings of recessions and expansions in the United States. Thanks to Mitchell's work, the *measurement* of business cycles was well advanced by 1930. But there was no widely accepted *theory* of business cycles.

In the absence of any clear theory, conflicts arose among policy-makers on how to respond to a recession. Some economists favoured expansionary monetary and fiscal policies to fight a recession. Others believed that such policies would worsen the slump or merely postpone the inevitable. For example, in 1934 Harvard's Joseph Schumpeter, now famous for his early recognition of the importance of technological change, warned that any attempt to alleviate the Great Depression with expansionary monetary policy "would, in the end, lead to a collapse worse than the one it was called in to remedy." When the Great Depression hit, policy was paralyzed by this lack of consensus. In many cases, economists now believe, policy moved in the wrong direction.

Necessity was, however, the mother of invention. As we'll explain next, the Great Depression provided a strong incentive for economists to develop theories that could serve as a guide to policy—and economists responded.

---

[1]The primary difference between the short run and long run in macroeconomics is the behaviour of prices. Many macroeconomists feel that in the short run, prices are sticky (not fully flexible); while in the long run, prices are fully or perfectly flexible. This leads to a short-run aggregate supply curve that is upward sloping, and a long-run aggregate supply curve that is perfectly vertical.

ECONOMICS ▶IN ACTION

WHEN DID THE BUSINESS CYCLE BEGIN?

The modern business cycle probably originated in Britain—home of the Industrial Revolution—which was already a largely industrial and urban society by 1820. The British recession of 1846–1847 had a particularly modern feel: it followed a bout of "irrational exuberance" in which firms spent heavily on an exciting new technology—railways—and then realized they had overdone it.

But when did Canada have its first business cycle? Unfortunately, we can't know for sure. There are two reasons for this. The first reason is that the further back in time we go, the less economic data are available. We have GDP data only from 1926 and output by industry from 1919. The other is that business cycles, in the modern sense, depend upon having a predominantly industrial society. We know that Canada had an overwhelmingly rural, agricultural economy throughout most of the 1800s. But by 1919—the first year for which we have data—industrial activities were already 1.5 times more important than agriculture. So we can't say precisely when Canada became sufficiently industrialized to experience a modern business cycle. Figure 18-1 shows the estimates of the changing percentages of GDP coming from agriculture and from manufacturing and mining over the period from 1919 to 1969. The figure shows that the importance of agriculture in national output declined, while manufacturing continued to gain in economic importance in these 50 years.

But why does the modern business cycle depend on having a predominantly industrialized society? Fluctuations in aggregate output in agricultural economies are very different from the business cycles we know today. That's because the prices of agricultural goods tend to be highly flexible. As a result, the short-run aggregate supply curve of a mainly agricultural economy is probably close to vertical, so demand shocks don't cause output fluctuations—they cause price fluctuations (volatility). Instead, fluctuations on the farm are driven mainly by weather, making shifts of the short-run aggregate supply curve the primary source of output and employment fluctuations. In contrast, with the modern business cycle fluctuations in output and employment are largely the result of shifts in the aggregate demand curve.

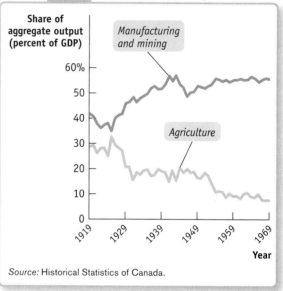

FIGURE 18-1 The Changing Character of the Canadian Economy

Source: Historical Statistics of Canada.

CHECK YOUR UNDERSTANDING 18-1

1. When Ben Bernanke, in his tribute to Milton Friedman, said that "Regarding the Great Depression … we did it," he was referring to the fact that the U.S. Federal Reserve at the time did not pursue expansionary monetary policy. Why would a classical economist have thought that action by the Federal Reserve would not have made a difference in the length or depth of the Great Depression?

Solutions appear at back of book.

▼ **Quick Review**

- Classical macroeconomists focused on the long-run effects of monetary policy on the aggregate price level, ignoring any short-run effects on aggregate output.

- By the time of the Great Depression, the measurement of business cycles was well advanced, but there was no widely accepted theory about why they happened.

The Great Depression and the Keynesian Revolution

The Great Depression demonstrated, once and for all, that economists cannot safely ignore the short run. Not only was the economic pain severe; it threatened to destabilize societies and political systems. In particular, the economic plunge helped Adolf Hitler rise to power in Germany.

The whole world wanted to know how this economic disaster could be happening and what should be done about it. But because there was no widely accepted theory of the business cycle, economists gave conflicting and, we now believe, often harmful advice. Some believed that only a huge change in the economic system—such as having the government take over much of private industry and replace markets with a command economy—could end the slump. Others argued that slumps were natural—even beneficial—and that nothing should be done.

Some economists, however, argued that the slump both could and should be cured—without giving up on the basic idea of a market economy. In 1930 the British economist John Maynard Keynes compared the problems of the U.S. and British economies to those of a car with a defective starter. Getting the economy running, he argued, would require only a modest repair, not a complete overhaul.

Nice metaphor. But what was the nature of the trouble?

Keynes's Theory

In 1936 Keynes presented his analysis of the Great Depression—his explanation of what was wrong with the economy's starter—in a book titled *The General Theory of Employment, Interest, and Money*. In 1946 the great American economist Paul Samuelson wrote that "it is a badly written book, poorly organized ... . Flashes of insight and intuition intersperse tedious algebra ... . We find its analysis to be obvious and at the same time new. In short, it is a work of genius." *The General Theory* isn't easy reading, but it stands with Adam Smith's *The Wealth of Nations* as one of the most influential books on economics ever written.

As Samuelson's description suggests, Keynes's book is a vast stew of ideas. *Keynesian economics* is principally based on two innovations. First, Keynes emphasized the short-run effects of changes in aggregate demand on aggregate output, rather than the long-run determination of the aggregate price level. As Keynes's famous remark about being dead in the long run suggests, until his book appeared most economists had treated short-run macroeconomics as a minor issue. Keynes focused the attention of economists on situations in which the short-run aggregate supply curve slopes upward and shifts in the aggregate demand curve affect aggregate output and employment as well as aggregate prices.

FIGURE   18-2   Classical versus Keynesian Macroeconomics

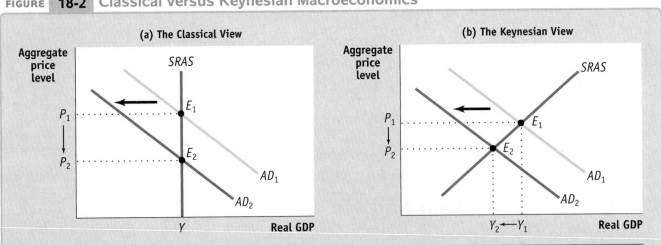

One important difference between classical and Keynesian economics involves the short-run aggregate supply curve. Panel (a) shows the classical view: the *SRAS* curve is vertical, so shifts in aggregate demand affect the aggregate price level but not aggregate output. Panel (b) shows the Keynesian view: in the short run the *SRAS* curve slopes upward, so shifts in aggregate demand affect aggregate output as well as aggregate prices.

Figure 18-2 illustrates the difference between Keynesian and classical macroeconomics. Both panels of the figure show the short-run aggregate supply curve, *SRAS*; in both it is assumed that for some reason the aggregate demand curve shifts leftward from AD_1 to AD_2—let's say in response to a fall in stock market prices that leads households to reduce consumer spending.

Panel (a) shows the classical view: the short-run aggregate supply curve is vertical. The decline in aggregate demand leads to a fall in the aggregate price level, from P_1 to P_2, but no change in aggregate output. Panel (b) shows the Keynesian view: the short-run aggregate supply curve slopes upward, so the decline in aggregate demand leads to both a fall in the aggregate price level, from P_1 to P_2, and a fall in aggregate output, from Y_1 to Y_2.

As we've already explained, many classical macroeconomists would have agreed that panel (b) was an accurate story in the short run—but they regarded the short run as unimportant. Keynes disagreed. [Just to be clear, there isn't any diagram that looks like panel (b) of Figure 18-2 in Keynes's *General Theory*. But Keynes's discussion of aggregate supply, translated into modern terminology, clearly implies an upward-sloping *SRAS* curve.]

Classical economists emphasized the role of changes in the money supply in shifting the aggregate demand curve, paying little attention to other factors. Keynes's second innovation was his argument that other factors, especially changes in "animal spirits"—these days usually referred to with the bland term *business confidence*—are mainly responsible for business cycles. Before Keynes, economists often argued that a decline in business confidence would have no effect on either the aggregate price level or aggregate output, as long as the money supply stayed constant. Keynes offered a very different picture.

Keynesian economics has penetrated deeply into the public consciousness, to the extent that many people who have never heard of Keynes, or have heard of him but think they disagree with his theory, use Keynesian ideas all the time. For example, suppose that a business commentator says something like this: "Because of a decline in business confidence, investment spending slumped, causing a recession." Whether the commentator knows it or not, that statement is pure Keynesian economics.

> **Keynesian economics** rests on two main tenets: changes in aggregate demand affect aggregate output, employment, and prices; and changes in business confidence cause the business cycle.

💭 FOR INQUIRING MINDS

THE POLITICS OF KEYNES

The term Keynesian economics is sometimes used as a synonym for left-wing economics: authors seem to believe that because Keynes offered a rationale for some kinds of government activism, he was a leftist of some kind, maybe even a socialist. But the truth is more complicated.

As we explain in the text, Keynesian ideas have actually been accepted across a broad range of the political spectrum. In 2004 the American president was a conservative, as was his top economist, N. Gregory Mankiw; but Mankiw is also the editor of a collection of readings titled *New Keynesian Economics*.

And Keynes himself was no socialist— and not much of a leftist. At the time *The General Theory* was published, many intellectuals in Britain believed that the Great Depression was the final crisis of the capitalist economic system and that only a government takeover of industry

Some people consider *Keynesian economics* a synonym for *left-wing economics*. But this is misguided because in reality the ideas of John Maynard Keynes have been accepted across a broad sweep of the political spectrum.

could save the economy. Keynes, in contrast, argued that all the system needed was a narrow technical fix. In that sense, his ideas were pro-capitalist and politically conservative.

What is true is that the rise of Keynesian economics in the 1940s, 1950s, and 1960s went along with a general enlargement of the role of government in the economy, and those who favoured a larger role for government tended to be enthusiastic Keynesians. Conversely, a swing of the pendulum back toward free-market policies in the 1970s and 1980s was accompanied by a series of challenges to Keynesian ideas, which we describe later in this chapter. But it's perfectly possible to have conservative political preferences while respecting Keynes's contribution and equally possible to be very liberal while questioning Keynes's ideas.

Macroeconomic policy activism is the use of monetary and fiscal policy to smooth out the business cycle.

Keynes himself more or less predicted that his ideas would become part of what "everyone knows." In another famous passage, this from the end of *The General Theory*, he wrote: "Practical men, who believe themselves to be quite exempt from any intellectual influences, are usually the slaves of some defunct economist."

Policy to Fight Recessions

The main practical consequence of Keynes's work was that it legitimized **macroeconomic policy activism**—the use of monetary and fiscal policy to smooth out the business cycle.

Macroeconomic policy activism wasn't something completely new. Before Keynes, many economists had argued for using monetary expansion to fight economic downturns—though others were fiercely opposed. Some economists had even argued that temporary budget deficits were a good thing in times of recession—though others disagreed strongly. In practice, during the 1930s many governments followed policies that we would now call Keynesian. In Canada, the Bennett government provided some welfare programs to fight the depression, which made the federal government run larger budget deficits.

However, these efforts were half-hearted. Worried about its budget deficit, the Bennett government began to cut spending in 1932. Given that the economy was still depressed, these spending cuts worsened economic conditions.

After World War II, Keynesian ideas were broadly accepted by economists. There were, however, a series of challenges to those ideas, which led to a considerable shift in views even among those economists who continued to believe that Keynes was broadly right about the causes of recessions. In the upcoming section, we'll learn about those challenges and the schools, *new classical economics* and *new Keynesian economics*, that emerged.

ECONOMICS ► IN ACTION·

THE END OF THE GREAT DEPRESSION

It would make a good story if Keynes's ideas had led to a change in economic policy that brought the Great Depression to an end. Unfortunately, that's not what happened. Still, the way the Depression ended did a lot to convince economists that Keynes was right.

The basic message many of the young economists who adopted Keynes's ideas in the 1930s took from his work was that economic recovery requires aggressive fiscal expansion—deficit spending on a large scale to create jobs. And that is what they eventually got; but it wasn't because politicians were persuaded. Instead, what happened was a very large war, World War II.

Figure 18-3 shows the Canadian unemployment rate and the federal budget deficit as a percentage of GDP from 1930 to 1950. As you can see, during the 1930s, deficit spending occurred on a very modest scale. It was only after Canada entered World War II in 1939 that federal deficit spending

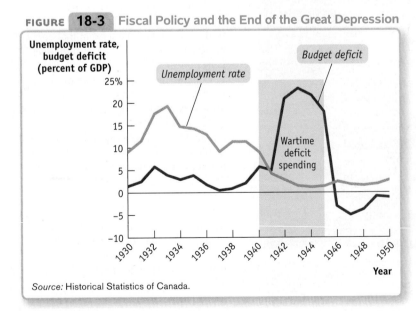

FIGURE 18-3 Fiscal Policy and the End of the Great Depression

Source: Historical Statistics of Canada.

really began to increase—eventually reaching truly mammoth proportions (23% of GDP) by 1943.[2]

And the economy recovered. World War II wasn't intended as a Keynesian fiscal policy, but it demonstrated that expansionary fiscal policy can, in fact, create jobs in the short run.

> **CHECK YOUR UNDERSTANDING**   18-2

1. The Canadian Federation of Independent Business (CFIB) calculates an index of business confidence known as the Business Barometer. In February 2013, the CFIB stated, "After a lacklustre November and December, Canadian entrepreneurs are feeling more optimistic in early 2013 … The Business Barometer index continued January's upward trend by rising another half a point to 66.2 in February." Ted Mallett, CFIB's chief economist and vice-president reported, "For the first time in a while, small business owners are reporting index numbers that indicate the economy is growing nearer its potential. The January and February results suggest Canadians are seeing modest, but widespread economic growth." Do these statements support Keynesian theory? Which conclusion would a Keynesian economist draw for the need for public policy?

Solution appears at back of book.

Challenges to Keynesian Economics

Keynes's ideas fundamentally changed the way economists think about business cycles. They did not, however, go unquestioned. In the decades that followed the publication of *The General Theory*, Keynesian economics faced a series of challenges. As a result, the consensus of macroeconomists retreated somewhat from the strong version of Keynesianism that prevailed in the 1950s. In particular, economists became much more aware of the limits to macroeconomic policy activism.

The Revival of Monetary Policy

Keynes's *The General Theory* suggested that monetary policy wouldn't be very effective in depression conditions. Many modern macroeconomists agree: in Chapter 16 we introduced the concept of a *liquidity trap*, a situation in which monetary policy is ineffective because the interest rate is down against the zero bound. In the 1930s, when Keynes wrote, interest rates were, in fact, very close to 0%. (The term *liquidity trap* was first introduced by the British economist John Hicks in a 1937 paper, "Mr. Keynes and The Classics: A Suggested Interpretation," that summarized Keynes's ideas.)

But even when the era of near-0% interest rates came to an end after World War II, many economists continued to emphasize fiscal policy and downplay the usefulness of monetary policy. Eventually, however, macroeconomists

Milton Friedman and Anna Schwartz played a key role in convincing macroeconomists of the importance of monetary policy. Both economists continued to contribute into their nineties.

---

[2]Unfortunately the Bennett government attempted to balance the budget through much of the 1930s. This makes them responsible for unnecessarily deepening and prolonging the Great Depression. They ignored Keynes's recommendation that in times of economic downturn, good government fiscal policy prescribes running a deficit in order to give the economy a needed boost. According to this view, good government fiscal policy is about more than balancing the books. Keynes argued that good budgetary policy should be about smoothing out the inevitable boom-and-bust cycles of market economies— running deficits during downturns and surpluses in good times.

reassessed the importance of monetary policy. A key milestone in this reassessment was the 1963 publication of *A Monetary History of the United States, 1867–1960* by Milton Friedman, of the University of Chicago, and Anna Schwartz, of the U.S. National Bureau of Economic Research. Friedman and Schwartz showed that business cycles had historically been associated with fluctuations in the money supply. In particular, the money supply fell sharply during the onset of the Great Depression. Friedman and Schwartz persuaded many, though not all, economists that the Great Depression could have been avoided if the U.S. Federal Reserve had acted to prevent that monetary contraction. They persuaded most economists that monetary policy should play a key role in economic management.

The revival of interest in monetary policy was significant because it suggested that the burden of managing the economy could be shifted away from fiscal policy—meaning that economic management could largely be taken out of the hands of politicians. Fiscal policy, which must involve changing tax rates or government spending, necessarily involves political choices. If the government tries to stimulate the economy by cutting taxes, it must decide whose taxes will be cut. If it tries to stimulate the economy with government spending, it must decide what to spend the money on.

Monetary policy, in contrast, does not involve such choices: when the central bank cuts interest rates to fight a recession, it cuts everyone's interest rate at the same time. So a shift from relying on fiscal policy to relying on monetary policy makes macroeconomics a more technical, less political issue. In fact, as we learned in Chapter 14, monetary policy in most major economies is set by an independent central bank that is insulated from the political process.

Monetarism

After the publication of *A Monetary History,* Milton Friedman led a movement that sought to eliminate macroeconomic policy activism while maintaining the importance of monetary policy. **Monetarism** asserts that GDP will grow steadily if the money supply grows steadily. The monetarist policy prescription was to have the central bank target a constant rate of growth of the money supply, such as 3% per year, and maintain that target regardless of any fluctuations in the economy.

It's important to realize that monetarism retained many Keynesian ideas. Like Keynes, Friedman asserted that the short run is important and that short-run changes in aggregate demand affect aggregate output as well as aggregate prices. Like Keynes, he argued that policy should have been much more expansionary during the Great Depression.

Monetarists argued, however, that most of the efforts of policy-makers to smooth out the business cycle actually make things worse. In Chapter 13 we discussed concerns over the usefulness of *discretionary fiscal policy*—changes in taxes or government spending, or both, in response to the state of the economy. As we explained, government perceptions about the economy often lag behind reality, and there are further lags in changing fiscal policy and in its effects on the economy. As a result, discretionary fiscal policies intended to fight a recession often end up feeding a boom, and vice versa. According to monetarists, **discretionary monetary policy,** changes in the interest rate or the money supply by the central bank in order to stabilize the economy, faces the same problem of lags as fiscal policy, but to a lesser extent.

Friedman also argued that if the central bank followed his advice and refused to change the money supply in response to fluctuations in the economy, fiscal policy would be much less effective than Keynesians believed. In Chapter 10 we analyzed the phenomenon of *crowding out,* in which government deficits drive up interest rates and lead to reduced investment spending. Friedman and others pointed out that if the money supply is held fixed while the government pursues an expansionary fiscal policy, crowding out will occur and will limit the effect of the fiscal expansion on aggregate demand.

Figure 18-4 illustrates this argument. Panel (a) shows aggregate output and the aggregate price level. AD_1 is the initial aggregate demand curve and *SRAS*

Monetarism asserts that GDP will grow steadily if the money supply grows steadily.

Discretionary monetary policy is the use of changes in the interest rate or the money supply to stabilize the economy.

FIGURE **18-4** **Fiscal Policy with a Fixed Money Supply**

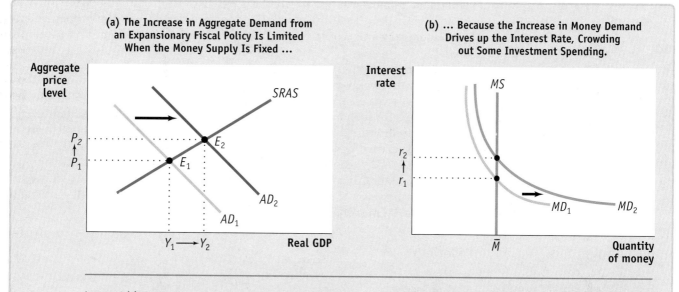

In panel (a) an expansionary fiscal policy shifts the *AD* curve rightward, driving up both the aggregate price level and aggregate output. However, this leads to an increase in the demand for money. If the money supply is held fixed, as in panel (b), the increase in money demand drives up the interest rate, reducing investment spending and offsetting part of the fiscal expansion. So the shift of the *AD* curve is less than it would otherwise be: fiscal policy becomes less effective when the money supply is held fixed.

is the short-run aggregate supply curve. At the initial equilibrium, E_1, the level of aggregate output is Y_1 and the aggregate price level is P_1. Panel (b) shows the money market. *MS* is the money supply curve and MD_1 is the initial money demand curve, so the initial interest rate is r_1.

Now suppose the government increases purchases of goods and services. We know that this will shift the *AD* curve rightward, as illustrated by the shift from AD_1 to AD_2, and that aggregate output will rise, from Y_1 to Y_2, and the aggregate price level will rise, from P_1 to P_2. Both the rise in aggregate output and the rise in the aggregate price level will, however, increase the demand for money, shifting the money demand curve rightward from MD_1 to MD_2. This drives up the equilibrium interest rate to r_2. Friedman's point was that this rise in the interest rate reduces investment spending, partially offsetting the initial rise in government spending. As a result, the rightward shift of the *AD* curve is smaller than the multiplier analysis in Chapter 13 indicated. And Friedman argued that with a constant money supply, the multiplier is so small that there's not much point in using fiscal policy, even in a depressed economy.

But Friedman didn't favour activist monetary policy either. He argued that the problems of time lags that limit the ability of discretionary fiscal policy to stabilize the economy also apply to discretionary monetary policy. Friedman's solution was to put monetary policy on "autopilot." The central bank, he argued, should follow a **monetary policy rule,** a formula that determines its actions and leaves it relatively little discretion. During the 1960s and 1970s, most monetarists favoured a monetary policy rule of slow, steady growth in the money supply. Underlying this view was the concept of the **velocity of money,** the ratio of nominal GDP to the money supply. Velocity is a measure of the number of times the average dollar bill in the economy turns over per year between buyers and sellers (e.g., I tip the Starbucks barista a dollar, she uses it to buy lunch, and so on). This concept gives rise to the *velocity equation:*

(18-1) $M \times V = P \times Y$

where *M* is the money supply, *V* is velocity, *P* is the aggregate price level, and *Y* is real GDP.

A **monetary policy rule** is a formula that determines the central bank's actions.

The **velocity of money** is the ratio of nominal GDP to the money supply.

Monetarists believed, with considerable historical justification, that the velocity of money was stable in the short run and changes only slowly in the long run. As a result, they claimed, steady growth in the money supply by the central bank would ensure steady growth in spending, and therefore in GDP.

Monetarism strongly influenced actual monetary policy in the late 1970s and early 1980s. It quickly became clear, however, that steady growth in the money supply didn't ensure steady growth in the economy: the velocity of money wasn't stable enough for such a simple policy rule to work. Figure 18-5 shows how events eventually undermined the monetarists' view. The figure shows the velocity of money, as measured by the ratio of nominal GDP to M1, from 1967 to 2011. As you can see, until 1982, velocity followed a fairly smooth, seemingly predictable trend. After the Bank of Canada began to adopt monetarist ideas in the late 1970s and early 1980s, however, the velocity of money began moving erratically—probably due to financial market innovations.

FIGURE 18-5 The Velocity of Money

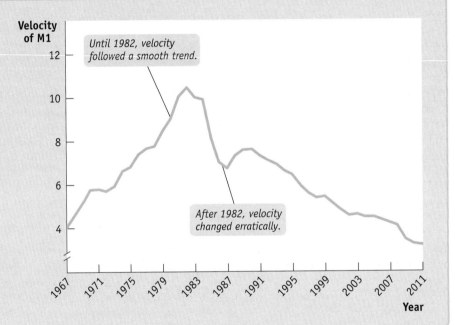

From 1967 to 1982, the velocity of money was stable, leading monetarists to believe that steady growth in the money supply would lead to a stable economy. After 1982, however, velocity began moving erratically, undermining the case for traditional monetarism. As a result, traditional monetarism fell out of favour.
Source: Statistics Canada.

Traditional monetarists—those who believe that GDP will grow steadily if the money supply grows steadily—are hard to find among today's macroeconomists. As we'll see later in the chapter, however, the concern that originally motivated the monetarists—that too much discretionary monetary policy can actually destabilize the economy—has become widely accepted.

Inflation and the Natural Rate of Unemployment

At the same time that monetarists were challenging Keynesian views about how macroeconomic policy should be conducted, other economists—some, but not all of them, monetarists—were emphasizing the limits to what activist macroeconomic policy could achieve.

In the 1940s and 1950s, many Keynesian economists believed that expansionary fiscal policy could be used to achieve full employment on a permanent basis. In the 1960s, however, many economists realized that expansionary policies could cause problems with inflation, but they still believed policy-makers could choose to trade off low unemployment for higher inflation even in the long run.

In 1968, however, Milton Friedman and Edmund Phelps of Columbia University, working independently, proposed the concept of the natural rate of unemployment, which we discussed in Chapter 8. And in Chapter 16 we showed that the natural rate of unemployment is also the non-accelerating inflation rate of unemployment, or NAIRU. According to the **natural rate hypothesis,** because inflation is eventually embedded into expectations, to avoid accelerating inflation over time, the unemployment rate must be high enough that the actual inflation rate equals the expected rate of inflation. Attempts to keep the unemployment rate below the natural rate will lead the expected inflation rate to exceed the actual inflation rate, and generate an ever-rising inflation rate.

The natural rate hypothesis limits the role of activist macroeconomic policy compared to earlier theories. Because the government can't keep unemployment below the natural rate, its task is not to keep unemployment low but to keep it *stable*—to prevent large fluctuations in unemployment in either direction.

The Friedman–Phelps hypothesis made a strong prediction: that the apparent trade-off between unemployment and inflation would not survive an extended period of rising prices. Once inflation was embedded into the public's expectations, it would continue even in the face of high unemployment. Sure enough, that's exactly what happened in the 1970s. This accurate prediction was one of the triumphs of macroeconomic analysis, and it convinced the great majority of economists that the natural rate hypothesis was correct. In contrast to traditional monetarism, which declined in influence as more evidence accumulated, the natural rate hypothesis has become almost universally accepted among macroeconomists, with a few qualifications. (Some macroeconomists believe that at very low or negative rates of inflation the hypothesis doesn't work.)

The Political Business Cycle

One final challenge to Keynesian economics focused not on the validity of the economic analysis but on its political consequences. A number of economists and political scientists pointed out that activist macroeconomic policy lends itself to political manipulation.

Statistical evidence suggests that election results tend to be determined by the state of the economy in the months just before the election. For example, in the United States, if the economy is growing rapidly and the unemployment rate is falling in the six months or so before Election Day, the incumbent party tends to be re-elected even if the economy performed poorly in the preceding three years.

This creates an obvious temptation to abuse activist macroeconomic policy: pump up the economy in an election year, and pay the price in higher inflation and/or higher unemployment later. The result can be unnecessary instability in the economy, a **political business cycle** caused by the use of macroeconomic policy to serve political ends.

An often-cited example is the combination of expansionary fiscal and monetary policy that led to rapid growth in the U.S. economy just before the 1972 election and a sharp acceleration in inflation after the election. Kenneth Rogoff, a highly respected macroeconomist who served as chief economist at the International Monetary Fund, has proclaimed Richard Nixon, the president at the time, "the all-time hero of political business cycles."

As we learned in Chapter 14, one way to avoid a political business cycle is to place monetary policy in the hands of an independent central bank, insulated from political pressure. The political business cycle is also a reason to limit the use of discretionary fiscal policy to extreme circumstances.

According to the **natural rate hypothesis,** because inflation is eventually embedded into expectations, to avoid accelerating inflation over time the unemployment rate must be high enough that the actual inflation rate equals the expected inflation rate.

A **political business cycle** results when politicians use macroeconomic policy to serve political ends.

ECONOMICS ▸ IN ACTION

THE BANK OF CANADA'S FLIRTATION WITH MONETARISM

Between 1975 and 1982, the Bank of Canada flirted with monetarism. Previously, the Bank had mainly targeted interest rates, adjusting its target based on the state of the economy. In 1975, however, the Bank began announcing target ranges for several measures of the money supply. It also stopped setting targets for interest rates. Most people saw these changes as a strong move toward monetarism.

In November 1982, however, the Bank of Canada announced that "the recorded M1 series is not a useful guide to policy at this time. In these circumstances the Bank no longer has a target for it." In effect, at that point the Bank turned its back on monetarism. After 1982, the Bank went back to using interest rates as its primary policy instrument. And since 1991, movements in interest rates have been determined by the goal of keeping inflation within its target bounds. If you visit the Bank of Canada's website today, you can find statements bluntly declaring that "the Bank of Canada can't directly increase or decrease the money supply at will."

Why did the Bank flirt with monetarism, and then give it up? The turn to monetarism largely reflected the events of the 1970s, when a sharp rise in inflation had the effect of discrediting traditional economic policies. Also, the fact that the natural rate hypothesis had successfully predicted a worsening of the trade-off between unemployment and inflation increased the prestige of Milton Friedman and his intellectual followers. So policy-makers were willing to try Friedman's policy proposals.

The turn away from monetarism also reflected events: as we saw in Figure 18-5, the velocity of money, which had followed a smooth trend before 1982, became erratic after 1982. This made monetarism seem like a much less good idea.

▼ Quick Review

- Early Keynesianism downplayed the effectiveness of monetary as opposed to fiscal policy, but later macroeconomists realized that monetary policy is effective except in the case of a liquidity trap.

- According to monetarism, **discretionary monetary policy** does more harm than good and a simple **monetary policy rule** is the best way to stabilize the economy. Monetarists believe that the **velocity of money** was stable and therefore steady growth of the money supply would lead to steady growth of GDP. This doctrine was popular for a time but has receded in influence.

- The **natural rate hypothesis,** now very widely accepted, places sharp limits on what macroeconomic policy can achieve.

- Concerns about a **political business cycle** suggest that the central bank should be independent and that discretionary fiscal policy should be avoided except in extreme circumstances like a liquidity trap.

CHECK YOUR UNDERSTANDING 18-3

1. Consider Figure 18-5.
   a. If the Bank of Canada had pursued a monetarist policy of a constant rate of growth in the money supply, what would have happened to output at the end of 2008 according to the velocity equation?
   b. In fact, the Bank of Canada accelerated the rate of growth in M1 rapidly at the end of 2008, partly in order to counteract a large increase in unemployment. Would a monetarist have agreed with this policy? What limits are there, according to a monetarist point of view, to changing the unemployment rate?

2. What are the limits of macroeconomic policy activism?

Solutions appear at back of book.

Rational Expectations, Real Business Cycles, and New Classical Macroeconomics

As we have seen, one key difference between classical economics and Keynesian economics is that classical economists believed that the short-run aggregate supply curve is vertical, while Keynesian economics claims that the aggregate supply curve slopes upward in the short run. As a result of the upward-sloping supply curve, Keynes argued that demand shocks—shifts in the aggregate short-run aggregate demand curve—can cause fluctuations in aggregate output.

The challenges to Keynesian economics that arose in the 1950s and 1960s from monetarists and from natural rate theorists didn't rely on classical economics ideas. In other words, the challengers still accepted that an increase in aggregate demand leads to a rise in aggregate output in the short run and that a decrease in aggregate demand leads to a fall in aggregate output in the short run. Instead, they argued that the policy medicine—activist macroeconomic policy—could worsen the disease—economic fluctuations.

In the 1970s and 1980s, however, some economists developed an approach to the business cycle known as **new classical macroeconomics,** which revived the classical view that shifts in the aggregate demand curve affect only the aggregate price level, not aggregate output. The new approach evolved in two steps. First, some economists challenged traditional arguments about the slope of the short-run aggregate supply curve based on the concept of *rational expectations.* Second, some economists suggested that changes in productivity cause economic fluctuations, a view known as *real business cycle theory.*

Rational Expectations

In the 1970s a concept known as *rational expectations* had a powerful impact on macroeconomics. **Rational expectations,** originally introduced by John Muth in 1961, is the view that individuals and firms make decisions optimally, using all available information. Since these expectations are optimal, agents learn from past errors and thus do not systematically repeat past mistakes.

For example, workers and employers bargaining over long-term wage contracts need to estimate the inflation rate they expect over the life of that contract. Rational expectations says that in making estimates of future inflation, they won't just look at past rates of inflation; they will also take into account available information about monetary and fiscal policy. Suppose that prices didn't rise last year, but that the monetary and fiscal policies announced by policy-makers make it clear to economic analysts that there will be substantial inflation over the next few years. According to rational expectations, long-term wage contracts being negotiated in this environment will be adjusted today to reflect this future inflation, even though prices didn't rise in the past.

Adopting rational expectations can significantly alter policy-makers' beliefs about the effectiveness of government policy. According to the original version of the natural rate hypothesis, a government attempt to trade off higher inflation for lower unemployment would work in the short run but would eventually fail because higher inflation would get built into expectations. According to rational expectations, we should remove the word *eventually* and replace it with *immediately:* if it's clear that the government intends to trade off higher inflation for lower unemployment, the public will understand this, and expected inflation will immediately rise. So, under rational expectations, government intervention fails in the short run and the long run.

In the 1970s Robert Lucas of the University of Chicago, in a series of highly influential papers, used the logic of rational expectations to argue that monetary policy can change the level of output and unemployment only if it comes as a surprise to the public. Otherwise, attempts to lower unemployment will simply result in higher prices. According to Lucas's **rational expectations model** of the economy, monetary policy isn't useful in stabilizing the economy after all. In 1995 Lucas won the Nobel Prize in economics for this work, which remains widely admired. However, many—perhaps most—macroeconomists, especially those advising policy-makers, now believe that his conclusions were overstated. The Bank of Canada certainly thinks that it can play a useful role in economic stabilization.

Why, in the view of many macroeconomists, doesn't Lucas's rational expectations model of macroeconomics accurately describe how the economy actually behaves? **New Keynesian economics,** a set of ideas that became influential in the 1990s, provides an explanation. It argues that market imperfections interact to make many prices in the economy temporarily sticky. For example, one new Keynesian argument

New classical macroeconomics is an approach to the business cycle that returns to the classical view that shifts in the aggregate demand curve affect only the aggregate price level, not aggregate output.

Rational expectations is the view that individuals and firms make decisions optimally, using all available information.

According to the **rational expectations model** of the economy, expected changes in monetary policy have no effect on unemployment and output and only affect the price level.

According to **new Keynesian economics,** market imperfections can lead to price stickiness for the economy as a whole.

Real business cycle theory claims that fluctuations in the rate of growth of total factor productivity cause the business cycle.

points out that monopolists don't have to be too careful about setting prices exactly "right": if they set a price a bit too high, they'll lose some sales but make more profit on each sale; if they set the price too low, they'll reduce the profit per sale but sell more. As a result, even small costs to changing prices, so-called *menu costs* we described in Chapter 8, can lead to substantial price stickiness in the short run. This stickiness results in an upward sloping short-run aggregate supply curve and makes the economy as a whole behave in a Keynesian fashion.

Over time, new Keynesian ideas combined with actual experience have reduced the practical influence of the rational expectations concept. Nonetheless, the idea of rational expectations served as a useful caution for macroeconomists who had become excessively optimistic about their ability to manage the economy.

Real Business Cycles

In Chapter 9 we introduced the concept of *total factor productivity*, the amount of output that can be generated with a given level of factor inputs. Total factor productivity grows over time, but that growth isn't smooth. In the 1980s a number of economists argued that slowdowns in productivity growth, which they attributed to pauses in technological progress, are the main cause of recessions. **Real business cycle theory** claims that fluctuations in the rate of growth of total factor productivity cause the business cycle.

Believing that the aggregate supply curve is vertical, real business cycle theorists attribute the source of business cycles to shifts of the aggregate supply curve: a recession occurs when a slowdown in total factor productivity growth shifts the aggregate supply curve leftward, and a recovery occurs when a pickup in total factor

---

💭 FOR INQUIRING MINDS

SUPPLY-SIDE ECONOMICS

During the 1970s a group of economic writers began propounding a view of economic policy that came to be known as "supply-side economics." The core of this view was the belief that reducing tax rates, and so increasing the incentives to work and invest, would have a powerful positive effect on the growth rate of potential output. The supply-siders urged the government to cut taxes without worrying about matching spending cuts: economic growth, they argued, would offset any negative effects from budget deficits. Some supply-siders even argued that a cut in tax *rates* would have such a miraculous effect on economic growth that tax *revenues*—the total amount taxpayers pay to the government—would actually rise. That is, some supply-siders argued that the United States was on the wrong side of the *Laffer curve,* a hypothetical relationship between tax rates and total tax revenue that slopes upward at low tax rates but turns downward when tax rates are very high.

In the 1970s supply-side economics was enthusiastically supported by

the editors of the *Wall Street Journal* and other figures in the media, and it became popular with politicians. In 1980 Ronald Reagan made supply-side economics the basis of his U.S. presidential campaign.

Because supply-side economics emphasizes supply rather than demand, and because the supply-siders themselves are harshly critical of Keynesian economics, it might seem as if supply-side theory belongs in our discussion of new classical macroeconomics. But unlike rational expectations and real business cycle theory, supply-side economics is generally dismissed by economic researchers.

The main reason for this dismissal is lack of supporting evidence. Almost all economists agree that tax cuts increase incentives to work and invest. But attempts to estimate these incentive effects indicate that at current Canadian and U.S.

Although many have claimed that the Reagan tax cuts were pro-growth, data from the U.S. Congressional Budget Office and others show no sign of an acceleration in growth after the cuts were implemented.

tax levels, the positive incentive effects aren't nearly strong enough to support the strong claims made by supply-siders. In particular, the supply-side doctrine implies that large tax cuts, such as those implemented by Ronald Reagan in the early 1980s, should sharply raise potential output. Yet estimates of potential output by the U.S. Congressional Budget Office and others show no sign of an acceleration in growth after the Reagan tax cuts.

productivity growth shifts the aggregate supply curve rightward. In the early days of real business cycle theory, the theory's proponents denied that changes in aggregate demand—and, likewise, macroeconomic policy activism—have any effect on aggregate output.

This theory was strongly influential, as shown by the fact that two of the founders of real business cycle theory, Finn Kydland of Carnegie Mellon University and Edward Prescott of the Federal Reserve Bank of Minneapolis, won the 2004 Nobel Prize in economics. The current status of real business cycle theory, however, is somewhat similar to that of rational expectations. The theory is widely recognized as having made valuable contributions to our understanding of the economy, and it serves as a useful caution against too much emphasis on aggregate demand. But many of the real business cycle theorists themselves now acknowledge that their models need an upward-sloping aggregate supply curve to fit the economic data—and that this gives aggregate demand a potential role in determining aggregate output. And as we have seen, policy-makers strongly believe that aggregate demand policy has an important role to play in fighting recessions.

ECONOMICS > IN ACTION

TOTAL FACTOR PRODUCTIVITY AND THE BUSINESS CYCLE

Real business cycle theory argues that fluctuations in the rate of growth of total factor productivity are the principal cause of business cycles. Although many macroeconomists dispute that claim, the theory did draw attention to the fact that there is a strong correlation between the rate of total factor productivity growth and the business cycle. Figure 18-6 shows the annual rate of total factor productivity growth estimated by Statistics Canada. The shaded areas represent recessions. Clearly, recessions tend also to be periods in which the growth of total factor productivity slows sharply or even turns negative. And real business cycle theorists deserve a lot of credit for drawing economists' attention to this fact.

There are, however, disputes about how to interpret this correlation. In the early days of real business cycle theory, proponents argued that productivity fluctuations are entirely the result of uneven technological progress. Critics pointed out, however, that in really severe recessions, like those of the early 1980s, 1990–1991, or 2008–2009, total factor productivity actually declines.[3] If real business cycle theorists were correct, then the level of technology actually regressed during those periods—something that is hard to believe.

So what accounts for declining total factor productivity during recessions? Some economists argue that it is a result, not a cause, of economic downturns. An example may be helpful. Suppose we measure productivity at the local post office by the number of pieces of mail handled, divided by the number of postal workers. Since the post office doesn't lay off workers whenever there's a slow mail day, days in which there is a fall in the amount of mail to process will seem to be days in which workers are especially unproductive. In other words, the slump in business is causing the apparent decline in productivity, not the other way around.

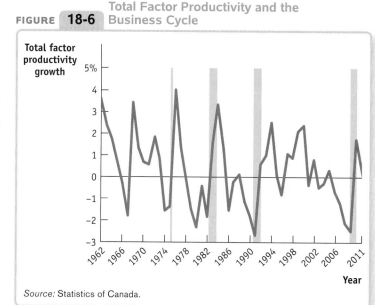

FIGURE 18-6 Total Factor Productivity and the Business Cycle

Source: Statistics of Canada.

---

[3]Canada experienced slowdowns in output in 1967, 1970, 1972, 1975, 1980, 1986, and 1995. These did not qualify as recessions using the common technical definition of a recession as two or more consecutive quarters of falling real output.

The **Great Moderation** is the period from 1992 to 2007 when the Canadian economy experienced relatively small fluctuations and low inflation.

The **Great Moderation consensus** combines a belief in monetary policy as the main tool of stabilization, with skepticism toward the use of fiscal policy, and an acknowledgement that monetary policy generally only has short-run real economic effects.

It's now widely accepted that some of the correlation between total factor productivity and the business cycle is the result of the effect of the business cycle on productivity, rather than the reverse. But the main direction of causation is a subject of continuing research.

CHECK YOUR UNDERSTANDING 18-4

1. In late 2008, as it became clear that Canada, like the United States, was experiencing a recession, the Bank of Canada reduced its target for the overnight interest rate to near zero, as part of a larger aggressively expansionary monetary policy stance. (In the United States the Fed made similar moves, including what they called "quantitative easing.") Most observers agreed that the BOC's aggressive monetary expansion helped reduce the length and severity of the 2008–2009 recession.
   a. What would rational expectations theorists say about this conclusion?
   b. What would real business cycle theorists say?

Solutions appear at back of book.

Consensus and Conflict in Modern Macroeconomics

The 1970s and the first half of the 1980s were a stormy period for the Canadian economy (and for other major economies, too). There were several slowdowns in output that threatened to push the economy into recession, especially in 1975 and again in 1980, followed by a severe recession in 1982–1983 that sent the annual unemployment rate to 12% in 1983. At the same time, the inflation rate soared into double digits—and then plunged. As we have seen, these events left a strong mark on macroeconomic thought.

After about 1991, however, the economy settled down. The recession of 1990–1991 was much milder than the 1982–1983 recession, and the inflation rate stayed below 3%. The period of relative calm in the economy from 1992 to 2007 came to be known as the **Great Moderation.**[4] And the calmness of the economy was to a large extent marked by a similar calm in macroeconomic policy discussion. In fact, it seemed that a broad consensus had emerged about several key macroeconomic issues.

The Great Moderation was, unfortunately, followed by the *Great Recession*, the severe and persistent slump that followed the worldwide 2008 financial crisis. We'll talk shortly about the policy disputes caused by the Great Recession. First, however, let's examine the apparent consensus that emerged during the Great Moderation, which we call the **Great Moderation consensus.** It combines a belief in monetary policy as the main tool of stabilization, with skepticism toward the use of fiscal policy, and an acknowledgement of the policy constraints imposed by the natural rate of unemployment and the political business cycle. To understand where it came from and what still remains in dispute, we'll look at how macroeconomists have changed their answers to five key questions about macroeconomic policy. The five questions and the various answers given by schools of macroeconomics over the decades are summarized in Table 18-1. (In the table, new classical economics is subsumed under classical economics, and new Keynesian economics is subsumed under the Great Moderation consensus.) Notice that classical macroeconomics said no to each question; basically, classical macroeconomists didn't think macroeconomic policy could accomplish very much. But let's go through the questions one by one.

[4]Most major developed economies experienced their own Great Moderation, a period of generally positive output growth coupled with a relatively low and stable rate of inflation. Although each specific country's period of moderation may have started in a different year, generally in the mid-1980s to early 1990s, most ended in 2007 due to the world financial crisis. For example, the U.S.'s Great Moderation ran from 1985 to 2007.

TABLE 18-1   Five Key Questions About Macroeconomic Policy

	Classical macroeconomics	Keynesian macroeconomics	Monetarism	Great Moderation consensus
1. Is expansionary monetary policy helpful in fighting recessions?	No	Not very	Yes	Yes, except in special circumstances
2. Is expansionary fiscal policy effective in fighting recessions?	No	Yes	No	Yes
3. Can monetary and/or fiscal policy reduce unemployment in the long run?	No	Yes	No	No
4. Should fiscal policy be used in a discretionary way?	No	Yes	No	No, except possibly in special circumstances
5. Should monetary policy be used in a discretionary way?	No	Yes	No	Still in dispute

Question 1: Is Expansionary Monetary Policy Helpful in Fighting Recessions?

As we've seen, classical macroeconomists generally believed that expansionary monetary policy was ineffective or even harmful in fighting recessions. In the early years of Keynesian economics, macroeconomists weren't against monetary expansion during recessions, but they tended to believe that it was of doubtful effectiveness. Milton Friedman and his monetarist followers convinced economists that monetary policy is effective after all.

Nearly all macroeconomists now agree that monetary policy can be used to shift the aggregate demand curve and to reduce economic instability. The classical view that changes in the money supply affect only aggregate prices, not aggregate output, has few supporters today. The view held by early Keynesian economists—that changes in the money supply have little effect—has equally few supporters. Now it is generally agreed that in the short run monetary policy is ineffective only in the case of a liquidity trap.

Question 2: Is Expansionary Fiscal Policy Effective in Fighting Recessions?

Classical macroeconomists were, if anything, even more opposed to fiscal expansion than monetary expansion. Keynesian economists, on the other hand, gave fiscal policy a central role in fighting recessions. Monetarists argued that fiscal policy was ineffective if the money supply was held constant. But that strong view has become relatively rare.

Most macroeconomists now agree that fiscal policy, like monetary policy, can shift the aggregate demand curve. Most macroeconomists also agree that the government should not seek to balance the budget regardless of the state of the economy: they agree that the role of the budget as an automatic stabilizer helps keep the economy on an even keel.

Question 3: Can Monetary and/or Fiscal Policy Reduce Unemployment in the Long Run?

Classical macroeconomists didn't believe the government could do anything about unemployment. Some Keynesian economists moved to the opposite extreme, arguing that expansionary policies could be used to achieve a permanently low unemployment rate, perhaps at the cost of some inflation. Monetarists believed that unemployment could not be kept below the natural rate.

Almost all macroeconomists now accept the natural rate hypothesis. This hypothesis leads them to accept sharp limits to what monetary and fiscal policy can accomplish. Effective monetary and fiscal policy, most macroeconomists believe, can limit the size of fluctuations of the actual unemployment rate around the natural rate, but they can't be used to continually keep unemployment below the natural rate in the longer term.

Question 4: Should Fiscal Policy Be Used in a Discretionary Way?

As we've already seen, views about the effectiveness of fiscal policy have gone back and forth, from rejection by classical macroeconomists, to a positive view by Keynesian economists, to a negative view once again by monetarists. Today most macroeconomists believe that tax cuts and spending increases are at least somewhat effective in increasing aggregate demand.

Many, but not all, macroeconomists, however, believe that *discretionary fiscal policy* is usually counterproductive, for the reasons discussed in Chapter 13: the lags in adjusting fiscal policy mean that, all too often, policies intended to fight a slump end up intensifying a boom.

As a result, the macroeconomic consensus gives monetary policy the lead role in economic stabilization. Some, but not all, economists believe that fiscal policy must be brought back into the mix under special circumstances, in particular when interest rates are at or near the zero lower bound and the economy is in a liquidity trap. As we'll see shortly, the proper role of fiscal policy became a huge point of contention after 2008.

Question 5: Should Monetary Policy Be Used in a Discretionary Way?

Classical macroeconomists didn't think that monetary policy should be used to fight recessions; Keynesian economists didn't oppose discretionary monetary policy, but they were skeptical about its effectiveness. Monetarists argued that discretionary monetary policy was doing more harm than good. Where are we today? This remains an area of dispute. Today, under the Great Moderation consensus, most macreconomists agree on these three points:

- Monetary policy should play the main role in stabilization policy.
- The central bank should be independent, insulated from political pressures, in order to avoid a political business cycle and/or a bias to create unexpected bouts of inflation so as to lower the real cost of past government borrowing (debt).
- Discretionary fiscal policy should be used sparingly, both because of policy lags and because of the risks of a political business cycle.

However, the Great Moderation was upended by events that posed very difficult questions—questions that rage as this book goes to press. We'll now examine what happened and why the ongoing debate is so fierce.

Crisis and Aftermath

The Great Recession shattered any sense among macroeconomists that they had entered a permanent era of agreement over key policy questions. Given the nature of the slump, however, this should not have come as a surprise. Why? Because the severity of the slump arguably made the policies that seemed to work during the Great Moderation inadequate.

Under the Great Moderation consensus, there had been broad agreement that the job of stabilizing the economy was best carried out by having the Bank of

Canada and its counterparts abroad raise or lower interest rates as the economic situation warranted. But what should be done if the economy is deeply depressed, but the interest rates the Bank of Canada normally controls are already close to zero and can go no lower (that is, when the economy is in a liquidity trap)? Some economists called for the aggressive use of discretionary fiscal policy and/or unconventional monetary policies that might achieve results despite the zero lower bound. Others strongly opposed these measures, arguing either that they would be ineffective or that they would produce undesirable side effects.

The Debate over Fiscal Policy In 2009 a number of governments, including that of Canada, responded with expansionary fiscal policy, or "stimulus," generally taking the form of a mix of temporary spending measures and temporary tax cuts. From the start, however, these efforts were highly controversial.

Supporters of fiscal stimulus offered three main arguments for breaking with the normal presumption against discretionary fiscal policy:

1. They argued that discretionary fiscal expansion was needed because the usual tool for stabilizing the economy, monetary policy, could no longer be used now that interest rates were near zero.

2. They argued that one normal concern about expansionary fiscal policy— that deficit spending would drive up interest rates, crowding out private investment spending—was unlikely to be a problem in a depressed economy. Again, this was because interest rates were close to zero and likely to stay there as long as the economy was depressed.

3. Finally, they argued that another concern about discretionary fiscal policy—that it might take a long time to get going—was less of a concern than usual given the likelihood that the economy would be depressed for an extended period.

These arguments generally won the day in early 2009. However, opponents of fiscal stimulus raised two main objections:

1. They argued that households and firms would see any rise in government spending as a sign that tax burdens were likely to rise in the future, leading to a fall in private spending that would undo any positive effect. (This is the *Ricardian equivalence* argument that we encountered in Chapter 13.)

2. They also warned that spending programs might undermine investors' faith in the government's ability to repay its debts, leading to an increase in long-term interest rates despite loose monetary policy.

In fact, by 2010 a number of economists were arguing that the best way to boost the economy was actually to cut government spending, which they argued would increase private-sector confidence and lead to a rise in output and employment. This notion, often referred to as the doctrine of "expansionary austerity," was especially popular in Europe, where it was supported by officials at the European Central Bank and became the official policy of the Cameron government in Britain, which took office in the spring of 2010.

One might have hoped that events would resolve this dispute. At the time this book went to press, however, the debate was still raging throughout the world. For instance, critics of fiscal stimulus pointed out that the U.S. stimulus had failed to deliver a convincing fall in unemployment; stimulus advocates, however, had warned from the start that this was likely to happen because the stimulus was too small compared with the depth of the slump. Meanwhile, austerity programs in Britain and elsewhere had also failed to deliver an economic turnaround and, in fact, had seemed to deepen the slump; supporters of these programs, however, argued that they were nonetheless necessary to head off a potential collapse of confidence.

One thing that was clear, however, was that those who had predicted a sharp rise in Canadian interest rates due to budget deficits, leading to conventional crowding out, had been wrong: by the fall of 2011, long-term rates were hitting record lows despite continuing large deficits.

The Debate over Monetary Policy As we saw in Chapter 16, a central bank that wants to increase aggregate demand conventionally buys short-term government debt, which pushes short-term interest rates down, and in turn causes spending to rise. Fortunately for Canada, the downturn in our economy caused by the Great Recession was "relatively" minor, so the Bank of Canada was able to pursue an expansionary monetary policy using conventional means. However, countries and economic regions that were more seriously affected by the recession could not use this method because the relevant interest rates were so close to zero. That is to say, interest rates could not be pushed down any further. So, central banks in this predicament began to look for other alternatives.

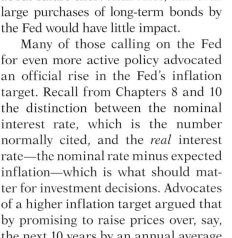

In 2008, the U.S. Federal Reserve took a series of unconventional monetary policy actions in response to the deepening recession and financial crisis.

Beginning in 2008, a number of central banks, including the Bank of England, the Bank of Japan, the Central European Bank, and the U.S. Federal Reserve pursued one such alternative, known as "quantitative easing," which involved buying assets other than short-term government debt, notably long-term debt whose interest rate was still significantly above zero. For example, in November 2010 the Fed began buying $600 billion worth of longer-term U.S. debt in a program generally referred to as "QE2" (quantitative easing 2). The idea was to drive down longer-term interest rates, which arguably matter more for private spending than short-term rates. In September 2011 the Fed announced another program, this time one that would involve selling shorter-term assets with interest rates already near zero and buying longer-term assets instead. This program was called "Operation Twist" as it would have the effect of lowering long-term interest rates while simultaneously raising short-term rates. Again the aim was to encourage increased borrowing/spending by households and firms.

The policy of quantitative easing was controversial, facing criticisms both from those who believed that the Fed was doing too much and from those who believed it was doing too little. Those who believed that the Fed was doing too much were concerned about possible future inflation; they argued that the Fed would find its unconventional measures hard to reverse as the economy recovered and that the end result would be a much too expansionary monetary policy.

Critics from the other side argued that the Fed's actions were likely to be ineffective: long-term interest rates, they suggested, mainly reflected expectations about future short-term rates, and even large purchases of long-term bonds by the Fed would have little impact.

Many of those calling on the Fed for even more active policy advocated an official rise in the Fed's inflation target. Recall from Chapters 8 and 10 the distinction between the nominal interest rate, which is the number normally cited, and the *real* interest rate—the nominal rate minus expected inflation—which is what should matter for investment decisions. Advocates of a higher inflation target argued that by promising to raise prices over, say, the next 10 years by an annual average

"I'll pause for a moment so you can let this information sink in."

rate of 3% or 4%, the Fed could push the real interest rate down even though the nominal rate was up against the zero lower bound.

Such proposals, however, led to fierce disputes. Some economists pointed out that the Fed had fought hard to drive inflation expectations down and argued that changing course would undermine hard-won credibility. Others argued that given the enormous economic and human damage being done by high unemployment, it was time for extraordinary measures, and inflation-fighting could no longer be given first priority.

At the time of writing, these disputes were still raging, and it seemed unlikely that a new consensus about macroeconomic policy would emerge any time soon.

ECONOMICS ▶ IN ACTION

AN IRISH ROLE MODEL?

Over the course of 2010 and 2011 a fierce debate raged, among both economists and policy-makers, about whether countries suffering large budget deficits should move quickly to reduce those deficits if they were also suffering from high unemployment. Many economists argued that spending cuts and/or tax increases should be delayed until economies had recovered. As we explained in the text, however, others argued that fast action on deficits would actually help the economy even in the short run, by improving confidence—a claim that came to be known as "expansionary austerity."

How could this dispute be settled? Researchers turned their attention to historical episodes, in particular to cases in which nations had managed to combine sharp reductions in budget deficits with strong economic growth. One case in particular became a major intellectual battleground: Ireland in the second half of the 1980s.

Panel (a) of Figure 18-7 shows why Ireland's experience drew attention. It compares Ireland's cyclically adjusted budget deficit as a percentage of GDP with its growth rate. Between 1986 and 1989 Ireland drastically reduced its underlying deficits with a combination of spending cuts and tax hikes, and the Irish economy's growth sharply accelerated. A number of observers suggested that nations facing large deficits in the aftermath of the 2008 financial crisis should seek to emulate that experience.

FIGURE **18-7** Economic Indicators for Ireland

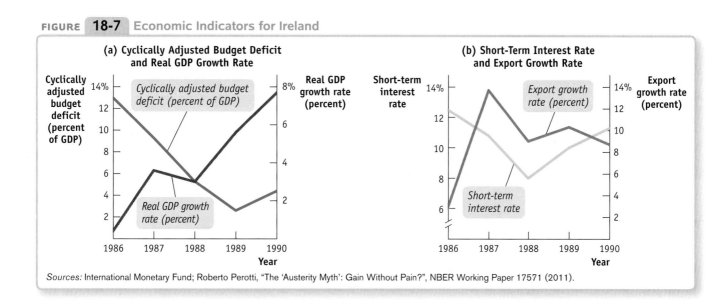

Sources: International Monetary Fund; Roberto Perotti, "The 'Austerity Myth': Gain Without Pain?", NBER Working Paper 17571 (2011).

A closer look, however, suggested that Ireland's situation in the 1980s was very different from that facing Western economies in 2010 and 2011. Panel (b) of Figure 18-7 shows two other economic indicators for Ireland from 1986 to 1990: short-term interest rates and export growth. Ireland entered into fiscal austerity with high interest rates, which fell sharply between 1986 and 1988 as investors gained more confidence in its solvency (although they rose thereafter). At the same time, Ireland had a major export boom, partly due to rapid economic growth in neighbouring Britain. Both factors helped offset any contractionary effects from lower spending and higher taxes.

The point was that these "cushioning" factors would not be available if, say, Canada were to slash spending. Short-term interest rates were already near zero and couldn't fall further, and Canada had no booming neighbours to export to.

By the end of 2011 careful study of the historical record had convinced most, though not all, economists studying the issue that hopes for expansionary austerity were probably misplaced. However, the debate about what Canada and other troubled economies should actually do raged on.

CHECK YOUR UNDERSTANDING 18-5

1. Why did the Great Recession lead to the decline of the Great Moderation consensus? Given events, why is it predictable that a new consensus has not emerged?

Solutions appear at back of book.

SUMMARY

1. Classical macroeconomics asserted that monetary policy affected only the aggregate price level, not aggregate output, and that the short run was unimportant. By the 1930s, measurement of business cycles was a well-established subject, but there was no widely accepted theory of business cycles.

2. Keynesian economics attributed the business cycle to shifts of the aggregate demand curve, often the result of changes in business confidence. Keynesian economics also offered a rationale for **macroeconomic policy activism.**

3. In the decades that followed Keynes's work, economists came to agree that monetary policy as well as fiscal policy is effective under certain conditions. **Monetarism,** a doctrine that called for a **monetary policy rule** as opposed to **discretionary monetary policy** and that argued—based on a belief that the **velocity of money** was stable—that GDP would grow steadily if the money supply grew steadily, was influential for a time but was eventually rejected by many macroeconomists.

4. The **natural rate hypothesis** became almost universally accepted, limiting the role of macroeconomic policy to stabilizing the economy rather than seeking a permanently lower unemployment rate. Fears of a **political business cycle** led to a consensus that monetary policy should be insulated from politics.

5. **Rational expectations** claims that individuals and firms make decisions using all available information. According to the **rational expectations model** of the economy, only unexpected changes in monetary policy affect aggregate output and employment; expected changes merely alter the price level. **Real business cycle theory** claims that changes in the rate of growth of total factor productivity are the main cause of business cycles. Both of these versions of **new classical macroeconomics** received wide attention and respect, but policy-makers and many economists haven't accepted the conclusion that monetary and fiscal policy are ineffective in changing aggregate output.

6. **New Keynesian economics** argues that market imperfections can lead to price stickiness, which makes the short-run aggregate supply curve upward sloping, so that changes in aggregate demand have effects on aggregate output in the short run after all.

7. The **Great Moderation** from 1992 to 2007 generated the **Great Moderation consensus:** belief in monetary policy as the main tool of stabilization; skepticism toward use of fiscal policy, except possibly in exceptional circumstances such as a liquidity trap; and acknowledgement of the policy constraints imposed by the natural rate of unemployment and the political business cycle. But the Great Moderation consensus was challenged by the post-2008 crisis events, as monetary policy lost its effectiveness in the midst of a liquidity trap. As a result, many advocated the use of fiscal policy to address the deep recession.

8. In 2009, a number of governments, including those of Canada and the United States, used fiscal stimulus to support their deeply depressed economies in the face of a liquidity trap. The use of fiscal policy remained highly controversial. In the United States, it failed to significantly reduce unemployment, with critics citing that as proof of its general ineffectiveness, while supporters argued the size of the stimulus was too small. Yet the crowding out predicted by its critics failed to occur.

9. Monetary policy was also hotly debated in the wake of the Great Recession, as the U.S. Federal Reserve pursued "quantitative easing" and other unconventional monetary policies to address the liquidity trap. Critics claimed the Fed was doing too much and would sacrifice its hard-won credibility as an inflation fighter. Others countered that the Fed was doing too little, yet others claimed the Fed's actions would have little impact. Some proposed the Fed adopt a higher inflation target to push the real interest rate down.

KEY TERMS

Keynesian economics, p. 591
Macroeconomic policy activism, p. 592
Monetarism, p. 594
Discretionary monetary policy, p. 594
Monetary policy rule, p. 595

Velocity of money, p. 595
Natural rate hypothesis, p. 597
Political business cycle, p. 597
New classical macroeconomics, p. 599
Rational expectations, p. 599

Rational expectations model, p. 599
New Keynesian economics, p. 599
Real business cycle theory, p. 600
Great Moderation, p. 602
Great Moderation consensus, p. 602

PROBLEMS

1. Since the crash of its stock market in 1989, the Japanese economy has seen little economic growth and some deflation. The accompanying table from the Organisation for Economic Cooperation and Development (OECD) shows some key macroeconomic data for Japan for 1991 (a "normal" year) and 1995–2003.

   a. From the data, determine the type of policies Japan's policy-makers undertook at that time to promote growth.

   b. We can safely consider a short-term interest rate that is less than 0.1% to effectively be a 0% interest rate. What is this situation called? What does it imply about the effectiveness of monetary policy? Of fiscal policy?

Year	Real GDP annual growth rate	Short-term interest rate	Government debt (percent of GDP)	Government budget deficit (percent of GDP)
1991	3.4%	7.38%	64.8%	−1.81%
1995	1.9	1.23	87.1	4.71
1996	3.4	0.59	93.9	5.07
1997	1.9	0.60	100.3	3.79
1998	−1.1	0.72	112.2	5.51
1999	0.1	0.25	125.7	7.23
2000	2.8	0.25	134.1	7.48
2001	0.4	0.12	142.3	6.13
2002	−0.3	0.06	149.3	7.88
2003	2.5	0.04	157.5	7.67

2. In 2012, Canada's C.D. Howe Institute (cdhowe.org/business-cycle-council) formed a Business Cycle Council to act as an arbiter of when Canadian business cycles begin and end. Similarly, in the United States, the National Bureau of Economic Research (NBER) Business Cycle Dating Committee (nber.org/cycles/cyclesmain.html) acts as arbiter of when recessions start and end. The NBER maintains the official chronology of past U.S. business cycles. Go to the websites of these organizations to help answer the following questions.

   a. How many business cycles have occurred in Canada since the end of World War II in 1945? How many have occurred in the United States during the same time? Did the two countries have about the same number of recessions, and if so did they happen at roughly the same times?

   b. From 1945 until the end of the most recent recession, what was the average duration of a business cycle when measured from the end of one expansion (its peak) to the end of the next? That is, what was the average duration of a business cycle as measured from the beginning of one recession until the start of the next one? Over time, has the length of a business cycle been getting shorter, longer, or staying the same?

   c. Recall from Chapter 6 that a recession is sometimes defined as two or more consecutive quarters of falling output. In contrast, the C.D. Howe Institute and the NBER both use more complex indicators of aggregate economic activity, in particular output and employment, to determine when a recession begins or ends. Briefly describe the pros and cons of each approach in determining the duration of a recession.

3. The fall of America's military rival, the Soviet Union, in 1989 allowed the United States to significantly reduce its defence spending in subsequent years. Using the data in the following table from the Economic Report of the President, replicate Figure 18-3 for the 1990–2000 period. Given the strong economic growth in the United States during the late 1990s, why would a Keynesian see the reduction in defence spending during the 1990s as a good thing?

Year	Budget deficit (percent of GDP)	Unemployment rate
1990	3.9%	5.6%
1991	4.5	6.8
1992	4.7	7.5
1993	3.9	6.9
1994	2.9	6.1
1995	2.2	5.6
1996	1.4	5.4
1997	0.3	4.9
1998	−0.8	4.5
1999	−1.4	4.2
2000	−2.4	4.0

4. In the modern world, central banks are free to increase or reduce the money supply as they see fit. However, some people hearken back to the "good old days" of the gold standard. Under the gold standard, the money supply could expand only when the amount of available gold increased.

   a. Under the gold standard, if the velocity of money were stable when the economy was expanding, what would have had to happen to keep prices stable?

   b. Why would modern macroeconomists consider the gold standard a bad idea?

5. For a period of time, monetarists believed that the velocity of money was stable within a country. However, with financial innovation, the velocity began shifting around erratically after 1980. As might be expected, the velocity of money can differ from one country to another—it tends to be faster in countries with more highly developed financial systems. The accompanying

table provides money supply and GDP information in 2005 (a typical pre-crisis year) for seven countries.

Country	National currency	M1 (billions in national currency)	Nominal GDP (billions in national currency)
Canada	Canadian dollars	306	1 374
Egypt	Egyptian pounds	101	539
India	Indian rupees	7 213	35 662
Kenya	Kenyan pounds	231	1 416
South Korea	Korean won	332 345	865 241
Thailand	Thai baht	863	7 093
United States	U.S. dollars	1 369	12 623

Sources: World Economic Outlook (IMF); Datastream; Statistics Canada.

a. Calculate the velocity of money for each of these countries.

The accompanying table shows GDP per capita for each of these countries in 2005 in Canadian dollars.

Country	Nominal GDP per capita (Canadian dollars)
Canada	$40 838
Egypt	1 488
India	846
Kenya	635
South Korea	20 359
Thailand	3 277
United States	49 450

Source: World Economic Outlook (IMF).

b. Rank the countries in descending order of per capita income and velocity of money. Do wealthy countries or poor countries tend to "turn over" their money more times per year? Would you expect wealthy countries to have more sophisticated financial systems?

6. The chapter explains that Kenneth Rogoff proclaimed Richard Nixon "the all-time hero of political business cycles." Using the following table of data from the Economic Report of the President, explain why Nixon may have earned that title. (*Note:* Nixon entered office in January 1969 and was re-elected in November 1972. He resigned in August 1974.)

7. The economy of Albernia is facing a recessionary gap, and the leader of that nation calls together five of its best economists representing the classical, Keynesian, monetarist, real business cycle, and Great Moderation consensus views of the macroeconomy. Explain what policies each economist would recommend and why.

8. Which of the following policy recommendations are consistent with the classical, Keynesian, monetarist, and/or Great Moderation consensus views of the macroeconomy?

a. Since the long-run growth of GDP is 2%, the money supply should grow at 2%.

b. Decrease government spending in order to decrease inflationary pressure.

c. Increase the money supply in order to alleviate a recessionary gap.

d. Always maintain a balanced budget.

e. Decrease the budget deficit as a percent of GDP when facing a recessionary gap.

9. Using a graph like Figure 18-4, show how a monetarist can argue that a contractionary fiscal policy need not lead to a fall in real GDP given a fixed money supply. Explain.

Year	Government receipts (billions of dollars)	Government spending (billions of dollars)	Government budget balance (billions of dollars)	M1 growth	M2 growth	3-month treasury bill rate
1969	$186.9	$183.6	$3.2	3.3%	3.7%	6.68%
1970	192.8	195.6	−2.8	5.1	6.6	6.46
1971	187.1	210.2	−23.0	6.5	13.4	4.35
1972	207.3	230.7	−23.4	9.2	13.0	4.07
1973	230.8	245.7	−14.9	5.5	6.6	7.04

Open-Economy Macroeconomics

SWITZERLAND DOESN'T WANT YOUR MONEY

In 2011, the Swiss National Bank undertook extraordinary actions to protect itself from the consequences of being an open economy.

WHAT YOU WILL LEARN IN THIS CHAPTER

❭ The meaning of the **balance of payments accounts**

❭ The determinants of international capital flows

❭ The role of the **foreign exchange market** and the **exchange rate**

❭ The importance of **real exchange rates** and their role in the **current account**

❭ Considerations that lead countries to choose different **exchange rate regimes,** such as **fixed exchange rates** and **floating exchange rates**

❭ Why open-economy considerations affect macroeconomic policy

ARKING YOUR MONEY IN A Swiss bank is no way to get rich, given the low interest rates Swiss bankers offer. Recently, in fact, Swiss banks have paid negative interest on deposits, charging customers for the service of keeping their funds.

But for generations, Swiss bank accounts have been seen as a way to *stay* rich, a safe place to store your wealth. In the troubled years that followed the 2008 financial crisis, the Swiss reputation for safety became especially important. European investors, in particular, poured money into Switzerland.

And the Swiss hated it—the result of the inflow of foreign funds was a surge in the value of the Swiss franc that wreaked havoc with Swiss exports.

At the beginning of 2008, one Swiss franc traded for about 0.6 euro. By mid-2011, the franc was trading for around 0.9 euro. That meant that Swiss exports, other things equal, had seen a 50% rise in their labour costs relative to competitors elsewhere in Europe. Thanks

to its reputation for quality, Switzerland has been remarkably successful over the years at selling goods to the world market, despite high labour costs. Nobody expects to get a bargain on Swiss watches or Swiss chocolate. But this was pushing matters to the breaking point.

So what was to be done? Starting in early 2009, the Swiss National Bank, Switzerland's equivalent of the Bank of Canada, began selling francs on the foreign exchange market in an attempt to hold down the franc's value. In return for these francs, it received other currencies, mainly U.S. dollars and euros, which it added to its reserves. We're talking about a *lot* of sales: over a period of 2½ years, the bank added about US$180 billion to its foreign exchange reserves, which was about a third of Switzerland's GDP—the equivalent of Canada selling C$600 billion.

Yet even that wasn't enough to stop the franc's rise. In September 2011, as the franc seemed headed for a value of 1 euro or more, the Swiss National Bank announced

that it would do whatever it took—sell an unlimited amount of francs—to keep the franc below a maximum of 0.833 euro per franc (that is, 1.2 francs per euro, which was the way the target was stated). That announcement finally seemed to stop the franc's rise, at least at first.

What the extraordinary efforts of the Swiss National Bank illustrated was the importance of a dimension of macroeconomics that we haven't emphasized so far—the fact that modern national economies are *open economies* that trade goods, services, and assets with the rest of the world. Open-economy macroeconomics is a branch of macroeconomics that deals with the relationships between national economies. In this chapter we'll learn about some of the key issues in open-economy macroeconomics: the determinants of a country's *balance of payments,* the factors affecting *exchange rates,* the different forms of *exchange rate policy* adopted by various countries, and the relationship between exchange rates and macroeconomic policy. ■

A country's **balance of payments accounts** are a summary of the country's transactions with other countries.

Capital Flows and the Balance of Payments

Countries are willing to trade with other countries because they can gain from the exchange. Without international trade, a country is restricted to consuming at a point on its production possibilities frontier, and not beyond. When a country produces a good for which it has a comparative advantage (a lower opportunity cost) and sells that good in exchange for a good for which it has a comparative disadvantage (higher opportunity cost), the country can consume a bundle of goods that lies beyond its production possibilities frontier. Therefore, international trade raises, or improves, the social welfare of a country. In 2012, people living in Canada sold about $810 billion worth of stuff to people living in other countries and bought about $810 billion worth of stuff in return. What kind of stuff? All kinds. Residents of Canada (including firms operating in Canada) sold airplanes, bonds, wheat, and many other items to residents of other countries. Residents of Canada bought cars, stocks, oil, and many other items from residents of other countries.

How can we keep track of these transactions? In Chapter 7 we learned that economists keep track of the domestic economy using the national income and product accounts. Economists keep track of international transactions using a different but related set of numbers, the *balance of payments accounts*.

Balance of Payments Accounts

A country's **balance of payments accounts** are a summary of the country's transactions with other countries.

To understand the basic idea behind the balance of payments accounts, let's consider a small-scale example: not a country, but a family farm. Let's say that we know the following about how last year went financially for the Lemieux family, who own a small apple farm in Nova Scotia:

- They made $100 000 by selling apples.
- They spent $70 000 on running the farm, including purchases of new farm machinery, and another $40 000 buying food, paying utility bills, replacing their worn-out car, and so on.
- They received $500 in interest on their bank account but paid $10 000 in interest on their mortgage.
- They took out a new $25 000 loan to help pay for farm improvements but didn't use all the money immediately. So they put the extra in the bank.

How could we summarize the Lemieux's year? One way would be with a table like Table 19-1, which shows sources of cash coming in and money going out, characterized under a few broad headings. The first row of Table 19-1 shows sales and purchases of goods and services: sales of apples; purchases of groceries, heating oil, that new car, and so on. The second row shows interest payments: the interest the Lemieux family received from their bank account and the interest they paid on their mortgage. The third row shows cash coming in from new borrowing versus money deposited in the bank.

TABLE 19-1 The Lemieux's Financial Year

	Sources of cash	Uses of cash	Net
Purchases or sales of goods and services	Apple sales: $100 000	Farm operation and living expenses: $110 000	−$10 000
Interest payments	Interest received on bank account: $500	Interest paid on mortgage: $10 000	−$9 500
Loans and deposits	Funds received from new loan: $25 000	Funds deposited in bank: $5 500	+$19 500
Total	$125 500	$125 500	$0

In each row we show the net inflow of cash from that type of transaction. So the net in the first row is –$10 000, because the Lemieux family spent $10 000 more than they earned. The net in the second row is –$9500, the difference between the interest the Lemieux family received on their bank account and the interest they paid on the mortgage. The net in the third row is $19 500: the Lemieux family brought in $25 000 with their new loan but put only $5500 of that sum in the bank.

The last row shows the sum of cash coming in from all sources and the sum of all cash used. These sums are equal, by definition: every dollar has a source, and every dollar received gets used somewhere. (What if the Lemieux family hid money under the mattress? Then that would be counted as another "use" of cash.)

A country's balance of payments accounts summarize its transactions with the world with a table basically similar to the way we just summarized the Lemieux's financial year.

Table 19-2 shows a simplified version of the Canadian balance of payments accounts for 2012. Where the Lemieux family's accounts show sources and uses of cash, the balance of payments accounts show payments from foreigners—in effect, sources of cash for Canada as a whole—and payments to foreigners.

Row 1 of Table 19-2 shows payments that arise from sales and purchases of goods and services. For example, the value of Canadian wheat exports and the fees foreigners pay to Canadian engineering companies appear in the second column; the value of Canadian electronic product imports and the fees Canadian companies pay to overseas call centres—the people who often answer your 1-800 calls—appear in the third column.

Row 2 shows *factor income*—the income countries pay for the use of factors of production owned by residents of other countries. Mostly this means investment income: interest paid on loans from overseas, the profits of foreign-owned corporations, and so on. For example, the profits earned by Bombardier Transportation Germany, which is owned by Canadian-based Bombardier Inc., appear in the second column; the profits earned by the Canadian operations of Japanese auto companies appear in the third column. This category also includes some labour income. For example, the wages of a Canadian engineer who works temporarily on a construction site in Dubai are counted in the second column.

Row 3 shows *international transfers*—funds sent by residents of one country to residents of another. The main element here is the remittances that immigrants send to their families in their country of origin.

Rows 4 and 5 of Table 19-2 show payments resulting from sales and purchases of assets, broken down by who is doing the buying and selling. Row 4 shows transactions that involve governments or government agencies, mainly central banks. Row 5 shows private sales and purchases of assets. For example, the 2012 purchase of Canadian oil firm Nexen Inc. by the Chinese state-owned firm China National Offshore Oil Corporation (CNOOC Ltd.) would show up in the second column of row 5; purchases of European stocks by Canadian investors show up in the third column.

In laying out Table 19-2, we have separated rows 1, 2, and 3 into one group and rows 4 and 5 into another. This reflects a fundamental difference in how these two groups of transactions affect the future.

TABLE 19-2 Canadian Balance of Payments in 2012 (billions of dollars)

		Payments from foreigners	Payments to foreigners	Net
1	Sales and purchases of goods and services	$545.8	$582.3	–$36.5
2	Factor incomes	69.5	96.3	–26.8
3	Transfers	8.9	12.6	–3.7
	Current account (1 + 2 + 3)	624.2	–691.2	–67.0
4	Official asset sales and purchases	0	1.7	–1.7
5	Private sales and purchases of assets	182.7	117.4	65.3
	Financial account (4 + 5)	182.7	119.1	63.6
	Total (BOP = CA + FA)	806.9	810.3	–3.4

Source: Statistics Canada.

A country's **balance of payments on current account,** or **current account,** is its balance of payments on goods and services plus net international transfer payments and factor income.

A country's **balance of payments on goods and services** is the difference between its exports and its imports during a given period.

The **merchandise trade balance,** or **trade balance,** is the difference between a country's exports and imports of goods.

A country's **balance of payments on financial account,** or simply its **financial account,** is the difference between its sales of assets to foreigners and its purchases of assets from foreigners during a given period.

When a Canadian resident sells a good such as wheat to a foreigner, that's the end of the transaction. But a financial asset, such as a bond, is different. Remember, a bond is a promise to pay interest and principal in the future. So when a Canadian resident sells a bond to a foreigner, that sale creates a liability: the Canadian resident will have to pay interest and repay principal in the future. The balance of payments accounts distinguish between transactions that don't create liabilities and those that do.

Transactions that don't create liabilities are considered part of the **balance of payments on current account,** often referred to simply as the **current account:** the balance of payments on goods and services plus net international transfer payments and factor income. The balance of row 1 of Table 19-2, –$36.5 billion, corresponds to the most important part of the current account: the **balance of payments on goods and services,** the difference between the value of exports and the value of imports during a given period.

By the way, if you read news reports on the economy, you may well see references to another measure, the **merchandise trade balance,** sometimes referred to as the **trade balance** for short. This is the difference between a country's exports and imports of goods alone—not including services. Economists sometimes focus on the merchandise trade balance, even though it's an incomplete measure, because data on international trade in services aren't as accurate as data on trade in physical goods, and they are also slower to arrive.

The current account, as we've just learned, consists of international transactions that don't create liabilities. Transactions that involve the sale or purchase of assets, and therefore do create future liabilities, are considered part of the **balance of payments on financial account,** or the **financial account** for short. (Until a few years ago, economists often referred to the financial account as the *capital account.* We'll use the modern term, but you may run across the older term.)

So how does it all add up? The shaded rows of Table 19-2 show the bottom lines: the overall Canadian current account and financial account for 2012. As you can see, in 2012 Canada ran a current account deficit: the amount it paid to foreigners for goods, services, factors, and transfers was more than the amount it received. Simultaneously, it ran a financial account surplus: the value of the assets it sold to foreigners was more than the value of the assets it bought from foreigners.

In the 2012 official data, the Canadian current account deficit and financial account surplus didn't offset each other: the financial account surplus in 2012 was $3.4 billion smaller than the current account deficit. But that's just a statistical error, reflecting the imperfection of official data. (That $3.4 billion discrepancy probably reflected foreign purchases of Canadian assets that official data somehow missed.) In fact, it's a basic rule of balance of payments accounting that the current account and the financial account must sum to zero:

(19-1) Current account (CA) + Financial account (FA) = 0

or

$$CA = -FA$$

Why must Equation 19-1 be true? We already saw the fundamental explanation in Table 19-1, which showed the accounts of the Lemieux family: in total, the sources of cash must equal the uses of cash. The same applies to balance of payments accounts. Figure 19-1, a variant on the circular-flow diagram we have found useful in discussing domestic macroeconomics, may help you visualize how this adding up works. Instead of showing the flow of money

FIGURE 19-1 The Balance of Payments

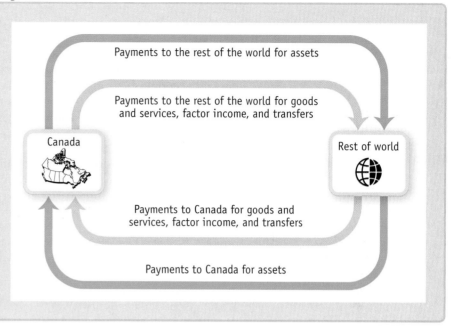

The green arrows represent payments that are counted in the current account. The yellow arrows represent payments that are counted in the financial account. Because the total flow into Canada must equal the total flow out of Canada, the sum of the current account plus the financial account is zero.

Payments to the rest of the world for assets

Payments to the rest of the world for goods and services, factor income, and transfers

Canada

Rest of world

Payments to Canada for goods and services, factor income, and transfers

Payments to Canada for assets

within a national economy, Figure 19-1 shows the flow of money *between* national economies.

Money flows into Canada from the rest of the world as payment for Canadian exports of goods and services, as payment for the use of Canadian-owned factors of production, and as transfer payments. These flows (indicated by the lower green arrow) are the positive components of the Canadian current account. Money also flows into Canada from foreigners who purchase Canadian assets (as shown by the lower yellow arrow)—the positive component of the Canadian financial account.

FOR INQUIRING MINDS

GDP, GNP, AND THE CURRENT ACCOUNT

When we discussed national income accounting in Chapter 7, we derived the basic equation relating GDP to the components of spending:

$$Y = C + I + G + X - IM$$

where X and IM are exports and imports, respectively, of goods and services. But as we've learned, the balance of payments on goods and services is only one component of the current account balance. Why doesn't the national income equation use the current account as a whole?

The answer is that gross domestic product, Y, is the value of goods and services produced domestically. So

it doesn't include international factor income and international transfers, two sources of income that are included in the calculation of the current account balance. The profits of Bombardier's European subsidiaries aren't included in Canada's GDP, and the funds immigrants send home to their families aren't subtracted from GDP.

Shouldn't we have a broader measure that does include these sources of income? Actually, gross *national* product—GNP—does include international factor income. Estimates of Canadian GNP differ slightly from estimates of GDP because GNP adds in items such as the earnings of Canadian companies abroad and

subtracts items such as the interest payments on bonds owned by residents of China and Japan. There isn't, however, any regularly calculated measure that includes transfer payments.

Why do economists use GDP rather than a broader measure? Two reasons. First, the original purpose of the national accounts was to track production rather than income. Second, data on international factor income and transfer payments are generally considered somewhat unreliable. So if you're trying to keep track of movements in the economy, it makes sense to focus on GDP, which doesn't rely on these unreliable data.

At the same time, money flows from Canada to the rest of the world as payment for Canadian imports of goods and services, as payment for the use of foreign-owned factors of production, and as transfer payments. These flows, indicated by the upper green arrow, are the negative components of the Canadian current account. Money also flows from Canada to purchase foreign assets, as shown by the upper yellow arrow—the negative component of the Canadian financial account. As in all circular-flow diagrams, the flow into a box and the flow out of a box are equal. This means that the sum of the yellow and green arrows going into Canada is equal to the sum of the yellow and green arrows going out of Canada. That is,

(19-2) Positive entries on current account (lower green arrow) + Positive entries on financial account (lower yellow arrow) = Negative entries on current account (upper green arrow) + Negative entries on financial account (upper yellow arrow)

Equation 19-2 can be rearranged as follows:

(19-3) Positive entries on current account – Negative entries on current account + Positive entries on financial account – Negative entries on financial account = 0

Equation 19-3 is equivalent to Equation 19-1: the current account plus the financial account—both equal to positive entries minus negative entries—is equal to zero.

But what determines the current account and the financial account?

Modelling the Financial Account

A country's financial account measures its net sales of assets to foreigners. There is, however, another way to think about the financial account: it's a measure of *capital inflows,* of foreign savings that are available to finance domestic investment spending.

What determines these capital inflows?

Part of our explanation will have to wait for a little while because some international capital flows are carried out by governments and central banks, which sometimes act very differently from private investors. But we can gain insight into the motivations for capital flows that are the result of private decisions by using the *loanable funds model* we developed in Chapter 10. In using this model, we make two important simplifications:

- We simplify the reality of international capital flows by assuming that all flows are in the form of loans. In reality, capital flows take many forms, including purchases of shares of stock in foreign companies and foreign real estate as well as *direct foreign investment,* in which companies build factories or acquire other productive assets abroad.

- We also ignore the effects of expected changes in *exchange rates,* the relative values of different national currencies. We analyze the determination of exchange rates later in the chapter.

FIGURE **19-2** The Loanable Funds Model Revisited

According to the loanable funds model of the interest rate, the equilibrium interest rate is determined by the intersection of the supply of loanable funds curve, S, and the demand for loanable funds curve, D. At point E, the equilibrium interest rate is 4%.

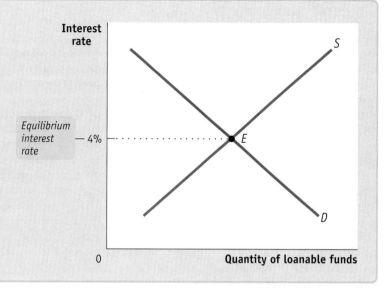

Figure 19-2 recaps the loanable funds model for a closed economy. Equilibrium corresponds to point *E*, at an interest rate of 4%, where the supply of loanable funds curve, *S*, intersects the demand for loanable funds curve, *D*. But if international capital flows are possible, this diagram changes and *E* may no longer be the equilibrium. We can analyze the causes and effects of international capital flows using Figure 19-3, which places the loanable funds market diagrams for two countries side by side.

Figure 19-3 illustrates a world consisting of only two countries, Canada and Britain. Panel (a) shows the loanable funds market in Canada, where the equilibrium in the absence of international capital flows is at point E_{Can} with an interest rate of 6%. Panel (b) shows the loanable funds market in Britain, where the equilibrium in the absence of international capital flows is at point E_B with an interest rate of 2%.

FIGURE **19-3** Loanable Funds Markets in a Two-Country World

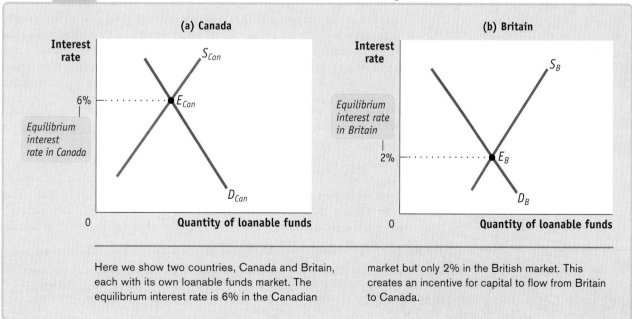

Here we show two countries, Canada and Britain, each with its own loanable funds market. The equilibrium interest rate is 6% in the Canadian market but only 2% in the British market. This creates an incentive for capital to flow from Britain to Canada.

GLOBAL COMPARISON   BIG SURPLUSES

From 2000 to 2008, Canada experienced current account surpluses. In some years, the surplus was more than 2% of GDP in magnitude. All this came to an end with the recession that began in late 2008: in 2009, 2010, and 2011, Canada experienced current account deficits equal to about 3% of GDP. Our southern neighbour, the United States, generally runs a large deficit in its current account. In fact, the United States leads the world in its current account deficit; other countries run bigger deficits as a share of GDP, but they have much smaller economies, so the U.S. deficit is much bigger in absolute terms.

For the world as a whole, however, deficits on the part of some countries must be matched with surpluses on the part of other countries. So who are the surplus nations that are offsetting Canada and United States, and what, if anything, do they have in common?

The accompanying figure shows the average current account surplus of the six countries that ran the largest surpluses in the decade from 2002 to 2011: China, Japan, Germany, Russia, Norway, and Saudi Arabia. You may not be surprised to learn that China tops the list.[1] As we explain later in this chapter, China's surplus is largely the result of its policy of keeping its currency weak relative to other currencies. But what about the others?

Japan and Germany each ran current account surpluses for more or less the same reasons: both are rich nations with high savings rates, which means they have lots of money to invest. Some of that money goes abroad, with the result that they run deficits on their financial accounts and surpluses on their current accounts.

The other three countries are all major oil exporters. (You may not think of Russia or Norway as "petro-economies," but Russia derives about two-thirds of its export revenue from oil, and Norway owns huge oil fields in the North Sea.) These three countries are all deliberately building up assets abroad to help them sustain their spending when the oil runs out.

All in all, the surplus countries are a diverse group. If your picture of the world is simply one of American and (sometimes) Canadian deficits versus Chinese surpluses, you're missing a large part of the story.

Source: International Monetary Fund.

Will the actual interest rate in Canada remain at 6% and that in Britain at 2%? Not if it is easy for British residents to make loans to Canadians. In that case, British lenders, attracted by high Canadian interest rates, will send some of their loanable funds to Canada. This capital inflow will increase the quantity of loanable funds supplied to Canadian borrowers, pushing the Canadian interest rate down. At the same time, it will reduce the quantity of loanable funds supplied to British borrowers, pushing the British interest rate up. So international capital flows will narrow the gap between Canadian and British interest rates.

Let's further suppose that British lenders regard a loan to a Canadian as being just as good as a loan to one of their own compatriots, and Canadian borrowers regard a debt to a British lender as no more costly than a debt to a Canadian lender. In that case, the flow of funds from Britain to Canada will continue until the gap between their interest rates is eliminated. In other words, when residents

---

[1]In fact, over this period, Taiwan and Hong Kong also experienced current account surpluses that averaged $33 and $20 billion 2011 U.S. dollars respectively. These surpluses are not counted in the official balance of payments statistics for China, since these data are for mainland China only.

FIGURE **19-4** International Capital Flows in a Two-Country World

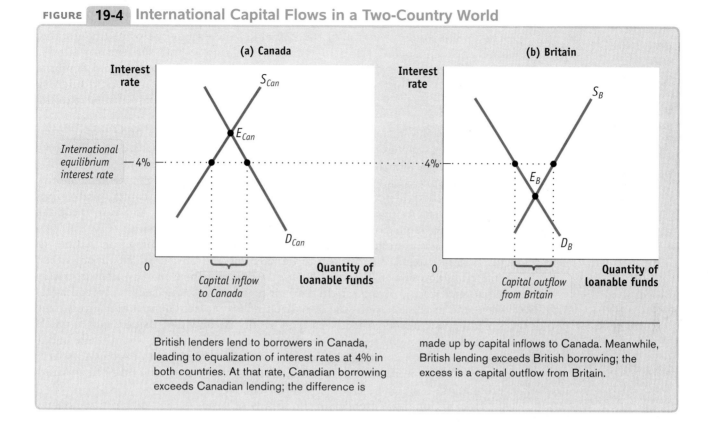

British lenders lend to borrowers in Canada, leading to equalization of interest rates at 4% in both countries. At that rate, Canadian borrowing exceeds Canadian lending; the difference is made up by capital inflows to Canada. Meanwhile, British lending exceeds British borrowing; the excess is a capital outflow from Britain.

of the two countries believe that a foreign asset is as good as a domestic one and that a foreign liability is as good as a domestic one, then international capital flows will equalize the interest rates in the two countries.

Figure 19-4 shows an international equilibrium in the loanable funds markets where the equilibrium interest rate is 4% in both Canada and Britain. At this interest rate, the quantity of loanable funds demanded by Canadian borrowers exceeds the quantity of loanable funds supplied by Canadian lenders. This gap is filled by "imported" funds—a capital inflow from Britain. At the same time, the quantity of loanable funds supplied by British lenders is greater than the quantity of loanable funds demanded by British borrowers. This excess is "exported" in the form of a capital outflow to Canada. And the two markets are in equilibrium at a common interest rate of 4%—at that interest rate, the total quantity of loans demanded by borrowers across the two markets is equal to the total quantity of loans supplied by lenders across the two markets.

Recall, in Chapter 10, we defined net foreign investment (NFI) as the net effect of international outflows and inflows of funds on total savings available for investment in any given. NFI is equal to the total outflows of domestic funds *minus* the total inflows of foreign funds. Why? As shown in Figure 19-4, at the international equilibrium interest rate of 4%, the domestic demand for funds in Canada (investment in Canada) exceeds the domestic supply of funds (national saving in Canada). Canada needs to borrow from Britain to make up the difference and Canada's net foreign investment turns negative. The reverse holds true for Britain. In other words, net foreign investment = −net capital inflows.

In short, international flows of capital are like international flows of goods and services. Capital moves from places where it would be cheap in the absence of international capital flows to places where it would be expensive in the absence of such flows.

Underlying Determinants of International Capital Flows

The open-economy version of the loanable funds model helps us understand international capital flows in terms of the supply and demand for funds. But what underlies differences across countries in the supply and demand for funds? Why, in the absence of international capital flows, would interest rates differ internationally, creating an incentive for international capital flows?

International differences in the demand for funds reflect underlying differences in investment opportunities. In particular, a country with a rapidly growing economy, other things equal, tends to offer more investment opportunities than a country with a slowly growing economy. So a rapidly growing economy typically—though not always—has a higher demand for capital and offers higher returns to investors than a slowly growing economy. As a result, capital tends to flow from slowly growing to rapidly growing economies.

The classic example, described in the upcoming Economics in Action, is the flow of capital from Britain to Canada and the United States, among other countries, between 1870 and 1914. During that era, the Canadian and American economies were growing rapidly as their populations increased and spread westward and as these nations industrialized. This created a demand for investment spending on railroads, factories, and so on. Meanwhile, Britain had a much more slowly growing population, was already industrialized, and already had a railroad network covering the country. This left Britain with savings to spare, much of which were lent out to Canada, the United States, and other New World economies.

International differences in the supply of funds reflect differences in savings across countries. These may be the result of differences in private savings rates, which vary widely among countries. For example, in 2010 gross private savings were 32.7% of Japan's GDP, but only 24.6% of Canada's GDP and 23% of U.S. GDP. They may also reflect differences in savings by governments. In particular, government budget deficits, which reduce overall national savings, can lead to capital inflows.

FOR INQUIRING MINDS

A GLOBAL SAVINGS GLUT?

In the early years of the twenty-first century, the United States moved into massive deficit on its current account, which meant that it became the recipient of huge capital inflows from the rest of the world (especially China, other Asian countries, and the Middle East). Why did that happen?

In an influential speech early in 2005, Ben Bernanke—who was at that time a governor of the Federal Reserve and who would soon become the Fed's chairman—offered a hypothesis: the United States wasn't responsible. The "principal causes of the U.S. current account deficit," he declared, lie "outside the country's borders." Specifically, he argued that special factors had

created a "global savings glut" that had pushed down interest rates worldwide and thereby led to an excess of investment spending over savings in the United States.

What caused this global savings glut? According to Bernanke, the main cause was the series of financial crises that began in Thailand in 1997; ricocheted across much of Asia; then hit Russia in 1998, Brazil in 1999, and Argentina in 2002. The ensuing fear and economic devastation led to a fall in investment spending and a rise in savings in a number of relatively poor countries. As a result, a number of these countries, which had previously been the recipients of capital inflows from advanced

countries like the United States, began experiencing large capital outflows. For the most part, the capital flowed to the United States, perhaps because "the depth and sophistication of the country's financial markets" made it an attractive destination.

When Bernanke gave his speech, it was viewed as reassuring: basically, he argued that the United States was responding in a sensible way to the availability of cheap money in world financial markets. Later, however, it would become clear that the cheap money from abroad helped fuel a U.S. housing bubble, which caused widespread financial and economic damage when it burst.

Two-Way Capital Flows

The loanable funds model helps us understand the direction of *net* capital flows— the excess of inflows into a country over outflows, or vice versa. The direction of net flows, other things equal, is determined by differences in interest rates between countries. As we saw in Table 19-2, however, *gross* flows take place in both directions: for example, Canada both sells assets to foreigners and buys assets from foreigners. Why does capital move in both directions?

The answer to this question is that in the real world, as opposed to the simple model we've just learned, there are other motives for international capital flows besides seeking a higher rate of interest.

Individual investors often seek to diversify against risk by buying stocks in a number of countries. Stocks in Europe may do well when stocks in Canada do badly, or vice versa, so investors in Europe try to reduce their risk by buying some Canadian stocks, as investors in Canada try to reduce their risk by buying some European stocks. The result is capital flows in both directions.

Meanwhile, corporations often engage in international investment as part of their business strategy—for example, auto companies may find that they can compete better in a national market if they assemble some of their cars locally. Such business investments can also lead to two-way capital flows, as, say, Japanese car makers build plants in Canada even as Canadian transportation companies open support facilities in Japan.

Finally, some countries, including Canada, are international banking centres: people from all over the world put money in Canadian financial institutions, which then invest many of those funds overseas.

The result of these two-way flows is that modern economies are typically both debtors (countries that owe money to the rest of the world) and creditors (countries to which the rest of the world owes money). Due to years of both capital inflows and outflows, at the end of 2012, Canada had accumulated foreign assets worth $2.7 trillion, and foreigners had accumulated assets in Canada worth the same amount, $2.7 trillion.

ECONOMICS ▸ IN ACTION

THE GOLDEN AGE OF CAPITAL FLOWS

Technology, it's often said, shrinks the world. Jet planes have put most of the world's cities within a few hours of one another; modern telecommunications transmit information instantly around the globe. So you might think that international capital flows must now be larger than ever.

But if capital flows are measured as a share of world savings and investment, that belief turns out not to be true. The golden age of capital flows actually preceded World War I—from 1870 to 1914.

These capital flows went mainly from European countries, especially Britain, to what were then known as "zones of recent settlement," countries that were attracting large numbers of European immigrants. Among the big recipients of capital inflows were Australia, Argentina, Canada, and the United States.

The large capital flows reflected differences in investment opportunities. Britain, a mature industrial economy with limited natural resources and a slowly growing population, offered relatively limited opportunities for new investment. The zones of recent settlement, with rapidly growing populations and abundant natural resources, offered investors a higher return and attracted capital inflows. Estimates suggest that over this period Britain sent about 40% of its savings abroad, largely to finance railroads and other large projects. No country has matched that record in modern times.

- The **balance of payments accounts,** which track a country's international transactions, are composed of the **balance of payments on current account,** or the **current account,** plus the **balance of payments on financial account,** or the **financial account.** The most important component of the current account is the **balance of payments on goods and services,** which itself includes the **merchandise trade balance,** or the **trade balance.**

- Because the sources of payments must equal the uses of payments, the current account plus the financial account sum to zero.

- Capital moves to equalize interest rates across countries. Countries can experience two-way capital flows because factors other than interest rates also affect investors' decisions.

- Capital flows reflect international differences in savings behaviour and in investment opportunities that lead to differences in interest rates across countries.

Why can't we match the capital flows of our great-great-grandparents? Economists aren't completely sure, but they have pointed to two causes: migration restrictions and political risks.

During the golden age of capital flows, capital movements were complementary to population movements: the big recipients of capital from Europe were also places to which large numbers of Europeans were moving. These large-scale population movements were possible before World War I because there were few legal restrictions on immigration. In today's world, by contrast, migration is limited by extensive legal barriers, as anyone considering a move to Canada, the United States, or Europe can tell you.

The other factor that has changed is political risk. Modern governments often limit foreign investment because they fear it will diminish their national autonomy. And due to political or security concerns, governments sometimes seize foreign property, a risk that deters investors from sending more than a relatively modest share of their wealth abroad. In the nineteenth century such actions were rare, partly because some major destinations of investment were still European colonies, partly because in those days governments had a habit of sending troops and gunboats to enforce the claims of their investors.

● ●◁

CHECK YOUR UNDERSTANDING **19-1**

1. Which of the balance of payments accounts do the following events affect?
   a. Bombardier, a Canadian-based company, sells a newly built airplane to China.
   b. Chinese investors buy stock in Bomdardier from Canadians.
   c. A Chinese company buys a used airplane from Air Canada and ships it to China.
   d. A Chinese investor buys an energy exploration plant in Alberta.

2. What effect do you think the collapse of the U.S. housing bubble and the ensuing recession had on international capital flows into the United States? What effect would this have had on international capital flows into Canada?

Solutions appear at back of book.

The Role of the Exchange Rate

We've just seen how differences in the supply of loanable funds from savings and the demand for loanable funds for investment spending lead to international capital flows. We've also learned that a country's balance of payments on current account plus its balance of payments on financial account add to zero: a country that receives net capital inflows must run a matching current account deficit, and a country that generates net capital outflows must run a matching current account surplus.

The behaviour of the financial account—reflecting inflows or outflows of capital—is best described by equilibrium in the international loanable funds market. At the same time, the balance of payments on goods and services, the main component of the current account, is determined by decisions in the international markets for goods and services. So given that the financial account reflects the movement of capital and the current account reflects the movement of goods and services, what ensures that the balance of payments really do balance? That is, what ensures that the two accounts actually offset each other?

Not surprisingly, a price is what makes these two accounts balance. Specifically, that price is the *exchange rate,* which is determined in the *foreign exchange market.*

Understanding Exchange Rates

In general, goods, services, and assets produced in a country must be paid for in that country's currency. Canadian products must be paid for in dollars; European products must be paid for in euros; Japanese products must be paid for in yen. Occasionally, sellers will accept payment in foreign currency, but they will usually then exchange that currency for their own domestic money.

International transactions, then, require a market—the **foreign exchange market**—in which currencies can be exchanged for each other. This market determines **exchange rates,** the prices at which currencies trade. (The foreign exchange market is, in fact, not located in any one geographic spot. Rather, it is a global electronic market that traders around the world use to buy and sell currencies.)

Table 19-3 shows exchange rates among the Canadian dollar and the world's three most important currencies, as of March 21, 2013. Each

TABLE **19-3**   Exchange Rates, March 21, 2013

	Canadian dollars	U.S. dollars	Yen	Euros
One Canadian dollar exchanged for	1	0.9765	92.850	0.7553
One U.S. dollar exchanged for	1.0241	1	95.088	0.7735
One yen exchanged for	0.01077	0.010517	1	0.008182
One euro exchanged for	1.3239	1.2927	122.92	1

Source: PACIFIC Exchange Rate Service (UBC).

entry shows the price of the "row" currency in terms of the "column" currency. For example, at that time C$1 exchanged for €0.7553, so it took €0.7553 to buy C$1. Similarly, it took C$1.3239 to buy €1. These two numbers reflect the same rate of exchange between the euro and the Canadian dollar: 1/1.3239 = 0.7553.

There are two ways to write any given exchange rate. In this case, there were €0.7553 to C$1 and C$1.3239 to €1. Which is the correct way to write it? The answer is that there is no fixed rule. In many countries, people express the exchange rate as the price of a unit of foreign currency in terms of domestic currency. However, this rule isn't universal, and the Canadian dollar–euro rate is commonly quoted both ways. The important thing is to be sure you know which one you are using! (See the Pitfalls section on the next page.)

When discussing movements in exchange rates, economists use specialized terms to avoid confusion. When a currency increases in value in terms of other currencies, economists say that the currency **appreciates.** When a currency decreases in value in terms of other currencies, it is said to **depreciate.** Suppose, for example, that the value of €1 went from $1 to $1.25, which means that the value of C$1 went from €1 to €0.80 (because 1/1.25 = 0.80). In this case, we would say that the euro appreciated and the Canadian dollar depreciated.

Movements in exchange rates, other things equal, affect the relative prices of goods, services, and assets in different countries. Suppose, for example, that the price of a Canadian hotel room is C$100 and the price of a French hotel room is €100. If the exchange rate were €1 = C$1, then these hotel rooms would have the same price. If the exchange rate were €1.25 = C$1, then the French hotel room would be 20% cheaper than the Canadian hotel room. If the exchange rate were €0.80 = C$1, then the French hotel room would be 25% more expensive than the Canadian hotel room.

The Equilibrium Exchange Rate

Imagine, for the sake of simplicity, that there are only two currencies in the world: Canadian dollars and euros. Europeans wanting to purchase Canadian goods, services, and assets come to the foreign exchange market, wanting to exchange euros for Canadian dollars. That is, Europeans demand Canadian dollars from the foreign exchange market and, correspondingly, supply euros to that market. Canadians wanting to buy European goods, services, and assets come to the foreign exchange market to exchange Canadian dollars for euros. That is, Canadians supply Canadian dollars to the foreign exchange market and, correspondingly, demand euros from that market. (International transfers and payments of factor

Currencies are traded in the **foreign exchange market.**

The prices at which currencies trade are known as **exchange rates.**

When a currency becomes more valuable in terms of other currencies, it **appreciates.**

When a currency becomes less valuable in terms of other currencies, it **depreciates.**

FIGURE **19-5** The Foreign Exchange Market

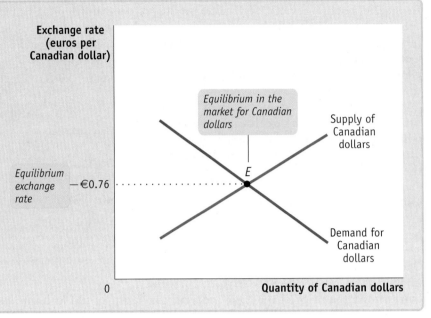

The foreign exchange market matches up the demand for a currency from foreigners who want to buy domestic goods, services, and assets with the supply of a currency from domestic residents who want to buy foreign goods, services, and assets. Here the equilibrium in the market for dollars is at point *E*, corresponding to an equilibrium exchange rate of €0.76 per C$1.

⚠ **PITFALLS**

WHICH WAY IS UP?

Suppose someone says, "The Canadian exchange rate is up." What does that person mean?

It isn't clear. Sometimes the exchange rate is measured as the price of a dollar in terms of foreign currency, sometimes as the price of foreign currency in terms of dollars. So the statement could mean either that the dollar appreciated or that it depreciated!

You have to be particularly careful when using published statistics. Most countries other than Canada state their exchange rates in terms of the price of a dollar in their domestic currency—for example, Mexican officials will say that the exchange rate is 10, meaning 10 pesos per dollar. But Britain, for historical reasons, usually states its exchange rate the other way. On March 21, 2013, C$1 was worth £0.6433, and £1 was worth C$1.5545. More often than not, this number is reported as an exchange rate of 1.5545. But on occasion, professional economists and consultants embarrass themselves by getting the direction in which the pound is moving wrong!

By the way, Canadians generally follow the lead of other countries: we usually say that the exchange rate against Mexico is 10 pesos per dollar but that the exchange rate against Britain is 1.55 dollars per pound.

But this rule isn't reliable; exchange rates against both the U.S. dollar and the euro are often stated both ways.

So it's always important to check before using exchange rate data: which way is the exchange rate being measured?

income also enter into the foreign exchange market, but to make things simple we'll ignore these.)

Figure 19-5 shows how the foreign exchange market works. The quantity of dollars demanded and supplied at any given euro–Canadian dollar exchange rate is shown on the horizontal axis, and the euro–Canadian dollar exchange rate is shown on the vertical axis. The exchange rate plays the same role as the price of a good or service in an ordinary supply-and-demand diagram. Throughout this chapter, we will express the exchange rate as the number of units of foreign currency needed to exchange for one unit of domestic currency.

The figure shows two curves, the demand curve for Canadian dollars and the supply curve for Canadian dollars. The key to understanding the slopes of these curves is that the level of the exchange rate affects exports and imports. When a country's currency appreciates, exports fall and imports rise. When it depreciates, exports rise and imports fall. To understand why the demand curve for Canadian dollars slopes downward, recall that the exchange rate, other things equal, determines the prices of Canadian goods, services, and assets relative to those of European goods, services, and assets. If the Canadian dollar rises against the euro (the dollar appreciates), Europeans will find Canadian products to be relatively more expensive. So, they will buy less from Canada and will acquire fewer dollars in the foreign exchange market: the quantity of Canadian dollars demanded falls as the number of euros needed to buy a Canadian dollar rises. In contrast, if the Canadian dollar falls against the euro (the dollar depreciates), Europeans will find Canadian products to be relatively cheaper. So, they will buy more from Canada and acquire more dollars in the foreign exchange market: the quantity of Canadian dollars demanded rises as the number of euros needed to buy a Canadian dollar falls.

A similar argument explains why the supply curve of Canadian dollars in Figure 19-5 slopes upward: the more euros required to buy a Canadian dollar, the more dollars Canadians will supply. Again, the reason is the effect of the exchange rate on relative prices. If the Canadian dollar rises against the euro, European products look cheaper to Canadians—who will demand more of them. This will require Canadians to convert more dollars into euros.

The **equilibrium exchange rate** is the exchange rate at which the quantity of Canadian dollars demanded in the foreign exchange market is equal to the quantity of Canadian dollars supplied. In Figure 19-5, the equilibrium is at point *E*, and the equilibrium exchange rate is 0.76. That is, at an exchange rate of €0.76 per C$1, the quantity of Canadian dollars supplied to the foreign exchange market is equal to the quantity of Canadian dollars demanded.

The **equilibrium exchange rate** is the exchange rate at which the quantity of a currency demanded in the foreign exchange market is equal to the quantity supplied.

To understand the significance of the equilibrium exchange rate, it's helpful to consider a numerical example of what equilibrium in the foreign exchange market looks like. A hypothetical example is shown in Table 19-4. The first row shows European purchases of Canadian dollars, either to buy Canadian goods and services or to buy Canadian assets. The second row shows Canadian sales of Canadian dollars, either to buy European goods and services or to buy European assets. At the equilibrium exchange rate, the total quantity of Canadian dollars Europeans want to buy is equal to the total quantity of Canadian dollars Canadians want to sell.

TABLE 19-4   A Hypothetical Equilibrium in the Foreign Exchange Market

European purchases of Canadian dollars (billions of Can. dollars)	To buy Canadian goods and services: 80.0	To buy Canadian assets: 8.5	Total purchases of Canadian dollars: 88.5
Canadian sales of Canadian dollars (billions of Can. dollars)	To buy European goods and services: 86.0	To buy European assets: 2.5	Total sales of Canadian dollars: 88.5
	Canadian balance of payments on current account: −6.0	Canadian balance of payments on financial account: +6.0	

Remember that the balance of payments accounts divide international transactions into two types. Purchases and sales of goods and services are counted in the current account. (Again, we're leaving out transfers and factor income to keep things simple.) Purchases and sales of assets are counted in the financial account. At the equilibrium exchange rate, then, we have the situation shown in Table 19-4: the sum of the balance of payments on current account plus the balance of payments on financial account is zero.

Now let's briefly consider how a shift in the demand for Canadian dollars affects equilibrium in the foreign exchange market. Suppose that for some reason capital flows from Europe to Canada increase—say, due to a change in the preferences of European investors. The effects are shown in Figure 19-6. The demand for Canadian dollars in the foreign exchange market increases as European investors convert euros into dollars to fund their new investments in Canada. This is shown by the shift of the demand curve from D_1 to D_2. As a result, the Canadian dollar appreciates against the euro: the number of euros per Canadian dollar at the equilibrium exchange rate rises from XR_1 to XR_2.

What are the consequences of this increased capital inflow for the balance of payments? The total quantity of Canadian dollars supplied to the foreign exchange market still must equal the total quantity of Canadian dollars demanded. So the increased capital inflow to Canada—an increase in the balance of payments on financial account—must be matched by a decline in the balance of payments on current account. What causes the balance of payments on current account to decline? The appreciation of the Canadian dollar. A rise in the number of euros per Canadian dollar leads Canadians to buy more European goods and services and Europeans to buy fewer Canadian goods and services.

Table 19-5 shows a hypothetical example of how this might work. Europeans are buying more Canadian assets, increasing the balance of payments on financial account from 0.5 to 1.0. This is offset by a reduction in European purchases of Canadian goods and services and a rise in Canadian purchases of European

TABLE **19-5** A Hypothetical Example of the Effects of Increased Capital Inflows

European purchases of Canadian dollars (billions of Can. dollars)	To buy Canadian goods and services: 75.0 (down 5.0)	To buy Canadian assets: 18.5 (up 10.0)	Total purchases of Canadian dollars: 93.5
Canadian sales of Canadian dollars (billions of Can. dollars)	To buy European goods and services: 91.0 (up 5.0)	To buy European assets: 2.5 (no change)	Total sales of Canadian dollars: 93.5
	Canadian balance of payments on current account: −16.0 (down 10.0)	Canadian balance of payments on financial account: +16.0 (up 10.0)	

goods and services, both the result of the dollar's appreciation. *So, any change in the Canadian balance of payments on financial account generates an equal and opposite reaction in the balance of payments on current account.* Movements in the exchange rate ensure that changes in the financial account and in the current account offset each other.

Let's briefly run this process in reverse. Suppose there is a reduction in capital flows from Europe to Canada—again due to a change in the preferences of European investors. The demand for Canadian dollars in the foreign exchange market falls, and the dollar depreciates: the number of euros per Canadian dollar at the equilibrium exchange rate falls. This leads Canadians to buy fewer European products and Europeans to buy more Canadian products. Ultimately, this generates an increase in the Canadian balance of payments on current account. So, a fall in capital flows into Canada leads to a weaker dollar, which in turn generates an increase in Canadian net exports.

FIGURE **19-6** An Increase in the Demand for Canadian Dollars

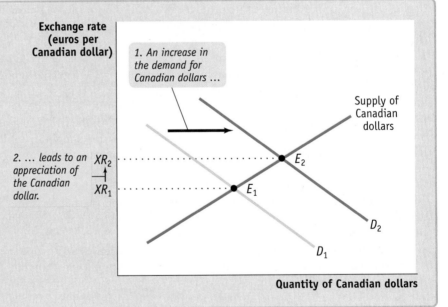

An increase in the demand for Canadian dollars might result from a change in the preferences of European investors. The demand curve for Canadian dollars shifts from D_1 to D_2. So the equilibrium number of euros per Canadian dollar rises— the dollar appreciates against the euro. As a result, the balance of payments on current account falls as the balance of payments on financial account rises.

Inflation and Real Exchange Rates

In 1993, one Canadian dollar exchanged, on average, for 2.35 Mexican pesos. By 2012, the peso had fallen against the Canadian dollar by almost 82%, with an average exchange rate in 2012 of 13.16 pesos per Canadian dollar. Did Mexican products also become much cheaper relative to Canadian products over that 19-year period? That is, did Mexican products also fall in price by almost 82%, in terms of Canadian dollars? The answer is no, because Mexico had much higher inflation than Canada did over that period. So, although the exchange rate changed considerably, the relative price of Canadian and Mexican products changed little between 1993 and 2012.

To take account of the effects of differences in inflation rates, economists calculate **real exchange rates,** exchange rates adjusted for international differ-

Real exchange rates are exchange rates adjusted for international differences in aggregate price levels.

ences in aggregate price levels. Suppose that the exchange rate we are looking at is the number of Mexican pesos per Canadian dollar. Let P_{Can} and P_{Mex} be indexes of the aggregate price levels in Canada and Mexico, respectively. Then the real exchange rate between the Mexican peso and the Canadian dollar is defined as:

(19-4) Real exchange rate = Mexican pesos per Canadian dollar $\times \dfrac{P_{Can}}{P_{Mex}}$

To distinguish it from the real exchange rate, the exchange rate unadjusted for aggregate price levels is sometimes called the *nominal* exchange rate. To understand the significance of the difference between the real and nominal exchange rates, let's consider the following example. Suppose that the Mexican peso depreciates against the Canadian dollar, with the exchange rate going from 10 pesos per Canadian dollar to 15 pesos per Canadian dollar, a 50% change. But suppose that the price of everything in Mexico, measured in pesos, simultaneously increases by 50%, so that the Mexican price index rises from 100 to 150. Further suppose that at the same time, Canadian prices do not change, so that the Canadian price index remains at 100. Then the initial real exchange rate is:

$$\text{Pesos per dollar before depreciation} \times \frac{P_{Can}}{P_{Mex}} = 10 \times \frac{100}{100} = 10$$

After the peso depreciates and the Mexican price level increases, the real exchange rate is:

$$\text{Pesos per dollar after depreciation} \times \frac{P_{Can}}{P_{Mex}} = 15 \times \frac{100}{150} = 10$$

In this example, the peso has depreciated substantially in terms of the Canadian dollar, but the *real* exchange rate between the peso and the Canadian dollar hasn't changed at all. And because the real peso–Canadian dollar exchange rate hasn't changed, the nominal depreciation of the peso against the Canadian dollar will have no effect, either on the real quantity of goods and services exported by Mexico to Canada or on the real quantity of goods and services imported by Mexico from Canada.

To see why, consider again the example of a hotel room. Suppose that this room initially costs 1000 pesos per night, which is $100 at an exchange rate of 10 pesos per dollar. After both Mexican prices and the number of pesos per dollar rise by 50%, the hotel room costs 1500 pesos per night—but 1500 pesos divided by 15 pesos per dollar is $100, so the Mexican hotel room still costs $100. As a result, a Canadian tourist considering a trip to Mexico will have no reason to change plans.

The same is true for all goods and services that enter into trade: *the current account responds only to changes in the real exchange rate, not the nominal exchange rate.* A country's products become cheaper to foreigners only when that country's currency depreciates in real terms, and those products become more expensive to foreigners only when the currency appreciates in real terms. As a consequence, economists who analyze movements in exports and imports of goods and services focus on the real exchange rate, not the nominal exchange rate.

Figure 19-7 illustrates just how important it can be to distinguish between nominal and real exchange rates. The line labelled "Nominal exchange rate" shows the number of pesos it took to buy a Canadian dollar from July 1993 to December 2012. As you can see, in nominal terms, the peso depreciated massively over that period. But the line labelled "Real exchange rate" shows the real exchange rate: it was calculated using Equation 19-4, with price indexes for both Mexico and Canada set so that 1993 = 100. In real terms, the peso depreciated between 1994 and 1995, but not by nearly as much as the nominal depreciation. By the end of 2012, the real peso–Canadian dollar exchange rate was just about back where it started.

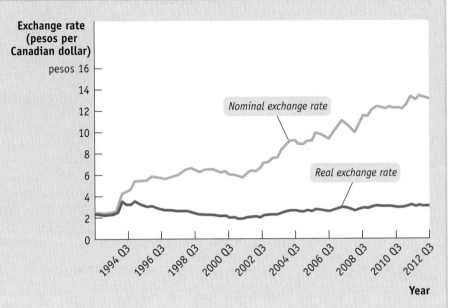

FIGURE 19-7 Real versus Nominal Exchange Rates, 1993–2012

Between 1993 and 2012, the price of a dollar in Mexican pesos increased dramatically. But because Mexico had higher inflation than Canada, the real exchange rate, which measures the relative price of Mexican goods and services, ended up roughly where it started.

Sources: Statistics Canada; TradingEconomics.com; CanadianForex.ca.

Purchasing Power Parity

A useful tool for analyzing exchange rates, closely connected to the concept of the real exchange rate, is known as *purchasing power parity*. The **purchasing power parity** between two countries' currencies is the nominal exchange rate at which a given basket of goods and services would cost the same amount in each country. Purchasing power parity is an example of the economic concept of the Law of One Price, the idea that perfectly substitutable goods, in this case baskets, must sell for the same price in equilibrium. Suppose, for example, that a basket of goods and services that costs C$100 in Canada and the same basket costs US$97.55 in the United States. Then the implied purchasing power parity exchange rate is 0.9755 U.S. dollars per Canadian dollar: at that exchange rate, US$97.55 = C$100, the market basket costs the same amount in both countries. In other words, if purchasing power parity holds, the nominal exchange rate is given by the relative price ratio between two countries. In this case:

$$\text{Nominal exchange rate (US\$ per C\$)} = \frac{P_{US}}{P_{Can}}$$

Calculations of purchasing power parities are usually made by estimating the cost of buying broad market baskets containing many goods and services—everything from automobiles and groceries to housing and telephone calls. But as the For Inquiring Minds below explains, once a year the magazine *The Economist* publishes a list of purchasing power parities based on the cost of buying a market basket that contains only one item—a McDonald's Big Mac.

Nominal exchange rates almost always differ from purchasing power parities. Some of these differences are systematic: in general, aggregate price levels are lower in poor countries than in rich countries because services tend to be cheaper in poor countries. But even among countries at roughly the same level of economic development, nominal exchange rates vary quite a lot from purchasing power parity. Figure 19-8 shows the nominal exchange rate between the U.S. dollar and the Canadian dollar, measured as the number of U.S. dollars per Canadian dollar, from 1990 to 2012, together with an estimate of the purchasing power parity exchange rate between Canada and the United States over the same period. The purchasing power parity didn't change much over the whole period because Canada and the United States had about the same rate of inflation. At the beginning of the period the nominal exchange

The **purchasing power parity** between two countries' currencies is the nominal exchange rate at which a given basket of goods and services would cost the same amount in each country.

FOR INQUIRING MINDS

BURGERNOMICS

Since 1986, the British magazine *The Economist* has produced an annual comparison of the cost in different countries of one particular consumption item that is found around the world—a McDonald's Big Mac. The magazine finds the price of a Big Mac in local currency, then computes two numbers: the price of a Big Mac in U.S. dollars using the prevailing exchange rate and the exchange rate at which the price of a Big Mac would equal the U.S. price. If purchasing power parity held for Big Macs, the U.S. dollar price of a Big Mac would be the same everywhere. If purchasing power parity is a good theory for the long run, the exchange rate at which a Big Mac's price matches the U.S. price should offer some guidance about where the exchange rate will eventually end up.

Table 19-6 shows *The Economist's* estimates for selected countries as of February 2, 2013. Instead of showing the price of a Big Mac in U.S. dollars, instead we show the price in selected countries in Canadian dollars and have ranked them in increasing order. The countries with the cheapest Big Macs, and therefore by this measure with the most undervalued currencies, are India and China, both developing countries. But not all developing countries have low-priced Big Macs: the price of a Big Mac in Brazil, converted into Canadian dollars, is considerably higher than in Canada. This reflects a sharp appreciation of the *real*, Brazil's currency, in recent years as the country has become a favourite of international invest-

ors (the country has experienced huge capital inflows and these inflows have raised the demand for the real—causing it to appreciate). And topping the list, with a Big Mac that is about 45% more expensive than in Canada, is Norway. The Norwegian currency, the *kroner*, was overvalued because of the country's abundance of natural resources. Because Norway is the world's fifth largest oil exporter and third largest gas exporter, there will always be plenty of demand for the country's currency and this will help the value of the kroner remain strong.

Switzerland's currency is overvalued by about 32% against the Canadian

dollar. As described in this chapter's opening story, Switzerland's reputation as a safe haven for investors has resulted in a significant increase in financial capital inflows—resulting in considerable upward pressure on the Swiss franc on foreign exchange markets. From 2009 through 2011, Swiss officials took extraordinary actions in an attempt to prevent the Swiss franc from appreciating even more—these measures essentially helped depreciate its currency. One can only imagine how much more overvalued the Swiss franc would have been without these measures, or how much it would have cost to buy a Big Mac in Zurich.

TABLE 19-6   Purchasing Power Parity and the Price of a Big Mac

Country	Big Mac price		Local currency per Canadian dollar		Degree of under-/over-valuation of local currency (versus C$)
	In local currency	In Canadian dollars	Implied PPP (local currency divided by $5.41)	Actual exchange rate	
India	Rupee 89	1.68	16.4510	53.0504	−69.0%
China	Yuan 16	2.58	2.9575	6.1996	−59.4%
Mexico	Peso 37	2.91	6.8392	12.7065	−46.2 %
Japan	¥320	3.53	59.1497	90.7441	−34.8 %
Britain	£2.69	4.26	0.4972	0.6312	−21.2 %
United States	US$4.37	4.38	0.8078	0.9967	−19.0 %
Euro area	€3.59	4.89	0.6636	0.7348	−9.7 %
Canada	C$5.41	5.41	–	1.0000	0 %
Brazil	Real 11.25	5.68	2.0795	1.9802	5.0 %
Switzerland	SFr 6.5	7.15	1.2015	0.9094	32.1 %
Norway	Kroner 43	7.86	7.9482	5.4675	45.4 %

Sources: The Economist; PACIFIC Exchange Rate Service (UBC).

rate was above purchasing power parity, so a given market basket cost more in Canada than in the United States. But in 2002, the nominal exchange rate was below the purchasing power parity, so a market basket cost less in Canada than in the United States.

Over the long run, however, purchasing power parities are pretty good at predicting actual changes in nominal exchange rates. In particular, nominal exchange rates between countries at similar levels of economic development tend to fluctuate around levels that lead to similar costs for a given market basket. In fact, by 2005 the nominal exchange rate between Canada and the United States was US$0.824 per C$1, just about the purchasing power parity. And in recent years the cost of living was higher in Canada than in the United States.

The purchasing power parity between Canada and the United States—the exchange rate at which a basket of goods and services would have cost the same amount in both countries—changed very little over the period shown, staying near US$0.82 per C$1. But the nominal exchange rate fluctuated widely.

Source: OECD.

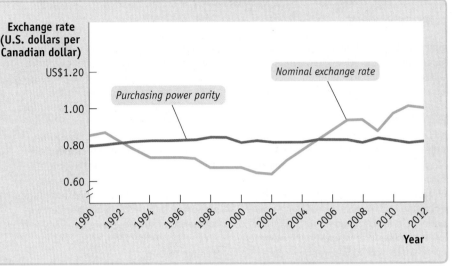

ECONOMICS ▸ IN ACTION

LET'S ALL SHOP (IN AMERICA)!

In recent years, you may have observed line-ups at the Canada–U.S. borders getting longer. Sometimes, Canadians have to wait more than an hour to cross the border. Many of them, if asked, were going to the United States to shop. Similarly, you may hear about how many of your friends and relatives are buying books, clothing, and other items from online U.S.-based retailers. Even you yourself may have taken part in such cross-border shopping. At the same time, you may have noticed that the number of American visitors to Canada has dropped recently. More Americans now prefer spending their vacations in their homeland to travelling in Canada, and many businesses, especially those located near the border, bitterly complain about lower and slower sales. What causes these changes? These changes are the result of many factors including changes in economic environments, duty-free limits, and passport regulations. But many believe the primary driving force of these trends is movements in the exchange rate.

Does the exchange rate matter when it comes to cross-border shopping and travel decisions? The answer, it seems, is yes. Panel (a) of Figure 19-9 shows the exchange rate between the U.S. dollar and the Canadian dollar between January 1995 and December 2012, while panel (b) shows the number of U.S. travellers entering Canada and number of Canadian travellers entering the United States over the same period. When the value of the Canadian dollar was low and declining somewhat in the mid-1990s and the early 2000s, the number of Americans travelling to Canada showed a steady rising trend, while the number of Canadians entering the United States

FIGURE **19-9** The Effect of the Exchange Rate on Cross-Border Travel

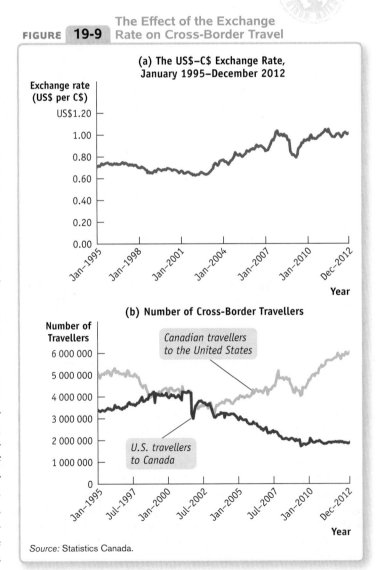

Source: Statistics Canada.

showed a downward trend. As the Canadian dollar got stronger against the U.S. dollar in recent years, these trends reversed directions. Holding all else constant, when the Canadian dollar appreciates American goods become more attractive. Indeed, in recent years Canadians considered goods bought in the United States to be such good bargains that they were willing to spend hours waiting in lines to cross the border. Not only will Canadians travel to shop, we also can find the merchandise offered on American websites to be very attractive. For example, sometimes we can observe a considerable difference in the price of a book available on Amazon.com and the same book on Amazon.ca. Even after taking duties, shipping and handling, and other transaction costs into account, we may still find goods from south of the border to be cheaper. The reversal of Canada's trade balance could be, in part, due to our stronger dollar and more frequent trips to the United States.

CHECK YOUR UNDERSTANDING 19-2

1. The province of Alberta discovers huge reserves of oil and starts exporting oil to the United States. Describe how this situation would affect each of the following items.

   a. The nominal U.S. dollar–Canadian dollar exchange rate

   b. Canadian exports of other goods and services

   c. Canadian imports of goods and services

2. Consider a basket of goods and services that costs C\$100 in Canada and US\$96 in the United States. The current nominal exchange rate is 0.9724 U.S. dollars per Canadian dollar. Over the next five years, the cost of that market basket rises to C\$120 in Canada and US\$120 in the United States, although the nominal exchange rate remains at 0.9724 U.S. dollars per Canadian dollar. Calculate each of the following items.

   a. The real exchange rate now and five years from now, if today's price index in both countries is 100

   b. Purchasing power parity (nominal exchange rate) today and five years from now

Solutions appear at back of book.

Exchange Rate Policy

The nominal exchange rate, like other prices, is determined by supply and demand. Unlike the price of wheat or oil, however, the exchange rate is the price of a country's money (in terms of another country's money). Money isn't a good or service produced by the private sector; it's an asset whose quantity is determined by government policy. As a result, governments have much more power to influence nominal exchange rates than they have to influence ordinary prices.

The nominal exchange rate is a very important price for many countries: the exchange rate determines the price of imports and the price of exports; in economies where exports and imports are large percentages of GDP, movements in the exchange rate can have major effects on aggregate output and the aggregate price level. What do governments do with their power to influence this important price?

The answer is, it depends. At different times and in different places, governments have adopted a variety of *exchange rate regimes*. Let's talk about these regimes, how they are enforced, and how governments choose a regime. (From now on, we'll adopt the convention that we mean the nominal exchange rate when we refer to the exchange rate.)

Exchange rates play a very important role in the global economy.

Exchange Rate Regimes

An **exchange rate regime** is a rule governing policy toward the exchange rate. There are two main kinds of exchange rate regimes. A country has a **fixed exchange rate** when the government keeps the exchange rate against some other currency at or near a particular target. For example, Hong Kong has an official policy of setting an exchange rate of HK$7.80 per US$1. In contrast, a country has a **floating exchange rate** when the government lets market forces determine the exchange rate. This is the policy followed by Canada, the United States, and Britain.

Fixed exchange rates and floating exchange rates aren't the only possibilities. At various times, countries have adopted compromise policies that lie somewhere between fixed and floating exchange rates. These include exchange rates that are fixed at any given time but are adjusted frequently, exchange rates that aren't fixed but are "managed" by the government to avoid wide swings, and exchange rates that float within a "target zone" but are prevented from leaving that zone. In this book, however, we'll focus on the two main exchange rate regimes.

The immediate question about a fixed exchange rate is how it is possible for governments to fix the exchange rate when the exchange rate is determined by supply and demand.

How Can an Exchange Rate Be Held Fixed?

To understand how it is possible for a country to fix its exchange rate, let's consider a hypothetical country, Genovia, which for some reason has decided to fix the value of its currency, the genov, at C$1.50.[2]

The obvious problem is that C$1.50 may not be the equilibrium exchange rate in the foreign exchange market: the equilibrium rate may be either higher or lower than the target exchange rate. Figure 19-10 shows the foreign exchange market for genovs, with the quantities of genovs supplied and demanded on the horizontal axis and the exchange rate of the genov, measured in Canadian dollars per genov, on the vertical axis. Panel (a) shows the case in which the equilibrium value of the genov is *below* the target exchange rate. Panel (b) shows the case in which the equilibrium value of the genov is *above* the target exchange rate.

Consider first the case in which the equilibrium value of the genov is below the target exchange rate. As panel (a) shows, at the target exchange rate of C$1.50 per genov, there is a surplus of genovs in the foreign exchange market, which would normally push the value of the genov down. How can the Genovian government support the value of the genov to keep the rate where it wants? There are three possible answers, all of which have been used by governments at some point.

One way the Genovian government can support the genov is to "soak up" the surplus of genovs by buying its own currency in the foreign exchange market. Government purchases or sales of currency in the foreign exchange market are called **exchange market intervention.** To buy genovs in the foreign exchange market, of course, the Genovian government must have Canadian dollars to exchange for genovs. In fact, most countries maintain **foreign exchange reserves,** stocks of foreign currency (usually U.S. dollars or euros) that they can use to buy their own currency to support its price. Nowadays, U.S. dollars and euros account for about 85% of reserve currency holdings worldwide.

We mentioned earlier in the chapter that an important part of international capital flows is the result of purchases and sales of foreign assets by governments and central banks. Now we can see why governments sell foreign assets: they are supporting their currency through exchange market intervention. As we'll see in a moment, governments that keep the value of their currency *down* through

An **exchange rate regime** is a rule governing policy toward the exchange rate.

A country has a **fixed exchange rate** when the government keeps the exchange rate against some other currency at or near a particular target.

A country has a **floating exchange rate** when the government lets market forces determine the exchange rate.

Government purchases or sales of currency in the foreign exchange market are **exchange market intervention.**

Foreign exchange reserves are stocks of foreign currency that governments maintain to buy their own currency on the foreign exchange market.

---

[2]In this section, we treat Genovia as the home country, so the exchange rate is quoted as the number of Canadian dollars needed to exchange for one genov.

FIGURE **19-10** Exchange Market Intervention

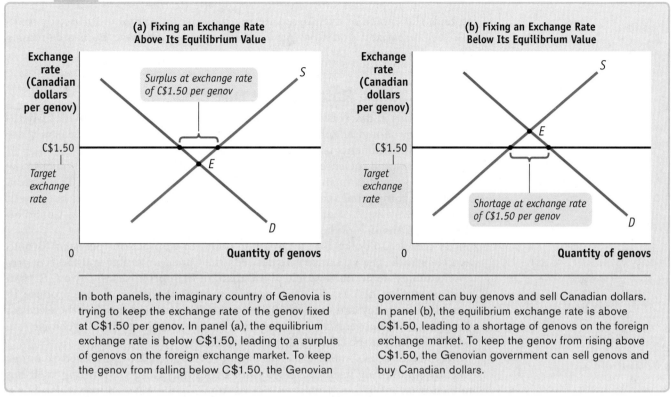

In both panels, the imaginary country of Genovia is trying to keep the exchange rate of the genov fixed at C$1.50 per genov. In panel (a), the equilibrium exchange rate is below C$1.50, leading to a surplus of genovs on the foreign exchange market. To keep the genov from falling below C$1.50, the Genovian

government can buy genovs and sell Canadian dollars. In panel (b), the equilibrium exchange rate is above C$1.50, leading to a shortage of genovs on the foreign exchange market. To keep the genov from rising above C$1.50, the Genovian government can sell genovs and buy Canadian dollars.

exchange market intervention must *buy* foreign assets. First, however, let's talk about the other ways governments fix exchange rates.

A second way for the Genovian government to support the genov is to try to shift the supply and demand curves for the genov in the foreign exchange market. Governments usually do this by changing monetary policy. For example, to support the genov the Genovian central bank can raise the Genovian interest rate. This will increase capital flows into Genovia, increasing the demand for genovs, at the same time that it reduces capital flows out of Genovia, reducing the supply of genovs. So, other things equal, an increase in a country's interest rate will increase the value of its currency.

Third, the Genovian government can support the genov by reducing the supply of genovs to the foreign exchange market. It can do this by requiring domestic residents who want to buy foreign currency to get a licence and giving these licences only to people engaging in approved transactions (such as the purchase of imported goods the Genovian government thinks are essential). Licensing systems that limit the right of individuals to buy foreign currency are called **foreign exchange controls.** Other things equal, foreign exchange controls increase the value of a country's currency.

So far we've been discussing a situation in which the government is trying to prevent a depreciation of the genov. Suppose, instead, that the situation is as shown in panel (b) of Figure 19-10, where the equilibrium value of the genov is *above* the target exchange rate of C$1.50 per genov and there is a shortage of genovs. To maintain the target exchange rate, the Genovian government can apply the same three basic options in the reverse direction. It can intervene in the foreign exchange market, in this case *selling* genovs and acquiring Canadian dollars, which it can add to its foreign exchange reserves. It can *reduce* interest rates to increase the supply of genovs and reduce the demand. Or it can impose foreign exchange controls that limit the ability of foreigners to buy genovs. All of these actions, other things equal, will reduce the value of the genov.

Foreign exchange controls are licensing systems that limit the right of individuals to buy foreign currency.

As we said, all three techniques have been used to manage fixed exchange rates. But we haven't said whether fixing the exchange rate is a good idea. In fact, the choice of exchange rate regime poses a dilemma for policy-makers, because fixed and floating exchange rates each have both advantages and disadvantages.

The Exchange Rate Regime Dilemma

Few questions in macroeconomics produce as many arguments as that of whether a country should adopt a fixed or a floating exchange rate. The reason there are so many arguments is that both sides have a case.

To understand the case for a fixed exchange rate, consider for a moment how easy it is to conduct business across provincial borders in Canada. There are a number of things that make interprovincial commerce trouble-free, but one of them is the absence of any uncertainty about the value of money: a Canadian dollar is a Canadian dollar, in both Toronto and Calgary.

By contrast, a dollar isn't a Canadian dollar in transactions between Toronto and New York. The exchange rate between the Canadian dollar and the U.S. dollar fluctuates, sometimes widely. If a Canadian firm promises to pay a U.S. firm a given number of U.S. dollars a year from now, the value of that promise in Canadian currency can vary by 10% or more. This uncertainty has the effect of deterring trade between the two countries. So one benefit of a fixed exchange rate is certainty about the future value of a currency.

There is also, in some cases, an additional benefit to adopting a fixed exchange rate: by committing itself to a fixed rate, a country is also committing itself not to engage in inflationary policies. For example, in 1991 Argentina, which has a long history of irresponsible policies leading to severe inflation, adopted a fixed exchange rate of US$1 per Argentine peso in an attempt to commit itself to non-inflationary policies in the future. (Argentina's fixed exchange rate regime collapsed disastrously in late 2001. But that's another story.)

The point is that there is some economic value in having a stable exchange rate. Indeed, as the upcoming For Inquiring Minds explains, the presumed benefits of stable exchange rates motivated the international system of fixed exchange rates created after World War II. It was also a major reason for the creation of the euro.

In 1945, at the end of World War II, most of the major world powers, including Canada and the United States, adopted a system of fixed exchange rates. Known as the *Bretton Woods* system, after the place where it was negotiated, this system was an attempt to return to a fixed exchange rate system that had the stability of the gold standard. In the Bretton Woods agreement, all of the exchange rates were set against the U.S. dollar, instead of the gold standard. This made the American dollar the world's reserve currency. To boost confidence, the U.S. dollar was linked to, and was convertible into, gold at the rate of $35 per ounce of gold. All of the participating countries agreed to peg their currency against the U.S. dollar and to actively trade their currency with U.S. dollars in order to keep their market exchange rate within 1% of the peg. The Bretton Woods system worked well until 1971, when it failed owing to a loss of confidence in the U.S. dollar: the United States was forced to abandon convertibility into gold and, along with it, the fixed exchange rate regime. Many of the participating nations were happy to stay with the Bretton Woods system while it was in effect. But Canada decided to do something a little different. As Figure 9-11 shows, in 1950 Canada abandoned the Bretton Woods fixed exchange rate regime and allowed the dollar to "float" in value. However, in the early 1960s the Canadian dollar depreciated significantly and in 1962 Canada was forced back into the fixed exchange rate system, with the dollar fixed

This graph plots the monthly average value of the Canada–U.S. exchange rate from October 1950 until April 2013. The exchange rate is quoted as the number of U.S. dollars that can be bought with one Canadian dollar. The shaded area shows when the Canadian dollar exchange rate was fixed against the U.S. dollar from 1962 to 1970. The Canadian dollar was allowed to float in value from 1950 to 1962 and again starting in 1970.

Source: Bank of Canada.

at US$0.925. This value was substantially lower than levels of the late 1950s and early 1960s, causing significant political pressure that helped to defeat Prime Minister Diefenbaker's conservative government in the 1963 election. Canada stayed with this fixed rate until it again abandoned the fixed rates of Bretton Woods in 1970 to fight inflation, which was coming largely from the United States and the fixed exchange rate.[3]

However, there are also costs to fixing the exchange rate. To stabilize an exchange rate through intervention, a country must keep large quantities of foreign currency on hand—usually a low-return investment. Furthermore, even large reserves can be quickly exhausted when there are large capital flows out of a country. If a country chooses to stabilize an exchange rate by adjusting monetary policy rather than through intervention, it must divert monetary policy from other goals, notably stabilizing the economy and managing the inflation rate. Finally, foreign exchange controls, like import quotas and tariffs, distort incentives for importing and exporting goods and services. They can also create substantial costs in terms of red tape and corruption.

So there's a dilemma. Should a country let its currency float, which leaves monetary policy available for macroeconomic stabilization but creates uncertainty for business? Or should it fix the exchange rate, which eliminates the

[3]For further information on selected highs and lows of the Canadian dollar between 1950 and 2007, consult www.cbc.ca/news/interactives/map-history-dollar. Click on each key point to see the commentary associated with it.

FOR INQUIRING MINDS

FROM BRETTON WOODS TO THE EURO

In 1944, while World War II was still raging, representatives of Allied nations met in Bretton Woods, New Hampshire, to establish a post-war international monetary system of fixed exchange rates among major currencies. The system was highly successful at first, but it broke down in 1971. After a confusing interval during which policy-makers tried unsuccessfully to establish a new fixed exchange rate system, by 1973 most economically advanced countries had moved to floating exchange rates.

In Europe, however, many policy-makers were unhappy with floating exchange rates, which they believed created too much uncertainty for business. From the late 1970s onward they tried several times to create a system of more

or less fixed exchange rates in Europe, culminating in an arrangement known as the Exchange Rate Mechanism. (The Exchange Rate Mechanism was, strictly speaking, a "target zone" system—European exchange rates were free to move within a narrow band, but not outside it.) And in 1991 they agreed to move to the ultimate in fixed exchange rates: a common European currency, the euro. To the surprise of many analysts, they pulled it off: at the time of writing 17 European countries have abandoned their national currencies for the euro.

Figure 19-12 illustrates the history of European exchange rate arrangements. It shows the exchange rate between the French franc and the German mark, measured as francs per mark, from

1971 until their replacement by the euro. The exchange rate fluctuated widely at first. The "plateaus" you can see in the data—eras when the exchange rate fluctuated only modestly—are periods when attempts to restore fixed exchange rates were in process. The Exchange Rate Mechanism, after a couple of false starts, became effective in 1987, stabilizing the exchange rate at about 3.4 francs per mark. (The wobbles in the early 1990s reflect two *currency crises*—episodes in which widespread expectations of imminent devaluations led to large but temporary capital flows.)

In 1999 the exchange rate was "locked"—no further fluctuations were allowed as the countries prepared to switch from francs and marks to the euro. At the end of 2001, the franc and the mark ceased to exist.

The transition to the euro has not been without costs. Countries that adopted the euro sacrificed some important policy tools: they could no longer tailor monetary policy to their specific economic circumstances, and they could no longer lower their costs relative to other European nations simply by letting their currencies depreciate. At the time this book went to press, the euro area was under serious stress, with several nations—including Greece, Spain, and Italy, three big economies—facing widespread skepticism about their ability to make needed economic adjustments without defaulting on their debts and abandoning the euro.

FIGURE 19-12 The Road to the Euro

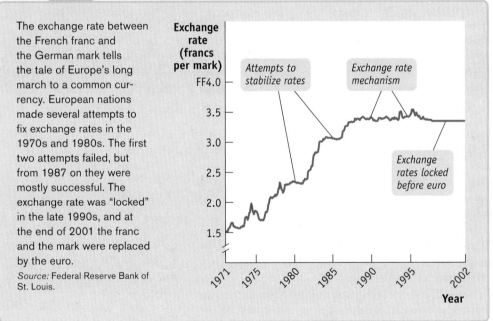

The exchange rate between the French franc and the German mark tells the tale of Europe's long march to a common currency. European nations made several attempts to fix exchange rates in the 1970s and 1980s. The first two attempts failed, but from 1987 on they were mostly successful. The exchange rate was "locked" in the late 1990s, and at the end of 2001 the franc and the mark were replaced by the euro.

Source: Federal Reserve Bank of St. Louis.

uncertainty but means giving up monetary policy, adopting exchange controls, or both? Different countries reach different conclusions at different times. Most European countries, but notably not Britain, have long believed that exchange rates among major European economies, which do most of their international trade with each other, should be fixed. But Canada seems happy with a floating exchange rate with the United States, even though the United States accounts for most of our trade.

Fortunately we don't have to resolve this dilemma. For the rest of the chapter, we'll take exchange rate regimes as given and ask how they affect macroeconomic policy.

ECONOMICS ➤ IN ACTION

CHINA PEGS THE YUAN

In the early years of the twenty-first century, China provided a striking example of the lengths to which countries sometimes go to maintain a fixed exchange rate. Here's the background: China's spectacular success as an exporter led to a rising surplus on current account. At the same time, non-Chinese private investors became increasingly eager to shift funds into China, to invest in its growing domestic economy. These capital flows were somewhat limited by foreign exchange controls—but kept coming in anyway. As a result of the current account surplus and private capital inflows, China found itself in the position described by panel (b) of Figure 19-10: at the target exchange rate, the demand for yuan exceeded the supply. Yet the Chinese government was determined to keep the exchange rate fixed at a value below its equilibrium level. Although China allowed a small revaluation of the yuan in 2005, at the time of this writing in 2013, many economists estimated the level of the undervaluation of the yuan at 15 to 25%. If the Big Mac Index (Table 19-6) were used to measure the value of the yuan against the U.S. dollar, then the level of the undervaluation of the yuan would be around 40%.

China provides a striking example of the lengths to which countries sometimes go to maintain a fixed exchange rate.

To keep the rate fixed, China had to engage in large-scale exchange market intervention, selling yuan, buying up other countries' currencies (mainly U.S. dollars) on the foreign exchange market, and adding them to its reserves. From 2011 to 2012, China added US$130.44 billion to its foreign exchange reserves, and by December 2012, those reserves had risen to $3.3 trillion. To get a sense of how big these totals are, in 2012 China's GDP was approximately US$8.25 trillion. This means that in 2012 China bought U.S. dollars and other currencies equal to about 1.6% of its GDP, making its accumulated reserves approximately equal to 40% of its GDP. Not surprisingly, China's exchange rate policy has led to some friction with its trading partners, who feel that China is, in effect, subsidizing Chinese exports.

CHECK YOUR UNDERSTANDING 19-3

1. Draw a diagram, similar to Figure 19-10, representing the foreign exchange situation of China when it kept the exchange rate fixed. (*Hint:* Express the exchange rate as Canadian dollars per yuan.) Then show with a diagram how each of the following policy changes might eliminate the disequilibrium in the market.
   a. An appreciation of the yuan
   b. Placing restrictions on foreigners who want to invest in China
   c. Removing restrictions on Chinese who want to invest abroad
   d. Imposing taxes on Chinese exports, such as shipments of clothing, that are causing a political backlash in the importing countries

Solutions appear at back of book.

> ▼ **Quick Review**
>
> ● Countries choose different **exchange rate regimes.** The two main regimes are **fixed exchange rates** and **floating exchange rates.**
>
> ● Exchange rates can be fixed through **exchange market intervention,** using **foreign exchange reserves.** Countries can also use domestic policies to shift supply and demand in the foreign exchange market (usually monetary policy), or they can impose **foreign exchange controls.**
>
> ● Choosing an exchange rate regime poses a dilemma: stable exchange rates are good for business. But holding large foreign exchange reserves is costly, using domestic policy to fix the exchange rate makes it hard to pursue other objectives, and foreign exchange controls distort incentives.

Exchange Rates and Macroeconomic Policy

When the euro was created in 1999, there were celebrations across the nations of Europe—with a few notable exceptions. You see, some countries chose not to adopt the new currency. The most important of these was Britain, but other European countries, such as Sweden, also decided that the euro was not for them.

A **devaluation** is a reduction in the value of a currency that is set under a fixed exchange rate regime.

A **revaluation** is an increase in the value of a currency that is set under a fixed exchange rate regime.

Why did Britain say no? Part of the answer was national pride: if Britain gave up the pound, it would also have to give up currency that bears the portrait of the queen. But there were also serious economic concerns about giving up the pound in favour of the euro. British economists who favoured adoption of the euro argued that if Britain used the same currency as its neighbours, the country's international trade would expand and its economy would become more productive. But other economists pointed out that adopting the euro would take away Britain's ability to have an independent monetary policy and might lead to macroeconomic problems.

As this discussion suggests, the fact that modern economies are open to international trade and capital flows adds a new level of complication to our analysis of macroeconomic policy. Let's look at three policy issues raised by open-economy macroeconomics.

1. Devaluation and Revaluation of Fixed Exchange Rates

Historically, fixed exchange rates haven't been permanent commitments. Sometimes countries with a fixed exchange rate switch to a floating rate, as Argentina did in 2001. In other cases, they retain a fixed rate but change the target exchange rate. Such adjustments in the target were common during the Bretton Woods era described in the preceding For Inquiring Minds. For example, in 1967 Britain changed the exchange rate of the pound against the U.S. dollar from US$2.80 per £1 to US$2.40 per £1. A modern example is Argentina, which maintained a fixed exchange rate against the dollar from 1991 to 2001 but switched to a floating exchange rate at the end of 2001.

A reduction in the value of a currency that is set under a fixed exchange rate regime is called a **devaluation.** As we've already learned, a *depreciation* is a downward move in a currency. A devaluation is a depreciation that is due to a revision in a fixed exchange rate target. An increase in the value of a currency that is set under a fixed exchange rate regime is called a **revaluation.**

A devaluation, like any depreciation, makes domestic goods cheaper in terms of foreign currency, which leads to higher exports. At the same time, it makes foreign goods more expensive in terms of domestic currency, which reduces imports. The effect is to increase the balance of payments on current account. Similarly, a revaluation makes domestic goods more expensive in terms of foreign currency, which reduces exports, and makes foreign goods cheaper in domestic currency, which increases imports. So a revaluation reduces the balance of payments on current account.

Devaluations and revaluations serve two purposes under fixed exchange rates. First, they can be used to eliminate shortages or surpluses in the foreign exchange market. For example, in 2010 some economists and politicians were urging China to revalue the yuan because they believed that China's exchange rate policy unfairly aided Chinese exports.

Second, devaluation and revaluation can be used as tools of macro-economic policy. A devaluation, by increasing exports and reducing imports, increases aggregate demand. So a devaluation can be used to reduce or eliminate a recessionary gap. A revaluation has the opposite effect, reducing aggregate demand. So a revaluation can be used to reduce or eliminate an inflationary gap.

2. Monetary Policy Under Floating Exchange Rates

Under a floating exchange rate regime, a country's central bank retains its ability to pursue monetary policy that is independent of other countries: it can increase aggregate demand by cutting the interest rate or decrease aggregate demand by raising the interest rate.[4] A floating exchange rate regime permits a country to conduct monetary policy that is independent of other countries.

But the exchange rate adds another dimension to the effects of monetary policy. To see why, let's return to the hypothetical country of Genovia and ask what happens if the central bank cuts the interest rate.

Just as in a closed economy, a lower interest rate leads to higher investment spending and higher consumer spending. But the decline in the interest rate also affects the foreign exchange market. Foreigners have less incentive to move funds into Genovia because they will receive a lower interest rate on their loans. As a result, they have less need to exchange Canadian dollars for genovs, so the demand for genovs falls. At the same time, Genovians have *more* incentive to move funds abroad because the interest rate on loans at home has fallen, making investments outside the country more attractive. As a result, they need to exchange more genovs for Canadian dollars, so the supply of genovs rises.

Figure 19-13 shows the effect of an interest rate reduction on the foreign exchange market. The demand curve for genovs shifts leftward, from D_1 to D_2, and the supply curve shifts rightward, from S_1 to S_2. The equilibrium exchange rate, as measured in Canadian dollars per genov, falls from XR_1 to XR_2. That is, a reduction in the Genovian interest rate causes the genov to *depreciate*.

FIGURE 19-13 Monetary Policy and the Exchange Rate

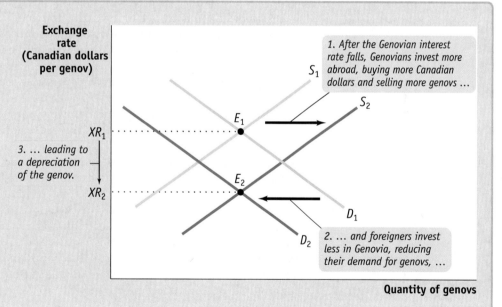

Here we show what happens in the foreign exchange market if Genovia cuts its interest rate. Residents of Genovia have a reduced incentive to keep their funds at home, so they invest more abroad. As a result, the supply of genovs shifts rightward, from S_1 to S_2. Meanwhile, foreigners have less incentive to put funds into Genovia, so the demand for genovs shifts leftward, from D_1 to D_2. The genov depreciates: the equilibrium exchange rate falls from XR_1 to XR_2.

1. After the Genovian interest rate falls, Genovians invest more abroad, buying more Canadian dollars and selling more genovs ...

2. ... and foreigners invest less in Genovia, reducing their demand for genovs, ...

3. ... leading to a depreciation of the genov.

Exchange rate (Canadian dollars per genov)

Quantity of genovs

---

[4]The Bank of Canada does not have complete independence in deciding on its policies. Generally, the governor of the BOC is given a large degree of autonomy from the federal government. However, as a result of the "Coyne Affair" in 1961, the government does have the theoretical authority to remove the governor of the BOC from his or her post. In 1961, the federal government chose to pursue expansionary fiscal policies and asked the Bank of Canada to lower interest rates so as to help the economy expand. James Coyne, the governor of the Bank of Canada, refused this request because in his opinion the country would benefit more from a contractionary policy. This public feud caused great controversy. In the end, Coyne resigned. Shortly afterward, a mechanism was introduced to prevent a re-occurrence of this fiasco. Today, it is theoretically possible for the minister of finance to order, in writing, the governor and the Bank to conduct specific monetary policies. If the governor refuses to follow these orders, the government can remove the governor.

The depreciation of the genov, in turn, affects aggregate demand. We've already seen that a devaluation—a depreciation that is the result of a change in a fixed exchange rate—increases exports and reduces imports, thereby increasing aggregate demand. A depreciation that results from an interest rate cut has the same effect: it increases exports and reduces imports, increasing aggregate demand.

In other words, monetary policy under floating rates has effects beyond those we've described in looking at closed economies. In a closed economy, a reduction in the interest rate leads to a rise in aggregate demand because it leads to more investment spending and consumer spending. In an open economy with a floating exchange rate, the interest rate reduction leads to increased investment spending and consumer spending, but it also increases aggregate demand in another way: it leads to a currency depreciation, which increases exports and reduces imports, and further increases aggregate demand.

3. International Business Cycles

Up to this point, we have discussed macroeconomics, even in an open economy, as if all demand shocks originate from the domestic economy. In reality, however, economies sometimes face shocks coming from abroad. For example, recessions in the United States have historically led to economic slowdowns in Canada.

The key point is that changes in aggregate demand affect the demand for goods and services produced abroad as well as at home: other things equal, a recession leads to a fall in imports and an expansion leads to a rise in imports. And one country's imports are another country's exports. This link between aggregate demand in different national economies is one reason business cycles in different countries sometimes—but not always—seem to be synchronized. The prime example is the Great Depression, which affected countries around the world.

The extent of this link depends, however, on the exchange rate regime. To see why, think about what happens if a recession abroad reduces the demand for Genovia's exports. A reduction in foreign demand for Genovian goods and services is also a reduction in demand for genovs in the foreign exchange market. If Genovia has a fixed exchange rate, it responds to this decline with exchange market intervention. But if Genovia has a floating exchange rate, the genov depreciates. Because Genovian goods and services become cheaper to foreigners when the demand for exports falls, the quantity of goods and services exported doesn't fall by as much as it would under a fixed rate. At the same time, the fall in the genov makes imports more expensive to Genovians, leading to a fall in imports. Both effects limit the decline in Genovia's aggregate demand compared to what it would have been under a fixed exchange rate.

One of the virtues of a floating exchange rate, according to advocates of such exchange rates, is that they help insulate countries from recessions originating abroad. This theory looked pretty good in the early 2000s: Britain, with a floating exchange rate, managed to stay out of a recession that affected the rest of Europe, and Canada, which also has a floating rate, suffered a less severe recession than the United States.

In 2008, however, the financial crisis that began in the United States led to a recession in virtually every country. In this case, it appears that the international linkages among financial markets were much stronger than any insulation from overseas disturbances provided by floating exchange rates.

ECONOMICS ▶ IN ACTION

THE JOY OF A DEVALUED POUND

Earlier in the chapter, we mentioned the Exchange Rate Mechanism, the system of European fixed exchange rates that paved the way for the creation of the euro in 1999. Britain joined that system in 1990 but dropped out in 1992. The story of Britain's exit from the Exchange Rate Mechanism is a classic example of open-economy macroeconomic policy.

Britain originally fixed its exchange rate for both the reasons we described earlier in the chapter: British leaders believed that a fixed exchange rate would help promote international trade, and they also hoped that it would help fight inflation. But by 1992 Britain was suffering from high unemployment: the unemployment rate in September 1992 was over 10%. And as long as the country had a fixed exchange rate, there wasn't much the government could do. In particular, the government wasn't able to cut interest rates because it was using high interest rates to help support the value of the pound.

In the summer of 1992, investors began speculating against the pound—selling pounds in the expectation that the currency would drop in value. As its foreign reserves dwindled, this speculation forced the British government's hand. On September 16, 1992, Britain abandoned its fixed exchange rate. The pound promptly dropped 20% against the German mark, the most important European currency at the time.

At first, the devaluation of the pound greatly damaged the prestige of the British government. But the Chancellor of the Exchequer—the counterpart of Canada's federal minister of finance—claimed to be happy about it. "My wife has never before heard me singing in the bath," he told reporters. There were several reasons for his joy. One was that the British government would no longer have to engage in large-scale exchange market intervention to support the pound's value. Another was that devaluation increases aggregate demand, so the pound's fall would help reduce British unemployment. Finally, because Britain no longer had a fixed exchange rate, it was free to pursue an expansionary monetary policy to fight its slump.

Indeed, events made it clear that the chancellor's joy was well founded. British unemployment fell over the next two years, even as the unemployment rate rose in France and Germany. One person who did not share in the improving employment picture, however, was the chancellor himself. Soon after his remark about singing in the bath, he was fired.

CHECK YOUR UNDERSTANDING   19-4

1. Look at the data in Figure 19-12. Where do you see devaluations and revaluations of the franc against the mark?

2. In the late 1980s Canadian economists argued that the high interest rate policies of the Bank of Canada weren't just causing high unemployment—they were also making it hard for Canadian manufacturers to compete with the United States. Explain this complaint, using our analysis of how monetary policy works under floating exchange rates.

Solutions appear at back of book.

▼ Quick Review

- Countries can change fixed exchange rates. **Devaluation** or **revaluation** can help reduce surpluses or shortages in the foreign exchange market and can increase or reduce aggregate demand.

- In an open economy with a floating exchange rate, interest rates also affect the exchange rate, and so monetary policy affects aggregate demand through the effects of the exchange rate on imports and exports.

- Because one country's imports are another country's exports, business cycles are sometimes synchronized across countries. However, floating exchange rates may reduce this link.

BUSINESS CASE : War of the Earthmovers

AP Photo/Douglas C. Pizac

Visit a construction site almost anywhere in the world, and odds are that the earthmoving equipment you see—the tractors, dump trucks, excavators, graders, scrapers, and so on—is made by one of two companies, America's Caterpillar or Japan's Komatsu. Caterpillar and Komatsu both rely heavily on exports, rather than selling only to their domestic markets, and have been fierce competitors for three decades, with first one company, then the other, seemingly on the ropes.

Ask the companies' leaders to explain the course of this seesawing competitive struggle, and they will tell a tale of corporate cultures and management decisions. Caterpillar, the story goes, entered the 1980s filled with complacency thanks to its longtime dominance of the earthmoving industry, only to face a shock from Komatsu that almost drove it to the brink. Then Caterpillar reformed its management practices, regaining the upper hand in the 1990s, and Komatsu found itself in danger of failing, until reinvigorated management stabilized the company again.

But is this the whole story? Not exactly. Management decisions were no doubt crucial to both firms, but so were movements in the exchange rate. Figure 19-14 shows the real exchange rate between the United States and Japan, using consumer prices, from 1980 to 2011. The figure immediately suggests one reason Caterpillar was able to recover from the shock of competition in the 1980s: a sharp appreciation of the Japanese yen beginning in 1985. And Komatsu's ability to survive Caterpillar's resurgence was surely helped by the slide in the yen after 1995, and especially after 2000.

The two companies seemed to have settled into relatively stable positions, with Caterpillar the bigger firm but Komatsu is also doing well thanks in part to rapid growth in demand from China. At the time of writing, many argue that the United States and Japan are themselves engaged in a currency war—with each nation racing to lower the value of (devalue) their currencies in an attempt to boost their trade balance and stimulate aggregate demand. This kind of currency war will definitely have an impact on the Caterpillar/Komatsu rivalry.

FIGURE 19-14 Comparing Real Exchange Rates, 1980–2011

Source: Federal Reserve Bank of St. Louis.

QUESTIONS FOR THOUGHT

1. Why does the yen–dollar exchange rate matter so much for the fortunes of Caterpillar and Komatsu?

2. Why does the figure present the real rather than the nominal exchange rate? Do you think this makes an important difference to the story?

3. In 2011, Japanese policy-makers were discussing possible sales of yen on the foreign exchange market. How would this affect the Caterpillar/Komatsu rivalry?

4. The so-called currency war between the United States and Japan will not only have effects on their own trade balances; it will also indirectly affect other countries' trade balance. How will this currency war affect Canada's trade balance?

SUMMARY

1. A country's **balance of payments accounts** summarize its transactions with the rest of the world. The **balance of payments on current account,** or **current account,** includes the **balance of payments on goods and services** together with balances on factor income and transfers. The **merchandise trade balance,** or **trade balance,** is a frequently cited component of the balance of payments on goods and services. The **balance of payments on financial account,** or **financial account,** measures capital flows. By definition, the balance of payments on current account plus the balance of payments on financial account is zero.

2. Capital flows respond to international differences in interest rates and other rates of return; they can be usefully analyzed using an international version of the loanable funds model, which shows how a country where the interest rate would be low in the absence of capital flows sends funds to a country where the interest rate would be high in the absence of capital flows. The underlying determinants of capital flows are international differences in savings and opportunities for investment spending.

3. Currencies are traded in the **foreign exchange market;** the prices at which they are traded are **exchange rates.** When a currency rises against another currency, it **appreciates;** when it falls, it **depreciates.** The **equilibrium exchange rate** matches the quantity of that currency supplied to the foreign exchange market to the quantity demanded.

4. To correct for international differences in inflation rates, economists calculate **real exchange rates,** which multiply the exchange rate between two countries' currencies by the ratio of the countries' price levels. The current account responds only to changes in the real exchange rate, not the nominal exchange rate. **Purchasing power parity** is the exchange rate that makes the cost of a basket of goods and services equal in two countries. While purchasing power parity and the nominal exchange rate almost always differ,

purchasing power parity is a good predictor of actual changes in the nominal exchange rate.

5. Countries adopt different **exchange rate regimes,** rules governing exchange rate policy. The main types are **fixed exchange rates,** where the government takes action to keep the exchange rate at a target level, and **floating exchange rates,** where the exchange rate is free to fluctuate. Countries can fix exchange rates using **exchange market intervention,** which requires them to hold **foreign exchange reserves** that they use to buy any surplus of their currency. Alternatively, they can change domestic policies, especially monetary policy, to shift the demand and supply curves in the foreign exchange market. Finally, they can use **foreign exchange controls.**

6. Exchange rate policy poses a dilemma: there are economic payoffs to stable exchange rates, but the policies used to fix the exchange rate have costs. Exchange market intervention requires large reserves, and exchange controls distort incentives. If monetary policy is used to help fix the exchange rate, it isn't available to use for domestic policy.

7. Fixed exchange rates aren't always permanent commitments: countries with a fixed exchange rate sometimes engage in **devaluations,** a reduction in the target value of the currency, or **revaluations,** an increase in the target value of the currency. In addition to helping eliminate a surplus of domestic currency on the foreign exchange market, a devaluation increases aggregate demand. Similarly, a revaluation reduces shortages of domestic currency and reduces aggregate demand.

8. Under floating exchange rates, expansionary monetary policy works in part through the exchange rate: cutting domestic interest rates leads to a depreciation, and through that to higher exports and lower imports, which increases aggregate demand. Contractionary monetary policy has the reverse effect.

9. The fact that one country's imports are another country's exports creates a link between the business cycle in different countries. Floating exchange rates, however, may reduce the strength of that link.

KEY TERMS

Balance of payments accounts, p. 614
Balance of payments on current account (current account), p. 616
Balance of payments on goods and services, p. 616
Merchandise trade balance (trade balance), p. 616
Balance of payments on financial account (financial account), p. 616

Foreign exchange market, p. 625
Exchange rates, p. 625
Appreciate, p. 625
Depreciate, p. 625
Equilibrium exchange rate, p. 627
Real exchange rate, p. 628
Purchasing power parity, p. 630
Exchange rate regime, p. 634

Fixed exchange rate, p. 634
Floating exchange rate, p. 634
Exchange market intervention, p. 634
Foreign exchange reserves, p. 634
Foreign exchange controls, p. 635
Devaluation, p. 640
Revaluation, p. 640

PROBLEMS

1. How would each of the following transactions be categorized in Canada's balance of payments accounts? Would it be entered in the current account (as a payment to, or from, a foreigner) or the financial account (as a sale of assets to, or purchase of assets from, a foreigner)? How will the balance of payments on the current and financial accounts change?

   a. A French importer buys a case of Ontario ice wine for $500.

   b. A Canadian who works for a French company deposits her paycheque, drawn on a Paris bank, into her bank in Regina.

   c. A Canadian buys a bond from a Japanese company for $10 000.

   d. A Canadian charity sends $100 000 to Africa to help local residents buy food after a harvest shortfall.

2. The accompanying diagram shows Canadian-owned assets abroad and foreign-owned assets in Canada, both as a percentage of Canada's GDP. As you can see from the diagram, both have trended upward from 1981 to 2011, especially Canadian-owned assets abroad.

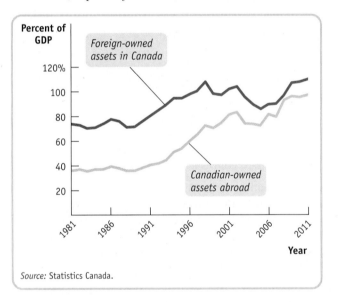

Source: Statistics Canada.

   a. Since Canadian-owned assets abroad increased as a percentage of GDP, does this mean that Canada, over the period, experienced net capital outflows?

   b. Compare the net capital flows in in the early 1980s to the net capital flows in the late 2000s. Did the net capital flows increase or decrease? Why?

3. In the economy of Scottopia in 2012, exports equalled $400 billion of goods and $300 billion of services, imports equalled $500 billion of goods and $350 billion of services, and the rest of the world purchased $250 billion of Scottopia's assets. What was the merchandise trade balance for Scottopia? What was the balance of payments on current account in Scottopia? What was the balance of payments on financial account? What was the value of Scottopia's purchases of assets from the rest of the world?

4. In the economy of Popania in 2012, total Popanian purchases of assets in the rest of the world equalled $300 billion, purchases of Popanian assets by the rest of the world equalled $400 billion, and Popania exported goods and services equal to $350 billion. What was Popania's balance of payments on financial account in 2010? What was its balance of payments on current account? What was the value of its imports?

5. Suppose that Northlandia and Southlandia are the only two trading countries in the world, that each nation runs a balance of payments on both current and financial accounts equal to zero, and that each nation sees the other's assets as identical to its own. Using the accompanying diagrams, explain how the demand and supply of loanable funds, the interest rate, and the balance of payments on current and financial accounts will change in each country if international capital flows are possible.

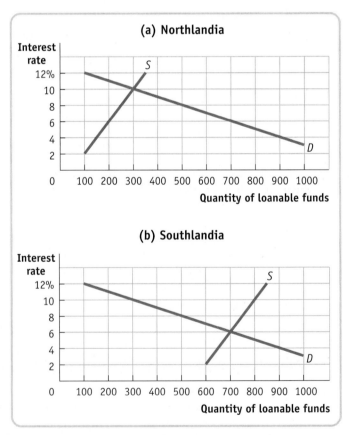

6. Based on the exchange rates for the first trading days of 2012 and 2013, as shown in the accompanying table, did the Canadian dollar appreciate or depreciate during 2012? Did the movement in the value of the Canadian dollar make Canadian goods and services more or less attractive to foreigners?

January 3, 2012	January 2, 2013
0.9549 Australian dollars to buy C$1	0.9617 Australian dollars to buy C$1
1.8185 Brazilian real to buy C$1	1.9841 Brazilian real to buy C$1
0.6331 British pounds to buy C$1	0.6360 British pounds to buy C$1
6.2383 Chinese yuan to buy C$1	6.2344 Chinese yuan to buy C$1
0.7588 euro to buy C$1	0.7314 euro to buy C$1
75.988 Japanese yen to buy C$1	92.678 Japanese yen to buy C$1
0.9236 Swiss franc to buy C$1	0.9043 Swiss franc to buy C$1
0.9911 U.S. dollars to buy C$1	1.0013 U.S. dollars to buy C$1

Source: Pacific Exchange Rate Service (UBC).

7. Go to fx.sauder.ubc.ca. Use the table "The Most Recent Cross-Rates of Major Currencies" to determine whether the British pound (GBP), the U.S. dollar (USD), the Japanese yen (JPY), the euro (EUR), and the Swiss franc (CHF) have appreciated or depreciated against the Canadian dollar (CAD) since January 2, 2013. The exchange rates on January 2, 2013, are listed in the table accompanying Problem 6 above.

8. Suppose Canada and the United States are the only two trading countries in the world. What will happen to the value of the Canadian dollar if each of the following events occurs, other things equal?

   a. The United States relaxes some of its import restrictions.

   b. Canada imposes import tariffs on American goods.

   c. Interest rates in Canada rise dramatically.

   d. A report indicates that Canadian wheat is of better quality than American wheat. In particular, consumers of Canadian grown wheat will enjoy much better health.

9. From January 2001 to June 2003, the U.S. federal funds rate decreased from 6.5% to 1%. During the same period, the target for the overnight rate at the Bank of Canada decreased from 4.75% to 3.25%.

   a. Considering the change in interest rates over the period and using the loanable funds model, would you have expected funds to flow from Canada to the United States or from the United States to Canada over this period?

   b. The accompanying diagram shows the exchange rate between the U.S. dollar and the Canadian dollar from January 1, 2001, through September 2008. Is the movement of the exchange rate over the period January 2001 to June 2003 consistent with the movement in funds predicted in part (a)?

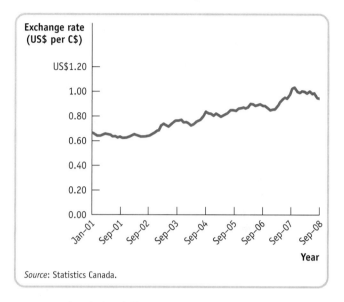

Source: Statistics Canada.

10. In each of the following scenarios, suppose that the two nations mentioned are the only trading nations in the world. Given inflation and the change in the nominal exchange rate, which nation's goods become more attractive?

    a. Inflation is 10% in Canada and 5% in Japan; the Canadian dollar–Japanese yen exchange rate remains the same.

    b. Inflation is 3% in Canada and 8% in Mexico; the price of the Canadian dollar falls from 12.50 to 10.25 Mexican pesos.

    c. Inflation is 5% in Canada and 3% in the eurozone; the price of the euro falls from C$1.30 to C$1.20.

    d. Inflation is 8% in the United States and 4% in Canada; the price of the Canadian dollar rises from US$0.60 to US$0.75.

11. Starting from a position of equilibrium in the foreign exchange market under a fixed exchange rate regime, how must a government react to an increase in the demand for the nation's goods and services by the rest of the world to keep the exchange rate at its fixed value?

12. Suppose that Albernia's central bank has fixed the value of its currency, the bern, to the Canadian dollar (at a rate of C$1.50 to 1 bern) and is committed to that exchange rate. Initially, the foreign exchange market for the bern is also in equilibrium, as shown in the accompanying diagram. However, both Albernians and Canadians begin to believe that there are big risks in holding Albernian assets; as a result, they become unwilling to hold Albernian assets unless they receive a higher rate of return on them than they do on Canadian

assets. How would this affect the diagram? If the Albernian central bank tries to keep the exchange rate fixed using monetary policy, how will this affect the Albernian economy?

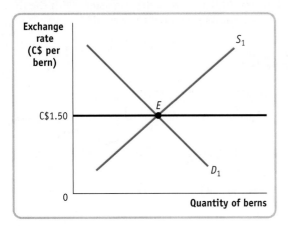

13. Your study partner asks you, "If central banks lose the ability to use discretionary monetary policy under fixed exchange rates, why would nations agree to a fixed exchange rate system?" How d o you respond?

MACROECONOMIC
DATA TABLES

Table I.
MACROECONOMIC DATA FOR CANADA 1970–2010[1]

	1970	1971	1972	1973	1974	1975
Nominal GDP and its Components						
1. + Consumption	50.419	54.871	61.410	70.256	81.937	94.750
2. + Investment (I)	19.406	22.102	24.806	30.843	39.607	43.363
3. + Government purchases of goods and services (G)	18.542	20.462	22.703	25.735	31.246	37.903
4. + Exports	20.124	21.110	23.820	29.892	37.760	38.950
5. − Imports	17.831	19.490	22.824	28.075	37.544	41.994
6. + Statistical discrepancy	−0.481	−0.626	−0.002	0.305	1.032	0.649
7. = **Gross domestic product (GDP)**	**90.179**	**98.429**	**109.913**	**128.956**	**154.038**	**173.621**
8. + Net factor income earned abroad	−1.341	−1.458	−1.475	−1.814	−2.310	−2.654
9. = **Gross national product (GNP)**	**88.838**	**96.971**	**108.438**	**127.142**	**151.728**	**170.967**
Real GDP and Growth Measures						
10. Real GDP (billions of 2002 dollars)	420.4	437.7	461.5	493.7	511.9	521.2
11. Real GDP growth (percent change from previous year)	3.0%	4.1%	5.4%	7.0%	3.7%	1.8%
12. Real GDP per capita (in 2002 dollars)	19 740	19 930	20 773	21 950	22 444	22 522
13. Real GDP per capita growth (percent change from previous year)	1.6%	1.0%	4.2%	5.7%	2.3%	0.3%
Prices and Inflation						
14. Consumer price index (2002 = 100)	20.3	20.9	21.9	23.6	26.2	29.0
15. CPI inflation rate	3.0%	3.0%	4.8%	7.8%	11.0%	10.7%
16. Industry price index (2002 = 100)	21.5	21.9	22.9	25.4	30.2	33.7
17. Industry price index inflation rate	2.9%	1.9%	4.6%	10.9%	18.9%	11.6%
18. GDP deflator (2002 = 100)	21.5	22.5	23.8	26.1	30.1	33.3
19. GDP deflator inflation rate	4.4%	4.7%	5.8%	9.7%	15.3%	10.6%
Population and Employment						
20. Population (thousands)	21 297	21 962	22 218	22 492	22 808	23 143
21. Labour force (thousands)	8 373	8 891	9 279	9 661	10 015	10 491.3
22. Unemployed (thousands)	495	552	562	520	525	707
23. Unemployment rate	5.9%	6.2%	6.1%	5.4%	5.2%	6.7%
Government Finance and Money						
24. (General) Government budget balance	−0.325	−1.000	−1.070	0.772	1.691	−6.143
25. (General) Government budget balance (percent of GDP)	−0.36%	−1.02%	−0.97%	0.60%	1.10%	−3.54%
26. M1	15.628	16.939	19.284	21.663	23.224	25.384
27. M2	32.945	36.986	41.294	47.592	57.537	66.049
28. M2+	39.653	44.54	50.711	59.098	71.461	82.994
29. Bank rate (yearly average)	7.12%	5.19%	4.75%	6.12%	8.50%	8.50%
30. Long-term interest rate (Government of Canada marketable bonds, over 10 years)	7.91%	6.95%	7.23%	7.56%	8.90%	9.04%
International Trade						
31. Current account balance	0.494	−1.046	−2.385	−2.055	−4.475	−8.319
32. Exchange rate (US$ per C$)	0.9591	0.9901	1.0096	1.0001	1.0224	0.9832

Source: Organisation for Economic Co-operation and Development.

[1]Data in billions of current dollars unless otherwise indicated.

1976	1977	1978	1979	1980	1981	1983	1983
107.818	120.185	134.370	150.091	168.479	190.430	204.121	224.100
49.166	52.258	55.927	68.623	72.259	89.438	73.280	81.343
43.499	49.349	53.491	59.045	67.083	76.448	86.939	93.417
44.293	51.229	61.336	75.153	88.288	97.027	97.586	104.735
45.723	51.613	60.424	73.585	82.462	94.413	82.791	91.339
0.941	−0.435	0.177	0.250	0.743	1.541	0.724	−0.870
199.994	**220.973**	**244.877**	**279.577**	**314.390**	**360.471**	**379.859**	**411.386**
−3.613	−4.683	−6.090	−7.636	−8.549	−12.136	−13.249	−12.236
196.381	**216.290**	**238.787**	**271.941**	**305.841**	**348.335**	**366.610**	**399.150**
548.3	567.3	589.7	612.2	625.4	647.3	628.8	645.9
5.2%	3.5%	4.0%	3.8%	2.2%	3.5%	−2.9%	2.7%
23 384	23 911	24 610	25 295	25 511	26 081	25 036	25 463
3.8%	2.3%	2.9%	2.8%	0.9%	2.2%	−4.0%	1.7%
31.1	33.6	36.6	40.0	44.0	49.5	54.9	58.1
7.2%	8.0%	8.9%	9.3%	10.0%	12.5%	10.9%	5.8%
35.4	38.2	41.7	47.8	54.1	59.6	63.6	65.8
5.0%	7.9%	9.2%	14.6%	13.2%	10.2%	6.7%	3.5%
36.5	38.9	41.5	45.7	50.3	55.7	60.4	63.7
9.6%	6.6%	6.7%	10.1%	10.1%	10.7%	8.4%	5.5%
23 450	23 726	23 963	24 202	24 516	24 820	25 117	25 366
10 495.8	10 790.7	11 159.8	11 536	11 873	12 236	12 320	12 527
744	870	935	866	893	932	1369	1502.6
7.1%	8.1%	8.4%	7.5%	7.5%	7.6%	11.1%	12.0%
−5.567	−9.054	−11.686	−9.542	−12.787	−10.195	−26.693	−33.613
−2.78%	−4.10%	−4.77%	−3.41%	−4.07%	−2.83%	−7.03%	−8.17%
26.904	28.754	31.455	32.996	34.803	35.822	36.226	40.915
75.480	87.212	98.439	114.320	135.924	156.337	169.101	179.994
96.05	112.175	128.884	150.554	176.584	202.969	219.833	236.221
9.29%	7.71%	8.98%	12.10%	12.89%	17.93%	13.96%	9.55%
9.18%	8.70%	9.27%	10.21%	12.48%	15.22%	14.26%	11.79%
−7.544	−7.407	−9.35	−9.832	−7.12	−14.994	2.302	−3.132
1.0133	0.9373	0.8746	0.8546	0.8544	0.8339	0.8091	0.8108

(continued on next page)

Table I, continued
MACROECONOMIC DATA FOR CANADA 1970–2010[1]

	1984	1985	1986	1987	1988	1989
Nominal GDP and its Components						
1. + Consumption	244.218	266.683	288.591	312.325	338.518	365.520
2. + Investment (I)	92.204	101.567	108.133	123.463	140.143	153.148
3. + Government purchases of goods and services (G)	98.085	106.065	111.411	117.868	127.912	138.461
4. + Exports	128.759	137.379	142.758	149.913	163.842	168.936
5. − Imports	112.913	126.077	137.782	143.316	159.117	168.723
6. + Statistical discrepancy	−0.771	0.097	−0.57	−1.304	1.796	0.386
7. = Gross domestic product (GDP)	**449.582**	**485.714**	**512.541**	**558.949**	**613.094**	**657.728**
8. + Net factor income earned abroad	−14.172	−15.076	−17.446	−17.305	−19.801	−22.543
9. = Gross national product (GNP)	**435.410**	**470.638**	**495.095**	**541.644**	**593.293**	**635.185**
Real GDP and Growth Measures						
10. Real GDP (billions of 2002 dollars)	683.5	716.1	733.5	764.7	802.7	823.7
11. Real GDP growth (percent change from previous year)	5.8%	4.8%	2.4%	4.3%	5.0%	2.6%
12. Real GDP per capita (in 2002 dollars)	26 690	27 712	28 102	28 914	29 961	30 199
13. Real GDP per capita growth (percent change from previous year)	4.8%	3.8%	1.4%	2.9%	3.6%	0.8%
Prices and Inflation						
14. Consumer price index (2002 = 100)	60.6	63.0	65.6	68.5	71.2	74.8
15. CPI inflation rate	4.3%	4.0%	4.1%	4.4%	3.9%	5.1%
16. Industry price index (2002 = 100)	68.8	70.7	71.3	73.3	76.5	78
17. Industry price index inflation rate	4.6%	2.8%	0.8%	2.8%	4.4%	2.0%
18. GDP deflator (2002 = 100)	65.8	67.8	69.9	73.1	76.4	79.8
19. GDP deflator inflation rate	3.3%	3.0%	3.1%	4.6%	4.5%	4.5%
Population and Employment						
20. Population (thousands)	25 607	25 842	26 100	26 447	26 792	27 277
21. Labour force (thousands)	12 753	13 024	13 279	13 522	13 781	14 049
22. Unemployed (thousands)	1451	1368	1275	1190	1069	1054
23. Unemployment rate	11.4%	10.5%	9.6%	8.8%	7.8%	7.5%
Government Finance and Money						
24. (General) Government budget balance	−34.957	−41.711	−36.605	−30.307	−26.572	−30.235
25. (General) Government budget balance (percent of GDP)	−7.78%	−8.59%	−7.14%	−5.42%	−4.33%	−4.60%
26. M1	45.338	59.275	73.065	83.074	83.468	86.602
27. M2	191.184	210.049	231.474	260.119	283.266	322.231
28. M2+	252.408	277.592	306.466	341.146	373.457	425.458
29. Bank rate (yearly average)	11.31%	9.65%	9.21%	8.40%	9.69%	12.29%
30. Long-term interest rate (Government of Canada marketable bonds, over 10 years)	12.75%	11.04%	9.52%	9.95%	10.22%	9.92%
International Trade						
31. Current account balance	−1.673	−7.828	−15.514	−17.806	−18.328	−25.812
32. Exchange rate (US$ per C$)	0.7713	0.7312	0.7189	0.7561	0.8154	0.8453

Source: Organisation for Economic Co-operation and Development.

[1] Data in billions of current dollars unless otherwise indicated.

1990	1991	1992	1993	1994	1995	1996	1997
385.413	398.314	411.167	428.219	445.857	460.906	480.427	510.695
142.180	128.739	124.669	129.776	145.482	152.027	152.207	183.02
151.418	162.234	168.787	171.163	171.59	172.459	171.161	171.756
175.513	172.161	189.784	219.664	262.127	302.48	321.248	348.604
174.624	176.093	192.393	219.673	253.014	276.618	287.553	331.271
0.021	0.012	−1.534	−1.965	−1.169	−0.828	−0.626	−0.071
679.921	**685.367**	**700.480**	**727.184**	**770.873**	**810.426**	**836.864**	**882.733**
−24.444	−22.854	−25.397	−25.169	−27.994	−28.550	−28.330	−27.704
655.477	**662.513**	**675.083**	**702.015**	**742.879**	**781.876**	**808.534**	**855.029**
825.3	808.1	815.1	834.2	874.3	898.8	913.4	952.0
0.2%	−2.1%	0.9%	2.3%	4.8%	2.8%	1.6%	4.2%
29 804	28 820	28 731	29 081	30 146	30 674	30 846	31 832
−1.3%	−3.3%	−0.3%	1.2%	3.7%	1.8%	0.6%	3.2%
78.4	82.8	84	85.6	85.7	87.6	88.9	90.4
4.8%	5.6%	1.4%	1.9%	0.1%	2.2%	1.5%	1.7%
78.3	77.5	77.8	80.6	85.5	91.9	92.3	92.9
0.4%	−1.0%	0.4%	3.6%	6.1%	7.5%	0.4%	0.7%
82.4	84.8	85.9	87.2	88.2	90.2	91.6	92.8
3.3%	2.9%	1.3%	1.5%	1.1%	2.3%	1.6%	1.3%
27 691	28 037	28 371	28 685	29 001	29 302	29 610	29 906
14 245	14 334	14 338	14 439	14 574	14 688	14 848	15 075
1162	1478	1609	1641	1513	1391	1429	1370
8.2%	10.3%	11.2%	11.4%	10.4%	9.5%	9.6%	9.1%
−39.633	−57.257	−63.928	−63.354	−51.684	−43.181	−23.421	1.640
−5.83%	−8.35%	−9.13%	−8.71%	−6.70%	−5.33%	−2.80%	0.19%
89.014	93.343	98.923	105.027	116.27	126.41	140.555	157.563
358.338	382.108	396.267	407.073	415.93	433.649	447.098	447.178
476.521	516.716	547.143	569.274	580.093	602.519	628.825	634.067
13.04%	9.03%	6.78%	5.09%	5.77%	7.31%	4.53%	3.52%
10.85%	9.76%	8.76%	7.84%	8.63%	8.28%	7.50%	6.42%
−23.135	−25.629	−25.36	−28.093	−17.73	−6.099	4.6	−11.397
0.8569	0.8729	0.8241	0.7733	0.7300	0.7311	0.7334	0.7200

(continued on next page)

Table I, continued
MACROECONOMIC DATA FOR CANADA 1970–2010[1]

	1998	1999	2000	2001	2002	2003
Nominal GDP and its Components						
1. + Consumption	531.169	560.884	596.009	620.614	655.722	686.552
2. + Investment (I)	186.542	199.457	217.801	212.538	222.455	242.517
3. + Government purchases of goods and services (G)	179.317	186.054	200.084	211.706	224.428	238.416
4. + Exports	379.203	424.258	490.688	482.463	479.185	462.473
5. – Imports	360.871	388.303	428.754	418.836	428.301	416.856
6. + Statistical discrepancy	−0.387	0.091	0.749	−0.437	−0.584	0.073
7. = Gross domestic product (GDP)	**914.973**	**982.441**	**1076.577**	**1108.048**	**1152.905**	**1213.175**
8. + Net factor income earned abroad	−30.420	−33.232	−28.032	−31.353	−28.868	−28.590
9. = Gross national product (GNP)	**884.553**	**949.209**	**1048.545**	**1076.695**	**1124.037**	**1184.585**
Real GDP and Growth Measures						
10. Real GDP (billions of 2002 dollars)	991.0	1045.8	1100.5	1120.1	1152.9	1174.6
11. Real GDP growth (percent change from previous year)	4.1%	5.5%	5.2%	1.8%	2.9%	1.9%
12. Real GDP per capita (in 2002 dollars)	32 862	34 399	35 864	36 112	36 771	37 124
13. Real GDP per capita growth (percent change from previous year)	3.2%	4.7%	4.3%	0.7%	1.8%	1.0%
Prices and Inflation						
14. Consumer price index (2002 = 100)	91.3	92.9	95.4	97.8	100	102.8
15. CPI inflation rate	1.0%	1.8%	2.7%	2.5%	2.2%	2.8%
16. Industry price index (2002 = 100)	93.3	94.9	99	100	100	98.8
17. Industry price index inflation rate	0.4%	1.7%	4.3%	1.0%	0.0%	−1.2%
18. GDP deflator (2002 = 100)	92.3	93.9	97.8	98.9	100	103.3
19. GDP deflator inflation rate	−0.5%	1.7%	4.2%	1.1%	1.1%	3.3%
Population and Employment						
20. Population (thousands)	30 155	30 401	30 686	31 019	31 354	31 640
21. Labour force (thousands)	15 316	15 586	15 849	16 110	16 566	16 946
22. Unemployed (thousands)	1269	1179	1084	1171	1269	1287
23. Unemployment rate	8.3%	7.6%	6.8%	7.3%	7.7%	7.6%
Government Finance and Money						
24. (General) Government budget balance	0.765	15.855	31.705	7.292	−1.088	−1.024
25. (General) Government budget balance (percent of GDP)	0.08%	1.61%	2.94%	0.66%	−0.09%	−0.08%
26. M1	169.744	180.482	208.934	229.89	252.192	263.276
27. M2	443.043	459.281	491.783	518.358	549.29	581.903
28. M2+	626.099	652.358	690.586	736.336	789.395	827.238
29. Bank rate (yearly average)	5.10%	4.92%	5.77%	4.31%	2.71%	3.19%
30. Long-term interest rate (Government of Canada marketable bonds, over 10 years)	5.46%	5.69%	5.89%	5.78%	5.66%	5.28%
International Trade						
31. Current account balance	−11.363	2.57	29.269	25.104	19.778	14.649
32. Exchange rate (US$ per C$)	0.6713	0.6750	0.6733	0.6446	0.6374	0.7195

Source: Organisation for Economic Co-operation and Development.

[1]Data in billions of current dollars unless otherwise indicated.

2004	2005	2006	2007	2008	2009	2010
719.917	758.966	801.742	851.603	890.601	898.215	940.620
267.518	303.277	333.895	355.472	372.598	319.047	360.735
247.397	259.857	277.608	293.608	315.977	337.735	353.569
495.980	519.435	524.075	534.718	563.075	439.527	478.132
440.314	468.27	487.674	505.055	538.654	465.328	508.653
0.408	0.58	0.759	−0.757	−0.179	−0.211	0.205
1290.906	**1373.845**	**1450.405**	**1529.589**	**1603.418**	**1528.985**	**1624.608**
−26.306	−25.748	−14.239	−19.556	−20.258	−23.690	−28.214
1264.600	**1348.097**	**1436.166**	**1510.033**	**1583.160**	**1505.295**	**1596.394**
1211.2	1247.8	1283.0	1311.3	1320.3	1283.7	1325.0
3.1%	3.0%	2.8%	2.2%	0.7%	−2.8%	3.2%
37 922	38 697	39 386	39 823	39 627	38 062	38 826
2.1%	2.0%	1.8%	1.1%	−0.5%	−3.9%	2.0%
104.7	107.0	109.1	111.5	114.1	114.4	116.5
1.8%	2.2%	2.0%	2.2%	2.3%	0.3%	1.8%
102	103.6	106	107.6	112.3	108.4	109.5
3.2%	1.6%	2.3%	1.5%	4.4%	−3.5%	1.0%
106.6	110.1	113	116.6	121.4	119.1	122.6
3.2%	3.3%	2.6%	3.2%	4.1%	−1.9%	2.9%
31 941	32 245	32 576	32 928	33 318	33 727	34 127
17 156	17 296	17 517	17 885	18 201	18 335	18 526
1230	1167	1105	1082	1119	1519	1479
7.2%	6.7%	6.3%	6.0%	6.1%	8.3%	8.0%
11.146	21.248	23.780	21.551	−6.317	−74.724	−90.244
0.86%	1.55%	1.64%	1.41%	−0.39%	−4.89%	−5.55%
286.07	306.247	331.512	361.182	393.311	444.044	495.937
619.299	654.903	703.761	759.808	832.347	945.356	1003.887
868.069	910.926	969.446	1049.307	1158.573	1292.87	1344.35
2.50%	2.92%	4.31%	4.60%	3.21%	0.65%	0.85%
5.08%	4.39%	4.30%	4.34%	4.04%	3.89%	3.66%
29.837	25.902	20.49	12.772	5.276	−45.236	−50.864
0.7716	0.8271	0.8847	0.9375	0.9343	0.8798	0.9657

Table II.
MACROECONOMIC DATA FOR SELECT COUNTRIES
GDP (Billions of U.S. Dollars)

Country	1985	1986	1987	1988	1989	1990	1991	1992	1993
Argentina	88.18	106.04	108.72	127.34	81.70	141.33	189.58	228.76	236.49
Australia	176.88	183.57	216.18	274.38	310.98	328.20	328.79	321.64	312.89
Austria	68.03	96.53	120.71	132.41	132.06	165.26	172.78	193.52	188.39
Bangladesh	21.34	22.37	24.68	26.64	29.34	30.50	31.43	31.44	32.95
Belgium	85.76	118.88	147.79	160.47	162.45	203.31	208.53	231.79	222.26
Brazil	253.08	293.58	319.55	356.98	490.05	507.78	445.24	426.52	478.62
Bulgaria	27.39	24.24	28.10	45.92	46.77	20.62	2.02	8.20	4.45
Canada	355.71	368.87	421.53	498.16	555.52	582.74	598.20	579.52	563.68
Chile	16.49	17.72	20.90	24.64	28.39	31.56	36.43	44.47	47.69
China	307.02	297.59	323.97	404.15	451.31	390.28	409.17	488.22	613.22
Colombia	48.68	48.75	50.75	54.71	55.17	56.19	57.54	68.75	77.85
Cyprus	2.43	3.09	3.71	4.27	4.56	5.59	5.77	6.91	6.61
Czech Republic	n/a	n/a	n/a	n/a	n/a	n/a	n/a	n/a	n/a
Denmark	61.20	86.37	107.37	113.23	110.06	135.84	136.70	150.20	140.63
Dominican Republic	6.49	7.88	8.30	7.60	8.58	7.99	9.79	11.49	12.95
Ecuador	16.18	11.87	11.10	10.55	10.36	10.52	11.80	12.90	15.07
Egypt	46.45	51.43	73.57	88.00	109.71	91.38	46.06	42.01	47.10
Estonia	n/a	n/a	n/a	n/a	n/a	n/a	n/a	n/a	1.73
Finland	55.25	72.33	90.12	107.26	116.73	139.12	125.66	110.72	87.39
France	547.90	761.35	923.68	1 004.44	1 009.84	1 248.56	1 249.22	1 374.07	1 292.12
Germany	639.70	913.64	1 136.93	1 225.73	1 216.80	1 547.03	1 815.06	2 066.73	2 005.56
Ghana	5.33	6.03	4.76	5.15	5.94	6.53	6.85	6.66	5.97
Greece	45.13	53.10	61.78	71.95	74.56	92.20	99.42	109.56	102.61
Guatemala	10.39	5.62	6.50	7.04	8.12	7.07	8.70	9.60	10.46
Hungary	21.14	24.35	26.77	29.29	29.90	33.89	34.27	38.19	39.57
Iceland	2.94	3.93	5.44	6.02	5.59	6.36	6.80	6.97	6.12
India	229.56	252.45	278.20	304.46	302.14	325.93	289.36	291.86	285.33
Ireland	20.99	28.14	33.36	36.55	37.70	47.77	48.42	54.44	50.44
Israel	25.32	31.17	37.23	46.06	46.81	55.09	62.10	69.03	69.19
Italy	437.10	619.08	777.01	860.86	895.34	1 135.54	1 198.99	1 271.91	1 022.66
Jamaica	2.16	2.57	2.90	3.46	4.01	5.06	4.75	4.25	5.92
Japan	1 352.06	2 003.32	2 429.60	2 950.00	2 951.77	3 030.05	3 464.93	3 781.78	4 340.89
Kenya	8.75	10.39	11.39	11.81	11.71	12.18	11.50	11.33	7.87
Korea	98.50	113.74	143.38	192.11	236.23	270.41	315.58	338.17	372.21
Latvia	n/a	n/a	n/a	n/a	n/a	n/a	n/a	1.55	2.47

Source: International Monetary Fund, World Economic Outlook Database, October 2010.
2010 is estimated as of 4/13/2011.

1994	1995	1996	1997	1998	1999	2000	2001	2002	2003	2004
257.43	258.02	272.22	292.99	299.08	283.76	284.54	269.10	102.72	129.54	153.01
356.64	382.25	428.03	428.44	382.28	413.57	400.87	379.42	426.47	543.19	658.55
201.64	238.55	234.23	207.13	212.44	211.21	191.76	190.32	206.68	252.52	289.42
35.80	39.58	41.52	43.39	44.76	46.53	47.05	47.19	49.56	54.48	59.12
242.62	284.79	275.17	249.76	255.57	254.38	233.14	232.34	253.29	311.70	360.98
596.76	769.74	840.05	871.52	841.30	573.12	642.42	552.84	500.27	555.54	665.55
7.82	13.11	9.90	10.37	12.85	12.98	12.60	13.60	15.60	19.99	24.65
564.48	590.50	613.78	637.53	616.78	661.25	724.91	715.44	734.65	865.90	992.23
55.16	71.35	75.77	82.81	79.37	72.99	75.20	68.56	67.25	73.99	95.65
559.22	727.95	856.08	952.65	1 019.48	1 083.28	1 198.48	1 324.81	1 453.83	1 640.96	1 931.65
97.87	110.81	120.00	112.70	109.12	96.89	100.36	98.75	98.23	94.97	118.86
7.45	9.25	9.35	8.90	9.56	9.78	9.32	9.68	10.56	13.32	15.82
n/a	55.26	62.01	57.14	61.85	60.19	56.72	61.84	75.28	91.36	109.53
153.59	181.99	184.44	170.44	173.65	173.94	160.08	160.48	173.88	212.62	244.73
13.99	15.52	17.07	19.19	20.08	21.48	23.72	24.62	24.93	20.18	21.56
18.59	20.22	21.29	23.66	23.28	16.69	15.95	21.27	24.72	28.41	32.65
51.88	60.16	67.63	75.87	84.82	89.94	99.16	95.40	87.51	81.38	78.80
2.42	3.78	4.73	5.05	5.59	5.71	5.68	6.24	7.32	9.85	12.03
100.99	130.85	128.28	123.07	129.84	130.39	122.07	124.67	135.56	164.44	189.17
1 366.16	1 572.38	1 574.32	1 425.80	1 474.24	1 458.37	1 333.28	1 341.25	1 463.46	1 804.41	2 060.58
2 151.03	2 524.95	2 439.35	2 163.23	2 187.48	2 146.43	1 905.80	1 892.60	2 024.06	2 446.89	2 748.82
5.45	6.46	6.93	6.89	7.48	7.72	4.98	5.32	6.17	7.63	8.88
109.82	128.90	136.27	133.13	133.87	137.83	127.60	131.14	147.91	194.99	231.02
11.84	13.32	14.20	16.09	17.31	16.49	17.19	18.70	20.78	21.92	23.96
42.55	45.79	46.59	47.18	48.75	49.13	47.29	53.37	66.77	83.88	102.61
6.29	7.01	7.31	7.42	8.27	8.73	8.68	7.90	8.91	10.97	13.23
323.94	367.73	378.99	424.14	427.55	456.52	479.87	491.44	514.25	595.44	690.32
55.35	67.13	74.09	81.29	88.12	96.42	97.04	104.91	123.21	158.33	185.68
78.37	96.06	105.37	108.39	109.89	110.79	124.75	123.06	113.01	118.90	126.84
1 054.90	1 126.63	1 259.95	1 193.62	1 218.67	1 202.40	1 100.56	1 118.32	1 223.24	1 510.06	1 730.10
7.66	5.81	7.84	8.20	8.62	8.76	8.95	9.13	9.56	9.49	10.17
4 778.99	5 264.38	4 642.55	4 261.84	3 857.03	4 368.73	4 667.45	4 095.48	3 918.33	4 229.10	4 605.94
9.42	11.94	12.05	13.28	13.77	12.88	12.32	13.06	13.19	15.04	16.09
435.59	531.14	573.00	532.24	357.51	461.81	533.39	504.58	575.93	643.76	721.98
4.15	4.96	5.68	6.25	6.73	7.29	7.83	8.31	9.32	11.19	13.76

(continued on next page)

Table II, continued
MACROECONOMIC DATA FOR SELECT COUNTRIES
GDP (Billions of U.S. Dollars)

Country	2005	2006	2007	2008	2009	2010
Argentina	183.00	214.04	262.04	328.03	310.06	351.02
Australia	738.08	783.67	951.77	1 058.05	994.25	1 219.72
Austria	303.45	322.64	372.83	416.62	382.07	366.26
Bangladesh	61.13	65.20	73.97	84.46	94.60	105.40
Belgium	377.77	399.98	459.25	506.72	472.10	461.33
Brazil	890.05	1 093.49	1 366.22	1 635.52	1 574.04	2 023.53
Bulgaria	27.19	31.66	39.55	49.90	47.10	44.84
Canada	1 133.76	1 278.61	1 424.07	1 499.11	1 336.07	1 563.66
Chile	118.22	146.75	164.21	170.86	161.62	199.18
China	2 256.92	2 712.92	3 494.24	4 519.95	4 984.73	5 745.13
Colombia	146.62	161.01	210.52	233.73	232.40	283.11
Cyprus	17.00	18.42	21.84	25.38	23.60	22.75
Czech Republic	124.55	142.61	174.22	216.09	190.32	195.23
Denmark	257.68	274.38	310.72	340.80	310.09	304.56
Dominican Republic	33.53	35.67	40.99	45.52	46.71	50.87
Ecuador	36.94	41.71	45.50	54.28	55.55	61.49
Egypt	89.79	107.38	130.35	162.44	187.95	216.83
Estonia	13.90	16.81	21.69	23.70	19.31	19.22
Finland	195.97	207.99	246.31	271.75	238.61	231.98
France	2 147.77	2 270.36	2 598.77	2 865.23	2 656.38	2 555.44
Germany	2 793.23	2 921.27	3 333.93	3 651.62	3 338.68	3 305.90
Ghana	10.73	12.74	15.02	16.50	15.33	18.06
Greece	243.38	264.26	310.36	351.95	330.78	305.01
Guatemala	27.21	30.23	34.11	39.15	37.66	40.77
Hungary	110.17	112.91	138.37	155.48	129.54	132.28
Iceland	16.34	16.73	20.43	16.80	12.14	12.77
India	809.72	908.04	1 151.65	1 260.62	1 236.94	1 430.02
Ireland	202.20	222.68	259.56	264.89	222.36	204.14
Israel	134.26	145.84	168.00	202.30	195.39	201.25
Italy	1 780.78	1 865.11	2 119.25	2 307.43	2 118.26	2 036.69
Jamaica	11.08	11.97	12.90	13.53	12.64	13.74
Japan	4 552.19	4 362.58	4 377.96	4 886.95	5 068.89	5 390.90
Kenya	19.37	23.30	28.89	26.62	30.14	32.42
Korea	844.87	951.77	1 049.24	931.41	832.51	986.26
Latvia	16.04	19.94	28.80	33.87	25.93	23.39

Source: International Monetary Fund, World Economic Outlook Database, October 2010.
2010 is estimated as of 4/13/2011.

Country	1985	1986	1987	1988	1989	1990	1991	1992	1993
Lithuania	n/a	n/a	n/a	n/a	n/a	n/a	n/a	1.99	2.81
Luxembourg	4.57	6.65	8.26	9.36	9.96	12.71	13.77	15.42	15.81
Malaysia	31.77	28.24	32.18	35.27	38.85	44.03	49.88	60.05	67.90
Mexico	211.52	146.45	160.60	196.48	239.44	282.56	338.74	392.84	436.13
Netherlands	133.17	185.60	226.44	241.38	238.18	295.46	303.46	334.65	324.39
New Zealand	22.38	27.23	36.29	44.67	43.07	44.68	42.79	40.62	43.94
Nigeria	25.97	20.56	21.91	24.31	23.49	31.48	28.34	25.52	15.79
Norway	64.26	77.20	92.45	100.06	100.77	117.62	119.67	128.32	118.17
Peru	17.21	25.82	42.64	33.73	41.63	28.98	34.55	35.95	34.82
Philippines	30.73	29.87	33.20	37.89	42.65	44.16	45.32	52.98	54.37
Poland	70.78	73.68	63.71	68.61	66.90	62.08	80.45	88.71	90.37
Portugal	26.78	37.25	46.61	54.52	58.82	78.13	88.43	106.34	93.57
Romania	47.80	51.77	57.89	59.93	53.69	38.24	28.85	19.58	26.36
Russia	n/a	n/a	n/a	n/a	n/a	n/a	n/a	85.59	183.82
Saudi Arabia	103.89	86.95	85.70	88.26	95.34	116.78	131.34	136.30	132.15
Singapore	18.46	18.73	21.55	26.48	31.41	38.84	45.19	52.01	60.47
South Africa	57.27	65.42	85.79	92.24	95.98	112.00	120.24	130.53	130.45
Spain	176.69	244.48	309.75	363.91	401.39	520.71	560.80	613.02	514.95
Sweden	106.38	140.79	171.61	193.88	204.45	244.55	257.90	267.17	202.04
Switzerland	99.47	142.60	178.58	193.20	186.53	238.22	241.00	250.98	244.09
Thailand	38.90	43.10	50.54	61.67	72.25	85.64	96.19	109.43	121.80
Turkey	90.38	101.80	117.18	122.13	144.03	202.38	202.72	213.58	242.14
Ukraine	n/a	n/a	n/a	n/a	n/a	n/a	n/a	20.78	32.71
United Arab Emirates	27.35	21.67	23.80	24.19	27.92	35.99	33.19	33.49	36.72
United Kingdom	468.96	570.88	702.54	852.40	861.29	1 017.79	1 059.26	1 098.30	982.62
United States	4 217.48	4 460.05	4 736.35	5 100.43	5 482.13	5 800.53	5 992.10	6 342.30	6 667.33
Vietnam	15.00	33.87	42.05	23.23	6.29	6.47	7.64	9.87	13.18

(continued on next page)

Table II, continued
MACROECONOMIC DATA FOR SELECT COUNTRIES
GDP (Billions of U.S. Dollars)

Country	1994	1995	1996	1997	1998	1999	2000	2001	2002
Lithuania	4.40	6.47	8.17	9.96	11.23	10.97	11.43	12.16	14.16
Luxembourg	17.59	20.70	20.59	18.54	19.38	21.22	20.33	20.22	22.66
Malaysia	75.61	90.17	102.38	101.68	73.27	80.34	93.79	92.78	100.85
Mexico	456.12	310.10	360.06	434.23	455.59	520.45	628.85	672.82	702.02
Netherlands	348.91	419.35	418.11	387.01	403.20	412.00	386.20	401.00	439.36
New Zealand	51.77	61.06	67.80	67.69	55.60	57.61	52.96	51.94	60.75
Nigeria	18.09	36.95	46.02	35.39	32.75	35.94	46.39	44.14	59.12
Norway	124.48	148.92	160.00	158.23	151.14	159.05	168.29	170.93	191.92
Peru	44.92	53.66	55.85	59.14	56.76	51.53	53.34	53.94	56.76
Philippines	64.08	75.53	84.37	83.74	66.60	76.16	75.91	71.22	76.81
Poland	103.68	139.10	156.66	157.08	172.00	167.79	171.26	190.42	198.21
Portugal	98.05	116.24	121.01	115.67	122.73	126.28	117.36	120.14	132.35
Romania	30.07	35.48	35.32	35.29	42.12	35.59	37.34	40.59	45.99
Russia	276.90	313.45	391.78	404.95	271.04	195.91	259.70	306.58	345.13
Saudi Arabia	134.33	142.46	157.74	164.99	145.97	161.17	188.69	183.26	188.80
Singapore	73.24	87.06	95.18	99.30	85.01	84.88	94.31	87.70	90.64
South Africa	135.82	151.12	143.83	148.84	134.22	133.11	132.96	118.56	111.36
Spain	516.72	597.28	622.65	573.38	601.63	618.69	582.38	609.63	688.68
Sweden	217.55	253.68	276.46	253.18	254.72	258.81	247.26	227.36	250.96
Switzerland	270.22	315.95	304.75	264.58	272.63	268.22	249.91	254.99	278.62
Thailand	144.31	168.02	181.95	150.89	111.86	122.63	122.73	115.54	126.88
Turkey	174.45	227.51	243.90	255.07	269.13	249.82	266.44	195.55	232.28
Ukraine	36.76	37.01	44.56	50.15	41.88	31.58	31.26	38.01	42.39
United Arab Emirates	37.44	40.73	48.01	51.22	48.51	55.18	70.22	69.23	74.30
United Kingdom	1 061.38	1 157.44	1 220.85	1 359.44	1 456.16	1 502.89	1 480.53	1 471.40	1 614.70
United States	7 085.15	7 414.63	7 838.48	8 332.35	8 793.48	9 353.50	9 951.48	10 286.18	10 642.30
Vietnam	16.28	20.80	24.69	26.89	27.23	28.70	31.18	32.52	35.10

Source: International Monetary Fund, World Economic Outlook Database, October 2010.
2010 is estimated as of 4/13/2011.

2003	2004	2005	2006	2007	2008	2009	2010
18.61	22.55	25.98	30.08	39.10	47.17	37.12	35.73
29.21	34.14	37.72	42.88	51.35	57.91	52.43	52.43
110.20	124.75	138.02	157.05	187.01	222.27	192.96	218.95
700.32	759.78	848.95	952.54	1 025.58	1 089.88	874.81	1 004.04
539.34	610.69	639.58	678.32	783.69	877.47	796.65	770.31
80.80	99.65	111.43	107.68	131.00	131.07	117.79	138.00
67.66	87.85	112.25	145.43	165.92	207.12	168.85	216.80
225.12	258.56	302.01	336.72	387.58	446.32	378.59	413.51
61.34	69.70	79.40	92.31	107.14	127.41	126.77	153.55
79.63	86.93	98.83	117.53	144.07	167.17	161.20	189.06
216.81	253.02	303.98	341.67	425.32	529.40	430.74	438.88
161.73	185.04	191.51	201.25	231.28	253.02	233.48	223.70
59.47	75.79	99.17	122.70	170.62	204.32	161.52	158.39
430.29	591.18	763.70	989.93	1 299.70	1 666.95	1 231.89	1 476.91
214.86	250.67	315.76	356.63	385.20	476.94	376.27	434.44
95.96	112.70	125.43	145.07	176.77	193.33	182.23	217.38
168.22	219.43	246.96	261.18	285.94	276.77	287.22	354.41
885.36	1 045.67	1 132.13	1 235.92	1 444.02	1 601.41	1 467.89	1 374.78
314.71	362.09	370.58	399.08	462.51	487.58	406.07	444.59
325.05	362.99	372.48	391.23	434.12	502.45	491.92	522.44
142.64	161.34	176.35	207.23	247.11	272.43	263.98	312.61
303.26	392.21	482.69	529.19	649.13	730.32	614.47	729.05
50.13	64.88	86.18	107.75	142.72	180.12	117.40	136.56
87.61	105.60	137.99	175.22	206.41	254.39	223.87	239.65
1 862.77	2 203.58	2 282.89	2 447.68	2 812.05	2 679.01	2 178.86	2 258.57
11 142.18	11 867.75	12 638.38	13 398.93	14 061.80	14 369.08	14 119.05	14 624.18
39.56	45.45	52.93	60.93	71.11	90.27	93.16	101.99

Table III.
MACROECONOMIC DATA FOR SELECT COUNTRIES
GDP PER PERSON (U.S. dollars)

Country	1985	1986	1987	1988	1989	1990	1991	1992	1993
Argentina	2 905.51	3 449.53	3 496.89	4 046.48	2 564.37	4 344.56	5 750.17	6 845.08	6 972.55
Australia	11 183.47	11 438.51	13 264.12	16 552.99	18 459.18	19 114.91	18 909.99	18 294.44	17 617.49
Austria	9 000.85	12 758.60	15 933.79	17 455.89	17 332.21	21 524.07	22 280.00	24 680.90	23 830.11
Bangladesh	207.17	211.96	228.35	240.83	259.41	263.74	266.08	260.66	267.72
Belgium	8 690.74	12 042.73	14 959.01	16 158.07	16 330.38	20 377.96	20 821.48	23 052.22	22 018.45
Brazil	1 902.86	2 161.63	2 305.75	2 526.14	3 403.20	3 463.91	2 986.31	2 814.44	3 108.22
Bulgaria	3 056.86	2 711.70	3 156.34	5 187.98	5 321.33	2 365.24	233.86	958.73	525.83
Canada	13 779.84	14 149.88	15 965.78	18 621.91	20 412.25	21 088.87	21 374.10	20 460.27	19 673.56
Chile	1 368.47	1 447.21	1 678.64	1 945.73	2 203.77	2 409.14	2 734.64	3 283.03	3 463.35
China	290.05	276.81	296.41	364.01	400.44	341.35	353.27	416.68	517.41
Colombia	1 580.94	1 550.93	1 581.29	1 669.79	1 649.49	1 646.60	1 651.75	1 935.07	2 150.17
Cyprus	4 492.97	5 641.41	6 694.01	7 640.24	8 042.04	9 647.73	9 697.76	11 322.67	10 562.59
Czech Republic	n/a	n/a	n/a	n/a	n/a	n/a	n/a	n/a	n/a
Denmark	11 974.67	16 880.56	20 950.32	22 075.41	21 454.88	26 451.43	26 560.90	29 095.51	27 144.62
Dominican Republic	1 017.32	1 206.08	1 238.83	1 108.08	1 224.38	1 117.44	1 345.60	1 556.04	1 729.10
Ecuador	1 778.51	1 272.70	1 160.39	1 077.26	1 032.55	1 024.51	1 123.61	1 201.21	1 372.53
Egypt	997.96	1 077.02	1 507.61	1 767.07	2 155.49	1 779.26	878.62	785.04	862.41
Estonia	n/a	n/a	n/a	n/a	n/a	n/a	n/a	n/a	1 144.63
Finland	11 249.99	14 684.85	18 247.74	21 649.39	23 467.10	27 832.32	24 986.08	21 902.56	17 209.10
France	9 910.66	13 706.55	16 546.25	17 898.68	17 897.45	22 017.09	21 925.58	24 005.52	22 484.47
Germany	8 405.08	11 996.27	14 925.38	15 993.71	15 720.09	19 610.39	22 713.25	25 703.34	24 795.78
Ghana	422.86	466.03	358.82	378.62	425.84	456.27	467.04	442.89	386.81
Greece	4 543.20	5 325.16	6 174.09	7 163.53	7 387.00	9 073.37	9 701.56	10 581.02	9 802.05
Guatemala	1 432.21	755.05	852.62	900.56	1 012.88	860.72	1 034.67	1 112.81	1 181.69
Hungary	1 994.90	2 306.36	2 547.02	2 799.19	2 869.34	3 266.35	3 303.76	3 681.66	3 817.42
Iceland	12 137.93	16 098.36	21 968.44	23 881.42	22 020.74	24 873.07	26 173.66	26 553.26	23 100.27
India	296.30	318.80	343.82	368.31	357.86	378.04	328.74	324.86	311.26
Ireland	5 928.40	7 947.96	9 407.19	10 351.70	10 741.39	13 626.12	13 732.85	15 314.37	14 112.47
Israel	6 171.41	7 480.52	8 797.63	10 700.08	10 645.01	12 204.03	13 328.51	14 291.12	13 796.30
Italy	7 724.27	10 938.18	13 729.40	15 207.03	15 804.94	20 029.19	21 129.68	22 403.30	17 997.61
Jamaica	952.72	1 122.37	1 256.68	1 488.94	1 723.04	2 138.61	2 007.47	1 796.23	2 499.47
Japan	11 192.50	16 495.61	19 909.75	24 072.15	23 992.61	24 547.04	27 959.09	30 408.22	34 791.19
Kenya	440.14	504.64	534.26	535.29	513.27	517.14	473.71	453.40	306.68
Korea	2 413.94	2 759.70	3 444.79	4 570.73	5 565.10	6 307.66	7 288.84	7 729.98	8 422.05
Latvia	n/a	n/a	n/a	n/a	n/a	n/a	n/a	580.22	925.32

Source: International Monetary Fund World Economic Outlook Database, October 2010.
As of 4/13/2011, 2010 is estimated.

1994	1995	1996	1997	1998	1999	2000	2001	2002	2003	2004
7 493.51	7 418.73	7 734.46	8 229.00	8 306.54	7 795.95	7 735.45	7 242.35	2 738.14	3 420.78	4 002.64
19 866.96	21 007.40	23 237.05	23 022.91	20 318.73	21 723.22	20 800.18	19 423.73	21 570.51	27 143.21	32 517.69
25 407.63	30 012.70	29 429.96	25 994.61	26 632.13	26 426.20	23 935.54	23 664.72	25 572.99	31 104.80	35 426.97
285.09	309.01	317.86	325.86	329.85	336.60	334.23	329.36	339.92	367.38	392.24
23 959.92	28 077.11	27 057.22	24 505.34	25 021.15	24 844.32	22 716.46	22 535.48	24 461.05	29 982.38	34 556.38
3 814.87	4 844.95	5 207.26	5 321.32	5 060.36	3 396.19	3 750.70	3 180.47	2 836.12	3 103.85	3 665.23
934.04	1 579.64	1 203.66	1 269.92	1 584.72	1 608.63	1 546.08	1 723.30	1 988.37	2 561.75	3 175.83
19 491.61	20 179.05	20 756.80	21 345.18	20 474.85	21 775.27	23 653.36	23 100.42	23 466.71	27 402.39	31 103.90
3 941.21	5 020.86	5 254.90	5 663.02	5 354.81	4 860.15	4 943.71	4 451.12	4 314.00	4 698.20	5 981.58
466.60	601.01	699.48	770.59	817.15	861.21	945.60	1 038.04	1 131.80	1 269.83	1 486.02
2 654.98	2 955.78	3 149.58	2 919.74	2 783.75	2 440.62	2 491.52	2 419.86	2 376.85	2 269.41	2 805.54
11 664.17	14 338.35	14 246.56	13 360.48	14 152.07	14 322.69	13 492.90	13 874.97	14 965.10	18 631.71	21 665.13
n/a	5 348.65	6 011.54	5 545.14	6 033.68	5 880.87	5 548.48	6 077.48	7 401.06	8 974.90	10 742.47
29 556.47	34 891.63	35 123.93	32 309.47	32 796.45	32 735.73	30 033.99	29 999.92	32 389.91	39 495.21	45 339.87
1 843.49	2 017.01	2 187.81	2 425.07	2 501.54	2 637.74	2 870.64	2 926.64	2 910.91	2 315.29	2 430.13
1 656.84	1 764.01	1 819.83	1 982.04	1 912.04	1 344.85	1 261.24	1 749.73	1 952.33	2 212.13	2 506.02
930.63	1 057.35	1 162.07	1 277.18	1 397.39	1 450.67	1 566.42	1 474.48	1 325.85	1 209.27	1 148.71
1 637.68	2 607.15	3 316.00	3 592.78	4 015.81	4 141.60	4 139.67	4 565.18	5 380.73	7 260.34	8 905.06
19 806.46	25 571.65	24 993.62	23 909.01	25 164.25	25 213.82	23 561.05	23 998.34	26 038.26	31 503.61	36 123.79
23 693.93	27 183.03	27 131.27	24 495.14	25 244.77	24 853.95	22 574.15	22 551.09	24 434.17	29 922.03	33 927.70
26 458.85	30 934.66	29 807.01	26 395.70	26 675.98	26 166.43	23 220.16	23 039.41	24 590.61	29 697.87	33 366.36
344.14	398.31	416.53	403.72	427.40	429.90	270.63	281.47	318.41	384.32	436.04
10 383.31	12 077.84	12 676.58	12 311.89	12 323.38	12 639.03	11 661.88	11 950.44	13 446.40	17 692.57	20 922.08
1 302.34	1 426.10	1 481.22	1 634.38	1 712.17	1 588.87	1 531.10	1 625.82	1 762.06	1 813.32	1 933.79
4 111.21	4 430.16	4 514.34	4 580.14	4 741.95	4 791.44	4 626.82	5 231.78	6 562.39	8 270.33	10 142.61
23 558.97	26 159.28	27 086.75	27 226.44	29 988.74	31 299.76	30 620.91	27 566.39	30 902.26	37 743.87	45 075.15
346.47	385.80	390.22	428.80	424.58	445.47	460.27	463.46	477.00	543.40	620.08
15 434.63	18 639.10	20 431.52	22 184.24	23 795.57	25 769.39	25 607.31	27 269.11	31 454.28	39 781.12	45 901.32
15 070.23	17 875.72	19 040.69	19 072.88	18 877.51	18 607.53	20 504.11	19 813.45	17 841.75	18 423.14	19 297.47
18 557.95	19 819.03	22 164.10	20 985.09	21 433.76	21 129.57	19 293.34	19 541.08	21 317.48	26 308.26	30 119.03
3 139.30	2 351.98	3 145.77	3 254.03	3 392.79	3 440.54	3 484.89	3 525.27	3 663.65	3 605.50	3 846.28
38 196.39	41 968.58	36 930.26	33 821.23	30 526.86	34 511.71	36 800.44	32 214.33	30 756.08	33 134.47	36 058.72
358.16	443.68	437.42	471.61	478.82	438.03	409.18	423.09	418.53	467.47	490.45
9 757.49	11 778.76	12 586.60	11 582.11	7 723.84	9 906.50	11 346.66	10 654.82	12 093.73	13 451.10	15 028.82
1 579.60	1 982.47	2 300.75	2 557.51	2 781.22	3 037.84	3 294.83	3 516.14	3 970.89	4 798.01	5 933.75

(continued on next page)

Table III, continued
MACROECONOMIC DATA FOR SELECT COUNTRIES
GDP PER PERSON (U.S. dollars)

Country	2005	2006	2007	2008	2009	2010
Argentina	4 741.91	5 492.40	6 658.16	8 253.18	7 725.46	8 662.99
Australia	35 926.70	37 543.54	44 761.03	48 706.88	45 285.02	54 868.92
Austria	36 892.02	39 022.92	44 913.74	49 975.21	45 685.88	43 723.32
Bangladesh	399.21	419.42	468.89	527.89	583.16	640.85
Belgium	35 940.82	37 787.60	43 102.15	47 224.21	43 794.31	42 596.55
Brazil	4 832.39	5 892.81	7 281.00	8 625.58	8 220.36	10 470.90
Bulgaria	3 522.32	4 122.32	5 301.52	6 560.72	6 223.25	5 954.72
Canada	35 204.73	39 301.50	43 302.01	45 051.11	39 657.92	45 887.74
Chile	7 285.82	8 940.63	9 901.11	10 200.76	9 515.93	11 587.09
China	1 726.05	2 063.87	2 644.56	3 403.53	3 734.61	4 282.89
Colombia	3 418.72	3 709.42	4 792.52	5 258.21	5 167.05	6 220.60
Cyprus	22 686.38	24 039.80	28 044.01	32 161.20	29 619.50	27 721.84
Czech Republic	12 175.43	13 892.90	16 880.48	20 734.15	18 256.16	18 721.63
Denmark	47 617.09	50 553.52	57 043.54	62 237.76	56 263.43	55 112.71
Dominican Republic	3 712.32	3 879.03	4 378.59	4 776.68	4 815.80	5 152.05
Ecuador	2 795.47	3 080.13	3 314.28	3 899.22	3 935.26	4 295.64
Egypt	1 282.77	1 505.96	1 771.00	2 160.04	2 450.39	2 771.41
Estonia	10 317.77	12 499.60	16 160.24	17 651.19	14 402.46	14 416.52
Finland	37 287.22	39 414.66	46 468.58	51 020.39	44 581.06	43 134.00
France	35 104.94	36 858.07	41 940.89	45 991.04	42 412.63	40 591.43
Germany	33 922.40	35 512.83	40 570.06	44 524.95	40 831.66	40 511.83
Ghana	513.76	594.51	683.57	732.16	663.39	761.98
Greece	21 997.32	23 835.36	27 930.40	31 601.66	29 634.92	27 264.83
Guatemala	2 142.56	2 322.56	2 557.00	2 863.23	2 687.57	2 839.03
Hungary	10 910.85	11 205.35	13 746.16	15 477.50	12 914.01	13 210.40
Iceland	54 471.92	54 374.91	65 181.13	53 107.81	37 991.40	39 562.89
India	716.18	791.15	988.58	1 066.46	1 031.59	1 176.06
Ireland	48 914.67	52 521.45	59 820.87	59 901.95	49 863.42	45 642.49
Israel	20 062.28	21 413.04	24 134.52	28 437.13	26 874.40	27 085.13
Italy	30 662.59	31 917.69	35 992.66	38 887.23	35 435.15	33 828.55
Jamaica	4 172.01	4 483.25	4 808.00	5 024.31	4 683.71	5 055.00
Japan	35 633.04	34 150.33	34 267.77	38 271.30	39 740.27	42 325.23
Kenya	579.05	684.49	833.69	754.86	840.00	887.92
Korea	17 550.88	19 706.59	21 653.27	19 161.95	17 074.33	20 164.85
Latvia	6 955.25	8 689.98	12 622.47	14 912.93	11 465.61	10 377.78

Source: International Monetary Fund, World Economic Outlook Database, October 2010.
As of 4/13/2011, 2010 is estimated.

Country	1985	1986	1987	1988	1989	1990	1991	1992	1993
Lithuania	n/a	n/a	n/a	n/a	n/a	n/a	n/a	531.34	743.92
Luxembourg	12 469.15	18 059.15	22 284.20	25 026.75	26 386.38	33 267.96	35 561.42	39 298.54	39 723.15
Malaysia	2 026.29	1 753.14	1 946.87	2 082.17	2 238.90	2 431.97	2 713.63	3 200.32	3 470.94
Mexico	2 802.90	1 901.55	2 044.18	2 452.40	2 931.82	3 395.13	3 994.92	4 548.33	4 958.68
Netherlands	9 189.30	12 736.41	15 441.07	16 353.76	16 040.23	19 760.56	20 136.83	22 119.79	21 286.59
New Zealand	6 891.89	8 310.97	10 975.98	13 388.89	12 778.44	13 098.57	12 222.46	11 483.85	12 274.65
Nigeria	331.05	254.85	263.86	284.38	266.90	347.63	304.17	266.62	160.53
Norway	15 449.40	18 496.04	22 020.51	23 706.45	23 805.31	27 677.27	27 999.23	29 848.03	27 323.01
Peru	881.80	1 293.35	2 088.49	1 616.57	1 953.19	1 331.97	1 557.50	1 590.72	1 513.25
Philippines	562.18	533.36	578.33	645.41	709.60	718.11	719.38	822.70	825.01
Poland	1 895.37	1 960.94	1 687.17	1 815.14	1 767.95	1 625.24	2 100.56	2 310.23	2 346.24
Portugal	2 673.82	3 713.27	4 644.50	5 438.56	5 873.95	7 816.33	8 868.71	10 671.01	9 381.23
Romania	2 073.64	2 233.82	2 483.98	2 558.08	2 283.52	1 624.61	1 227.46	836.15	1 132.02
Russia	n/a	n/a	n/a	n/a	n/a	n/a	n/a	575.22	1 236.98
Saudi Arabia	8 732.75	6 960.55	6 532.88	6 407.38	6 592.09	7 689.19	8 235.57	8 042.29	7 648.99
Singapore	6 748.29	6 853.03	7 767.00	9 303.40	10 715.16	12 745.06	14 412.55	16 099.09	18 240.07
South Africa	1 735.62	1 937.54	2 485.04	2 614.36	2 662.24	3 039.44	3 192.05	3 389.85	3 315.64
Spain	4 600.34	6 347.03	8 022.62	9 405.61	10 353.62	13 407.90	14 401.90	15 691.09	13 140.00
Sweden	12 726.98	16 804.10	20 413.72	22 959.79	24 048.59	28 543.17	29 899.78	30 791.92	23 148.90
Switzerland	15 373.83	21 923.98	27 285.00	29 301.51	28 062.55	35 490.19	35 441.76	36 504.10	35 179.84
Thailand	750.97	813.60	938.09	1 122.03	1 306.77	1 518.17	1 686.61	1 899.10	2 087.83
Turkey	1 837.97	2 024.85	2 281.01	2 416.97	2 810.23	3 859.52	3 788.04	3 915.63	4 355.54
Ukraine	n/a	n/a	n/a	n/a	n/a	n/a	n/a	400.70	632.56
United Arab Emirates	19 818.48	15 051.53	15 865.98	13 513.74	15 011.58	19 514.64	17 220.53	16 652.45	17 628.87
United Kingdom	8 292.22	10 071.35	12 367.79	14 976.44	15 090.29	17 782.06	18 441.42	19 072.63	17 025.60
United States	17 689.60	18 537.76	19 511.17	20 820.82	22 169.18	23 197.70	23 647.57	24 699.63	25 629.13
Vietnam	251.20	556.02	674.88	365.89	97.16	98.03	113.65	144.15	189.26

(continued on next page)

Table III, continued
MACROECONOMIC DATA FOR SELECT COUNTRIES
GDP PER PERSON (U.S. dollars)

Country	1994	1995	1996	1997	1998	1999	2000	2001	2002
Lithuania	1 168.11	1 741.55	2 268.54	2 787.02	3 163.68	3 113.15	3 267.38	3 492.73	4 082.09
Luxembourg	43 570.22	50 515.36	49 539.13	44 037.74	45 439.25	49 053.28	46 360.39	45 789.99	50 781.69
Malaysia	3 759.35	4 358.45	4 836.12	4 693.25	3 303.27	3 537.53	4 029.68	3 863.93	4 111.69
Mexico	5 093.73	3 402.30	3 889.58	4 623.09	4 783.03	5 388.50	6 419.10	6 713.54	6 912.25
Netherlands	22 742.86	27 187.80	26 985.21	24 860.92	25 756.79	26 141.54	24 249.91	24 990.55	27 206.45
New Zealand	14 269.23	16 579.55	18 123.50	17 871.13	14 558.72	15 003.34	13 708.73	13 343.55	15 338.96
Nigeria	178.95	355.76	431.26	322.73	290.68	310.48	389.95	361.11	470.70
Norway	28 626.25	34 077.70	36 424.60	35 853.71	34 036.54	35 554.37	37 390.55	37 821.70	42 206.16
Peru	1 953.74	2 298.39	2 356.06	2 456.54	2 322.06	2 076.04	2 115.87	2 107.06	2 183.50
Philippines	949.21	1 104.99	1 206.14	1 170.32	910.44	1 018.88	986.56	906.42	957.57
Poland	2 686.41	3 603.96	4 056.01	4 064.24	4 448.54	4 339.99	4 453.74	4 978.57	5 184.50
Portugal	9 814.38	11 603.35	12 049.01	11 483.23	12 139.97	12 442.64	11 511.28	11 712.97	12 813.29
Romania	1 299.35	1 542.01	1 543.54	1 550.48	1 859.90	1 579.31	1 664.36	1 811.50	2 110.08
Russia	1 864.66	2 116.48	2 641.77	2 749.13	1 852.62	1 345.51	1 793.52	2 095.58	2 376.90
Saudi Arabia	7 588.63	7 855.13	8 489.58	8 667.04	7 483.87	8 065.43	9 216.39	8 736.41	8 785.13
Singapore	21 419.97	24 702.00	25 929.64	26 158.10	21 647.26	21 441.38	22 790.80	21 001.23	22 027.88
South Africa	3 382.24	3 684.84	3 439.25	3 495.07	3 100.05	3 029.06	2 986.45	2 632.83	2 445.22
Spain	13 149.72	15 164.36	15 772.03	14 485.63	15 146.23	15 495.85	14 464.24	14 971.13	16 811.64
Sweden	24 750.02	28 710.50	31 238.76	28 591.84	28 750.48	29 188.77	27 841.74	25 531.88	28 090.69
Switzerland	38 637.47	44 874.60	43 093.25	37 323.36	38 344.56	37 544.78	34 786.15	35 284.34	38 246.93
Thailand	2 441.76	2 825.74	3 037.52	2 496.14	1 828.67	1 984.94	1 966.75	1 835.78	1 999.30
Turkey	3 084.88	3 956.36	4 170.26	4 390.31	4 560.43	4 169.85	4 245.22	3 064.26	3 581.58
Ukraine	716.46	727.45	884.10	1 003.56	845.35	642.99	642.40	787.90	886.45
United Arab Emirates	16 788.85	16 891.58	19 650.32	19 850.98	17 118.62	18 193.68	23 446.15	21 858.84	22 184.77
United Kingdom	18 343.34	19 947.19	20 989.85	23 312.43	24 902.18	25 609.93	25 142.25	24 891.24	27 218.78
United States	26 906.53	27 826.60	29 076.55	30 541.33	31 857.84	33 501.68	35 251.93	36 064.52	36 949.99
Vietnam	229.85	288.87	337.52	361.91	360.93	374.72	401.57	413.34	440.21

Source: International Monetary Fund, World Economic Outlook Database, October 2010.
As of 4/13/2011, 2010 is estimated.

2003	2004	2005	2006	2007	2008	2009	2010
5 387.33	6 562.97	7 608.24	8 863.07	11 582.13	14 047.47	11 115.07	10 765.34
64 675.97	74 516.56	81 092.71	90 714.82	106 983.25	118 570.05	105 917.79	104 390.27
4 409.42	4 898.40	5 318.53	5 950.56	6 967.10	8 142.62	6 950.47	7 754.99
6 807.90	7 294.27	8 167.17	9 084.16	9 694.42	10 216.02	8 133.87	9 243.03
33 241.45	37 507.13	39 189.91	41 497.70	47 838.63	53 354.89	48 208.83	46 418.33
20 016.70	24 333.02	26 902.63	25 685.01	30 927.30	30 652.74	27 258.94	31 588.78
524.26	662.47	823.82	1 038.76	1 153.40	1 401.24	1 111.75	1 389.31
49 228.14	56 219.31	65 203.29	72 074.46	82 086.88	93 235.22	78 178.34	84 543.44
2 323.97	2 600.45	2 916.98	3 339.59	3 796.51	4 445.84	4 356.04	5 195.98
972.59	1 040.35	1 159.13	1 351.39	1 624.13	1 848.02	1 747.82	2 011.00
5 675.00	6 626.66	7 964.70	8 958.02	11 157.27	13 886.66	11 302.08	11 521.64
15 539.29	17 665.23	18 188.19	19 040.18	21 820.44	23 830.05	21 969.76	21 030.61
2 736.09	3 497.02	4 586.27	5 684.47	7 921.82	9 501.33	7 523.11	7 390.71
2 967.51	4 099.70	5 321.98	6 932.30	9 139.96	11 739.11	8 681.41	10 521.79
9 758.02	11 126.52	13 657.95	15 049.63	15 858.75	19 156.86	14 744.61	16 641.41
23 029.40	26 418.80	28 497.52	31 615.67	36 526.53	39 266.25	36 378.74	42 652.76
3 656.18	4 722.82	5 266.90	5 511.06	5 975.57	5 684.68	5 823.58	7 100.81
21 250.10	24 693.89	26 305.39	28 244.15	32 468.29	35 364.24	32 030.27	29 875.09
35 096.99	40 218.82	40 997.73	43 946.23	50 558.90	52 882.38	43 668.36	47 667.02
44 291.00	49 112.67	50 084.28	52 275.88	57 490.59	65 699.35	63 535.95	67 074.31
2 228.54	2 479.01	2 708.51	3 174.43	3 758.91	4 107.79	3 940.97	4 620.71
4 602.81	5 862.20	7 108.45	7 766.97	9 422.08	10 484.26	8 711.16	10 206.79
1 056.72	1 377.56	1 843.51	2 318.97	3 089.69	3 921.02	2 568.65	3 002.80
24 672.25	28 076.55	33 607.69	41 433.45	45 990.64	53 388.04	45 614.54	47 406.66
31 277.10	36 820.75	37 897.81	40 399.45	46 118.06	43 651.55	35 257.45	36 298.39
38 324.38	40 450.62	42 680.64	44 822.96	46 577.19	47 155.32	45 934.47	47 131.95
489.03	554.07	636.91	724.05	835.08	1 047.54	1 068.26	1 155.57

Solutions to Check Your Understanding Questions

This section offers suggested answers to the "Check Your Understanding" questions found within chapters.

Chapter One

1-1 CHECK YOUR UNDERSTANDING

1. **a.** This illustrates the concept of opportunity cost. Given that a person can only eat so much at one sitting, having a slice of chocolate cake requires that you forgo eating something else, such as a slice of coconut cream pie.

   b. This illustrates the concept that resources are scarce. Even if there were more resources in the world, the total amount of those resources would be limited. As a result, scarcity would still arise. For there to be no scarcity, there would have to be unlimited amounts of everything (including unlimited time in a human life), which is clearly impossible.

   c. This illustrates the concept that people usually exploit opportunities to make themselves better off. Students will seek to make themselves better off by signing up for the tutorials of teaching assistants with good reputations and avoiding those teaching assistants with poor reputations. It also illustrates the concept that resources are scarce. If there were unlimited spaces in tutorials with good teaching assistants, they would not fill up.

   d. This illustrates the concept of marginal analysis. Your decision about allocating your time is a "how much" decision: how much time spent exercising versus how much time spent studying. You make your decision by comparing the benefit of an additional hour of exercising to its cost, the effect on your grades of one fewer hour spent studying.

2. **a.** Yes. The increased time spent commuting is a cost you will incur if you accept the new job. That additional time spent commuting—or equivalently, the benefit you would get from spending that time doing something else—is an opportunity cost of the new job.

   b. Yes. One of the benefits of the new job is that you will be making $50 000. But if you take the new job, you will have to give up your current job; that is, you have to give up your current salary of $45 000. So $45 000 is one of the opportunity costs of taking the new job.

   c. No. A more spacious office is an additional benefit of your new job and does not involve forgoing something else. So it is not an opportunity cost.

1-2 CHECK YOUR UNDERSTANDING

1. **a.** This illustrates the concept that markets usually lead to efficiency. Any seller who wants to sell a book for at least $30 does indeed sell to someone who is willing to buy a book for $30. As a result, there is no way to change how used textbooks are distributed among buyers and sellers in a way that would make one person better off without making someone else worse off.

   b. This illustrates the concept that there are gains from trade. Students trade tutoring services based on their different abilities in academic subjects.

   c. This illustrates the concept that when markets don't achieve efficiency, government intervention can improve society's welfare. In this case the market, left alone, will permit bars and nightclubs to impose costs on their neighbours in the form of loud music, costs that the bars and nightclubs have no incentive to take into account. This is an inefficient outcome because society as a whole can be made better off if bars and nightclubs are induced to reduce their noise.

   d. This illustrates the concept that resources should be used as efficiently as possible to achieve society's goals. By closing neighbourhood clinics and shifting funds to the main hospital, better health care can be provided at a lower cost.

   e. This illustrates the concept that markets move toward equilibrium. Here, because books with the same amount of wear and tear sell for about the same price, no buyer or seller can be made better off by engaging in a different trade than he or she undertook. This means that the market for used textbooks has moved to an equilibrium.

2. **a.** This does not describe an equilibrium situation. Many students should want to change their behaviour and switch to eating at the restaurants. Therefore, the situation described is not an equilibrium. An equilibrium will be established when students are equally as well off eating at the restaurants as eating at the dining hall—which would happen if, say, prices at the restaurants were higher than at the dining hall.

   b. This does describe an equilibrium situation. By changing your behaviour and riding a bicycle, you would not be made better off. Therefore, you have no incentive to change your behaviour.

1-3 CHECK YOUR UNDERSTANDING

1. **a.** This illustrates the principle that government policies can change spending. The tax cut would increase people's after-tax incomes, leading to higher consumer spending.

   b. This illustrates the principle that one person's spending is another person's income. As oil companies increase their spending on labour by hiring more workers, or pay existing workers higher wages, those workers' incomes rise. In turn, these workers increase their consumer spending, which becomes income to restaurants and other consumer businesses.

   c. This illustrates the principle that overall spending sometimes gets out of line with the economy's productive capacity. In this case, spending on housing was too high relative to the economy's capacity to create new housing. This first led to a rise in house prices, and then—as a result—to a rise in overall prices, or *inflation*.

Chapter Two

2-1 CHECK YOUR UNDERSTANDING

1. a. False. An increase in the resources available to Bombardier for use in producing CSeries jets and subway trains changes the production possibility frontier by shifting it outward. This is because Bombardier can now produce more CSeries jets and subway trains than before. In the accompanying figure, the line labelled "Bombardier's original *PPF*" represents Boeing's original production possibility frontier, and the line labelled "Bombardier's new *PPF*" represents the new production possibility frontier that results from an increase in resources available to Boeing.

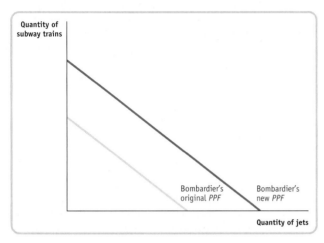

b. True. A technological change that allows Bombardier to build more subway trains for any amount of CSeries jets built results in a change in its production possibility frontier. This is illustrated in the accompanying figure: the new production possibility frontier is represented by the line labelled "Bombardier's new *PPF*," and the original production frontier is represented by the line labelled "Bombardier's original *PPF*." Since the maximum quantity of CSeries jets that Bombardier can build is the same as before, the new production possibility frontier intersects the horizontal axis at the same point as the original frontier. But since the maximum possible quantity of subway trains is now greater than before, the new frontier intersects the vertical axis above the original frontier.

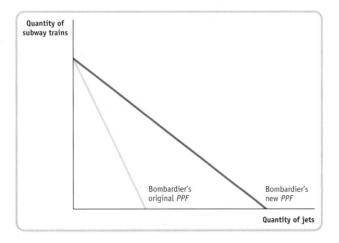

c. False. The production possibility frontier illustrates how much of one good an economy must give up to get more of another good only when resources are used efficiently in production. If an economy is producing inefficiently—that is, inside the frontier—then it does not have to give up a unit of one good in order to get another unit of the other good. Instead, by becoming more efficient in production, this economy can have more of both goods.

2. a. Canada has an absolute advantage in automobile production because it takes fewer Canadians (6) to produce a car in one day than Italians (8). Canada also has an absolute advantage in washing machine production because it takes fewer Canadians (2) to produce a washing machine in one day than Italians (3).

b. In Italy the opportunity cost of a washing machine in terms of an automobile is $3/8$: $3/8$ of a car can be produced with the same number of workers and in the same time it takes to produce 1 washing machine. In Canada the opportunity cost of a washing machine in terms of an automobile is $2/6 = 1/3$: $1/3$ of a car can be produced with the same number of workers and in the same time it takes to produce 1 washing machine. Since $1/3 < 3/8$, Canada has a comparative advantage in the production of washing machines: to produce a washing machine, only $1/3$ of a car must be given up in Canada but $3/8$ of a car must be given up in Italy. This means that Italy has a comparative advantage in automobiles. This can be checked as follows. The opportunity cost of an automobile in terms of a washing machine in Italy is $8/3$, equal to $2\,2/3$: $2\,2/3$ washing machines can be produced with the same number of workers and in the time it takes to produce 1 car in Italy. And the opportunity cost of an automobile in terms of a washing machine in Canada is $6/2$, equal to 3: 3 washing machines can be produced with the same number of workers and in the time it takes to produce 1 car in Canada. Since $2\,2/3 < 3$, Italy has a comparative advantage in producing automobiles.

c. The greatest gains are realized when each country specializes in producing the good for which it has a comparative advantage. Therefore, Canada should specialize in washing machines and Italy should specialize in automobiles.

3. At a trade of 7 Canadian jets for 29 Brazilian subway trains, Brazil gives up less for a jet than it would if it were building the jets itself. Without trade, Brazil gives up 6 subway trains for each jet it produces. With trade, Brazil gives up only $29/7$ subway trains for each jet from Canada. Likewise, Canada gives up less for a subway train than it would if it were producing subway train itself. Without trade, Canada gives up $2/7$ of jet for each subway train. With trade, Canada gives up only $7/29$ of a jet for each subway train from Brazil.

4. An increase in the amount of money spent by households results in an increase in the flow of goods to households. This, in turn, generates an increase in demand for factors of production by firms. So, there is an increase in the number of jobs in the economy.

2-2 CHECK YOUR UNDERSTANDING

1. a. This is a normative statement because it stipulates what should be done. In addition, it may have no "right" answer. That is, should people be prevented from all dangerous personal behaviour if they enjoy that behaviour—like skydiving? Your answer will depend on your point of view.

b. This is a positive statement because it is a description of fact.

2. a. True. Economists often have different value judgments about the desirability of a particular social goal. But despite those differences in value judgments, they will tend to agree that society, once it has decided to pursue a given social goal, should adopt the most efficient policy to achieve that goal. Therefore economists are likely to agree on adopting policy choice B.

b. False. Disagreements between economists are more likely to arise because they base their conclusions on different models or because they have different value judgments about the desirability of the policy.

c. False. Deciding which goals a society should try to achieve is a matter of value judgments, not a question of economic analysis.

Chapter Three
3-1 CHECK YOUR UNDERSTANDING

1. a. The quantity of umbrellas demanded is higher at any given price on a rainy day than on a dry day. This is a rightward *shift of* the demand curve, since at any given price the quantity demanded rises. This implies that any specific quantity can now be sold at a higher price.

b. The quantity of weekend calls demanded rises in response to a price reduction. This is a *movement along* the demand curve for weekend calls.

c. The demand for roses increases the week of Valentine's Day. This is a rightward *shift of* the demand curve.

d. The quantity of gasoline demanded falls in response to a rise in price. This is a *movement along* the demand curve.

3-2 CHECK YOUR UNDERSTANDING

1. a. The quantity of houses supplied rises as a result of an increase in prices. This is a *movement along* the supply curve.

b. The quantity of strawberries supplied is higher at any given price. This is a rightward *shift of* the supply curve.

c. The quantity of labour supplied is lower at any given wage. This is a leftward *shift of* the supply curve compared to the supply curve during school vacation. So, in order to attract workers, fast-food chains have to offer higher wages.

d. The quantity of wheat supplied is higher at any given price. This is a rightward *shift* of the supply curve.

e. The quantity of cabins supplied is higher at any given price. This is a rightward *shift of* the supply curve.

3-3 CHECK YOUR UNDERSTANDING

1. a. The supply curve shifts rightward. At the original equilibrium price of the year before, the quantity of grapes supplied exceeds the quantity demanded. This is a case of surplus. The price of grapes will fall.

b. The demand curve shifts leftward. At the original equilibrium price, the quantity of hotel rooms supplied exceeds the quantity demanded. This is a case of surplus. The rates for hotel rooms will fall.

c. The demand curve for second-hand snowblowers shifts rightward. At the original equilibrium price, the quantity of second-hand snowblowers demanded exceeds the quantity supplied. This is a case of shortage. The equilibrium price of second-hand snowblowers will rise.

3-4 CHECK YOUR UNDERSTANDING

1. a. The market for large cars: this is a rightward shift in demand caused by a decrease in the price of a complement, gasoline. As a result of the shift, the equilibrium price of large cars will rise and the equilibrium quantity of large cars bought and sold will also rise.

b. The market for fresh paper made from recycled stock: this is a rightward shift in supply due to a technological innovation. As a result of this shift, the equilibrium price of fresh paper made from recycled stock will fall and the equilibrium quantity bought and sold will rise.

c. The market for movies at a local movie theatre: this is a leftward shift in demand caused by a fall in the price of a substitute, on-demand films. As a result of this shift, the equilibrium price of movie tickets will fall and the equilibrium number of people who go to the movies will also fall.

2. Upon the announcement of the new chip, the demand curve for computers using the earlier chip shifts leftward, as demand decreases, and the supply curve for these computers shifts rightward, as supply increases.

a. If demand decreases relatively more than supply increases, then the equilibrium quantity falls, as shown here:

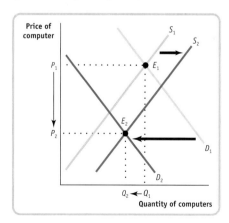

b. If supply increases relatively more than demand decreases, then the equilibrium quantity rises, as shown here:

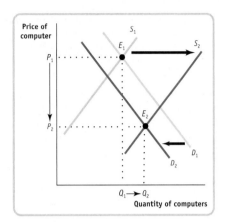

In both cases, the equilibrium price falls.

Chapter Four

4-1 CHECK YOUR UNDERSTANDING

1. a. Fewer homeowners are willing to rent out their driveways because the price ceiling has reduced the payment they receive. This is an example of a fall in price leading to a fall in the quantity supplied. It is shown in the accompanying diagram by the movement from point E to point A along the supply curve, a reduction in quantity of 400 parking spaces.

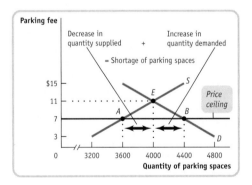

b. The quantity demanded increases by 400 spaces as the price decreases. At a lower price, more fans are willing to drive and rent a parking space. It is shown in the diagram by the movement from point E to point B along the demand curve.

c. Under a price ceiling, the quantity demanded exceeds the quantity supplied; as a result, shortages arise.

In this case, there will be a shortage of 800 parking spaces. It is shown by the horizontal distance between points A and B.

d. Price ceilings result in wasted resources. The additional time fans spend to guarantee a parking space is wasted time.

e. Price ceilings lead to inefficient allocation of a good— here, the parking spaces—to consumers.

f. Price ceilings lead to black markets.

2. a. False. By lowering the price that producers receive, a price ceiling leads to a decrease in the quantity supplied.

b. True. A price ceiling leads to a lower quantity supplied than in an efficient, unregulated market. As a result, some people who would have been willing to pay the market price, and so would have gotten the good in an unregulated market, are unable to obtain it when a price ceiling is imposed.

c. True. Those producers who still sell the product now receive less for it and are therefore worse off. Other producers will no longer find it worthwhile to sell the product at all and so will also be made worse off.

4-2 CHECK YOUR UNDERSTANDING

1. a. Some gas station owners will benefit from getting a higher price. Q_F indicates the sales made by these owners. But some will lose; there are those who make sales at the market equilibrium price of P_E but do not make sales at the regulated price of P_F. These missed sales are indicated on the graph by the fall in the quantity demanded along the demand curve, from point E to point A.

b. Those who buy gas at the higher price of P_F will probably receive better service; this is an example of *inefficiently high quality* caused by a price floor as gas station owners compete on quality rather than price. But opponents are correct to claim that consumers are generally worse off—those who buy at P_F would have been happy to buy at P_E, and many who were willing to buy at a price between P_E and P_F are now unwilling to buy. This is indicated on the graph by the fall in the quantity demanded along the demand curve, from point E to point A.

c. Proponents are wrong because consumers and some gas station owners are hurt by the price floor. Every price floor creates "missed opportunities"—desirable transactions between consumers and station owners that never take place. Moreover, the inefficiency of wasted resources arises as consumers spend time and money driving to other provinces or to the United States. The price floor also tempts people to engage in black market activity. With the price floor, only Q_F units are sold. But at prices between P_E and P_F, there are drivers who cumulatively want to buy more than Q_F and owners who are willing to sell to them, a situation likely to lead to illegal activity.

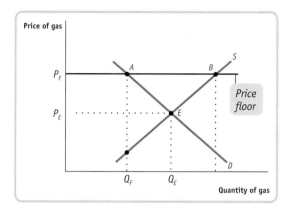

4-3 CHECK YOUR UNDERSTANDING

1. a. The price of a ride is $7 since the quantity demanded at this price is 6 million: $7 is the *demand price* of 6 million rides. This is represented by point *A* in the accompanying figure.

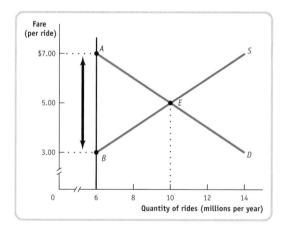

b. At 6 million rides, the supply price is $3 per ride, represented by point *B* in the figure. The wedge between the demand price of $7 per ride and the supply price of $3 per ride is the quota rent per ride, $4. This is represented in the figure above by the vertical distance between points *A* and *B*.

2. At 9 million rides, the demand price is $5.50 per ride, indicated by point *C* in the accompanying figure, and the supply price is $4.50 per ride, indicated by point *D*. The quota rent is the difference between the demand price and the supply price: $1.

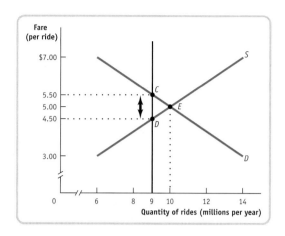

3. The accompanying figure shows a decrease in demand by 4 million rides, represented by a leftward shift of the demand curve from D_1 to D_2: at any given price, the quantity demanded falls by 4 million rides. (For example, at a price of $5, the quantity demanded falls from 10 million to 6 million rides per year.) This eliminates the effect of a quota limit of 8 million rides. At point E_2, the new market equilibrium, the equilibrium quantity is equal to the quota limit; as a result, the quota has no effect on the market.

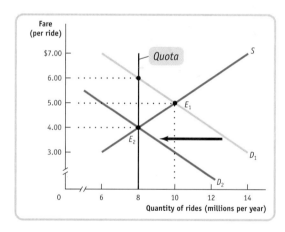

Chapter Five

5-1 CHECK YOUR UNDERSTANDING

1. a. To determine comparative advantage, we must compare the two countries' opportunity costs for a given good. Take the opportunity cost of 1 tonne of wheat in terms of bicycles. In China, the opportunity cost of 1 bicycle is 0.01 tonne of wheat; so the opportunity cost of 1 tonne of wheat is 1/0.01 bicycles = 100 bicycles. Canada has the comparative advantage in wheat since its opportunity cost in terms of bicycles is 50, a smaller number.

Similarly, the opportunity cost in Canada of 1 bicycle in terms of wheat is 1/50 tonne of wheat = 0.02 tonne of wheat. This is greater than 0.01, the Chinese opportunity cost of 1 bicycle in terms of wheat, implying that China has a comparative advantage in bicycles.

b. Given that Canada can produce 200 000 bicycles if no wheat is produced, it can produce 200 000 bicycles × 0.02 tonne of wheat/bicycle = 4000 tonnes of wheat when no bicycles are produced. Likewise, if China can produce 3000 tonnes of wheat if no bicycles are produced, it can produce 3000 tonnes of wheat × 100 bicycles/tonne of wheat = 300 000 bicycles if no wheat is produced. These points determine the vertical and horizontal intercepts of the Canadian and Chinese production possibility frontiers, as shown in the accompanying diagram.

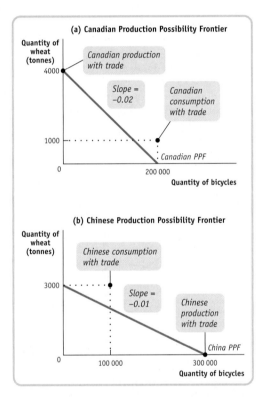

(a) Canadian Production Possibility Frontier

(b) Chinese Production Possibility Frontier

c. The diagram shows the production and consumption points of the two countries. Each country is clearly better off with international trade because each now consumes a bundle of the two goods that lies outside its own production possibility frontier, indicating that these bundles were unattainable in autarky.

2. a. According to the Heckscher–Ohlin model, this pattern of trade occurs because Canada has a relatively larger endowment of factors of production, such as human capital and physical capital, that are suited to the production of lumber, but France has a relatively larger endowment of factors of production suited to wine-making, such as vineyards and the human capital of vintners.

b. According to the Heckscher–Ohlin model, this pattern of trade occurs because Canada has a relatively larger endowment of factors of production, such as human and physical capital, that are suited to making machinery, but Brazil has a relatively larger endowment of factors of production suited to shoe-making, such as unskilled labour and leather.

5-2 CHECK YOUR UNDERSTANDING

1. In the accompanying diagram, P_A is the Canadian price of grapes in autarky and P_W is the world price of grapes under international trade. With trade, Canadian consumers pay a price of P_W for grapes and consume quantity Q_D, Canadian grape producers produce quantity Q_S, and the difference, $Q_D - Q_S$, represents imports of Mexican grapes. As a consequence of the strike by truckers, imports are halted, the price paid by Canadian consumers rises to the autarky price, P_A, and Canadian consumption falls to the autarky quantity, Q_A.

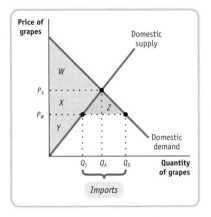

a. Before the strike, Canadian consumers enjoyed consumer surplus equal to areas $W + X + Z$. After the strike, their consumer surplus shrinks to W. So consumers are worse off, losing consumer surplus represented by $X + Z$.

b. Before the strike, Canadian producers had producer surplus equal to the area Y. After the strike, their producer surplus increases to $Y + X$. So Canadian producers are better off, gaining producer surplus represented by X.

c. Canadian total surplus falls as a result of the strike by an amount represented by area Z, the loss in consumer surplus that does not accrue to producers.

2. Mexican grape producers are worse off because they lose sales of exported grapes to Canada, and Mexican grape pickers are worse off because they lose the wages that were associated with the lost sales. The lower demand for Mexican grapes caused by the strike implies that the price Mexican consumers pay for grapes falls, making them better off. Canadian grape pickers are better off because their wages increase as a result of the increase of $Q_A - Q_S$ in Canadian sales.

5-3 CHECK YOUR UNDERSTANDING

1. a. If the tariff is $2.00, the price paid by domestic consumers for a kilogram of imported butter is $2.00 + $2.00 = $4.00, the same price as a kilogram of domestic butter. Imported butter will no longer have a price advantage over domestic butter, imports will cease, and domestic producers will capture all the feasible sales to domestic consumers, selling amount

Q_A in the accompanying figure. But if the tariff is less than $2.00—say, only $1.00—the price paid by domestic consumers for a kilogram of imported butter is $2.00 + $1.00 = $3.00, $1.00 cheaper than a kilogram of domestic butter. Canadian butter producers will gain sales in the amount of $Q_2 - Q_1$ as a result of the $1.00 tariff. But this is smaller than the amount they would have gained under the $2.00 tariff, the amount $Q_A - Q_1$.

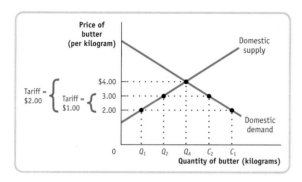

b. As long as the tariff is at least $2.00, increasing it more has no effect. At a tariff of $2.00, all imports are effectively blocked.

2. All imports are effectively blocked at a tariff of $2.00. So such a tariff corresponds to an import quota of 0.

5-4 CHECK YOUR UNDERSTANDING

1. There are many fewer businesses that use steel as an input than there are consumers who buy eggs or clothing. So it will be easier for such businesses to communicate and coordinate among themselves to lobby against tariffs than it will be for consumers. In addition, each business will perceive that the cost of a steel tariff is quite costly to its profits, but an individual consumer is either unaware of or perceives little loss from tariffs on eggs or clothing.

2. Countries are often tempted to protect domestic industries by claiming that an import poses a quality, health, or environmental danger to domestic consumers. A WTO official should examine whether domestic producers are subject to the same stringency in the application of quality, health, or environmental regulations as foreign producers. If they are, then it is more likely that the regulations are for legitimate, non–trade protection purposes; if they are not, then it is more likely that the regulations are intended as trade protection measures.

Chapter Six
6-1 CHECK YOUR UNDERSTANDING

1. a. This is a microeconomic question because it addresses decisions made by consumers about a particular product.

b. This is a macroeconomic question because it addresses consumer spending in the overall economy.

c. This is a macroeconomic question because it addresses changes in the overall economy.

d. This is a microeconomic question because it addresses changes in a particular market, in this case the market for geologists.

e. This is a microeconomic question because it addresses choices made by consumers and producers about which mode of transportation to use.

f. This is a microeconomic question because it addresses changes in a particular market.

g. This is a macroeconomic question because it addresses changes in a measure of the economy's overall price level.

2. a. When people can't get credit to finance their purchases, they will be unable to spend money. This will weaken the economy, and as others see the economy weaken, they will also cut back on their spending in order to save for future bad times. As a result, the credit shortfall will spark a compounding effect through the economy as people cut back their spending, making the economy worse, leading to more cutbacks in spending, and so on.

b. If you believe the economy is self-regulating, then you would advocate doing nothing in response to the slump.

c. If you believe in Keynesian economics, you would advocate that policy-makers undertake monetary and fiscal policies to stimulate spending in the economy.

6-2 CHECK YOUR UNDERSTANDING

1. We talk about business cycles for the economy as a whole because recessions and expansions are not confined to a few industries—they reflect downturns and upturns for the economy as a whole. In downturns, almost every sector of the economy reduces output and the number of people employed. Moreover, business cycles are an international phenomenon, sometimes moving in rough synchrony across countries.

2. Recessions cause a great deal of pain across the entire society. They cause large numbers of workers to lose their jobs and make it hard to find new jobs. Recessions hurt the standard of living of many families and are usually associated with a rise in the number of people living below the poverty line, an increase in the number of people who lose their houses because they can't afford their mortgage payments, and a fall in the percentage of Americans with health insurance. Recessions also hurt the profits of firms.

6-3 CHECK YOUR UNDERSTANDING

1. Countries with high rates of population growth will have to maintain higher growth rates of total output than countries with low rates of population growth in order to achieve an increased standard of living per person because aggregate output will have to be divided among a larger number of people.

2. No, Argentina is not poorer than it was in the past. Both Argentina and Canada have experienced long-run growth. However, after World War II, Argentina did not make as much progress as Canada, perhaps because of political instability and bad macroeconomic policies. Canada's economy grew much faster than Argentina's.

Although Canada is now about three times as rich as Argentina, Argentina still had long-run growth of its economy.

6-4 CHECK YOUR UNDERSTANDING

1. a. As some prices have risen but other prices have fallen, there may be overall inflation or deflation. The answer is ambiguous.

b. As all prices have risen significantly, this sounds like inflation.

c. As most prices have fallen and others have not changed, this sounds like deflation.

6-5 CHECK YOUR UNDERSTANDING

1. a. This situation reflects comparative advantage. Canada's comparative advantage results from the development of oil—Canada now has an abundance of oil.

b. This situation reflects comparative advantage. China's comparative advantage results from an abundance of labour; China is good at labour-intensive activities such as assembly.

c. This situation reflects macroeconomic forces. Germany has been running a huge trade surplus because of underlying decisions regarding savings and investment spending with its savings in excess of its investment spending.

d. This situation reflects macroeconomic forces. Canada's trade balance changed from a surplus to a deficit in 2009 because the 2008 financial crisis had reduced the foreign demand for Canadian goods, which lowered Canada's exports. Alternatively, the 2008 financial crisis lowered national output in Canada, which also reduced savings. Holding all else constant, the reduction in savings makes investment spending outstrip Canada's savings.

Chapter Seven
7-1 CHECK YOUR UNDERSTANDING

1. Let's start by considering the relationship between the total value added of all domestically produced final goods and services and aggregate spending on domestically produced final goods and services. These two quantities are equal because every final good and service produced in the economy is either purchased by someone or added to inventories. And additions to inventories are counted as spending by firms. Next, consider the relationship between aggregate spending on domestically produced final goods and services and total factor income. These two quantities are equal because all spending that is channelled to firms to pay for purchases of domestically produced final goods and services is revenue for firms. Those revenues must be paid out by firms to their factors of production in the form of wages, profit, interest, and rent. Taken together, this means that all three methods of calculating GDP are equivalent.

2. Firms make sales to other firms, households, the government, and the rest of the world. Households are linked to firms through the sale of factors of production to firms, through purchases from firms of final goods and services, and through lending funds to firms in the financial markets. Households are linked to the government through their payment of taxes, their receipt of transfers, and their lending of funds to the government via the financial markets. Finally, households are linked to the rest of the world through their purchases of imports and transactions with foreigners in financial markets.

3. You would be counting the value of the steel twice— once as it was sold by Canadian Steel to Canadian Motors and once as part of the car sold by Canadian Motors.

7-2 CHECK YOUR UNDERSTANDING

1. a. In 2011 nominal GDP was (1 000 000 × $0.40) + (800 000 × $0.60) = $400 000 + $480 000 = $880 000. A 25% rise in the price of french fries from 2011 to 2012 means that the 2012 price of french fries was 1.25 × $0.40 = $0.50. A 10% fall in servings means that 1 000 000 × 0.9 = 900 000 servings were sold in 2012. As a result, the total value of sales of french fries in 2012 was 900 000 × $0.50 = $450 000. A 15% fall in the price of onion rings from 2011 to 2012 means that the 2012 price of onion rings was 0.85 × $0.60 = $0.51. A 5% rise in servings sold means that 800 000 × 1.05 = 840 000 servings were sold in 2012. As a result, the total value of sales of onion rings in 2012 was 840 000 × $0.51 = $428 400. Nominal GDP in 2012 was $450 000 + $428 400 = $878 400. To find real GDP in 2012, we must calculate the value of sales in 2012 using 2011 prices: (900 000 french fries × $0.40) + (840 000 onion rings × $0.60) = $360 000 + $504 000 = $864 000.

b. A comparison of nominal GDP in 2011 to nominal GDP in 2012 shows a decline of (($880 000 − $878 400) / $880 000) × 100 = 0.18%. But a comparison using real GDP shows a decline of (($880 000 − $864 000) / $880 000) × 100 = 1.8%. That is, a calculation based on real GDP shows a drop 10 times larger (1.8%) than a calculation based on nominal GDP (0.18%). In this case, the calculation based on nominal GDP underestimates the true magnitude of the change.

2. A price index based on 2005 prices will contain a relatively high price of electronics and a relatively low price of housing compared to a price index based on 2010 prices. This means that a 2005 price index used to calculate real GDP in 2012 will magnify the value of electronics production in the economy, but a 2010 price index will magnify the value of housing production in the economy.

7-3 CHECK YOUR UNDERSTANDING

1. This market basket costs, pre-frost, (100× $0.20) + (50 × $0.60) + (200 × $0.25) = $20 + $30 + $50 = $100. The same market basket, post-frost, costs (100 × $0.40) + (50 × $1.00) + (200 × $0.45) = $40 + $50 + $90 = $180. So the price index is ($100/$100) × 100 = 100 before the frost and ($180/$100) × 100 = 180 after the frost, implying a rise in the price index of 80%. This increase in the price index is less than the 84.2% increase calculated in the text. The reason for this difference is that the new market basket of 100 oranges, 50 grapefruit, and 200 lemons contains proportionately more of the items that have experienced relatively lower price increases (the lemons, whose price has increased by 80%) and proportionately fewer of the items that have experienced relatively large price increases (the oranges, whose price has increased by 100%). This shows that the price index can be very sensitive to the composition of the market basket. If the market basket contains a large proportion of goods whose prices have risen faster than the prices of other goods, it will lead to a higher estimate of the increase in the price level. If it contains a large proportion of goods whose prices have risen more slowly than the prices of other goods, it will lead to a lower estimate of the increase in the price level.

2. **a.** A market basket determined 10 years ago will contain fewer cars than at present. Given that the average price of a car has grown faster than the average prices of other goods, this basket will underestimate the true increase in the cost of living because it contains relatively too few cars.

   b. A market basket determined 10 years ago will not contain broadband Internet access. So it cannot track the fall in prices of Internet access over the past few years. As a result, it will overestimate the true increase in the cost of living.

3. Using Equation 7-3, the inflation rate from 2009 to 2010 is $((116.5 - 114.4)/114.4) \times 100 = 1.8\%$.

Chapter Eight

8-1 CHECK YOUR UNDERSTANDING

1. The advent of websites that enable job-seekers to find jobs more quickly will reduce the unemployment rate over time. However, websites that induce discouraged workers to begin actively looking for work again will lead to an increase in the unemployment rate over time.

2. **a.** Rosa is not counted as unemployed because she is not actively looking for work, but she is counted in broader measures of labour underutilization as a discouraged worker.

   b. Anthony is not counted as unemployed; he is considered employed because he has a job.

   c. Grace is unemployed; she is not working and is actively looking for work.

   d. Sergio is not unemployed, but underemployed; he is working part time for economic reasons. He is counted in broader measures of labour underutilization.

   e. Natasha is not unemployed, but marginally attached. She is counted in broader measures of labour underutilization.

3. Both parts a and b are consistent with the relationship, illustrated in Figure 8-5, between above-average or below-average growth in real GDP and changes in the unemployment rate: during years of above-average growth, the unemployment rate falls, and during years of below-average growth, the unemployment rate rises.

However, part c is not consistent: it implies that a recession is associated with a fall in the unemployment rate, which is incorrect.

8-2 CHECK YOUR UNDERSTANDING

1. **a.** When the pace of technological advance quickens, there will be higher rates of job creation and destruction as old industries disappear and new ones emerge. As a result, frictional unemployment will be higher as workers leave jobs in declining industries in search of jobs in expanding industries.

   b. When the pace of technological advance quickens, there will be greater mismatch between the skills employees have and the skills employers are looking for, leading to higher structural unemployment.

   c. When the unemployment rate is low, frictional unemployment will account for a larger share of total unemployment because other sources of unemployment will be diminished. So the share of total unemployment composed of the frictionally unemployed will rise.

2. A binding minimum wage represents a price floor below which wages cannot fall. As a result, actual wages cannot move toward equilibrium. So a minimum wage causes the quantity of labour supplied to exceed the quantity of labour demanded. Because this surplus of labour reflects unemployed workers, it affects the unemployment rate. Collective bargaining has a similar effect—unions are able to raise the wage above the equilibrium level to a level like W_U in the accompanying diagram. This will act like a minimum wage by causing the number of job-seekers to be larger than the number of workers firms are willing to hire. Collective bargaining causes the unemployment rate to be higher than it otherwise would be, as shown in the accompanying diagram.

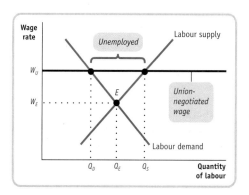

3. An increase in unemployment benefits at the peak of the business cycle reduces the cost to individuals of being unemployed, causing them to spend more time searching for new jobs. So the natural rate of unemployment would increase.

8-3 CHECK YOUR UNDERSTANDING

1. Shoe-leather costs as a result of inflation will be lower because it is now less costly for individuals to manage their assets in order to economize on their money holdings. This reduction in the costs associated with converting other assets into money translates into lower shoe-leather costs.

2. If inflation came to an unexpected and complete stop over the next 15 or 20 years, the inflation rate would be zero, which of course is less than the expected inflation rate of 2%. Because the real interest rate is the nominal interest rate minus the inflation rate, the real interest rate on a loan would be higher than expected, and lenders would gain at the expense of borrowers. Borrowers would have to repay their loans with funds that have a higher real value than had been expected.

Chapter Nine

9-1 CHECK YOUR UNDERSTANDING

1. Economic progress raises the living standards of the average resident of a country. An increase in overall real GDP does not accurately reflect an increase in an average resident's living standard because it does not account for growth in the number of residents. If, for example, real GDP rises by 10% but population grows by 20%, the living standard of the average resident falls: after the change, the average resident has only $(110/120) \times 100 = 91.6\%$ as much real income as before the change. Similarly, an increase in nominal GDP per capita does not accurately reflect an increase in living standards because it does not account for any change in prices. For example, a 5% increase in nominal GDP per capita generated by a 5% increase in prices implies that there has been no change in living standards. Real GDP per capita accounts for both changes in the population and changes in prices, which provides a better measure.

2. Using the Rule of 70, Canada will double its real GDP per capita in $(70/2.2) = 32$ years; China in $(70/8.9) = 8$ years; India in $(70/4.2) = 17$ years; Ireland in $(70/3.1) = 23$ years; the United States in $(70/1.7) = 41$ years; France in $(70/1.3) = 54$ years; and Argentina in $(70/1.2) = 58$ years. Since the Rule of 70 can only be applied to a positive growth rate, it cannot be applied in the case of Zimbabwe, which experienced negative growth. If India continues to have a higher growth rate of real GDP per capita than Canada, then India's real GDP per capita will eventually surpass that of Canada.

3. Canada began growing rapidly over a century ago, but China and India have begun growing rapidly only recently. As a result, the living standard of the typical Chinese or Indian household has not yet caught up with that of the typical Canadian household.

9-2 CHECK YOUR UNDERSTANDING

1. a. Significant technological progress will result in a positive growth rate of productivity even though physical capital per worker and human capital per worker are unchanged.

   b. The growth rate of productivity will fall but remain positive due to diminishing returns to physical capital.

2. a. If output has grown 3% per year and the labour force has grown 1% per year, then productivity—output per person—has grown at approximately 3% − 1% = 2% per year.

   b. If physical capital has grown 4% per year and the labour force has grown 1% per year, then physical capital per worker has grown at approximately 4% − 1% = 3% per year.

   c. According to estimates, each 1% rise in physical capital, other things equal, increases productivity by 0.3%. So, as physical capital per worker has increased by 3%, productivity growth that can be attributed to an increase in physical capital per worker is $0.3 \times 3\% = 0.9\%$. As a percentage of total productivity growth, this is $0.9\%/2\% \times 100\% = 45\%$.

   d. If the rest of productivity growth is due to technological progress, then technological progress has contributed 2% − 0.9% = 1.1% to productivity growth. As a percentage of total productivity growth, this is $1.1\%/2\% \times 100\% = 55\%$.

3. It will take a period time for workers to learn how to use the new computer system and to adjust their routines. And because there are often setbacks in learning a new system, such as accidentally erasing your computer files, productivity at Multinomics may decrease for a period of time.

9-3 CHECK YOUR UNDERSTANDING

1. A country that has high domestic savings is able to achieve a high rate of investment spending as a percent of GDP. This, in turn, allows the country to achieve a high growth rate.

2. By accumulating more human capital, the economy would have more productive resources and grow faster. The government can speed up the accumulation of human capital by subsidizing education and R&D, and protecting property rights.

3. It is likely that these events resulted in a fall in the country's growth rate because the lack of property rights would have dissuaded people from making investments in productive capacity.

9-4 CHECK YOUR UNDERSTANDING

1. The conditional version of the convergence hypothesis says that countries grow faster, other things equal, when they start from relatively low GDP per capita. From this we can infer that they grow more slowly, other things equal, when their real GDP per capita is relatively higher. This points to lower future Asian growth. However, other things might not be equal: if Asian economies continue investing in human capital, if savings rates continue to be high, if governments invest in infrastructure, and so on, growth might continue at an accelerated pace.

2. The regions of East Asia, Western Europe, Canada, and the United States support the convergence hypothesis because a comparison among them shows that the growth rate of real GDP per capita falls as real GDP per capita rises. Eastern Europe, West Asia, Latin America, and Africa do not support the hypothesis because they all have much lower real GDP per capita than the United States but have either approximately the same growth rate (West Asia and Eastern Europe) or a lower growth rate (Africa and Latin America).

3. The evidence suggests that both sets of factors matter: better infrastructure is important for growth, but so is

political and financial stability. Policies should try to address both areas.

9-5

1. Economists are typically more concerned about environmental degradation than resource scarcity. The reason is that in modern economies the price response tends to alleviate the limits imposed by resource scarcity through conservation and the development of alternatives. However, because environmental degradation involves a negative externality—a cost imposed by individuals or firms on others without the requirement to pay compensation—effective government intervention is required to address it. As a result, economists are more concerned about the limits to growth imposed by environmental degradation because a market response would be inadequate.

2. Growth increases a country's greenhouse gas emissions. The current best estimates are that a large reduction in emissions will result in only a modest reduction in growth. The international burden sharing of greenhouse gas emissions reduction is contentious because rich countries are reluctant to pay the costs of reducing their emissions only to see newly emerging countries like China rapidly increase their emissions. Yet most of the current accumulation of gases is due to the past actions of rich countries. Poorer countries like China are equally reluctant to sacrifice their growth to pay for the past actions of rich countries.

Chapter Ten
10-1

1. a. When the government reduces its subsidy on investment, this makes undertaking investment becomes less attractive, and the demand for loanable funds decreases. This is illustrated by the shift of the demand curve from D_1 to D_2 in the accompanying diagram. As the equilibrium moves from E_1 to E_2, the equilibrium interest rate falls from i_1 to i_2, and the equilibrium quantity of loanable funds decreases from Q_1 to Q_2.

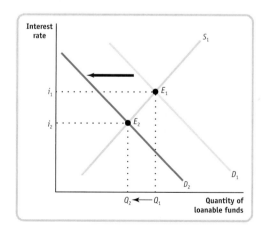

b. Savings fall due to the higher proportion of retired people, and the supply of loanable funds decreases. This is illustrated by the leftward shift of the supply curve from S_1 to S_2 in the accompanying diagram. The equilibrium moves from E_1 to E_2, the equilibrium interest rate rises from i_1 to i_2, and the equilibrium quantity of loanable funds falls from Q_1 to Q_2.

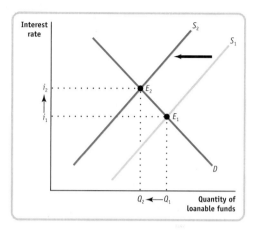

2. We know from the loanable funds market that as the interest rate rises, households want to save more and consume less. But at the same time, an increase in the interest rate lowers the number of investment spending projects with returns at least as high as the interest rate. The statement "households will want to save more money than businesses will want to invest" cannot represent an equilibrium in the loanable funds market because it says that the quantity of loanable funds offered exceeds the quantity of loanable funds demanded. If that were to occur, the interest rate must fall to make the quantity of loanable funds offered equal to the quantity of loanable funds demanded.

3. a. The real interest rate will not change. According to the Fisher effect, an increase in expected inflation drives up the nominal interest rate, leaving the real interest rate unchanged.

b. The nominal interest rate will rise by 3%. Each additional percentage point of expected inflation drives up the nominal interest rate by 1 percentage point.

c. As we saw in Figure 10-7, as long as inflation is expected, it does not affect the equilibrium quantity of loanable funds. Both the supply and demand curves for loanable funds are pushed upward, leaving the equilibrium quantity of loanable funds unchanged.

10-2

1. The transaction costs for (a) a bank deposit and (b) a share of a mutual fund are approximately equal because each can typically be accomplished by making a phone call, going online, or visiting a branch office. Transaction costs are highest for (c) a share of a family business, since finding a buyer for the share consumes time and resources. The level of risk is lowest for (a) a bank deposit, since these deposits are insured by the Canada Deposit Insurance Corporation (CDIC) up to $100 000, somewhat higher for (b) a share of a mutual fund, since despite diversification, there is still risk associated with holding mutual funds; and highest for (c) a share of a family business, since this investment

is not diversified. The level of liquidity is highest for (a) a bank deposit, since withdrawals can usually be made immediately; somewhat lower for (b) a share of a mutual fund, since it may take a few days between selling your shares and the payment being processed; and lowest for (c) a share of a family business, since it can only be sold with the unanimous agreement of other members and it will take some time to find a buyer.

2. Economic development and growth are the result of, among other factors, investment spending on physical capital. Since investment spending is equal to savings, the greater the amount saved, the higher investment spending will be, and so the higher growth and economic development will be. So the existence of institutions that facilitate savings will help a country's growth and economic development. As a result, a country with a financial system that provides low transaction costs, opportunities for diversification of risk, and high liquidity to its savers will experience faster growth and economic development than a country that doesn't.

10-3 CHECK YOUR UNDERSTANDING

1. a. Today's stock prices reflect the market's expectation of future stock prices, and according to the efficient markets hypothesis, stock prices always take account of all available information. The fact that this year's profits are low is not new information, so it is already built into the share price. However, when it becomes known that the company's profits will be high next year, the price of a share of its stock will rise today, reflecting this new information.

b. The expectations of investors about high profits were already built into the stock price. Since profits will be lower than expected, the market's expectations about the company's future stock price will be revised downward. This new information will lower the stock price.

c. When other companies in the same industry announce that sales are unexpectedly slow this year, investors are likely to conclude that sales will also be unexpectedly slow for this company. As a result, investors will revise downward their expectations of future profits and of the future stock price. This new information will result in a lower stock price today.

d. This announcement will either have no effect on the company's stock price or will increase it only slightly. It does not add any new information, beyond removing some uncertainty about whether the profit forecast was correct. It should therefore result in either no increase or only a small increase in the stock price.

2. The efficient markets hypothesis states that all available information is immediately taken into account in stock prices. So if investors consistently bought stocks the day after the TSX rose by 1%, a smart investor would *sell* on that day because demand—and so stock prices—would be high. If a profit can be made that way, eventually many investors would be selling, and it would no longer be true that investors always bought stocks the day after the TSX rose by 1%.

Chapter Eleven
11-1 CHECK YOUR UNDERSTANDING

1. A decline in investment spending, like a rise in investment spending, has a multiplier effect on real GDP—the only difference in this case is that real GDP falls instead of rises. The fall in *I* leads to an initial fall in real GDP, which leads to a fall in disposable income, which leads to lower consumer spending, which leads to another fall in real GDP, and so on. So consumer spending falls as an indirect result of the fall in investment spending.

2. When the *MPC* is 0.5, the multiplier is equal to $1/(1 − 0.5) = 1/0.5 = 2$. When the *MPC* is 0.8, the multiplier is equal to $1/(1 − 0.8) = 1/0.2 = 5$.

3. The greater the share of GDP that is saved rather than spent, the lower the *MPC*. Disposable income that goes to savings is like a "leak" in the system, reducing the amount of spending that fuels a further expansion. So it is likely that Amerigo will have the larger multiplier.

11-2 CHECK YOUR UNDERSTANDING

1. a. Angelina's autonomous consumer spending is $8000. When her current disposable income rises by $10 000, her consumer spending rises by $12 000 − $8000 = $4000. So her *MPC* is $4000/$10 000 = 0.4 and her consumption function is $c = \$8000 + 0.4 \times yd$. Felicia's autonomous consumer spending is $6500. When her current disposable income rises by $10 000, her consumer spending rises by $14 500 − $6500 = $8000. So her *MPC* is $8000/$10 000 = 0.8 and her consumption function is $c = \$6500 + 0.8 \times yd$. Marina's autonomous consumer spending is $7250. When her current disposable income rises by $10 000, her consumer spending rises by $14 250 − $7250 = $7000. So her *MPC* is $7000/$10 000 = 0.7 and her consumption function is $c = \$7250 + 0.7 \times yd$.

b. The aggregate autonomous consumer spending in this economy is $8000 + $6500 + $7250 = $21 750. A $30 000 increase in disposable income (3 × $10 000) leads to a $4000 + $8000 + $7000 = $19 000 increase in consumer spending. So the economy-wide *MPC* is $19 000/$30 000 = 0.63 and the aggregate consumption function is $C = \$21\,750 + 0.63 \times YD$.

2. If you expect your future disposable income to fall, you would like to save some of today's disposable income to tide you over in the future. But you cannot do this if you cannot save. If you expect your future disposable income to rise, you would like to spend some of tomorrow's higher income today. But you cannot do this if you cannot borrow. If you cannot save or borrow, your expected future disposable income will have no effect on your consumer spending today. In fact, your *MPC* must always equal 1: you must consume all your current disposable income today, and you will be unable to smooth your consumption over time.

11-3 CHECK YOUR UNDERSTANDING

1. a. An unexpected increase in consumer spending will result in a reduction in inventories as producers sell items from their inventories to satisfy this short-term increase in demand. This is negative unplanned inventory investment: it reduces the value of producers' inventories.

b. A rise in the cost of borrowing is equivalent to a rise in the interest rate: fewer investment spending projects are now profitable to producers, whether they are financed through borrowing or retained earnings. As a result, producers will reduce the amount of planned investment spending.

c. A sharp increase in the rate of real GDP growth leads to a higher level of planned investment spending by producers, according to the accelerator principle, as they increase production capacity to meet higher demand.

d. As sales fall, producers sell less, and their inventories grow. This leads to positive unplanned inventory investment.

2. Since the marginal propensity to consume is less than 1—because consumers normally spend part but not all of an additional dollar of disposable income—consumer spending does not fully respond to fluctuations in current disposable income. This behaviour diminishes the effect of fluctuations in the economy on consumer spending. In contrast, by the accelerator principle, investment spending is directly related to the expected future growth rate of GDP. As a result, investment spending will magnify fluctuations in the economy: a higher expected future growth rate of real GDP leads to higher planned investment spending; a lower expected future growth rate of real GDP leads to lower planned investment spending.

3. When consumer spending is sluggish, firms with excess production capacity will cut back on planned investment spending because they think their existing capacities are sufficient for expected future sales. Similarly, when consumer spending is sluggish and firms have a large amount of unplanned inventory investment, they are likely to cut back their production of output because they think their existing inventories are sufficient for expected future sales. So an inventory overhang is likely to depress current economic activity as firms cut back on their planned investment spending and on their output.

11-4 CHECK YOUR UNDERSTANDING

1. A slump in planned investment spending will lead to a fall in real GDP in response to an unanticipated increase in inventories. The fall in real GDP will translate into a fall in households' disposable income, and households will respond by reducing consumer spending. The decrease in consumer spending leads producers to further decrease output, further lowering disposable income and leading to further reductions in consumer spending. So although the slump originated in investment spending, it will cause a reduction in consumer spending.

2. a. After an autonomous fall in planned aggregate expenditure, the economy is no longer in equilibrium: real GDP is greater than planned aggregate expenditure. The accompanying figure shows this autonomous fall in planned aggregate expenditure by the shift of the aggregate expenditure curve from AE_1 to AE_2. The difference

between the two results in positive unplanned inventory investment: there is an unanticipated increase in inventories. Firms will respond by reducing production. This will eventually move the economy to a new equilibrium. In the accompanying figure, this is illustrated by the movement from the initial income–expenditure equilibrium at E_1 to the new income–expenditure equilibrium at E_2. As the economy moves to its new equilibrium, real GDP falls from its initial income–expenditure equilibrium level at Y_1^* to its new lower level, Y_2^*.

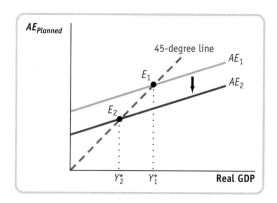

b. We know that the change in income–expenditure equilibrium GDP is given by Equation 11-17: $\Delta Y^* =$ Multiplier $\times \Delta AAE_{Planned}$. Here, the multiplier = $1/(1 - 0.5) = 1/0.5 = 2$. So a $300 million autonomous reduction in planned aggregate expenditure will lead to a $2 \times$ $300 million = $600 million ($0.6 billion) fall in income–expenditure equilibrium GDP. The new Y^* will be $500 billion – $0.6 billion = $499.4 billion.

Chapter Twelve
12-1 CHECK YOUR UNDERSTANDING

1. a. This is a shift of the aggregate demand curve. A decrease in the quantity of money raises the interest rate, since people now want to borrow more and lend less. A higher interest rate reduces investment and consumer spending at any given aggregate price level. So the aggregate demand curve shifts to the left.

b. This is a movement up along the aggregate demand curve. As the aggregate price level rises, the real value of money holdings falls. This is the interest rate effect of a change in the aggregate price level: as the value of money falls, people want to hold more money. They do so by borrowing more and lending less. This leads to a rise in the interest rate and a reduction in consumer and investment spending. So it is a movement along the aggregate demand curve.

c. This is a shift of the aggregate demand curve. Expectations of a poor job market, and so lower average disposable incomes, will reduce people's consumer spending today at any given aggregate price level. So the aggregate demand curve shifts to the left.

d. This is a shift of the aggregate demand curve. A fall in tax rates raises people's disposable income. At any given aggregate price level, consumer spending is now higher. So the aggregate demand curve shifts to the right.

e. This is a movement down along the aggregate demand curve. As the aggregate price level falls, the real value of assets rises. This is the wealth effect of a change in the aggregate price level: as the value of assets rises, people will increase their consumption plans. This leads to higher consumer spending. So it is a movement along the aggregate demand curve.

f. This is a shift of the aggregate demand curve. A rise in the real value of assets in the economy due to a surge in real estate values raises consumer spending at any given aggregate price level. So the aggregate demand curve shifts to the right.

12-2 CHECK YOUR UNDERSTANDING

1. a. This represents a movement along the *SRAS* curve because the CPI—like the GDP deflator—is a measure of the aggregate price level, the overall price level of final goods and services in the economy.

b. This represents a shift of the *SRAS* curve because oil is a commodity. The *SRAS* curve will shift to the right because production costs are now lower, leading to a higher quantity of aggregate output supplied at any given aggregate price level.

c. This represents a shift of the *SRAS* curve because it involves a change in nominal wages. An increase in legally mandated benefits to workers is equivalent to an increase in nominal wages. As a result, the *SRAS* curve will shift leftward because production costs are now higher, leading to a lower quantity of aggregate output supplied at any given aggregate price level.

2. You would need to know what happened to the aggregate price level. If the increase in the quantity of aggregate output supplied was due to a movement along the *SRAS* curve, the aggregate price level would have increased at the same time as the quantity of aggregate output supplied increased. If the increase in the quantity of aggregate output supplied was due to a rightward shift of the *LRAS* curve, the aggregate price level might not rise. Alternatively, you could make the determination by observing what happened to aggregate output in the long run. If it fell back to its initial level in the long run, then the temporary increase in aggregate output was due to a movement along the *SRAS* curve. If it stayed at the higher level in the long run, the increase in aggregate output was due to a rightward shift of the *LRAS* curve.

12-3 CHECK YOUR UNDERSTANDING

1. a. An increase in the minimum wage raises the nominal wage and, as a result, shifts the short-run aggregate supply curve to the left. As a result of this negative supply shock, the aggregate price level rises and aggregate output falls.

b. Increased investment spending shifts the aggregate demand curve to the right. As a result of this positive demand shock, both the aggregate price level and aggregate output rise.

c. An increase in taxes and a reduction in government spending both result in negative demand shocks, shifting the aggregate demand curve to the left. As a

result, both the aggregate price level and aggregate output fall.

d. This is a negative supply shock, shifting the short-run aggregate supply curve to the left. As a result, the aggregate price level rises and aggregate output falls.

2. As the rise in productivity increases potential output, the long-run aggregate supply curve shifts to the right. If, in the short run, there is now a recessionary gap (aggregate output is less than potential output), nominal wages will fall, shifting the short-run aggregate supply curve to the right. This results in a fall in the aggregate price level and a rise in aggregate output. As prices fall, we move along the aggregate demand curve due to the wealth and interest rate effects of a change in the aggregate price level. Eventually, as long-run macroeconomic equilibrium is reestablished, aggregate output will rise to be equal to potential output.

12-4 CHECK YOUR UNDERSTANDING

1. a. An economy is overstimulated when an inflationary gap is present. This will arise if an expansionary monetary or fiscal policy is implemented when the economy is currently in long-run macroeconomic equilibrium. This shifts the aggregate demand curve to the right, in the short run raising the aggregate price level and aggregate output and creating an inflationary gap. Eventually nominal wages will rise and shift the short-run aggregate supply curve to the left, and aggregate output will fall back to potential output while the aggregate price level will be higher. This is the scenario envisaged by the speaker.

b. No, this is not a valid argument. When the economy is not currently in long-run macroeconomic equilibrium, an expansionary monetary or fiscal policy does not lead to the outcome described above. Suppose a negative demand shock has shifted the aggregate demand curve to the left, resulting in a recessionary gap. An expansionary monetary or fiscal policy can shift the aggregate demand curve back to its original position in long-run macroeconomic equilibrium. In this way, the short-run fall in aggregate output and deflation caused by the original negative demand shock can be avoided. So, if used in response to demand shocks, fiscal or monetary policy is an effective policy tool.

2. Those within the BOC who advocated lowering interest rates were focused on boosting aggregate demand in order to counteract the negative demand shock caused by the collapse of the U.S. housing bubble. Lowering interest rates will result in a rightward shift of the aggregate demand curve, increasing aggregate output but raising the aggregate price level. Those within the BOC who advocated holding interest rates steady were focused on the fact that fighting the slump in aggregate demand in the face of a negative supply shock could result in a rise in inflation. Holding interest rates steady relies on the ability of the economy to self-correct in the long run, with the aggregate price level and aggregate output only gradually returning to their levels before the negative supply shock.

Chapter Thirteen

13-1 CHECK YOUR UNDERSTANDING

1. a. This is a contractionary fiscal policy because it is a reduction in government purchases of goods and services.

b. This is an expansionary fiscal policy because it is an increase in government transfers that will increase disposable income.

c. This is a contractionary fiscal policy because it is an increase in taxes that will reduce disposable income.

2. Federal disaster relief that is quickly disbursed is more effective than legislated aid because there is very little time lag between the time of the disaster and the time it is received by victims. So it will stabilize the economy after a disaster. In contrast, legislated aid is likely to entail a time lag in its disbursement, potentially destabilizing the economy.

3. This statement implies that expansionary fiscal policy will result in crowding out of the private sector, and that the opposite, contractionary fiscal policy, will lead the private sector to grow. Whether this statement is true or not depends upon whether the economy is at full employment; it is only then that we should expect expansionary fiscal policy to lead to crowding out. If, instead, the economy has a recessionary gap, then we should expect instead that the private sector grows along with the fiscal expansion, and contracts along with a fiscal contraction.

13-2 CHECK YOUR UNDERSTANDING

1. A $500 million increase in government purchases of goods and services directly increases aggregate expenditure by $500 million, which then starts the multiplier in motion. It will increase real GDP by $500 million × $1/(1 - MPC)$. A $500 million increase in government transfers increases aggregate expenditure only to the extent that it leads to an increase in consumer spending. Consumer spending rises by $MPC × \$1$ for every $1 increase in disposable income, where MPC is less than 1. So a $500 million increase in government transfers will cause a rise in real GDP only MPC times as much as a $500 million increase in government purchases of goods and services. It will increase real GDP by $500 million × $MPC/(1 - MPC)$.

2. This is the same issue as in Problem 1, but in reverse. If government purchases of goods and services fall by $500 million, the initial fall in aggregate expenditure is $500 million. If there is a $500 million reduction in government transfers, the initial fall in aggregate expenditure is $MPC × \$500$ million, which is less than $500 million.

3. Boldovia will experience greater variation in its real GDP than Moldovia because Moldovia has automatic stabilizers while Boldovia does not. In Moldovia the effects of slumps will be lessened by unemployment insurance benefits that will support residents' incomes, while the effects of booms will be diminished because tax revenues will go up. In contrast, incomes will not be supported in Boldovia during slumps because there is no unemployment insurance. In addition, because Boldovia has lump-sum taxes, its booms will not be diminished by increases in tax revenue.

13-3 CHECK YOUR UNDERSTANDING

1. The actual budget balance takes into account the effects of the business cycle on the budget deficit. During recessionary gaps, it incorporates the effect of lower tax revenues and higher transfers on the budget balance; during inflationary gaps, it incorporates the effect of higher tax revenues and reduced transfers. In contrast, the cyclically adjusted budget balance factors out the effects of the business cycle and assumes that real GDP is at potential output. Since, in the long run, real GDP tends to potential output, the cyclically adjusted budget balance is a better measure of the long-run sustainability of government policies.

2. In recessions, real GDP falls. This implies that consumers' incomes, consumer spending, and producers' profits also fall. So in recessions, government's tax revenue (which depends in large part on consumers' incomes, consumer spending, and producers' profits) falls. In order to balance the budget, government has to cut spending or raise taxes. But that deepens the recession. Without a balanced-budget requirement, government could use expansionary fiscal policy during a recession to lessen the fall in real GDP.

13-4 CHECK YOUR UNDERSTANDING

1. a. A higher growth rate of real GDP implies that tax revenue will increase. If government spending remains constant and the government runs a budget surplus, the size of the public debt will be less than it would otherwise have been.

b. If retirees live longer, the average age of the population increases. As a result, the implicit liabilities of the government increase because spending on programs for older Canadians, such as health care, Old Age Security, and Guaranteed Income Supplement and Allowance, will rise.

c. A decrease in tax revenue without offsetting reductions in government spending will cause the public debt to increase.

d. Public debt will increase as a result of government borrowing to pay interest on its current public debt.

2. In order to stimulate the economy in the short run, the government can use fiscal policy to increase real GDP. This entails borrowing, increasing the size of the public debt further and leading to undesirable consequences: in extreme cases, governments can be forced to default on their debts. Even in less extreme cases, a large public debt is undesirable because government borrowing crowds out borrowing for private investment spending. This reduces the amount of investment spending, reducing the long-run growth of the economy.

3. Fiscal austerity is the same as a contractionary fiscal policy. It reduces government spending, which in turn reduces income and reduces tax revenue. With less tax revenue, the government is less able to pay its debts. Also, a failing economy causes lenders to have less confidence that a government is able to pay its debts and leads them to raise interest rates on the debt. Higher interest rates on the debt make it even less likely the government can repay.

Chapter Fourteen
14-1 CHECK YOUR UNDERSTANDING

1. The defining characteristic of money is its liquidity: how easily it can be used to purchase goods and services. Although a gift certificate can easily be used to purchase a very defined set of goods or services (the goods or services available at the store issuing the gift certificate), it cannot be used to purchase any other goods or services. A gift certificate is therefore not money, since it cannot easily be used to purchase all goods and services.

2. Again, the important characteristic of money is its liquidity: how easily it can be used to purchase goods and services. M1, the narrowest definition of the money supply, contains only currency in circulation and demand deposits (chequable bank deposits at the chartered banks). GICs aren't chequable—and they can't be made chequable without incurring a cost because there's a penalty for early withdrawal. This makes them less liquid than the assets counted in M1.

3. Commodity-backed money uses resources more efficiently than simple commodity money, like gold and silver coins, because commodity-backed money ties up fewer valuable resources. Although a bank must keep some of the commodity—generally gold and silver—on hand, it only has to keep enough to satisfy demand for redemptions. It can then lend out the remaining gold and silver, which allows society to use these resources for other purposes, with no loss in the ability to achieve gains from trade.

14-2 CHECK YOUR UNDERSTANDING

1. Even though you know that the rumour about the bank is not true, you are concerned about other depositors pulling their money out of the bank. And you know that if enough other depositors pull their money out, the bank will fail. In that case, it is rational for you to pull your money out before the bank fails. All depositors will think like this, so even if they all know that the rumour is false, they may still rationally pull their money out, leading to a bank run. Deposit insurance leads depositors to worry less about the possibility of a bank run. Even if a bank fails, the CDIC will currently pay each depositor up to $100 000 per account. This will make you much less likely to pull your money out in response to a rumour. Since other depositors will think the same, there will be no bank run.

2. The aspects of modern bank regulation that would frustrate this scheme are *capital requirements* and *reserve requirements*. (In Canada, banks are no longer required to hold minimum reserves). Capital requirements mean that a bank has to have a certain amount of capital—the difference between its assets (loans plus reserves) and its liabilities (deposits). So the con artist could not open a bank without putting any of his own wealth in

because the bank needs a certain amount of capital—that is, it needs to hold more assets (loans plus reserves) than deposits. So the con artist would be at risk of losing his own wealth if his loans turn out badly.

14-3 CHECK YOUR UNDERSTANDING

1. Since they only have to hold $100 in reserves, instead of $200, banks now lend out $100 of their reserves. Whoever borrows the $100 will deposit it in a bank, which will lend out $100 × (1 − rr) = $100 × 0.9 = $90. Whoever borrows the $90 will put it into a bank, which will lend out $90 × 0.9 = $81, and so on. Overall, deposits will increase by $100/0.1 = $1000.

2. Silas puts $1000 in the bank, of which the bank lends out $1000 × (1 − rr) = $1000 × 0.9 = $900. Whoever borrows the $900 will keep $450 in cash and deposit $450 in a bank. The bank will lend out $450 × 0.9 = $405. Whoever borrows the $405 will keep $202.50 in cash and deposit $202.50 in a bank. The bank will lend out $202.50 × 0.9 = $182.25, and so on. Overall, this leads to an increase in deposits of $1000 + $450 + $202.50 + … But it decreases the amount of currency in circulation: the amount of cash is reduced by the $1000 Silas puts into the bank. This is offset, but not fully, by the amount of cash held by each borrower. The amount of currency in circulation therefore changes by −$1000 + $450 + $202.50 + … The money supply therefore increases by the sum of the increase in deposits and the change in currency in circulation, which is $1000 − $1000 + $450 + $450 + $202.50 + $202.50 + … and so on.

14-4 CHECK YOUR UNDERSTANDING

1. An open-market purchase of $100 million by the BOC increases banks' reserves by $100 million as the BOC credits their accounts with additional reserves. In other words, this open-market purchase increases the monetary base (currency in circulation plus bank reserves) by $100 million. Banks lend out the additional $100 million. Whoever borrows the money puts it back into the banking system in the form of deposits. Of these deposits, banks lend out $100 million × (1 − rr) = $100 million × 0.9 = $90 million. Whoever borrows the money deposits it back into the banking system. And banks lend out $90 million × 0.9 = $81 million, and so on. As a result, bank deposits increase by $100 million + $90 million + $81 million + … = $100 million/rr = $100 million/0.1 = $1000 million = $1 billion. Since in this simplified example all money lent out is deposited back into the banking system, there is no increase of currency in circulation, so the increase in bank deposits is equal to the increase in the money supply. In other words, the money supply increases by $1 billion. This is greater than the increase in the monetary base by a factor of 10: in this simplified model in which deposits are the only component of the money supply and in which banks hold no excess reserves, the money multiplier is 1/rr = 10.

14-5 CHECK YOUR UNDERSTANDING

1. It is because the financial risks were spread out more evenly across Canada than in the United States. In the

United States, the financial risks were localized as the American banks were localized banks, i.e., they were providing services in specific state. In Canada, banks were operated across the country, which allowed them to diversify their risks. Also, the Canadian banking system is more concentrated than the American system, so the Canadian banks are well capitalized and diversified. Therefore, there were fewer and smaller sized bank runs in Canada than in the United States.

2. A home price bubble refers to the situation in which the housing prices keep rising to unrealistic levels that they suddenly collapse. Real estate developers who can sell the houses at higher prices and financial institutions that quickly sold mortgages to other investors would gain from the creation of these bubbles. The society should be concerned about home price bubbles because the bursting of these bubbles could cause huge damage to the economy such as the collapse of trust in the financial system, huge losses incurred by financial institutions, and all these lead to the vicious cycle of deleveraging and the tightening in the credit market.

3. The balance sheet effect occurs when asset sales cause declines in asset prices, which then reduce the value of other firms' net worth as the value of the assets on their balance sheets declines. In the vicious cycle of deleveraging, the balance sheet effect on firms forces their creditors to call in their loan contracts, forcing the firms to sell assets to pay back their loans, leading to further asset sales and price declines. Because the vicious cycle of deleveraging occurs across different firms and no single firm can stop it, it is necessary for the government to step in to stop it.

Chapter Fifteen
15-1 CHECK YOUR UNDERSTANDING

1. a. By increasing the opportunity cost of holding money, a high interest rate reduces the quantity of money demanded. This is a movement up and to the left along the money demand curve.

   b. A 10% fall in prices reduces the quantity of money demanded at any given interest rate, shifting the money demand curve leftward.

   c. This technological change reduces the quantity of money demanded at any given interest rate. So it shifts the money demand curve leftward.

   d. This will increase the demand for money at any given interest rate. With more of the economy's assets in overseas bank accounts that are difficult to access, people will want to hold more cash to finance purchases.

2. a. A 1% processing fee on debit/credit card transactions for purchases less than $50 reduces the opportunity cost of holding cash because consumers will save money by paying with cash.

   b. An increase in the interest paid on one-year GICs raises the opportunity cost of holding cash because holding cash requires forgoing the higher interest paid.

   c. When prices fall, the demand for money falls and the money demand curve shifts to the left. In this case, the

interest rate would need to fall in order for people to hold the same quantity of money that they did before the prices were slashed.

   d. When prices rise, the demand for money rises and the money demand curve shifts to the right. In this case, the interest rate would need to rise in order for people to hold the same quantity of money that they did before the prices increased; thus the opportunity cost of holding cash rises.

15-2 CHECK YOUR UNDERSTANDING

1. In the accompanying diagram, the increase in the demand for money is shown as a rightward shift of the money demand curve, from MD_1 to MD_2. This raises the equilibrium interest rate from i_1 to i_2.

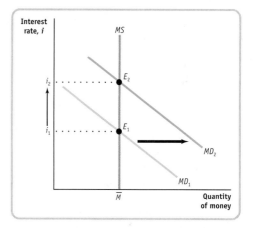

2. In order to prevent the interest rate from rising, the Bank of Canada must make an open-market purchase of Treasury bills, shifting the money supply curve rightward. This is shown in the accompanying diagram as the move from MS_1 to MS_2.

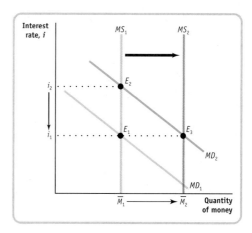

3. a. Frannie is better off buying a one-year bond today and a one-year bond tomorrow because this allows her to get the higher interest rate one year from now.

   b. Frannie is better off buying a two-year bond today because it gives her a higher interest rate in the second year than if she bought two one-year bonds.

15-3 CHECK YOUR UNDERSTANDING

1. a. The money supply curve shifts to the right.

  b. The equilibrium interest rate falls.

  c. Investment spending rises, due to the fall in the interest rate.

  d. Consumer spending rises, due to the multiplier process.

  e. Aggregate output rises because of the rightward shift of the aggregate demand curve.

2. The central bank that uses a backward-looking policy is likely to respond more directly to a financial crisis than one that uses inflation targeting because with a backward-looking policy the central bank does not have to set policy to meet a prespecified inflation target.

15-4 CHECK YOUR UNDERSTANDING

1. a. Aggregate output rises in the short run, then falls back to equal potential output in the long run.

  b. The aggregate price level rises in the short run, but by less than 25%. It rises further in the long run, for a total increase of 25%.

  c. The interest rate falls in the short run, then rises back to its original level in the long run.

2. In the short run, a change in the interest rate alters the economy because it affects investment spending, which in turn affects aggregate demand and real GDP through the multiplier process. However, in the long run, changes in consumer spending and investment spending will eventually result in changes in nominal wages and the nominal prices of other factors of production. For example, an expansionary monetary policy will eventually cause a rise in factor prices; a contractionary policy will eventually cause a fall in factor prices. In response, the short-run aggregate supply curve will shift to move the economy back to long-run equilibrium. So in the long run monetary policy has no effect on the economy.

Chapter Sixteen
16-1 CHECK YOUR UNDERSTANDING

1. The inflation rate is more likely to quickly reflect changes in the money supply when the economy has had an extended period of high inflation. That's because an extended period of high inflation sensitizes workers and firms to raise nominal wages and prices of intermediate goods when the aggregate price level rises. As a result, there will be little or no increase in real output in the short run after an increase in the money supply, and the increase in the money supply will simply be reflected in an equal-sized percent increase in prices. In an economy where people are not sensitized to high inflation because of low inflation in the past, an increase in the money supply will lead to an increase in real output in the short run. This illustrates the fact that the classical model of the price level best applies to economies with *persistently* high inflation, not those with little

or no history of high inflation even though they may currently have high inflation.

2. Yes, there can still be an inflation tax because the tax is levied on people who hold money. As long as people hold money, regardless of whether prices are indexed or not, the government is able to use seignorage to capture real resources from the public.

16-2 CHECK YOUR UNDERSTANDING

1. When real GDP equals potential output, cyclical unemployment is zero and the unemployment rate is equal to the natural rate. This is given by point E_1 in Figure 16-7. Assuming a 0% expected inflation rate, this also corresponds to a 6% unemployment rate on curve $SRPC_0$ in Figure 16-9. Any unemployment in excess of this 6% rate, or less than the 6% rate, represents cyclical unemployment. An increase in aggregate demand leads to a fall in the unemployment rate below the natural rate (negative cyclical unemployment) and an increase in the inflation rate. This is given by the movement from E_1 to E_2 in Figure 16-7 and traces a movement upward along the short-run Phillips curve. A reduction in aggregate demand leads to a rise in the unemployment rate above the natural rate (positive cyclical unemployment) and a fall in the inflation rate. This would be represented by a movement down along the short-run Phillips curve from point E_1. So for a given expected inflation rate, the short-run Phillips curve illustrates the relationship between cyclical unemployment and the actual inflation rate.

2. A fall in commodities prices leads to a positive supply shock, which lowers the aggregate price level and reduces inflation. As a result, any given level of unemployment can be sustained with a lower inflation rate now—meaning that the short-run Phillips curve has shifted downward. In contrast, a surge in commodities prices leads to a negative supply shock, which raises the aggregate price level and increases inflation. Any given level of unemployment can be sustained only with a higher inflation rate—meaning that the short-run Phillips curve has shifted upward.

16-3 CHECK YOUR UNDERSTANDING

1. There is no long-run trade-off between inflation and unemployment because once expectations of inflation adjust, wages will also adjust, returning employment and the unemployment rate to their equilibrium (natural) levels. This implies that once expectations of inflation fully adjust to any change in actual inflation, the unemployment rate will return to the natural rate of unemployment, or NAIRU. This also implies that the long-run Phillips curve is vertical.

2. There are two possible explanations for this. First, negative supply shocks (for example, increases in the price of oil) will cause an increase in unemployment and an increase in inflation. Second, it is possible that British policy-makers attempted to peg the unemployment rate below the natural rate of unemployment. Any attempt to peg unemployment below the natural rate will result in an increase in inflation.

3. Disinflation is costly because to reduce the inflation rate, aggregate output in the short run must typically fall below potential output. This, in turn, results in an increase in the unemployment rate above the natural rate. In general, we would observe a reduction in real GDP. The costs of disinflation can be reduced by not allowing inflation to increase in the first place. Second, the costs of any disinflation will be lower if the central bank is credible and it announces in advance its policy to reduce inflation. In this situation, the adjustment to the disinflationary policy will be more rapid, resulting in a smaller loss of aggregate output.

16-4 CHECK YOUR UNDERSTANDING

1. If the nominal interest rate is negative, an individual is better off simply holding cash, which has a 0% nominal rate of return. If the options facing an individual are to lend and receive a negative nominal interest rate or to hold cash and receive a 0% nominal interest rate, the individual will hold cash. Such a scenario creates the possibility of a liquidity trap, in which monetary policy is ineffective because the nominal interest rate cannot fall below zero. Once the nominal interest rate falls to zero, further increases in the money supply will lead firms and individuals to simply hold the additional cash.

Chapter Seventeen
17-1 CHECK YOUR UNDERSTANDING

1. **a.** This is not an example of maturity transformation because no short-term liabilities are being turned into long-term assets. So it is not subject to a bank run.

   b. This is an example of maturity transformation: Dana incurs a short-term liability, credit card debt, to fund the acquisition of a long-term asset, better job skills. It can result in a bank-run-like phenomenon if her credit card lender becomes fearful of her ability to repay and stops lending to her. If this happens, she will not be able to finish her course and, as a result, will not be able to get the better job that would allow her to pay off her credit card loans.

   c. This is not an example of maturity transformation because there are no short-term liabilities. The partnership itself has no obligation to repay an individual partner's investment and so has no liabilities, short term or long term.

   d. This is an example of maturity transformation: the checking accounts are short-term liabilities of the student union savings bank, and the student loans are long-term assets.

17-2 CHECK YOUR UNDERSTANDING

1. **a.** The asset bubble occurred in Irish real estate.

   b. The channel of the financial contagion was the short-term lending that Irish banks depended on from the wholesale interbank lending market. When lenders began to worry about the soundness of the Irish banks, they refused to lend any more money, leading to a type of bank run and putting the Irish banks at great risk of failure.

2. Because the bank run started with fears among lenders to Irish banks, the Irish government sought to eliminate those fears by guaranteeing the lenders that they would be repaid in full. It was a questionable strategy, though, because it put the Irish taxpayers on the hook for potentially very large losses, so large that they threatened the solvency of the Irish government.

17-3 CHECK YOUR UNDERSTANDING

1. The Federal Reserve was able to prevent a replay of the Great Depression because, unlike in the 1930s, it acted as a lender of last resort to stabilize the banking sector and halt the contagion. But it was unable to significantly reduce the surge in unemployment because the United States experienced a credit crunch and a vicious circle of deleveraging, leaving monetary policy relatively ineffective.

2. In the aftermath of a severe banking crisis, businesses and households have high debt and reduced assets. They cut back on spending to try to reduce their debt. So they are unwilling to borrow regardless of how low the interest rate is.

17-4 CHECK YOUR UNDERSTANDING

1. According to standard macroeconomics, a government should adopt expansionary policies to increase aggregate demand to address an economic slump. France, however, did just the opposite, responding to a weaker economy with a contractionary fiscal policy that would make the economy even weaker. This shows that the French government had adopted the austerity view, believing that it was more important to try to assure markets of its solvency than to support the economy.

17-5 CHECK YOUR UNDERSTANDING

1. Because shadow banks like Lehman relied on short-term borrowing to fund their operations, fears about their soundness could quickly lead lenders to immediately cut off their credit and force them into failure. And without membership in the lender-of-last-resort system, shadow banks like Lehman could not borrow from the Federal Reserve to make up for the short-term loans it had lost.

2. If there had been only a formal depository banking sector, several factors would have mitigated the potential and scope of a banking crisis. First, there would have been no repo financing; the only short-term liabilities would have been customers' deposits, and these would have been largely covered by deposit insurance. Second, capital requirements would have reduced banks' willingness to take on excessive risk, such as holding onto subprime mortgages. Also, direct oversight by the Office of the Superintendent of Financial Institutions would have prevented so much concentration of risk within the banking sector. Finally, depository banks are within

the lender-of-last-resort system; as a result, depository banks had another layer of protection against the fear of depositors and other creditors that they couldn't meet their obligations. All of these factors would have reduced the potential and scope of a banking crisis.

3. Because the shadow banking sector had become such a critical part of the U.S. economy, the crisis of 2007–2009 made it clear that in the event of another crisis the government would find it necessary to guarantee a wide range of financial institution debts, including those of shadow banks as well as depository banks. This created an incentive problem because it would induce shadow banks to take more risk, knowing that the government would bail them out in the event of a meltdown. To counteract this, the Dodd-Frank bill gave the government the power to regulate "systemically important" shadow banks (those likely to require bailing out) in order to reduce their risk taking. It also gave the government the power to seize control of failing shadow banks in a way that was fair to taxpayers and didn't unfairly enrich the owners of the banks.

Chapter Eighteen
18-1 CHECK YOUR UNDERSTANDING

1. A classical economist would have said that although expansionary monetary policy would probably have some effect in the short run, the short run was unimportant. Instead, a classical economist would have stressed the long run, claiming expansionary monetary policy would result only in an increase in the aggregate price level without affecting aggregate output.

18-2 CHECK YOUR UNDERSTANDING

1. The statements support Keynesian theory. According to Keynes, business confidence (which he called "animal spirits") is mainly responsible for recessions. If business confidence is rising, a Keynesian economist would think that investment would rise and aggregate demand would shift to the right. As the economy is recovering from a recession, a Keynesian economist would think of this as a case for macroeconomic policy activism: that the government should use expansionary monetary and fiscal policy to help the economy reaches its potential output faster (i.e., to speed up the recovery).

18-3 CHECK YOUR UNDERSTANDING

1. **a.** According to the velocity equation, $M \times V = P \times Y$, where M is the money supply, V the velocity of money, P the aggregate price level, and Y real GDP. If the Bank of Canada had pursued a monetary policy rule of constant money supply growth, the decline in the velocity of money at the end of 2008 and visible in Figure 18-5 would have resulted in a dramatic decline in aggregate output.

   b. Although monetarists generally believe that monetary policy is not only effective but, in fact, more effective than fiscal policy, they also generally do not favour macroeconomic policy activism. Instead, monetarists gener-

ally advocate monetary policy rules, such as a low but constant rate of money supply growth. In addition, the natural rate hypothesis states that although monetary policy may be effective in helping return unemployment to its natural rate, it cannot permanently reduce unemployment below the natural rate.

2. Fiscal policy is limited by time lags in recognizing economic problems, forming a response, passing legislation, and implementing the policies. Monetary policy is also limited by time lags, but these lags are not as severe as those for fiscal policy because the Bank of Canada tends to act more quickly than the Parliament. Attempts to reduce unemployment below the natural rate via both fiscal and monetary policy are limited by predictions of the natural rate hypothesis: that these attempts will result in accelerating inflation. Also, both fiscal and monetary policy are limited by concerns about the political business cycle: that they will be used to satisfy political ends and will end up destabilizing the economy.

18-4 CHECK YOUR UNDERSTANDING

1. **a.** Rational expectations theorists would argue that only unexpected changes in the money supply would have any short-run effect on economic activity. They would also argue that expected changes in the money supply would affect only the aggregate price level, with no short-run effect on aggregate output. So such theorists would give credit to the BOC for limiting the severity of the 2008–2009 recession only if the BOC's monetary policy had been more aggressive than individuals expected during this period.

   b. Real business cycle theorists would argue that the BOC's policy had no effect on ending the 2008–2009 recession because they believe that fluctuations in aggregate output are caused largely by changes in total factor productivity.

18-5 CHECK YOUR UNDERSTANDING

1. The liquidity trap brought on by the Great Recession greatly diminished the Great Moderation consensus because it considered monetary policy to be the main policy tool and monetary policy was now largely ineffective. The continuing disagreements over fiscal policy were now brought to the forefront as fiscal policy was used by policy-makers to support their deeply depressed economies. A new consensus is unlikely to emerge anytime soon because results of the various policies have been unclear or disappointing: fiscal stimulus like the one in the United States has failed to bring down the U.S. unemployment substantially (although some say the stimulus was too small); conventional monetary policy does not work; and the Fed's unconventional monetary policy seemed to have relatively little effect.

Chapter Nineteen
19-1 CHECK YOUR UNDERSTANDING

1. **a.** The sale of the new airplane to China represents an export of a good to China and so enters the current account.

b. The sale of Bombardier stock to Chinese investors is a sale of a Canadian asset and so enters the financial account.

c. Even though the plane already exists, when it is shipped to China it is an export of a good from Canada. So the sale of the plane enters the current account.

d. Because the plant is in Alberta, the Chinese investor is undertaking foreign direct investment (i.e., buying a Canadian physical asset). So the sale of energy exploration plant enter the financial account.

2. The collapse of the U.S. housing bubble and the ensuing recession led to a dramatic fall in interest rates in the United States because of the deeply depressed economy. Consequently, capital inflows into the United States dried up. The collapse of the U.S. housing bubble also led to a recession in Canada between 2008 and 2009. To stimulate the economy, the Bank of Canada lowered interest rates to historical low levels. Consequently, international capital flows into Canada began to fall.

19-2 CHECK YOUR UNDERSTANDING

1. a. The increased sale of Alberta's oil will cause U.S. individuals (and firms) to increase their demand for the Canadian dollar (C$). To purchase the Canadian dollar, individuals will increase their demand for C$ in the foreign exchange market, causing a rightward shift in the demand curve for C$. This will cause the US$ price of the C$ to rise (the amount of US$ per C$ will rise). The C$ has appreciated and the U.S. dollar has depreciated as a result.

b. This appreciation of the C$ means it will take more U.S. dollars to obtain the same quantity of Canadian dollars. If we assume that the price level (measured in C$) of other Canadian goods and services does not change, other Canadian goods and services become more expensive to U.S. households and firms. The U.S. dollar cost of other Canadian goods and services will rise as the C$ appreciates. So Canadian exports of goods and services other than oil will fall.

c. U.S. goods and services become cheaper in terms of C$, so Canadian imports of goods and services will rise.

2. a. The real exchange rate equals

$$\text{US\$ per C\$} \times \frac{\text{Aggregate price level in Canada}}{\text{Aggregate price level in the United States}}$$

Today, the real exchange rate today is 0.9724 × (100/100) = 0.9724.

The aggregate price level in five years in the United States will be 100 × (120/96) = 125, and in Canada it will be 100 × (120/100) = 120. The real exchange rate in five years, assuming the nominal exchange rate does not change, will be 0.9724 × (120/125) = 0.9335.

b. Today, a basket of goods and services that costs C$100 costs US$96, so the purchasing power parity is 0.96 US$ per C$. In five years, a basket that costs C$120 will cost US$120, so the purchasing power parity will be 1 US$ per C$.

19-3 CHECK YOUR UNDERSTANDING

1. The accompanying diagram shows the supply of and demand for the yuan, with the U.S. dollar price of the yuan on the vertical axis. In 2005, prior to the revaluation, the exchange rate was pegged at 8.28 yuan per U.S. dollar or, equivalently, 0.121 U.S. dollars per yuan ($0.121). At the target exchange rate of $0.121, the quantity of yuan demanded exceeded the quantity of yuan supplied, creating the shortage depicted in the diagram. Without any intervention by the Chinese government, the U.S. dollar price of the yuan would be bid up, causing an appreciation of the yuan. The Chinese government, however, intervened to prevent this appreciation.

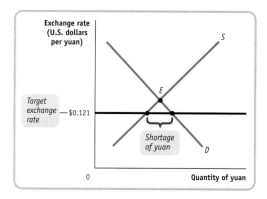

a. If the exchange rate were allowed to move freely, the U.S. dollar price of the exchange rate would move toward the equilibrium exchange rate (labelled XR^* in the accompanying diagram). This would occur as a result of the shortage, when buyers of the yuan would bid up its U.S. dollar price. As the exchange rate increases, the quantity of yuan demanded would fall and the quantity of yuan supplied would increase. If the exchange rate were to increase to XR^*, the disequilibrium would be entirely eliminated.

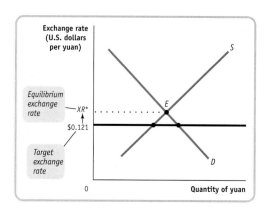

b. Placing restrictions on foreigners who want to invest in China would reduce the demand for the yuan, causing the demand curve to shift in the accompanying diagram from D_1 to something like D_2. This would cause a reduction in the shortage of the yuan. If demand fell to D_3, the disequilibrium would be completely eliminated.

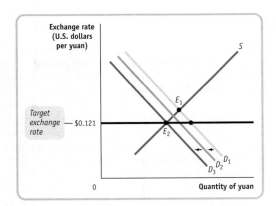

c. Removing restrictions on Chinese who wish to invest abroad would cause an increase in the supply of the yuan and a rightward shift in the supply curve. This increase in supply would also cause a reduction in the size of the shortage. If, for example, supply increased from S_1 to S_2, the disequilibrium would be eliminated completely in the accompanying diagram.

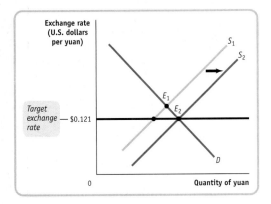

d. Imposing a tax on exports (Chinese goods sold to foreigners) would raise the price of these goods and decrease the amount of Chinese goods purchased. This would also decrease the demand for the yuan. The graphical analysis here is virtually identical to that found in the figure accompanying part b.

19-4 CHECK YOUR UNDERSTANDING

1. The devaluations and revaluations most likely occurred in those periods when there was a sudden change in the franc–mark exchange rate: 1974, 1976, the early 1980s, 1986, and 1993–1994.

2. The high Canadian interest rates would likely have caused an increase in capital inflows to Canada. To obtain these assets (which yielded a relatively higher interest rate) in Canada, investors would first have had to obtain Canadian dollars. The increase in the demand for the Canadian dollar would have caused the Canadian dollar to appreciate. This appreciation of the Canadian currency would have raised the price of Canadian goods to foreigners (measured in terms of the foreign currency). This would have made it more difficult for Canadian firms to compete in other markets.

Italicized terms within definitions are key terms that are defined elsewhere in this glossary.

A

absolute advantage the advantage conferred on an individual or country in an activity if the individual or country can do it better than others. A country with an absolute advantage can produce more output per worker than other countries.

absolute value the value of a number without regard to a plus or minus sign.

accelerator principle the proposition that a higher rate of growth in *real GDP* results in a higher level of *planned investment spending*, and a lower growth rate in *real GDP* leads to lower planned investment spending.

actual investment spending the sum of *planned investment spending* and *unplanned inventory investment*.

AD–AS model the basic *model* used to understand fluctuations in *aggregate output* and the *aggregate price level*. It uses the *aggregate supply curve* and the *aggregate demand curve* together to analyze the behaviour of the *economy* in response to shocks or government policy.

aggregate consumption function the relationship for the *economy* as a whole between aggregate current *disposable income* and aggregate *consumer spending*.

aggregate demand curve a graphical representation that shows the relationship between the *aggregate price level* and the quantity of *aggregate output* demanded by *households*, *firms*, the government, and the rest of the world. The aggregate demand curve has a negative slope due to the *wealth effect of a change in the aggregate price level* and the *interest rate effect of a change in the aggregate price level*.

aggregate expenditure the sum of *consumer spending*, *investment spending*, *government purchases of goods and services*, and *exports* minus *imports*, is the total spending on domestically produced final goods and services in the *economy*.

aggregate output the total quantity of *final goods and services* the *economy* produces for a given time period, usually a year. *Real GDP* is the numerical measure of aggregate output typically used by economists.

aggregate price level a single number that represents the overall price level for *final goods and services* in the *economy*.

aggregate production function a relationship that shows how the aggregate real quantity of output is produced using the available *factors of production* (the *inputs*: labour, *physical capital*, and human capital) and *technology* [A and the function F(…)].

aggregate supply curve a graphical representation that shows the relationship between the *aggregate price level* and the total quantity of *aggregate output* supplied.

appreciation a rise in the value of one currency in terms of other currencies.

asset bubble the price of an asset pushed to an unreasonably high level due to expectations of further price gains.

autarky a situation in which a country does not trade with other countries.

automatic stabilizers government spending and taxation rules that cause *fiscal policy* to be automatically expansionary when the *economy* contracts and automatically contractionary when the economy expands without requiring any deliberate actions by policy-makers. Taxes that depend on *disposable income* are the most important example of *automatic stabilizers*.

autonomous change in aggregate expenditure an initial rise or fall in *aggregate expenditure* at a given level of *real GDP*.

average productivity of labour (AP_L) (real) output per worker or, in some cases, output per hour. Also referred to as *labour productivity* or simply *productivity*.

B

balance of payments accounts a summary of a country's transactions with other countries, including two main elements: the *balance of payments on current account* and the *balance of payments on financial account*.

balance of payments on current account (current account) transactions that don't create *liabilities;* a country's *balance of payments on goods and services* plus net international transfer payments and *factor income*.

balance of payments on financial account (financial account) international transactions that involve the sale or purchase of assets, and therefore create future *liabilities*.

balance of payments on goods and services the difference between the value of *exports* and the value of *imports* during a given period.

balance sheet effect the reduction in a *firm's* net worth from falling asset prices.

bank a *financial intermediary* that provides *liquid* assets in the form of *bank deposits* to lenders and uses those funds to finance the *illiquid* investments or *investment spending* needs of borrowers.

bank deposit a claim on a *bank* that obliges the bank to give the depositor his or her cash when demanded.

bank rate the rate of interest a central bank charges on loans to banks. In many countries, this rate of interest is known as the *discount rate*.

bank reserves currency held by *banks* in their vaults plus their deposits at the Bank of Canada.

bank run a phenomenon in which many of a *bank's* depositors try to withdraw their funds due to fears of a bank failure.

banking crisis episode when a large part of the depository banking sector or the shadow banking sector fails or threatens to fail.

bar graph a graph that uses bars of varying heights or lengths to show the comparative sizes of different observations of a *variable*.

barter the direct exchange of goods or services for other goods or services without the use of money.

black market a market in which goods or services are bought and sold illegally, either because it is illegal to sell them at all or because the prices charged are legally prohibited by a *price ceiling*.

bond a legal document based on borrowing in the form of an IOU that pays interest.

budget balance the difference between tax revenue and government spending. A positive budget balance is referred to as a *budget surplus*; a negative budget balance is referred to as a *budget deficit*; also known as *public savings*.

budget deficit the difference between tax revenue and government spending when government spending exceeds tax revenue; dissaving by the government in the form of a *budget deficit* is a negative contribution to *national savings*.

budget surplus the difference between tax revenue and government spending when tax revenue exceeds government spending; saving by the government in the form of a *budget surplus* is a positive contribution to *national savings*.

business cycle the short-run alternation between economic downturns, known as *recessions*, and economic upturns, known as *expansions*.

business-cycle peak the point in time at which the *economy* shifts from *expansion* to *recession*.

business-cycle trough the point in time at which the *economy* shifts from *recession* to *expansion*.

C

capital requirements government rules imposed on a bank to ensure the bank holds more assets than the value of its deposits, thus reducing the possibility of a *bank run*.

causal relationship the relationship between two *variables* in which the value taken by one variable directly influences or determines the value taken by the other variable.

central bank an institution that oversees and regulates the banking system and controls the *monetary base*.

chained dollars method of calculating *real GDP* using the average between the growth rate calculated using an early base year and the growth rate calculated using a late base year.

chequeable deposits *bank* accounts on which people can write cheques.

circular-flow diagram a diagram that represents the transactions in an *economy* by two kinds of flows around a circle: flows of physical things such as goods or labour in one direction and flows of money to pay for these physical things in the opposite direction.

classical model of the price level a simplified financial *model* of the price level in which the real quantity of money, M/P, is always at its long-run *equilibrium* level. This model ignores the distinction between the short run and the long run but is useful for analyzing the case of high *inflation*.

commercial bank a *bank* that accepts deposits and is covered by *deposit insurance*.

commodity money a *medium of exchange* that is a good, normally gold or silver, that has intrinsic value in other uses.

commodity-backed money a *medium of exchange* that has no intrinsic value whose ultimate value is guaranteed by a promise that it can be converted into valuable goods on demand.

comparative advantage the advantage conferred on an individual or country in producing a good or service if the *opportunity cost* of producing the good or service is lower for that individual or country than for other producers.

competitive market a market in which there are many buyers and sellers of the same good or service, none of whom can influence the price at which the good or service is sold.

complements pairs of goods for which a rise in the price of one good leads to a decrease in the demand for the other good.

consumer price index (CPI) a measure of prices; calculated by surveying market prices for a *market basket* intended to represent the consumption of a typical Canadian family. The CPI is the most commonly used measure of prices in the Canada.

consumer spending (consumption) *household* spending on goods and services from domestic and foreign *firms*.

consumer surplus a term often used to refer both to *individual consumer surplus* and to *total consumer surplus*.

contractionary fiscal policy *fiscal policy* that reduces aggregate demand by decreasing government purchases, increasing taxes, or decreasing transfers.

contractionary monetary policy *monetary policy* that, through the raising of the *interest rate,* reduces aggregate demand and therefore output.

convergence hypothesis a principle of economic growth that holds that international differences in *real GDP* per capita tend to narrow over time because countries that start with lower real GDP per capita tend to have higher growth rates.

cost (of potential seller) the lowest price at which a seller is willing to sell a good.

credit crunch a reduction in the availability of credit in which potential borrowers can't get credit at all or must pay very high *interest rates*.

crowding out the negative effect of *budget deficits* on private investment, which occurs because *government borrowing* drives up *interest rates*.

currency in circulation actual cash held by the public.

current account (balance of payments on current account) transactions that don't create *liabilities*; a country's *balance of payments on goods and services* plus net international transfer payments and *factor income*.

curve a line on a graph, which may be curved or straight, that depicts a relationship between two *variables*.

cyclical unemployment the difference between the actual rate of *unemployment* and the *natural rate of unemployment* due to downturns and upturns in the *business cycle*.

cyclically adjusted budget balance an estimate of what the *budget balance* would be if *real GDP* were exactly equal to *potential output*.

D

deadweight loss the loss in total *surplus* that occurs whenever an action or a policy reduces the quantity transacted below the efficient market *equilibrium quantity*.

debt deflation the reduction in aggregate demand arising from the increase in the real burden of outstanding debt caused by *deflation*; occurs because borrowers, whose real debt rises as a result of deflation, are likely to cut spending sharply, and lenders, whose real assets are now more valuable, are less likely to increase spending.

debt overhang high debt but diminished assets, resulting from a vicious circle of deleveraging.

debt-to-GDP ratio government debt as a percentage of *GDP*, frequently used as a measure of a government's ability to pay its debts.

default the failure of a borrower to make payments as specified by the *bond* or *loan* contract.

deflation a fall in the overall level of prices.

demand curve a graphical representation of the *demand schedule,* showing the relationship between *quantity demanded* and price.

demand price the price of a given quantity at which consumers will demand that quantity.

demand schedule a list or table showing how much of a good or service consumers will want to buy at different prices.

demand shock an event that shifts the *aggregate demand curve*. A positive demand shock is associated with higher demand for *aggregate output* at any price level and shifts the curve to the right. A negative demand shock is associated with lower demand for aggregate output at any price level and shifts the curve to the left.

dependent variable the determined *variable* in a *causal relationship*.

deposit insurance a guarantee that a *bank*'s depositors will be paid even if the bank can't come up with the funds, up to a maximum amount per account.

deposit switching the shifting of government deposits between the Bank of Canada and the *commercial banks*. It is a major tool used by the Bank of Canada in its day-to-day operations.

depreciation a fall in the value of one currency in terms of other currencies.

desired (or voluntary) reserve ratio the fraction of *bank deposits* that *banks* want to hold as reserves.

devaluation a reduction in the value of a currency that is set under a *fixed exchange rate regime*.

diminishing marginal productivity of (physical) capital (dim MP_K) in a *per worker production function* when, holding the amount of *human capital* per worker and the state of *technology* fixed, each successive increase in the amount of *physical capital* per worker leads to a smaller increase in *productivity*.

diminishing returns to physical capital in an *aggregate production function* when the amount of *human capital* per worker and the state of *technology* are held fixed, each successive increase in the amount of *physical capital* per worker leads to a smaller increase in productivity; also referred to as *diminishing marginal productivity of (physical) capital (dim MP_K)*.

discount rate the rate of interest a central bank, such as the Bank of Canada, charges on loans to *banks*; also referred to as the *bank rate*.

discouraged workers individuals who want to work but who have stated to government researchers that they aren't currently searching for a job because they see little prospect of finding one given the state of the job market.

discretionary fiscal policy *fiscal policy* that is the direct result of deliberate actions by policy-makers rather than rules.

discretionary monetary policy policy actions, either changes in *interest rates* or changes in the *money supply*, undertaken by the *central bank* based on its assessment of the state of the *economy*.

disinflation the process of bringing down *inflation* that has become embedded in expectations.

disposable income income plus *government transfers* minus taxes; the total amount of *household* income available to spend on *consumption* and to save.

diversification investment in several different assets with unrelated, or independent, risks, so that the possible losses are independent events.

domestic demand curve a *demand curve* that shows how the quantity of a good demanded by domestic consumers depends on the price of that good.

domestic supply curve a *supply curve* that shows how the quantity of a good supplied by domestic producers depends on the price of that good.

E

economic growth the growing ability of the *economy* to produce goods and services.

economics the social science that studies the production, distribution, and *consumption* of goods and services.

economy a system for coordinating society's productive activities.

efficiency wages wages that employers set above the *equilibrium* wage rate as an incentive for workers to deliver better performance.

efficient description of a market or *economy* that takes all opportunities to make some people better off without making other people worse off.

efficient markets hypothesis a principle of asset price determination that holds that asset prices embody all publicly available information. The hypothesis implies that *stock* prices should be unpredictable, or follow a *random walk*, since changes should occur only in response to new information about fundamentals.

employment the total number of people (aged 15 and older) currently employed for pay in the *economy*, either full time or part time.

equilibrium an economic situation in which no individual would be better off doing something different.

equilibrium exchange rate the *exchange rate* at which the quantity of a currency demanded in the *foreign exchange market* is equal to the quantity supplied.

equilibrium price the price at which the market is in *equilibrium*, that is, the quantity of a good or service demanded equals the quantity of that good or service supplied; also referred to as the *market-clearing price*.

equilibrium quantity the quantity of a good or service bought and sold at the *equilibrium* (or *market-clearing*) *price*.

equity fairness; everyone gets his or her fair share. Since people can disagree about what's "fair," equity isn't as well defined a concept as efficiency.

excess reserves a *bank*'s *reserves* over and above its *desired (or voluntary) reserve ratio*.

exchange market intervention government purchases or sales of currency in the *foreign exchange market*.

exchange rate the price at which currencies trade, determined by the *foreign exchange market*.

exchange rate regime a rule governing policy toward the *exchange rate*.

expansion period of economic upturn in which output and *employment* are rising; most economic numbers are following their normal upward trend; also referred to as a recovery.

expansionary fiscal policy *fiscal policy* that increases aggregate demand by increasing government purchases, decreasing taxes, or increasing transfers.

expansionary monetary policy *monetary policy* that, through the lowering of the *interest rate*, increases aggregate demand and therefore output.

expected rate of inflation the rate of inflation employers and workers expect in the near future.

exporting industries industries that produce goods or services that are sold abroad.

exports goods and services sold to other countries.

F

factor incomes incomes earned by *factors of production*, which include wages, interest, rent dividends, and profits.

factor intensity the difference in the ratio of factors used to produce a good in various industries. For example, oil refining is capital-intensive compared to auto seat production because oil refiners use a higher ratio of capital to labour than do producers of auto seats.

factor markets markets in which *firms* buy the *resources* they need to produce goods and services.

factors of production the *resources* used to produce goods and services. Labour and capital are examples of factors.

fiat money a *medium of exchange* whose value derives entirely from its official status as a means of payment.

final goods and services goods and services sold to the final, or end, user.

financial account (balance of payments on financial account) international transactions that involve the sale or purchase of assets, and therefore create future *liabilities*.

financial asset a paper claim that entitles the buyer to future income from the seller. *Loans, stocks, bonds,* and *bank deposits* are types of financial assets.

financial contagion a vicious downward spiral among depository banks or *shadow banks:* each bank's failure worsens fears and increases the likelihood that another bank will fail.

financial intermediary an institution, such as a *mutual fund, pension fund, life insurance company,* or *bank,* that transforms the funds it gathers from many individuals into *financial assets.*

financial markets the banking, *stock,* and *bond* markets, which channel *private savings* and foreign lending into *investment spending, government borrowing,* and foreign borrowing.

financial panic a sudden and widespread disruption of the *financial markets* that occurs when people suddenly lose faith in the liquidity of financial institutions and markets.

financial risk uncertainty about future outcomes that involve financial losses or gains.

firm an organization that produces goods and services for sale.

fiscal policy changes in government spending and taxes designed to affect overall spending.

fiscal year the time period used for much of government accounting, running from April 1 to March 31. Fiscal years are labelled by the calendar year in which they end.

Fisher effect the principle by which an increase in expected future *inflation* drives up the *nominal interest rate,* leaving the expected *real interest rate* unchanged.

fixed exchange rate an *exchange rate regime* in which the government keeps the *exchange rate* against some other currency at or near a particular target.

floating exchange rate an *exchange rate regime* in which the government lets market forces determine the *exchange rate.*

forecast a simple prediction of the future.

foreign exchange controls licensing systems that limit the right of individuals to buy foreign currency.

foreign exchange market the market in which currencies can be exchanged for each other.

foreign exchange reserves *stocks* of foreign currency that governments can use to buy their own currency on the *foreign exchange market.*

free trade *trade* that is unregulated by government *tariffs* or other artificial barriers; the levels of *exports* and *imports* occur naturally, as a result of supply and demand.

frictional unemployment *unemployment* due to time workers spend in *job search.*

G

gains from trade gains achieved by dividing tasks and trading; in this way people can get more of what they want through *trade* than they could if they tried to be self-sufficient.

GDP deflator a price measure for a given year that is equal to 100 times the ratio of *nominal GDP* to *real GDP* in that year.

GDP per capita GDP divided by the size of the population; equivalent to the average GDP per person.

globalization the phenomenon of growing economic linkages among countries.

government borrowing the total amount of funds borrowed by federal, provincial, and local governments in *financial markets* to buy goods and services.

government purchases of goods and services total purchases by federal, provincial, and local governments on goods and services.

government transfers payments by the government to individuals for which no good or service is provided in return.

Great Moderation the period from 1985 to 2007 when the Canadian *economy* experienced small fluctuations and low *inflation.*

Great Moderation consensus a belief in *monetary policy* as the main tool of stabilization combined with skepticism toward the use of *fiscal policy* and an acknowledgment of the policy constraints imposed by the *natural rate of unemployment* and the *political business cycle.*

gross domestic product (GDP) the total value of all *final goods and services* produced in the *economy* during a given period, usually a year.

growth accounting accounting that estimates the contribution of each major factor in the *per worker production function* to economic growth.

H

Heckscher–Ohlin model a *model* of international trade in which a country has a *comparative advantage* in a good whose production is intensive in the factors that are abundantly available in that country.

horizontal axis the horizontal number line of a graph along which values of the *x*-variable are measured; also referred to as the *x-axis.*

horizontal intercept the point at which a *curve* hits the *horizontal axis;* it indicates the value of the *x*-variable when the value of the *y*-variable is zero.

household a person or a group of people who share their income.

human capital the improvement in labour created by the education and knowledge embodied in the workforce.

I

illiquid describes an asset that cannot be quickly converted into cash with relatively little loss of value.

implicit liabilities spending promises made by governments that are effectively a debt despite the fact that they are not included in the usual debt statistics. Canada's largest implicit liabilities come from transfer programs, including the Canada Health Transfer (CHT), the Canada Social Transfer (CST), and benefits for retired and elderly people.

import quota a legal limit on the quantity of a good that can be imported.

import-competing industries industries that produce goods or services that are also imported.

imports goods and services purchased from other countries.

incentive anything that offers rewards to people who change their behaviour.

income distribution the way in which total income is divided among the owners of the various *factors of production.*

income–expenditure (level of) equilibrium a situation in which *aggregate output,* measured by *real GDP,* is equal to *planned aggregate expenditure* and *firms* have no incentive to change output.

income–expenditure equilibrium GDP the level of *real GDP* at which real GDP equals *planned aggregate expenditure.*

independent variable the determining *variable* in a *causal relationship.*

indexing a way to correct the effect of *inflation* on the purchasing power of a unit of currency by adjusting the nominal/dollar value of an item to the *inflation rate.*

individual choice the decision by an individual of what to do, which necessarily involves a decision of what not to do.

individual consumer surplus the net gain to an individual buyer from the purchase of a good; equal to the difference between the buyer's *willingness to pay* and the price paid.

individual consumption function an equation showing how an individual *household's consumer spending* varies with the household's current *disposable income*.

individual demand curve a graphical representation of the relationship between *quantity demanded* and price for an individual consumer.

individual producer surplus the net gain to an individual seller from selling a good; equal to the difference between the price received and the seller's *cost*.

individual supply curve a graphical representation of the relationship between *quantity supplied* and price for an individual producer.

industrial producer price index (IPPI) an index that measures changes in the prices of goods purchased by producers.

inefficient allocation of sales among sellers a form of inefficiency in which sellers who would be willing to sell a good at the lowest price are not always those who actually manage to sell it; often the result of a *price floor*.

inefficient allocation to consumers a form of inefficiency in which people who badly want a good and are willing to pay a high price don't get it, and those who care relatively little about the good and are only willing to pay a low price do get it; often a result of a *price ceiling*.

inefficiently high quality a form of inefficiency in which sellers offer high-quality goods at a high price even though buyers would prefer a lower quality at a lower price; often the result of a *price floor*.

inefficiently low quality a form of inefficiency in which sellers offer low-quality goods at a low price even though buyers would prefer a higher quality at a higher price; often a result of a *price ceiling*.

inferior good a good for which a rise in income decreases the demand for the good.

inflation a rise in the overall level of prices.

inflation rate the annual percent change in a *price index*—typically the *consumer price index*. The *inflation rate* is positive when the *aggregate price level* is rising (*inflation*) and negative when the aggregate price level is falling (*deflation*).

inflation targeting an approach to *monetary policy* that requires that the *central bank* try to keep the *inflation rate* near a predetermined target rate.

inflation tax the reduction in the value of money held by the public caused by *inflation*.

inflationary gap a state that exists when *aggregate output* is above *potential output*.

infrastructure *physical capital*, such as roads, power lines, ports, information networks, and other parts of an *economy*, that provides the underpinnings, or foundation, for economic activity.

input a good or service used to produce another good or service.

interaction (of choices) the effect of one individual's choices upon another's; a feature of most economic situations. The results of this interaction are often quite different from what the individuals intend.

interest rate the price, calculated as a percentage of the amount borrowed, that a lender charges a borrower for the use of their savings for one year.

interest rate effect of a change in the aggregate price level the effect on *consumer spending* and *investment spending* caused by a change in the purchasing power of consumers' money holdings when the *aggregate price level* changes. A rise (fall) in the aggregate price level decreases (increases) the purchasing power of consumers' money holdings. In response, consumers try to increase (decrease) their money holdings, which drives up (down) *interest rates*, thereby decreasing (increasing) *consumption* and *investment*.

intermediate goods and services goods and services—bought from one *firm* by another firm—that are *inputs* for production of *final goods and services*.

international trade agreements treaties by which countries agree to lower *trade protections* against one another.

inventories stocks of goods and raw materials held to facilitate business operations.

inventory investment the value of the change in total *inventories* held in the *economy* during a given period. Unlike other types of *investment spending*, inventory investment can be negative, if inventories fall.

investment bank a *bank* that trades in *financial assets* and is not covered by *deposit insurance*.

investment spending (investment) spending on productive *physical capital*—such as machinery and construction of buildings—and on changes to *inventories*.

invisible hand a phrase used by Adam Smith to refer to the way in which an individual's pursuit of self-interest can lead, without the individual's intending it, to good results for society as a whole.

invisible underemployment the number of people who have jobs that do not fully use their skills or that have one or more substandard job characteristics, such as low pay.

J

job search when workers spend time looking for *employment*.

jobless recovery a period in which the *real GDP* growth rate is positive but the *unemployment rate* is still rising.

K

Keynesian cross a diagram that identifies *income–expenditure equilibrium* as the point where the *planned aggregate expenditure* line crosses the 45-degree line.

Keynesian economics a school of thought emerging out of the works of John Maynard Keynes; according to Keynesian economics, a depressed *economy* is the result of inadequate spending and government intervention can help a depressed economy through *monetary policy* and *fiscal policy*. Changes in aggregate demand affect *aggregate output, employment,* and prices. Changes in business confidence cause the *business cycle*.

L

labour force the sum of *employment* and *unemployment*; that is, the number of people who are currently working plus the number of people who are currently looking for work.

labour force participation rate the percentage of the population age 15 or older that is in the *labour force*.

labour productivity output per worker; also referred to as Average Productivity of Labour (AP_L) or simply *productivity*. Increases in labour productivity are the only source of *long-run economic growth*.

law of demand the principle that a higher price for a good or service, *other things equal*, leads people to demand a smaller quantity of that good or service.

lender of last resort an institution, usually a country's *central bank,* that provides funds to financial institutions when they are unable to borrow from private credit markets.

leverage the degree to which a financial institution is financing its investments with borrowed funds.

liability a requirement to pay income in the future.

licence the right, conferred by the government or an owner, to supply a good.

life insurance company a *financial intermediary* that sells policies guaranteeing a payment to a policyholder's beneficiaries when the policyholder dies.

linear relationship the relationship between two *variables* in which the *slope* is constant and therefore is depicted on a graph by a *curve* that is a straight line.

liquid describes an asset that can be quickly converted into cash with relatively little loss of value.

liquidity preference model of the interest rate a *model* of the market for money in which the *interest rate* is determined by the supply and demand for money.

liquidity trap a state of the *economy* where *monetary policy* is ineffective because *nominal interest rates* are up against the *zero bound.*

loan a lending agreement between an individual lender and an individual borrower. Loans are usually tailored to the individual borrower's needs and ability to pay but carry relatively high *transaction costs.*

loan-backed securities assets created by pooling individual *loans* and selling shares in that pool.

loanable funds market a hypothetical market that brings together those who want to lend money (savers) and those who want to borrow (*firms* with *investment spending* projects).

long-run aggregate supply curve a graphical representation that shows the relationship between the *aggregate price level* and the quantity of *aggregate output* supplied that would exist if all prices, including *nominal wages,* were fully flexible. The *long-run aggregate supply curve* is vertical because the aggregate price level has no effect on aggregate output in the long run; in the long run, aggregate output is determined by the *economy's potential output.*

long-run economic growth the sustained rise in the quantity of goods and services the *economy* produces.

long-run macroeconomic equilibrium the point at which the *short-run macroeconomic equilibrium* is on the *long-run aggregate supply curve;* so *short-run equilibrium aggregate output* is equal to *potential output.*

long-run Phillips curve a graphical representation of the relationship between *unemployment* and *inflation* in the long run after expectations of inflation have had time to adjust to experience.

long-term interest rate the *interest rate* on *financial assets* that mature a number of years into the future.

lump-sum taxes taxes that don't depend on the taxpayer's income.

M

macroeconomic policy activism the use of *monetary policy* and *fiscal policy* to smooth out the *business cycle.*

macroeconomics the branch of *economics* that is concerned with the overall ups and downs in the *economy.*

marginal analysis the study of *marginal decisions.*

marginal decision a decision made at the "margin" of an activity to do a bit more or a bit less of that activity.

marginal propensity to consume (*MPC*) the increase in *consumer spending* when *disposable income* rises by \$1. Because consumers normally spend part but not all of an additional dollar of disposable income, *MPC* is between 0 and 1.

marginal propensity to save (*MPS*) the fraction of an additional dollar of *disposable income* that is saved; *MPS* is equal to 1 − *MPC*.

marginally attached workers nonworking individuals who say they would like a job and have looked for work in the recent past but are not currently looking for work.

market basket a hypothetical *consumption* bundle of consumer purchases of goods and services, used to measure changes in overall price level.

market economy an *economy* in which decisions about production and *consumption* are made by individual producers and consumers.

market failure the failure of a market to be *efficient.*

market-clearing price the price at which the market is in *equilibrium,* that is, the quantity of a good or service demanded equals the quantity of that good or service supplied; also referred to as the *equilibrium price.*

markets for goods and services markets in which *firms* sell goods and services that they produce to *households.*

maturity transformation the conversion of short-term *liabilities* into long-term assets.

maximum the highest point on a *nonlinear curve,* where the *slope* changes from positive to negative.

medium of exchange an asset that individuals acquire for the purpose of trading for goods and services rather than for their own *consumption.*

menu cost the real cost of changing a listed price.

merchandise trade balance (trade balance) the difference between a country's *exports* and *imports* of goods alone—not including services.

microeconomics the branch of *economics* that studies how people make decisions and how those decisions interact.

minimum the lowest point on a *nonlinear curve,* where the *slope* changes from negative to positive.

minimum wage a legal floor on the wage rate. The wage rate is the market price of labour.

model a simplified representation of a real situation that is used to better understand real-life situations.

monetarism a theory of *business cycles,* associated primarily with Milton Friedman, that asserts that GDP will grow steadily if the *money supply* grows steadily.

monetary aggregate an overall measure of the *money supply.* The most common *monetary aggregates* in Canada range from M1, the narrowest category (cash and all chequeable deposits at chartered banks), to M3, the broadest category (cash, all deposits in financial institutions, and money market funds).

monetary base the sum of *currency in circulation* and *bank reserves.*

monetary neutrality the concept that changes in the *money supply* have no real effects on the *economy* in the long run and only result in a proportional change in the price level.

monetary policy changes in the quantity of money in circulation designed to alter *interest rates* and affect the level of overall spending.

monetary policy rule a formula that determines the *central bank's* actions.

monetary transmission mechanism the channels through which a change in *interest rates* (or *money supply*) will cause a shift in the *aggregate demand curve* (and ultimately affect the *economy's* output and *inflation rate*).

money any asset that can easily be used to purchase goods and services.

money demand curve a graphical representation of the relationship between the *interest rate* and the quantity of money demanded. The money demand curve slopes downward because, other things equal, a higher *interest rate* increases the *opportunity cost* of holding money.

money multiplier the ratio of the *money supply* to the *monetary base*.

money supply the total value of *financial assets* in the *economy* that are considered *money*.

money supply curve a graphical representation of the relationship between the quantity of money supplied and the *interest rate*.

movement along the demand curve a change in the *quantity demanded* of a good that results from a change in the price of that good.

movement along the supply curve a change in the *quantity supplied* of a good that results from a change in the price of that good.

multiplier the ratio of total change in *real GDP* caused by an *autonomous change in aggregate expenditure* to the size of that autonomous change.

mutual fund a *financial intermediary* that creates a *stock* portfolio by buying and holding shares in companies and then selling shares of this portfolio to individual investors.

N

national income and product accounts (national accounts) method of calculating and keeping track of *consumer spending*, sales of producers, business *investment spending*, government purchases, and a variety of other flows of money between different sectors of the *economy*.

national savings the sum of *private savings* and the government's *budget balance;* the total amount of savings generated within the *economy*.

natural rate hypothesis the hypothesis that because *inflation* is eventually embedded into expectations, to avoid accelerating inflation over time the *unemployment rate* must be high enough that the actual *inflation rate* equals the expected inflation rate.

natural rate of unemployment the normal *unemployment rate* around which the actual unemployment rate fluctuates; the unemployment rate that arises from the effects of *frictional* and *structural unemployment*.

near moneys financial assets that can't be directly used as a *medium of exchange* but can be readily converted into cash or *chequeable deposits*.

negative relationship a relationship between two *variables* in which an increase in the value of one variable is associated with a decrease in the value of the other variable. It is illustrated by a *curve* that slopes downward from left to right.

net exports the difference between the value of *exports* and the value of *imports*. A positive value for net exports indicates that a country is a net exporter of goods and services; a negative value indicates that a country is a net importer of goods and services.

Net foreign investment (NFI) the total outflows of funds out of a country minus the total inflows of funds into that country; the difference between the amount of foreign investment undertaken by the country and the amount of domestic investment undertaken by foreigners.

new classical macroeconomics an approach to the *business cycle* that returns to the classical view that shifts in the *aggregate demand curve* affect only the *aggregate price level*, not *aggregate output*.

new Keynesian economics theory that argues that market imperfections can lead to price stickiness for the *economy* as a whole.

nominal GDP the value of all *final goods and services* produced in the *economy* during a given year, calculated using the prices (current) in the year in which the output is produced.

nominal interest rate the *interest rate* in dollar terms.

nominal wage the dollar amount of any given wage paid.

non-accelerating inflation rate of unemployment (NAIRU) the *unemployment rate* at which, *other things equal*, inflation does not change over time.

non-factor payments the difference between the prices paid for *final goods and services* and the amount received by *factors of production*, which include net indirect taxes and capital depreciation.

non-linear curve a *curve* in which the *slope* is not the same between every pair of points.

non-linear relationship the relationship between two *variables* in which the *slope* is not constant and therefore is depicted on a graph by a *curve* that is not a straight line.

non-monetary assets assets that are not made up of money, nor function as money.

normal good a good for which a rise in income increases the demand for that good—the "normal" case.

normative economics the branch of economic analysis that makes prescriptions about the way the *economy* should work.

North American Free Trade Agreement (NAFTA) a *trade* agreement among Canada, the United States, and Mexico.

O

offshore outsourcing the practice of businesses hiring people in another country to perform various tasks.

Okun's law the negative relationship between the *output gap* and the *unemployment rate*, whereby each additional percentage point of *output gap* reduces the *unemployment rate* by about ½ of a percentage point.

omitted variable an unobserved *variable* that, through its influence on other variables, may create the erroneous appearance of a direct *causal relationship* among those variables.

open economy an *economy* that trades goods and services with other countries.

open-market operation the purchase or sale of assets by a *central bank*. For the Bank of Canada, normally these assets are Government of Canada *bonds*, but they may also be foreign exchange.

opportunity cost the real cost of an item: what one must give up in order to get it.

origin the point where the axes of a two-*variable* graph meet.

other things equal assumption in the development of a *model*, the assumption that all relevant factors except the one under study remain unchanged.

output gap the percentage difference between actual *aggregate output* and *potential output*.

overnight funds market a *financial market* in which financial institutions, such as *banks* that are short of reserves can borrow funds from *banks* with *excess reserves*.

overnight rate the *interest rate* determined in the *overnight funds market*.

P

pension fund a type of *mutual fund* that holds assets in order to provide retirement income to its members.

per worker production function is a hypothetical function that shows how productivity (*real GDP* per worker) depends on the quantities of *physical capital* per worker and *human capital* per worker as well as the state of *technology*.

physical asset a claim on a tangible object that can be used to generate future income.

physical capital manufactured resources, such as buildings and machines.

pie chart a circular graph that shows how some total is divided among its components, usually expressed in percentages.

planned aggregate expenditure the total amount of planned spending in the *economy*; includes *consumer spending* and *planned investment spending*.

planned investment spending the *investment spending* that *firms* intend to undertake during a given period. Planned investment spending may differ from actual investment spending due to *unplanned inventory investment*.

political business cycle a *business cycle* that results from the use of macroeconomic policy to serve political ends.

positive economics the branch of economic analysis that describes the way the *economy* actually works.

positive marginal productivity of physical capital (positive MP_K) the amount by which *productivity* is increased as the result of a small increase in *physical capital* used.

positive relationship a relationship between two *variables* in which an increase in the value of one variable is associated with an increase in the value of the other variable. It is illustrated by a *curve* that slopes upward from left to right.

potential output the level of *real GDP* the *economy* would produce if all prices, including *nominal wages*, were fully flexible.

present value (of Y dollars) the amount of money needed today in order to receive X dollars at a future date given the *interest rate*.

price ceiling the maximum price sellers are allowed to charge for a good or service; a form of *price control*.

price controls legal restrictions on how high or low a market price may go.

price floor the minimum price buyers are required to pay for a good or service; a form of *price control*.

price index a measure of the cost of purchasing a given *market basket* in a given year, where that cost is normalized so that it is equal to 100 in the selected base year; a measure of overall price level.

price stability a situation in which the overall cost of living is changing slowly or not at all.

private savings *disposable income* minus *consumer spending*; *disposable income* that is not spent on *consumption* but rather goes into *financial markets*.

producer surplus a term often used to refer to either *individual producer surplus* or *total producer surplus*.

production possibility frontier a *model* that illustrates the *trade-offs* facing an *economy* that produces only two goods. It shows the maximum quantity of one good that can be produced for any given quantity produced of the other.

productivity output per worker; a shortened form of the term *labour productivity*.

protection policies that limit *imports*; an alternative term for *trade protection*.

public debt government debt held by individuals and institutions outside the government.

public savings the difference between net tax revenue ($T - TR$) and government spending on goods and services, i.e., $T - TR - G$. A positive *budget balance* is a *budget surplus*, a negative budget balance is a *budget deficit*, and a zero budget balance is a balanced budget.

purchasing power parity (between two countries' currencies) the nominal *exchange rate* at which a given basket of goods and services would cost the same amount in each country.

Q

quantitative easing (QE) a monetary policy in which a government tries to drive down *interest rates*, thus exerting an expansionary effect on the *economy*, by buying longer-term government *bonds*, instead of the shorter-term bonds it would buy usually.

quantity control an upper limit, set by the government, on the quantity of some good that can be bought or sold; also referred to as a *quota*.

quantity demanded the actual amount of a good or service consumers are willing to buy at some specific price.

quantity supplied the actual amount of a good or service producers are willing to sell at some specific price.

quota an upper limit, set by the government, on the quantity of some good that can be bought or sold; also referred to as a *quantity control*.

quota limit the total amount of a good under a *quota* or *quantity control* that can be legally transacted.

quota rent the difference between the *demand price* and the *supply price* at the *quota limit*; this difference, the earnings that accrue to the licence holder, is equal to the market price of the *licence* when the licence is traded.

R

random walk the movement over time of an unpredictable *variable*.

rational expectations a theory of expectation formation that holds that individuals and *firms* make decisions optimally, using all available information.

rational expectations model a *model* of the *economy* in which expected changes in *monetary policy* have no effect on *unemployment* and output and only affect the price level.

real business cycle theory a theory of *business cycles* that asserts that fluctuations in the growth rate of *total factor productivity* cause the *business cycle*.

real exchange rate the *exchange rate* adjusted for international differences in *aggregate price levels*.

real GDP the total value of all *final goods and services* produced in the *economy* during a given year, calculated using the prices of a selected base year.

real income income divided by the price level.

real interest rate the *nominal interest rate* minus the *inflation rate*.

real wage the wage rate divided by the price level.

recession a downturn in the *economy* when output and *employment* are falling.

recessionary gap a state that exists when *aggregate output* is below *potential output*.

research and development (R&D) spending to create new technologies and prepare them for practical use.

reserve ratio the fraction of *bank deposits* that a *bank* holds as reserves. In Canada, banks maintain whatever reserve ratio they think is appropriate to avoid running out of cash.

reserve requirements rules set by the *central bank* that determine the minimum *reserve ratio* for *banks*.

resource anything, such as land, labour, and capital, that can be used to produce something else; includes natural resources (from the physical environment) and human resources (labour, skill, intelligence).

revaluation an increase in the value of a currency that is set under a *fixed exchange rate regime*.

reverse causality the error committed when the true direction of causality between two *variables* is reversed, and the *independent variable* and the *dependent variable* are incorrectly identified.

Ricardian model of international trade a *model* that analyzes international *trade* under the assumption that *opportunity costs* are constant.

Rule of 70 a mathematical formula that states that the time it takes *real GDP* per capita, or any other *variable* that grows gradually over time, to double is approximately 70 divided by that variable's annual growth rate.

S

savings–investment spending identity an accounting fact that states that savings and *investment spending* are always equal for the *economy* as a whole.

scarce in short supply; a *resource* is scarce when there is not enough of the resource available to satisfy all the various ways a society wants to use it.

scatter diagram a graph that shows points that correspond to actual observations of the *x*- and *y*-variables; a *curve* is usually fitted to the scatter of points to indicate the trend in the data.

securitization the pooling of *loans* and mortgages made by a financial institution and the sale of shares in such a pool to other investors.

self-correcting describes an *economy* in which shocks to aggregate demand affect *aggregate output* in the short run but not in the long run.

self-regulating economy an *economy* in which problems such as *unemployment* are resolved without government intervention, through the working of the *invisible hand*, and in which government attempts to improve the economy's performance would be ineffective at best, and would probably make things worse.

shadow bank a non-depository financial institution that engages in *maturity transformation*.

shift of the demand curve a change in the *quantity demanded* at any given price, represented graphically by the change of the original *demand curve* to a new position, denoted by a new demand curve.

shift of the supply curve a change in the *quantity supplied* of a good or service at any given price, represented graphically by the change of the original *supply curve* to a new position, denoted by a new supply curve.

shoe-leather costs (of inflation) the increased costs of transactions caused by inflation.

shortage the insufficiency of a good or service that occurs when the *quantity demanded* exceeds the *quantity supplied*; shortages occur when the price is below the *equilibrium price*.

short-run aggregate supply curve a graphical representation that shows the positive relationship between the *aggregate price level* and the quantity of *aggregate output* supplied that exists in the short run, the time period when many production costs, particularly *nominal wages*, can be taken as fixed. The *short-run aggregate supply curve* has a positive slope because a rise in the aggregate price level leads to a rise in profits, and therefore output, when production costs are fixed.

short-run equilibrium aggregate output the quantity of *aggregate output* produced in *short-run macroeconomic equilibrium*.

short-run equilibrium aggregate price level the *aggregate price level* in *short-run macroeconomic equilibrium*.

short-run macroeconomic equilibrium the point at which the quantity of *aggregate output* supplied is equal to the *quantity demanded*.

short-run Phillips curve a graphical representation of the negative short-run relationship between the *unemployment rate* and the *inflation rate*.

short-term interest rate the *interest rate* on *financial assets* that mature within less than a year.

slope a measure of how steep a line or *curve* is. The slope of a line is measured by "rise over run"—the change in the *y*-variable between two points on the line divided by the change in the *x*-variable between those same points.

social insurance government programs—like the Canada/Quebec Pension Plan (CPP/QPP), Old Age Security (OAS), and welfare—intended to protect families against economic hardship.

specialization the situation in which each person specializes in the task that he or she is good at performing.

stabilization policy the use of government policy to reduce the severity of *recessions* and to rein in excessively strong *expansions*. There are two main tools of stabilization policy: *monetary policy* and *fiscal policy*.

stagflation the combination of *inflation* and falling *aggregate output*.

sticky wages *nominal wages* that are slow to fall even in the face of high *unemployment* and slow to rise even in the face of labour *shortages*.

stock a share in the ownership of a company held by a shareholder.

store of value an asset that is a means of holding purchasing power over time.

structural unemployment *unemployment* that results when there are more people seeking jobs in a particular labour market than there are jobs available at the current wage rate, even when the economy is at the peak of the *business cycle*.

sub-prime lending lending to homebuyers who don't meet the usual criteria for borrowing.

substitutes pairs of goods for which a rise in the price of one of the goods leads to an increase in the demand for the other good.

supply and demand model a *model* of how a *competitive market* behaves.

supply curve a graphical representation of the *supply schedule*, showing the relationship between *quantity supplied* and price.

supply price the price of a given quantity at which producers will supply that quantity.

supply schedule a list or table showing how much of a good or service producers will supply at different prices.

supply shock an event that shifts the *short-run aggregate supply curve*. A negative *supply shock* raises production costs and reduces the *quantity supplied* at any *aggregate price level*, shifting the curve leftward. A positive *supply shock* decreases production costs and increases the quantity supplied at any aggregate price level, shifting the curve rightward.

surplus the excess of a good or service that occurs when the *quantity supplied* exceeds the *quantity demanded*; surpluses occur when the price is above the *equilibrium price*.

sustainable long-run economic growth long-run growth that can continue in the face of the limited supply of natural *resources* and the impact of growth on the environment.

T

T-account a simple tool that summarizes a business's financial position by showing, in a single table, the business's assets and *liabilities*, with assets on the left and liabilities and equity on the right.

tangent line a straight line that just touches a *non-linear curve* at a particular point; the *slope* of the tangent line is equal to the slope of the non-linear curve at that point.

target for the overnight rate the Bank of Canada's official key policy *interest rate*.

tariff a tax levied on *imports*.

technological progress an advance in the technical means of production of goods and services.

technology the technical means for producing goods and services.

time-series graph a two-*variable* graph that has dates on the *horizontal axis* and values of a variable that occurred on those dates on the *vertical axis*.

total consumer surplus the sum of the *individual consumer surpluses* of all the buyers of a good in a market.

total factor productivity the parameter *A* in the aggregate production function $Y = A \times F(K, L, H)$; a term that accounts for output that is not a result of the productive inputs. That is, it captures all inputs and technological features left out of the aggregate production function.

total producer surplus the sum of the *individual producer surpluses* of all the sellers of a good in a market.

total surplus the total net gain to consumers and producers from trading in a market; the sum of the *consumer surplus* and the *producer surplus*.

trade the practice, in a *market economy*, in which individuals provide goods and services to others and receive goods and services in return.

trade balance (merchandise trade balance) the difference between a country's *exports* and *imports* of goods alone—not including services.

trade deficit when the value of the goods and services bought from other countries is more than the value of the goods and services sold to consumers abroad.

trade protection policies that limit *imports*; also known simply as *protection*.

trade surplus when the value of goods and services bought from other countries is less than the value of the goods and services sold to them.

trade-off a comparison of costs and benefits of doing something.

transaction costs the expenses of negotiating and executing a deal.

truncated cut; in a truncated axis, some of the range of values are omitted, usually to save space.

U

underemployment the number of people who have jobs that, in certain ways, fall short of what they want.

unemployment the total number of people (aged 15 and older) who are actively looking for work but aren't currently employed.

unemployment rate the percentage of the total number of people in the *labour force* who are unemployed, calculated as *unemployment/(unemployment + employment)*.

unexpected inflation the difference between the actual and expected *inflation rates*.

unit of account a measure used to set prices and make economic calculations.

unit-of-account costs (of inflation) costs arising from the way *inflation* makes money a less reliable unit of measurement.

unplanned inventory investment unplanned changes in *inventories*, which occur when actual sales are more or less than businesses expected.

V

value added (of a producer) the value of a producer's sales minus the value of its purchases of intermediate goods and services.

variable a quantity that can take on more than one value.

velocity of money the ratio of *nominal GDP* to the *money supply*.

vertical axis the vertical number line of a graph along which values of the *y*-variable are measured; also referred to as the *y-axis*.

vertical intercept the point at which a *curve* hits the *vertical axis*; it shows the value of the *y*-variable when the value of the *x*-variable is zero.

vicious cycle of deleveraging describes the sequence of events that takes place when a *firm's* asset sales to cover losses produce negative *balance sheet effects* on other firms and force creditors to call in their *loans*, forcing sales of more assets and causing further declines in asset prices.

visible underemployment the number of people who involuntarily work part time because they cannot find full-time jobs.

W

wasted resources a form of inefficiency in which people expend money, effort, and time to cope with the shortages caused by a *price ceiling*.

wealth (of a household) the value of accumulated savings.

wealth effect of a change in the aggregate price level the effect on *consumer spending* caused by the change in the purchasing power of consumers' assets when the *aggregate price level* changes. A rise in the aggregate price level decreases the purchasing power of consumers' assets, so consumers decrease their *consumption*; a fall in the aggregate price level increases the purchasing power of consumers' assets, so consumers increase their consumption.

wedge the difference between the *demand price* of the quantity transacted and the *supply price* of the quantity transacted for a good when the supply of the good is legally restricted. Often created by a *quantity control*, or *quota*.

willingness to pay the maximum price a consumer is prepared to pay for a good.

world price the price at which a good can be bought or sold abroad.

World Trade Organization (WTO) an international organization of member countries that oversees *international trade agreements* and rules on disputes between countries over those agreements.

X

*x***-axis** the horizontal number line of a graph along which values of the *x*-variable are measured; also referred to as the *horizontal axis*.

Y

*y***-axis** the vertical number line of a graph along which values of the *y*-variable are measured; also referred to as the *vertical axis*.

Z

zero bound the lower bound of zero on the *nominal interest rate*.

zero lower bound for interest rates statement of the fact that *interest rates* cannot fall below zero.

—